D1345551

LONDON

THE PHOTOGRAPHIC ATLAS

getmapping.com™ + HarperCollins*Illustrated*

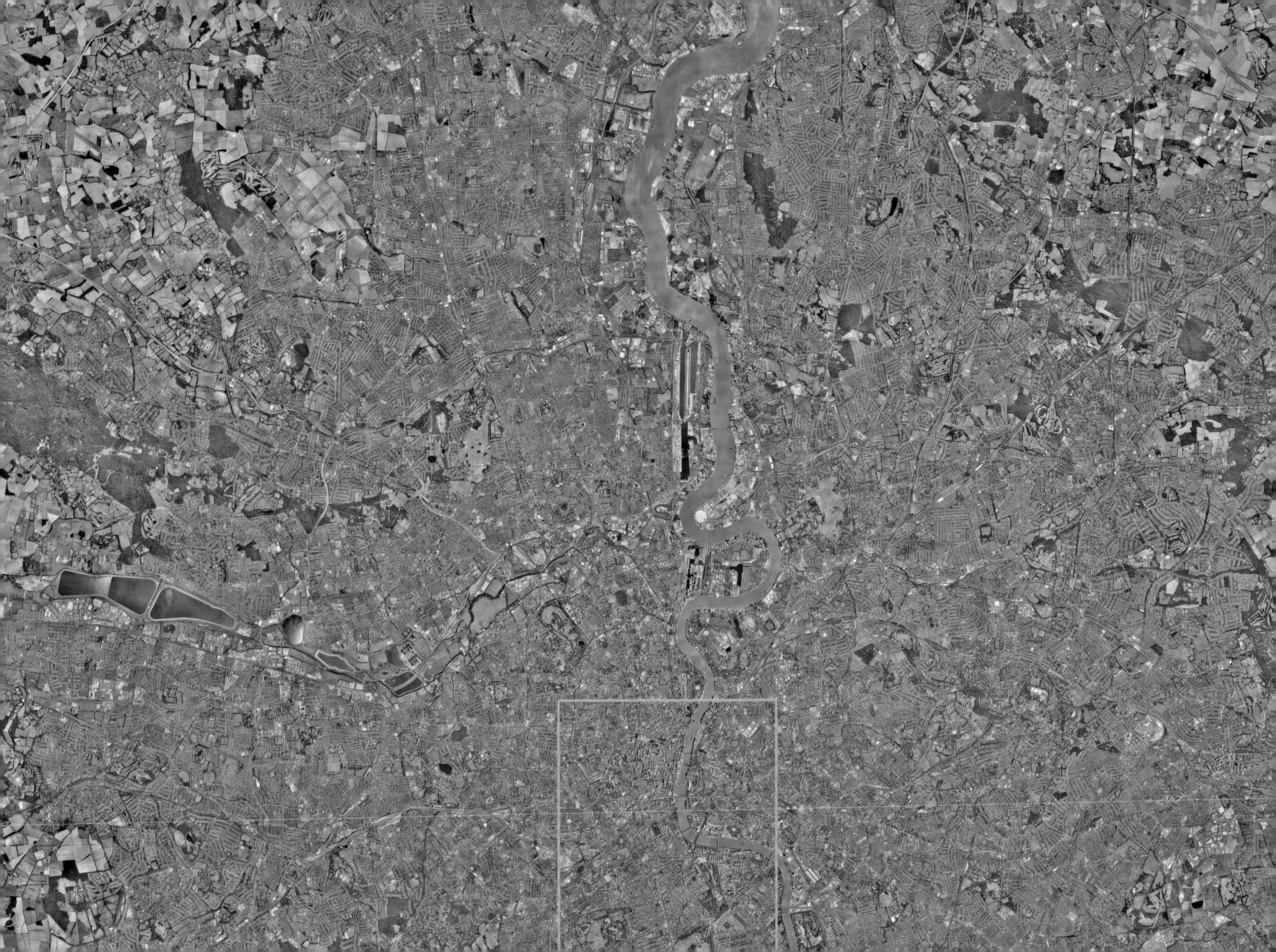

First published in 2000 by
HarperCollinsIllustrated,
an imprint of HarperCollinsPublishers
77–85 Fulham Palace Road
London W6 8JB

The HarperCollins website address is
www.**fire**and**water**.com

Photography © 2000 Getmapping.com plc
Cartography © 2000 HarperCollinsPublishers Ltd

Getmapping.com plc hereby asserts its moral right to be identified as the author of this work.

Getmapping can produce an individual print of any area shown in this book, or of any area within the United Kingdom. The image can be centred wherever you choose, printed at any size from A6 to 7.5 metres square, and at any scale up to 1:1,000. For further information, please contact Getmapping on 0845 0551550, or log on to www.getmapping.com

All cartography in this book is generated from the Bartholomew digital databases, and is also available for purchase, in digital format. For further information, please contact Bartholomew Data Sales on 01242 233887, or email bartholomew@harpercollins.co.uk

All rights reserved. No part of this publication may be reproduced, stored in a retrieval system, or transmitted in any form or by any means, mechanical, photocopying, recording or otherwise, without the prior written permission of the copyright owners.

The publisher regrets that it can accept no responsibility for any errors or omissions within this publication, or for any expense or loss thereby caused.

The representation of a road, track or footpath is no evidence of a right of way.

A CIP catalogue record for this book is available from the British Library.

ISBN: 0 00 710841 9

04 03 02 01 00
9 8 7 6 5 4 3 2

Book design by SMITH

Photographic image processing by Wildgoose Publications Ltd

Colour origination by Colourscan, Singapore
Additional colour origination by Saxon Photolitho, Norwich
Printed and bound in Great Britain by Bath Press Colourbooks

Introduction

This book is startlingly simple; it consists of aerial photographs of London. Not just the famous landmarks and the great parks; and not just the photogenic parts, captured from the best angles and in the best light. It contains aerial photographs of every square metre of Greater London, taken from an altitude of 5,500 feet by automatically-triggered survey cameras. This treatment lets you see the city as it really is, not flattering any particular aspect, but revealing each area in its true proportions and each building in its proper place.

If you live in London, you will already have a personal stake in the book – within its pages you will be able to find your house, perhaps locate your car parked in the street, trace your route to work, and visit some of your favourite places. Aerial photography is interesting because it shows a familiar environment from an unfamiliar perspective, forcing you, the viewer, to interpret the scene anew. From these photographs you will notice patterns that are invisible from the ground, discover surprising links between unconnected areas, find large areas of greenery that you never knew existed, and explore new neighbourhoods for the first time.

Even if you are not familiar with London, you will still find this a fascinating book. The window seats on aeroplanes are always the first to be taken because looking down is intriguing, whether you know the place below or not. If you do, you seek out familiar landmarks; if not, you imagine what it must be like, and try to reconcile the view with your preconceptions.

These photographs of London are taken from the Millennium Map, a survey of the whole of the United Kingdom – a record of every mountain, field, lake, house, hedge and tree in the land. I began making the Millennium Map in 1999 with my partner Joe Studholme. For my part I embarked on the project because I knew that no truly comprehensive survey had ever been undertaken. The RAF had photographed most of the

country in 1947, but the negatives were not in good condition and had never been assembled into a coherent whole. Since then the UK had only been surveyed piecemeal by various authorities and organisations, although a consistent survey of Scotland (in black and white) was undertaken in 1987. The fragmented nature of the existing surveys made it difficult for most users to find the information that they needed; I therefore believed that a complete new survey would be a useful – and profitable – commodity.

Joe's inspiration was rather different. In 1984 he had embarked on making the first true facsimile of William the Conqueror's great Domesday survey of 1086. This epic task was not completed until 1999 and, to celebrate the millennium, Joe decided to make an electronic version of the Domesday Book that would incorporate modern aerial photographs of all the settlements originally listed. Joe and I first discussed this project in 1996, but it was not until late 1998 that our ideas evolved into the Millennium Map. We conceived this modern-day counterpart to the Domesday survey as a benchmark against which future generations would be able to measure the evolution of the country. Drawing on this resource, environmentalists would be able to measure coastal erosion and changes to natural habitats; sociologists and town planners to monitor the rate of urban development; and surveyors to date alterations to individual buildings. Still further into the future, our descendants would be able to step back in time to revisit the country at the turn of the millennium. Just imagine how interesting it would be to study a photographic record of London in the time of Shakespeare, Pepys or Dickens.

Our plan is to keep the Millennium Map updated by re-flying it every five years. This means that by 2050 you will be able to log in to the Map on the internet, choose to view any part of the country at any scale, and then fly backwards and forwards in time through ten layers of the Map to experience the changes in the landscape.

Inevitably, creating the Millennium Map has posed many technical challenges. The key point is that the whole survey is digital. We use film nine inches wide (to date, almost thirty kilometres of it) to take individual photographs that are then scanned at high resolution. After scanning, the files undergo a process known as geo-correction, which removes the geometric distortions caused by the tilt of the aircraft and the contours of the ground. The individual files are then colour-balanced and spliced together to form a single map-accurate 'mosaic' of the entire country. If the complete mosaic of the United Kingdom were published in the same format as this book, reproduced at the scale used for Central London, it would fill around five hundred volumes; and if it were laid out on the ground at a scale of 1:1,000, the Map would measure eight hundred metres long by six hundred metres wide. We are actively looking for a suitable site for this venture.

Despite its size, the idea behind the Millennium Map – to create a complete and accessible photographic record of the whole of the United Kingdom – is such a simple one that it seems almost incredible that this is the first time it has ever been done. London: The Photographic Atlas records the vast and intricate capital with unprecedented clarity, and I hope that through these pages you will see the city as you've never seen it before.

Tristram Cary

Managing Director, Getmapping.com plc

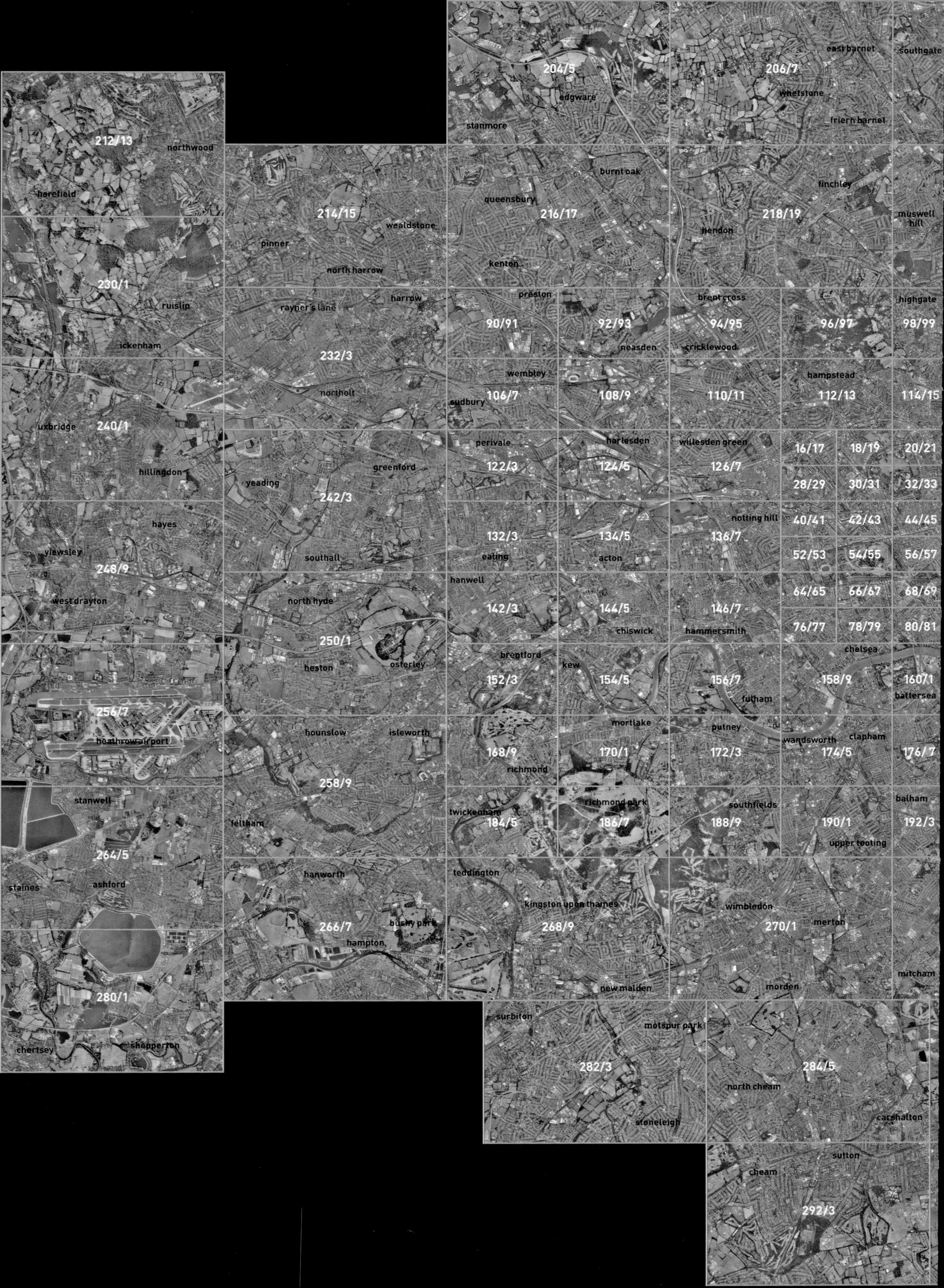
204/5
edgware
stanmore
206/7
east barnet
southgate
whetstone
friern barnet
212/13
northwood
harefield
burnt oak
queensbury
214/15
wealdstone
216/17
218/19
finchley
muswell hill
hendon
pinner
north harrow
kenton
230/1
ruislip
ickenham
harrow
rayner's lane
preston
brent cross
highgate
90/91
92/93
94/95
96/97
98/99
neasden
cricklewood
232/3
wembley
hampstead
northolt
sudbury
106/7
108/9
110/11
112/13
114/15
uxbridge
240/1
perivale
harlesden
willesden green
16/17
18/19
20/21
greenford
122/3
124/5
126/7
hillingdon
yeading
242/3
28/29
30/31
32/33
hayes
notting hill
40/41
42/43
44/45
132/3
134/5
136/7
yiewsley
southall
ealing
acton
52/53
54/55
56/57
248/9
hanwell
64/65
66/67
68/69
north hyde
west drayton
142/3
144/5
146/7
250/1
chiswick
hammersmith
76/77
78/79
80/81
heston
osterley
brentford
kew
chelsea
152/3
154/5
156/7
158/9
160/1
256/7
fulham
battersea
heathrow airport
hounslow
isleworth
mortlake
putney
wandsworth
clapham
168/9
170/1
172/3
174/5
176/7
richmond
258/9
stanwell
balham
twickenham
richmond park
southfields
feltham
184/5
186/7
188/9
190/1
192/3
upper tooting
264/5
hanworth
teddington
staines
ashford
kingston upon thames
wimbledon
266/7
bushy park
268/9
270/1
merton
hampton
mitcham
new malden
morden
280/1
surbiton
motspur park
chertsey
shepperton
282/3
284/5
north cheam
carshalton
stoneleigh
sutton
cheam
292/3

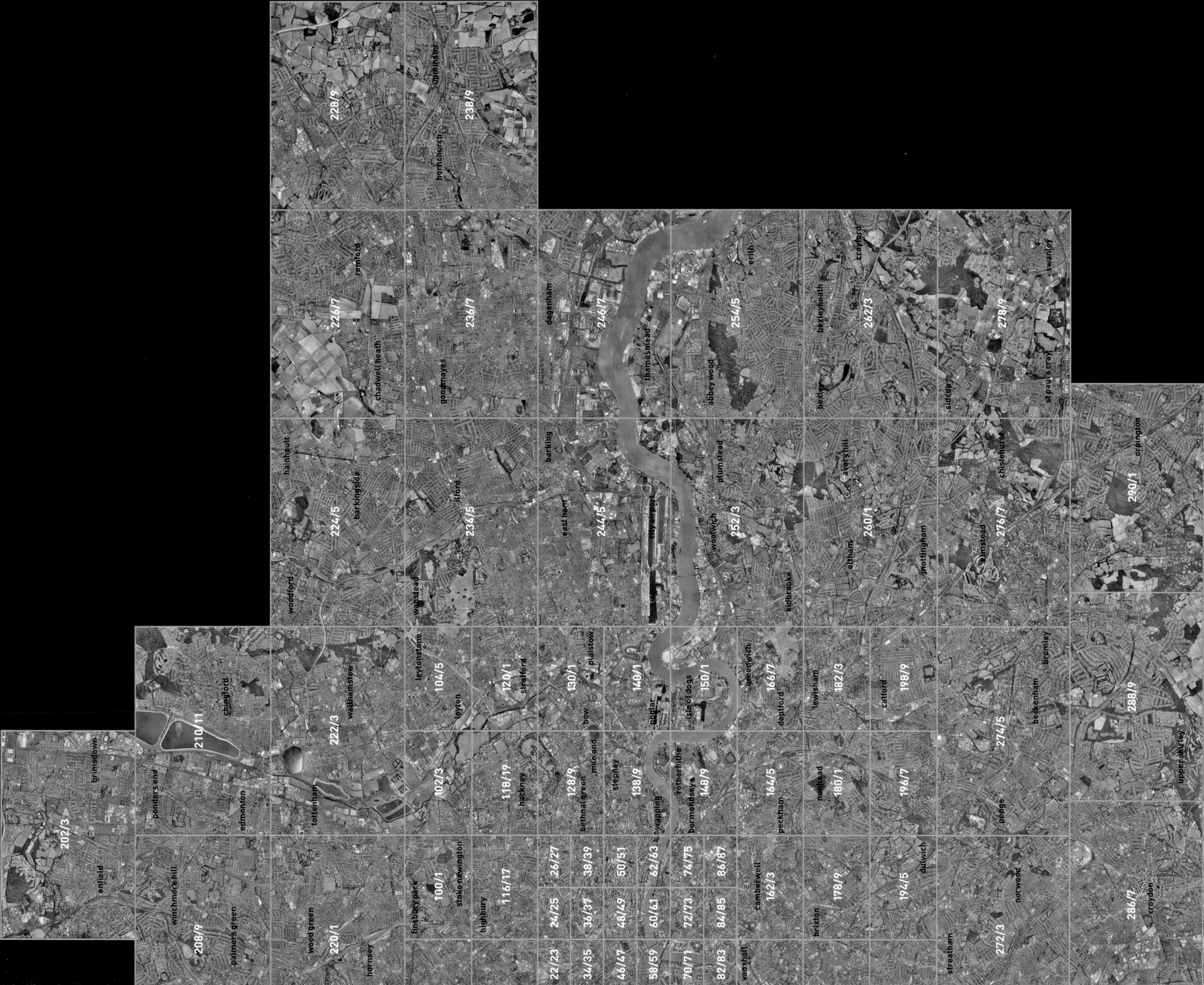

228/9
upminster
238/9
hornchurch
romford
226/7
chadwell heath
236/7
goodmayes
dagenham
246/7
thamesmead
erith
254/5
abbey wood
bexleyheath
crayford
262/3
bexley
swanley
278/9
sidcup
st paul's cray
hainault
barkingside
224/5
woodford
ilford
234/5
wanstead
barking
east ham
244/5
city airport
plumstead
woolwich
252/3
kidbrooke
avery hill
260/1
eltham
mottingham
chislehurst
276/7
elmstead
orpington
290/1
chingford
210/11
walthamstow
222/3
leytonstone
104/5
leyton
120/1
stratford
130/1
plaistow
bow
140/1
poplar
isle of dogs
150/1
greenwich
166/7
deptford
lewisham
182/3
catford
198/9
bromley
beckenham
274/5
288/9
upper shirley
brimsdown
ponders end
edmonton
tottenham
102/3
118/19
hackney
128/9
mile end
bethnal green
stepney
138/9
wapping
rotherhithe
bermondsey
148/9
164/5
peckham
nunhead
180/1
196/7
penge
202/3
enfield
winchmore hill
208/9
palmers green
wood green
220/1
hornsey
finsbury park
100/1
stoke newington
highbury
116/17
26/27
24/25
22/23
38/39
36/37
34/35
50/51
48/49
46/47
62/63
60/61
58/59
74/75
72/73
70/71
86/87
84/85
82/83
vauxhall
camberwell
162/3
brixton
178/9
194/5
dulwich
streatham
272/3
norwood
286/7
croydon
sanderstead
294/5
purley

Central London

The key to photography on page 12 indicates complete area of coverage
The corresponding cartography page reference is located at the bottom left of each spread
The photography and the cartography share the same standard grid system
The grid interval throughout the book is 500 metres

16 kilburn/st john's wood
18 st john's wood/primrose hill/regent's park
20 regent's park/camden town
22 king's cross/islington
24 islington
26 hoxton/haggerston
28 west kilburn/maida vale
30 st john's wood/regent's park/marylebone
32 regent's park/euston
34 euston/st pancras
36 finsbury/clerkenwell
38 hoxton/shoreditch
40 westbourne green/paddington
42 paddington/marylebone
44 marylebone/oxford circus
46 bloomsbury/holborn/covent garden
48 farringdon/smithfield/barbican/st paul's
50 broadgate/bank/spitalfields/whitechapel
52 notting hill/bayswater/kensington
54 kensington gardens/hyde park/marble arch
56 mayfair/st james's
58 soho/covent garden/charing cross/whitehall
60 embankment/blackfriars/southwark
62 southwark/tower bridge/st katharine's dock/butler's wharf
64 kensington/south kensington
66 south kensington/hyde park/knightsbridge
68 hyde park corner/buckingham palace/belgravia/victoria
70 st james's park/westminster/waterloo
72 waterloo/lambeth/the borough/elephant and castle
74 bricklayer's arms/bermondsey
76 earls court/west brompton
78 south kensington/chelsea
80 chelsea/victoria/pimlico
82 pimlico/lambeth/vauxhall
84 lambeth/kennington/newington/walworth
86 newington/walworth/old kent road

1:3,000

16
kilburn/london marriott hotel
Scale 1:3,000 see cartography pages 314/315
127
28
112
DA
DB

17
kilburn/st john's wood/saatchi gallery
18
112
29
DB
DC

17
30
113
DD
DE
Scale 1:3,000 see cartography pages 314/315
st john's wood/st john's wood barracks

67
20
68
DF
113
31
DE

Scale 1:3,000 see cartography pages 316/317
19
32
114
DG
DH

22
114
33
DJ
DH

Scale 1:3,000 see cartography pages 316/317
21
34
115
DK
DL

24
115
35
DL
DL

24.
islington/royal mail depot/business design centre/the angel centre
Scale 1:3,000 see cartography pages 316/317
23
36
116

26
116
37

25
38
117
Scale 1:3,000 see cartography pages 316/317

128
117
39

Scale 1:3,000 see cartography pages 314/315

127
40
16

30
DC
DC
17
41
DB
DB

Scale 1:3,000 see cartography pages 314/315

regent's park/london central mosque/london business school/boating lake/marylebone station

Scale 1:3,000 see cartography pages 316/317
31
44
20

34
21
45

34
euston station/british library/st pancras station/university college london
Scale 1:3,000 see cartography pages 316/317
33
46
22

36
23
47

35
24
48
Scale 1:3,000 see cartography pages 316/317

38
25
49

37
50
26

Scale 1:3,000 see cartography pages 316/317

128
27
51

Scale 1:3,000 see cartography pages 314/315

42
DC
DC
29
53

Scale 1:3,000 see cartography pages 314/315

44
31
55

43
56
32
Scale 1:3,000 see cartography pages 316/317

46
33
57

46
university of london/russell square/bedford square/british museum/centrepoint/soho square/seven dials
Scale 1:3,000 see cartography pages 316/317
45
58
34

48
35
59

Scale 1:3,000 see cartography pages 316/317

50
37
61

Scale 1:3,000 see cartography pages 316/317

138
39
63

137
64
40
Scale 1:3,000 see cartography pages 314/315

54
41
65

Scale 1:3,000 see cartography pages 314/315

56
73
74
43
67
DE
DF

55
68
44
Scale 1:3,000 see cartography pages 316/317

58

45
69

57
70
46

Scale 1:3,000 see cartography pages 316/317

60
73
47
71

Scale 1:3,000 see cartography pages 316/317

62

millennium bridge under construction/southwark bridge/tate modern under construction/shakespeare's globe

49
73

61

74

50

Scale 1:3,000 see cartography pages 316/317

138
73
DT
51
75

147
64
king's college/town hall/kensington roof gardens/commonwealth institute
Scale 1:3,000 see cartography pages 314/315
76
52

66
53
77

Scale 1:3,000 see cartography pages 314/315

68
55
79

Scale 1:3,000 see cartography pages 316/317

green park/buckingham palace and gardens/the mall/st james's park/victoria station/westminster rc cathedral

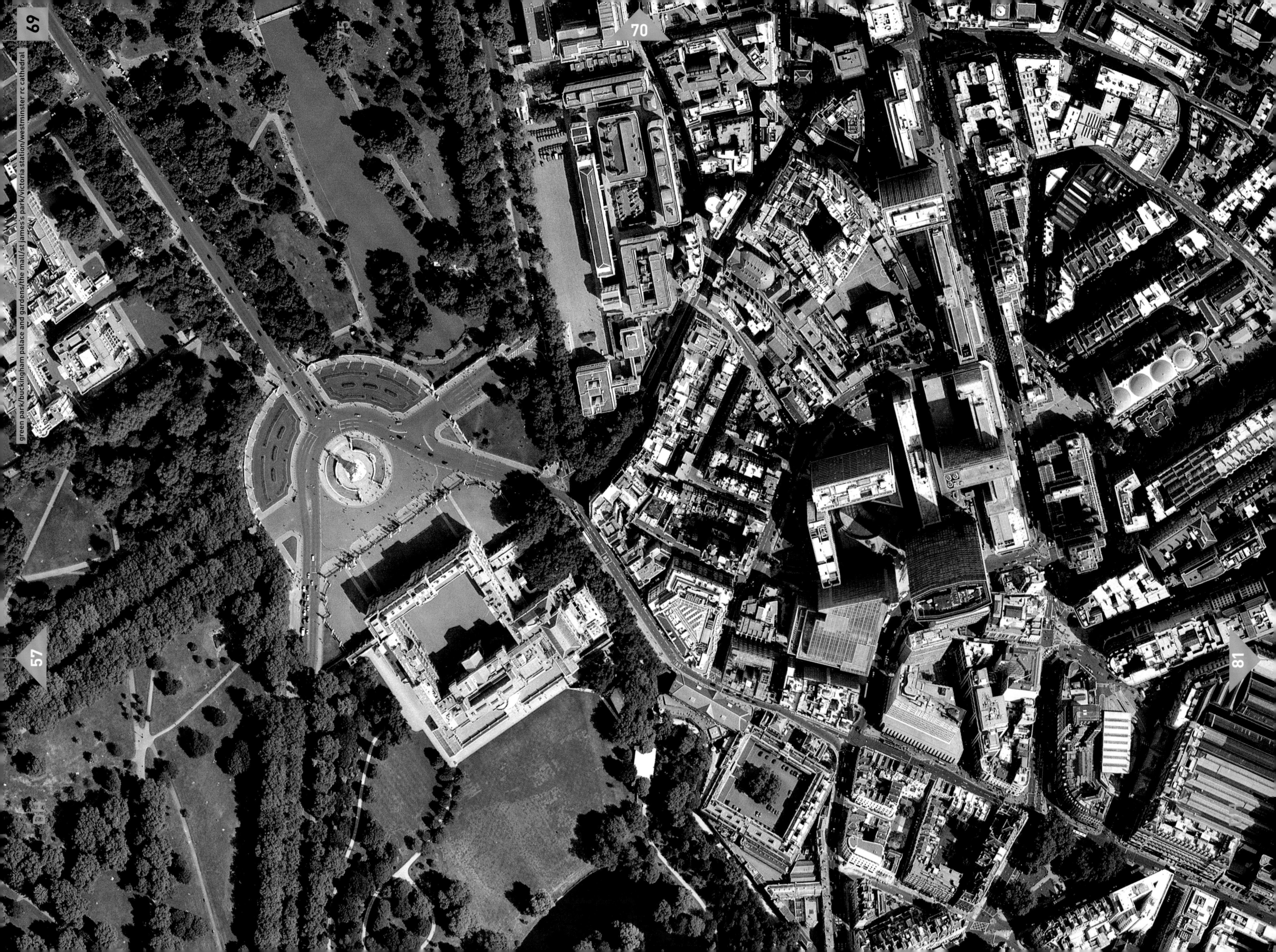

70
57
81

Scale 1:3,000 see cartography pages 316/317

houses of parliament/westminster bridge/london eye under construction/county hall/waterloo international station/st thomas' hospital/lambeth palace

72
59
83

waterloo station/lambeth/imperial war museum/st george's circus
Scale 1:3,000 see cartography pages 316/317
71
84
60
DN
DN

74
76
DQ
61
85

Scale 1:3,000 see cartography pages 316/317

148
63
87

Scale 1:3,000 see cartography pages 314/315

78
65
158
DB

Scale 1:3,000 see cartography pages 314/315

80
67
159
78
DF

79
78
160
89
Scale 1:3,000 see cartography pages 316/317

82
77
78
69
160

81
161
70
DK
Scale 1:3,000 see cartography pages 316/317

84
78
71
161
DM
DL

Scale 1:3,000 see cartography pages 316/317
78
83
162
72

86
73
162

Scale 1:3,000 see cartography pages 316/317

148
75
163
DT
DT
DS
DS

Inner London

The key to photography on page 12 indicates complete area of coverage
The corresponding cartography page reference is located at the bottom left of each spread
The photography and the cartography share the same standard grid system
The grid interval throughout the book is 500 metres

90 north wembley/preston/wembley park
92 brent/wembley park/west hendon/neasden
94 staples corner/brent cross/golders green/cricklewood
96 golders green/childs hill/hampstead heath
98 highgate/archway/upper holloway/stroud green
100 finsbury park/stamford hill/stoke newington
102 upper clapton/walthamstow marshes/hackney marsh
104 leyton/leytonstone
106 sudbury/wembley
108 wembley stadium/tokyngton/neasden/church end
110 dollis hill/willesden green/cricklewood/brondesbury
112 west hampstead/hampstead/belsize park
114 kentish town/camden lock/tufnell park/holloway
116 highbury/barnsbury/dalston
118 hackney/lower clapton/homerton/victoria park
120 hackney wick/stratford/west ham
122 perivale/alperton
124 stonebridge/park royal/harlesden
126 willesden green/kensal rise/west kilburn
128 bethnal green/victoria park/old ford/mile end
130 bow/bromley-by-bow/plaistow
132 ealing
134 acton
136 wormwood scrubs/white city/north kensington/notting hill
138 whitechapel/wapping/stepney/limehouse/rotherhithe
140 poplar/isle of dogs/canary wharf/canning town/millennium dome
142 hanwell/ealing/gunnersbury park
144 south acton/gunnersbury/bedford park/chiswick
146 shepherd's bush/hammersmith/holland park/olympia
148 bermondsey/rotherhithe/surrey quays/deptford
150 isle of dogs/north greenwich peninsula
152 brentford/syon park/kew gardens/north sheen
154 kew/north sheen/grove park/chiswick/barnes
156 castelnau/barnes/fulham
158 west brompton/parsons green/chelsea/battersea
160 battersea/vauxhall/south lambeth
162 kennington/camberwell/peckham
164 peckham/new cross gate/new cross
166 deptford/greenwich/greenwich park/blackheath
168 st margaret's/old deer park/richmond
170 north sheen/mortlake/east sheen
172 roehampton/putney
174 wandsworth/clapham
176 clapham common/stockwell/brixton
178 brixton/brockwell park/herne hill/east dulwich
180 east dulwich/peckham rye/nunhead/brockley/honor oak park
182 lewisham/ladywell/hither green/lee
184 twickenham/eel pie island/ham/richmond/petersham
186 richmond park
188 putney heath/wimbledon common/southfields/wimbledon park
190 southfields/earlsfield/balham/upper tooting
192 balham/tooting bec/streatham hill/streatham
194 streatham hill/tulse hill/west norwood/dulwich
196 east dulwich/forest hill
198 catford/bellingham/grove park

1:6,000

Scale 1:6,000 see cartography pages 304/305

preston/wembley park/gec estate and sports ground

Scale 1:6,000 see cartography pages 304/305

94
217
109
CT
CS
CR
60

staples corner business park/M1-A406 interchange/brent cross shopping centre/dollis hill

Scale 1:6,000 see cartography pages 304/305

96
218
111

95
96
golders green/london underground depot/childs hill/west heath/sandy heath
Scale 1:6,000 see cartography pages 304/305
DA
DA
DB
DC
DC
112
219

98
219
113

Scale 1:6,000 see cartography pages 306/307

100
DM
DM
DL
DL
220
115
DK
DK

Scale 1:6,000 see cartography pages 306/307

102
221
117

Scale 1:6,000 see cartography pages 306/307

101

118

222

104
61
62
DZ
DY
222
119
DX

Scale 1:6,000 see cartography pages 306/307
103
120
223
EA
EB

leytonstone/st patrick's rc cemetery/wanstead flats

234
223
121

106
sudbury/wasps rufc/sudbury golf course
Scale 1:6,000 see cartography pages 304/305
233
66
65
CG
CG
CH
122
90

108
99
91
123
CM
CL
CK
CM
CK

Scale 1:6,000 see cartography pages 304/305

110
93
125

gladstone park/dollis hill/willesden jewish cemetery/willesden green
Scale 1:6,000 see cartography pages 304/305
109
126
94
CU
CV
CW
CU
CV
CW

112
95
127
CZ
CY
CX

Scale 1:6,000 see cartography pages 304/305
111
16
17
96
DA
DB

114
19
18
97
DE
DE

113
114
gospel oak/kentish town/round house/camden lock
Scale 1:6,000 see cartography pages 306/307
20
21
98

tufnell park/holloway prison/holloway/caledonian park/pentonville prison

115
116
highbury/highbury fields/highbury stadium/barnsbury/canonbury
Scale 1:6,000 see cartography pages 306/307
24
25
100

118
27
26
101
DT

Scale 1:6,000 see cartography pages 306/307
117
128
102

120
103
129
63
64
DZ
DZ
DY

119
130
104
Scale 1:6,000 see cartography pages 306/307

234
105
131
EE
ED
EF

Scale 1:6,000 see cartography pages 314/315

124
107
133
CM
CK
CK
68
69
70

stonebridge/park royal/guinness brewery and sports ground

126
109
135

126
willesden green/king edward vii sports ground/st mary's rc cemetery/kensal green cemetery
Scale 1:6,000 see cartography pages 314/315
125
136
110

16
28
111
137

128
haggerston park/bethnal green/weavers fields
Scale 1:6,000 see cartography pages 316/317
39
27
138
118

130
70
DZ
DY
119
139

Scale 1:6,000 see cartography pages 316/317

244
EF
EE
121
141
ED
ED

Scale 1:6,000 see cartography pages 314/315

134
123
143
CM
CL
CK

Scale 1:6,000 see cartography pages 314/315
133
144
124

136
125
145
CT
CS
CR

135
146
126

40
52
127
147

Scale 1:6,000 see cartography pages 316/317
63
51
148
128
DU
DV
DW

140
129
149

Scale 1:6,000 see cartography pages 316/317
139
150
130
EB

244
131
151
EF
EF
ED

142
hanwell/ealing/lammas park/little ealing/london playing fields/M4
Scale 1:6,000 see cartography pages 314/315
251
152
132

144
133
153

Scale 1:6,000 see cartography pages 314/315

145
bedford park/chiswick
146
135
155
CT
CS
CR

Scale 1:6,000 see cartography pages 314/315
145
156
136
CV

64
76
137
157

Scale 1:6,000 see cartography pages 316/317

151
north greenwich peninsula/millennium dome/blackwall tunnel southern approach
149
rotherhithe/surrey quays shopping centre/greenland dock/deptford park
150
141
139
165
EF
DZ
ED
DY
77
78

CG
CH
142
79
TESCO
80
251
81
CG
CH
168
CJ
Scale 1:6,000 see cartography pages 314/315
EA
EB
166
EC
Scale 1:6,000 see cartography pages 316/317

Scale 1:6,000 see cartography pages 314/315
155
170
172
146
CV

155
153
154
chiswick/hogarth roundabout/chiswick house/duke's meadow/barnes bridge/barnes/leg of mutton nature reserve
brentford/kew gardens/royal mid-surrey golf course/kew bridge/north sheen
CT
CM
CS
CR
145
143
169
CM

fulham/craven cottage stadium/bishop's park/fulham palace

Scale 1:6,000 see cartography pages 314/315

160
79
78
175
DF
DD

159
80
81
176
182
Scale 1:6,000 see cartography pages 316/317

162
83
82
177
DK
DL
DM

163
180
148

167
greenwich/royal naval college/queen's house/greenwich park/blackheath
165
new cross gate/new cross/telegraph hill park
166
151
149
181

st margaret's/richmond foot bridge/twickenham bridge/isleworth ait/kew observatory/old deer park
Scale 1:6,000 see cartography pages 316/317
Scale 1:6,000 see cartography pages 322/323
259
184
182
152

170
86
153
185

170
north sheen/mortlake/east sheen/east sheen common/richmond park
Scale 1:6,000 see cartography pages 322/323
169
186
154
86
85
CN
CN
CP
CP
CQ
CQ

172
155
187

171
188
156
85
86
CU
CV
CW
Scale 1:6,000 see cartography pages 322/323

putney bridge/hurlingham club/putney/wandsworth park

174
157
189

173
190
158
Scale 1:6,000 see cartography pages 322/323

176
159
191
DD
DE

175
192
160
Scale 1:6,000 see cartography pages 324/325

178
161
193

Scale 1:6,000 see cartography pages 324/325
177
194
162

180
163
195
DT
DS
DR

Scale 1:6,000 see cartography pages 324/325

182
165
197

Scale 1:6,000 see cartography pages 324/325
181
198
166
EA
EB
EC

260
167
199
EF

Scale 1:6,000 see cartography pages 322/323

186
169
268

richmond/petersham/ham/sudbrook park/richmond golf course

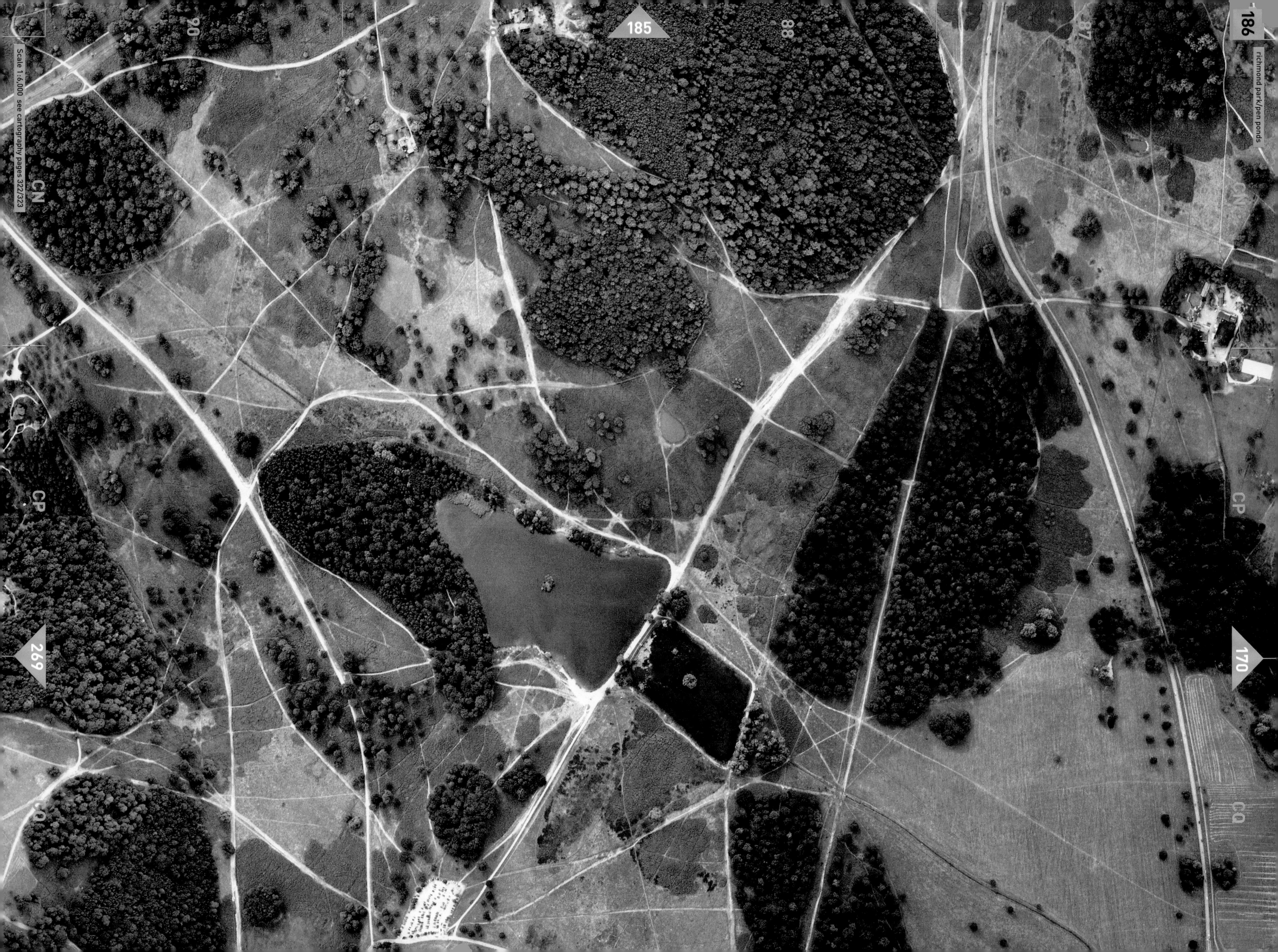
185
90
88
87
Scale 1:6,000 see cartography pages 322/323
CN
CP
CQ
269
170

187
richmond park/white lodge/putney vale
188
88
89
90
CT
CS
171
269
CR

187
270
172
Scale 1:6,000 see cartography pages 322/323

southfields/wimbledon park/all england lawn tennis and croquet club

189
Scale 1:6,000 see cartography pages 322/323
271
174

191
wandsworth prison/wandsworth common/earlsfield/balham/upper tooting
192
DE
175
DE
271
DD

191
272
176
DG
DH
Scale 1:6,000 see cartography pages 324/325

194
177
272

Scale 1:6,000 see cartography pages 324/325
193
273
178

dulwich/dulwich park/dulwich college/dulwich and sydenham golf course

196
179
273

Scale 1:6,000 see cartography pages 324/325

198
181
274

198
catford/bellingham/forster memorial park
Scale 1:6,000 see cartography pages 324/325
197
275
182
EA
EB
87
88
89
90

260
183
275

Outer London

The key to photography on page 12 indicates complete area of coverage
The corresponding cartography page reference is located at the bottom left of each spread
The photography and the cartography share the same standard grid system
The grid interval throughout the book is 500 metres

202 whitewebbs park/enfield/brimsdown
204 elstree/stanmore/edgware
206 chipping barnet/totteridge/mill hill/east barnet/oakleigh park/whetstone/friern barnet
208 oakwood/winchmore hill/southgate/palmers green/edmonton
210 ponders end/edmonton/chingford/highams park
212 batchworth/harefield/moor park/eastbury/northwood
214 pinner/eastcote/wealdstone/headstone/north harrow
216 belmont/queensbury/kenton/burnt oak/kingsbury
218 mill hill/hendon/finchley/east finchley/hampstead garden suburb
220 wood green/muswell hill/hornsey/crouch end/noel park/tottenham/harringay
222 tottenham/hale end/epping forest/walthamstow/south woodford
224 woodford/clayhall/hainault/barkingside/aldborough hatch/gants hill
226 mark's gate/chadwell heath/collier row/romford
228 romford/gidea park/upminster
230 south harefield/denham/ruislip/ickenham
232 ruislip manor/rayner's lane/south ruislip/harrow
234 wanstead/cranbrook/aldersbrook/ilford/loxford
236 goodmayes/beacontree/rush green/beacontree heath
238 hornchurch/havering/upminster
240 uxbridge/north hillingdon/hillingdon
242 yeading/southall/greenford/dormer's wells
244 upton park/east ham/royal docks/city airport/barking/beckton
246 barking/dagenham/thamesmead/south hornchurch
248 yiewsley/thorney/west drayton/hayes
250 north hyde/heston/osterley/lampton/spring grove
252 silvertown/charlton/thamesmead west/plumstead/shooter's hill
254 abbey wood/east wickham/bexleyheath/belvedere/erith
256 heathrow airport
258 hounslow/feltham/hanworth/isleworth
260 kidbrooke/blackheath park/eltham/mottingham/falconwood/avery hill
262 welling/bexley/bexleyheath/crayford/old bexley
264 stanwell/staines/ashford/east bedfont/lower feltham
266 felthamhill/hanworth/hampton/bushy park/east molesey
268 teddington/hampton wick/kingston upon thames/coombe/norbiton/new malden
270 wimbledon common/wimbledon/collier's wood/merton/morden
272 streatham/mitcham/norwood/thornton heath
274 sydenham/crystal palace/penge/southend/beckenham/bromley
276 elmstead/sundridge/widmore/bickley/chislehurst/petts wood
278 sidcup/foots cray/st paul's cray/swanley
280 laleham/chertsey/littleton/upper halliford/shepperton
282 long ditton/surbiton/tolworth/motspur park/old malden/worcester park/stoneleigh
284 morden park/north cheam/st helier/beddington corner/hackbridge/the wrythe/carshalton
286 broad green/beddington/waddon/selhurst/croydon/addiscombe
288 upper elmer's end/shirley/addington/park langley/west wickham/hayes
290 southborough/bromley common/farnborough/petts wood/orpington
292 cheam/east ewell/belmont/carshalton/little woodcote
294 south beddington/woodcote/purley/south croydon/sanderstead

1:12,000

202
whitewebbs park/hillyfields park/enfield golf course/enfield town
Scale 1:12,000 see cartography pages 300/301
209
DN
DP
DQ
DS
DT
40
39
38
37
36
35

35
36
38
39
40
41
42
DY
DX
DW
DV
DU
210

204
elstree/aldenham reservoir and park/M1/royal national orthopaedic hospital/stanmore
Scale 1:12,000 see cartography pages 298/299
216
CK
CK
CK

scratch wood/mill hill golf course/scratchwood services/M1/edgware

206
217

205
Scale 1:12,000 see cartography pages 298/299
CU
CV
218

208
219

208
oakwood/winchmore hill/southgate/new southgate
Scale 1:12,000 see cartography pages 300/301
207
220

210
202
221
DT
DS
DR
DQ
DP
DN

209
245
203
222
Scale 1:12,000 see cartography pages 300/301

EF
EE
ED
EC
EA
45
48
223

212
springwell lake/stocker's lake/bury lake/batchworth/park wood/bishop's wood/harefield
Scale 1:12,000 see cartography pages 302/303
51
50
BG
BK
BL
BM
230

214
231

pinner hill golf course/hatch end/pinner green/pinner/eastcote village/eastcote
Scale 1:12,000 see cartography pages 302/303
231
213
232
BU
BV
BW
BX
BY
BZ

216
55
CE
CD
CC
CB
233

215
90
91
204
55
CC
CH
CL
CL
Scale 1:12,000 see cartography pages 304/305

217
burnt oak/M1/the hyde/kingsbury
218
93
92
205

Scale 1:12,000 see cartography pages 304/305

220
55
56
57
58
97
96
207

Scale 1:12,000 see cartography pages 306/307

222
101
100
209

221
102
103
210

Scale 1:12,000 see cartography pages 306/307

224
105
104
211
EE
ED
EC
EB
EA

223
224
woodford/woodford bridge/M11-A406 interchange/clayhall/wanstead
Scale 1:12,000 see cartography pages 308/309
234

52
53
54
226
55
57
58
EO
235

Scale 1:12,000 see cartography pages 308/309
225
236
57
56
55
54
53
EW
EZ

51
228
FE
237
FB
FA

Scale 1:12,000 see cartography pages 310/311

harold park/M25/upminster

239

Scale 1:12,000 see cartography pages 302/303 & 312/313

214
232
213
241
BT
BS
BR
BQ
BP
BN

Scale 1:12,000 see cartography pages 312/313

90
106
215
243
59
60
65
66
CF
CE
CA

Scale 1:12,000 see cartography pages 308/309

121
105
244
224

236
225
245

235
246
226
Scale 1:12,000 see cartography pages 308/309

238
227
247
FF
FE
FD
FC
FB
FA

237
228
Scale 1:12,000 see cartography pages 310/311

229

240
M40 junction 1/uxbridge/uxbridge moor/brunel university
Scale 1:12,000 see cartography pages 312/313
248
230

232
242
231
249

248
yiewsley/thorney/west drayton/M25-M4 interchange
Scale 1:12,000 see cartography pages 312/313 & 320/321
78
256
240

242
250
241
257

Scale 1:12,000 see cartography pages 320/321

142
152
243
259

Scale 1:12,000 see cartography pages 318/319

254
245
261
76
79
81
ET
ES
ER
EQ
EP
EN

253
262
246
EV
EW
EX
Scale 1:12,000 see cartography pages 318/319

247
263

Scale 1:12,000 see cartography pages 320/321

264

248

250
258
249
265
80
81
82
83
84
85
86
BT
BS
BQ
BP
BN

Scale 1:12,000 see cartography pages 320/321
265
257
266
250
BU
BW

168
184
251
267

Scale 1:12,000 see cartography pages 326/327

262
253
277
ER
EQ
ER
EP
EN

Scale 1:12,000 see cartography pages 320/321 & 328/329

258
266
257
281
BT
BS
BP
BN

Scale 1:12,000 see cartography pages 328/329

268
259

Scale 1:12,000 see cartography pages 322/323

270
187
186
283
CP
CN
CN

270
wimbledon common/wimbledon/copse hill/cottenham park/raynes park
Scale 1:12,000 see cartography pages 322/323
269
188
189
284

272
191
190
285
DE
DD
DF
DD
DA

271
192
193
286
DG
DH
Scale 1:12,000 see cartography pages 324/325

274
195
194
287
DT
DT
DS
DQ
96
95

273
196
197
288
DU
DV
DW
DX
DY
DZ
Scale 1:12,000 see cartography pages 324/325

southend/beckenham place park/plaistow/beckenham/bromley park/shortlands
276
199
198
289
EE
ED
EC
EB

275
290
260
Scale 1:12,000 see cartography pages 326/327

278
261
291

Scale 1:12,000 see cartography pages 326/327

91
92
95
FF
FE
FD
FC
FB
263

280
queen mary reservoir/laleham/shepperton studios/laleham park and golf course/M3/chertsey
Scale 1:12,000 see cartography pages 328/329
BG
BH
BJ
BK
BL
BM
264

266
265
96
98
100
BQ
BP
BN

282
long ditton/berrylands/surbiton/tolworth/tolworth roundabout/chessington
Scale 1:12,000 see cartography pages 330/331
268

284
269

Scale 1:12,000 see cartography pages 330/331 & 332/333

286
271
293
DH
DG
DF
DE
DD

Scale 1:12,000 see cartography pages 332/333

288
273
295
DV
DU
DT

upper elmers end/monks orchard/shirley/shirley park golf course/addington golf course
Scale 1:12,000 see cartography pages 332/333 & 334/335
287
274

290
275
101
102
104
105
EH
EG
EF
ED
EC

Scale 1:12,000 see cartography pages 334/335
289
276

291
petts wood/orpington/farnborough
277

292
nonsuch park/cheam/sutton/east ewell/belmont/banstead downs
Scale 1:12,000 see cartography pages 330/331 & 332/333
284

294
285
110
111
112
114
DG
DF
DE
DD

293
286
Scale 1:12,000 see cartography pages 332/333

295
south croydon/croham hurst woods and golf course/sanderstead/purley downs golf course
DV
DU
109
113
287

Greater London

The orange grid laid over the cartography indicates corresponding photography page reference

The cartography and the photography share the same standard grid system

The grid interval throughout the book is 500 metres

1:24,000

Scale 1:24,000
303
304
BOREHAMWOOD
ELSTREE
EDGWARE
STANMORE
RADLETT
ALDENHAM COUNTRY PARK
ALDENHAM RESERVOIR
ELSTREE OPEN SPACE
DEACONS HILL OPEN SPACE
SCRATCH WOOD
MILL HILL GOLF COURSE
MOAT MOUNT OPEN SPACE
ROYAL NATIONAL ORTHOPAEDIC HOSPITAL
ELSTREE GOLF COURSE
Green Street
Well End
Rowley Green
Ridge
Junction 4
Scratchwood Services
HA7
WD6
WD7
NW7
M1
A1
A41
A5
A411
A5183
WATLING STREET
BARNET WAY
BARNET LANE
EDGWARE WAY
ALDENHAM WATER PARK
AERODROME
Flying School
BIRCH WOOD
LITTLEPLUMPSTED WOOD

299
300
305
ENF
COCKFOSTERS
EAST BARNET
OAK HILL PARK
BRUNSWICK PARK
OAKLEIGH PARK
FRIERN BARNET
BETHUNE GOLF COURSE
NORTH MIDDLESEX GOLF COURSE
NORTH FINCHLEY
HADLEY WOOD
HADLEY WOOD GOLF COURSE
BEECH HILL LAKE
MONKEN HADLEY COMMON
NEW BARNET
WHETSTONE
TOTTERIDGE & WHETSTONE
BROOK FARM OPEN SPACE
SOUTH HERTS GOLF COURSE
N20
N12
FINCHLEY
HERTFORDSHIRE
ENFIELD
Junction 24
Ganwick Corner
COMMUNITY HOSPITAL
WROTHAM PARK
Bentley Heath
Kitt's End
MONKEN HADLEY
HADLEY
BARNET
HIGH BARNET
CHIPPING BARNET
Underhill
OLD FOLD MANOR GOLF COURSE
BRIDGEDOWN GOLF COURSE
EN5
Dancers Hill
DYRHAM PARK GOLF COURSE
DYRHAM PARK
Junction 1 A1(M)
Junction 23 (M25)
Ducks Island
WHITINGS HILL OPEN SPACE
ARKLEY
TOTTERIDGE
DARLANDS LAKE NATURE RESERVE
MILL HILL
TOTTERIDGE FIELDS NATURE RESERVE
OLD CHOLELEIAN SPORTS GROUND
OLD ELIZABETHANS (BARNET) MEMORIAL PLAYING FIELD
GREAT NORTH ROAD
ST ALBANS ROAD
COCKFOSTERS ROAD
A1000
A111
A1081
A110
A109
A5109
M25
A1(M)
Consolata Missionary College
National Inst for Medical Research
CONVENT
MILL HILL CEMETERY
INGLIS
35
36
37
38
39
DF
DE
DD
DC
DB
DA
CZ
CY
CX
CW
CV
CU

ENFIELD CHASE
Botany Bay
CREWS HILL GOLF COURSE
Crews Hills
WHITEWEBBS PARK
WHITE WEBBS GOLF COURSE
Clay Hill
Forty Hill
HILLYFIELDS PARK
EN2
CHASE FARM & ENFIELD TRUST (CHASE FARM HOSPITAL)
TRENT PARK COUNTRY PARK
TRENT PARK GOLF COURSE
Middlesex University
World's End
ENFIELD GOLF COURSE
GRANGE PARK
BUSH HILL PARK GOLF COURSE
BUSH HILL PARK
HIGHLANDS HOSPITAL
OAKWOOD
OAKWOOD PARK
N21
N14
WINCHMORE HILL
GROVELANDS PARK
GROVELANDS PRIORY HOSP
OSIDGE
SOUTHGATE
BRUNSWICK PARK
NEW SOUTHGATE CEMETERY & CREMATORIUM
PALMERS GREEN
NEW SOUTHGATE
EDMONTON CEMETERY
N13
N18
N11
BOWES PARK
NORTH MIDDLESEX HOSPITAL
299
306
Scale 1:24,000

301
307
WALTHAM ABBEY
SEWARDSTONEBURY
SEWARDSTONE
WEST ESSEX GOLF COURSE
CHINGFORD GOLF COURSE
Chingford Green
LEE VALLEY PARK
KING GEORGE'S RESERVOIR
WILLIAM GIRLING RESERVOIR
LEE VALLEY LEISURE GOLF COURSE
DEEPHAMS SEWAGE WORKS
CHINGFORD
CHINGFORD HATCH
SOUTH CHINGFORD
FRIDAY HILL
HIGHAMS PARK
WOODFORD GREEN
Freezy Water
Enfield Lock
Enfield Wash
Enfield Highway
Brimsdown
Ponders End
Bullsmoor
EN3
EN1
E4
N9
Junction 25

302
312
Scale 1:24,000
RICKMANSWORTH
BATCHWORTH
MONEYHILL
CROXLEY GREEN
HOLYWELL
HAREFIELD
SOUTH HAREFIELD
UB9
HA6
NORTHWOOD
MOOR PARK
EASTBURY
RUISLIP
RUISLIP COMMON
NEWYEARS GREEN
Hill End
PARK WOOD
COPSE WOOD
MAD BESS WOOD
BAYHURST WOOD COUNTRY PARK
BISHOP'S WOOD
HAREFIELD HOSPITAL
MOOR PARK GOLF COURSE
SANDY LODGE GOLF COURSE
NORTHWOOD GOLF COURSE
HASTE HILL GOLF COURSE
BATCHWORTH PARK GOLF COURSE
RICKMANSWORTH GOLF COURSE
GRAND UNION CANAL
BURY LAKE
BATCHWORTH LAKE
STOCKER'S LAKE
SPRINGWELL LAKE
RUISLIP LIDO
COMMON MOOR
HERTFORDSHIRE
HILLINGDON
THREE RIVERS
RECYCLING CENTRE

303
298
304
313
HILFIELD PARK RESERVOIR
STANMORE COMMON
BENTLEY PRIORY OPEN SPACE
BUSHEY HEATH
HARROW WEALD
HARROW WEALD COMMON
WEALDSTONE
HA3
Merry Hill
BUSHEY
BUSHEY GOLF AND COUNTRY CLUB GOLF COURSE
HARTSBOURNE GOLF AND COUNTRY CLUB GOLF COURSE
GRIMS DYKE GOLF COURSE
CARPENDERS PARK
HEADSTONE
NORTH HARROW
PINNER PARK
HATCH END
PINNER
Watford Heath
OXHEY
SOUTH OXHEY
OXHEY PARK
OXHEY WOOD
PINNER HILL GOLF COURSE
Pinnerwood Park
PINNER GREEN
HA5
EASTCOTE
EASTCOTE VILLAGE
WATFORD
WD1
OXHEY PARK GOLF COURSE
SOUTH OXHEY PLAYING FIELDS
PINNER NEW CEMETERY
HERTFORDSHIRE
HARROW
THREE RIVERS
UXBRIDGE ROAD
OXHEY LANE
PINNER ROAD
GEORGE V AVENUE
BROOKSHILL
COMMON ROAD
HIGH STREET
LONDON ROAD
RICKMANSWORTH ROAD
ST THOMAS' DRIVE
ELSTREE ROAD
SPARROWS HERNE
DEACONS HILL
WIGGENHALL ROAD

Scale 1:24,000
313
303
298
314
SUDBURY
NORTH WEMBLEY
WEMBLEY
WEMBLEY PARK
PRESTON
KENTON
KINGSBURY
QUEENSBURY
BELMONT
TOKYNGTON
NEASDEN
CHURCH END
BURNT OAK
FRYENT COUNTRY PARK
STANMORE GOLF COURSE
SUDBURY GOLF COURSE
NORTHWICK PARK GOLF COURSE
CANONS PARK
WEALDSTONE CEM
WEST HENDON
WELSH HARP
HA0
HA1
HA3
HA8
HA9
NW9

305
306
299
315
NORTH FINCHLEY
FINCHLEY
EAST FINCHLEY
N2
N3
N6
NW11
NW4
NW2
NW6
HAMPSTEAD
HAMPSTEAD HEATH
HAMPSTEAD GARDEN SUBURB
HAMPSTEAD HEATH EXTENSION
HAMPSTEAD GOLF CLUB
HIGHGATE GOLF COURSE
KENWOOD
PARLIAMENT HILL
SANDY HEATH
WEST HEATH
GOLDERS GREEN
GOLDERS HILL PARK
CHILDS HILL
WEST HAMPSTEAD
SOUTH HAMPSTEAD
BELSIZE PARK
PRIMROSE HILL
ROYAL FREE HOSPITAL
FREUD MUSEUM
ATHLONE HOUSE
BIG WOOD
COLDFALL WOOD
COPPETTS WOOD
ST PANCRAS AND ISLINGTON CEMETERY
EAST FINCHLEY CEMETERY
HENDON CEMETERY
HAMPSTEAD CEMETERY
FINCHLEY MEMORIAL HOSPITAL
FINCHLEY GOLF COURSE
CHURCH END
HOLDERS HILL
MILL HILL EAST
MILL HILL
HENDON
HENDON PARK
HENDON GOLF COURSE
SUNNY HILL PARK
COPTHALL STADIUM
COPTHALL SPORTS CENTRE
CLITTERHOUSE PLAYING FIELDS
BRENT CROSS
Brent Cross Shopping Centre
CRICKLEWOOD
DOLLIS HILL
GLADSTONE PARK
BRONDESBURY
BRONDESBURY PARK
WILLESDEN GREEN
UNIVERSITY COLLEGE SPORTS GROUND
Junction 1
Junction 2
M1
A1
A41
A406
A598
A1000
A504
A5
NORTH CIRCULAR ROAD
FINCHLEY ROAD
EDGWARE ROAD
GREAT NORTH WAY
HENDON WAY
WATFORD WAY
REGENTS PARK ROAD
HIGH ROAD
FALLODEN WAY
LYTTELTON ROAD
NORTH END WAY
KILBURN HIGH ROAD
CRICKLEWOOD BROADWAY
HAVERSTOCK HILL

306
305
316
300
Scale 1:24,000
HIGHGATE WOOD
QUEEN'S WOOD
HIGHGATE CEMETERY
DARTMOUTH PARK
GOSPEL OAK
NW5
KENTISH TOWN
TUFNELL PARK
UPPER HOLLOWAY
N19
CROUCH END
MUSWELL HILL
N10
N11
MUSWELL HILL GOLF COURSE
ALEXANDRA PARK
ALEXANDRA PALACE
HORNSEY
N8
WOOD GREEN
N22
BOWES PARK
N7
HOLLOWAY
LOWER HOLLOWAY
PENTONVILLE PRISON
KING'S CROSS
CALEDONIAN PARK
BARNSBURY
STROUD GREEN
N4
HARRINGAY
NOEL PARK
FINSBURY PARK
HIGHBURY
N5
CLISSOLD PARK
STOKE NEWINGTON
ABNEY PARK CEMETERY
N16
STAMFORD HILL
N15
WEST GREEN
LORDSHIP RECREATION GROUND
TOTTENHAM
TOTTENHAM CEMETERY
SOUTH TOTTENHAM
DALSTON
KINGSLAND HIGH ST
STOKE NEWINGTON ROAD
STOKE NEWINGTON HIGH ST
GREAT CAMBRIDGE ROAD
HIGH ROAD
SEVEN SISTERS ROAD

307
308
301
317
SOUTH WOODFORD
E18
SNARESBROOK
EPPING FOREST
E11
LEYTONSTONE
WEST HAM
HIGHAMS PARK
HALE END
UPPER WALTHAMSTOW
WALTHAMSTOW
E17
LEYTON
E10
STRATFORD
E15
HACKNEY WICK
HACKNEY MARSH
HOMERTON
CLAPTON PARK
LOWER CLAPTON
UPPER CLAPTON
E5
LEA BRIDGE
HACKNEY
E9
SOUTH HACKNEY
CHINGFORD
HIGHAM HILL
BANBURY RESERVOIR
LOCKWOOD RESERVOIR
HIGH MAYNARD RESERVOIR
LOW MAYNARD RESERVOIR
WARWICK RESERVOIR (EAST)
WARWICK RESERVOIR (WEST)
WALTHAMSTOW MARSHES
TOTTENHAM HALE
N17
EDMONTON
LLOYD PARK
MARKHOUSE ROAD
CHINGFORD ROAD
FOREST ROAD
HIGH ROAD LEYTON
LEA BRIDGE ROAD
WHIPPS CROSS
SPRINGFIELD PARK
LONDON FIELDS
VICTORIA PARK

308
307
318
Scale 1:24,000
WEST HAM
WEST HAM PARK
FOREST GATE
UPTON
WANSTEAD FLATS
ALDERSBROOK
MANOR PARK CEMETERY
MANOR PARK
CITY OF LONDON CEMETERY
WANSTEAD PARK
WANSTEAD GOLF COURSE
WANSTEAD
HERONRY POND
SHOULDER OF MUTTON POND
WOODFORD
WOODFORD BRIDGE
RODING VALLEY PARK
CLAYHALL
CLAYHALL PARK
REDBRIDGE
CRANBROOK
GANTS HILL
VALENTINES PARK
BARKINGSIDE
FULLWELL CROSS
GRANGE HILL
CLAYBURY HOSPITAL (Closed)
HAINAULT
FAIRLOP WATERS GOLF COURSE
ALDBOROUGH
NEWBURY PARK
KING GEORGE HOSP
SEVEN KINGS
ILFORD
LITTLE ILFORD
PLASHET PARK
PLASHET CEMETERY
WOODGRANGE PARK CEM
LOXFORD PARK
BARKING PARK
BARKING HOSPITAL
SOUTH PARK
E7
E12
E18
IG1
IG2
IG3
IG4
IG5
IG6

309
310
319
RISEBRIDGE GOLF COURSE
BEDFORDS PARK
CHASE CROSS
RISE PARK
RAPHAEL PARK
VICTORIA HOSP
ROMFORD
RM1
RM5
RM6
RM7
RM8
RM9
RM10
HAVERING PARK
COLLIER ROW
LAWNS REC GRD
KING GEORGE'S PLAYING FIELDS
COTTONS PARK
OLDCHURCH HOSPITAL
OLDCHURCH PARK
ROMFORD CEMETERY
RUSH GREEN
RUSH GREEN HOSPITAL (Closed)
Barking College of Technology
EASTBROOKEND COUNTRY PARK
SPORTS GROUNDS
BRITTONS PLAYING FIELDS
SOUTH HORNCHURCH
CENTRAL PARK
DAGENHAM CIVIC CENTRE
BEACONTREE HEATH
WESTLANDS PLAYING FIELDS
TRAINING GROUND
DAGENHAM
OLD DAGENHAM PARK
PARSLOES PARK
VALENCE PARK
BEACONTREE
CHADWELL HEATH
MARKS GATE CEM
Mark's Gate
WHALEBONE LANE NORTH
WHALEBONE LANE SOUTH
EASTERN AVENUE
HEATHWAY
RAINHAM ROAD NORTH
RAINHAM ROAD SOUTH
GREEN LANE
WOOD LANE
LONGBRIDGE ROAD
HAINAULT ROAD
Redbridge College
KING GEORGE HOSPITAL
GOODMAYES
GOODMAYES PARK
MAYESBROOK PARK SPORTS GROUND
BOATING LAKE
ALLOTMENTS
CASTLE GREEN
HAVERING
REDBRIDGE
EZ
EY
EX
EW
FA
FB
FC
FD
FE
226/7
236/7
A12
A118
A124
A125
A1112
A1240
A1153

310
309
319
Scale 1:24,000
PARSLOES PARK
BEACONTREE
BEACONTREE HEATH
DAGENHAM
CENTRAL PARK
EASTBROOKEND COUNTRY PARK
RUSH GREEN
ROMFORD
COLLIER ROW
HAVERING PARK
CHASE CROSS
GIDEA PARK
RISEBRIDGE GOLF COURSE
ROMFORD GOLF COURSE
BEDFORDS PARK
Ardleigh Green
HARROW LODGE PARK
ELM PARK
HORNCHURCH
SOUTH HORNCHURCH
HORNCHURCH COUNTRY PARK
RM1
RM2
RM5
RM6
RM7
RM9
RM10
RM12

51
52
53
54
55
56
58
59
60
61
62
63
64
65
66
FX
FW
FV
FU
FT
FS
FR
FQ
FP
FN
FM
FL
Great Warley
Junction 29
M25
CM13
RM14
RM11
RM3
CRANHAM
UPMINSTER
North Ockendon
Corbets Tey
Hacton
EMERSON PARK
HAROLD WOOD
HAROLD PARK
HAROLD HILL
TYLERS COMMON
UPMINSTER GOLF COURSE
PARKLANDS OPEN SPACE
SAND & GRAVEL PIT
REFUSE TRANSFER STATION
WARLEY HOSPITAL
HAROLD WOOD HOSPITAL
HOLDEN'S WOOD
BARRACK WOOD
WARLEY PARK GOLF COURSE
TOP MEADOW GOLF COURSE
COYS LAKE
RUSSELL'S LAKE
FOXBURROW WOOD
CRANHAM PLAYING FIELDS
FRANKS WOOD
UPMINSTER HALL PLAYING FIELDS
CLAY TYE WOOD
ESSEX
THURROCK
HAVERING
BRENTWOOD
SOUTHEND ARTERIAL ROAD
A127
WARLEY STREET
CLAY TYE ROAD
OCKENDON ROAD
ST. MARY'S LANE
HALL LANE

312
302
320
Scale 1:24,000
UB9
UB8
UB10
UB11
HA4
UXBRIDGE
UXBRIDGE MOOR
HILLINGDON
NORTH HILLINGDON
ICKENHAM
YIEWSLEY
COWLEY
DENHAM
RUISLIP
RUISLIP GARDENS
HAYES
HAYES TOWN
HAYES END
NEWYEARS GREEN
BUCKINGHAMSHIRE
GRAND UNION CANAL
M25
M40
A40
A437
A408
Junction 1
WESTERN AVENUE
LONG LANE
STOCKLEY PARK GOLF COURSE
HILLINGDON GOLF COURSE
RUISLIP PUBLIC GOLF COURSE
DENHAM GOLF COURSE
HAREFIELD PLACE GOLF COURSE
DENHAM COUNTRY PARK
HUNTSMOOR PARK
HILLINGDON AND UXBRIDGE CEMETERY
UNIVERSITY PLAYING FIELDS
HILLINGDON HOUSE FARM SPORTS GROUND
HILLINGDON COURT PARK
NORTHOLT AE

313
304
314
303
321
HARROW ON THE HILL
HA1
HARROW SCHOOL
HARROW
WEST HARROW
SOUTH HARROW
ROXETH
RAYNERS LANE
HA2
NORTHOLT
UB5
UB6
GREENFORD
UB1
W7
HANWELL
SOUTHALL
DORMER'S WELLS
BROOKSIDE
YEADING
SOUTH RUISLIP
RUISLIP MANOR
EASTCOTE
UB4
SPORTS GROUND
GREAT BRAMSTONES
BERKELEY FIELDS
PERIVALE PARK GOLF COURSE
BRENT VALLEY PARK
BRENT VALLEY GOLF COURSE
WEST MIDDLESEX GOLF COURSE
GREENFORD PARK CEMETERY
RECTORY PARK
LONDON GOLF CENTRE
LIME TREE PARK
WEST LONDON SHOOTING GROUNDS
GRAND UNION CANAL
HAYES BYPASS
WESTERN AVENUE
ALEXANDRA AVENUE
UXBRIDGE ROAD

304
313
321
322
PERIVALE
ALPERTON
STONEBRIDGE
HARLESDEN
PARK ROYAL
EALING GOLF COURSE
NORTH ACTON
OLD OAK COMMON
W5
W3
W13
EALING
WEST ACTON
EAST ACTON
ACTON
HANWELL
SOUTH ACTON
BEDFORD PARK
LITTLE EALING
GUNNERSBURY PARK
GUNNERSBURY
W4
TW8
BRENTFORD
CHISWICK
KEW
ROYAL BOTANIC GARDENS
SYON PARK
GROVE PARK
TW9
NORTH SHEEN
MORTLAKE
OLD DEER
ROYAL MID-SURREY GOLF COURSE
RIVER THAMES
Scale 1:24,000

315
316
305
323
REGENT'S PARK
PRIMROSE HILL
HYDE PARK
THE SERPENTINE
THE LONG WATER
KENSINGTON GARDENS
ROUND POND
KENSINGTON PALACE
HOLLAND PARK
HOLLAND HOUSE
BATTERSEA PARK
MARYLEBONE
PADDINGTON
BAYSWATER
NOTTING HILL
KENSINGTON
SOUTH KENSINGTON
BROMPTON
CHELSEA
EARLS COURT
WEST BROMPTON
WALHAM GREEN
PARSONS GREEN
SANDS END
FULHAM
HAMMERSMITH
SHEPHERD'S BUSH
NORTH KENSINGTON
WESTBOURNE GREEN
MAIDA VALE
MAIDA HILL
KILBURN
WEST KILBURN
ST. JOHN'S WOOD
KENSAL RISE
KENSAL GREEN
KENSAL TOWN
QUEEN'S PARK
WILLESDEN GREEN
WORMWOOD SCRUBS
CASTELNAU
BARNES
BARN ELMS WILDFOWL RESERVE
NW8
NW6
NW10
W2
W9
W10
W11
W8
W14
W6
W12
SW1
SW3
SW5
SW6
SW7
SW10
SW11
SW13
WESTWAY
WEST CROSS ROUTE
HAMMERSMITH & FULHAM
RICHMOND UPON THAMES

316
306
315
324
Scale 1:24,000
REGENT'S PARK
CAMDEN TOWN
KING'S CROSS
ISLINGTON
HOXTON
PENTONVILLE
FINSBURY
CLERKENWELL
ST. PANCRAS
BLOOMSBURY
FITZROVIA
HOLBORN
SOHO
MAYFAIR
STRAND
GREEN PARK
ST. JAMES'S PARK
WESTMINSTER
BELGRAVIA
PIMLICO
SOUTHWARK
THE BOROUGH
NEWINGTON
LAMBETH
WALWORTH
KENNINGTON
VAUXHALL
NINE ELMS
SOUTH LAMBETH
CAMBERWELL
BATTERSEA
RIVER THAMES

317
318
307
325
PLAISTOW
RIVER
MILLENNIUM EXPERIENCE
BLACKWALL TUNNEL APPROACH
GREENWICH PARK
BLACKHEATH
ISLE OF DOGS
MILLWALL
POPLAR
CUBITT TOWN
MUDCHUTE PARK
WEST INDIA DOCKS
CANARY WHARF
BROMLEY
BOW
OLD FORD
VICTORIA PARK
MILE END
LIMEHOUSE
STEPNEY
SHADWELL
WAPPING
ROTHERHITHE
SOUTHWARK PARK
DEPTFORD
NEW CROSS
NEW CROSS GATE
SOUTH HACKNEY
BETHNAL GREEN
GREENWICH
LIMEHOUSE REACH
TOWER HAMLETS CEMETERY PARK
SE10
SE8
SE14
SE15
SE16
E1
E2
E3
E14

WEST HAM
UPTON
UPTON PARK
E13
EAST HAM CENTRAL PARK
EAST HAM JEWISH CEMETERY
E6
BARKING
IG11
NORTH BECKTON
BECKTON
CUSTOM HOUSE
CANNING TOWN
E16
ROYAL VICTORIA DOCK
ROYAL ALBERT DOCK
LONDON CITY AIRPORT
KING GEORGE V DOCK
CYPRUS
ALBERT BASIN
SILVERTOWN
NORTH WOOLWICH
THAMES
WOOLWICH REACH
THAMES FLOOD BARRIER
GALLIONS REACH
SE28
HM PRISON BELMARSH
THAMESMEAD WEST
NEW CHARLTON
MARYON PARK
MARYON WILSON PARK
CHARLTON
SE7
CHARLTON PARK
WOOLWICH
WOOLWICH COMMON
QUEEN ELIZABETH HOSPITAL
SE18
PLUMSTEAD
PLUMSTEAD COMMON
WINN'S COMMON
SHREWSBURY PARK
SHOOTER'S HILL
SHOOTER'S HILL GOLF COURSE
ELTHAM COMMON
OXLEAS WOOD
CASTLE WOOD
JACK WOOD
KIDBROOKE
SE3
GREENWICH CEMETERY
HILLVIEW CEMETERY
Scale 1:24,000
317
308
326

SOUTH HORNCHURCH
HORNCHURCH MARSHES
FORD MOTOR WORKS
RM9
CASTLE GREEN
RIVER THAMES
ERITH REACH
ERITH
DA8
NORTHUMBERLAND HEATH
BARNEHURST
DA7
BELVEDERE
LESSNESS HEATH
DA17
ERITH MARSHES
DA18
CROSSNESS SEWAGE TREATMENT WORKS
CROSSNESS LIGHTHOUSE
THAMESMEAD NORTH
THAMESMEAD
ABBEY WOOD
LESNES ABBEY WOOD
WEST HEATH
SE2
BOSTALL HEATH
BOSTALL WOODS
PLUMSTEAD CEMETERY
EAST WICKHAM
71
72
73
74
75
76
77
78
309
327

HEATHROW AIRPORT
(LONDON)
TW6
HARMONDSWORTH
SIPSON
HARLINGTON
LONGFORD
WEST DRAYTON
UB7
UB3
UB11
YIEWSLEY
HAYES TOWN
THORNEY
STANWELL MOOR
STANWELL
TW19
KING GEORGE VI RESERVOIR
STAINES RESERVOIRS
PERRY OAKS SEWAGE TREATMENT WORKS
EAST BEDFONT
LOWER FELTHAM
STAINES
Junction 15(M25)
Junction 4b(M4)
Junction 4
Junction 4a
CARGO TERMINAL
TERMINAL 1
TERMINAL 2
TERMINAL 3
TERMINAL 4
HEATHROW TERMINALS 1,2&3
HEATHROW TERMINAL 4
H.M. YOUNG OFFENDER INSTITUTION AND REMAND CENTRE
IMPERIAL COLLEGE SPORTS GROUND
LITTLE HARLINGTON FIELD
HOLIDAY INN GOLF COURSE
CHERRY LANE CEMETERY
GOVERNMENT BUILDINGS
BATH ROAD
STANWELL MOOR RD
STAINES ROAD
GREAT SOUTH WEST ROAD
STOCKLEY ROAD
HOLLOWAY LANE
HATCH LANE
SURREY
HILLINGDON
SPELTHORNE
HOUNSLOW
BERKSHIRE
SOUTH BUCKS
Scale 1:24,000
312
328
256/7
264/5

321
314
322
313
329
HANWELL
OSTERLEY PARK
OSTERLEY
WYKE GREEN GOLF COURSE
SPRING GROVE
WOODLANDS
ISLEWORTH
MOGDEN WATER TREATMENT WORKS
TW7
TW3
TW2
TW4
TW5
TW13
STRAWBERRY HILL
WHITTON
LAMPTON
HOUNSLOW
HOUNSLOW HEATH
HOUNSLOW WEST
HESTON
NORWOOD GREEN
NORTH HYDE
UB2
FULWELL GOLF COURSE
TWICKENHAM GOLF COURSE
HOUNSLOW HEATH GOLF COURSE
AIRLINKS GOLF COURSE
Heston Services
Junction 3
CRANFORD
FELTHAM
HANWORTH PARK
M4
GREAT WEST ROAD
WELLINGTON ROAD N
STAINES ROAD
HARLINGTON ROAD WEST
THE PARKWAY
MERRICK ROAD

Scale 1:24,000
329
321
330
314
HAMPTON COURT
PARK
HAMPTON WICK
TEDDINGTON
TW11
TWICKENHAM
TW1
MARBLE HILL PARK
ST MARGARETS
OLD DEER PARK
ROYAL MID-SURREY GOLF COURSE
RICHMOND
HAM
PETERSHAM
SUDBROOK PARK
HAM COMMON
KINGSTON UPON THAMES
KT1
KT2
NORBITON
KINGSTON HOSPITAL
COOMBE WOOD GOLF COURSE
COOMBE
COOMBE HILL GOLF COURSE
KINGSTON VALE
NEW MALDEN
KT3
MALDEN GOLF COURSE
RICHMOND PARK
TW10
ISABELLA PLANTATION
SIDMOUTH WOOD
PEN PONDS
DEER PARK
RICHMOND CEMETERY
EAST SHEEN COMMON
EAST SHEEN
SW14
MORTLAKE
NORTH SHEEN
PUTNEY VALE
ROEHAMPTON GOLF COURSE
RICHMOND PARK (PUBLIC) GOLF COURSE
THAMES

323
324
315
331
WANDSWORTH COMMON
BALHAM
UPPER TOOTING
TOOTING GRAVENEY
SW17
COLLIER'S WOOD
CARSHALTON
SW18
EARLSFIELD
SUMMERSTOWN
LAMBETH CEMETERY
WIMBLEDON CEMETERY
SOUTHFIELDS
WANDSWORTH
SOUTH WIMBLEDON
MERTON
MERTON PARK
MORDEN
MORDEN HALL PARK
WIMBLEDON PARK
ALL ENGLAND LAWN TENNIS & CROQUET CLUB
WIMBLEDON
SW19
PUTNEY
SW15
PUTNEY HEATH
ROEHAMPTON
WIMBLEDON COMMON
COPSE HILL
COTTENHAM PARK
SW20
RAYNES PARK
WEST BARNES
BUSHEY MEAD
BARNES
HURLINGHAM PARK
RIVER WANDLE
ROYAL WIMBLEDON GOLF COURSE
PUTNEY VALE CEMETERY
KINGSTON BY-PASS

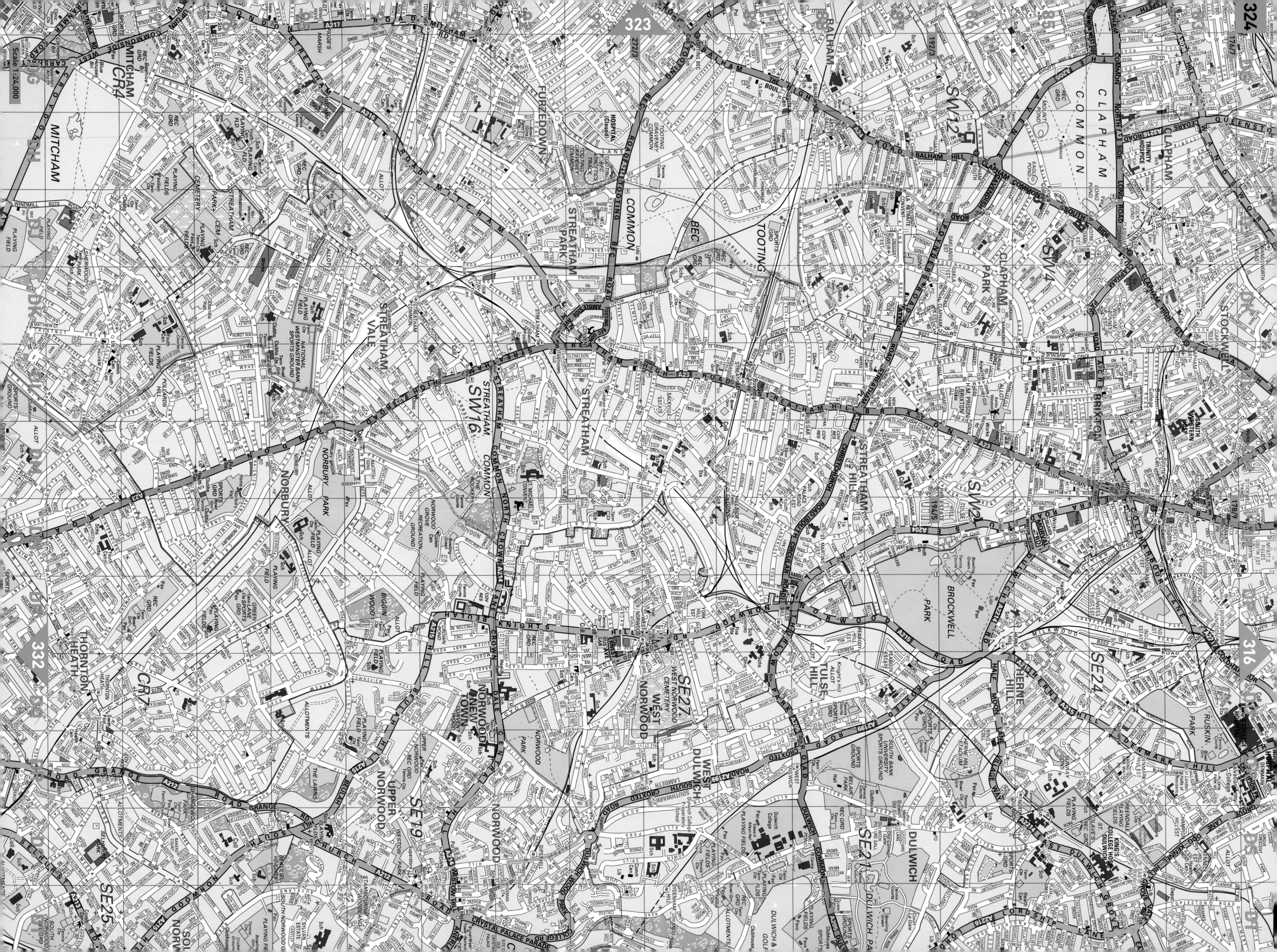
323
332
316
Scale 1:24,000
MITCHAM
CR4
FURZEDOWN
TOOTING BEC COMMON
BALHAM
SW12
CLAPHAM COMMON
CLAPHAM
CLAPHAM PARK
SW4
STOCKWELL
STREATHAM PARK
STREATHAM VALE
STREATHAM
STREATHAM COMMON
SW16
STREATHAM HILL
BRIXTON
SW2
NORBURY
NORBURY PARK
BROCKWELL PARK
HERNE HILL
SE24
RUSKIN PARK
TULSE HILL
WEST NORWOOD
SE27
NORWOOD NEW TOWN
UPPER NORWOOD
SE19
THORNTON HEATH
CR7
SE25
WEST DULWICH
DULWICH
SE21
DULWICH PARK
STREATHAM HIGH ROAD
BALHAM HIGH ROAD
LONDON ROAD
CROYDON ROAD
GRANGE ROAD
NORWOOD ROAD
DENMARK HILL
CRYSTAL PALACE PARADE
A23
A24
A215
A205
A214
A212
A204

325
326
317
333
BLACKHEATH
LEE
HITHER GREEN
GROVE PARK
DOWNHAM
PLAISTOW
BROMLEY
SHORTLANDS
BROMLEY PARK
LEWISHAM
SE13
LADYWELL
CATFORD
SE6
SOUTHEND
BELLINGHAM
BECKENHAM PLACE PARK
BECKENHAM
BR3
EDEN PARK
HILLY FIELDS
SE4
BROCKLEY
HONOR OAK PARK
BELL GREEN
NEW BECKENHAM
CATOR PARK
ELMERS END
SE23
FOREST HILL
LOWER SYDENHAM
HONOR OAK
NUNHEAD
SE22
SE26
SYDENHAM
PENGE
SE20
ANERLEY
CRYSTAL PALACE PARK
SOUTH NORWOOD COUNTRY PARK
BECKENHAM CEMETERY
NUNHEAD CEMETERY
PECKHAM RYE PARK
PECKHAM RYE COMMON
CAMBERWELL NEW CEMETERY
CAMBERWELL OLD CEMETERY
BROCKLEY CEMETERY
LADYWELL CEMETERY

Scale 1:24,000
325
334
318
WIDMORE
BICKLEY
SUNDRIDGE
BR1
SUNDRIDGE PARK GOLF COURSE
ELMSTEAD
ELMSTEAD WOOD
GROVE PARK
SE12
MOTTINGHAM
ELTHAM
ELTHAM PALACE
SE9
BLACKHEATH PARK
KIDBROOKE
SUTCLIFFE PARK
CHISLEHURST
CHISLEHURST WEST
CAMDEN PARK CHISLEHURST GOLF COURSE
CHISLEHURST COMMON
BR7
NEW ELTHAM
ROYAL BLACKHEATH GOLF COURSE
AVERY HILL
AVERY HILL PARK
ELTHAM PARK SOUTH
ELTHAM PARK NORTH
OXLEAS MEADOW
OXLEAS WOOD
FALCONWOOD
DA16
DA15
BLACKFEN
LONGLANDS
PETTS WOOD
BR5
HAWKWOOD ESTATE NT
ST PAUL'S CRAY COMMON
PARK WOOD
SIDCUP BY-PASS
WELL HALL ROAD (SOUTH CIRCULAR)
ROCHESTER WAY RELIEF ROAD
BURNT ASH HILL
BARING ROAD
MOTTINGHAM LANE
SIDCUP ROAD
COURT ROAD
WHITE HORSE HILL
BROMLEY LANE
FOOTSCRAY ROAD
ORPINGTON ROAD
WIDMORE ROAD
BICKLEY PARK ROAD
ELTHAM HIGH ST
SHEPHERDLEAS WOOD

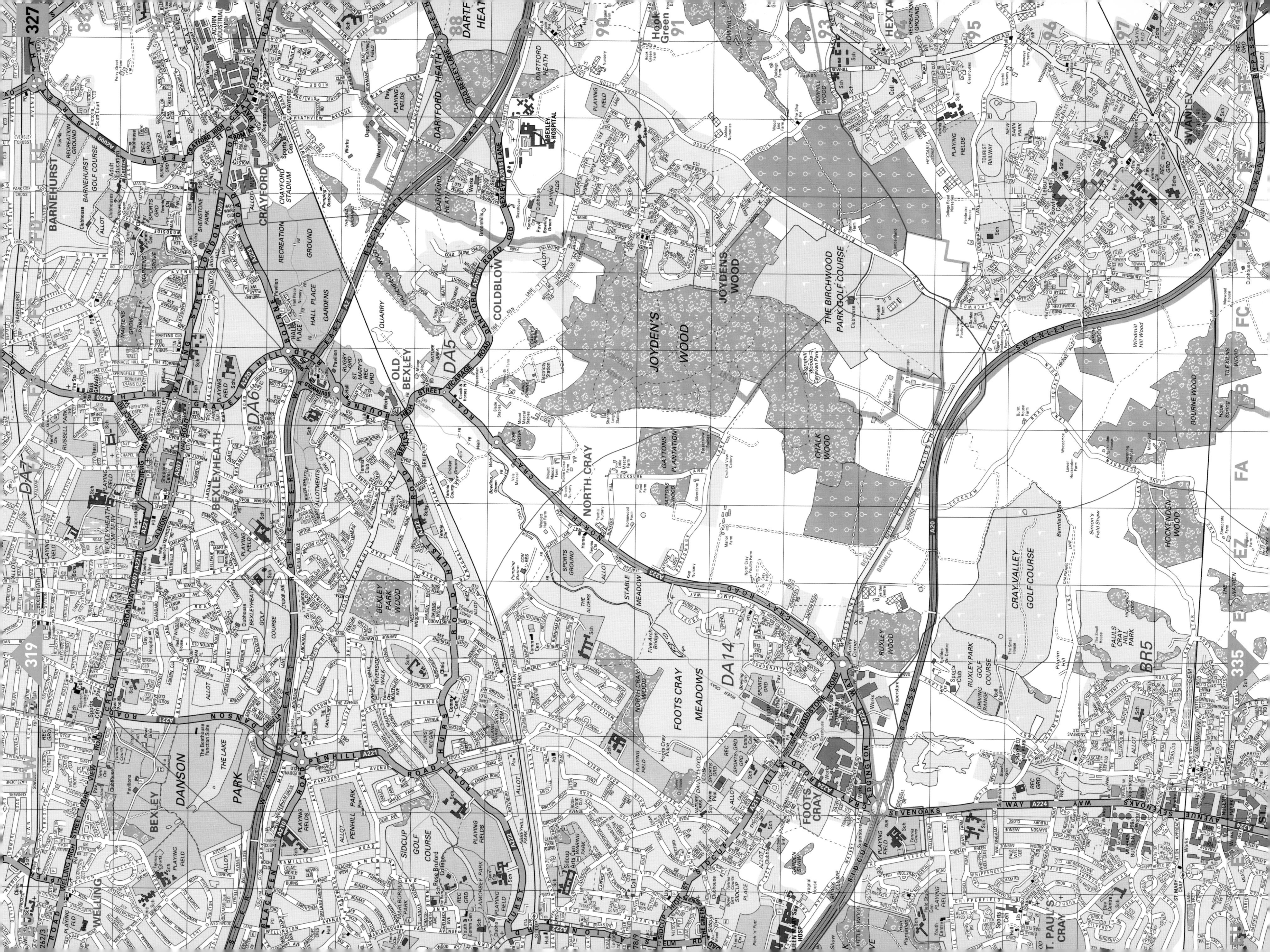
CRAYFORD
BARNEHURST
BEXLEYHEATH
OLD BEXLEY
COLDBLOW
NORTH CRAY
JOYDEN'S WOOD
JOYDENS WOOD
CHALK WOOD
GATTONS PLANTATION
THE BIRCHWOOD PARK GOLF COURSE
DARTFORD HEATH
BEXLEY HOSPITAL
SWANLEY
HEXTABLE
BOURNE WOOD
HOCKENDEN WOOD
CRAY VALLEY GOLF COURSE
RUXLEY PARK GOLF COURSE
RUXLEY WOOD
PAULS CRAY HILL PARK
ST. PAUL'S CRAY
FOOTS CRAY
FOOTS CRAY MEADOWS
NORTH CRAY WOOD
STABLE MEADOW
THE ALDERS
SIDCUP GOLF COURSE
SIDCUP
DANSON PARK
THE LAKE
BEXLEY
WELLING
BEXLEY PARK WOOD
BEXLEYHEATH GOLF COURSE
HALL PLACE GARDENS
RECREATION GROUND
CRAYFORD STADIUM
BARNEHURST GOLF COURSE
MARTENS GROVE PARK
SHENSTONE PARK
PENHILL PARK
LAMORBEY PARK
QUEEN MARY'S HOSP
GARDEN SHAW
DA5
DA6
DA7
DA14
BR5
EW
EX
EY
EZ
FA
FB
FC
FD
FE
88
90
91
93
94
95
96
97
Hook Green
319
335
262/3
78/9
A2
A20
A220
A221
A222
A223
A224
A207
A2018
A2000
SEVENOAKS WAY
ROCHESTER WAY
MAIDSTONE ROAD
NORTH CRAY ROAD
SWANLEY BY-PASS
BEXLEY LANE
DARTFORD ROAD
WATLING STREET
BROADWAY

STAINES
FELTHAM
ASHFORD
ASHFORD MANOR GOLF COURSE
TW15
TW18
TW17
QUEEN MARY RESERVOIR
LALEHAM
LALEHAM GOLF COURSE
LALEHAM PARK
LITTLETON
UPPER HALLIFORD
SUNBURY GOLF COURSE
SHEPPERTON
DESBOROUGH ISLAND
THAMES MEADOW
CHERTSEY
CHERTSEY MEADS
ADDLESTONE MOOR
ADDLESTONE
WOBURN PARK
WEYBRIDGE
OATLANDS PARK
ASHFORD COMMON WATER TREATMENT WORKS
LAKESIDE SPORTS GRD
PENTON HOOK ISLAND
Junction 1
M3
A308
A244
A317
A3050
320
Scale 1:24,000

329
322
330
321
BUSHY PARK
HAMPTON COURT PARK
THAMES DITTON
WESTON GREEN
HINCHLEY WOOD
STRAWBERRY HILL
HAMPTON HILL
EAST MOLESEY
KT7
KT8
KT10
KT12
TW12
TW13
TW16
LITTLEWORTH COMMON
FULWELL GOLF COURSE
HAMPTON
ISLAND BARN RESERVOIR
SANDOWN PARK GOLF COURSE
RACECOURSE
ESHER
LOWER GREEN
MOORE PLACE PUBLIC GOLF COURSE
CLARE HILL GOLF COURSE
WEST MOLESEY
MOLESEY RESERVOIRS
STAIN HILL RESERVOIRS
BESSBOROUGH RESERVOIR
KNIGHTS RESERVOIR
QUEEN ELIZABETH II RESERVOIR
HANWORTH
KEMPTON PARK RACECOURSE
SUNBURY
RYDENS
HERSHAM
WEST END
RIVER THAMES
RIVER MOLE
RIVER EMBER
WATER TREATMENT WORKS
GRAVEL PIT
CORONATION PLAYING FIELDS
MINISTRY OF DEFENCE
NATIONAL PHYSICAL LABORATORY
HERSHAM TRADING ESTATE
RICHMOND UPON THAMES
HOUNSLOW
HAMPTON COURT WAY
UXBRIDGE ROAD
HURST ROAD
UPPER SUNBURY ROAD
STAINES ROAD EAST
HERSHAM ROAD
PORTSMOUTH ROAD
KINGSTON BYPASS
ESHER BYPASS
95
96
97
98
103
105
106
BX
BY
BW
CA
CB
CC
CD

322
329
HOME PARK GOLF COURSE
BERRYLANDS
KT5
SURBITON
KT6
LONG DITTON
TOLWORTH
OLD MALDEN
WORCESTER PARK
SURBITON GOLF COURSE
CHESSINGTON
KT9
CHESSINGTON WORLD OF ADVENTURE
HORTON COUNTRY PARK
HORTON PARK COUNTRY CLUB GOLF COURSE
HORTON
KT19
ST. EBBA'S HOSPITAL
WEST EWELL
MALDEN RUSHETT
WEST PARK HOSPITAL
THE MANOR HOSPITAL (closed)
HORTON HOSPITAL
EPSOM COMMON
THE FOREST
EPSOM
PRINCE'S COVERTS
Scale 1:24,000

331
332
323
292/3
284/5
107
108
109
110
111
112
113
DC
DB
DA
CZ
CY
CX
CW
CV
CARSHALTON
CARSHALTON BEECHES
THE WRYTHE
ST. HELIER
ROSEHILL
BENHILTON
SUTTON
BELMONT
LITTLE WOODCOTE
THE OAKS PARK
OAKS SPORTS CENTRE GOLF COURSE
BANSTEAD DOWNS
CUDDINGTON GOLF COURSE
NORTH CHEAM
CHEAM
EAST EWELL
NORTH LOOE
NONSUCH PARK
MORDEN PARK
MORDEN CEMETERY
STONELEIGH
WEST BARNES
MOTSPUR PARK
EWELL
EPSOM DOWNS
SM1
SM2
SM3
SM4
KT4
KT17
ROSEHILL RECREATION GROUND
COLLINGWOOD PARK
OVERTON PARK
CHEAM PARK
CHEAM RECREATION GROUND
KING GEORGE'S FIELD
MORDEN PARK SPORTS GROUND
MORDEN PLAYING FIELDS
RAYNES PARK PLAYING FIELDS
DOWNVIEW PRISON
HIGHDOWN PRISON
SUTTON HOSPITAL
THE ROYAL MARSDEN HOSPITAL
ST. HELIER HOSPITAL
QUEEN MARY'S HOSPITAL FOR CHILDREN
CARSHALTON SPORTS ARENA
ST. HELIER OPEN SPACE
ROSEHILL PARK EAST
PERRETS FIELD
SUTTON CEMETERY
NONSUCH MANSION HOUSE
CUDDINGTON RECREATION GROUND
MERTON & SUTTON JOINT CEMETERY
THE SIR JOSEPH HOOD MEMORIAL PLAYING FIELDS
UNIVERSITY OF LONDON ATHLETICS GROUND
ST. DUNSTAN'S HILL
BRIGHTON ROAD
REIGATE AVENUE
EPSOM ROAD
LONDON ROAD
MALDEN ROAD
CHEAM COMMON ROAD
CENTRAL ROAD
EWELL ROAD
CHEAM ROAD
WOODMANSTERNE ROAD
CROYDON ROAD
BANSTEAD ROAD
SUTTON COMMON ROAD
A24
A217
A232
A240
A2022
A297
A2043
B278
B2218
B2230

Scale 1:24,000
331
324
SM5
SM6
CR5
CR8
LITTLE WOODCOTE
CARSHALTON ON THE HILL
WOODCOTE PARK GOLF COURSE
WOODCOTE
WALLINGTON
SOUTH BEDDINGTON
BEDDINGTON
BEDDINGTON CORNER
BEDDINGTON PARK
HACKBRIDGE
MITCHAM
MITCHAM (PUBLIC) GOLF COURSE
COMMON
ROUNDSHAW OPEN SPACE
PURLEY
PURLEY WAY PLAYING FIELDS
DUPPAS HILL
WADDON
WANDLE PARK
BROAD GREEN
CROYDON CEMETERY
QUEEN'S ROAD CEMETERY
THORNTON HEATH
CROYDON
SOUTH CROYDON
SELHURST
PURLEY DOWNS GOLF COURSE
RIDDLESDOWN
FOXLEY WOOD
CROHAM HURST
SANDERSTEAD
PURLEY WAY
BRIGHTON ROAD
LONDON ROAD
MAYDAY HOSPITAL

333
334
325
106
107
108
109
110
111
112
113
114
EF
EE
ED
EC
EB
EA
DZ
DY
DX
DW
DU
PARK LANGLEY
LANGLEY PARK GOLF COURSE
WEST WICKHAM
SPRING PARK
BR4
EDEN PARK
UPPER ELMERS END
MONKS ORCHARD
BETHLEM ROYAL HOSPITAL
NEW ADDINGTON
ROWDOWN FIELDS
ADDINGTON COURT (PUBLIC) GOLF COURSES
FORESTDALE
ADDINGTON
ADDINGTON GOLF COURSE
ADDINGTON PALACE GOLF COURSE
ADDINGTON PARK
FARLEIGH COURT GOLF COURSE
FARLEIGH
SELSDON WOOD NT
SELSDON
SELSDON PARK HOTEL GOLF COURSE
KINGS WOOD
SHIRLEY
SHIRLEY PARK GOLF COURSE
CR0
CR2
ADDINGTON HILLS
LITTLEHEATH WOODS
LLOYD PARK
ASHBURTON PLAYING FIELDS
SHIRLEY OAKS HOSPITAL
ALLOTMENTS
NORWOOD COUNTRY PARK
WOODSIDE
BROMLEY
SURREY
TANDRIDGE

326
333
HAYES
BR2
BR5
BR6
HAYES COMMON
CROYDON ROAD
OAKLEY ROAD
WESTERHAM ROAD
LEAVES GREEN ROAD
MAIN ROAD
FARNBOROUGH ROAD
FARNBOROUGH COMMON
CROFTON ROAD
HASTINGS ROAD
SOUTHBOROUGH
BROMLEY COMMON
BROMLEY PUBLIC GOLF COURSE
NORMAN PARK RECREATION GROUND
Bromley College of Technology
PETTS WOOD
FARNBOROUGH
FARNBOROUGH HOSPITAL
GREEN STREET GREEN
HIGH ELMS GOLF COURSE
DOWNE
WEST KENT GOLF COURSE
BIGGIN HILL CIVIL AIRPORT
KESTON COMMON
SOUTH PARK
JUBILEE COUNTRY PARK
CROFTON HEATH
SPARROW WOOD
CUCKOO WOOD
HAYES GROVE PRIORY HOSPITAL
Scale 1:24,000

CROCKENHILL
LULLINGSTONE PARK GOLF COURSE
SWANLEY
BR8
BR6
Well Hill
Maypole
BADGERS MOUNT
HALSTEAD
Knockholt Pound
PRATT'S BOTTOM
CHELSFIELD
CHELSFIELD PARK HOSPITAL
CHELSFIELD DOWN GOLF COURSE
BROKE HILL GOLF COURSE
GODDINGTON
GODDINGTON PARK
RAMSDEN
DERRY DOWNS
ST. MARY CRAY
SHOREHAM
DARENT VALLEY
PILOTS WOOD
MEENFIELD WOOD
ANDREW'S WOOD
WEST WOOD
CROWN WOOD
GRIFF'S WOOD
KYNASTON WOOD
TILE KILNS WOOD
BOURNE WOOD
Junction 4
M25
A224
A21
A20
A232
ORPINGTON BYPASS
KENT
BROMLEY
SEVENOAKS
327

Index

The index reads in this sequence: street name/postal district or post town/photography page number/cartography page number/grid reference.

The index also contains some roads for which there is insufficient space to name within the cartography. These are printed in light type.

General abbreviations used within the cartography and index

All	Alley
Allot	Allotments
Amb	Ambulance
App	Approach
Arc	Arcade
Ave	Avenue
Bdy	Broadway
Bldgs	Buildings
Boul	Boulevard
Bowl	Bowling
Bri	Bridge
Bus	Business
C of E	Church of England
Cath	Cathedral
Cem	Cemetery
Cen	Central, Centre
Cft	Croft
Cfts	Crofts
Ch	Church
Chyd	Churchyard
Cin	Cinema
Circ	Circus
Clo	Close
Co	County
Coll	College
Comm	Community
Conv	Convent
Cor	Corner
Cors	Corners
Coron	Coroners
Cotts	Cottages
Cov	Covered
Crem	Crematorium
Cres	Crescent
Ct	Court
Ctyd	Courtyard
Dep	Depot
Dr	Drive
Dws	Dwellings
E	East
Ed	Education
Elec	Electricity
Emb	Embankment
Est	Estate
Ex	Exchange
FB	Footbridge
FC	Football Club
Fld	Field
Flds	Fields
Fm	Farm
Gall	Gallery
Gar	Garage
Gdn	Garden
Gdns	Gardens
Govt	Government
Gra	Grange
Grd	Ground
Grds	Grounds
Grn	Green
Grns	Greens
Gro	Grove
Gros	Groves
Ho	House
Hos	Houses
Hosp	Hospital
Ind	Industrial
Junct	Junction
La	Lane
Las	Lanes
Lo	Lodge
Lwr	Lower
Mag	Magistrates
Mans	Mansions
Meml	Memorial
Met	Metropolitan
Mkt	Market
Mkts	Markets
Ms	Mews
Mt	Mount
Mus	Museum
N	North
North	Northern
PH	Public House
Par	Parade
Pas	Passage
Pav	Pavilion
Pia	Piazza
Pk	Park
Pl	Place
Prec	Precinct
Prom	Promenade
Pt	Point
Quad	Quadrant
RC	Roman Catholic
Rd	Road
Rds	Roads
Rec	Recreation
Res	Reservoir
Ri	Rise
S	South
Sch	School
Shop	Shopping
Sq	Square
St	Street
St.	Saint
Sta	Station
Sts	Streets
Sub	Subway
Swim	Swimming
TA	Territorial Army
Tenn	Tennis
Ter	Terrace
Thea	Theatre
Trd	Trading
Twr	Tower
Twrs	Towers
Tun	Tunnel
Vill	Villas
Vw	View
W	West
Wd	Wood
Wds	Woods
Wf	Wharf
Wk	Walk
Wks	Walks
Yd	Yard

Post town abbreviations used within the index

Ashf.	Ashford
Bans.	Banstead
Bark.	Barking
Barn.	Barnet
Beck.	Beckenham
Bedd.	Beddington
Belv.	Belvedere
Bexh.	Bexleyheath
Borwd.	Borehamwood
Brent.	Brentford
Brom.	Bromley
Brwd.	Brentwood
Cars.	Carshalton
Cher.	Chertsey
Chess.	Chessington
Chig.	Chigwell
Chis.	Chislehurst
Couls.	Coulsdon
Croy.	Croydon
Dag.	Dagenham
Dart.	Dartford
E.Mol.	East Molesey
Edg.	Edgware
Enf.	Enfield
Felt.	Feltham
Grnf.	Greenford
Har.	Harrow
Hav.	Havering
Hmptn.	Hampton
Horn.	Hornchurch
Houns.	Hounslow
Ilf.	Ilford
Islw.	Isleworth
Ken.	Kenley
Kes.	Keston
Kings.T.	Kingston upon Thames
Mitch.	Mitcham
Mord.	Morden
N.Mal.	New Malden
Nthlt.	Northolt
Nthwd.	Northwood
Orp.	Orpington
Pnr.	Pinner
Pur.	Purley
Rain.	Rainham
Rich.	Richmond
Rick.	Rickmansworth
Rom.	Romford
Ruis.	Ruislip
S.Croy.	South Croydon
Shep.	Shepperton
Sid.	Sidcup
Stai.	Staines
Stan.	Stanmore
Sthl.	Southall
Sun.	Sunbury-on-Thames
Surb.	Surbiton
Sutt.	Sutton
Swan.	Swanley
Tedd.	Teddington
Th.Hth.	Thornton Heath
Twick.	Twickenham
Uxb.	Uxbridge
W.Mol.	West Molesey
W.Wick.	West Wickham
Wal.Abb.	Waltham Abbey
Wal.Cr.	Waltham Cross
Wall.	Wallington
Walt.	Walton-on-Thames
Wat.	Watford
Wdf.Grn.	Woodford Green
Well.	Welling
Wem.	Wembley
West Dr.	West Drayton
Wor.Pk.	Worcester Park

Abberley Ms. SW4 176 324 DH83
Abberton Wk., Rain. 237 309 FE66
Abbess Clo. E6 244 318 EL71
Abbess Clo. SW2 194 324 DN88
Abbeville Rd. N8 220 306 DK56
Abbeville Rd. SW4 176 324 DJ86
Abbey Ave., Wem. 123 314 CL68
Abbey Clo., Hayes 242 313 BV74
Abbey Clo., Nthlt. 242 313 BZ69
Abbey Clo., Pnr. 214 303 BV55
Abbey Clo., Rom. 228 310 FG58
Abbey Cres., Belv. 255 319 FA77
Abbey Dr. SW17 272 324 DG92
Abbey Dr., Stai. 280 328 BJ97
Abbey Gdns. NW8 17 315 DC68
Abbey Gdns. SE16 148 317 DU77
Abbey Gdns. W6 157 315 CY79
Abbey Gdns., Cher. 280 328 BG100
Abbey Grn., Cher. 280 328 BG100
Abbey Gro. SE2 254 319 EV77
Abbey La. E15 130 317 EC68
Abbey La., Beck. 275 325 EA94
Abbey Manufact. Est., Wem. 123 314 CM67
Abbey Ms. E17 223 307 EA57
Abbey Orchard St. SW1 70 316 DK76
Abbey Par. W5 123 314 CM69
Abbey Pk., Beck. 275 325 EA94
Abbey Rd. E15 131 317 ED68
Abbey Rd. NW6 112 305 DB66
Abbey Rd. NW8 16/7 315 DB67
Abbey Rd. NW10 124 314 CP68
Abbey Rd. SE2 254 319 EX77
Abbey Rd. SW19 271 323 DC94
Abbey Rd., Bark. 235 308 EP66
Abbey Rd., Belv. 254 319 EX77
Abbey Rd., Bexh. 262 327 EY84
Abbey Rd., Cher. 280 328 BH101
Abbey Rd., Croy. 286 332 DP104
Abbey Rd., Enf. 209 300 DS43
Abbey Rd., Ilf. 225 308 ER57
Abbey Rd., Shep. 281 328 BN102
Abbey Rd. Est. NW8 16/7 315 DB67
Abbey St. E13 244 318 EG70
Abbey St. SE1 75 316 DT76
Abbey Ter. SE2 254 319 EW77
Abbey Vw. NW7 205 298 CT48
Abbey Wk., W.Mol. 267 329 CB97
Abbey Way SE2 254 319 EX75
Abbey Wf. Ind. Est., Bark. 245 318 ER68
Abbey Wd. Rd. SE2 254 319 EV77
Abbeydale Rd., Wem. 124 314 CN67
Abbeyfield Est. SE16 148 317 DW77
Abbeyfield Rd. SE16 148 317 DW77
Abbeyfields Clo. NW10 124 314 CN69
Abbeyhill Rd., Sid. 262 327 EW89
Abbot Clo., Stai. 264 328 BK94
Abbot St. E8 117 306 DT65
Abbots Clo. N1 116 306 DQ65
Abbots Clo., Orp. 291 334 EQ102
Abbots Clo., Ruis. 232 313 BX62
Abbots Clo., Uxb. 248 312 BK71
Abbots Cres., Enf. 202 300 DP40
Abbots Dr., Har. 233 313 CA61
Abbots Gdns. N2 219 305 DD56
Abbots Gdns. W8 64/5 315 DB76
Abbots La. SE1 62/3 316 DS74
Abbots Manor Est. SW1 80/1 316 DH78
Abbots Pk. SW2 194 324 DN88
Abbot's Pl. NW6 16/7 315 DB67
Abbot's Rd. E6 244 318 EK67
Abbots Rd., Edg. 217 304 CQ52
Abbots Ter. N8 220 306 DL58
Abbots Wk. W8 64/5 315 DB76
Abbots Way, Beck. 288 333 DY99
Abbotsbury Clo. E15 130 317 EC68
Abbotsbury Clo. W14 147 315 CZ75
Abbotsbury Gdns., Pnr. 214 303 BW58
Abbotsbury Ms. SE15 180 325 DW83
Abbotsbury Rd. W14 147 315 CY75
Abbotsbury Rd., Brom. 289 333 EF103
Abbotsbury Rd., Mord. 284 331 DB99
Abbotsford Ave. N15 221 306 DQ56
Abbotsford Gdns., Wdf.Grn. 224 308 EG52
Abbotsford Lo., Nthwd. 213 302 BS50
Abbotsford Rd., Ilf. 236 309 EU61
Abbotshade Rd. SE16 139 317 DX74
Abbotshall Ave. N14 208 300 DJ48
Abbotshall Rd. SE6 199 325 ED88
Abbotsleigh Clo., Sutt. 292 331 DB108
Abbotsleigh Rd. SW16 272 324 DJ91
Abbotsmede Clo., Twick. 259 321 CF89
Abbotstone Rd. SW15 172 323 CW83
Abbotswell Rd. SE4 181 325 DZ85
Abbotswood Clo., Belv. 254 319 EY76
Abbotswood Gdns., Ilf. 224 308 EM55
Abbotswood Rd. SE22 179 324 DS84
Abbotswood Rd. SW16 193 324 DK90
Abbotswood Way, Hayes 242 313 BV74
Abbott Ave. SW20 270 323 CX95
Abbott Clo., Hmptn. 266 329 BY93
Abbott Clo., Nthlt. 232 313 BZ65
Abbott Rd. E14 140 317 EC72
Abbotts Clo. SE28 246 319 EW73
Abbotts Clo., Rom. 227 309 FB55
Abbotts Cres. E4 211 301 ED49
Abbotts Dr., Wem. 90 304 CH61
Abbotts Pk. Rd. E10 104 307 EC59
Abbotts Rd., Mitch. 272 324 DJ98
Abbotts Rd., Sthl. 242 313 BY74
Abbotts Rd., Sutt. 284 331 CY105
Abbotts Wk., Bexh. 254 319 EX80
Abbs Cross Gdns., Horn. 238 310 FJ60
Abbs Cross La., Horn. 238 310 FJ63
Abchurch La. EC4 62 316 DR73
Abchurch Yd. EC4 62 316 DR73
Abdale Rd. W12 136 315 CV74
Abenglen Ind. Est., Hayes 249 320 BR75
Aberavon Rd. E3 129 317 DY69
Abercairn Rd. SW16 272 324 DJ94
Aberconway Rd., Mord. 271 323 DB97
Abercorn Clo. NW7 218 305 CY52
Abercorn Clo. NW8 29 315 DC69
Abercorn Cres., Har. 233 313 CB61
Abercorn Gdns., Har. 91 304 CK59
Abercorn Gdns., Rom. 226 309 EV58
Abercorn Gro., Ruis. 231 302 BR56
Abercorn Pl. NW8 29 315 DC69
Abercorn Rd. NW7 218 305 CY52
Abercorn Rd., Stan. 216 304 CJ52
Abercorn Way SE1 148 317 DU78
Abercrombie Dr., Enf. 203 301 DU39
Abercrombie St. SW11 159 315 DE82
Aberdare Clo., W.Wick. 289 333 EC103
Aberdare Gdns. NW6 112 305 DB66
Aberdare Gdns. NW7 218 305 CX52
Aberdare Rd., Enf. 203 301 DW42
Aberdeen La. N5 116 306 DQ64
Aberdeen Par. N18 210 301 DV50
Aberdeen Pk. N5 116 306 DQ64
Aberdeen Pk. Ms. N5 116 306 DQ63
Aberdeen Pl. NW8 30 315 DD70
Aberdeen Rd. N5 116 306 DQ63
Aberdeen Rd. N18 210 301 DV50
Aberdeen Rd. NW10 109 304 CT64
Aberdeen Rd., Croy. 287 332 DQ105
Aberdeen Rd., Har. 215 303 CF54
Aberdeen Sq. E14 139 317 DZ74
Aberdeen Ter. SE3 167 317 ED82
Aberdour Rd., Ilf. 236 309 EV62
Aberdour St. SE1 86/7 316 DS77
Aberfeldy St. E14 140 317 EC72
Aberford Gdns. SE18 252 318 EL81
Aberfoyle Rd. SW16 272 324 DK93
Abergeldie Rd. SE12 260 326 EH86
Abernethy Rd. SE13 183 325 EE84
Abersham Rd. E8 117 306 DT64
Abery St. SE18 253 318 ES77
Abingdon Clo. NW1 115 306 DK65
Abingdon Clo. SE1 87 316 DT77
Abingdon Clo. SW19 271 323 DC93
Abingdon Clo., Uxb. 240 312 BM67
Abingdon Rd. N3 219 305 DC54
Abingdon Rd. SW16 272 324 DL96
Abingdon Rd. W8 64 315 DA76
Abingdon St. SW1 70/1 316 DL76
Abingdon Vil. W8 64 315 DA76
Abingdon Way, Orp. 291 335 EV105
Abinger Ave., Sutt. 292 331 CW109
Abinger Clo., Bark. 236 309 EU63
Abinger Clo., Brom. 276 326 EL97
Abinger Clo., Wall. 286 332 DL106
Abinger Gdns., Islw. 259 321 CE83
Abinger Gro. SE8 165 317 DZ79
Abinger Ms. W9 28 315 DA70
Abinger Rd. W4 145 314 CS76
Ablett St. SE16 148 317 DW78
Abney Gdns. N16 101 306 DT61
Aboyne Dr. SW20 270 323 CU96
Aboyne Est. SW17 191 323 DD90
Aboyne Rd. NW10 93 304 CR62
Aboyne Rd. SW17 191 323 DD90
Abridge Clo., Wal.Cr. 203 301 DX35
Abridge Gdns., Rom. 227 309 FA51
Abridge Way, Bark. 246 319 EV68
Abyssinia Clo. SW11 175 323 DE84
Acacia Ave. N17 221 306 DR52
Acacia Ave., Brent. 152 314 CH80
Acacia Ave., Hayes 249 312 BT72
Acacia Ave., Horn. 237 309 FF61
Acacia Ave., Mitch. 272 324 DH96
Acacia Ave., Ruis. 232 313 BU60
Acacia Ave., Shep. 281 328 BN99
Acacia Ave., Wem. 107 304 CL64
Acacia Ave., West Dr. 248 312 BM73
Acacia Clo. SE20 274 325 DU96
Acacia Clo., Orp. 291 334 ER99
Acacia Clo., Stan. 215 303 CE51
Acacia Dr., Bans. 292 331 CX114
Acacia Dr., Sutt. 284 331 CZ102
Acacia Dr., Upmin. 239 311 FN62
Acacia Gdns. NW8 18 315 DD68
Acacia Gdns., Upmin. 239 311 FT59
Acacia Gdns., W.Wick. 289 333 EC103
Acacia Gro. SE21 195 324 DR89
Acacia Gro., N.Mal. 269 322 CS97
Acacia Ms., West Dr. 256 320 BK79
Acacia Pl. NW8 18 315 DD68
Acacia Rd. E11 105 307 EE61
Acacia Rd. E17 222 307 DY58
Acacia Rd. N22 221 306 DN53
Acacia Rd. NW8 18 315 DD68
Acacia Rd. SW16 272 324 DL95
Acacia Rd. W3 134 314 CQ73
Acacia Rd., Beck. 274 325 DZ97
Acacia Rd., Enf. 202 300 DR39
Acacia Rd., Hmptn. 267 329 CA93
Acacia Rd., Mitch. 272 324 DG96
Acacia Rd., Stai. 264 328 BH92
Acacia Wk., Swan. 279 327 FD96
Acacia Way, Sid. 261 326 ET88
Academy Gdns., Croy. 287 332 DT102
Academy Gdns., Nthlt. 242 313 BX68
Academy Pl. SE18 252 318 EM81
Academy Rd. SE18 252 318 EM81
Acanthus Dr. SE1 148 317 DU78
Acanthus Rd. SW11 176 324 DG83
Accommodation La., West Dr. 256 320 BG81
Accommodation Rd. NW11 95 305 CZ59
Acer Ave., Hayes 242 313 BY71
Acfold Rd. SW6 158 315 DB81
Achilles Clo. SE1 148 317 DU78
Achilles Rd. NW6 112 305 DA64
Achilles St. SE14 165 317 DY80
Achilles Way W1 56 316 DG74
Acklam Rd. W10 137 315 CZ71
Acklington Dr. NW9 217 304 CS53
Ackmar Rd. SW6 158 315 DA81
Ackroyd Dr. E3 139 317 DZ71
Ackroyd Rd. SE23 197 325 DX87
Ackworth Clo. N9 210 301 DW45
Acland Clo. SE18 253 318 ER80
Acland Cres. SE5 179 324 DR84
Acland Rd. NW2 110 305 CV65
Acol Cres., Ruis. 232 313 BV64
Acol Rd. NW6 112 305 DA66
Aconbury Rd., Dag. 246 319 EV67
Acorn Clo. E4 211 301 EB50
Acorn Clo., Chis. 277 326 EQ92
Acorn Clo., Enf. 202 300 DP39
Acorn Clo., Stan. 216 304 CH52
Acorn Ct., Ilf. 225 308 ES58
Acorn Gdns. SE19 273 324 DT95
Acorn Gdns. W3 135 314 CR71
Acorn Gro., Hayes 257 320 BT80
Acorn Gro., Ruis. 241 312 BT63
Acorn Par. SE15 164 317 DV80
Acorn Rd., Dart. 263 327 FF85
Acorn Wk. SE16 139 317 DY74
Acorn Way SE23 197 325 DX90
Acorn Way, Orp. 290 334 EP105
Acorns Clo., Hmptn. 267 329 CB93
Acre La. SW2 177 324 DL84
Acre La., Cars. 285 332 DG105
Acre La., Wall. 285 332 DG105
Acre Path, Nthlt. 232 313 BY65
Acre Rd. SW19 271 323 DD93
Acre Rd., Dag. 237 309 FB66
Acre Rd., Kings.T. 268 322 CL95
Acre Vw., Horn. 228 311 FL56
Acre Way, Nthwd. 213 302 BT53
Acris St. SW18 174 323 DC85
Acton Clo. N9 210 301 DU47
Acton La. NW10 124 314 CQ69
Acton La. W3 144 314 CQ75
Acton La. W4 144 314 CQ77
Acton Ms. E8 27 316 DT67
Acton Pk. Ind. Est. W3 145 314 CR75
Acton St. WC1 35 316 DM69
Acuba Rd. SW18 190 323 DB88
Acworth Clo. N9 210 301 DW45
Ada Gdns. E14 141 317 ED72
Ada Gdns. E15 131 317 EF67
Ada Pl. E2 128 317 DU67
Ada Rd. SE5 163 316 DS80
Ada Rd., Wem. 90 304 CJ62
Ada St. E8 128 317 DV67
Adair Clo. SE25 274 325 DV97
Adair Rd. W10 127 315 CY70
Adair Twr. W10 127 315 CY70
Adam & Eve Ct. W1 45 316 DJ72
Adam & Eve Ms. W8 64 315 DA76
Adam Ct. SW7 77 315 DC77
Adam Pl. N16 101 306 DT61
Adam Rd. E4 222 307 DZ51
Adam St. WC2 58/9 316 DL73
Adam Wk. SW6 156 315 CW80
Adams Clo. N3 219 305 DA52
Adams Clo. NW9 92 304 CP61
Adams Clo., Surb. 282 330 CM100
Adams Ct. EC2 50 316 DR72
Adams Gdns. Est. SE16 148 317 DW75
Adams Pl. E14 140 317 EB74
Adams Pl. N7 115 306 DM64
Adams Rd. N17 221 306 DR54
Adams Rd., Beck. 288 333 DY99
Adams Row W1 56 316 DG73
Adams Sq., Bexh. 262 327 EY83
Adams Way, Croy. 287 332 DT100
Adamson Rd. E16 244 318 EG72
Adamson Rd. NW3 113 305 DD66
Adamsrill Clo., Enf. 209 300 DR43
Adamsrill Rd. SE26 274 325 DY91
Adare Wk. SW16 193 324 DM90
Adastral Est. NW9 217 304 CS53
Adcock Wk., Orp. 291 334 ET105
Adderley Gdns. SE9 277 326 EN91
Adderley Gro. SW11 176 324 DG85
Adderley Rd., Har. 215 303 CF53
Adderley St. E14 140 317 EC72
Addington Ct. SW14 171 322 CR83
Addington Dr. N12 219 305 DC51
Addington Gro. SE26 274 325 DY91
Addington Rd. E3 130 317 EA69
Addington Rd. E16 131 317 EE70
Addington Rd. N4 221 306 DN58
Addington Rd., Croy. 286 332 DN102
Addington Rd., S.Croy. 295 333 DU112
Addington Rd., W.Wick. 289 333 EC105
Addington Sq. SE5 163 316 DR79
Addington St. SE1 71 316 DM75
Addis Clo., Enf. 203 301 DX39
Addiscombe Ave., Croy. 287 333 DU101
Addiscombe Clo., Har. 216 304 CJ57
Addiscombe Ct. Rd., Croy. 287 332 DS102
Addiscombe Gro., Croy. 287 332 DS103
Addiscombe Rd., Croy. 287 332 DS103
Addison Ave. N14 208 300 DH44
Addison Ave. W11 137 315 CY74
Addison Ave., Houns. 251 321 CC81
Addison Bri. Pl. W14 147 315 CZ77
Addison Clo., Nthwd. 214 303 BU53
Addison Clo., Orp. 291 334 EQ100
Addison Cres. W14 147 315 CY76
Addison Dr. SE12 260 326 EH85
Addison Gdns. W14 147 315 CX76
Addison Gdns., Surb. 268 322 CM98
Addison Gro. W4 145 314 CS76
Addison Pl. W11 137 315 CY74
Addison Pl., Sthl. 243 313 CA73
Addison Rd. E11 224 308 EG58
Addison Rd. E17 223 307 EB57
Addison Rd. SE25 274 325 DU98
Addison Rd. W14 147 315 CY76
Addison Rd., Brom. 290 334 EJ99
Addison Rd., Enf. 203 301 DW39
Addison Rd., Ilf. 225 308 EQ53
Addison Rd., Tedd. 268 322 CH93
Addison Way NW11 218 305 CZ56
Addison Way, Hayes 242 313 BU72
Addison Way, Nthwd. 213 302 BT53
Addison's Clo., Croy. 288 333 DZ103
Addle Hill EC4 48/9 316 DP72
Addle St. EC2 49 316 DQ71
Adecroft Way, W.Mol. 267 329 CC97
Adela Ave., N.Mal. 283 331 CV99
Adela St. W10 127 315 CY70
Adelaide Ave. SE4 181 325 DZ84
Adelaide Clo., Enf. 202 300 DS38
Adelaide Clo., Stan. 204 298 CG49
Adelaide Cotts. W7 251 321 CF75
Adelaide Gdns., Rom. 226 309 EY57
Adelaide Gro. W12 136 315 CU74
Adelaide Rd. E10 104 307 EC62
Adelaide Rd. NW3 113 305 DD66
Adelaide Rd. SW18 174 323 DA85
Adelaide Rd. W13 132 314 CG74
Adelaide Rd., Ashf. 264 328 BK92
Adelaide Rd., Chis. 277 326 EP92
Adelaide Rd., Houns. 250 321 BY81
Adelaide Rd., Ilf. 235 308 EP61
Adelaide Rd., Rich. 169 322 CM84
Adelaide Rd., Sthl. 250 321 BY77
Adelaide Rd., Surb. 282 330 CL99
Adelaide Rd., Tedd. 267 329 CF93
Adelaide St. WC2 58/9 316 DL73
Adelaide Ter., Brent. 143 314 CK78
Adelaide Wk. SW9 178 324 DN84
Adelina Gro. E1 138 317 DW71
Adelina Ms. SW12 193 324 DK88
Adeline Pl. WC1 46 316 DK71
Adelphi Cres., Hayes 241 312 BT69
Adelphi Cres., Horn. 238 310 FG61
Adelphi Ter. WC2 58/9 316 DL73
Adelphi Way, Hayes 241 312 BT69
Aden Gro. N16 117 306 DR63
Aden Rd., Enf. 203 301 DY42
Aden Rd., Ilf. 235 308 EP59
Aden Ter. N16 117 306 DR63
Adeney Clo. W6 157 315 CX79
Adenmore Rd. SE6 198 325 EA87
Adie Rd. W6 146 315 CW76
Adine Rd. E13 244 318 EH70
Adler St. E1 138 317 DU72
Adley St. E5 119 307 DY63
Adlington Clo. N18 209 300 DS50
Admaston Rd. SE18 253 318 EQ79
Admiral Clo., Orp. 278 327 EX98
Admiral Pl. SE16 139 317 DY74
Admiral Seymour Rd. SE9 260 326 EM84
Admiral Sq. SW10 158 315 DC81
Admiral St. SE8 166 317 EA81
Admirals Clo. E18 224 308 EH56
Admirals Wk. NW3 96 305 DC62
Admirals Way E14 150 317 EA75
Admiralty Clo. SE8 166 317 EA80
Admiralty Rd., Tedd. 267 329 CF93
Adnams Wk., Rain. 237 309 FF65
Adolf St. SE6 275 325 EB91
Adolphus Rd. N4 100 306 DP61
Adolphus St. SE8 165 317 DZ80

Adomar Rd., Dag.	236	309	EX62
Adpar St. W2	42	315	DD71
Adrian Ave. NW2	94	305	CV60
Adrian Clo., Uxb.	212	302	BK53
Adrian Ms. SW10	158	315	DB79
Adrienne Ave., Sthl.	242	313	BZ69
Advance Rd. SE27	273	324	DQ91
Advent Way N18	210	301	DX50
Adys Rd. SE15	179	324	DT83
Aerodrome Rd. NW4	218	305	CU55
Aerodrome Rd. NW9	217	304	CT55
Aerodrome Way, Houns.	250	321	BW79
Aeroville NW9	217	304	CS54
Affleck St. N1	23	316	DM68
Afghan Rd. SW11	159	315	DE82
Aftab Ter. E1	128	317	DV70
Agamemnon Rd. NW6	111	305	CZ64
Agar Clo., Surb.	282	330	CM103
Agar Gro. NW1	114	306	DJ66
Agar Gro. Est. NW1	114	306	DJ66
Agar Pl. NW1	114	306	DJ66
Agar St. WC2	58/9	316	DL73
Agate Clo. E16	244	318	EK72
Agate Rd. W6	146	315	CW76
Agatha Clo. E1	138	317	DV74
Agaton Rd. SE9	261	326	EQ89
Agave Rd. NW2	110	305	CW63
Agdon St. EC1	36/7	316	DP70
Agincourt Rd. NW3	113	305	DF63
Agnes Ave., Ilf.	235	308	EP63
Agnes Clo. E6	245	318	EN73
Agnes Gdns., Dag.	236	309	EX63
Agnes Rd. W3	135	314	CT74
Agnes St. E14	139	317	DZ72
Agnesfield Clo. N12	219	305	DE51
Agnew Rd. SE23	197	325	DX87
Agricola Pl., Enf.	209	300	DT43
Aidan Clo., Dag.	236	309	EY63
Aileen Wk. E15	121	307	EF66
Ailsa Ave., Twick.	168	322	CG85
Ailsa Rd., Twick.	168	322	CH85
Ailsa St. E14	140	317	EC71
Ainger Ms. NW3	113	305	DF66
Ainger Rd. NW3	113	305	DF66
Ainsdale Clo., Orp.	291	334	ER102
Ainsdale Cres., Pnr.	215	303	CA55
Ainsdale Rd. W5	123	314	CK70
Ainsley Ave., Rom.	227	309	FB58
Ainsley Clo. N9	209	300	DS46
Ainsley St. E2	128	317	DV69
Ainslie Wk. SW12	192	324	DH87
Ainslie Wd. Cres. E4	211	301	EB50
Ainslie Wd. Gdns. E4	211	301	EB50
Ainslie Wd. Rd. E4	211	301	EA50
Ainsty Est. SE16	149	317	DX75
Ainsworth Clo. NW2	94	305	CU62
Ainsworth Rd. E9	118	307	DW66
Ainsworth Rd., Croy.	286	332	DP103
Ainsworth Way NW8	17	315	DC67
Aintree Ave. E6	244	318	EL67
Aintree Clo., Uxb.	249	312	BP72
Aintree Cres., Ilf.	225	308	EQ54
Aintree Est. SW6	157	315	CY80
Aintree Gro., Upmin.	238	311	FM62
Aintree Rd., Grnf.	122	314	CH68
Aintree St. SW6	157	315	CY80
Air St. W1	57	316	DJ73
Airdrie Clo. N1	115	306	DM66
Airdrie Clo., Hayes	242	313	BY71
Airedale Ave. W4	145	314	CT77
Airedale Ave. S. W4	145	314	CT78
Airedale Rd. SW12	191	323	DF87
Airedale Rd. W5	142	314	CJ76
Airfield Way, Horn.	238	310	FH65
Airlie Gdns. W8	52	315	DA74
Airlie Gdns., Ilf.	235	308	EP60
Airlinks Est., Houns.	250	321	BW78
Airport Roundabout E16	244	318	EK74
Airthrie Rd., Ilf.	236	309	EV61
Aisgill Ave. W14	147	315	CZ78
Aisher Rd. SE28	246	319	EW73
Aislibie Rd. SE12	183	325	EE84
Aitken Clo. E8	128	317	DU67
Aitken Clo., Mitch.	285	331	DF101
Aitken Rd. SE6	198	325	EB89
Aitken Rd., Barn.	206	299	CW43
Ajax Ave. NW9	217	304	CS55
Ajax Rd. NW6	111	305	CZ64
Akabusi Clo., Croy.	287	333	DU100
Akehurst St. SW15	172	323	CU86
Akenside Rd. NW3	113	305	DD64
Akerman Rd. SW9	162	316	DP82
Akerman Rd., Surb.	282	330	CJ100
Alabama St. SE18	253	318	ER80
Alacross Rd. W5	142	314	CJ75
Alan Dr., Barn.	206	299	CY44
Alan Gdns., Rom.	237	309	FA59
Alan Hocken Way E15	131	317	EE68
Alan Rd. SW19	270	323	CY92
Alandale Dr., Pnr.	214	303	BV54
Alanthus Clo. SE12	183	325	EF85
Alaska St. SE1	60	316	DN74
Alba Clo., Hayes	242	313	BX70
Alba Gdns. NW11	218	305	CY58
Alba Pl. W11	137	315	CZ72
Albacore Cres. SE13	182	325	EB86
Albain Cres., Ashf.	264	320	BL89
Alban Highwalk EC2	49	316	DQ71
Albany, The W1	57	316	DJ73
Albany, The, Wdf.Grn.	211	301	EF49
Albany Clo. N15	221	306	DP56
Albany Clo. SW14	170	322	CP84
Albany Clo., Bex.	262	327	EW87
Albany Clo., Uxb.	241	312	BN64
Albany Ct. E4	211	301	EB44
Albany Ctyd. W1	57	316	DJ73
Albany Cres., Edg.	217	304	CN52
Albany Mans. SW11	159	315	DE80
Albany Ms. N1	116	306	DN66
Albany Ms. SE5	162	316	DQ79
Albany Ms., Brom.	276	326	EG93
Albany Ms., Kings.T.	268	322	CK93
Albany Ms., Sutt.	284	331	DB106
Albany Pk. Ave., Enf.	203	301	DW39
Albany Pk. Rd., Kings.T.	268	322	CK93
Albany Pas., Rich.	169	322	CM85
Albany Pl. N7	116	306	DN63
Albany Pl., Brent.	153	314	CL79
Albany Rd. E10	104	307	EA59
Albany Rd. E12	234	308	EK63
Albany Rd. E17	222	307	DY58
Albany Rd. N4	220	306	DM58
Albany Rd. N18	210	301	DV50
Albany Rd. SE5	163	316	DR79
Albany Rd. SW19	271	323	DB92
Albany Rd. W13	132	314	CH73
Albany Rd., Belv.	254	319	EZ79
Albany Rd., Bex.	262	327	EW87
Albany Rd., Brent.	153	314	CK79
Albany Rd., Chis.	277	326	EP92
Albany Rd., Enf.	203	301	DX37
Albany Rd., Horn.	238	310	FG60
Albany Rd., N.Mal.	269	322	CR98
Albany Rd., Rich.	169	322	CM85
Albany Rd., Rom.	226	309	EZ58
Albany St. NW1	20/1	316	DH68
Albany Ter. NW1	32/3	316	DH70
Albatross St. SE18	253	318	ES80
Albatross Way SE16	149	317	DX75
Albemarle SW19	189	323	CX89
Albemarle App., Ilf.	225	308	EP58
Albemarle Ave., Twick.	258	321	BZ88
Albemarle Gdns., Ilf.	225	308	EP58
Albemarle Gdns., N.Mal.	269	322	CR98
Albemarle Pk., Stan.	204	298	CJ50
Albemarle Rd., Barn.	207	299	DE45
Albemarle Rd., Beck.	275	325	EB95
Albemarle St. W1	56/7	316	DH73
Albemarle Way EC1	36/7	316	DP70
Alberon Gdns. NW11	218	305	CZ56
Albert Ave. E4	211	301	EA49
Albert Ave. SW8	161	316	DM80
Albert Ave., Cher.	280	328	BG97
Albert Bri. SW3	159	315	DE79
Albert Bri. SW11	159	315	DE80
Albert Bri. Rd. SW11	159	315	DE80
Albert Carr Gdns. SW16	272	324	DL92
Albert Clo. E9	128	317	DV67

Albert Clo. N22	220	306	DK53
Albert Ct. SW7	66	315	DD75
Albert Cres. E4	211	301	EA49
Albert Dr. SW19	189	323	CY89
Albert Embk. SE1	82/3	316	DL78
Albert Gdns. E1	139	317	DX72
Albert Gate SW1	67	315	DF75
Albert Gro. SW20	270	323	CX95
Albert Hall Mans. SW7	66	315	DD75
Albert Mans. SW11	159	315	DF81
Albert Ms. E14	139	317	DY73
Albert Ms. W8	65	315	DC76
Albert Pl. N3	219	305	DA53
Albert Pl. N17	221	306	DT55
Albert Pl. W8	64/5	315	DB75
Albert Rd. E10	104	307	EC61
Albert Rd. E16	244	318	EL74
Albert Rd. E17	223	307	EA57
Albert Rd. E18	224	308	EH55
Albert Rd. N4	99	306	DM60
Albert Rd. N15	221	306	DS58
Albert Rd. N22	220	306	DJ53
Albert Rd. NW4	218	305	CX56
Albert Rd. NW6	127	315	CZ68
Albert Rd. NW7	205	298	CT50
Albert Rd. SE9	260	326	EL90
Albert Rd. SE20	274	325	DX93
Albert Rd. SE25	274	325	DU98
Albert Rd. W5	122	314	CH70
Albert Rd., Ashf.	264	328	BM92
Albert Rd., Belv.	254	319	EZ78
Albert Rd., Bex.	263	327	FA86
Albert Rd., Brom.	290	334	EK99
Albert Rd., Dag.	237	309	FA60
Albert Rd., Hmptn.	267	329	CC92
Albert Rd., Har.	215	303	CC55
Albert Rd., Hayes	249	320	BS76
Albert Rd., Houns.	259	321	CA84
Albert Rd., Ilf.	235	308	EP62
Albert Rd., Kings.T.	268	322	CM96
Albert Rd., Mitch.	271	323	DF97
Albert Rd., N.Mal.	269	322	CT98
Albert Rd., Orp.	291	335	EU106
Albert Rd. (St. Mary Cray), Orp.	291	335	EV100
Albert Rd., Rich.	169	322	CL85
Albert Rd., Rom.	227	309	FF57
Albert Rd., Sthl.	250	321	BX76
Albert Rd., Sutt.	285	331	DD106
Albert Rd., Tedd.	267	329	CF93
Albert Rd., Twick.	259	321	CF88
Albert Rd., West Dr.	248	312	BL74
Albert Rd. Est., Belv.	254	319	EZ78
Albert Sq. E15	121	307	EE64
Albert Sq. SW8	161	316	DM80
Albert St. N12	207	299	DC50
Albert St. NW1	20/1	316	DH67
Albert Ter. NW1	20	316	DG67
Albert Ter. NW10	125	314	CR67
Albert Ter. Ms. NW1	20	316	DG67
Albert Wk. E16	253	318	EN75
Alberta Ave., Sutt.	284	331	CY105
Alberta Est. SE17	84/5	316	DP78
Alberta Rd., Enf.	209	300	DT44
Alberta Rd., Erith	255	319	FC81
Alberta St. SE17	84/5	316	DP78
Albion Ave. N10	220	306	DG53
Albion Ave. SW8	161	316	DK82
Albion Bldgs. EC1	49	316	DQ71
Albion Clo. W2	54/5	315	DE73
Albion Clo., Rom.	227	309	FD58
Albion Dr. E8	117	306	DT66
Albion Est. SE16	148	317	DW75
Albion Gdns. W6	146	315	CV77
Albion Gro. N16	117	306	DS63
Albion Hill SE13	166	317	EB82
Albion Ms. N1	116	306	DN66
Albion Ms. NW6	111	305	CZ66
Albion Ms. W2	42/3	315	DE72
Albion Par. N16	117	306	DR63
Albion Pl. EC1	48/9	316	DP71
Albion Pl. SE25	274	325	DU97
Albion Pl. W6	146	315	CV77
Albion Rd. E17	223	307	EC55
Albion Rd. N16	117	306	DR63
Albion Rd. N17	222	307	DU54
Albion Rd., Bexh.	262	327	EZ84
Albion Rd., Hayes	249	312	BS72
Albion Rd., Houns.	259	321	CA84
Albion Rd., Kings.T.	269	322	CQ95
Albion Rd., Sutt.	293	331	DD107
Albion Rd., Twick.	259	321	CE88
Albion Sq. E8	117	306	DT66
Albion St. SE16	148	317	DW75
Albion St. W2	42/3	315	DE72
Albion St., Croy.	286	332	DP102
Albion Ter. E8	117	306	DT66
Albion Vil. Rd. SE26	196	325	DW90
Albion Way EC1	49	316	DQ71
Albion Way SE13	182	325	EC84
Albion Way, Wem.	92	304	CP62
Albion Yd. E1	138	317	DV71
Albright Ind. Est., Rain.	247	319	FF71
Albrighton Rd. SE22	179	324	DS83
Albuhera Clo., Enf.	202	300	DN39
Albury Ave., Bexh.	254	319	EY82
Albury Ave., Islw.	251	321	CF80
Albury Ave., Sutt.	292	331	CW109
Albury Clo., Hmptn.	267	329	CA93
Albury Dr., Pnr.	214	303	BW53
Albury Ms. E12	234	308	EJ60
Albury Rd., Chess.	282	330	CL106
Albury St. SE8	166	317	EA79
Albyfield, Brom.	276	326	EM97
Albyn Rd. SE8	166	317	EA81
Albyns Clo., Rain.	238	310	FG66
Alcester Cres. E5	102	307	DV61
Alcester Rd., Wall.	285	332	DH105
Alcock Clo., Wall.	294	332	DK108
Alcock Rd., Houns.	250	321	BX80
Alconbury Rd. E5	102	307	DU61
Alcorn Clo., Sutt.	284	331	DA103
Alcott Clo. W7	243	313	CF71
Alcuin Ct., Stan.	216	304	CJ51
Aldborough Rd., Dag.	237	309	FC65
Aldborough Rd., Upmin.	238	311	FM61
Aldborough Rd. N., Ilf.	225	308	ET57
Aldborough Rd. S., Ilf.	235	308	ES60
Aldbourne Rd. W12	135	314	CT74
Aldbridge St. SE17	86/7	316	DS78
Aldburgh Ms. W1	44	316	DG72
Aldbury Ave., Wem.	108	304	CP66
Aldbury Ms. N9	209	300	DR45
Aldebert Ter. SW8	161	316	DL80
Aldeburgh Clo. E5	102	307	DV61
Aldeburgh St. SE10	252	318	EG78
Alden Ave. E15	131	317	EF70
Aldenham Dr., Uxb.	241	312	BP70
Aldenham St. NW1	21	316	DJ68
Aldensley Rd. W6	146	315	CV76
Alder Ave., Upmin.	238	311	FM63
Alder Clo. SE15	163	316	DT79
Alder Gro. NW2	94	305	CU61
Alder Ind. Est., Hayes	249	320	BR75
Alder Ms. N19	98	306	DJ61
Alder Rd. SW14	171	322	CR83
Alder Rd., Sid.	261	326	ET90
Alder Rd., Uxb.	240	312	BJ65
Alder Wk., Ilf.	235	308	EQ64
Alder Way, Swan.	279	327	FD96
Alderbrook Rd. SW12	176	324	DH86
Alderbury Rd. SW13	156	315	CU79
Aldergrove Gdns., Houns.	250	321	BY82
Aldergrove Wk., Horn.	238	310	FJ65
Alderholt Way SE15	163	316	DT80
Alderman Ave., Bark.	246	319	EU69
Alderman Judge Mall, Kings.T.	268	322	CL96
Aldermanbury EC2	49	316	DQ72
Aldermanbury Sq. EC2	49	316	DQ71
Aldermans Hill N13	208	300	DL49
Alderman's Wk. EC2	50/1	316	DS71
Aldermary Rd., Brom.	276	326	EG95
Aldermoor Rd. SE6	197	325	DZ90
Alderney Ave., Houns.	251	321	CB80
Alderney Gdns., Nthlt.	232	313	BZ66
Alderney Rd. E1	129	317	DX70
Alderney St. SW1	80/1	316	DH77
Alders, The N21	209	300	DN44
Alders, The, Felt.	266	329	BY91

Alders, The, Houns.	250	321	BZ79
Alders, The, W.Wick.	288	333	EB102
Alders Ave., Wdf.Grn.	223	307	EE51
Alders Clo. E11	234	308	EH61
Alders Clo. W5	143	314	CK76
Alders Clo., Edg.	205	298	CQ50
Alders Rd., Edg.	205	298	CQ50
Aldersbrook Ave., Enf.	202	300	DS40
Aldersbrook Dr., Kings.T.	268	322	CM93
Aldersbrook La. E12	234	308	EM62
Aldersbrook Rd. E11	234	308	EH61
Aldersbrook Rd. E12	234	308	EH61
Aldersey Gdns., Bark.	235	308	ER65
Aldersford Clo. SE4	181	325	DX85
Aldersgate St. EC1	49	316	DQ71
Aldersgrove Ave. SE9	260	326	EJ90
Aldershot Rd. NW6	127	315	CZ67
Aldersmead Ave., Croy.	288	333	DX100
Aldersmead Rd., Beck.	274	325	DY94
Alderson Pl., Sthl.	243	313	CC74
Alderson St. W10	127	315	CY70
Alderton Clo. NW10	93	304	CR62
Alderton Cres. NW4	218	305	CV57
Alderton Rd. SE24	178	324	DQ83
Alderton Rd., Croy.	287	332	DT101
Alderton Way NW4	218	305	CV57
Alderville Rd. SW6	157	315	CZ82
Alderwick Dr., Houns.	259	321	CD83
Alderwood Rd. SE9	261	326	ER86
Aldford St. W1	56	316	DG74
Aldgate EC3	50/1	316	DS72
Aldgate Ave. E1	51	316	DT72
Aldgate High St. EC3	51	316	DT72
Aldine Ct. W12	136	315	CW74
Aldine Pl. W12	136	315	CW74
Aldine St. W12	136	315	CW74
Aldingham Ct., Horn.	238	310	FG64
Aldingham Gdns., Horn.	238	310	FG64
Aldington Clo., Dag.	236	309	EW59
Aldington Rd. SE18	252	318	EK76
Aldis Ms. SW17	271	323	DE92
Aldis St. SW17	271	323	DE92
Aldred Rd. NW6	112	305	DA64
Aldren Rd. SW17	190	323	DC90
Aldrich Gdns., Sutt.	284	331	CZ104
Aldrich Ter. SW18	190	323	DC89
Aldriche Way E4	223	307	EC51
Aldridge Ave., Edg.	205	298	CP48
Aldridge Ave., Ruis.	232	313	BX61
Aldridge Ave., Stan.	216	304	CL53
Aldridge Ri., N.Mal.	283	330	CS101
Aldridge Rd. Vil. W11	137	315	CZ71
Aldridge Wk. N14	208	300	DL45
Aldrington Rd. SW16	272	324	DJ91
Aldsworth Clo. W9	28/9	315	DB70
Aldwick Clo. SE9	261	326	ER90
Aldwick Rd., Croy.	286	332	DM104
Aldworth Gro. SE13	182	325	EC86
Aldworth Rd. E15	121	307	EE66
Aldwych WC2	59	316	DM73
Aldwych Ave., Ilf.	225	308	EQ56
Aldwych Clo., Horn.	238	310	FG61
Alers Rd., Bexh.	262	327	EX85
Aleston Beck Rd. E16	244	318	EK72
Alexa Ct. W8	76	315	DA77
Alexander Ave. NW10	110	305	CV66
Alexander Clo., Brom.	289	334	EG102
Alexander Clo., Sid.	261	326	ES86
Alexander Clo., Sthl.	243	313	CC74
Alexander Clo., Twick.	259	321	CF89
Alexander Evans Ms. SE23	197	325	DX88
Alexander Ms. W2	40/1	315	DB72
Alexander Pl. SW7	78/9	315	DE77
Alexander Rd. N19	99	306	DL62
Alexander Rd., Bexh.	254	319	EX82
Alexander Rd., Chis.	277	326	EP92
Alexander Sq. SW3	78/9	315	DE77
Alexander St. W2	40	315	DA72
Alexandra Ave. N22	220	306	DK53
Alexandra Ave. SW11	160	316	DG81
Alexandra Ave. W4	155	314	CR80
Alexandra Ave., Har.	232	313	BZ60
Alexandra Ave., Sthl.	242	313	BZ73
Alexandra Ave., Sutt.	284	331	DA104
Alexandra Clo., Ashf.	265	328	BR94
Alexandra Clo., Har.	233	313	CA62
Alexandra Clo., Stai.	264	328	BK93
Alexandra Clo., Swan.	279	327	FE96
Alexandra Cotts. SE14	165	317	DZ81
Alexandra Ct. N14	208	300	DJ43
Alexandra Ct., Ashf.	265	328	BR93
Alexandra Ct., Wem.	107	304	CM63
Alexandra Cres., Brom.	275	325	EF93
Alexandra Dr. SE19	273	324	DS92
Alexandra Dr., Surb.	282	330	CN101
Alexandra Est. NW8	16/7	315	DB67
Alexandra Gdns. N10	220	306	DH56
Alexandra Gdns. W4	155	314	CS80
Alexandra Gdns., Cars.	293	332	DG109
Alexandra Gdns., Houns.	251	321	CB82
Alexandra Gro. N4	100	306	DP60
Alexandra Gro. N12	207	299	DB50
Alexandra Ms. N2	219	305	DF55
Alexandra Ms. SW19	271	323	DA93
Alexandra Palace Way N22	220	306	DJ56
Alexandra Pk. Rd. N10	220	306	DH54
Alexandra Pk. Rd. N22	220	306	DJ53
Alexandra Pl. NW8	17	315	DC67
Alexandra Pl. SE25	287	332	DR99
Alexandra Pl., Croy.	287	332	DS102
Alexandra Rd. E6	245	318	EN69
Alexandra Rd. E10	104	307	EC62
Alexandra Rd. E17	222	307	DZ58
Alexandra Rd. E18	224	308	EH55
Alexandra Rd. N8	221	306	DN55
Alexandra Rd. N9	210	301	DV45
Alexandra Rd. N10	220	306	DH53
Alexandra Rd. N15	221	306	DR57
Alexandra Rd. NW4	218	305	CX56
Alexandra Rd. NW8	112	305	DC66
Alexandra Rd. SE26	274	325	DX93
Alexandra Rd. SW14	171	322	CR83
Alexandra Rd. SW19	270	323	CZ93
Alexandra Rd. W4	145	314	CR75
Alexandra Rd., Ashf.	265	328	BR94
Alexandra Rd., Brent.	153	314	CK79
Alexandra Rd., Croy.	287	332	DS102
Alexandra Rd., Enf.	203	301	DX42
Alexandra Rd., Erith	255	319	FF79
Alexandra Rd., Houns.	251	321	CB82
Alexandra Rd., Kings.T.	269	322	CN94
Alexandra Rd., Mitch.	271	323	DE94
Alexandra Rd., Rain.	247	319	FF67
Alexandra Rd., Rich.	153	314	CM82
Alexandra Rd., Rom.	227	309	FF58
Alexandra Rd. (Chadwell Heath), Rom.	226	309	EX58
Alexandra Rd., Twick.	168	322	CJ86
Alexandra Rd., Uxb.	240	312	BK68
Alexandra Sq., Mord.	284	331	DA99
Alexandra St. E16	244	318	EG71
Alexandra St. SE14	165	317	DY80
Alexandra Wk. SE19	273	324	DS92
Alexandria Rd. W13	132	314	CG73
Alexis St. SE16	148	317	DU77
Alfan La., Dart.	279	327	FD92
Alfearn Rd. E5	118	307	DW63
Alford Pl. N1	25	316	DQ68
Alford Rd. SW8	161	316	DK81
Alford Rd., Erith	255	319	FC78
Alfoxton Ave. N15	221	306	DP56
Alfred Gdns., Sthl.	242	313	BY73
Alfred Ms. W1	46	316	DK71
Alfred Pl. WC1	46	316	DK71
Alfred Prior Ho. E12	235	308	EN63
Alfred Rd. E15	121	307	EF64
Alfred Rd. SE25	287	333	DU99
Alfred Rd. W2	40	315	DA71
Alfred Rd. W3	134	314	CQ74
Alfred Rd., Belv.	254	319	EZ78
Alfred Rd., Felt.	258	321	BW89
Alfred Rd., Kings.T.	268	322	CL97
Alfred Rd., Sutt.	285	331	DC106
Alfred St. E3	129	317	DZ69
Alfred St. E16	141	317	EF73
Alfreda St. SW11	160	316	DH81
Alfred's Gdns., Bark.	245	318	ES68
Alfreds Way, Bark.	245	318	EQ69

Alfreds Way Ind. Est., Bark.	246	319	EU67
Alfreton Clo. SW19	189	323	CX90
Alfriston Ave., Croy.	286	332	DL101
Alfriston Ave., Har.	215	303	CA58
Alfriston Clo., Surb.	282	330	CM99
Alfriston Rd. SW11	175	323	DF85
Algar Clo., Islw.	168	322	CG83
Algar Rd., Islw.	168	322	CG83
Algarve Rd. SW18	190	323	DB88
Algernon Rd. NW4	218	305	CU58
Algernon Rd. NW6	16	315	DA67
Algernon Rd. SE13	182	325	EB83
Algiers Rd. SE13	182	325	EA84
Alibon Gdns., Dag.	237	309	FA64
Alibon Rd., Dag.	236	309	EZ64
Alice Gilliatt Ct. W14	147	315	CZ78
Alice La. E3	129	317	DZ67
Alice Ms., Tedd.	267	329	CF92
Alice St. SE1	74/5	316	DS76
Alice Thompson Clo. SE12	260	326	EJ89
Alice Walker Clo. SE24	178	324	DP84
Alice Way, Houns.	259	321	CB84
Alicia Ave., Har.	216	304	CH56
Alicia Clo., Har.	216	304	CJ56
Alicia Gdns., Har.	216	304	CH56
Alie St. E1	51	316	DT72
Alington Cres. NW9	92	304	CQ60
Alington Gro., Wall.	294	332	DJ109
Alison Clo. E6	245	318	EN72
Alison Clo., Croy.	288	333	DX102
Aliwal Rd. SW11	175	323	DE84
Alkerden Rd. W4	145	314	CS78
Alkham Rd. N16	101	306	DT60
All Hallows Rd. N17	221	306	DS53
All Saints Clo. N9	210	301	DU47
All Saints Dr. SE3	167	317	EE82
All Saints Dr., S.Croy.	295	332	DT112
All Saints Ms., Stan.	215	303	CE51
All Saints Pas. SW18	174	323	DB85
All Saints Rd. SW19	271	323	DC94
All Saints Rd. W3	144	314	CQ76
All Saints Rd. W11	137	315	CZ72
All Saints Rd., Sutt.	284	331	DB104
All Saints St. N1	23	316	DM68
All Saints Twr. E10	104	307	EB59
All Souls Ave. NW10	126	315	CV68
All Souls Pl. W1	44/5	316	DH71
Allan Barclay Clo. N15	221	306	DT58
Allan Clo., N.Mal.	283	330	CR99
Allan Way W3	134	314	CQ71
Allandale Ave. N3	218	305	CY55
Allandale Rd., Enf.	203	301	DX36
Allandale Rd., Horn.	237	309	FF59
Allard Gdns. SW4	177	324	DK85
Allardyce St. SW4	177	324	DM84
Allbrook Clo., Tedd.	267	329	CE92
Allcot Clo., Felt.	265	320	BT88
Allcroft Rd. NW5	114	306	DG64
Allen Clo., Mitch.	272	324	DH95
Allen Clo., Sun.	266	329	BV95
Allen Ct., Grnf.	233	313	CF64
Allen Edwards Dr. SW8	161	316	DL81
Allen Pl., Twick.	184	322	CG88
Allen Rd. E3	129	317	DZ68
Allen Rd. N16	117	306	DS63
Allen Rd., Beck.	274	325	DX96
Allen Rd., Croy.	286	332	DM102
Allen Rd., Sun.	266	329	BV95
Allen St. W8	64	315	DA76
Allenby Ave., S.Croy.	295	332	DQ109
Allenby Clo., Grnf.	243	313	CA69
Allenby Dr., Horn.	238	311	FL60
Allenby Rd. SE23	197	325	DY90
Allenby Rd., Sthl.	243	313	CA69
Allendale Ave., Sthl.	243	313	CA72
Allendale Clo. SE5	163	316	DR81
Allendale Clo. SE26	274	325	DX92
Allendale Rd., Grnf.	106	304	CH65
Allens Rd., Enf.	210	301	DW43
Allensbury Pl. NW1	115	306	DK66
Allenswood Rd. SE9	260	326	EL83
Allerford Ct., Har.	215	303	CB57
Allerford Rd. SE6	198	325	EB90
Allerton Rd. N16	100	306	DQ61
Allerton Wk. N7	99	306	DM61
Allestree Rd. SW6	157	315	CY80
Alleyn Cres. SE21	195	324	DR89
Alleyn Pk. SE21	195	324	DR89
Alleyn Pk., Sthl.	251	321	CA78
Alleyn Rd. SE21	195	324	DR90
Alleyndale Rd., Dag.	236	309	EW61
Allfarthing La. SW18	174	323	DB86
Allgood Clo., Mord.	284	331	CX100
Allgood St. E2	27	316	DT68
Allhallows La. EC4	62	316	DR73
Allhallows Rd. E6	244	318	EL71
Alliance Clo., Wem.	107	304	CK63
Alliance Rd. E13	244	318	EJ70
Alliance Rd. SE18	254	319	EU79
Alliance Rd. W3	124	314	CP70
Allied Ind. Est. W3	145	314	CS75
Allied Way W3	145	314	CS75
Allingham Clo. W7	243	313	CF73
Allingham St. N1	25	316	DQ68
Allington Ave. N17	221	306	DS51
Allington Clo. SW19	270	323	CX92
Allington Clo., Grnf.	233	313	CC66
Allington Ct. SW19	270	323	CX92
Allington Ct., Enf.	210	301	DX43
Allington Rd. NW4	218	305	CV57
Allington Rd. W10	127	315	CY68
Allington Rd., Har.	215	303	CC57
Allington Rd., Orp.	291	334	ER103
Allington St. SW1	68/9	316	DH76
Allison Clo. SE10	166	317	EC81
Allison Gro. SE21	195	324	DS88
Allison Rd. N8	221	306	DN57
Allison Rd. W3	134	314	CQ72
Allitsen Rd. NW8	18/9	315	DE68
Allnutt Way SW4	177	324	DK85
Alloa Rd. SE8	149	317	DY78
Alloa Rd., Ilf.	236	309	EU61
Allonby Dr., Ruis.	231	312	BP59
Allonby Gdns., Wem.	90	304	CJ60
Alloway Rd. E3	129	317	DY69
Allsop Pl. NW1	31	315	DF70
Allum La., Borwd.	204	298	CK43
Allum Way N20	207	299	DC46
Allwood Clo. SE26	274	325	DX91
Alma Ave. E4	223	307	EC52
Alma Ave., Horn.	238	311	FL63
Alma Cres., Sutt.	284	331	CY106
Alma Gro. SE1	87	316	DT77
Alma Pl. NW10	126	315	CV69
Alma Pl. SE19	273	324	DT94
Alma Pl., Th.Hth.	286	332	DN99
Alma Rd. N10	220	306	DH52
Alma Rd. SW18	174	323	DC84
Alma Rd., Cars.	285	331	DE106
Alma Rd., Enf.	203	301	DY41
Alma Rd., Sid.	262	327	EU90
Alma Rd., Sthl.	242	313	BY73
Alma Row, Har.	215	303	CD53
Alma Sq. NW8	29	315	DC69
Alma St. E15	121	307	ED65
Alma St. NW5	114	306	DH65
Alma Ter. SW18	191	323	DD87
Almack Rd. E5	118	307	DW63
Almeida St. N1	116	306	DP66
Almer Rd. SW20	270	323	CU94
Almeric Rd. SW11	175	323	DF84
Almington St. N4	99	306	DL60
Almond Ave. W5	143	314	CL76
Almond Ave., Cars.	285	331	DF103
Almond Ave., Uxb.	231	312	BP62
Almond Ave., West Dr.	249	320	BN76
Almond Clo. SE15	164	317	DU82
Almond Clo., Brom.	290	334	EN101
Almond Clo., Hayes	249	312	BS73
Almond Clo., Ruis.	231	312	BT62
Almond Clo., Shep.	281	328	BQ96
Almond Dr., Swan.	279	327	FD96
Almond Gro., Brent.	152	314	CH80
Almond Rd. N17	222	307	DU52
Almond Rd. SE16	148	317	DV77
Almond Way, Brom.	290	334	EN101
Almond Way, Har.	215	303	CB54
Almond Way, Mitch.	286	332	DK99

Almorah Rd. N1	117	306	DR66
Almorah Rd., Houns.	250	321	BX81
Almshouse La., Enf.	203	301	DV37
Alnwick Gro., Mord.	271	323	DB98
Alnwick Rd. E16	244	318	EJ72
Alnwick Rd. SE12	260	326	EH87
Alperton La., Grnf.	123	314	CK68
Alperton La., Wem.	123	314	CK68
Alperton St. W10	127	315	CY70
Alpha Clo. NW1	30/1	315	DE69
Alpha Gro. E14	150	317	EA75
Alpha Pl. NW6	16	315	DA68
Alpha Pl. SW3	159	315	DE79
Alpha Rd. E4	211	301	EA48
Alpha Rd. N18	222	307	DU51
Alpha Rd. SE14	165	317	DZ81
Alpha Rd., Croy.	287	332	DS102
Alpha Rd., Enf.	203	301	DY42
Alpha Rd., Surb.	282	330	CM100
Alpha Rd., Tedd.	267	329	CD92
Alpha Rd., Uxb.	241	312	BP70
Alpha St. SE15	164	317	DU82
Alphabet Gdns., Cars.	285	331	DD100
Alphabet Sq. E3	140	317	EA71
Alphea Clo. SW19	271	323	DE94
Alpine Ave., Surb.	283	330	CQ103
Alpine Clo., Croy.	287	332	DS104
Alpine Copse, Brom.	277	326	EN96
Alpine Rd. SE16	148	317	DW77
Alpine Vw., Sutt.	285	331	DE106
Alpine Way E6	245	318	EN71
Alric Ave. NW10	109	304	CR66
Alric Ave., N.Mal.	269	322	CS97
Alroy Rd. N4	100	306	DN59
Alsace Rd. SE17	86/7	316	DS78
Alscot Rd. SE1	87	316	DT77
Alscot Way SE1	87	316	DT77
Alsike Rd. SE2	254	319	EX76
Alsike Rd., Erith	254	319	EY76
Alsom Ave., Wor.Pk.	283	330	CT105
Alston Rd. N18	210	301	DV50
Alston Rd. SW17	271	323	DD91
Alt Gro. SW19	270	323	CZ94
Altair Clo. N17	221	306	DT51
Altair Way, Nthwd.	213	302	BT50
Altash Way SE9	260	326	EM89
Altenburg Ave. W13	142	314	CH76
Altenburg Gdns. SW11	175	323	DF84
Altham Rd., Pnr.	214	303	BY52
Althea St. SW6	158	315	DB82
Althorne Gdns. E18	223	307	EF56
Althorne Way, Dag.	237	309	FA61
Althorp Rd. SW17	191	323	DF88
Althorpe Gro. SW11	159	315	DD81
Althorpe Ms. SW11	159	315	DD81
Althorpe Rd., Har.	215	303	CC57
Altmore Ave. E6	234	308	EM66
Alton Ave., Stan.	215	303	CF52
Alton Clo., Bex.	262	327	EY88
Alton Clo., Islw.	251	321	CF82
Alton Gdns., Beck.	275	325	EA94
Alton Gdns., Twick.	259	321	CD86
Alton Rd. N17	221	306	DR55
Alton Rd. SW15	188	323	CU88
Alton Rd., Croy.	286	332	DN104
Alton Rd., Rich.	169	322	CL84
Alton St. E14	140	317	EB71
Altyre Clo., Beck.	288	333	DZ99
Altyre Rd., Croy.	287	332	DR103
Altyre Way, Beck.	288	333	DZ100
Alvanley Gdns. NW6	112	305	DB64
Alverstoke Rd., Rom.	228	311	FL52
Alverston Gdns. SE25	287	332	DS99
Alverstone Ave. SW19	190	323	DA89
Alverstone Ave., Barn.	207	299	DE45
Alverstone Gdns. SE9	261	326	EQ88
Alverstone Rd. E12	235	308	EN63
Alverstone Rd. NW2	110	305	CW66
Alverstone Rd., N.Mal.	269	322	CT98
Alverstone Rd., Wem.	91	304	CM60
Alverton St. SE8	149	317	DZ78
Alveston Ave., Har.	216	304	CH55
Alvey Est. SE17	86/7	316	DS77
Alvey St. SE17	86/7	316	DS78
Alvia Gdns., Sutt.	285	331	DC105
Alvington Cres. E8	117	306	DT64
Alway Ave., Epsom	283	330	CQ106
Alwold Cres. SE12	260	326	EH86
Alwyn Ave. W4	145	314	CR78
Alwyn Clo., Borwd.	204	298	CM44
Alwyn Gdns. NW4	218	305	CU56
Alwyn Gdns. W3	134	314	CP72
Alwyne La. N1	116	306	DP66
Alwyne Pl. N1	116	306	DQ65
Alwyne Rd. N1	116	306	DQ66
Alwyne Rd. SW19	270	323	CZ93
Alwyne Rd. W7	243	313	CE73
Alwyne Sq. N1	116	306	DQ65
Alwyne Vil. N1	116	306	DP66
Alwyns Clo., Cher.	280	328	BG100
Alyth Gdns. NW11	219	305	DA58
Alzette Ho. E2	129	317	DX68
Amalgamated Dr., Brent.	152	314	CG79
Amanda Clo., Ilf.	225	308	ER51
Amazon St. E1	138	317	DV72
Ambassador Clo., Houns.	250	321	BY82
Ambassador Gdns. E6	244	318	EM71
Ambassador Sq. E14	150	317	EB77
Ambassador's Ct. SW1	57	316	DJ74
Amber Ave. E17	222	307	DY53
Amber Gro. NW2	95	305	CX60
Amber St. E15	121	307	ED65
Amberden Ave. N3	219	305	DA55
Ambergate St. SE17	84/5	316	DP78
Amberley Clo., Orp.	291	334	ET106
Amberley Clo., Pnr.	214	303	BZ55
Amberley Ct., Sid.	278	327	EW92
Amberley Gdns., Enf.	209	300	DS45
Amberley Gdns., Epsom	283	330	CT105
Amberley Gro. SE26	274	325	DV92
Amberley Gro., Croy.	287	332	DT101
Amberley Rd. E10	104	307	EA59
Amberley Rd. N13	208	300	DM47
Amberley Rd. SE2	254	319	EX79
Amberley Rd. W9	40	315	DA71
Amberley Rd., Enf.	209	300	DT45
Amberley Way, Houns.	258	321	BW85
Amberley Way, Mord.	284	331	CZ101
Amberley Way, Rom.	227	309	FB56
Amberley Way, Uxb.	240	312	BL69
Amberside Clo., Islw.	259	321	CD86
Amberwood Ri., N.Mal.	283	330	CS100
Amblecote Clo. SE12	260	326	EH90
Amblecote Meadows SE12	260	326	EH90
Amblecote Rd. SE12	260	326	EH90
Ambler Rd. N4	100	306	DP62
Ambleside, Brom.	275	325	ED93
Ambleside Ave. SW16	272	324	DK91
Ambleside Ave., Beck.	288	333	DY99
Ambleside Ave., Horn.	238	310	FH64
Ambleside Clo. E9	118	307	DW64
Ambleside Clo. E10	104	307	EB59
Ambleside Cres., Enf.	203	301	DX41
Ambleside Dr., Felt.	265	320	BT88
Ambleside Gdns., Ilf.	224	308	EL56
Ambleside Gdns., Sutt.	293	331	DC107
Ambleside Gdns., Wem.	91	304	CK60
Ambleside Rd. NW10	109	304	CT66
Ambleside Rd., Bexh.	255	319	FA82
Ambrey Way, Wall.	294	332	DK109
Ambrooke Rd., Belv.	255	319	FA76
Ambrosden Ave. SW1	69	316	DJ76
Ambrose Ave. NW11	95	305	CY59
Ambrose Clo. E6	244	318	EL71
Ambrose Clo., Dart.	263	327	FF84
Ambrose Clo., Orp.	291	334	ET104
Ambrose Ms. SW11	159	315	DF82
Ambrose St. SE16	148	317	DV77
Ambrose Wk. E3	130	317	EA68
Amelia St. SE17	84/5	316	DP78
Amen Cor. EC4	48/9	316	DP72
Amen Cor. SW17	271	323	DF93
Amen Ct. EC4	48/9	316	DP72
Amenity Way, Mord.	284	331	CW101
America Sq. EC3	63	316	DT73
America St. SE1	61	316	DQ74
Amerland Rd. SW18	173	323	CZ85
Amersham Ave. N18	221	306	DR51

ame

Amersham Clo., Rom. 228 311 FM51
Amersham Dr., Rom. 228 311 FL51
Amersham Gro. SE14 165 317 DZ80
Amersham Rd. SE14 165 317 DZ81
Amersham Rd., Croy. 287 332 DQ100
Amersham Rd., Rom. 228 311 FL51
Amersham Vale SE14 165 317 DZ80
Amersham Wk., Rom. 228 311 FM51
Amery Gdns. NW10 126 315 CV67
Amery Gdns., Rom. 228 310 FK55
Amery Rd., Har. 90 304 CG61
Amesbury Ave. SW2 193 324 DL89
Amesbury Clo., Wor.Pk. 248 331 CW102
Amesbury Dr. E4 211 301 EB44
Amesbury Rd., Brom. 276 326 EK97
Amesbury Rd., Dag. 236 309 EX66
Amesbury Rd., Felt. 258 321 BX89
Amethyst Rd. E15 121 307 ED63
Amherst Ave. W13 132 314 CJ72
Amherst Clo., Orp. 278 327 EU98
Amherst Dr., Orp. 277 326 ET98
Amherst Rd. W13 132 314 CJ72
Amherst Gdns., Islw. 251 321 CF81
Amhurst Par. N16 101 306 DT59
Amhurst Pk. N16 101 306 DR59
Amhurst Pas. E8 118 307 DU64
Amhurst Rd. E8 118 307 DV64
Amhurst Rd. N16 117 306 DT63
Amhurst Ter. E8 118 307 DU63
Amhurst Wk. SE28 246 319 EU74
Amidas Gdns., Dag. 236 309 EV63
Amiel St. E1 128 317 DW70
Amies St. SW11 175 323 DF83
Amina Way SE16 148 317 DU76
Amity Gro. SW20 270 323 CW95
Amity Rd. E15 131 317 EF67
Ammanford Gdn. NW9 217 304 CS58
Amner Rd. SW11 176 324 DG86
Amoco Ho. W5 123 314 CL69
Amor Rd. W6 146 315 CW76
Amott Rd. SE15 180 325 DU83
Amoy Pl. E14 140 317 EA72
Ampere Way, Croy. 286 332 DL101
Ampleforth Rd. SE2 254 319 EV75
Ampthill Sq. Est. NW1 21 316 DJ68
Ampton Pl. WC1 35 316 DM69
Ampton St. WC1 35 316 DM69
Amroth Clo. SE23 196 325 DV88
Amsterdam Rd. E14 150 317 EC76
Amwell Clo., Enf. 209 300 DR43
Amwell Ct. Est. N4 100 306 DQ60
Amwell St. EC1 36 316 DN69
Amy Warne Clo. E6 244 318 EL70
Amyand Cotts., Twick. 168 322 CH86
Amyand La., Twick. 184 322 CH87
Amyand Pk. Gdns., Twick. 184 322 CH87
Amyand Pk. Rd., Twick. 184 322 CG87
Amyruth Rd. SE4 182 325 EA85
Anatola Rd. N19 98 306 DH61
Ancaster Cres., N.Mal. 283 331 CU100
Ancaster Ms., Beck. 274 325 DX97
Ancaster Rd., Beck. 274 325 DX97
Ancaster St. SE18 253 318 ES80
Anchor & Hope La. SE7 252 318 EJ77
Anchor Ms. SW12 176 324 DH86
Anchor St. SE16 148 317 DV77
Anchor Wf. E3 140 317 EB71
Anchor Yd. EC1 37 316 DQ70
Anchorage Clo. SW19 271 323 DA92
Ancill Clo. W6 157 315 CY79
Ancona Rd. NW10 126 315 CU68
Ancona Rd. SE18 253 318 ER78
Andace Pk. Gdns., Brom. 276 326 EJ95
Andalus Rd. SW9 177 324 DL83
Ander Clo., Wem. 107 304 CK63
Anderson Clo. W3 135 314 CR72
Anderson Clo., Uxb. 212 302 BG53
Anderson Dr., Ashf. 265 328 BQ91
Anderson Ho., Bark. 245 318 ER68
Anderson Pl., Houns. 259 321 CB84
Anderson Rd. E9 119 307 DX65
Anderson Rd., Wdf.Grn. 224 308 EK55
Anderson St. SW3 79 315 DF78
Anderson Way, Belv. 255 319 FB75
Anderton Clo. SE5 179 324 DR83
Andover Ave. E16 244 318 EK72
Andover Clo., Felt. 265 320 BT88
Andover Clo., Grnf. 243 313 CB70
Andover Clo., Uxb. 240 312 BH68
Andover Pl. NW6 16/7 315 DB68
Andover Rd. N7 99 306 DM61
Andover Rd., Orp. 291 334 ES103
Andover Rd., Twick. 259 321 CD88
Andre St. E8 118 307 DU64
Andrew Borde St. WC2 46 316 DK72
Andrew Clo., Bex. 263 327 FD85
Andrew Clo., Dart. 263 327 FD85
Andrew Clo., Ilf. 225 308 ER51
Andrew Pl. SW8 161 316 DK81
Andrew St. E14 140 317 EC72
Andrewes Gdns. E6 244 318 EL72
Andrewes Ho. EC2 49 316 DQ71
Andrews Clo. E6 244 318 EL72
Andrews Clo., Har. 233 313 CD59
Andrews Clo., Orp. 278 327 EX97
Andrews Clo., Wor.Pk. 284 331 CW103
Andrews Crosse WC2 48 316 DN72
Andrews Pl. SE9 261 326 EP86
Andrew's Rd. E8 128 317 DV67
Andrews Wk. SE17 162 316 DP79
Andwell Clo. SE2 254 319 EV75
Anerley Gro. SE19 273 324 DT94
Anerley Hill SE19 273 324 DT93
Anerley Pk. SE20 274 325 DU94
Anerley Pk. Rd. SE20 274 325 DV94
Anerley Rd. SE19 274 325 DU94
Anerley Rd. SE20 274 325 DU94
Anerley Sta. Rd. SE20 274 325 DV95
Anerley St. SW11 159 315 DF82
Anerley Vale SE19 273 324 DT94
Anfield Clo. SW12 192 324 DJ87
Angel All. E1 138 317 DU72
Angel Clo. N18 209 300 DT50
Angel Ct. EC2 50 316 DR72
Angel Ct. SW1 57 316 DJ74
Angel Ct. SW17 271 323 DF91
Angel Hill, Sutt. 284 331 DB104
Angel Hill Dr., Sutt. 284 331 DB104
Angel La. E15 121 307 ED65
Angel La., Hayes 249 312 BR71
Angel Ms. N1 24 316 DN68
Angel Pas. EC4 62 316 DR73
Angel Pl. N18 210 301 DU50
Angel Pl. SE1 74 316 DR75
Angel Rd. N18 210 301 DU50
Angel Rd., Har. 215 303 CE58
Angel Rd. Wks. N18 210 301 DW50
Angel Sq. EC1 24 316 DN68
Angel St. EC1 49 316 DQ72
Angel Wk. W6 146 315 CW78
Angel Way, Rom. 227 309 FE57
Angelfield, Houns. 259 321 CB84
Angelica Dr. E6 245 318 EN71
Angelica Gdns., Croy. 288 333 DX102
Angell Pk. Gdns. SW9 178 324 DN83
Angell Rd. SW9 178 324 DN83
Angerstein La. SE3 167 317 EF81
Angle Clo., Uxb. 241 312 BN67
Angle Grn., Dag. 236 309 EW60
Anglers Clo., Rich. 268 322 CJ91
Angler's La. NW5 114 306 DH65
Angles Rd. SW16 272 324 DL91
Anglesea Ave. SE18 253 318 EP77
Anglesea Rd. SE18 253 318 EP77
Anglesea Rd., Kings.T. 268 322 CK98
Anglesea Ter. W6 146 315 CV76
Anglesey Clo., Ashf. 265 328 BN91
Anglesey Ct. Rd., Cars. 293 332 DG107
Anglesey Gdns., Cars. 293 332 DG107
Anglesey Rd., Enf. 203 301 DV42
Anglesmede Cres., Pnr. 214 303 CA55
Anglesmede Way, Pnr. 214 303 BY55
Anglia Clo. N17 222 307 DV52
Anglia Ho. E14 139 317 DY72
Anglia Wk. E6 244 318 EM67
Anglian Ind. Est., Bark. 246 319 EU71
Anglian Rd. E11 105 307 ED62
Anglo Rd. E3 129 317 DZ68

Angrave Ct. E8 27 316 DT67
Angrave Pas. E8 27 316 DT67
Angus Clo., Chess. 282 330 CN106
Angus Dr., Ruis. 232 313 BW63
Angus Gdns. NW9 217 304 CR53
Angus Rd. E13 244 318 EJ69
Angus St. SE14 165 317 DY80
Anhalt Rd. SW11 159 315 DE80
Ankerdine Cres. SE18 253 318 EP81
Anlaby Rd., Tedd. 267 329 CE92
Anley Rd. W14 147 315 CX75
Anmersh Gro., Stan. 216 304 CK53
Ann La. SW10 158 315 DD80
Ann Moss Way SE16 148 317 DW76
Ann St. SE18 253 318 EQ78
Anna Clo. E8 27 316 DT67
Anna Neagle Clo. E7 234 308 EG63
Annabel Clo. E14 140 317 EB72
Annan Way, Rom. 227 309 FD53
Annandale Gro., Uxb. 231 312 BQ62
Annandale Rd. SE10 151 317 EF78
Annandale Rd. W4 145 314 CS78
Annandale Rd., Croy. 287 333 DU103
Annandale Rd., Sid. 261 326 ES87
Anne Boleyn's Wk., Kings.T. 268 322 CL92
Anne Boleyn's Wk., Sutt. 292 331 CX108
Anne Case Ms., N.Mal. 269 322 CR97
Anne St. E13 244 318 EG70
Anne Way, Ilf. 225 308 EQ51
Anne Way, W.Mol. 267 329 CB98
Annesley Ave. NW9 217 304 CR55
Annesley Clo. NW10 93 304 CS62
Annesley Dr., Croy. 288 333 DZ105
Annesley Rd. SE3 252 318 EH81
Annesley Wk. N19 98 306 DJ61
Annett Clo., Shep. 281 328 BS98
Annette Clo., Har. 215 303 CE54
Annette Cres. N1 116 306 DQ66
Annette Rd. N7 99 306 DM62
Annie Besant Clo. E3 129 317 DZ67
Anning St. EC2 38/9 316 DS70
Annington Rd. N2 219 305 DF55
Annis Rd. E9 119 307 DY65
Ann's Clo. SW1 67 315 DF75
Ann's Pl. E1 51 316 DT71
Annsworthy Ave., Th.Hth. 273 324 DR97
Annsworthy Cres. SE25 273 324 DR96
Ansdell Rd. SE15 164 317 DW82
Ansdell St. W8 64/5 315 DB76
Ansdell Ter. W8 64/5 315 DB76
Ansell Gro., Cars. 285 332 DG102
Ansell Rd. SW17 191 323 DE90
Anselm Clo., Croy. 287 332 DT104
Anselm Rd. SW6 158 315 DA79
Anselm Rd., Pnr. 214 303 BZ52
Ansford Rd., Brom. 275 325 EC92
Ansleigh Pl. W11 137 315 CX73
Ansley Clo., S.Croy. 295 333 DV114
Anson Clo., Rom. 227 309 FB54
Anson Rd. N7 114 306 DJ63
Anson Rd. NW2 110 305 CV64
Anson Ter., Nthlt. 233 313 CB65
Anson Wk., Nthwd. 213 302 BP49
Anstey Rd. SE15 180 325 DU83
Anstey Wk. N15 221 306 DP56
Anstice Clo. W4 155 314 CS80
Anstridge Path SE9 261 326 ER86
Anstridge Rd. SE9 261 326 ER86
Antelope Rd. SE18 252 318 EM76
Anthony Clo. NW7 205 298 CS49
Anthony Rd. SE25 287 333 DU100
Anthony Rd., Grnf. 243 313 CE68
Anthony Rd., Well. 254 319 EU81
Anthony St. E1 138 317 DV72
Anthus Ms., Nthwd. 213 302 BS52
Antigua Clo. SE19 273 324 DR92
Antigua Wk. SE19 273 324 DR92
Antill Rd. E3 129 317 DY69
Antill Rd. N15 222 307 DU56
Antill Ter. E1 139 317 DX72
Anton Cres., Sutt. 284 331 DA104
Anton St. E8 118 307 DU64
Antoneys Clo., Pnr. 214 303 BX54
Antrim Gro. NW3 113 305 DF65
Antrim Mans. NW3 113 305 DF65
Antrim Rd. NW3 113 305 DF65
Antrobus Clo., Sutt. 284 331 CZ106
Antrobus Rd. W4 144 314 CQ77
Anvil Rd., Sun. 266 329 BU98
Anworth Clo., Wdf.Grn. 224 308 EH51
Apeldoorn Dr., Wall. 294 332 DL109
Aperfield Rd., Erith 255 319 FF79
Apex Clo., Beck. 275 325 EB95
Apex Cor. NW7 205 298 CR49
Apex Twr., N.Mal. 269 322 CS97
Aplin Way, Islw. 251 321 CE81
Apollo Ave., Brom. 276 326 EH95
Apollo Clo., Horn. 238 310 FH61
Apollo Pl. E11 105 307 EE62
Apollo Pl. SW10 158 315 DD80
Apollo Way SE28 253 318 ER76
Apostle Way, Th.Hth. 273 324 DP96
Apothecary St. EC4 48/9 316 DP72
Appach Rd. SW2 178 324 DN85
Apple Garth, Brent. 143 314 CK77
Apple Gro., Chess. 282 330 CL105
Apple Gro., Enf. 202 300 DS41
Apple Mkt., Kings.T. 268 322 CK96
Apple Orchard, Swan. 279 327 FD98
Apple Rd. E11 105 307 EE62
Apple Tree Ave., Uxb. 248 312 BM72
Apple Tree Ave., West Dr. 248 312 BM72
Apple Tree Yd. SW1 57 316 DJ74
Appleby Clo. E4 223 307 EB51
Appleby Clo. N15 221 306 DR57
Appleby Clo., Twick. 265 321 CD89
Appleby Gdns., Felt. 259 320 BT88
Appleby Rd. E8 118 307 DU66
Appleby Rd. E16 141 317 EF72
Appleby St. E2 27 316 DT68
Appledore Ave., Bexh. 255 319 FC81
Appledore Ave., Ruis. 232 313 BW62
Appledore Clo. SW17 191 323 DF89
Appledore Clo., Brom. 289 333 EF99
Appledore Clo., Edg. 217 304 CN53
Appledore Clo., Rom. 228 310 FJ53
Appledore Cres., Sid. 261 326 ES90
Appleford Rd. W10 127 315 CY70
Applegarth Dr., Ilf. 225 308 ET56
Applegarth Rd. SE28 246 319 EV74
Applegarth Rd. W14 147 315 CX76
Appleton Gdns., N.Mal. 283 331 CU100
Appleton Rd. SE9 260 326 EL83
Appleton Sq., Mitch. 271 323 DE95
Appleton Way, Horn. 238 310 FK60
Appletree Clo. SE20 274 325 DV95
Applewood Clo. N20 207 299 DE46
Applewood Clo. NW2 94 305 CV62
Appold St. EC2 50/1 316 DS71
Appold St., Erith 255 319 FF79
Apprentice Way E5 118 307 DV63
Approach, The NW4 218 305 CX57
Approach, The W3 135 314 CR72
Approach, The, Enf. 203 301 DV40
Approach, The, Orp. 291 334 ET103
Approach, The, Upmin. 239 311 FP62
Approach Clo. N16 117 306 DS64
Approach Rd. E2 128 317 DW68
Approach Rd. SW20 270 323 CW96
Approach Rd., Ashf. 265 328 BQ93
Approach Rd., Pur. 294 332 DP112
Aprey Gdns. NW4 218 305 CW56
April Clo. W7 243 313 CE73
April Clo., Felt. 258 321 BU90
April Clo., Orp. 291 334 ET106
April Glen SE23 197 325 DX90
April St. E8 117 306 DT63
Apsley Clo., Har. 215 303 CC57
Apsley Rd. SE25 274 325 DV98
Apsley Rd., N.Mal. 269 322 CQ97
Apsley Way NW2 94 305 CU61
Apsley Way W1 68 316 DG75
Aquila St. NW8 18 315 DD68
Aquinas St. SE1 60 316 DN74
Arabella Dr. SW15 171 322 CS84
Arabia Clo. E4 211 301 EC45
Arabin Rd. SE4 181 325 DY84
Aragon Clo., Brom. 290 334 EM102

Aragon Clo., Rom. 227 309 FB51
Aragon Clo., Sun. 265 328 BT94
Aragon Dr., Ilf. 225 308 EQ52
Aragon Dr., Ruis. 232 313 BX60
Aragon Ms. E1 138 317 DU74
Aragon Rd., Kings.T. 268 322 CL92
Aragon Rd., Mord. 284 331 CX100
Aran Dr., Stan. 204 298 CJ49
Arandora Cres., Rom. 236 309 EV59
Arbery Rd. E3 129 317 DY69
Arbor Clo., Beck. 275 325 EB96
Arbor Ct. N16 101 306 DR61
Arbor Rd. E4 211 303 ED48
Arbour Rd., Enf. 203 301 DX42
Arbour Sq. E1 139 317 DX72
Arbour Way, Horn. 238 310 FH64
Arbroath Rd. SE9 260 326 EL83
Arbrook Clo., Orp. 278 327 EU97
Arbury Ter. SE26 196 325 DV90
Arbuthnot La., Bex. 262 327 EY86
Arbuthnot Rd. SE14 165 317 DX82
Arbutus St. E8 27 316 DT67
Arcade, The EC2 50/1 316 DS71
Arcade Pl., Rom. 227 309 FE57
Arcadia Ave. N3 219 305 DA53
Arcadia Clo., Cars. 285 332 DG105
Arcadia St. E14 140 317 EA72
Arcadian Ave., Bex. 262 327 EY86
Arcadian Clo., Bex. 262 327 EY86
Arcadian Gdns. N22 220 306 DM52
Arcadian Rd., Bex. 262 327 EY86
Arch St. SE1 73 316 DQ76
Archangel St. SE16 149 317 DX75
Archbishops Pl. SW2 177 324 DM86
Archdale Pl., N.Mal. 269 322 CP97
Archdale Rd. SE22 179 324 DT85
Archel Rd. W14 157 315 CZ79
Archer Clo., Kings.T. 268 322 CL94
Archer Ho. SW11 159 315 DD81
Archer Ms., Hmptn. 267 329 CC93
Archer Rd. SE25 274 325 DV98
Archer Rd., Orp. 291 335 EU99
Archer St. W1 58 316 DK73
Archer Ter., West Dr. 248 312 BL73
Archer Way, Swan. 279 327 FF96
Archers Dr., Enf. 203 301 DW40
Archery Clo. W2 163 316 DT81
Archery Clo., Har. 42/3 315 DE72
Archery Rd. SE9 215 303 CF55
Arches, The SW6 260 326 EM85
Arches, The WC2 157 315 CZ82
Arches, The, Har. 58/9 316 DL74
Archibald Ms. W1 233 313 CB61
Archibald Rd. N7 56 316 DG73
Archibald Rd., Rom. 115 306 DK63
Archibald St. E3 229 311 FN53
Archie Clo., West Dr. 130 317 EA70
Archway, Rom. 249 320 BN75
Archway Clo. N19 228 310 FH51
Archway Clo. SW19 98 306 DJ61
Archway Clo., Wall. 271 323 DB91
Archway Mall N19 286 332 DK104
Archway Rd. N6 98 306 DJ61
Archway Rd. N19 219 305 DF57
Archway St. SW13 98 306 DJ60
Arcola St. E8 171 322 CS83
Arctic St. NW5 117 306 DT64
Arcus Rd., Brom. 114 306 DG64
Ardbeg Rd. SE24 275 325 EE93
Arden Clo., Har. 179 324 DR85
Arden Ct. Gdns. N2 233 313 CD62
Arden Cres. E14 219 305 DD58
Arden Cres., Dag. 150 317 EA77
Arden Est. N1 236 309 EW66
Arden Gro., Orp. 26/7 316 DS68
Arden Ms. E17 290 334 EP105
Arden Mhor, Pnr. 223 307 EB57
Arden Rd. N3 214 303 BV56
Arden Rd. W13 218 305 CY55
Ardent Clo. SE25 132 314 CJ73
Ardfern Ave. SW16 273 324 DS97
Ardfillan Rd. SE6 273 324 DN97
Ardgowan Rd. SE6 199 325 ED88
Ardilaun Rd. N5 199 325 EE87
Ardingly Clo., Croy. 116 306 DQ63
Ardleigh Clo., Horn. 288 333 DX104
Ardleigh Gdns., Sutt. 228 310 FK55
Ardleigh Grn. Rd., Horn. 284 331 DA101
Ardleigh Ho., Bark. 228 310 FK58
Ardleigh Ms., Ilf. 245 318 EQ67
Ardleigh Rd. E17 235 308 EP62
Ardleigh Rd. N1 222 307 DZ53
Ardleigh Ter. E17 117 306 DS65
Ardley Clo. NW10 222 307 DZ53
Ardley Clo. SE6 93 304 CS62
Ardley Clo., Ruis. 197 325 DY90
Ardlui Rd. SE27 231 312 BQ59
Ardmay Gdns., Surb. 194 324 DQ89
Ardmere Rd. SE13 282 330 CL99
Ardoch Rd. SE6 183 325 ED86
Ardra Rd. N9 199 325 ED89
Ardross Ave., Nthwd. 210 301 DX48
Ardrossan Gdns., Wor.Pk. 213 302 BS50
Ardshiel Clo. SW15 283 331 CU104
Ardwell Ave., Ilf. 173 323 CX83
Ardwell Rd. SW2 225 308 EQ57
Ardwick Rd. NW2 193 324 DL89
Arena Ind. Est., Enf. 112 305 DA63
Argall Ave. E10 203 301 DZ38
Argent St. SE1 103 307 DX59
Argenta Way NW10 72/3 316 DP75
Argon Ms. SW6 108 304 CP66
Argon Rd. N18 158 315 DA80
Argosy La., Stai. 210 301 DX50
Argus Clo., Rom. 264 320 BK87
Argus Way W3 227 309 FB53
Argus Way, Nthlt. 144 314 CP76
Argyle Ave., Houns. 242 313 BY69
Argyle Clo. W13 259 321 CA86
Argyle Gdns., Upmin. 122 314 CG70
Argyle Pas. N17 239 311 FR61
Argyle Pl. W6 221 306 DT53
Argyle Rd. E1 146 315 CV77
Argyle Rd. E15 129 317 DX70
Argyle Rd. E16 121 307 EE64
Argyle Rd. N12 141 318 EH72
Argyle Rd. N17 207 299 DA50
Argyle Rd. N18 222 307 DU53
Argyle Rd. W13 210 301 DU49
Argyle Rd., Grnf. 132 314 CG71
Argyle Rd., Har. 243 313 CF69
Argyle Rd., Houns. 215 303 CB58
Argyle Rd., Ilf. 259 321 CB85
Argyle Rd., Tedd. 235 308 EN61
Argyle Sq. WC1 267 329 CE92
Argyle St. WC1 34/5 316 DL69
Argyle Wk. WC1 34/5 316 DL69
Argyle Way SE16 34/5 316 DL69
Argyll Ave., Sthl. 148 317 DU78
Argyll Clo. SW9 243 313 CB74
Argyll Gdns., Edg. 177 324 DM83
Argyll Rd. W8 217 304 CP54
Argyll St. W1 64 315 DA75
Arica Rd. SE4 45 316 DJ72
Ariel Rd. NW6 181 325 DY84
Ariel Way W12 112 305 DA65
Ariel Way, Houns. 136 315 CW74
Aristotle Rd. SW4 258 321 BV83
Arkell Gro. SE19 177 324 DK83
Arkindale Rd. SE6 273 324 DP94
Arkley Cres. E17 198 325 EC90
Arkley Rd. E17 222 307 DZ57
Arklow Ms., Surb. 222 307 DZ57
Arklow Rd. SE14 282 330 CL103
Arkwright Rd. NW3 165 317 DZ79
Arkwright Rd., S.Croy. 112 305 DC64
Arlesey Clo. SW15 295 332 DT110
Arlesford Rd. SW9 173 323 CY86
Arlingford Rd. SW2 177 324 DL83
Arlington N12 178 324 DN85
Arlington Ave. N1 207 299 DA48
Arlington Clo., Sid. 25 316 DQ67
Arlington Clo., Sutt. 261 326 ES87
Arlington Clo., Twick. 284 331 DA103
Arlington Ct., Hayes 168 322 CJ86
Arlington Dr., Cars. 249 320 BR78
Arlington Dr., Ruis. 285 331 DF103
231 302 BR58

Arlington Gdns. W4 144 314 CQ78
Arlington Gdns., Ilf. 235 308 EN60
Arlington Gdns., Rom. 228 311 FL53
Arlington Lo. SW2 177 324 DM84
Arlington Ms., Twick. 168 322 CH86
Arlington Pl. SE10 166 317 EC80
Arlington Rd. N14 208 300 DH47
Arlington Rd. NW1 20/1 316 DH67
Arlington Rd. W13 132 314 CH72
Arlington Rd., Ashf. 264 328 BM92
Arlington Rd., Rich. 185 322 CK89
Arlington Rd., Surb. 282 330 CK100
Arlington Rd., Tedd. 267 329 CF91
Arlington Rd., Twick. 168 322 CJ86
Arlington Rd., Wdf.Grn. 224 308 EG52
Arlington Sq. N1 25 316 DQ67
Arlington St. SW1 57 316 DJ74
Arlington Way EC1 36 316 DN69
Arliss Way, Nthlt. 242 313 BW67
Arlow Rd. N21 209 300 DN46
Armada Ct. SE8 166 317 EA79
Armada St. SE8 166 317 EA79
Armada Way E6 245 318 EQ73
Armadale Clo. N17 222 307 DV56
Armadale Rd. SW6 158 315 DA80
Armadale Rd., Felt. 258 321 BU85
Armagh Rd. E3 129 317 DZ67
Armfield Cres., Mitch. 271 323 DF96
Armfield Rd., Enf. 202 300 DR39
Arminger Rd. W12 136 315 CV74
Armitage Rd. NW11 95 305 CY60
Armitage Rd. SE10 151 317 EF78
Armour Clo. N7 115 306 DM65
Armoury Rd. SE8 166 317 EB82
Armoury Way SW18 174 323 DA85
Armstead Wk., Dag. 237 309 FA66
Armstrong Ave., Wdf.Grn. 223 307 EE51
Armstrong Clo. E6 244 318 EM72
Armstrong Clo., Dag. 236 309 EX60
Armstrong Clo., Pnr. 214 303 BU58
Armstrong Rd. SW7 66 315 DD76
Armstrong Rd. W3 135 314 CT74
Armstrong Rd., Felt. 266 329 BY92
Armstrong Way, Sthl. 251 321 CB75
Armytage Rd., Houns. 250 321 BX80
Arnal Cres. SW18 189 323 CY87
Arncroft Ct., Bark. 246 319 EV69
Arndale Cen., The SW18 174 323 DB86
Arndale Wk. SW18 174 323 DB85
Arne Gro., Orp. 291 334 ET104
Arne St. WC2 46/7 316 DL72
Arne Wk. SE3 183 325 EF84
Arnett Sq. E4 222 307 DZ51
Arneway St. SW1 70 316 DK76
Arneways Ave., Rom. 226 309 EX56
Arnewood Clo. SW15 188 323 CU88
Arney's La., Mitch. 285 332 DG100
Arngask Rd. SE6 199 325 ED87
Arnhem Pl. E14 150 317 EA76
Arnhem Way SE22 179 324 DS85
Arnison Rd., E.Mol. 267 329 CD98
Arnold Ave. W., Enf. 203 301 DZ38
Arnold Circ. E2 39 316 DT69
Arnold Clo., Har. 91 304 CM59
Arnold Cres., Islw. 259 321 CD85
Arnold Est. SE1 75 316 DT75
Arnold Gdns. N13 209 300 DP50
Arnold Rd. E3 130 317 EA69
Arnold Rd. N15 221 306 DT55
Arnold Rd. SW17 184 322 CF94
Arnold Rd., Dag. 236 309 EZ66
Arnold Rd., Nthlt. 232 313 BX65
Arnold Rd., Stai. 264 328 BJ94
Arnos Gro. N14 208 300 DK49
Arnos Rd. N11 208 300 DJ50
Arnott Clo. SE28 246 319 EW73
Arnott Clo. W4 145 314 CR77
Arnould Ave. SE5 179 324 DR84
Arnsberg Way, Bexh. 263 327 FA84
Arnside Gdns., Wem. 91 304 CK60
Arnside Rd., Bexh. 255 319 FA81
Arnside St. SE17 162 316 DQ79
Arnulf St. SE6 275 325 EB91
Arnulls Rd. SW16 273 324 DN93
Arodene Rd. SW2 177 324 DM86
Arosa Rd., Twick. 169 322 CK86
Aragon Gdns. SW16 272 324 DL94
Arragon Gdns., W.Wick. 288 333 EB104
Arragon Rd. E6 244 318 EK67
Arragon Rd. SW18 190 323 DA88
Arragon Rd., Twick. 184 322 CG87
Arran Clo., Erith 255 319 FD79
Arran Clo., Wall. 286 332 DJ105
Arran Dr. E12 234 308 EK60
Arran Ms. W5 133 314 CM74
Arran Rd. SE6 198 325 EB89
Arran Wk. N1 116 306 DQ66
Arras Ave., Mord. 285 331 DC99
Arrol Rd., Beck. 274 325 DW97
Arrow Rd. E3 130 317 EB69
Arrowscout Wk., Nthlt. 242 313 BY69
Arsenal Rd. SE9 252 318 EM82
Arterberry Rd. SW20 270 323 CW94
Artesian Clo. NW10 109 304 CR66
Artesian Clo., Horn. 227 309 FF58
Artesian Rd. W2 40 315 DA72
Artesian Wk. E11 105 307 EE62
Arthingworth St. E15 131 317 EE67
Arthur Ct. W2 40/1 315 DB72
Arthur Gro. SE18 253 318 EQ77
Arthur Henderson Ho. SW6 157 315 CZ82
Arthur Rd. E6 244 318 EM68
Arthur Rd. N7 115 306 DM63
Arthur Rd. N9 209 300 DT47
Arthur Rd. SW19 270 323 CY92
Arthur Rd., Kings.T. 269 322 CN94
Arthur Rd., N.Mal. 283 331 CV99
Arthur Rd., Rom. 226 309 EX58
Arthur St. EC4 62 316 DR73
Arthur St., Erith 255 319 FF80
Arthurdon Rd. SE4 182 325 EA85
Artichoke Hill E1 138 317 DV73
Artichoke Pl. SE5 163 316 DR81
Artillery Clo., Ilf. 225 308 EQ58
Artillery La. E1 50/1 316 DS71
Artillery La. W12 136 315 CU72
Artillery Pas. E1 50/1 316 DS71
Artillery Pl. SE18 252 318 EM77
Artillery Pl. SW1 70 316 DK76
Artillery Row SW1 70 316 DK76
Artington Clo., Orp. 291 334 EQ105
Artisan Clo. E6 245 318 EP72
Artizan St. E1 50/1 316 DS72
Arundel Ave., Mord. 270 323 CZ98
Arundel Ave., S.Croy. 295 333 DU110
Arundel Clo. E15 121 307 EE63
Arundel Clo. SW11 175 323 DE85
Arundel Clo., Bex. 262 327 EZ86
Arundel Clo., Croy. 286 332 DP104
Arundel Clo., Hmptn. 267 329 CB92
Arundel Ct. N12 219 305 DE51
Arundel Ct., Har. 233 313 CA63
Arundel Dr., Borwd. 205 298 CP43
Arundel Dr., Har. 232 313 BZ63
Arundel Dr., Orp. 291 335 EV106
Arundel Dr., Wdf.Grn. 224 308 EG52
Arundel Gdns. N21 209 300 DN46
Arundel Gdns. W11 137 315 CZ73
Arundel Gdns., Edg. 217 304 CR52
Arundel Gdns., Ilf. 236 309 EU61
Arundel Great Ct. WC2 59 316 DM73
Arundel Gro. N16 117 306 DS64
Arundel Pl. N1 116 306 DN65
Arundel Rd., Croy. 287 332 DR100
Arundel Rd., Houns. 257 321 BW83
Arundel Rd., Kings.T. 269 322 CP96
Arundel Rd., Rom. 228 311 FM52
Arundel Rd., Sutt. 292 331 CY108
Arundel Rd., Uxb. 240 312 BH68
Arundel Sq. N7 116 306 DN65
Arundel St. WC2 59 316 DM73
Arundel Ter. SW13 156 315 CV79
Arvon Rd. N5 116 306 DN64
Asbaston Ter., Ilf. 235 308 EQ64
Ascalon St. SW8 160 316 DJ80
Ascension Rd., Rom. 227 309 FC51
Ascham Dr. E4 223 307 EB52
Ascham End E17 222 307 DY53

Ascham St. NW5 114 306 DJ64
Aschurch Rd., Croy. 287 332 DT101
Ascot Clo., Borwd. 205 298 CN43
Ascot Clo., Ilf. 225 308 ES51
Ascot Clo., Nthlt. 233 313 CA65
Ascot Gdns., Enf. 203 301 DW37
Ascot Gdns., Horn. 238 311 FL63
Ascot Gdns., Sthl. 242 313 BZ70
Ascot Ms., Wall. 294 332 DJ109
Ascot Rd. E6 244 318 EM69
Ascot Rd. N15 221 306 DR57
Ascot Rd. N18 210 301 DU49
Ascot Rd. SW17 272 324 DG93
Ascot Rd., Felt. 265 320 BN89
Ascot Rd., Orp. 277 326 ET98
Ascott Ave. W5 143 314 CL75
Ash Clo. SE20 274 325 DW96
Ash Clo., Cars. 285 331 DF103
Ash Clo., Edg. 205 298 CQ49
Ash Clo., N.Mal. 269 322 CR96
Ash Clo., Orp. 291 334 ER99
Ash Clo., Rom. 227 309 FB52
Ash Clo., Sid. 262 327 EV90
Ash Clo., Stan. 216 304 CG51
Ash Clo., Swan. 279 327 FC96
Ash Clo., Uxb. 212 302 BK53
Ash Ct., Epsom 283 330 CQ105
Ash Grn., Uxb. 240 312 BH65
Ash Gro. E8 128 317 DV67
Ash Gro. N13 209 300 DQ48
Ash Gro. NW2 111 305 CX63
Ash Gro. SE20 274 325 DW96
Ash Gro. W5 143 314 CL75
Ash Gro., Enf. 209 300 DS45
Ash Gro., Felt. 265 320 BS88
Ash Gro., Hayes 249 312 BR73
Ash Gro., Houns. 250 321 BX81
Ash Gro., Sthl. 243 313 CA71
Ash Gro., Stai. 264 328 BJ93
Ash Gro., Uxb. 212 302 BK53
Ash Gro., Wem. 106 304 CG63
Ash Gro., West Dr. 248 312 BM73
Ash Gro., W.Wick. 289 333 EC103
Ash Hill Dr., Pnr. 214 303 BW55
Ash Island, E.Mol. 267 329 CD97
Ash La., Croy. 286 332 DP105
Ash La., Horn. 229 311 FN56
Ash La., Rom. 228 310 FG51
Ash Ride, Enf. 202 300 DN35
Ash Rd. E15 121 307 EE64
Ash Rd., Croy. 288 333 EA103
Ash Rd., Shep. 281 328 BN98
Ash Rd., Sutt. 284 331 CY101
Ash Row, Brom. 290 334 EN101
Ash Tree Clo., Croy. 288 333 DY100
Ash Tree Clo., Surb. 282 330 CL102
Ash Tree Dell NW9 217 304 CR57
Ash Tree Way, Croy. 288 333 DY99
Ash Vw. Clo., Ashf. 264 328 BL93
Ash Vw. Gdns., Ashf. 264 328 BL92
Ash Wk. SW2 193 324 DM88
Ash Wk., Wem. 90 304 CJ62
Ashan Ct., Ashf. 265 328 BS94
Ashbourne Ave. E18 224 308 EH56
Ashbourne Ave. N20 207 299 DF47
Ashbourne Ave. NW11 218 305 CZ57
Ashbourne Ave., Bexh. 254 319 EY80
Ashbourne Ave., Har. 213 313 CD61
Ashbourne Clo. N12 207 299 DB49
Ashbourne Clo. W5 134 314 CN71
Ashbourne Ct. E5 119 307 DY63
Ashbourne Gro. NW7 205 298 CR50
Ashbourne Gro. SE22 179 324 DT85
Ashbourne Gro. W4 145 314 CS78
Ashbourne Ri., Orp. 291 334 ER105
Ashbourne Rd. W5 123 314 CM70
Ashbourne Rd., Mitch. 272 324 DG93
Ashbourne Sq., Nthwd. 213 302 BS51
Ashbourne Ter. SW19 271 323 DA94
Ashbourne Way NW11 218 305 CZ57
Ashbridge Rd. E11 105 307 EE59
Ashbridge St. NW8 30/1 315 DE70
Ashbrook Rd. N19 99 306 DK60
Ashbrook Rd., Dag. 237 309 FB62
Ashburn Gdns. SW7 77 315 DC77
Ashburn Pl. SW7 77 315 DC77
Ashburnham Ave., Har. 215 303 CF58
Ashburnham Clo. N2 219 305 DD55
Ashburnham Dr., Wat. 213 302 CF59
Ashburnham Gdns., Har. 233 313 CF59
Ashburnham Gdns., Upmin. 239 311 FP60
Ashburnham Gro. SE10 166 317 EB80
Ashburnham Pl. SE10 166 317 EB80
Ashburnham Retreat SE10 166 317 EB80
Ashburnham Rd. NW10 126 315 CW69
Ashburnham Rd. SW10 158 315 DC80
Ashburnham Rd., Belv. 255 319 FC77
Ashburnham Rd., Rich. 184 322 CH89
Ashburton Ave., Croy. 287 333 DV102
Ashburton Ave., Ilf. 235 308 ES63
Ashburton Clo., Croy. 287 333 DU102
Ashburton Ct., Pnr. 214 303 BX55
Ashburton Gdns., Croy. 287 333 DU103
Ashburton Gro. N7 116 306 DN63
Ashburton Rd. E16 244 318 EG72
Ashburton Rd., Croy. 287 333 DU103
Ashburton Rd., Ruis. 232 313 BU61
Ashburton Ter. E13 244 318 EG68
Ashbury Dr., Uxb. 231 312 BP61
Ashbury Gdns., Rom. 226 309 EX57
Ashbury Rd. SW11 175 323 DF83
Ashby Clo., Horn. 229 311 FN60
Ashby Gro. N1 116 306 DQ66
Ashby Ms. SE4 165 317 DZ82
Ashby Rd. N15 222 307 DU57
Ashby Rd. SE4 165 317 DZ82
Ashby St. EC1 36/7 316 DP69
Ashby Wk., Croy. 287 332 DQ100
Ashby Way, West Dr. 257 320 BN80
Ashchurch Gro. W12 146 315 CU76
Ashchurch Pk. Vil. W12 146 315 CU76
Ashchurch Ter. W12 146 315 CU76
Ashcombe Ave., Surb. 282 330 CK101
Ashcombe Gdns., Edg. 205 298 CN49
Ashcombe Pk. NW2 93 304 CS62
Ashcombe Rd. SW19 271 323 DA92
Ashcombe Rd., Cars. 293 332 DG107
Ashcombe Sq., N.Mal. 269 322 CQ97
Ashcombe St. SW6 158 315 DB82
Ashcroft, Pnr. 215 303 CA51
Ashcroft Ave., Sid. 262 327 EU86
Ashcroft Cres., Sid. 262 327 EU86
Ashcroft Rd. E3 129 317 DY69
Ashcroft Rd., Chess. 282 330 CM104
Ashcroft Sq. W6 146 315 CW77
Ashdale Clo., Stai. 264 320 BL89
Ashdale Clo., Twick. 259 321 CC87
Ashdale Gro., Stan. 215 303 CF51
Ashdale Rd. SE12 276 326 EH88
Ashdale Way, Twick. 259 321 CC87
Ashdene SE15 164 317 DV81
Ashdene, Pnr. 214 303 BW55
Ashdene Clo., Ashf. 265 328 BQ94
Ashdon Clo., Wdf.Grn. 224 308 EH51
Ashdon Rd. NW10 125 314 CT67
Ashdown Clo., Beck. 275 325 EB96
Ashdown Clo., Bex. 263 327 FC87
Ashdown Cres. NW5 114 306 DG64
Ashdown Est. E11 121 307 EE63
Ashdown Rd., Enf. 203 301 DW41
Ashdown Rd., Kings.T. 268 322 CL96
Ashdown Rd., Uxb. 241 312 BN68
Ashdown Wk. E14 150 317 EA77
Ashdown Wk., Rom. 227 309 FB54
Ashdown Way SW17 192 324 DG89
Ashen E6 245 318 EN72
Ashen Gro. SW19 190 323 DA90
Ashenden Rd. E5 119 307 DY64
Asher Way E1 138 317 DU74
Ashfield Ave., Felt. 258 321 BV88
Ashfield Clo., Beck. 275 325 EA94
Ashfield Clo., Rich. 185 322 CL88
Ashfield La., Chis. 277 326 EQ93
Ashfield Par. N14 208 300 DK46
Ashfield Rd. N4 221 306 DQ58
Ashfield Rd. N14 208 300 DJ48
Ashfield Rd. W3 135 314 CT74
Ashfield St. E1 138 317 DV71
Ashford Ave. N8 220 306 DL56

Ashford Ave., Ashf.	265	328	BP93
Ashford Ave., Hayes	242	313	BX72
Ashford Clo. E17	222	307	DZ58
Ashford Clo., Ashf.	264	328	BL91
Ashford Cres., Ashf.	264	320	BL90
Ashford Cres., Enf.	203	301	DW40
Ashford Ind. Est., Ashf.	265	328	BQ91
Ashford Rd. E6	235	308	EN65
Ashford Rd. E18	224	308	EH54
Ashford Rd. NW2	111	305	CX63
Ashford Rd., Ashf.	265	328	BP94
Ashford Rd., Felt.	265	328	BR91
Ashford Rd., Stai.	280	328	BK95
Ashford St. N1	38/9	316	DS69
Ashgrove Rd., Ashf.	265	328	BQ92
Ashgrove Rd., Brom.	275	325	ED93
Ashgrove Rd., Ilf.	235	308	ET60
Ashingdon Clo. E4	211	301	EC48
Ashington Rd. SW6	157	315	CZ82
Ashlake Rd. SW16	272	324	DL91
Ashland Pl. W1	44	316	DG71
Ashlar Pl. SE18	253	318	EP77
Ashleigh Gdns., Sutt.	284	331	DB103
Ashleigh Gdns., Upmin.	239	311	FR62
Ashleigh Rd. SE20	274	325	DV97
Ashleigh Rd. SW14	171	322	CS83
Ashley Ave., Ilf.	225	308	EP54
Ashley Ave., Mord.	284	331	DA99
Ashley Clo. NW4	218	305	CW54
Ashley Clo., Pnr.	214	303	BV54
Ashley Clo., Walt.	281	328	BS102
Ashley Cres. N22	221	306	DN54
Ashley Cres. SW11	176	324	DG83
Ashley Dr., Bans.	292	331	DA114
Ashley Dr., Borwd.	205	298	CQ43
Ashley Dr., Islw.	251	321	CE79
Ashley Dr., Twick.	259	321	CB88
Ashley Gdns. N13	209	300	DQ49
Ashley Gdns. SW1	69	316	DJ76
Ashley Gdns., Orp.	291	334	ES106
Ashley Gdns., Rich.	185	322	CK89
Ashley Gdns., Wem.	91	304	CL61
Ashley La. NW4	218	305	CW54
Ashley La., Croy.	286	332	DP105
Ashley Pk. Cres., Walt.	281	328	BT102
Ashley Pl. SW1	69	316	DJ76
Ashley Rd. E4	211	301	EA50
Ashley Rd. E7	234	308	EJ66
Ashley Rd. N17	222	307	DU55
Ashley Rd. N19	99	306	DL60
Ashley Rd. SW19	271	323	DB93
Ashley Rd., Enf.	203	301	DW40
Ashley Rd., Hmptn.	267	329	CA95
Ashley Rd., Rich.	169	322	CL83
Ashley Rd., Th.Hth.	272	324	DM98
Ashley Rd., Uxb.	240	312	BH68
Ashley Wk. NW7	218	305	CW52
Ashlin Rd. E15	121	307	ED63
Ashling Rd., Croy.	287	333	DU102
Ashlone Rd. SW15	172	323	CW83
Ashlyn Gro., Horn.	228	310	FK55
Ashmead N14	208	300	DJ43
Ashmead Dr., Uxb.	230	312	BG61
Ashmead Gate, Brom.	276	326	EJ95
Ashmead La., Uxb.	230	312	BG61
Ashmead Rd. SE8	166	317	EA82
Ashmead Rd., Felt.	258	321	BU88
Ashmere Ave., Beck.	275	325	ED96
Ashmere Clo., Sutt.	284	331	CW106
Ashmere Gro. SW2	177	324	DL84
Ashmill St. NW1	42/3	315	DE71
Ashmole Pl. SW8	161	316	DM79
Ashmole St. SW8	161	316	DM79
Ashmore Ct., Houns.	251	321	CA79
Ashmore Gro., Well.	261	326	ER83
Ashmore Rd. W9	127	315	CZ68
Ashmount Rd. N15	221	306	DT57
Ashmount Rd. N19	98	306	DJ59
Ashmount Ter. W5	143	314	CK77
Ashmour Gdns., Rom.	227	309	FD54
Ashneal Gdns., Har.	233	313	CD62
Ashness Gdns., Grnf.	106	304	CH65
Ashness Rd. SW11	175	323	DF85
Ashridge Clo., Har.	216	304	CJ58
Ashridge Cres. SE18	253	318	EQ80
Ashridge Gdns. N13	208	300	DK50
Ashridge Gdns., Pnr.	214	303	BY56
Ashridge Way, Mord.	270	323	CZ97
Ashridge Way, Sun.	266	329	BU93
Ashstead Rd. E5	102	307	DU59
Ashton Clo., Sutt.	284	331	DA105
Ashton Gdns., Houns.	258	321	BZ84
Ashton Gdns., Rom.	226	309	EY58
Ashton Rd. E15	121	307	ED64
Ashton Rd., Enf.	203	301	DY36
Ashton Rd., Rom.	228	310	FK52
Ashton St. E14	140	317	EC73
Ashtree Ave., Mitch.	271	323	DD96
Ashtree Clo., Orp.	290	334	EP105
Ashurst Clo. SE20	274	325	DV95
Ashurst Clo., Dart.	263	327	FF83
Ashurst Clo., Nthwd.	213	302	BS52
Ashurst Dr., Ilf.	225	308	EP58
Ashurst Dr., Shep.	280	328	BL99
Ashurst Rd. N12	207	299	DE50
Ashurst Rd., Barn.	207	299	DF43
Ashurst Wk., Croy.	287	333	DV103
Ashvale Dr., Upmin.	239	311	FS61
Ashvale Gdns., Upmin.	239	311	FS61
Ashvale Rd. SW17	271	323	DF92
Ashville Rd. E11	105	307	ED61
Ashwater Rd. SE12	260	326	EG88
Ashwell Clo. E6	244	318	EL72
Ashwin St. E8	117	306	DT65
Ashwood Ave., Uxb.	249	312	BN72
Ashwood Gdns., Hayes	249	320	BT77
Ashwood Rd. E4	211	301	ED48
Ashworth Clo. SE5	163	316	DR82
Ashworth Rd. W9	28/9	315	DB69
Aske St. N1	38/9	316	DS69
Askern Clo., Bexh.	262	327	EX84
Askew Cres. W12	145	314	CT75
Askew Rd. W12	135	314	CT74
Askew Rd., Nthwd.	213	302	BR47
Askham Ct. W12	136	315	CU74
Askham Rd. W12	136	315	CU74
Askill Dr. SW15	173	323	CY85
Askwith Rd., Rain.	247	319	FD69
Asland Rd. E15	131	317	ED67
Aslett St. SW18	190	323	DB87
Asmara Rd. NW2	111	305	CY64
Asmuns Hill NW11	219	305	DA57
Asmuns Pl. NW11	218	305	CZ57
Aspen Clo. N19	98	306	DJ61
Aspen Clo. W5	143	314	CM75
Aspen Clo., Orp.	291	335	EU106
Aspen Clo., Swan.	279	327	FD95
Aspen Clo., West Dr.	248	312	BM74
Aspen Copse, Brom.	276	326	EM96
Aspen Ct., Hayes	249	320	BS77
Aspen Dr., Wem.	106	304	CG63
Aspen Gdns. W6	146	315	CV78
Aspen Gdns., Mitch.	285	332	DG99
Aspen Grn., Erith	254	319	EZ76
Aspen Gro., Upmin.	239	311	FN63
Aspen La., Nthlt.	242	313	BY69
Aspen Way E14	141	317	EB73
Aspen Way, Bans.	292	331	CX114
Aspen Way, Enf.	203	301	DX35
Aspen Way, Felt.	258	321	BV90
Aspenlea Rd. W6	157	315	CX79
Aspern Gro. NW3	113	305	DE64
Aspinall Rd. SE4	181	325	DX83
Aspinden Rd. SE16	148	317	DV77
Aspley Rd. SW18	174	323	DB85
Aspley Way NW2	94	305	CU61
Asplins Rd. N17	222	307	DU53
Asquith Clo., Dag.	236	309	EW60
Assam St. E1	138	317	DU72
Assata Ms. N1	116	306	DP65
Assembly Pas. E1	138	317	DW71
Assembly Wk., Cars.	285	331	DE101
Assurance Cotts., Belv.	254	319	EZ78
Astall Clo., Har.	215	303	CE53
Astbury Rd. SE15	164	317	DW81
Aste St. E14	150	317	EC75
Astell St. SW3	78/9	315	DE78
Asteys Row N1	116	306	DP66
Asthall Gdns., Ilf.	225	308	EQ56
Astle St. SW11	160	316	DG82
Astleham Rd., Shep.	280	328	BL97
Astley Ave. NW2	110	305	CW64
Aston Ave., Har.	90	304	CJ59
Aston Clo., Sid.	262	327	EU90
Aston Grn., Houns.	250	321	BW82
Aston Ms., Rom.	236	309	EW59
Aston Rd. SW20	270	323	CW96
Aston Rd. W5	133	314	CK72
Aston St. E14	139	317	DY72
Astons Rd., Nthwd.	213	302	BQ48
Astonville St. SW18	190	323	DA88
Astor Ave., Rom.	227	309	FC58
Astor Clo., Kings.T.	269	322	CP93
Astoria Wk. SW9	178	324	DN83
Astra Clo., Horn.	238	310	FH65
Astrop Ms. W6	146	315	CW76
Astrop Ter. W6	146	315	CW75
Astwood Ms. SW7	76/7	315	DB77
Asylum Rd. SE15	164	317	DV80
Atalanta Clo., Pur.	294	332	DN110
Atalanta St. SW6	157	315	CX81
Atbara Ct., Tedd.	268	322	CH93
Atbara Rd., Tedd.	268	322	CH93
Atcham Rd., Houns.	259	321	CC84
Atcost Rd., Bark.	246	319	EU71
Atheldene Rd. SW18	190	323	DC87
Athelney St. SE6	198	325	EA90
Athelstan Clo., Rom.	228	311	FM54
Athelstan Rd., Kings.T.	268	322	CM98
Athelstan Rd., Rom.	228	311	FM53
Athelstan Way, Orp.	278	327	EU95
Athelstane Gro. E3	129	317	DZ68
Athelstane Ms. N4	100	306	DN60
Athelstone Rd., Har.	215	303	CD54
Athena Clo., Har.	233	313	CE61
Athena Clo., Kings.T.	268	322	CM97
Athena Pl., Nthwd.	213	302	BT53
Athenaeum Pl. N10	220	306	DH55
Athenaeum Rd. N20	207	299	DC46
Athenlay Rd. SE15	181	325	DX85
Athens Gdns. W9	28	315	DA70
Atherden Rd. E5	118	307	DW63
Atherfold Rd. SW9	177	324	DL83
Atherley Way, Houns.	258	321	BZ87
Atherstone Ms. SW7	77	315	DC77
Atherton Clo., Stai.	256	320	BK86
Atherton Dr. SW19	270	323	CX91
Atherton Hts., Wem.	106	304	CJ65
Atherton Ms. E7	121	307	EF65
Atherton Pl., Har.	215	303	CD55
Atherton Pl., Sthl.	243	313	CB73
Atherton Rd. E7	121	307	EF65
Atherton Rd. SW13	156	315	CU80
Atherton Rd., Ilf.	224	308	EL54
Atherton St. SW11	159	315	DE82
Athlon Rd., Wem.	123	314	CK68
Athlone Clo. E5	118	307	DV63
Athlone Rd. SW2	193	324	DM87
Athlone St. NW5	114	306	DG65
Athol Clo., Pnr.	214	303	BV53
Athol Gdns., Pnr.	214	303	BV53
Athol Rd., Erith	255	319	FC78
Athol Sq. E14	140	317	EC72
Athol Way, Uxb.	241	312	BN69
Athole Gdns., Enf.	209	300	DS43
Atholl Rd., Ilf.	236	309	EU59
Atkins Dr., W.Wick.	289	333	ED103
Atkins Rd. E10	223	307	EB58
Atkins Rd. SW12	193	324	DK87
Atkinson Clo., Orp.	291	335	EU106
Atkinson Rd. E16	244	318	EJ71
Atlanta Boul., Rom.	227	309	FE58
Atlantic Rd. SW9	178	324	DN84
Atlas Gdns. SE7	252	318	EJ77
Atlas Ms. E8	117	306	DT65
Atlas Ms. N7	115	306	DM65
Atlas Rd. E13	244	318	EG68
Atlas Rd. NW10	125	314	CS69
Atlas Rd., Wem.	108	304	CQ63
Atley Rd. E3	130	317	EA67
Atlip Rd., Wem.	123	314	CL67
Atney Rd. SW15	173	323	CY84
Atterbury Rd. N4	221	306	DN58
Atterbury St. SW1	82/3	316	DL77
Attewood Ave. NW10	93	304	CS62
Attewood Rd., Nthlt.	232	313	BY65
Attfield Clo. N20	207	299	DD47
Attle Clo., Uxb.	241	312	BN68
Attlee Clo., Hayes	242	313	BV69
Attlee Clo., Th.Hth.	287	332	DQ100
Attlee Rd. SE28	246	319	EV73
Attlee Rd., Hayes	242	313	BU69
Attlee Ter. E17	223	307	EB56
Attneave St. WC1	36	316	DN69
Atwood Clo., S.Croy.	295	333	DV114
Atwater Clo. SW2	194	324	DN88
Atwell Clo. E10	223	307	EB58
Atwell Rd. SE15	164	317	DU82
Atwood Ave., Rich.	154	314	CN82
Atwood Rd. W6	146	315	CV77
Aubert Pk. N5	116	306	DN63
Aubert Rd. N5	116	306	DP63
Aubretia Clo., Rom.	228	311	FL53
Aubrey Pl. NW8	17	315	DC68
Aubrey Rd. E17	223	307	EA55
Aubrey Rd. N8	220	306	DL57
Aubrey Rd. W8	137	315	CZ74
Aubrey Wk. W8	137	315	CZ74
Aubyn Hill SE27	273	324	DQ91
Aubyn Sq. SW15	172	323	CU84
Auckland Ave., Rain.	247	319	FF69
Auckland Clo. SE19	273	324	DT95
Auckland Clo., Enf.	203	301	DV37
Auckland Gdns. SE19	273	324	DS95
Auckland Hill SE27	273	324	DQ91
Auckland Ri. SE19	273	324	DS95
Auckland Rd. E10	104	307	EB62
Auckland Rd. SE19	273	324	DT95
Auckland Rd. SW11	175	323	DE84
Auckland Rd., Ilf.	235	308	EP60
Auckland Rd., Kings.T.	268	322	CM98
Auckland St. SE11	83	316	DM78
Auden Pl. NW1	20	316	DG67
Audleigh Pl., Chig.	225	308	EN51
Audley Clo. N10	220	306	DH52
Audley Clo. SW11	176	324	DG83
Audley Ct. E18	223	307	EF56
Audley Ct., Pnr.	214	303	BW54
Audley Gdns., Ilf.	235	308	ET61
Audley Pl., Sutt.	292	331	DB108
Audley Rd. NW4	218	305	CU58
Audley Rd. W5	134	314	CM71
Audley Rd., Enf.	202	300	DP40
Audley Rd., Rich.	169	322	CM85
Audley Sq. W1	56	316	DG74
Audrey Clo., Beck.	288	333	EB100
Audrey Gdns., Wem.	90	304	CH61
Audrey Rd., Ilf.	235	308	EP62
Audrey St. E2	128	317	DU68
Audric Clo., Kings.T.	269	322	CN95
Augurs La. E13	244	318	EH69
Augusta Clo., W.Mol.	266	329	BZ97
Augusta Rd., Twick.	259	321	CC89
Augusta St. E14	140	317	EB72
Augustine Rd. W14	146	315	CX76
Augustine Rd., Har.	215	303	CB53
Augustine Rd., Orp.	278	327	EX97
Augustus Clo., Brent.	153	314	CK80
Augustus La., Orp.	291	335	EU103
Augustus Rd. SW19	189	323	CX88
Augustus St. NW1	20/1	316	DH68
Aulton Pl. SE11	84	316	DN78
Aultone Way, Cars.	285	331	DF104
Aultone Way, Sutt.	284	331	DB103
Aurelia Gdns., Croy.	286	332	DM99
Aurelia Rd., Croy.	286	332	DL100
Auriel Ave., Dag.	237	309	FD65
Auriga Ms. N16	117	306	DR64
Auriol Clo., Wor.Pk.	283	330	CS104
Auriol Dr., Grnf.	233	313	CD66
Auriol Dr., Uxb.	241	312	BP65
Auriol Pk. Rd., Wor.Pk.	283	330	CS104
Auriol Rd. W14	147	315	CY77
Austell Gdns. NW7	205	298	CS48
Austen Clo. SE28	246	319	EV74
Austen Ho. NW6	28	315	DA69
Austen Rd., Erith	255	319	FB81
Austen Rd., Har.	233	313	CB61
Austin Ave., Brom.	290	334	EL99
Austin Clo. SE23	197	325	DZ87
Austin Clo., Twick.	168	322	CJ85
Austin Ct. E6	244	318	EJ67
Austin Friars EC2	50	316	DR72
Austin Friars Pas. EC2	50	316	DR72
Austin Friars Sq. EC2	50	316	DR72
Austin Rd. SW11	160	316	DG81
Austin Rd., Hayes	249	320	BT75
Austin Rd., Orp.	291	335	EU100
Austin St. E2	39	316	DT69
Austin Waye, Uxb.	240	312	BJ67
Austin's La., Uxb.	231	312	BQ62
Austral Clo., Sid.	261	326	ET90
Austral Dr., Horn.	238	310	FK59
Austral St. SE11	84/5	316	DP77
Australia Rd. W12	136	315	CV73
Austyn Gdns., Surb.	282	330	CP102
Autumn Clo., Enf.	203	301	DU39
Autumn Dr., Sutt.	292	331	DB109
Autumn St. E3	130	317	EA67
Avalon Clo. SW20	270	323	CY96
Avalon Clo. W13	132	314	CG71
Avalon Clo., Enf.	202	300	DN40
Avalon Rd. SW6	158	315	DB81
Avalon Rd. W13	122	314	CG70
Avalon Rd., Orp.	291	335	EV103
Avard Gdns., Orp.	291	334	EQ105
Avarn Rd. SW17	271	323	DF93
Ave Maria La. EC4	48/9	316	DP72
Avebury Ct. N1	26	316	DR67
Avebury Pk., Surb.	282	330	CK101
Avebury Rd. E11	105	307	ED60
Avebury Rd. SW19	270	323	CZ95
Avebury Rd., Orp.	291	334	ER104
Avebury St. N1	26	316	DR67
Aveley Rd., Rom.	227	309	FD56
Aveley Rd., Upmin.	239	311	FP65
Aveline St. SE11	84	316	DN78
Aveling Clo., Pur.	294	332	DM113
Aveling Pk. Rd. E17	223	307	EA54
Avelon Rd., Rom.	227	309	FD51
Avenell Rd. N5	100	306	DP62
Avening Rd. SW18	190	323	DA87
Avening Ter. SW18	174	323	DA86
Avenons Rd. E13	244	318	EG70
Avenue, The E4	223	307	ED51
Avenue, The (Leytonstone) E11	105	307	EF61
Avenue, The (Wanstead) E11	224	308	EH58
Avenue, The N3	219	305	DA54
Avenue, The N8	221	306	DN55
Avenue, The N10	220	306	DJ54
Avenue, The N11	208	300	DH50
Avenue, The N17	221	306	DS54
Avenue, The NW6	127	315	CX67
Avenue, The SE7	252	318	EJ80
Avenue, The SE10	167	317	ED80
Avenue, The SW4	176	324	DG85
Avenue, The SW11	191	323	DF87
Avenue, The SW18	191	323	DE87
Avenue, The W4	145	314	CS76
Avenue, The W13	132	314	CH73
Avenue, The, Beck.	275	325	EB95
Avenue, The, Bex.	262	327	EX86
Avenue, The, Brom.	276	326	EK97
Avenue, The, Cars.	293	332	DG108
Avenue, The, Croy.	287	332	DS104
Avenue, The, Hmptn.	266	329	BZ93
Avenue, The, Har.	215	303	CF53
Avenue, The, Horn.	238	310	FJ61
Avenue, The, Houns.	259	321	CB85
Avenue, The (Cranford), Houns.	250	321	BU81
Avenue, The, Islw.	251	321	CD80
Avenue, The, Kes.	290	334	EK104
Avenue, The, Nthwd.	213	302	BQ51
Avenue, The, Orp.	291	334	ET103
Avenue, The (St. Paul's Cray), Orp.	278	327	EV94
Avenue, The, Pnr.	214	303	BZ58
Avenue, The (Hatch End), Pnr.	214	303	BZ51
Avenue, The, Rich.	153	314	CM82
Avenue, The, Rom.	227	309	FD56
Avenue, The, Stai.	280	328	BH95
Avenue, The, Sun.	266	329	BV95
Avenue, The, Surb.	282	330	CM100
Avenue, The, Sutt.	292	331	CY109
Avenue, The, Twick.	168	322	CH85
Avenue, The (Cowley), Uxb.	240	312	BK70
Avenue, The (Ickenham), Uxb.	241	312	BN63
Avenue, The, Wem.	91	304	CL60
Avenue, The, West Dr.	248	320	BL76
Avenue, The, W.Wick.	289	333	EC101
Avenue, The, Wor.Pk.	283	330	CT103
Avenue Clo. N14	208	300	DJ44
Avenue Clo. NW8	18/9	315	DE67
Avenue Clo., Houns.	250	321	BU81
Avenue Clo., Rom.	228	311	FM52
Avenue Clo., West Dr.	248	320	BK76
Avenue Cres. W3	144	314	CP75
Avenue Cres., Houns.	250	321	BV80
Avenue Elmers, Surb.	282	330	CL99
Avenue Gdns. SE25	274	325	DU97
Avenue Gdns. SW14	171	322	CS83
Avenue Gdns. W3	144	314	CP75
Avenue Gdns., Houns.	250	321	BU80
Avenue Gdns., Tedd.	267	329	CF94
Avenue Ind. Est. E4	222	307	DZ51
Avenue Ms. N10	220	306	DH55
Avenue Pk. Rd. SE27	194	324	DP89
Avenue Rd. E7	234	308	EH63
Avenue Rd. N6	98	306	DJ59
Avenue Rd. N12	207	299	DC49
Avenue Rd. N14	208	300	DH45
Avenue Rd. N15	221	306	DR57
Avenue Rd. NW3	113	305	DD66
Avenue Rd. NW8	113	305	DD66
Avenue Rd. NW10	125	314	CT68
Avenue Rd. SE20	274	325	DW95
Avenue Rd. SE25	273	324	DT96
Avenue Rd. SW16	272	324	DK96
Avenue Rd. SW20	270	323	CV96
Avenue Rd. W3	144	314	CP75
Avenue Rd., Beck.	274	325	DX95
Avenue Rd., Belv.	255	319	FC77
Avenue Rd., Bexh.	262	327	EY84
Avenue Rd., Brent.	142	314	CJ78
Avenue Rd., Erith	255	319	FC80
Avenue Rd., Felt.	265	320	BT90
Avenue Rd., Hmptn.	267	329	CB95
Avenue Rd., Islw.	251	321	CF81
Avenue Rd., Kings.T.	268	322	CL97
Avenue Rd., N.Mal.	269	322	CS98
Avenue Rd., Pnr.	214	303	BY55
Avenue Rd. (Chadwell Heath), Rom.	236	309	EV60
Avenue Rd. (Harold Wd.), Rom.	228	311	FM52
Avenue Rd., Sthl.	250	321	BZ75
Avenue Rd., Sutt.	292	331	DA110
Avenue Rd., Tedd.	268	322	CG94
Avenue Rd., Wall.	294	332	DJ108
Avenue Rd., Wdf.Grn.	224	308	EJ51
Avenue S., Surb.	282	330	CM101
Avenue Ter., N.Mal.	269	322	CQ97
Averil Gro. SW16	273	324	DP93
Averill St. W6	157	315	CX79
Avern Gdns., W.Mol.	267	329	CB98
Avern Rd., W.Mol.	267	329	CB98
Avery Fm. Row SW1	80/1	316	DH77
Avery Gdns., Ilf.	224	308	EM57
Avery Hill Rd. SE9	261	326	ER86
Avery Row W1	56/7	316	DH73
Aviary Clo. E16	141	317	EF71
Aviemore Clo., Beck.	288	333	DZ99
Aviemore Way, Beck.	288	333	DY99
Avignon Rd. SE4	181	325	DX83
Avington Ct. SE1	86/7	316	DS77
Avington Gro. SE20	274	325	DW94
Avington Way SE15	163	316	DT80
Avior Dr., Nthwd.	213	302	BT49
Avis Sq. E1	139	317	DX72
Avoca Rd. SW17	272	324	DG91
Avocet Ms. SE28	253	318	ER76
Avon Clo., Hayes	242	313	BW70
Avon Clo., Sutt.	285	331	DC105
Avon Clo., Wor.Pk.	283	331	CU103
Avon Ct., Grnf.	243	313	CB70
Avon Ms., Pnr.	214	303	BZ53
Avon Path, S.Croy.	295	332	DQ107
Avon Pl. SE1	73	316	DQ75
Avon Rd. E17	223	307	ED55
Avon Rd. SE4	182	325	EA83
Avon Rd., Grnf.	243	313	CA70
Avon Rd., Sun.	265	328	BT94
Avon Rd., Upmin.	229	311	FR58
Avon Way E18	224	308	EG55
Avondale Ave. N12	207	299	DB50
Avondale Ave. NW2	93	304	CS62
Avondale Ave., Barn.	207	299	DF46
Avondale Ave., Wor.Pk.	283	330	CT102
Avondale Ct. E11	105	307	EE60
Avondale Ct. E16	141	317	EE71
Avondale Ct. E18	224	308	EH53
Avondale Cres., Enf.	203	301	DY41
Avondale Cres., Ilf.	224	308	EK57
Avondale Dr., Hayes	242	313	BU74
Avondale Gdns., Houns.	258	321	BZ85
Avondale Ms., Brom.	276	326	EG93
Avondale Pk. Gdns. W11	137	315	CY73
Avondale Pk. Rd. W11	137	315	CY73
Avondale Pavement SE1	148	317	DU78
Avondale Ri. SE15	179	324	DT83
Avondale Rd. E16	141	317	EE71
Avondale Rd. E17	104	307	EA59
Avondale Rd. N3	219	305	DC53
Avondale Rd. N13	209	300	DN47
Avondale Rd. N15	221	306	DP57
Avondale Rd. SE9	260	326	EL89
Avondale Rd. SW14	171	322	CR83
Avondale Rd. SW19	271	323	DB92
Avondale Rd., Ashf.	264	320	BK90
Avondale Rd., Brom.	275	325	EE93
Avondale Rd., Har.	215	303	CF55
Avondale Rd., S.Croy.	295	332	DQ108
Avondale Rd., Well.	254	319	EW82
Avondale Sq. SE1	148	317	DU78
Avonley Rd. SE14	164	317	DW80
Avonmore Gdns. W14	147	315	CY77
Avonmore Pl. W14	147	315	CY77
Avonmore Rd. W14	147	315	CY77
Avonmouth St. SE1	73	316	DQ76
Avonwick Rd., Houns.	251	321	CB82
Avril Way E4	211	301	EC50
Avro Way, Wall.	294	332	DL108
Award Gdns., Orp.	291	334	EQ105
Awlfield Ave. N17	221	306	DR53
Awliscombe Rd., Well.	253	318	ET82
Axe St., Bark.	245	318	EQ67
Axholme Ave., Edg.	217	304	CN53
Axminster Cres., Well.	254	319	EW81
Axminster Rd. N7	99	306	DL62
Aybrook St. W1	44	316	DG71
Aycliffe Clo., Brom.	276	326	EM98
Aycliffe Rd. W12	135	314	CT74
Aylands Clo., Wem.	91	304	CL61
Aylands Rd., Enf.	203	301	DX36
Ayles Rd., Hayes	242	313	BV69
Aylesbury Clo. E7	121	307	EF65
Aylesbury Est. SE17	86	316	DR78
Aylesbury Rd. SE17	86	316	DR78
Aylesbury Rd., Brom.	276	326	EG97
Aylesbury St. EC1	36/7	316	DP70
Aylesbury St. NW10	93	304	CR62
Aylesford Ave., Beck.	288	333	DY99
Aylesford St. SW1	82	316	DK78
Aylesham Clo. NW7	218	305	CU52
Aylesham Rd., Orp.	291	334	ET101
Aylestone Ave. NW6	111	305	CX66
Aylett Rd. SE25	274	325	DV98
Aylett Rd., Islw.	251	321	CE82
Aylett Rd., Upmin.	239	311	FQ61
Ayley Cft., Enf.	210	301	DU43
Ayliffe Clo., Kings.T.	269	322	CN96
Aylmer Clo., Stan.	204	298	CG49
Aylmer Dr., Stan.	204	298	CG49
Aylmer Par. N2	219	305	DF57
Aylmer Rd. E11	105	307	EF60
Aylmer Rd. N2	219	305	DE57
Aylmer Rd. W12	145	314	CT75
Aylmer Rd., Dag.	236	309	EY62
Ayloffe Rd., Dag.	236	309	EZ65
Ayloffs Clo., Horn.	228	311	FL57
Ayloffs Wk., Horn.	228	310	FK57
Aylsham Dr., Uxb.	231	312	BQ61
Aylton Est. SE16	148	317	DW75
Aylward Rd. SE23	197	325	DX89
Aylward Rd. SW20	270	323	CZ96
Aylward St. E1	138	317	DW72
Aylwards Ri., Stan.	204	298	CG49
Aylwyn Est. SE1	74/5	316	DS76
Aynhoe Rd. W14	147	315	CX77
Aynscombe Angle, Orp.	291	335	EU101
Aynscombe La. SW14	170	322	CQ83
Aynscombe Path SW14	154	314	CQ82
Ayr Ct. W3	134	314	CN71
Ayr Grn., Rom.	227	309	FE52
Ayr Way, Rom.	227	309	FE52
Ayres Clo. E13	244	318	EG69
Ayres Cres. NW10	109	304	CR66
Ayres St. SE1	73	316	DQ75
Ayrsome Rd. N16	101	306	DS62
Ayrton Rd. SW7	66	315	DD76
Aysgarth Rd. SE21	179	324	DS86
Aytoun Pl. SW9	161	316	DM82
Aytoun Rd. SW9	161	316	DM82
Azalea Clo. W7	243	313	CF74
Azalea Clo., Ilf.	235	308	EP64
Azalea Ct., Wdf.Grn.	223	307	EE52
Azalea Dr., Swan.	279	327	FD98
Azalea Wk., Pnr.	214	303	BV57
Azalea Wk., Sthl.	251	321	CC75
Azenby Rd. SE15	163	316	DT82
Azile Everitt Ho. SE18	253	318	EQ78
Azof St. SE10	151	317	EE77
Baalbec Rd. N5	116	306	DP64
Babbacombe Clo., Chess.	282	330	CK106
Babbacombe Gdns., Ilf.	224	308	EL56
Babbacombe Rd., Brom.	276	326	EG95
Baber Dr., Felt.	258	321	BW86
Babington Ri., Wem.	108	304	CN65
Babington Rd. NW4	218	305	CV56
Babington Rd. SW16	272	324	DK92
Babington Rd., Dag.	236	309	EW64
Babington Rd., Horn.	238	310	FH60
Babmaes St. SW1	58	316	DK74
Bacchus Wk. N1	26/7	316	DS68
Baches St. N1	38	316	DR69
Back Ch. La. E1	138	317	DU73
Back Hill EC1	36	316	DN70
Back La. N8	220	306	DL57
Back La. NW3	112	305	DC63
Back La., Bex.	263	327	FA87
Back La., Brent.	153	314	CK79
Back La., Edg.	217	304	CQ53
Back La., Rich.	184	322	CJ90
Back La., Rom.	236	309	EY59
Back Rd., Sid.	278	327	EU91
Backhouse Pl. SE17	86/7	316	DS77
Backley Gdns. SE25	287	333	DU100
Bacon Gro. SE1	75	316	DT76
Bacon La. NW9	217	304	CP56
Bacon La., Edg.	217	304	CN53
Bacon Link, Rom.	227	309	FB51
Bacon St. E1	39	316	DT70
Bacon St. E2	39	316	DT70
Bacon Ter., Dag.	236	309	EV64
Bacons La. N6	98	306	DG60
Bacons Mead, Uxb.	230	312	BG61
Bacton NW5	114	306	DG64
Bacton St. E2	128	317	DW69
Baddow Clo., Dag.	247	319	FA67
Baddow Clo., Wdf.Grn.	224	308	EK51
Baddow Wk. N1	26	316	DQ67
Baden Clo., Stai.	264	328	BG94
Baden Pl. SE1	74	316	DR75
Baden Powell Clo., Surb.	282	330	CM103
Baden Rd. N8	220	306	DK56
Baden Rd., Ilf.	235	308	EP64
Bader Way, Rain.	238	310	FG65
Badger Clo., Felt.	258	321	BU90
Badger Clo., Houns.	258	321	BW83
Badger Clo., Ilf.	235	308	EQ59
Badgers Clo., Ashf.	264	328	BM92
Badgers Clo., Enf.	202	300	DP41
Badgers Clo., Har.	215	303	CD58
Badgers Clo., Hayes	249	312	BS74
Badgers Copse, Orp.	291	334	ET103
Badgers Copse, Wor.Pk.	283	330	CT103
Badgers Cft. N20	206	299	CY46
Badgers Cft. SE9	261	326	EN90
Badgers Hole, Croy.	288	333	DX105
Badgers Wk., N.Mal.	269	322	CS96
Badgers Wk., Pur.	294	332	DJ111
Badlis Rd. E17	223	307	EA54
Badlow Clo., Erith	255	319	FE80
Badminton Clo., Har.	215	303	CE56
Badminton Clo., Nthlt.	233	313	CA66
Badminton Ms. E16	141	317	EE72
Badminton Rd. SW12	176	324	DG86
Badsworth Rd. SE5	162	316	DQ81
Baffin Way E14	141	317	ED73
Bagley Clo., West Dr.	248	320	BL75
Bagley's La. SW6	158	315	DB81
Bagleys Spring, Rom.	226	309	EY56
Bagshot Ct. SE18	253	318	EN81
Bagshot Rd., Enf.	209	300	DT45
Bagshot St. SE17	86/7	316	DS78
Baildon St. SE8	166	317	EA80
Bailey Clo. E4	211	301	EC49
Bailey Pl. SE26	274	325	DX93
Baillies Wk. W5	143	314	CK75
Bainbridge Rd., Dag.	236	309	EZ63
Bainbridge St. WC1	46	316	DK72
Baird Ave., Sthl.	243	313	CB73
Baird Clo. NW9	217	304	CQ58
Baird Gdns. SE19	273	324	DS91
Baird Rd., Enf.	203	301	DV42
Baird St. EC1	37	316	DQ70
Baizdon Rd. SE3	167	317	EE82
Baker La., Mitch.	272	324	DG96
Baker Pas. NW10	125	314	CS67
Baker Rd. NW10	125	314	CS67
Baker Rd. SE18	252	318	EL81
Baker St. NW1	31	315	DF70
Baker St. W1	43	315	DF71
Baker St., Enf.	202	300	DR41
Bakers Ave. E17	223	307	EB58
Bakers Ct. SE25	273	324	DS97
Bakers End SW20	270	323	CY96
Bakers Fld. N7	115	306	DK63
Bakers Gdns., Cars.	285	331	DE103
Bakers Hill E5	102	307	DV60
Bakers La. N6	219	305	DF58
Baker's Ms. W1	44	316	DG72
Bakers Pas. NW3	112	305	DC63
Baker's Rents E2	39	316	DT69
Bakers Rd., Uxb.	240	312	BK66
Bakers Row E15	131	317	EE68
Baker's Row EC1	36	316	DN70
Baker's Yd. EC1	36	316	DN70
Baker's Yd., Uxb.	240	312	BK66
Bakery Clo. SW9	161	316	DM81
Bakery Path, Edg.	217	304	CP51
Bakery Pl. SW11	175	323	DF84
Bakewell Way, N.Mal.	269	322	CS96
Bala Gdn. NW9	217	304	CS58
Balaam St. E13	244	318	EG70
Balaams La. N14	208	300	DK47
Balaclava Rd. SE1	87	316	DT77
Balaclava Rd., Surb.	282	330	CJ101
Balben Path E9	119	307	DX66
Balcaskie Rd. SE9	260	326	EM85
Balchen Rd. SE3	252	318	EK82
Balchier Rd. SE22	180	325	DV86
Balcombe Clo., Bexh.	262	327	EX84
Balcombe St. NW1	31	315	DF70
Balcorne St. E9	118	307	DW66
Balder Ri. SE12	260	326	EH89
Balderton St. W1	44	316	DG72
Baldock St. E3	130	317	EB68
Baldry Gdns. SW16	272	324	DL93
Baldwin Cres. SE5	162	316	DQ81
Baldwin St. EC1	38	316	DR69
Baldwin Ter. N1	25	316	DQ68
Baldwin's Gdns. EC1	48	316	DN71
Baldwyn Gdns. W3	135	314	CR73
Baldwyns Pk., Bex.	263	327	FD89
Baldwyns Rd., Bex.	263	327	FD89
Balfe St. N1	22/3	316	DL68
Balfern Gro. W4	145	314	CS78
Balfern St. SW11	159	315	DE82
Balfont Clo., S.Croy.	295	333	DU113
Balfour Ave. W7	243	313	CF74
Balfour Gro. N20	207	299	DF48
Balfour Ho. W10	137	315	CX71
Balfour Ms. N9	210	301	DU48
Balfour Ms. W1	56	316	DG74
Balfour Pl. SW15	172	323	CV84
Balfour Pl. W1	56	316	DG73
Balfour Rd. N5	116	306	DQ63
Balfour Rd. SE25	287	333	DU99
Balfour Rd. SW19	271	323	DB94
Balfour Rd. W3	134	314	CQ71
Balfour Rd. W13	142	314	CG75
Balfour Rd., Brom.	290	334	EK99
Balfour Rd., Cars.	293	331	DF108
Balfour Rd., Har.	215	303	CD57
Balfour Rd., Houns.	259	321	CB83
Balfour Rd., Ilf.	235	308	EP61
Balfour Rd., Sthl.	250	321	BX76
Balfour St. SE17	86	316	DR77
Balgonie Rd. E4	211	301	ED46
Balgores Cres., Rom.	228	310	FH55
Balgores La., Rom.	228	310	FH55
Balgores Sq., Rom.	228	310	FH56
Balgowan Clo., N.Mal.	269	322	CS98
Balgowan Rd., Beck.	274	325	DY97
Balgowan St. SE18	253	318	ET77
Balham Gro. SW12	192	324	DG87
Balham High Rd. SW12	192	324	DG90
Balham High Rd. SW17	192	324	DG90
Balham Hill SW12	192	324	DH87
Balham New Rd. SW12	192	324	DH87
Balham Pk. Rd. SW12	191	323	DF88
Balham Rd. N9	210	301	DU47
Balham Sta. Rd. SW12	192	324	DH88
Balkan Wk. E1	138	317	DV73
Balladier Wk. E14	140	317	EB71
Ballamore Rd., Brom.	260	326	EG90
Ballance Rd. E9	119	307	DX65
Ballantine St. SW18	174	323	DC84
Ballard Clo., Kings.T.	269	322	CR94
Ballards Clo., Dag.	247	319	FB67
Ballards Fm. Rd., Croy.	295	333	DU107
Ballards Fm. Rd., S.Croy.	295	333	DU107
Ballards La. N3	219	305	DA53
Ballards La. N12	219	305	DC51
Ballards Ms., Edg.	217	304	CN51
Ballards Ri., S.Croy.	295	333	DU107
Ballards Rd. NW2	94	305	CU61
Ballards Rd., Dag.	247	319	FB68
Ballards Way, Croy.	295	333	DV107
Ballards Way, S.Croy.	295	333	DU107
Ballast Quay SE10	151	317	ED78
Ballater Rd. SW2	177	324	DL84
Ballater Rd., S.Croy.	287	332	DT106
Ballina St. SE23	197	325	DX87
Ballingdon Rd. SW11	176	324	DG86
Ballinger Pt. E3	130	317	EB69
Balliol Ave. E4	211	301	EE49
Balliol Rd. N17	221	306	DS53
Balliol Rd. W10	137	315	CX72
Balliol Rd., Well.	254	319	EV82
Balloch Rd. SE6	199	325	ED88
Ballogie Ave. NW10	109	304	CS63
Ballow Clo. SE5	163	316	DS80
Balls Pond Pl. N1	117	306	DR65
Balls Pond Rd. N1	117	306	DR65
Balmain Clo. W5	133	314	CK74
Balmer Rd. E3	129	317	DZ68
Balmes Rd. N1	26	316	DR67
Balmoral Ave. N11	208	300	DG50
Balmoral Ave., Beck.	274	325	DY98
Balmoral Clo. SW15	173	323	CX86
Balmoral Cres., W.Mol.	267	329	CA97
Balmoral Dr., Borwd.	205	298	CR43
Balmoral Dr., Hayes	241	312	BS70
Balmoral Dr., Sthl.	242	313	BZ70
Balmoral Gdns. W13	142	314	CG76
Balmoral Gdns., Bex.	262	327	EZ87
Balmoral Gdns., Ilf.	235	308	ET60
Balmoral Gro. N7	115	306	DM65
Balmoral Ms. W12	145	314	CT76

Balmoral Rd. E7 234 308 EJ63
Balmoral Rd. E10 104 307 EB61
Balmoral Rd. NW2 110 305 CV65
Balmoral Rd., Enf. 203 301 DX36
Balmoral Rd., Har. 233 313 CA63
Balmoral Rd., Horn. 238 310 FK62
Balmoral Rd., Kings.T. 268 322 CM98
Balmoral Rd., Rom. 228 310 FH57
Balmoral Rd., Wor.Pk. 283 331 CV104
Balmoral Way, Sutt. 292 331 DA110
Balmore Cres., Barn. 208 300 DG43
Balmore St. N19 98 306 DH61
Balmuir Gdns. SW15 172 323 CW84
Balnacraig Ave. NW10 109 304 CS63
Balniel Gate SW1 82 316 DK78
Baltic Clo. SW19 271 323 DD94
Baltic Ct. SE16 149 317 DX75
Baltic St. E. EC1 37 316 DQ70
Baltic St. W. EC1 37 316 DQ70
Baltimore Pl., Well. 253 318 ET82
Balvernie Gro. SW18 189 323 CZ87
Bamber Ho., Bark. 245 318 EQ67
Bamborough Gdns. W12 146 315 CW75
Bamford Ave., Wem. 123 314 CM67
Bamford Ct. E15 120 307 EB64
Bamford Rd., Bark. 235 308 EQ65
Bamford Rd., Brom. 275 325 EC92
Bampfylde Clo., Wall. 286 332 DJ104
Bampton Rd. SE23 197 325 DX90
Bampton Rd., Rom. 228 311 FL52
Banavie Gdns., Beck. 275 325 EC95
Banbury Clo., Enf. 202 300 DP39
Banbury Ct. WC2 58/9 316 DL73
Banbury Ct., Sutt. 292 331 DA108
Banbury Enterprise Cen., Croy. 286 332 DP103
Banbury Rd. E9 119 307 DX66
Banbury Rd. E17 222 307 DY53
Banbury St. SW11 159 315 DE82
Banbury Wk., Nthlt. 243 313 CA68
Banchory Rd. SE3 252 318 EH80
Bancroft Ave. N2 219 305 DE57
Bancroft Clo., Ashf. 265 328 BN92
Bancroft Ct., Nthlt. 242 313 BW67
Bancroft Gdns., Har. 215 303 CC53
Bancroft Gdns., Orp. 291 334 ET102
Bancroft Rd. E1 129 317 DX69
Bancroft Rd., Har. 215 303 CC53
Bandon Ri., Wall. 286 332 DK106
Bangalore St. SW15 172 323 CW83
Bangor Clo., Nthlt. 233 313 CB64
Banim St. W6 146 315 CV77
Banister Rd. W10 127 315 CX69
Bank, The N6 98 306 DH60
Bank Ave., Mitch. 271 323 DD96
Bank End SE1 61 316 DQ74
Bank La. SW15 171 322 CS85
Bank La., Kings.T. 268 322 CL94
Bank Ms., Sutt. 292 331 DA111
Bankfoot Rd., Brom. 275 325 EE91
Bankhurst Rd. SE6 197 325 DZ87
Banks La., Bexh. 262 327 EZ84
Banksia Rd. N18 210 301 DW50
Banksian Wk., Islw. 251 321 CE81
Bankside SE1 61 316 DQ73
Bankside, Enf. 202 300 DP39
Bankside, S.Croy. 295 332 DT107
Bankside, Sthl. 242 313 BX74
Bankside Ave., Nthlt. 242 313 BU68
Bankside Clo., Bex. 279 327 FD91
Bankside Clo., Cars. 293 331 DE107
Bankside Clo., Islw. 259 321 CF84
Bankside Way SE19 273 324 DS93
Bankton Rd. SW2 178 324 DN84
Bankwell Rd. SE13 183 325 EE84
Banner St. EC1 37 316 DQ70
Bannerman Ho. SW8 161 316 DM79
Banning St. SE10 151 317 EE78
Bannister Clo. SW2 194 324 DN88
Bannister Clo., Grnf. 233 313 CD64
Bannister Gdns., Orp. 278 327 EW97
Bannister Ho. E9 119 307 DX64
Bannockburn Rd. SE18 253 318 ES77
Banstead Gdns. N9 209 300 DS48
Banstead Rd., Bans. 292 331 CX112
Banstead Rd., Cars. 293 331 DE107
Banstead Rd., Pur. 294 332 DN111
Banstead Rd. S., Sutt. 293 331 DC111
Banstead St. SE15 180 325 DW83
Banstead Way, Wall. 286 332 DL106
Banstock Rd., Edg. 217 304 CP51
Banting Dr. N21 208 300 DM43
Banton Clo., Enf. 203 301 DV40
Bantry St. SE5 163 316 DR80
Banwell Rd., Bex. 262 327 EX86
Banyard Rd. SE16 148 317 DV76
Banyards, Horn. 228 311 FL56
Bapchild Pl., Orp. 278 327 EW98
Baptist Gdns. NW5 114 306 DG65
Barandon Wk. W11 137 315 CX73
Barb Ms. W6 146 315 CW76
Barbara Brosnan Ct. NW8 18 315 DD68
Barbara Clo., Shep. 281 328 BP99
Barbara Hucklesby Clo. N22 221 306 DP54
Barbauld Rd. N16 101 306 DS62
Barber Clo. N21 209 300 DN45
Barberry Clo., Rom. 228 310 FJ51
Barber's All. E13 244 318 EH69
Barbers Rd. E15 130 317 EB68
Barbican, The EC2 49 316 DQ71
Barbican Rd., Grnf. 243 313 CB72
Barbon Clo. WC1 46/7 316 DL71
Barbot Clo. N9 210 301 DU48
Barchard St. SW18 174 323 DB85
Barchester Clo. W7 243 313 CF74
Barchester Clo., Uxb. 240 312 BJ70
Barchester Rd., Har. 215 303 CD54
Barchester St. E14 140 317 EB71
Barclay Clo. SW6 158 315 DA80
Barclay Path E17 223 307 EC57
Barclay Rd. E11 105 307 EE60
Barclay Rd. E13 244 318 EJ70
Barclay Rd. E17 223 307 EC57
Barclay Rd. N18 221 306 DR51
Barclay Rd. SW6 158 315 DA80
Barclay Rd., Croy. 287 332 DR104
Barclay Way SE22 196 325 DU87
Barcombe Ave. SW2 193 324 DL89
Barcombe Clo., Orp. 278 327 EU97
Bard Rd. W10 137 315 CX73
Barden Clo., Uxb. 212 302 BJ52
Barden St. SE18 253 318 ES80
Bardfield Ave., Rom. 226 309 EX55
Bardney Rd., Mord. 271 323 DB98
Bardolph Rd. N7 115 306 DL63
Bardolph Rd., Rich. 169 322 CM83
Bardsey Pl. E1 138 317 DW71
Bardsey Wk. N1 116 306 DQ65
Bardsley Clo., Croy. 287 332 DT104
Bardsley La. SE10 166 317 EC79
Barfett St. W10 127 315 CZ70
Barfield Ave. N20 207 299 DF47
Barfield Rd. E11 105 307 EF60
Barfield Rd., Brom. 277 326 EN97
Barford Clo. NW4 218 305 CU53
Barford St. N1 24 316 DN67
Barforth Rd. SE15 180 325 DV83
Barfreston Way SE20 274 325 DV95
Bargate Clo. SE18 253 318 ET78
Bargate Clo., N.Mal. 283 331 CU101
Barge Ho. Rd. E16 253 318 EP75
Barge Ho. St. SE1 60 316 DN74
Barge Wk., E.Mol. 267 329 CD97
Barge Wk., Kings.T. 268 322 CK96
Barge Wk., Walt. 266 329 BW97
Bargery Rd. SE6 198 325 EB88
Bargrove Clo. SE20 274 325 DU94
Bargrove Cres. SE6 197 325 DZ89
Barham Clo., Brom. 290 334 EL102
Barham Clo., Chis. 277 326 EP92
Barham Clo., Rom. 227 309 FB54
Barham Clo., Wem. 106 304 CH65
Barham Rd. SW20 270 323 CU94
Barham Rd., Chis. 277 326 EP92
Barham Rd., S.Croy. 287 332 DQ105
Baring Clo. SE12 260 326 EG89
Baring Rd. SE12 260 326 EG87
Baring Rd., Croy. 287 333 DU102
Baring St. N1 26 316 DR67
Bark Hart Rd., Orp. 291 335 EV102
Bark Pl. W2 52/3 315 DB73
Barker Dr. NW1 114 306 DJ66
Barker Ms. SW4 176 324 DH84
Barker St. SW10 158 315 DC79
Barker Wk. SW16 193 324 DK90
Barker Way SE22 196 325 DU88
Barkham Rd. N17 221 306 DR52
Barking Ind. Pk., Bark. 245 318 ET67
Barking Rd. E6 244 318 EK68
Barking Rd. E13 244 318 EG70
Barking Rd. E16 141 317 EE71
Barkis Way SE16 148 317 DV78
Barkston Gdns. SW5 76/7 315 DB77
Barkway Ct. N4 100 306 DQ62
Barkwood Clo., Rom. 227 309 FC57
Barkworth Rd. SE16 148 317 DV78
Barlborough St. SE14 165 317 DX80
Barlby Gdns. W10 127 315 CX70
Barlby Rd. W10 136 315 CW71
Barlee Cres., Uxb. 248 312 BJ71
Barley La., Ilf. 236 309 EU59
Barley La., Rom. 226 309 EV56
Barley Mow Pas. EC1 48/9 316 DP71
Barley Mow Pas. W4 145 314 CR78
Barley Mow Way, Shep. 281 328 BN98
Barley Shotts Business Pk. W10 137 315 CZ71
Barleycorn Way E14 139 317 DZ73
Barleycorn Way, Horn. 228 311 FM58
Barleyfields Clo., Rom. 226 309 EV58
Barlow Clo., Wall. 294 332 DL107
Barlow Pl. W1 56/7 316 DH73
Barlow Rd. NW6 111 305 CZ65
Barlow Rd. W3 134 314 CP74
Barlow Rd., Hmptn. 267 329 CA94
Barlow St. SE17 86 316 DR77
Barlow Way, Rain. 247 319 FD71
Barmeston Rd. SE6 198 325 EB89
Barmor Clo., Har. 215 303 CB54
Barmouth Ave., Grnf. 243 313 CF68
Barmouth Rd. SW18 174 323 DC86
Barmouth Rd., Croy. 288 333 DX103
Barn Clo., Ashf. 265 328 BP92
Barn Clo., Nthlt. 242 313 BW68
Barn Cres., Pur. 295 332 DR113
Barn Cres., Stan. 216 304 CJ51
Barn Elms Pk. SW15 156 315 CW82
Barn Hill, Wem. 92 304 CN60
Barn Ms., Har. 233 313 CA62
Barn Ri., Wem. 92 304 CN60
Barn St. N16 101 306 DS62
Barn Way, Wem. 92 304 CN60
Barnabas Ct. N21 209 300 DN43
Barnabas Rd. E9 119 307 DX64
Barnaby Clo., Har. 233 313 CC61
Barnaby Pl. SW7 78 315 DD77
Barnacre Clo., Uxb. 248 312 BK72
Barnard Clo. SE18 253 318 EN76
Barnard Clo., Chis. 277 326 ER95
Barnard Clo., Sun. 266 329 BV94
Barnard Clo., Wall. 294 332 DK108
Barnard Gdns., Hayes 242 313 BV70
Barnard Gdns., N.Mal. 270 323 CU98
Barnard Gro. E15 121 307 EF66
Barnard Hill N10 220 306 DH53
Barnard Ms. SW11 175 323 DE84
Barnard Rd. SW11 175 323 DE84
Barnard Rd., Enf. 203 301 DV40
Barnard Rd., Mitch. 272 324 DG97
Barnardo Dr., Ilf. 225 308 EQ56
Barnardo St. E1 139 317 DX72
Barnard's Inn EC1 48 316 DN72
Barnards Pl., S.Croy. 294 332 DP109
Barnby Sq. E15 131 317 EE67
Barnby St. E15 131 317 EE67
Barnby St. NW1 33 316 DJ69
Barncroft Clo., Uxb. 249 312 BP71
Barnehurst Ave., Bexh. 255 319 FC81
Barnehurst Ave., Erith 255 319 FC81
Barnehurst Clo., Erith 255 319 FC81
Barnehurst Rd., Bexh. 255 319 FC82
Barnes All., Hmptn. 267 329 CC96
Barnes Ave. SW13 156 315 CU80
Barnes Ave., Sthl. 250 321 BZ77
Barnes Bri. SW13 155 314 CS82
Barnes Bri. W4 155 314 CS82
Barnes Clo. E12 234 308 EK63
Barnes Ct. E16 244 318 EJ71
Barnes End, N.Mal. 283 331 CU99
Barnes High St. SW13 155 314 CT82
Barnes Ho., Bark. 245 318 ER67
Barnes Rd. N18 210 301 DW49
Barnes Rd., Ilf. 235 308 EQ64
Barnes St. E14 139 317 DY72
Barnes Ter. SE8 149 317 DZ78
Barnesbury Ho. SW4 177 324 DK86
Barnesdale Cres., Orp. 291 335 EU100
Barnet Dr., Brom. 290 334 EL103
Barnet Gate La., Barn. 205 298 CT44
Barnet Gro. E2 128 317 DU69
Barnet Ho. N20 207 299 DC47
Barnet La. N20 206 299 CZ46
Barnet La., Barn. 207 299 DA44
Barnet La., Borwd. 204 298 CK44
Barnet Rd. (Arkley), Barn. 205 298 CR44
Barnet Way NW7 205 298 CR48
Barnet Wd. Rd., Brom. 289 334 EH103
Barnett Clo., Erith 255 319 FF82
Barnett St. E1 138 317 DV72
Barney Clo. SE7 252 318 EJ78
Barnfield, Bans. 292 331 DB114
Barnfield, N.Mal. 283 330 CS100
Barnfield Ave., Croy. 288 333 DW103
Barnfield Ave., Kings.T. 268 322 CL92
Barnfield Ave., Mitch. 272 324 DH98
Barnfield Clo. N4 99 306 DL59
Barnfield Clo. SW17 190 323 DC90
Barnfield Gdns. SE18 253 318 EP79
Barnfield Gdns., Kings.T. 268 322 CL92
Barnfield Pl. E14 150 317 EA77
Barnfield Rd. SE18 253 318 EP79
Barnfield Rd. W5 122 314 CJ70
Barnfield Rd., Belv. 254 319 EZ79
Barnfield Rd., Edg. 217 304 CQ53
Barnfield Rd., Orp. 278 327 EX97
Barnfield Rd., S.Croy. 295 332 DS109
Barnfield Wd. Clo., Beck. 289 333 ED100
Barnfield Wd. Rd., Beck. 289 333 ED100
Barnham Rd., Grnf. 243 313 CC69
Barnham St. SE1 74/5 316 DS75
Barnhill, Pnr. 214 303 BW57
Barnhill Ave., Brom. 289 333 EF99
Barnhill La., Hayes 242 313 BV70
Barnhill Rd., Hayes 242 313 BV70
Barnhill Rd., Wem. 92 304 CQ62
Barningham Way NW9 217 304 CR58
Barnlea Clo., Felt. 258 321 BY89
Barnmead Gdns., Dag. 236 309 EZ64
Barnmead Rd., Beck. 274 325 DY95
Barnmead Rd., Dag. 236 309 EZ64
Barnsbury Clo., N.Mal. 269 322 CQ98
Barnsbury Cres., Surb. 282 330 CP102
Barnsbury Est. N1 24 316 DN67
Barnsbury Gro. N7 115 306 DM65
Barnsbury La., Surb. 282 330 CP103
Barnsbury Pk. N1 116 306 DN66
Barnsbury Rd. N1 24 316 DN68
Barnsbury Sq. N1 116 306 DN66
Barnsbury St. N1 116 306 DN66
Barnsbury Ter. N1 115 306 DM66
Barnscroft SW20 270 323 CV97
Barnsdale Ave. E14 150 317 EB77
Barnsdale Rd. W9 127 315 CZ70
Barnsfield Pl., Uxb. 240 312 BJ67
Barnsley Rd., Rom. 228 311 FM52
Barnsley St. E1 128 317 DV70
Barnstaple Rd., Ruis. 232 313 BW62
Barnston Wk. N1 25 316 DQ67
Barnwell Rd. SW2 178 324 DN85
Barnwood Clo. W9 28/9 315 DB70
Barnwood Clo., Ruis. 231 312 BR61
Barnwood Ct. E16 244 318 EG74
Baron Clo. N11 208 300 DG50
Baron Clo., Sutt. 292 331 DB110
Baron Gdns., Ilf. 225 308 EQ55
Baron Gro., Mitch. 271 323 DE98
Baron Rd., Dag. 236 309 EX60
Baron St. N1 24 316 DN68
Baron Wk. E16 141 317 EF71
Baron Wk., Mitch. 271 323 DE98
Baroness Rd. E2 39 316 DT69
Baronet Gro. N17 222 307 DU53
Baronet Rd. N17 222 307 DU53
Barons, The, Twick. 168 322 CH86
Barons Ct., Wall. 286 332 DK104
Barons Ct. Rd. W14 147 315 CY78
Barons Gate, Barn. 207 299 DE44
Barons Keep W14 147 315 CY78
Barons Mead, Har. 215 303 CE56
Barons Pl. SE1 72 316 DN75
Barons Wk., Croy. 288 333 DY100
Baronsfield Rd., Twick. 168 322 CH86
Baronsmead Rd. SW13 156 315 CU81
Baronsmede W5 143 314 CM75
Baronsmere Rd. N2 219 305 DE56
Barque Ms. SE8 166 317 EA79
Barra Hall Circ., Hayes 249 312 BS72
Barra Hall Rd., Hayes 249 312 BS73
Barrack Rd., Houns. 258 321 BX84
Barratt Ave. N22 220 306 DM54
Barratt Ind. Pk., Sthl. 251 321 CA75
Barratt Way, Har. 215 303 CD55
Barrenger Rd. N10 219 305 DF53
Barrett Clo., Rom. 228 310 FH52
Barrett Rd. E17 223 307 EC56
Barrett St. W1 44 316 DG72
Barretts Grn. Rd. NW10 124 314 CQ69
Barretts Gro. N16 117 306 DS64
Barrhill Rd. SW2 193 324 DL89
Barrie Est. W2 54 315 DD73
Barrie Twr. W3 144 314 CQ75
Barriedale SE14 165 317 DY82
Barrier App. SE7 252 318 EK76
Barringer Sq. SW17 272 324 DG91
Barrington Clo. NW5 114 306 DG64
Barrington Clo., Ilf. 224 308 EM53
Barrington Dr., Uxb. 212 302 BG52
Barrington Rd. E12 235 308 EN65
Barrington Rd. N8 220 306 DK57
Barrington Rd. SW9 178 324 DP83
Barrington Rd., Bexh. 254 319 EX82
Barrington Rd., Pur. 294 332 DJ112
Barrington Rd., Sutt. 284 331 DA102
Barrington Vil. SE18 253 318 EN81
Barrow Ave., Cars. 293 331 DF108
Barrow Clo. N21 209 300 DP48
Barrow Hedges Clo., Cars. 293 331 DE108
Barrow Hedges Way, Cars. 293 331 DE108
Barrow Hill, Wor.Pk. 283 330 CS103
Barrow Hill Clo., Wor.Pk. 283 330 CS103
Barrow Hill Rd. NW8 18/9 315 DE68
Barrow Pt. Ave., Pnr. 214 303 BY54
Barrow Pt. La., Pnr. 214 303 BY54
Barrow Rd. SW16 272 324 DK93
Barrow Rd., Croy. 286 332 DN106
Barrow Wk., Brent. 142 314 CJ78
Barrow Way N7 99 306 DM62
Barrowdene Clo., Pnr. 214 303 BY54
Barrowell Grn. N21 209 300 DP47
Barrowfield Clo. N9 210 301 DV48
Barrowgate Rd. W4 144 314 CQ78
Barrowsfield, S.Croy. 295 332 DT112
Barrs Rd. NW10 109 304 CR66
Barry Ave. N15 221 306 DT58
Barry Ave., Bexh. 254 319 EY80
Barry Clo., Orp. 291 334 ES104
Barry Rd. E6 244 318 EL72
Barry Rd. NW10 108 304 CQ66
Barry Rd. SE22 180 325 DU86
Barset Rd. SE15 180 325 DW83
Barson Clo. SE20 274 325 DW94
Barston Rd. SE27 194 324 DQ89
Barstow Cres. SW2 193 324 DM88
Barter St. WC1 46/7 316 DL71
Barters Wk., Pnr. 214 303 BY55
Barth Rd. SE18 253 318 ES77
Bartholomew Clo. EC1 49 316 DQ71
Bartholomew Clo. SW18 174 323 DC84
Bartholomew Dr., Rom. 228 310 FK54
Bartholomew La. EC2 50 316 DR72
Bartholomew Pl. EC1 49 316 DQ71
Bartholomew Rd. NW5 114 306 DJ65
Bartholomew Sq. E1 128 317 DV70
Bartholomew Sq. EC1 37 316 DQ70
Bartholomew St. SE1 74 316 DR76
Bartholomew Vil. NW5 114 306 DJ65
Bartholomew Way, Swan. 279 327 FE97
Bartle Ave. E6 244 318 EL68
Bartle Rd. W11 137 315 CY72
Bartlett Clo. E14 140 317 EA72
Bartlett Ct. EC4 48 316 DN72
Bartlett St., S.Croy. 287 332 DR106
Bartlow Gdns., Rom. 227 309 FD53
Barton Ave., Rom. 237 309 FB60
Barton Clo. E6 244 318 EM72
Barton Clo. E9 118 307 DW64
Barton Clo. SE15 180 325 DV83
Barton Clo., Bexh. 262 327 EY85
Barton Clo., Shep. 281 328 BP100
Barton Grn., N.Mal. 269 322 CR96
Barton Meadows, Ilf. 225 308 EP56
Barton Rd. W14 147 315 CY78
Barton Rd., Horn. 238 310 FG60
Barton Rd., Sid. 278 327 EY93
Barton St. SW1 70/1 316 DL76
Bartons, The, Borwd. 204 298 CK44
Bartonway NW8 18 315 DD68
Bartram Clo., Uxb. 241 312 BP70
Bartram Rd. SE4 181 325 DY85
Barville Clo. SE4 181 325 DY84
Barwick Rd. E7 234 308 EH63
Barwood Ave., W.Wick. 288 333 EB102
Basden Gro., Felt. 259 321 CA89
Basedale Rd., Dag. 236 309 EV66
Baseing Clo. E6 245 318 EN73
Bashley Rd. NW10 125 314 CR70
Basil Ave. E6 244 318 EL68
Basil Gdns., Croy. 288 333 DX102
Basil St. SW3 67 315 DF76
Basildene Rd., Houns. 258 321 BX83
Basildon Ave., Ilf. 225 308 EN53
Basildon Clo., Sutt. 292 331 DB109
Basildon Rd. SE2 254 319 EU78
Basildon Rd., Bexh. 254 319 EY82
Basin S. E16 245 318 EP74
Basing Ct. SE15 163 316 DT81
Basing Dr., Bex. 262 327 EZ86
Basing Hill NW11 95 305 CZ60
Basing Hill, Wem. 91 304 CM61
Basing Ho., Bark. 245 318 ER67
Basing Ho. Yd. E2 38/9 316 DS69
Basing Pl. E2 38/9 316 DS69
Basing Rd., Bans. 292 331 CZ114
Basing St. W11 137 315 CZ72
Basing Way N3 219 305 DA55
Basingdon Way SE5 179 324 DR84
Basinghall Ave. EC2 50 316 DR71
Basinghall Gdns., Sutt. 292 331 DB109
Basinghall St. EC2 49 316 DQ71
Basire St. N1 25 316 DQ67
Baskerville Rd. SW18 191 323 DE87
Basket Gdns. SE9 260 326 EL85
Baslow Clo., Har. 215 303 CD53
Baslow Wk. E5 119 307 DX63
Basnett Rd. SW11 176 324 DG83
Basque Ct. SE16 149 317 DX75
Bassano St. SE22 179 324 DT85
Bassant Rd. SE18 253 318 ET79
Bassein Pk. Rd. W12 145 314 CT75
Basset Ho., Dag. 246 319 EV67
Bassett Clo., Sutt. 292 331 DB109
Bassett Gdns., Islw. 251 321 CC80
Bassett Rd. W10 137 315 CX72
Bassett Rd., Uxb. 240 312 BJ66
Bassett St. NW5 114 306 DG65
Bassett Way, Grnf. 243 313 CB72
Bassetts Clo., Orp. 290 334 EP104
Bassetts Way, Orp. 290 334 EP105
Bassingham Rd. SW18 190 323 DC87
Bassingham Rd., Wem. 107 304 CK65
Bassishaw Highwalk EC2 49 316 DQ71
Basswood Clo. SE15 180 325 DV83
Bastable Ave., Bark. 245 318 ES68
Bastion Highwalk EC2 49 316 DQ71
Bastion Ho. EC2 49 316 DQ71
Bastion Rd. SE2 254 319 EU78
Baston Manor Rd., Brom. 289 334 EH104
Baston Rd., Brom. 289 334 EH102
Bastwick St. EC1 37 316 DQ70
Basuto Rd. SW6 158 315 DA81
Batavia Clo., Sun. 266 329 BW95
Batavia Ms. SE14 165 317 DY80
Batavia Rd. SE14 165 317 DY80
Batavia Rd., Sun. 266 329 BV95
Batchelor St. N1 24 316 DN68
Batchwood Grn., Orp. 278 327 EU97
Batchworth Heath Hill, Rick. 213 302 BN49
Batchworth Hill, Rick. 212 302 BM48
Batchworth La., Nthwd. 213 302 BP50
Bate St. E14 139 317 DZ73
Bateman Clo., Bark. 235 308 EQ65
Bateman Ho. SE17 162 316 DP79
Bateman Rd. E4 223 307 EA51
Bateman St. W1 46 316 DK72
Bateman's Bldgs. W1 46 316 DK72
Bateman's Row EC2 38/9 316 DS70
Bates Cres. SW16 272 324 DJ94
Bates Cres., Croy. 286 332 DN106
Bates Rd., Rom. 229 311 FN52
Bateson St. SE18 253 318 ES77
Bath Clo. SE15 164 317 DV80
Bath Ct. EC1 36 316 DN70
Bath Ho. Rd., Croy. 286 332 DL102
Bath Pas., Kings.T. 268 322 CK96
Bath Pl. EC2 38/9 316 DS69
Bath Rd. E7 234 308 EK65
Bath Rd. N9 210 301 DV47
Bath Rd. W4 145 314 CS77
Bath Rd., Hayes 257 320 BS81
Bath Rd., Houns. 250 321 BX82
Bath Rd., Mitch. 271 323 DD97
Bath Rd., Rom. 226 309 EY58
Bath Rd., West Dr. 256 320 BK81
Bath St. EC1 37 316 DQ69
Bath Ter. SE1 73 316 DQ76
Bathgate Rd. SW19 189 323 CX90
Baths Rd., Brom. 276 326 EK98
Bathurst Ave. SW19 271 323 DB95
Bathurst Gdns. NW10 126 315 CV68
Bathurst Ms. W2 54 315 DD73
Bathurst Rd., Ilf. 235 308 EP60
Bathurst St. W2 54 315 DD73
Bathway SE18 253 318 EN77
Batley Clo., Mitch. 285 331 DF101
Batley Pl. N16 101 306 DT62
Batley Rd. N16 101 306 DT62
Batley Rd., Enf. 202 300 DR39
Batman Clo. W12 136 315 CV74
Batoum Gdns. W6 146 315 CW76
Batson St. W12 146 315 CU75
Batsworth Rd., Mitch. 271 323 DD97
Batten Clo. E6 244 318 EM72
Batten St. SW11 175 323 DE83
Battenburg Wk. SE19 273 324 DS92
Battersby Rd. SE6 199 325 ED89
Battersea Bri. SW3 159 315 DD80
Battersea Bri. SW11 159 315 DE80
Battersea Bri. Rd. SW11 159 315 DE80
Battersea Ch. Rd. SW11 159 315 DD81
Battersea High St. SW11 159 315 DD81
Battersea Pk. SW11 159 315 DF80
Battersea Pk. Rd. SW8 160 316 DH81
Battersea Pk. Rd. SW11 159 315 DE82
Battersea Ri. SW11 175 323 DD85
Battersea Sq. SW11 159 315 DD81
Battery Rd. SE28 253 318 ES75
Battis, The, Rom. 227 309 FE58
Battishill Gdns. N1 116 306 DP66
Battishill St. N1 116 306 DP66
Battle Bri. La. SE1 62/3 316 DS74
Battle Bri. Rd. NW1 22/3 316 DL68
Battle Clo. SW19 271 323 DC93
Battle Rd., Belv. 255 319 FC77
Battle Rd., Erith 255 319 FC77
Battledean Rd. N5 116 306 DP64
Batty St. E1 138 317 DU72
Baudwin Rd. SE6 199 325 EE89
Baugh Rd., Sid. 278 327 EW92
Baulk, The SW18 190 323 DA87
Bavant Rd. SW16 272 324 DM96
Bavaria Rd. N19 99 306 DL61
Bavent Rd. SE5 162 316 DQ82
Bawdale Rd. SE22 179 324 DT85
Bawdsey Ave., Ilf. 225 308 ET56
Bawtree Clo., Sutt. 293 331 DC110
Bawtree Rd. SE14 165 317 DY80
Bawtree Rd., Uxb. 240 312 BK65
Bawtry Rd. N20 207 299 DF48
Baxendale N20 207 299 DC47
Baxendale St. E2 128 317 DU69
Baxter Clo., Uxb. 241 312 BP69
Baxter Rd. E16 244 318 EJ72
Baxter Rd. N1 117 306 DR65
Baxter Rd. N18 210 301 DV49
Baxter Rd. NW10 125 314 CS70
Baxter Rd., Ilf. 235 308 EP64
Bay Ct. W5 143 314 CL76
Bay Tree Clo., Brom. 276 326 EJ95
Baydon Ct., Brom. 275 325 EF97
Bayes Clo. SE26 274 325 DW92
Bayfield Rd. SE9 260 326 EK84
Bayford Ms. E8 118 307 DV66
Bayford Rd. NW10 127 315 CX69
Bayford St. E8 118 307 DV66
Bayham Pl. NW1 21 316 DJ67
Bayham Rd. W4 145 314 CR76
Bayham Rd. W13 132 314 CH73
Bayham Rd., Mord. 271 323 DB98
Bayham St. NW1 21 316 DJ67
Bayhurst Dr., Nthwd. 213 302 BT51
Bayley St. WC1 46 316 DK71
Bayley Wk. SE2 254 319 EY78
Baylin Rd. SW18 174 323 DB86
Baylis Rd. SE1 72 316 DN75
Bayliss Ave. SE28 246 319 EX73
Bayliss Clo. N21 208 300 DL43
Bayne Clo. E6 244 318 EM72
Baynes Clo., Enf. 203 301 DU39
Baynes Ms. NW3 113 305 DD65
Baynes St. NW1 114 306 DJ66
Baynham Clo., Bex. 262 327 EZ86
Bayonne Rd. W6 157 315 CY79
Bayshill Ri., Nthlt. 233 313 CB65
Bayston Rd. N16 101 306 DT62
Bayswater Rd. W2 52/3 315 DB73
Baythorne St. E3 139 317 DZ71
Baytree Clo., Sid. 261 326 ET88
Baytree Rd. SW2 177 324 DM84
Bazalgette Clo., N.Mal. 283 330 CR99
Bazalgette Gdns., N.Mal. 283 330 CR99
Bazely St. E14 140 317 EC73
Bazile Rd. N21 209 300 DN44
Beach Gro., Felt. 259 321 CA89
Beacham Clo. SE7 252 318 EK78
Beachborough Rd., Brom. 275 325 EC91
Beachcroft Rd. E11 105 307 EE62
Beachcroft Way N19 99 306 DK60
Beachy Rd. E3 120 307 EA66
Beacon Clo., Uxb. 240 312 BK64
Beacon Gate SE14 165 317 DX82
Beacon Gro., Cars. 285 332 DG105
Beacon Hill N7 115 306 DL64
Beacon Rd. SE13 183 325 ED86
Beacon Rd., Houns. 257 320 BN86
Beacons Clo. E6 244 318 EL71
Beaconsfield Clo. N11 208 300 DG50
Beaconsfield Clo. SE3 252 318 EG79
Beaconsfield Clo. W4 144 314 CQ78
Beaconsfield Par. SE9 276 326 EL91
Beaconsfield Rd. E10 104 307 EC61
Beaconsfield Rd. E16 131 317 EF70
Beaconsfield Rd. E17 222 307 DZ58
Beaconsfield Rd. N9 210 301 DU48
Beaconsfield Rd. N11 208 300 DG48
Beaconsfield Rd. N15 221 306 DS56
Beaconsfield Rd. NW10 109 304 CT65
Beaconsfield Rd. SE3 167 317 EF80
Beaconsfield Rd. SE9 260 326 EL89
Beaconsfield Rd. SE17 163 316 DR79
Beaconsfield Rd. W4 145 314 CR76
Beaconsfield Rd. W5 142 314 CJ75
Beaconsfield Rd., Bex. 263 327 FD89
Beaconsfield Rd., Brom. 276 326 EK97
Beaconsfield Rd., Croy. 287 332 DR100
Beaconsfield Rd., Enf. 203 301 DX37
Beaconsfield Rd., Hayes 242 313 BW74
Beaconsfield Rd., N.Mal. 269 322 CR96
Beaconsfield Rd., Sthl. 242 313 BX74
Beaconsfield Rd., Surb. 282 330 CM101
Beaconsfield Rd., Twick. 168 322 CH86
Beaconsfield Ter., Rom. 226 309 EX58
Beaconsfield Ter. Rd. W14 147 315 CY76
Beaconsfield Wk. E6 245 318 EN72
Beaconsfield Wk. SW6 157 315 CZ81
Beacontree Ave. E17 223 307 ED53
Beacontree Rd. E11 105 307 EF59
Beadlow Clo., Cars. 285 331 DD100
Beadman Pl. SE27 273 324 DP91
Beadman St. SE27 273 324 DP91
Beadnell Rd. SE23 197 325 DX88
Beadon Rd. W6 146 315 CW77
Beadon Rd., Brom. 276 326 EG98
Beaford Gro. SW20 270 323 CY97
Beagle Clo., Felt. 266 329 BV91
Beak St. W1 57 316 DJ73
Beal Clo., Well. 254 319 EU81
Beal Rd., Ilf. 235 308 EN61
Beale Clo. N13 209 300 DP50
Beale Pl. E3 129 317 DZ68
Beale Rd. E3 129 317 DZ67
Beam Ave., Dag. 247 319 FB67
Beam Way, Dag. 237 309 FD66
Beaminster Gdns., Ilf. 225 308 EP54
Beamish Rd. N9 210 301 DU46
Bean Rd., Bexh. 262 327 EX84
Beanacre Clo. E9 119 307 DZ65
Beanshaw SE9 277 326 EN91
Beansland Gro., Rom. 226 309 EY54
Bear All. EC4 48/9 316 DP72
Bear Clo., Rom. 227 309 FB58
Bear Gdns. SE1 61 316 DQ74
Bear La. SE1 60/1 316 DP74
Bear Rd., Felt. 266 329 BX92
Bear St. WC2 58 316 DK73
Beard Rd., Kings.T. 268 322 CM92
Beardell St. SE19 273 324 DT93
Beardow Gro. N14 208 300 DJ44
Beard's Hill, Hmptn. 267 329 CA95
Beard's Hill Clo., Hmptn. 267 329 CA95
Beards Rd., Ashf. 265 328 BS93
Beardsfield E13 244 318 EG67
Beardsley Ter., Dag. 236 309 EV64
Beardsley Way W3 145 314 CR75
Bearfield Rd., Kings.T. 268 322 CL94
Bearstead Ri. SE4 181 325 DZ85
Bearstead Ter., Beck. 275 325 EA95
Beasley's Ait La., Sun. 281 328 BT100
Beasleys Yd., Uxb. 240 312 BJ66
Beatrice Ave. SW16 272 324 DM96
Beatrice Ave., Wem. 107 304 CL64
Beatrice Clo. E13 244 318 EG70
Beatrice Clo., Pnr. 214 303 BU56
Beatrice Pl. W8 64/5 315 DB76
Beatrice Rd. E17 223 307 EA57
Beatrice Rd. N4 100 306 DN59
Beatrice Rd. N9 210 301 DW45
Beatrice Rd. SE1 148 317 DU77
Beatrice Rd., Rich. 169 322 CM85
Beatrice Rd., Sthl. 242 313 BZ74
Beatson Wk. SE16 139 317 DY74
Beattock Ri. N10 220 306 DH56
Beatty Rd. N16 117 306 DS63
Beatty Rd., Stan. 216 304 CJ51
Beatty St. NW1 21 316 DJ68
Beattyville Gdns., Ilf. 225 308 EN55
Beauchamp Clo. W4 144 314 CQ76
Beauchamp Pl. SW3 66/7 315 DE76
Beauchamp Rd. E7 234 308 EH66
Beauchamp Rd. SE19 273 324 DR95
Beauchamp Rd. SW11 175 323 DE84
Beauchamp Rd., Sutt. 284 331 DA105
Beauchamp Rd., Twick. 184 322 CG87
Beauchamp St. EC1 48 316 DN71
Beauchamp Ter. SW15 172 323 CV83
Beauclerc Rd. W6 146 315 CV76
Beauclerk Clo., Felt. 258 321 BV88
Beaudesert Ms., West Dr. 248 320 BL75
Beaufort E6 245 318 EN71
Beaufort Ave., Har. 216 304 CG56
Beaufort Clo. E4 223 307 EB51
Beaufort Clo. SW15 188 323 CV87
Beaufort Clo. W5 133 314 CM71
Beaufort Clo., Rom. 227 309 FC56
Beaufort Ct., Rich. 268 322 CJ91
Beaufort Dr. NW11 219 305 DA56
Beaufort Gdns. NW4 218 305 CW58
Beaufort Gdns. SW3 66/7 315 DE76
Beaufort Gdns. SW16 272 324 DM94
Beaufort Gdns., Houns. 250 321 BY81
Beaufort Gdns., Ilf. 235 308 EN60
Beaufort Ms. SW6 157 315 CZ79
Beaufort Pk. NW11 219 305 DA56
Beaufort Rd. W5 133 314 CM71
Beaufort Rd., Kings.T. 268 322 CL98
Beaufort Rd., Rich. 268 322 CJ91
Beaufort Rd., Ruis. 231 312 BR61
Beaufort Rd., Twick. 184 322 CJ87
Beaufort St. SW3 159 315 DD79
Beaufoy Rd. N17 221 306 DS52
Beaufoy Wk. SE11 83 316 DM77
Beaulieu Ave. SE26 274 325 DV91
Beaulieu Clo. NW9 217 304 CS55
Beaulieu Clo. SE5 179 324 DR83
Beaulieu Clo., Houns. 258 321 BZ85
Beaulieu Clo., Mitch. 272 324 DG95
Beaulieu Clo., Twick. 169 322 CK86
Beaulieu Dr., Pnr. 214 303 BX58
Beaulieu Gdns. N21 209 300 DQ45
Beaulieu Pl. W4 144 314 CQ76
Beauly Way, Rom. 227 309 FE53
Beaumanor Gdns. SE9 277 326 EN91
Beaumaris Dr., Wdf.Grn. 224 308 EK52
Beaumont Ave. W14 147 315 CZ78
Beaumont Ave., Har. 215 303 CB58
Beaumont Ave., Rich. 169 322 CM83
Beaumont Ave., Wem. 106 304 CJ64
Beaumont Clo., Kings.T. 269 322 CN94
Beaumont Clo., Rom. 228 310 FJ54
Beaumont Cres. W14 147 315 CZ78
Beaumont Cres., Rain. 238 310 FG65
Beaumont Dr., Ashf. 265 328 BR92
Beaumont Gdns. NW3 96 305 DA62
Beaumont Gro. E1 129 317 DX70
Beaumont Ms. W1 44 316 DG71
Beaumont Pl. W1 33 316 DJ70
Beaumont Pl., Islw. 259 321 CF85
Beaumont Ri. N19 99 306 DK59
Beaumont Rd. E10 104 307 EB59
Beaumont Rd. E13 244 318 EH69
Beaumont Rd. SE19 273 324 DQ93
Beaumont Rd. SW19 189 323 CY87
Beaumont Rd. W4 144 314 CQ76
Beaumont Rd., Orp. 291 334 ER100
Beaumont Rd., Pur. 294 332 DN113
Beaumont Sq. E1 129 317 DX70
Beaumont St. W1 44 316 DG71
Beaumont Wk. NW3 113 305 DF66
Beauvais Ter., Nthlt. 242 313 BX69
Beauval Rd. SE22 179 324 DT86
Beaver Clo. SE20 274 325 DU94
Beaver Clo., Hmptn. 267 329 CB95
Beaver Gro., Nthlt. 242 313 BY69
Beaverbank Rd. SE9 261 326 ER88
Beavers Cres., Houns. 258 321 BX84
Beavers La., Houns. 250 321 BW82
Beavers La. Camp, Houns. 258 321 BW83
Beaverwood Rd., Chis. 277 326 ES93
Beavor Gro. W6 146 315 CU77
Beavor La. W6 146 315 CU77
Bebbington Rd. SE18 253 318 ES77
Bebletts Clo., Orp. 291 334 ET106
Bec Clo., Ruis. 232 313 BX62
Beccles Dr., Bark. 235 308 ES65
Beccles St. E14 139 317 DZ73
Beck Clo. SE13 166 317 EB81
Beck Ct., Beck. 274 325 DX97
Beck La., Beck. 274 325 DX97
Beck River Pk., Beck. 275 325 EA95
Beck Rd. E8 128 317 DV67
Beck Way, Beck. 274 325 DZ97
Beckenham Gdns. N9 209 300 DS48
Beckenham Gro., Brom. 275 325 ED96

Beckenham Hill Rd. SE6 275 325 EC92
Beckenham Hill Rd., Beck. 275 325 EB92
Beckenham La., Brom. 275 325 EE96
Beckenham Pl. Pk., Beck. 275 325 EB94
Beckenham Rd., Beck. 274 325 DX95
Beckenham Rd., W.Wick. 288 333 EB101
Beckers, The N16 102 307 DU62
Becket Ave. E6 245 318 EN69
Becket Clo. SE25 287 333 DU100
Becket Fold, Har. 215 303 CF57
Becket Rd. N18 210 301 DW49
Becket St. SE1 74 316 DR76
Beckett Clo. NW10 109 304 CR65
Beckett Clo. SW16 193 324 DK89
Beckett Clo., Belv. 254 319 EY76
Beckett Wk., Beck. 274 325 DY93
Becketts Clo., Felt. 258 321 BV86
Becketts Clo., Orp. 291 334 ET104
Becketts Pl., Kings.T. 268 322 CK95
Beckford Dr., Orp. 291 334 ER101
Beckford Pl. SE17 85 316 DQ78
Beckford Rd., Croy. 287 332 DT100
Becklow Gdns. W12 146 315 CU75
Becklow Rd. W12 145 314 CT75
Becks Rd., Sid. 262 327 EU90
Beckton Pk. Roundabout E16 252 318 EK76
Beckton Retail Pk. E6 245 318 EN71
Beckton Rd. E16 141 317 EF71
Beckway Rd. SW16 272 324 DK96
Beckway St. SE17 86 316 DR77
Beckwith Rd. SE24 179 324 DR86
Beclands Rd. SW17 272 324 DG93
Becmead Ave. SW16 272 324 DK91
Becmead Ave., Har. 216 304 CH57
Becondale Rd. SE19 273 324 DS92
Becontree Ave., Dag. 236 309 EV63
Bective Pl. SW15 173 323 CZ84
Bective Rd. E7 234 308 EG63
Bective Rd. SW15 173 323 CY84
Becton Pl., Erith 255 319 FB80
Bedale Rd., Enf. 202 300 DQ38
Bedale St. SE1 62 316 DR74
Beddington Fm. Rd., Croy. 286 332 DL101
Beddington Gdns., Cars. 293 332 DG107
Beddington Gdns., Wall. 293 332 DH107
Beddington Grn., Orp. 277 326 ET95
Beddington Gro., Wall. 286 332 DK106
Beddington La., Croy. 286 332 DJ99
Beddington Path, Orp. 277 326 ET95
Beddington Rd., Ilf. 235 308 ET59
Beddington Rd., Orp. 277 326 ES95
Beddington Trd. Pk. W., Croy. 286 332 DL102
Bede Clo., Pnr. 214 303 BX53
Bede Rd., Rom. 226 309 EW58
Bedenham Way SE15 163 316 DT80
Bedens Rd., Sid. 278 327 EY93
Bedfont Clo., Felt. 257 320 BQ86
Bedfont Clo., Mitch. 272 324 DG96
Bedfont Ct., Stai. 256 320 BH84
Bedfont Ct. Est., Stai. 256 320 BG83
Bedfont Grn. Clo., Felt. 265 320 BQ88
Bedfont La., Felt. 265 320 BS87
Bedfont Rd., Felt. 265 320 BQ88
Bedfont Rd., Stai. 256 320 BL86
Bedford Ave. WC1 46 316 DK71
Bedford Ave., Barn. 206 299 CZ43
Bedford Ave., Hayes 242 313 BV72
Bedford Clo. N10 220 306 DG52
Bedford Clo. W4 155 314 CS79
Bedford Cor. W4 145 314 CS77
Bedford Ct. WC2 58/9 316 DL73
Bedford Cres., Enf. 203 301 DY35
Bedford Gdns. W8 52 315 DA74
Bedford Gdns., Horn. 238 310 FJ61
Bedford Hill SW12 192 324 DH88
Bedford Hill SW16 192 324 DH88
Bedford Ho. SW4 177 324 DL84
Bedford Pk., Croy. 287 332 DQ102
Bedford Pas. SW6 157 315 CY80
Bedford Pl. WC1 46/7 316 DL71
Bedford Pl., Croy. 287 332 DR102
Bedford Rd. E6 245 318 EN67
Bedford Rd. E17 223 307 EA54
Bedford Rd. E18 224 308 EG54
Bedford Rd. N2 219 305 DE55
Bedford Rd. N8 220 306 DK58
Bedford Rd. N9 210 301 DV45
Bedford Rd. N15 221 306 DS56
Bedford Rd. N22 220 306 DL53
Bedford Rd. NW7 205 298 CS47
Bedford Rd. SW4 177 324 DL83
Bedford Rd. W4 145 314 CR76
Bedford Rd. W13 132 314 CH73
Bedford Rd., Har. 215 303 CC58
Bedford Rd., Ilf. 235 308 EP62
Bedford Rd., Nthwd. 213 302 BQ48
Bedford Rd., Orp. 291 335 EV103
Bedford Rd., Ruis. 241 312 BT63
Bedford Rd., Sid. 261 326 ES90
Bedford Rd., Twick. 259 321 CD90
Bedford Rd., Wor.Pk. 284 331 CW103
Bedford Row WC1 47 316 DM71
Bedford Sq. WC1 46 316 DK71
Bedford St. WC2 58/9 316 DL73
Bedford Ter. SW2 177 324 DL85
Bedford Way WC1 34 316 DK70
Bedfordbury WC2 58/9 316 DL73
Bedgebury Gdns. SW19 189 323 CY89
Bedgebury Rd. SE9 260 326 EK84
Bedivere Rd., Brom. 260 326 EG90
Bedlow Way, Croy. 286 332 DM105
Bedonwell Rd. SE2 254 319 EY79
Bedonwell Rd., Belv. 254 319 EY79
Bedonwell Rd., Bexh. 254 319 EZ81
Bedser Clo. SE11 161 316 DM79
Bedser Clo., Th.Hth. 273 324 DQ97
Bedser Dr., Grnf. 233 313 CD64
Bedster Gdns., W.Mol. 267 329 CB96
Bedwardine Rd. SE19 273 324 DS94
Bedwell Gdns., Hayes 249 320 BS78
Bedwell Rd. N17 221 306 DS53
Bedwell Rd., Belv. 255 319 FA78
Bedwin Way SE16 148 317 DV78
Beeby Rd. E16 244 318 EH71
Beech Ave. N20 207 299 DE46
Beech Ave. W3 135 314 CS74
Beech Ave., Brent. 152 314 CH80
Beech Ave., Enf. 202 300 DN35
Beech Ave., Ruis. 232 313 BV60
Beech Ave., Sid. 262 327 EU87
Beech Ave., S.Croy. 295 332 DR111
Beech Ave., Swan. 279 327 FF98
Beech Ave., Upmin. 239 311 FP62
Beech Clo. N9 210 301 DU44
Beech Clo. SE8 165 317 DZ79
Beech Clo. SW15 188 323 CU87
Beech Clo. SW19 270 323 CW93
Beech Clo., Ashf. 265 328 BR92
Beech Clo., Cars. 285 331 DF103
Beech Clo., Horn. 238 310 FH62
Beech Clo., Stai. 264 320 BK87
Beech Clo., Sun. 266 329 BX96
Beech Clo., West Dr. 249 320 BN76
Beech Copse, Brom. 276 326 EM96
Beech Copse, S.Croy. 287 332 DS106
Beech Ct. E17 223 307 ED55
Beech Ct. SE9 260 326 EL86
Beech Ct., Ilf. 235 308 EN62
Beech Dell, Kes. 290 334 EM105
Beech Dr. N2 219 305 DF54
Beech Gdns. EC2 49 316 DQ71
Beech Gdns. W5 143 314 CL75
Beech Gdns., Dag. 237 309 FB66
Beech Gro., Ilf. 225 308 ES51
Beech Gro., Mitch. 286 332 DK99
Beech Gro., N.Mal. 269 322 CR97
Beech Hall Cres. E4 223 307 ED52
Beech Hall Rd. E4 223 307 EC52
Beech Ho. Rd., Croy. 287 332 DR104
Beech Lawns N12 207 299 DD50
Beech Rd. N11 220 306 DL51
Beech Rd. SW16 272 324 DL96
Beech Rd., Felt. 265 320 BS87
Beech Row, Rich. 268 322 CL91
Beech St. EC2 49 316 DQ71
Beech St., Rom. 227 309 FC56
Beech Tree Glade E4 211 301 EF46
Beech Wk. NW7 217 304 CS51
Beech Way NW10 109 304 CR66
Beech Way, Twick. 259 321 CA90
Beechcroft, Chis. 277 326 EN94
Beechcroft Ave. NW11 95 305 CZ59
Beechcroft Ave., Bexh. 255 319 FD81
Beechcroft Ave., Har. 233 313 CA59
Beechcroft Ave., N.Mal. 269 322 CQ95
Beechcroft Ave., Sthl. 242 313 BZ74
Beechcroft Clo., Houns. 250 321 BY80
Beechcroft Clo., Orp. 291 334 ER105
Beechcroft Gdns., Wem. 91 304 CM62
Beechcroft Rd. E18 224 308 EH54
Beechcroft Rd. SW14 170 322 CQ83
Beechcroft Rd. SW17 191 323 DE89
Beechcroft Rd., Chess. 282 330 CM105
Beechcroft Rd., Orp. 291 334 ER105
Beechdale N21 208 300 DM47
Beechdale Rd. SW2 177 324 DM86
Beechen Cliff Way, Islw. 251 321 CF81
Beechen Gro., Pnr. 214 303 BZ55
Beeches, The, Houns. 251 321 CB81
Beeches Ave., Cars. 293 331 DE108
Beeches Clo. SE20 274 325 DW95
Beeches Ct., Brom. 276 326 EG93
Beeches Rd. SW17 191 323 DE90
Beeches Rd., Sutt. 284 331 CY102
Beeches Wk., Cars. 293 331 DD109
Beechfield, Bans. 292 331 DB113
Beechfield Cotts., Brom. 276 326 EJ96
Beechfield Gdns., Rom. 237 309 FC59
Beechfield Rd. N4 221 306 DQ58
Beechfield Rd. SE6 197 325 DZ88
Beechfield Rd., Brom. 276 326 EJ96
Beechfield Rd., Erith 255 319 FE80
Beechhill Rd. SE9 261 326 EN85
Beechmont Clo., Brom. 275 325 EE92
Beechmore Gdns., Sutt. 284 331 CX103
Beechmore Rd. SW11 159 315 DF81
Beechmount Ave. W7 243 313 CD71
Beecholme, Bans. 292 331 CY114
Beecholme Ave., Mitch. 272 324 DH95
Beecholme Est. E5 102 307 DV62
Beechtree Clo., Stan. 204 298 CJ50
Beechtree Pl., Sutt. 284 331 DB106
Beechvale Clo. N12 207 299 DE50
Beechway, Bex. 262 327 EX86
Beechwood Ave. N3 218 305 CZ55
Beechwood Ave., Grnf. 243 313 CB69
Beechwood Ave., Har. 233 313 CB62
Beechwood Ave., Hayes 249 312 BR73
Beechwood Ave., Orp. 291 334 ES106
Beechwood Ave., Rich. 154 314 CN81
Beechwood Ave., Ruis. 231 312 BT61
Beechwood Ave., Stai. 264 328 BH93
Beechwood Ave., Sun. 266 329 BU93
Beechwood Ave., Th.Hth. 273 324 DP98
Beechwood Ave., Uxb. 248 312 BM72
Beechwood Clo. NW7 205 298 CR50
Beechwood Clo., Surb. 282 330 CK101
Beechwood Ct., Cars. 285 331 DF105
Beechwood Ct., Sun. 266 329 BU93
Beechwood Cres., Bexh. 262 327 EX83
Beechwood Dr., Kes. 290 334 EK105
Beechwood Dr., Wdf.Grn. 211 301 EF50
Beechwood Gdns. NW10 123 314 CM69
Beechwood Gdns., Har. 233 313 CB62
Beechwood Gdns., Ilf. 224 308 EM57
Beechwood Gro. W3 135 314 CS73
Beechwood Gro., Surb. 282 330 CJ101
Beechwood Ms. N9 210 301 DU47
Beechwood Pk. E18 224 308 EG55
Beechwood Ri., Chis. 277 326 EP91
Beechwood Rd. E8 117 306 DT65
Beechwood Rd. N8 220 306 DK56
Beechwood Rd., S.Croy. 295 332 DS110
Beechwoods Ct. SE19 273 324 DT92
Beechworth Clo. NW3 96 305 DA61
Beecroft Rd. SE4 181 325 DY85
Beehive Clo. E8 117 306 DT66
Beehive Clo., Borwd. 204 298 CK44
Beehive Clo., Uxb. 240 312 BM66
Beehive La., Ilf. 224 308 EM57
Beehive Pas. EC3 50/1 316 DS72
Beehive Pl. SW9 178 324 DN83
Beeken Dene, Orp. 291 334 EQ105
Beeleigh Rd., Mord. 271 323 DB98
Beeston Clo. E8 118 307 DU64
Beeston Pl. SW1 68/9 316 DH76
Beeston Rd., Barn. 207 299 DD44
Beeston Way, Felt. 258 321 BW86
Beethoven Rd., Borwd. 204 298 CJ44
Beethoven St. W10 127 315 CY69
Beeton Clo., Pnr. 215 303 CA52
Begbie Rd. SE3 252 318 EJ81
Beggars Hollow, Enf. 202 300 DR37
Beggars Roost La., Sutt. 292 331 DA107
Begonia Clo. E6 244 318 EL71
Begonia Pl., Hmptn. 267 329 CA93
Begonia Wk. W12 135 314 CT72
Beira St. SW12 192 324 DH87
Bekesbourne St. E14 139 317 DY72
Belcroft Clo., Brom. 275 325 EF94
Beldham Gdns., W.Mol. 267 329 CB97
Belfairs Dr., Rom. 236 309 EW59
Belfast Rd. N16 101 306 DT61
Belfast Rd. SE25 274 325 DV98
Belfont Wk. N7 115 306 DL63
Belford Gro. SE18 253 318 EN77
Belfort Rd. SE15 164 317 DW82
Belfry Ave., Uxb. 212 302 BG53
Belgrade Rd. N16 101 306 DS63
Belgrade Rd., Hmptn. 267 329 CB95
Belgrave Ave., Rom. 228 310 FJ55
Belgrave Clo. N14 208 300 DJ43
Belgrave Clo. W3 144 314 CQ75
Belgrave Clo., Orp. 278 327 EW98
Belgrave Cres., Sun. 266 329 BV95
Belgrave Gdns. N14 208 300 DK43
Belgrave Gdns. NW8 16/7 315 DB67
Belgrave Gdns., Stan. 204 298 CJ50
Belgrave Ms., Uxb. 240 312 BK70
Belgrave Ms. N. SW1 68 316 DG76
Belgrave Ms. S. SW1 68 316 DG76
Belgrave Ms. W. SW1 68 316 DG76
Belgrave Pl. SW1 68 316 DG76
Belgrave Rd. E10 104 307 EC60
Belgrave Rd. E11 234 308 EG61
Belgrave Rd. E13 244 318 EJ69
Belgrave Rd. E17 223 307 EA57
Belgrave Rd. SE25 274 325 DU98
Belgrave Rd. SW1 80/1 316 DH77
Belgrave Rd. SW13 155 314 CT80
Belgrave Rd., Houns. 258 321 BZ83
Belgrave Rd., Ilf. 234 308 EM60
Belgrave Rd., Mitch. 271 323 DD97
Belgrave Rd., Sun. 266 329 BV95
Belgrave Sq. SW1 68 316 DG76
Belgrave St. E1 139 317 DX71
Belgrave Wk., Mitch. 271 323 DD97
Belgrave Yd. SW1 68/9 316 DH76
Belgravia Gdns., Brom. 275 325 EE93
Belgravia Ho. SW4 177 324 DK86
Belgravia Ms., Kings.T. 268 322 CK98
Belgrove St. WC1 34/5 316 DL69
Belham Wk. SE5 163 316 DR81
Belinda Rd. SW9 178 324 DP83
Belitha Vil. N1 115 306 DM66
Bell Ave., Rom. 228 310 FH53
Bell Ave., West Dr. 249 320 BM76
Bell Clo., Pnr. 214 303 BW54
Bell Clo., Ruis. 231 312 BT62
Bell Ct., Surb. 282 330 CP103
Bell Dr. SW18 189 323 CY87
Bell Fm. Ave., Dag. 237 309 FC62
Bell Gdns. E17 222 307 DZ57
Bell Grn. SE26 197 325 DZ90
Bell Grn. La. SE26 274 325 DZ92
Bell Hill, Croy. 287 332 DQ104
Bell Ho. Rd., Rom. 237 309 FC60
Bell Inn Yd. EC3 50 316 DR72
Bell La. E1 51 316 DT71
Bell La. E16 244 318 EG74
Bell La. NW4 218 305 CW56
Bell La., Enf. 203 301 DX38
Bell La., Twick. 184 322 CG88
Bell La., Wem. 91 304 CK61
Bell Meadow SE19 273 324 DS91
Bell Rd., Enf. 202 300 DR39
Bell Rd., Houns. 259 321 CB83
Bell St. NW1 42/3 315 DE71
Bell Water Gate SE18 253 318 EN76
Bell Wf. La. EC4 61 316 DQ73
Bell Yd. WC2 48 316 DN72
Bellamy Clo. W14 147 315 CZ78
Bellamy Clo., Edg. 205 298 CQ48
Bellamy Clo., Uxb. 231 312 BN62
Bellamy Dr., Stan. 216 304 CH53
Bellamy Rd. E4 223 307 EB51
Bellamy Rd., Enf. 202 300 DR40
Bellamy St. SW12 192 324 DH87
Bellasis Ave. SW2 193 324 DL89
Bellclose Rd., West Dr. 248 320 BL75
Belle Staines Pleasaunce E4 211 301 EA47
Belle Vue, Grnf. 243 313 CD67
Belle Vue Clo., Stai. 280 328 BG95
Belle Vue Est. NW4 218 305 CW56
Belle Vue Rd. E17 223 307 ED54
Belle Vue Rd. NW4 218 305 CW56
Bellefield Rd., Orp. 291 335 EV99
Bellefields Rd. SW9 177 324 DM83
Bellegrove Clo., Well. 253 318 ET82
Bellegrove Rd., Well. 253 318 ES82
Bellenden Rd. SE15 179 324 DT83
Belleville Rd. SW11 175 323 DE85
Bellevue Ms. N11 208 300 DG50
Bellevue Par. SW17 191 323 DE88
Bellevue Pk., Th.Hth. 273 324 DQ97
Bellevue Pl. E1 128 317 DW70
Bellevue Rd. N11 208 300 DG49
Bellevue Rd. SW13 156 315 CU82
Bellevue Rd. SW17 191 323 DE88
Bellevue Rd. W13 122 314 CH70
Bellevue Rd., Bexh. 262 327 EZ85
Bellevue Rd., Horn. 238 311 FM60
Bellevue Rd., Kings.T. 268 322 CL97
Bellevue Rd., Rom. 227 309 FC51
Bellew St. SW17 190 323 DC90
Bellflower Clo. E6 244 318 EL71
Bellflower Path, Rom. 228 310 FJ52
Bellgate Ms. NW5 98 306 DH62
Bellingham Ct., Bark. 246 319 EV69
Bellingham Grn. SE6 198 325 EA90
Bellingham Rd. SE6 198 325 EC90
Bello Clo. SE24 194 324 DP87
Bellot Gdns. SE10 151 317 EE78
Bellot St. SE10 151 317 EE78
Bellring Clo., Belv. 255 319 FA79
Bells All. SW6 158 315 DA82
Bells Gdn. Est. SE15 164 317 DU80
Bells Hill, Barn. 206 299 CX43
Belltrees Gro. SW16 272 324 DM92
Bellwood Rd. SE15 181 325 DX84
Belmarsh Rd. SE28 253 318 ES75
Belmont Ave. N9 210 301 DU46
Belmont Ave. N13 208 300 DL50
Belmont Ave. N17 221 306 DQ55
Belmont Ave., Barn. 207 299 DF43
Belmont Ave., N.Mal. 283 331 CU99
Belmont Ave., Sthl. 250 321 BY76
Belmont Ave., Upmin. 238 311 FM61
Belmont Ave., Well. 253 318 ES82
Belmont Ave., Wem. 123 314 CM67
Belmont Circle, Har. 216 304 CH54
Belmont Clo. E4 211 301 ED50
Belmont Clo. N20 207 299 DB46
Belmont Clo. SW4 176 324 DJ83
Belmont Clo., Uxb. 240 312 BK65
Belmont Ct. NW11 218 305 CZ57
Belmont Gro. SE13 183 325 ED83
Belmont Hall Ct. SE13 183 325 ED83
Belmont Hill SE13 182 325 EC83
Belmont La., Chis. 277 326 ER92
Belmont La., Stan. 216 304 CJ52
Belmont Pk. SE13 183 325 ED84
Belmont Pk. Clo. SE13 183 325 ED84
Belmont Pk. Rd. E10 223 307 EB58
Belmont Ri., Sutt. 292 331 CZ107
Belmont Rd. N15 221 306 DQ56
Belmont Rd. N17 221 306 DQ55
Belmont Rd. SE25 287 333 DV99
Belmont Rd. SW4 176 324 DJ83
Belmont Rd. W4 145 314 CR77
Belmont Rd., Beck. 274 325 DZ96
Belmont Rd., Chis. 277 326 EP92
Belmont Rd., Erith 255 319 FA80
Belmont Rd., Har. 215 303 CF55
Belmont Rd., Horn. 238 310 FK62
Belmont Rd., Ilf. 235 308 EQ62
Belmont Rd., Sutt. 292 331 DA110
Belmont Rd., Twick. 259 321 CD89
Belmont Rd., Uxb. 240 312 BK66
Belmont Rd., Wall. 285 332 DH106
Belmont St. NW1 114 306 DG66
Belmont Ter. W4 145 314 CR77
Belmor, Borwd. 205 298 CN43
Belmore Ave., Hayes 242 313 BU72
Belmore La. N7 115 306 DK64
Belmore St. SW8 161 316 DK81
Beloe Clo. SW15 172 323 CU83
Belper Ct. E5 119 307 DX63
Belsham St. E9 118 307 DW65
Belsize Ave. N13 220 306 DM51
Belsize Ave. NW3 113 305 DD65
Belsize Ave. W13 142 314 CH76
Belsize Cres. NW3 113 305 DD64
Belsize Gdns., Sutt. 284 331 DB105
Belsize Gro. NW3 113 305 DE65
Belsize La. NW3 113 305 DD65
Belsize Ms. NW3 113 305 DD65
Belsize Pk. NW3 113 305 DD65
Belsize Pk. Gdns. NW3 113 305 DD65
Belsize Pk. Ms. NW3 113 305 DD65
Belsize Pl. NW3 113 305 DD65
Belsize Rd. NW6 16/7 315 DB67
Belsize Rd., Har. 215 303 CD52
Belsize Sq. NW3 113 305 DD65
Belsize Ter. NW3 113 305 DD65
Belson Rd. SE18 252 318 EM77
Beltane Dr. SW19 189 323 CX90
Belthorn Cres. SW12 192 324 DJ87
Beltinge Rd., Rom. 228 311 FM54
Belton Rd. E7 234 308 EH66
Belton Rd. E11 121 307 EE63
Belton Rd. N17 221 306 DS55
Belton Rd. NW2 110 305 CU65
Belton Rd., Sid. 278 327 EU91
Belton Way E3 140 317 EA71
Beltran Rd. SW6 158 315 DB82
Beltwood Rd., Belv. 255 319 FC77
Belvedere Ave. SW19 270 323 CY92
Belvedere Ave., Ilf. 225 308 EP54
Belvedere Bldgs. SE1 72/3 316 DP75
Belvedere Clo., Tedd. 267 329 CE92
Belvedere Ct. N2 219 305 DD57
Belvedere Dr. SW19 270 323 CY92
Belvedere Gro. SW19 270 323 CY92
Belvedere Ho., Felt. 258 321 BU88
Belvedere Ind. Est., Belv. 255 319 FC76
Belvedere Ms. SE15 180 325 DW83
Belvedere Pl. SE1 72/3 316 DP75
Belvedere Rd. E10 103 307 DY60
Belvedere Rd. SE1 71 316 DM75
Belvedere Rd. SE2 246 319 EX74
Belvedere Rd. SE19 273 324 DT94
Belvedere Rd. W7 251 321 CE76
Belvedere Rd., Bexh. 262 327 EZ83
Belvedere Sq. SW19 270 323 CY92
Belvedere Strand NW9 217 304 CT54
Belvedere Way, Har. 216 304 CL58
Belvoir Clo. SE9 260 326 EL90
Belvoir Rd. SE22 196 325 DU87
Belvue Clo., Nthlt. 233 313 CA66
Belvue Rd., Nthlt. 233 313 CA66
Bembridge Clo. NW6 111 305 CY66
Bembridge Gdns., Ruis. 231 312 BR61
Bemerton Est. N1 115 306 DL66
Bemerton St. N1 23 316 DM67
Bemish Rd. SW15 173 323 CX83
Bempton Dr., Ruis. 232 313 BV61
Bemsted Rd. E17 222 307 DZ55
Ben Hale Clo., Stan. 204 298 CH49
Ben Jonson Rd. E1 139 317 DX71
Ben Smith Way SE16 148 317 DU76
Ben Tillet Clo. E16 246 318 EM74
Ben Tillet Clo., Bark. 236 309 EU66
Benares Rd. SE18 253 318 ET77
Benbow Rd. W6 146 315 CV76
Benbow St. SE8 166 317 EA79
Benbow Waye, Uxb. 248 312 BJ71
Benbury Clo., Brom. 275 325 EC92
Bench Fld., S.Croy. 295 332 DT107
Bencombe Rd., Pur. 294 332 DN114
Bencroft Rd. SW16 272 324 DJ94
Bencurtis Pk., W.Wick. 289 333 ED104
Bendall Ms. NW1 42/3 315 DE71
Bendemeer Rd. SW15 173 323 CX83
Bendish Rd. E6 234 308 EL66
Bendmore Ave. SE2 254 319 EU78
Bendon Valley SW18 190 323 DB87
Benedict Clo., Belv. 254 319 EY76
Benedict Clo., Orp. 291 334 ES104
Benedict Dr., Felt. 265 320 BR87
Benedict Rd. SW9 177 324 DM83
Benedict Rd., Mitch. 271 323 DD97
Benedict Way N2 219 305 DC55
Benenden Grn., Brom. 289 333 EF99
Benets Rd., Horn. 239 311 FN60
Benett Gdns. SW16 272 324 DL96
Benfleet Clo., Sutt. 285 331 DC104
Bengal Ct. EC3 50 316 DR72
Bengal Rd., Ilf. 235 308 EP63
Bengarth Dr., Har. 215 303 CD54
Bengarth Rd., Nthlt. 242 313 BX67
Bengeworth Rd. SE5 178 324 DQ83
Bengeworth Rd., Har. 90 304 CG61
Benham Clo. SW11 175 323 DD83
Benham Gdns., Houns. 258 321 BZ84
Benham Rd. W7 243 313 CE71
Benhams Pl. NW3 112 305 DC63
Benhill Ave., Sutt. 284 331 DB105
Benhill Rd. SE5 163 316 DR80
Benhill Rd., Sutt. 285 331 DC104
Benhill Wd. Rd., Sutt. 285 331 DC105
Benhilton Gdns., Sutt. 284 331 DB104
Benhurst Ave., Horn. 238 310 FH63
Benhurst Ct. SW16 273 324 DN92
Benhurst La. SW16 273 324 DN92
Benin St. SE13 199 325 ED87
Benjafield Clo. N18 210 301 DV49
Benjamin Clo. E8 128 317 DU67
Benjamin Clo., Horn. 228 310 FG58
Benjamin St. EC1 48/9 316 DP71
Benledi St. E14 141 317 ED72
Benn St. E9 119 307 DY65
Bennerley Rd. SW11 175 323 DE85
Bennet's Hill EC4 60/1 316 DP73
Bennetsfield Rd., Uxb. 249 312 BP74
Bennett Clo., Kings.T. 268 322 CJ95
Bennett Clo., Nthwd. 213 302 BT52
Bennett Clo., Well. 254 319 EU82
Bennett Gro. SE13 166 317 EB81
Bennett Pk. SE3 183 325 EF83
Bennett Rd. E13 244 318 EJ70
Bennett Rd. N16 117 306 DS63
Bennett Rd., Rom. 226 309 EY58
Bennett St. SW1 57 316 DJ74
Bennett St. W4 155 314 CS79
Bennetts Ave., Croy. 288 333 DY103
Bennetts Ave., Grnf. 243 313 CE67
Bennetts Castle La., Dag. 236 309 EW63
Bennetts Clo. N17 221 306 DT51
Bennetts Clo., Mitch. 272 324 DH95
Bennetts Copse, Chis. 276 326 EL93
Bennetts Way, Croy. 288 333 DY103
Bennetts Yd. SW1 70 316 DK76
Benningholme Rd., Edg. 217 304 CS51
Bennington Rd. N17 221 306 DS53
Bennington Rd., Wdf.Grn. 223 307 EE52
Bennions Clo., Horn. 238 310 FK65
Bennison Dr., Rom. 228 310 FK54
Benn's Wk., Rich. 169 322 CL84
Benrek Clo., Ilf. 225 308 EQ53
Bensbury Clo. SW15 188 323 CW87
Bensham Clo., Th.Hth. 273 324 DQ98
Bensham Gro., Th.Hth. 273 324 DQ96
Bensham La., Croy. 286 332 DP101
Bensham La., Th.Hth. 273 324 DP98
Bensham Manor Rd., Th.Hth. 273 324 DQ98
Bensington Ct., Felt. 257 320 BR86
Bensley Clo. N11 207 299 DF50
Benson Ave. E6 244 318 EJ68
Benson Clo., Houns. 259 321 CA84
Benson Clo., Uxb. 248 312 BL71
Benson Quay E1 138 317 DW73
Benson Rd. SE23 196 325 DW88
Benson Rd., Croy. 286 332 DN104
Bentfield Gdns. SE9 260 326 EJ90
Benthal Rd. N16 102 307 DU61
Bentham Rd. E9 119 307 DX65
Bentham Rd. SE28 246 319 EV73
Bentham Wk. NW10 108 304 CQ64
Bentinck Ms. W1 44 316 DG72
Bentinck Pl. NW8 18/9 315 DE68
Bentinck Rd., West Dr. 248 312 BK74
Bentinck St. W1 44 316 DG72
Bentley Dr., Ilf. 225 308 EQ58
Bentley Rd. N1 117 306 DS65
Bentley Way, Stan. 204 298 CG50
Benton Rd., Ilf. 235 308 ER60
Bentons La. SE27 273 324 DQ91
Bentons Ri. SE27 273 324 DR92
Bentry Clo., Dag. 236 309 EY61
Bentry Rd., Dag. 236 309 EY61
Bentworth Rd. W12 136 315 CV72
Benwell Ct., Sun. 266 329 BU95
Benwell Rd. N7 116 306 DN63
Benwick Clo. SE16 148 317 DV77
Benworth St. E3 129 317 DZ69
Benyon Rd. N1 26 316 DR67
Beomonds Row, Cher. 280 328 BG101
Berber Rd. SW11 175 323 DF85
Berberis Wk., West Dr. 248 320 BL77
Bercta Rd. SE9 261 326 EQ89
Berdens La., Brwd. 229 311 FT55
Bere St. E1 139 317 DX73
Beredens La., Brwd. 229 311 FT55
Berenger Wk. SW10 159 315 DD80
Berens Rd. NW10 127 315 CX69
Berens Way, Chis. 277 326 ET98
Beresford Ave. N20 207 299 DF47
Beresford Ave. W7 243 313 CD71
Beresford Ave., Surb. 282 330 CP102
Beresford Ave., Twick. 168 322 CJ86
Beresford Ave., Wem. 123 314 CM67
Beresford Dr., Brom. 276 326 EL97
Beresford Gdns., Enf. 202 300 DS42
Beresford Gdns., Houns. 258 321 BZ85
Beresford Gdns., Rom. 226 309 EY57
Beresford Rd. E4 211 301 EE46
Beresford Rd. E17 223 307 EB53
Beresford Rd. N2 219 305 DE55
Beresford Rd. N5 117 306 DR64
Beresford Rd. N8 221 306 DN57
Beresford Rd., Har. 215 303 CD57
Beresford Rd., Kings.T. 268 322 CM95
Beresford Rd., N.Mal. 269 322 CQ98
Beresford Rd., Sthl. 242 313 BX74
Beresford Rd., Sutt. 292 331 CZ108
Beresford Sq. SE18 253 318 EP77
Beresford St. SE18 253 318 EP76
Beresford Ter. N5 116 306 DQ64
Berestede Rd. W6 145 314 CT78
Bergen Sq. SE16 149 317 DY76
Berger Clo., Orp. 291 334 ER100
Berger Rd. E9 119 307 DX65
Berghem Ms. W14 147 315 CX76
Bergholt Ave., Ilf. 224 308 EL57
Bergholt Cres. N16 101 306 DS59
Bergholt Ms. NW1 114 306 DJ66
Bering Wk. E16 244 318 EK72
Berisford Ms. SW18 174 323 DC86
Berkeley Ave., Bexh. 254 319 EX81
Berkeley Ave., Grnf. 233 313 CE65
Berkeley Ave., Houns. 250 321 BU81
Berkeley Ave., Ilf. 225 308 EN54
Berkeley Ave., Rom. 227 309 FC52
Berkeley Clo., Borwd. 205 298 CN43
Berkeley Clo., Horn. 239 311 FP61
Berkeley Clo., Kings.T. 268 322 CL94
Berkeley Clo., Orp. 291 334 ES101
Berkeley Clo., Ruis. 232 313 BU62
Berkeley Ct. N14 208 300 DJ44
Berkeley Ct., Wall. 286 332 DJ104
Berkeley Cres., Barn. 207 299 DD43
Berkeley Dr., Horn. 239 311 FN60
Berkeley Gdns. N21 209 300 DR45
Berkeley Gdns. W8 52 315 DA74
Berkeley Gdns., Walt. 281 328 BT101
Berkeley Ho. E3 130 317 EA69
Berkeley Ms. W1 43 315 DF72
Berkeley Pl. SW19 270 323 CX93
Berkeley Rd. E12 234 308 EL64
Berkeley Rd. N8 220 306 DK57
Berkeley Rd. N15 221 306 DR58
Berkeley Rd. NW9 217 304 CN56
Berkeley Rd. SW13 156 315 CU81
Berkeley Rd., Uxb. 241 312 BQ66
Berkeley Sq. W1 56/7 316 DH73
Berkeley St. W1 56/7 316 DH74
Berkeley Wk. N7 99 306 DM61
Berkeley Waye, Houns. 250 321 BX80
Berkhampstead Rd., Belv. 255 319 FA78
Berkhamsted Ave., Wem. 107 304 CM65
Berkley Dr., W.Mol. 266 329 BZ97
Berkley Gro. NW1 113 305 DF66
Berkley Rd. NW1 113 305 DF66
Berkshire Gdns. N13 221 306 DN51
Berkshire Gdns. N18 210 301 DV50
Berkshire Rd. E9 119 307 DZ65
Berkshire Sq., Mitch. 272 324 DL98
Berkshire Way, Horn. 229 311 FN57
Berkshire Way, Mitch. 272 324 DL98
Bermans Way NW10 109 304 CS63
Bermondsey Sq. SE1 74/5 316 DS76
Bermondsey St. SE1 74/5 316 DS75
Bermondsey Wall E. SE16 148 317 DU75
Bermondsey Wall W. SE16 148 317 DU75
Bernal Clo. SE28 246 319 EX73
Bernard Ashley Dr. SE7 252 318 EH78
Bernard Ave. W13 142 314 CH76
Bernard Cassidy St. E16 141 317 EF71
Bernard Gdns. SW19 270 323 CZ92
Bernard Rd. N15 221 306 DT57
Bernard Rd., Rom. 237 309 FC59
Bernard Rd., Wall. 285 332 DH106
Bernard St. WC1 34/5 316 DL70
Bernards Clo., Ilf. 225 308 EQ52
Bernays Clo., Stan. 216 304 CJ51
Bernays Gro. SW9 177 324 DM84
Berne Rd., Th.Hth. 286 332 DQ99
Bernel Dr., Croy. 288 333 DZ104
Berners Dr. W13 132 314 CG72
Berners Ms. W1 45 316 DJ71
Berners Pl. W1 45 316 DJ72
Berners Rd. N1 24 316 DN67
Berners Rd. N22 221 306 DN53
Berners St. W1 45 316 DJ71
Bernersmede SE3 260 326 EG83
Berney Rd., Croy. 287 332 DR101
Bernville Way, Har. 216 304 CM57
Bernwell Rd. E4 211 301 EE48
Berridge Grn., Edg. 217 304 CP52
Berridge Rd. SE19 273 324 DS92
Berriman Rd. N7 99 306 DM62
Berriton Rd., Har. 232 313 BZ60
Berry Clo. N21 209 300 DP46
Berry Clo. NW10 109 304 CS66
Berry Clo., Horn. 238 310 FJ64
Berry Ct., Houns. 258 321 BZ85
Berry Hill, Stan. 204 298 CK49
Berry La. SE21 273 324 DR91
Berry Pl. EC1 36/7 316 DP69
Berry St. EC1 36/7 316 DP70
Berry Way W5 143 314 CL76
Berrybank Clo. E4 211 301 EC47
Berrydale Rd., Hayes 242 313 BY70
Berryfield Clo. E17 223 307 EB56
Berryfield Clo., Brom. 276 326 EL95
Berryfield Rd. SE17 84/5 316 DP78
Berryhill SE9 261 326 EP84
Berryhill Gdns. SE9 261 326 EP84
Berrylands SW20 270 323 CW97
Berrylands, Surb. 282 330 CM100
Berrylands Rd., Surb. 282 330 CM100
Berryman Clo., Dag. 236 309 EW62
Berrymans La. SE26 274 325 DX91
Berrymead Gdns. W3 144 314 CQ75
Berrymede Rd. W4 145 314 CR76
Berryscroft Ct., Stai. 264 328 BJ94
Berryscroft Rd., Stai. 264 328 BJ94
Bert Rd., Th.Hth. 287 332 DQ99
Bertal Rd. SW17 271 323 DD91
Berther Rd., Horn. 238 310 FK59
Berthon St. SE8 166 317 EA80
Bertie Rd. NW10 110 305 CU65
Bertie Rd. SE26 274 325 DX93
Bertram Cotts. SW19 271 323 DA94
Bertram Rd. NW4 218 305 CU58
Bertram Rd., Enf. 203 301 DU42
Bertram Rd., Kings.T. 269 322 CN94
Bertram St. N19 98 306 DH61
Bertram Way, Enf. 202 300 DT42
Bertrand St. SE13 182 325 EB83
Bertrand Way SE28 246 319 EV73
Berwick Ave., Hayes 242 313 BX72
Berwick Clo., Stan. 215 303 CF52
Berwick Cres., Sid. 261 326 ES86
Berwick Pond Rd., Upmin. 238 311 FM66
Berwick Rd. E16 244 318 EH72
Berwick Rd. N22 221 306 DP53
Berwick Rd., Well. 254 319 EV81
Berwick St. W1 45 316 DJ72
Berwick Way, Orp. 291 335 EU102
Berwyn Ave., Houns. 251 321 CB81
Berwyn Rd. SE24 194 324 DP88
Berwyn Rd., Rich. 170 322 CP84
Beryl Ave. E6 244 318 EL71
Beryl Rd. W6 147 315 CX78
Berystede, Kings.T. 269 322 CP94
Besant Ct. N1 117 306 DR64
Besant Rd. NW2 111 305 CY63
Besant Wk. N7 99 306 DM61
Besant Way NW10 108 304 CQ64
Besley St. SW16 272 324 DJ94
Bessant Dr., Rich. 154 314 CP81
Bessborough Gdns. SW1 82 316 DK78
Bessborough Pl. SW1 82 316 DK78
Bessborough Rd. SW15 188 323 CU88
Bessborough Rd., Har. 233 313 CD60
Bessborough St. SW1 82 316 DK78
Bessemer Rd. SE5 162 316 DQ82
Bessie Lansbury Clo. E6 245 318 EN72
Bessingby Rd., Ruis. 232 313 BV61
Bessingham Wk. SE4 181 325 DX84
Besson St. SE14 164 317 DW81
Bessy St. E2 128 317 DW69
Bestwood St. SE8 149 317 DX77
Beswick Ms. NW6 112 305 DB65
Betam Rd., Hayes 249 320 BR75
Betchworth Clo., Sutt. 285 331 DD106
Betchworth Rd., Ilf. 235 308 ES61
Betham Rd., Grnf. 243 313 CD69
Bethany Waye, Felt. 265 320 BS87
Bethecar Rd., Har. 215 303 CE57
Bethel Rd., Well. 262 327 EW83
Bethell Ave. E16 131 317 EF70
Bethell Ave., Ilf. 235 308 EN59
Bethersden Clo., Beck. 274 325 DZ94
Bethnal Grn. Rd. E1 39 316 DT70
Bethnal Grn. Rd. E2 39 316 DT70
Bethune Ave. N11 207 299 DF49
Bethune Rd. N16 101 306 DR59
Bethune Rd. NW10 125 314 CR70
Bethwin Rd. SE5 162 316 DP80
Betjeman Clo., Pnr. 215 303 CA56
Betony Clo., Croy. 288 333 DX102
Betony Rd., Rom. 228 310 FK51
Betoyne Ave. E4 211 301 EE49
Betsham Rd., Erith 255 319 FF80
Betstyle Rd. N11 208 300 DH49
Betterton Dr., Sid. 262 327 EY89
Betterton Rd., Rain. 247 319 FE69
Betterton St. WC2 46/7 316 DL72
Bettles Clo., Uxb. 240 312 BJ68
Bettons Pk. E15 131 317 EE67
Bettridge Rd. SW6 157 315 CZ82
Betts Clo., Beck. 274 325 DY96
Betts Ms. E17 222 307 DZ58
Betts Rd. E16 244 318 EH73
Betts St. E1 138 317 DV73
Betts Way SE20 274 325 DV95
Beulah Ave., Th.Hth. 272 324 DM98

Bonnington Rd., Horn.	238	310	FK64
Bonnington Sq. SW8	161	316	DM79
Bonnington Twr., Brom.	290	334	EL100
Bonny St. NW1	114	306	DJ66
Bonser Rd., Twick.	259	321	CF89
Bonsor St. SE5	163	316	DS80
Bonville Gdns. NW4	218	305	CU56
Bonville Rd., Brom.	275	325	EF92
Book Ms. WC2	45	316	DK72
Booker Clo. E14	139	317	DZ71
Booker Rd. N18	210	301	DU50
Boone Ct. N9	210	301	DW48
Boone St. SE13	183	325	EE84
Boones Rd. SE13	183	325	EE84
Boord St. SE10	151	317	EE76
Boot St. N1	38/9	316	DS69
Booth Clo. SE28	246	319	EV73
Booth Dr., Stai.	264	328	BK93
Booth Rd. NW9	217	304	CR54
Booth Rd., Croy.	286	332	DP103
Boothby Rd. N19	99	306	DK61
Booth's Pl. W1	45	316	DJ71
Bordars Rd. W7	243	313	CE71
Bordars Wk. W7	243	313	CE71
Borden Ave., Enf.	209	300	DR44
Border Cres. SE26	274	325	DV92
Border Gdns., Croy.	288	333	EB105
Border Rd. SE26	274	325	DV92
Bordergate, Mitch.	271	323	DF95
Bordesley Rd., Mord.	271	323	DB98
Bordon Wk. SW15	188	323	CU87
Boreas Wk. N1	24/5	316	DP68
Boreham Ave. E16	244	318	EG72
Boreham Clo. E11	104	307	EC60
Boreham Rd. N22	221	306	DQ54
Borer's Pas. E1	50/1	316	DS72
Borgard Rd. SE18	252	318	EM77
Borkwood Pk., Orp.	291	334	ET105
Borkwood Way, Orp.	291	334	ES105
Borland Rd. SE15	180	325	DW84
Borland Rd., Tedd.	268	322	CH93
Borneo St. SW15	172	323	CW83
Borough High St. SE1	73	316	DQ75
Borough Hill, Croy.	286	332	DP104
Borough Rd. SE1	72/3	316	DP76
Borough Rd., Islw.	251	321	CE81
Borough Rd., Kings.T.	269	322	CN95
Borough Rd., Mitch.	271	323	DE96
Borough Sq. SE1	73	316	DQ75
Borrett Clo. SE17	85	316	DQ78
Borrodaile Rd. SW18	174	323	DB86
Borrowdale Ave., Har.	216	304	CG54
Borrowdale Clo., Ilf.	224	308	EL56
Borrowdale Clo., S.Croy.	295	332	DT113
Borrowdale Ct., Enf.	202	300	DQ39
Borrowdale Dr., S.Croy.	295	332	DT112
Borthwick Ms. E15	121	307	EE63
Borthwick Rd. E15	121	307	EE63
Borthwick Rd. NW9	217	304	CT58
Borthwick St. SE8	150	317	EA78
Borwick Ave. E17	222	307	DZ55
Bosanquet Clo., Uxb.	240	312	BK70
Bosbury Rd. SE6	198	325	EC90
Boscastle Rd. NW5	98	306	DH62
Bosco Clo., Orp.	291	334	ET105
Boscobel Pl. SW1	80	316	DG77
Boscobel St. NW8	30	315	DD70
Boscombe Ave. E10	105	307	ED59
Boscombe Ave., Horn.	238	310	FK60
Boscombe Clo. E5	119	307	DY64
Boscombe Gdns. SW16	272	324	DL93
Boscombe Rd. SW17	272	324	DG93
Boscombe Rd. SW19	271	323	DA95
Boscombe Rd. W12	136	315	CU74
Boscombe Rd., Wor.Pk.	284	331	CW102
Bosgrove E4	211	301	EC46
Boss St. SE1	75	316	DT75
Bostal Row, Bexh.	262	327	EZ83
Bostall Heath SE2	254	319	EW78
Bostall Hill SE2	254	319	EU78
Bostall La. SE2	254	319	EW78
Bostall Manorway SE2	254	319	EV77
Bostall Pk. Ave., Bexh.	254	319	EY80
Bostall Rd., Orp.	278	327	EV94
Boston Gdns. W4	155	314	CS79
Boston Gdns. W7	142	314	CG77
Boston Gro., Ruis.	231	302	BQ58
Boston Manor Rd., Brent.	142	314	CH77
Boston Pk. Rd., Brent.	142	314	CJ78
Boston Pl. NW1	31	315	DF70
Boston Rd. E6	244	318	EL69
Boston Rd. E17	223	307	EA58
Boston Rd. W7	142	313	CE74
Boston Rd., Croy.	286	332	DM100
Boston Rd., Edg.	217	304	CQ52
Boston St. E2	128	317	DU68
Boston Vale W7	142	314	CG77
Bostonthorpe Rd. W7	251	321	CE75
Boswell Ct. WC1	46/7	316	DL71
Boswell Path, Hayes	249	320	BT77
Boswell Rd., Th.Hth.	273	324	DQ98
Boswell St. WC1	46/7	316	DL71
Bosworth Clo. E17	222	307	DZ53
Bosworth Cres., Rom.	228	310	FJ51
Bosworth Rd. N11	220	306	DK51
Bosworth Rd. W10	127	315	CY70
Bosworth Rd., Dag.	237	309	FA62
Botany Bay La., Chis.	277	326	EQ96
Boteley Clo. E4	211	301	ED47
Botha Rd. E13	244	318	EH71
Botham Clo., Edg.	217	304	CQ52
Bothwell Clo. E16	141	317	EF71
Bothwell St. W6	157	315	CX79
Botolph All. EC3	62/3	316	DS73
Botolph La. EC3	62/3	316	DS73
Botsford Rd. SW20	270	323	CY96
Botts Ms. W2	40	315	DA72
Botts Pas. W2	40	315	DA72
Botwell Common Rd., Hayes	249	312	BR73
Botwell Cres., Hayes	249	312	BS72
Botwell La., Hayes	249	312	BS73
Boucher Clo., Tedd.	267	329	CF92
Bouchier Wk., Rain.	238	310	FG65
Boughton Ave., Brom.	289	333	EF101
Boughton Rd. SE28	253	318	ES76
Boulcott St. E1	139	317	DX72
Boulevard, The SW17	192	324	DG89
Boulevard, The, Pnr.	215	303	CA56
Boulmer Rd., Uxb.	240	312	BJ69
Boulogne Rd., Croy.	287	332	DQ100
Boulter Gdns., Rain.	238	310	FG65
Boulton Ho., Brent.	143	314	CL78
Boulton Rd., Dag.	236	309	EY62
Boultwood Rd. E6	244	318	EM72
Bounces La. N9	210	301	DV47
Bounces Rd. N9	210	301	DV47
Boundaries Rd. SW12	191	323	DF89
Boundaries Rd., Felt.	258	321	BW88
Boundary Ave. E17	103	307	DZ59
Boundary Clo. SE20	274	325	DU96
Boundary Clo., Ilf.	235	308	ES63
Boundary Clo., Kings.T.	269	322	CP97
Boundary Clo., Sthl.	251	321	CA78
Boundary La. E13	244	318	EK69
Boundary La. SE17	162	316	DQ79
Boundary Par. N8	220	306	DL58
Boundary Pas. E2	39	316	DT70
Boundary Rd. E13	244	318	EJ68
Boundary Rd. E17	103	307	DZ59
Boundary Rd. N9	210	301	DW44
Boundary Rd. N22	221	306	DP55
Boundary Rd. NW8	17	315	DC67
Boundary Rd. SW19	271	323	DD93
Boundary Rd., Ashf.	264	328	BJ92
Boundary Rd., Bark.	245	318	ER67
Boundary Rd., Cars.	293	332	DG108
Boundary Rd., Pnr.	232	313	BX59
Boundary Rd., Rom.	228	310	FG58
Boundary Rd., Sid.	261	326	ES85
Boundary Rd., Upmin.	239	311	FN62
Boundary Rd., Wall.	293	332	DH107
Boundary Rd., Wem.	91	304	CL62
Boundary Row SE1	72/3	316	DP75
Boundary St. E2	39	316	DT70
Boundary St., Erith	255	319	FF80
Boundary Way, Croy.	288	333	EA106
Boundfield Rd. SE6	199	325	EE90
Bounds Grn. Rd. N11	220	306	DJ51
Bounds Grn. Rd. N22	220	306	DL52
Bourchier St. W1	58	316	DK73
Bourdon Pl. W1	56/7	316	DH73
Bourdon Rd. SE20	274	325	DW96
Bourdon St. W1	56/7	316	DH73
Bourke Clo. NW10	109	304	CS65
Bourke Clo. SW4	177	324	DL86
Bourlet Clo. W1	45	316	DJ71
Bourn Ave. N15	221	306	DR56
Bourn Ave., Barn.	207	299	DD43
Bourn Ave., Uxb.	241	312	BN70
Bournbrook Rd. SE3	260	326	EK83
Bourne, The N14	208	300	DK46
Bourne Ave. N14	208	300	DL47
Bourne Ave., Cher.	280	328	BG97
Bourne Ave., Hayes	249	320	BQ76
Bourne Ave., Ruis.	232	313	BW64
Bourne Ct., Ruis.	232	313	BV64
Bourne Dr., Mitch.	271	323	DD96
Bourne End, Horn.	239	311	FN59
Bourne End Rd., Nthwd.	213	302	BS49
Bourne Est. EC1	48	316	DN71
Bourne Gdns. E4	211	301	EB49
Bourne Hill N13	208	300	DM47
Bourne Ind. Pk., Dart.	263	327	FE85
Bourne Mead, Bex.	263	327	FC85
Bourne Pl. W4	145	314	CR78
Bourne Rd. E7	105	307	EF62
Bourne Rd. N8	220	306	DL58
Bourne Rd., Bex.	263	327	FB87
Bourne Rd., Brom.	276	326	EK98
Bourne Rd., Dart.	263	327	FD85
Bourne St. SW1	80	316	DG77
Bourne St., Croy.	286	332	DP103
Bourne Ter. W2	40/1	315	DB71
Bourne Vale, Brom.	289	333	EF102
Bourne Vw., Grnf.	233	313	CF65
Bourne Way, Brom.	289	333	EE103
Bourne Way, Epsom	283	330	CQ105
Bourne Way, Sutt.	284	331	CZ106
Bourne Way, Swan.	279	327	FC97
Bournemead Ave., Nthlt.	242	313	BU68
Bournemead Clo., Nthlt.	242	313	BU69
Bournemead Way, Nthlt.	242	313	BV68
Bournemouth Rd. SE15	164	317	DU82
Bournemouth Rd. SW19	271	323	DA95
Bourneside Cres. N14	208	300	DK46
Bourneside Gdns. SE6	275	325	EC92
Bournevale Rd. SW16	272	324	DL91
Bournewood Rd. SE18	254	319	EU80
Bournewood Rd., Orp.	291	335	EV101
Bournville Rd. SE6	198	325	EA87
Bourton Clo., Hayes	242	313	BU74
Bousfield Rd. SE14	165	317	DX82
Boutflower Rd. SW11	175	323	DE84
Bouverie Gdns., Har.	216	304	CK58
Bouverie Ms. N16	101	306	DS61
Bouverie Pl. W2	42	315	DD72
Bouverie Rd. N16	101	306	DS60
Bouverie Rd., Har.	215	303	CC58
Bouverie St. EC4	48	316	DN72
Bouvier Rd., Enf.	203	301	DW38
Boveney Rd. SE23	197	325	DX87
Bovill Rd. SE23	197	325	DX87
Bovingdon Ave., Wem.	108	304	CN65
Bovingdon Clo. N19	97	306	DJ61
Bovingdon La. NW9	217	304	CS53
Bovingdon Rd. SW6	158	315	DB81
Bovingdon Sq., Mitch.	272	324	DL98
Bow Bri. Est. E3	130	317	EB68
Bow Chyd. EC4	49	316	DQ72
Bow Common La. E3	129	317	DY70
Bow Ind. Est. E15	120	307	EB66
Bow La. EC4	49	316	DQ72
Bow La. N12	219	305	DC52
Bow La., Mord.	284	331	CY100
Bow Rd. E3	129	317	DZ69
Bow St. E15	121	307	EE64
Bow St. WC2	46/7	316	DL72
Bowater Clo. NW9	217	304	CR57
Bowater Clo. SW2	177	324	DL86
Bowater Pl. SE3	252	318	EH80
Bowater Rd. SE18	252	318	EK76
Bowden Clo., Felt.	265	320	BS88
Bowden Dr., Horn.	238	311	FL60
Bowden St. SE11	84	316	DN78
Bowditch SE8	149	317	DZ78
Bowdon Rd. E17	104	307	EA59
Bowen Dr. SE21	195	324	DS90
Bowen Rd., Har.	214	303	CC59
Bowen St. E14	140	317	EB72
Bower Ave. SE10	167	317	EE81
Bower Clo., Nthlt.	242	313	BW68
Bower Clo., Rom.	227	309	FD52
Bower St. E1	139	317	DX72
Bowerdean St. SW6	158	315	DB81
Bowerman Ave. SE14	165	317	DY79
Bowers Wk. E6	244	318	EM72
Bowes Clo., Sid.	262	327	EV86
Bowes Rd. N11	208	300	DH50
Bowes Rd. N13	208	300	DL50
Bowes Rd. W3	135	314	CS73
Bowes Rd., Dag.	236	309	EW63
Bowfell Rd. W6	156	315	CW79
Bowford Ave., Bexh.	254	319	EY81
Bowhill Clo. SW9	162	316	DN80
Bowie Clo. SW4	193	324	DK87
Bowl Ct. EC2	38/9	316	DS70
Bowland Rd. SW4	177	324	DK84
Bowland Rd., Wdf.Grn.	224	308	EJ51
Bowland Yd. SW1	67	316	DF75
Bowles Grn., Enf.	203	301	DV36
Bowles Rd. SE1	164	317	DU79
Bowley Clo. SE19	273	324	DT93
Bowley La. SE19	273	324	DT92
Bowling Grn. Clo. SW15	188	323	CV87
Bowling Grn. La. EC1	36	316	DN70
Bowling Grn. Pl. SE1	74	316	DR75
Bowling Grn. Row SE18	252	318	EM76
Bowling Grn. St. SE11	162	316	DN79
Bowling Grn. Wk. N1	38/9	316	DS69
Bowls Clo., Stan.	204	298	CH50
Bowman Ave. E16	141	317	EF73
Bowman Ms. SW18	189	323	CZ88
Bowmans Clo. W13	132	314	CH74
Bowmans Lea SE23	196	325	DW87
Bowmans Meadow, Wall.	293	332	DH104
Bowmans Ms. E1	138	317	DU72
Bowmans Ms. N7	99	306	DL62
Bowmans Pl. N7	99	306	DL62
Bowmans Rd., Dart.	263	327	FF87
Bowman's Trd. Est. NW9	216	304	CM55
Bowmead SE9	260	326	EM89
Bowmore Wk. NW1	115	306	DK66
Bowness Clo. E8	117	306	DT65
Bowness Cres. SW15	269	322	CS92
Bowness Dr., Houns.	258	321	BY84
Bowness Rd. SE6	198	325	EB87
Bowness Rd., Bexh.	255	319	FB82
Bowness Way, Horn.	238	310	FG64
Bowood Rd. SW11	190	323	DG85
Bowood Rd., Enf.	203	301	DX40
Bowrons Ave., Wem.	107	304	CK66
Bowyer Clo. E6	244	318	EM71
Bowyer Pl. SE5	162	316	DQ80
Bowyer St. SE5	162	316	DQ80
Box La., Bark.	246	319	EV68
Box Ridge Ave., Pur.	294	332	DM112
Boxall Rd. SE21	179	324	DS86
Boxgrove Rd. SE2	254	319	EV75
Boxley Rd., Mord.	271	323	DC98
Boxley St. E16	140	318	EH74
Boxmoor Rd., Har.	216	304	CH56
Boxoll Rd., Dag.	236	309	EZ63
Boxtree La., Har.	215	303	CC53
Boxtree Rd., Har.	215	303	CD52
Boxwood Clo., West Dr.	248	320	BM75
Boxworth Clo. N12	207	299	DD50
Boxworth Gro. N1	23	316	DM67
Boyard Rd. SE18	253	318	EP78
Boyce St. SE1	59	316	DM74
Boyce Way E13	244	318	EG70
Boycroft Ave. NW9	217	304	CQ58
Boyd Ave., Sthl.	242	313	BZ74
Boyd Clo., Kings.T.	269	322	CN94
Boyd Rd. SW19	271	323	DD93
Boyd St. E1	138	317	DU72
Boydell Ct. NW8	113	305	DD66
Boyfield St. SE1	72/3	316	DP75
Boyland Rd., Brom.	275	325	EF92
Boyle Ave., Stan.	216	304	CG51
Boyle St. W1	57	316	DJ73
Boyne Ave. NW4	218	305	CX56
Boyne Rd. SE13	182	325	EC83
Boyne Rd., Dag.	237	309	FA62
Boyne Ter. Ms. W11	137	315	CZ74
Boyseland Ct., Edg.	205	298	CQ47
Boyson Rd. SE17	163	316	DR79
Boythorn Way SE16	148	317	DV78
Boyton Clo. E1	129	317	DX70
Boyton Clo. N8	220	306	DL55
Boyton Rd. N8	220	306	DL55
Brabant Ct. EC3	62/3	316	DS73
Brabant Rd. N22	220	306	DM54
Brabazon Ave., Wall.	294	332	DL108
Brabazon Rd., Houns.	250	321	BW80
Brabazon Rd., Nthlt.	243	313	CA68
Brabazon St. E14	140	317	EB72
Brabourn Gro. SE15	164	317	DW82
Brabourne Clo. SE19	273	324	DS92
Brabourne Cres., Bexh.	254	319	EZ79
Brabourne Hts. NW7	205	298	CS48
Brabourne Ri., Beck.	289	333	EC99
Bracewell Ave., Grnf.	106	304	CG65
Bracewell Rd. W10	136	315	CW71
Bracewood Gdns., Croy.	287	332	DT104
Bracey Ms. N4	99	306	DL61
Bracey St. N4	99	306	DL61
Bracken, The E4	211	301	EC47
Bracken Ave. SW12	176	324	DG86
Bracken Ave., Croy.	288	333	EA104
Bracken Clo. E6	244	318	EM71
Bracken Clo., Sun.	265	328	BT93
Bracken Clo., Twick.	259	321	CA87
Bracken Dr., Chig.	225	308	EP51
Bracken End, Islw.	259	321	CD85
Bracken Gdns. SW13	156	315	CU82
Bracken Hill Clo., Brom.	275	325	EF95
Bracken Hill La., Brom.	275	325	EF95
Bracken Ind. Est., Ilf.	225	308	ET52
Bracken Ms. E4	211	301	EC47
Bracken Ms., Rom.	227	309	FB58
Brackenbridge Dr., Ruis.	232	313	BX62
Brackenbury Gdns. W6	146	315	CV76
Brackenbury Rd. N2	219	305	DC55
Brackenbury Rd. W6	146	315	CV76
Brackendale N21	208	300	DM47
Brackendale Clo., Houns.	251	321	CB81
Brackendale Gdns., Upmin.	239	311	FQ63
Brackendene, Dart.	279	327	FE91
Brackenfield Clo. E5	118	307	DV63
Brackens, The, Enf.	209	300	DS45
Brackens, The, Orp.	291	335	EU106
Brackenwood, Sun.	266	329	BU95
Brackley Clo., Wall.	294	332	DL108
Brackley Rd. W4	145	314	CS78
Brackley Rd., Beck.	274	325	DZ94
Brackley Sq., Wdf.Grn.	224	308	EK52
Brackley St. EC1	49	316	DQ71
Brackley Ter. W4	145	314	CS78
Bracklyn Clo. N1	26	316	DR68
Bracklyn Ct. N1	26	316	DR68
Bracklyn St. N1	26	316	DR68
Bracknell Clo. N22	221	306	DN53
Bracknell Gdns. NW3	112	305	DB63
Bracknell Gate NW3	112	305	DB64
Bracknell Way NW3	112	305	DB63
Bracondale Rd. SE2	254	319	EU77
Brad St. SE1	60	316	DN74
Bradbourne Rd., Bex.	263	327	FA87
Bradbourne St. SW6	158	315	DA82
Bradbury Clo., Sthl.	250	321	BZ77
Bradbury Ms. N16	117	306	DS64
Bradbury St. N16	117	306	DS64
Braddock Clo., Islw.	259	321	CF83
Braddon Rd., Rich.	169	322	CM83
Braddyll St. SE10	151	317	EE78
Braden St. W9	28/9	315	DB70
Bradenham Ave., Well.	262	327	EU84
Bradenham Clo. SE17	163	316	DR79
Bradenham Rd., Har.	216	304	CH56
Bradenham Rd., Hayes	241	312	BS69
Bradfield Dr., Bark.	236	309	EU64
Bradfield Rd. E16	252	318	EG75
Bradfield Rd., Ruis.	232	313	BY64
Bradford Clo. SE26	274	325	DV91
Bradford Clo., Brom.	290	334	EM102
Bradford Rd. W3	145	314	CS75
Bradford Rd., Ilf.	235	308	ER60
Bradgate Rd. SE6	182	325	EA86
Brading Cres. E11	234	308	EH61
Brading Rd. SW2	193	324	DM87
Brading Rd., Croy.	286	332	DM100
Bradiston Rd. W9	127	315	CZ69
Bradley Clo. N7	115	306	DM65
Bradley Clo., Sutt.	292	331	DA110
Bradley Gdns. W13	132	314	CH72
Bradley Ms. SW17	191	323	DF88
Bradley Rd. N22	220	306	DM54
Bradley Rd. SE19	273	324	DQ93
Bradley Rd., Enf.	203	301	DY37
Bradley Stone Rd. E6	244	318	EM71
Bradley's Clo. N1	24	316	DN68
Bradman Row, Edg.	217	304	CQ52
Bradmead SW8	160	316	DH80
Bradmore Ho. E1	138	317	DW71
Bradmore Pk. Rd. W6	146	315	CV77
Bradshaw Clo. SW19	271	323	DA93
Bradshawe Waye, Uxb.	248	312	BL71
Bradshaws Clo. SE25	274	325	DU97
Bradstock Rd. E9	119	307	DX65
Bradstock Rd., Epsom	283	331	CU106
Bradwell Ave., Dag.	237	309	FA61
Bradwell Clo. E18	223	307	EF56
Bradwell Clo., Horn.	238	310	FH65
Bradwell Ms. N18	210	301	DU49
Bradwell St. E1	129	317	DX69
Brady St. E1	128	317	DV70
Bradymead E6	245	318	EP72
Braemar Ave. N22	220	306	DL53
Braemar Ave. NW10	93	304	CR62
Braemar Ave. SW19	190	323	DA89
Braemar Ave., Bexh.	263	327	FC84
Braemar Ave., S.Croy.	295	332	DQ110
Braemar Ave., Th.Hth.	273	324	DN97
Braemar Ave., Wem.	107	304	CK66
Braemar Gdns. NW9	217	304	CR53
Braemar Gdns., Horn.	229	311	FN58
Braemar Gdns., Sid.	261	326	ER90
Braemar Gdns., W.Wick.	289	333	EC102
Braemar Rd. E13	131	317	EF70
Braemar Rd. N15	221	306	DS57
Braemar Rd., Brent.	153	314	CK79
Braemar Rd., Wor.Pk.	283	331	CV104
Braes St. N1	116	306	DP66
Braeside, Beck.	275	325	EA92
Braeside Ave. SW19	270	323	CY95
Braeside Clo., Pnr.	215	303	CA52
Braeside Cres., Bexh.	263	327	FC84
Braeside Rd. SW16	272	324	DJ94
Braesyde Clo., Belv.	254	319	EZ77
Brafferton Rd., Croy.	287	332	DQ105
Braganza St. SE17	84/5	316	DP78
Braham St. E1	51	316	DT72
Braid Ave. W3	135	314	CS72
Braid Clo., Felt.	258	321	BZ89
Braidwood Rd. SE6	199	325	ED88
Braidwood St. SE1	62/3	316	DS74
Brailsford Clo., Mitch.	271	323	DE94
Brailsford Rd. SW2	178	324	DN85
Brainton Ave., Felt.	258	321	BV87
Braintree Ave., Ilf.	224	308	EL56
Braintree Rd., Dag.	237	309	FA62
Braintree Rd., Ruis.	232	313	BV63
Braintree St. E2	128	317	DW70
Braithwaite Ave., Rom.	237	309	FA59
Braithwaite Gdns., Stan.	216	304	CJ53
Braithwaite Rd., Enf.	203	301	DZ41
Bramah Grn. SW9	162	316	DN81
Bramalea Clo. N6	220	306	DG58
Bramall Clo. E15	121	307	EF64
Bramber Ct. W5	143	314	CL77
Bramber Rd. N12	207	299	DE50
Bramber Rd. W14	157	315	CZ79
Bramble Banks, Cars.	293	332	DG109
Bramble Clo., Croy.	288	333	EA105
Bramble Clo., Shep.	281	328	BR98
Bramble Clo., Stan.	216	304	CK52
Bramble Clo., Uxb.	248	312	BM71
Bramble Cft., Erith	255	319	FC77
Bramble Gdns. W12	135	314	CT73
Bramble La., Hmptn.	266	329	BZ93
Brambleacres Clo., Sutt.	292	331	DA108
Bramblebury Rd. SE18	253	318	EQ78
Brambledown, Stai.	281	328	BH95
Brambledown Clo., W.Wick.	289	333	EE99
Brambledown Rd., Cars.	293	332	DG108
Brambledown Rd., S.Croy.	295	332	DS108
Brambledown Rd., Wall.	293	332	DH108
Brambles, The, Chig.	225	308	EQ51
Brambles, The, West Dr.	248	320	BK77
Brambles Clo., Islw.	152	314	CH80
Brambles Fm. Dr., Uxb.	241	312	BN69
Bramblewood Clo., Cars.	285	331	DF102
Bramblings, The E4	211	301	ED49
Bramcote Ave., Mitch.	271	323	DF98
Bramcote Gro. SE16	148	317	DW78
Bramcote Rd. SW15	172	323	CV84
Bramdean Cres. SE12	260	326	EG88
Bramdean Gdns. SE12	260	326	EG88
Bramerton Rd., Beck.	274	325	DZ97
Bramerton St. SW3	159	315	DE79
Bramfield Ct. N4	100	306	DQ61
Bramfield Rd. SW11	175	323	DE86
Bramford Ct. N14	208	300	DK47
Bramford Rd. SW18	174	323	DC84
Bramham Gdns. SW5	76/7	315	DB78
Bramham Gdns., Chess.	282	330	CK105
Bramhope La. SE7	252	318	EH79
Bramlands Clo. SW11	175	323	DE83
Bramley Clo. E17	222	307	DY54
Bramley Clo. N14	208	300	DH43
Bramley Clo., Cher.	280	328	BH102
Bramley Clo., Hayes	242	313	BU73
Bramley Clo., Orp.	290	334	EP102
Bramley Clo., S.Croy.	286	332	DP106
Bramley Clo., Stai.	264	328	BJ93
Bramley Clo., Swan.	279	327	FE98
Bramley Clo., Twick.	259	321	CC86
Bramley Ct., Well.	254	319	EV81
Bramley Cres. SW8	161	316	DK80
Bramley Cres., Ilf.	225	308	EN58
Bramley Hill, S.Croy.	286	332	DP106
Bramley Rd. N14	208	300	DH43
Bramley Rd. W5	142	314	CJ76
Bramley Rd. W10	137	315	CX73
Bramley Rd., Sutt.	285	331	DD106
Bramley Rd. (Cheam), Sutt.	292	331	CX109
Bramley Way, Houns.	258	321	BZ85
Bramley Way, W.Wick.	288	333	EB103
Brampton Clo. E5	102	307	DV61
Brampton Gdns. N15	221	306	DQ57
Brampton Gro. NW4	218	305	CV56
Brampton Gro., Har.	216	304	CG56
Brampton Gro., Wem.	91	304	CM60
Brampton La. NW4	218	305	CW56
Brampton Pk. Rd. N22	221	306	DN55
Brampton Rd. E6	244	318	EK70
Brampton Rd. N15	221	306	DQ57
Brampton Rd. NW9	217	304	CN56
Brampton Rd. SE2	254	319	EW79
Brampton Rd., Bexh.	262	327	EX83
Brampton Rd., Croy.	287	332	DT101
Brampton Rd., Uxb.	241	312	BP68
Bramshaw Ri., N.Mal.	283	330	CS100
Bramshaw Rd. E9	119	307	DX65
Bramshill Gdns. NW5	98	306	DH62
Bramshill Rd. NW10	125	314	CS68
Bramshot Ave. SE7	252	318	EG79
Bramston Clo., Ilf.	225	308	ET51
Bramston Rd. NW10	126	315	CU68
Bramston Rd. SW17	190	323	DC90
Bramwell Clo., Sun.	266	329	BX96
Bramwell Ms. N1	23	316	DM67
Brancaster Dr. NW7	218	305	CU52
Brancaster La., Pur.	295	332	DQ110
Brancaster Rd. E12	234	308	EM63
Brancaster Rd. SW16	193	324	DL90
Brancaster Rd., Ilf.	225	308	ER58
Branch Hill NW3	96	305	DC62
Branch Pl. N1	26	316	DR67
Branch Rd. E14	139	317	DY73
Branch St. SE15	163	316	DS80
Brancker Clo., Wall.	294	332	DL108
Brancker Rd., Har.	216	304	CK55
Brancroft Way, Enf.	203	301	DY39
Brand St. SE10	166	317	EC80
Brandlehow Rd. SW15	173	323	CZ84
Brandon Est. SE17	162	316	DP79
Brandon Ms. EC2	50	316	DR71
Brandon Rd. E17	223	307	EC55
Brandon Rd. N7	115	306	DL66
Brandon Rd., Sthl.	250	321	BZ78
Brandon Rd., Sutt.	284	331	DB105
Brandon St. SE17	85	316	DQ77
Brandram Rd. SE13	183	325	EE83
Brandreth Rd. E6	244	318	EM72
Brandreth Rd. SW17	192	324	DH89
Brandries, The, Wall.	286	332	DK104
Brandville Gdns., Ilf.	225	308	EP56
Brandville Rd., West Dr.	248	320	BL75
Brandy Way, Sutt.	292	331	DA108
Branfill Rd., Upmin.	239	311	FP61
Brangbourne Rd., Brom.	275	325	EC92
Brangton Rd. SE11	83	316	DM78
Brangwyn Cres. SW19	271	323	DC96
Branksea St. SW6	157	315	CY80
Branksome Ave. N18	221	306	DT51
Branksome Rd. SW2	177	324	DL85
Branksome Rd. SW19	271	323	DA95
Branksome Way, Har.	216	304	CL58
Branksome Way, N.Mal.	269	322	CQ95
Branscombe Gdns. N21	209	300	DN45
Branscombe St. SE13	182	325	EB83
Bransdale Clo. NW6	16/7	315	DB67
Bransgrove Rd., Edg.	216	304	CM53
Branston Cres., Orp.	291	334	ER102
Branstone Rd., Rich.	153	314	CM81
Brants Wk. W7	243	313	CE70
Brantwood Ave., Erith	255	319	FC80
Brantwood Ave., Islw.	168	322	CG84
Brantwood Clo. E17	223	307	EB55
Brantwood Gdns., Ilf.	224	308	EL56
Brantwood Rd. N17	221	306	DT51
Brantwood Rd. SE24	178	324	DQ85
Brantwood Rd., Bexh.	255	319	FB82
Brantwood Rd., S.Croy.	295	332	DQ109
Brantwood Way, Orp.	278	327	EW97
Brasher Clo., Grnf.	233	313	CD64
Brass Tally All. SE16	149	317	DX75
Brassey Clo., Felt.	265	320	BT88
Brassey Rd. NW6	111	305	CZ65
Brassey Sq. SW11	176	324	DG83
Brassie Ave. W3	135	314	CS72
Brasted Clo. SE26	274	325	DW91
Brasted Clo., Bexh.	262	327	EX85
Brasted Clo., Orp.	291	335	EU103
Brasted Clo., Sutt.	292	331	DA110
Brasted Rd., Erith	255	319	FF78
Brathway Rd. SW18	190	323	DA87
Bratley St. E1	128	317	DU70
Braund Ave., Grnf.	243	313	CB70
Braundton Ave., Sid.	261	326	ET88
Braunston Dr., Hayes	242	313	BY70
Bravington Clo., Shep.	280	328	BM99
Bravington Pl. W9	127	315	CZ70
Bravington Rd. W9	127	315	CZ69
Brawne Ho. SE17	162	316	DP79
Braxfield Rd. SE4	181	325	DY84
Braxted Pk. SW16	272	324	DM93
Bray NW3	113	305	DE66
Bray Cres. SE16	149	317	DX75
Bray Dr. E16	141	317	EF73
Bray Pas. E16	141	317	EF73
Bray Pl. SW3	79	315	DF77
Bray Rd. NW7	218	305	CX52
Brayards Rd. SE15	164	317	DV82
Brayards Rd. Est. SE15	164	317	DV82
Braybourne Clo., Uxb.	240	312	BJ65
Braybourne Dr., Islw.	251	321	CF80
Braybrook St. W12	135	314	CT71
Braybrooke Gdns. SE19	273	324	DT94
Brayburne Ave. SW4	160	316	DJ82
Braydon Rd. N16	102	307	DU59
Brayfield Ter. N1	116	306	DN66
Brayford Sq. E1	139	317	DY72
Braywood Rd. SE9	261	326	ER84
Brazil Clo., Croy.	286	332	DL101
Breach La., Dag.	247	319	FA69
Bread St. EC4	61	316	DQ73
Breakspear Rd., Ruis.	231	312	BP59
Breakspear Rd. N., Uxb.	212	302	BJ53
Breakspear Rd. S., Uxb.	230	312	BM62
Breakspears Dr., Orp.	278	327	EU95
Breakspears Ms. SE4	166	317	EA82
Breakspears Rd. SE4	181	325	DZ83
Bream Clo. N17	222	307	DV56
Bream Gdns. E6	245	318	EN69
Bream St. E3	120	307	EA66
Breamore Clo. SW15	188	323	CU88
Breamore Rd., Ilf.	235	308	ET61
Bream's Bldgs. EC4	48	316	DN72
Breamwater Gdns., Rich.	184	322	CH90
Brearley Clo., Edg.	217	304	CQ52
Brearley Clo., Uxb.	240	312	BL65
Breasley Clo. SW15	172	323	CV84
Brechin Pl. SW7	77	315	DC77
Brecknock Rd. N7	115	306	DK64
Brecknock Rd. N19	114	306	DJ63
Brecknock Rd. Est. N7	114	306	DJ63
Brecon Clo., Mitch.	272	324	DL97
Brecon Clo., Wor.Pk.	284	331	CW103
Brecon Rd. W6	157	315	CY79
Brecon Rd., Enf.	203	301	DW42
Brede Clo. E6	245	318	EN69
Bredgar Rd. N19	98	306	DJ61
Bredhurst Clo. SE20	274	325	DW93
Bredon Rd. SE5	178	324	DQ83
Bredon Rd., Croy.	287	332	DT101
Breer St. SW6	174	323	DB83
Breezers Hill E1	138	317	DU73
Brember Rd., Har.	233	313	CC61
Bremer Ms. E17	223	307	EB56
Bremer Rd., Stai.	264	320	BG90
Bremner Rd. SW7	65	315	DC76
Brenchley Clo., Brom.	289	333	EF100
Brenchley Clo., Chis.	277	326	EN95
Brenchley Gdns. SE23	180	325	DW86
Brenchley Rd., Orp.	277	326	ES95
Brenda Rd. SW17	191	323	DF89
Brendans Clo., Horn.	238	311	FL60
Brende Gdns., W.Mol.	267	329	CB98
Brendon Ave. NW10	94	304	CS63
Brendon Clo., Erith	255	319	FE81
Brendon Clo., Hayes	257	320	BQ80
Brendon Gdns., Har.	233	313	CB63
Brendon Gdns., Ilf.	225	308	ES57
Brendon Gro. N2	219	305	DC54
Brendon Rd. SE9	261	326	ER89
Brendon Rd., Dag.	236	309	EZ60
Brendon St. W1	42/3	315	DE72
Brendon Way, Enf.	209	300	DS45
Brenley Clo., Mitch.	272	324	DG97
Brenley Gdns. SE9	260	326	EK84
Brent Clo., Bex.	262	327	EY88
Brent Cres. NW10	123	314	CM68
Brent Cross Gdns. NW4	218	305	CX58
Brent Cross Shop. Cen. NW4	94	305	CW59
Brent Grn. NW4	218	305	CW57
Brent Grn. Wk., Wem.	92	304	CQ62
Brent Lea, Brent.	152	314	CJ80
Brent Pk. NW10	109	304	CR64
Brent Pk. Rd. NW4	94	305	CV59
Brent Pk. Rd. NW9	94	305	CV59
Brent Pl., Barn.	207	299	DA43
Brent Rd. E16	244	318	EG71
Brent Rd. SE18	253	318	EP80
Brent Rd., Brent.	152	314	CJ79
Brent Rd., S.Croy.	295	333	DV109
Brent Rd., Sthl.	250	321	BW76
Brent St. NW4	218	305	CW56
Brent Ter. NW2	94	305	CW60
Brent Vw. Rd. NW9	218	305	CU58
Brent Way N3	219	305	DA51
Brent Way, Brent.	153	314	CK80
Brent Way, Wem.	108	304	CP65
Brentcot Clo. W13	122	314	CH70
Brentfield NW10	108	304	CP66
Brentfield Clo. NW10	109	304	CR65
Brentfield Gdns. NW2	95	305	CX59
Brentfield Rd. NW10	109	304	CR65
Brentford Business Cen., Brent.	152	314	CJ80
Brentford Clo., Hayes	242	313	BX70
Brentham Way W5	123	314	CK70
Brenthouse Rd. E9	118	307	DW65
Brenthurst Rd. NW10	109	304	CT65
Brentmead Clo. W7	243	313	CE73
Brentmead Gdns. NW10	123	314	CM68
Brentmead Pl. NW11	218	305	CX58
Brenton St. E14	139	317	DY72
Brentside, Brent.	152	314	CJ79
Brentside Clo. W13	122	314	CG70
Brentside Executive Cen., Brent.	152	314	CH79
Brentvale Ave., Sthl.	243	313	CD74
Brentvale Ave., Wem.	123	314	CM67
Brentwick Gdns., Brent.	143	314	CL77
Brentwood Clo. SE9	261	326	EQ88
Brentwood Ho. SE18	252	318	EK80
Brentwood Rd., Rom.	227	309	FF58
Brereton Rd. N17	221	306	DT52
Bressenden Pl. SW1	68/9	316	DH76
Bressey Ave., Enf.	203	301	DU39
Bressey Gro. E18	223	307	EF54
Brett Clo. N16	101	306	DS61
Brett Clo., Nthlt.	242	313	BX69
Brett Ct. N9	210	301	DW47
Brett Cres. NW10	109	304	CR66
Brett Gdns., Dag.	236	309	EY66
Brett Ho. Clo. SW15	173	323	CX86
Brett Pas. E8	118	307	DV64
Brett Rd. E8	118	307	DV64
Brett Rd., Barn.	206	299	CW43
Brettell St. SE17	86	316	DR78
Brettenham Ave. E17	223	307	EA53
Brettenham Rd. E17	223	307	EA54
Brettenham Rd. N18	210	301	DU49
Brewer St. W1	57	316	DJ73
Brewer's Grn. SW1	69	316	DJ76
Brewers Hall Gdns. EC2	49	316	DQ71
Brewers La., Rich.	169	322	CK85
Brewery Clo., Wem.	106	304	CG64
Brewery La., Twick.	259	321	CF87
Brewery Rd. N7	115	306	DL66
Brewery Rd. SE18	253	318	ER78
Brewery Rd., Brom.	290	334	EL102
Brewery Sq. SE1	63	316	DT74
Brewhouse La. E1	138	317	DV74
Brewhouse Rd. SE18	252	318	EM77
Brewhouse St. SW15	173	323	CY83
Brewhouse Wk. SE16	139	317	DY74
Brewhouse Yd. EC1	36/7	316	DP70
Brewood Rd., Dag.	236	309	EV65
Brewster Gdns. W10	136	315	CW71
Brewster Ho. E14	139	317	DZ73
Brewster Rd. E10	104	307	EB60
Brian Ave., S.Croy.	295	332	DS112
Brian Clo., Horn.	238	310	FH63
Brian Rd., Rom.	226	309	EW57
Briant St. SE14	165	317	DX81
Briants Clo., Pnr.	214	303	BZ54
Briar Ave. SW16	272	324	DM94
Briar Banks, Cars.	293	332	DG109
Briar Clo. N2	219	305	DB54
Briar Clo. N13	209	300	DQ48
Briar Clo., Hmptn.	266	329	BZ92
Briar Clo., Islw.	259	321	CF85
Briar Ct., Sutt.	284	331	CW105
Briar Cres., Nthlt.	233	313	CB65
Briar Gdns., Brom.	289	333	EF102
Briar Gro., S.Croy.	295	333	DU113
Briar Hill, Pur.	294	332	DL111
Briar La., Cars.	293	332	DG109
Briar La., Croy.	288	333	EB105
Briar Pas. SW16	272	324	DL97
Briar Pl. SW16	272	324	DM97
Briar Rd. NW2	110	305	CW63
Briar Rd. SW16	272	324	DL97
Briar Rd., Bex.	263	327	FD90
Briar Rd., Har.	216	304	CJ57
Briar Rd., Rom.	228	310	FJ52
Briar Rd., Shep.	280	328	BM99

Briar Rd., Twick.	259	321	CE88
Briar Wk. SW15	172	323	CV84
Briar Wk. W10	127	315	CY70
Briar Wk., Edg.	217	304	CQ52
Briar Way, West Dr.	249	320	BN75
Briarbank Rd. W13	132	314	CG72
Briardale Gdns. NW3	96	305	DA62
Briarfield Ave. N3	219	305	DB54
Briaris Clo. N17	222	307	DV52
Briarleas Gdns., Upmin.	239	311	FS59
Briars Wk., Rom.	228	311	FM54
Briarswood Way, Orp.	291	334	ET106
Briarwood Clo. NW9	217	304	CQ58
Briarwood Clo., Felt.	265	320	BS90
Briarwood Dr., Nthwd.	214	303	BU54
Briarwood Rd. SW4	177	324	DK85
Briary Clo. NW3	113	305	DE66
Briary Ct., Sid.	278	327	EV92
Briary Gdns., Brom.	276	326	EH92
Briary Gro., Edg.	217	304	CP54
Briary La. N9	209	300	DT48
Brick Ct. EC4	48	316	DN72
Brick Fm. Clo., Rich.	154	314	CP81
Brick La. E1	39	316	DT70
Brick La. E2	39	316	DT69
Brick La., Enf.	203	301	DV40
Brick La., Stan.	216	304	CK52
Brick St. W1	56/7	316	DH74
Brickett Clo., Ruis.	231	302	BQ57
Brickfield Clo., Brent.	152	314	CJ80
Brickfield Cotts. SE18	253	318	ET79
Brickfield Fm. Gdns., Orp.	291	334	EQ105
Brickfield La., Barn.	205	298	CT44
Brickfield La., Hayes	257	320	BR79
Brickfield Rd. SW19	271	323	DB91
Brickfield Rd., Th.Hth.	273	324	DP95
Brickfields, Har.	233	313	CD61
Brickfields Way, West Dr.	248	320	BM76
Bricklayer's Arms SE1	86/7	316	DS77
Brickwall La., Ruis.	231	312	BS60
Brickwood Clo. SE26	196	325	DV90
Brickwood Rd., Croy.	287	332	DS103
Bride Ct. EC4	48/9	316	DP72
Bride La. EC4	48/9	316	DP72
Bride St. N7	115	306	DM65
Brideale Clo. SE15	163	316	DT80
Bridewain St. SE1	75	316	DT76
Bridewell Pl. E1	138	317	DV74
Bridewell Pl. EC4	48/9	316	DP72
Bridford Ms. W1	44/5	316	DH71
Bridge, The, Har.	215	303	CE55
Bridge App. NW1	114	306	DG66
Bridge Ave. W6	146	315	CV78
Bridge Ave. W7	243	313	CD71
Bridge Ave., Upmin.	239	311	FN61
Bridge Clo. W10	137	315	CX72
Bridge Clo., Enf.	203	301	DV40
Bridge Clo., Rom.	227	309	FE58
Bridge Clo., Walt.	281	328	BT101
Bridge Dr. N13	208	300	DM50
Bridge End E17	223	307	EC53
Bridge Gdns., Ashf.	265	328	BQ94
Bridge Gdns., E.Mol.	267	329	CD98
Bridge Gate N21	209	300	DQ45
Bridge Ho. Quay E14	140	317	EC74
Bridge La. NW11	218	305	CY56
Bridge La. SW11	159	315	DE81
Bridge Meadows SE14	165	317	DX79
Bridge Pk. SW18	174	323	DA85
Bridge Pl. SW1	80/1	316	DH77
Bridge Pl., Croy.	287	332	DR102
Bridge Rd. E6	234	308	EM66
Bridge Rd. E15	131	317	ED67
Bridge Rd. E17	103	307	DZ59
Bridge Rd. N9	210	301	DU48
Bridge Rd. N22	220	306	DL53
Bridge Rd. NW10	109	304	CS65
Bridge Rd., Beck.	274	325	DZ94
Bridge Rd., Bexh.	254	319	EY82
Bridge Rd., Cher.	280	328	BH101
Bridge Rd., Chess.	282	330	CK106
Bridge Rd., Croy.	287	332	DQ104
Bridge Rd., Erith	255	319	FF82
Bridge Rd., Houns.	259	321	CD83
Bridge Rd., Islw.	259	321	CD83
Bridge Rd., Orp.	291	335	EV100
Bridge Rd., Sthl.	250	321	BZ75
Bridge Rd., Sutt.	292	331	DB107
Bridge Rd., Twick.	168	322	CH86
Bridge Rd., Uxb.	240	312	BJ67
Bridge Rd., Wall.	285	332	DH106
Bridge Rd., Wem.	92	304	CN62
Bridge Row, Croy.	287	332	DR102
Bridge St. SW1	70/1	316	DL75
Bridge St. W4	145	314	CR77
Bridge St., Pnr.	214	303	BY55
Bridge St., Rich.	169	322	CK85
Bridge St., Walt.	281	328	BS102
Bridge Ter. E15	121	307	ED66
Bridge Vw. W6	146	315	CW78
Bridge Way N11	208	300	DJ48
Bridge Way NW11	218	305	CZ57
Bridge Way, Twick.	259	321	CC87
Bridge Way, Uxb.	241	312	BP64
Bridge Way, Wem.	107	304	CL66
Bridge Wf., Cher.	280	328	BJ102
Bridge Wf. Rd., Islw.	168	322	CH83
Bridge Wks. Ind. Est., Uxb.	240	312	BJ70
Bridge Yd. SE1	62	316	DR74
Bridgefield Rd., Sutt.	292	331	DA107
Bridgefoot SE1	82/3	316	DL78
Bridgeland Rd. E16	244	318	EG73
Bridgeman Rd. N1	115	306	DM66
Bridgeman Rd. W4	144	314	CQ76
Bridgeman Rd., Tedd.	268	322	CG93
Bridgeman St. NW8	18/9	315	DE68
Bridgen Rd., Bex.	262	327	EY86
Bridgend Rd. SW18	174	323	DC84
Bridgend Rd., Enf.	203	301	DW35
Bridgenhall Rd., Enf.	202	300	DT39
Bridgeport Pl. E1	138	317	DU74
Bridges Ct. SW11	175	323	DD83
Bridges La., Croy.	286	332	DL105
Bridges Ms. SW19	271	323	DB93
Bridges Pl. SW6	157	315	CZ81
Bridges Rd. SW19	271	323	DB93
Bridges Rd. Ms. SW19	271	323	DB93
Bridgetown Clo. SE19	273	324	DS92
Bridgeview Ct., Ilf.	225	308	ER51
Bridgewater Clo., Chis.	277	326	ES97
Bridgewater Gdns., Edg.	216	304	CM54
Bridgewater Rd., Ruis.	232	313	BU63
Bridgewater Rd., Wem.	106	304	CJ65
Bridgewater Sq. EC2	49	316	DQ71
Bridgewater St. EC2	49	316	DQ71
Bridgeway, Bark.	235	308	ET66
Bridgeway St. NW1	21	316	DJ68
Bridgewood Clo. SE20	274	325	DV94
Bridgewood Rd. SW16	272	324	DK94
Bridgewood Rd., Wor.Pk.	283	331	CU104
Bridgford St. SW18	190	323	DC90
Bridgwater Rd. E15	130	317	EC67
Bridle Clo., Enf.	203	301	DZ37
Bridle Clo., Epsom	283	330	CR106
Bridle Clo., Kings.T.	268	322	CK98
Bridle Clo., Sun.	266	329	BU97
Bridle La. W1	57	316	DJ73
Bridle La., Twick.	168	322	CH86
Bridle Path, Croy.	286	332	DL104
Bridle Path, Wdf.Grn.	223	307	EE52
Bridle Rd., Croy.	288	333	EA104
Bridle Rd., Pnr.	214	303	BW58
Bridle Rd., The, Pur.	294	332	DL110
Bridle Way, Croy.	288	333	EA106
Bridle Way, Orp.	291	334	EQ105
Bridle Way, The, Wall.	286	332	DJ105
Bridlepath Way, Felt.	265	320	BS87
Bridleway Clo., Epsom	292	331	CW110
Bridlington Rd. N9	210	301	DV45
Bridport Ave., Rom.	227	309	FB58
Bridport Pl. N1	26	316	DR67
Bridport Rd. N18	209	300	DS50
Bridport Rd., Grnf.	243	313	CB67
Bridport Rd., Th.Hth.	273	324	DN97
Bridport Ter. SW8	161	316	DK81
Bridstow Pl. W2	40	315	DA72
Brief St. SE5	162	316	DP81
Brierley Ave. N9	210	301	DW46
Brierley Clo. SE25	274	325	DU98
Brierley Clo., Horn.	228	310	FJ58
Brierley Rd. E11	121	307	ED63
Brierley Rd. SW12	192	324	DJ89
Brierly Gdns. E2	128	317	DW68
Brig Ms. SE8	166	317	EA79
Brigade Clo., Har.	233	313	CD61
Brigade St. SE3	167	317	EF82
Brigadier Ave., Enf.	202	300	DQ38
Brigadier Hill, Enf.	202	300	DQ38
Briggeford Clo. E5	102	307	DU61
Briggs Clo., Mitch.	272	324	DH95
Bright Clo., Belv.	254	319	EX77
Bright St. E14	140	317	EB72
Brightfield Rd. SE12	183	325	EF85
Brightling Rd. SE4	181	325	DZ86
Brightlingsea Pl. E14	139	317	DZ73
Brightman Rd. SW18	191	323	DD88
Brighton Ave. E17	222	307	DZ57
Brighton Clo., Uxb.	241	312	BP66
Brighton Dr., Nthlt.	233	313	CA65
Brighton Gro. SE14	165	317	DY81
Brighton Rd. E6	245	318	EN69
Brighton Rd. N2	219	305	DC54
Brighton Rd. N16	117	306	DS63
Brighton Rd., Pur.	294	332	DN111
Brighton Rd., S.Croy.	287	332	DQ106
Brighton Rd., Surb.	282	330	CJ100
Brighton Rd., Sutt.	293	331	DC108
Brighton Ter. SW9	177	324	DM84
Brightside, The, Enf.	203	301	DX39
Brightside Ave., Stai.	264	328	BJ94
Brightside Rd. SE13	183	325	ED86
Brightwell Clo., Croy.	286	332	DN102
Brightwell Cres. SW17	271	323	DF92
Brigstock Rd., Belv.	255	319	FB77
Brigstock Rd., Th.Hth.	286	332	DN99
Brill Pl. NW1	22	316	DK68
Brim Hill N2	219	305	DC56
Brimpsfield Clo. SE2	254	319	EV76
Brimsdown Ave., Enf.	203	301	DY40
Brimsdown Ind. Est., Enf.	203	301	DZ40
Brindle Gate, Sid.	261	326	ES88
Brindles, Horn.	228	311	FL56
Brindley Clo., Bexh.	263	327	FB83
Brindley St. SE14	165	317	DZ81
Brindley Way, Brom.	276	326	EG92
Brindley Way, Sthl.	243	313	CB73
Brindwood Rd. E4	210	301	DZ48
Brinkburn Clo. SE2	254	319	EU77
Brinkburn Clo., Edg.	217	304	CP54
Brinkburn Gdns., Edg.	217	304	CN55
Brinkley Rd., Wor.Pk.	283	331	CV103
Brinklow Cres. SE18	253	318	EP80
Brinklow Ho. W2	40/1	315	DB71
Brinkworth Rd., Ilf.	224	308	EL55
Brinkworth Way E9	119	307	DZ65
Brinsdale Rd. NW4	218	305	CX55
Brinsley Rd., Har.	215	303	CD54
Brinsley St. E1	138	317	DV72
Brinsmead Rd., Rom.	229	311	FN54
Brinsworth Clo., Twick.	259	321	CD88
Brinton Wk. SE1	60/1	316	DP74
Brion Pl. E14	140	317	EC71
Brisbane Ave. SW19	271	323	DB95
Brisbane Ct. N10	220	306	DH52
Brisbane Rd. E10	104	307	EB61
Brisbane Rd. W13	142	314	CG75
Brisbane Rd., Ilf.	235	308	EP59
Brisbane St. SE5	163	316	DR80
Briscoe Clo. E11	105	307	EF61
Briscoe Rd. SW19	271	323	DD93
Briset Rd. SE9	260	326	EK83
Briset St. EC1	48/9	316	DP71
Briset Way N7	99	306	DM61
Bristol Clo., Stai.	256	320	BL86
Bristol Gdns. W9	28/9	315	DB70
Bristol Ms. W9	28/9	315	DB70
Bristol Pk. Rd. E17	222	307	DY56
Bristol Rd. E7	234	308	EJ65
Bristol Rd., Grnf.	243	313	CB67
Bristol Rd., Mord.	285	331	DC99
Briston Gro. N8	220	306	DL58
Briston Ms. NW7	218	305	CU52
Bristow Rd. SE19	273	324	DS92
Bristow Rd., Bexh.	254	319	EY81
Bristow Rd., Croy.	286	332	DL105
Bristow Rd., Houns.	259	321	CB83
Britannia Clo. SW4	177	324	DK84
Britannia Clo., Nthlt.	242	313	BX69
Britannia Gate E16	141	317	EE72
Britannia La., Twick.	259	321	CC87
Britannia Rd. E14	150	317	EA77
Britannia Rd. N12	207	299	DC48
Britannia Rd. SW6	158	315	DB80
Britannia Rd., Ilf.	235	308	EP62
Britannia Rd., Surb.	282	330	CM101
Britannia Row N1	24/5	316	DP67
Britannia St. WC1	35	316	DM69
Britannia Wk. N1	38	316	DR69
Britannia Way NW10	124	314	CP70
Britannia Way SW6	158	315	DB81
Britannia Way, Stai.	264	320	BK87
British Gro. W4	145	314	CT78
British Gro. Pas. W4	145	314	CT78
British Gro. S. W4	145	314	CT78
British Legion Rd. E4	211	301	EF47
British St. E3	129	317	DZ69
Briton Clo., S.Croy.	295	332	DS111
Briton Cres., S.Croy.	295	332	DS111
Briton Hill Rd., S.Croy.	295	332	DS110
Brittain Rd., Dag.	236	309	EY62
Britten Clo. NW11	96	305	DB60
Britten Clo., Borwd.	204	298	CK44
Britten Dr., Sthl.	243	313	CA72
Britten St. SW3	78/9	315	DE78
Britten's Ct. E1	138	317	DV73
Britton Clo. SE6	199	325	ED87
Britton St. EC1	36/7	316	DP70
Brixham Cres., Ruis.	232	313	BU60
Brixham Gdns., Ilf.	235	308	ES64
Brixham Rd., Well.	254	319	EX81
Brixham St. E16	244	318	EM74
Brixton Est., Edg.	217	304	CP54
Brixton Hill SW2	193	324	DL87
Brixton Hill Pl. SW2	193	324	DL87
Brixton Oval SW2	178	324	DN84
Brixton Rd. SW9	178	324	DN83
Brixton Sta. Rd. SW9	178	324	DN83
Brixton Water La. SW2	178	324	DN85
Broad Ct. WC2	46/7	316	DL72
Broad Grn. Ave., Croy.	286	332	DP101
Broad La. EC2	50/1	316	DS71
Broad La. N8	220	306	DM57
Broad La. N15	221	306	DT56
Broad La., Hmptn.	266	329	BZ94
Broad Lawn SE9	261	326	EN89
Broad Oak Clo. E4	211	301	EA50
Broad Oak Clo., Orp.	278	327	EU96
Broad Sanctuary SW1	70	316	DK75
Broad St., Dag.	237	309	FA66
Broad St., Tedd.	267	329	CF93
Broad St. Ave. EC2	50/1	316	DS71
Broad St. Pl. EC2	50	316	DR71
Broad Vw. NW9	217	304	CN58
Broad Wk. N21	208	300	DM47
Broad Wk. NW1	20	316	DG68
Broad Wk. SE3	252	318	EJ82
Broad Wk. W1	56	316	DG74
Broad Wk., Houns.	250	321	BX81
Broad Wk., Rich.	153	314	CM80
Broad Wk., The W8	53	315	DC74
Broad Wk., The, E.Mol.	267	329	CF98
Broad Wk., The, Nthwd.	213	302	BQ54
Broad Wk. La. NW11	95	305	CZ59
Broad Yd. EC1	36/7	316	DP70
Broadacre, Stai.	264	328	BG92
Broadacre Clo., Uxb.	231	312	BP62
Broadbent Clo. N6	98	306	DH60
Broadbent St. W1	56/7	316	DH73
Broadberry Ct. N18	222	307	DV51
Broadbridge Clo. SE3	252	318	EG80
Broadcroft Ave., Stan.	216	304	CK54
Broadcroft Rd., Orp.	291	334	ER101
Broadfield Clo. NW2	94	305	CW62
Broadfield Clo., Croy.	286	332	DM103
Broadfield Clo., Rom.	227	309	FF57
Broadfield La. NW1	115	306	DL66
Broadfield Rd. SE6	199	325	EE87
Broadfield Sq., Enf.	203	301	DV40
Broadfields, Har.	215	303	CB53
Broadfields Ave. N21	209	300	DN45
Broadfields Ave., Edg.	205	298	CP49
Broadfields Hts., Edg.	205	298	CP49
Broadfields Way NW10	109	304	CT64
Broadgate E13	244	318	EJ68
Broadgate EC2	50/1	316	DS71
Broadgate Circle EC2	50/1	316	DS71
Broadgate Rd. E16	244	318	EK72
Broadgates Rd. SW18	191	323	DD88
Broadhead Strand NW9	217	304	CT53
Broadheath Dr., Chis.	276	326	EM92
Broadhinton Rd. SW4	176	324	DH83
Broadhurst Ave., Edg.	205	298	CP49
Broadhurst Ave., Ilf.	235	308	ET63
Broadhurst Clo. NW6	112	305	DC65
Broadhurst Clo., Rich.	169	322	CM85
Broadhurst Gdns. NW6	112	305	DB65
Broadhurst Gdns., Ruis.	232	313	BW61
Broadhurst Wk., Rain.	238	310	FG65
Broadlands, The, Felt.	258	321	BZ90
Broadlands Ave. SW16	193	324	DL89
Broadlands Ave., Enf.	203	301	DV41
Broadlands Ave., Shep.	281	328	BQ100
Broadlands Clo. N6	98	306	DG59
Broadlands Clo. SW16	193	324	DL89
Broadlands Clo., Enf.	203	301	DW41
Broadlands Rd. N6	97	305	DF59
Broadlands Rd., Brom.	276	326	EH91
Broadlands Way, N.Mal.	283	330	CT100
Broadlawns Ct., Har.	215	303	CF53
Broadley St. NW8	42	315	DD71
Broadley Ter. NW1	30/1	315	DE70
Broadmayne SE17	86	316	DR78
Broadmead SE6	198	325	EA90
Broadmead Ave., Wor.Pk.	283	331	CU101
Broadmead Clo., Hmptn.	267	329	CA93
Broadmead Clo., Pnr.	214	303	BY52
Broadmead Est., Wdf.Grn.	224	308	EJ52
Broadmead Rd., Hayes	242	313	BY70
Broadmead Rd., Nthlt.	242	313	BY70
Broadmead Rd., Wdf.Grn.	224	308	EG51
Broadoak Ave., Enf.	203	301	DX35
Broadoak Rd., Erith	255	319	FD80
Broadoaks, Surb.	282	330	CP102
Broadoaks Way, Brom.	289	333	EF99
Broadstone Pl. W1	44	316	DG71
Broadstone Rd., Horn.	238	310	FG61
Broadview Est., Stai.	257	320	BN86
Broadview Rd. SW16	272	324	DK94
Broadwalk E18	223	307	EF55
Broadwalk, Har.	215	303	CA57
Broadwall SE1	60	316	DN74
Broadwater Gdns., Orp.	290	334	EP105
Broadwater Gdns., Uxb.	230	302	BH56
Broadwater La., Uxb.	230	302	BH56
Broadwater Rd. N17	221	306	DS53
Broadwater Rd. SE28	253	318	EQ76
Broadwater Rd. SW17	271	323	DE91
Broadway E15	121	307	ED66
Broadway N20	207	299	DC47
Broadway SW1	70	316	DK76
Broadway, Bark.	235	308	EQ66
Broadway, Bexh.	262	327	EY84
Broadway, Grnf.	243	313	CC70
Broadway, Rom.	228	310	FG54
Broadway, Stai.	264	328	BH92
Broadway, Surb.	282	330	CP102
Broadway, The E4	223	307	EC51
Broadway, The E13	244	318	EH68
Broadway, The N8	220	306	DL58
Broadway, The N9	210	301	DU48
Broadway, The N14	208	300	DK46
Broadway, The N22	221	306	DN54
Broadway, The NW7	205	298	CS50
Broadway, The SW13	155	314	CS82
Broadway, The SW19	271	323	DA94
Broadway, The W5	133	314	CK73
Broadway, The W7	243	313	CE74
Broadway, The W13	132	314	CG74
Broadway, The, Croy.	286	332	DL105
Broadway, The, Dag.	236	309	EZ61
Broadway, The, Epsom	283	331	CU106
Broadway, The, Har.	215	303	CE54
Broadway, The, Horn.	238	310	FH63
Broadway, The, Pnr.	214	303	BZ52
Broadway, The, Sthl.	242	313	BX73
Broadway, The, Stai.	280	328	BJ97
Broadway, The, Stan.	204	298	CJ50
Broadway, The, Sutt.	292	331	CY107
Broadway, The, Wem.	91	304	CL62
Broadway, The, Wdf.Grn.	224	308	EH51
Broadway Ave., Croy.	287	332	DR99
Broadway Ave., Twick.	168	322	CH86
Broadway Clo., S.Croy.	295	333	DV114
Broadway Clo., Wdf.Grn.	224	308	EH51
Broadway Ct. SW19	271	323	DA93
Broadway E., Uxb.	230	312	BG59
Broadway Gdns., Mitch.	271	323	DE98
Broadway Mkt. E8	128	317	DV67
Broadway Mkt. Ms. E8	128	317	DU67
Broadway Ms. E5	101	306	DT59
Broadway Ms. N13	208	300	DM50
Broadway Ms. N21	209	300	DP46
Broadway Par. N8	220	306	DL58
Broadway Pl. SW19	270	323	CZ93
Broadwick St. W1	45	316	DJ72
Broadwood Ave., Ruis.	231	302	BS58
Brocas Clo. NW3	113	305	DE66
Brock Pl. E3	130	317	EB70
Brock Rd. E13	244	318	EH71
Brock St. SE15	180	325	DW83
Brockdish Ave., Bark.	235	308	ET64
Brockenhurst Ave., Wor.Pk.	283	330	CS102
Brockenhurst Gdns. NW7	217	304	CS51
Brockenhurst Gdns., Ilf.	235	308	EQ64
Brockenhurst Rd., Croy.	287	333	DV101
Brockenhurst Way SW16	272	324	DK96
Brockham Clo. SW19	270	323	CZ92
Brockham Dr. SW2	193	324	DM87
Brockham Dr., Ilf.	225	308	EP58
Brockham St. SE1	73	316	DQ76
Brockhurst Clo., Stan.	215	303	CF51
Brockill Cres. SE4	181	325	DY84
Brocklebank Rd. SE7	252	318	EH77
Brocklebank Rd. SW18	190	323	DC87
Brocklehurst St. SE14	165	317	DX80
Brocklesby Rd. SE25	274	325	DV98
Brockley Ave., Stan.	204	298	CL48
Brockley Clo., Stan.	204	298	CL49
Brockley Cres., Rom.	227	309	FC52
Brockley Cross SE4	181	325	DY83
Brockley Footpath SE15	180	325	DW84
Brockley Gdns. SE4	165	317	DZ82
Brockley Gro. SE4	181	325	DZ85
Brockley Hall Rd. SE4	181	325	DY85
Brockley Hill, Stan.	204	298	CJ46
Brockley Ms. SE4	181	325	DY85
Brockley Pk. SE23	197	325	DY87
Brockley Ri. SE23	197	325	DY87
Brockley Rd. SE4	181	325	DZ83
Brockley Vw. SE23	197	325	DY87
Brockley Way SE4	181	325	DX85
Brockleyside, Stan.	204	298	CL49
Brockman Ri., Brom.	275	325	ED91
Brocks Dr., Sutt.	284	331	CY104
Brockshot Clo., Brent.	143	314	CK78
Brockton Clo., Rom.	227	309	FF56
Brockway Clo. E11	105	307	EE61
Brockwell Clo., Orp.	277	326	ET98
Brockwell Pk. Gdns. SE24	194	324	DN87
Brockworth Clo. SE15	163	316	DS79
Brodia Rd. N16	101	306	DS62
Brodie Rd. E4	211	301	EC46
Brodie Rd., Enf.	202	300	DQ38
Brodie St. SE1	87	316	DT78
Brodlove La. E1	139	317	DX73
Brodrick Gro. SE2	254	319	EV77
Brodrick Rd. SW17	191	323	DE89
Brograve Gdns., Beck.	275	325	EB96
Broke Wk. E8	128	317	DU67
Broken Wf. EC4	61	316	DQ73
Brokesley St. E3	129	317	DZ69
Bromar Rd. SE5	179	324	DS83
Brome Rd. SE9	260	326	EM83
Bromefield, Stan.	216	304	CJ53
Bromehead Rd. E1	138	317	DW72
Bromell's Rd. SW4	176	324	DJ84
Bromfelde Rd. SW4	177	324	DK83
Bromfelde Wk. SW4	161	316	DL82
Bromfield St. N1	24	316	DN68
Bromhall Rd., Dag.	236	309	EV65
Bromhedge SE9	260	326	EM90
Bromholm Rd. SE2	254	319	EV76
Bromleigh Ct. SE23	196	325	DV89
Bromley Ave., Brom.	275	325	EE94
Bromley Common, Brom.	276	326	EJ98
Bromley Cres., Brom.	275	325	EF97
Bromley Cres., Ruis.	241	312	BT63
Bromley Gdns., Brom.	275	325	EF97
Bromley Gro., Brom.	275	325	ED96
Bromley Hall Rd. E14	140	317	EC71
Bromley High St. E3	130	317	EB69
Bromley Hill, Brom.	275	325	EE93
Bromley La., Chis.	277	326	EQ94
Bromley Pl. W1	45	316	DJ71
Bromley Rd. E10	223	307	EB58
Bromley Rd. E17	223	307	EA54
Bromley Rd. N17	221	306	DT53
Bromley Rd. N18	209	300	DR48
Bromley Rd. SE6	198	325	EB89
Bromley Rd., Beck.	275	325	EB96
Bromley Rd., Brom.	275	325	EB96
Bromley Rd. (Downham), Brom.	275	325	ED91
Bromley Rd., Chis.	277	326	EP95
Bromley St. E1	139	317	DX71
Brompton Arc. SW3	67	315	DF75
Brompton Clo. SE20	274	325	DU96
Brompton Clo., Houns.	258	321	BZ85
Brompton Gro. N2	219	305	DE56
Brompton Pk. Cres. SW6	158	315	DB79
Brompton Pl. SW3	66/7	315	DE76
Brompton Rd. SW1	67	315	DF75
Brompton Rd. SW3	78/9	315	DE77
Brompton Rd. SW7	66/7	315	DE76
Brompton Sq. SW3	66/7	315	DE76
Brompton Ter. SE18	253	318	EN81
Bromwich Ave. N6	98	306	DG61
Bromyard Ave. W3	135	314	CS73
Bromyard Ho. SE15	164	317	DV80
Brondesbury Ct. NW2	111	305	CX65
Brondesbury Ms. NW6	112	305	DA66
Brondesbury Pk. NW2	110	305	CW66
Brondesbury Pk. NW6	111	305	CX66
Brondesbury Rd. NW6	127	315	CZ68
Brondesbury Vil. NW6	127	315	CZ68
Bronsart Rd. SW6	157	315	CY80
Bronson Rd. SW20	270	323	CX96
Bronte Clo. E7	234	308	EG63
Bronte Clo., Erith	255	319	FB81
Bronte Clo., Ilf.	225	308	EN56
Bronte Ho. NW6	28	315	DA69
Bronti Clo. SE17	85	316	DQ78
Bronze St. SE8	166	317	EA80
Brook Ave., Dag.	237	309	FB66
Brook Ave., Edg.	217	304	CP51
Brook Ave., Wem.	92	304	CN62
Brook Clo. NW7	218	305	CY52
Brook Clo. SW20	270	323	CV97
Brook Clo. W3	134	314	CN74
Brook Clo., Chis.	277	326	EN95
Brook Clo., Rom.	227	309	FF53
Brook Clo., Ruis.	231	312	BS59
Brook Clo., Stai.	264	320	BM87
Brook Cres. E4	211	301	EA49
Brook Cres. N9	210	301	DV49
Brook Dr. SE11	72	316	DN76
Brook Dr., Har.	215	303	CC56
Brook Dr., Ruis.	231	302	BS58
Brook Dr., Sun.	265	328	BS92
Brook Gdns. E4	211	301	EB49
Brook Gdns. SW13	171	322	CT83
Brook Gdns., Kings.T.	269	322	CQ95
Brook Gate W1	55	315	DF73
Brook Grn. W6	146	315	CW76
Brook Ind. Est., Hayes	242	313	BX74
Brook La. SE3	252	318	EH82
Brook La., Bex.	262	327	EX86
Brook La., Brom.	276	326	EG93
Brook La. N., Brent.	143	314	CK78
Brook Meadow N12	207	299	DB48
Brook Meadow Clo., Wdf.Grn.	223	307	EE51
Brook Ms. N. W2	54	315	DD73
Brook Pk. Clo. N21	209	300	DP44
Brook Pl., Barn.	207	299	DA43
Brook Rd. N8	220	306	DL56
Brook Rd. N22	220	306	DM55
Brook Rd. NW2	93	304	CT61
Brook Rd., Ilf.	225	308	ES58
Brook Rd., Rom.	227	309	FF53
Brook Rd., Surb.	282	330	CL103
Brook Rd., Swan.	279	327	FD97
Brook Rd., Th.Hth.	273	324	DQ98
Brook Rd., Twick.	168	322	CG86
Brook Rd. S., Brent.	153	314	CK79
Brook St. N17	221	306	DT54
Brook St. W1	56	316	DG73
Brook St. W2	54	315	DD73
Brook St., Belv.	255	319	FB78
Brook St., Erith	255	319	FB79
Brook St., Kings.T.	268	322	CL96
Brook Wk. N2	219	305	DD53
Brook Wk., Edg.	217	304	CR51
Brookbank Ave. W7	243	313	CD71
Brookbank Rd. SE13	182	325	EA83
Brookdale N11	208	300	DJ49
Brookdale Ave., Upmin.	239	311	FN62
Brookdale Clo., Upmin.	239	311	FP62
Brookdale Rd. E17	223	307	EA55
Brookdale Rd. SE6	182	325	EB86
Brookdale Rd., Bex.	262	327	EY86
Brookdene Dr., Nthwd.	213	302	BT52
Brookdene Rd. SE18	253	318	ET77
Brooke Ave., Har.	233	313	CC62
Brooke Rd. E5	102	307	DU62
Brooke Rd. E17	223	307	EC56
Brooke Rd. N16	101	306	DT62
Brooke St. EC1	48	316	DN71
Brookehowse Rd. SE6	198	325	EA89
Brookend Rd., Sid.	261	326	ES88
Brooke's Ct. EC1	48	316	DN71
Brookes Mkt. EC1	48	316	DN71
Brookfield N6	98	306	DG62
Brookfield Ave. E17	223	307	EC56
Brookfield Ave. NW7	218	305	CV51
Brookfield Ave. W5	123	314	CK70
Brookfield Ave., Sutt.	285	331	DE105
Brookfield Clo. NW7	218	305	CV51
Brookfield Ct., Grnf.	243	313	CC69
Brookfield Ct., Har.	216	304	CK57
Brookfield Cres. NW7	218	305	CV51
Brookfield Cres., Har.	216	304	CL57
Brookfield Pk. NW5	98	306	DH62
Brookfield Path, Wdf.Grn.	223	307	EE51
Brookfield Rd. E9	119	307	DY65
Brookfield Rd. N9	210	301	DU48
Brookfield Rd. W4	145	314	CR75
Brookfields, Enf.	203	301	DX42
Brookfields Ave., Mitch.	285	331	DE99
Brookhill Clo. SE18	253	318	EP78
Brookhill Clo., Barn.	207	299	DE43
Brookhill Rd. SE18	253	318	EP77
Brookhill Rd., Barn.	207	299	DD43
Brookhouse Gdns. E4	211	301	EE49
Brooking Rd. E7	234	308	EG64
Brookland Clo. NW11	219	305	DB56
Brookland Garth NW11	219	305	DB56
Brookland Hill NW11	219	305	DB56
Brookland Ri. NW11	219	305	DA56
Brooklands App., Rom.	227	309	FD56
Brooklands Ave. SW19	190	323	DB89
Brooklands Ave., Sid.	261	326	ER89
Brooklands Clo., Rom.	227	309	FD56
Brooklands Clo., Sun.	281	328	BS95
Brooklands Dr., Grnf.	122	314	CJ67
Brooklands Gdns., Horn.	228	310	FJ57
Brooklands La., Rom.	227	309	FD56
Brooklands Pk. SE3	260	326	EG83
Brooklands Rd., Rom.	227	309	FD56
Brooklea Clo. NW9	217	304	CS53
Brooklyn Ave. SE25	274	325	DV98
Brooklyn Clo., Cars.	285	331	DE103
Brooklyn Gro. SE25	274	325	DV98
Brooklyn Rd. SE25	274	325	DV98
Brooklyn Rd., Brom.	290	334	EK99
Brooklyn Way, West Dr.	248	320	BK76
Brookmans Clo., Upmin.	239	311	FS59
Brookmarsh Ind. Est. SE10	166	317	EB80
Brookmead Ave., Brom.	290	334	EM99
Brookmead Clo., Orp.	291	335	EV101
Brookmead Rd., Croy.	286	332	DJ100
Brookmead Way, Orp.	291	335	EV100
Brookmeads Est., Mitch.	285	331	DE99
Brookmill Rd. SE8	166	317	EA81
Brooks Ave. E6	244	318	EM70
Brooks Clo. SE9	261	326	EN89
Brooks Ct. E15	120	307	EB64
Brooks La. W4	154	314	CN79
Brook's Ms. W1	56/7	316	DH73
Brooks Rd. E13	244	318	EG67
Brooks Rd. W4	144	314	CN78
Brooks Way, Orp.	278	327	EW96
Brooksbank St. E9	118	307	DW65
Brooksby Ms. N1	116	306	DN66
Brooksby St. N1	116	306	DN66
Brooksby's Wk. E9	119	307	DX64
Brookscroft Rd. E17	223	307	EB53
Brookside N21	208	300	DM44
Brookside, Barn.	207	299	DE44
Brookside, Cars.	285	332	DG106
Brookside, Horn.	228	311	FL57
Brookside, Ilf.	225	308	EQ51
Brookside, Orp.	291	334	ET101
Brookside, Uxb.	240	312	BM66
Brookside Ave., Ashf.	264	328	BJ92
Brookside Clo., Barn.	206	299	CY44
Brookside Clo., Felt.	258	321	BU90
Brookside Clo., Har.	216	304	CK57
Brookside Clo. (Kenton), Har.	232	313	BY63
Brookside Cres., Wor.Pk.	283	331	CU102
Brookside Gdns., Enf.	203	301	DW37
Brookside Rd. N9	210	301	DV49
Brookside Rd. N19	98	306	DJ61
Brookside Rd. NW11	218	305	CY58
Brookside Rd., Hayes	242	313	BW73
Brookside S., Barn.	208	300	DG45
Brookside Wk. N3	218	305	CX55
Brookside Wk. N12	219	305	DA51
Brookside Wk. NW4	218	305	CY56
Brookside Wk. NW11	218	305	CY56
Brookside Way, Croy.	288	333	DX100
Brooksville Ave. NW6	127	315	CY67
Brookvale, Erith	255	319	FB81
Brookview Rd. SW16	272	324	DJ92
Brookville Rd. SW6	157	315	CZ80
Brookway SE3	260	326	EG83
Brookwood Ave. SW13	171	322	CT83
Brookwood Clo., Brom.	275	325	EF98
Brookwood Rd. SW18	189	323	CZ88
Brookwood Rd., Houns.	251	321	CB81
Broom Ave., Orp.	278	327	EV96
Broom Clo., Brom.	290	334	EL100
Broom Clo., Tedd.	268	322	CK94
Broom Gdns., Croy.	288	333	EA104
Broom Lock, Tedd.	268	322	CJ93
Broom Mead, Bexh.	263	327	FA85
Broom Pk., Tedd.	268	322	CK94
Broom Rd., Croy.	288	333	EA104
Broom Rd., Tedd.	268	322	CH92
Broom Water, Tedd.	268	322	CJ93
Broom Water W., Tedd.	268	322	CJ92
Broomcroft Ave., Nthlt.	242	313	BW69
Broome Rd., Hmptn.	266	329	BZ94
Broome Way SE5	162	316	DQ80
Broomfield E17	103	307	DZ59
Broomfield, Stai.	264	328	BG93
Broomfield, Sun.	266	329	BU95
Broomfield Ave. N13	208	300	DM50
Broomfield Clo., Rom.	227	309	FD52
Broomfield La. N13	208	300	DL49
Broomfield Pl. W13	132	314	CH74
Broomfield Rd. N13	208	300	DL50
Broomfield Rd. W13	132	314	CH74
Broomfield Rd., Beck.	274	325	DY98
Broomfield Rd., Bexh.	263	327	FA85
Broomfield Rd., Rich.	153	314	CM81
Broomfield Rd., Rom.	236	309	EX59
Broomfield Rd., Surb.	282	330	CM102
Broomfield Rd., Tedd.	268	322	CJ93
Broomfield St. E14	140	317	EA71
Broomgrove Gdns., Edg.	217	304	CN53
Broomgrove Rd. SW9	161	316	DM82
Broomhall Rd., S.Croy.	295	332	DR109
Broomhill Ri., Bexh.	263	327	FA85
Broomhill Rd. SW18	174	323	DA85
Broomhill Rd., Ilf.	236	309	EU61
Broomhill Rd., Orp.	291	335	EU101
Broomhill Rd., Wdf.Grn.	224	308	EG51
Broomhill Wk., Wdf.Grn.	223	307	EF52
Broomhouse La. SW6	158	315	DA82
Broomhouse Rd. SW6	158	315	DA82
Broomloan La., Sutt.	284	331	DA103
Broomsleigh St. NW6	111	305	CZ64
Broomwood Clo., Croy.	288	333	DX99
Broomwood Rd. SW11	175	323	DF86
Broomwood Rd., Orp.	278	327	EV96
Broseley Gro. SE26	274	325	DY92
Broster Gdns. SE25	273	324	DT97
Brough Clo. SW8	161	316	DL80
Brough Clo., Kings.T.	268	322	CK92
Brougham Rd. E8	128	317	DU67
Brougham Rd. W3	134	314	CQ72
Brougham St. SW11	159	315	DF82
Broughton Ave. N3	218	305	CY55
Broughton Ave., Rich.	184	322	CH90
Broughton Dr. SW9	178	324	DN84
Broughton Gdns. N6	220	306	DJ58
Broughton Rd. SW6	158	315	DB82
Broughton Rd. W13	132	314	CH73
Broughton Rd., Orp.	291	334	ER103
Broughton Rd., Th.Hth.	286	332	DN100
Broughton Rd. App. SW6	158	315	DB82
Broughton St. SW8	160	316	DG82
Brouncker Rd. W3	144	314	CQ75
Browells La., Felt.	258	321	BV89
Brown Clo., Wall.	294	332	DL108
Brown Hart Gdns. W1	56	316	DG73
Brown St. W1	43	315	DF72
Brownfield St. E14	140	317	EB72
Browngraves Rd., Hayes	257	320	BQ80
Brownhill Rd. SE6	198	325	EB87
Browning Ave. W7	243	313	CF72
Browning Ave., Sutt.	285	331	DE105
Browning Ave., Wor.Pk.	283	331	CV102
Browning Clo. E17	223	307	EC56
Browning Clo. W9	29	315	DC70
Browning Clo., Hmptn.	266	329	BZ91
Browning Clo., Rom.	226	309	EZ52
Browning Clo., Well.	253	318	ES81
Browning Est. SE17	85	316	DQ78
Browning Ho. W12	136	315	CW72
Browning Ms. W1	44	316	DG71
Browning Rd. E11	105	307	EF59
Browning Rd. E12	234	308	EM65
Browning Rd., Enf.	202	300	DR37
Browning St. SE17	85	316	DQ78
Browning Way, Houns.	250	321	BX81
Brownlea Gdns., Ilf.	236	309	EU61
Brownlow Ms. WC1	35	316	DM70
Brownlow Rd. E7	234	308	EH63
Brownlow Rd. E8	27	316	DT67
Brownlow Rd. N3	219	305	DB52
Brownlow Rd. N11	220	306	DL51
Brownlow Rd. NW10	109	304	CS66
Brownlow Rd. W13	132	314	CG74
Brownlow Rd., Croy.	287	332	DS105
Brownlow St. WC1	47	316	DM71
Brownrigg Rd., Ashf.	265	328	BN91
Brown's Bldgs. EC3	50/1	316	DS72
Browns La. NW5	114	306	DH64
Browns Rd. E17	223	307	EA55
Browns Rd., Surb.	282	330	CM101
Brownspring Dr. SE9	277	326	EP91
Brownswell Rd. N2	219	305	DD54
Brownswood Rd. N4	100	306	DP62
Broxash Rd. SW11	176	324	DG86
Broxbourne Ave. E18	224	308	EH56
Broxbourne Rd. E7	234	308	EG62
Broxbourne Rd., Orp.	291	334	ET102
Broxholm Rd. SE27	194	324	DN90
Broxted Rd. SE6	197	325	DZ89
Broxwood Way NW8	18/9	315	DE67

Bruce Ave., Horn.	238	310	FJ61
Bruce Ave., Shep.	281	328	BQ100
Bruce Castle Rd. N17	221	306	DT53
Bruce Clo. W10	137	315	CY71
Bruce Clo., Well.	254	319	EV81
Bruce Gdns. N20	207	299	DF48
Bruce Gro. N17	221	306	DS53
Bruce Gro., Orp.	291	335	EU101
Bruce Hall Ms. SW17	272	324	DG91
Bruce Rd. E3	130	317	EB69
Bruce Rd. NW10	109	304	CR66
Bruce Rd. SE25	273	324	DR98
Bruce Rd., Har.	215	303	CE54
Bruce Rd., Mitch.	272	324	DG94
Bruckner St. W10	127	315	CZ69
Brudenell Rd. SW17	191	323	DF90
Bruffs Meadow, Nthlt.	232	313	BY65
Bruges Pl. NW1	114	306	DJ66
Brumfield Rd., Epsom	283	330	CQ106
Brummel Clo., Bexh.	263	327	FC83
Brundley Way, Brom.	276	326	EG92
Brune St. E1	51	316	DT71
Brunel Clo. SE19	273	324	DT93
Brunel Clo., Houns.	250	321	BV80
Brunel Clo., Nthlt.	242	313	BZ69
Brunel Est. W2	40	315	DA71
Brunel Pl., Sthl.	243	313	CB72
Brunel Rd. E17	222	307	DY58
Brunel Rd. SE16	148	317	DW75
Brunel Rd. W3	135	314	CS71
Brunel St. E16	141	317	EF72
Brunel Wk. N15	221	306	DS56
Brunel Wk., Twick.	259	321	CA87
Brunner Clo. NW11	219	305	DB57
Brunner Rd. E17	222	307	DY57
Brunner Rd. W5	123	314	CK70
Bruno Pl. NW9	92	304	CQ61
Brunswick Ave. N11	208	300	DG48
Brunswick Ave., Upmin.	239	311	FS59
Brunswick Cen. WC1	34/5	316	DL70
Brunswick Clo., Bexh.	262	327	EX84
Brunswick Clo., Pnr.	214	303	BY58
Brunswick Clo., Twick.	259	321	CD90
Brunswick Ct. EC1	36/7	316	DP69
Brunswick Ct. SE1	74/5	316	DS75
Brunswick Ct., Barn.	207	299	DD43
Brunswick Cres. N11	208	300	DG48
Brunswick Gdns. W5	123	314	CL70
Brunswick Gdns. W8	52	315	DA74
Brunswick Gdns., Ilf.	225	308	EQ52
Brunswick Gro. N11	208	300	DG48
Brunswick Ind. Pk. N11	208	300	DH49
Brunswick Ms. SW16	272	324	DK93
Brunswick Ms. W1	43	315	DF72
Brunswick Pk. SE5	163	316	DR81
Brunswick Pk. Gdns. N11	208	300	DG47
Brunswick Pk. Rd. N11	208	300	DG46
Brunswick Pl. N1	38	316	DR69
Brunswick Pl. SE19	274	325	DU94
Brunswick Quay SE16	149	317	DX76
Brunswick Rd. E10	104	307	EC60
Brunswick Rd. E14	140	317	EC72
Brunswick Rd. N15	221	306	DS56
Brunswick Rd. W5	123	314	CK70
Brunswick Rd., Bexh.	262	327	EX84
Brunswick Rd., Kings.T.	269	322	CN95
Brunswick Rd., Sutt.	284	331	DB105
Brunswick Sq. N17	221	306	DT51
Brunswick Sq. WC1	34/5	316	DL70
Brunswick St. E17	223	307	EC57
Brunswick Vil. SE5	163	316	DS81
Brunswick Way N11	208	300	DH49
Brunton Pl. E14	139	317	DY72
Brushfield St. E1	50/1	316	DS71
Brussels Rd. SW11	175	323	DD84
Bruton Clo., Chis.	276	326	EM94
Bruton La. W1	56/7	316	DH73
Bruton Pl. W1	56/7	316	DH73
Bruton Rd., Mord.	271	323	DC98
Bruton St. W1	56/7	316	DH73
Bruton Way W13	132	314	CG71
Bryan Ave. NW10	110	305	CV66
Bryan Clo., Sun.	266	329	BU94
Bryan Rd. SE16	149	317	DZ75
Bryan's All. SW6	158	315	DB82
Bryanston Ave., Twick.	259	321	CB88
Bryanston Clo., Sthl.	250	321	BZ77
Bryanston Ms. E. W1	43	315	DF71
Bryanston Ms. W. W1	43	315	DF71
Bryanston Pl. W1	43	315	DF71
Bryanston Sq. W1	43	315	DF71
Bryanston St. W1	43	315	DF72
Bryanstone Rd. N8	220	306	DK57
Bryant Ave., Rom.	228	310	FK53
Bryant Clo., Barn.	206	299	CZ43
Bryant Ct. E2	27	316	DT68
Bryant Ind. Est., Rom.	228	310	FK54
Bryant Rd., Nthlt.	242	313	BW69
Bryant St. E15	121	307	ED66
Bryantwood Rd. N7	116	306	DN64
Bryce Rd., Dag.	236	309	EW63
Brycedale Cres. N14	208	300	DJ49
Bryden Clo. SE26	274	325	DY92
Brydges Pl. WC2	58/9	316	DL73
Brydges Rd. E15	121	307	ED64
Brydon Wk. N1	22/3	316	DL67
Bryer Ct. EC2	49	316	DQ71
Bryett Rd. N7	99	306	DL62
Brymay Clo. E3	130	317	EA68
Bryn-y-Mawr Rd., Enf.	202	300	DT42
Brynmaer Rd. SW11	159	315	DF81
Bryony Clo., Uxb.	248	312	BM71
Bryony Rd. W12	136	315	CU73
Bryony Way, Sun.	265	328	BT93
Buchan Clo., Uxb.	240	312	BJ69
Buchan Rd. SE15	180	325	DW83
Buchanan Clo. N21	208	300	DM43
Buchanan Gdns. NW10	126	315	CV68
Bucharest Rd. SW18	190	323	DC87
Buck Hill Wk. W2	54	315	DD73
Buck La. NW9	217	304	CR56
Buck St. NW1	114	306	DH66
Buck Wk. E17	223	307	ED56
Buckbean Path, Rom.	228	310	FJ52
Buckden Clo. N2	219	305	DF56
Buckden Clo. SE12	183	325	EF86
Buckfast Rd., Mord.	271	323	DB98
Buckfast St. E2	128	317	DU69
Buckhold Rd. SW18	174	323	DA86
Buckhurst Ave., Cars.	285	331	DE102
Buckhurst St. E1	128	317	DV70
Buckingham Arc. WC2	58/9	316	DL73
Buckingham Ave. N20	207	299	DC45
Buckingham Ave., Felt.	258	321	BV86
Buckingham Ave., Grnf.	122	314	CG67
Buckingham Ave., Th.Hth.	273	324	DN95
Buckingham Ave., Well.	261	326	ES84
Buckingham Ave., W.Mol.	267	329	CB97
Buckingham Clo. W5	132	314	CJ71
Buckingham Clo., Enf.	202	300	DS40
Buckingham Clo., Hmptn.	266	329	BZ92
Buckingham Clo., Horn.	228	310	FK58
Buckingham Clo., Orp.	291	334	ES101
Buckingham Ct. NW4	218	305	CU55
Buckingham Dr., Chis.	277	326	EP92
Buckingham Gdns., Edg.	216	304	CL52
Buckingham Gdns., Th.Hth.	273	324	DN96
Buckingham Gdns., W.Mol.	267	329	CB96
Buckingham Gate SW1	68/9	316	DH76
Buckingham Gro., Uxb.	241	312	BN68
Buckingham La. SE23	197	325	DY87
Buckingham Ms. NW10	125	314	CT68
Buckingham Ms. SW1	69	316	DJ76
Buckingham Palace Rd. SW1	80/1	316	DH77
Buckingham Pl. SW1	69	316	DJ76
Buckingham Rd. E10	104	307	EB62
Buckingham Rd. E11	224	308	EJ57
Buckingham Rd. E15	121	307	EF64
Buckingham Rd. E18	223	307	EF53
Buckingham Rd. N1	117	306	DS65
Buckingham Rd. N22	220	306	DL53
Buckingham Rd. NW10	125	314	CT68
Buckingham Rd., Edg.	216	304	CM52
Buckingham Rd., Hmptn.	266	329	BZ91
Buckingham Rd., Har.	215	303	CD57
Buckingham Rd., Ilf.	235	308	ER61
Buckingham Rd., Kings.T.	268	322	CM98
Buckingham Rd., Mitch.	286	332	DL99
Buckingham Rd., Rich.	185	322	CK89
Buckingham St. WC2	58/9	316	DL73
Buckingham Way, Wall.	294	332	DJ109
Buckland Cres. NW3	113	305	DD66
Buckland Ri., Pnr.	214	303	BW53
Buckland Rd. E10	104	307	EC61
Buckland Rd., Chess.	282	330	CM106
Buckland Rd., Orp.	291	334	ES105
Buckland Rd., Sutt.	292	331	CW110
Buckland St. N1	26	316	DR68
Buckland Wk., Mord.	271	323	DC98
Buckland Way, Wor.Pk.	284	331	CW102
Bucklands Rd., Tedd.	268	322	CJ93
Buckle St. E1	51	316	DT72
Buckleigh Ave. SW20	270	323	CY97
Buckleigh Rd. SW16	272	324	DK93
Buckleigh Way SE19	273	324	DT95
Buckler Gdns. SE9	260	326	EM90
Bucklers All. SW6	158	315	DA79
Bucklers Way, Cars.	285	331	DF104
Bucklersbury EC4	50	316	DR72
Buckles Ct., Belv.	254	319	EX76
Buckley Clo., Dart.	255	319	FF82
Buckley Rd. NW6	111	305	CZ66
Buckley St. SE1	59	316	DM74
Buckmaster Rd. SW11	175	323	DE84
Bucknall St. WC2	46	316	DK72
Bucknell Clo. SW2	177	324	DM84
Buckner Rd. SW2	177	324	DM84
Buckrell Rd. E4	211	301	ED47
Buckstone Clo. SE23	180	325	DW86
Buckstone Rd. N18	210	301	DU50
Buckters Rents SE16	139	317	DY74
Buckthorne Rd. SE4	181	325	DY86
Budd Clo. N12	207	299	DB49
Buddings Circ., Wem.	92	304	CQ62
Budd's All., Twick.	168	322	CJ85
Budebury Rd., Stai.	264	328	BG92
Budge La., Mitch.	285	331	DF101
Budge Row EC4	62	316	DR73
Budge's Wk. W2	54	315	DD73
Budich Ct., Ilf.	236	309	EU61
Budleigh Cres., Well.	254	319	EW81
Budoch Dr., Ilf.	236	309	EU61
Buer Rd. SW6	157	315	CY82
Buff Ave., Bans.	292	331	DB114
Bugsby's Way SE7	252	318	EG77
Bugsby's Way SE10	151	317	EF77
Bulganak Rd., Th.Hth.	273	324	DQ98
Bulinga St. SW1	82	316	DK77
Bull All., Well.	262	327	EV83
Bull Inn Ct. WC2	58/9	316	DL73
Bull La. N18	209	300	DS50
Bull La., Chis.	277	326	ER94
Bull La., Dag.	237	309	FB62
Bull Rd. E15	131	317	EF68
Bull Wf. La. EC4	61	316	DQ73
Bull Yd. SE15	164	317	DU81
Bullace Row SE5	162	316	DQ81
Bullards Pl. E2	129	317	DX69
Bullbanks Rd., Belv.	255	319	FC77
Bullen St. SW11	159	315	DE82
Buller Clo. SE15	164	317	DU80
Buller Rd. N17	222	307	DU54
Buller Rd. N22	221	306	DN54
Buller Rd. NW10	127	315	CX69
Buller Rd., Bark.	235	308	ES66
Buller Rd., Th.Hth.	273	324	DR96
Bullers Clo., Sid.	278	327	EY92
Bullers Wd. Dr., Chis.	276	326	EM94
Bullescroft Rd., Edg.	205	298	CN48
Bullied Way SW1	80/1	316	DH77
Bullivant St. E14	140	317	EC72
Bullrush Gro., Uxb.	240	312	BJ70
Bull's All. SW14	155	314	CR82
Bulls Bri. Ind. Est., Sthl.	250	321	BV76
Bulls Bri. Rd., Sthl.	250	321	BV76
Bulls Cross, Enf.	203	301	DU37
Bulls Cross Ride, Wal.Cr.	203	301	DU35
Bulls Gdns. SW3	78/9	315	DE77
Bull's Head Pas. EC3	50/1	316	DS72
Bullsbrook Rd., Hayes	242	313	BW74
Bullsmoor Clo., Wal.Cr.	203	301	DW35
Bullsmoor Gdns., Wal.Cr.	203	301	DV35
Bullsmoor La., Enf.	203	301	DW35
Bullsmoor La., Wal.Cr.	203	301	DU35
Bullsmoor Ride, Wal.Cr.	203	301	DW35
Bullsmoor Way, Wal.Cr.	203	301	DV35
Bulmer Gdns., Har.	91	304	CK59
Bulmer Ms. W11	52	315	DA73
Bulmer Pl. W11	52	315	DA74
Bulow Est. SW6	158	315	DB82
Bulstrode Ave., Houns.	250	321	BZ82
Bulstrode Gdns., Houns.	258	321	BZ83
Bulstrode Pl. W1	44	316	DG71
Bulstrode Rd., Houns.	259	321	CA83
Bulstrode St. W1	44	316	DG72
Bulwer Ct. Rd. E11	105	307	ED60
Bulwer Rd. E11	105	307	ED59
Bulwer Rd. N18	209	300	DS49
Bulwer St. W12	136	315	CW74
Bunces La., Wdf.Grn.	223	307	EF52
Bungalow Rd. SE25	273	324	DS98
Bungalows, The SW16	272	324	DH94
Bungalows, The, Wall.	285	332	DH106
Bunhill Row EC1	38	316	DR70
Bunhouse Pl. SW1	80	316	DG78
Bunkers Hill NW11	96	305	DC59
Bunkers Hill, Belv.	255	319	FA77
Bunkers Hill, Sid.	262	327	EZ90
Bunning Way N7	115	306	DL66
Bunns La. NW7	217	304	CS51
Bunsen St. E3	129	317	DY68
Bunting Clo. N9	210	301	DX46
Bunting Clo., Mitch.	285	331	DF99
Buntingbridge Rd., Ilf.	225	308	ER57
Bunton St. SE18	253	318	EN76
Bunyan Ct. EC2	49	316	DQ71
Bunyan Rd. E17	222	307	DY55
Buonaparte Ms. SW1	82	316	DK78
Burbage Clo. SE1	74	316	DR76
Burbage Rd. SE21	195	324	DR87
Burbage Rd. SE24	178	324	DQ86
Burberry Clo., N.Mal.	269	322	CS96
Burbidge Rd., Shep.	281	328	BN98
Burbridge Way N17	221	306	DT54
Burcham St. E14	140	317	EB72
Burcharbro Rd. SE2	254	319	EX79
Burchell Rd. E10	104	307	EB60
Burchell Rd. SE15	164	317	DV81
Burchett Way, Rom.	226	309	EZ58
Burchetts Way, Shep.	281	328	BP100
Burchwall Clo., Rom.	227	309	FC52
Burcote Rd. SW18	191	323	DD87
Burcott Rd., Pur.	294	332	DN114
Burden Clo., Brent.	142	314	CJ78
Burden Way E11	234	308	EH61
Burdenshott Ave., Rich.	170	322	CP84
Burder Clo. N1	117	306	DS65
Burder Rd. N1	117	306	DS65
Burdett Ave. SW20	270	323	CU95
Burdett Clo., Sid.	278	327	EY92
Burdett Ms. NW3	113	305	DD65
Burdett Ms. W2	40/1	315	DB72
Burdett Rd. E3	129	317	DY70
Burdett Rd. E14	139	317	DZ71
Burdett Rd., Croy.	287	332	DR100
Burdett Rd., Rich.	153	314	CM82
Burdett St. SE1	72	316	DN76
Burdetts Rd., Dag.	246	319	EZ67
Burdock Clo., Croy.	288	333	DX102
Burdock Rd. N17	222	307	DU55
Burdon La., Sutt.	292	331	CY108
Burdon Pk., Sutt.	292	331	CZ109
Burfield Clo. SW17	271	323	DD91
Burford Clo., Dag.	236	309	EW62
Burford Clo., Ilf.	225	308	EQ56
Burford Clo., Uxb.	240	312	BL63
Burford Gdns. N13	208	300	DM48
Burford La., Epsom	292	331	CW111
Burford Rd. E6	244	318	EL69
Burford Rd. E15	121	307	ED66
Burford Rd. SE6	197	325	DZ89
Burford Rd., Brent.	143	314	CL78
Burford Rd., Brom.	276	326	EL98
Burford Rd., Sutt.	284	331	DA103
Burford Rd., Wor.Pk.	283	330	CT101
Burford Wk. SW6	158	315	DB80
Burgate Clo., Dart.	263	327	FF83
Burge St. SE1	74	316	DR76
Burges Clo., Horn.	228	311	FM58
Burges Ct. E6	235	308	EN66
Burges Gro. SW13	156	315	CV80
Burges Rd. E6	234	308	EL66
Burges Way, Stai.	264	328	BG92
Burgess Ave. NW9	217	304	CR58
Burgess Clo., Felt.	266	329	BY91
Burgess Hill NW2	112	305	DA63
Burgess Rd. E15	121	307	EE63
Burgess Rd., Sutt.	284	331	DB105
Burgess St. E14	140	317	EA71
Burgh St. N1	24/5	316	DP68
Burghill Rd. SE26	274	325	DY91
Burghley Ave., Borwd.	205	298	CQ43
Burghley Ave., N.Mal.	269	322	CR95
Burghley Pl., Mitch.	285	331	DF99
Burghley Rd. E11	105	307	EE60
Burghley Rd. N8	221	306	DN55
Burghley Rd. NW5	114	306	DH63
Burghley Rd. SW19	270	323	CX91
Burghley Twr. W3	135	314	CT73
Burgon St. EC4	48/9	316	DP72
Burgos Gro. SE10	166	317	EB81
Burgoyne Rd. N4	221	306	DP58
Burgoyne Rd. SE25	273	324	DT98
Burgoyne Rd. SW9	177	324	DM83
Burgoyne Rd., Sun.	265	328	BS93
Burham Clo. SE20	274	325	DW94
Burhill Gro., Pnr.	214	303	BY54
Burke Clo. SW15	171	322	CS84
Burke St. E16	141	317	EF72
Burket Clo., Sthl.	250	321	BZ77
Burland Rd. SW11	175	323	DF85
Burland Rd., Rom.	227	309	FC51
Burleigh Ave., Sid.	261	326	ET85
Burleigh Ave., Wall.	285	332	DG104
Burleigh Gdns. N14	208	300	DJ46
Burleigh Gdns., Ashf.	265	328	BQ92
Burleigh Ho. W10	137	315	CX71
Burleigh Pl. SW15	173	323	CX85
Burleigh Pl., Mitch.	285	331	DF99
Burleigh Rd., Enf.	202	300	DS42
Burleigh Rd., Sutt.	284	331	CY102
Burleigh Rd., Uxb.	241	312	BP67
Burleigh St. WC2	58/9	316	DL73
Burleigh Wk. SE6	198	325	EC88
Burleigh Way, Enf.	202	300	DR41
Burley Clo. E4	211	301	EA50
Burley Clo. SW16	272	324	DK96
Burley Orchard, Cher.	280	328	BG100
Burley Rd. E16	244	318	EJ71
Burlington Arc. W1	57	316	DJ73
Burlington Ave., Rich.	154	314	CN81
Burlington Ave., Rom.	227	309	FB58
Burlington Clo. E6	244	318	EL72
Burlington Clo. W9	127	315	CZ70
Burlington Clo., Felt.	265	320	BR87
Burlington Clo., Orp.	290	334	EP103
Burlington Clo., Pnr.	214	303	BV55
Burlington Gdns. W1	57	316	DJ73
Burlington Gdns. W3	134	314	CQ74
Burlington Gdns. W4	144	314	CQ78
Burlington Gdns., Rom.	236	309	EY59
Burlington La. W4	155	314	CS80
Burlington Ms. W3	134	314	CQ74
Burlington Pl. SW6	157	315	CY82
Burlington Ri., Barn.	207	299	DE46
Burlington Rd. N10	220	306	DG54
Burlington Rd. N17	222	307	DU53
Burlington Rd. SW6	157	315	CY82
Burlington Rd. W4	144	314	CQ78
Burlington Rd., Enf.	202	300	DR39
Burlington Rd., Islw.	251	321	CD81
Burlington Rd., N.Mal.	269	322	CT98
Burlington Rd., Th.Hth.	273	324	DQ96
Burma Rd. N16	117	306	DR63
Burmester Rd. SW17	190	323	DC90
Burn Side N9	210	301	DW48
Burnaby Cres. W4	154	314	CQ79
Burnaby Gdns. W4	154	314	CP79
Burnaby St. SW10	158	315	DC80
Burnbrae Clo. N12	219	305	DB51
Burnbury Rd. SW12	192	324	DJ88
Burncroft Ave., Enf.	203	301	DW40
Burne Jones Ho. W14	147	315	CZ77
Burne St. NW1	42/3	315	DE71
Burnell Ave., Rich.	268	322	CJ92
Burnell Ave., Well.	254	319	EU82
Burnell Gdns., Stan.	216	304	CK53
Burnell Rd., Sutt.	284	331	DB105
Burnell Wk. SE1	87	316	DT78
Burnels Ave. E6	245	318	EN69
Burness Clo. N7	115	306	DM65
Burness Clo., Uxb.	240	312	BK68
Burnett Clo. E9	118	307	DW64
Burney Ave., Surb.	282	330	CM99
Burney St. SE10	166	317	EC80
Burnfoot Ave. SW6	157	315	CY81
Burnfoot Ct. SE22	196	325	DV88
Burnham NW3	113	305	DE66
Burnham Ave., Uxb.	241	312	BQ63
Burnham Clo. NW7	218	305	CU52
Burnham Clo. SE1	87	316	DT77
Burnham Clo., Enf.	202	300	DS38
Burnham Ct. NW4	218	305	CW56
Burnham Cres. E11	224	308	EJ56
Burnham Dr., Wor.Pk.	284	331	CX103
Burnham Gdns., Croy.	287	332	DT101
Burnham Gdns., Hayes	249	320	BR76
Burnham Gdns., Houns.	250	321	BV81
Burnham Rd. E4	210	301	DZ50
Burnham Rd., Dag.	236	309	EV66
Burnham Rd., Mord.	284	331	DB99
Burnham Rd., Rom.	227	309	FD55
Burnham Rd., Sid.	262	327	EY89
Burnham St. E2	128	317	DW69
Burnham St., Kings.T.	269	322	CN95
Burnham Way SE26	274	325	DZ92
Burnham Way W13	142	314	CH77
Burnhill Rd., Beck.	275	325	EA96
Burnley Rd. NW10	109	304	CT64
Burnley Rd. SW9	161	316	DM82
Burns Ave., Felt.	258	321	BU86
Burns Ave., Rom.	236	309	EW59
Burns Ave., Sid.	262	327	EU86
Burns Ave., Sthl.	243	313	CA73
Burns Clo. SW19	271	323	DD93
Burns Clo., Erith	255	319	FF81
Burns Clo., Hayes	249	312	BT71
Burns Clo., Well.	253	318	ET81
Burns Dr., Bans.	292	331	CY114
Burns Rd. NW10	125	314	CT67
Burns Rd. SW11	159	315	DF82
Burns Rd. W13	142	314	CH75
Burns Rd., Wem.	123	314	CL68
Burns Way, Houns.	250	321	BX82
Burnsall St. SW3	78/9	315	DE78
Burnside Ave. E4	222	307	DZ51
Burnside Clo. SE16	139	317	DX74
Burnside Clo., Twick.	168	322	CG86
Burnside Cres., Wem.	123	314	CK67
Burnside Rd., Dag.	236	309	EW61
Burnt Ash Hill SE12	183	325	EF86
Burnt Ash La., Brom.	276	326	EG94
Burnt Ash Rd. SE12	183	325	EF85
Burnt Oak Bdy., Edg.	217	304	CP52
Burnt Oak Flds., Edg.	217	304	CQ53
Burnt Oak La., Sid.	262	327	EU89
Burnthwaite Rd. SW6	157	315	CZ80
Burntwood Ave., Horn.	228	310	FK58
Burntwood Clo. SW18	191	323	DD88
Burntwood Gra. Rd. SW18	191	323	DD88
Burntwood La. SW17	190	323	DC90
Burntwood Vw. SE19	273	324	DT92
Burnway, Horn.	238	311	FL59
Buross St. E1	138	317	DV72
Burr Clo. E1	138	317	DU74
Burr Clo., Bexh.	262	327	EZ83
Burr Rd. SW18	190	323	DA88
Burrage Gro. SE18	253	318	EQ77
Burrage Pl. SE18	253	318	EP78
Burrage Rd. SE18	253	318	EQ77
Burrard Rd. E16	244	318	EH72
Burrard Rd. NW6	112	305	DA64
Burrell Clo., Croy.	288	333	DY100
Burrell Clo., Edg.	205	298	CP47
Burrell Row, Beck.	275	325	EA96
Burrell St. SE1	60/1	316	DP74
Burrell Twr. E10	104	307	EA59
Burrells Wf. Sq. E14	150	317	EB78
Burritt Rd., Kings.T.	269	322	CN96
Burroughs, The NW4	218	305	CV56
Burroughs Gdns. NW4	218	305	CV56
Burrow Rd. SE22	179	324	DS84
Burrow Wk. SE21	194	324	DQ87
Burrows Hill Clo., Houns.	256	320	BJ84
Burrows Hill La., Houns.	256	320	BH84
Burrows Ms. SE1	72/3	316	DP75
Burrows Rd. NW10	126	315	CW69
Bursdon Clo., Sid.	261	326	ET89
Bursland Rd., Enf.	203	301	DX42
Burslem Ave., Ilf.	226	309	EU51
Burslem St. E1	138	317	DU72
Burstock Rd. SW15	173	323	CY84
Burston Rd. SW15	173	323	CX85
Burston Vil. SW15	173	323	CX85
Burstow Rd. SW20	270	323	CY95
Burt Rd. E16	244	318	EJ74
Burtley Clo. N4	100	306	DQ60
Burton Ct. SW3	79	315	DF78
Burton Gdns., Houns.	250	321	BZ81
Burton Gro. SE17	86	316	DR78
Burton La. SW9	162	316	DN82
Burton Ms. SW1	80	316	DG77
Burton Pl. WC1	34	316	DK69
Burton Rd. E18	224	308	EH55
Burton Rd. NW6	111	305	CZ66
Burton Rd. SW9	162	316	DP82
Burton Rd., Kings.T.	268	322	CL94
Burton St. WC1	34	316	DK69
Burtonhole Clo. NW7	206	299	CX49
Burtonhole La. NW7	206	299	CW50
Burtons Rd., Hmptn.	267	329	CB91
Burtwell La. SE27	273	324	DR91
Burwash Ho. SE1	74	316	DR75
Burwash Rd. SE18	253	318	ER78
Burway Cres., Cher.	280	328	BG97
Burwell Ave., Grnf.	233	313	CE65
Burwell Clo. E1	138	317	DV72
Burwell Rd. E10	103	307	DY60
Burwell Wk. E3	130	317	EA70
Burwood Ave., Brom.	289	334	EH103
Burwood Ave., Ken.	294	332	DP114
Burwood Ave., Pnr.	214	303	BV57
Burwood Clo., Surb.	282	330	CN102
Burwood Gdns., Rain.	247	319	FF69
Burwood Pl. W2	42/3	315	DE72
Bury Ave., Hayes	241	312	BS68
Bury Ave., Ruis.	231	302	BQ58
Bury Clo. SE16	139	317	DX74
Bury Ct. EC3	50/1	316	DS72
Bury Gro., Mord.	284	331	DB99
Bury Pl. WC1	46/7	316	DL71
Bury Rd. N22	221	306	DN55
Bury Rd., Dag.	237	309	FB64
Bury St. EC3	50/1	316	DS72
Bury St. N9	209	300	DT45
Bury St. SW1	57	316	DJ74
Bury St., Ruis.	231	302	BQ57
Bury St. W. N9	209	300	DR45
Bury Wk. SW3	78/9	315	DE77
Busbridge Ho. E14	140	317	EA71
Busby Ms. NW5	115	306	DK65
Busby Pl. NW5	115	306	DK65
Busby St. E2	39	316	DT70
Bush Clo., Ilf.	225	308	ER57
Bush Cotts. SW18	174	323	DA85
Bush Ct. W12	147	315	CX75
Bush Elms Rd., Horn.	238	310	FG59
Bush Gro. NW9	92	304	CQ59
Bush Gro., Stan.	216	304	CK52
Bush Hill N21	209	300	DQ45
Bush Hill Rd. N21	209	300	DR44
Bush Hill Rd., Har.	216	304	CM58
Bush Ind. Est. NW10	125	314	CR70
Bush La. EC4	62	316	DR73
Bush Rd. E8	128	317	DV67
Bush Rd. E11	105	307	EF59
Bush Rd. SE8	149	317	DX77
Bush Rd., Rich.	153	314	CM79
Bush Rd., Shep.	280	328	BM99
Bushbaby Clo. SE1	74/5	316	DS76
Bushberry Rd. E9	119	307	DY65
Bushell Clo. SW2	193	324	DM89
Bushell St. E1	138	317	DU74
Bushell Way, Chis.	277	326	EN92
Bushey Ave. E18	223	307	EF55
Bushey Ave., Orp.	291	334	ER101
Bushey Clo. E4	211	301	EC48
Bushey Clo., Uxb.	231	312	BN61
Bushey Ct. SW20	270	323	CV97
Bushey Down SW12	192	324	DH89
Bushey Hill Rd. SE5	163	316	DS81
Bushey La., Sutt.	284	331	DA104
Bushey Lees, Sid.	261	326	ET86
Bushey Rd. E13	244	318	EJ68
Bushey Rd. N15	221	306	DS58
Bushey Rd. SW20	270	323	CV97
Bushey Rd., Croy.	288	333	EA103
Bushey Rd., Hayes	249	320	BS77
Bushey Rd., Sutt.	284	331	DA105
Bushey Rd., Uxb.	231	312	BN61
Bushey Way, Beck.	289	333	ED100
Bushfield Clo., Edg.	205	298	CP47
Bushfield Cres., Edg.	205	298	CP47
Bushgrove Rd., Dag.	236	309	EX63
Bushmead Clo. N15	221	306	DT56
Bushmoor Cres. SE18	253	318	EQ80
Bushnell Rd. SW17	192	324	DH89
Bushway, Dag.	236	309	EX63
Bushwood E11	105	307	EF60
Bushwood Dr. SE1	87	316	DT77
Bushwood Rd., Rich.	154	314	CN79
Bushy Pk., Hmptn.	267	329	CF95
Bushy Pk., Tedd.	267	329	CF95
Bushy Pk. Gdns., Tedd.	267	329	CD92
Bushy Pk. Rd., Tedd.	268	322	CH94
Bushy Rd., Tedd.	267	329	CF93
Butcher Row E1	139	317	DX73
Butcher Row E14	139	317	DX73
Butchers Rd. E16	244	318	EG72
Bute Ave., Rich.	185	322	CL89
Bute Ct., Wall.	286	332	DJ106
Bute Gdns. W6	147	315	CX77
Bute Gdns., Wall.	286	332	DJ106
Bute Gdns. W., Wall.	286	332	DJ106
Bute Rd., Croy.	286	332	DN102
Bute Rd., Ilf.	225	308	EP57
Bute Rd., Wall.	286	332	DJ105
Bute St. SW7	78	315	DD77
Bute Wk. N1	117	306	DR65
Butler Ave., Har.	233	313	CD59
Butler Pl. SW1	70	316	DK76
Butler Rd. NW10	109	304	CT66
Butler Rd., Dag.	236	309	EV63
Butler Rd., Har.	233	313	CC59
Butler St. E2	128	317	DW69
Butler St., Uxb.	241	312	BP70
Butlers Wf. SE1	75	316	DT75
Butter Hill, Cars.	285	332	DG104
Butter Hill, Wall.	285	332	DG104
Buttercup Clo., Rom.	228	310	FK53
Buttercup Sq., Stai.	264	320	BK88
Butterfield Clo. SE16	148	317	DV75
Butterfield Clo., Twick.	259	321	CF86
Butterfield Sq. E6	244	318	EM72
Butterfields E17	223	307	EC57
Butterfly La. SE9	261	326	EP86
Butterfly Wk. SE5	163	316	DR81
Butteridges Clo., Dag.	246	319	EZ67
Buttermere Clo. SE1	87	316	DT77
Buttermere Clo., Felt.	265	320	BT88
Buttermere Clo., Mord.	284	331	CX100
Buttermere Dr. SW15	173	323	CY85
Buttermere Gdns., Pur.	295	332	DR113
Buttermere Rd., Orp.	278	327	EX98
Buttermere Wk. E8	117	306	DT65
Butterwick W6	146	315	CW77
Buttesland St. N1	38	316	DR69
Buttfield Clo., Dag.	237	309	FB65
Buttmarsh Clo. SE18	253	318	EP78
Butts, The, Brent.	152	314	CJ79
Butts, The, Sun.	266	329	BW97
Butts Cotts., Felt.	258	321	BZ90
Butts Cres., Felt.	259	321	CA90
Butts Grn. Rd., Horn.	228	310	FK58
Butts Piece, Nthlt.	242	313	BV68
Butts Rd., Brom.	275	325	EE92
Buttsbury Rd., Ilf.	235	308	EQ64
Buttsmead, Nthwd.	213	302	BQ52
Buxted Rd. E8	117	306	DT66
Buxted Rd. N12	207	299	DE50
Buxted Rd. SE22	179	324	DS84
Buxton Clo., Wdf.Grn.	224	308	EK51
Buxton Ct. N1	37	316	DQ69
Buxton Cres., Sutt.	284	331	CY105
Buxton Dr. E11	223	307	EE56
Buxton Dr., N.Mal.	269	322	CR96
Buxton Gdns. W3	134	314	CP73
Buxton Rd. E4	211	301	ED45
Buxton Rd. E6	244	318	EL69
Buxton Rd. E15	121	307	EE64
Buxton Rd. E17	222	307	DY56
Buxton Rd. N19	99	306	DK60
Buxton Rd. NW2	110	305	CV65
Buxton Rd. SW14	171	322	CS83
Buxton Rd., Ashf.	264	328	BK92
Buxton Rd., Erith	255	319	FD80
Buxton Rd., Ilf.	225	308	ES58
Buxton Rd., Th.Hth.	286	332	DP99
Buxton St. E1	39	316	DT70
Buzzard Creek Ind. Est., Bark.	245	318	ET71
Byam St. SW6	158	315	DC82
Byards Cft. SW16	272	324	DK95
Byatt Wk., Hmptn.	266	329	BY93
Bychurch End, Tedd.	267	329	CF92
Bycroft Rd., Sthl.	243	313	CA70
Bycroft St. SE20	274	325	DX94
Bycullah Ave., Enf.	202	300	DP41
Bycullah Rd., Enf.	202	300	DP40
Bye, The W3	135	314	CS72
Bye Way, The, Har.	215	303	CF53
Bye Ways, Twick.	259	321	CB90
Byegrove Rd. SW19	271	323	DD93
Byeway, The SW14	170	322	CQ83
Byeway, The, Epsom	283	330	CT105
Byeway, The, Rick.	212	302	BL47
Byeways, The, Surb.	282	330	CN99
Byfeld Gdns. SW13	156	315	CU81
Byfield Clo. SE16	149	317	DY75
Byfield Rd., Islw.	168	322	CG83
Byford Clo. E15	121	307	EE66
Bygrove St. E14	140	317	EB72
Byland Clo. N21	208	300	DM45
Bylands Clo. SE2	254	319	EV76
Bylands Clo. SE16	139	317	DX74
Byne Rd. SE26	274	325	DW93
Byne Rd., Cars.	285	331	DE103
Bynes Rd., S.Croy.	295	332	DR108
Byng Pl. WC1	34	316	DK70
Byng St. E14	150	317	EA75
Bynon Ave., Bexh.	262	327	EZ83
Byre, The N14	208	300	DH44
Byre Rd. N14	208	300	DG44
Byrne Rd. SW12	192	324	DH88
Byron Ave. E12	234	308	EL65
Byron Ave. E18	223	307	EF55
Byron Ave. NW9	217	304	CP56
Byron Ave., Borwd.	205	298	CN43
Byron Ave., Houns.	250	321	BU82
Byron Ave., N.Mal.	283	331	CU99
Byron Ave., Sutt.	285	331	DD105
Byron Ave. E., Sutt.	285	331	DD105
Byron Clo. E8	128	317	DU67
Byron Clo. SE26	274	325	DY91
Byron Clo. SE28	246	319	EW74
Byron Clo., Hmptn.	266	329	BZ91
Byron Ct. W9	28	315	DA70
Byron Ct., Enf.	202	300	DP40
Byron Dr. N2	219	305	DD58
Byron Dr., Erith	255	319	FB81
Byron Gdns., Sutt.	285	331	DD105
Byron Hill Rd., Har.	233	313	CD60
Byron Ho., Beck.	275	325	EB93
Byron Ms. NW3	113	305	DE63
Byron Ms. W9	28	315	DA70
Byron Rd. E10	104	307	EB60
Byron Rd. E17	223	307	EA55
Byron Rd. NW2	94	305	CV61
Byron Rd. NW7	206	299	CU50
Byron Rd. W5	133	314	CM74
Byron Rd., Har.	215	303	CE58
Byron Rd. (Wealdstone), Har.	215	303	CF54
Byron Rd., S.Croy.	295	333	DV110
Byron Rd., Wem.	90	304	CJ61
Byron St. E14	140	317	EC72
Byron Ter. N9	210	301	DW45
Byron Way, Hayes	241	312	BS70
Byron Way, Nthlt.	242	313	BY69
Byron Way, Rom.	228	310	FJ53
Byron Way, West Dr.	248	320	BM77
Bysouth Clo., Ilf.	225	308	EP53
Bythorn St. SW9	177	324	DM84
Byton Rd. SW17	271	323	DF93
Byward Ave., Felt.	258	321	BW86
Byward St. EC3	62/3	316	DS73
Bywater Pl. SE16	139	317	DY74
Bywater St. SW3	79	315	DF78
Byway, The, Sutt.	293	331	DD109
Bywell Pl. W1	45	316	DJ71
Bywood Ave., Croy.	288	333	DW100
Byworth Wk. N19	99	306	DK60
C.I. Twr., N.Mal.	269	322	CS97
Cabbell St. NW1	42/3	315	DE71
Cabinet Way E4	222	307	DZ51
Cable Pl. SE10	166	317	EC81
Cable St. E1	138	317	DU73
Cabot Sq. E14	140	317	EA74
Cabot Way E6	244	318	EK67
Cabul Rd. SW11	159	315	DE82
Cactus Wk. W12	135	314	CT73
Cadbury Clo., Islw.	152	314	CG81
Cadbury Clo., Sun.	265	328	BS94
Cadbury Rd., Sun.	265	328	BS94
Cadbury Way SE16	148	317	DU76
Caddington Clo., Barn.	207	299	DE43
Caddington Rd. NW2	95	305	CY62
Caddis Clo., Stan.	215	303	CF52
Cade Rd. SE10	167	317	ED81
Cadell Clo. E2	39	316	DT69
Cader Rd. SW18	174	323	DC86
Cadet Dr. SE1	87	316	DT78
Cadet Pl. SE10	151	317	EE78
Cadiz Rd., Dag.	237	309	FC66
Cadiz St. SE17	85	316	DQ78
Cadley Ter. SE23	196	325	DW89
Cadmer Clo., N.Mal.	269	322	CS98
Cadmus Clo. SW4	177	324	DK83
Cadogan Clo., Beck.	275	325	ED95
Cadogan Clo., Har.	233	313	CB63
Cadogan Clo., Tedd.	267	329	CE92
Cadogan Ct., Sutt.	292	331	DB107
Cadogan Gdns. E18	224	308	EH55
Cadogan Gdns. N3	219	305	DB53
Cadogan Gdns. N21	209	300	DN43
Cadogan Gdns. SW3	79	315	DF77
Cadogan Gate SW1	79	315	DF77
Cadogan La. SW1	68	316	DG76
Cadogan Pl. SW1	67	315	DF76
Cadogan Rd., Surb.	282	330	CK99
Cadogan Sq. SW1	67	315	DF76
Cadogan St. SW3	79	315	DF77
Cadogan Ter. E9	119	307	DZ65
Cadoxton Ave. N15	221	306	DT58
Cadwallon Rd. SE9	261	326	EP89
Caedmon Rd. N7	115	306	DM63
Caerleon Clo., Sid.	278	327	EW92
Caerleon Ter. SE2	254	319	EV77
Caernarvon Clo., Horn.	239	311	FN60
Caernarvon Clo., Mitch.	272	324	DL97
Caernarvon Dr., Ilf.	225	308	EN53
Caesars Wk., Mitch.	285	331	DF99
Caesars Way, Shep.	281	328	BR100
Cage Rd. E16	141	317	EE71
Cahill St. EC1	37	316	DQ70
Cahir St. E14	150	317	EB77
Cains La., Felt.	257	320	BR85
Caird St. W10	127	315	CY69
Cairn Ave. W5	133	314	CK74
Cairn Way, Stan.	215	303	CF51
Cairndale Clo., Brom.	275	325	EF94

Cairnfield Ave. NW2 93 304 CS62
Cairngorm Clo., Tedd. 268 322 CG92
Cairns Ave., Wdf.Grn. 224 308 EL51
Cairns Rd. SW11 175 323 DE85
Cairo New Rd., Croy. 286 332 DP103
Cairo Rd. E17 223 307 EA56
Caistor Ms. SW12 192 324 DH87
Caistor Pk. Rd. E15 131 317 EF67
Caistor Rd. SW12 192 324 DH87
Caithness Gdns., Sid. 261 326 ET86
Caithness Rd. W14 147 315 CX76
Caithness Rd., Mitch. 272 324 DH94
Calabria Rd. N5 116 306 DP65
Calais Gate SE5 162 316 DP81
Calais St. SE5 162 316 DP81
Calbourne Ave., Horn. 238 310 FH64
Calbourne Rd. SW12 191 323 DF87
Calcott Wk. SE9 276 326 EL91
Caldbeck Ave., Wor.Pk. 283 331 CU103
Caldecot Rd. SE5 162 316 DQ82
Caldecott Way E5 103 307 DX62
Calder Ave., Grnf. 243 313 CF68
Calder Clo., Enf. 202 300 DS41
Calder Gdns., Edg. 217 304 CN55
Calder Rd., Mord. 285 331 DC99
Calderon Pl. W10 136 315 CW71
Calderon Rd. E11 120 307 EC63
Caldervale Rd. SW4 177 324 DK85
Calderwood St. SE18 253 318 EN77
Caldicot Grn. NW9 217 304 CS58
Caldwell St. SW9 161 316 DM80
Caldwell Yd. EC4 61 316 DQ73
Caldy Rd., Belv. 255 319 FB76
Caldy Wk. N1 116 306 DQ65
Cale St. SW3 78/9 315 DE78
Caleb St. SE1 73 316 DQ75
Caledon Rd. E6 244 318 EL67
Caledon Rd., Wall. 285 332 DG105
Caledonia Rd., Stai. 264 320 BL87
Caledonia St. N1 22/3 316 DL68
Caledonian Clo., Ilf. 236 309 EV60
Caledonian Rd. N1 22/3 316 DL68
Caledonian Rd. N7 115 306 DM63
Caledonian Wf. Rd. E14 151 317 ED77
Caletock Way SE10 151 317 EF78
Calico Row SW11 174 323 DC83
Calidore Clo. SW2 177 324 DM86
California Rd., N.Mal. 269 322 CQ97
Callaby Ter. N1 117 306 DR65
Callaghan Clo. SE13 183 325 EE84
Callander Rd. SE6 198 325 EB89
Callard Ave. N13 209 300 DP50
Callcott Rd. NW6 111 305 CZ66
Callcott St. W8 52 315 DA74
Callendar Rd. SW7 66 315 DD76
Callingham Clo. E14 139 317 DZ71
Callis Fm. Clo., Stai. 256 320 BL86
Callis Rd. E17 222 307 DZ58
Callow Fld., Pur. 294 332 DN113
Callow St. SW3 159 315 DD79
Calmington Rd. SE5 86/7 316 DS78
Calmont Rd., Brom. 275 325 ED93
Calmore Clo., Horn. 238 310 FJ64
Calne Ave., Ilf. 225 308 EP53
Calonne Rd. SW19 270 323 CX91
Calshot Rd., Houns. 257 320 BN82
Calshot St. N1 23 316 DM68
Calshot Way, Enf. 202 300 DP41
Calthorpe Gdns., Edg. 204 298 CL50
Calthorpe Gdns., Sutt. 285 331 DC104
Calthorpe St. WC1 35 316 DM70
Calton Ave. SE21 179 324 DS86
Calton Rd., Barn. 207 299 DC44
Calverley Clo., Beck. 275 325 EB93
Calverley Cres., Dag. 237 309 FA61
Calverley Gdns., Har. 91 304 CK59
Calverley Gro. N19 99 306 DK60
Calvert Ave. E2 38/9 316 DS69
Calvert Clo., Belv. 255 319 FA77
Calvert Clo., Sid. 278 327 EY93
Calvert Rd. SE10 151 317 EF78
Calvert St. NW1 20 316 DG67
Calverton SE5 163 316 DS79
Calverton Rd. E6 245 318 EN67
Calvert's Bldgs. SE1 62 316 DR74
Calvin Clo., Orp. 278 327 EX97
Calvin St. E1 39 316 DT70
Calydon Rd. SE7 252 318 EH78
Calypso Way SE16 149 317 DZ77
Cam Rd. E15 131 317 ED67
Camac Rd., Twick. 259 321 CD88
Cambalt Rd. SW15 173 323 CX85
Camberley Ave. SW20 270 323 CV96
Camberley Ave., Enf. 202 300 DS42
Camberley Clo., Sutt. 284 331 CX104
Camberley Rd., Houns. 257 320 BN83
Cambert Way SE3 260 326 EH84
Camberwell Ch. St. SE5 163 316 DR81
Camberwell Glebe SE5 163 316 DS81
Camberwell Grn. SE5 163 316 DR81
Camberwell Gro. SE5 163 316 DR81
Camberwell New Rd. SE5 162 316 DN79
Camberwell Pas. SE5 162 316 DQ81
Camberwell Rd. SE5 162 316 DQ79
Camberwell Sta. Rd. SE5 162 316 DQ81
Cambeys Rd., Dag. 237 309 FB64
Camborne Ave. W13 142 314 CH75
Camborne Ave., Rom. 228 310 FK52
Camborne Ms. W11 137 315 CY72
Camborne Rd. SW18 190 323 DA87
Camborne Rd., Croy. 287 333 DU101
Camborne Rd., Houns. 257 320 BN83
Camborne Rd., Mord. 284 331 CX99
Camborne Rd., Sid. 262 327 EW90
Camborne Rd., Sutt. 292 331 DA108
Camborne Rd., Well. 253 318 ET82
Camborne Way, Houns. 251 321 CA81
Camborne Way, Rom. 228 311 FL52
Cambourne Ave. N9 210 301 DX45
Cambray Rd. SW12 192 324 DJ88
Cambray Rd., Orp. 291 334 ET101
Cambria Clo., Houns. 259 321 CA84
Cambria Clo., Sid. 261 326 ER88
Cambria Ct., Felt. 258 321 BV87
Cambria Gdns., Stai. 264 320 BL87
Cambria Rd. SE5 178 324 DQ83
Cambria St. SW6 158 315 DB80
Cambrian Ave., Ilf. 225 308 ES57
Cambrian Clo. SE27 194 324 DP90
Cambrian Rd. E10 104 307 EA59
Cambrian Rd., Rich. 169 322 CM86
Cambridge Ave. NW6 16 315 DA68
Cambridge Ave., Grnf. 233 313 CF64
Cambridge Ave., N.Mal. 269 322 CS96
Cambridge Ave., Rom. 228 310 FJ55
Cambridge Ave., Well. 261 326 ET84
Cambridge Barracks Rd. SE18 252 318 EM77
Cambridge Circ. WC2 46 316 DK72
Cambridge Clo. N22 221 306 DN53
Cambridge Clo. NW10 92 304 CQ62
Cambridge Clo. SW20 270 323 CV95
Cambridge Clo., Houns. 258 321 BY84
Cambridge Clo., West Dr. 256 320 BK79
Cambridge Cotts., Rich. 154 314 CN79
Cambridge Cres. E2 128 317 DV68
Cambridge Cres., Tedd. 268 322 CG92
Cambridge Dr. SE12 260 326 EG85
Cambridge Dr., Ruis. 232 313 BX61
Cambridge Gdns. N10 220 306 DG53
Cambridge Gdns. N13 209 300 DN50
Cambridge Gdns. N17 221 306 DR52
Cambridge Gdns. N21 209 300 DR45
Cambridge Gdns. NW6 16 315 DA68
Cambridge Gdns. W10 137 315 CX72
Cambridge Gdns., Enf. 203 301 DU40
Cambridge Gdns., Kings.T. 269 322 CN96
Cambridge Gate NW1 32/3 316 DH70
Cambridge Gate Ms. NW1 32/3 316 DH70
Cambridge Grn. SE9 261 326 EP88
Cambridge Gro. SE20 274 325 DV95
Cambridge Gro. W6 146 315 CV77
Cambridge Gro. Rd., Kings.T. 269 322 CN97
Cambridge Heath Rd. E1 128 317 DV70
Cambridge Heath Rd. E2 128 317 DW70
Cambridge Mans. SW11 159 315 DF81
Cambridge Par., Enf. 203 301 DU39
Cambridge Pk. E11 234 308 EG59
Cambridge Pk., Twick. 168 322 CJ86
Cambridge Pk. Rd. E11 105 307 EF59
Cambridge Pl. W8 64/5 315 DB75
Cambridge Rd. E4 211 301 ED46
Cambridge Rd. E11 223 307 EF58
Cambridge Rd. NW6 28 315 DA69
Cambridge Rd. SE20 274 325 DV97
Cambridge Rd. SW11 159 315 DF81
Cambridge Rd. SW13 155 314 CT82
Cambridge Rd. SW20 270 323 CV95
Cambridge Rd. W7 251 321 CF75
Cambridge Rd., Ashf. 265 328 BQ94
Cambridge Rd., Bark. 235 308 EQ66
Cambridge Rd., Brom. 276 326 EG94
Cambridge Rd., Cars. 293 331 DE107
Cambridge Rd., Hmptn. 266 329 BZ94
Cambridge Rd., Har. 215 303 CA57
Cambridge Rd., Houns. 258 321 BY84
Cambridge Rd., Ilf. 235 308 ES60
Cambridge Rd., Kings.T. 269 322 CN96
Cambridge Rd., Mitch. 272 324 DH97
Cambridge Rd., N.Mal. 269 322 CR98
Cambridge Rd., Rich. 154 314 CN80
Cambridge Rd., Sid. 277 326 ES91
Cambridge Rd., Sthl. 242 313 BZ74
Cambridge Rd., Tedd. 267 329 CF91
Cambridge Rd., Twick. 169 322 CK86
Cambridge Rd., Uxb. 240 312 BK65
Cambridge Rd., W.Mol. 266 329 BZ98
Cambridge Rd. Est., Kings.T. 269 322 CN96
Cambridge Rd. N. W4 144 314 CP78
Cambridge Rd. S. W4 144 314 CP78
Cambridge Row SE18 253 318 EP78
Cambridge Sq. W2 42/3 315 DE72
Cambridge St. SW1 80/1 316 DH77
Cambridge Ter. N13 209 300 DN50
Cambridge Ter. NW1 32/3 316 DH69
Cambridge Ter. Ms. NW1 32/3 316 DH69
Cambus Clo., Hayes 242 313 BY71
Cambus Rd. E16 244 318 EG71
Camdale Rd. SE18 253 318 ET80
Camden Ave., Felt. 258 321 BW89
Camden Ave., Hayes 242 313 BX73
Camden Clo., Chis. 277 326 EQ95
Camden Est. SE15 163 316 DT81
Camden Gdns. NW1 114 306 DH66
Camden Gdns., Sutt. 284 331 DB106
Camden Gdns., Th.Hth. 273 324 DP97
Camden Gro., Chis. 277 326 EP93
Camden High St. NW1 20/1 316 DH67
Camden Hill Rd. SE19 273 324 DS93
Camden La. N7 115 306 DK65
Camden Lock Pl. NW1 114 306 DH66
Camden Ms. NW1 114 306 DJ66
Camden Pk. Rd. NW1 115 306 DK65
Camden Pk. Rd., Chis. 276 326 EM94
Camden Pas. N1 24/5 316 DP67
Camden Rd. E11 224 308 EH58
Camden Rd. E17 222 307 DZ58
Camden Rd. N7 115 306 DL63
Camden Rd. NW1 114 306 DJ66
Camden Rd., Bex. 262 327 EY88
Camden Rd., Cars. 285 331 DF105
Camden Rd., Sutt. 284 331 DA106
Camden Row SE3 167 317 EE82
Camden Sq. NW1 115 306 DK65
Camden Sq. SE15 163 316 DT81
Camden St. NW1 114 306 DJ66
Camden Ter. NW1 115 306 DK65
Camden Wk. N1 24/5 316 DP67
Camden Way, Chis. 276 326 EM94
Camden Way, Th.Hth. 273 324 DP97
Camdenhurst St. E14 139 317 DY72
Camel Gro., Kings.T. 268 322 CK92
Camel Rd. E16 244 318 EK74
Camelford Wk. W11 137 315 CY72
Camellia Clo., Rom. 228 311 FL53
Camellia Ct., Wdf.Grn. 223 307 EE52
Camellia Pl., Twick. 259 321 CB87
Camellia St. SW8 161 316 DL80
Camelot Clo. SE28 253 318 ER75
Camelot Clo. SW19 271 323 DA91
Camelot St. SE15 164 317 DV80
Camera Pl. SW10 159 315 DD79
Cameron Clo. N18 210 301 DV49
Cameron Clo. N20 207 299 DE47
Cameron Clo., Bex. 263 327 FD90
Cameron Pl. E1 138 317 DV72
Cameron Rd. SE6 197 325 DZ89
Cameron Rd., Brom. 276 326 EG98
Cameron Rd., Croy. 286 332 DP100
Cameron Rd., Ilf. 235 308 ES60
Cameron Sq., Mitch. 271 323 DE95
Camerton Clo. E8 117 306 DT65
Camgate Est., Stai. 256 320 BM86
Camilla Clo., Sun. 265 328 BS93
Camilla Rd. SE16 148 317 DV77
Camille Clo. SE25 274 325 DU97
Camlan Rd., Brom. 275 325 EF91
Camlet St. E2 39 316 DT70
Camley St. NW1 115 306 DK66
Camm Gdns., Kings.T. 268 322 CM96
Camomile Ave., Mitch. 271 323 DF95
Camomile St. EC3 50/1 316 DS72
Camp Rd. SW19 270 323 CV92
Camp Vw. SW19 270 323 CV92
Campana Rd. SW6 158 315 DA81
Campbell Ave., Ilf. 225 308 EP56
Campbell Clo. SE18 253 318 EN81
Campbell Clo. SW16 272 324 DK92
Campbell Clo.
(Havering-atte-Bower), Rom. 227 309 FE51
Campbell Clo., Ruis. 214 303 BU58
Campbell Clo., Twick. 259 321 CD89
Campbell Ct. N17 221 306 DT53
Campbell Cft., Edg. 205 298 CN50
Campbell Gordon Way NW2 110 305 CV63
Campbell Rd. E3 130 317 EA69
Campbell Rd. E6 244 318 EL67
Campbell Rd. E15 121 307 EF63
Campbell Rd. E17 222 307 DZ56
Campbell Rd. N17 221 306 DT53
Campbell Rd. W7 243 313 CE73
Campbell Rd., Croy. 286 332 DP101
Campbell Rd., E.Mol. 267 329 CF97
Campbell Rd., Twick. 259 321 CD88
Campbell Wk. N1 22/3 316 DL67
Campdale Rd. N7 99 306 DK62
Campden Cres., Dag. 236 309 EV63
Campden Cres., Wem. 90 304 CH62
Campden Gro. W8 64 315 DA75
Campden Hill W8 64 315 DA75
Campden Hill Gdns. W8 52 315 DA74
Campden Hill Gate W8 64 315 DA75
Campden Hill Pl. W11 137 315 CZ74
Campden Hill Rd. W8 52 315 DA74
Campden Hill Sq. W8 137 315 CZ74
Campden Ho. Clo. W8 64 315 DA75
Campden Rd., S.Croy. 287 332 DS106
Campden Rd., Uxb. 230 312 BM62
Campden St. W8 52 315 DA74
Campen Clo. SW19 189 323 CY89
Camperdown St. E1 51 316 DT72
Campfield Rd. SE9 260 326 EK87
Campion Clo. E6 244 318 EM73
Campion Clo., Croy. 287 332 DS105
Campion Clo., Har. 216 304 CM58
Campion Clo. (Denham), Uxb. 230 312 BG62
Campion Clo. (Hillingdon), Uxb. 248 312 BM71
Campion Pl. SE28 246 319 EV74
Campion Rd. SW15 172 323 CW84
Campion Rd., Islw. 251 321 CF81
Campion Ter. NW2 111 305 CX63
Camplin Rd., Har. 216 304 CL57
Camplin St. SE14 165 317 DX80
Campsbourne, The N8 220 306 DL56
Campsbourne Rd. N8 220 306 DL55
Campsey Gdns., Dag. 236 309 EV66
Campsey Rd., Dag. 236 309 EV66
Campsfield Rd. N8 220 306 DL55
Campshill Pl. SE13 182 325 EC85
Campshill Rd. SE13 182 325 EC85
Campus Rd. E17 222 307 DZ58
Camrose Ave., Edg. 216 304 CM54
Camrose Ave., Erith 255 319 FB79
Camrose Ave., Felt. 266 329 BV91
Camrose Clo., Croy. 288 333 DY101
Camrose Clo., Mord. 271 323 DA98
Camrose St. SE2 254 319 EU78
Canada Ave. N18 221 306 DQ51
Canada Cres. W3 124 314 CQ70
Canada Est. SE16 148 317 DW76
Canada Gdns. SE13 182 325 EC85
Canada Rd. W3 134 314 CQ71
Canada Sq. E14 140 317 EB74
Canada St. SE16 149 317 DX75
Canada Way W12 136 315 CV73
Canada Yd. S. SE16 149 317 DX76
Canadian Ave. SE6 198 325 EB88
Canal App. SE8 149 317 DY78
Canal Clo. E1 129 317 DY70
Canal Clo. W10 127 315 CX70
Canal Gro. SE15 164 317 DU79
Canal Head SE15 164 317 DU81
Canal Path E2 27 316 DT67
Canal Rd. E3 129 317 DY70
Canal St. SE5 163 316 DR79
Canal Wk. N1 26 316 DR67
Canal Wk. SE26 274 325 DW92
Canal Wk., Croy. 287 332 DS100
Canal Way NW1 20 316 DG67
Canal Way NW10 125 314 CR68
Canal Way W10 127 315 CX70
Canal Way, Wem. 123 314 CM67
Canal Way Wk. W10 127 315 CY70
Canary Wf. E14 140 317 EA74
Canberra Clo. NW4 218 305 CU55
Canberra Clo., Dag. 237 309 FD66
Canberra Clo., Horn. 238 310 FJ63
Canberra Cres., Dag. 237 309 FD66
Canberra Dr., Nthlt. 242 313 BW69
Canberra Rd. E6 244 318 EM67
Canberra Rd. SE7 252 318 EJ79
Canberra Rd. W13 132 314 CG74
Canberra Rd., Bexh. 254 319 EX79
Canberra Rd., Houns. 257 320 BN83
Canbury Ave., Kings.T. 268 322 CM95
Canbury Ms. SE26 196 325 DU90
Canbury Pk. Rd., Kings.T. 268 322 CL95
Canbury Pas., Kings.T. 268 322 CK95
Canbury Path, Orp. 278 327 EU97
Cancell Rd. SW9 162 316 DN81
Candahar Rd. SW11 159 315 DE82
Candler St. N15 221 306 DR58
Candover Clo., West Dr. 256 320 BK80
Candover Rd., Horn. 238 310 FH60
Candover St. W1 45 316 DJ71
Candy St. E3 129 317 DZ67
Cane Clo., Wall. 294 332 DL108
Cane Hill, Rom. 228 310 FK54
Caney Ms. NW2 95 305 CX61
Canfield Dr., Ruis. 232 313 BV64
Canfield Gdns. NW6 112 305 DB66
Canfield Pl. NW6 112 305 DC65
Canfield Rd., Rain. 247 319 FF67
Canfield Rd., Wdf.Grn. 224 308 EL52
Canford Ave., Nthlt. 242 313 BY67
Canford Clo., Enf. 202 300 DN40
Canford Gdns., N.Mal. 283 330 CS100
Canford Pl., Tedd. 268 322 CH93
Canford Rd. SW11 176 324 DG85
Canham Rd. SE25 273 324 DS97
Canham Rd. W3 145 314 CS75
Canmore Gdns. SW16 272 324 DJ94
Cann Hall Rd. E11 121 307 EE63
Canning Cres. N22 220 306 DM53
Canning Cross SE5 163 316 DS82
Canning Pas. W8 65 315 DC75
Canning Pl. W8 65 315 DC76
Canning Pl. Ms. W8 65 315 DC76
Canning Rd. E15 131 317 EE68
Canning Rd. E17 222 307 DY56
Canning Rd. N5 100 306 DP62
Canning Rd., Croy. 287 332 DT103
Canning Rd., Har. 215 303 CE55
Cannington Rd., Dag. 236 309 EW65
Cannizaro Rd. SW19 270 323 CW92
Cannon Clo. SW20 270 323 CW97
Cannon Clo., Hmptn. 267 329 CB93
Cannon Dr. E14 140 317 EA73
Cannon Hill N14 208 300 DK48
Cannon Hill NW6 112 305 DA64
Cannon Hill La. SW20 270 323 CY97
Cannon La. NW3 97 305 DD62
Cannon La., Pnr. 214 303 BY57
Cannon Pl. NW3 96 305 DC62
Cannon Pl. SE7 252 318 EL78
Cannon Rd. N14 208 300 DL48
Cannon Rd., Bexh. 254 319 EY81
Cannon St. EC4 49 316 DQ72
Cannon St. Rd. E1 138 317 DV72
Cannon Way, W.Mol. 267 329 CA98
Cannonbury Ave., Pnr. 214 303 BX58
Canon Ave., Rom. 226 309 EW57
Canon Beck Rd. SE16 148 317 DW75
Canon Mohan Clo. N14 208 300 DH44
Canon Rd., Brom. 276 326 EJ97
Canon Row SW1 70/1 316 DL75
Canon St. N1 25 316 DQ67
Canon Trd. Est., The, Wem. 108 304 CP63
Canonbie Rd. SE23 196 325 DW87
Canonbury Cres. N1 116 306 DQ66
Canonbury Gro. N1 116 306 DQ66
Canonbury La. N1 116 306 DP66
Canonbury Pk. N. N1 116 306 DQ65
Canonbury Pk. S. N1 116 306 DQ65
Canonbury Pl. N1 116 306 DP65
Canonbury Rd. N1 116 306 DP65
Canonbury Rd., Enf. 202 300 DS39
Canonbury Sq. N1 116 306 DP66
Canonbury St. N1 116 306 DQ66
Canonbury Vil. N1 116 306 DP66
Canonbury Yd. N1 25 316 DQ67
Canons Clo. N2 97 305 DD59
Canons Clo., Edg. 216 304 CM51
Canons Cor., Edg. 204 298 CL49
Canons Dr., Edg. 216 304 CL51
Canons Wk., Croy. 288 333 DX104
Canonsleigh Rd., Dag. 236 309 EV66
Canopus Way, Stai. 264 320 BL87
Canrobert St. E2 128 317 DV69
Cantelowes Rd. NW1 115 306 DK65
Canterbury Ave., Ilf. 234 308 EL59
Canterbury Ave., Sid. 262 327 EW89
Canterbury Ave., Upmin. 239 311 FT60
Canterbury Clo. E6 244 318 EM72
Canterbury Clo., Beck. 275 325 EB95
Canterbury Clo., Grnf. 243 313 CB72
Canterbury Clo., Nthwd. 213 302 BT51
Canterbury Cres. SW9 178 324 DN83
Canterbury Gro. SE27 273 324 DN91
Canterbury Pl. SE17 84/5 316 DP77
Canterbury Rd. E10 104 307 EC59
Canterbury Rd. NW6 127 315 CZ68
Canterbury Rd., Croy. 286 332 DN101
Canterbury Rd., Felt. 258 321 BY90
Canterbury Rd., Har. 215 303 CB57
Canterbury Rd., Mord. 284 331 DB101
Canterbury Ter. NW6 16 315 DA68
Cantley Gdns. SE19 273 324 DT95
Cantley Gdns., Ilf. 225 308 EQ58
Cantley Rd. W7 142 314 CG76
Canton St. E14 140 317 EA72
Cantrell Rd. E3 129 317 DZ70
Cantwell Rd. SE18 253 318 EP80
Canute Gdns. SE16 149 317 DX77
Canvey St. SE1 60/1 316 DP74
Cape Clo., Bark. 235 308 EQ65
Cape Rd. N17 222 307 DU55
Cape Yd. E1 138 317 DU74
Capel Ave., Wall. 286 332 DM106
Capel Clo. N20 207 299 DC48
Capel Clo., Brom. 290 334 EM102
Capel Ct. EC2 50 316 DR72
Capel Ct. SE20 274 325 DW95
Capel Gdns., Ilf. 235 308 ET63
Capel Gdns., Pnr. 214 303 BZ56
Capel Pt. E7 234 308 EH63
Capel Rd. E7 234 308 EH63
Capel Rd. E12 234 308 EK63
Capel Rd., Barn. 207 299 DE44
Capel Rd., Enf. 203 301 DV36
Capella Rd., Nthwd. 213 302 BT49
Capener's Clo. SW1 68 316 DG75
Capern Rd. SW18 190 323 DC88
Capital Business Cen., Wem. 123 314 CK67
Capital Interchange Way, Brent. 144 314 CN78
Capital Pl., Croy. 286 332 DM106
Capitol Ind. Est. NW9 217 304 CQ55
Capitol Way NW9 217 304 CQ55
Capland St. NW8 30 315 DD70
Caple Rd. NW10 125 314 CT68
Capper St. WC1 33 316 DJ70
Caprea Clo., Hayes 242 313 BX71
Capri Rd., Croy. 287 332 DT102
Capstan Clo., Rom. 226 309 EV58
Capstan Ride, Enf. 202 300 DN40
Capstan Rd. SE8 149 317 DZ77
Capstan Sq. E14 150 317 EC75
Capstan Way SE16 139 317 DY74
Capstone Rd., Brom. 275 325 EF91
Capthorne Ave., Har. 232 313 BY60
Capuchin Clo., Stan. 216 304 CH51
Capulet Ms. E16 141 317 EE72
Capworth St. E10 104 307 EA60
Caradoc Clo. W2 40 315 DA72
Caradoc St. SE10 151 317 EE78
Caradon Clo. E11 105 307 EE61
Caradon Way N15 221 306 DR56
Caravel Clo. E14 150 317 EA76
Caravel Ms. SE8 166 317 EA79
Caravelle Gdns., Nthlt. 242 313 BX69
Caraway Clo. E13 244 318 EH71
Caraway Pl., Wall. 285 332 DH104
Carberry Rd. SE19 273 324 DS93
Carbery Ave. W3 143 314 CM75
Carbis Clo. E4 211 301 ED46
Carbis Rd. E14 139 317 DZ72
Carbuncle Pas. Way N17 222 307 DU54
Carburton St. W1 44/5 316 DH71
Carbury Clo., Horn. 238 310 FJ65
Cardale St. E14 150 317 EC76
Carden Rd. SE15 180 325 DV83
Cardiff Rd. W7 142 314 CG76
Cardiff Rd., Enf. 203 301 DV42
Cardiff St. SE18 253 318 ES80
Cardigan Gdns., Ilf. 236 309 EU61
Cardigan Rd. E3 129 317 DZ68
Cardigan Rd. SW13 156 315 CU82
Cardigan Rd. SW19 271 323 DC93
Cardigan Rd., Rich. 169 322 CL86
Cardigan St. SE11 84 316 DN78
Cardigan Wk. N1 116 306 DQ66
Cardinal Ave., Kings.T. 268 322 CL92
Cardinal Ave., Mord. 284 331 CY100
Cardinal Bourne St. SE1 74 316 DR76
Cardinal Clo., Chis. 277 326 ER95
Cardinal Clo., Mord. 284 331 CY100
Cardinal Clo., Wor.Pk. 283 331 CU105
Cardinal Cres., N.Mal. 269 322 CQ96
Cardinal Dr., Ilf. 225 308 EQ51
Cardinal Pl. SW15 173 323 CX84
Cardinal Rd., Felt. 258 321 BV88
Cardinal Rd., Ruis. 232 313 BX60
Cardinal Way, Har. 215 303 CE55
Cardinals Wk., Hmptn. 267 329 CC94
Cardinals Wk., Sun. 265 328 BS93
Cardinals Way N19 99 306 DK60
Cardine Ms. SE15 164 317 DV80
Cardington Sq., Houns. 258 321 BX84
Cardington St. NW1 33 316 DJ69
Cardozo Rd. N7 115 306 DL64
Cardrew Ave. N12 207 299 DD50
Cardrew Clo. N12 207 299 DD50
Cardross St. W6 146 315 CV76
Cardwell Rd. N7 115 306 DL63
Cardwell Rd. SE18 252 318 EM77
Carew Clo. N7 99 306 DM61
Carew Rd. N17 222 307 DU54
Carew Rd. W13 142 314 CJ75
Carew Rd., Ashf. 265 328 BQ93
Carew Rd., Mitch. 272 324 DG96
Carew Rd., Nthwd. 213 302 BS51
Carew Rd., Th.Hth. 273 324 DP97
Carew Rd., Wall. 294 332 DJ107
Carew St. SE5 162 316 DQ82
Carey Ct., Bexh. 263 327 FB85
Carey Gdns. SW8 160 316 DJ81
Carey La. EC2 49 316 DQ72
Carey Pl. SW1 82 316 DK77
Carey Rd., Dag. 236 309 EY63
Carey St. WC2 47 316 DM72
Carey Way, Wem. 108 304 CQ63
Carfax Pl. SW4 177 324 DK84
Carfax Rd., Hayes 249 320 BT78
Carfax Rd., Horn. 237 309 FF63
Carfree Clo. N1 116 306 DN66
Cargill Rd. SW18 190 323 DB88
Cargreen Pl. SE25 273 324 DT98
Cargreen Rd. SE25 273 324 DT98
Carholme Rd. SE23 197 325 DZ88
Carisbrook Clo., Stan. 216 304 CK54
Carisbrooke Ave., Bex. 262 327 EX88
Carisbrooke Clo., Enf. 202 300 DT39
Carisbrooke Clo., Horn. 239 311 FN60
Carisbrooke Gdns. SE15 163 316 DT80
Carisbrooke Rd. E17 222 307 DY56
Carisbrooke Rd., Brom. 276 326 EJ98
Carisbrooke Rd., Mitch. 272 324 DK98
Carker's La. NW5 114 306 DH64
Carleton Ave., Wall. 294 332 DK108
Carleton Rd. N7 115 306 DK64
Carleton Vil. NW5 114 306 DJ64
Carlile Clo. E3 129 317 DZ68
Carlingford Gdns., Mitch. 271 323 DF94
Carlingford Rd. N15 221 306 DP55
Carlingford Rd. NW3 113 305 DD63
Carlingford Rd., Mord. 284 331 CX100
Carlisle Ave. EC3 51 316 DT72
Carlisle Ave. W3 135 314 CS72
Carlisle Clo., Kings.T. 269 322 CN95
Carlisle Gdns., Har. 91 304 CK59
Carlisle Gdns., Ilf. 224 308 EL58
Carlisle La. SE1 71 316 DM76
Carlisle Ms. NW8 42 315 DD71
Carlisle Pl. N11 208 300 DH49
Carlisle Pl. SW1 69 316 DJ76
Carlisle Rd. E10 104 307 EA60
Carlisle Rd. N4 100 306 DN59
Carlisle Rd. NW6 127 315 CY67
Carlisle Rd. NW9 217 304 CQ55
Carlisle Rd., Hmptn. 267 329 CB94
Carlisle Rd., Rom. 227 309 FF57
Carlisle Rd., Sutt. 284 331 CZ106
Carlisle St. W1 46 316 DK72
Carlisle Wk. E8 117 306 DT65
Carlisle Way SW17 272 324 DG92
Carlos Pl. W1 56 316 DG73
Carlow St. NW1 21 316 DJ68
Carlton Ave. N14 208 300 DK43
Carlton Ave., Felt. 258 321 BW86
Carlton Ave., Har. 216 304 CH57
Carlton Ave., Hayes 249 320 BS77
Carlton Ave., S.Croy. 295 332 DS108
Carlton Ave. E., Wem. 91 304 CK61
Carlton Ave. W., Wem. 90 304 CH61
Carlton Clo. NW3 96 305 DA61
Carlton Clo., Edg. 205 298 CN50
Carlton Clo., Upmin. 239 311 FP61
Carlton Ct. SW9 162 316 DP81
Carlton Ct., Ilf. 225 308 ER55
Carlton Ct., Uxb. 248 312 BK71
Carlton Cres., Sutt. 284 331 CY105
Carlton Dr. SW15 173 323 CX85
Carlton Dr., Ilf. 225 308 ER55
Carlton Gdns. SW1 58 316 DK74
Carlton Gdns. W5 132 314 CJ72
Carlton Gro. SE15 164 317 DV81
Carlton Hill NW8 16/7 315 DB68
Carlton Ho. Ter. SW1 58 316 DK74
Carlton Par., Orp. 291 335 EV101
Carlton Pk. Ave. SW20 270 323 CX96
Carlton Pl., Felt. 265 320 BT87
Carlton Pl., Nthwd. 213 302 BP50
Carlton Rd. E11 105 307 EF60
Carlton Rd. E12 234 308 EK63
Carlton Rd. E17 222 307 DY53
Carlton Rd. N4 100 306 DN59
Carlton Rd. N11 208 300 DG50
Carlton Rd. SW14 170 322 CQ83
Carlton Rd. W4 145 314 CR75
Carlton Rd. W5 132 314 CJ73
Carlton Rd., Erith 255 319 FB79
Carlton Rd., N.Mal. 269 322 CS96
Carlton Rd., Rom. 227 309 FF57
Carlton Rd., Sid. 277 326 ET92
Carlton Rd., S.Croy. 295 332 DR107
Carlton Rd., Sun. 265 328 BT94
Carlton Rd., Well. 262 327 EV83
Carlton Sq. E1 129 317 DX70
Carlton St. SW1 58 316 DK73
Carlton Ter. E11 224 308 EH57
Carlton Ter. N18 209 300 DR48
Carlton Ter. SE26 196 325 DW90
Carlton Twr. Pl. SW1 67 315 DF76
Carlton Vale NW6 16 315 DA68
Carlton Vil. SW15 172 323 CW85
Carlwell St. SW17 271 323 DE92
Carlyle Ave., Brom. 276 326 EK97
Carlyle Ave., Sthl. 242 313 BZ73
Carlyle Clo. N2 219 305 DC58
Carlyle Clo. NW10 125 314 CR67
Carlyle Clo., W.Mol. 267 329 CB96
Carlyle Gdns., Sthl. 242 313 BZ73
Carlyle Pl. SW15 173 323 CX84
Carlyle Rd. E12 234 308 EL63
Carlyle Rd. SE28 246 319 EV73
Carlyle Rd. W5 142 314 CJ77
Carlyle Rd., Croy. 287 333 DU103
Carlyle Sq. SW3 78 315 DD78
Carlyon Ave., Har. 232 313 BZ63
Carlyon Clo., Wem. 123 314 CL67
Carlyon Rd., Hayes 242 313 BW71
Carlyon Rd., Wem. 123 314 CL68
Carmalt Gdns. SW15 172 323 CW84
Carmarthen Gdn. NW9 217 304 CS58
Carmel Ct. W8 64/5 315 DB75
Carmel Ct., Wem. 92 304 CP61
Carmelite Clo., Har. 215 303 CC53
Carmelite Rd., Har. 215 303 CC53
Carmelite St. EC4 60 316 DN73
Carmelite Wk., Har. 215 303 CC53
Carmelite Way, Har. 215 303 CC54
Carmen St. E14 140 317 EB72
Carmichael Clo. SW11 175 323 DD83
Carmichael Clo., Ruis. 232 313 BU63
Carmichael Ms. SW18 175 323 DD86
Carmichael Rd. SE25 274 325 DU98
Carminia Rd. SW17 192 324 DH89
Carnaby St. W1 45 316 DJ72
Carnac St. SE27 273 324 DR91
Carnanton Rd. E17 223 307 ED53
Carnarvon Ave., Enf. 202 300 DT41
Carnarvon Dr., Hayes 249 320 BQ77
Carnarvon Rd. E10 223 307 EC58
Carnarvon Rd. E15 121 307 EF65
Carnarvon Rd. E18 223 307 EF54
Carnation St. SE2 254 319 EV78
Carnbrook Rd. SE3 260 326 EK83
Carnecke Gdns. SE9 260 326 EL85
Carnegie Clo., Surb. 282 330 CM103
Carnegie Pl. SW19 189 323 CX90
Carnegie St. N1 23 316 DM67
Carnforth Gdns., Horn. 238 310 FG64
Carnforth Rd. SW16 272 324 DK94
Carnie Lo. SW17 192 324 DH90
Carnoustie Dr. N1 115 306 DM66
Carnwath Rd. SW6 174 323 DA83
Carol St. NW1 21 316 DJ67
Carolina Clo. E15 121 307 EE64
Carolina Rd., Th.Hth. 273 324 DP96
Caroline Clo. N10 220 306 DH54
Caroline Clo. SW16 272 324 DM91
Caroline Clo. W2 52/3 315 DB73
Caroline Clo., Croy. 287 332 DS105
Caroline Clo., Islw. 251 321 CE80
Caroline Clo., West Dr. 248 320 BK75
Caroline Ct., Ashf. 265 328 BP93
Caroline Ct., Stan. 216 304 CG51
Caroline Gdns. SE15 164 317 DV80
Caroline Pl. SW11 160 316 DG82
Caroline Pl. W2 52/3 315 DB73
Caroline Pl., Hayes 257 320 BS80
Caroline Pl. Ms. W2 52/3 315 DB73
Caroline Rd. SW19 270 323 CZ94
Caroline St. E1 139 317 DX72
Caroline Ter. SW1 80 316 DG77
Caroline Wk. W6 157 315 CY79
Carolyn Dr., Orp. 291 335 EU104
Carpenter Gdns. N21 209 300 DP47
Carpenter St. W1 56/7 316 DH73
Carpenters Ct., Twick. 259 321 CE89
Carpenters Pl. SW4 177 324 DK84
Carpenters Rd. E15 120 307 EA65
Carpenters Rd., Enf. 203 301 DW36
Carr Gro. SE18 252 318 EL77
Carr Rd. E17 222 307 DZ54
Carr Rd., Nthlt. 233 313 CA65
Carr St. E14 139 317 DY71
Carrara Wk. SW9 178 324 DN84
Carriage Dr. E. SW11 160 316 DG80
Carriage Dr. N. SW11 159 315 DF80
Carriage Dr. S. SW11 159 315 DF81
Carriage Dr. W. SW11 159 315 DF80
Carrick Clo., Islw. 168 322 CG83
Carrick Dr., Ilf. 225 308 EQ53
Carrick Gdns. N17 221 306 DS52
Carrick Ms. SE8 166 317 EA79
Carrill Way, Belv. 254 319 EX77
Carrington Ave., Borwd. 205 298 CP43
Carrington Ave., Houns. 259 321 CB85
Carrington Clo., Barn. 206 299 CU43
Carrington Clo., Borwd. 205 298 CQ43
Carrington Clo., Croy. 288 333 DY101
Carrington Clo., Kings.T. 269 322 CQ92
Carrington Gdns. E7 234 308 EH63
Carrington Rd., Rich. 170 322 CN84
Carrington Sq., Har. 215 303 CC52
Carrington St. W1 56/7 316 DH74
Carrol Clo. NW5 114 306 DH63
Carroll Clo. E15 121 307 EF64
Carron Clo. E14 140 317 EB72
Carronade Pl. SE28 253 318 EQ76
Carroun Rd. SW8 161 316 DM80
Carrow Rd., Dag. 236 309 EV66
Carroway La., Grnf. 243 313 CD69
Carrs La. N21 209 300 DQ43
Carshalton Gro., Sutt. 285 331 DD105
Carshalton Pk. Rd., Cars. 293 331 DF107
Carshalton Pl., Cars. 285 332 DG105
Carshalton Rd., Bans. 293 331 DF114
Carshalton Rd., Cars. 285 331 DE106
Carshalton Rd., Mitch. 272 324 DG98
Carshalton Rd., Sutt. 285 331 DC106
Carslake Rd. SW15 172 323 CW86
Carson Rd. E16 244 318 EG70
Carson Rd. SE21 194 324 DQ89
Carstairs Rd. SE6 198 325 EC90
Carston Clo. SE12 183 325 EF85
Carswell Clo., Ilf. 224 308 EK56
Carswell Rd. SE6 198 325 EC87
Cart La. E4 211 301 ED45
Carter Clo., Rom. 227 309 FB52
Carter Clo., Wall. 294 332 DK108
Carter Ct. EC4 48/9 316 DP72
Carter Dr., Rom. 227 309 FB52
Carter La. EC4 48/9 316 DP72
Carter Pl. SE17 85 316 DQ78
Carter Rd. E13 244 318 EH67
Carter Rd. SW19 271 323 DD93
Carter St. SE17 162 316 DQ79
Carteret St. SW1 70 316 DK75
Carteret Way SE8 149 317 DY77
Carterhatch La., Enf. 202 300 DT38
Carterhatch Rd., Enf. 203 301 DW39
Carters Clo., Wor.Pk. 284 331 CX103
Carters Hill Clo. SE9 260 326 EJ88
Carters La. SE23 197 325 DY89
Carters Yd. SW18 174 323 DA85
Carthew Rd. W6 146 315 CV76
Carthew Vil. W6 146 315 CV76
Carthusian St. EC1 49 316 DQ71
Cartier Circle E14 140 317 EB74
Carting La. WC2 58/9 316 DL73
Cartmel Clo. N17 222 307 DV52
Cartmel Rd., Bexh. 255 319 FA81
Cartmell Gdns., Mord. 285 331 DC99
Carton St. W1 43 315 DF72
Cartwright Gdns. WC1 34/5 316 DL69
Cartwright Rd., Dag. 236 309 EY66
Cartwright St. E1 63 316 DT73
Cartwright Way SW13 156 315 CV80
Carver Rd. SE24 178 324 DQ86

Carville Cres., Brent. 143 314 CL77
Cary Rd. E11 121 307 EE63
Carysfort Rd. N8 220 306 DK57
Carysfort Rd. N16 101 306 DR62
Cascade Ave. N10 220 306 DJ56
Cascade Clo., Orp. 278 327 EW97
Casella Rd. SE14 165 317 DX80
Casewick Rd. SE27 273 324 DN92
Casimir Rd. E5 102 307 DV62
Casino Ave. SE24 179 324 DR85
Caspian St. SE5 163 316 DR80
Caspian Wk. E16 244 318 EK72
Caspian Wf. E3 140 317 EB71
Cassandra Clo., Nthlt. 233 313 CD63
Casselden Rd. NW10 109 304 CR66
Cassidy Rd. SW6 158 315 DA80
Cassilda Rd. SE2 254 319 EU77
Cassilis Rd., Twick. 168 322 CH85
Cassiobury Ave., Felt. 257 320 BT86
Cassiobury Rd. E17 222 307 DX57
Cassland Rd. E9 119 307 DX66
Cassland Rd., Th.Hth. 273 324 DR98
Casslee Rd. SE6 197 325 DZ87
Cassocks Sq., Shep. 281 328 BR101
Casson St. E1 138 317 DU71
Casstine Clo., Swan. 279 327 FF94
Castalia Sq. E14 150 317 EC75
Castalia St. E14 150 317 EC75
Castellain Rd. W9 28/9 315 DB70
Castellan Ave., Rom. 228 310 FH55
Castellane Clo., Stan. 215 303 CF52
Castello Ave. SW15 172 323 CW85
Castelnau SW13 156 315 CU81
Castelnau Pl. SW13 156 315 CV79
Castelnau Row SW13 156 315 CV79
Casterbridge NW6 16/7 315 DB67
Casterbridge Rd. SE3 260 326 EG83
Casterton St. E8 118 307 DV65
Castile Rd. SE18 253 318 EN77
Castillon Rd. SE6 199 325 EE89
Castlands Rd. SE6 197 325 DZ89
Castle Ave. E4 211 301 ED50
Castle Ave., Rain. 237 309 FE66
Castle Ave., West Dr. 248 312 BL73
Castle Baynard St. EC4 60/1 316 DP73
Castle Clo. E9 119 307 DY64
Castle Clo. SW19 189 323 CX90
Castle Clo., Brom. 275 325 EE97
Castle Clo., Sun. 265 328 BS94
Castle Ct. EC3 50 316 DR72
Castle Ct. SE26 274 325 DY91
Castle Dr., Ilf. 224 308 EL58
Castle La. SW1 69 316 DJ76
Castle Ms. N12 207 299 DC50
Castle Ms. NW1 114 306 DH65
Castle Pl. NW1 114 306 DH65
Castle Pl. W4 145 314 CS77
Castle Pt. E6 244 318 EJ68
Castle Rd. N12 207 299 DC50
Castle Rd. NW1 114 306 DH65
Castle Rd., Dag. 246 319 EV67
Castle Rd., Enf. 203 301 DY39
Castle Rd., Islw. 251 321 CF82
Castle Rd., Nthlt. 233 313 CB65
Castle Rd., Sthl. 250 321 BZ76
Castle St. E6 244 318 EJ68
Castle St., Kings.T. 268 322 CL96
Castle Wk., Sun. 266 329 BW97
Castle Way SW19 189 323 CX90
Castle Way, Felt. 266 329 BW91
Castle Yd. N6 98 306 DG59
Castle Yd. SE1 60/1 316 DP74
Castle Yd., Rich. 169 322 CK85
Castlebar Hill W5 132 314 CH71
Castlebar Ms. W5 132 314 CJ71
Castlebar Pk. W5 122 314 CH70
Castlebar Rd. W5 132 314 CJ72
Castlecombe Dr. SW19 189 323 CX87
Castlecombe Rd. SE9 276 326 EL91
Castledine Rd. SE20 274 325 DV94
Castleford Ave. SE9 261 326 EP88
Castlegate, Rich. 169 322 CM83
Castlehaven Rd. NW1 114 306 DH66
Castleleigh Ct., Enf. 209 300 DR43
Castlemaine Ave., S.Croy. 287 332 DT106
Castlemaine Twr. SW11 159 315 DF82
Castlereagh St. W1 42/3 315 DE72
Castleton Ave., Bexh. 255 319 FD81
Castleton Ave., Wem. 107 304 CL63
Castleton Clo., Croy. 288 333 DY100
Castleton Gdns., Wem. 91 304 CL62
Castleton Rd. E17 223 307 ED54
Castleton Rd. SE9 276 326 EK91
Castleton Rd., Ilf. 236 309 EU60
Castleton Rd., Mitch. 272 324 DK98
Castleton Rd., Ruis. 232 313 BX60
Castletown Rd. W14 147 315 CY78
Castleview Gdns., Ilf. 224 308 EL58
Castlewood Dr. SE9 252 318 EM82
Castlewood Rd. N15 222 307 DU58
Castlewood Rd. N16 102 307 DU59
Castor La. E14 140 317 EB73
Cat Hill, Barn. 207 299 DF43
Caterham Ave., Ilf. 224 308 EM54
Caterham Rd. SE13 182 325 EC83
Catesby St. SE17 86 316 DR77
Catford Bdy. SE6 198 325 EB87
Catford Hill SE6 197 325 DZ88
Catford Ms. SE6 198 325 EB87
Catford Rd. SE6 198 325 EA87
Cathall Rd. E11 105 307 ED61
Cathay St. SE16 148 317 DV75
Cathay Wk., Nthlt. 243 313 CA68
Cathcart Dr., Orp. 291 334 ES103
Cathcart Hill N19 98 306 DJ62
Cathcart Rd. SW10 158 315 DB79
Cathcart St. NW5 114 306 DH65
Cathedral Pl. EC4 49 316 DQ72
Cathedral St. SE1 62 316 DR74
Catherall Rd. N5 100 306 DQ62
Catherine Clo. SE16 139 317 DX74
Catherine Ct. N14 208 300 DJ43
Catherine Dr., Rich. 169 322 CL84
Catherine Dr., Sun. 265 328 BT93
Catherine Gdns., Houns. 259 321 CD84
Catherine Griffiths Ct. EC1 36 316 DN70
Catherine Gro. SE10 166 317 EB81
Catherine Pl. SW1 69 316 DJ76
Catherine Rd., Enf. 203 301 DY36
Catherine Rd., Rom. 228 310 FH57
Catherine Rd., Surb. 282 330 CK99
Catherine St. WC2 59 316 DM73
Catherine Wheel All. E1 50/1 316 DS71
Catherine Wheel Rd., Brent. 153 314 CK80
Catherine Wheel Yd. SW1 57 316 DJ74
Catherine's Clo., West Dr. 248 320 BK76
Cathles Rd. SW12 176 324 DH86
Cathnor Hill Ct. W12 146 315 CV76
Cathnor Rd. W12 146 315 CV75
Catisfield Rd., Enf. 203 301 DY37
Catlin Cres., Shep. 281 328 BR99
Catlin St. SE16 148 317 DU78
Catling Clo. SE23 196 325 DW90
Catlins La., Pnr. 214 303 BV55
Cato Rd. SW4 177 324 DK83
Cato St. W1 42/3 315 DE71
Cator La., Beck. 274 325 DZ95
Cator Rd. SE26 274 325 DX93
Cator Rd., Cars. 285 331 DF106
Cator St. SE15 163 316 DT79
Cattistock Rd. SE9 276 326 EL92
Catton St. WC1 47 316 DM71
Caulfield Rd. E6 244 318 EL67
Caulfield Rd. SE15 164 317 DV82
Causeway, The N2 219 305 DE56
Causeway, The SW18 174 323 DB85
Causeway, The SW19 270 323 CW92
Causeway, The, Cars. 285 332 DG104
Causeway, The, Chess. 282 330 CL105
Causeway, The, Felt. 258 321 BU84
Causeway, The, Sutt. 293 331 DC109
Causeway, The, Tedd. 267 329 CF93
Causeyware Rd. N9 210 301 DV45
Causton Rd. N6 98 306 DH59
Causton St. SW1 82 316 DK77
Cautley Ave. SW4 176 324 DJ85
Cavalier Clo., Rom. 226 309 EX56
Cavalier Gdns., Hayes 249 312 BR72
Cavalry Barracks, Houns. 258 321 BX83
Cavalry Cres., Houns. 258 321 BX84
Cavalry Gdns. SW15 173 323 CZ85
Cavaye Pl. SW10 77 315 DC78
Cave Rd. E13 244 318 EH68
Cave Rd., Rich. 268 322 CJ91
Cave St. N1 23 316 DM68
Cavell Cres., Rom. 228 311 FL54
Cavell Dr., Enf. 202 300 DN40
Cavell Rd. N17 221 306 DR52
Cavell St. E1 138 317 DV71
Cavendish Ave. N3 219 305 DA54
Cavendish Ave. NW8 18 315 DD68
Cavendish Ave. W13 132 314 CG71
Cavendish Ave., Erith 255 319 FC80
Cavendish Ave., Har. 233 313 CD63
Cavendish Ave., Horn. 238 310 FH65
Cavendish Ave., N.Mal. 283 331 CU99
Cavendish Ave., Ruis. 232 313 BV64
Cavendish Ave., Sid. 262 327 EU87
Cavendish Ave., Well. 261 326 ET83
Cavendish Ave., Wdf.Grn. 224 308 EH53
Cavendish Clo. N18 210 301 DV50
Cavendish Clo. NW6 111 305 CZ66
Cavendish Clo. NW8 30 315 DD69
Cavendish Clo., Hayes 249 312 BS71
Cavendish Clo., Sun. 265 328 BT93
Cavendish Ct. EC3 50/1 316 DS72
Cavendish Ct., Sun. 265 328 BT93
Cavendish Cres., Horn. 238 310 FH65
Cavendish Dr. E11 105 307 ED60
Cavendish Dr., Edg. 216 304 CM51
Cavendish Gdns., Bark. 235 308 ES64
Cavendish Gdns., Ilf. 235 308 EN60
Cavendish Gdns., Rom. 226 309 EY57
Cavendish Ms. N. W1 44/5 316 DH71
Cavendish Ms. S. W1 44/5 316 DH71
Cavendish Pl. W1 44/5 316 DH72
Cavendish Rd. E4 223 307 EC52
Cavendish Rd. N4 221 306 DN58
Cavendish Rd. N18 210 301 DV50
Cavendish Rd. NW6 111 305 CY66
Cavendish Rd. SW12 176 324 DH86
Cavendish Rd. SW19 271 323 DD94
Cavendish Rd. W4 154 314 CQ81
Cavendish Rd., Croy. 286 332 DP102
Cavendish Rd., N.Mal. 283 330 CS99
Cavendish Rd., Sun. 265 328 BT93
Cavendish Rd., Sutt. 293 331 DC108
Cavendish Sq. W1 44/5 316 DH72
Cavendish St. N1 26 316 DR68
Cavendish Ter., Felt. 258 321 BU89
Cavendish Way, W.Wick. 288 333 EB102
Cavenham Gdns., Horn. 228 310 FJ57
Cavenham Gdns., Ilf. 235 308 ER62
Caverleigh Way, Wor.Pk. 283 331 CU102
Caversham Ave. N13 209 300 DN48
Caversham Ave., Sutt. 284 331 CY103
Caversham Flats SW3 159 315 DF79
Caversham Rd. N15 221 306 DQ56
Caversham Rd. NW5 114 306 DJ65
Caversham Rd., Kings.T. 268 322 CM96
Caversham St. SW3 159 315 DF79
Caverswall St. W12 136 315 CW72
Caveside Clo., Chis. 277 326 EN95
Cawdor Cres. W7 142 314 CG77
Cawnpore St. SE19 273 324 DS92
Caxton Dr., Uxb. 240 312 BK68
Caxton Gro. E3 130 317 EA69
Caxton Ms., Brent. 153 314 CK79
Caxton Rd. N22 220 306 DM54
Caxton Rd. SW19 271 323 DC92
Caxton Rd. W12 137 315 CX74
Caxton Rd., Sthl. 250 321 BX76
Caxton St. SW1 69 316 DJ76
Caxton St. N. E16 141 317 EF73
Caygill Clo., Brom. 275 325 EF98
Cayley Clo., Wall. 294 332 DL108
Cayton Pl. EC1 38 316 DR69
Cayton Rd., Grnf. 243 313 CE68
Cayton St. EC1 38 316 DR69
Cazenove Rd. E17 223 307 EA53
Cazenove Rd. N16 101 306 DT61
Cearns Ho. E6 244 318 EK67
Cecil Ave., Bark. 235 308 ER66
Cecil Ave., Enf. 202 300 DT42
Cecil Ave., Horn. 228 310 FK55
Cecil Ave., Wem. 107 304 CM64
Cecil Clo., Ashf. 265 328 BQ93
Cecil Clo., Chess. 282 330 CK105
Cecil Ct. WC2 58/9 316 DL73
Cecil Pk., Pnr. 214 303 BY56
Cecil Pl., Mitch. 285 331 DF99
Cecil Rd. E11 105 307 EE62
Cecil Rd. E13 244 318 EG67
Cecil Rd. E17 223 307 EA53
Cecil Rd. N10 220 306 DH54
Cecil Rd. N14 208 300 DJ46
Cecil Rd. NW9 217 304 CR55
Cecil Rd. NW10 125 314 CS67
Cecil Rd. SW19 271 323 DB94
Cecil Rd. W3 134 314 CQ71
Cecil Rd., Ashf. 265 328 BQ94
Cecil Rd., Croy. 286 332 DL100
Cecil Rd., Enf. 202 300 DQ42
Cecil Rd., Har. 215 303 CE55
Cecil Rd., Houns. 251 321 CC82
Cecil Rd., Ilf. 235 308 EP63
Cecil Rd., Rom. 236 309 EX59
Cecil Rd., Sutt. 292 331 CZ107
Cecil Way, Brom. 289 334 EG102
Cecile Pk. N8 220 306 DL58
Cecilia Clo. N2 219 305 DC55
Cecilia Rd. E8 117 306 DT64
Cedar Ave., Barn. 207 299 DE45
Cedar Ave., Enf. 203 301 DW40
Cedar Ave., Hayes 242 313 BU72
Cedar Ave., Rom. 226 309 EY57
Cedar Ave., Ruis. 232 313 BW65
Cedar Ave., Sid. 262 327 EU87
Cedar Ave., Twick. 259 321 CB86
Cedar Ave., Upmin. 239 311 FN62
Cedar Ave., West Dr. 248 312 BM74
Cedar Clo. SE21 194 324 DQ88
Cedar Clo. SW15 269 322 CR91
Cedar Clo., Brom. 290 334 EL104
Cedar Clo., Cars. 293 331 DF107
Cedar Clo., E.Mol. 267 329 CE98
Cedar Clo., Rom. 227 309 FC56
Cedar Clo., Stai. 280 328 BJ96
Cedar Clo., Swan. 279 327 FC96
Cedar Copse, Brom. 276 326 EM96
Cedar Ct. E8 117 306 DT66
Cedar Ct. N1 116 306 DQ66
Cedar Ct. SE9 260 326 EL86
Cedar Ct. SW19 189 323 CX90
Cedar Cres., Brom. 290 334 EL104
Cedar Dr. N2 219 305 DE56
Cedar Dr., Pnr. 215 303 CA52
Cedar Gdns., Sutt. 293 331 DC107
Cedar Gdns., Upmin. 239 311 FQ62
Cedar Gro. W5 143 314 CL76
Cedar Gro., Bex. 262 327 EW86
Cedar Gro., Sthl. 243 313 CA71
Cedar Hts., Rich. 185 322 CL88
Cedar Ho., Sun. 265 328 BT94
Cedar Lawn Ave., Barn. 206 299 CY43
Cedar Mt. SE9 260 326 EK88
Cedar Pk. Gdns., Rom. 236 309 EX59
Cedar Pk. Rd., Enf. 202 300 DQ38
Cedar Pl. SE7 252 318 EJ78
Cedar Pl., Nthwd. 213 302 BQ51
Cedar Ri. N14 208 300 DG45
Cedar Rd. N17 221 306 DT53
Cedar Rd. NW2 110 305 CW63
Cedar Rd., Brom. 276 326 EJ96
Cedar Rd., Croy. 287 332 DR103
Cedar Rd., E.Mol. 267 329 CE98
Cedar Rd., Enf. 202 300 DP38
Cedar Rd., Felt. 265 320 BR88
Cedar Rd., Horn. 238 310 FJ62
Cedar Rd., Houns. 250 321 BW82
Cedar Rd., Rom. 227 309 FC56
Cedar Rd., Sutt. 293 331 DC107
Cedar Rd., Tedd. 268 322 CG92
Cedar Ter., Rich. 169 322 CL84
Cedar Tree Gro. SE27 273 324 DP92
Cedar Vista, Rich. 153 314 CL81
Cedar Way NW1 115 306 DK66
Cedar Way, Sun. 265 328 BS94
Cedarcroft Rd., Chess. 282 330 CM105
Cedarhurst, Brom. 275 325 EE94
Cedarhurst Dr. SE9 260 326 EJ85
Cedarne Rd. SW6 158 315 DB80
Cedars, Bans. 293 331 DF114
Cedars, The E15 131 317 EF67
Cedars, The W13 132 314 CJ72
Cedars, The, Tedd. 267 329 CF93
Cedars Ave. E17 223 307 EA57
Cedars Ave., Mitch. 272 324 DG98
Cedars Clo. NW4 218 305 CX55
Cedars Ct. N9 209 300 DS47
Cedars Dr., Uxb. 240 312 BM68
Cedars Ms. SW4 176 324 DH84
Cedars Pl. SE7 252 318 EJ78
Cedars Rd. E15 121 307 EE65
Cedars Rd. N9 210 301 DU47
Cedars Rd. N21 209 300 DP47
Cedars Rd. SW4 176 324 DH83
Cedars Rd. SW13 155 314 CT82
Cedars Rd. W4 154 314 CQ79
Cedars Rd., Beck. 274 325 DY96
Cedars Rd., Croy. 286 332 DL104
Cedars Rd., Kings.T. 268 322 CJ95
Cedars Rd., Mord. 271 323 DA98
Cedarville Gdns. SW16 272 324 DM93
Cedra Ct. N16 102 307 DU60
Cedric Ave., Rom. 227 309 FE55
Cedric Rd. SE9 261 326 EQ90
Celadon Clo., Enf. 203 301 DY41
Celandine Clo. E14 140 317 EA71
Celandine Dr. SE28 246 319 EV74
Celandine Way E15 131 317 EE69
Celbridge Ms. W2 40/1 315 DB72
Celestial Gdns. SE13 183 325 ED84
Celia Cres., Ashf. 264 328 BK93
Celia Rd. N19 114 306 DJ63
Celtic Ave., Brom. 275 325 EE97
Celtic St. E14 140 317 EB71
Cemetery La. SE7 252 318 EL79
Cemetery La., Shep. 281 328 BP101
Cemetery Rd. E7 121 307 EF63
Cemetery Rd. N17 221 306 DS52
Cemetery Rd. SE2 254 319 EV80
Cenacle Clo. NW3 96 305 DA62
Centaur St. SE1 71 316 DM76
Centaurs Business Pk., Islw. 152 314 CG79
Centenary Rd., Enf. 203 301 DZ42
Centenary Trd. Est., Enf. 203 301 DZ42
Central Ave. E11 105 307 ED61
Central Ave. N2 219 305 DD54
Central Ave. N9 209 300 DS48
Central Ave. SW11 159 315 DF80
Central Ave., Enf. 203 301 DV40
Central Ave., Hayes 249 312 BT74
Central Ave., Houns. 259 321 CC84
Central Ave., Pnr. 214 303 BZ58
Central Ave., Wall. 286 332 DL106
Central Ave., Well. 253 318 ET82
Central Ave., W.Mol. 266 329 BZ98
Central Circ. NW4 218 305 CV57
Central Dr., Horn. 238 311 FL62
Central Gdns., Mord. 285 331 DC99
Central Hill SE19 273 324 DR92
Central Mkts. EC1 49 316 DQ71
Central Par., Felt. 258 321 BW87
Central Par., Surb. 282 330 CL100
Central Pk. Ave., Dag. 237 309 FB62
Central Pk. Est., Houns. 258 321 BX85
Central Pk. Rd. E6 244 318 EK68
Central Pl. SE25 274 325 DV98
Central Rd., Mord. 284 331 DA100
Central Rd., Wem. 106 304 CH64
Central Rd., Wor.Pk. 283 331 CU102
Central Sq. NW11 219 305 DA57
Central Sq., Wem. 107 304 CL64
Central Sq., W.Mol. 266 329 BZ98
Central St. EC1 37 316 DQ69
Central Way NW10 124 314 CQ69
Central Way SE28 246 319 EU74
Central Way, Cars. 293 331 DE108
Central Way, Felt. 258 321 BU85
Centre, The, Felt. 258 321 BU89
Centre Ave. W3 135 314 CR74
Centre Ave. W10 126 315 CW69
Centre Common Rd., Chis. 277 326 EQ93
Centre Rd. E7 234 308 EG61
Centre Rd. E11 234 308 EG61
Centre Rd., Dag. 247 319 FB68
Centre St. E2 128 317 DV68
Centre Way E17 223 307 EC52
Centre Way N9 210 301 DW47
Centreway NW7 218 305 CU52
Centreway, Ilf. 235 308 EQ61
Centric Clo. NW1 20/1 316 DH67
Centurion Clo. N7 115 306 DM66
Centurion Ct., Wall. 285 332 DH103
Centurion La. E3 129 317 DZ68
Centurion Way, Erith 255 319 FA76
Century Rd. E17 222 307 DY55
Cephas Ave. E1 128 317 DW70
Cephas St. E1 128 317 DW70
Ceres Rd. SE18 253 318 ET77
Cerise Rd. SE15 164 317 DU81
Cerne Clo., Hayes 242 313 BW73
Cerne Rd., Mord. 285 331 DC100
Cerney Ms. W2 54 315 DD73
Cervantes Ct. W2 40/1 315 DB72
Cervantes Ct., Nthwd. 213 302 BT52
Cester St. E2 128 317 DU67
Ceylon Rd. W14 147 315 CX76
Chadacre Ave., Ilf. 224 308 EM55
Chadbourn St. E14 140 317 EB71
Chadd Dr., Brom. 276 326 EL97
Chadd Grn. E13 244 318 EG67
Chadview Ct., Rom. 236 309 EX59
Chadville Gdns., Rom. 226 309 EX57
Chadway, Dag. 236 309 EW60
Chadwell Ave., Rom. 236 309 EV59
Chadwell Heath La., Rom. 226 309 EV56
Chadwell St. EC1 36 316 DN69
Chadwick Ave. E4 211 301 ED49
Chadwick Ave. SW19 271 323 DA93
Chadwick Clo., Tedd. 268 322 CG93
Chadwick Dr., Rom. 228 310 FK54
Chadwick Rd. E11 105 307 EE59
Chadwick Rd. NW10 125 314 CT67
Chadwick Rd. SE15 163 316 DT82
Chadwick Rd., Ilf. 235 308 EP62
Chadwick St. SW1 70 316 DK76
Chadwick Way SE28 246 319 EX73
Chadwin Rd. E13 244 318 EH71
Chaffinch Ave., Croy. 288 333 DX100
Chaffinch Clo. N9 210 301 DX46
Chaffinch Clo., Croy. 288 333 DX99
Chaffinch Clo., Surb. 282 330 CN104
Chaffinch Rd., Beck. 274 325 DY95
Chafford Way, Rom. 226 309 EW56
Chagford St. NW1 31 315 DF70
Chailey Ave., Enf. 202 300 DT40
Chailey Clo., Houns. 250 321 BX81
Chailey St. E5 102 307 DW62
Chalcombe Rd. SE2 254 319 EV76
Chalcot Clo., Sutt. 292 331 DA108
Chalcot Cres. NW1 19 315 DF67
Chalcot Gdns. NW3 113 305 DF65
Chalcot Ms. SW16 193 324 DL90
Chalcot Rd. NW1 114 306 DG66
Chalcot Sq. NW1 114 306 DG66
Chalcott Gdns., Surb. 282 330 CJ102
Chalcroft Rd. SE13 183 325 EE85
Chaldon Path, Th.Hth. 273 324 DP98
Chaldon Rd. SW6 157 315 CY80
Chale Rd. SW2 177 324 DL86
Chale Wk., Sutt. 292 331 DB109
Chalet Clo., Bex. 279 327 FD91
Chalet Est. NW7 206 299 CU49
Chalfont Ave., Wem. 108 304 CP65
Chalfont Ct. NW9 217 304 CT55
Chalfont Grn. N9 209 300 DS48
Chalfont Rd. N9 209 300 DS48
Chalfont Rd. SE25 273 324 DT97
Chalfont Rd., Hayes 250 321 BU75
Chalfont Wk., Pnr. 214 303 BW54
Chalfont Way W13 142 314 CH76
Chalford Clo., W.Mol. 267 329 CA98
Chalford Rd. SE21 195 324 DR90
Chalford Wk., Wdf.Grn. 224 308 EK53
Chalforde Gdns., Rom. 228 310 FH56
Chalgrove Ave., Mord. 284 331 DA99
Chalgrove Cres., Ilf. 224 308 EL54
Chalgrove Gdns. N3 218 305 CY55
Chalgrove Rd. E9 118 307 DW65
Chalgrove Rd. N17 222 307 DV53
Chalgrove Rd., Sutt. 293 331 DD108
Chalice Clo., Wall. 294 332 DK107
Chalk Cres. SE12 260 326 EH90
Chalk Fm. Rd. NW1 114 306 DG66
Chalk Hill Rd. W6 147 315 CX77
Chalk Pit Ave., Orp. 278 327 EW97
Chalk Pit Way, Sutt. 285 331 DC106
Chalk Rd. E13 244 318 EH71
Chalk Wk., Sutt. 292 331 DB109
Chalkenden Clo. SE20 274 325 DV94
Chalkhill Rd., Wem. 92 304 CN62
Chalklands, The, Wem. 92 304 CQ62
Chalkley Clo., Mitch. 271 323 DF96
Chalkmill Rd., Enf. 203 301 DV41
Chalkstone Clo., Well. 254 319 EU81
Chalkwell Pk. Ave., Enf. 202 300 DS42
Challenge Rd., Ashf. 265 320 BR90
Challice Way SW2 193 324 DM88
Challin St. SE20 274 325 DW95
Challis Rd., Brent. 143 314 CK78
Challoner Clo. N2 219 305 DD54
Challoner Cres. W14 147 315 CZ78
Challoner St. W14 147 315 CZ78
Challoners Clo., E.Mol. 267 329 CD98
Chalmers Rd., Ashf. 265 328 BP91
Chalmers Rd. E., Ashf. 265 328 BP91
Chalmers Wk. SE17 162 316 DP79
Chalmers Way, Felt. 258 321 BU85
Chaloner Ct. SE1 74 316 DR75
Chalsey Rd. SE4 181 325 DZ84
Chalton Dr. N2 219 305 DC58
Chalton St. NW1 21 316 DJ68
Chamber St. E1 63 316 DT73
Chamberlain Clo. SE28 253 318 ER76
Chamberlain Cotts. SE5 163 316 DR81
Chamberlain Cres., W.Wick. 288 333 EB102
Chamberlain La., Pnr. 214 303 BU56
Chamberlain Pl. E17 222 307 DY55
Chamberlain Rd. N2 219 305 DC54
Chamberlain Rd. N9 210 301 DU48
Chamberlain Rd. W13 142 314 CG75
Chamberlain St. NW1 113 305 DF66
Chamberlain Wk., Felt. 266 329 BY91
Chamberlain Way, Pnr. 214 303 BV55
Chamberlain Way, Surb. 282 330 CL101
Chamberlayne Rd. NW10 126 315 CW67
Chambers Gdns. N2 219 305 DD53
Chambers La. NW10 110 305 CV66
Chambers Rd. N7 115 306 DL63
Chambers St. SE16 148 317 DU75
Chambord St. E2 39 316 DT69
Champion Cres. SE26 274 325 DY91
Champion Gro. SE5 179 324 DR83
Champion Hill SE5 179 324 DR83
Champion Hill Est. SE5 179 324 DS83
Champion Pk. SE5 163 316 DR82
Champion Pk. Est. SE5 179 324 DR83
Champion Rd. SE26 274 325 DY91
Champion Rd., Upmin. 239 311 FP61
Champness Clo. SE27 273 324 DR91
Champneys Clo., Sutt. 292 331 CZ108
Chance St. E1 39 316 DT70
Chance St. E2 39 316 DT70
Chancel St. SE1 60/1 316 DP74
Chancellor Gdns., S.Croy. 294 332 DP109
Chancellor Gro. SE21 194 324 DQ89
Chancellor Pas. E14 140 317 EA74
Chancellor Pl. NW9 217 304 CT54
Chancellors Rd. W6 146 315 CW78
Chancellors St. W6 146 315 CW78
Chancelot Rd. SE2 254 319 EV77
Chancery La. WC2 48 316 DN72
Chancery La., Beck. 275 325 EB96
Chanctonbury Clo. SE9 261 326 EP90
Chanctonbury Gdns., Sutt. 292 331 DB108
Chanctonbury Way N12 207 299 DA49
Chandler Ave. E16 244 318 EG71
Chandler Clo., Hmptn. 267 329 CA95
Chandler St. E1 138 317 DV74
Chandler Way SE15 163 316 DT80
Chandlers Clo., Felt. 265 320 BT87
Chandlers Dr., Erith 255 319 FD77
Chandlers Ms. E14 150 317 EA75
Chandlers Way SW2 194 324 DN87
Chandlers Way, Rom. 227 309 FE57
Chandos Ave. E17 223 307 EA54
Chandos Ave. N14 208 300 DJ48
Chandos Ave. N20 207 299 DC46
Chandos Ave. W5 143 314 CK77
Chandos Cres., Edg. 216 304 CM52
Chandos Par., Edg. 216 304 CM52
Chandos Pl. WC2 58/9 316 DL73
Chandos Rd. E15 121 307 ED64
Chandos Rd. N2 219 305 DD54
Chandos Rd. N17 221 306 DS54
Chandos Rd. NW2 110 305 CW64
Chandos Rd. NW10 125 314 CS70
Chandos Rd., Har. 215 303 CC57
Chandos Rd., Pnr. 232 313 BX59
Chandos St. W1 44/5 316 DH71
Chandos Way NW11 96 305 DB60
Change All. EC3 50 316 DR72
Channel Clo., Houns. 251 321 CA81
Channel Gate Rd. NW10 125 314 CT69
Channelsea Rd. E15 131 317 ED67
Channing Clo., Horn. 238 311 FM59
Chant Sq. E15 121 307 ED66
Chant St. E15 121 307 ED66
Chanton Dr., Sutt. 292 331 CW110
Chantrey Rd. SW9 177 324 DM83
Chantry, The, Uxb. 240 312 BM69
Chantry Clo., Enf. 202 300 DQ38
Chantry Clo., Har. 216 304 CM57
Chantry Clo., Sid. 278 327 EY92
Chantry Clo., West Dr. 248 312 BK73
Chantry La., Brom. 290 334 EK99
Chantry Pl., Har. 215 303 CB53
Chantry Pt. W9 127 315 CZ70
Chantry Rd., Cher. 280 328 BJ101
Chantry Rd., Chess. 282 330 CM106
Chantry Rd., Har. 215 303 CB53
Chantry St. N1 24/5 316 DP67
Chantry Way, Mitch. 271 323 DD97
Chantry Way, Rain. 247 319 FD68
Chapel Clo., Dart. 263 327 FE85
Chapel Ct. N2 219 305 DE55
Chapel Ct. SE1 74 316 DR75
Chapel Fm. Rd. SE9 260 326 EM90
Chapel Hill, Dart. 263 327 FE85
Chapel Ho. St. E14 150 317 EB78
Chapel La., Pnr. 214 303 BX55
Chapel La., Rom. 236 309 EX59
Chapel La., Uxb. 249 312 BN72
Chapel Mkt. N1 24 316 DN68
Chapel Path E11 224 308 EH58
Chapel Pl. EC2 38/9 316 DS69
Chapel Pl. N1 24 316 DN68
Chapel Pl. N17 221 306 DT52
Chapel Pl. W1 44/5 316 DH72
Chapel Rd. SE27 273 324 DP91
Chapel Rd. W13 132 314 CH74
Chapel Rd., Bexh. 263 327 FA84
Chapel Rd., Houns. 259 321 CB83
Chapel Rd., Ilf. 235 308 EN62
Chapel Rd., Twick. 184 322 CH87
Chapel Row, Uxb. 212 302 BJ53
Chapel Side W2 52/3 315 DB73
Chapel Stones N17 221 306 DT53
Chapel St. E15 121 307 ED66
Chapel St. NW1 42/3 315 DE71
Chapel St. SW1 68 316 DG76
Chapel St., Enf. 202 300 DR41
Chapel St., Uxb. 240 312 BJ67
Chapel Wk. NW4 218 305 CV56
Chapel Wk., Croy. 287 332 DQ103
Chapel Way N7 99 306 DM62
Chapel Yd. SW18 174 323 DA85
Chapelmount Rd., Wdf.Grn. 224 308 EM51
Chaplaincy Gdns., Horn. 238 311 FL60
Chaplin Clo. SE1 72 316 DN75
Chaplin Cres., Sun. 265 328 BS93
Chaplin Rd. E15 131 317 EE67
Chaplin Rd. N17 221 306 DT55
Chaplin Rd. NW2 110 305 CU65
Chaplin Rd., Dag. 236 309 EY66
Chaplin Rd., Wem. 106 304 CJ65
Chaplin Sq. N12 219 305 DD52
Chapman Clo., West Dr. 248 320 BM76
Chapman Cres., Har. 216 304 CL57
Chapman Rd. E9 119 307 DZ65
Chapman Rd., Belv. 255 319 FA78
Chapman Rd., Croy. 286 332 DN102
Chapman St. E1 138 317 DV73
Chapman's La. SE2 254 319 EW77
Chapmans La., Belv. 254 319 EX77
Chapmans La., Orp. 278 327 EW96
Chapmans Pk. Ind. Est. NW10 109 304 CT65
Chapone Pl. W1 46 316 DK72
Chapter Clo. W4 144 314 CQ76
Chapter Clo., Uxb. 240 312 BM66
Chapter Ho. Ct. EC4 48/9 316 DP72
Chapter Rd. NW2 110 305 CU64
Chapter Rd. SE17 84/5 316 DP78
Chapter St. SW1 82 316 DK77
Chapter Way, Hmptn. 267 329 CA91
Chara Pl. W4 155 314 CR79
Charcroft Gdns., Enf. 203 301 DX42
Chardin Rd. W4 145 314 CS77
Chardmore Rd. N16 102 307 DU60
Chardwell Clo. E6 244 318 EL72
Charecroft Way W12 147 315 CX75
Charfield Ct. W9 28/9 315 DB70
Charford Rd. E16 244 318 EG71
Chargeable La. E13 131 317 EF70
Chargeable St. E16 131 317 EF70
Chargrove Clo. SE16 149 317 DX75
Charing Clo., Orp. 291 334 ET105
Charing Cross WC2 58/9 316 DL74
Charing Cross Rd. WC2 46 316 DK72
Charlbert St. NW8 18/9 315 DE68
Charlbury Ave., Stan. 204 298 CK50
Charlbury Clo., Rom. 228 310 FJ51
Charlbury Cres., Rom. 228 310 FJ51
Charlbury Gdns., Ilf. 235 308 ET61
Charlbury Gro. W5 132 314 CJ72
Charlbury Rd., Uxb. 230 312 BM62
Charldane Rd. SE9 261 326 EP90
Charlecote Gro. SE26 196 325 DV90
Charlecote Rd., Dag. 236 309 EY62
Charlemont Rd. E6 244 318 EM69
Charles Barry Clo. SW4 176 324 DJ83
Charles Burton Ct. E5 119 307 DY64
Charles Clo., Sid. 278 327 EV91
Charles Coveney Rd. SE15 163 316 DT81
Charles Cres., Har. 233 313 CD59
Charles Dickens Ho. E2 128 317 DV69
Charles Grinling Wk. SE18 253 318 EN77
Charles Ho. N17 221 306 DT52
Charles La. NW8 18 315 DD68
Charles Pl. NW1 33 316 DJ69
Charles Rd. E7 234 308 EJ66
Charles Rd. SW19 271 323 DA95
Charles Rd. W13 132 314 CG72
Charles Rd., Dag. 237 309 FD65
Charles Rd., Rom. 236 309 EX59
Charles Rd., Stai. 264 328 BK93
Charles II St. SW1 58 316 DK74
Charles Sevright Dr. NW7 206 299 CX50
Charles Sq. N1 38 316 DR69
Charles Sq. Est. N1 38 316 DR69
Charles St. E16 244 318 EK74
Charles St. SW13 155 314 CS82
Charles St. W1 56/7 316 DH74
Charles St., Croy. 287 332 DQ104
Charles St., Enf. 209 300 DT43
Charles St., Houns. 250 321 BY82
Charles St., Uxb. 241 312 BP70
Charlesfield SE9 260 326 EJ90
Charleston Clo., Felt. 258 321 BU90
Charleston St. SE17 85 316 DQ77
Charleville Circ. SE26 274 325 DU92
Charleville Rd. W14 147 315 CY78
Charlieville Rd., Erith 255 319 FC80
Charlmont Rd. SW17 271 323 DF93
Charlotte Clo., Bexh. 262 327 EY85
Charlotte Despard Ave. SW11 160 316 DG81
Charlotte Gdns., Rom. 227 309 FB51
Charlotte Ms. W1 45 316 DJ71
Charlotte Ms. W14 147 315 CY77
Charlotte Pl. NW9 217 304 CQ57
Charlotte Pl. SW1 81 316 DJ77
Charlotte Pl. W1 45 316 DJ71
Charlotte Rd. EC2 38/9 316 DS70
Charlotte Rd. SW13 155 314 CT81
Charlotte Rd., Dag. 237 309 FB65
Charlotte Rd., Wall. 294 332 DJ107
Charlotte Row SW4 176 324 DJ83
Charlotte Sq., Rich. 169 322 CM86
Charlotte St. W1 45 316 DJ71
Charlotte Ter. N1 23 316 DM67
Charlow Clo. SW6 158 315 DC82
Charlton Ch. La. SE7 252 318 EJ78
Charlton Clo., Uxb. 231 312 BP61
Charlton Cres., Bark. 245 318 ET68
Charlton Dene SE7 252 318 EJ80
Charlton Kings Rd. NW5 115 306 DK64
Charlton La. SE7 252 318 EK78
Charlton La., Shep. 281 328 BQ97
Charlton Pk. La. SE7 252 318 EK80
Charlton Pk. Rd. SE7 252 318 EK79
Charlton Pl. N1 24/5 316 DP68
Charlton Rd. N9 210 301 DX46
Charlton Rd. NW10 125 314 CS67
Charlton Rd. SE3 252 318 EH80
Charlton Rd. SE7 252 318 EJ79
Charlton Rd., Har. 216 304 CK57
Charlton Rd., Shep. 281 328 BQ97
Charlton Rd., Wem. 91 304 CM60
Charlton Way SE3 167 317 EE81
Charlwood Clo., Har. 215 303 CE52
Charlwood Pl. SW1 81 316 DJ77
Charlwood Rd. SW15 173 323 CX84
Charlwood Sq., Mitch. 271 323 DD97
Charlwood St. SW1 81 316 DJ78
Charlwood Ter. SW15 173 323 CX84
Charmian Ave., Stan. 216 304 CK55
Charminster Ave. SW19 271 323 DA96
Charminster Ct., Surb. 282 330 CK100
Charminster Rd. SE9 276 326 EK91
Charminster Rd., Wor.Pk. 284 331 CX102
Charmouth Rd., Well. 254 319 EV81
Charnock, Swan. 279 327 FE98
Charnock Rd. E5 102 307 DV62
Charnwood Ave. SW19 271 323 DA96
Charnwood Clo., N.Mal. 269 322 CS98
Charnwood Dr. E18 224 308 EH55
Charnwood Gdns. E14 150 317 EA77
Charnwood Pl. N20 207 299 DC48
Charnwood Rd. SE25 287 332 DR99
Charnwood Rd., Enf. 203 301 DV36
Charnwood Rd., Uxb. 241 312 BN69
Charnwood St. E5 102 307 DV61
Charrington Rd., Croy. 286 332 DP103
Charrington St. NW1 22 316 DK68
Charsley Rd. SE6 198 325 EB89
Chart Clo., Brom. 275 325 EE95
Chart Clo., Croy. 288 333 DW100
Chart St. N1 38 316 DR69
Charter Ave., Ilf. 235 308 ER60
Charter Ct., N.Mal. 269 322 CS97
Charter Cres., Houns. 258 321 BY84
Charter Dr., Bex. 262 327 EY87
Charter Pl., Uxb. 240 312 BJ66
Charter Rd., Kings.T. 269 322 CP97
Charter Rd., The, Wdf.Grn. 223 307 EE51
Charter Sq., Kings.T. 269 322 CP96
Charter Way N3 218 305 CZ56
Charter Way N14 208 300 DJ44
Charterhouse Ave., Wem. 106 304 CJ63
Charterhouse Bldgs. EC1 36/7 316 DP70
Charterhouse Ms. EC1 48/9 316 DP71
Charterhouse Rd., Orp. 291 335 EU104
Charterhouse Sq. EC1 48/9 316 DP71
Charterhouse St. EC1 48 316 DN71
Charteris Rd. N4 100 306 DN60
Charteris Rd. NW6 127 315 CZ67
Charteris Rd., Wdf.Grn. 224 308 EH52
Charters Clo. SE19 273 324 DS92

Chartfield Ave. SW15	172	323	CV85
Chartfield Sq. SW15	173	323	CX85
Chartham Gro. SE27	194	324	DN90
Chartham Rd. SE25	274	325	DV97
Chartley Ave. NW2	93	304	CS62
Chartley Ave., Stan.	215	303	CF51
Charton Clo., Belv.	254	319	EZ79
Chartridge Clo., Barn.	206	299	CU43
Chartwell Clo. SE9	261	326	EQ89
Chartwell Clo., Croy.	287	332	DR102
Chartwell Clo., Grnf.	243	313	CB67
Chartwell Dr., Orp.	291	334	ER106
Chartwell Gdns., Sutt.	284	331	CZ104
Chartwell Pl., Har.	233	313	CD60
Chartwell Pl., Sutt.	284	331	CZ104
Chartwell Rd., Nthwd.	213	302	BT51
Chartwell Way SE20	274	325	DV95
Charville La., Hayes	241	312	BQ69
Charville La. W., Uxb.	241	312	BP69
Charwood SW16	273	324	DN91
Chase, The E12	234	308	EK63
Chase, The SW4	176	324	DH83
Chase, The SW16	272	324	DM94
Chase, The SW20	270	323	CY95
Chase, The, Bexh.	263	327	FB83
Chase, The, Brom.	276	326	EH97
Chase, The, Couls.	294	332	DJ114
Chase, The, Edg.	217	304	CP53
Chase, The, Horn.	237	309	FF62
Chase, The, Pnr.	214	303	BZ56
Chase, The (Eastcote), Pnr.	214	303	BW58
Chase, The, Rom.	227	309	FE55
Chase, The (Chadwell Heath), Rom.	226	309	EY58
Chase, The (Rush Grn.), Rom.	237	309	FD62
Chase, The, Stan.	204	298	CG50
Chase, The, Sun.	266	329	BV95
Chase, The, Upmin.	239	311	FS62
Chase, The, Uxb.	241	312	BN64
Chase, The, Wall.	286	332	DL106
Chase Ct. Gdns., Enf.	202	300	DQ41
Chase Cross Rd., Rom.	227	309	FC52
Chase Gdns. E4	211	301	EA49
Chase Gdns., Twick.	259	321	CD86
Chase Grn., Enf.	202	300	DQ41
Chase Grn. Ave., Enf.	202	300	DP40
Chase Hill, Enf.	202	300	DQ41
Chase Ho. Gdns., Horn.	228	311	FM57
Chase La., Ilf.	225	308	ER57
Chase Ridings, Enf.	202	300	DN40
Chase Rd. N14	208	300	DJ43
Chase Rd. NW10	125	314	CR70
Chase Rd. W3	125	314	CR70
Chase Side N14	208	300	DG43
Chase Side, Enf.	202	300	DQ41
Chase Side Ave. SW20	270	323	CY96
Chase Side Ave., Enf.	202	300	DQ40
Chase Side Cres., Enf.	202	300	DQ39
Chase Side Pl., Enf.	202	300	DQ41
Chase Way N14	208	300	DH47
Chasefield Rd. SW17	271	323	DF91
Chaseley Dr. W4	154	314	CP81
Chaseley Dr., S.Croy.	295	332	DR110
Chaseley St. E14	139	317	DY72
Chasemore Clo., Mitch.	285	331	DF101
Chasemore Gdns., Croy.	286	332	DP106
Chaseside Clo., Rom.	227	309	FE51
Chaseside Gdns., Cher.	280	328	BH101
Chaseville Pk. Rd. N21	208	300	DL43
Chasewood Ave., Enf.	202	300	DP40
Chastilian Rd., Dart.	263	327	FF87
Chatfield Rd. SW11	174	323	DC83
Chatfield Rd., Croy.	286	332	DP102
Chatham Ave., Brom.	289	333	EF101
Chatham Clo. NW11	219	305	DA57
Chatham Clo., Sutt.	284	331	CZ101
Chatham Pl. E9	118	307	DW65
Chatham Rd. E17	222	307	DY55
Chatham Rd. E18	223	307	EF54
Chatham Rd. SW11	175	323	DF86
Chatham Rd., Kings.T.	269	322	CN96
Chatham Rd., Orp.	291	334	EQ106
Chatham St. SE17	86	316	DR77
Chatsfield Pl. W5	133	314	CL72
Chatsworth Ave. NW4	218	305	CW54
Chatsworth Ave. SW20	270	323	CY95
Chatsworth Ave., Brom.	276	326	EH92
Chatsworth Ave., Sid.	262	327	EU88
Chatsworth Ave., Wem.	107	304	CM64
Chatsworth Clo. NW4	218	305	CW54
Chatsworth Clo., W.Wick.	289	333	EF103
Chatsworth Ct. W8	76	315	DA77
Chatsworth Cres., Houns.	259	321	CD84
Chatsworth Dr., Enf.	210	301	DU45
Chatsworth Est. E5	119	307	DX63
Chatsworth Gdns. W3	134	314	CP74
Chatsworth Gdns., Har.	233	313	CB60
Chatsworth Gdns., N.Mal.	283	330	CT99
Chatsworth Pl., Mitch.	271	323	DF97
Chatsworth Pl., Tedd.	268	322	CG91
Chatsworth Ri. W5	123	314	CM70
Chatsworth Rd. E5	102	307	DW62
Chatsworth Rd. E15	121	307	EF64
Chatsworth Rd. NW2	111	305	CX65
Chatsworth Rd. W4	154	314	CQ79
Chatsworth Rd. W5	123	314	CM70
Chatsworth Rd., Croy.	287	332	DR105
Chatsworth Rd., Hayes	242	313	BV70
Chatsworth Rd., Sutt.	284	331	CX106
Chatsworth Way SE27	194	324	DP90
Chatteris Ave., Rom.	228	310	FJ51
Chattern Hill, Ashf.	265	328	BP91
Chattern Rd., Ashf.	265	328	BQ91
Chatterton Rd. N4	100	306	DP62
Chatterton Rd., Brom.	276	326	EK98
Chatto Rd. SW11	175	323	DF85
Chaucer Ave., Hayes	242	313	BU71
Chaucer Ave., Houns.	250	321	BV82
Chaucer Ave., Rich.	170	322	CN83
Chaucer Clo. N11	208	300	DJ50
Chaucer Clo., Bans.	292	331	CY114
Chaucer Ct. N16	117	306	DS63
Chaucer Dr. SE1	87	316	DT77
Chaucer Gdns., Sutt.	284	331	DA104
Chaucer Grn., Croy.	288	333	DW101
Chaucer Rd. E7	234	308	EG65
Chaucer Rd. E11	224	308	EG58
Chaucer Rd. E17	223	307	EC54
Chaucer Rd. SE24	178	324	DN85
Chaucer Rd. W3	134	314	CQ74
Chaucer Rd., Ashf.	264	328	BL91
Chaucer Rd., Rom.	228	310	FH52
Chaucer Rd., Sid.	262	327	EW88
Chaucer Rd., Sutt.	284	331	DA105
Chaucer Rd., Well.	253	318	ET81
Chaucer Way SW19	271	323	DD93
Chauncey Clo. N9	210	301	DU48
Chaundrye Clo. SE9	260	326	EL86
Chauntler Clo. E16	244	318	EH72
Cheam Common Rd., Wor.Pk.	283	331	CV103
Cheam Mans., Sutt.	292	331	CY108
Cheam Pk. Way, Sutt.	292	331	CY107
Cheam Rd., Sutt.	292	331	CZ107
Cheam Rd. (East Ewell), Sutt.	292	331	CX110
Cheam St. SE15	180	325	DV83
Cheapside EC2	49	316	DQ72
Cheddar Rd., Houns.	257	320	BN82
Cheddar Waye, Hayes	242	313	BV72
Cheddington Rd. N18	209	300	DS48
Chedworth Clo. E16	141	317	EF72
Cheeseman Clo., Hmptn.	266	329	BY93
Cheesemans Ter. W14	147	315	CZ78
Chelford Rd., Brom.	275	325	ED92
Chelmer Cres., Bark.	246	319	EV68
Chelmer Rd. E9	119	307	DX64
Chelmer Rd., Upmin.	229	311	FR58
Chelmsford Ave., Rom.	227	309	FD52
Chelmsford Clo. E6	244	318	EM72
Chelmsford Clo. W6	157	315	CX79
Chelmsford Clo., Sutt.	292	331	DA109
Chelmsford Dr., Upmin.	238	311	FM62
Chelmsford Gdns., Ilf.	234	308	EL59
Chelmsford Rd. E11	105	307	ED60
Chelmsford Rd. E17	223	307	EA58
Chelmsford Rd. E18	223	307	EF53
Chelmsford Rd. N14	208	300	DJ45
Chelmsford Sq. NW10	126	315	CW67
Chelsea Bri. SW1	160	316	DH79
Chelsea Bri. SW8	160	316	DH79
Chelsea Bri. Rd. SW1	80	316	DG78
Chelsea Cloisters SW3	78/9	315	DE77
Chelsea Clo. NW10	125	314	CR67
Chelsea Clo., Edg.	217	304	CN54
Chelsea Clo., Hmptn.	267	329	CC93
Chelsea Embk. SW3	159	315	DE79
Chelsea Gdns., Sutt.	284	331	CY105
Chelsea Harbour SW10	159	315	DD81
Chelsea Harbour Dr. SW10	158	315	DC81
Chelsea Manor Gdns. SW3	78/9	315	DE78
Chelsea Manor St. SW3	78/9	315	DE78
Chelsea Pk. Gdns. SW3	159	315	DD79
Chelsea Sq. SW3	78	315	DD78
Chelsea Wf. SW10	159	315	DD80
Chelsfield Ave. N9	210	301	DX45
Chelsfield Gdns. SE26	196	325	DW90
Chelsfield Grn. N9	210	301	DX45
Chelsham Rd. SW4	177	324	DK83
Chelsham Rd., S.Croy.	295	332	DR107
Chelston App., Ruis.	232	313	BU61
Chelston Rd., Ruis.	232	313	BU60
Chelsworth Clo., Rom.	228	311	FM53
Chelsworth Dr. SE18	253	318	ER79
Chelsworth Dr., Rom.	228	311	FL53
Cheltenham Ave., Twick.	184	322	CG87
Cheltenham Clo., N.Mal.	269	322	CQ97
Cheltenham Clo., Nthlt.	233	313	CB65
Cheltenham Gdns. E6	244	318	EL68
Cheltenham Pl. W3	134	314	CP74
Cheltenham Pl., Har.	216	304	CL56
Cheltenham Rd. E10	223	307	EC58
Cheltenham Rd. SE15	180	325	DW84
Cheltenham Rd., Orp.	291	335	EU104
Cheltenham Ter. SW3	79	315	DF78
Chelverton Rd. SW15	173	323	CX84
Chelwood Clo. E4	211	301	EB44
Chelwood Clo., Nthwd.	213	302	BQ52
Chelwood Gdns., Rich.	154	314	CN82
Chelwood Wk. SE4	181	325	DY84
Chenappa Clo. E13	244	318	EG69
Cheney Rd. NW1	22/3	316	DL68
Cheney Row E17	222	307	DZ53
Cheney St., Pnr.	214	303	BW57
Cheneys Rd. E11	105	307	EE62
Chenies, The, Dart.	279	327	FE91
Chenies, The, Orp.	291	334	ES100
Chenies Ms. WC1	34	316	DK70
Chenies Pl. NW1	22	316	DK68
Chenies St. WC1	46	316	DK71
Cheniston Gdns. W8	64/5	315	DB76
Chepstow Ave., Horn.	238	311	FL62
Chepstow Clo. SW15	173	323	CY86
Chepstow Cres. W11	52	315	DA73
Chepstow Cres., Ilf.	225	308	ES58
Chepstow Gdns., Sthl.	242	313	BZ72
Chepstow Pl. W2	40	315	DA72
Chepstow Ri., Croy.	287	332	DS104
Chepstow Rd. W2	40	315	DA72
Chepstow Rd. W7	142	314	CG76
Chepstow Rd., Croy.	287	332	DS104
Chepstow Vil. W11	137	315	CZ73
Chepstow Way SE15	163	316	DT80
Chequer St. EC1	37	316	DQ70
Chequers Clo., Orp.	277	326	ET98
Chequers Gdns. N13	209	300	DP50
Chequers La., Dag.	246	319	EZ71
Chequers Par. SE9	260	326	EM86
Chequers Sq., Uxb.	240	312	BJ66
Chequers Way N13	209	300	DP50
Cherbury Clo. SE28	246	319	EX72
Cherbury Ct. N1	26	316	DR68
Cherbury St. N1	26	316	DR68
Cherchefelle Ms., Stan.	204	298	CH50
Cherimoya Gdns., W.Mol.	267	329	CB97
Cherington Rd. W7	243	313	CF74
Cheriton Ave., Brom.	289	333	EF99
Cheriton Ave., Ilf.	224	308	EM54
Cheriton Clo. W5	132	314	CJ71
Cheriton Dr. SE18	253	318	ER80
Cheriton Sq. SW17	192	324	DG89
Cherry Ave., Sthl.	242	313	BX74
Cherry Ave., Swan.	279	327	FD97
Cherry Clo. E17	223	307	EB57
Cherry Clo. SW2	194	324	DN87
Cherry Clo. W5	143	314	CK76
Cherry Clo., Bans.	292	331	CX114
Cherry Clo., Cars.	285	331	DF103
Cherry Clo., Mord.	270	323	CY98
Cherry Clo., Ruis.	231	312	BT62
Cherry Cres., Brent.	152	314	CH80
Cherry Gdn. St. SE16	148	317	DV75
Cherry Gdns., Dag.	236	309	EZ64
Cherry Gdns., Nthlt.	233	313	CB66
Cherry Garth, Brent.	143	314	CK78
Cherry Gro., Hayes	242	313	BV74
Cherry Gro., Uxb.	249	312	BP71
Cherry Hill, Barn.	207	299	DB44
Cherry Hill, Har.	215	303	CE52
Cherry Hill Gdns., Croy.	286	332	DM105
Cherry La., West Dr.	248	320	BM77
Cherry Laurel Wk. SW2	177	324	DM86
Cherry Orchard, Stai.	264	328	BG92
Cherry Orchard, West Dr.	248	320	BL75
Cherry Orchard Gdns., Croy.	287	332	DR103
Cherry Orchard Gdns., W.Mol.	266	329	BZ97
Cherry Orchard Rd., Brom.	290	334	EL103
Cherry Orchard Rd., Croy.	287	332	DR103
Cherry Orchard Rd., W.Mol.	266	329	BZ97
Cherry Rd., Enf.	203	301	DW38
Cherry St., Rom.	227	309	FD57
Cherry Tree Ave., Stai.	264	328	BH93
Cherry Tree Ave., West Dr.	248	312	BM72
Cherry Tree Clo., Wem.	233	313	CF63
Cherry Tree Ct. NW9	217	304	CQ56
Cherry Tree Dr. SW16	193	324	DL90
Cherry Tree Grn., S.Croy.	295	333	DV114
Cherry Tree La., Dart.	263	327	FF90
Cherry Tree La., Rain.	247	319	FE69
Cherry Tree Rd. E15	121	307	EE63
Cherry Tree Rd. N2	219	305	DF56
Cherry Tree Wk. EC1	37	316	DQ70
Cherry Tree Wk., Beck.	274	325	DZ98
Cherry Tree Wk., W.Wick.	289	333	EF105
Cherry Tree Way, Stan.	216	304	CH51
Cherry Wk., Brom.	289	334	EG102
Cherry Wk., Rain.	247	319	FF68
Cherry Way, Shep.	281	328	BR98
Cherry Wd. Way W5	134	314	CN71
Cherrycot Hill, Orp.	291	334	ER105
Cherrycot Ri., Orp.	291	334	EQ105
Cherrycroft Gdns., Pnr.	214	303	BZ52
Cherrydown Ave. E4	210	301	DZ48
Cherrydown Clo. E4	210	301	DZ48
Cherrydown Rd., Sid.	262	327	EX89
Cherrydown Wk., Rom.	227	309	FB54
Cherrytree La., Iver	240	312	BG67
Cherrywood Clo. E3	129	317	DY69
Cherrywood Clo., Kings.T.	269	322	CN94
Cherrywood Dr. SW15	173	323	CX85
Cherrywood La., Mord.	270	323	CY98
Chertsey Bri. Rd., Cher.	280	328	BK101
Chertsey Dr., Sutt.	284	331	CY103
Chertsey Rd. E11	105	307	ED61
Chertsey Rd., Ashf.	265	328	BR94
Chertsey Rd., Felt.	265	328	BS92
Chertsey Rd., Ilf.	235	308	ER63
Chertsey Rd., Shep.	280	328	BK101
Chertsey Rd., Sun.	265	328	BR94
Chertsey Rd., Twick.	259	321	CF86
Chertsey St. SW17	272	324	DG92
Chervil Clo., Felt.	258	321	BU90
Chervil Ms. SE28	246	319	EV74
Cherwell Ct., Epsom	283	330	CQ105
Cherwell Way, Ruis.	231	302	BQ58
Cheryls Clo. SW6	158	315	DB81
Cheseman St. SE26	196	325	DV90
Chesfield Rd., Kings.T.	268	322	CL94
Chesham Ave., Orp.	290	334	EP100
Chesham Clo. SW1	68	316	DG76
Chesham Clo., Rom.	227	309	FD56
Chesham Clo., Sutt.	292	331	CY110
Chesham Ct., Nthwd.	213	302	BT51
Chesham Cres. SE20	274	325	DW96
Chesham Ms. SW1	68	316	DG76
Chesham Pl. SW1	68	316	DG76
Chesham Rd. SE20	274	325	DW96
Chesham Rd. SW19	271	323	DD92
Chesham Rd., Kings.T.	269	322	CN96
Chesham St. NW10	93	304	CR62
Chesham St. SW1	68	316	DG76
Chesham Ter. W13	142	314	CH75
Cheshire Clo. SE4	165	317	DZ82
Cheshire Clo., Horn.	229	311	FN57
Cheshire Clo., Mitch.	272	324	DL97
Cheshire Rd. N22	220	306	DM51
Cheshire St. E2	39	316	DT70
Chesholm Rd. N16	101	306	DS62
Cheshunt Rd. E7	234	308	EH65
Cheshunt Rd., Belv.	255	319	FA78
Chesil Ct. E2	128	317	DW68
Chesil Way, Hayes	241	312	BT69
Chesilton Rd. SW6	157	315	CZ81
Chesley Gdns. E6	244	318	EK68
Chesney St. SW11	160	316	DG81
Chesnut Est. N17	221	306	DT55
Chesnut Gro. N17	221	306	DT55
Chesnut Rd. N17	221	306	DT55
Chessholme Ct., Sun.	265	328	BS94
Chessholme Rd., Ashf.	265	328	BQ93
Chessington Ave. N3	218	305	CY55
Chessington Ave., Bexh.	254	319	EY80
Chessington Ct., Pnr.	214	303	BZ56
Chessington Hill Pk., Chess.	282	330	CN106
Chessington Lo. N3	218	305	CZ55
Chessington Way, W.Wick.	288	333	EB103
Chesson Rd. W14	157	315	CZ79
Chesswood Way, Pnr.	214	303	BX54
Chester Ave., Rich.	169	322	CM86
Chester Ave., Twick.	258	321	BZ88
Chester Ave., Upmin.	239	311	FS61
Chester Clo. SW1	68/9	316	DH75
Chester Clo. SW13	172	323	CV83
Chester Clo., Ashf.	265	328	BR92
Chester Clo., Sutt.	284	331	DA103
Chester Clo., Uxb.	249	312	BP72
Chester Clo. N. NW1	32/3	316	DH69
Chester Clo. S. NW1	32/3	316	DH69
Chester Cotts. SW1	80	316	DG77
Chester Ct. NW1	32/3	316	DH69
Chester Ct. SE5	163	316	DR80
Chester Cres. E8	117	306	DT65
Chester Dr., Har.	214	303	BZ58
Chester Gdns. W13	132	314	CH72
Chester Gdns., Enf.	210	301	DV44
Chester Gdns., Mord.	285	331	DC100
Chester Gate NW1	32/3	316	DH69
Chester Ms. SW1	68/9	316	DH76
Chester Pl. NW1	32/3	316	DH69
Chester Rd. E7	234	308	EK66
Chester Rd. E11	224	308	EH58
Chester Rd. E16	131	317	EE70
Chester Rd. E17	222	307	DX57
Chester Rd. N9	210	301	DV46
Chester Rd. N17	221	306	DR55
Chester Rd. N19	98	306	DH61
Chester Rd. NW1	32	316	DG69
Chester Rd. SW19	270	323	CW93
Chester Rd., Houns.	258	321	BV83
Chester Rd. (Heathrow Airport), Houns.	257	320	BN83
Chester Rd., Ilf.	235	308	ET60
Chester Rd., Nthwd.	213	302	BS52
Chester Rd., Sid.	261	326	ES85
Chester Row SW1	80	316	DG77
Chester Sq. SW1	80	316	DG77
Chester Sq. Ms. SW1	68/9	316	DH76
Chester St. E2	128	317	DU70
Chester St. SW1	68	316	DG76
Chester Ter. NW1	32/3	316	DH69
Chester Way SE11	84	316	DN77
Chesterfield Clo., Orp.	278	327	EX98
Chesterfield Gdns. N4	221	306	DP57
Chesterfield Gdns. SE10	167	317	ED80
Chesterfield Gdns. W1	56/7	316	DH74
Chesterfield Gro. SE22	179	324	DT85
Chesterfield Hill W1	56/7	316	DH74
Chesterfield Ms. N4	221	306	DP57
Chesterfield Ms., Ashf.	264	328	BL91
Chesterfield Rd. E10	223	307	EC58
Chesterfield Rd. N3	219	305	DA51
Chesterfield Rd. W4	154	314	CQ79
Chesterfield Rd., Ashf.	264	328	BL91
Chesterfield Rd., Barn.	206	299	CX43
Chesterfield Rd., Enf.	203	301	DY37
Chesterfield St. W1	56/7	316	DH74
Chesterfield Wk. SE10	167	317	ED81
Chesterfield Way SE15	164	317	DW80
Chesterfield Way, Hayes	250	321	BU75
Chesterford Gdns. NW3	112	305	DB63
Chesterford Ho. SE18	252	318	EK80
Chesterford Rd. E12	234	308	EM64
Chesters, The, N.Mal.	269	322	CS95
Chesterton Clo. SW18	174	323	DA85
Chesterton Clo., Grnf.	243	313	CB68
Chesterton Dr., Stai.	264	320	BM88
Chesterton Rd. E13	244	318	EG69
Chesterton Rd. W10	137	315	CX71
Chesterton Ter. E13	244	318	EG69
Chesterton Ter., Kings.T.	269	322	CN96
Chesthunte Rd. N17	221	306	DQ53
Chestnut All. SW6	157	315	CZ79
Chestnut Ave. E7	234	308	EH63
Chestnut Ave. N8	220	306	DL57
Chestnut Ave. SW14	171	322	CR83
Chestnut Ave., Brent.	143	314	CK77
Chestnut Ave., E.Mol.	267	329	CF97
Chestnut Ave., Edg.	216	304	CL51
Chestnut Ave., Epsom	283	330	CS105
Chestnut Ave., Hmptn.	267	329	CA94
Chestnut Ave., Horn.	237	309	FF61
Chestnut Ave., Nthwd.	213	302	BT54
Chestnut Ave., Tedd.	267	329	CF96
Chestnut Ave., Wem.	106	304	CH64
Chestnut Ave., West Dr.	248	312	BM73
Chestnut Ave., W.Wick.	289	333	EE106
Chestnut Ave. N. E17	223	307	EC56
Chestnut Ave. S. E17	223	307	EC56
Chestnut Clo. N14	208	300	DJ43
Chestnut Clo. N16	101	306	DR61
Chestnut Clo. SE6	275	325	EC92
Chestnut Clo. SE14	181	325	DZ83
Chestnut Clo. SW16	273	324	DN91
Chestnut Clo., Ashf.	265	328	BP91
Chestnut Clo., Cars.	285	331	DF102
Chestnut Clo., Hayes	249	312	BS73
Chestnut Clo., Horn.	238	310	FJ63
Chestnut Clo., Orp.	291	335	EU106
Chestnut Clo., Sid.	262	327	EU88
Chestnut Clo., Sun.	265	328	BT93
Chestnut Clo., West Dr.	257	320	BP80
Chestnut Ct. SW6	157	315	CZ79
Chestnut Dr. E11	224	308	EG58
Chestnut Dr., Bexh.	262	327	EX83
Chestnut Dr., Har.	215	303	CF52
Chestnut Dr., Pnr.	214	303	BX58
Chestnut Glen, Horn.	238	310	FG61
Chestnut Gro. SE20	274	325	DV94
Chestnut Gro. SW12	192	324	DG87
Chestnut Gro. W5	143	314	CK76
Chestnut Gro., Barn.	207	299	DF43
Chestnut Gro., Dart.	279	327	FD91
Chestnut Gro., Ilf.	225	308	ES51
Chestnut Gro., Islw.	168	322	CG84
Chestnut Gro., Mitch.	286	332	DK99
Chestnut Gro., N.Mal.	269	322	CR97
Chestnut Gro., S.Croy.	295	333	DV108
Chestnut Gro., Stai.	264	328	BJ93
Chestnut Gro., Wem.	106	304	CH64
Chestnut La. N20	206	299	CY46
Chestnut Manor Clo., Stai.	264	328	BH92
Chestnut Ri. SE18	253	318	ES78
Chestnut Rd. SE27	194	324	DP90
Chestnut Rd. SW20	270	323	CX96
Chestnut Rd., Ashf.	265	328	BP91
Chestnut Rd., Enf.	203	301	DY36
Chestnut Rd., Kings.T.	268	322	CL94
Chestnut Rd., Twick.	259	321	CE89
Chestnut Wk., Shep.	281	328	BS99
Chestnut Way, Felt.	258	321	BV90
Cheston Ave., Croy.	288	333	DY103
Chestwood Gro., Uxb.	240	312	BM66
Cheswick Clo., Dart.	263	327	FF84
Chesworth Clo., Erith	255	319	FE81
Chettle Clo. SE1	74	316	DR76
Chettle Ct. N8	221	306	DN58
Chetwode Rd. SW17	191	323	DF90
Chetwood Wk. E6	244	318	EL71
Chetwynd Ave., Barn.	207	299	DF46
Chetwynd Dr., Uxb.	240	312	BM68
Chetwynd Rd. NW5	114	306	DH63
Cheval Pl. SW7	66/7	315	DE76
Cheval St. E14	150	317	EA76
Cheveley Clo., Rom.	228	311	FM53
Cheveney Wk., Brom.	276	326	EG97
Chevening Rd. NW6	127	315	CX68
Chevening Rd. SE10	151	317	EF78
Chevening Rd. SE19	273	324	DR93
Chevenings, The, Sid.	262	327	EW90
Cheverton Rd. N19	99	306	DK60
Chevet St. E9	119	307	DY64
Chevington Way, Horn.	238	310	FK63
Cheviot Clo., Bexh.	255	319	FE82
Cheviot Clo., Enf.	202	300	DR40
Cheviot Clo., Hayes	257	320	BR80
Cheviot Clo., Sutt.	293	331	DD109
Cheviot Gdns. NW2	95	305	CX61
Cheviot Gate NW2	95	305	CY61
Cheviot Rd. SE27	273	324	DN92
Cheviot Rd., Horn.	238	310	FG59
Cheviot Way, Ilf.	225	308	ES56
Chevron Clo. E16	244	318	EG72
Chevy Rd., Sthl.	251	321	CC75
Chewton Rd. E17	222	307	DY56
Cheyham Gdns., Sutt.	292	331	CX110
Cheyham Way, Sutt.	292	331	CY110
Cheyne Ave. E18	223	307	EF55
Cheyne Ave., Twick.	258	321	BZ88
Cheyne Clo. NW4	218	305	CW58
Cheyne Clo., Brom.	290	334	EL104
Cheyne Ct. SW3	159	315	DF79
Cheyne Gdns. SW3	159	315	DE79
Cheyne Hill, Surb.	268	322	CM98
Cheyne Ms. SW3	159	315	DE79
Cheyne Path W7	243	313	CF72
Cheyne Pl. SW3	159	315	DF79
Cheyne Rd., Ashf.	265	328	BR93
Cheyne Row SW3	159	315	DE79
Cheyne Wk. N21	209	300	DP43
Cheyne Wk. NW4	218	305	CW58
Cheyne Wk. SW3	159	315	DE79
Cheyne Wk. SW10	159	315	DD80
Cheyne Wk., Croy.	287	333	DU103
Cheyney Rd., Ashf.	265	328	BR93
Cheyneys Ave., Edg.	216	304	CK51
Chichele Gdns., Croy.	287	332	DT105
Chichele Rd. NW2	111	305	CX64
Chicheley Gdns., Har.	215	303	CC52
Chicheley Rd., Har.	215	303	CC52
Chicheley St. SE1	71	316	DM75
Chichester Ave., Ruis.	231	312	BR61
Chichester Clo. E6	244	318	EL72
Chichester Clo. SE3	252	318	EJ81
Chichester Clo., Hmptn.	266	329	BZ93
Chichester Ct., Stan.	216	304	CL55
Chichester Dr., Pur.	294	332	DM112
Chichester Gdns., Ilf.	234	308	EL59
Chichester Ms. SE27	273	324	DN91
Chichester Rents WC2	48	316	DN72
Chichester Rd. E11	105	307	EE62
Chichester Rd. N9	210	301	DU47
Chichester Rd. NW6	16	315	DA68
Chichester Rd. W2	40/1	315	DB71
Chichester Rd., Croy.	287	332	DS104
Chichester St. SW1	81	316	DJ78
Chichester Way E14	151	317	ED77
Chichester Way, Felt.	258	321	BW87
Chicksand St. E1	51	316	DT71
Chiddingfold N12	207	299	DA48
Chiddingstone Ave., Bexh.	254	319	EZ80
Chiddingstone Clo., Sutt.	292	331	DA110
Chiddingstone St. SW6	158	315	DA82
Chieveley Rd., Bexh.	263	327	FB84
Chignell Pl. W13	132	314	CG74
Chigwell Hill E1	138	317	DV73
Chigwell Hurst Ct., Pnr.	214	303	BX54
Chigwell Rd. E18	224	308	EH55
Chigwell Rd., Wdf.Grn.	224	308	EK52
Chigwell Vw., Rom.	227	309	FA51
Chilcot Clo. E14	140	317	EB72
Childebert Rd. SW17	192	324	DH89
Childeric Rd. SE14	165	317	DY80
Childerley St. SW6	157	315	CX81
Childers St. SE8	165	317	DY79
Childs Ave., Uxb.	212	302	BJ54
Childs Clo., Horn.	228	310	FJ58
Childs Hill Wk. NW2	95	305	CZ62
Childs La. SE19	273	324	DS93
Child's Pl. SW5	76	315	DA77
Child's St. SW5	76	315	DA77
Child's Wk. SW5	76	315	DA77
Childs Way NW11	218	305	CZ57
Chilham Clo., Bex.	262	327	EZ87
Chilham Clo., Grnf.	122	314	CG68
Chilham Rd. SE9	276	326	EL91
Chilham Way, Brom.	289	334	EG101
Chillerton Rd. SW17	272	324	DG92
Chillingworth Gdns., Twick.	259	321	CF90
Chillingworth Rd. N7	116	306	DN64
Chilmark Gdns., N.Mal.	283	330	CT101
Chilmark Rd. SW16	272	324	DK96
Chiltern Ave., Twick.	259	321	CA88
Chiltern Clo., Bexh.	255	319	FE81
Chiltern Clo., Croy.	287	332	DS104
Chiltern Clo., Uxb.	231	312	BN61
Chiltern Clo., Wor.Pk.	284	331	CW103
Chiltern Dr., Surb.	282	330	CN100
Chiltern Gdns. NW2	95	305	CX62
Chiltern Gdns., Brom.	275	325	EF98
Chiltern Gdns., Horn.	238	310	FJ62
Chiltern Rd. E3	130	317	EA70
Chiltern Rd., Ilf.	225	308	ES56
Chiltern Rd., Pnr.	214	303	BW57
Chiltern Rd., Sutt.	292	331	DB109
Chiltern St. W1	44	316	DG71
Chiltern Vw. Rd., Uxb.	240	312	BJ68
Chilterns, The, Sutt.	292	331	DB109
Chilthorne Clo. SE6	197	325	DZ87
Chilton Ave. W5	143	314	CK77
Chilton Gro. SE8	149	317	DX77
Chilton Rd., Edg.	217	304	CN51
Chilton Rd., Rich.	170	322	CN83
Chilton St. E2	39	316	DT70
Chiltonian Ind. Est. SE12	183	325	EF86
Chiltons, The E18	224	308	EG54
Chilver St. SE10	151	317	EF78
Chilworth Ct. SW19	189	323	CX88
Chilworth Gdns., Sutt.	285	331	DC104
Chilworth Ms. W2	42	315	DD72
Chilworth St. W2	41	315	DC72
Chimes Ave. N13	209	300	DN50
Chinbrook Cres. SE12	260	326	EH90
Chinbrook Est. SE9	260	326	EK90
Chinbrook Rd. SE12	260	326	EH90
Chinchilla Dr., Houns.	250	321	BW82
Chine, The N10	220	306	DJ56
Chine, The N21	209	300	DP44
Chine, The, Wem.	106	304	CH64
Ching Ct. WC2	46/7	316	DL72
Ching Way E4	222	307	DZ51
Chingdale Rd. E4	211	301	EE48
Chingford Ave. E4	211	301	EA48
Chingford Hall Est. E4	222	307	DZ51
Chingford Ind. Est. E4	210	301	DY50
Chingford La., Wdf.Grn.	211	301	EE49
Chingford Mt. Rd. E4	211	301	EA49
Chingford Rd. E4	223	307	EA51
Chingford Rd. E17	223	307	EB53
Chingley Clo., Brom.	275	325	EE93
Chinnery Clo., Enf.	202	300	DT39
Chinnor Cres., Grnf.	243	313	CB68
Chip St. SW4	177	324	DK84
Chipka St. E14	150	317	EC75
Chipley St. SE14	165	317	DY79
Chipmunk Gro., Nthlt.	242	313	BY69
Chippendale All., Uxb.	240	312	BK66
Chippendale St. E5	103	307	DX62
Chippendale Waye, Uxb.	240	312	BK66
Chippenham Ave., Wem.	108	304	CP64
Chippenham Clo., Pnr.	231	302	BT56
Chippenham Gdns. NW6	28	315	DA69
Chippenham Ms. W9	28	315	DA70
Chippenham Rd. W9	28	315	DA70
Chippenham Rd., Rom.	228	310	FK51
Chippenham Wk., Rom.	228	310	FK51
Chipperfield Clo., Upmin.	239	311	FS60
Chipperfield Rd., Orp.	278	327	EU95
Chipstead Ave., Th.Hth.	273	324	DP98
Chipstead Clo. SE19	273	324	DT94
Chipstead Clo., Sutt.	292	331	DB109
Chipstead Gdns. NW2	94	305	CV61
Chipstead Rd., Erith	255	319	FE80
Chipstead Rd., Houns.	257	320	BN83
Chipstead St. SW6	158	315	DA81
Chirk Clo., Hayes	242	313	BY70
Chisenhale Rd. E3	129	317	DY68
Chisholm Rd., Croy.	287	332	DS103
Chisholm Rd., Rich.	169	322	CM86
Chisledon Wk. E9	119	307	DZ65
Chislehurst Ave. N12	219	305	DC52
Chislehurst Rd., Brom.	276	326	EK96
Chislehurst Rd., Chis.	276	326	EK96
Chislehurst Rd., Orp.	291	334	ES100
Chislehurst Rd., Rich.	169	322	CL85
Chislehurst Rd., Sid.	278	327	EU92
Chislet Clo., Beck.	275	325	EA94
Chisley Rd. N15	221	306	DS58
Chiswell Sq. SE3	252	318	EH82
Chiswell St. EC1	50	316	DR71
Chiswick Bri. SW14	154	314	CQ82
Chiswick Bri. W4	154	314	CQ82
Chiswick Clo., Croy.	286	332	DM104
Chiswick Common Rd. W4	145	314	CR77
Chiswick Ct., Pnr.	214	303	BZ55
Chiswick Gdns. W4	154	314	CQ81
Chiswick High Rd. W4	144	314	CN78
Chiswick High Rd., Brent.	144	314	CN78
Chiswick Ho. Grds. W4	155	314	CR79
Chiswick La. W4	145	314	CS78
Chiswick La. S. W4	145	314	CT78
Chiswick Mall W4	155	314	CT79
Chiswick Mall W6	146	315	CU78
Chiswick Quay W4	154	314	CQ81
Chiswick Rd. N9	210	301	DU47
Chiswick Rd. W4	144	314	CQ77
Chiswick Sq. W4	155	314	CS79
Chiswick Staithe W4	154	314	CQ81
Chiswick Ter. W4	144	314	CQ77
Chiswick Village W4	154	314	CP79
Chiswick Wf. W4	155	314	CT79
Chitterfield Gate, West Dr.	257	320	BN80
Chitty St. W1	45	316	DJ71
Chitty's La., Dag.	236	309	EX61
Chivalry Rd. SW11	175	323	DE85
Chivenor Gro., Kings.T.	268	322	CK92
Chivers Rd. E4	211	301	EB49
Choats Manor Way, Bark.	246	319	EV70
Choats Rd., Bark.	246	319	EW68
Choats Rd., Dag.	246	319	EY69
Chobham Gdns. SW19	189	323	CX89
Chobham Rd. E15	121	307	ED64
Cholmeley Cres. N6	98	306	DH59
Cholmeley Pk. N6	98	306	DH60
Cholmley Gdns. NW6	112	305	DA64
Cholmondeley Ave. NW10	126	315	CU68
Cholmondeley Wk., Rich.	168	322	CJ85
Choppins Ct. E1	138	317	DV74
Chopwell Clo. E15	121	307	ED66
Chorleywood Cres., Orp.	277	326	ET96
Choumert Gro. SE15	164	317	DU82
Choumert Rd. SE15	179	324	DT83
Choumert Sq. SE15	164	317	DU82
Chow Sq. E8	117	306	DT64
Chrislaine Clo. (Stanwell), Stai.	256	320	BK86
Chrisp St. E14	140	317	EB71
Christ Ch. Ave., Erith	255	319	FD79
Christ Ch. Pas. EC1	48/9	316	DP72
Christ Ch. Rd. SW14	170	322	CP85
Christ Ch. Rd., Beck.	275	325	EA96
Christ Ch. Rd., Surb.	282	330	CM101
Christchurch Ave. N12	219	305	DC51
Christchurch Ave. NW6	127	315	CX67
Christchurch Ave., Har.	215	303	CF56
Christchurch Ave., Rain.	247	319	FF68
Christchurch Ave., Tedd.	268	322	CG92
Christchurch Ave., Wem.	107	304	CL65
Christchurch Clo. SW19	271	323	DD94
Christchurch Gdns., Har.	216	304	CG56
Christchurch Grn., Wem.	107	304	CL65
Christchurch Hill NW3	97	305	DD62
Christchurch Ind. Cen., Har.	215	303	CF56
Christchurch Pk., Sutt.	293	331	DC108
Christchurch Pas. NW3	97	305	DD62
Christchurch Rd. N8	220	306	DL58
Christchurch Rd. SW2	193	324	DM88
Christchurch Rd. SW19	271	323	DD95
Christchurch Rd., Houns.	257	320	BN82
Christchurch Rd., Ilf.	235	308	EP60
Christchurch Rd., Pur.	294	332	DP110
Christchurch Rd., Sid.	277	326	ET91
Christchurch Sq. E9	128	317	DW67
Christchurch St. SW3	159	315	DF79
Christchurch Ter. SW3	159	315	DF79
Christchurch Way SE10	151	317	EE78
Christian Ct. SE16	139	317	DZ74
Christian Flds. SW16	273	324	DN94
Christian St. E1	138	317	DU72
Christie Dr., Croy.	287	332	DT100
Christie Gdns., Rom.	226	309	EV58
Christie Rd. E9	119	307	DY65
Christina Sq. N4	100	306	DP60
Christina St. EC2	38/9	316	DS70
Christopher Ave. W7	142	314	CG76
Christopher Clo. SE16	149	317	DX75
Christopher Clo., Horn.	238	310	FK63
Christopher Clo., Sid.	261	326	ET85
Christopher Gdns., Dag.	236	309	EX64
Christopher Pl. NW1	34	316	DK69
Christopher Rd., Sthl.	250	321	BV77
Christopher St. EC2	38	316	DR70
Christopher's Ms. W11	137	315	CY74
Chryssell Rd. SW9	162	316	DN80
Chubworthy St. SE14	165	317	DY79
Chudleigh Cres., Ilf.	235	308	ES63
Chudleigh Gdns., Sutt.	285	331	DC104
Chudleigh Rd. NW6	111	305	CX66
Chudleigh Rd. SE4	181	325	DZ85
Chudleigh Rd., Twick.	259	321	CE86
Chudleigh St. E1	139	317	DX72
Chudleigh Way, Ruis.	232	313	BU60
Chulsa Rd. SE26	274	325	DV92
Chumleigh St. SE5	163	316	DS79
Chumleigh Wk., Surb.	268	322	CM98
Church All., Croy.	286	332	DP101
Church App. SE21	195	324	DR90
Church App., Stai.	256	320	BK86
Church Ave. E4	223	307	ED51
Church Ave. NW1	114	306	DH65
Church Ave. SW14	171	322	CR83
Church Ave., Beck.	275	325	EA95
Church Ave., Nthlt.	232	313	BZ66
Church Ave., Pnr.	214	303	BY58
Church Ave., Ruis.	231	312	BR60
Church Ave., Sid.	278	327	EU92
Church Ave., Sthl.	250	321	BY76
Church Clo. N20	207	299	DE48
Church Clo. W8	64/5	315	DB75
Church Clo., Edg.	205	298	CQ50
Church Clo., Hayes	249	312	BR71
Church Clo., Nthwd.	213	302	BT52
Church Clo., Stai.	280	328	BJ97
Church Clo., Uxb.	240	312	BH68
Church Clo., West Dr.	248	320	BL76
Church Ct., Rich.	169	322	CK85
Church Cres. E9	119	307	DX66
Church Cres. N3	218	305	CZ53
Church Cres. N10	220	306	DH56
Church Cres. N20	207	299	DE48
Church Dr. NW9	93	304	CR60
Church Dr., Har.	214	303	BZ58
Church Dr., W.Wick.	289	333	EE104
Church Elm La., Dag.	237	309	FA65
Church End E17	223	307	EB56
Church End NW4	218	305	CV55
Church Entry EC4	48/9	316	DP72
Church Fm. La., Sutt.	292	331	CY107
Church Gdns. W5	143	314	CK75
Church Gdns., Wem.	106	304	CG63
Church Gate SW6	173	323	CY83
Church Grn., Hayes	249	312	BT72
Church Gro. SE13	182	325	EB84
Church Gro., Kings.T.	268	322	CJ95

Church Hill E17 223 307 EA56
Church Hill N21 208 300 DM45
Church Hill SE18 252 318 EM76
Church Hill SW19 270 323 CZ92
Church Hill, Cars. 285 331 DF106
Church Hill (Crayford), Dart. 263 327 FE84
Church Hill, Har. 233 313 CE60
Church Hill, Orp. 291 335 EU101
Church Hill, Pur. 294 332 DL110
Church Hill, Uxb. 230 302 BJ55
Church Hill Rd. E17 223 307 EB56
Church Hill Rd., Barn. 207 299 DE44
Church Hill Rd., Surb. 268 330 CL99
Church Hill Rd., Sutt. 284 331 CX105
Church Hill Wd., Orp. 291 335 EU99
Church Hyde SE18 253 318 ES79
Church La. E11 105 307 EE60
Church La. E17 223 307 EB56
Church La. N2 219 305 DC55
Church La. N8 220 306 DM56
Church La. N9 210 301 DU47
Church La. N17 221 306 DS53
Church La. NW9 217 304 CQ58
Church La. SW17 272 324 DH92
Church La. SW19 270 323 CZ95
Church La. W5 142 314 CJ75
Church La., Brom. 290 334 EL102
Church La., Chis. 277 326 EQ95
Church La., Dag. 237 309 FB65
Church La., Enf. 202 300 DR41
Church La., Har. 215 303 CF53
Church La., Pnr. 214 303 BY55
Church La., Rich. 185 322 CL88
Church La., Rom. 227 309 FE56
Church La., Tedd. 267 329 CF92
Church La., Twick. 184 322 CG88
Church La., Uxb. 240 312 BH68
Church La., Wall. 286 332 DK104
Church Manor Est. SW9 162 316 DN80
Church Manorway SE2 254 319 EU78
Church Manorway, Erith 255 319 FD76
Church Meadow, Surb. 282 330 CJ103
Church Mt. N2 219 305 DD57
Church Pas. EC2 49 316 DQ72
Church Pas., Surb. 282 330 CL99
Church Path E11 224 308 EG57
Church Path E17 223 307 EB56
Church Path N12 207 299 DC50
Church Path N17 221 306 DS52
Church Path N20 207 299 DC49
Church Path NW10 109 304 CS66
Church Path SW14 171 322 CR83
Church Path SW19 270 323 CZ96
Church Path W4 144 314 CQ76
Church Path W7 243 313 CE74
Church Path, Croy. 287 332 DQ103
Church Path, Mitch. 271 323 DE97
Church Path, Sthl. 250 321 BZ76
Church Pl. SW1 57 316 DJ73
Church Pl. W5 143 314 CK75
Church Pl., Mitch. 271 323 DE97
Church Pl., Twick. 184 322 CH88
Church Pl., Uxb. 231 312 BQ62
Church Ri. SE23 197 325 DX89
Church Rd. E10 104 307 EA60
Church Rd. E12 234 308 EL64
Church Rd. E17 222 307 DY54
Church Rd. N6 220 306 DG58
Church Rd. N17 221 306 DS53
Church Rd. NW4 218 305 CV56
Church Rd. NW10 109 304 CS66
Church Rd. SE19 273 324 DS95
Church Rd. SW13 155 314 CT82
Church Rd. (Wimbledon) SW19 270 323 CY92
Church Rd. W3 134 314 CQ74
Church Rd. W7 243 313 CD73
Church Rd., Ashf. 264 320 BM90
Church Rd., Bark. 235 308 EQ65
Church Rd., Bexh. 262 327 EZ83
Church Rd., Brom. 276 326 EG96
Church Rd. (Shortlands), Brom. 275 325 EE97
Church Rd., Croy. 286 332 DP103
Church Rd., E.Mol. 267 329 CD98
Church Rd., Enf. 210 301 DW44
Church Rd., Erith 255 319 FC78
Church Rd., Felt. 266 329 BX92
Church Rd., Hayes 249 312 BT74
Church Rd. (Cranford), Houns. 250 321 BV78
Church Rd. (Heston), Houns. 251 321 CA80
Church Rd., Ilf. 225 308 ES58
Church Rd., Islw. 251 321 CD81
Church Rd., Kings.T. 268 322 CM96
Church Rd., Mitch. 271 323 DD97
Church Rd., Nthlt. 242 313 BX68
Church Rd., Nthwd. 213 302 BT52
Church Rd. (Farnborough), Orp. 291 334 EQ106
Church Rd., Pur. 294 332 DL110
Church Rd., Rich. 169 322 CL84
Church Rd. (Ham), Rich. 268 322 CK91
Church Rd. (Harold Wd.), Rom. 229 311 FN53
Church Rd., Shep. 281 328 BP101
Church Rd., Sid. 278 327 EU91
Church Rd., Sthl. 250 321 BZ76
Church Rd., Stan. 204 298 CH50
Church Rd., Surb. 282 330 CJ102
Church Rd., Sutt. 292 331 CY107
Church Rd., Tedd. 267 329 CE91
Church Rd. (Cowley), Uxb. 240 312 BK70
Church Rd. (Harefield), Uxb. 230 302 BJ55
Church Rd., Wall. 286 332 DJ104
Church Rd., Well. 254 319 EV82
Church Rd., West Dr. 248 320 BK76
Church Rd., Wor.Pk. 283 330 CS103
Church Rd. Merton SW19 271 323 DD95
Church Row NW3 112 305 DC63
Church Row, Chis. 277 326 EQ95
Church Sq., Shep. 281 328 BP101
Church St. E15 131 317 EE68
Church St. E16 245 318 EP74
Church St. N9 209 300 DT47
Church St. NW8 42 315 DD71
Church St. W2 42 315 DD71
Church St. W4 155 314 CT79
Church St., Croy. 287 332 DQ103
Church St., Dag. 237 309 FB65
Church St., Enf. 202 300 DQ41
Church St., Hmptn. 267 329 CC96
Church St., Islw. 168 322 CH83
Church St., Kings.T. 268 322 CK96
Church St., Sun. 266 329 BU97
Church St., Sutt. 284 331 DB106
Church St., Twick. 184 322 CG88
Church St. Est. NW8 30 315 DD70
Church St. N. E15 131 317 EE67
Church St. Pas. E15 131 317 EE67
Church Stretton Rd., Houns. 259 321 CC85
Church Ter. NW4 218 305 CV55
Church Ter. SE13 183 325 EE83
Church Ter. SW8 161 316 DK82
Church Ter., Rich. 169 322 CK85
Church Vale N2 219 305 DF55
Church Vale SE23 196 325 DW89
Church Vw., Swan. 279 327 FD97
Church Vw., Upmin. 239 311 FN61
Church Wk. N6 98 306 DG62
Church Wk. N16 117 306 DR63
Church Wk. NW2 95 305 CZ62
Church Wk. NW4 218 305 CW55
Church Wk. NW9 93 304 CR61
Church Wk. SW13 156 315 CU81
Church Wk. SW15 172 323 CV85
Church Wk. SW16 272 324 DJ96
Church Wk. SW20 270 323 CW97
Church Wk., Brent. 152 314 CJ79
Church Wk., Cher. 280 328 BG100
Church Wk., Hayes 249 312 BS72
Church Wk., Rich. 169 322 CK85
Church Way, Edg. 217 304 CN51
Church Way, S.Croy. 295 332 DT110
Churchbury Clo., Enf. 202 300 DS40
Churchbury La., Enf. 202 300 DR41
Churchbury Rd. SE9 260 326 EK87
Churchbury Rd., Enf. 202 300 DR40
Churchcroft Clo. SW12 192 324 DG87
Churchdown, Brom. 275 325 EE91
Churchfield Ave. N12 219 305 DC51
Churchfield Clo., Har. 215 303 CC56
Churchfield Clo., Hayes 249 312 BT73
Churchfield Rd. W3 134 314 CQ74
Churchfield Rd. W7 251 321 CE75
Churchfield Rd. W13 132 314 CH74
Churchfield Rd., Well. 262 327 EU83
Churchfields E18 224 308 EG53
Churchfields SE10 166 317 EC79
Churchfields, W.Mol. 267 329 CA97
Churchfields Ave., Felt. 258 321 BZ90
Churchfields Rd., Beck. 274 325 DX96
Churchill Ave., Har. 216 304 CH58
Churchill Ave., Uxb. 241 312 BP69
Churchill Clo., Felt. 265 320 BT88
Churchill Clo., Uxb. 241 312 BP69
Churchill Ct. W5 123 314 CM70
Churchill Ct., Nthlt. 233 313 CA64
Churchill Ct., Stai. 264 328 BJ93
Churchill Gdns. SW1 81 316 DJ78
Churchill Gdns. W3 134 314 CN72
Churchill Gdns. Rd. SW1 80/1 316 DH78
Churchill Ms., Wdf.Grn. 223 307 EF51
Churchill Pl. E14 140 317 EB74
Churchill Pl., Har. 215 303 CE56
Churchill Rd. E16 244 318 EJ72
Churchill Rd. NW2 110 305 CV65
Churchill Rd. NW5 114 306 DH63
Churchill Rd., Edg. 216 304 CM51
Churchill Rd., S.Croy. 295 332 DQ109
Churchill Ter. E4 211 301 EA49
Churchill Wk. E9 118 307 DW64
Churchill Way, Brom. 276 326 EG97
Churchill Way, Sun. 266 329 BU92
Churchley Rd. SE26 274 325 DV91
Churchmead Clo., Barn. 207 299 DE44
Churchmead Rd. NW10 110 305 CU65
Churchmore Rd. SW16 272 324 DJ95
Churchview Rd., Twick. 259 321 CD88
Churchway NW1 24 316 DK69
Churchwell Path E9 118 307 DW65
Churchyard Row SE11 84/5 316 DP77
Churston Ave. E13 244 318 EH67
Churston Clo. SW2 194 324 DP88
Churston Dr., Mord. 284 331 CX99
Churston Gdns. N11 220 306 DJ51
Churton Pl. SW1 81 316 DJ77
Churton St. SW1 81 316 DJ77
Chusan Pl. E14 139 317 DZ72
Chyngton Clo., Sid. 261 327 ET90
Cibber Rd. SE23 197 325 DX89
Cicada Rd. SW18 174 323 DC86
Cicely Rd. SE15 164 317 DU81
Cinderford Way, Brom. 275 325 EE91
Cinema Par. W5 123 314 CM70
Cinnamon Clo., Croy. 286 332 DL101
Cinnamon Row SW11 174 323 DC83
Cinnamon St. E1 138 317 DV74
Cintra Pk. SE19 273 324 DT94
Circle, The NW2 93 304 CS62
Circle, The NW7 205 298 CR50
Circle Gdns. SW19 271 323 DA96
Circuits, The, Pnr. 214 303 BW56
Circular Rd. N17 221 306 DT55
Circular Way SE18 252 318 EM79
Circus Ms. W1 43 315 DF71
Circus Pl. EC2 50 316 DR71
Circus Rd. NW8 30 315 DD69
Circus St. SE10 166 317 EC80
Cirencester St. W2 40/1 315 DB71
Cissbury Ring N. N12 206 299 CZ50
Cissbury Ring S. N12 206 299 CZ50
Cissbury Rd. N15 221 306 DR57
Citadel Pl. SE11 83 316 DM78
Citizen Rd. N7 100 306 DN62
Citron Ter. SE15 180 325 DV83
City Gdn. Row N1 24/5 316 DP68
City Rd. EC1 24/5 316 DP68
Civic Way, Ilf. 225 308 EQ56
Civic Way, Ruis. 232 313 BX64
Clabon Ms. SW1 67 315 DF76
Clack St. SE16 148 317 DW75
Clacton Rd. E6 244 318 EK69
Clacton Rd. E17 222 307 DY58
Clacton Rd. N17 221 306 DT54
Claigmar Gdns. N3 219 305 DB53
Claire Ct. N12 207 299 DC48
Claire Ct., Pnr. 214 303 BZ52
Claire Pl. E14 150 317 EA76
Clairvale, Horn. 238 311 FL59
Clairvale Rd., Houns. 250 321 BX81
Clairview Rd. SW16 272 324 DH92
Clairville Gdns. W7 243 313 CE74
Clairville Pt. SE23 197 325 DX90
Clammas Way, Uxb. 248 312 BJ71
Clancarty Rd. SW6 158 315 DA82
Clandon Clo. W3 144 314 CP75
Clandon Gdns. N3 219 305 DA55
Clandon Rd., Ilf. 235 308 ES61
Clandon St. SE8 166 317 EA82
Clanfield Way SE15 163 316 DS80
Clanricarde Gdns. W2 52 315 DA73
Clap La., Dag. 237 309 FB62
Clapham Common N. Side SW4 175 323 DF84
Clapham Common S. Side SW4 176 324 DH86
Clapham Common W. Side SW4 175 323 DF84
Clapham Cres. SW4 177 324 DK84
Clapham High St. SW4 177 324 DK84
Clapham Junct. Est. SW11 175 323 DE84
Clapham Manor St. SW4 176 324 DJ83
Clapham Pk. Est. SW4 177 324 DK86
Clapham Pk. Rd. SW4 177 324 DK84
Clapham Rd. SW9 177 324 DL83
Clapham Rd. Est. SW4 177 324 DK83
Claps Gate La. E6 245 318 EP70
Claps Gate La., Bark. 245 318 EP70
Clapton Common E5 101 306 DT59
Clapton Pk. Est. E5 119 307 DY63
Clapton Pas. E5 118 307 DW64
Clapton Sq. E5 118 307 DW64
Clapton Ter. N16 102 307 DU60
Clapton Way E5 118 307 DU63
Clara Pl. SE18 253 318 EN77
Clare Clo. N2 219 305 DC55
Clare Clo., Borwd. 204 298 CM44
Clare Cor. SE9 261 326 EP87
Clare Ct., Nthwd. 213 302 BS50
Clare Gdns. E7 234 308 EG63
Clare Gdns. W11 137 315 CY72
Clare Gdns., Bark. 235 308 ET65
Clare Gdns., Stan. 204 298 CJ50
Clare La. N1 116 306 DQ66
Clare Lawn Ave. SW14 171 322 CR85
Clare Mkt. WC2 47 316 DM72
Clare Ms. SW6 158 315 DB80
Clare Pl. SW15 172 323 CT86
Clare Rd. E11 223 307 ED58
Clare Rd. NW10 110 305 CU66
Clare Rd. SE14 165 317 DZ82
Clare Rd., Grnf. 233 313 CD65
Clare Rd., Houns. 258 321 BZ83
Clare Rd., Stai. 264 320 BK88
Clare St. E2 128 317 DV68
Clare Way, Bexh. 254 319 EY81
Claredale St. E2 128 317 DU68
Claremont Ave., Har. 216 304 CL57
Claremont Ave., N.Mal. 283 331 CV99
Claremont Ave., Sun. 266 329 BV95
Claremont Clo. E16 245 318 EN74
Claremont Clo. N1 24 316 DN68
Claremont Clo. SW2 193 324 DL88
Claremont Clo., Orp. 290 334 EN105
Claremont Cres., Dart. 263 327 FE84
Claremont Dr., Shep. 281 328 BP100
Claremont Gdns., Ilf. 235 308 ES61
Claremont Gdns., Surb. 282 330 CL99
Claremont Gdns., Upmin. 239 311 FR60
Claremont Gro. W4 155 314 CS80
Claremont Gro., Wdf.Grn. 224 308 EJ51
Claremont Pk. N3 218 305 CY53
Claremont Rd. E7 234 308 EH64
Claremont Rd. E17 222 307 DY54
Claremont Rd. N6 98 306 DH59
Claremont Rd. NW2 94 305 CW59
Claremont Rd. W9 127 315 CZ68
Claremont Rd. W13 132 314 CG71
Claremont Rd., Brom. 276 326 EL98
Claremont Rd., Croy. 287 333 DU102
Claremont Rd., Har. 215 303 CE54
Claremont Rd., Horn. 228 310 FG58
Claremont Rd., Surb. 282 330 CL100
Claremont Rd., Swan. 279 327 FE94
Claremont Rd., Tedd. 267 329 CF92
Claremont Rd., Twick. 168 322 CH86
Claremont Sq. N1 24 316 DN68
Claremont St. E16 245 318 EN74
Claremont St. N18 222 307 DU51
Claremont St. SE10 166 317 EB79
Claremont Way NW2 94 305 CW60
Clarence Ave. SW4 193 324 DK87
Clarence Ave., Brom. 276 326 EL98
Clarence Ave., Ilf. 225 308 EN58
Clarence Ave., N.Mal. 269 322 CQ96
Clarence Ave., Upmin. 239 311 FN61
Clarence Cres. SW4 177 324 DK86
Clarence Cres., Sid. 262 327 EV90
Clarence Gdns. NW1 32/3 316 DH69
Clarence La. SW15 171 322 CS86
Clarence Ms. E5 118 307 DV64
Clarence Ms. SE16 139 317 DX74
Clarence Pas. NW1 22/3 316 DL68
Clarence Pl. E5 118 307 DV64
Clarence Rd. E5 118 307 DV63
Clarence Rd. E12 234 308 EK64
Clarence Rd. E16 131 317 EE70
Clarence Rd. E17 222 307 DX54
Clarence Rd. N15 221 306 DQ57
Clarence Rd. N22 220 306 DL52
Clarence Rd. NW6 111 305 CZ66
Clarence Rd. SE9 260 326 EL89
Clarence Rd. SW19 271 323 DB93
Clarence Rd. W4 144 314 CN78
Clarence Rd., Bexh. 262 327 EY84
Clarence Rd., Brom. 276 326 EK97
Clarence Rd., Croy. 287 332 DR101
Clarence Rd., Enf. 210 301 DV43
Clarence Rd., Rich. 153 314 CM81
Clarence Rd., Sid. 262 327 EV90
Clarence Rd., Sutt. 284 331 DB105
Clarence Rd., Tedd. 267 329 CF93
Clarence Rd., Wall. 285 332 DH106
Clarence St., Kings.T. 268 322 CL96
Clarence St., Rich. 169 322 CL84
Clarence St., Sthl. 250 321 BX76
Clarence Ter. NW1 31 315 DF70
Clarence Ter., Houns. 259 321 CB84
Clarence Wk. SW4 161 316 DL82
Clarence Way NW1 114 306 DH66
Clarence Way Est. NW1 114 306 DH66
Clarenden Pl., Dart. 279 327 FE92
Clarendon Clo. W2 54/5 315 DE73
Clarendon Clo., Orp. 278 327 EU97
Clarendon Cres. W11 137 315 CY73
Clarendon Cres., Twick. 259 321 CD90
Clarendon Cross W11 137 315 CY73
Clarendon Dr. SW15 172 323 CW83
Clarendon Gdns. NW4 218 305 CU55
Clarendon Gdns. W9 29 315 DC70
Clarendon Gdns., Ilf. 234 308 EM60
Clarendon Gdns., Wem. 91 304 CK62
Clarendon Grn., Orp. 278 327 EU97
Clarendon Gro. NW1 34 316 DK69
Clarendon Gro., Mitch. 271 323 DF97
Clarendon Gro., Orp. 278 327 EU98
Clarendon Ms. W2 54/5 315 DE73
Clarendon Ms., Bex. 263 327 FB88
Clarendon Path, Orp. 278 327 EU97
Clarendon Pl. W2 54/5 315 DE73
Clarendon Ri. SE13 182 325 EC83
Clarendon Rd. E11 105 307 ED60
Clarendon Rd. E17 223 307 EB58
Clarendon Rd. E18 224 308 EG55
Clarendon Rd. N8 220 306 DM55
Clarendon Rd. N15 221 306 DP56
Clarendon Rd. N18 222 307 DU51
Clarendon Rd. N22 220 306 DM54
Clarendon Rd. SW19 271 323 DE94
Clarendon Rd. W5 123 314 CL70
Clarendon Rd. W11 137 315 CY73
Clarendon Rd., Ashf. 264 328 BM91
Clarendon Rd., Croy. 286 332 DP103
Clarendon Rd., Har. 215 303 CE58
Clarendon Rd., Hayes 249 320 BT75
Clarendon Rd., Wall. 294 332 DJ107
Clarendon St. SW1 80/1 316 DH78
Clarendon Ter. W9 29 315 DC70
Clarendon Wk. W11 137 315 CY72
Clarendon Way N21 209 300 DQ44
Clarendon Way, Chis. 277 326 ET97
Clarendon Way, Orp. 278 327 EU97
Clarens St. SE6 197 325 DZ89
Claret Gdns. SE25 273 324 DS98
Clareville Gro. SW7 77 315 DC77
Clareville Rd., Orp. 291 334 EQ103
Clareville St. SW7 77 315 DC77
Clarewood Wk. SW9 178 324 DN84
Clarges Ms. W1 56/7 316 DH74
Clarges St. W1 56/7 316 DH74
Claribel Rd. SW9 162 316 DP82
Clarice Way, Wall. 294 332 DL109
Claridge Rd., Dag. 236 309 EX60
Clarina Rd. SE20 274 325 DX94
Clarissa Rd., Rom. 236 309 EX59
Clarissa St. E8 27 316 DT67
Clark St. E1 138 317 DV71
Clark Way, Houns. 250 321 BX80
Clarke Path N16 102 307 DU60
Clarkes Ave., Wor.Pk. 284 331 CX102
Clarkes Dr., Uxb. 248 312 BL71
Clarke's Ms. W1 44 316 DG71
Clarks Pl. EC2 50/1 316 DS72
Clarks Rd., Ilf. 235 308 ER61
Clarkson Rd. E16 141 317 EF72
Clarkson St. E2 128 317 DV69
Clarksons, The, Bark. 245 318 EQ68
Classon Clo., West Dr. 248 320 BL75
Claston Clo., Dart. 263 327 FE84
Claude Rd. E10 104 307 EC61
Claude Rd. E13 244 318 EH67
Claude Rd. SE15 164 317 DV82
Claude St. E14 150 317 EA77
Claudia Jones Way SW2 177 324 DL86
Claudia Pl. SW19 189 323 CY88
Claughton Rd. E13 244 318 EJ68
Clauson Ave., Nthlt. 233 313 CB64
Clave St. E1 138 317 DV74
Clavell St. SE10 166 317 EC79
Claverdale Rd. SW2 193 324 DM87
Clavering Ave. SW13 156 315 CV79
Clavering Clo., Twick. 268 322 CG91
Clavering Rd. E12 234 308 EK60
Claverings Ind. Est. N9 210 301 DX47
Claverley Gro. N3 219 305 DB53
Claverley Vil. N3 219 305 DB52
Claverton St. SW1 81 316 DJ78
Claxton Gro. W6 147 315 CX78
Clay Ave., Mitch. 272 324 DH96
Clay Hill, Enf. 202 300 DP37
Clay La., Edg. 205 298 CP47
Clay La., Stai. 264 320 BM87
Clay St. W1 43 315 DF71
Claybank Gro. SE13 182 325 EB83
Claybourne Ms. SE19 273 324 DS94
Claybridge Rd. SE12 276 326 EJ91
Claybrook Clo. N2 219 305 DD55
Claybrook Rd. W6 157 315 CX79
Claybury Bdy., Ilf. 224 308 EL55
Claybury Rd., Wdf.Grn. 224 308 EL52
Claydon Dr., Croy. 286 332 DL105
Clayfarm Rd. SE9 261 326 EQ89
Claygate Clo., Horn. 238 310 FG63
Claygate Rd. W13 142 314 CH76
Clayhall Ave., Ilf. 224 308 EL55
Clayhill, Surb. 282 330 CN99
Clayhill Cres. SE9 276 326 EK91
Claylands Pl. SW8 162 316 DN80
Claylands Rd. SW8 161 316 DM79
Claymill Ho. SE18 253 318 EQ78
Claymore Clo., Mord. 284 331 DA101
Claypole Dr., Houns. 250 321 BY81
Claypole Rd. E15 130 317 EC68
Clayponds Ave., Brent. 143 314 CL77
Clayponds Gdns. W5 143 314 CK77
Clayponds La., Brent. 143 314 CL78
Clays La. E15 120 307 EB64
Clays La. Clo. E15 120 307 EB64
Clayton Ave., Upmin. 239 311 FP64
Clayton Ave., Wem. 107 304 CL66
Clayton Clo. E6 244 318 EM72
Clayton Cres., Brent. 143 314 CK78
Clayton Fld. NW9 217 304 CS52
Clayton Ms. SE10 167 317 ED81
Clayton Rd. SE15 164 317 DU81
Clayton Rd., Chess. 282 330 CJ105
Clayton Rd., Hayes 249 320 BS75
Clayton Rd., Islw. 259 321 CE83
Clayton Rd., Rom. 237 309 FC60
Clayton St. SE11 162 316 DN79
Clayton Ter., Hayes 242 313 BX71
Clayton Way, Uxb. 240 312 BK70
Claywood Clo., Orp. 291 334 ES101
Clayworth Clo., Sid. 262 327 EV86
Cleanthus Clo. SE18 253 318 EP81
Cleanthus Rd. SE18 253 318 EP81
Clearbrook Way E1 139 317 DX72
Clearwater Ter. W11 147 315 CX75
Clearwell Dr. W9 28/9 315 DB70
Cleave Ave., Hayes 249 320 BS77
Cleaveland Rd., Surb. 282 330 CK99
Cleaver Sq. SE11 84 316 DN78
Cleaver St. SE11 84 316 DN78
Cleaverholme Clo. SE25 287 333 DV100
Cleeve Ct., Felt. 265 320 BS88
Cleeve Hill SE23 196 325 DV88
Cleeve Pk. Gdns., Sid. 262 327 EV89
Clegg St. E1 138 317 DV74
Clegg St. E13 244 318 EG68
Clem Attlee Ct. SW6 157 315 CZ79
Clem Attlee Par. SW6 157 315 CZ79
Clematis Clo., Rom. 228 310 FJ52
Clematis St. W12 136 315 CU73
Clemence St. E14 139 317 DZ71
Clement Ave. SW4 177 324 DK84
Clement Clo. NW6 110 305 CW66
Clement Clo. W4 145 314 CR77
Clement Gdns., Hayes 249 320 BS77
Clement Rd. SW19 270 323 CY92
Clement Rd., Beck. 274 325 DX96
Clement Way, Upmin. 238 311 FM62
Clementhorpe Rd., Dag. 236 309 EW65
Clementina Rd. E10 103 307 DZ60
Clementine Clo. W13 142 314 CH75
Clements Ave. E16 244 318 EG73
Clements Ct., Houns. 258 321 BX84
Clements Ct., Ilf. 235 308 EP62
Clement's Inn WC2 47 316 DM72
Clement's Inn Pas. WC2 47 316 DM72
Clements La. EC4 62 316 DR73
Clements La., Ilf. 235 308 EP62
Clements Pl., Brent. 143 314 CK78
Clements Rd. E6 234 308 EL66
Clements Rd. SE16 148 317 DU76
Clements Rd., Ilf. 235 308 EP62
Clendon Way SE18 253 318 ER77
Clennam St. SE1 73 316 DQ75
Clensham La., Sutt. 284 331 DA103
Clenston Ms. W1 43 315 DF72
Clephane Rd. N1 116 306 DQ65
Clere St. EC2 38 316 DR70
Clerics Wk., Shep. 281 328 BR100
Clerkenwell Clo. EC1 36 316 DN70
Clerkenwell Grn. EC1 36 316 DN70
Clerkenwell Rd. EC1 36 316 DN70
Clermont Rd. E9 128 317 DW67
Cleve Rd. NW6 112 305 DA66
Cleve Rd., Sid. 262 327 EX90
Clevedon Clo. N16 101 306 DT62
Clevedon Gdns., Hayes 249 320 BR76
Clevedon Gdns., Houns. 250 321 BV81
Clevedon Rd. SE20 274 325 DX95
Clevedon Rd., Kings.T. 269 322 CN96
Clevedon Rd., Twick. 169 322 CK86
Cleveland Ave. SW20 270 323 CZ96
Cleveland Ave. W4 145 314 CT77
Cleveland Ave., Hmptn. 266 329 BZ94
Cleveland Cres., Borwd. 205 298 CQ43
Cleveland Dr., Stai. 280 328 BH96
Cleveland Gdns. N4 221 306 DQ57
Cleveland Gdns. NW2 95 305 CX61
Cleveland Gdns. SW13 155 314 CT82
Cleveland Gdns. W2 41 315 DC72
Cleveland Gdns., Wor.Pk. 283 330 CS103
Cleveland Gro. E1 128 317 DW70
Cleveland Ms. W1 45 316 DJ71
Cleveland Pk., Stai. 256 320 BL86
Cleveland Pk. Ave. E17 223 307 EA56
Cleveland Pk. Cres. E17 223 307 EA56
Cleveland Pl. SW1 57 316 DJ74
Cleveland Ri., Mord. 284 331 CX101
Cleveland Rd. E18 224 308 EG55
Cleveland Rd. N1 117 306 DR66
Cleveland Rd. N9 210 301 DV45
Cleveland Rd. SW13 155 314 CT82
Cleveland Rd. W4 144 314 CQ76
Cleveland Rd. W13 132 314 CG71
Cleveland Rd., Ilf. 235 308 EP62
Cleveland Rd., Islw. 168 322 CG84
Cleveland Rd., N.Mal. 269 322 CS98
Cleveland Rd., Uxb. 240 312 BK68
Cleveland Rd., Well. 253 318 ET82
Cleveland Rd., Wor.Pk. 283 330 CS103
Cleveland Row SW1 57 316 DJ74
Cleveland Sq. W2 41 315 DC72
Cleveland St. W1 32/3 316 DH70
Cleveland Ter. W2 41 315 DC72
Cleveland Way E1 128 317 DW70
Cleveley Clo. SE7 252 318 EK77
Cleveley Cres. W5 123 314 CL68
Cleveleys Rd. E5 102 307 DV62
Cleverley Est. W12 136 315 CU74
Cleves Rd. E6 244 318 EK67
Cleves Rd., Rich. 184 322 CJ90
Cleves Wk., Ilf. 225 308 EQ52
Cleves Way, Hmptn. 266 329 BZ94
Cleves Way, Ruis. 232 313 BX60
Cleves Way, Sun. 265 328 BT93
Clewer Cres., Har. 214 303 CD53
Clichy Est. E1 138 317 DW71
Clifden Rd. E5 118 307 DW64
Clifden Rd., Brent. 153 314 CK79
Clifden Rd., Twick. 259 321 CF88
Cliff End, Pur. 294 332 DP112
Cliff Rd. NW1 115 306 DK65
Cliff Ter. SE8 166 317 EA82
Cliff Vil. NW1 115 306 DK65
Cliff Wk. E16 131 317 EF70
Cliffe Rd., S.Croy. 287 332 DR106
Cliffe Wk., Sutt. 285 331 DC106
Clifford Ave. SW14 170 322 CP83
Clifford Ave., Chis. 276 326 EM93
Clifford Ave., Ilf. 225 308 EP53
Clifford Ave., Wall. 286 332 DJ105
Clifford Clo., Nthlt. 242 313 BY67
Clifford Dr. SW9 178 324 DP84
Clifford Gdns. NW10 126 315 CW68
Clifford Gro., Ashf. 265 328 BN91
Clifford Rd. E16 131 317 EF70
Clifford Rd. E17 223 307 EC54
Clifford Rd. N9 210 301 DW44
Clifford Rd. SE25 274 325 DU98
Clifford Rd., Houns. 258 321 BX83
Clifford Rd., Rich. 185 322 CK89
Clifford Rd., Wem. 123 314 CK67
Clifford St. W1 57 316 DJ73
Clifford Way NW10 109 304 CT63
Clifford's Inn Pas. EC4 48 316 DN72
Cliffview Rd. SE13 182 325 EA83
Clifton Ave. E17 222 307 DX55
Clifton Ave. N3 218 305 CZ53
Clifton Ave. W12 145 314 CT75
Clifton Ave., Felt. 258 321 BW90
Clifton Ave., Stan. 216 304 CH54
Clifton Ave., Sutt. 292 331 DB111
Clifton Ave., Wem. 107 304 CM65
Clifton Clo., Orp. 291 334 EQ106
Clifton Ct. N4 100 306 DN61
Clifton Ct. NW8 30 315 DD70
Clifton Cres. SE15 164 317 DV80
Clifton Est. SE15 164 317 DV81
Clifton Gdns. N15 221 306 DT58
Clifton Gdns. NW11 218 305 CZ58
Clifton Gdns. W4 145 314 CR77
Clifton Gdns. W9 29 315 DC70
Clifton Gdns., Uxb. 241 312 BP68
Clifton Gro. E8 118 307 DU65
Clifton Hill NW8 16/7 315 DB68
Clifton Pk. Ave. SW20 270 323 CW96
Clifton Pl. SE16 148 317 DW75
Clifton Pl. W2 42 315 DD72
Clifton Ri. SE14 165 317 DY80
Clifton Rd. E7 234 308 EK65
Clifton Rd. E16 141 317 EE71
Clifton Rd. N3 219 305 DC53
Clifton Rd. N22 220 306 DJ53
Clifton Rd. NW10 126 315 CU68
Clifton Rd. SE25 273 324 DR98
Clifton Rd. SW19 270 323 CX93
Clifton Rd. W9 29 315 DC70
Clifton Rd., Grnf. 243 313 CC70
Clifton Rd., Har. 216 304 CM57
Clifton Rd., Horn. 228 310 FG58
Clifton Rd., Ilf. 225 308 ER58
Clifton Rd., Islw. 251 321 CD82
Clifton Rd., Kings.T. 268 322 CM94
Clifton Rd., Sid. 277 326 ES91
Clifton Rd., Sthl. 250 321 BY77
Clifton Rd., Tedd. 267 329 CE91
Clifton Rd., Wall. 285 332 DH106
Clifton Rd., Well. 262 327 EW83
Clifton St. EC2 50/1 316 DS71
Clifton Ter. N4 100 306 DN61
Clifton Vil. W9 41 315 DC71
Clifton Wk. E6 244 318 EL71
Clifton Way SE15 164 317 DW80
Clifton Way, Wem. 123 314 CL67
Clinch Ct. E16 244 318 EG71
Cline Rd. N11 220 306 DJ51
Clinger Ct. N1 26/7 316 DS67
Clink St. SE1 61 316 DQ74
Clinton Ave., E.Mol. 267 329 CC98
Clinton Ave., Well. 262 327 EU84
Clinton Cres., Ilf. 225 308 ES51
Clinton Rd. E3 129 317 DY69
Clinton Rd. E7 234 308 EG63
Clinton Rd. N15 221 306 DR56
Clipper Clo. SE16 149 317 DX75
Clipper Way SE13 182 325 EC84
Clipstone Ms. W1 45 316 DJ71
Clipstone Rd., Houns. 259 321 CA83
Clipstone St. W1 44/5 316 DH71
Clissold Clo. N2 219 305 DF55
Clissold Ct. N4 100 306 DQ61
Clissold Cres. N16 117 306 DR63
Clissold Rd. N16 101 306 DR62
Clitheroe Ave., Har. 233 313 CA60
Clitheroe Rd. SW9 161 316 DL82
Clitherow Ave. W7 142 314 CG76
Clitherow Pas., Brent. 142 314 CH78
Clitherow Rd., Brent. 142 314 CH78
Clitterhouse Cres. NW2 94 305 CW60
Clitterhouse Rd. NW2 94 305 CW60
Clive Ave. N18 222 307 DU51
Clive Ave., Dart. 263 327 FF86
Clive Ct. W9 29 315 DC70
Clive Par., Nthwd. 213 302 BS52
Clive Pas. SE21 195 324 DR90
Clive Rd. SE21 195 324 DR90
Clive Rd. SW19 271 323 DE93
Clive Rd., Belv. 255 319 FA77
Clive Rd., Enf. 203 301 DU42
Clive Rd., Felt. 258 321 BU86
Clive Rd., Rom. 228 310 FH57
Clive Rd., Twick. 267 329 CF91
Clive Way, Enf. 203 301 DU42
Cliveden Clo. N12 207 299 DC49
Cliveden Pl. SW1 80 316 DG77
Cliveden Pl., Shep. 281 328 BQ100
Cliveden Rd. SW19 270 323 CZ95
Clivedon Ct. W13 132 314 CH71
Clivedon Rd. E4 211 301 EE50
Clivesdale Dr., Hayes 242 313 BU74
Cloak La. EC4 61 316 DQ73
Clock Ho. Rd., Beck. 274 325 DY97
Clock Twr. Ms. N1 25 316 DQ67
Clock Twr. Pl. N7 115 306 DL65
Clock Twr. Rd., Islw. 259 321 CF83
Clockhouse Ave., Bark. 245 318 EQ67
Clockhouse Clo. SW19 188 323 CW90
Clockhouse La., Ashf. 265 328 BN91
Clockhouse La., Felt. 265 320 BP90
Clockhouse La., Rom. 227 309 FB52
Cloister Clo., Tedd. 268 322 CH92
Cloister Gdns. SE25 287 333 DV100
Cloister Gdns., Edg. 205 298 CQ50
Cloister Rd. NW2 95 305 CZ62
Cloister Rd. W3 134 314 CQ71
Cloisters Ave., Brom. 290 334 EM99
Cloisters Mall, Kings.T. 268 322 CK96
Clonard Way, Pnr. 215 303 CA51
Clonbrock Rd. N16 117 306 DS63
Cloncurry St. SW6 157 315 CX82
Clonmel Clo., Har. 233 313 CD61
Clonmel Rd. SW6 157 315 CZ80
Clonmel Rd., Tedd. 267 329 CD91
Clonmell Rd. N17 221 306 DR55
Clonmore St. SW18 189 323 CZ88
Cloonmore Ave., Orp. 291 334 ET105
Clorane Gdns. NW3 96 305 DA62
Close, The E4 223 307 EC52
Close, The N14 208 300 DK47
Close, The N20 206 299 CZ47
Close, The SE3 167 317 ED82
Close, The, Barn. 207 299 DF44
Close, The, Beck. 274 325 DY98
Close, The, Bex. 263 327 FA86
Close, The, Cars. 293 331 DE109
Close, The, Har. 215 303 CC54
Close, The, Islw. 251 321 CD82
Close, The, Mitch. 271 323 DF98
Close, The, N.Mal. 269 322 CQ96
Close, The, Orp. 291 334 ES100
Close, The (Eastcote), Pnr. 232 313 BW59
Close, The (Rayners La.), Pnr. 232 313 BZ59
Close, The (Pampisford Rd.), Pur. 294 332 DP110
Close, The (Russell Hill), Pur. 294 332 DM110
Close, The, Rich. 170 322 CP83
Close, The, Rom. 226 309 EY58
Close, The, Sid. 278 327 EV91
Close, The, Sutt. 284 331 CZ101
Close, The, Uxb. 240 312 BL66
Close, The (Hillingdon), Uxb. 241 312 BN67
Close, The (Barnhill Rd.), Wem. 92 304 CQ62
Close, The (Lyon Pk. Ave.), Wem. 107 304 CL65
Closemead Clo., Nthwd. 213 302 BQ51
Cloth Ct. EC1 48/9 316 DP71
Cloth Fair EC1 48/9 316 DP71
Cloth St. EC1 49 316 DQ71
Clothier St. E1 50/1 316 DS72
Clothworkers Rd. SE18 253 318 ER80
Cloudberry Rd., Rom. 228 310 FK51
Cloudesdale Rd. SW17 192 324 DH89
Cloudesley Pl. N1 24 316 DN67
Cloudesley Rd. N1 24 316 DN67
Cloudesley Rd., Bexh. 254 319 EZ81
Cloudesley Rd., Erith 255 319 FF81
Cloudesley Sq. N1 24 316 DN67
Cloudesley St. N1 24 316 DN67
Clouston Clo., Wall. 286 332 DL106
Clova Rd. E7 121 307 EF65
Clove Cres. E14 141 317 ED73
Clove Hitch Quay SW11 174 323 DC83
Clove St. E13 244 318 EG70
Clovelly Ave. NW9 217 304 CT56
Clovelly Ave., Uxb. 241 312 BQ63
Clovelly Clo., Pnr. 214 303 BV55
Clovelly Clo., Uxb. 241 312 BQ63
Clovelly Ct., Horn. 238 311 FM61
Clovelly Gdns. SE19 273 324 DT95
Clovelly Gdns., Enf. 209 300 DS45
Clovelly Gdns., Rom. 227 309 FB53
Clovelly Rd. N8 220 306 DK56
Clovelly Rd. W4 145 314 CR75
Clovelly Rd. W5 142 314 CJ75
Clovelly Rd., Bexh. 254 319 EY79
Clovelly Rd., Houns. 250 321 BZ82
Clovelly Way E1 138 317 DW72
Clovelly Way, Har. 232 313 BZ61
Clovelly Way, Orp. 291 334 ET100
Clover Clo. E11 105 307 ED61
Clover Ms. SW3 159 315 DF79
Clover Way, Wall. 285 332 DG102

Cloverdale Gdns., Sid. 261 326 ET86
Clowders Rd. SE6 197 325 DZ90
Clowser Clo., Sutt. 285 331 DC106
Cloyster Wd., Edg. 216 304 CK52
Cloysters Grn. E1 138 317 DU74
Club Gdns. Rd., Brom. 289 334 EG101
Club Row E1 39 316 DT70
Club Row E2 39 316 DT70
Clumps, The, Ashf. 265 328 BR91
Clumps, The, Felt. 265 328 BR91
Clunas Gdns., Rom. 228 310 FK55
Clunbury Ave., Sthl. 250 321 BZ78
Clunbury St. N1 26 316 DR68
Cluny Est. SE1 74/5 316 DS76
Cluny Ms. SW5 76 315 DA77
Cluny Pl. SE1 74/5 316 DS76
Cluse Ct. N1 25 316 DQ68
Clutton St. E14 140 317 EB71
Clydach Rd., Enf. 202 300 DT42
Clyde Circ. N15 221 306 DS56
Clyde Cres., Upmin. 229 311 FS58
Clyde Pl. E10 104 307 EB59
Clyde Rd. N15 221 306 DS56
Clyde Rd. N22 220 306 DK53
Clyde Rd., Croy. 287 332 DT103
Clyde Rd., Stai. 264 320 BK88
Clyde Rd., Sutt. 284 331 DA106
Clyde Rd., Wall. 294 332 DJ107
Clyde St. SE8 165 317 DZ79
Clyde Ter. SE23 196 325 DW89
Clyde Vale SE23 196 325 DW89
Clyde Way, Rom. 227 309 FE52
Clydesdale, Enf. 203 301 DX42
Clydesdale Ave., Stan. 216 304 CK55
Clydesdale Clo., Borwd. 205 298 CR43
Clydesdale Clo., Islw. 259 321 CF83
Clydesdale Gdns., Rich. 170 322 CP84
Clydesdale Rd. W11 137 315 CZ72
Clydesdale Rd., Horn. 237 309 FF59
Clydon Clo., Erith 255 319 FE79
Clyfford Rd., Ruis. 241 312 BT63
Clymping Dene, Felt. 258 321 BV87
Clyston St. SW8 160 316 DJ82
Coach & Horses Yd. W1 57 316 DJ73
Coach Ho. La. N5 116 306 DP63
Coach Ho. La. SW19 270 323 CX91
Coach Ho. Ms. SE23 180 325 DW86
Coach Ho. Yd. SW18 174 323 DB84
Coachhouse Ms. SE20 274 325 DV94
Coal Wf. Rd. W12 147 315 CX75
Coaldale Wk. SE21 194 324 DQ87
Coalecroft Rd. SW15 172 323 CW84
Coate St. E2 128 317 DU68
Coates Hill Rd., Brom. 277 326 EN96
Coates Rd., Borwd. 204 298 CK45
Coates Wk., Brent. 143 314 CL78
Cobb Clo., Borwd. 205 298 CQ43
Cobb St. E1 51 316 DT71
Cobbett Clo., Enf. 203 301 DW36
Cobbett Rd. SE9 260 326 EL83
Cobbett Rd., Twick. 259 321 CA88
Cobbett St. SW8 161 316 DM80
Cobbetts Ave., Ilf. 224 308 EK57
Cobblers Wk., E.Mol. 268 322 CH95
Cobblers Wk., Hmptn. 267 329 CC95
Cobblers Wk., Kings.T. 268 322 CG95
Cobblers Wk., Tedd. 267 329 CD94
Cobbles, The, Upmin. 239 311 FT59
Cobblestone Pl., Croy. 287 332 DQ102
Cobbold Est. NW10 109 304 CT65
Cobbold Ms. W12 145 314 CT75
Cobbold Rd. E11 105 307 EF62
Cobbold Rd. NW10 109 304 CT65
Cobbold Rd. W12 145 314 CT75
Cobb's Ct. EC4 48/9 316 DP72
Cobb's Rd., Houns. 258 321 BZ84
Cobden Clo., Uxb. 240 312 BJ67
Cobden Rd. E11 105 307 EE62
Cobden Rd. SE25 287 333 DU99
Cobden Rd., Orp. 291 334 ER105
Cobham Ave., N.Mal. 283 331 CU99
Cobham Clo. SW11 175 323 DE86
Cobham Clo., Brom. 290 334 EL101
Cobham Clo., Sid. 262 327 EV86
Cobham Clo., Wall. 294 332 DL107
Cobham Ho., Bark. 245 318 EQ67
Cobham Pl., Bexh. 262 327 EY85
Cobham Rd. E17 223 307 EC53
Cobham Rd. N22 221 306 DP55
Cobham Rd., Houns. 250 321 BW80
Cobham Rd., Ilf. 235 308 ES61
Cobham Rd., Kings.T. 269 322 CN96
Cobill Clo., Horn. 228 310 FJ56
Cobland Rd. SE12 276 326 EJ91
Coborn Rd. E3 129 317 DZ69
Coborn St. E3 129 317 DZ69
Cobourg Rd. SE5 163 316 DT79
Cobourg St. NW1 33 316 DJ69
Coburg Clo. SW1 81 316 DJ77
Coburg Cres. SW2 193 324 DM88
Coburg Gdns., Ilf. 224 308 EK54
Coburg Rd. N22 220 306 DM55
Cochrane Ms. NW8 18 315 DD68
Cochrane Rd. SW19 270 323 CZ94
Cochrane St. NW8 18 315 DD68
Cock Hill E1 50/1 316 DS71
Cock La. EC1 48/9 316 DP71
Cockayne Way SE8 149 317 DY77
Cocker Rd., Enf. 203 301 DW36
Cockerell Rd. E17 222 307 DY58
Cockpit Steps SW1 70 316 DK75
Cockpit Yd. WC1 47 316 DM71
Cocks Cres., N.Mal. 269 322 CT98
Cock's Yd., Uxb. 240 312 BJ66
Cockspur Ct. SW1 58 316 DK74
Cockspur St. SW1 58 316 DK74
Cocksure La., Sid. 263 327 FA90
Code St. E1 39 316 DT70
Codicote Ter. N4 100 306 DQ61
Codling Clo. E1 138 317 DU74
Codling Way, Wem. 107 304 CK63
Codrington Hill SE23 197 325 DY87
Codrington Ms. W11 137 315 CY72
Cody Clo., Har. 216 304 CK55
Cody Clo., Wall. 294 332 DK108
Cody Rd. E16 131 317 ED70
Coe Ave. SE25 287 333 DU100
Cofers Circle, Wem. 92 304 CP62
Cogan Ave. E17 222 307 DY53
Coin St. SE1 60 316 DN74
Coity Rd. NW5 114 306 DG65
Coke St. E1 138 317 DU72
Cokers La. SE21 195 324 DR88
Colas Ms. NW6 16 315 DA67
Colbeck Ms. SW7 76/7 315 DB77
Colbeck Rd., Har. 233 313 CC59
Colberg Pl. N16 101 306 DS59
Colborne Way, Wor.Pk. 284 331 CW104
Colbrook Ave., Hayes 249 320 BR76
Colbrook Clo., Hayes 249 320 BR76
Colburn Ave., Pnr. 214 303 BY51
Colburn Way, Sutt. 285 331 DD104
Colby Rd. SE19 273 324 DS92
Colchester Ave. E12 234 308 EM62
Colchester Dr., Pnr. 214 303 BX57
Colchester Rd. E10 104 307 EC59
Colchester Rd. E17 223 307 EA58
Colchester Rd., Edg. 217 304 CQ52
Colchester Rd., Nthwd. 214 303 BU54
Colchester Rd., Rom. 228 310 FK53
Colchester St. E1 51 316 DT72
Cold Blow Cres., Bex. 263 327 FD88
Cold Blow La. SE14 165 317 DX80
Cold Blows, Mitch. 271 323 DF97
Cold Harbour E14 150 317 EC75
Coldbath Sq. EC1 36 316 DN70
Coldbath St. SE13 166 317 EB81
Coldershaw Rd. W13 132 314 CG74
Coldfall Ave. N10 219 305 DF54
Coldham Gro., Enf. 203 301 DY37
Coldharbour La. SE5 178 324 DQ83
Coldharbour La. SW9 178 324 DN84
Coldharbour La., Hayes 249 320 BT75
Coldharbour La., Pur. 294 332 DN110
Coldharbour La., Rain. 247 319 FE72
Coldharbour Pl. SE5 162 316 DQ82
Coldharbour Rd., Croy. 286 332 DN106
Coldharbour Way, Croy. 286 332 DN106
Coldstream Gdns. SW18 173 323 CZ86
Cole Clo. SE28 246 319 EV74
Cole Gdns., Houns. 250 321 BU80
Cole Pk. Gdns., Twick. 168 322 CG86
Cole Pk. Rd., Twick. 184 322 CG87
Cole Pk. Vw., Twick. 168 322 CG86
Cole Rd., Twick. 168 322 CG86
Cole St. SE1 73 316 DQ75
Colebeck Ms. N1 116 306 DP65
Colebert Ave. E1 128 317 DW70
Colebrook Clo. SW15 189 323 CX87
Colebrook Ho. E14 140 317 EB72
Colebrook Rd. SW16 272 324 DL95
Colebrook Way N11 208 300 DH50
Colebrooke Ave. W13 132 314 CH72
Colebrooke Dr. E11 234 308 EH59
Colebrooke Pl. N1 24/5 316 DP67
Colebrooke Ri., Brom. 275 325 EE96
Colebrooke Row N1 24/5 316 DP68
Coleby Path SE5 163 316 DR80
Coledale Dr., Stan. 216 304 CJ53
Coleford Rd. SW18 174 323 DC85
Colegrave Rd. E15 121 307 ED64
Colegrove Rd. SE15 163 316 DT79
Coleherne Ct. SW5 76/7 315 DB78
Coleherne Ms. SW10 76/7 315 DB78
Coleherne Rd. SW10 76/7 315 DB78
Colehill Gdns. SW6 157 315 CY82
Colehill La. SW6 157 315 CY81
Coleman Clo. SE25 274 325 DU96
Coleman Flds. N1 25 316 DQ67
Coleman Rd. SE5 163 316 DS80
Coleman Rd., Belv. 255 319 FA77
Coleman Rd., Dag. 236 309 EY65
Coleman St. EC2 50 316 DR72
Colemans Heath SE9 261 326 EN90
Colenso Rd. E5 118 307 DW63
Colenso Rd., Ilf. 235 308 ES60
Colepits Wd. Rd. SE9 261 326 ER85
Coleraine Rd. N8 221 306 DN55
Coleraine Rd. SE3 167 317 EF79
Coleridge Ave. E12 234 308 EL65
Coleridge Ave., Sutt. 285 331 DE105
Coleridge Clo. SW8 160 316 DH82
Coleridge Gdns. NW6 112 305 DC66
Coleridge La. N8 220 306 DL58
Coleridge Rd. E17 222 307 DZ56
Coleridge Rd. N4 100 306 DN61
Coleridge Rd. N8 220 306 DK58
Coleridge Rd. N12 207 299 DC50
Coleridge Rd., Ashf. 264 328 BL91
Coleridge Rd., Croy. 288 333 DW100
Coleridge Rd., Rom. 228 310 FH52
Coleridge Sq. W13 132 314 CG72
Coleridge Wk. NW11 219 305 DA56
Coleridge Way, Hayes 242 313 BU72
Coleridge Way, Orp. 291 335 EU100
Coleridge Way, West Dr. 248 320 BL77
Coles Cres., Har. 233 313 CB61
Coles Grn. Ct. NW2 94 305 CU61
Coles Grn. Rd. NW2 94 305 CU60
Colesburg Rd., Beck. 274 325 DZ97
Coleshill Rd., Tedd. 267 329 CE93
Colestown St. SW11 159 315 DE82
Colet Clo. N13 221 306 DP51
Colet Gdns. W14 147 315 CX78
Coley St. WC1 35 316 DM70
Colfe Rd. SE23 197 325 DY88
Colham Ave., West Dr. 248 312 BL74
Colham Grn. Rd., Uxb. 249 312 BN71
Colham Mill Rd., West Dr. 248 320 BK75
Colham Rd., Uxb. 240 312 BM70
Colin Clo. NW9 217 304 CS56
Colin Clo., Croy. 288 333 DZ104
Colin Clo., W.Wick. 289 333 EF104
Colin Cres. NW9 217 304 CT56
Colin Dr. NW9 217 304 CT57
Colin Gdns. NW9 217 304 CT57
Colin Par. NW9 217 304 CS56
Colin Pk. Rd. NW9 217 304 CS55
Colin Rd. NW10 110 305 CU65
Colina Ms. N15 221 306 DP57
Colina Rd. N15 221 306 DP57
Colindale Ave. NW9 217 304 CR55
Colindale Business Pk. NW9 217 304 CQ55
Colindeep Gdns. NW4 218 305 CU57
Colindeep La. NW4 218 305 CU56
Colindeep La. NW9 217 304 CS55
Colinette Rd. SW15 172 323 CW84
Colinton Rd., Ilf. 236 309 EV61
Coliston Pas. SW18 190 323 DA87
Coliston Rd. SW18 190 323 DA87
Collamore Ave. SW18 191 323 DE88
Collapit Clo., Har. 215 303 CB58
College App. SE10 166 317 EC79
College Ave., Har. 215 303 CE53
College Clo. E9 118 307 DW64
College Clo. N18 209 300 DT50
College Clo., Har. 215 303 CE52
College Clo., Twick. 259 321 CD88
College Cres. NW3 113 305 DD65
College Cross N1 116 306 DN66
College Dr., Ruis. 232 313 BU59
College Gdns. E4 211 301 EB45
College Gdns. N18 209 300 DT50
College Gdns. SE21 195 324 DS88
College Gdns. SW17 191 323 DE89
College Gdns., Enf. 202 300 DR39
College Gdns., Ilf. 224 308 EL57
College Gdns., N.Mal. 283 330 CT99
College Grn. SE19 273 324 DS94
College Gro. NW1 22 316 DK67
College Hill EC4 61 316 DQ73
College Hill Rd., Har. 215 303 CE52
College La. NW5 114 306 DH63
College Ms. SW1 70/1 316 DL76
College Ms. SW18 174 323 DB85
College Pk. Clo. SE13 183 325 ED84
College Pk. Rd. N17 221 306 DT51
College Pl. E17 223 307 EE56
College Pl. NW1 21 316 DJ67
College Pl. SW10 158 315 DC80
College Pt. E15 121 307 EF65
College Rd. E17 223 307 EC57
College Rd. N17 221 306 DT51
College Rd. N21 209 300 DN47
College Rd. NW10 126 315 CW68
College Rd. SE19 273 324 DT92
College Rd. SE21 195 324 DS87
College Rd. SW19 271 323 DD93
College Rd. W13 132 314 CH72
College Rd., Brom. 276 326 EG95
College Rd., Croy. 287 332 DR103
College Rd., Enf. 202 300 DR39
College Rd. (Harrow on the Hill), Har. 215 303 CE58
College Rd. (Harrow Weald), Har. 215 303 CE53
College Rd., Islw. 251 321 CF81
College Rd., Swan. 279 327 FE95
College Rd., Wem. 91 304 CK60
College Row E9 119 307 DX64
College Slip, Brom. 276 326 EG95
College St. EC4 62 316 DR73
College Ter. E3 129 317 DZ69
College Ter. N3 218 305 CZ54
College Vw. SE9 260 326 EK88
College Wk., Kings.T. 268 322 CL96
College Way, Ashf. 264 328 BM91
College Way, Nthwd. 213 302 BR51
College Yd. NW5 114 306 DH63
Collent St. E9 118 307 DW65
Colless Rd. N15 221 306 DT57
Collett Rd. SE16 148 317 DU76
Collett Way, Sthl. 243 313 CB74
Collier Clo. E6 245 318 EP72
Collier Dr., Edg. 217 304 CN54
Collier Row La., Rom. 227 309 FB52
Collier Row Rd., Rom. 227 309 FA53
Collier St. N1 23 316 DM68
Colliers Shaw, Kes. 290 334 EK106
Colliers Water La., Th.Hth. 286 332 DN99
Collindale Ave., Erith 255 319 FB79
Collindale Ave., Sid. 262 327 EU88
Collingbourne Rd. W12 136 315 CV74
Collingham Gdns. SW5 76/7 315 DB77
Collingham Pl. SW5 76/7 315 DB77
Collingham Rd. SW5 76/7 315 DB77
Collings Clo. N22 220 306 DM51
Collingtree Rd. SE26 274 325 DW91
Collingwood Ave. N10 220 306 DG55
Collingwood Ave., Surb. 283 330 CQ102
Collingwood Clo. SE20 274 325 DV95
Collingwood Clo., Twick. 259 321 CA87
Collingwood Rd. E17 223 307 EA58
Collingwood Rd. N15 221 306 DS56
Collingwood Rd., Mitch. 271 323 DE96
Collingwood Rd., Sutt. 284 331 CZ104
Collingwood Rd., Uxb. 241 312 BP70
Collingwood St. E1 128 317 DV70
Collins Ave., Stan. 216 304 CL54
Collins Dr., Ruis. 232 313 BW61
Collins Rd. N5 116 306 DQ63
Collins Sq. SE3 167 317 EF82
Collins St. SE3 167 317 EE82
Collin's Yd. N1 24/5 316 DP67
Collinson St. SE1 73 316 DQ75
Collinson Wk. SE1 73 316 DQ75
Collinwood Ave., Enf. 203 301 DW41
Collinwood Gdns., Ilf. 224 308 EM57
Colls Rd. SE15 164 317 DW81
Collyer Ave., Croy. 286 332 DL105
Collyer Pl. SE15 164 317 DU81
Collyer Rd., Croy. 286 332 DL105
Colman Rd. E16 244 318 EJ71
Colmar Clo. E1 129 317 DX70
Colmer Pl., Har. 215 303 CD52
Colmer Rd. SW16 272 324 DL95
Colmore Ms. SE15 164 317 DV81
Colmore Rd., Enf. 203 301 DW42
Colnbrook Bypass, West Dr. 256 320 BH80
Colnbrook St. SE1 72/3 316 DP76
Colne Ave., Rick. 212 302 BG47
Colne Ave., West Dr. 248 320 BJ75
Colne Ct., Epsom 283 330 CQ105
Colne Dr., Rom. 228 311 FM51
Colne Ho., Bark. 235 308 EP65
Colne Mead, Rick. 212 302 BG47
Colne Pk. Caravan Pk., West Dr. 248 320 BJ77
Colne Rd. E5 119 307 DY63
Colne Rd. N21 209 300 DQ45
Colne Rd., Twick. 259 321 CE88
Colne St. E13 244 318 EG69
Colne Valley, Upmin. 229 311 FS58
Colnedale Rd., Uxb. 240 312 BK64
Colney Hatch La. N10 220 306 DG52
Colney Hatch La. N11 219 305 DF51
Cologne Rd. SW11 175 323 DD84
Colomb St. SE10 151 317 EE78
Colombo Rd., Ilf. 235 308 EQ60
Colombo St. SE1 60/1 316 DP74
Colonels La., Cher. 280 328 BG100
Colonels Wk., Enf. 202 300 DP40
Colonial Ave., Twick. 259 321 CC85
Colonial Rd., Felt. 265 320 BS87
Colonnade WC1 34/5 316 DL70
Colonnade Wk. SW1 80/1 316 DH77
Colonnades, The W2 40/1 315 DB72
Colson Rd., Croy. 287 332 DS103
Colson Way SW16 272 324 DJ91
Colsterworth Rd. N15 221 306 DT56
Colston Ave., Cars. 285 331 DE105
Colston Clo., Cars. 285 331 DF105
Colston Rd. E7 234 308 EK65
Colston Rd. SW14 170 322 CQ84
Coltishall Rd., Horn. 238 310 FJ65
Coltness Cres. SE2 254 319 EV78
Colton Gdns. N17 221 306 DQ55
Colton Rd., Har. 215 303 CE57
Coltsfoot Dr., West Dr. 248 312 BL72
Coltsfoot Path, Rom. 228 310 FK51
Columbia Ave., Edg. 217 304 CP53
Columbia Ave., Ruis. 232 313 BV60
Columbia Ave., Wor.Pk. 283 330 CT101
Columbia Ctyd. E14 140 317 EA74
Columbia Rd. E2 39 316 DT69
Columbia Rd. E13 131 317 EF70
Columbia Sq. SW14 170 322 CQ84
Columbine Ave. E6 244 318 EL71
Columbine Ave., S.Croy. 294 332 DP108
Columbine Way SE13 166 317 EC82
Columbine Way, Rom. 228 311 FL53
Columbus Ct. SE16 138 317 DW74
Columbus Gdns., Nthwd. 214 303 BU53
Columbus Sq., Erith 255 319 FF79
Colva Wk. N19 98 306 DH61
Colvestone Cres. E8 117 306 DT64
Colview Ct. SE9 260 326 EK88
Colville Est. N1 26/7 316 DS67
Colville Gdns. W11 137 315 CZ72
Colville Hos. W11 137 315 CZ72
Colville Ms. W11 137 315 CZ72
Colville Pl. W1 45 316 DJ71
Colville Rd. E11 104 307 EC62
Colville Rd. E17 222 307 DY54
Colville Rd. N9 210 301 DV46
Colville Rd. W3 144 314 CP76
Colville Rd. W11 137 315 CZ72
Colville Sq. W11 137 315 CZ72
Colville Sq. Ms. W11 137 315 CZ72
Colville Ter. W11 137 315 CZ72
Colvin Clo. SE26 274 325 DW92
Colvin Gdns. E4 211 301 EC48
Colvin Gdns. E11 224 308 EH56
Colvin Gdns., Ilf. 225 308 EQ53
Colvin Gdns., Wal.Cr. 203 301 DX35
Colvin Rd. E6 234 308 EL66
Colvin Rd., Th.Hth. 286 332 DN99
Colwell Rd. SE22 179 324 DT85
Colwick Clo. N6 99 306 DK59
Colwith Rd. W6 156 315 CW79
Colwood Gdns. SW19 271 323 DD94
Colworth Gro. SE17 85 316 DQ77
Colworth Rd. E11 223 307 EE58
Colworth Rd., Croy. 287 333 DU102
Colwyn Ave., Grnf. 243 313 CF68
Colwyn Clo. SW16 272 324 DJ92
Colwyn Cres., Houns. 251 321 CC81
Colwyn Grn. NW9 217 304 CS58
Colwyn Rd. NW2 94 305 CV62
Colyer Clo. SE9 261 326 EP89
Colyers Clo., Erith 255 319 FD81
Colyers La., Erith 255 319 FC81
Colyers Wk., Erith 255 319 FE81
Colyton Clo., Well. 254 319 EX81
Colyton Clo., Wem. 106 304 CJ65
Colyton Rd. SE22 180 325 DV85
Colyton Way N18 210 301 DU50
Combe Ave. SE3 167 317 EF80
Combe Lea, Brom. 276 326 EL97
Combe Lo. SE7 252 318 EJ79
Combe Ms. SE3 167 317 EF80
Combedale Rd. SE10 252 318 EG78
Combemartin Rd. SW18 189 323 CY87
Comber Clo. NW2 94 305 CV62
Comber Gro. SE5 162 316 DQ80
Combermere Rd. SW9 177 324 DM83
Combermere Rd., Mord. 284 331 DB99
Comberton Rd. E5 102 307 DV61
Combeside SE18 253 318 ET80
Combwell Cres. SE2 254 319 EU76
Comely Bank Rd. E17 223 307 EC57
Comer Cres., Sthl. 251 321 CC75
Comeragh Ms. W14 147 315 CY78
Comeragh Rd. W14 147 315 CY78
Comerford Rd. SE4 181 325 DY84
Comet Clo. E12 234 308 EK63
Comet Pl. SE8 166 317 EA80
Comet Rd., Stai. 264 320 BK87
Comet St. SE8 166 317 EA80
Commerce Rd. N22 220 306 DM53
Commerce Rd., Brent. 152 314 CJ79
Commerce Way, Croy. 286 332 DM103
Commercial Rd. E1 138 317 DU72
Commercial Rd. E14 139 317 DY72
Commercial Rd. N17 221 306 DS51
Commercial Rd. N18 209 300 DS50
Commercial Rd., Stai. 264 328 BG93
Commercial St. E1 39 316 DT70
Commercial Way NW10 124 314 CP68
Commercial Way SE15 163 316 DT80
Commerell St. SE10 151 317 EE78
Commodity Quay E1 63 316 DT73
Commodore Sq. SW10 158 315 DC81
Commodore St. E1 129 317 DY70
Common, The W5 133 314 CL73
Common, The, Rich. 185 322 CK90
Common, The, Sthl. 250 321 BW77
Common Rd. SW13 172 323 CU83
Commondale SW15 172 323 CW83
Commonfield La. SW17 271 323 DE92
Commonfield Rd., Bans. 292 331 DA114
Commonside, Kes. 290 334 EJ105
Commonside Clo., Sutt. 292 331 DB111
Commonside E., Mitch. 272 324 DG97
Commonside W., Mitch. 271 323 DF97
Commonwealth Ave. W12 136 315 CV73
Commonwealth Ave., Hayes 249 312 BR72
Commonwealth Rd. N17 222 307 DU52
Commonwealth Way SE2 254 319 EV78
Community Clo., Houns. 250 321 BV81
Community Clo., Uxb. 231 312 BQ62
Community La. N7 115 306 DK64
Community Rd. E15 121 307 ED64
Community Rd., Grnf. 243 313 CC67
Como Rd. SE23 197 325 DY89
Como St., Rom. 227 309 FD57
Compass Hill, Rich. 169 322 CK86
Compayne Gdns. NW6 112 305 DB66
Compton Ave. E6 244 318 EK68
Compton Ave. N1 116 306 DP65
Compton Ave. N6 97 305 DE59
Compton Ave., Rom. 228 310 FH55
Compton Clo. E3 140 317 EA71
Compton Clo. NW1 32/3 316 DH69
Compton Clo. W13 132 314 CG72
Compton Clo., Edg. 217 304 CQ52
Compton Ct. SE19 273 324 DS92
Compton Cres. N17 221 306 DQ52
Compton Cres. W4 154 314 CQ79
Compton Cres., Nthlt. 242 313 BX67
Compton Pas. EC1 36/7 316 DP70
Compton Pl. WC1 34/5 316 DL70
Compton Pl., Erith 255 319 FF79
Compton Ri., Pnr. 214 303 BY57
Compton Rd. N1 116 306 DP65
Compton Rd. N21 209 300 DN46
Compton Rd. NW10 127 315 CX69
Compton Rd. SW19 270 323 CZ93
Compton Rd., Croy. 287 333 DV102
Compton Rd., Hayes 249 312 BS73
Compton St. EC1 36/7 316 DP70
Compton Ter. N1 116 306 DP65
Comreddy Clo., Enf. 202 300 DP39
Comus Pl. SE17 86/7 316 DS77
Comyn Rd. SW11 175 323 DE84
Comyns Clo. E16 141 317 EF71
Comyns Rd., Dag. 237 309 FA66
Conant Ms. E1 138 317 DU73
Concanon Rd. SW2 177 324 DM84
Concert Hall App. SE1 59 316 DM74
Concord Clo., Nthlt. 242 313 BX69
Concord Rd. W3 124 314 CP70
Concord Rd., Enf. 210 301 DV43
Concorde Clo., Houns. 251 321 CB82
Concorde Clo., Uxb. 240 312 BL68
Concorde Dr. E6 244 318 EM71
Concourse, The N9 210 301 DU47
Concourse, The NW9 217 304 CT53
Condell Rd. SW8 160 316 DJ81
Conder St. E14 139 317 DY72
Conderton Rd. SE5 178 324 DQ83
Condor Path, Nthlt. 243 313 CA68
Condor Rd., Stai. 280 328 BH97
Condor Wk., Horn. 238 310 FH66
Condover Cres. SE18 253 318 EP80
Condray Pl. SW11 159 315 DE80
Conduit Ct. WC2 58/9 316 DL73
Conduit La. N18 210 301 DW50
Conduit La., Croy. 287 333 DU106
Conduit La., Enf. 210 301 DY44
Conduit La., S.Croy. 287 333 DU106
Conduit Ms. W2 42 315 DD72
Conduit Pas. W2 42 315 DD72
Conduit Pl. W2 42 315 DD72
Conduit Rd. SE18 253 318 EP78
Conduit St. W1 56/7 316 DH73
Conduit Way NW10 108 304 CQ66
Conewood St. N5 100 306 DP62
Coney Acre SE21 194 324 DQ88
Coney Burrows E4 211 301 EE47
Coney Gro., Uxb. 241 312 BN69
Coney Hill Rd., W.Wick. 289 333 EE103
Coney Way SW8 161 316 DM79
Coneygrove Path, Nthlt. 232 313 BY65
Conference Clo. E4 211 301 EC47
Conference Rd. SE2 254 319 EW77
Congleton Gro. SE18 253 318 EQ78
Congo Rd. SE18 253 318 ER78
Congress Rd. SE2 254 319 EW77
Congreve Rd. SE9 260 326 EM83
Congreve St. SE17 86/7 316 DS77
Congreve Wk. E16 244 318 EK71
Conical Cor., Enf. 202 300 DQ40
Conifer Clo., Orp. 291 334 ER105
Conifer Gdns. SW16 193 324 DL90
Conifer Gdns., Enf. 209 300 DR44
Conifer Gdns., Sutt. 284 331 DB104
Conifer Way, Hayes 242 313 BU73
Conifer Way, Swan. 279 327 FC95
Conifer Way, Wem. 90 304 CJ62
Conifers Clo., Tedd. 268 322 CJ94
Coniger Rd. SW6 158 315 DA82
Coningham Ms. W12 136 315 CU74
Coningham Rd. W12 136 315 CV74
Coningsby Cotts. W5 143 314 CK75
Coningsby Gdns. E4 223 307 EB51
Coningsby Rd. N4 100 306 DP59
Coningsby Rd. W5 143 314 CK75
Coningsby Rd., S.Croy. 295 332 DQ109
Conington Rd. SE13 166 317 EB82
Conisbee Ct. N14 208 300 DJ43
Conisborough Cres. SE6 198 325 EC90
Coniscliffe Rd. N13 209 300 DQ48
Coniston Ave., Bark. 235 308 ES66
Coniston Ave., Grnf. 122 314 CH69
Coniston Ave., Upmin. 239 311 FQ63
Coniston Ave., Well. 261 326 ES83
Coniston Clo. N20 207 299 DC48
Coniston Clo. SW13 155 314 CT80
Coniston Clo. SW20 284 331 CX100
Coniston Clo. W4 154 314 CQ80
Coniston Clo., Bark. 235 308 ES66
Coniston Clo., Bexh. 255 319 FC81
Coniston Clo., Erith 255 319 FE80
Coniston Gdns. N9 210 301 DW46
Coniston Gdns. NW9 217 304 CR57
Coniston Gdns., Ilf. 224 308 EL56
Coniston Gdns., Pnr. 214 303 BU56
Coniston Gdns., Sutt. 293 331 DD107
Coniston Gdns., Wem. 90 304 CJ60
Coniston Ho. SE5 162 316 DQ80
Coniston Rd. N10 220 306 DH54
Coniston Rd. N17 222 307 DU51
Coniston Rd., Bexh. 255 319 FC81
Coniston Rd., Brom. 275 325 ED93
Coniston Rd., Croy. 287 333 DU101
Coniston Rd., Twick. 259 321 CB86
Coniston Wk. E9 118 307 DW64
Coniston Way, Chess. 282 330 CL104
Coniston Way, Horn. 238 310 FG64
Conistone Way N7 115 306 DL66
Conlan St. W10 127 315 CY70
Conley Rd. NW10 109 304 CS65
Conley St. SE10 151 317 EE78
Connaught Ave. E4 211 301 ED45
Connaught Ave. SW14 170 322 CQ83
Connaught Ave., Ashf. 264 328 BL91
Connaught Ave., Barn. 207 299 DF46
Connaught Ave., Enf. 202 300 DS40
Connaught Ave., Houns. 258 321 BY85
Connaught Bri. E16 244 318 EK73
Connaught Clo. E10 103 307 DY61
Connaught Clo. W2 42/3 315 DE72
Connaught Clo., Enf. 202 300 DS40
Connaught Clo., Sutt. 293 331 DD107
Connaught Clo., Uxb. 241 312 BQ70
Connaught Dr. NW11 219 305 DA56
Connaught Gdns. N10 220 306 DH57
Connaught Gdns. N13 209 300 DP49
Connaught Gdns., Mord. 271 323 DC98
Connaught La., Ilf. 235 308 ER61
Connaught Ms. SE18 253 318 EN78
Connaught Ms. W2 43 315 DF72
Connaught Ms., Ilf. 235 308 ER61
Connaught Pl. W2 55 315 DF73
Connaught Rd. E4 211 301 EE45
Connaught Rd. E11 105 307 ED60
Connaught Rd. E17 223 307 EA57
Connaught Rd. N4 100 306 DN59
Connaught Rd. NW10 125 314 CS67
Connaught Rd. SE18 253 318 EN78
Connaught Rd. W13 132 314 CH73
Connaught Rd., Barn. 206 299 CX44
Connaught Rd., Har. 215 303 CF53
Connaught Rd., Horn. 238 310 FK62
Connaught Rd., Ilf. 235 308 ER61
Connaught Rd., N.Mal. 269 322 CS98
Connaught Rd., Rich. 169 322 CM85
Connaught Rd., Sutt. 285 331 DD103
Connaught Rd., Tedd. 267 329 CD92
Connaught Roundabout E16 244 318 EK73
Connaught Sq. W2 43 315 DF72
Connaught St. W2 42/3 315 DE72
Connaught Way N13 209 300 DP49
Connell Cres. W5 123 314 CM70
Connemara Clo., Borwd. 205 298 CR44
Connington Cres. E4 211 301 ED48
Connop Rd., Enf. 203 301 DX38
Connor Rd., Dag. 236 309 EZ63
Connor St. E9 129 317 DX67
Conolly Rd. W7 243 313 CE74
Conrad Dr., Wor.Pk. 284 331 CW102
Conrad Ho. N16 117 306 DS64
Cons St. SE1 72 316 DN75
Consfield Ave., N.Mal. 270 323 CU98
Consort Ms., Islw. 259 321 CD85
Consort Rd. SE15 164 317 DV81
Constable Clo. NW11 219 305 DB58
Constable Clo., Hayes 241 312 BQ69
Constable Cres. N15 222 307 DU57
Constable Gdns., Edg. 217 304 CN53
Constable Gdns., Islw. 259 321 CD85
Constable Ms., Dag. 236 309 EV63
Constable Wk. SE21 195 324 DT90
Constance Cres., Brom. 289 333 EF101
Constance Rd., Croy. 286 332 DP101
Constance Rd., Enf. 209 300 DS44
Constance Rd., Sutt. 285 331 DC105
Constance Rd., Twick. 259 321 CB87
Constance St. E16 244 318 EL74
Constantine Rd. NW3 113 305 DE63
Constitution Hill SW1 68/9 316 DH75
Constitution Ri. SE18 253 318 EN81
Consul Ave., Dag. 247 319 FC69
Content St. SE17 85 316 DQ77
Contessa Clo., Orp. 291 334 ES106
Control Twr. Rd., Houns. 257 320 BN83
Convair Wk., Nthlt. 242 313 BX69
Convent Clo., Beck. 275 325 EC94
Convent Gdns. W5 142 314 CJ77
Convent Gdns. W11 137 315 CZ72
Convent Hill SE19 273 324 DQ93
Convent Rd., Ashf. 265 328 BN92
Convent Way, Sthl. 250 321 BW77
Conway Clo., Rain. 238 310 FG66
Conway Clo., Stan. 216 304 CG51
Conway Cres., Grnf. 243 313 CE68
Conway Cres., Rom. 226 309 EW58
Conway Dr., Ashf. 265 328 BQ93
Conway Dr., Hayes 249 320 BQ76
Conway Dr., Sutt. 292 331 DB107
Conway Gdns., Enf. 202 300 DS38
Conway Gdns., Mitch. 272 324 DK98
Conway Gdns., Wem. 90 304 CJ59
Conway Gro. W3 135 314 CR71
Conway Ms. W1 33 316 DJ70
Conway Rd. N14 208 300 DL48
Conway Rd. N15 221 306 DP57
Conway Rd. NW2 94 305 CW61
Conway Rd. SE18 253 318 ER77
Conway Rd. SW20 270 323 CW95
Conway Rd., Felt. 266 329 BX92
Conway Rd., Houns. 258 321 BZ87
Conway Rd. (Heathrow Airport), Houns. 257 320 BP83
Conway St. E13 244 318 EG70
Conway St. W1 33 316 DJ70
Conway Wk., Hmptn. 266 329 BZ93
Conybeare NW3 113 305 DE66
Conyer St. E3 129 317 DY68
Conyers Clo., Wdf.Grn. 223 307 EE51
Conyers Rd. SW16 272 324 DK92
Cooden Clo., Brom. 276 326 EH94
Cooderidge Clo. N17 221 306 DT51
Cook Ct. SE16 138 317 DW74
Cook Rd., Dag. 246 319 EY67
Cook Sq., Erith 255 319 FF80
Cooke Clo. E14 140 317 EA74
Cookes Clo. E11 105 307 EF61
Cookes La., Sutt. 292 331 CY107
Cookham Cres. SE16 149 317 DX75
Cookham Dene Clo., Chis. 277 326 ER95
Cookham Rd., Sid. 279 327 FA95
Cookham Rd., Swan. 279 327 FA95
Cookhill Rd. SE2 254 319 EV75
Cooks Clo., Rom. 227 309 FC53
Cook's Hole Rd., Enf. 202 300 DP38
Cook's Rd. E15 130 317 EB68
Cooks Rd. SE17 162 316 DP79
Cookson Gro., Erith 255 319 FB80
Cool Oak La. NW9 93 304 CS59
Coolfin Rd. E16 244 318 EG72
Coolgardie Ave. E4 211 301 ED50
Coolgardie Rd., Ashf. 265 328 BQ92
Coolhurst Rd. N8 220 306 DK58
Coomassie Rd. W9 127 315 CZ70
Coombe Ave., Croy. 287 332 DS105
Coombe Bank, Kings.T. 269 322 CS95
Coombe Clo., Edg. 216 304 CM54
Coombe Clo., Houns. 259 321 CA84
Coombe Cor. N21 209 300 DP46
Coombe Cres., Hmptn. 266 329 BY94
Coombe Dr., Kings.T. 269 322 CR94
Coombe Dr., Ruis. 232 313 BV60
Coombe End, Kings.T. 269 322 CR94
Coombe Gdns. SW20 270 323 CU96
Coombe Gdns., N.Mal. 269 322 CT98
Coombe Hts., Kings.T. 269 322 CS94
Coombe Hill Glade, Kings.T. 269 322 CS94
Coombe Hill Rd., Kings.T. 269 322 CS94
Coombe Ho. Chase, N.Mal. 269 322 CR95
Coombe La. SW20 269 322 CT95
Coombe La., Croy. 287 333 DV106
Coombe La. W., Kings.T. 269 322 CP95
Coombe Lea, Brom. 276 326 EL97
Coombe Neville, Kings.T. 269 322 CR94
Coombe Pk., Kings.T. 269 322 CR92
Coombe Ridings, Kings.T. 269 322 CQ92
Coombe Ri., Kings.T. 269 322 CQ95
Coombe Rd. N22 221 306 DN54
Coombe Rd. NW10 93 304 CR62
Coombe Rd. SE26 274 325 DV91
Coombe Rd. W4 145 314 CS78
Coombe Rd. W13 142 314 CH76
Coombe Rd., Croy. 287 332 DQ105
Coombe Rd., Hmptn. 266 329 BZ93
Coombe Rd., Kings.T. 269 322 CN95
Coombe Rd., N.Mal. 269 322 CS96
Coombe Rd., Rom. 228 311 FM55
Coombe Wk., Sutt. 284 331 DB104
Coombe Wd. Hill, Pur. 295 332 DQ112
Coombe Wd. Rd., Kings.T. 269 322 CQ92
Coombefield Clo., N.Mal. 283 330 CS99
Coomber Way, Croy. 286 332 DK101
Coombes Rd., Dag. 246 319 EZ67
Coombewood Dr., Rom. 227 309 FA58
Coombs St. N1 24/5 316 DP68
Coomer Ms. SW6 157 315 CZ79
Coomer Pl. SW6 157 315 CZ79
Coomer Rd. SW6 157 315 CZ79
Cooms Wk., Edg. 217 304 CQ53
Cooper Ave. E17 222 307 DY53
Cooper Clo. SE1 72 316 DN75
Cooper Ct. E15 120 307 EB64
Cooper Cres., Cars. 285 331 DF104
Cooper Rd. NW10 110 305 CU64
Cooper Rd., Croy. 286 332 DP105
Cooper St. E16 141 317 EF71
Cooperage Clo. N17 221 306 DT51
Coopers Clo. E1 128 317 DW70
Coopers Clo., Dag. 237 309 FB65

Coopers La. E10	104	307	EB60
Coopers La. NW1	22	316	DK68
Cooper's La. SE12	260	326	EH89
Coopers Rd. SE1	87	316	DT78
Cooper's Row EC3	63	316	DT73
Cooper's Yd. SE19	273	324	DS93
Coopersale Clo., Wdf.Grn.	224	308	EJ52
Coopersale Rd. E9	119	307	DX64
Coote Gdns., Dag.	236	309	EZ62
Coote Rd., Bexh.	254	319	EZ81
Coote Rd., Dag.	236	309	EZ62
Cope Pl. W8	64	315	DA76
Cope St. SE16	149	317	DX77
Copeland Dr. E14	150	317	EA77
Copeland Rd. E17	223	307	EB57
Copeland Rd. SE15	164	317	DU82
Copeman Clo. SE26	274	325	DW92
Copenhagen Gdns. W4	145	314	CR75
Copenhagen Pl. E14	139	317	DZ72
Copenhagen St. N1	22/3	316	DL67
Copers Cope Rd., Beck.	274	325	DZ94
Copford Clo., Wdf.Grn.	224	308	EL51
Copford Wk. N1	25	316	DQ67
Copinger Wk., Edg.	217	304	CP53
Copland Ave., Wem.	107	304	CK64
Copland Clo., Wem.	106	304	CJ64
Copland Ms., Wem.	107	304	CL65
Copland Rd., Wem.	107	304	CL65
Copleston Ms. SE15	163	316	DT82
Copleston Pas. SE15	163	316	DT82
Copleston Rd. SE15	179	324	DT83
Copley Clo. SE17	162	316	DP79
Copley Clo. W7	243	313	CF70
Copley Dene, Brom.	276	326	EK95
Copley Pk. SW16	272	324	DM93
Copley Rd., Stan.	204	298	CJ50
Copley St. E1	139	317	DX71
Copnor Way SE15	163	316	DS80
Copped Hall SE21	195	324	DR89
Coppelia Rd. SE3	183	325	EF84
Coppen Rd., Dag.	236	309	EZ59
Copper Beech Clo. NW3	113	305	DD65
Copper Beech Clo., Ilf.	225	308	EN53
Copper Beeches, Islw.	251	321	CD81
Copper Clo. SE19	273	324	DT94
Copper Mead Clo. NW2	94	305	CW62
Copper Mill Dr., Islw.	251	321	CF82
Copper Mill La. SW17	271	323	DC91
Copper Row SE1	63	316	DT74
Copperas St. SE8	166	317	EB79
Copperbeech Clo. NW3	113	305	DD64
Copperdale Rd., Hayes	250	321	BU75
Copperfield App., Chig.	225	308	ER51
Copperfield Ave., Uxb.	249	312	BN71
Copperfield Clo., S.Croy.	295	332	DQ111
Copperfield Ct., Pnr.	214	303	BZ56
Copperfield Dr. N15	221	306	DT56
Copperfield Ms. N18	209	300	DS50
Copperfield Rd. E3	129	317	DY70
Copperfield Rd. SE28	246	319	EW72
Copperfield St. SE1	72/3	316	DP75
Copperfield Way, Chis.	277	326	EQ93
Copperfield Way, Pnr.	214	303	BZ56
Copperfields Way, Rom.	228	310	FK53
Coppergate Clo., Brom.	276	326	EH95
Coppermill La. E17	222	307	DW58
Coppetts Clo. N12	219	305	DE52
Coppetts Rd. N10	219	305	DF52
Coppice, The, Ashf.	265	328	BP93
Coppice, The, Enf.	202	300	DP42
Coppice, The, West Dr.	248	312	BL72
Coppice Clo. SW20	270	323	CW97
Coppice Clo., Ruis.	231	302	BR58
Coppice Clo., Stan.	215	303	CF51
Coppice Dr. SW15	172	323	CU86
Coppice Wk. N20	207	299	DA48
Coppice Way E18	223	307	EF56
Coppies Gro. N11	208	300	DH49
Copping Clo., Croy.	287	332	DS105
Coppins, The, Har.	215	303	CE51
Coppock Clo. SW11	159	315	DE82
Coppsfield, W.Mol.	267	329	CA97
Copse, The E4	211	301	EF46
Copse Ave., W.Wick.	288	333	EB104
Copse Clo. SE7	252	318	EH79
Copse Clo., Nthwd.	213	302	BQ54
Copse Clo., West Dr.	248	320	BK76
Copse Glade, Surb.	282	330	CK102
Copse Hill SW20	270	323	CU95
Copse Hill, Pur.	294	332	DL113
Copse Hill, Sutt.	292	331	DB108
Copse Wd. Way, Nthwd.	213	302	BP53
Copsewood Clo., Sid.	261	326	ES86
Coptefield Dr., Belv.	254	319	EX76
Copthall Ave. EC2	50	316	DR72
Copthall Bldgs. EC2	50	316	DR72
Copthall Clo. EC2	50	316	DR72
Copthall Dr. NW7	218	305	CU52
Copthall Gdns. NW7	218	305	CU52
Copthall Gdns., Twick.	259	321	CF88
Copthall Rd. E., Uxb.	231	312	BN61
Copthall Rd. W., Uxb.	231	312	BN61
Copthorne Ave. SW12	193	324	DK87
Copthorne Ave., Brom.	290	334	EM103
Copthorne Ave., Ilf.	225	308	EP51
Copthorne Chase, Ashf.	264	328	BM91
Copthorne Clo., Shep.	281	328	BQ100
Copthorne Gdns., Horn.	229	311	FN57
Copthorne Ms., Hayes	249	320	BS77
Copthorne Ri., S.Croy.	295	332	DR113
Coptic St. WC1	46/7	316	DL71
Copwood Clo. N12	207	299	DD49
Coral Clo., Rom.	226	309	EW55
Coral Row SW11	174	323	DC83
Coral St. SE1	72	316	DN75
Coraline Clo., Sthl.	242	313	BZ69
Coralline Wk. SE2	254	319	EW75
Coram St. WC1	34/5	316	DL70
Coran Clo. N9	210	301	DX45
Corban Rd., Houns.	259	321	CA83
Corbet Clo., Wall.	285	332	DG102
Corbet Ct. EC3	50	316	DR72
Corbet Pl. E1	51	316	DT71
Corbets Ave., Upmin.	239	311	FP64
Corbets Tey Rd., Upmin.	239	311	FP63
Corbett Gro. N22	220	306	DL52
Corbett Rd. E11	224	308	EJ58
Corbett Rd. E17	223	307	EC55
Corbetts La. SE16	148	317	DW77
Corbetts Pas. SE16	148	317	DW77
Corbicum E11	105	307	EE59
Corbiere Ct. SW19	270	323	CX93
Corbiere Ho. N1	26/7	316	DS67
Corbins La., Har.	233	313	CB62
Corbridge Cres. E2	128	317	DV68
Corby Rd. NW10	125	314	CR68
Corby Way E3	130	317	EA70
Corbylands Rd., Sid.	261	326	ES87
Corbyn St. N4	99	306	DL60
Cord Way E14	150	317	EA76
Cordelia Clo. SE24	178	324	DP84
Cordelia Gdns., Stai.	264	320	BL87
Cordelia Rd., Stai.	264	320	BL87
Cordelia St. E14	140	317	EB72
Cording St. E14	140	317	EB71
Cordingley Rd., Ruis.	231	312	BR61
Cordova Rd. E3	129	317	DY69
Cordwainers Wk. E13	244	318	EG68
Cordwell Rd. SE13	183	325	EE85
Corelli Rd. SE3	252	318	EL81
Corfe Ave., Har.	233	313	CA63
Corfe Clo., Hayes	242	313	BW72
Corfe Twr. W3	144	314	CQ75
Corfield Rd. N21	208	300	DM43
Corfield St. E2	128	317	DV69
Corfton Rd. W5	133	314	CL72
Coriander Ave. E14	141	317	ED72
Cories Clo., Dag.	236	309	EX61
Corinium Clo., Wem.	107	304	CM63
Corinne Rd. N19	114	306	DJ63
Corinth Par., Hayes	249	312	BT71
Corinthian Manorway, Erith	255	319	FD77
Corinthian Rd., Erith	255	319	FD77
Cork Sq. E1	138	317	DV74
Cork St. W1	57	316	DJ73
Cork St. Ms. W1	57	316	DJ73
Cork Tree Way E4	210	301	DY50
Corker Wk. N7	99	306	DM61
Corkran Rd., Surb.	282	330	CK101
Corkscrew Hill, W.Wick.	289	333	EC103
Corlett St. NW1	42/3	315	DE71
Cormont Rd. SE5	162	316	DP81
Cormorant Clo. E17	222	307	DX53
Cormorant Rd. E7	121	307	EF64
Cormorant Wk., Horn.	238	310	FH65
Corn Mill Dr., Orp.	291	335	EU101
Corn Way E11	105	307	ED62
Cornbury Rd., Edg.	216	304	CK52
Cornelia Pl., Erith	255	319	FE79
Cornelia St. N7	115	306	DM65
Cornell Clo., Sid.	278	327	EY93
Corner Grn. SE3	252	318	EG82
Corner Ho. St. WC2	58/9	316	DL74
Corner Mead NW9	217	304	CT52
Cornerside, Ashf.	265	328	BQ94
Corney Reach Way W4	155	314	CS80
Corney Rd. W4	155	314	CS79
Cornfield Clo., Uxb.	240	312	BK68
Cornflower La., Croy.	288	333	DX102
Cornflower Ter. SE22	180	325	DV86
Cornflower Way, Rom.	228	311	FL53
Cornford Clo., Brom.	289	334	EG99
Cornford Gro. SW12	192	324	DH89
Cornhill EC3	50	316	DR72
Cornish Ct. N9	210	301	DV45
Cornish Gro. SE20	274	325	DV95
Cornish Ho. SE17	162	316	DP79
Cornish Ho., Brent.	143	314	CM78
Cornmill La. SE13	182	325	EC83
Cornmow Dr. NW10	110	305	CU63
Cornshaw Rd., Dag.	236	309	EX60
Cornthwaite Rd. E5	102	307	DW62
Cornwall Ave. E2	128	317	DW69
Cornwall Ave. N3	219	305	DA52
Cornwall Ave. N22	220	306	DL53
Cornwall Ave., Sthl.	242	313	BZ71
Cornwall Ave., Well.	261	326	ES83
Cornwall Clo., Bark.	235	308	ET65
Cornwall Clo., Horn.	229	311	FN56
Cornwall Cres. W11	137	315	CY72
Cornwall Dr., Orp.	278	327	EW94
Cornwall Gdns. NW10	110	305	CV65
Cornwall Gdns. SW7	64/5	315	DB76
Cornwall Gdns. Wk. SW7	64/5	315	DB76
Cornwall Gro. W4	145	314	CS78
Cornwall Ms. S. SW7	65	315	DC76
Cornwall Ms. W. SW7	64/5	315	DB76
Cornwall Rd. N4	100	306	DN59
Cornwall Rd. N15	221	306	DR57
Cornwall Rd. N18	210	301	DU50
Cornwall Rd. SE1	60	316	DN74
Cornwall Rd., Croy.	286	332	DP103
Cornwall Rd., Har.	215	303	CC58
Cornwall Rd., Pnr.	214	303	BZ52
Cornwall Rd., Ruis.	231	312	BT62
Cornwall Rd., Sutt.	292	331	CZ108
Cornwall Rd., Twick.	184	322	CG87
Cornwall Rd., Uxb.	240	312	BK65
Cornwall St. E1	138	317	DV73
Cornwall Ter. NW1	31	315	DF70
Cornwall Ter. Ms. NW1	31	315	DF70
Cornwallis Ave. N9	210	301	DV47
Cornwallis Ave. SE9	261	326	ER89
Cornwallis Clo., Erith	255	319	FF79
Cornwallis Gro. N9	210	301	DV47
Cornwallis Rd. E17	222	307	DX56
Cornwallis Rd. N9	210	301	DV47
Cornwallis Rd. N19	99	306	DL61
Cornwallis Rd., Dag.	236	309	EX63
Cornwallis Sq. N19	99	306	DL61
Cornwallis Wk. SE9	260	326	EM83
Cornwood Clo. N2	219	305	DD57
Cornwood Dr. E1	138	317	DW72
Cornworthy Rd., Dag.	236	309	EW64
Corona Rd. SE12	260	326	EG87
Coronation Ave. N16	101	306	DT62
Coronation Clo., Bex.	262	327	EX86
Coronation Clo., Ilf.	225	308	EQ56
Coronation Dr., Horn.	238	310	FH63
Coronation Rd. E13	244	318	EJ69
Coronation Rd. NW10	123	314	CM69
Coronation Rd., Hayes	249	320	BT77
Coronation Wk., Twick.	259	321	CA88
Coronet St. N1	38/9	316	DS69
Corporation Ave., Houns.	258	321	BY84
Corporation Row EC1	36	316	DN70
Corporation St. E15	131	317	EE68
Corporation St. N7	115	306	DL64
Corrance Rd. SW2	177	324	DL84
Corri Ave. N14	208	300	DK49
Corrib Dr., Sutt.	285	331	DE106
Corrigan Ave., Couls.	293	332	DG114
Corringham Ct. NW11	96	305	DB59
Corringham Rd. NW11	96	305	DA59
Corringham Rd., Wem.	92	304	CN61
Corringway NW11	96	305	DB59
Corringway W5	133	314	CM71
Corsair Clo., Stai.	264	320	BK87
Corsair Rd., Stai.	264	320	BL87
Corscombe Clo., Kings.T.	269	322	CQ92
Corsehill St. SW16	272	324	DJ93
Corsham St. N1	38	316	DR69
Corsica St. N5	116	306	DP65
Corsley Way E9	119	307	DZ65
Cortayne Rd. SW6	157	315	CZ82
Cortis Rd. SW15	172	323	CV86
Cortis Ter. SW15	172	323	CV86
Corunna Rd. SW8	160	316	DJ81
Corunna Ter. SW8	160	316	DJ81
Corvette Sq. SE10	167	317	ED79
Corwell Gdns., Uxb.	249	312	BQ72
Corwell La., Uxb.	249	312	BQ72
Coryton Path W9	127	315	CZ70
Cosbycote Ave. SE24	178	324	DQ85
Cosdach Ave., Wall.	294	332	DK108
Cosedge Cres., Croy.	286	332	DN106
Cosgrove Clo. N21	209	300	DQ47
Cosgrove Clo., Hayes	249	313	BY70
Cosmo Pl. WC1	46/7	316	DL71
Cosmur Clo. W12	145	314	CT76
Cossall Wk. SE15	164	317	DV81
Cosser St. SE1	72	316	DN76
Costa St. SE15	164	317	DU82
Coston Wk. SE4	181	325	DX84
Costons Ave., Grnf.	243	313	CD69
Costons La., Grnf.	243	313	CD69
Cosway St. NW1	42/3	315	DE71
Cotall St. E14	140	317	EA72
Coteford Clo., Pnr.	214	303	BU57
Coteford St. SW17	271	323	DF91
Cotelands, Croy.	287	332	DS104
Cotesbach Rd. E5	102	307	DW62
Cotesmore Gdns., Dag.	236	309	EW63
Cotford Rd., Th.Hth.	273	324	DQ98
Cotham St. SE17	85	316	DQ77
Cotherstone Rd. SW2	193	324	DM88
Cotleigh Ave., Bex.	262	327	EX89
Cotleigh Rd. NW6	112	305	DA66
Cotleigh Rd., Rom.	227	309	FD58
Cotman Clo. NW11	219	305	DC58
Cotman Clo. SW15	172	323	CW86
Cotman Gdns., Edg.	217	304	CN54
Cotman Ms., Dag.	236	309	EW64
Cotmandene Cres., Orp.	278	327	EU96
Cotmans Clo., Hayes	242	313	BU74
Coton Rd., Well.	262	327	EU83
Cotsford Ave., N.Mal.	283	330	CQ99
Cotswold Clo., Bexh.	255	319	FE82
Cotswold Clo., Kings.T.	269	322	CP93
Cotswold Clo., Stai.	264	328	BG92
Cotswold Clo., Uxb.	240	312	BJ67
Cotswold Ct. N11	208	300	DG49
Cotswold Gdns. E6	244	318	EK69
Cotswold Gdns. NW2	95	305	CX61
Cotswold Gdns., Ilf.	235	308	ER59
Cotswold Gate NW2	95	305	CY60
Cotswold Ms. SW11	159	315	DD81
Cotswold Ri., Orp.	291	334	ET100
Cotswold Rd., Hmptn.	267	329	CA93
Cotswold Rd., Rom.	228	311	FM54
Cotswold Rd., Sutt.	292	331	DB110
Cotswold St. SE27	273	324	DP91
Cotswold Way, Wor.Pk.	284	331	CW103
Cottage Ave., Brom.	290	334	EL102
Cottage Clo., Ruis.	231	312	BR60
Cottage Fld. Clo., Sid.	262	327	EW88
Cottage Grn. SE5	163	316	DR80
Cottage Gro. SW9	177	324	DL83
Cottage Gro., Surb.	282	330	CK100
Cottage Homes NW7	206	299	CU49
Cottage Homes Chalet Est. NW7	206	299	CU49
Cottage Pl. SW3	66/7	315	DE76
Cottage St. E14	140	317	EB73
Cottage Wk. N16	101	306	DT62
Cottage Wk. SE15	163	316	DT80
Cottenham Dr. NW9	217	304	CT55
Cottenham Dr. SW20	270	323	CV94
Cottenham Par. SW20	270	323	CV96
Cottenham Pk. Rd. SW20	270	323	CV95
Cottenham Pl. SW20	270	323	CV94
Cottenham Rd. E17	222	307	DZ56
Cotterill Rd., Surb.	282	330	CL103
Cottesbrook St. SE14	165	317	DY80
Cottesloe Ms. SE1	72	316	DN76
Cottesmore Ave., Ilf.	225	308	EN54
Cottesmore Gdns. W8	64/5	315	DB76
Cottingham Chase, Ruis.	232	313	BU62
Cottingham Rd. SE20	274	325	DX94
Cottingham Rd. SW8	161	316	DM80
Cottington Rd., Felt.	266	329	BX91
Cottington St. SE11	84	316	DN78
Cottle St. SE16	148	317	DW75
Cotton Ave. W3	135	314	CR72
Cotton Hill, Brom.	275	325	ED91
Cotton Row SW11	175	323	DD83
Cotton St. E14	140	317	EC73
Cottongrass Clo., Croy.	288	333	DX102
Cottons App., Rom.	227	309	FD57
Cottons Ct., Rom.	227	309	FD57
Cottons Gdns. E2	38/9	316	DS69
Cottons La. SE1	62	316	DR74
Couchmore Ave., Ilf.	224	308	EM54
Coulgate St. SE4	181	325	DY83
Coulson Clo., Dag.	236	309	EW59
Coulson St. SW3	79	315	DF78
Coulter Rd. W6	146	315	CV76
Coultree Clo., Hayes	242	313	BY70
Councillor St. SE5	162	316	DQ80
Counter Ct. SE1	62	316	DR74
Counter St. SE1	62/3	316	DS74
Countess Clo., Uxb.	212	302	BJ54
Countess Rd. NW5	114	306	DJ64
Countisbury Ave., Enf.	209	300	DT45
Country Way, Felt.	266	329	BV93
Country Way, Sun.	266	329	BU94
County Gdns., Bark.	245	318	ES68
County Gate SE9	261	326	EQ90
County Gate, Barn.	207	299	DB44
County Gro. SE5	162	316	DQ81
County Rd. E6	245	318	EP71
County Rd., Th.Hth.	273	324	DP96
County St. SE1	73	316	DQ76
Coupland Pl. SE18	253	318	EQ78
Courage Clo., Horn.	228	310	FJ58
Courcy Rd. N8	221	306	DN55
Courier Rd., Dag.	247	319	FC70
Courland Gro. SW8	161	316	DK82
Courland St. SW8	161	316	DK81
Course, The SE9	261	326	EN90
Court, The, Ruis.	232	313	BY63
Court Ave., Belv.	254	319	EZ78
Court Ave., Rom.	229	311	FN52
Court Clo., Har.	216	304	CK55
Court Clo., Twick.	259	321	CB90
Court Clo., Wall.	294	332	DK108
Court Clo. Ave., Twick.	259	321	CB90
Court Cres., Chess.	288	330	CK106
Court Cres., Swan.	279	327	FE98
Court Downs Rd., Beck.	275	325	EB96
Court Dr., Croy.	286	332	DM105
Court Dr., Stan.	204	298	CL49
Court Dr., Sutt.	285	331	DE105
Court Dr., Uxb.	240	312	BM67
Court Fm. Ave., Epsom	283	330	CR106
Court Fm. Ind. Est., Stai.	256	320	BM86
Court Fm. Rd. SE9	260	326	EK89
Court Fm. Rd., Nthlt.	233	313	CA66
Court Gdns. N7	116	306	DN65
Court Hill, S.Croy.	295	332	DS112
Court Ho. Gdns. N3	219	305	DA51
Court La. SE21	179	324	DS86
Court La., Iver	248	312	BG74
Court La. Gdns. SE21	195	324	DS87
Court Mead, Nthlt.	242	313	BZ69
Court Par., Wem.	90	304	CH62
Court Rd. SE9	260	326	EM86
Court Rd. SE25	273	324	DT96
Court Rd., Orp.	291	335	EV101
Court Rd., Sthl.	250	321	BZ77
Court Rd., Uxb.	241	312	BP64
Court St. E1	138	317	DV71
Court St., Brom.	276	326	EG96
Court Way NW9	217	304	CS56
Court Way W3	134	314	CQ71
Court Way, Ilf.	225	308	EQ55
Court Way, Rom.	228	311	FL54
Court Way, Twick.	259	321	CF87
Court Yd. SE9	260	326	EM86
Courtauld Clo. SE28	246	319	EU74
Courtauld Rd. N19	99	306	DK60
Courtenay Ave. N6	97	305	DE59
Courtenay Ave., Har.	215	303	CC52
Courtenay Ave., Sutt.	292	331	DA109
Courtenay Dr., Beck.	275	325	ED96
Courtenay Gdns., Har.	215	303	CC54
Courtenay Gdns., Upmin.	239	311	FQ61
Courtenay Ms. E17	222	307	DY57
Courtenay Pl. E17	222	307	DY57
Courtenay Rd. E11	105	307	EF62
Courtenay Rd. E17	222	307	DX56
Courtenay Rd. SE20	274	325	DX94
Courtenay Rd., Wem.	91	304	CK62
Courtenay Rd., Wor.Pk.	284	331	CW104
Courtenay Sq. SE11	84	316	DN78
Courtenay St. SE11	84	316	DN78
Courtens Ms., Stan.	216	304	CJ52
Courtfield W5	132	314	CJ71
Courtfield Ave., Har.	215	303	CF57
Courtfield Cres., Har.	215	303	CF57
Courtfield Gdns. SW5	76/7	315	DB77
Courtfield Gdns. W13	132	314	CG72
Courtfield Gdns., Ruis.	231	312	BT61
Courtfield Gdns., Uxb.	230	312	BG62
Courtfield Ms. SW5	76/7	315	DB77
Courtfield Ri., W.Wick.	289	333	ED104
Courtfield Rd. SW7	77	315	DC77
Courtfield Rd., Ashf.	265	328	BP93
Courthill Rd. SE13	182	325	EC84
Courthope Rd. NW3	113	305	DF63
Courthope Rd. SW19	270	323	CY92
Courthope Rd., Grnf.	243	313	CD68
Courthope Vil. SW19	270	323	CY94
Courthouse Rd. N12	219	305	DB51
Courtland Ave. E4	211	301	EF47
Courtland Ave. NW7	205	299	CR48
Courtland Ave. SW16	272	324	DM94
Courtland Ave., Ilf.	234	308	EM61
Courtland Gro. SE28	246	319	EX73
Courtland Rd. E6	244	318	EL67
Courtlands, Rich.	170	322	CN85
Courtlands Ave. SE12	260	326	EH85
Courtlands Ave., Brom.	289	333	EE102
Courtlands Ave., Hmptn.	266	329	BZ93
Courtlands Ave., Rich.	154	314	CP82
Courtlands Clo., Ruis.	231	312	BT59
Courtlands Clo., S.Croy.	295	332	DT110
Courtlands Rd., Surb.	282	330	CN101
Courtleet Dr., Erith	255	319	FB81
Courtleigh Gdns. NW11	218	305	CY56
Courtman Rd. N17	221	306	DQ52
Courtmead Clo. SE24	178	324	DQ86
Courtnell St. W2	40	315	DA72
Courtney Clo. SE19	273	324	DS93
Courtney Cres., Cars.	293	331	DF108
Courtney Pl., Croy.	286	332	DN104
Courtney Rd. N7	116	306	DN64
Courtney Rd. SW19	271	323	DE94
Courtney Rd., Croy.	286	332	DN104
Courtney Rd., Houns.	257	320	BN83
Courtrai Rd. SE23	181	325	DY86
Courtside N8	220	306	DK58
Courtyard, The N1	115	306	DM66
Cousin La. EC4	62	316	DR73
Cousins Clo., West Dr.	248	312	BL73
Couthurst Rd. SE3	252	318	EH79
Coutts Ave., Chess.	282	330	CL106
Coutts Cres. NW5	98	306	DG62
Coval Gdns. SW14	170	322	CP84
Coval La. SW14	170	322	CP84
Coval Rd. SW14	170	322	CP84
Covelees Wall E6	245	318	EN72
Covell Ct. SE8	166	317	EA80
Covent Gdn. WC2	58/9	316	DL73
Coventry Clo. E6	244	318	EM72
Coventry Clo. NW6	16	315	DA67
Coventry Cross E3	130	317	EB70
Coventry Rd. E1	128	317	DV70
Coventry Rd. E2	128	317	DV70
Coventry Rd. SE25	274	325	DU98
Coventry Rd., Ilf.	235	308	EP61
Coventry St. W1	58	316	DK73
Coverack Clo. N14	208	300	DJ44
Coverack Clo., Croy.	288	333	DY101
Coverdale Clo., Stan.	204	298	CH50
Coverdale Ct., Enf.	203	301	DY37
Coverdale Gdns., Croy.	287	332	DT104
Coverdale Rd. NW2	111	305	CX66
Coverdale Rd. W12	146	315	CV75
Coverdales, The, Bark.	245	318	ER68
Coverley Clo. E1	138	317	DU71
Covert, The, Nthwd.	213	302	BQ52
Covert, The, Orp.	291	334	ES100
Covert Rd., Chig.	225	308	ET51
Coverton Rd. SW17	271	323	DE92
Covet Wd. Clo., Orp.	291	334	ET100
Covington Gdns. SW16	273	324	DP94
Covington Way SW16	272	324	DM93
Cow La., Grnf.	243	313	CD68
Cow Leaze E6	245	318	EN72
Cowan Clo. E6	244	318	EL71
Cowbridge La., Bark.	235	308	EP66
Cowbridge Rd., Har.	216	304	CM56
Cowcross St. EC1	48/9	316	DP71
Cowden Rd., Orp.	291	334	ET101
Cowden St. SE6	275	325	EA91
Cowdenbeath Path N1	23	316	DM67
Cowdray Rd., Uxb.	241	312	BQ67
Cowdray Way, Horn.	237	309	FF63
Cowdrey Clo., Enf.	202	300	DS40
Cowdrey Rd. SW19	271	323	DB92
Cowdry Rd. E9	119	307	DY65
Cowen Ave., Har.	233	313	CC61
Cowgate Rd., Grnf.	243	313	CD68
Cowick Rd. SW17	271	323	DF91
Cowings Mead, Nthlt.	232	313	BY65
Cowland Ave., Enf.	203	301	DW42
Cowleaze Rd., Kings.T.	268	322	CL95
Cowley Cres., Uxb.	248	312	BJ71
Cowley La. E11	105	307	EE62
Cowley Mill Rd., Uxb.	240	312	BH68
Cowley Pl. NW4	218	305	CW57
Cowley Rd. E11	224	308	EH57
Cowley Rd. SW9	162	316	DN81
Cowley Rd. SW14	171	322	CS83
Cowley Rd. W3	135	314	CT74
Cowley Rd., Ilf.	234	308	EM59
Cowley Rd., Rom.	228	310	FH52
Cowley Rd., Uxb.	240	312	BJ67
Cowley St. SW1	70/1	316	DL76
Cowling Clo. W11	137	315	CY74
Cowper Ave. E6	234	308	EL66
Cowper Ave., Sutt.	285	331	DD105
Cowper Clo., Brom.	276	326	EK98
Cowper Clo., Well.	262	327	EU85
Cowper Gdns. N14	208	300	DH44
Cowper Gdns., Wall.	294	332	DJ107
Cowper Rd. N14	208	300	DH46
Cowper Rd. N16	117	306	DS64
Cowper Rd. N18	210	301	DU50
Cowper Rd. SW19	271	323	DC93
Cowper Rd. W3	135	314	CR74
Cowper Rd. W7	243	313	CF73
Cowper Rd., Belv.	255	319	FA77
Cowper Rd., Brom.	276	326	EK98
Cowper Rd., Kings.T.	268	322	CM92
Cowper St. EC2	38	316	DR70
Cowper Ter. W10	137	315	CX71
Cowslip Clo., Uxb.	240	312	BL66
Cowslip Rd. E18	224	308	EH54
Cowthorpe Rd. SW8	161	316	DK81
Cox La., Chess.	282	330	CL105
Cox La., Epsom	282	330	CP105
Coxley Ri., Pur.	295	332	DQ113
Coxmount Rd. SE7	252	318	EK78
Cox's Wk. SE21	196	325	DU88
Coxson Pl. SE1	75	316	DT75
Coxwell Rd. SE18	253	318	ER78
Coxwell Rd. SE19	273	324	DS94
Crab Hill, Beck.	275	325	ED94
Crabbs Cft. Clo., Orp.	291	334	EQ106
Crabtree Ave., Rom.	226	309	EX56
Crabtree Ave., Wem.	123	314	CL68
Crabtree Clo. E2	27	316	DT68
Crabtree Ct. E15	120	307	EB64
Crabtree La. SW6	157	315	CX80
Crabtree Manorway N., Belv.	255	319	FC75
Crabtree Manorway S., Belv.	255	319	FC76
Crabtree Wk. SE15	163	316	DT81
Crace St. NW1	34	316	DK69
Craddock Rd., Enf.	202	300	DT41
Craddock St. NW5	114	306	DG65
Cradley Rd. SE9	261	326	ER88
Craig Dr., Uxb.	249	312	BP72
Craig Gdns. E18	223	307	EF54
Craig Pk. Rd. N18	210	301	DV49
Craig Rd., Rich.	268	322	CJ91
Craigdale Rd., Horn.	227	309	FF58
Craigen Ave., Croy.	287	333	DV102
Craigerne Rd. SE3	252	318	EH80
Craigholm SE18	253	318	EN82
Craigmuir Pk., Wem.	123	314	CM67
Craignair Rd. SW2	194	324	DN87
Craignish Ave. SW16	272	324	DM96
Craigs Ct. SW1	58/9	316	DL74
Craigton Rd. SE9	260	326	EM84
Craigweil Clo., Stan.	204	298	CK50
Craigweil Dr., Stan.	204	298	CK50
Craigwell Ave., Felt.	258	321	BU90
Craik Ct. NW6	127	315	CZ68
Crail Row SE17	86	316	DR77
Cramer St. W1	44	316	DG71
Crammond Clo. W6	157	315	CY79
Cramond Ct., Felt.	265	320	BR88
Crampton Rd. SE20	274	325	DW93
Crampton St. SE17	85	316	DQ77
Cranberry Clo., Nthlt.	242	313	BX68
Cranberry La. E16	131	317	EE70
Cranborne Ave., Sthl.	251	321	CA77
Cranborne Gdns., Upmin.	239	311	FP61
Cranborne Rd., Bark.	245	318	ER67
Cranborne Waye, Hayes	242	313	BW72
Cranbourn All. WC2	58	316	DK73
Cranbourn Pas. SE16	148	317	DV75
Cranbourn St. WC2	58	316	DK73
Cranbourne Ave. E11	224	308	EH56
Cranbourne Ave., Surb.	282	330	CN104
Cranbourne Clo. SW16	272	324	DL97
Cranbourne Dr., Pnr.	214	303	BX57
Cranbourne Gdns. NW11	218	305	CY57
Cranbourne Gdns., Ilf.	225	308	EQ55
Cranbourne Rd. E12	234	308	EL64
Cranbourne Rd. E15	120	307	EC63
Cranbourne Rd. N10	220	306	DH54
Cranbourne Rd., Nthwd.	231	302	BT55
Cranbrook Clo., Brom.	289	334	EG100
Cranbrook Dr., Rom.	228	310	FH56
Cranbrook Dr., Twick.	259	321	CB88
Cranbrook Est. E2	129	317	DX68
Cranbrook Ms. E17	222	307	DZ57
Cranbrook Pk. N22	220	306	DM53
Cranbrook Pt. E16	244	318	EG74
Cranbrook Ri., Ilf.	224	308	EM58
Cranbrook Rd. SE8	166	317	EA81
Cranbrook Rd. SW19	270	323	CY94
Cranbrook Rd. W4	145	314	CS78
Cranbrook Rd., Barn.	207	299	DD44
Cranbrook Rd., Bexh.	254	319	EZ81
Cranbrook Rd., Houns.	258	321	BZ84
Cranbrook Rd., Ilf.	225	308	EN57
Cranbrook Rd., Th.Hth.	273	324	DQ96
Cranbrook St. E2	129	317	DX68
Cranbury Rd. SW6	158	315	DB82
Crane Ave. W3	134	314	CQ73
Crane Ave., Islw.	168	322	CG85
Crane Clo., Dag.	237	309	FA65
Crane Clo., Har.	233	313	CC62
Crane Ct. EC4	48	316	DN72
Crane Ct., Epsom	283	330	CQ105
Crane Gdns., Hayes	249	320	BT77
Crane Gro. N7	116	306	DN65
Crane Lo. Rd., Houns.	250	321	BV79
Crane Mead SE16	149	317	DX77
Crane Pk. Rd., Twick.	259	321	CB89
Crane Rd., Twick.	259	321	CE88
Crane St. SE10	151	317	ED78
Crane St. SE15	163	316	DT81
Crane Way, Twick.	259	321	CC87
Cranebrook, Twick.	259	321	CC89
Craneford Clo., Twick.	259	321	CF87
Craneford Way, Twick.	259	321	CE87
Cranes Dr., Surb.	268	322	CL98
Cranes Pk., Surb.	268	322	CL98
Cranes Pk. Ave., Surb.	268	322	CL98
Cranes Pk. Cres., Surb.	268	322	CM98
Cranes Way, Borwd.	205	298	CQ43
Craneswater, Hayes	257	320	BT80
Craneswater Pk., Sthl.	250	321	BZ78
Cranfield Clo. SE27	194	324	DQ90
Cranfield Dr. NW9	217	304	CS52
Cranfield Rd. SE4	181	325	DZ83
Cranfield Rd. E., Cars.	293	332	DG109
Cranfield Rd. W., Cars.	293	331	DF109
Cranfield Row SE1	72	316	DN76
Cranford Ave. N13	208	300	DL50
Cranford Ave., Stai.	264	320	BL87
Cranford Clo. SW20	270	323	CV94
Cranford Clo., Pur.	295	332	DQ113
Cranford Clo., Stai.	264	320	BL87
Cranford Cotts. E1	139	317	DX73
Cranford Dr., Hayes	249	320	BT77
Cranford La., Hayes	257	320	BR79
Cranford La. (Cranford), Houns.	257	320	BT81
Cranford La. (Hatton Cross), Houns.	257	320	BT83
Cranford La. (Heston), Houns.	250	321	BV80
Cranford Pk. Rd., Hayes	249	320	BT77
Cranford St. E1	139	317	DX73
Cranford Way N8	220	306	DM57
Cranham Gdns., Upmin.	239	311	FS60
Cranham Rd., Horn.	228	310	FH58
Cranhurst Rd. NW2	110	305	CW64
Cranleigh Clo. SE20	274	325	DV96
Cranleigh Clo., Bex.	263	327	FB86
Cranleigh Clo., Orp.	291	335	EU104
Cranleigh Clo., S.Croy.	295	333	DU112
Cranleigh Gdns. N21	209	300	DN43
Cranleigh Gdns. SE25	273	324	DS97
Cranleigh Gdns., Bark.	235	308	ER66
Cranleigh Gdns., Har.	216	304	CL57
Cranleigh Gdns., Kings.T.	268	322	CM93
Cranleigh Gdns., S.Croy.	295	333	DU112
Cranleigh Gdns., Sthl.	242	313	BZ72
Cranleigh Gdns., Sutt.	284	331	DB103
Cranleigh Ms. SW11	159	315	DE82
Cranleigh Rd. N15	221	306	DQ57
Cranleigh Rd. SW19	270	323	CZ97
Cranleigh Rd., Felt.	265	328	BT91
Cranleigh St. NW1	21	316	DJ68
Cranley Dene Ct. N10	220	306	DH56
Cranley Dr., Ilf.	235	308	EQ59
Cranley Dr., Ruis.	231	312	BT61
Cranley Gdns. N10	220	306	DH56
Cranley Gdns. N13	208	300	DM48
Cranley Gdns. SW7	77	315	DC78
Cranley Gdns., Wall.	294	332	DJ108
Cranley Ms. SW7	77	315	DC78
Cranley Par. SE9	276	326	EL91
Cranley Pl. SW7	78	315	DD77
Cranley Rd. E13	244	318	EH71
Cranley Rd., Ilf.	225	308	EQ58
Cranmer Ave. W13	142	314	CH76
Cranmer Clo., Mord.	284	331	CX100
Cranmer Clo., Ruis.	232	313	BX60
Cranmer Clo., Stan.	216	304	CJ52
Cranmer Ct. SW3	78/9	315	DE77
Cranmer Ct. SW4	177	324	DK83
Cranmer Ct., Hmptn.	267	329	CB92
Cranmer Fm. Clo., Mitch.	271	323	DF98
Cranmer Gdns., Dag.	237	309	FC63
Cranmer Rd. E7	234	308	EH63
Cranmer Rd. SW9	162	316	DN80
Cranmer Rd., Croy.	286	332	DP104
Cranmer Rd., Edg.	205	298	CP48
Cranmer Rd., Hmptn.	267	329	CB92
Cranmer Rd., Hayes	249	312	BR72
Cranmer Rd., Kings.T.	268	322	CL92
Cranmer Rd., Mitch.	271	323	DF98
Cranmer Ter. SW17	271	323	DD92
Cranmore Ave., Islw.	251	321	CC80
Cranmore Rd., Brom.	199	325	EF90
Cranmore Rd., Chis.	276	326	EM92
Cranmore Way N10	220	306	DJ56
Cranston Clo., Houns.	250	321	BY82
Cranston Clo., Uxb.	231	312	BR61
Cranston Est. N1	26	316	DR68
Cranston Gdns. E4	211	301	EB50
Cranston Pk. Ave., Upmin.	239	311	FP63
Cranston Rd. SE23	197	325	DY88
Cranswick Rd. SE16	148	317	DV78
Crantock Rd. SE6	198	325	EB89
Cranwell Clo. E3	130	317	EB70
Cranwell Gro., Shep.	280	328	BM98
Cranwell Rd., Houns.	257	320	BP82
Cranwich Ave. N21	209	300	DR45
Cranwich Rd. N16	101	306	DR59
Cranwood St. EC1	38	316	DR69
Cranworth Cres. E4	211	301	ED46
Cranworth Gdns. SW9	162	316	DN81
Craster Rd. SW2	193	324	DM87
Crathie Rd. SE12	260	326	EH86
Crathorn St. SE13	182	325	EC83
Cravan Ave., Felt.	258	321	BU89
Craven Ave. W5	132	314	CJ73
Craven Ave., Sthl.	242	313	BZ71
Craven Clo., Hayes	242	313	BU72
Craven Gdns. SW19	271	323	DA92
Craven Gdns., Bark.	245	318	ES68
Craven Gdns., Ilf.	225	308	ER54
Craven Gdns. (Harold Wd.), Rom.	229	311	FQ51
Craven Hill W2	53	315	DC73
Craven Hill Gdns. W2	53	315	DC73
Craven Hill Ms. W2	53	315	DC73
Craven Ms. SW11	176	324	DG83
Craven Pk. NW10	125	314	CS67
Craven Pk. Ms. NW10	125	314	CS67
Craven Pk. Rd. N15	221	306	DT58
Craven Pk. Rd. NW10	125	314	CS67
Craven Pas. WC2	58/9	316	DL74
Craven Rd. NW10	125	314	CR67
Craven Rd. W2	41	315	DC72
Craven Rd. W5	132	314	CJ73
Craven Rd., Croy.	287	333	DV102
Craven Rd., Kings.T.	268	322	CM95
Craven St. WC2	58/9	316	DL74
Craven Ter. W2	53	315	DC73
Craven Wk. N16	102	307	DU59
Crawford Ave., Wem.	107	304	CK64
Crawford Clo., Islw.	251	321	CE82
Crawford Compton Clo., Horn.	238	310	FJ65
Crawford Est. SE5	162	316	DQ82
Crawford Gdns. N13	209	300	DP48
Crawford Gdns., Nthlt.	242	313	BZ69
Crawford Ms. W1	43	315	DF71
Crawford Pas. EC1	36	316	DN70
Crawford Pl. W1	42/3	315	DE72
Crawford Rd. SE5	162	316	DQ81
Crawford St. W1	43	315	DF71
Crawfords, Swan.	279	327	FE94
Crawley Rd. E10	104	307	EB60
Crawley Rd. N22	221	306	DQ54
Crawley Rd., Enf.	209	300	DS45
Crawshaw Ct. SW9	162	316	DN81
Crawthew Gro. SE22	179	324	DT84
Cray Ave., Orp.	291	335	EV100
Cray Riverway, Dart.	263	327	FF85
Cray Rd., Belv.	255	319	FA79
Cray Rd., Sid.	278	327	EW94
Cray Valley Rd., Orp.	291	335	EU99
Craybrooke Rd., Sid.	278	327	EV91

Craybury End SE9	261	326	EQ89
Craydene Rd., Erith	255	319	FF81
Crayford Clo. E6	244	318	EL71
Crayford High St., Dart.	263	327	FE85
Crayford Rd. N7	115	306	DK63
Crayford Rd., Dart.	263	327	FE85
Crayford Way, Dart.	263	327	FF85
Craylands, Orp.	278	327	EW97
Crayonne Clo., Sun.	281	328	BS95
Crealock Gro., Wdf.Grn.	211	301	EF50
Crealock St. SW18	174	323	DB86
Creasey Clo., Horn.	238	310	FH61
Creasy Est. SE1	74/5	316	DS76
Crebor St. SE22	180	325	DU86
Credenhall Dr., Brom.	290	334	EM102
Credenhill St. SW16	272	324	DJ93
Crediton Hill NW6	112	305	DB64
Crediton Rd. E16	244	318	EG72
Crediton Rd. NW10	127	315	CX67
Credon Rd. E13	244	318	EJ68
Credon Rd. SE16	148	317	DV78
Cree Way, Rom.	227	309	FE52
Creechurch La. EC3	50/1	316	DS72
Creechurch Pl. EC3	50/1	316	DS72
Creed Ct. EC4	48/9	316	DP72
Creed La. EC4	48/9	316	DP72
Creek Rd. SE8	166	317	EA79
Creek Rd. SE10	166	317	EB79
Creek Rd., Bark.	245	318	ET69
Creek Rd., E.Mol.	267	329	CE98
Creekside SE8	166	317	EB80
Creekside, Rain.	247	319	FE70
Creeland Gro. SE6	197	325	DZ88
Crefeld Clo. W6	157	315	CX79
Creffield Rd. W3	133	314	CM73
Creffield Rd. W5	133	314	CM73
Creighton Ave. E6	244	318	EK68
Creighton Ave. N2	219	305	DE55
Creighton Ave. N10	219	305	DF54
Creighton Clo. W12	136	315	CV73
Creighton Rd. N17	221	306	DS52
Creighton Rd. NW6	127	315	CX68
Creighton Rd. W5	143	314	CK76
Cremer St. E2	27	316	DT68
Cremorne Est. SW10	159	315	DD79
Cremorne Rd. SW10	158	315	DC80
Crescent, The E17	222	307	DY57
Crescent, The EC3	63	316	DT73
Crescent, The N11	208	300	DG49
Crescent, The NW2	94	305	CV62
Crescent, The SW13	155	314	CT82
Crescent, The SW19	190	323	DA90
Crescent, The W3	135	314	CS72
Crescent, The, Ashf.	264	328	BM92
Crescent, The, Beck.	275	325	EA95
Crescent, The, Bex.	262	327	EW87
Crescent, The, Cher.	280	328	BG97
Crescent, The, Croy.	287	332	DR99
Crescent, The, Har.	233	313	CC60
Crescent, The, Hayes	257	320	BQ80
Crescent, The, Ilf.	225	308	EN58
Crescent, The, N.Mal.	269	322	CQ96
Crescent, The, Shep.	281	328	BT101
Crescent, The, Sid.	277	326	ET91
Crescent, The, Sthl.	250	321	BZ75
Crescent, The, Surb.	282	330	CL99
Crescent, The, Sutt.	285	331	DD106
Crescent, The (Belmont), Sutt.	292	331	DA111
Crescent, The, Upmin.	239	311	FS59
Crescent, The, Wem.	90	304	CG61
Crescent, The, W.Mol.	267	329	CA98
Crescent, The, W.Wick.	289	333	EE100
Crescent Ave., Horn.	237	309	FF61
Crescent Dr., Orp.	290	334	EP100
Crescent Gdns. SW19	190	323	DA90
Crescent Gdns., Ruis.	232	313	BV59
Crescent Gdns., Swan.	279	327	FC96
Crescent Gro. SW4	176	324	DJ84
Crescent Gro., Mitch.	271	323	DE98
Crescent La. SW4	176	324	DJ84
Crescent Pl. SW3	78/9	315	DE77
Crescent Ri. N22	220	306	DK53
Crescent Ri., Barn.	207	299	DE43
Crescent Rd. E4	211	301	EE45
Crescent Rd. E6	244	318	EJ67
Crescent Rd. E10	104	307	EB61
Crescent Rd. E13	244	318	EG67
Crescent Rd. E18	224	308	EJ54
Crescent Rd. N3	218	305	CZ53
Crescent Rd. N8	220	306	DK58
Crescent Rd. N9	210	301	DU46
Crescent Rd. N11	207	299	DF49
Crescent Rd. N15	221	306	DP55
Crescent Rd. N22	220	306	DK53
Crescent Rd. SE18	253	318	EP78
Crescent Rd. SW20	270	323	CX95
Crescent Rd., Beck.	275	325	EB96
Crescent Rd., Brom.	276	326	EG94
Crescent Rd., Dag.	237	309	FB62
Crescent Rd., Enf.	202	300	DP42
Crescent Rd., Erith	255	319	FF79
Crescent Rd., Kings.T.	269	322	CN94
Crescent Rd., Shep.	281	328	BQ99
Crescent Rd., Sid.	261	326	ET90
Crescent Row EC1	37	316	DQ70
Crescent Stables SW15	173	323	CY84
Crescent St. N1	115	306	DM66
Crescent Way N12	219	305	DE51
Crescent Way SE4	182	325	EA83
Crescent Way SW16	272	324	DM93
Crescent Way, Orp.	291	334	ES106
Crescent Wd. Rd. SE26	196	325	DU90
Cresford Rd. SW6	158	315	DB81
Crespigny Rd. NW4	218	305	CV58
Cressage Clo., Sthl.	243	313	CA70
Cresset Rd. E9	118	307	DW65
Cresset St. SW4	177	324	DK83
Cressfield Clo. NW5	114	306	DG64
Cressida Rd. N19	98	306	DJ60
Cressingham Gro., Sutt.	285	331	DC105
Cressingham Rd. SE13	182	325	EC83
Cressingham Rd., Edg.	217	304	CR51
Cressington Clo. N16	117	306	DS64
Cresswell Gdns. SW5	77	315	DC78
Cresswell Pk. SE3	183	325	EF83
Cresswell Pl. SW10	77	315	DC78
Cresswell Rd. SE25	274	325	DU98
Cresswell Rd., Felt.	266	329	BY91
Cresswell Rd., Twick.	169	322	CK86
Cresswell Way N21	209	300	DN45
Cressy Ct. E1	138	317	DW71
Cressy Ct. W6	146	315	CV76
Cressy Pl. E1	138	317	DW71
Cressy Rd. NW3	113	305	DF64
Crest, The N13	209	300	DN49
Crest, The NW4	218	305	CW57
Crest, The, Surb.	282	330	CN99
Crest Dr., Enf.	203	301	DW38
Crest Gdns., Ruis.	232	313	BW62
Crest Rd. NW2	93	304	CT62
Crest Rd., Brom.	289	333	EF101
Crest Rd., S.Croy.	295	333	DV108
Crest Vw., Pnr.	214	303	BX56
Crest Vw. Dr., Orp.	290	334	EP99
Crestbrook Ave. N13	209	300	DP48
Crestfield St. WC1	34/5	316	DL69
Creston Way, Wor.Pk.	284	331	CX102
Crestway SW15	172	323	CU86
Crestwood Way, Houns.	258	321	BZ85
Creswick Rd. W3	134	314	CP73
Creswick Wk. E3	130	317	EA69
Creswick Wk. NW11	218	305	CZ56
Creton St. SE18	253	318	EN76
Crewdson Rd. SW9	162	316	DN80
Crewe Pl. NW10	125	314	CT69
Crews St. E14	150	317	EA77
Crewys Rd. NW2	95	305	CZ61
Crewys Rd. SE15	164	317	DV82
Crichton Ave., Wall.	286	332	DK106
Crichton Rd., Cars.	293	331	DF108
Cricket Fld. Rd., Uxb.	240	312	BK67
Cricket Grn., Mitch.	271	323	DF97
Cricket Grd. Rd., Chis.	277	326	EP95
Cricket La., Beck.	274	325	DY92
Cricketers Arms Rd., Enf.	202	300	DQ40
Cricketers Clo. N14	208	300	DJ45
Cricketers Clo., Chess.	282	330	CK105
Cricketers Clo., Erith	255	319	FE78
Cricketers Ct. SE11	84/5	316	DP77
Cricketers Ter., Cars.	285	331	DE104
Cricketfield Rd. E5	118	307	DV63
Cricketfield Rd., West Dr.	248	320	BJ77
Cricklade Ave. SW2	193	324	DL89
Cricklade Ave., Rom.	228	310	FK51
Cricklewood Bdy. NW2	94	305	CW62
Cricklewood La. NW2	111	305	CX63
Cricklewood Trd. Est. NW2	95	305	CY62
Cridland St. E15	131	317	EF67
Crieff Ct., Tedd.	268	322	CJ94
Crieff Rd. SW18	174	323	DC86
Criffel Ave. SW2	193	324	DK89
Crimscott St. SE1	74/5	316	DS76
Crimsworth Rd. SW8	161	316	DK81
Crinan St. N1	22/3	316	DL68
Cringle St. SW8	160	316	DJ80
Cripplegate St. EC2	49	316	DQ71
Crisp Rd. W6	146	315	CW78
Crispe Ho., Bark.	245	318	ER68
Crispen Rd., Felt.	266	329	BY91
Crispian Clo. NW10	109	304	CS63
Crispin Clo., Croy.	286	332	DL103
Crispin Cres., Croy.	286	332	DK103
Crispin Rd., Edg.	217	304	CQ51
Crispin St. E1	51	316	DT71
Cristowe Rd. SW6	157	315	CZ82
Criterion Ms. N19	99	306	DK61
Crockerton Rd. SW17	191	323	DF89
Crockham Way SE9	277	326	EN91
Crocus Clo., Croy.	288	333	DX102
Crocus Fld., Barn.	206	299	CZ44
Croft, The NW10	125	314	CT68
Croft, The W5	133	314	CL71
Croft, The, Houns.	250	321	BY79
Croft, The, Pnr.	232	313	BZ59
Croft, The, Ruis.	232	313	BW63
Croft, The, Swan.	279	327	FC97
Croft, The, Wem.	106	304	CJ64
Croft Ave., W.Wick.	289	333	EC102
Croft Clo. NW7	205	298	CS48
Croft Clo., Belv.	254	319	EZ78
Croft Clo., Chis.	276	326	EM91
Croft Clo., Hayes	257	320	BQ80
Croft Clo., Uxb.	241	312	BN66
Croft Gdns. W7	142	314	CG75
Croft Gdns., Ruis.	231	312	BS60
Croft Lo. Clo., Wdf.Grn.	224	308	EH51
Croft Ms. N12	207	299	DC48
Croft Rd. SW16	273	324	DN95
Croft Rd. SW19	271	323	DC94
Croft Rd., Brom.	276	326	EG93
Croft Rd., Enf.	203	301	DY39
Croft Rd., Sutt.	285	331	DE106
Croft St. SE8	149	317	DY77
Croft Way NW3	112	305	DA63
Croft Way, Sid.	261	326	ES90
Croftdown Rd. NW5	98	306	DG62
Crofters Clo., Islw.	259	321	CD85
Crofters Ct. SE8	149	317	DY77
Crofters Rd., Nthwd.	213	302	BS49
Crofters Way NW1	22	316	DK67
Crofton Ave. W4	154	314	CQ80
Crofton Ave., Bex.	262	327	EX87
Crofton Ave., Orp.	291	334	EQ103
Crofton Gro. E4	211	301	ED49
Crofton La., Orp.	291	334	ER103
Crofton Pk. Rd. SE4	181	325	DZ86
Crofton Rd. E13	244	318	EH70
Crofton Rd. SE5	163	316	DS81
Crofton Rd., Orp.	290	334	EN104
Crofton Ter. E5	119	307	DY64
Crofton Ter., Rich.	169	322	CM84
Crofton Way, Barn.	207	299	DB44
Crofton Way, Enf.	202	300	DN40
Croftongate Way SE4	181	325	DY85
Crofts, The, Shep.	281	328	BS98
Crofts La. N22	221	306	DN52
Crofts Rd., Har.	216	304	CG58
Crofts St. E1	138	317	DU73
Croftside SE25	274	325	DU97
Croftway NW3	112	305	DA63
Croftway, Rich.	184	322	CH90
Crogsland Rd. NW1	114	306	DG66
Croham Clo., S.Croy.	295	332	DS108
Croham Manor Rd., S.Croy.	295	332	DS108
Croham Mt., S.Croy.	295	332	DS108
Croham Pk. Ave., S.Croy.	287	332	DS106
Croham Rd., S.Croy.	287	332	DR106
Croham Valley Rd., S.Croy.	295	332	DT107
Croindene Rd. SW16	272	324	DL95
Cromartie Rd. N19	99	306	DK59
Cromarty Rd., Edg.	205	298	CP47
Crombie Clo., Ilf.	224	308	EM57
Crombie Rd., Sid.	261	326	ER88
Cromer Clo., Uxb.	249	312	BQ72
Cromer Pl., Orp.	291	334	ER102
Cromer Rd. E10	223	307	ED58
Cromer Rd. N17	222	307	DU54
Cromer Rd. SE25	274	325	DV97
Cromer Rd. SW17	272	324	DG93
Cromer Rd., Horn.	238	310	FK59
Cromer Rd., Houns.	257	320	BN83
Cromer Rd., Rom.	227	309	FC58
Cromer Rd. (Chadwell Heath), Rom.	226	309	EY58
Cromer Rd. W., Houns.	257	320	BN83
Cromer St. WC1	34/5	316	DL69
Cromer Ter. E8	118	307	DU64
Cromer Vil. Rd. SW18	173	323	CZ86
Cromford Clo., Orp.	291	334	ES104
Cromford Path E5	119	307	DX63
Cromford Rd. SW18	174	323	DA85
Cromford Way, N.Mal.	269	322	CR95
Cromlix Clo., Chis.	277	326	EP96
Crompton St. W2	30	315	DD70
Cromwell Ave. N6	98	306	DH60
Cromwell Ave. W6	146	315	CV77
Cromwell Ave., Brom.	276	326	EH97
Cromwell Ave., N.Mal.	283	330	CT99
Cromwell Clo. E1	138	317	DU74
Cromwell Clo. N2	219	305	DD56
Cromwell Clo. W3	134	314	CQ74
Cromwell Clo., Brom.	276	326	EH98
Cromwell Cres. SW5	76	315	DA77
Cromwell Gdns. SW7	66	315	DD76
Cromwell Gro. W6	146	315	CW76
Cromwell Ind. Est. E10	103	307	DY60
Cromwell Ms. SW7	78	315	DD77
Cromwell Pl. N6	98	306	DH60
Cromwell Pl. SW7	78	315	DD77
Cromwell Pl. SW14	170	322	CQ83
Cromwell Pl. W3	134	314	CQ74
Cromwell Rd. E7	234	308	EJ66
Cromwell Rd. E17	223	307	EC57
Cromwell Rd. N3	219	305	DC54
Cromwell Rd. N10	220	306	DG52
Cromwell Rd. SW5	76/7	315	DB77
Cromwell Rd. SW7	76/7	315	DB77
Cromwell Rd. SW9	162	316	DP81
Cromwell Rd. SW19	271	323	DA92
Cromwell Rd., Beck.	274	325	DY96
Cromwell Rd., Croy.	287	332	DR101
Cromwell Rd., Felt.	258	321	BV88
Cromwell Rd., Hayes	249	312	BR72
Cromwell Rd., Houns.	259	321	CA84
Cromwell Rd., Kings.T.	268	322	CL95
Cromwell Rd., Tedd.	268	322	CG93
Cromwell Rd., Wem.	123	314	CL68
Cromwell Rd., Wor.Pk.	283	330	CR104
Cromwell St., Houns.	259	321	CA84
Cromwell Twr. EC2	49	316	DQ71
Cromwells Mere, Rom.	227	309	FD51
Crondace Rd. SW6	158	315	DA81
Crondall St. N1	26	316	DR68
Crook Log, Bexh.	262	327	EX83
Crooke Rd. SE8	149	317	DY78
Crooked Billet SW19	270	323	CW93
Crooked Billet Roundabout E17	223	307	EA52
Crooked Billet Yd. E2	38/9	316	DS69
Crooked Usage N3	218	305	CY55
Crookham Rd. SW6	157	315	CZ81
Crookston Rd. SE9	261	326	EN83
Croombs Rd. E16	244	318	EJ71
Crooms Hill SE10	166	317	EC80
Crooms Hill Gro. SE10	166	317	EC80
Cropley Ct. N1	26	316	DR68
Cropley St. N1	26	316	DR68
Croppath Rd., Dag.	237	309	FA63
Cropthorne Ct. W9	29	315	DC69
Crosby Clo., Felt.	266	329	BY91
Crosby Ct. SE1	74	316	DR75
Crosby Rd. E7	234	308	EG65
Crosby Rd., Dag.	247	319	FB68
Crosby Row SE1	74	316	DR75
Crosby Sq. EC3	50/1	316	DS72
Crosby Wk. E8	117	306	DT65
Crosby Wk. SW2	194	324	DN87
Crosier Rd., Uxb.	241	312	BQ63
Crosier Way, Ruis.	231	312	BS62
Crosland Pl. SW11	176	324	DG83
Cross Ave. SE10	167	317	ED79
Cross Deep, Twick.	259	321	CF90
Cross Deep Gdns., Twick.	259	321	CF89
Cross Keys Clo. W1	44	316	DG71
Cross Keys Sq. EC1	49	316	DQ71
Cross Lances Rd., Houns.	259	321	CB84
Cross La. EC3	62/3	316	DS73
Cross La. N8	220	306	DM55
Cross La., Bex.	262	327	EZ87
Cross Rd. E4	211	301	EE46
Cross Rd. N11	208	300	DH50
Cross Rd. N22	221	306	DN52
Cross Rd. SE5	163	316	DS82
Cross Rd. SW19	271	323	DA94
Cross Rd., Brom.	290	334	EL103
Cross Rd., Croy.	287	332	DR102
Cross Rd., Enf.	202	300	DT42
Cross Rd., Felt.	266	329	BY91
Cross Rd., Har.	215	303	CD56
Cross Rd. (South Harrow), Har.	233	313	CB62
Cross Rd. (Wealdstone), Har.	216	304	CG54
Cross Rd., Kings.T.	268	322	CM94
Cross Rd., Orp.	291	335	EV99
Cross Rd., Pur.	294	332	DP113
Cross Rd., Rom.	227	309	FA56
Cross Rd. (Chadwell Heath), Rom.	236	309	EW59
Cross Rd., Sid.	278	327	EV91
Cross Rd., Sutt.	285	331	DD106
Cross Rd. (Belmont), Sutt.	292	331	DA110
Cross Rd., Uxb.	240	312	BJ66
Cross Rd., Wdf.Grn.	224	308	EM51
Cross St. N1	24/5	316	DP67
Cross St. SW13	155	314	CS82
Cross St., Erith	255	319	FE78
Cross St., Hmptn.	267	329	CC92
Cross St., Uxb.	240	312	BJ66
Cross Way, Pnr.	214	303	BV54
Cross Way, The, Har.	215	303	CE54
Crossbrook Rd. SE3	252	318	EL82
Crossfield Rd. N17	221	306	DQ55
Crossfield Rd. NW3	113	305	DD65
Crossfield St. SE8	166	317	EA80
Crossford St. SW9	161	316	DL82
Crossgate, Edg.	205	298	CN48
Crossgate, Grnf.	106	304	CH65
Crossland Rd., Th.Hth.	286	332	DP99
Crosslands Ave. W5	133	314	CM74
Crosslands Ave., Sthl.	250	321	BZ78
Crosslet St. SE17	86	316	DR77
Crosslet Vale SE10	166	317	EB81
Crossley St. N7	116	306	DN65
Crossmead SE9	260	326	EM88
Crossmead Ave., Grnf.	243	313	CA69
Crossmount Ho. SE5	162	316	DQ80
Crossness La. SE28	246	319	EX73
Crossness Rd., Bark.	245	318	ET69
Crossthwaite Ave. SE5	179	324	DR84
Crosswall EC3	63	316	DT73
Crossway N12	219	305	DD51
Crossway N16	117	306	DS64
Crossway N22	221	306	DP52
Crossway NW9	217	304	CT56
Crossway SE28	246	319	EW72
Crossway SW20	270	323	CW98
Crossway W13	122	314	CG70
Crossway, Dag.	236	309	EW62
Crossway, Enf.	209	300	DS45
Crossway, Hayes	242	313	BU74
Crossway, Orp.	277	326	ER98
Crossway, Ruis.	232	313	BW63
Crossway, The SE9	260	326	EK89
Crossway, The, Uxb.	240	312	BM68
Crossways N21	209	300	DQ44
Crossways, Rom.	228	310	FH55
Crossways, Sun.	265	328	BT94
Crossways, Sutt.	293	331	DD109
Crossways, The, Houns.	250	321	BZ80
Crossways, The, Wem.	92	304	CN61
Crossways Rd., Beck.	275	325	EA98
Crossways Rd., Mitch.	272	324	DH97
Crosswell Clo., Shep.	281	328	BQ96
Croston St. E8	128	317	DU67
Crothall Clo. N13	208	300	DM48
Crouch Ave., Bark.	246	319	EV68
Crouch Clo., Beck.	275	325	EA93
Crouch Cft. SE9	261	326	EN90
Crouch End Hill N8	99	306	DK59
Crouch Hall Rd. N8	220	306	DK58
Crouch Hill N4	99	306	DL59
Crouch Hill N8	220	306	DL58
Crouch Rd. NW10	109	304	CR66
Crouch Valley, Upmin.	239	311	FR59
Crouchman's Clo. SE26	195	324	DT90
Crow La., Rom.	236	309	EZ59
Crowborough Rd. SW17	272	324	DG93
Crowden Way SE28	246	319	EW73
Crowder St. E1	138	317	DV73
Crowfoot Clo. E9	119	307	DZ64
Crowhurst Clo. SW9	162	316	DN82
Crowland Ave., Hayes	249	320	BS77
Crowland Gdns. N14	208	300	DL45
Crowland Rd. N15	221	306	DT57
Crowland Rd., Th.Hth.	273	324	DR98
Crowland Ter. N1	117	306	DR66
Crowland Wk., Mord.	284	331	DB100
Crowlands Ave., Rom.	227	309	FB58
Crowley Cres., Croy.	286	332	DN106
Crowline Wk. N1	117	306	DR65
Crowmarsh Gdns. SE23	196	325	DW87
Crown Arc., Kings.T.	268	322	CK96
Crown Clo. E3	130	317	EA67
Crown Clo. NW6	112	305	DB65
Crown Clo. NW7	205	298	CT47
Crown Clo., Hayes	249	320	BT75
Crown Clo., Orp.	291	335	EU105
Crown Ct. EC2	49	316	DQ72
Crown Ct. SE12	260	326	EH86
Crown Ct. WC2	46/7	316	DL72
Crown Ct., Brom.	290	334	EK99
Crown Dale SE19	273	324	DP93
Crown Hill, Croy.	287	332	DQ103
Crown La. N14	208	300	DJ46
Crown La. SW16	273	324	DN92
Crown La., Brom.	290	334	EK99
Crown La., Chis.	277	326	EQ95
Crown La., Mord.	271	323	DA97
Crown La. Gdns. SW16	273	324	DN92
Crown La. Spur, Brom.	290	334	EK100
Crown Ms. E13	244	318	EJ67
Crown Ms. W6	146	315	CU77
Crown Office Row EC4	60	316	DN73
Crown Par., Hayes	249	312	BT71
Crown Pas. SW1	57	316	DJ74
Crown Pl. NW5	114	306	DH65
Crown Pt. Par. SE19	273	324	DP93
Crown Rd. N10	220	306	DG52
Crown Rd., Enf.	203	301	DU41
Crown Rd., Ilf.	225	308	ER56
Crown Rd., Mord.	271	323	DA98
Crown Rd., N.Mal.	269	322	CQ95
Crown Rd., Orp.	291	335	EU106
Crown Rd., Ruis.	232	313	BX64
Crown Rd., Sutt.	284	331	DA105
Crown Rd., Twick.	168	322	CH86
Crown St. SE5	162	316	DQ80
Crown St. W3	134	314	CP74
Crown St., Dag.	237	309	FC65
Crown St., Har.	233	313	CD60
Crown Ter., Rich.	169	322	CM84
Crown Wk., Uxb.	240	312	BJ66
Crown Wk., Wem.	91	304	CM62
Crown Way, West Dr.	248	312	BM74
Crown Wds. La. SE9	253	318	EQ82
Crown Wds. La. SE18	253	318	EP82
Crown Wds. Way SE9	261	326	ER85
Crown Yd., Houns.	259	321	CC83
Crowndale Rd. NW1	21	316	DJ68
Crownfield Ave., Ilf.	225	308	ES58
Crownfield Rd. E15	121	307	ED63
Crownhill Rd. NW10	125	314	CT67
Crownhill Rd., Wdf.Grn.	224	308	EL52
Crownmead Way, Rom.	227	309	FB56
Crownstone Rd. SW2	178	324	DN85
Crowntree Clo., Islw.	251	321	CF79
Crows Rd. E15	131	317	ED69
Crowshott Ave., Stan.	216	304	CJ54
Crowther Ave., Brent.	143	314	CL77
Crowther Rd. SE25	274	325	DU98
Crowthorne Clo. SW18	189	323	CZ88
Crowthorne Rd. W10	137	315	CX72
Croxden Clo., Edg.	216	304	CM55
Croxden Wk., Mord.	285	331	DC100
Croxford Gdns. N22	221	306	DP52
Croxford Way, Rom.	237	309	FD60
Croxley Clo., Orp.	278	327	EV96
Croxley Grn., Orp.	278	327	EV95
Croxley Rd. W9	127	315	CZ69
Croxted Clo. SE21	194	324	DQ87
Croxted Rd. SE21	194	324	DQ87
Croxted Rd. SE24	194	324	DQ87
Croyde Ave., Grnf.	243	313	CC69
Croyde Ave., Hayes	249	320	BS77
Croyde Clo., Sid.	261	326	ER87
Croydon Flyover, The, Croy.	286	332	DP105
Croydon Gro., Croy.	286	332	DP102
Croydon La., Bans.	292	331	DB114
Croydon La. S., Bans.	292	331	DB114
Croydon Rd. E13	131	317	EF70
Croydon Rd. SE20	274	325	DV96
Croydon Rd., Beck.	274	325	DY97
Croydon Rd., Brom.	290	334	EJ104
Croydon Rd., Croy.	285	332	DH105
Croydon Rd., Houns.	257	320	BP82
Croydon Rd., Kes.	290	334	EM104
Croydon Rd., Mitch.	272	324	DG98
Croydon Rd., Wall.	285	332	DH105
Croydon Rd., W.Wick.	289	333	EE104
Croyland Rd. N9	210	301	DU46
Croylands Dr., Surb.	282	330	CL101
Croysdale Ave., Sun.	266	329	BU97
Crozier Dr., S.Croy.	295	333	DV109
Crozier Ter. E9	119	307	DX64
Crucible Clo., Rom.	226	309	EV58
Crucifix La. SE1	74/5	316	DS75
Cruden Ho. SE17	162	316	DP79
Cruden St. N1	24/5	316	DP67
Cruikshank Rd. E15	121	307	EE63
Cruikshank St. WC1	36	316	DN69
Crummock Gdns. NW9	217	304	CS57
Crumpsall St. SE2	254	319	EW77
Crundale Ave. NW9	217	304	CN57
Crunden Rd., S.Croy.	295	332	DR108
Crusader Gdns., Croy.	287	332	DS104
Crusoe Rd., Erith	255	319	FD78
Crusoe Rd., Mitch.	271	323	DF94
Crutched Friars EC3	62/3	316	DS73
Crutchley Rd. SE6	199	325	EE89
Crystal Ave., Horn.	238	311	FL63
Crystal Ct. SE19	273	324	DT92
Crystal Palace Par. SE19	273	324	DT93
Crystal Palace Pk. Rd. SE26	274	325	DU92
Crystal Palace Rd. SE22	179	324	DT86
Crystal Palace Sta. Rd. SE19	274	325	DU93
Crystal Ter. SE19	273	324	DR93
Crystal Vw. Ct., Brom.	275	325	ED91
Crystal Way, Dag.	236	309	EW60
Crystal Way, Har.	215	303	CF57
Cuba Dr., Enf.	203	301	DW40
Cuba St. E14	150	317	EA75
Cubitt Sq., Sthl.	243	313	CC74
Cubitt Steps E14	140	317	EA74
Cubitt St. WC1	35	316	DM69
Cubitt St., Croy.	286	332	DM106
Cubitt Ter. SW4	176	324	DJ83
Cubitts Yd. WC2	58/9	316	DL73
Cuckoo Ave. W7	243	313	CE70
Cuckoo Dene W7	243	313	CD71
Cuckoo Hall La. N9	210	301	DW45
Cuckoo Hill, Pnr.	214	303	BW55
Cuckoo Hill Dr., Pnr.	214	303	BW55
Cuckoo Hill Rd., Pnr.	214	303	BW56
Cuckoo La. W7	243	313	CE73
Cuckoo Pound, Shep.	281	328	BS99
Cudas Clo., Epsom	283	330	CT105
Cuddington Ave., Wor.Pk.	283	330	CT104
Cuddington Pk. Clo., Bans.	292	331	CZ113
Cuddington Way, Sutt.	292	331	CX112
Cudham Clo., Sutt.	292	331	DA110
Cudham St. SE6	198	325	EC87
Cudworth St. E1	128	317	DV70
Cuff Cres. SE9	260	326	EK86
Cuff Pt. E2	39	316	DT69
Culford Gdns. SW3	79	315	DF77
Culford Gro. N1	117	306	DS65
Culford Ms. N1	117	306	DS65
Culford Rd. N1	117	306	DS66
Cullen Way NW10	124	314	CQ70
Cullera Clo., Nthwd.	213	302	BT51
Culling Rd. SE16	148	317	DW76
Cullington Clo., Har.	216	304	CG56
Cullingworth Rd. NW10	110	305	CU64
Culloden Clo. SE16	148	317	DU78
Culloden Rd., Enf.	202	300	DP40
Culloden St. E14	140	317	EC72
Cullum St. EC3	62/3	316	DS73
Culmington Rd. W13	132	314	CJ74
Culmington Rd., S.Croy.	295	332	DQ108
Culmore Cross SW12	192	324	DH88
Culmore Rd. SE15	164	317	DV80
Culmstock Rd. SW11	176	324	DG85
Culpeper Clo., Ilf.	225	308	EP51
Culross Clo. N15	221	306	DQ56
Culross St. W1	56	316	DG73
Culsac Rd., Surb.	282	330	CL103
Culver Gro., Stan.	216	304	CJ54
Culverden Rd. SW12	192	324	DJ89
Culverhouse Gdns. SW16	193	324	DM90
Culverlands Clo., Stan.	204	298	CH49
Culverley Rd. SE6	198	325	EB88
Culvers Ave., Cars.	285	331	DE103
Culvers Retreat, Cars.	285	331	DF102
Culvers Way, Cars.	285	331	DF104
Culverstone Clo., Brom.	289	333	EF100
Culvert La., Uxb.	240	312	BH68
Culvert Pl. SW11	160	316	DG82
Culvert Rd. N15	221	306	DS57
Culvert Rd. SW11	159	315	DF81
Culworth St. NW8	18/9	315	DE68
Cumberland Ave. NW10	124	314	CP69
Cumberland Ave., Horn.	238	311	FL62
Cumberland Ave., Well.	261	326	ES83
Cumberland Clo. E8	117	306	DT65
Cumberland Clo. SW20	270	323	CX94
Cumberland Clo., Horn.	238	311	FL62
Cumberland Clo., Ilf.	225	308	EQ53
Cumberland Clo., Twick.	168	322	CH86
Cumberland Cres. W14	147	315	CY77
Cumberland Dr., Bexh.	254	319	EY80
Cumberland Dr., Chess.	282	330	CM104
Cumberland Gdns. NW4	218	305	CX54
Cumberland Gdns. WC1	35	316	DM69
Cumberland Gate W1	55	315	DF73
Cumberland Mkt. NW1	32/3	316	DH69
Cumberland Mkt. Est. NW1	32/3	316	DH69
Cumberland Mills Sq. E14	151	317	ED78
Cumberland Pk. W3	134	314	CQ73
Cumberland Pl. NW1	32/3	316	DH69
Cumberland Pl. SE6	199	325	EF88
Cumberland Pl., Sun.	266	329	BU98
Cumberland Rd. E12	234	308	EK63
Cumberland Rd. E13	244	318	EH71
Cumberland Rd. E17	222	307	DY54
Cumberland Rd. N9	210	301	DW46
Cumberland Rd. N22	220	306	DM54
Cumberland Rd. SE25	287	333	DV100
Cumberland Rd. SW13	155	314	CT81
Cumberland Rd. W3	134	314	CQ73
Cumberland Rd. W7	251	321	CF75
Cumberland Rd., Ashf.	264	320	BK90
Cumberland Rd., Brom.	275	325	EE98
Cumberland Rd., Har.	215	303	CB57
Cumberland Rd., Rich.	154	314	CN80
Cumberland Rd., Stan.	216	304	CM55
Cumberland St. SW1	80/1	316	DH78
Cumberland Ter. NW1	20/1	316	DH68
Cumberland Ter. Ms. NW1	20/1	316	DH68
Cumberland Vil. W3	134	314	CQ73
Cumberlow Ave. SE25	273	324	DT97
Cumbernauld Gdns., Sun.	265	328	BT92
Cumberton Rd. N17	221	306	DR53
Cumbrae Gdns., Surb.	282	330	CJ102
Cumbrian Ave., Bexh.	255	319	FE81
Cumbrian Gdns. NW2	95	305	CX61
Cumbrian Way, Uxb.	240	312	BK66
Cumming St. N1	23	316	DM68
Cumnor Rd., Sutt.	293	331	DC107
Cunard Cres. N21	209	300	DR44
Cunard Pl. EC3	50/1	316	DS72
Cunard Rd. NW10	125	314	CR69
Cunard St. SE5	163	316	DS79
Cunard Wk. SE16	149	317	DX77
Cundy Rd. E16	244	318	EJ72
Cundy St. SW1	80	316	DG77
Cundy St. Est. SW1	80	316	DG77
Cunliffe Rd., Wor.Pk.	283	330	CT105
Cunliffe St. SW16	272	324	DJ93
Cunningham Ave., Enf.	203	301	DY36
Cunningham Clo., Rom.	226	309	EW57
Cunningham Clo., W.Wick.	288	333	EB103
Cunningham Pk., Har.	215	303	CC57
Cunningham Pl. NW8	30	315	DD70
Cunningham Rd. N15	222	307	DU56
Cunnington St. W4	144	314	CQ77
Cupar Rd. SW11	160	316	DH81
Cupola Clo., Brom.	276	326	EH92
Cureton St. SW1	82	316	DK77
Curfew Ho., Bark.	245	318	EQ67
Curlew Clo. SE28	246	319	EX73
Curlew Ct., Surb.	282	330	CM104
Curlew St. SE1	75	316	DT75
Curlew Way, Hayes	242	313	BX71
Curnick's La. SE27	273	324	DQ91
Curnock Est. NW1	21	316	DJ67
Curran Ave., Sid.	261	326	ET85
Curran Ave., Wall.	285	332	DG104
Curran Clo., Uxb.	240	312	BJ70
Currey Rd., Grnf.	233	313	CC65
Curricle St. W3	135	314	CS74
Currie Hill Clo. SW19	270	323	CZ91
Curry Ri. NW7	218	305	CX51
Cursitor St. EC4	48	316	DN72
Curtain Pl. EC2	38/9	316	DS69
Curtain Rd. EC2	38/9	316	DS69
Curtis Dr. W3	135	314	CR72
Curtis Fld. Rd. SW16	272	324	DM91
Curtis La., Wem.	107	304	CL65
Curtis Rd., Epsom	283	330	CQ105
Curtis Rd., Horn.	238	311	FM60
Curtis Rd., Houns.	258	321	BY87
Curtis St. SE1	87	316	DT77
Curtis Way SE1	87	316	DT77
Curtis Way SE28	246	319	EV73
Curtismill Clo., Orp.	278	327	EV97
Curtismill Way, Orp.	278	327	EV97
Curve, The W12	136	315	CU73
Curwen Ave. E7	234	308	EH63
Curwen Rd. W12	146	315	CU75
Curzon Ave., Enf.	210	301	DX43
Curzon Ave., Stan.	216	304	CG53
Curzon Clo., Orp.	291	334	ER105
Curzon Cres. NW10	109	304	CS66
Curzon Cres., Bark.	245	318	ET68
Curzon Gate W1	56	316	DG74
Curzon Pl. W1	56	316	DG74
Curzon Pl., Pnr.	214	303	BW57
Curzon Rd. N10	220	306	DH54
Curzon Rd. W5	122	314	CH70
Curzon Rd., Th.Hth.	286	332	DN100
Curzon St. W1	56	316	DG74
Cusack Clo., Twick.	267	329	CF91
Custom Ho. Quay EC3	62/3	316	DS73
Custom Ho. Reach SE16	149	317	DZ75
Custom Ho. Wk. EC3	62/3	316	DS73
Cut, The SE1	72	316	DN75
Cutcombe Rd. SE5	162	316	DQ82
Cuthbert Gdns. SE25	273	324	DS97
Cuthbert Rd. E17	223	307	EC55
Cuthbert Rd. N18	210	301	DU50
Cuthbert Rd., Croy.	286	332	DP103
Cuthbert St. W2	30	315	DD70
Cuthill Wk. SE5	163	316	DR81
Cutler St. E1	50/1	316	DS72
Cutlers Gdns. E1	50/1	316	DS72
Cutlers Gdns. Arc. EC2	50/1	316	DS72
Cutlers Sq. E14	150	317	EA77
Cutthroat All., Rich.	184	322	CJ89
Cuxton Clo., Bexh.	262	327	EY85
Cyclamen Clo., Hmptn.	267	329	CA93
Cyclamen Rd., Swan.	279	327	FD98
Cyclamen Way, Epsom	283	330	CQ106
Cyclops Ms. E14	150	317	EA77
Cygnet Ave., Felt.	258	321	BW87
Cygnet Clo. NW10	109	304	CR64
Cygnet Clo., Nthwd.	213	302	BQ52
Cygnet St. E1	39	316	DT70
Cygnet Way, Hayes	242	313	BX71
Cygnets, The, Felt.	266	329	BY91
Cymbeline Ct., Har.	215	303	CF58
Cynthia St. N1	23	316	DM68
Cyntra Pl. E8	118	307	DV66
Cypress Ave., Enf.	202	300	DN35
Cypress Ave., Twick.	259	321	CC87
Cypress Gro., Ilf.	225	308	ES51
Cypress Path, Rom.	228	310	FK52
Cypress Pl. W1	33	316	DJ70
Cypress Rd. SE25	273	324	DS96
Cypress Rd., Har.	215	303	CD54
Cypress Tree Clo., Sid.	261	326	ET87
Cypress Way, Bans.	292	331	CX114
Cyprus Ave. N3	218	305	CY54
Cyprus Clo. N4	221	306	DP58
Cyprus Gdns. N3	218	305	CY54
Cyprus Pl. E2	128	317	DW68
Cyprus Pl. E6	245	318	EN73
Cyprus Rd. N3	218	305	CZ54
Cyprus Rd. N9	209	300	DT47
Cyprus Roundabout E16	252	318	EK77
Cyprus St. E2	128	317	DW68
Cyrena Rd. SE22	179	324	DT86
Cyril Mans. SW11	159	315	DF81
Cyril Rd., Bexh.	254	319	EY82
Cyril Rd., Orp.	291	335	EU101
Cyrus St. EC1	36/7	316	DP70
Czar St. SE8	166	317	EA79
Dabbs Hill La., Nthlt.	233	313	CA64
Dabin Cres. SE10	166	317	EC81
Dacca St. SE8	165	317	DZ79
Dace Rd. E3	130	317	EA67
Dacre Ave., Ilf.	225	308	EN54
Dacre Clo., Grnf.	243	313	CB68
Dacre Gdns. SE13	183	325	EE84
Dacre Gdns., Borwd.	205	298	CR43
Dacre Pk. SE13	183	325	EE83
Dacre Pl. SE13	183	325	EE83
Dacre Rd. E11	105	307	EF60
Dacre Rd. E13	244	318	EH67
Dacre Rd., Croy.	286	332	DL101
Dacre St. SW1	70	316	DK76
Dacres Rd. SE23	197	325	DX90
Dade Way, Sthl.	250	321	BZ78
Daerwood Clo., Brom.	290	334	EM102
Daffodil Clo., Croy.	288	333	DX102
Daffodil Gdns., Ilf.	235	308	EP64
Daffodil Pl., Hmptn.	267	329	CA93
Daffodil St. W12	135	314	CT73
Dafforne Rd. SW17	191	323	DF90
Dagenham Ave., Dag.	246	319	EY67
Dagenham Rd. E10	103	307	DZ60
Dagenham Rd., Dag.	237	309	FB63
Dagenham Rd., Rain.	237	309	FD66
Dagenham Rd., Rom.	237	309	FD59
Dagger La., Borwd.	204	298	CG44
Dagmar Ave., Wem.	107	304	CM63
Dagmar Gdns. NW10	127	315	CX68
Dagmar Pas. N1	24/5	316	DP67
Dagmar Rd. N4	100	306	DN59
Dagmar Rd. N15	221	306	DR56
Dagmar Rd. N22	220	306	DK53
Dagmar Rd. SE5	163	316	DS81

Dagmar Rd. SE25 287 332 DS99
Dagmar Rd., Dag. 237 309 FC66
Dagmar Rd., Kings.T. 268 322 CM95
Dagmar Rd., Sthl. 250 321 BY76
Dagmar Ter. N1 24/5 316 DP67
Dagnall Cres., Uxb. 248 312 BJ71
Dagnall Pk. SE25 287 332 DS100
Dagnall Rd. SE25 287 332 DS99
Dagnall St. SW11 159 315 DF82
Dagnam Pk. Gdns., Rom. 229 311 FN51
Dagnam Pk. Sq., Rom. 229 311 FP51
Dagnan Rd. SW12 192 324 DH87
Dagonet Gdns., Brom. 260 326 EG90
Dagonet Rd., Brom. 260 326 EG90
Dahlia Dr., Swan. 279 327 FF96
Dahlia Gdns., Ilf. 235 308 EP65
Dahlia Gdns., Mitch. 272 324 DK98
Dahlia Rd. SE2 254 319 EV77
Dahomey Rd. SW16 272 324 DJ93
Daimler Way, Wall. 294 332 DL108
Daines Clo. E12 234 308 EM62
Dainford Clo., Brom. 275 325 ED92
Dainton Clo., Brom. 276 326 EH95
Daintry Clo., Har. 216 304 CG56
Daintry Lo., Nthwd. 213 302 BT52
Daintry Way E9 119 307 DZ65
Dairsie Rd. SE9 261 326 EN83
Dairy Clo., Th.Hth. 273 324 DQ96
Dairy La. SE18 252 318 EM77
Dairy Ms. SW9 177 324 DL83
Dairy Wk. SW19 270 323 CY91
Daisy Clo., Croy. 293 324 DX102
Daisy Dobbins Wk. N19 99 306 DL59
Daisy La. SW6 174 323 DA83
Daisy Rd. E16 131 317 EE70
Daisy Rd. E18 224 308 EH54
Dakota Gdns. E6 244 318 EL70
Dakota Gdns., Nthlt. 242 313 BY69
Dalberg Rd. SW2 178 324 DN85
Dalberg Way SE2 254 319 EX76
Dalby Rd. SW18 174 323 DC84
Dalby St. NW5 114 306 DH65
Dalcross Rd., Houns. 250 321 BY82
Dale, The, Kes. 290 334 EK105
Dale Ave., Edg. 216 304 CM53
Dale Ave., Houns. 258 321 BY83
Dale Clo. SE3 260 326 EG83
Dale Clo., Barn. 207 299 DB44
Dale Clo., Dart. 263 327 FF86
Dale Clo., Pnr. 214 303 BV53
Dale Dr., Hayes 241 312 BT70
Dale End, Dart. 263 327 FF86
Dale Grn. Rd. N11 208 300 DH48
Dale Gro. N12 207 299 DC50
Dale Pk. Ave., Cars. 285 331 DF103
Dale Pk. Rd. SE19 273 324 DQ95
Dale Rd. NW5 114 306 DG64
Dale Rd. SE17 162 316 DP79
Dale Rd., Dart. 263 327 FF86
Dale Rd., Grnf. 243 313 CB71
Dale Rd., Pur. 294 332 DN112
Dale Rd., Sun. 265 328 BT94
Dale Rd., Sutt. 284 331 CZ105
Dale Rd., Swan. 279 327 FC96
Dale Rd., Walt. 281 328 BT101
Dale Row W11 137 315 CY72
Dale St. W4 145 314 CS78
Dale Vw., Erith 255 319 FF82
Dale Vw. Ave. E4 211 301 EC47
Dale Vw. Cres. E4 211 301 EC47
Dale Vw. Gdns. E4 211 301 ED48
Dale Wd. Rd., Orp. 291 334 ES101
Dalebury Rd. SW17 191 323 DE89
Dalegarth Gdns., Pur. 295 332 DR113
Daleham Dr., Uxb. 249 312 BP72
Daleham Gdns. NW3 113 305 DD64
Daleham Ms. NW3 113 305 DD65
Dalehead NW1 21 316 DJ68
Dalemain Ms. E16 141 317 EE72
Dales Path, Borwd. 205 298 CR43
Dales Rd., Borwd. 205 298 CR43
Daleside, Orp. 291 335 EU106
Daleside Rd. SW16 272 324 DH92
Dalestone Ms., Rom. 228 310 FH51
Daleview Rd. N15 221 306 DS58
Dalewood Clo., Horn. 238 311 FL59
Dalewood Gdns., Wor.Pk. 283 331 CV103
Daley St. E9 119 307 DX65
Daley Thompson Way SW8 176 324 DH83
Dalgarno Gdns. W10 136 315 CW71
Dalgarno Gdns. Est. W10 126 315 CW70
Dalgarno Way W10 126 315 CW70
Dalgleish St. E14 139 317 DY72
Daling Way E3 129 317 DY68
Dalkeith Gro., Stan. 204 298 CK50
Dalkeith Rd. SE21 194 324 DQ88
Dalkeith Rd., Ilf. 235 308 EQ62
Dallas Rd. NW4 94 305 CU59
Dallas Rd. SE26 274 325 DV91
Dallas Rd. W5 133 314 CM71
Dallas Rd., Sutt. 292 331 CY107
Dallas Ter., Hayes 249 320 BT76
Dallega Clo., Hayes 249 312 BR73
Dallin Rd. SE18 253 318 EP80
Dallin Rd., Bexh. 262 327 EX84
Dalling Rd. W6 146 315 CV77
Dallinger Rd. SE12 183 325 EF86
Dallington St. EC1 36/7 316 DP70
Dalmain Rd. SE23 197 325 DX88
Dalmally Rd., Croy. 287 332 DT101
Dalmeny Ave. N7 115 306 DK63
Dalmeny Ave. SW16 273 324 DN96
Dalmeny Clo., Wem. 106 304 CJ65
Dalmeny Cres., Houns. 259 321 CD84
Dalmeny Rd. N7 99 306 DK62
Dalmeny Rd., Barn. 207 299 DC44
Dalmeny Rd., Cars. 293 332 DG108
Dalmeny Rd., Erith 255 319 FB81
Dalmeny Rd., Wor.Pk. 283 331 CV104
Dalmeyer Rd. NW10 109 304 CT65
Dalmore Rd. SE21 194 324 DQ89
Dalrymple Clo. N14 208 300 DK45
Dalrymple Rd. SE4 181 325 DY84
Dalston Cross Shop. Cen. E8 117 306 DT65
Dalston Gdns., Stan. 216 304 CL53
Dalston La. E8 117 306 DT65
Dalton Ave., Mitch. 271 323 DE96
Dalton Clo., Hayes 241 312 BR70
Dalton Clo., Orp. 291 334 ES104
Dalton Clo., Pur. 295 332 DQ112
Dalton Rd., Har. 215 303 CD54
Dalton St. SE27 194 324 DP89
Dalwood St. SE5 163 316 DS81
Daly Ct. E15 120 307 EC64
Dalyell Rd. SW9 177 324 DM83
Damascene Wk. SE21 194 324 DQ88
Damask Cres. E16 131 317 EE70
Dame St. N1 25 316 DQ68
Damer Ter. SW10 158 315 DC80
Dames Rd. E7 234 308 EG62
Damien St. E1 138 317 DV72
Damon Clo., Sid. 262 327 EV90
Damson Ct., Swan. 279 327 FD98
Damson Way, Cars. 293 331 DF110
Damsonwood Clo., Sthl. 251 321 CA76
Dan Leno Wk. SW6 158 315 DB80
Danbrook Rd. SW16 272 324 DL95
Danbury Clo., Rom. 226 309 EX55
Danbury Ms., Wall. 285 332 DH105
Danbury Rd., Rain. 247 319 FF67
Danbury St. N1 24/5 316 DP68
Danbury Way, Wdf.Grn. 224 308 EJ51
Danby St. SE15 179 324 DT83
Dancer Rd. SW6 157 315 CZ81
Dancer Rd., Rich. 170 322 CN83
Dando Cres. SE3 260 326 EH83
Dandridge Clo. SE10 151 317 EF78
Dane Clo., Bex. 263 327 FA87
Dane Clo., Orp. 291 334 ER106
Dane Pl. E3 129 317 DY68
Dane Rd. N18 210 301 DW49
Dane Rd. SW19 271 323 DC95
Dane Rd. W13 132 314 CJ74
Dane Rd., Ashf. 265 328 BQ93
Dane Rd., Ilf. 235 308 EQ64
Dane Rd., Sthl. 242 313 BY73
Dane St. WC1 47 316 DM71
Danebury Ave. SW15 171 322 CS86
Daneby Rd. SE6 198 325 EB90
Danecourt Gdns., Croy. 287 332 DT104
Danecroft Rd. SE24 178 324 DQ85
Danehill Wk., Sid. 262 327 EU90
Danehurst Gdns., Ilf. 224 308 EL57
Danehurst St. SW6 157 315 CY81
Daneland, Barn. 207 299 DF43
Danemead Gro., Nthlt. 233 313 CB64
Danemere St. SW15 172 323 CW83
Danes Ct., Wem. 92 304 CP62
Danes Gate, Har. 215 303 CE55
Danes Rd., Rom. 237 309 FC59
Danesbury Rd., Felt. 258 321 BV88
Danescombe SE12 260 326 EG88
Danescourt Cres., Sutt. 285 331 DC103
Danescroft NW4 218 305 CX57
Danescroft Ave. NW4 218 305 CX57
Danescroft Gdns. NW4 218 305 CX57
Danesdale Rd. E9 119 307 DY65
Danesfield SE5 163 316 DS79
Daneswood Ave. SE6 198 325 EC90
Danethorpe Rd., Wem. 107 304 CK65
Danette Gdns., Dag. 236 309 EZ61
Daneville Rd. SE5 163 316 DR81
Dangan Rd. E11 224 308 EG58
Daniel Bolt Clo. E14 140 317 EB71
Daniel Clo. N18 210 301 DW49
Daniel Clo. SW17 271 323 DE93
Daniel Gdns. SE15 163 316 DT80
Daniel Pl. NW4 218 305 CV58
Daniel Rd. W5 133 314 CM73
Daniel Way, Bans. 292 331 DB114
Daniell Way, Croy. 286 332 DM102
Daniels Ms. SE4 181 325 DZ84
Daniels Rd. SE15 180 325 DW83
Dansey Pl. W1 58 316 DK73
Dansington Rd., Well. 262 327 EU84
Danson Cres., Well. 262 327 EV83
Danson La., Well. 262 327 EU84
Danson Mead, Well. 262 327 EW83
Danson Pk., Bexh. 262 327 EW84
Danson Rd., Bex. 262 327 EX85
Danson Rd., Bexh. 262 327 EX85
Dante Pl. SE11 84/5 316 DP77
Dante Rd. SE11 84/5 316 DP77
Danube St. SW3 78/9 315 DE78
Danvers Rd. N8 220 306 DK56
Danvers St. SW3 159 315 DD79
Daphne Gdns. E4 211 301 EC48
Daphne St. SW18 174 323 DC86
Daplyn St. E1 138 317 DU71
D'Arblay St. W1 45 316 DJ72
Darby Cres., Sun. 266 329 BW96
Darby Gdns., Sun. 266 329 BW96
Darcy Ave., Wall. 286 332 DJ105
Darcy Clo. N20 207 299 DD47
D'Arcy Dr., Har. 216 304 CK56
D'Arcy Gdns., Dag. 246 319 EZ67
D'Arcy Gdns., Har. 216 304 CL56
Darcy Rd. SW16 272 324 DL96
Darcy Rd., Islw. 152 314 CG81
D'Arcy Rd., Sutt. 284 331 CX105
Dare Gdns., Dag. 236 309 EY62
Darell Rd., Rich. 170 322 CN83
Darenth Rd. N16 101 306 DT59
Darenth Rd., Well. 254 319 EU81
Darfield Rd. SE4 181 325 DZ85
Darfield Way W10 137 315 CX72
Darfur St. SW15 173 323 CX83
Dargate Clo. SE19 273 324 DT94
Darien Rd. SW11 175 323 DD83
Darlan Rd. SW6 157 315 CZ80
Darlaston Rd. SW19 270 323 CX94
Darley Clo., Croy. 288 333 DY100
Darley Dr., N.Mal. 269 322 CR96
Darley Gdns., Mord. 285 331 DC100
Darley Rd. N9 209 300 DT46
Darley Rd. SW11 175 323 DF86
Darling Rd. SE4 182 325 EA83
Darling Row E1 128 317 DV70
Darlington Rd. SE27 273 324 DP92
Darlton Clo., Dart. 263 327 FF83
Darmaine Clo., S.Croy. 295 332 DQ108
Darndale Clo. E17 222 307 DZ54
Darnley Ho. E14 139 317 DY72
Darnley Rd. E9 118 307 DW65
Darnley Rd., Wdf.Grn. 224 308 EG53
Darnley Ter. W11 137 315 CY74
Darrell Rd. SE22 180 325 DU85
Darren Clo. N4 99 306 DM59
Darrick Wd. Rd., Orp. 291 334 ER103
Darris Clo., Hayes 242 313 BY70
Darsley Dr. SW8 161 316 DL81
Dart Clo., Upmin. 229 311 FR58
Dart St. W10 127 315 CY69
Dartfields, Rom. 228 310 FK51
Dartford Ave. N9 210 301 DW44
Dartford Rd., Bex. 263 327 FC88
Dartford St. SE17 162 316 DQ79
Dartmoor Wk. E14 150 317 EA77
Dartmouth Clo. W11 40 315 DA72
Dartmouth Gro. SE10 166 317 EC81
Dartmouth Hill SE10 166 317 EC81
Dartmouth Pk. Ave. NW5 98 306 DH62
Dartmouth Pk. Hill N19 98 306 DH60
Dartmouth Pk. Hill NW5 98 306 DJ62
Dartmouth Pk. Rd. NW5 114 306 DH63
Dartmouth Pl. SE23 196 325 DW89
Dartmouth Pl. W4 155 314 CS79
Dartmouth Rd. E16 244 318 EG72
Dartmouth Rd. NW2 111 305 CX65
Dartmouth Rd. NW4 218 305 CU58
Dartmouth Rd. SE23 196 325 DW89
Dartmouth Rd. SE26 196 325 DV90
Dartmouth Rd., Brom. 289 334 EG101
Dartmouth Rd., Ruis. 232 313 BU62
Dartmouth Row SE10 166 317 EC81
Dartmouth St. SW1 70 316 DK75
Dartmouth Ter. SE10 167 317 ED81
Dartnell Rd., Croy. 287 332 DT101
Dartrey Wk. SW10 159 315 DD80
Dartville Rd. N16 101 306 DT62
Darwell Clo. E6 245 318 EN68
Darwin Clo. N11 208 300 DH48
Darwin Clo., Orp. 291 334 ER106
Darwin Dr., Sthl. 243 313 CB72
Darwin Rd. N22 221 306 DP53
Darwin Rd. W5 142 314 CJ78
Darwin Rd., Well. 261 326 ET83
Darwin St. SE17 86 316 DR77
Darwin St. SE17 86 316 DS77
Daryngton Dr., Grnf. 243 313 CD68
Dashwood Clo., Bexh. 263 327 FA85
Dashwood Rd. N8 220 306 DM58
Dassett Rd. SE27 273 324 DP92
Datchelor Pl. SE5 163 316 DR81
Datchet Rd. SE6 197 325 DZ90
Datchworth Ct. N4 100 306 DQ62
Date St. SE17 85 316 DQ78
Daubeney Gdns. N17 221 306 DQ52
Daubeney Rd. E5 119 307 DY63
Daubeney Rd. N17 221 306 DQ52
Daubeney Twr. SE8 149 317 DZ77
Dault Rd. SW18 174 323 DC86
Davema Clo., Chis. 277 326 EN95
Davenant Rd. N19 99 306 DK61
Davenant Rd., Croy. 286 332 DP105
Davenant St. E1 138 317 DU71
Davenham Ave., Nthwd. 213 302 BT49
Davenport Clo., Tedd. 268 322 CG93
Davenport Rd. SE6 182 325 EC86
Davenport Rd., Sid. 262 327 EX89
Daventer Dr., Stan. 215 303 CF52
Daventry Ave. E17 223 307 EA57
Daventry St. NW1 42/3 315 DE71
Davern Clo. SE10 151 317 EF77
Davey Clo. N7 115 306 DM65
Davey Rd. E9 120 307 EA66
Davey St. SE15 163 316 DT79
David Ave., Grnf. 243 313 CE69
David Clo., Hayes 257 320 BR80
David Dr., Rom. 229 311 FN51
David Ms. W1 44 316 DG71
David Rd., Dag. 236 309 EY61
David St. E15 121 307 ED65
Davidge St. SE1 72/3 316 DP75
Davids Rd. SE23 196 325 DW88
David's Way, Ilf. 225 308 ES52
Davidson Gdns. SW8 161 316 DL80
Davidson La., Har. 233 313 CF59
Davidson Rd., Croy. 287 332 DS102
Davidson Way, Rom. 227 309 FE58
Davies Clo., Croy. 287 332 DT100
Davies La. E11 105 307 EE61
Davies Ms. W1 56/7 316 DH73
Davies St. W1 56/7 316 DH73
Davington Gdns., Dag. 236 309 EV64
Davington Rd., Dag. 236 309 EV65
Davinia Clo., Wdf.Grn. 224 308 EM51
Davis Rd. W3 135 314 CT74
Davis Rd., Chess. 282 330 CN105
Davis St. E13 244 318 EH68
Davisville Rd. W12 146 315 CU75
Dawes Ave., Horn. 238 310 FK62
Dawes Ave., Islw. 168 322 CG85
Dawes Ho. SE17 86 316 DR77
Dawes Rd. SW6 157 315 CY80
Dawes Rd., Uxb. 240 312 BL68
Dawes St. SE17 86 316 DR78
Dawley Ave., Uxb. 249 312 BQ72
Dawley Par., Hayes 249 312 BQ73
Dawley Rd., Hayes 249 312 BQ73
Dawlish Ave. N13 208 300 DL49
Dawlish Ave. SW18 190 323 DB89
Dawlish Ave., Grnf. 234 312 CG68
Dawlish Dr., Ilf. 235 308 ES63
Dawlish Dr., Pnr. 214 303 BY57
Dawlish Dr., Ruis. 232 313 BU61
Dawlish Rd. E10 104 307 EC60
Dawlish Rd. N17 222 307 DU55
Dawlish Rd. NW2 111 305 CX65
Dawlish Wk., Rom. 228 310 FJ53
Dawn Clo., Houns. 258 321 BY83
Dawnay Gdns. SW18 191 323 DD89
Dawnay Rd. SW18 190 323 DC89
Dawpool Rd. NW2 93 304 CT61
Daws La. NW7 205 298 CT50
Dawson Ave., Bark. 235 308 ET66
Dawson Ave., Orp. 278 327 EV96
Dawson Clo. SE18 253 318 EQ77
Dawson Clo., Hayes 249 312 BR71
Dawson Dr., Rain. 238 310 FH66
Dawson Dr., Swan. 279 327 FE93
Dawson Gdns., Bark. 235 308 ET66
Dawson Hts. Est. SE22 196 325 DU87
Dawson Pl. W2 52 315 DA73
Dawson Rd. NW2 110 305 CW64
Dawson Rd., Kings.T. 268 322 CM97
Dawson St. E2 27 316 DT68
Dax Ct., Sun. 266 329 BW97
Daybrook Rd. SW19 271 323 DB96
Daylesford Ave. SW15 172 323 CU84
Daymer Gdns., Pnr. 214 303 BV56
Days Acre, S.Croy. 295 332 DT110
Days La., Sid. 261 326 ES87
Daysbrook Rd. SW2 193 324 DM89
Dayton Gro. SE15 164 317 DW81
De Barowe Ms. N5 116 306 DP63
De Beauvoir Cres. N1 26/7 316 DS67
De Beauvoir Est. N1 26 316 DR67
De Beauvoir Rd. N1 26/7 316 DS67
De Beauvoir Sq. N1 117 306 DS66
De Bohun Ave. N14 208 300 DH44
De Brome Rd., Felt. 258 321 BW88
De Crespigny Pk. SE5 163 316 DR82
De Frene Rd. SE26 274 325 DX91
De Havilland Rd., Edg. 217 304 CN54
De Havilland Rd., Houns. 250 321 BW80
De Havilland Rd., Wall. 294 332 DL108
De Havilland Way, Stai. 256 320 BK86
De Laune St. SE17 84/5 316 DP78
De Luci Rd., Erith 255 319 FC78
De Lucy St. SE2 254 319 EV77
De Mandeville Gate, Enf. 203 301 DU42
De Montfort Rd. SW16 193 324 DL90
De Morgan Rd. SW6 174 323 DB83
De Quincey Ms. E16 141 317 EE72
De Quincey Rd. N17 221 306 DR53
De Salis Rd., Uxb. 241 312 BQ70
De Vere Cotts. W8 65 315 DC76
De Vere Gdns. W8 65 315 DC75
De Vere Gdns., Ilf. 234 308 EM61
De Vere Ms. W8 65 315 DC76
De Walden St. W1 44 316 DG71
Deacon Clo., Pur. 294 332 DL109
Deacon Ms. N1 117 306 DR66
Deacon Rd. NW2 110 305 CU64
Deacon Rd., Kings.T. 268 322 CM95
Deacon Way SE17 85 316 DQ77
Deacon Way, Wdf.Grn. 224 308 EM52
Deacons Clo., Pnr. 214 303 BV54
Deacons Leas, Orp. 291 334 ER105
Deacons Wk., Hmptn. 266 329 BZ91
Deal Porters Way SE16 148 317 DW76
Deal Rd. SW17 272 324 DG93
Deal St. E1 138 317 DU71
Deal's Gateway SE10 166 317 EB81
Dealtry Rd. SW15 172 323 CW84
Dean Bradley St. SW1 70/1 316 DL76
Dean Clo. E9 118 307 DW64
Dean Clo. SE16 139 317 DX74
Dean Clo., Uxb. 240 312 BM66
Dean Ct., Wem. 90 304 CH62
Dean Dr., Stan. 216 304 CL54
Dean Farrar St. SW1 70 316 DK76
Dean Gdns. E17 223 307 ED56
Dean Gdns. W13 132 314 CH74
Dean Rd. NW2 110 305 CW65
Dean Rd., Croy. 287 332 DR105
Dean Rd., Hmptn. 266 329 BZ92
Dean Rd., Houns. 259 321 CB85
Dean Ryle St. SW1 82/3 316 DL77
Dean Stanley St. SW1 70/1 316 DL76
Dean St. E7 234 308 EG64
Dean St. W1 44 316 DK72
Dean Trench St. SW1 70/1 316 DL76
Dean Wk., Edg. 217 304 CQ51
Dean Way, Sthl. 251 321 CB75
Deancross St. E1 138 317 DW72
Deane Ave., Ruis. 232 313 BV64
Deane Cft. Rd., Pnr. 214 303 BV58
Deane Way, Ruis. 214 303 BV58
Deanery Clo. N2 219 305 DE56
Deanery Ms. W1 56 316 DG74
Deanery Rd. E15 121 307 EE65
Deanery St. W1 56 316 DG74
Deanhill Rd. SW14 170 322 CP84
Deans Bldgs. SE17 86 316 DR77
Deans Clo. W4 154 314 CP79
Dean's Clo., Croy. 287 332 DT104
Deans Clo., Edg. 217 304 CQ51
Deans Ct. EC4 48/9 316 DP72
Deans Dr. N13 221 306 DP51
Deans Dr., Edg. 205 298 CR50
Dean's Gate Clo. SE23 197 325 DX90
Deans La., Edg. 217 304 CQ51
Deans Ms. W1 44/5 316 DH72
Dean's Pl. SW1 82 316 DK78
Deans Rd. W7 243 313 CF74
Deans Rd., Sutt. 284 331 DB104
Deans Way, Edg. 205 298 CQ50
Dean's Yd. SW1 70 316 DK76
Deansbrook Clo., Edg. 217 304 CQ51
Deansbrook Rd., Edg. 217 304 CP52
Deanscroft Ave. NW9 92 304 CQ61
Deansway N2 219 305 DD56
Deansway N9 209 300 DS48
Dearn Gdns., Mitch. 271 323 DE97
Dearne Clo., Stan. 204 298 CG50
Dearsley Ho., Rain. 247 319 FD68
Dearsley Rd., Enf. 203 301 DV41
Deason St. E15 130 317 EC67
Debden Clo., Kings.T. 268 322 CK92
Debden Clo., Wdf.Grn. 224 308 EK52
Debden Wk., Horn. 238 310 FH65
Debnams Rd. SE16 148 317 DW77
Deborah Clo., Islw. 251 321 CE81
Deborah Cres., Ruis. 231 312 BR59
Debrabant Clo., Erith 255 319 FD79
Deburgh Rd. SW19 271 323 DC94
Decima St. SE1 74/5 316 DS76
Deck Clo. SE16 149 317 DX75
Decoy Ave. NW11 218 305 CY57
Dee Clo., Upmin. 229 311 FS58
Dee Rd., Rich. 169 322 CM84
Dee St. E14 140 317 EC72
Dee Way, Rom. 227 309 FE52
Deeley Rd. SW8 161 316 DK81
Deena Clo. W3 133 314 CM72
Deepdale SW19 270 323 CX91
Deepdale Ave., Brom. 275 325 EF98
Deepdene W5 123 314 CM70
Deepdene Ave., Croy. 287 332 DT104
Deepdene Clo. E11 224 308 EG56
Deepdene Ct. N21 209 300 DP44
Deepdene Gdns. SW2 193 324 DM87
Deepdene Rd. SE5 179 324 DR84
Deepdene Rd., Well. 262 327 EU83
Deepwell Clo., Islw. 152 314 CG81
Deepwood La., Grnf. 243 313 CD69
Deer Pk. Clo., Kings.T. 269 322 CP94
Deer Pk. Gdns., Mitch. 271 323 DD97
Deer Pk. Rd. SW19 271 323 DB96
Deer Pk. Way, W.Wick. 289 333 EE103
Deerbrook Rd. SE24 194 324 DP88
Deerdale Rd. SE24 178 324 DQ84
Deere Ave., Rain. 238 310 FG65
Deerhurst Clo., Felt. 266 329 BU91
Deerhurst Cres., Hmptn. 267 329 CC92
Deerhurst Rd. NW2 111 305 CX65
Deerhurst Rd. SW16 272 324 DM92
Deerings Dr., Pnr. 214 303 BU57
Deerleap Gro. E4 211 301 EB43
Deeside Rd. SW17 191 323 DD90
Defiance Wk. SE18 252 318 EM76
Defiant Way, Wall. 294 332 DL108
Defoe Ave., Rich. 154 314 CN80
Defoe Clo. SE16 149 317 DZ75
Defoe Clo. SW17 271 323 DE93
Defoe Clo., Erith 255 319 FE81
Defoe Ho. EC2 49 316 DQ71
Defoe Rd. N16 101 306 DS61
Defoe Way, Rom. 227 309 FA51
Degema Rd., Chis. 277 326 EP92
Dehar Cres. NW9 93 304 CT59
Dekker Rd. SE21 179 324 DS86
Delacourt Rd. SE3 252 318 EH80
Delafield Rd. SE7 252 318 EH78
Delaford Clo., Iver 249 312 BG72
Delaford Rd. SE16 148 317 DV78
Delaford St. SW6 157 315 CY80
Delamere Cres., Croy. 288 333 DW100
Delamere Gdns. NW7 217 304 CR51
Delamere Rd. SW20 270 323 CX95
Delamere Rd. W5 133 314 CL74
Delamere Rd., Hayes 242 313 BX73
Delamere Ter. W2 40/1 315 DB71
Delancey Pas. NW1 20/1 316 DH67
Delancey St. NW1 20/1 316 DH67
Delaware Rd. W9 28/9 315 DB70
Delawyk Cres. SE24 178 324 DQ86
Delcombe Ave., Wor.Pk. 284 331 CW102
Delft Way SE22 179 324 DS85
Delhi Rd., Enf. 209 300 DT45
Delhi St. N1 22/3 316 DL67
Delia St. SW18 190 323 DB87
Delius Clo., Borwd. 204 298 CJ44
Delius Gro. E15 130 317 EC68
Dell, The SE2 254 319 EU78
Dell, The SE19 273 324 DT95
Dell, The, Bex. 263 327 FE88
Dell, The, Brent. 152 314 CJ79
Dell, The, Felt. 258 321 BV87
Dell, The, Nthwd. 213 302 BS47
Dell, The, Pnr. 214 303 BX54
Dell, The, Wem. 106 304 CH64
Dell Clo. E15 131 317 ED67
Dell Clo., Wall. 286 332 DJ105
Dell Fm. Rd., Ruis. 231 302 BR57
Dell La., Epsom 283 331 CU106
Dell Rd., Enf. 203 301 DW38
Dell Rd., West Dr. 248 320 BM76
Dell Wk., N.Mal. 269 322 CS96
Dell Way W13 132 314 CJ72
Della Path E5 102 307 DV62
Dellbow Rd., Felt. 258 321 BV85
Dellfield Clo., Beck. 275 325 EC94
Dellfield Cres., Uxb. 240 312 BK70
Dellfield Par. (Cowley), Uxb. 240 312 BJ70
Dellors Clo., Barn. 206 299 CX43
Dellow Clo., Ilf. 235 308 ER59
Dellow St. E1 138 317 DV73
Dells Clo. E4 211 301 EB45
Dell's Ms. SW1 81 316 DJ77
Dellside, Uxb. 230 312 BJ57
Dellwood Gdns., Ilf. 225 308 EN55
Delmare Clo. SW9 177 324 DM84
Delme Cres. SE3 252 318 EH82
Delmey Clo., Croy. 287 332 DT104
Deloraine St. SE8 166 317 EA81
Delorme St. W6 157 315 CX79
Delta Clo., Wor.Pk. 283 330 CT104
Delta Ct. NW2 94 305 CU61
Delta Gro., Nthlt. 242 313 BX69
Delta Rd., Wor.Pk. 283 330 CS104
Delta St. E2 128 317 DU69
Delvan Clo. SE18 253 318 EN80
Delvers Mead, Dag. 237 309 FC63
Delverton Rd. SE17 84/5 316 DP78
Delvino Rd. SW6 158 315 DA81
Demesne Rd., Wall. 286 332 DK105
Demeta Clo., Wem. 92 304 CQ62
Dempster Clo., Surb. 282 330 CJ101
Dempster Rd. SW18 174 323 DC85
Den Clo., Beck. 275 325 ED97
Den Rd., Brom. 275 325 ED97
Denberry Dr., Sid. 262 327 EV90
Denbigh Clo. NW10 109 304 CS66
Denbigh Clo. W11 52 315 CZ73
Denbigh Clo., Chis. 276 326 EM93
Denbigh Clo., Horn. 229 311 FN56
Denbigh Clo., Ruis. 231 312 BT61
Denbigh Clo., Sthl. 242 313 BZ72
Denbigh Clo., Sutt. 284 331 CZ106
Denbigh Dr., Hayes 249 320 BQ75
Denbigh Gdns., Rich. 169 322 CM85
Denbigh Ms. SW1 81 316 DJ77
Denbigh Pl. SW1 81 316 DJ78
Denbigh Rd. E6 244 318 EK69
Denbigh Rd. W11 137 315 CZ73
Denbigh Rd. W13 132 314 CH73
Denbigh Rd., Houns. 251 321 CB82
Denbigh Rd., Sthl. 242 313 BZ72
Denbigh St. SW1 81 316 DJ77
Denbigh Ter. W11 137 315 CZ73
Denbridge Rd., Brom. 276 326 EM96
Dendridge Clo., Enf. 203 301 DV37
Dene, The W13 132 314 CH71
Dene, The, Croy. 288 333 DX105
Dene, The, Sutt. 292 331 CZ111
Dene, The, Wem. 107 304 CL63
Dene Ave., Houns. 258 321 BZ83
Dene Ave., Sid. 262 327 EV87
Dene Clo. SE4 181 325 DY83
Dene Clo., Brom. 289 333 EF102
Dene Clo., Dart. 279 327 FE91
Dene Clo., Wor.Pk. 283 330 CT103
Dene Dr., Orp. 291 335 EV104
Dene Gdns., Stan. 204 298 CJ50
Dene Rd. N11 207 299 DF46
Dene Rd., Nthwd. 302 BQ51
Denecroft Cres., Uxb. 241 312 BP67
Denehurst Gdns. NW4 218 305 CW58
Denehurst Gdns. W3 134 314 CP74
Denehurst Gdns., Rich. 170 322 CN84
Denehurst Gdns., Twick. 259 321 CD87
Denewood, Barn. 207 299 DC43
Denewood Rd. N6 219 305 DF58
Dengie Wk. N1 25 316 DQ67
Denham Clo., Uxb. 230 312 BG62
Denham Clo., Well. 262 327 EW83
Denham Ct. Rd., Uxb. 230 312 BG63
Denham Cres., Mitch. 271 323 DF98
Denham Dr., Ilf. 225 308 EQ58
Denham Grn. Clo., Uxb. 230 312 BG59
Denham Rd. N20 207 299 DF48
Denham Rd., Felt. 258 321 BW86
Denham St. SE10 252 318 EG78
Denham Way, Bark. 245 318 ES67
Denham Way, Uxb. 230 312 BG62
Denholme Rd. W9 237 309 FF65
Denholme Wk., Rain. 237 309 FF65
Denison Clo. N2 219 305 DC55
Denison Rd. SW19 271 323 DD93
Denison Rd. W5 122 314 CJ70
Denison Rd., Felt. 265 328 BT91
Deniston Ave., Bex. 262 327 EY88
Denleigh Gdns. N21 209 300 DN46
Denman Dr. NW11 219 305 DA57
Denman Dr., Ashf. 265 328 BP93
Denman Dr. N. NW11 219 305 DA57
Denman Dr. S. NW11 219 305 DA57
Denman Rd. SE15 163 316 DT81
Denman St. W1 58 316 DK73
Denmark Ave. SW19 270 323 CY94
Denmark Ct., Mord. 284 331 DA99
Denmark Gdns., Cars. 285 331 DF104
Denmark Gro. N1 24 316 DN68
Denmark Hill SE5 163 316 DR81
Denmark Hill Dr. NW9 217 304 CT56
Denmark Hill Est. SE5 179 324 DR84
Denmark Pl. WC2 46 316 DK72
Denmark Rd. N8 221 306 DN56
Denmark Rd. NW6 127 315 CZ68
Denmark Rd. SE5 162 316 DQ81
Denmark Rd. SE25 287 333 DU99
Denmark Rd. SW19 270 323 CX93
Denmark Rd. W13 132 314 CH73
Denmark Rd., Brom. 276 326 EH95
Denmark Rd., Cars. 285 331 DF104
Denmark Rd., Kings.T. 268 322 CL97
Denmark Rd., Twick. 259 321 CD90
Denmark St. E11 105 307 EE62
Denmark St. E13 244 318 EH71
Denmark St. N17 222 307 DV53
Denmark St. WC2 46 316 DK72
Denmark Wk. SE27 273 324 DQ91
Denmead Ho. SW15 171 322 CT86
Denmead Rd., Croy. 286 332 DP102
Denmead Way SE15 163 316 DT80
Dennan Rd., Surb. 282 330 CM102
Denne Ter. E8 27 316 DT67
Denner Rd. E4 211 301 EA47
Dennett Rd., Croy. 286 332 DN102
Dennetts Gro. SE14 165 317 DX82
Dennetts Rd. SE14 164 317 DW81
Denning Ave., Croy. 286 332 DN105
Denning Clo. NW8 29 315 DC69
Denning Clo., Hmptn. 266 329 BZ93
Denning Rd. NW3 113 305 DD63
Dennington Clo. E5 102 307 DV61
Dennington Pk. Rd. NW6 112 305 DA65
Denningtons, The, Wor.Pk. 283 330 CS103
Dennis Ave., Wem. 107 304 CM64
Dennis Clo., Ashf. 265 328 BR93
Dennis Gdns., Stan. 204 298 CJ50
Dennis La., Stan. 204 298 CH48
Dennis Pk. Cres. SW20 270 323 CY95
Dennis Reeve Clo., Mitch. 271 323 DF95
Dennis Rd., E.Mol. 267 329 CC98
Dennis Way SW4 177 324 DK83
Dennison Pt. E15 120 307 EC66
Denny Clo. E6 244 318 EL71
Denny Cres. SE11 84 316 DN78
Denny Gdns., Dag. 236 309 EV66
Denny Rd. N9 210 301 DV46
Denny St. SE11 84 316 DN78
Densbridge Ind. Est., Uxb. 240 312 BJ65
Densham Rd. E15 131 317 EE67
Densole Clo., Beck. 274 325 DY95
Densworth Gro. N9 210 301 DW47
Denton Clo., Barn. 206 299 CW43
Denton Rd. N8 220 306 DM57
Denton Rd. N18 209 300 DS49
Denton Rd., Bex. 263 327 FD89
Denton Rd., Dart. 263 327 FF87
Denton Rd., Twick. 169 322 CK86
Denton Rd., Well. 254 319 EW80
Denton St. SW18 174 323 DB86
Denton Ter., Bex. 263 327 FE89
Denton Way E5 103 307 DX62
Dents Rd. SW11 175 323 DF86
Denver Clo., Orp. 291 334 ES100
Denver Ind. Est., Rain. 247 319 FF71
Denver Rd. N16 101 306 DS59
Denyer St. SW3 78/9 315 DE77
Denzil Rd. NW10 109 304 CT64
Denziloe Ave., Uxb. 241 312 BP69
Deodar Rd. SW15 173 323 CY84
Deodara Clo. N20 207 299 DE48
Depot Rd., Houns. 259 321 CD83
Deptford Bri. SE8 166 317 EA81
Deptford Bdy. SE8 166 317 EA81
Deptford Ch. St. SE8 166 317 EA79
Deptford Ferry Rd. E14 150 317 EA77
Deptford Grn. SE8 166 317 EA79
Deptford High St. SE8 166 317 EA79
Deptford Strand SE8 149 317 DZ77
Deptford Wf. SE8 149 317 DZ77
Derby Ave. N12 207 299 DC50
Derby Ave., Har. 215 303 CD53
Derby Ave., Rom. 227 309 FC58
Derby Ave., Upmin. 238 311 FM62
Derby Ct. E5 119 307 DX63
Derby Est., Houns. 259 321 CA84
Derby Gate SW1 70/1 316 DL75
Derby Hill SE23 196 325 DW89
Derby Hill Cres. SE23 196 325 DW89
Derby Rd. E7 234 308 EK66
Derby Rd. E9 129 317 DX67
Derby Rd. E18 223 307 EF53
Derby Rd. N18 210 301 DW50
Derby Rd. SW14 170 322 CP84
Derby Rd. SW19 271 323 DA94
Derby Rd., Croy. 286 332 DP103
Derby Rd., Enf. 210 301 DV43
Derby Rd., Grnf. 243 313 CB67
Derby Rd., Houns. 259 321 CB84
Derby Rd., Surb. 282 330 CN102
Derby Rd., Sutt. 292 331 CZ107
Derby Rd., Uxb. 240 312 BJ68
Derby St. W1 56 316 DG74
Derbyshire St. E2 128 317 DU69
Dereham Pl. EC2 38/9 316 DS69
Dereham Rd., Bark. 235 308 ET65
Derek Ave., Wall. 285 332 DH104
Derek Ave., Wem. 108 304 CP66
Derek Clo., Epsom 282 330 CP106
Derek Walcott Clo. SE24 178 324 DP85
Derham Gdns., Upmin. 239 311 FQ62
Dericote St. E8 128 317 DU67
Deridene Clo., Stai. 256 320 BL86
Derifall Clo. E6 244 318 EM71
Dering Pl., Croy. 287 332 DQ105
Dering Rd., Croy. 287 332 DQ105
Dering St. W1 44/5 316 DH72
Derinton Rd. SW17 271 323 DF91
Derley Rd., Sthl. 250 321 BW76
Dermody Gdns. SE13 183 325 ED85
Dermody Rd. SE13 183 325 ED85
Deronda Rd. SE24 194 324 DP88
Deroy Clo., Cars. 293 331 DF107
Derrick Ave., S.Croy. 295 332 DQ110
Derrick Gdns. SE7 252 318 EJ77
Derrick Rd., Beck. 274 325 DZ97
Derry Rd., Croy. 286 332 DL104
Derry St. W8 64/5 315 DB75
Dersingham Ave. E12 234 308 EM63
Dersingham Rd. NW2 95 305 CY62
Derwent Ave. N18 209 300 DR50
Derwent Ave. NW7 217 304 CR51
Derwent Ave. SW15 269 322 CS91
Derwent Ave., Barn. 207 299 DF46
Derwent Ave., Pnr. 214 303 BY51
Derwent Ave., Uxb. 231 312 BN61
Derwent Clo., Felt. 265 320 BT88
Derwent Cres. N20 207 299 DC48
Derwent Cres., Bexh. 255 319 FA82
Derwent Cres., Stan. 216 304 CJ54
Derwent Dr. NW9 217 304 CS57
Derwent Dr., Hayes 249 312 BS71
Derwent Dr., Orp. 291 334 ER101
Derwent Dr., Pur. 295 332 DR113
Derwent Gdns., Ilf. 224 308 EL56
Derwent Gdns., Wem. 90 304 CJ59
Derwent Gro. SE22 179 324 DT84
Derwent Ri. NW9 217 304 CS58
Derwent Rd. N13 208 300 DM49
Derwent Rd. SE20 274 325 DU96
Derwent Rd. SW20 284 331 CX100
Derwent Rd. W5 142 314 CJ76
Derwent Rd., Sthl. 242 313 BZ72
Derwent Rd., Twick. 259 321 CB86

Derwent St. SE10 151 317 EE78
Derwent Wk., Wall. 293 332 DH108
Derwent Way, Horn. 238 310 FH64
Derwent Yd. W5 142 314 CJ76
Derwentwater Rd. W3 134 314 CQ74
Desborough Clo., Shep. 281 328 BN102
Desborough St. W2 40/1 315 DB71
Desenfans Rd. SE21 179 324 DS86
Desford Ct., Ashf. 264 320 BM89
Desford Ms. E16 131 317 EE70
Desford Rd. E16 131 317 EE70
Desford Way, Ashf. 264 320 BM89
Desmond St. SE14 165 317 DY79
Despard Rd. N19 98 306 DJ60
Detling Clo., Horn. 238 310 FJ64
Detling Rd., Brom. 276 326 EG92
Detling Rd., Erith 255 319 FD80
Detmold Rd. E5 102 307 DW61
Devalls Clo. E6 245 318 EN73
Devana End, Cars. 285 331 DF104
Devas Rd. SW20 270 323 CW95
Devas St. E3 130 317 EB70
Devenay Rd. E15 121 307 EF66
Devenish Rd. SE2 254 319 EU75
Deventer Cres. SE22 179 324 DS85
Deverell St. SE1 74 316 DR76
Devereux Ct. WC2 48 316 DN72
Devereux La. SW13 156 315 CV80
Devereux Rd. SW11 175 323 DF86
Deverill Ct. SE20 274 325 DW95
Deveron Way, Rom. 227 309 FE53
Devey Clo., Kings.T. 269 322 CS94
Devizes St. N1 26 316 DR67
Devon Ave., Twick. 259 321 CC88
Devon Clo. N17 221 306 DT55
Devon Clo., Grnf. 122 314 CJ67
Devon Gdns. N4 221 306 DP58
Devon Ri. N2 219 305 DD56
Devon Rd., Bark. 245 318 ES67
Devon Rd., Sutt. 292 331 CY109
Devon St. SE15 164 317 DV79
Devon Way, Chess. 282 330 CJ106
Devon Way, Epsom 282 330 CP106
Devon Way, Uxb. 240 312 BM68
Devon Waye, Houns. 250 321 BZ80
Devoncroft Gdns., Twick. 184 322 CG87
Devonia Gdns. N18 221 306 DQ51
Devonia Rd. N1 24/5 316 DP68
Devonport Gdns., Ilf. 224 308 EM58
Devonport Ms. W12 136 315 CV74
Devonport Rd. W12 146 315 CV75
Devonport St. E1 139 317 DX72
Devons Est. E3 130 317 EB69
Devons Rd. E3 140 317 EA71
Devonshire Ave., Sutt. 293 331 DC108
Devonshire Clo. E15 121 307 EE63
Devonshire Clo. N13 209 300 DN48
Devonshire Clo. W1 44/5 316 DH71
Devonshire Cres. NW7 218 305 CX52
Devonshire Dr. SE10 166 317 EB80
Devonshire Dr., Surb. 282 330 CK103
Devonshire Gdns. N17 221 306 DQ51
Devonshire Gdns. N21 209 300 DQ45
Devonshire Gdns. W4 154 314 CQ80
Devonshire Gro. SE15 164 317 DV79
Devonshire Hill La. N17 221 306 DP51
Devonshire Ms. W4 145 314 CS78
Devonshire Ms. N. W1 44/5 316 DH71
Devonshire Ms. S. W1 44/5 316 DH71
Devonshire Ms. W. W1 32 316 DG70
Devonshire Pas. W4 145 314 CS78
Devonshire Pl. NW2 96 305 DA62
Devonshire Pl. W1 32 316 DG70
Devonshire Pl. W4 145 314 CS78
Devonshire Pl. W8 64/5 315 DB76
Devonshire Pl. Ms. W1 32 316 DG70
Devonshire Rd. E15 121 307 EE63
Devonshire Rd. E16 244 318 EH72
Devonshire Rd. E17 223 307 EA58
Devonshire Rd. N9 210 301 DW46
Devonshire Rd. N13 208 300 DM49
Devonshire Rd. N17 221 306 DQ51
Devonshire Rd. NW7 218 305 CX52
Devonshire Rd. SE9 260 326 EL89
Devonshire Rd. SE23 196 325 DW88
Devonshire Rd. SW19 271 323 DE94
Devonshire Rd. W4 145 314 CS78
Devonshire Rd. W5 142 314 CJ76
Devonshire Rd., Bexh. 262 327 EY84
Devonshire Rd., Cars. 285 332 DG105
Devonshire Rd., Croy. 287 332 DR101
Devonshire Rd., Felt. 258 321 BY90
Devonshire Rd., Har. 215 303 CD58
Devonshire Rd., Horn. 238 310 FJ61
Devonshire Rd., Ilf. 235 308 ER59
Devonshire Rd., Orp. 291 335 EU101
Devonshire Rd. (Eastcote), Pnr. 214 303 BW58
Devonshire Rd. (Hatch End), Pnr. 214 303 BZ53
Devonshire Rd., Sthl. 243 313 CA71
Devonshire Rd., Sutt. 293 331 DC108
Devonshire Row EC2 50/1 316 DS71
Devonshire Row Ms. W1 32/3 316 DH70
Devonshire Sq. EC2 50/1 316 DS71
Devonshire Sq., Brom. 276 326 EH98
Devonshire St. W1 44/5 316 DH71
Devonshire St. W4 145 314 CS78
Devonshire Ter. W2 41 315 DC72
Devonshire Way, Croy. 288 333 DY103
Devonshire Way, Hayes 242 313 BV72
Dewar St. SE15 180 325 DU83
Dewberry Gdns. E6 244 318 EL71
Dewberry St. E14 140 317 EC71
Dewey Rd. N1 24 316 DN68
Dewey Rd., Dag. 237 309 FB65
Dewey St. SW17 271 323 DF92
Dewgrass Gro., Wal.Cr. 203 301 DX35
Dewhurst Rd. W14 147 315 CX76
Dewsbury Clo., Pnr. 214 303 BY58
Dewsbury Clo., Rom. 228 311 FL51
Dewsbury Ct. W4 144 314 CQ77
Dewsbury Gdns., Rom. 228 310 FK51
Dewsbury Gdns., Wor.Pk. 283 331 CU104
Dewsbury Rd. NW10 110 305 CU64
Dewsbury Rd., Rom. 228 310 FK51
Dewsbury Ter. NW1 20/1 316 DH67
Dexter Rd., Barn. 206 299 CX44
Dexter Rd., Uxb. 212 302 BJ54
Deyncourt Gdns., Upmin. 239 311 FQ61
Deyncourt Rd. N17 221 306 DQ53
Deynecourt Gdns. E11 224 308 EJ56
D'Eynsford Rd. SE5 163 316 DR81
Diadem Ct. W1 46 316 DK72
Dial Wk., The W8 64/5 315 DB75
Diamedes Ave., Stai. 264 320 BK87
Diameter Rd., Orp. 290 334 EP101
Diamond Clo., Dag. 236 309 EW60
Diamond Rd., Ruis. 232 313 BX63
Diamond St. SE15 163 316 DS80
Diamond Ter. SE10 166 317 EC81
Diana Clo. E18 224 308 EH53
Diana Gdns., Surb. 282 330 CM103
Diana Ho. SW13 155 314 CT81
Diana Pl. NW1 32/3 316 DH70
Diana Rd. E17 222 307 DZ55
Dianna Way, Barn. 207 299 DE43
Dianthus Clo. SE2 254 319 EV78
Diban Ave., Horn. 238 310 FH63
Dibden Row SE1 72 316 DN76
Dibden St. N1 25 316 DQ67
Dibdin Clo., Sutt. 284 331 DA104
Dibdin Rd., Sutt. 284 331 DA104
Dicey Ave. NW2 110 305 CW63
Dick Turpin Way, Felt. 257 320 BT84
Dickens Ave. N3 219 305 DC53
Dickens Ave., Uxb. 249 312 BP72
Dickens Clo., Erith 255 319 FB81
Dickens Clo., Hayes 249 320 BS77
Dickens Clo., Rich. 185 322 CL89
Dickens Dr., Chis. 277 326 EQ93
Dickens Est. SE1 75 316 DT75
Dickens Est. SE16 75 316 DT75
Dickens La. N18 209 300 DS50
Dickens Rd. E6 244 318 EK68
Dickens Sq. SE1 73 316 DQ76
Dickens St. SW8 160 316 DH82
Dickenson Clo. N9 210 301 DU46
Dickenson Rd. N8 99 306 DL59
Dickenson Rd., Felt. 266 329 BX92
Dickenson St. NW5 114 306 DH65
Dickensons La. SE25 287 333 DU99
Dickensons Pl. SE25 287 333 DU100
Dickerage La., N.Mal. 269 322 CQ97
Dickerage Rd., Kings.T. 269 322 CQ95
Dickerage Rd., N.Mal. 269 322 CQ95
Dickson Fold, Pnr. 214 303 BX56
Dickson Rd. SE9 260 326 EL83
Didsbury Clo. E6 244 318 EM67
Digby Cres. N4 100 306 DQ61
Digby Gdns., Dag. 247 319 FA67
Digby Pl., Croy. 287 332 DT104
Digby Rd. E9 119 307 DX64
Digby Rd., Bark. 235 308 ET66
Digby St. E2 128 317 DW69
Digby Wk., Horn. 238 310 FJ65
Dighton Ct. SE5 162 316 DQ79
Dighton Rd. SW18 174 323 DC85
Digswell St. N7 116 306 DN65
Dilhorne Clo. SE12 260 326 EH90
Dilke St. SW3 159 315 DF79
Dillwyn Clo. SE26 274 325 DY91
Dilston Clo., Nthlt. 242 313 BW69
Dilston Gro. SE16 148 317 DW77
Dilton Gdns. SW15 188 323 CV88
Dimes Pl. W6 146 315 CV77
Dimmock Dr., Grnf. 233 313 CD64
Dimond Clo. E7 234 308 EG63
Dimsdale Dr. NW9 92 304 CQ60
Dimsdale Dr., Enf. 210 301 DU44
Dimsdale Wk. E13 244 318 EG67
Dimson Cres. E3 130 317 EA70
Dingle, The, Uxb. 241 312 BP69
Dingle Clo., Barn. 205 298 CT44
Dingle Gdns. E14 140 317 EA73
Dingle Rd., Ashf. 265 328 BP92
Dingley La. SW16 193 324 DK89
Dingley Pl. EC1 37 316 DQ69
Dingley Rd. EC1 37 316 DQ69
Dingwall Ave., Croy. 287 332 DQ103
Dingwall Gdns. NW11 219 305 DA58
Dingwall Pl., Croy. 287 332 DR103
Dingwall Rd. SW18 190 323 DC87
Dingwall Rd., Cars. 293 331 DF109
Dingwall Rd., Croy. 287 332 DR102
Dinmont St. E2 128 317 DV68
Dinsdale Gdns. SE25 287 332 DS99
Dinsdale Gdns., Barn. 207 299 DB43
Dinsdale Rd. SE3 167 317 EF79
Dinsmore Rd. SW12 192 324 DH87
Dinton Rd. SW19 271 323 DD93
Dinton Rd., Kings.T. 268 322 CM94
Diploma Ave. N2 219 305 DE56
Dirleton Rd. E15 131 317 EF67
Disbrowe Rd. W6 157 315 CY79
Discovery Wk. E1 138 317 DV74
Dishforth La. NW9 217 304 CS53
Disney Ms. N4 221 306 DP57
Disney Pl. SE1 73 316 DQ75
Disney St. SE1 73 316 DQ75
Dison Clo., Enf. 203 301 DX39
Disraeli Clo. SE28 246 319 EW74
Disraeli Clo. W4 145 314 CR77
Disraeli Gdns. SW15 173 323 CZ84
Disraeli Rd. E7 234 308 EG65
Disraeli Rd. NW10 125 314 CR68
Disraeli Rd. SW15 173 323 CY84
Disraeli Rd. W5 133 314 CK74
Diss St. E2 39 316 DT69
Distaff La. EC4 61 316 DQ73
Distillery La. W6 146 315 CW78
Distillery Rd. W6 146 315 CW78
Distillery Wk., Brent. 153 314 CL79
Distin St. SE11 84 316 DN77
District Rd., Wem. 106 304 CH64
Ditch All. SE10 166 317 EB81
Ditchburn St. E14 140 317 EC73
Ditchfield Rd., Hayes 242 313 BY70
Dittisham Rd. SE9 276 326 EL91
Ditton Gra. Clo., Surb. 282 330 CK102
Ditton Gra. Dr., Surb. 282 330 CK102
Ditton Hill, Surb. 282 330 CJ102
Ditton Hill Rd., Surb. 282 330 CJ102
Ditton Pl. SE20 274 325 DV95
Ditton Rd., Bexh. 262 327 EX85
Ditton Rd., Sthl. 250 321 BZ78
Ditton Rd., Surb. 282 330 CK103
Divis Way SW15 172 323 CV86
Dixon Clark Ct. N1 116 306 DP65
Dixon Clo. E6 244 318 EM72
Dixon Pl., W.Wick. 288 333 EB102
Dixon Rd. SE14 165 317 DY81
Dixon Rd. SE25 273 324 DS97
Dixon's All. SE16 148 317 DV75
Dobbin Clo., Har. 216 304 CG54
Dobell Rd. SE9 260 326 EM85
Dobree Ave. NW10 110 305 CV66
Dobson Clo. NW6 113 305 DD66
Dock Hill Ave. SE16 149 317 DX75
Dock Rd. E16 141 317 EF73
Dock Rd., Brent. 153 314 CK80
Dock St. E1 138 317 DU73
Dockers Tanner Rd. E14 150 317 EA77
Dockett Eddy La., Shep. 280 328 BM102
Dockhead SE1 75 316 DT75
Dockland St. E16 245 318 EN74
Dockley Rd. SE16 148 317 DU76
Dockwell Clo., Felt. 258 321 BU84
Doctor Johnson Ave. SW17 192 324 DH90
Doctors Clo. SE26 274 325 DW92
Docwra's Bldgs. N1 117 306 DS65
Dod St. E14 140 317 EA72
Dodbrooke Rd. SE27 194 324 DN90
Doddington Gro. SE17 162 316 DP79
Doddington Pl. SE17 162 316 DP79
Dodsley Pl. N9 210 301 DW48
Dodson St. SE1 72 316 DN75
Doebury Wk. SE18 254 319 EU79
Doel Clo. SW19 271 323 DC94
Dog Kennel Hill SE22 179 324 DS83
Dog Kennel Hill Est. SE22 179 324 DS83
Dog La. NW10 109 304 CS63
Doggets Ct., Barn. 207 299 DE43
Doggett Rd. SE6 198 325 EA87
Doghurst Ave., Hayes 257 320 BP80
Doghurst Dr., West Dr. 257 320 BP80
Doherty Rd. E13 244 318 EG70
Dolben St. SE1 60/1 316 DP74
Dolby Ct. EC4 61 316 DQ73
Dolby Rd. SW6 157 315 CZ82
Dolland St. SE11 83 316 DM78
Dollis Ave. N3 218 305 CZ53
Dollis Brook Wk., Barn. 206 299 CY44
Dollis Cres., Ruis. 232 313 BW60
Dollis Hill Ave. NW2 94 305 CV62
Dollis Hill Est. NW2 94 305 CU62
Dollis Hill La. NW2 109 304 CT63
Dollis Ms. N3 218 305 CZ53
Dollis Pk. N3 218 305 CZ53
Dollis Rd. N3 218 305 CY53
Dollis Rd. NW7 218 305 CY52
Dollis Valley Grn. Wk. N20 207 299 DC47
Dollis Valley Grn. Wk., Barn. 206 299 CY44
Dollis Valley Way, Barn. 206 299 CZ43
Dolman Clo. N3 219 305 DC54
Dolman Rd. W4 145 314 CR77
Dolman St. SW4 177 324 DM84
Dolphin App., Rom. 227 309 FF56
Dolphin Clo. SE16 149 317 DX75
Dolphin Clo. SE28 246 319 EX72
Dolphin Clo., Surb. 282 330 CK100
Dolphin Ct. NW11 218 305 CY58
Dolphin Ct., Stai. 264 320 BG90
Dolphin Ct. N., Stai. 264 320 BG90
Dolphin Est., The, Sun. 281 328 BS95
Dolphin La. E14 140 317 EB73
Dolphin Rd., Nthlt. 242 313 BZ67
Dolphin Rd., Sun. 281 328 BS95
Dolphin Rd. N., Sun. 281 328 BS95
Dolphin Rd. S., Sun. 281 328 BR95
Dolphin Rd. W., Sun. 281 328 BS95
Dolphin Sq. SW1 81 316 DJ78
Dolphin Sq. W4 155 314 CS80
Dolphin St., Kings.T. 268 322 CL95
Dombey St. WC1 47 316 DM71
Dome Hill Pk. SE26 273 324 DT91
Domett Clo. SE5 179 324 DR84
Domfe Pl. E5 118 307 DW63
Domingo St. EC1 37 316 DQ70
Dominion Dr., Rom. 227 309 FB51
Dominion Rd., Croy. 287 332 DT101
Dominion Rd., Sthl. 250 321 BY76
Dominion St. EC2 50 316 DR71
Domonic Dr. SE9 277 326 EP91
Domville Clo. N20 207 299 DD47
Don Phelan Clo. SE5 163 316 DR81
Don Way, Rom. 227 309 FE52
Donald Dr., Rom. 226 309 EW57
Donald Rd. E13 244 318 EH67
Donald Rd., Croy. 286 332 DM100
Donald Wds. Gdns., Surb. 282 330 CP103
Donaldson Rd. NW6 127 315 CZ67
Donaldson Rd. SE18 253 318 EN81
Doncaster Dr., Nthlt. 232 313 BZ64
Doncaster Gdns. N4 221 306 DQ58
Doncaster Gdns., Nthlt. 232 313 BZ64
Doncaster Rd. N9 210 301 DV45
Doncaster Way, Upmin. 238 311 FM62
Doncel Ct. E4 211 301 ED45
Donegal St. N1 23 316 DM68
Doneraile St. SW6 157 315 CX82
Dongola Rd. E13 244 318 EH69
Dongola Rd. N17 221 306 DS55
Dongola Rd. W. E13 244 318 EH69
Donington Ave., Ilf. 225 308 EQ57
Donkey All. SE22 196 325 DU87
Donkey La., Enf. 203 301 DU40
Donne Ct. SE24 178 324 DQ86
Donne Pl. SW3 78/9 315 DE77
Donne Pl., Mitch. 272 324 DH98
Donne Rd., Dag. 236 309 EW61
Donnefield Ave., Edg. 216 304 CL52
Donnington Rd. NW10 110 305 CV66
Donnington Rd., Har. 216 304 CJ57
Donnington Rd., Wor.Pk. 283 331 CU103
Donnybrook Rd. SW16 272 324 DJ94
Donovan Ave. N10 220 306 DH55
Doon St. SE1 60 316 DN74
Doone Clo., Tedd. 268 322 CG93
Dora Rd. SW19 271 323 DA92
Dora St. E14 139 317 DZ72
Doral Way, Cars. 285 331 DF106
Doran Gro. SE18 253 318 ES80
Doran Mans. N2 219 305 DF57
Doran Wk. E15 120 307 EC66
Dorchester Ave. N13 209 300 DQ49
Dorchester Ave., Bex. 262 327 EX88
Dorchester Ave., Har. 215 303 CC58
Dorchester Clo., Nthlt. 233 313 CB64
Dorchester Clo., Orp. 278 327 EU94
Dorchester Ct. N14 208 300 DH45
Dorchester Ct. SE24 178 324 DQ85
Dorchester Dr. SE24 178 324 DQ85
Dorchester Dr., Felt. 257 320 BS86
Dorchester Gdns. E4 211 301 EA49
Dorchester Gdns. NW11 219 305 DA56
Dorchester Gro. W4 145 314 CS78
Dorchester Ms., N.Mal. 269 322 CR98
Dorchester Ms., Twick. 184 322 CJ87
Dorchester Rd., Mord. 284 331 DB101
Dorchester Rd., Nthlt. 233 313 CB64
Dorchester Rd., Wor.Pk. 284 331 CW102
Dorchester Way, Har. 216 304 CM58
Dorchester Waye, Hayes 242 313 BV72
Dorcis Ave., Bexh. 254 319 EY82
Dordrecht Rd. W3 135 314 CS74
Dore Ave. E12 235 308 EN64
Dore Gdns., Mord. 284 331 DB101
Doreen Ave. NW9 93 304 CR60
Dorell Clo., Sthl. 242 313 BZ71
Doria Rd. SW6 157 315 CZ82
Dorian Rd., Horn. 238 310 FG60
Doric Way NW1 34 316 DK69
Dorien Rd. SW20 270 323 CX96
Doris Ave., Erith 255 319 FC81
Doris Rd. E7 234 308 EG66
Doris Rd., Ashf. 265 328 BR93
Dorking Clo. SE8 165 317 DZ79
Dorking Clo., Wor.Pk. 284 331 CX103
Dorkins Way, Upmin. 239 311 FS59
Dorlcote Rd. SW18 191 323 DE87
Dorly Clo., Shep. 281 328 BS98
Dorma Trd. Est. E10 103 307 DX60
Dorman Pl. N9 210 301 DU47
Dorman Wk. NW10 109 304 CR64
Dorman Way NW8 18 315 DD67
Dormans Clo., Nthwd. 213 302 BR52
Dormay St. SW18 174 323 DB85
Dormer Clo. E15 121 307 EF65
Dormer Clo., Barn. 206 299 CX43
Dormers Ave., Sthl. 243 313 CA72
Dormers Ri., Sthl. 243 313 CB73
Dormers Wells La., Sthl. 243 313 CA72
Dormywood, Ruis. 231 302 BT57
Dornberg Clo. SE3 252 318 EG80
Dornberg Rd. SE3 252 318 EH80
Dorncliffe Rd. SW6 157 315 CY82
Dorney NW3 113 305 DE66
Dorney Ri., Orp. 277 326 ET98
Dorney Way, Houns. 258 321 BY85
Dornfell St. NW6 111 305 CZ64
Dornton Rd. SW12 192 324 DH89
Dornton Rd., S.Croy. 287 332 DR106
Dorothy Ave., Wem. 107 304 CL66
Dorothy Evans Clo., Bexh. 263 327 FB84
Dorothy Gdns., Dag. 236 309 EV63
Dorothy Rd. SW11 175 323 DF83
Dorrell Pl. SW9 178 324 DN84
Dorrien Wk. SW16 193 324 DK89
Dorrington Ct. SE25 273 324 DS96
Dorrington Gdns., Horn. 238 310 FK60
Dorrington Pt. E3 130 317 EB69
Dorrington St. EC1 48 316 DN71
Dorrit Ms. N18 209 300 DS50
Dorrit Way, Chis. 277 326 EQ93
Dors Clo. NW9 93 304 CR60
Dorset Ave., Hayes 241 312 BS69
Dorset Ave., Rom. 227 309 FD56
Dorset Ave., Sthl. 251 321 CA77
Dorset Ave., Well. 261 326 ET84
Dorset Bldgs. EC4 48/9 316 DP72
Dorset Clo. NW1 43 315 DF71
Dorset Clo., Hayes 241 312 BS69
Dorset Dr., Edg. 216 304 CM51
Dorset Est. E2 39 316 DT69
Dorset Gdns., Mitch. 272 324 DM98
Dorset Ms. N3 219 305 DA53
Dorset Ms. SW1 68/9 316 DH76
Dorset Pl. E15 121 307 ED65
Dorset Pl. SW1 82 316 DK78
Dorset Ri. EC4 48/9 316 DP72
Dorset Rd. E7 234 308 EJ66
Dorset Rd. N15 221 306 DR56
Dorset Rd. N22 220 306 DL53
Dorset Rd. SE9 260 326 EL89
Dorset Rd. SW8 161 316 DL80
Dorset Rd. SW19 271 323 DA95
Dorset Rd. W5 142 314 CJ76
Dorset Rd., Ashf. 264 320 BK90
Dorset Rd., Beck. 274 325 DX97
Dorset Rd., Har. 215 303 CC58
Dorset Rd., Mitch. 271 323 DE96
Dorset Rd., Sutt. 292 331 DA110
Dorset Sq. NW1 31 315 DF70
Dorset St. W1 43 315 DF71
Dorset Way, Twick. 259 321 CD88
Dorset Way, Uxb. 240 312 BM68
Dorset Waye, Houns. 250 321 BZ80
Dorville Cres. W6 146 315 CV76
Dorville Rd. SE12 183 325 EF85
Dothill Rd. SE18 253 318 ER80
Douai Gro., Hmptn. 267 329 CC95
Doughty Ms. WC1 35 316 DM70
Doughty St. WC1 35 316 DM70
Douglas Ave. E17 223 307 EA53
Douglas Ave., N.Mal. 270 323 CV98
Douglas Ave., Rom. 228 311 FL54
Douglas Ave., Wem. 107 304 CL66
Douglas Clo., Stan. 204 298 CG50
Douglas Clo., Wall. 294 332 DL107
Douglas Cres., Hayes 242 313 BW70
Douglas Dr., Croy. 288 333 EA104
Douglas Est. N1 116 306 DQ65
Douglas Ms. NW2 95 305 CY62
Douglas Pl. E14 150 317 EC78
Douglas Rd. E4 211 301 EE45
Douglas Rd. E16 244 318 EG71
Douglas Rd. N1 116 306 DQ66
Douglas Rd. N22 221 306 DN53
Douglas Rd. NW6 127 315 CZ67
Douglas Rd., Horn. 227 309 FF58
Douglas Rd., Houns. 259 321 CB83
Douglas Rd., Ilf. 236 309 EU59
Douglas Rd., Kings.T. 269 322 CP96
Douglas Rd., Stai. 256 320 BK86
Douglas Rd., Surb. 282 330 CM103
Douglas Rd., Well. 254 319 EV81
Douglas Sq., Mord. 284 331 DA100
Douglas St. SW1 82 316 DK77
Douglas Ter. E17 223 307 EA53
Douglas Way SE8 165 317 DZ80
Doulton Ms. NW6 112 305 DB65
Doultons, The, Stai. 264 328 BG94
Dounesforth Gdns. SW18 190 323 DB88
Douro Pl. W8 64/5 315 DB76
Douro St. E3 130 317 EA68
Douthwaite Sq. E1 138 317 DU74
Dove App. E6 244 318 EL71
Dove Clo., Nthlt. 242 313 BX70
Dove Ct. EC2 50 316 DR72
Dove Ho. Gdns. E4 211 301 EA47
Dove Ms. SW5 77 315 DC77
Dove Pk., Pnr. 215 303 CA52
Dove Rd. N1 117 306 DR65
Dove Row E2 128 317 DU67
Dove Wk. SW1 80 316 DG78
Dove Wk., Horn. 238 310 FH65
Dovecot Clo., Pnr. 214 303 BV57
Dovecote Ave. N22 221 306 DN55
Dovecote Gdns. SW14 171 322 CR83
Dovecott Gdns. SW14 171 322 CR83
Dovedale Ave., Har. 216 304 CJ58
Dovedale Ave., Ilf. 225 308 EN54
Dovedale Clo., Uxb. 212 302 BJ54
Dovedale Clo., Well. 254 319 EU81
Dovedale Ri., Mitch. 271 323 DF94
Dovedale Rd. SE22 180 325 DV85
Dovedon Clo. N14 208 300 DL47
Dovehouse Mead, Bark. 245 318 ER68
Dovehouse St. SW3 78 315 DD78
Doveney Clo., Orp. 278 327 EW97
Dover Clo. NW2 95 305 CX61
Dover Clo., Rom. 227 309 FC54
Dover Flats SE1 86/7 316 DS77
Dover Gdns., Cars. 285 331 DF104
Dover Ho. Rd. SW15 172 323 CU84
Dover Pk. Dr. SW15 172 323 CV86
Dover Rd. E12 234 308 EJ61
Dover Rd. N9 210 301 DW47
Dover Rd. SE19 273 324 DR93
Dover Rd., Rom. 226 309 EY58
Dover St. W1 56/7 316 DH73
Dover Yd. W1 56/7 316 DH74
Dovercourt Ave., Th.Hth. 286 332 DN99
Dovercourt Est. N1 117 306 DR65
Dovercourt Gdns., Stan. 204 298 CL50
Dovercourt La., Sutt. 285 331 DC104
Dovercourt Rd. SE22 179 324 DS86
Doverfield Rd. SW2 177 324 DL86
Doveridge Gdns. N13 209 300 DP49
Doves Clo., Brom. 290 334 EL103
Doveton Rd., S.Croy. 287 332 DR106
Doveton St. E1 128 317 DW70
Dowanhill Rd. SE6 199 325 ED88
Dowdeswell Clo. SW15 171 322 CS84
Dowding Pl., Stan. 216 304 CG51
Dowding Rd., Uxb. 240 312 BM66
Dowding Way, Horn. 238 310 FH66
Dower Ave., Wall. 293 332 DH109
Dowgate Hill EC4 62 316 DR73
Dowland St. W10 127 315 CY69
Dowlas Est. SE5 163 316 DS80
Dowlas St. SE5 163 316 DS80
Dowman Clo. SW19 271 323 DB95
Down Clo., Nthlt. 242 313 BV68
Down Hall Rd., Kings.T. 268 322 CK95
Down Pl. W6 146 315 CV78
Down Rd., Tedd. 268 322 CH93
Down St. W1 56/7 316 DH74
Down St. Ms. W1 56/7 316 DH74
Down Way, Nthlt. 242 313 BV69
Downage NW4 218 305 CW55
Downbank Ave., Bexh. 255 319 FD81
Downbarns Rd., Ruis. 232 313 BX62
Downbury Ms. SW18 174 323 DA86
Downderry Rd., Brom. 199 325 ED90
Downe Clo., Well. 254 319 EW80
Downe Rd., Mitch. 271 323 DF96
Downend SE18 253 318 EP80
Downers Cotts. SW4 176 324 DJ84
Downes Clo., Twick. 168 322 CH86
Downes Ct. N21 209 300 DN46
Downfield, Wor.Pk. 283 330 CT102
Downfield Clo. W9 28/9 315 DB70
Downham Clo., Rom. 227 309 FA52
Downham La., Brom. 275 325 ED92
Downham Rd. N1 117 306 DR66
Downham Way, Brom. 275 325 ED92
Downhills Ave. N17 221 306 DR55
Downhills Pk. Rd. N17 221 306 DQ55
Downhills Way N17 221 306 DQ54
Downhurst Ave. NW7 205 298 CR50
Downing Clo., Har. 215 303 CC55
Downing Dr., Grnf. 243 313 CD67
Downing Rd., Dag. 246 319 EZ67
Downing St. SW1 70/1 316 DL75
Downings E6 245 318 EN72
Downland Clo. N20 207 299 DC46
Downland Clo., Couls. 293 332 DH114
Downlands Rd., Pur. 294 332 DL114
Downleys Clo. SE9 260 326 EL89
Downman Rd. SE9 260 326 EL83
Downs, The SW20 270 323 CX94
Downs Ave., Chis. 276 326 EM92
Downs Ave., Pnr. 214 303 BZ58
Downs Bri. Rd., Beck. 275 325 ED95
Downs Ct. Rd., Pur. 294 332 DP112
Downs Hill, Beck. 275 325 ED94
Downs La. E5 118 307 DV63
Downs Pk. Rd. E5 118 307 DU64
Downs Pk. Rd. E8 117 306 DT64
Downs Rd. E5 118 307 DU63
Downs Rd., Beck. 275 325 EB96
Downs Rd., Enf. 202 300 DS42
Downs Rd., Pur. 294 332 DP111
Downs Rd., Sutt. 292 331 DB110
Downs Rd., Th.Hth. 273 324 DQ95
Downs Side, Sutt. 292 331 CZ111
Downs Vw., Islw. 251 321 CF81
Downs Way, Orp. 291 334 ES106
Downsbury Ms. SW18 174 323 DA85
Downsell Rd. E15 120 307 EC63
Downsfield Rd. E17 222 307 DY58
Downshall Ave., Ilf. 225 308 ES58
Downshire Hill NW3 113 305 DD63
Downside, Sun. 266 329 BU95
Downside, Twick. 259 321 CF90
Downside Clo. SW19 271 323 DC93
Downside Cres. NW3 113 305 DE64
Downside Cres. W13 122 314 CG70
Downside Rd., Sutt. 293 331 DD107
Downside Wk., Nthlt. 242 313 BZ69
Downsview Clo., Swan. 279 327 FF97
Downsview Gdns. SE19 273 324 DQ94
Downsview Rd. SE19 273 324 DQ94
Downsway, Orp. 291 334 ES106
Downsway, S.Croy. 295 332 DS111
Downsway, The, Sutt. 293 331 DC109
Downton Ave. SW2 193 324 DL89
Downtown Rd. SE16 149 317 DY75
Downway N12 219 305 DE52
Dowrey St. N1 24 316 DN67
Dowsett Rd. N17 221 306 DT54
Dowson Clo. SE5 179 324 DR84
Doyce St. SE1 73 316 DQ75
Doyle Clo., Erith 255 319 FE81
Doyle Gdns. NW10 126 315 CU67
Doyle Rd. SE25 274 325 DU98
D'Oyley St. SW1 80 316 DG77
Doynton St. N19 98 306 DH61
Draco St. SE17 162 316 DQ79
Dragmire La., Mitch. 271 323 DD97
Dragonfly Clo. E13 244 318 EH69
Dragoon Rd. SE8 149 317 DZ78
Dragor Rd. NW10 124 314 CQ70
Drake Clo. SE16 149 317 DX75
Drake Ct. SE19 273 324 DT92
Drake Ct., Har. 232 313 BZ60
Drake Cres. SE28 246 319 EW72
Drake Ms., Horn. 238 310 FG66
Drake Rd. SE4 182 325 EA83
Drake Rd., Chess. 282 330 CN106
Drake Rd., Croy. 286 332 DM101
Drake Rd., Har. 232 313 BZ61
Drake Rd., Mitch. 285 332 DG100
Drake St. WC1 47 316 DM71
Drake St., Enf. 202 300 DR39
Drakefell Rd. SE4 181 325 DY83
Drakefell Rd. SE14 165 317 DX82
Drakefield Rd. SW17 192 324 DG90
Drakeley Ct. N5 116 306 DP63
Drakes Ctyd. NW6 111 305 CZ66
Drakes Dr., Nthwd. 213 302 BP53
Drakes Wk. E6 245 318 EN67
Drakewood Rd. SW16 272 324 DK94
Draper Clo., Belv. 254 319 EZ77
Draper Pl. N1 24/5 316 DP67
Drapers Gdns. EC2 50 316 DR72
Drapers Rd. E15 121 307 ED63
Drapers Rd. N17 221 306 DT55
Drapers Rd., Enf. 202 300 DP40
Drappers Way SE16 148 317 DU77
Drawdock Rd. SE10 141 317 ED74
Drawell Clo. SE18 253 318 ES78
Drax Ave. SW20 270 323 CU94
Draxmont SW19 270 323 CY93
Dray Gdns. SW2 177 324 DM85
Draycot Rd. E11 224 308 EH58
Draycot Rd., Surb. 282 330 CN102
Draycott Ave. SW3 78/9 315 DE77
Draycott Ave., Har. 216 304 CH58
Draycott Clo., Har. 216 304 CH58
Draycott Ms. SW6 157 315 CZ82
Draycott Pl. SW3 79 315 DF77
Draycott Ter. SW3 79 315 DF77
Drayford Clo. W9 127 315 CZ70
Draymans Way, Islw. 259 321 CF83
Drayside Ms., Sthl. 250 321 BZ75
Drayson Ms. W8 64 315 DA75
Drayton Ave. W13 132 314 CG73
Drayton Ave., Orp. 290 334 EP102
Drayton Bri. Rd. W7 243 313 CF73
Drayton Bri. Rd. W13 132 314 CG72
Drayton Clo., Houns. 258 321 BZ85
Drayton Clo., Ilf. 235 308 ER60
Drayton Gdns. N21 209 300 DP45
Drayton Gdns. SW10 77 315 DC78
Drayton Gdns. W13 132 314 CG73
Drayton Gdns., West Dr. 248 320 BK75
Drayton Grn. W13 132 314 CG73
Drayton Grn. Rd. W13 132 314 CH73
Drayton Gro. W13 132 314 CG73
Drayton Pk. N5 116 306 DN64
Drayton Pk. Ms. N5 116 306 DN64
Drayton Rd. E11 105 307 ED60
Drayton Rd. N17 221 306 DS54
Drayton Rd. NW10 125 314 CT67
Drayton Rd. W13 132 314 CG73
Drayton Rd., Croy. 286 332 DP103
Drayton Waye, Har. 216 304 CH58
Dreadnought St. SE10 151 317 EE76
Drenon Sq., Hayes 249 312 BT73
Dresden Clo. NW6 112 305 DB65
Dresden Rd. N19 98 306 DJ60
Dressington Ave. SE4 182 325 EA86
Drew Ave. NW7 218 305 CY51
Drew Gdns., Grnf. 233 313 CF65
Drew Rd. E16 244 318 EL74
Drewstead Rd. SW16 193 324 DK89
Driffield Rd. E3 129 317 DY68
Drift, The, Brom. 290 334 EK104
Drift Way, Rich. 185 322 CM88
Driftway, The, Mitch. 272 324 DG95
Drill Hall Rd., Cher. 280 328 BG101
Drinkwater Rd., Har. 233 313 CB61
Drive, The E4 211 301 ED45
Drive, The E17 223 307 EB55
Drive, The E18 224 308 EG56
Drive, The N3 219 305 DA52
Drive, The N6 219 305 DF57
Drive, The N11 220 306 DJ51
Drive, The NW10 125 314 CT67
Drive, The NW11 95 305 CY59
Drive, The SW6 157 315 CY82
Drive, The SW16 272 324 DM97
Drive, The SW20 270 323 CW94
Drive, The W3 134 314 CQ72
Drive, The, Ashf. 265 328 BR94
Drive, The, Bark. 235 308 ET66
Drive, The (New Barnet), Barn. 207 299 DC44
Drive, The, Beck. 275 325 EA96
Drive, The, Bex. 262 327 EW86
Drive, The, Chis. 277 326 ET97
Drive, The, Couls. 294 332 DL114
Drive, The, Edg. 205 298 CN50
Drive, The, Enf. 202 300 DR39
Drive, The, Erith 255 319 FB80
Drive, The, Felt. 258 321 BW87
Drive, The, Har. 233 313 CA59
Drive, The, Houns. 251 321 CC82
Drive, The, Ilf. 224 308 EL58
Drive, The, Islw. 251 321 CD82
Drive, The, Kings.T. 269 322 CQ94
Drive, The, Mord. 285 331 DC99
Drive, The, Nthwd. 213 302 BS54
Drive, The, Orp. 291 334 ET103
Drive, The, Rom. 227 309 FC53
Drive, The (Harold Wd.), Rom. 228 311 FL53
Drive, The, Sid. 262 327 EV90
Drive, The, Surb. 282 330 CL101
Drive, The, Sutt. 292 331 CZ112
Drive, The, Th.Hth. 273 324 DR98
Drive, The, Uxb. 240 312 BL63
Drive, The, Wall. 294 332 DJ110
Drive, The, Wem. 92 304 CQ61
Drive, The, W.Wick. 289 333 ED101
Drive Mead, Couls. 294 332 DL114
Driveway, The E17 223 307 EB58
Droitwich Clo. SE26 196 325 DU90
Dromey Gdns., Har. 215 303 CF52
Dromore Rd. SW15 173 323 CY86
Dronfield Gdns., Dag. 236 309 EW64
Droop St. W10 127 315 CY70
Drover La. SE15 164 317 DV80
Drovers Pl. SE15 164 317 DV80
Drovers Rd., S.Croy. 287 332 DR106
Druce Rd. SE21 179 324 DS86
Druid St. SE1 74/5 316 DS75
Druids Way, Brom. 275 325 ED98
Drum St. E1 51 316 DT72
Drumaline Ridge, Wor.Pk. 283 330 CS103
Drummond Ave., Rom. 227 309 FD56
Drummond Clo., Erith 255 319 FE81
Drummond Cres. NW1 34 316 DK69
Drummond Dr., Stan. 215 303 CF52
Drummond Gate SW1 82 316 DK78
Drummond Pl., Rich. 169 322 CL84
Drummond Pl., Twick. 184 322 CH87
Drummond Rd. E11 224 308 EJ58
Drummond Rd. SE16 148 317 DV76
Drummond Rd., Croy. 287 332 DQ103
Drummond Rd., Rom. 227 309 FD56
Drummond St. NW1 33 316 DJ70
Drummonds Pl., Rich. 169 322 CL84
Drury Cres., Croy. 286 332 DN103
Drury Ind. Est. NW10 108 304 CQ64
Drury La. WC2 46/7 316 DL72
Drury Rd., Har. 233 313 CC59
Drury Way NW10 109 304 CR64
Dryad St. SW15 173 323 CX83
Dryburgh Gdns. NW9 217 304 CN55
Dryburgh Rd. SW15 172 323 CV83
Dryden Ave. W7 243 313 CF72
Dryden Clo., Ilf. 225 308 ET51
Dryden Ct. SE11 84 316 DN77
Dryden Rd. SW19 271 323 DC93
Dryden Rd., Enf. 209 300 DS44
Dryden Rd., Har. 233 313 CF63
Dryden Rd., Well. 253 318 ES81
Dryden St. WC2 46/7 316 DL72
Dryden Twrs., Rom. 228 310 FH52

Dryden Way, Orp.	291	335	EU102
Dryfield Clo. NW10	108	304	CQ65
Dryfield Rd., Edg.	217	304	CQ51
Dryfield Wk. SE8	166	317	EA79
Dryhill Rd., Belv.	254	319	EZ79
Dryland Ave., Orp.	291	334	ET105
Drylands Rd. N8	220	306	DL58
Drysdale Ave. E4	211	301	EB45
Drysdale Clo., Nthwd.	213	302	BS52
Drysdale Pl. N1	38/9	316	DS69
Drysdale St. N1	38/9	316	DS69
Du Burstow Ter. W7	251	321	CE75
Du Cane Clo. W12	136	315	CW72
Du Cane Ct. SW17	192	324	DG88
Du Cane Rd. W12	135	314	CT72
Du Cros Dr., Stan.	216	304	CK51
Du Cros Rd. W3	135	314	CS74
Dublin Ave. E8	128	317	DU67
Ducal St. E2	39	316	DT69
Duchess Clo. N11	208	300	DH50
Duchess Ms. W1	44/5	316	DH71
Duchess of Bedford's Wk. W8	64	315	DA75
Duchess St. W1	44/5	316	DH71
Duchy St. SE1	60	316	DN74
Ducie St. SW4	177	324	DM84
Duck La. W1	46	316	DK72
Duck Lees La., Enf.	203	301	DY42
Duckett Ms. N4	221	306	DP58
Duckett Rd. N4	221	306	DN58
Duckett St. E1	129	317	DX70
Ducketts Rd., Dart.	263	327	FF85
Ducking Stool Ct., Rom.	227	309	FE56
Ducks Hill, Nthwd.	213	302	BN54
Ducks Hill Rd., Nthwd.	213	302	BP54
Ducks Hill Rd., Ruis.	213	302	BP54
Ducks Wk., Twick.	168	322	CJ85
Dudden Hill La. NW10	109	304	CT63
Duddington Clo. SE9	276	326	EK91
Dudley Ave., Har.	216	304	CJ55
Dudley Ct. NW11	218	305	CZ56
Dudley Dr., Mord.	284	331	CY102
Dudley Dr., Ruis.	232	313	BV64
Dudley Gdns. W13	142	314	CH75
Dudley Gdns., Har.	233	313	CD60
Dudley Gdns., Rom.	228	310	FK51
Dudley Rd. E17	223	307	EA54
Dudley Rd. N3	219	305	DB54
Dudley Rd. NW6	127	315	CY68
Dudley Rd. SW19	271	323	DA93
Dudley Rd., Ashf.	264	328	BL92
Dudley Rd., Felt.	265	320	BQ88
Dudley Rd., Har.	233	313	CC61
Dudley Rd., Ilf.	235	308	EP63
Dudley Rd., Kings.T.	268	322	CM97
Dudley Rd., Rich.	153	314	CM82
Dudley Rd., Rom.	228	310	FK51
Dudley Rd., Sthl.	250	321	BX75
Dudley St. W2	42	315	DD71
Dudlington Rd. E5	102	307	DW61
Dudmaston Ms. SW3	78	315	DD78
Dudsbury Rd., Sid.	278	327	EV93
Dudset La., Houns.	250	321	BU81
Duff St. E14	140	317	EB72
Dufferin Ave. EC1	38	316	DR70
Dufferin St. EC1	37	316	DQ70
Duffield Clo., Har.	215	303	CF57
Duffield Dr. N15	221	306	DT56
Dufour's Pl. W1	45	316	DJ72
Duke Gdns., Ilf.	225	308	ER56
Duke Hill Rd. SE1	60/1	316	DP74
Duke Humphrey Rd. SE3	167	317	EE81
Duke of Cambridge Clo., Twick.	259	321	CD86
Duke of Edinburgh Rd., Sutt.	285	331	DD103
Duke of Wellington Pl. SW1	68	316	DG75
Duke of York St. SW1	57	316	DJ74
Duke Rd. W4	145	314	CR78
Duke Rd., Ilf.	225	308	ER56
Duke Shore Pl. E14	139	317	DZ73
Duke St. SW1	57	316	DJ74
Duke St. W1	44	316	DG72
Duke St., Rich.	169	322	CK85
Duke St., Sutt.	285	331	DD105
Duke St. Hill SE1	62	316	DR74
Dukes Ave. N3	219	305	DB53
Dukes Ave. N10	220	306	DJ55
Dukes Ave. W4	145	314	CR78
Dukes Ave., Edg.	216	304	CM51
Dukes Ave., Har.	214	303	BZ58
Dukes Ave. (Wealdstone), Har.	215	303	CE56
Dukes Ave., Houns.	258	321	BY84
Dukes Ave., Kings.T.	268	322	CJ91
Dukes Ave., N.Mal.	269	322	CT97
Dukes Ave., Nthlt.	232	313	BY66
Dukes Ave., Rich.	268	322	CJ91
Dukes Clo., Ashf.	265	328	BQ91
Dukes Clo., Hmptn.	266	329	BZ92
Dukes Clo., Kings.T.	268	322	CK91
Dukes Ct. E6	245	318	EN67
Dukes Grn. Ave., Felt.	258	321	BU85
Dukes La. W8	64/5	315	DB75
Dukes Lo., Nthwd.	213	302	BS50
Duke's Meadows W4	154	314	CQ82
Dukes Ms. N10	220	306	DH55
Duke's Ms. W1	44	316	DG72
Dukes Orchard, Bex.	263	327	FC88
Duke's Pas. E17	223	307	EC55
Dukes Pl. EC3	50/1	316	DS72
Dukes Ride, Uxb.	240	312	BL63
Dukes Rd. E6	245	318	EN67
Dukes Rd. W3	124	314	CN70
Duke's Rd. WC1	34	316	DK69
Dukes Way, W.Wick.	289	333	EE104
Duke's Yd. W1	56	316	DG73
Dukesthorpe Rd. SE26	274	325	DX91
Dulas St. N4	99	306	DM60
Dulford St. W11	137	315	CY73
Dulka Rd. SW11	175	323	DF85
Dulverton Rd. SE9	261	326	EQ89
Dulverton Rd., Rom.	228	310	FK51
Dulverton Rd., Ruis.	232	313	BU60
Dulwich Common SE21	195	324	DS88
Dulwich Common SE22	195	324	DT88
Dulwich Lawn Clo. SE22	179	324	DT85
Dulwich Oaks, The SE21	195	324	DT90
Dulwich Rd. SE24	178	324	DN85
Dulwich Village SE21	179	324	DS86
Dulwich Wd. Ave. SE19	273	324	DS91
Dulwich Wd. Pk. SE19	273	324	DS91
Dumbarton Rd. SW2	177	324	DL86
Dumbleton Clo., Kings.T.	269	322	CP95
Dumbreck Rd. SE9	260	326	EM84
Dumfries Clo., Wat.	213	302	BT48
Dumont Rd. N16	101	306	DS62
Dumpton Pl. NW1	114	306	DG66
Dunally Pk., Shep.	281	328	BR101
Dunbar Ave. SW16	273	324	DN96
Dunbar Ave., Beck.	274	325	DY98
Dunbar Ave., Dag.	237	309	FA62
Dunbar Clo., Hayes	242	313	BU71
Dunbar Ct., Sutt.	285	331	DD106
Dunbar Gdns., Dag.	237	309	FA64
Dunbar Rd. E7	234	308	EG65
Dunbar Rd. N22	221	306	DN53
Dunbar Rd., N.Mal.	269	322	CQ98
Dunbar St. SE27	194	324	DQ90
Dunblane Clo., Edg.	205	298	CP47
Dunblane Rd. SE9	252	318	EL82
Dunboe Pl., Shep.	281	328	BQ101
Dunboyne Rd. NW3	113	305	DF64
Dunbridge St. E2	128	317	DU70
Duncan Gro. W3	135	314	CS72
Duncan Rd. E8	128	317	DV67
Duncan Rd., Rich.	169	322	CL84
Duncan St. N1	24/5	316	DP68
Duncan Ter. N1	24/5	316	DP68
Duncannon St. WC2	58/9	316	DL73
Dunch St. E1	138	317	DV72
Duncombe Hill SE23	197	325	DY87
Duncombe Rd. N19	99	306	DK60
Duncrievie Rd. SE13	183	325	ED86
Duncroft SE18	253	318	ES80
Dundalk Rd. SE4	181	325	DY83
Dundas Gdns., W.Mol.	267	329	CB97
Dundas Rd. SE15	164	317	DW82
Dundee Rd. E13	244	318	EH68
Dundee Rd. SE25	287	333	DV99
Dundee St. E1	138	317	DV74
Dundela Gdns., Wor.Pk.	283	331	CV105
Dundonald Clo. E6	244	318	EL72
Dundonald Rd. NW10	127	315	CX67
Dundonald Rd. SW19	270	323	CY94
Dunedin Rd. E10	104	307	EB62
Dunedin Rd., Ilf.	235	308	EQ60
Dunedin Rd., Rain.	247	319	FE69
Dunedin Way, Hayes	242	313	BW70
Dunelm Gro. SE27	273	324	DQ91
Dunelm St. E1	139	317	DX72
Dunfield Gdns. SE6	275	325	EB92
Dunfield Rd. SE6	275	325	EB92
Dunford Rd. N7	115	306	DM63
Dungarvan Ave. SW15	172	323	CU84
Dunheved Clo., Th.Hth.	286	332	DN100
Dunheved Rd. N., Th.Hth.	286	332	DN100
Dunheved Rd. S., Th.Hth.	286	332	DN100
Dunheved Rd. W., Th.Hth.	286	332	DN100
Dunholme Grn. N9	209	300	DT48
Dunholme La. N9	209	300	DT48
Dunholme Rd. N9	209	300	DT48
Dunkeld Rd. SE25	273	324	DR98
Dunkeld Rd., Dag.	236	309	EV61
Dunkery Rd. SE9	276	326	EK91
Dunkirk St. SE27	273	324	DQ91
Dunlace Rd. E5	118	307	DW63
Dunleary Clo., Houns.	258	321	BZ87
Dunlin Ho. W13	243	313	CF70
Dunloe Ave. N17	221	306	DR55
Dunloe St. E2	27	316	DT68
Dunlop Pl. SE16	75	316	DT76
Dunlop Pt. E16	244	318	EG74
Dunmail Dr., Pur.	295	332	DS114
Dunmore Pt. E2	39	316	DT69
Dunmore Rd. NW6	127	315	CY67
Dunmore Rd. SW20	270	323	CW95
Dunmow Clo., Felt.	266	329	BX91
Dunmow Clo., Rom.	226	309	EW57
Dunmow Dr., Rain.	247	319	FF67
Dunmow Ho., Dag.	246	319	EV67
Dunmow Rd. E15	121	307	ED63
Dunmow Wk. N1	25	316	DQ67
Dunn Mead NW9	217	304	CT52
Dunn St. E8	117	306	DT64
Dunnale Cres. SE16	149	317	DY77
Dunningford Clo., Horn.	237	309	FF64
Dunnock Clo. N9	210	301	DX46
Dunnock Rd. E6	244	318	EL72
Dunns Pas. WC1	46/7	316	DL72
Dunollie Pl. NW5	114	306	DJ64
Dunollie Rd. NW5	114	306	DJ64
Dunoon Rd. SE23	196	325	DW87
Dunraven Dr., Enf.	202	300	DN40
Dunraven Rd. W12	136	315	CU74
Dunraven St. W1	55	315	DF73
Dunsany Rd. W14	147	315	CX76
Dunsbury Clo., Sutt.	292	331	DB109
Dunsfold Ri., Couls.	294	332	DK113
Dunsford Way SW15	172	323	CV86
Dunsmore Clo., Hayes	242	313	BY70
Dunsmure Rd. N16	101	306	DS60
Dunspring La., Ilf.	225	308	EP54
Dunstable Clo., Rom.	228	310	FK51
Dunstable Ms. W1	44	316	DG71
Dunstable Rd., Rich.	169	322	CL84
Dunstable Rd., Rom.	228	310	FK51
Dunstable Rd., W.Mol.	266	329	BZ98
Dunstall Rd. SW20	270	323	CV93
Dunstall Way, W.Mol.	267	329	CB97
Dunstan Clo. N2	219	305	DC55
Dunstan Rd. NW11	95	305	CZ60
Dunstans Gro. SE22	180	325	DV86
Dunstans Rd. SE22	196	325	DU87
Dunster Ave., Mord.	284	331	CX102
Dunster Clo., Rom.	227	309	FC54
Dunster Clo., Uxb.	212	302	BH53
Dunster Ct. EC3	62/3	316	DS73
Dunster Cres., Horn.	239	311	FN61
Dunster Dr. NW9	92	304	CQ60
Dunster Gdns. NW6	111	305	CZ66
Dunster Way, Har.	232	313	BY62
Dunsterville Way SE1	74	316	DR75
Dunston Rd. E8	27	316	DT67
Dunston Rd. SW11	176	324	DG83
Dunston St. E8	27	316	DT67
Dunton Clo., Surb.	282	330	CL102
Dunton Rd. E10	104	307	EB59
Dunton Rd. SE1	87	316	DT77
Dunton Rd., Rom.	227	309	FE56
Duntshill Rd. SW18	190	323	DB88
Dunvegan Clo., W.Mol.	267	329	CB98
Dunvegan Rd. SE9	260	326	EM84
Dunwich Rd., Bexh.	254	319	EZ81
Dunworth Ms. W11	137	315	CZ72
Duplex Ride SW1	67	315	DF75
Dupont Rd. SW20	270	323	CX96
Dupont St. E14	139	317	DY71
Duppas Ave., Croy.	286	332	DP105
Duppas Clo., Shep.	281	328	BR99
Duppas Hill La., Croy.	286	332	DP105
Duppas Hill Rd., Croy.	286	332	DN105
Duppas Hill Ter., Croy.	286	332	DP104
Duppas Rd., Croy.	286	332	DN104
Dupree Rd. SE7	252	318	EH78
Dura Den Clo., Beck.	275	325	EB94
Durand Clo., Cars.	285	331	DF102
Durand Gdns. SW9	161	316	DM81
Durand Way NW10	108	304	CQ66
Durands Wk. SE16	149	317	DY75
Durant St. E2	128	317	DU69
Durants Pk. Ave., Enf.	203	301	DX42
Durants Rd., Enf.	203	301	DW42
Durban Gdns., Dag.	237	309	FC66
Durban Rd. E15	131	317	EE69
Durban Rd. E17	222	307	DZ53
Durban Rd. N17	221	306	DS51
Durban Rd. SE27	273	324	DQ91
Durban Rd., Beck.	274	325	DZ96
Durban Rd., Ilf.	235	308	ES60
Durbin Rd., Chess.	282	330	CL105
Durdans Rd., Sthl.	242	313	BZ72
Durell Gdns., Dag.	236	309	EX64
Durell Rd., Dag.	236	309	EX64
Durford Cres. SW15	188	323	CV88
Durham Ave., Brom.	275	325	EF98
Durham Ave., Houns.	250	321	BZ79
Durham Ave., Rom.	228	310	FJ56
Durham Clo. SW20	270	323	CV96
Durham Hill, Brom.	275	325	EF91
Durham Ho. St. WC2	58/9	316	DL73
Durham Pl. SW3	79	315	DF78
Durham Pl., Ilf.	235	308	EQ63
Durham Ri. SE18	253	318	EQ78
Durham Rd. E12	234	308	EK63
Durham Rd. E16	131	317	EE70
Durham Rd. N2	219	305	DE55
Durham Rd. N7	99	306	DM61
Durham Rd. N9	210	301	DU47
Durham Rd. SW20	270	323	CV95
Durham Rd. W5	143	314	CK76
Durham Rd., Brom.	275	325	EF97
Durham Rd., Dag.	237	309	FC64
Durham Rd., Felt.	258	321	BW87
Durham Rd., Har.	215	303	CB57
Durham Rd., Sid.	278	327	EV92
Durham Row E1	139	317	DY71
Durham St. SE11	83	316	DM78
Durham Ter. W2	40/1	315	DB72
Durham Wf., Brent.	152	314	CJ80
Durham Yd. E2	128	317	DV69
Durley Ave., Pnr.	232	313	BY59
Durley Gdns., Orp.	291	335	EV105
Durley Rd. N16	101	306	DS59
Durlston Rd. E5	102	307	DU61
Durlston Rd., Kings.T.	268	322	CL93
Durnford St. N15	221	306	DS57
Durnford St. SE10	166	317	EC79
Durning Rd. SE19	273	324	DR92
Durnsford Ave. SW19	190	323	DA89
Durnsford Rd. N11	220	306	DK53
Durnsford Rd. SW19	190	323	DA89
Durrant Way, Orp.	291	334	ER106
Durrell Rd. SW6	157	315	CZ81
Durrell Way, Shep.	281	328	BR100
Durrington Ave. SW20	270	323	CW95
Durrington Pk. Rd. SW20	270	323	CW95
Durrington Rd. E5	119	307	DY63
Dursley Clo. SE3	252	318	EJ82
Dursley Gdns. SE3	252	318	EK81
Dursley Rd. SE3	252	318	EJ82
Durward St. E1	138	317	DV71
Durweston Ms. W1	43	315	DF71
Durweston St. W1	43	315	DF71
Dury Falls Clo., Horn.	238	311	FM60
Dutch Barn Clo., Stai.	256	320	BK86
Dutch Gdns., Kings.T.	269	322	CP93
Dutch Yd. SW18	174	323	DA85
Duthie St. E14	140	317	EC73
Dutton St. SE10	166	317	EC81
Duxberry Clo., Brom.	290	334	EL99
Duxford Clo., Horn.	238	310	FH65
Dwight Ct. SW6	157	315	CY82
Dye Ho. La. E3	130	317	EA67
Dyer's Bldgs. EC1	48	316	DN71
Dyers Hall Rd. E11	105	307	EE61
Dyers La. SW15	172	323	CV84
Dyers Way, Rom.	228	310	FH52
Dykes Way, Brom.	275	325	EF97
Dykewood Clo., Bex.	263	327	FE90
Dylan Clo., Borwd.	204	298	CK45
Dylan Rd. SE24	178	324	DP84
Dylan Rd., Belv.	255	319	FA76
Dylan Thomas Ho. N8	220	306	DM56
Dylways SE5	179	324	DR84
Dymchurch Clo., Ilf.	225	308	EN55
Dymchurch Clo., Orp.	291	334	ES105
Dymes Path SW19	189	323	CX89
Dymock St. SW6	174	323	DB83
Dymoke Rd., Horn.	237	309	FF59
Dymond Est. SW17	191	323	DE90
Dyne Rd. NW6	111	305	CY66
Dyneley Rd. SE12	276	326	EJ91
Dynevor Rd. N16	101	306	DT62
Dynevor Rd., Rich.	169	322	CL85
Dynham Rd. NW6	112	305	DA66
Dyott St. WC1	46	316	DK72
Dysart Ave., Kings.T.	268	322	CJ92
Dysart St. EC2	38/9	316	DS70
Dyson Rd. E11	223	307	EE58
Dyson Rd. E15	121	307	EF65
Dysons Rd. N18	210	301	DV50
Eade Rd. N4	100	306	DQ59
Eagans Clo. N2	219	305	DE55
Eagle Ave., Rom.	226	309	EY58
Eagle Clo. SE16	148	317	DW78
Eagle Clo., Enf.	203	301	DW42
Eagle Clo., Horn.	238	310	FH65
Eagle Clo., Wall.	294	332	DL107
Eagle Ct. EC1	48/9	316	DP71
Eagle Dr. NW9	217	304	CS54
Eagle Hill SE19	273	324	DR93
Eagle La. E11	224	308	EG56
Eagle Ms. N1	117	306	DS65
Eagle Pl. SW1	57	316	DJ73
Eagle Pl. SW7	77	315	DC78
Eagle Rd., Wem.	107	304	CK66
Eagle St. WC1	47	316	DM71
Eagle Ter., Wdf.Grn.	224	308	EH52
Eagle Wf. E14	140	317	EB71
Eagle Wf. Rd. N1	25	316	DQ68
Eaglesfield Rd. SE18	253	318	EP82
Ealdham Sq. SE9	260	326	EJ84
Ealing Downs Ct., Grnf.	122	314	CG69
Ealing Grn. W5	133	314	CK74
Ealing Pk. Gdns. W5	142	314	CJ77
Ealing Rd., Brent.	143	314	CK77
Ealing Rd., Nthlt.	243	313	CA67
Ealing Rd., Wem.	107	304	CL65
Ealing Village W5	133	314	CL72
Eamont Clo., Ruis.	231	312	BP59
Eamont St. NW8	18/9	315	DE68
Eardemont Clo., Dart.	263	327	FF84
Eardley Cres. SW5	76	315	DA78
Eardley Pt. SE18	253	318	EP77
Eardley Rd. SW16	272	324	DJ92
Eardley Rd., Belv.	255	319	FA78
Earl Clo. N11	208	300	DH50
Earl Ri. SE18	253	318	ER77
Earl Rd. SE1	87	316	DT78
Earl Rd. SW14	170	322	CQ84
Earl St. EC2	50	316	DR71
Earldom Rd. SW15	172	323	CW84
Earle Gdns., Kings.T.	268	322	CL94
Earlham Gro. E7	121	307	EF64
Earlham Gro. N22	220	306	DM52
Earlham St. WC2	46	316	DK72
Earls Ct. Gdns. SW5	76/7	315	DB77
Earls Ct. Rd. SW5	76	315	DA77
Earls Ct. Rd. W8	76	315	DA77
Earls Ct. Sq. SW5	76/7	315	DB78
Earls Cres., Har.	215	303	CE56
Earls Ter. W8	147	315	CZ76
Earls Wk. W8	64	315	DA76
Earls Wk., Dag.	236	309	EV63
Earls Way, Orp.	291	334	ET103
Earlsdown Ho., Bark.	245	318	ER68
Earlsferry Way N1	115	306	DM66
Earlsfield Rd. SW18	190	323	DC88
Earlshall Rd. SE9	260	326	EM84
Earlsmead, Har.	232	313	BZ63
Earlsmead Rd. N15	221	306	DT57
Earlsmead Rd. NW10	126	315	CW69
Earlsthorpe Ms. SW12	176	324	DG86
Earlsthorpe Rd. SE26	274	325	DX91
Earlstoke St. EC1	36/7	316	DP69
Earlston Gro. E9	128	317	DV67
Earlswood Ave., Th.Hth.	286	332	DN99
Earlswood Clo. SE10	151	317	EE78
Earlswood Gdns., Ilf.	225	308	EN55
Earlswood St. SE10	151	317	EE78
Early Ms. NW1	20/1	316	DH67
Earnshaw St. WC2	46	316	DK72
Earsby St. W14	147	315	CY77
Easby Cres., Mord.	284	331	DB100
Easebourne Rd., Dag.	236	309	EW64
Easedale Dr., Horn.	238	310	FG64
Easedale Ho., Islw.	259	321	CF85
Easley's Ms. W1	44	316	DG72
East Acton La. W3	135	314	CS73
East Arbour St. E1	139	317	DX72
East Ave. E12	234	308	EL66
East Ave. E17	223	307	EB56
East Ave., Hayes	249	320	BT75
East Ave., Sthl.	242	313	BZ73
East Ave., Wall.	286	332	DM106
East Bank N16	101	306	DS59
East Churchfield Rd. W3	135	314	CR74
East Clo. W5	124	314	CN70
East Clo., Grnf.	243	313	CC68
East Ct., Wem.	90	304	CJ61
East Cres. N11	207	299	DF49
East Cres., Enf.	209	300	DS43
East Cross Route E3	119	307	DZ66
East Dr., Cars.	293	331	DE109
East Dr., Nthwd.	213	302	BS47
East Dr., Orp.	291	335	EV100
East Duck Lees La., Enf.	203	301	DY42
East Dulwich Gro. SE22	179	324	DS85
East Dulwich Rd. SE15	180	325	DU84
East Dulwich Rd. SE22	179	324	DT84
East End Rd. N2	219	305	DB55
East End Rd. N3	218	305	CZ54
East End Way, Pnr.	214	303	BY55
East Entrance, Dag.	247	319	FB68
East Ferry Rd. E14	150	317	EB77
East Gdns. SW17	271	323	DE93
East Ham Ind. Est. E6	244	318	EK70
East Ham Manor Way E6	245	318	EN72
East Harding St. EC4	48	316	DN72
East Heath Rd. NW3	96	305	DC62
East Hill SW18	174	323	DB85
East Hill, S.Croy.	295	332	DS110
East Hill, Wem.	92	304	CN61
East Holme, Erith	255	319	FD81
East Holme, Hayes	242	313	BU74
East India Dock Rd. E14	140	317	EA72
East India Dock Wall Rd. E14	141	317	ED73
East La. SE16	148	317	DU75
East La., Kings.T.	268	322	CK97
East La., Wem.	90	304	CH62
East Mascalls SE7	252	318	EJ79
East Mead, Ruis.	232	313	BX62
East Mt. St. E1	138	317	DV71
East Pk. Clo., Rom.	226	309	EX57
East Pas. EC1	49	316	DQ71
East Pier E1	138	317	DV74
East Pl. SE27	273	324	DQ91
East Poultry Ave. EC1	48/9	316	DP71
East Ramp, Houns.	257	320	BP81
East Rd. E15	244	318	EG67
East Rd. N1	38	316	DR69
East Rd. SW19	271	323	DC93
East Rd., Barn.	208	300	DG46
East Rd., Edg.	217	304	CP53
East Rd., Enf.	203	301	DW38
East Rd., Felt.	265	320	BR87
East Rd., Kings.T.	268	322	CL95
East Rd. (Chadwell Heath), Rom.	226	309	EY57
East Rd. (Rush Grn.), Rom.	237	309	FD59
East Rd., Well.	254	319	EV82
East Rd., West Dr.	248	320	BM77
East Rochester Way SE9	261	326	ER84
East Rochester Way, Bex.	262	327	EX86
East Rochester Way, Sid.	261	326	ER84
East Row E11	224	308	EG58
East Row W10	127	315	CY70
East Sheen Ave. SW14	171	322	CR85
East Smithfield E1	63	316	DT73
East St. SE17	85	316	DQ78
East St., Bexh.	263	327	FA84
East St., Brent.	152	314	CJ80
East St., Brom.	276	326	EG96
East St., Cher.	280	328	BG101
East Surrey Gro. SE15	163	316	DT80
East Tenter St. E1	51	316	DT72
East Twrs., Pnr.	214	303	BX57
East Vw. E4	211	301	EC50
East Wk. NW7	218	305	CU52
East Wk., Barn.	208	300	DG45
East Wk., Hayes	242	313	BU74
East Way E11	224	308	EH57
East Way, Brom.	289	334	EG101
East Way, Croy.	288	333	DY103
East Way, Hayes	242	313	BU74
East Way, Ruis.	232	313	BU60
East Woodside, Bex.	262	327	EY88
Eastbank Rd., Hmptn.	267	329	CC92
Eastbourne Ave. W3	135	314	CR72
Eastbourne Gdns. SW14	170	322	CQ83
Eastbourne Ms. W2	41	315	DC72
Eastbourne Rd. E6	245	318	EN69
Eastbourne Rd. E15	131	317	EE67
Eastbourne Rd. N15	221	306	DS58
Eastbourne Rd. SW17	272	324	DG93
Eastbourne Rd. W4	154	314	CQ79
Eastbourne Rd., Brent.	143	314	CK78
Eastbourne Rd., Felt.	258	321	BX89
Eastbourne Ter. W2	41	315	DC72
Eastbournia Ave. N9	210	301	DV48
Eastbrook Ave. N9	210	301	DW45
Eastbrook Ave., Dag.	237	309	FC63
Eastbrook Dr., Rom.	237	309	FE62
Eastbrook Rd. SE3	252	318	EH81
Eastbury Ave., Bark.	245	318	ES67
Eastbury Ave., Enf.	202	300	DS39
Eastbury Ave., Nthwd.	213	302	BS50
Eastbury Clo., Nthwd.	213	302	BT50
Eastbury Ct., Bark.	245	318	ES67
Eastbury Gro. W4	145	314	CS78
Eastbury Ho., Bark.	245	318	ET67
Eastbury Pl., Nthwd.	213	302	BT50
Eastbury Rd. E6	245	318	EN70
Eastbury Rd., Kings.T.	268	322	CL94
Eastbury Rd., Nthwd.	213	302	BS50
Eastbury Rd., Orp.	291	334	ER100
Eastbury Rd., Rom.	227	309	FD58
Eastbury Sq., Bark.	245	318	ET67
Eastbury Ter. E1	129	317	DX70
Eastcastle St. W1	45	316	DJ72
Eastcheap EC3	62	316	DR73
Eastchurch Rd., Houns.	257	320	BS82
Eastcombe Ave. SE7	252	318	EH79
Eastcote, Orp.	291	334	ET102
Eastcote Ave., Grnf.	106	304	CG65
Eastcote Ave., Har.	233	313	CB61
Eastcote High Rd., Pnr.	214	303	BU58
Eastcote La., Har.	232	313	BY63
Eastcote La., Nthlt.	232	313	BZ64
Eastcote La. N., Nthlt.	232	313	BZ65
Eastcote Rd., Har.	233	313	CC62
Eastcote Rd., Pnr.	214	303	BX57
Eastcote Rd., Ruis.	231	312	BS59
Eastcote Rd., Well.	253	318	ER82
Eastcote St. SW9	161	316	DM82
Eastcote Vw., Pnr.	214	303	BW56
Eastdown Pk. SE13	183	325	ED84
Eastern Ave. E11	224	308	EH58
Eastern Ave., Cher.	280	328	BG97
Eastern Ave., Ilf.	225	308	EP58
Eastern Ave., Pnr.	232	313	BX59
Eastern Ave., Rom.	226	309	EW56
Eastern Ave. E., Rom.	227	309	FD55
Eastern Ave. W., Rom.	226	309	EY56
Eastern Ind. Est., Erith	254	319	EZ75
Eastern Pathway, Horn.	238	310	FK65
Eastern Perimeter Rd., Houns.	257	320	BS82
Eastern Rd. E13	244	318	EH68
Eastern Rd. E17	223	307	EC57
Eastern Rd. N2	219	305	DF55
Eastern Rd. N22	220	306	DL53
Eastern Rd. SE4	182	325	EA84
Eastern Rd., Rom.	227	309	FE57
Eastern Way SE2	246	319	EY74
Eastern Way SE28	254	319	EU75
Eastern Way, Erith	246	319	EY74
Easternville Gdns., Ilf.	225	308	EQ58
Eastfield Cotts., Hayes	249	320	BR78
Eastfield Gdns., Dag.	237	309	FA63
Eastfield Rd. E17	223	307	EA56
Eastfield Rd. N8	220	306	DL55
Eastfield Rd., Dag.	236	309	EZ63
Eastfield Rd., Enf.	203	301	DX38
Eastfields, Pnr.	214	303	BW57
Eastfields Rd. W3	134	314	CQ71
Eastfields Rd., Mitch.	272	324	DG96
Eastgate, Bans.	292	331	CZ114
Eastgate Clo. SE28	246	319	EX72
Eastglade, Nthwd.	213	302	BT50
Eastglade, Pnr.	214	303	BZ55
Eastham Clo., Barn.	206	299	CY43
Eastholm NW11	219	305	DB56
Eastlake Rd. SE5	162	316	DQ82
Eastlands Cres. SE21	179	324	DT86
Eastleigh Ave., Har.	233	313	CB61
Eastleigh Clo. NW2	93	304	CS62
Eastleigh Clo., Sutt.	292	331	DB108
Eastleigh Rd. E17	222	307	DZ54
Eastleigh Rd., Bexh.	255	319	FC82
Eastleigh Rd., Houns.	257	320	BT83
Eastleigh Wk. SW15	188	323	CU87
Eastleigh Way, Felt.	258	321	BU88
Eastman Rd. W3	145	314	CR75
Eastmead Ave., Grnf.	243	313	CB69
Eastmead Clo., Brom.	276	326	EL96
Eastmearn Rd. SE21	194	324	DQ89
Eastmoor Pl. SE7	252	318	EK76
Eastmoor St. SE7	252	318	EK76
Eastney Rd., Croy.	286	332	DP102
Eastney St. SE10	151	317	ED78
Eastnor Rd. SE9	261	326	EQ88
Easton St. WC1	36	316	DN69
Eastry Ave., Brom.	289	333	EF100
Eastry Rd., Erith	255	319	FA79
Eastside Rd. NW11	218	305	CZ56
Eastview Ave. SE18	253	318	ES80
Eastville Ave. NW11	218	305	CZ58
Eastway E9	119	307	DZ65
Eastway E10	120	307	EA63
Eastway, Mord.	284	331	CX99
Eastway, Wall.	286	332	DJ105
Eastwell Clo., Beck.	274	325	DY94
Eastwood Clo. E18	224	308	EG54
Eastwood Clo. N17	222	307	DV52
Eastwood Rd. E18	224	308	EG54
Eastwood Rd. N10	220	306	DG54
Eastwood Rd., Ilf.	236	309	EU59
Eastwood Rd., West Dr.	249	320	BN75
Eastwood St. SW16	272	324	DJ93
Eatington Rd. E10	223	307	ED57
Eaton Clo. SW1	80	316	DG77
Eaton Clo., Stan.	204	298	CH49
Eaton Dr. SW9	178	324	DP84
Eaton Dr., Kings.T.	269	322	CN94
Eaton Dr., Rom.	227	309	FB52
Eaton Gdns., Dag.	236	309	EY66
Eaton Gate SW1	80	316	DG77
Eaton Gate, Nthwd.	213	302	BQ51
Eaton La. SW1	68/9	316	DH76
Eaton Ms. N. SW1	68	316	DG76
Eaton Ms. S. SW1	80	316	DG77
Eaton Ms. W. SW1	80	316	DG77
Eaton Pk. Rd. N13	209	300	DN47
Eaton Pl. SW1	68	316	DG76
Eaton Ri. E11	224	308	EJ57
Eaton Ri. W5	132	314	CJ71
Eaton Rd. NW4	218	305	CW57
Eaton Rd., Enf.	202	300	DS41
Eaton Rd., Houns.	259	321	CD84
Eaton Rd., Sid.	262	327	EX89
Eaton Rd., Sutt.	293	331	DD107
Eaton Rd., Upmin.	239	311	FS61
Eaton Row SW1	68/9	316	DH76
Eaton Sq. SW1	80	316	DG77
Eaton Ter. SW1	80	316	DG77
Eaton Ter. Ms. SW1	80	316	DG77
Eaton Wk. SE15	163	316	DT80
Eatons Mead E4	211	301	EA47
Eatonville Rd. SW17	191	323	DF89
Eatonville Vil. SW17	191	323	DF89
Ebbisham Dr. SW8	161	316	DM79
Ebbisham Rd., Wor.Pk.	284	331	CW103
Ebbsfleet Rd. NW2	111	305	CY64
Ebdon Way SE3	260	326	EH83
Ebenezer St. N1	38	316	DR69
Ebenezer Wk. SW16	272	324	DJ95
Ebley Clo. SE15	163	316	DT79
Ebner St. SW18	174	323	DB85
Ebor St. E1	39	316	DT70
Ebrington Rd., Har.	216	304	CJ58
Ebsworth St. SE23	197	325	DX87
Eburne Rd. N7	99	306	DL62
Ebury Bri. SW1	80/1	316	DH78
Ebury Bri. Est. SW1	80/1	316	DH78
Ebury Bri. Rd. SW1	80	316	DG78
Ebury Clo., Kes.	290	334	EL104
Ebury Clo., Nthwd.	213	302	BQ50
Ebury Ms. SE27	194	324	DP90
Ebury Ms. SW1	80/1	316	DH77
Ebury Ms. E. SW1	68/9	316	DH76
Ebury Sq. SW1	80	316	DG77
Ebury St. SW1	80	316	DG77
Eccles Rd. SW11	175	323	DF84
Ecclesbourne Clo. N13	209	300	DN50
Ecclesbourne Gdns. N13	209	300	DN50
Ecclesbourne Rd. N1	116	306	DQ66
Ecclesbourne Rd., Th.Hth.	287	332	DQ99
Eccleston Bri. SW1	80/1	316	DH77
Eccleston Clo., Orp.	291	334	ER102
Eccleston Cres., Rom.	236	309	EU59
Eccleston Ms. SW1	68	316	DG76
Eccleston Pl. SW1	80/1	316	DH77
Eccleston Rd. W13	132	314	CG73
Eccleston Sq. SW1	80/1	316	DH77
Eccleston Sq. Ms. SW1	80/1	316	DH77
Eccleston St. SW1	80/1	316	DH77
Ecclestone Ct., Wem.	107	304	CL64
Ecclestone Pl., Wem.	107	304	CM64
Echelforde Dr., Ashf.	265	328	BN91
Echo Hts. E4	211	301	EB46
Eckersley St. E1	128	317	DU70
Eckford St. N1	24	316	DN68
Eckstein Rd. SW11	175	323	DE84
Eclipse Rd. E13	244	318	EH71
Ector Rd. SE6	199	325	EE89
Edbrooke Rd. W9	28	315	DA70
Eddiscombe Rd. SW6	157	315	CZ82
Eddy Clo., Rom.	227	309	FB58
Eddystone Rd. SE4	181	325	DY85
Eddystone Wk., Stai.	264	320	BL87
Ede Clo., Houns.	258	321	BZ83
Eden Clo. W8	64	315	DA76
Eden Clo., Bex.	279	327	FD91
Eden Clo., Wem.	123	314	CK67
Eden Gro. E17	223	307	EB57
Eden Gro. N7	115	306	DM64
Eden Ms. SW17	190	323	DC90
Eden Pk. Ave., Beck.	274	325	DY98
Eden Rd. E17	223	307	EB57
Eden Rd. SE27	273	324	DP92
Eden Rd., Beck.	274	325	DY98
Eden Rd., Bex.	279	327	FC91
Eden Rd., Croy.	287	332	DR105
Eden St., Kings.T.	268	322	CK96
Eden Wk., Kings.T.	268	322	CL96
Eden Way, Beck.	288	333	DZ99
Edenbridge Clo., Orp.	278	327	EX98
Edenbridge Rd. E9	119	307	DX66
Edenbridge Rd., Enf.	209	300	DS44
Edencourt Rd. SW16	272	324	DH93
Edendale Rd., Bexh.	255	319	FD81
Edenfield Gdns., Wor.Pk.	283	330	CT104
Edenham Way W10	137	315	CZ71
Edenhurst Ave. SW6	173	323	CZ83
Edensor Gdns. W4	155	314	CS80
Edensor Rd. W4	155	314	CS80
Edenvale Rd., Mitch.	272	324	DG94
Edenvale St. SW6	158	315	DB82
Ederline Ave. SW16	272	324	DM97
Edgar Clo., Swan.	279	327	FF97
Edgar Kail Way SE22	179	324	DS84
Edgar Rd. E3	130	317	EB69
Edgar Rd., Houns.	258	321	BZ87
Edgar Rd., Rom.	236	309	EX59
Edgar Rd., S.Croy.	295	332	DR110
Edgar Rd., West Dr.	248	312	BL73
Edgarley Ter. SW6	157	315	CY81
Edge Hill SE18	253	318	EP79
Edge Hill SW19	270	323	CX94
Edge Hill Ave. N3	219	305	DA56
Edge Hill Ct. SW19	270	323	CX94
Edge St. W8	52	315	DA74
Edgeborough Way, Brom.	276	326	EK94
Edgebury, Chis.	277	326	EP91
Edgebury Wk., Chis.	277	326	EQ91
Edgecombe Ho. SW19	189	323	CY88
Edgecoombe Clo., Kings.T.	269	322	CR94
Edgecot Gro. N15	221	306	DR57
Edgecote Clo. W3	134	314	CQ74
Edgefield Ave., Bark.	235	308	ET66
Edgehill Gdns., Dag.	237	309	FA63
Edgehill Rd. W13	132	314	CJ71
Edgehill Rd., Chis.	261	326	EQ90
Edgehill Rd., Mitch.	272	324	DH95
Edgehill Rd., Pur.	294	332	DN110
Edgel St. SW18	174	323	DB84
Edgeley La. SW4	177	324	DK83
Edgeley Rd. SW4	177	324	DK83
Edgepoint Clo. SE27	273	324	DP92
Edgewood Dr., Orp.	291	334	ET106
Edgewood Grn., Croy.	288	333	DX102
Edgeworth Ave. NW4	218	305	CU57
Edgeworth Clo. NW4	218	305	CU57
Edgeworth Cres. NW4	218	305	CU57
Edgeworth Rd. SE9	260	326	EJ84
Edgington Rd. SW16	272	324	DK93
Edgington Way, Sid.	278	327	EW94
Edgware Ct., Edg.	217	304	CN51
Edgware Rd. NW2	94	305	CV60
Edgware Rd. NW9	217	304	CQ54
Edgware Rd. W2	30	315	DD70
Edgware Way, Edg.	204	298	CM49
Edgwarebury Gdns., Edg.	205	298	CN50
Edgwarebury La., Borwd.	204	298	CL45
Edgwarebury La., Edg.	205	298	CN47
Edinburgh Clo. E2	128	317	DW68
Edinburgh Clo., Uxb.	241	312	BP63
Edinburgh Ct. SW20	284	331	CX99
Edinburgh Dr., Rom.	227	309	FC56
Edinburgh Dr., Stai.	264	328	BK93
Edinburgh Dr. (Ickenham), Uxb.	241	312	BP63
Edinburgh Gate SW1	67	315	DF75
Edinburgh Ho. W9	28/9	315	DB69
Edinburgh Rd. E13	244	318	EH68
Edinburgh Rd. E17	223	307	EA57
Edinburgh Rd. N18	210	301	DU50
Edinburgh Rd. W7	251	321	CF75
Edinburgh Rd., Sutt.	285	331	DC103
Edington Rd. SE2	254	319	EV76
Edington Rd., Enf.	203	301	DW40
Edis St. NW1	20	316	DG67
Edison Ave., Horn.	237	309	FF60

Edison Clo. E17	223	307	EA57
Edison Clo., Horn.	237	309	FF60
Edison Dr., Sthl.	243	313	CB72
Edison Gro. SE18	253	318	ET80
Edison Rd. N8	220	306	DK58
Edison Rd., Brom.	276	326	EG96
Edison Rd., Enf.	203	301	DZ40
Edison Rd., Well.	253	318	ET81
Edith Cavell Clo. N19	99	306	DK59
Edith Gdns., Surb.	282	330	CP101
Edith Gro. SW10	158	315	DC79
Edith Rd. E6	234	308	EK66
Edith Rd. E15	121	307	ED64
Edith Rd. N11	220	306	DK52
Edith Rd. SE25	287	332	DR99
Edith Rd. SW19	271	323	DB93
Edith Rd. W14	147	315	CY77
Edith Rd., Orp.	291	335	EU106
Edith Rd., Rom.	226	309	EX58
Edith Row SW6	158	315	DB81
Edith St. E2	27	316	DT68
Edith Ter. SW10	158	315	DC80
Edith Turbeville Ct. N19	99	306	DL59
Edith Vil. W14	147	315	CZ78
Edith Yd. SW10	158	315	DC80
Edithna St. SW9	177	324	DL83
Edmansons Clo. N17	221	306	DS53
Edmeston Clo. E9	119	307	DY65
Edmonds Ct., W.Mol.	267	329	CB98
Edmonton Grn. N9	210	301	DV47
Edmund Rd., Mitch.	271	323	DE97
Edmund Rd., Rain.	247	319	FE68
Edmund Rd., Well.	262	327	EU83
Edmund St. SE5	163	316	DR80
Edmunds Ave., Orp.	278	327	EX97
Edmunds Clo., Hayes	242	313	BW71
Edmunds Wk. N2	219	305	DE56
Edna Rd. SW20	270	323	CX96
Edna St. SW11	159	315	DE81
Edric Rd. SE14	165	317	DX80
Edrich Ho. SW4	161	316	DL81
Edrick Rd., Edg.	217	304	CQ51
Edrick Wk., Edg.	217	304	CQ51
Edridge Clo., Horn.	238	310	FK64
Edridge Rd., Croy.	287	332	DQ104
Edward Ave. E4	223	307	EB51
Edward Ave., Mord.	285	331	DD99
Edward Clo. N9	209	300	DT45
Edward Clo., Hmptn.	267	329	CC92
Edward Clo., Nthlt.	242	313	BW68
Edward Clo., Rom.	228	310	FJ55
Edward Ct. E16	244	318	EG71
Edward Ct., Stai.	264	328	BJ93
Edward Gro., Barn.	207	299	DD43
Edward Ms. NW1	20/1	316	DH68
Edward Pauling Ho., Felt.	265	320	BT87
Edward Pl. SE8	165	317	DZ79
Edward Rd. E17	222	307	DX56
Edward Rd. SE20	274	325	DX94
Edward Rd., Barn.	207	299	DD43
Edward Rd., Brom.	276	326	EH94
Edward Rd., Chis.	277	326	EP92
Edward Rd., Croy.	287	332	DS101
Edward Rd., Felt.	257	320	BR85
Edward Rd., Hmptn.	267	329	CC92
Edward Rd., Har.	215	303	CC55
Edward Rd., Nthlt.	242	313	BW68
Edward Rd., Rom.	226	309	EX58
Edward Sq. N1	23	316	DM67
Edward Sq. SE16	139	317	DY74
Edward St. E16	244	318	EG70
Edward St. SE8	165	317	DZ79
Edward St. SE14	165	317	DY80
Edward Temme Ave. E15	121	307	EF66
Edward Tyler Rd. SE12	260	326	EJ89
Edward Way, Ashf.	264	320	BM89
Edwardes Sq. W8	147	315	CZ76
Edward's Ave., Ruis.	232	313	BV65
Edwards Clo., Wor.Pk.	284	331	CX103
Edwards Cotts. N1	116	306	DP65
Edwards Dr. N11	220	306	DK52
Edwards Gdns., Swan.	279	327	FD98
Edwards La. N16	101	306	DR61
Edwards Ms. N1	116	306	DP66
Edwards Ms. W1	44	316	DG72
Edwards Rd., Belv.	255	319	FA77
Edwin Ave. E6	245	318	EN68
Edwin Clo., Bexh.	254	319	EZ79
Edwin Clo., Rain.	247	319	FF69
Edwin Pl., Croy.	287	332	DR102
Edwin Rd., Edg.	217	304	CR51
Edwin Rd., Twick.	259	321	CE88
Edwin St. E1	128	317	DW70
Edwin St. E16	244	318	EG71
Edwina Gdns., Ilf.	224	308	EL57
Edwins Mead E9	119	307	DY63
Edwyn Clo., Barn.	206	299	CW44
Eel Brook Studios SW6	158	315	DA80
Eel Pie Island, Twick.	184	322	CG88
Effie Pl. SW6	158	315	DA80
Effie Rd. SW6	158	315	DA80
Effingham Clo., Sutt.	292	331	DB108
Effingham Rd. N8	221	306	DN57
Effingham Rd. SE12	183	325	EE85
Effingham Rd., Croy.	286	332	DM101
Effort St. SW17	271	323	DE92
Effra Par. SW2	178	324	DN85
Effra Rd. SW2	178	324	DN84
Effra Rd. SW19	271	323	DA93
Egan Way SE16	148	317	DV78
Egan Way, Hayes	249	312	BS73
Egbert St. NW1	20	316	DG67
Egerton Ave., Swan.	279	327	FF94
Egerton Clo., Pnr.	214	303	BU54
Egerton Cres. SW3	78/9	315	DE77
Egerton Dr. SE10	166	317	EB81
Egerton Gdns. NW4	218	305	CV56
Egerton Gdns. NW10	126	315	CW67
Egerton Gdns. SW3	78/9	315	DE77
Egerton Gdns. W13	132	314	CH72
Egerton Gdns., Ilf.	235	308	ET62
Egerton Gdns. Ms. SW3	66/7	315	DE76
Egerton Pl. SW3	66/7	315	DE76
Egerton Rd. N16	101	306	DT59
Egerton Rd. SE25	273	324	DS97
Egerton Rd., N.Mal.	269	322	CT98
Egerton Rd., Twick.	259	321	CE87
Egerton Rd., Wem.	107	304	CM66
Egerton Ter. SW3	66/7	315	DE76
Egerton Way, Hayes	257	320	BP80
Egham Clo. SW19	189	323	CY89
Egham Clo., Sutt.	284	331	CY103
Egham Cres., Sutt.	284	331	CX104
Egham Rd. E13	244	318	EH71
Eglantine Rd. SW18	174	323	DC85
Egleston Rd., Mord.	284	331	DB100
Eglington Ct. SE17	162	316	DQ79
Eglington Rd. E4	211	301	ED45
Eglinton Hill SE18	253	318	EP79
Eglinton Rd. SE18	253	318	EP79
Egliston Ms. SW15	172	323	CW83
Egliston Rd. SW15	172	323	CW83
Eglon Ms. NW1	113	305	DF66
Egmont Ave., Surb.	282	330	CM102
Egmont Rd., N.Mal.	269	322	CT98
Egmont Rd., Surb.	282	330	CM102
Egmont Rd., Sutt.	293	331	DC108
Egmont St. SE14	165	317	DX80
Egremont Rd. SE27	194	324	DN90
Egret Way, Hayes	242	313	BX71
Eider Clo. E7	121	307	EF64
Eider Clo., Hayes	242	313	BX71
Eighteenth Rd., Mitch.	272	324	DL98
Eighth Ave. E12	234	308	EM63
Eighth Ave., Hayes	242	313	BU74
Eileen Rd. SE25	287	332	DR99
Eindhoven Clo., Cars.	285	332	DG102
Eisenhower Dr. E6	244	318	EL71
Elaine Gro. NW5	114	306	DG64
Elam Clo. SE5	162	316	DP82
Elam St. SE5	162	316	DP82
Eland Rd. SW11	175	323	DF83
Eland Rd., Croy.	286	332	DP104
Elba Pl. SE17	85	316	DQ77
Elbe St. SW6	158	315	DC82
Elberon Ave., Croy.	286	332	DJ100
Elborough Rd. SE25	287	333	DU99
Elborough St. SW18	190	323	DA88
Elbury Dr. E16	244	318	EG72
Elcho St. SW11	159	315	DE80
Elcot Ave. SE15	164	317	DU80
Elder Ave. N8	220	306	DL57
Elder Clo., West Dr.	248	312	BL73
Elder Oak Clo. SE20	274	325	DV95
Elder Rd. SE27	273	324	DQ92
Elder St. E1	51	316	DT71
Elder Wk. N1	24/5	316	DP67
Elderberry Gro. SE27	273	324	DQ92
Elderberry Rd. W5	143	314	CL75
Elderfield Rd. E5	119	307	DX63
Elderfield Wk. E11	224	308	EH57
Elderflower Way E15	121	307	EE66
Elderslie Clo., Beck.	288	333	EA99
Elderslie Rd. SE9	261	326	EN85
Elderton Rd. SE26	274	325	DY91
Eldertree Pl., Mitch.	272	324	DJ95
Eldertree Way, Mitch.	272	324	DJ95
Elderwood Pl. SE27	273	324	DQ92
Eldon Ave., Croy.	288	333	DW103
Eldon Ave., Houns.	251	321	CA80
Eldon Gro. NW3	113	305	DD64
Eldon Pk. SE25	274	325	DV98
Eldon Rd. E17	222	307	DZ56
Eldon Rd. N9	210	301	DW47
Eldon Rd. N22	221	306	DP53
Eldon Rd. W8	64/5	315	DB76
Eldon St. EC2	50	316	DR71
Eldon Way NW10	124	314	CP68
Eldonwall Trd. Est. NW2	94	305	CU60
Eldred Gdns., Upmin.	239	311	FS59
Eldred Rd., Bark.	245	318	ES67
Eldrick Ct., Felt.	265	320	BR88
Eldridge Clo., Felt.	258	321	BU88
Eleanor Clo. N15	221	306	DT55
Eleanor Clo. SE16	149	317	DX75
Eleanor Cres. NW7	206	299	CX49
Eleanor Gdns., Barn.	206	299	CX43
Eleanor Gdns., Dag.	236	309	EZ62
Eleanor Gro. SW13	171	322	CS83
Eleanor Gro., Uxb.	231	312	BP62
Eleanor Rd. E8	118	307	DV65
Eleanor Rd. E15	121	307	EF65
Eleanor Rd. N11	220	306	DL51
Eleanor St. E3	130	317	EA69
Eleanor Wk. SE18	252	318	EM77
Electric Ave. SW9	178	324	DN84
Electric La. SW9	178	324	DN84
Electric Par., Surb.	282	330	CK100
Elephant & Castle SE1	72/3	316	DP76
Elephant La. SE16	148	317	DW75
Elephant Rd. SE17	85	316	DQ77
Elers Rd. W13	142	314	CJ75
Elers Rd., Hayes	249	320	BR77
Eley Est. N18	210	301	DW49
Eley Rd. N18	210	301	DW49
Elf Row E1	138	317	DW73
Elfin Gro., Tedd.	267	329	CF92
Elfindale Rd. SE24	178	324	DQ85
Elford Clo. SE3	260	326	EJ84
Elfort Rd. N5	116	306	DN63
Elfrida Cres. SE6	275	325	EA91
Elfwine Rd. W7	243	313	CE71
Elgal Clo., Orp.	290	334	EP106
Elgar Ave. NW10	109	304	CR65
Elgar Ave. SW16	272	324	DL97
Elgar Ave. W5	143	314	CL75
Elgar Ave., Surb.	282	330	CN102
Elgar Clo. E13	244	318	EJ68
Elgar Clo. SE8	166	317	EA80
Elgar Clo., Borwd.	204	298	CJ45
Elgar Clo., Uxb.	231	312	BN61
Elgar St. SE16	149	317	DY75
Elgin Ave. W9	28	315	DA70
Elgin Ave., Ashf.	265	328	BQ93
Elgin Ave., Har.	216	304	CH54
Elgin Ave., Rom.	229	311	FP52
Elgin Cres. W11	137	315	CY73
Elgin Cres., Houns.	257	320	BS82
Elgin Dr., Nthwd.	213	302	BS52
Elgin Est. W9	28	315	DA70
Elgin Ms. W11	137	315	CY72
Elgin Ms. N. W9	28/9	315	DB69
Elgin Ms. S. W9	28/9	315	DB69
Elgin Rd. N22	220	306	DJ54
Elgin Rd., Croy.	287	332	DT103
Elgin Rd., Ilf.	235	308	ES60
Elgin Rd., Sutt.	285	331	DC104
Elgin Rd., Wall.	294	332	DJ107
Elgood Ave., Nthwd.	213	302	BT51
Elgood Clo. W11	137	315	CY73
Elham Clo., Brom.	276	326	EK94
Elia Ms. N1	24/5	316	DP68
Elia St. N1	24/5	316	DP68
Elias Pl. SW8	162	316	DN79
Elibank Rd. SE9	260	326	EM84
Elim Est. SE1	74	316	DR76
Elim Way E13	131	317	EF69
Eliot Bank SE23	196	325	DV89
Eliot Cotts. SE3	167	317	EE82
Eliot Dr., Har.	233	313	CB61
Eliot Gdns. SW15	172	323	CU84
Eliot Hill SE13	166	317	EC82
Eliot Ms. NW8	17	315	DC68
Eliot Pk. SE13	166	317	EC82
Eliot Pl. SE3	167	317	EE82
Eliot Rd., Dag.	236	309	EX63
Eliot Vale SE3	167	317	ED82
Elizabeth Ave. N1	116	306	DQ66
Elizabeth Ave., Enf.	202	300	DP41
Elizabeth Ave., Ilf.	235	308	ER61
Elizabeth Ave., Stai.	264	328	BJ93
Elizabeth Blackwell Ho. N22	221	306	DN53
Elizabeth Bri. SW1	80/1	316	DH77
Elizabeth Clo. E14	140	317	EB72
Elizabeth Clo. W9	29	315	DC70
Elizabeth Clo., Rom.	227	309	FB53
Elizabeth Clo., Sutt.	284	331	CZ105
Elizabeth Clyde Clo. N15	221	306	DS56
Elizabeth Cotts., Rich.	153	314	CM81
Elizabeth Ct. SW1	70	316	DK76
Elizabeth Est. SE17	163	316	DR79
Elizabeth Fry Rd. E8	118	307	DV66
Elizabeth Gdns. W3	135	314	CT74
Elizabeth Gdns., Stan.	216	304	CJ51
Elizabeth Gdns., Sun.	266	329	BW97
Elizabeth Ms. NW3	113	305	DF65
Elizabeth Pl. N15	221	306	DR56
Elizabeth Ride N9	210	301	DV45
Elizabeth Rd. E6	244	318	EK67
Elizabeth Rd. N15	221	306	DS57
Elizabeth Sq. SE16	139	317	DY73
Elizabeth St. SW1	80	316	DG77
Elizabeth Ter. SE9	260	326	EM86
Elizabeth Way SE19	273	324	DR94
Elizabeth Way, Felt.	266	329	BW91
Elizabethan Clo., Stai.	264	320	BK87
Elizabethan Way, Stai.	264	320	BK87
Elkington Rd. E13	244	318	EH70
Elkins, The, Rom.	227	309	FE54
Elkstone Rd. W10	137	315	CZ71
Ella Rd. N8	99	306	DL59
Ellaline Rd. W6	157	315	CX79
Ellanby Cres. N18	210	301	DV49
Elland Rd. SE15	180	325	DW84
Ellement Clo., Pnr.	214	303	BX57
Ellen Clo., Brom.	276	326	EK97
Ellen Ct. N9	210	301	DW47
Ellen St. E1	138	317	DU72
Ellen Webb Dr., Har.	215	303	CE55
Ellenborough Pl. SW15	172	323	CU84
Ellenborough Rd. N22	221	306	DQ53
Ellenborough Rd., Sid.	278	327	EX92
Ellenbridge Way, S.Croy.	295	332	DS109
Elleray Rd., Tedd.	267	329	CF93
Ellerby St. SW6	157	315	CX81
Ellerdale Clo. NW3	112	305	DC63
Ellerdale Rd. NW3	112	305	DC64
Ellerdale St. SE13	182	325	EB84
Ellerdine Rd., Houns.	259	321	CD84
Ellerker Gdns., Rich.	169	322	CL85
Ellerman Ave., Twick.	258	321	BZ88
Ellerslie Gdns. NW10	126	315	CU67
Ellerslie Rd. W12	136	315	CV74
Ellerslie Sq. Ind. Est. SW2	177	324	DL84
Ellerton Gdns., Dag.	236	309	EW66
Ellerton Rd. SW13	156	315	CU81
Ellerton Rd. SW18	191	323	DD88
Ellerton Rd. SW20	270	323	CU94
Ellerton Rd., Dag.	236	309	EW66
Ellerton Rd., Surb.	282	330	CM103
Ellery Rd. SE19	273	324	DR94
Ellery St. SE15	164	317	DV82
Ellesmere Ave. NW7	205	298	CR48
Ellesmere Ave., Beck.	275	325	EB96
Ellesmere Clo. E11	223	307	EF57
Ellesmere Clo., Ruis.	231	312	BQ59
Ellesmere Dr., S.Croy.	295	333	DV114
Ellesmere Gdns., Ilf.	224	308	EL57
Ellesmere Gro., Barn.	206	299	CZ43
Ellesmere Rd. E3	129	317	DY68
Ellesmere Rd. NW10	110	305	CU64
Ellesmere Rd. W4	155	314	CR79
Ellesmere Rd., Grnf.	243	313	CC70
Ellesmere Rd., Twick.	168	322	CJ86
Ellesmere St. E14	140	317	EB72
Ellingfort Rd. E8	118	307	DV66
Ellingham Rd. E15	121	307	ED63
Ellingham Rd. W12	146	315	CU75
Ellington Rd. N10	220	306	DH56
Ellington Rd., Felt.	265	328	BT91
Ellington Rd., Houns.	251	321	CB82
Ellington St. N7	116	306	DN65
Elliot Clo. E15	121	307	EE66
Elliot Rd. NW4	218	305	CV58
Elliot Rd., Stan.	216	304	CG51
Elliott Ave., Ruis.	232	313	BV61
Elliott Clo., Wem.	91	304	CM62
Elliott Gdns., Rom.	228	310	FH53
Elliott Gdns., Shep.	281	328	BN98
Elliott Rd. SW9	162	316	DP80
Elliott Rd. W4	145	314	CS77
Elliott Rd., Brom.	276	326	EK98
Elliott Rd., Th.Hth.	273	324	DP98
Elliott Sq. NW3	113	305	DE66
Elliotts Clo., Uxb.	248	312	BJ71
Elliott's Pl. N1	24/5	316	DP67
Elliotts Row SE11	84/5	316	DP77
Ellis Clo. SE9	261	326	EQ89
Ellis Ct. W7	243	313	CF71
Ellis Ms. SE7	252	318	EJ79
Ellis Rd., Mitch.	285	331	DF100
Ellis Rd., Sthl.	243	313	CC74
Ellis St. SW1	79	315	DF77
Elliscombe Rd. SE7	252	318	EJ78
Ellisfield Dr. SW15	187	322	CT87
Ellison Gdns., Sthl.	250	321	BZ77
Ellison Rd. SW13	155	314	CT82
Ellison Rd. SW16	272	324	DK94
Ellison Rd., Sid.	261	326	ER88
Elliston Ho. SE18	253	318	EN77
Ellmore Clo., Rom.	228	310	FH53
Ellora Rd. SW16	272	324	DK92
Ellsworth St. E2	128	317	DV69
Ellwood Ct. W9	28/9	315	DB70
Elm Ave. W5	133	314	CL74
Elm Ave., Cars.	293	331	DF110
Elm Ave., Ruis.	232	313	BU60
Elm Ave., Upmin.	239	311	FP62
Elm Bank N14	208	300	DL45
Elm Bank, Brom.	276	326	EK96
Elm Bank Gdns. SW13	155	314	CS82
Elm Clo. E11	224	308	EH58
Elm Clo. N19	98	306	DJ61
Elm Clo. NW4	218	305	CX57
Elm Clo. SW20	270	323	CW98
Elm Clo., Cars.	285	331	DF102
Elm Clo., Har.	215	303	CB58
Elm Clo., Hayes	242	313	BU72
Elm Clo., Rom.	227	309	FB53
Elm Clo., S.Croy.	295	332	DS107
Elm Clo., Stai.	264	320	BK88
Elm Clo., Surb.	283	330	CQ101
Elm Clo., Twick.	259	321	CB89
Elm Ct. EC4	60	316	DN73
Elm Ct., Mitch.	271	323	DF96
Elm Ct., Sun.	265	328	BT94
Elm Cres. W5	133	314	CL74
Elm Cres., Kings.T.	268	322	CL95
Elm Cft., Sutt.	284	331	CX104
Elm Dr., Har.	215	303	CB58
Elm Dr., Sun.	266	329	BW96
Elm Dr., Swan.	279	327	FD96
Elm Friars Wk. NW1	115	306	DK66
Elm Gdns. N2	219	305	DC55
Elm Gdns., Enf.	202	300	DR38
Elm Gdns., Mitch.	272	324	DK98
Elm Grn. W3	135	314	CS72
Elm Gro. N8	220	306	DL58
Elm Gro. NW2	111	305	CX63
Elm Gro. SE15	163	316	DT82
Elm Gro. SW19	270	323	CY94
Elm Gro., Erith	255	319	FD80
Elm Gro., Har.	233	313	CA59
Elm Gro., Horn.	228	311	FL58
Elm Gro., Kings.T.	268	322	CL95
Elm Gro., Orp.	291	334	ET102
Elm Gro., Sutt.	284	331	DB105
Elm Gro., West Dr.	248	312	BM73
Elm Gro., Wdf.Grn.	211	301	EF50
Elm Gro. Par., Wall.	285	332	DG104
Elm Gro. Rd. SW13	156	315	CU82
Elm Gro. Rd. W5	143	314	CL75
Elm Hall Gdns. E11	224	308	EH58
Elm La. SE6	197	325	DZ89
Elm Lawn Clo., Uxb.	240	312	BL66
Elm Ms., Rich.	169	322	CM86
Elm Pk. SW2	177	324	DM86
Elm Pk., Stan.	204	298	CH50
Elm Pk. Ave. N15	221	306	DT57
Elm Pk. Ave., Horn.	238	310	FG63
Elm Pk. Ct., Pnr.	214	303	BW55
Elm Pk. Gdns. NW4	218	305	CX57
Elm Pk. Gdns. SW10	78	315	DD78
Elm Pk. La. SW3	78	315	DD78
Elm Pk. Mans. SW10	158	315	DC79
Elm Pk. Rd. E10	103	307	DY60
Elm Pk. Rd. N3	218	305	CZ52
Elm Pk. Rd. N21	209	300	DQ45
Elm Pk. Rd. SE25	273	324	DT97
Elm Pk. Rd. SW3	159	315	DD79
Elm Pk. Rd., Pnr.	214	303	BW54
Elm Pl. SW7	78	315	DD78
Elm Quay Ct. SW8	161	316	DK79
Elm Rd. E7	121	307	EF65
Elm Rd. E11	105	307	ED61
Elm Rd. E17	223	307	EC57
Elm Rd. N22	221	306	DP53
Elm Rd. SW14	170	322	CQ83
Elm Rd., Beck.	274	325	DZ96
Elm Rd., Chess.	282	330	CL105
Elm Rd., Felt.	265	320	BR88
Elm Rd., Kings.T.	268	322	CM95
Elm Rd., N.Mal.	269	322	CR97
Elm Rd., Pur.	294	332	DP113
Elm Rd., Rom.	227	309	FB54
Elm Rd., Sid.	278	327	EU91
Elm Rd., Th.Hth.	273	324	DR98
Elm Rd., Wall.	285	332	DG102
Elm Rd., Wem.	107	304	CL64
Elm Rd. W., Sutt.	284	331	CZ101
Elm Row NW3	96	305	DC62
Elm St. WC1	35	316	DM70
Elm Ter. NW2	96	305	DA62
Elm Ter. NW3	113	305	DE63
Elm Ter. SE9	261	326	EN86
Elm Ter., Har.	215	303	CD53
Elm Tree Clo. NW8	30	315	DD69
Elm Tree Clo., Ashf.	265	328	BP92
Elm Tree Clo., Nthlt.	242	313	BZ68
Elm Tree Rd. NW8	30	315	DD69
Elm Wk. NW3	96	305	DA61
Elm Wk. SW20	270	323	CW98
Elm Wk., Orp.	290	334	EM104
Elm Wk., Rom.	228	310	FG55
Elm Way N11	220	306	DG51
Elm Way NW10	109	304	CS63
Elm Way, Epsom	283	330	CR106
Elm Way, Wor.Pk.	284	331	CW104
Elmar Rd. N15	221	306	DR56
Elmbank Way W7	243	313	CD71
Elmbourne Dr., Belv.	255	319	FB77
Elmbourne Rd. SW17	192	324	DG90
Elmbridge Ave., Surb.	282	330	CP99
Elmbridge Clo., Ruis.	214	303	BU58
Elmbridge Dr., Ruis.	231	302	BT57
Elmbridge Rd., Ilf.	226	309	EU51
Elmbridge Wk. E8	118	307	DU66
Elmbrook Clo., Sun.	266	329	BV95
Elmbrook Gdns. SE9	260	326	EL84
Elmbrook Rd., Sutt.	284	331	CZ105
Elmcourt Rd. SE27	194	324	DP89
Elmcroft Ave. E11	224	308	EH57
Elmcroft Ave. N9	210	301	DV44
Elmcroft Ave. NW11	95	305	CZ59
Elmcroft Ave., Sid.	261	326	ET87
Elmcroft Clo. E11	224	308	EH56
Elmcroft Clo. N8	220	306	DM57
Elmcroft Clo. W5	133	314	CK72
Elmcroft Clo., Chess.	282	330	CL104
Elmcroft Clo., Felt.	257	320	BT86
Elmcroft Cres. NW11	95	305	CX59
Elmcroft Cres., Har.	215	303	CA55
Elmcroft Dr., Ashf.	265	328	BN92
Elmcroft Dr., Chess.	282	330	CL104
Elmcroft Gdns. NW9	217	304	CN57
Elmcroft Rd., Orp.	291	335	EU101
Elmcroft St. E5	118	307	DW63
Elmdale Rd. N13	208	300	DM50
Elmdene, Surb.	283	330	CQ102
Elmdene Ave., Horn.	228	311	FM57
Elmdene Clo., Beck.	288	333	DZ99
Elmdene Rd. SE18	253	318	EP78
Elmdon Rd., Houns.	250	321	BX82
Elmdon Rd. (Hatton Cross), Houns.	257	320	BT83
Elmer Clo., Rain.	238	310	FG66
Elmer Gdns., Edg.	217	304	CP52
Elmer Gdns., Islw.	259	321	CD83
Elmer Gdns., Rain.	238	310	FG66
Elmer Rd. SE6	198	325	EC87
Elmers Dr., Tedd.	268	322	CH93
Elmers End Rd. SE20	274	325	DW96
Elmers End Rd., Beck.	274	325	DW96
Elmers Rd. SE25	287	333	DU101
Elmerside Rd., Beck.	274	325	DY98
Elmfield Ave. N8	220	306	DL57
Elmfield Ave., Mitch.	272	324	DG95
Elmfield Ave., Tedd.	267	329	CF92
Elmfield Clo., Har.	233	313	CE61
Elmfield Pk., Brom.	276	326	EG97
Elmfield Rd. E4	211	301	EC47
Elmfield Rd. E17	222	307	DX57
Elmfield Rd. N2	219	305	DD55
Elmfield Rd. SW17	192	324	DG89
Elmfield Rd., Brom.	276	326	EG97
Elmfield Rd., Sthl.	250	321	BY76
Elmfield Way W9	40	315	DA71
Elmfield Way, S.Croy.	295	332	DT109
Elmgate Ave., Felt.	258	321	BV90
Elmgate Gdns., Edg.	205	298	CR50
Elmgreen Clo. E15	131	317	EE67
Elmgrove Cres., Har.	215	303	CF57
Elmgrove Gdns., Har.	216	304	CG57
Elmgrove Rd., Croy.	287	333	DV101
Elmgrove Rd., Har.	215	303	CF57
Elmhurst, Belv.	254	319	EY79
Elmhurst Ave. N2	219	305	DD55
Elmhurst Ave., Mitch.	272	324	DG94
Elmhurst Dr. E18	224	308	EG54
Elmhurst Dr., Horn.	238	310	FJ60
Elmhurst Gdns. E18	224	308	EH53
Elmhurst Rd. E7	234	308	EH66
Elmhurst Rd. N17	221	306	DS54
Elmhurst Rd. SE9	260	326	EL89
Elmhurst Rd., Enf.	203	301	DW37
Elmhurst St. SW4	177	324	DK83
Elmington Clo., Bex.	263	327	FB86
Elmington Est. SE5	163	316	DR80
Elmington Rd. SE5	163	316	DR81
Elmira St. SE13	182	325	EB83
Elmlea Dr., Hayes	249	312	BS71
Elmlee Clo., Chis.	276	326	EM93
Elmley Clo. E6	244	318	EL71
Elmley St. SE18	253	318	ER77
Elmore Clo., Wem.	123	314	CL68
Elmore Rd. E11	104	307	EC62
Elmore Rd., Enf.	203	301	DX38
Elmore St. N1	117	306	DR66
Elms, The SW13	171	322	CT83
Elms Ave. N10	220	306	DH55
Elms Ave. NW4	218	305	CX57
Elms Ct., Wem.	106	304	CG63
Elms Cres. SW4	176	324	DJ86
Elms Fm. Rd., Horn.	238	310	FJ64
Elms Gdns., Dag.	236	309	EZ63
Elms Gdns., Wem.	106	304	CG63
Elms Ind. Est., Rom.	229	311	FP52
Elms La., Wem.	90	304	CG62
Elms Ms. W2	54	315	DD73
Elms Pk. Ave., Wem.	106	304	CG63
Elms Rd. SW4	176	324	DJ85
Elms Rd., Har.	215	303	CE52
Elms Wk. SE3	183	325	EF84
Elmscott Gdns. N21	209	300	DQ44
Elmscott Rd., Brom.	275	325	EE92
Elmscroft N8	220	306	DM57
Elmsdale Rd. E17	222	307	DZ56
Elmshaw Rd. SW15	172	323	CU85
Elmshurst Cres. N2	219	305	DC56
Elmside Rd., Wem.	92	304	CN62
Elmsleigh Ave., Har.	216	304	CH56
Elmsleigh Rd., Twick.	259	321	CD89
Elmslie Clo., Wdf.Grn.	224	308	EM51
Elmslie Pt. E3	139	317	DZ71
Elmstead Ave., Chis.	276	326	EM92
Elmstead Ave., Wem.	91	304	CL60
Elmstead Clo. N20	207	299	DA47
Elmstead Clo., Epsom	283	330	CS106
Elmstead Cres., Well.	254	319	EW79
Elmstead Gdns., Wor.Pk.	283	331	CU104
Elmstead Glade, Chis.	276	326	EM93
Elmstead La., Chis.	276	326	EL94
Elmstead Rd., Erith	255	319	FE81
Elmstead Rd., Ilf.	235	308	ES61
Elmstone Rd. SW6	158	315	DA81
Elmsway, Ashf.	264	328	BM92
Elmsworth Ave., Houns.	251	321	CB82
Elmton Way E5	102	307	DU62
Elmtree Rd., Tedd.	267	329	CE91
Elmwood Ave. N13	208	300	DL50
Elmwood Ave., Felt.	258	321	BU89
Elmwood Ave., Har.	216	304	CG57
Elmwood Clo., Wall.	285	332	DG103
Elmwood Ct., Wem.	90	304	CG62
Elmwood Cres. NW9	217	304	CQ56
Elmwood Dr., Bex.	262	327	EY87
Elmwood Gdns. W7	243	313	CE72
Elmwood Rd. SE24	179	324	DR85
Elmwood Rd. W4	154	314	CQ79
Elmwood Rd., Croy.	286	332	DP101
Elmwood Rd., Mitch.	271	323	DF97
Elmworth Gro. SE21	195	324	DR89
Elnathan Ms. W9	28/9	315	DB70
Elphinstone Rd. E17	222	307	DZ54
Elphinstone St. N5	116	306	DP63
Elrick Clo., Erith	255	319	FE79
Elrington Rd. E8	118	307	DU65
Elruge Clo., West Dr.	248	320	BK76
Elsa Rd., Well.	254	319	EV82
Elsa St. E1	139	317	DY71
Elsdale St. E9	118	307	DW65
Elsden Ms. E2	128	317	DW68
Elsden Rd. N17	221	306	DT53
Elsenham Rd. E12	235	308	EN64
Elsenham St. SW18	189	323	CZ88
Elsham Rd. E11	105	307	EE62
Elsham Rd. W14	147	315	CY75
Elsham Ter. W14	147	315	CY75
Elsie Rd. SE22	179	324	DT84
Elsiedene Rd. N21	209	300	DQ45
Elsiemaud Rd. SE4	181	325	DZ85
Elsinge Rd., Enf.	203	301	DV36
Elsinore Ave., Stai.	264	320	BL87
Elsinore Gdns. NW2	95	305	CY62
Elsinore Rd. SE23	197	325	DY88
Elsinore Way, Rich.	170	322	CP83
Elsley Rd. SW11	175	323	DF83
Elspeth Rd. SW11	175	323	DF84
Elspeth Rd., Wem.	107	304	CL64
Elsrick Ave., Mord.	284	331	DA99
Elstan Way, Croy.	288	333	DY101
Elsted St. SE17	86	316	DR77
Elstow Clo. SE9	261	326	EN85
Elstow Clo., Ruis.	232	313	BX59
Elstow Gdns., Dag.	246	319	EY67
Elstow Rd., Dag.	236	309	EY66
Elstree Gdns. N9	210	301	DV46
Elstree Gdns., Belv.	254	319	EY77
Elstree Gdns., Ilf.	235	308	EQ64
Elstree Hill, Brom.	275	325	EE94
Elstree Hill N., Borwd.	204	298	CK44
Elstree Hill S., Borwd.	204	298	CJ45
Elstree Rd., Borwd.	204	298	CH44
Elswick Rd. SE13	166	317	EB82
Elswick St. SW6	158	315	DC82
Elsworth Clo., Felt.	265	320	BS88
Elsworthy Ri. NW3	113	305	DE66
Elsworthy Rd. NW3	18	315	DD67
Elsworthy Ter. NW3	113	305	DE66
Elsynge Rd. SW18	175	323	DD85
Eltham Grn. SE9	260	326	EJ85
Eltham Grn. Rd. SE9	260	326	EJ84
Eltham High St. SE9	260	326	EM86
Eltham Hill SE9	260	326	EK85
Eltham Palace Rd. SE9	260	326	EJ86
Eltham Pk. Gdns. SE9	261	326	EN84
Eltham Rd. SE9	260	326	EJ85
Eltham Rd. SE12	260	326	EG85
Elthiron Rd. SW6	158	315	DA81
Elthorne Ave. W7	251	321	CF75
Elthorne Ct., Felt.	258	321	BW88
Elthorne Pk. Rd. W7	251	321	CF75
Elthorne Rd. N19	99	306	DK61
Elthorne Rd. NW9	93	304	CR59
Elthorne Rd., Uxb.	240	312	BK68
Elthorne Way NW9	217	304	CR58
Elthruda Rd. SE13	183	325	ED86
Eltisley Rd., Ilf.	235	308	EP63
Elton Ave., Barn.	206	299	CZ43
Elton Ave., Grnf.	233	313	CE65
Elton Ave., Wem.	106	304	CH64
Elton Clo., Kings.T.	268	322	CJ94
Elton Ho. E3	129	317	DZ67
Elton Pl. N16	117	306	DS64
Elton Rd., Kings.T.	268	322	CM95
Elton Rd., Pur.	294	332	DJ112
Eltringham St. SW18	174	323	DC84
Elvaston Ms. SW7	65	315	DC76
Elvaston Pl. SW7	65	315	DC76
Elveden Pl. NW10	124	314	CN68
Elveden Rd. NW10	124	314	CN68
Elvendon Rd. N13	220	306	DL51
Elver Gdns. E2	128	317	DU68
Elverson Rd. SE8	166	317	EB82
Elverton St. SW1	82	316	DK77
Elvet Ave., Rom.	228	310	FJ56
Elvington Grn., Brom.	289	333	EF99
Elvington La. NW9	217	304	CS53
Elvino Rd. SE26	274	325	DX92
Elvis Rd. NW2	110	305	CW65
Elwill Way, Beck.	275	325	EC98
Elwin St. E2	128	317	DU69
Elwood St. N5	100	306	DP62
Elwyn Gdns. SE12	260	326	EG87
Ely Clo., Erith	255	319	FF82
Ely Clo., N.Mal.	269	322	CT96
Ely Ct. EC1	48	316	DN71
Ely Gdns., Borwd.	205	298	CR43
Ely Gdns., Dag.	237	309	FC62
Ely Gdns., Ilf.	234	308	EL59
Ely Pl. EC1	48	316	DN71
Ely Pl., Wdf.Grn.	225	308	EN51
Ely Rd. E10	104	307	EC59
Ely Rd., Croy.	287	332	DR99
Ely Rd. (Heathrow Airport), Houns.	257	320	BT82
Ely Rd. (Hounslow W.), Houns.	258	321	BW83
Elyne Rd. N4	221	306	DN58
Elysian Ave., Orp.	291	334	ES100
Elysium Pl. SW6	157	315	CZ82
Elysium St. SW6	157	315	CZ82
Elystan Clo., Wall.	293	332	DH109
Elystan Pl. SW3	78/9	315	DE78
Elystan St. SW3	78/9	315	DE77
Elystan Wk. N1	24	316	DN67
Emanuel Ave. W3	134	314	CQ72
Emanuel Dr., Hmptn.	266	329	BZ92
Emba St. SE16	148	317	DU75
Embankment SW15	157	315	CX82
Embankment, The, Twick.	184	322	CG88
Embankment Gdns. SW3	159	315	DF79
Embankment Pl. WC2	58/9	316	DL74
Embassy Ct., Sid.	262	327	EV90
Embassy Ct., Well.	262	327	EV83
Ember Clo., Orp.	291	334	EQ101
Emberton SE5	163	316	DS79
Embleton Rd. SE13	182	325	EB84
Embleton Wk., Hmptn.	266	329	BZ93
Embley Pt. E5	118	307	DV63
Embry Clo., Stan.	204	298	CG49
Embry Dr., Stan.	216	304	CG51
Embry Way, Stan.	204	298	CG49
Emden Clo., West Dr.	249	320	BN75
Emden St. SW6	158	315	DB81
Emerald Clo. E16	244	318	EL72
Emerald Gdns., Dag.	237	309	FA60
Emerald St. WC1	47	316	DM71
Emerson Dr., Horn.	238	310	FK59
Emerson Gdns., Har.	216	304	CM58
Emerson Rd., Ilf.	235	308	EN59
Emerson St. SE1	61	316	DQ74
Emersons Ave., Swan.	279	327	FF94
Emerton Clo., Bexh.	262	327	EY84
Emery Hill St. SW1	69	316	DJ76
Emery St. SE1	72	316	DN76
Emes Rd., Erith	255	319	FC80
Emily Pl. N7	116	306	DN63
Emlyn Gdns. W12	145	314	CS75
Emlyn Rd. W12	145	314	CS75
Emma Rd. E13	131	317	EF68
Emma St. E2	128	317	DV68
Emmanuel Clo., Nthwd.	213	302	BT52
Emmanuel Rd. SW12	192	324	DJ88
Emmanuel Rd., Nthwd.	213	302	BT52
Emmott Ave., Ilf.	225	308	EQ57
Emmott Clo. E1	129	317	DY70
Emmott Clo. NW11	219	305	DC58
Emms Pas., Kings.T.	268	322	CK96
Emperor's Gate SW7	64/5	315	DB76
Empire Ave. N18	209	300	DQ50
Empire Ct., Wem.	92	304	CP62
Empire Rd., Grnf.	122	314	CH67
Empire Way, Wem.	107	304	CM63
Empire Wf. Rd. E14	151	317	ED77
Empire Yd. N7	99	306	DL62
Empress Ave. E4	223	307	EB52
Empress Ave. E12	234	308	EJ61
Empress Ave., Ilf.	234	308	EM61
Empress Ave., Wdf.Grn.	223	307	EF52
Empress Dr., Chis.	277	326	EP93
Empress Pl. SW6	76	315	DA78
Empress St. SE17	162	316	DQ79
Empson St. E3	130	317	EB70
Emsworth Clo. N9	210	301	DW46
Emsworth Rd., Ilf.	225	308	EP54
Emsworth St. SW2	193	324	DL89
Emu Rd. SW8	160	316	DH82
Ena Rd. SW16	272	324	DL97
Enbrook St. W10	127	315	CY69
End Way, Surb.	282	330	CN101
Endale Clo., Cars.	285	331	DF103
Endeavour Way SW19	271	323	DB91
Endeavour Way, Bark.	246	319	EU68
Endeavour Way, Croy.	286	332	DK101
Endell St. WC2	46/7	316	DL72
Enderby St. SE10	151	317	EE78
Enderley Clo., Har.	215	303	CE53
Enderley Rd., Har.	215	303	CE53
Endersby Rd., Barn.	206	299	CW43
Endersleigh Gdns. NW4	218	305	CU56
Endlebury Rd. E4	211	301	EC47
Endlesham Rd. SW12	192	324	DG87
Endsleigh Gdns. WC1	34	316	DK70
Endsleigh Gdns., Ilf.	234	308	EM61
Endsleigh Gdns., Surb.	282	330	CJ100
Endsleigh Pl. WC1	34	316	DK70
Endsleigh Rd. W13	132	314	CG73
Endsleigh Rd., Sthl.	250	321	BY77
Endsleigh St. WC1	34	316	DK70
Endwell Rd. SE4	165	317	DY82

Endymion Rd. N4	100	306	DN59
Endymion Rd. SW2	177	324	DM86
Enfield Clo., Uxb.	240	312	BK68
Enfield Retail Pk., Enf.	203	301	DU41
Enfield Rd. N1	117	306	DS66
Enfield Rd. W3	144	314	CP75
Enfield Rd., Brent.	143	314	CK78
Enfield Rd., Houns.	257	320	BS82
Enfield Wk., Brent.	143	314	CK78
Enford St. W1	43	315	DF71
Engadine Clo., Croy.	287	332	DT104
Engadine St. SW18	189	323	CZ88
Engate St. SE13	182	325	EC84
Engayne Gdns., Upmin.	239	311	FP60
Engel Pk. NW7	218	305	CW51
Engineer Clo. SE18	253	318	EN79
Engineers Way, Wem.	108	304	CN63
Englands La. NW3	113	305	DF65
Englefield Clo., Croy.	287	332	DQ100
Englefield Clo., Enf.	202	300	DN40
Englefield Clo., Orp.	277	326	ET98
Englefield Cres., Orp.	277	326	ET98
Englefield Path, Orp.	278	327	EU98
Englefield Rd. N1	117	306	DR66
Englefield Rd., Orp.	278	327	EU98
Engleheart Dr., Felt.	257	320	BT86
Engleheart Rd. SE6	198	325	EB87
Englewood Rd. SW12	176	324	DH86
English Grds. SE1	62/3	316	DS74
English St. E3	129	317	DZ70
Enid St. SE16	75	316	DT76
Enmore Ave. SE25	287	333	DU99
Enmore Gdns. SW14	171	322	CR85
Enmore Rd. SE25	287	333	DU99
Enmore Rd. SW15	172	323	CW84
Enmore Rd., Sthl.	243	313	CA70
Ennerdale Ave., Horn.	238	310	FG64
Ennerdale Ave., Stan.	216	304	CJ55
Ennerdale Clo., Felt.	265	320	BT88
Ennerdale Clo. (Cheam), Sutt.	284	331	CZ105
Ennerdale Dr. NW9	217	304	CS57
Ennerdale Gdns., Wem.	90	304	CJ60
Ennerdale Ho. E3	129	317	DZ70
Ennerdale Rd., Bexh.	255	319	FA81
Ennerdale Rd., Rich.	153	314	CM82
Ennersdale Rd. SE13	183	325	ED85
Ennis Rd. N4	100	306	DN60
Ennis Rd. SE18	253	318	EQ79
Ennismore Ave. W4	145	314	CT77
Ennismore Ave., Grnf.	233	313	CE65
Ennismore Gdns. SW7	66/7	315	DE75
Ennismore Gdns. Ms. SW7	66/7	315	DE76
Ennismore Ms. SW7	66/7	315	DE76
Ennismore St. SW7	66/7	315	DE76
Ensign Clo., Pur.	294	332	DN110
Ensign Clo., Stai.	264	320	BL88
Ensign Dr. N13	209	300	DQ48
Ensign St. E1	138	317	DU73
Ensign Way, Stai.	264	320	BK88
Enslin Rd. SE9	261	326	EN87
Ensor Ms. SW7	78	315	DD78
Enstone Rd., Enf.	203	301	DY41
Enstone Rd., Uxb.	230	312	BM62
Enterprise Clo., Croy.	286	332	DN102
Enterprise Way NW10	126	315	CU69
Enterprise Way SW18	174	323	DA84
Enterprise Way, Tedd.	267	329	CF92
Enterprize Way SE8	149	317	DZ77
Epirus Ms. SW6	158	315	DA80
Epirus Rd. SW6	157	315	CZ80
Epping Clo. E14	150	317	EA77
Epping Clo., Rom.	227	309	FB55
Epping Glade E4	211	301	EC44
Epping Pl. N1	116	306	DN65
Epping Way E4	211	301	EB44
Epple Rd. SW6	157	315	CZ81
Epsom Clo., Bexh.	263	327	FB83
Epsom Clo., Nthlt.	232	313	BZ64
Epsom Rd. E10	223	307	EC58
Epsom Rd., Croy.	286	332	DN105
Epsom Rd., Ilf.	225	308	ET58
Epsom Rd., Mord.	284	331	DA100
Epsom Rd., Sutt.	284	331	CZ101
Epsom Sq., Houns.	257	320	BT82
Epsom Way, Horn.	238	311	FM63
Epstein Rd. SE28	246	319	EU74
Epworth Rd., Islw.	152	314	CH81
Epworth St. EC2	38	316	DR70
Equity Sq. E2	39	316	DT69
Erasmus St. SW1	82	316	DK77
Erconwald St. W12	135	314	CT72
Eresby Dr., Beck.	288	333	EA102
Eresby Pl. NW6	112	305	DA66
Eric Clo. E7	234	308	EG63
Eric Rd. E7	234	308	EG63
Eric Rd. NW10	109	304	CT65
Eric Rd., Rom.	236	309	EX59
Eric St. E3	129	317	DZ70
Erica Ct., Swan.	279	327	FE98
Erica Gdns., Croy.	288	333	EA104
Erica St. W12	136	315	CU73
Ericcson Clo. SW18	174	323	DA85
Eridge Rd. W4	145	314	CR76
Erin Clo., Brom.	275	325	EE94
Erindale SE18	253	318	ER79
Erindale Ter. SE18	253	318	ER79
Erith Cres., Rom.	227	309	FC53
Erith High St., Erith	255	319	FE78
Erith Rd., Belv.	255	319	FA78
Erith Rd., Bexh.	263	327	FB84
Erith Rd., Erith	255	319	FC81
Erlanger Rd. SE14	165	317	DX81
Erlesmere Gdns. W13	142	314	CG76
Ermine Clo., Houns.	250	321	BW82
Ermine Ho. N17	221	306	DT52
Ermine Rd. N15	221	306	DT58
Ermine Rd. SE13	182	325	EB84
Ermine Side, Enf.	210	301	DU43
Ermington Rd. SE9	261	326	EQ89
Ernald Ave. E6	244	318	EL68
Erncroft Way, Twick.	259	321	CF86
Ernest Ave. SE27	273	324	DP91
Ernest Clo., Beck.	288	333	EA99
Ernest Gdns. W4	154	314	CP79
Ernest Gro., Beck.	288	333	DZ99
Ernest Rd., Horn.	228	311	FL58
Ernest Rd., Kings.T.	269	322	CP96
Ernest Sq., Kings.T.	269	322	CP96
Ernest St. E1	129	317	DX70
Ernle Rd. SW20	270	323	CV94
Ernshaw Pl. SW15	173	323	CY85
Erpingham Rd. SW15	172	323	CW83
Erridge Rd. SW19	271	323	DA96
Errington Rd. W9	127	315	CZ70
Errol Gdns., Hayes	242	313	BV70
Errol Gdns., N.Mal.	270	323	CU98
Errol St. EC1	37	316	DQ70
Erroll Rd., Rom.	227	309	FF56
Erskine Clo., Sutt.	285	331	DE104
Erskine Cres. N17	222	307	DV56
Erskine Hill NW11	219	305	DA57
Erskine Ms. NW3	113	305	DF66
Erskine Rd. E17	222	307	DZ56
Erskine Rd. NW3	113	305	DF66
Erskine Rd., Sutt.	285	331	DD105
Erwood Rd. SE7	252	318	EL78
Esam Way SW16	273	324	DN92
Escot Way, Barn.	206	299	CW43
Escott Gdns. SE9	276	326	EL91
Escreet Gro. SE18	253	318	EN77
Esdaile Gdns., Upmin.	239	311	FR59
Esher Ave., Rom.	227	309	FC58
Esher Ave., Sutt.	284	331	CX104
Esher Bypass, Chess.	282	330	CJ105
Esher Clo., Bex.	262	327	EY88
Esher Cres., Houns.	257	320	BS82
Esher Gdns. SW19	189	323	CX89
Esher Ms., Mitch.	271	323	DF97
Esher Rd., Ilf.	235	308	ES62
Esk Rd. E13	244	318	EG70
Esk Way, Rom.	227	309	FD52
Eskdale Ave., Nthlt.	242	313	BZ67
Eskdale Clo., Wem.	91	304	CK61
Eskdale Gdns., Pur.	295	332	DR114
Eskdale Rd., Bexh.	255	319	FA82
Eskdale Rd., Uxb.	240	312	BH68
Eskmont Ridge SE19	273	324	DS94
Esmar Cres. NW9	94	305	CU59
Esme Ho. SW15	171	322	CT84
Esmeralda Rd. SE1	148	317	DU77
Esmond Clo., Rain.	238	310	FH66
Esmond Rd. NW6	127	315	CZ67
Esmond Rd. W4	145	314	CR77
Esmond St. SW15	173	323	CY84
Esparto St. SW18	190	323	DB87
Essenden Rd., Belv.	255	319	FA78
Essenden Rd., S.Croy.	295	332	DS108
Essendine Rd. W9	28	315	DA69
Essex Ave., Islw.	259	321	CE83
Essex Clo. E17	222	307	DY56
Essex Clo., Mord.	284	331	CX101
Essex Clo., Rom.	227	309	FB56
Essex Clo., Ruis.	232	313	BX60
Essex Ct. EC4	48	316	DN72
Essex Ct. SW13	155	314	CT82
Essex Gdns. N4	221	306	DP58
Essex Gdns., Horn.	228	311	FM57
Essex Gro. SE19	73	324	DR93
Essex Ho. E14		317	EB72
Essex Pk. N3		305	DB51
Essex Pk. Ms. W3		314	CS74
Essex Pl. W4		314	CQ77
Essex Rd. E4		301	EE46
Essex Rd. E10	[illegible]	307	EC58
Essex Rd. E12	[illegible]	308	EL64
Essex Rd. E17	222	307	DY58
Essex Rd. E18	224	308	EH54
Essex Rd. N1	24/5	316	DP67
Essex Rd. NW10	109	304	CS66
Essex Rd. W3	134	314	CQ73
Essex Rd. W4	145	314	CR77
Essex Rd., Bark.	235	308	ER66
Essex Rd., Dag.	237	309	FC64
Essex Rd., Enf.	202	300	DR42
Essex Rd., Rom.	227	309	FA56
Essex Rd. (Chadwell Heath), Rom.	236	309	EW59
Essex Rd. S. E11	105	307	ED59
Essex St. E7	234	308	EG64
Essex St. WC2	60	316	DN73
Essex Twr. SE20	274	325	DV95
Essex Vil. W8	64	315	DA75
Essex Wf. E5	102	307	DW61
Essian St. E1	139	317	DY71
Essoldo Way, Edg.	216	304	CM55
Estate Way E10	103	307	DZ60
Estcourt Rd. SE25	287	333	DV100
Estcourt Rd. SW6	157	315	CZ80
Este Rd. SW11	175	323	DE83
Estella Ave., N.Mal.	270	323	CV98
Estelle Rd. NW3	113	305	DF63
Esterbrooke St. SW1	82	316	DK77
Esther Clo. N21	209	300	DN45
Esther Rd. E11	105	307	EE59
Estreham Rd. SW16	272	324	DK93
Estridge Clo., Houns.	259	321	CA84
Estuary Clo., Bark.	246	319	EV69
Eswyn Rd. SW17	271	323	DF91
Etchingham Pk. Rd. N3	219	305	DB52
Etchingham Rd. E15	120	307	EC63
Eternit Wk. SW6	156	315	CW81
Etfield Gro., Sid.	278	327	EV92
Ethel Rd. E16	244	318	EH72
Ethel Rd., Ashf.	264	328	BL92
Ethel St. SE17	85	316	DQ77
Ethelbert Clo., Brom.	276	326	EG97
Ethelbert Gdns., Ilf.	224	308	EM57
Ethelbert Rd. SW20	270	323	CX95
Ethelbert Rd., Brom.	276	326	EG97
Ethelbert Rd., Erith	255	319	FC80
Ethelbert Rd., Orp.	278	327	EX97
Ethelbert St. SW12	192	324	DH88
Ethelburga Rd., Rom.	228	311	FM53
Ethelburga St. SW11	159	315	DE81
Ethelden Rd. W12	136	315	CV74
Etheldene Ave. N10	220	306	DJ56
Etheridge Rd. NW2	94	305	CW59
Etherley Rd. N15	221	306	DQ57
Etherow St. SE22	180	325	DU86
Etherstone Grn. SW16	273	324	DN91
Etherstone Rd. SW16	273	324	DN91
Ethnard Rd. SE15	164	317	DV79
Ethronvi Rd., Bexh.	262	327	EY83
Etloe Rd. E10	104	307	EA61
Eton Ave. N12	219	305	DC52
Eton Ave. NW3	113	305	DD66
Eton Ave., Barn.	207	299	DE44
Eton Ave., Houns.	250	321	BZ79
Eton Ave., N.Mal.	283	330	CR99
Eton Ave., Wem.	106	304	CH64
Eton College Rd. NW3	113	305	DF65
Eton Ct. NW3	113	305	DD66
Eton Ct., Wem.	106	304	CJ63
Eton Garages NW3	113	305	DE65
Eton Gro. NW9	217	304	CN55
Eton Gro. SE13	183	325	EE83
Eton Hall NW3	113	305	DF65
Eton Pl. NW3	114	306	DG66
Eton Ri. NW3	113	305	DF65
Eton Rd. NW3	113	305	DF66
Eton Rd., Hayes	257	320	BT80
Eton Rd., Ilf.	235	308	EQ64
Eton Rd., Orp.	291	335	EV105
Eton St., Rich.	169	322	CL85
Eton Vil. NW3	113	305	DF65
Etta St. SE8	165	317	DY79
Etton Clo., Horn.	238	311	FL61
Ettrick St. E14	140	317	EC72
Etwell Pl., Surb.	282	330	CM100
Eugene Clo., Rom.	228	310	FJ56
Eugenia Rd. SE16	148	317	DW77
Eureka Rd., Kings.T.	269	322	CN96
Europa Pl. EC1	37	316	DQ69
Europe Rd. SE18	252	318	EM76
Eustace Rd. E6	244	318	EL69
Eustace Rd. SW6	158	315	DA80
Eustace Rd., Rom.	236	309	EX59
Euston Cen. NW1	33	316	DJ70
Euston Gro. NW1	34	316	DK69
Euston Rd. N1	32/3	316	DH70
Euston Rd. NW1	32/3	316	DH70
Euston Rd., Croy.	286	332	DN102
Euston Sq. NW1	34	316	DK69
Euston Sta. Colonnade NW1	34	316	DK69
Euston St. NW1	33	316	DJ69
Eva Rd., Rom.	236	309	EW59
Evandale Rd. SW9	162	316	DN82
Evangelist Rd. NW5	114	306	DH63
Evans Clo. E8	117	306	DT65
Evans Gro., Felt.	259	321	CA89
Evans Rd. SE6	199	325	EE89
Evansdale, Rain.	247	319	FF69
Evanston Ave. E4	223	307	EC52
Evanston Gdns., Ilf.	224	308	EL58
Eve Rd. E11	121	307	EE63
Eve Rd. E15	131	317	EE68
Eve Rd. N17	221	306	DS55
Eve Rd., Islw.	168	322	CG84
Evelina Rd. SE15	180	325	DW83
Evelina Rd. SE20	274	325	DX94
Eveline Lowe Est. SE16	148	317	DU76
Eveline Rd., Mitch.	271	323	DF95
Evelyn Ave. NW9	217	304	CR55
Evelyn Ave., Ruis.	231	312	BT59
Evelyn Clo., Twick.	259	321	CB87
Evelyn Ct. N1	26	316	DR68
Evelyn Cres., Sun.	281	328	BT95
Evelyn Denington Rd. E6	244	318	EM71
Evelyn Dr., Pnr.	214	303	BX52
Evelyn Fox Ct. W10	136	315	CW71
Evelyn Gdns. SW7	78	315	DD78
Evelyn Gdns., Rich.	169	322	CL84
Evelyn Gro. W5	133	314	CM74
Evelyn Gro., Sthl.	242	313	BZ72
Evelyn Rd. E16	244	318	EH74
Evelyn Rd. E17	223	307	EC56
Evelyn Rd. SW19	271	323	DB92
Evelyn Rd. W4	145	314	CR76
Evelyn Rd., Rich.	169	322	CL83
Evelyn Rd. (Ham), Rich.	184	322	CJ90
Evelyn Sharp Clo., Rom.	228	310	FK55
Evelyn St. SE8	149	317	DY78
Evelyn Ter., Rich.	169	322	CL83
Evelyn Wk. N1	26	316	DR68
Evelyn Way, Sun.	281	328	BT95
Evelyn Way, Wall.	286	332	DK105
Evelyn Yd. W1	46	316	DK72
Evelyns Clo., Uxb.	249	312	BN72
Evening Hill, Beck.	275	325	EC94
Evenwood Clo. SW15	173	323	CY85
Everard Ave., Brom.	289	334	EG102
Everard Way, Wem.	91	304	CL62
Everatt Clo. SW18	173	323	CZ86
Everdon Rd. SW13	156	315	CU79
Everest Pl. E14	140	317	EC71
Everest Pl., Swan.	279	327	FD98
Everest Rd. SE9	260	326	EM85
Everest Rd., Stai.	264	320	BK87
Everett Clo., Pnr.	231	302	BT55
Everett Wk., Belv.	254	319	EZ78
Everglade Strand NW9	217	304	CT53
Evergreen Ct., Stai.	264	320	BK87
Evergreen Way, Hayes	249	312	BT73
Evergreen Way, Stai.	264	320	BK87
Everilda St. N1	23	316	DM67
Evering Rd. E5	102	307	DU62
Evering Rd. N16	102	307	DU62
Everington Rd. N10	219	305	DF54
Everington St. W6	157	315	CX79
Everitt Rd. NW10	125	314	CR69
Everleigh St. N4	99	306	DM60
Eversfield Gdns. NW7	217	304	CS51
Eversfield Rd., Rich.	153	314	CM82
Evershed Wk. W4	145	314	CR76
Eversholt St. NW1	21	316	DJ68
Evershot Rd. N4	99	306	DM60
Eversleigh Gdns., Upmin.	239	311	FR60
Eversleigh Rd. E6	244	318	EK67
Eversleigh Rd. N3	218	305	CZ52
Eversleigh Rd. SW11	175	323	DF83
Eversleigh Rd., Barn.	207	299	DC43
Eversley Ave., Bexh.	255	319	FD82
Eversley Ave., Wem.	92	304	CN61
Eversley Clo. N21	208	300	DM44
Eversley Cres. N21	208	300	DM44
Eversley Cres., Islw.	251	321	CD81
Eversley Cres., Ruis.	231	312	BS61
Eversley Cross, Bexh.	255	319	FE82
Eversley Mt. N21	208	300	DM44
Eversley Pk. SW19	270	323	CV92
Eversley Pk. Rd. N21	208	300	DM44
Eversley Rd. SE7	252	318	EH79
Eversley Rd. SE19	273	324	DR94
Eversley Rd., Surb.	268	322	CM98
Eversley Way, Croy.	288	333	EA105
Everthorpe Rd. SE15	179	324	DT83
Everton Bldgs. NW1	33	316	DJ69
Everton Dr., Stan.	216	304	CM55
Everton Rd., Croy.	287	333	DU102
Evesham Ave. E17	223	307	EA54
Evesham Clo., Grnf.	243	313	CB68
Evesham Clo., Sutt.	292	331	DA108
Evesham Grn., Mord.	284	331	DB100
Evesham Rd. E15	121	307	EF66
Evesham Rd. N11	208	300	DJ50
Evesham Rd., Felt.	258	321	BW87
Evesham Rd., Mord.	284	331	DB100
Evesham St. W11	137	315	CX73
Evesham Wk. SE5	163	316	DR82
Evesham Wk. SW9	162	316	DN82
Evesham Way SW11	176	324	DG83
Evesham Way, Ilf.	225	308	EN55
Evry Rd., Sid.	278	327	EW93
Ewald Rd. SW6	157	315	CZ82
Ewan Rd., Rom.	228	310	FK54
Ewart Gro. N22	221	306	DN53
Ewart Pl. E3	129	317	DZ68
Ewart Rd. SE23	197	325	DX87
Ewe Clo. N7	115	306	DL65
Ewell Ct. Ave., Epsom	283	330	CS106
Ewell Rd., Surb.	282	330	CL99
Ewell Rd., Sutt.	292	331	CX108
Ewellhurst Rd., Ilf.	224	308	EL54
Ewelme Rd. SE23	196	325	DW88
Ewen Cres. SW2	194	324	DN87
Ewer St. SE1	61	316	DQ74
Ewhurst Ave., S.Croy.	295	332	DT109
Ewhurst Clo., Sutt.	292	331	CW109
Ewhurst Ho. E1	138	317	DW71
Ewhurst Rd. SE4	181	325	DZ86
Exbury Rd. SE6	198	325	EA89
Excel Ct. WC2	58	316	DK73
Excelsior Clo., Kings.T.	269	322	CN96
Excelsior Gdns. SE13	166	317	EC82
Exchange Arc. EC2	50/1	316	DS71
Exchange Bldgs. E1	50/1	316	DS72
Exchange Ct. WC2	58/9	316	DL73
Exchange Pl. EC2	50/1	316	DS71
Exchange Sq. EC2	50/1	316	DS71
Exchange St., Rom.	227	309	FE57
Exeforde Ave., Ashf.	265	328	BN91
Exeter Clo. E6	244	318	EM72
Exeter Gdns., Ilf.	234	308	EL60
Exeter Ho. SW15	172	323	CW86
Exeter Ms. NW6	112	305	DB65
Exeter Rd. E16	244	318	EG71
Exeter Rd. E17	223	307	EA57
Exeter Rd. N9	210	301	DW47
Exeter Rd. N14	208	300	DH46
Exeter Rd. NW2	111	305	CY64
Exeter Rd. SE15	163	316	DT81
Exeter Rd., Croy.	287	332	DS101
Exeter Rd., Dag.	237	309	FB65
Exeter Rd., Enf.	203	301	DX41
Exeter Rd., Felt.	258	321	BZ90
Exeter Rd., Har.	232	313	BY61
Exeter Rd., Well.	253	318	ET82
Exeter St. WC2	58/9	316	DL73
Exeter Way SE14	165	317	DZ80
Exford Gdns. SE12	260	326	EH88
Exford Rd. SE12	260	326	EH89
Exhibition Clo. W12	136	315	CW73
Exhibition Rd. SW7	66	315	DD75
Exmoor Clo., Ilf.	225	308	EQ53
Exmoor St. W10	137	315	CX71
Exmouth Mkt. EC1	36	316	DN70
Exmouth Ms. NW1	33	316	DJ69
Exmouth Pl. E8	118	307	DV66
Exmouth Rd. E17	222	307	DZ57
Exmouth Rd., Brom.	276	326	EH97
Exmouth Rd., Hayes	241	312	BS69
Exmouth Rd., Ruis.	232	313	BW62
Exmouth Rd., Well.	254	319	EW81
Exmouth St. E1	138	317	DW72
Exning Rd. E16	131	317	EF70
Exon St. SE17	86/7	316	DS77
Explorer Ave., Stai.	264	320	BL87
Express Dr., Ilf.	236	309	EV60
Exton Cres. NW10	108	304	CQ66
Exton Gdns., Dag.	236	309	EW64
Exton St. SE1	60	316	DN74
Eyebright Clo., Croy.	288	333	DX102
Eyhurst Ave., Horn.	238	310	FG62
Eyhurst Clo. NW2	94	305	CU61
Eylewood Rd. SE27	273	324	DQ92
Eynella Rd. SE22	195	324	DT87
Eynham Rd. W12	136	315	CW72
Eynsford Clo., Orp.	291	334	EQ101
Eynsford Cres., Bex.	262	327	EW88
Eynsford Rd., Ilf.	235	308	ES61
Eynsham Dr. SE2	254	319	EU77
Eynswood Dr., Sid.	278	327	EV92
Eyot Gdns. W6	145	314	CT78
Eyot Grn. W4	155	314	CT79
Eyre Clo., Rom.	228	310	FH56
Eyre Ct. NW8	18	315	DD68
Eyre St. Hill EC1	36	316	DN70
Eythorne Rd. SW9	162	316	DN81
Ezra St. E2	39	316	DT69
Faber Gdns. NW4	218	305	CU57
Fabian Rd. SW6	157	315	CZ80
Fabian St. E6	244	318	EM70
Factory La. N17	221	306	DT54
Factory La., Croy.	286	332	DN102
Factory Pl. E14	150	317	EB78
Factory Rd. E16	244	318	EL74
Factory Sq. SW16	272	324	DL93
Factory Yd. W7	243	313	CE74
Faesten Way, Bex.	263	327	FE90
Faggs Rd., Felt.	258	321	BU85
Fair Acres, Brom.	289	334	EG99
Fair St. SE1	74/5	316	DS75
Fair St., Houns.	259	321	CC83
Fairacre, N.Mal.	269	322	CS97
Fairacres SW15	172	323	CU85
Fairacres, Ruis.	231	312	BT59
Fairbairn Clo., Pur.	294	332	DN113
Fairbairn Grn. SW9	162	316	DN81
Fairbank Ave., Orp.	290	334	EP103
Fairbanks Rd. N17	221	306	DT55
Fairbourne Rd. N17	221	306	DS55
Fairbridge Rd. N19	99	306	DK61
Fairbrook Clo. N13	209	300	DN50
Fairbrook Rd. N13	221	306	DN51
Fairburn Ct. SW15	173	323	CY85
Fairby Rd. SE12	260	326	EH85
Fairchild Clo. SW11	159	315	DD82
Fairchild Pl. EC2	38/9	316	DS70
Fairchild St. EC2	38/9	316	DS70
Fairclough St. E1	138	317	DU72
Faircross Ave., Bark.	235	308	EQ65
Faircross Ave., Rom.	227	309	FD52
Fairdale Gdns. SW15	172	323	CV84
Fairdale Gdns., Hayes	250	321	BU75
Fairey Ave., Hayes	249	320	BT77
Fairfax Gdns. SE3	252	318	EJ81
Fairfax Pl. NW6	112	305	DC66
Fairfax Rd. N8	221	306	DN56
Fairfax Rd. NW6	112	305	DC66
Fairfax Rd. W4	145	314	CS76
Fairfax Rd., Tedd.	268	322	CG93
Fairfax Way N10	220	306	DG52
Fairfield Ave. NW4	218	305	CV58
Fairfield Ave., Edg.	217	304	CP51
Fairfield Ave., Ruis.	231	312	BQ59
Fairfield Ave., Twick.	259	321	CB88
Fairfield Ave., Upmin.	239	311	FQ62
Fairfield Clo. N12	207	299	DC49
Fairfield Clo., Enf.	203	301	DY42
Fairfield Clo., Epsom	283	330	CS106
Fairfield Clo., Horn.	238	310	FG60
Fairfield Clo., Mitch.	271	323	DE94
Fairfield Clo., Nthwd.	213	302	BP50
Fairfield Clo., Sid.	261	326	ET86
Fairfield Ct. NW10	126	315	CU67
Fairfield Cres., Edg.	217	304	CP51
Fairfield Dr. SW18	174	323	DB85
Fairfield Dr., Grnf.	122	314	CJ67
Fairfield Dr., Har.	215	303	CC55
Fairfield E., Kings.T.	268	322	CL96
Fairfield Gdns. N8	220	306	DL57
Fairfield Gro. SE7	252	318	EK79
Fairfield Ind. Est., Kings.T.	269	322	CN97
Fairfield N., Kings.T.	268	322	CL96
Fairfield Path, Croy.	287	332	DR104
Fairfield Pl., Kings.T.	268	322	CL97
Fairfield Rd. E3	130	317	EA68
Fairfield Rd. E17	222	307	DY54
Fairfield Rd. N8	220	306	DL57
Fairfield Rd. N18	210	301	DU49
Fairfield Rd. W7	142	314	CG76
Fairfield Rd., Beck.	275	325	EA96
Fairfield Rd., Bexh.	254	319	EZ82
Fairfield Rd., Brom.	276	326	EG94
Fairfield Rd., Croy.	287	332	DS104
Fairfield Rd., Ilf.	235	308	EP65
Fairfield Rd., Kings.T.	268	322	CL96
Fairfield Rd., Orp.	291	334	ER100
Fairfield Rd., Sthl.	242	313	BZ72
Fairfield Rd., Uxb.	240	312	BK65
Fairfield Rd., West Dr.	248	312	BL73
Fairfield Rd., Wdf.Grn.	224	308	EG51
Fairfield S., Kings.T.	268	322	CL97
Fairfield St. SW18	174	323	DB85
Fairfield Way, Barn.	207	299	DA43
Fairfield Way, Couls.	294	332	DK114
Fairfield Way, Epsom	283	330	CS106
Fairfield W., Kings.T.	268	322	CL96
Fairfields, Cher.	280	328	BG102
Fairfields Clo. NW9	217	304	CQ57
Fairfields Cres. NW9	217	304	CQ57
Fairfields Rd., Houns.	259	321	CC83
Fairfoot Rd. E3	130	317	EA70
Fairford Ave., Bexh.	255	319	FD81
Fairford Ave., Croy.	288	333	DX99
Fairford Clo., Croy.	288	333	DX99
Fairford Clo., Rom.	229	311	FP51
Fairford Gdns., Wor.Pk.	283	330	CT103
Fairford Way, Rom.	229	311	FP51
Fairgreen Rd., Th.Hth.	286	332	DP99
Fairhaven Ave., Croy.	288	333	DX100
Fairhazel Gdns. NW6	112	305	DB65
Fairholme, Felt.	265	320	BR87
Fairholme Ave., Rom.	228	310	FG57
Fairholme Clo. N3	218	305	CY56
Fairholme Cres., Hayes	241	312	BT70
Fairholme Gdns. N3	218	305	CY55
Fairholme Gdns., Upmin.	239	311	FT59
Fairholme Rd. W14	147	315	CY78
Fairholme Rd., Ashf.	264	328	BL92
Fairholme Rd., Croy.	286	332	DN101
Fairholme Rd., Har.	215	303	CF57
Fairholme Rd., Ilf.	234	308	EM59
Fairholme Rd., Sutt.	292	331	CZ107
Fairholt Clo. N16	101	306	DS60
Fairholt Rd. N16	101	306	DR60
Fairholt St. SW7	66/7	315	DE76
Fairkytes Ave., Horn.	238	310	FK60
Fairland Rd. E15	121	307	EF65
Fairlands Ave., Sutt.	284	331	DA103
Fairlands Ave., Th.Hth.	272	324	DM98
Fairlands Ct. SE9	261	326	EN86
Fairlawn SE7	252	318	EJ79
Fairlawn Ave. N2	219	305	DE56
Fairlawn Ave. W4	144	314	CQ77
Fairlawn Ave., Bexh.	254	319	EX82
Fairlawn Clo. N14	208	300	DJ44
Fairlawn Clo., Felt.	266	329	BZ91
Fairlawn Clo., Kings.T.	269	322	CQ93
Fairlawn Dr., Wdf.Grn.	224	308	EG52
Fairlawn Gdns., Sthl.	242	313	BZ73
Fairlawn Gro. W4	144	314	CQ77
Fairlawn Gro., Bans.	293	331	DD113
Fairlawn Pk. SE26	274	325	DY92
Fairlawn Rd. SW19	270	323	CZ94
Fairlawn Rd., Cars.	293	331	DC111
Fairlawns, Pnr.	214	303	BW54
Fairlawns, Sun.	266	329	BU97
Fairlawns, Twick.	168	322	CJ86
Fairlawns Clo., Horn.	238	311	FM59
Fairlawns Clo., Stai.	264	328	BH93
Fairlea Pl. W5	132	314	CJ71
Fairlie Gdns. SE23	196	325	DW87
Fairlight Ave. E4	211	301	ED47
Fairlight Ave. NW10	125	314	CS68
Fairlight Ave., Wdf.Grn.	224	308	EG51
Fairlight Clo. E4	211	301	ED47
Fairlight Clo., Wor.Pk.	284	331	CW105
Fairlight Dr., Uxb.	240	312	BK65
Fairlight Rd. SW17	271	323	DD91
Fairlop Clo., Horn.	238	310	FH65
Fairlop Gdns., Ilf.	225	308	EQ52
Fairlop Rd. E11	105	307	ED59
Fairlop Rd., Ilf.	225	308	EQ54
Fairmark Dr., Uxb.	241	312	BN65
Fairmead, Brom.	276	326	EM98
Fairmead, Surb.	282	330	CP102
Fairmead Clo., Brom.	276	326	EM98
Fairmead Clo., Houns.	250	321	BX80
Fairmead Clo., N.Mal.	269	322	CR97
Fairmead Cres., Edg.	205	298	CQ48
Fairmead Gdns., Ilf.	224	308	EL57
Fairmead Rd. N19	99	306	DK62
Fairmead Rd., Croy.	286	332	DM102
Fairmile Ave. SW16	272	324	DK92
Fairmont Clo., Belv.	254	319	EZ78
Fairmount Rd. SW2	177	324	DM86
Fairoak Clo., Orp.	290	334	EP101
Fairoak Dr. SE9	261	326	ER85
Fairoak Gdns., Rom.	227	309	FE54
Fairstead Wk. N1	25	316	DQ67
Fairthorn Rd. SE7	252	318	EG78
Fairview, Epsom	292	331	CW111
Fairview, Erith	255	319	FF80
Fairview Ave., Wem.	107	304	CK65
Fairview Clo. E17	222	307	DY53
Fairview Ct., Ashf.	265	328	BN92
Fairview Cres., Har.	233	313	CA60
Fairview Dr., Orp.	291	334	ER105
Fairview Dr., Shep.	280	328	BM99
Fairview Gdns., Wdf.Grn.	224	308	EH53
Fairview Ind. Pk., Rain.	247	319	FD71
Fairview Pl. SW2	193	324	DM87
Fairview Rd. N15	221	306	DT57
Fairview Rd. SW16	272	324	DM95
Fairview Rd., Enf.	202	300	DN39
Fairview Rd., Sutt.	285	331	DD106
Fairview Way, Edg.	205	298	CN49
Fairwater Ave., Well.	262	327	EU84
Fairway SW20	270	323	CW97
Fairway, Bexh.	262	327	EY85
Fairway, Cars.	293	331	DC111
Fairway, Cher.	280	328	BH102
Fairway, Orp.	291	334	ER99
Fairway, The N13	209	300	DQ48
Fairway, The N14	208	300	DH44
Fairway, The NW7	205	298	CR48
Fairway, The W3	135	314	CS72
Fairway, The, Barn.	207	299	DB44
Fairway, The, Brom.	290	334	EM99
Fairway, The, N.Mal.	269	322	CR95
Fairway, The, Nthlt.	233	313	CC65
Fairway, The, Nthwd.	213	302	BS49
Fairway, The, Ruis.	232	313	BW63
Fairway, The, Upmin.	239	311	FQ59
Fairway, The, Uxb.	240	312	BM69
Fairway, The, Wem.	90	304	CH62
Fairway, The, W.Mol.	267	329	CB97
Fairway Ave. NW9	217	304	CP55
Fairway Ave., West Dr.	248	312	BJ74
Fairway Clo. NW11	96	305	DC59
Fairway Clo., Croy.	288	333	DY99
Fairway Clo., Epsom	283	330	CQ105
Fairway Clo., Houns.	258	321	BW85
Fairway Clo., West Dr.	248	312	BK74
Fairway Ct. NW7	205	298	CR48
Fairway Dr. SE28	246	319	EX72
Fairway Dr., Grnf.	233	313	CB66
Fairway Est., Grnf.	233	313	CC66
Fairway Gdns., Beck.	289	333	ED100
Fairway Gdns., Ilf.	235	308	EQ64
Fairways, Ashf.	265	328	BP93
Fairways, Stan.	216	304	CL54
Fairways, Tedd.	268	322	CK94
Fairweather Clo. N15	221	306	DS56
Fairweather Rd. N16	222	307	DU58
Fairwyn Rd. SE26	274	325	DY91
Fakenham Clo. NW7	218	305	CU52
Fakenham Clo., Nthlt.	233	313	CA65
Fakruddin St. E1	128	317	DU70
Falcon Ave., Brom.	276	326	EL98
Falcon Clo. SE1	60/1	316	DP74
Falcon Clo. W4	154	314	CQ79
Falcon Clo., Nthwd.	213	302	BS52
Falcon Cres., Enf.	210	301	DX43
Falcon Dr., Stai.	256	320	BK86
Falcon Gro. SW11	175	323	DE83
Falcon Ho. W13	243	313	CF70
Falcon La. SW11	175	323	DE83
Falcon Rd. SW11	159	315	DE82
Falcon Rd., Enf.	210	301	DX43
Falcon Rd., Hmptn.	266	329	BZ94
Falcon St. E13	131	317	EF70
Falcon Ter. SW11	175	323	DE83
Falcon Trd. Est. NW10	109	304	CS63
Falcon Way E11	224	308	EG56
Falcon Way E14	150	317	EB77
Falcon Way NW9	217	304	CS54
Falcon Way, Felt.	258	321	BV85
Falcon Way, Har.	216	304	CL57
Falcon Way, Horn.	238	310	FG66
Falcon Way, Sun.	281	328	BS96
Falconberg Ct. W1	46	316	DK72
Falconberg Ms. W1	46	316	DK72
Falconer Wk. N7	99	306	DM61
Falconwood Ave., Well.	253	318	ER82
Falconwood Par., Well.	261	326	ES84
Falcourt Clo., Sutt.	284	331	DB106
Falkirk Clo., Horn.	239	311	FN60
Falkirk Ho. W9	28/9	315	DB69
Falkirk St. N1	26/7	316	DS68
Falkland Ave. N3	219	305	DA52
Falkland Ave. N11	208	300	DG49
Falkland Pk. Ave. SE25	273	324	DS97
Falkland Pl. NW5	114	306	DJ64
Falkland Rd. N8	221	306	DN56
Falkland Rd. NW5	114	306	DJ64
Fallaize Ave., Ilf.	235	308	EP63
Falling La., West Dr.	248	312	BL73
Falloden Way NW11	219	305	DA56
Fallow Ct. SE16	148	317	DU78
Fallow Ct. Ave. N12	219	305	DC52
Fallowfield, Stan.	204	298	CG49
Fallowfield Clo., Uxb.	212	302	BJ53
Fallowfield Ct., Stan.	204	298	CG48
Fallowfields Dr. N12	219	305	DE51
Fallows Clo. N2	219	305	DC54
Fallsbrook Rd. SW16	272	324	DH93
Falmer Rd. E17	223	307	EB55
Falmer Rd. N15	221	306	DQ57
Falmer Rd., Enf.	202	300	DS42
Falmouth Ave. E4	211	301	ED50
Falmouth Clo. N22	220	306	DM52
Falmouth Clo. SE12	183	325	EF85
Falmouth Gdns., Ilf.	224	308	EK56
Falmouth Rd. SE1	73	316	DQ76
Falmouth St. E15	121	307	ED64
Falstaff Ms., Hmptn.	267	329	CD92
Fambridge Clo. SE26	274	325	DZ91
Fambridge Rd., Dag.	237	309	FA60
Famet Ave., Pur.	295	332	DQ113
Famet Clo., Pur.	295	332	DQ113
Famet Wk., Pur.	295	332	DQ113
Fane St. W14	157	315	CZ79
Fann St. EC1	37	316	DQ70
Fann St. EC2	37	316	DQ70
Fanshaw St. N1	38/9	316	DS69
Fanshawe Ave., Bark.	235	308	EQ65
Fanshawe Cres., Dag.	236	309	EY64
Fanshawe Cres., Horn.	228	310	FK58
Fanshawe Rd., Rich.	268	322	CJ91
Fanthorpe St. SW15	172	323	CW83
Faraday Ave., Sid.	262	327	EU89
Faraday Clo. N7	115	306	DM65
Faraday Rd. E15	121	307	EF65
Faraday Rd. SW19	271	323	DA93
Faraday Rd. W3	134	314	CQ73
Faraday Rd. W10	137	315	CY71
Faraday Rd., Sthl.	243	313	CB73
Faraday Rd., Well.	262	327	EU83
Faraday Rd., W.Mol.	267	329	CA98
Faraday Way SE18	252	318	EK76
Faraday Way, Croy.	286	332	DM102
Faraday Way, Orp.	278	327	EV98
Fareham Rd., Felt.	258	321	BW87
Fareham St. W1	46	316	DK72
Farewell Pl., Mitch.	271	323	DE95
Faringdon Ave., Brom.	290	334	EN101
Faringdon Ave., Rom.	228	310	FJ53
Faringford Rd. E15	121	307	EE66
Farjeon Rd. SE3	252	318	EK81
Farleigh Ave., Brom.	289	333	EF100
Farleigh Pl. N16	117	306	DT63
Farleigh Rd. N16	117	306	DT63
Farley Dr., Ilf.	235	308	ES60
Farley Pl. SE25	274	325	DU98
Farley Rd. SE6	198	325	EC87
Farley Rd., S.Croy.	295	333	DU108
Farlington Pl. SW15	188	323	CV87
Farlow Rd. SW15	172	323	CW83
Farlton Rd. SW18	190	323	DB87
Farm Ave. NW2	95	305	CY62
Farm Ave. SW16	272	324	DL91
Farm Ave., Har.	232	313	BZ59
Farm Ave., Swan.	279	327	FC97
Farm Ave., Wem.	106	304	CJ65
Farm Clo., Barn.	206	299	CV43
Farm Clo., Dag.	237	309	FC66
Farm Clo., Shep.	281	328	BN101
Farm Clo., Sthl.	243	313	CB73
Farm Clo., Sutt.	293	331	DD108
Farm Clo., Uxb.	231	312	BP61
Farm Clo., Wall.	294	332	DJ110
Farm Clo., W.Wick.	289	333	EE104
Farm Ct. NW4	218	305	CU55
Farm Dr., Croy.	288	333	DZ103
Farm Dr., Pur.	294	332	DK112
Farm End E4	211	301	EE43
Farm End, Nthwd.	213	302	BP53

Farm Flds., S.Croy. 295 332 DS111
Farm La. N14 208 300 DG44
Farm La. SW6 158 315 DA79
Farm La., Cars. 293 331 DF110
Farm La., Croy. 288 333 DZ103
Farm La., Pur. 294 332 DJ110
Farm Pl. W8 52 315 DA74
Farm Rd. N21 209 300 DQ46
Farm Rd., Edg. 217 304 CP51
Farm Rd., Houns. 258 321 BY88
Farm Rd., Mord. 284 331 DB99
Farm Rd., Nthwd. 213 302 BQ50
Farm Rd., Stai. 264 328 BH93
Farm Rd., Sutt. 293 331 DD108
Farm St. W1 56/7 316 DH73
Farm Vale, Bex. 263 327 FB86
Farm Wk. NW11 218 305 CZ57
Farm Way, Horn. 238 310 FH63
Farm Way, Nthwd. 213 302 BS49
Farm Way, Wor.Pk. 284 331 CW104
Farman Gro., Nthlt. 242 313 BX69
Farmborough Clo., Har. 233 313 CD59
Farmcote Rd. SE12 260 326 EG88
Farmdale Rd. SE10 252 318 EG78
Farmdale Rd., Cars. 293 331 DE108
Farmer Rd. E10 104 307 EB60
Farmer St. W8 52 315 DA74
Farmers Rd. SE5 162 316 DP80
Farmfield Rd., Brom. 275 325 EE92
Farmhouse Rd. SW16 272 324 DJ94
Farmilo Rd. E17 103 307 DZ59
Farmington Ave., Sutt. 285 331 DD104
Farmland Wk., Chis. 277 326 EP92
Farmlands, Enf. 202 300 DN39
Farmlands, Pnr. 214 303 BU56
Farmlands, The, Nthlt. 233 313 CA65
Farmleigh N14 208 300 DJ45
Farmstead Rd. SE6 275 325 EB91
Farmstead Rd., Har. 215 303 CD53
Farmway, Dag. 236 309 EW62
Farnaby Rd. SE9 260 326 EJ84
Farnaby Rd., Brom. 275 325 ED94
Farnan Ave. E17 223 307 EA54
Farnan Rd. SW16 272 324 DL92
Farnborough Ave. E17 222 307 DY55
Farnborough Clo., Wem. 92 304 CP61
Farnborough Common, Orp. 290 334 EM104
Farnborough Cres., Brom. 289 333 EF102
Farnborough Hill, Orp. 291 334 ER106
Farnborough Way SE15 163 316 DS80
Farnborough Way, Orp. 290 334 EP106
Farncombe St. SE16 148 317 DU75
Farndale Ave. N13 209 300 DP48
Farndale Cres., Grnf. 243 313 CC69
Farnell Ms. SW5 76/7 315 DB78
Farnell Rd., Islw. 259 321 CD84
Farnell Rd., Stai. 264 320 BG90
Farnes Dr., Rom. 228 310 FJ54
Farnham Clo. N20 207 299 DC45
Farnham Gdns. SW20 270 323 CV96
Farnham Pl. SE1 60/1 316 DP74
Farnham Rd., Ilf. 235 308 ET59
Farnham Rd., Well. 254 319 EW82
Farnham Royal SE11 83 316 DM78
Farningham Rd. N17 222 307 DU52
Farnley Rd. E4 211 301 EE45
Farnley Rd. SE25 273 324 DR98
Faro Clo., Brom. 277 326 EN96
Faroe Rd. W14 147 315 CX76
Farorna Wk., Enf. 202 300 DN39
Farquhar Rd. SE19 273 324 DT92
Farquhar Rd. SW19 190 323 DA90
Farquharson Rd., Croy. 287 332 DQ102
Farr Ave., Bark. 246 319 EU68
Farr Rd., Enf. 202 300 DR39
Farrance Rd., Rom. 226 309 EY58
Farrance St. E14 140 317 EA72
Farrans Ct., Har. 90 304 CH59
Farrant Ave. N22 221 306 DN54
Farrell Ho. E1 138 317 DW72
Farren Rd. SE23 197 325 DY89
Farrer Ms. N8 220 306 DJ56
Farrer Rd. N8 220 306 DJ56
Farrer Rd., Har. 216 304 CL57
Farrier Clo., Sun. 266 329 BU98
Farrier Rd., Nthlt. 243 313 CA68
Farrier St. NW1 114 306 DH66
Farrier Wk. SW10 158 315 DC79
Farriers Way, Borwd. 205 298 CR43
Farringdon La. EC1 36 316 DN70
Farringdon Rd. EC1 36 316 DN70
Farringdon St. EC4 48/9 316 DP71
Farrington Ave., Orp. 278 327 EV97
Farrington Pl., Chis. 277 326 ER94
Farrins Rents SE16 139 317 DY74
Farrow La. SE14 164 317 DW80
Farrow Pl. SE16 149 317 DY76
Farthing All. SE1 148 317 DU75
Farthing Flds. E1 138 317 DV74
Farthingale Wk. E15 121 307 ED66
Farthings, The, Kings.T. 269 322 CN95
Farthings Clo. E4 211 301 EE48
Farthings Clo., Pnr. 214 303 BV58
Farwell Rd., Sid. 262 327 EV90
Farwig La., Brom. 275 325 EF95
Fashion St. E1 51 316 DT71
Fashoda Rd., Brom. 276 326 EJ98
Fassett Rd. E8 118 307 DU65
Fassett Rd., Kings.T. 268 322 CL98
Fassett Sq. E8 118 307 DU65
Fassnidge Way, Uxb. 240 312 BJ66
Fauconberg Rd. W4 154 314 CQ79
Faulkner Clo., Dag. 236 309 EX59
Faulkner St. SE14 164 317 DW81
Faulkner's All. EC1 48/9 316 DP71
Fauna Clo., Rom. 226 309 EW58
Faunce St. SE17 84/5 316 DP78
Favart Rd. SW6 158 315 DA81
Faversham Ave. E4 211 301 EE46
Faversham Ave., Enf. 209 300 DR44
Faversham Rd. SE6 197 325 DZ87
Faversham Rd., Beck. 274 325 DZ96
Faversham Rd., Mord. 284 331 DB100
Fawcett Clo. SW11 159 315 DD82
Fawcett Est. E5 102 307 DU60
Fawcett Rd. NW10 109 304 CT66
Fawcett Rd., Croy. 287 332 DQ104
Fawcett St. SW10 158 315 DB79
Fawe Pk. Rd. SW15 173 323 CZ84
Fawe St. E14 140 317 EB71
Fawley Rd. NW6 112 305 DB64
Fawn Rd. E13 244 318 EJ68
Fawnbrake Ave. SE24 178 324 DP85
Fawns Manor Clo., Felt. 265 320 BQ88
Fawns Manor Rd., Felt. 265 320 BR88
Fawood Ave. NW10 109 304 CR66
Faygate Cres., Bexh. 263 327 FA85
Faygate Rd. SW2 193 324 DM89
Fayland Ave. SW16 272 324 DJ92
Fearnley Cres., Hmptn. 266 329 BY92
Fearon St. SE10 252 318 EG78
Feathers Pl. SE10 167 317 ED79
Featherstone Ave. SE23 196 325 DV89
Featherstone Ind. Est., Sthl. 250 321 BY75
Featherstone Rd. NW7 218 305 CV51
Featherstone Rd., Sthl. 250 321 BY76
Featherstone St. EC1 38 316 DR70
Featherstone Ter., Sthl. 250 321 BY76
Featley Rd. SW9 178 324 DP83
Federal Rd., Grnf. 122 314 CJ68
Federation Rd. SE2 254 319 EV77
Felbridge Ave., Stan. 216 304 CG53
Felbridge Clo. SW16 273 324 DN91
Felbridge Clo., Sutt. 292 331 DB109
Felbrigge Rd., Ilf. 235 308 ET61
Felday Rd. SE13 182 325 EB86
Felden Clo., Pnr. 214 303 BY52
Felden St. SW6 157 315 CZ81
Feldman Clo. N16 102 307 DU60
Felgate Ms. W6 146 315 CV77
Felhampton Rd. SE9 261 326 EP89
Felhurst Cres., Dag. 237 309 FB63
Felix Ave. N8 220 306 DL58
Felix La., Shep. 281 328 BS100
Felix Rd. W13 132 314 CG73
Felix St. E2 128 317 DV68
Felixstowe Rd. N9 210 301 DU48
Felixstowe Rd. N17 221 306 DT55
Felixstowe Rd. NW10 126 315 CV69
Felixstowe Rd. SE2 254 319 EV76
Fell Rd., Croy. 287 332 DQ104
Fell Wk., Edg. 217 304 CP53
Fellbrigg Rd. SE22 179 324 DT85
Fellbrigg St. E1 128 317 DV70
Fellbrook, Rich. 184 322 CH90
Fellowes Clo., Hayes 242 313 BX70
Fellowes Rd., Cars. 285 331 DE104
Fellows Ct. E2 27 316 DT68
Fellows Rd. NW3 113 305 DD66
Felltram Way SE7 252 318 EG77
Felmersham Clo. SW4 177 324 DK84
Felmingham Rd. SE20 274 325 DW96
Fels Clo., Dag. 237 309 FB62
Fels Fm. Ave., Dag. 237 309 FC62
Felsberg Rd. SW2 177 324 DL86
Felsham Rd. SW15 173 323 CX83
Felspar Clo. SE18 253 318 ET78
Felstead Ave., Ilf. 225 308 EN53
Felstead Gdns. E14 150 317 EC78
Felstead Rd. E11 234 308 EG59
Felstead Rd., Orp. 291 335 EU103
Felstead Rd., Rom. 227 309 FC51
Felstead St. E9 119 307 DZ65
Felsted Rd. E16 244 318 EK72
Feltham Ave., E.Mol. 267 329 CE98
Feltham Hill Rd., Ashf. 265 328 BP92
Feltham Hill Rd., Felt. 266 329 BU91
Feltham Rd., Ashf. 265 328 BP91
Feltham Rd., Mitch. 271 323 DF96
Felthambrook Ind. Est., Felt. 258 321 BV90
Felthambrook Way, Felt. 258 321 BV90
Felton Clo., Orp. 290 334 EP100
Felton Gdns., Bark. 245 318 ES67
Felton Lea, Sid. 277 326 ET92
Felton Rd. W13 142 314 CJ75
Felton Rd., Bark. 245 318 ES68
Felton St. N1 26 316 DR67
Fen Ct. EC3 62/3 316 DS73
Fen Gro., Sid. 261 326 ET86
Fen St. E16 141 317 EF73
Fencepiece Rd., Ilf. 225 308 EQ51
Fenchurch Ave. EC3 50/1 316 DS72
Fenchurch Bldgs. EC3 50/1 316 DS72
Fenchurch Pl. EC3 62/3 316 DS73
Fenchurch St. EC3 62/3 316 DS73
Fendall Rd., Epsom 283 330 CQ106
Fendall St. SE1 74/5 316 DS76
Fendt Clo. E16 141 317 EF73
Fendyke Rd., Belv. 254 319 EX76
Fenelon Pl. W14 147 315 CZ77
Fenham Rd. SE15 164 317 DU80
Fenman Ct. N17 222 307 DV53
Fenman Gdns., Ilf. 236 309 EV60
Fenn Clo., Brom. 276 326 EG93
Fenn St. E9 118 307 DW64
Fennel Clo. E16 131 317 EE70
Fennel Clo., Croy. 288 333 DX102
Fennel St. SE18 253 318 EN79
Fenner Clo. SE16 148 317 DV77
Fenner Sq. SW11 175 323 DD83
Fenning St. SE1 74/5 316 DS75
Fenstanton Ave. N12 219 305 DD51
Fenswood Clo., Bex. 263 327 FA86
Fentiman Rd. SW8 161 316 DL79
Fentiman Way, Horn. 238 311 FL60
Fenton Ave., Stai. 264 328 BJ93
Fenton Clo. E8 117 306 DT65
Fenton Clo. SW9 161 316 DM82
Fenton Clo., Chis. 276 326 EM92
Fenton Rd. N17 221 306 DQ52
Fentons Ave. E13 244 318 EH68
Fenwick Clo. SE18 253 318 EN79
Fenwick Gro. SE15 180 325 DU83
Fenwick Pl. SW9 177 324 DL83
Fenwick Rd. SE15 180 325 DU83
Ferdinand Pl. NW1 114 306 DG66
Ferdinand St. NW1 114 306 DG66
Fergus Rd. N5 116 306 DP64
Ferguson Ave., Rom. 228 310 FJ54
Ferguson Ave., Surb. 282 330 CM99
Ferguson Clo. E14 150 317 EA77
Ferguson Clo., Brom. 275 325 ED97
Ferguson Ct., Rom. 228 310 FK54
Ferguson Dr. W3 135 314 CR72
Ferme Pk. Rd. N4 99 306 DM59
Ferme Pk. Rd. N8 220 306 DL57
Fermor Rd. SE23 197 325 DY88
Fermoy Rd. W9 127 315 CZ70
Fermoy Rd., Grnf. 243 313 CB70
Fern Ave., Mitch. 272 324 DK98
Fern Dene W13 132 314 CH71
Fern Gro., Felt. 258 321 BV87
Fern La., Houns. 250 321 BZ78
Fern St. E3 130 317 EA70
Fern Wk., Ashf. 264 328 BK92
Fernbank Ave., Horn. 238 310 FJ63
Fernbank Ave., Wem. 233 313 CF63
Fernbrook Ave., Sid. 261 326 ES85
Fernbrook Cres. SE13 183 325 EE86
Fernbrook Dr., Har. 233 313 CB59
Fernbrook Rd. SE13 183 325 EE86
Ferncliff Rd. E8 118 307 DU64
Ferncroft Ave. N12 219 305 DE51
Ferncroft Ave. NW3 96 305 DA62
Ferncroft Ave., Ruis. 232 313 BW61
Ferndale, Brom. 276 326 EJ96
Ferndale Ave. E17 223 307 ED57
Ferndale Ave., Houns. 258 321 BY83
Ferndale Ct. SE3 167 317 EF80
Ferndale Cres., Uxb. 240 312 BJ69
Ferndale Rd. E7 234 308 EH66
Ferndale Rd. E11 105 307 EE61
Ferndale Rd. N15 221 306 DT58
Ferndale Rd. SE25 287 333 DV99
Ferndale Rd. SW4 177 324 DM84
Ferndale Rd. SW9 177 324 DL84
Ferndale Rd., Ashf. 264 328 BK92
Ferndale Rd., Enf. 203 301 DY36
Ferndale Rd., Rom. 227 309 FC54
Ferndale St. E6 245 318 EP73
Ferndale Ter., Har. 215 303 CF56
Ferndale Way, Orp. 291 334 ER106
Ferndell Ave., Bex. 263 327 FD90
Fernden Way, Rom. 227 309 FB58
Ferndene Rd. SE24 178 324 DQ84
Ferndown, Horn. 228 311 FM58
Ferndown, Nthwd. 214 303 BU54
Ferndown Ave., Orp. 291 334 ER102
Ferndown Clo., Pnr. 214 303 BY52
Ferndown Clo., Sutt. 293 331 DD107
Ferndown Rd. SE9 260 326 EK87
Fernes Clo., Uxb. 248 312 BJ72
Ferney Meade Way, Islw. 152 314 CG82
Ferney Rd., Barn. 208 300 DG45
Fernhall Dr., Ilf. 224 308 EK57
Fernham Rd., Th.Hth. 273 324 DQ97
Fernhead Rd. W9 127 315 CZ69
Fernheath Way, Dart. 279 327 FD92
Fernhill Ct. E17 223 307 ED54
Fernhill Gdns., Kings.T. 268 322 CK92
Fernhill St. E16 244 318 EM74
Fernholme Rd. SE15 181 325 DX85
Fernhurst Gdns., Edg. 217 304 CN51
Fernhurst Rd. SW6 157 315 CY81
Fernhurst Rd., Ashf. 265 328 BQ91
Fernhurst Rd., Croy. 287 333 DU101
Fernlea Rd. SW12 192 324 DH88
Fernlea Rd., Mitch. 272 324 DG96
Fernleigh Clo., Croy. 286 332 DN105
Fernleigh Ct., Har. 215 303 CB54
Fernleigh Ct., Wem. 91 304 CL61
Fernleigh Rd. N21 209 300 DN47
Ferns Clo., Enf. 203 301 DY36
Ferns Clo., S.Croy. 295 333 DV110
Ferns Rd. E15 121 307 EF65
Fernsbury St. WC1 36 316 DN69
Fernshaw Rd. SW10 158 315 DC79
Fernside NW11 96 305 DA61
Fernside Ave. NW7 205 298 CR48
Fernside Ave., Felt. 266 329 BV91
Fernside Rd. SW12 191 323 DF88
Fernthorpe Rd. SW16 272 324 DJ93
Ferntower Rd. N5 117 306 DR64
Fernways, Ilf. 235 308 EP63
Fernwood Ave. SW16 272 324 DK91
Fernwood Ave., Wem. 106 304 CJ64
Fernwood Clo., Brom. 276 326 EJ96
Fernwood Cres. N20 207 299 DF48
Ferranti Clo. SE18 252 318 EK76
Ferraro Clo., Houns. 251 321 CA79
Ferrers Ave., Wall. 286 332 DK105
Ferrers Ave., West Dr. 248 320 BK75
Ferrers Rd. SW16 272 324 DK92
Ferrestone Rd. N8 220 306 DM56
Ferriby Clo. N1 116 306 DN66
Ferrier Pt. E16 244 318 EH71
Ferrier St. SW18 174 323 DB84
Ferring Clo., Har. 233 313 CC60
Ferrings SE21 195 324 DS89
Ferris Ave., Croy. 288 333 DZ104
Ferris Rd. SE22 180 325 DU84
Ferron Rd. E5 102 307 DV62
Ferry La. N17 222 307 DV56
Ferry La. SW13 155 314 CT79
Ferry La., Brent. 153 314 CL79
Ferry La., Cher. 280 328 BG100
Ferry La., Rain. 247 319 FE72
Ferry La., Rich. 153 314 CM79
Ferry La., Shep. 281 328 BN102
Ferry La. (Laleham), Stai. 280 328 BJ97
Ferry Pl. SE18 253 318 EN76
Ferry Rd. SW13 156 315 CU80
Ferry Rd., Tedd. 268 322 CH92
Ferry Rd., Twick. 184 322 CH88
Ferry Rd., W.Mol. 267 329 CA97
Ferry Sq., Brent. 153 314 CK79
Ferry Sq., Shep. 281 328 BP101
Ferry St. E14 150 317 EC78
Ferrymead Ave., Grnf. 243 313 CA69
Ferrymead Dr., Grnf. 243 313 CA69
Ferrymead Gdns., Grnf. 243 313 CC68
Ferrymoor, Rich. 184 322 CH90
Festing Rd. SW15 173 323 CX83
Festival Clo., Bex. 262 327 EX88
Festival Clo., Erith 255 319 FF80
Festival Clo., Uxb. 241 312 BP67
Fetter La. EC4 48 316 DN72
Ffinch St. SE8 166 317 EA80
Fiddicroft Ave., Bans. 292 331 DB114
Field Clo. E4 223 307 EB51
Field Clo., Brom. 276 326 EJ96
Field Clo., Chess. 282 330 CJ106
Field Clo., Hayes 257 320 BQ80
Field Clo., Houns. 250 321 BV81
Field Clo., Ruis. 231 312 BQ60
Field Clo., S.Croy. 295 333 DV114
Field Ct. WC1 47 316 DM71
Field End, Couls. 294 332 DK114
Field End, Nthlt. 232 313 BX65
Field End, Ruis. 232 313 BW65
Field End, Twick. 267 329 CF91
Field End Rd., Pnr. 214 303 BV57
Field End Rd., Ruis. 232 313 BW60
Field La., Brent. 152 314 CJ80
Field La., Tedd. 268 322 CG92
Field Mead NW7 217 304 CS52
Field Mead NW9 217 304 CS52
Field Pl., N.Mal. 283 330 CT100
Field Rd. E7 234 308 EG63
Field Rd. N17 221 306 DR55
Field Rd. W6 147 315 CY78
Field Rd., Felt. 258 321 BV86
Field St. WC1 35 316 DM69
Field Vw., Felt. 265 328 BR91
Field Way NW10 108 304 CQ66
Field Way, Grnf. 243 313 CB67
Field Way, Ruis. 231 312 BQ60
Field Way, Uxb. 240 312 BK70
Fieldend Rd. SW16 272 324 DJ95
Fielders Clo., Enf. 202 300 DS42
Fielders Clo., Har. 233 313 CC60
Fieldfare Rd. SE28 246 319 EW73
Fieldgate La., Mitch. 271 323 DE97
Fieldgate St. E1 138 317 DU71
Fieldhouse Rd. SW12 192 324 DJ88
Fielding Ave., Twick. 259 321 CC90
Fielding Ho. NW6 28 315 DA69
Fielding Ms. SW13 156 315 CV79
Fielding Rd. W4 145 314 CR76
Fielding Rd. W14 147 315 CX76
Fielding St. SE17 162 316 DQ79
Fieldings, The SE23 196 325 DW88
Fields Est. E8 118 307 DU66
Fields Pk. Cres., Rom. 226 309 EW57
Fieldsend Rd., Sutt. 284 331 CY106
Fieldside Clo., Orp. 291 334 EQ105
Fieldside Rd., Brom. 275 325 ED92
Fieldview SW18 191 323 DD88
Fieldway, Dag. 236 309 EW62
Fieldway, Orp. 291 334 ER100
Fieldway Cres. N5 116 306 DN64
Fiennes Clo., Dag. 236 309 EW60
Fiesta Dr., Dag. 247 319 FC70
Fife Rd. E16 244 318 EG71
Fife Rd. N22 221 306 DP52
Fife Rd. SW14 170 322 CQ85
Fife Rd., Kings.T. 268 322 CL96
Fife Ter. N1 23 316 DM68
Fifehead Clo., Ashf. 264 328 BL93
Fifield Path SE23 197 325 DX90
Fifth Ave. E12 234 308 EM63
Fifth Ave. W10 127 315 CY69
Fifth Ave., Hayes 249 312 BT74
Fifth Cross Rd., Twick. 259 321 CD89
Fifth Way, Wem. 108 304 CP63
Fig Tree Clo. NW10 125 314 CS67
Figges Rd., Mitch. 272 324 DG94
Filey Ave. N16 102 307 DU60
Filey Clo., Sutt. 293 331 DC108
Filey Waye, Ruis. 232 313 BU61
Fillebrook Ave., Enf. 202 300 DS40
Fillebrook Rd. E11 105 307 ED60
Filmer Rd. SW6 157 315 CY81
Filston Rd., Erith 255 319 FB78
Finborough Rd. SW10 76/7 315 DB78
Finborough Rd. SW17 271 323 DF93
Finch Ave. SE27 273 324 DR91
Finch Clo. NW10 109 304 CR64
Finch Clo., Barn. 207 299 DA43
Finch Dr., Felt. 258 321 BX87
Finch La. EC3 50 316 DR72
Finch Ms. SE15 163 316 DT81
Finchale Rd. SE2 254 319 EU76
Fincham Clo., Uxb. 231 312 BQ61
Finchdale Rd. SE2 254 319 EU76
Finchdean Way SE15 163 316 DT80
Finchingfield Ave., Wdf.Grn. 224 308 EJ52
Finchley Ct. N3 219 305 DB51
Finchley La. NW4 218 305 CW56
Finchley Pk. N12 207 299 DC49
Finchley Pl. NW8 18 315 DD68
Finchley Rd. NW2 96 305 DA62
Finchley Rd. NW3 112 305 DB64
Finchley Rd. NW8 113 305 DD66
Finchley Rd. NW11 218 305 CZ56
Finchley Way N3 219 305 DA52
Finck St. SE1 71 316 DM75
Finden Rd. E7 234 308 EH64
Findhorn Ave., Hayes 242 313 BV71
Findhorn St. E14 140 317 EC72
Findon Clo. SW18 174 323 DA86
Findon Clo., Har. 233 313 CB62
Findon Rd. N9 210 301 DV46
Findon Rd. W12 146 315 CU75
Fine Bush La., Uxb. 231 302 BP58
Fingal St. SE10 151 317 EF78
Finians Clo., Uxb. 240 312 BM66
Finland Quay SE16 149 317 DY76
Finland Rd. SE4 181 325 DY83
Finland St. SE16 149 317 DY76
Finlay St. SW6 157 315 CX81
Finlays Clo., Chess. 282 330 CN106
Finnis St. E2 128 317 DV69
Finnymore Rd., Dag. 236 309 EY66
Finsbury Ave. EC2 50 316 DR71
Finsbury Circ. EC2 50 316 DR71
Finsbury Cotts. N22 220 306 DL52
Finsbury Est. EC1 36 316 DN69
Finsbury Ho. N22 220 306 DL53
Finsbury Mkt. EC2 38/9 316 DS70
Finsbury Pk. Ave. N4 221 306 DQ58
Finsbury Pk. Rd. N4 100 306 DP61
Finsbury Pavement EC2 50 316 DR71
Finsbury Rd. N22 220 306 DM53
Finsbury Sq. EC2 50 316 DR71
Finsbury St. EC2 50 316 DR71
Finsbury Way, Bex. 262 327 EZ86
Finsen Rd. SE5 178 324 DQ83
Finstock Rd. W10 137 315 CX72
Finucane Gdns., Rain. 238 310 FG65
Fir Dene, Orp. 290 334 EM104
Fir Gro., N.Mal. 283 330 CT100
Fir Rd., Felt. 266 329 BX92
Fir Rd., Sutt. 284 331 CZ102
Fir Tree Ave., West Dr. 249 320 BN76
Fir Tree Clo. SW16 272 324 DJ92
Fir Tree Clo. W5 133 314 CL72
Fir Tree Clo., Epsom 283 330 CT105
Fir Tree Clo., Orp. 291 334 ET106
Fir Tree Clo., Rom. 227 309 FD55
Fir Tree Gdns., Croy. 288 333 EA105
Fir Tree Gro., Cars. 293 331 DF108
Fir Tree Pl., Ashf. 265 328 BN92
Fir Tree Rd., Bans. 292 331 CW114
Fir Tree Rd., Houns. 258 321 BY84
Fir Tree Wk., Dag. 237 309 FC62
Fir Tree Wk., Enf. 202 300 DR41
Fir Trees Clo. SE16 139 317 DY74
Firbank Clo. E16 244 318 EK71
Firbank Clo., Enf. 202 300 DQ42
Firbank Rd. SE15 164 317 DV82
Fircroft Ave., Chess. 282 330 CM105
Fircroft Gdns., Har. 233 313 CE62
Fircroft Rd. SW17 191 323 DF89
Firdene, Surb. 283 330 CQ102
Fire Bell All., Surb. 282 330 CL100
Firecrest Dr. NW3 96 305 DB62
Firefly Clo., Wall. 294 332 DL108
Firefly Gdns. E6 244 318 EL70
Firham Pk. Ave., Rom. 229 311 FN52
Firhill Rd. SE6 275 325 EA91
Firs, The N20 207 299 DD46
Firs, The W5 133 314 CK71
Firs, The, Bex. 263 327 FD88
Firs Ave. N10 220 306 DG55
Firs Ave. N11 219 305 DF51
Firs Ave. SW14 170 322 CQ84
Firs Clo. N10 220 306 DG55
Firs Clo. SE23 197 325 DX87
Firs Clo., Mitch. 272 324 DH96
Firs Dr., Houns. 250 321 BV81
Firs La. N13 209 300 DQ48
Firs La. N21 209 300 DQ47
Firs Pk. Ave. N21 209 300 DR46
Firs Pk. Gdns. N21 209 300 DQ46
Firs Wk., Nthwd. 213 302 BR51
Firsby Ave., Croy. 288 333 DX102
Firsby Rd. N16 101 306 DT60
Firscroft N13 209 300 DQ48
Firside Gro., Sid. 261 326 ET88
First Ave. E12 234 308 EL63
First Ave. E13 244 318 EG69
First Ave. E17 223 307 EA57
First Ave. N18 210 301 DW49
First Ave. NW4 218 305 CW56
First Ave. SW14 171 322 CS83
First Ave. W3 135 314 CT74
First Ave. W10 127 315 CZ70
First Ave., Bexh. 254 319 EW80
First Ave., Dag. 247 319 FB68
First Ave., Enf. 209 300 DT43
First Ave., Hayes 249 312 BT74
First Ave., Rom. 226 309 EW57
First Ave., Wem. 91 304 CK61
First Ave., W.Mol. 266 329 BZ98
First Clo., W.Mol. 267 329 CC97
First Cross Rd., Twick. 259 321 CE89
First St. SW3 78/9 315 DE77
First Way, Wem. 108 304 CP63
Firstway SW20 270 323 CW96
Firswood Ave., Epsom 283 330 CT106
Firth Gdns. SW6 157 315 CY81
Firtree Ave., Mitch. 272 324 DG96
Fish St. Hill EC3 62 316 DR73
Fisher Clo., Croy. 287 332 DT102
Fisher Clo., Grnf. 243 313 CA69
Fisher Rd., Har. 215 303 CF54
Fisher St. E16 244 318 EG71
Fisher St. WC1 47 316 DM71
Fisherman Clo., Rich. 268 322 CJ91
Fishermans Dr. SE16 149 317 DX75
Fisherman's Wk. E14 140 317 EA74
Fishers Ct. SE14 165 317 DX81
Fishers La. W4 145 314 CR77
Fishers Way, Belv. 247 319 FC74
Fisherton Est. NW8 30 315 DD70
Fisherton St. NW8 30 315 DD70
Fisherton St. Est. NW8 30 315 DD70
Fishponds Rd. SW17 271 323 DE91
Fishponds Rd., Kes. 290 334 EK106
Fisons Rd. E16 244 318 EG74
Fitzalan Rd. N3 218 305 CY55
Fitzalan St. SE11 83 316 DM77
Fitzgeorge Ave. W14 147 315 CY77
Fitzgeorge Ave., N.Mal. 269 322 CR95
Fitzgerald Ave. SW14 171 322 CS83
Fitzgerald Clo. E11 224 308 EG57
Fitzgerald Ho. E14 140 317 EB72
Fitzgerald Ho., Hayes 242 313 BV74
Fitzgerald Rd. E11 224 308 EG57
Fitzgerald Rd. SW14 171 322 CR83
Fitzhardinge St. W1 44 316 DG72
Fitzhugh Gro. SW18 175 323 DD86
Fitzhugh Gro. Est. SW18 175 323 DD86
Fitzilian Ave., Rom. 228 311 FM53
Fitzjames Ave. W14 147 315 CY77
Fitzjames Ave., Croy. 287 333 DU103
Fitzjohn Ave., Barn. 206 299 CY43
Fitzjohn's Ave. NW3 113 305 DD64
Fitzmaurice Pl. W1 56/7 316 DH74
Fitzneal St. W12 135 314 CT72
Fitzroy Clo. N6 97 305 DF60
Fitzroy Ct. W1 33 316 DJ70
Fitzroy Cres. W4 155 314 CR80
Fitzroy Gdns. SE19 273 324 DS94
Fitzroy Ms. W1 33 316 DJ70
Fitzroy Pk. N6 97 305 DF61
Fitzroy Rd. NW1 20 316 DG67
Fitzroy Sq. W1 33 316 DJ70
Fitzroy St. W1 33 316 DJ70
Fitzroy Yd. NW1 20 316 DG67
Fitzstephen Rd., Dag. 236 309 EV64
Fitzwarren Gdns. N19 98 306 DJ60
Fitzwilliam Ave., Rich. 153 314 CM82
Fitzwilliam Ms. E16 141 317 EE72
Fitzwilliam Rd. SW4 176 324 DJ83
Fitzwygram Clo., Hmptn. 267 329 CC92
Five Acre NW9 217 304 CT53
Five Bell All. E14 139 317 DZ73
Five Elms Rd., Brom. 289 334 EH104
Five Elms Rd., Dag. 236 309 EZ62
Five Oaks La., Chig. 226 309 EY51
Fiveacre Clo., Th.Hth. 286 332 DN100
Fiveways Rd. SW9 162 316 DN82
Fladbury Rd. N15 221 306 DR58
Fladgate Rd. E11 223 307 EE58
Flag Clo., Croy. 288 333 DX102
Flag Wk., Pnr. 214 303 BU58
Flambard Rd., Har. 216 304 CG58
Flamborough Rd., Ruis. 232 313 BU62
Flamborough St. E14 139 317 DY72
Flamingo Gdns., Nthlt. 242 313 BY69
Flamingo Wk., Horn. 238 310 FG66
Flamstead Gdns., Dag. 236 309 EW66
Flamstead Rd., Dag. 236 309 EW66
Flamsted Ave., Wem. 108 304 CN65
Flamsteed Rd. SE7 252 318 EL78
Flanchford Rd. W12 145 314 CT76
Flanders Cres. SW17 271 323 DF94
Flanders Rd. E6 244 318 EM68
Flanders Rd. W4 145 314 CS77
Flanders Way E9 119 307 DX65
Flank St. E1 138 317 DU73
Flash La., Enf. 202 300 DP37
Flask Cotts. NW3 113 305 DD63
Flask Wk. NW3 112 305 DC63
Flavell Ms. SE10 151 317 EE78
Flaxen Clo. E4 211 301 EB48
Flaxen Rd. E4 211 301 EB48
Flaxley Rd., Mord. 284 331 DB100
Flaxman Ct. W1 46 316 DK72
Flaxman Rd. SE5 178 324 DP83
Flaxman Ter. WC1 34 316 DK69
Flaxmore Pl., Beck. 289 333 ED100
Flaxton Rd. SE18 253 318 ER80
Fleece Dr. N9 210 301 DU49
Fleece Rd., Surb. 282 330 CJ102
Fleece Wk. N7 115 306 DL65
Fleeming Clo. E17 222 307 DZ54
Fleeming Rd. E17 222 307 DZ54
Fleet Ave., Upmin. 229 311 FR58
Fleet Clo., Ruis. 231 302 BQ58
Fleet Clo., Upmin. 229 311 FR58
Fleet Pl. EC4 48 316 DN72
Fleet Rd. NW3 113 305 DE64
Fleet Sq. WC1 35 316 DM69
Fleet St. EC4 48 316 DN72
Fleet St. Hill E1 128 317 DU70
Fleetway W. Business Pk., Grnf. 122 314 CH68
Fleetwood Clo. E16 244 318 EK71
Fleetwood Clo., Croy. 287 332 DS104
Fleetwood Ct. E6 244 318 EM71
Fleetwood Gro. W3 135 314 CS73
Fleetwood Rd. NW10 110 305 CU64
Fleetwood Rd., Kings.T. 269 322 CP97
Fleetwood Sq., Kings.T. 269 322 CP97
Fleetwood St. N16 101 306 DS61
Fleming Ave., Ruis. 232 313 BV61
Fleming Ct. W2 42 315 DD71
Fleming Ct., Croy. 286 332 DN106
Fleming Gdns., Rom. 228 310 FK54
Fleming Mead, Mitch. 271 323 DE94
Fleming Rd. SE17 162 316 DP79
Fleming Rd., Sthl. 243 313 CB72
Fleming Way SE28 246 319 EX73
Fleming Way, Islw. 259 321 CF83
Flemish Flds., Cher. 280 328 BG101
Flempton Rd. E10 103 307 DY60
Fletcher Clo. E6 245 318 EP72
Fletcher La. E10 104 307 EC59
Fletcher Path SE8 166 317 EA80
Fletcher Rd. W4 144 314 CQ76
Fletcher St. E1 138 317 DU73
Fletchers Clo., Brom. 276 326 EH98
Fletching Rd. E5 102 307 DW62
Fletching Rd. SE7 252 318 EJ79
Fletton Rd. N11 220 306 DL52
Fleur de Lis St. E1 38/9 316 DS70
Fleur Gates SW19 189 323 CX87
Flexmere Gdns. N17 221 306 DR53
Flexmere Rd. N17 221 306 DR53
Flight App. NW9 217 304 CT54
Flimwell Clo., Brom. 275 325 EE92
Flint Clo., Sutt. 292 331 DB114
Flint Down Clo., Orp. 278 327 EU95
Flint St. SE17 86 316 DR77
Flintlock Clo., Stai. 256 320 BG84
Flintmill Cres. SE3 252 318 EL82
Flinton St. SE17 86/7 316 DS78
Flitcroft St. WC2 46 316 DK72
Flock Mill Pl. SW18 190 323 DB88
Flockton St. SE16 148 317 DU75
Flodden Rd. SE5 162 316 DQ81
Flood La., Twick. 184 322 CG88
Flood Pas. SE18 252 318 EM77
Flood St. SW3 78/9 315 DE78
Flood Wk. SW3 159 315 DE79
Flora Clo. E14 140 317 EB72
Flora Gdns. W6 146 315 CV77
Flora Gdns., Rom. 226 309 EW58
Flora St., Belv. 254 319 EZ78
Floral St. WC2 58/9 316 DL73
Florence Ave., Enf. 202 300 DQ41
Florence Ave., Mord. 285 331 DC99
Florence Cantwell Wk. N19 99 306 DL59
Florence Clo., Horn. 238 311 FL61
Florence Dr., Enf. 202 300 DQ41
Florence Gdns. W4 154 314 CQ79
Florence Gdns., Stai. 264 328 BH94
Florence Nightingale Ho. N1 117 306 DR65
Florence Rd. E6 244 318 EJ67
Florence Rd. E13 131 317 EF68
Florence Rd. N4 100 306 DN60
Florence Rd. SE2 254 319 EW76
Florence Rd. SE14 165 317 DZ81
Florence Rd. SW19 271 323 DB93
Florence Rd. W4 145 314 CR76
Florence Rd. W5 133 314 CL73
Florence Rd., Beck. 274 325 DY96
Florence Rd., Brom. 276 326 EG95
Florence Rd., Felt. 258 321 BV88
Florence Rd., Kings.T. 268 322 CM94
Florence Rd., S.Croy. 295 332 DR109
Florence Rd., Sthl. 250 321 BX77
Florence St. E16 131 317 EF70
Florence St. N1 116 306 DP66
Florence St. NW4 218 305 CW56
Florence Ter. SE14 165 317 DZ81
Florence Way SW12 191 323 DF88
Florfield Pas. E8 118 307 DV65
Florfield Rd. E8 118 307 DV65
Florian Ave., Sutt. 285 331 DD105
Florian Rd. SW15 173 323 CY84
Florida Rd., Th.Hth. 273 324 DP95
Florida St. E2 128 317 DU69
Floriston Ave., Uxb. 241 312 BQ66
Floriston Clo., Stan. 216 304 CH53
Floriston Gdns., Stan. 216 304 CH53
Floss St. SW15 156 315 CW82
Flower & Dean Wk. E1 51 316 DT71
Flower La. NW7 205 298 CT50
Flower Wk., The SW7 65 315 DC75
Flowers Ms. N19 98 306 DJ61
Flowersmead SW17 192 324 DG89
Floyd Rd. SE7 252 318 EJ78
Fludyer St. SE13 183 325 EE84
Folair Way SE16 148 317 DV78
Foley St. W1 45 316 DJ71
Folgate St. E1 50/1 316 DS71
Foliot St. W12 135 314 CT72
Folkes La., Upmin. 229 311 FS57
Folkestone Rd. E6 245 318 EN68
Folkestone Rd. E17 223 307 EB56
Folkestone Rd. N18 210 301 DU49
Folkingham La. NW9 217 304 CR53
Folkington Cor. N12 206 299 CZ50
Follett St. E14 140 317 EC72
Folly La. E4 222 307 DY53
Folly La. E17 222 307 DY53
Folly Ms. W11 137 315 CZ72
Folly Wall E14 150 317 EC75
Follyfield Rd., Bans. 292 331 DA114
Font Hills N2 219 305 DC54
Fontaine Rd. SW16 272 324 DM94
Fontarabia Rd. SW11 176 324 DG84
Fontayne Ave., Rain. 237 309 FE66
Fontayne Ave., Rom. 227 309 FE55
Fontenoy Rd. SW12 192 324 DH89
Fonteyne Gdns., Wdf.Grn. 224 308 EK54
Fonthill Clo. SE20 274 325 DU96
Fonthill Ms. N4 100 306 DN61
Fonthill Rd. N4 99 306 DM60
Fontley Way SW15 188 323 CU87
Fontmell Clo., Ashf. 265 328 BN92
Fontmell Pk., Ashf. 264 328 BM92
Fontwell Clo., Har. 215 303 CE52
Fontwell Clo., Nthlt. 233 313 CA65
Fontwell Dr., Brom. 290 334 EN99
Fontwell Pk. Gdns., Horn. 238 311 FL63
Football La., Har. 233 313 CE60
Footbury Hill Rd., Orp. 291 335 EU101
Footpath, The SW15 172 323 CU85
Foots Cray High St., Sid. 278 327 EW93
Foots Cray La., Sid. 262 327 EW88
Footscray Rd. SE9 261 326 EN86
Footway, The SE9 261 326 EQ87
Forbes Clo. NW2 94 305 CU61
Forbes Clo., Horn. 238 310 FH60
Forbes Ct. SE19 273 324 DS92
Forbes St. E1 138 317 DU72
Forbes Way, Ruis. 232 313 BV61
Forburg Rd. N16 102 307 DU60
Ford Clo. E3 129 317 DY68
Ford Clo., Ashf. 264 328 BL93
Ford Clo., Har. 233 313 CD59
Ford Clo., Rain. 237 309 FF66
Ford Clo., Shep. 281 328 BN98
Ford Clo., Th.Hth. 286 332 DP99
Ford End, Wdf.Grn. 224 308 EH51
Ford La., Iver 248 312 BG72

Ford La., Rain. 237 309 FF66
Ford Rd. E3 129 317 DY67
Ford Rd., Ashf. 264 328 BM91
Ford Rd., Cher. 280 328 BH102
Ford Rd., Dag. 236 309 EZ66
Ford Sq. E1 138 317 DV71
Ford St. E16 141 317 EF72
Fordbridge Clo., Cher. 280 328 BH102
Fordbridge Rd., Ashf. 264 328 BL93
Fordbridge Rd., Shep. 281 328 BS100
Fordbridge Rd., Sun. 281 328 BS100
Fordcroft Rd., Orp. 291 335 EV99
Forde Ave., Brom. 276 326 EJ97
Fordel Rd. SE6 199 325 ED88
Fordham Clo., Horn. 239 311 FN59
Fordham St. E1 138 317 DU72
Fordhook Ave. W5 133 314 CM73
Fordingley Rd. W9 127 315 CZ69
Fordington Rd. N6 219 305 DF57
Fordmill Rd. SE6 198 325 EA89
Fords Gro. N21 209 300 DQ46
Fords Pk. Rd. E16 244 318 EG72
Fordwater Rd., Cher. 280 328 BH102
Fordwater Trd. Est., Cher. 280 328 BH102
Fordwich Clo., Orp. 291 334 ET101
Fordwych Rd. NW2 111 305 CY63
Fordyce Clo., Horn. 238 311 FM59
Fordyce Rd. SE13 182 325 EC86
Fordyke Rd., Dag. 236 309 EZ61
Fore St. EC2 49 316 DQ71
Fore St. N9 210 301 DU49
Fore St. N18 221 306 DT51
Fore St., Pnr. 214 303 BU57
Fore St. Ave. EC2 50 316 DR71
Foreland Ct. NW4 218 305 CX53
Foreland St. SE18 253 318 ER77
Foreman Ct. W6 146 315 CW77
Foremark Clo., Ilf. 225 308 ET51
Foreshore SE8 149 317 DZ77
Forest, The E11 223 307 EE56
Forest App. E4 211 301 EE45
Forest App., Wdf.Grn. 224 308 EG52
Forest Ave. E4 211 301 EE45
Forest Business Pk. E17 103 307 DY59
Forest Clo. E11 223 307 EF57
Forest Clo., Chis. 277 326 EN95
Forest Ct. E4 211 301 EF46
Forest Ct. E11 223 307 EE56
Forest Cft. SE23 196 325 DV89
Forest Dr. E12 234 308 EK62
Forest Dr., Kes. 290 334 EL105
Forest Dr., Sun. 265 328 BT94
Forest Dr., Wdf.Grn. 223 307 ED52
Forest Dr. E. E11 105 307 ED59
Forest Dr. W. E11 104 307 EC59
Forest Gdns. N17 221 306 DT54
Forest Gate NW9 217 304 CS57
Forest Glade E4 211 301 EE49
Forest Glade E11 223 307 EE58
Forest Gro. E8 117 306 DT65
Forest Hill Rd. SE22 180 325 DV85
Forest Hill Rd. SE23 180 325 DW86
Forest Ind. Est., Ilf. 225 308 ES53
Forest La. E7 234 308 EG64
Forest La. E15 121 307 EE65
Forest Mt. Rd., Wdf.Grn. 223 307 ED52
Forest Ridge, Beck. 275 325 EA97
Forest Ridge, Kes. 290 334 EL105
Forest Ri. E17 223 307 ED57
Forest Rd. E7 234 308 EG63
Forest Rd. E8 117 306 DT65
Forest Rd. E11 105 307 ED59
Forest Rd. E17 222 307 DW56
Forest Rd. N9 210 301 DV46
Forest Rd. N17 222 307 DW56
Forest Rd., Enf. 203 301 DY36
Forest Rd., Felt. 258 321 BW89
Forest Rd., Ilf. 225 308 ES53
Forest Rd., Rich. 154 314 CN80
Forest Rd., Rom. 227 309 FB55
Forest Rd., Sutt. 284 331 DA102
Forest Side E4 211 301 EF45
Forest Side E7 234 308 EH63
Forest Side, Wor.Pk. 283 330 CT102
Forest St. E7 234 308 EG64
Forest Vw. E4 211 301 ED45
Forest Vw. E11 105 307 EF59
Forest Vw. Ave. E10 223 307 ED57
Forest Vw. Rd. E12 234 308 EL63
Forest Vw. Rd. E17 223 307 EC53
Forest Way N19 98 306 DJ61
Forest Way, Orp. 291 334 ET99
Forest Way, Sid. 261 326 ER87
Forestdale N14 208 300 DK49
Forester Rd. SE15 180 325 DV84
Foresters Clo., Wall. 294 332 DK108
Foresters Cres., Bexh. 263 327 FB84
Foresters Dr. E17 223 307 ED56
Foresters Dr., Wall. 294 332 DK107
Forestholme Clo. SE23 196 325 DW89
Forfar Rd. N22 221 306 DP53
Forfar Rd. SW11 160 316 DG81
Forge Clo., Brom. 289 334 EG102
Forge Clo., Hayes 257 320 BR79
Forge Cotts. W5 133 314 CK74
Forge La., Felt. 266 329 BY92
Forge La., Nthwd. 213 302 BS52
Forge La., Sun. 266 329 BU97
Forge La., Sutt. 292 331 CY108
Forge Pl. NW1 114 306 DG65
Forman Pl. N16 117 306 DT63
Formby Ave., Stan. 216 304 CJ55
Formosa St. W9 28/9 315 DB70
Formunt Clo. E16 141 317 EF71
Forres Gdns. NW11 219 305 DA58
Forrest Gdns. SW16 272 324 DM97
Forrester Path SE26 274 325 DW91
Forris Ave., Hayes 249 312 BT74
Forset St. W1 42/3 315 DE72
Forstal Clo., Brom. 276 326 EG97
Forster Rd. E17 222 307 DY58
Forster Rd. N17 221 306 DT55
Forster Rd. SW2 193 324 DL87
Forster Rd., Beck. 274 325 DY97
Forster Rd., Croy. 287 332 DQ101
Forsters Clo., Rom. 226 309 EZ58
Forsters Way, Hayes 242 313 BV72
Forston St. N1 26 316 DR68
Forsyte Cres. SE19 273 324 DS95
Forsyth Gdns. SE17 162 316 DP79
Forsyth Pl., Enf. 209 300 DS43
Forsythia Clo., Ilf. 235 308 EP64
Fort Rd. SE1 87 316 DT77
Fort Rd., Nthlt. 233 313 CA66
Fort St. E1 50/1 316 DS71
Fort St. E16 244 318 EH74
Forterie Gdns., Ilf. 236 309 EU62
Fortescue Ave. E8 118 307 DV66
Fortescue Ave., Twick. 259 321 CC90
Fortescue Rd. SW19 271 323 DD94
Fortescue Rd., Edg. 217 304 CQ53
Fortess Gro. NW5 114 306 DH64
Fortess Rd. NW5 114 306 DH64
Fortess Wk. NW5 114 306 DH64
Forth Rd., Upmin. 229 311 FR58
Forthbridge Rd. SW11 176 324 DG84
Fortis Clo. E16 244 318 EJ72
Fortis Grn. N2 219 305 DE56
Fortis Grn. N10 220 306 DG55
Fortis Grn. Ave. N2 219 305 DF55
Fortis Grn. Rd. N10 220 306 DG55
Fortismere Ave. N10 220 306 DG55
Fortnam Rd. N19 99 306 DK61
Fortnums Acre, Stan. 215 303 CF51
Fortrose Gdns. SW2 193 324 DK88
Fortuna Clo. N7 115 306 DM65
Fortune Gate Rd. NW10 125 314 CS67
Fortune Grn. Rd. NW6 112 305 DA63
Fortune La., Borwd. 204 298 CK44
Fortune St. EC1 37 316 DQ70
Fortune Wk. SE28 253 318 ER76
Fortune Way NW10 126 315 CU69
Fortunes Mead, Nthlt. 232 313 BY65
Forty Acre La. E16 244 318 EG71
Forty Ave., Wem. 91 304 CM62
Forty Clo., Wem. 91 304 CM62
Forty Hill, Enf. 202 300 DS38
Forty La., Wem. 92 304 CP61
Forum, The, W.Mol. 267 329 CB98
Forum Way, Edg. 217 304 CN51
Forumside, Edg. 217 304 CN51
Forval Clo., Mitch. 285 331 DF99
Forward Dr., Har. 215 303 CF56
Fosbury Ms. W2 52/3 315 DB73
Foscote Ms. W9 40 315 DA71
Foscote Rd. NW4 218 305 CV57
Foskett Rd. SW6 157 315 CZ82
Foss Ave., Croy. 286 332 DN106
Foss Rd. SW17 271 323 DD91
Fossdene Rd. SE7 252 318 EH78
Fossdyke Clo., Hayes 242 313 BY71
Fosse Way W13 132 314 CG71
Fossil Rd. SE13 182 325 EA83
Fossington Rd., Belv. 254 319 EX77
Fossway, Dag. 236 309 EW61
Foster La. EC2 49 316 DQ72
Foster Rd. E13 244 318 EG70
Foster Rd. W3 135 314 CS73
Foster Rd. W4 145 314 CR78
Foster St. NW4 218 305 CW56
Foster Wk. NW4 218 305 CW56
Fosters Clo. E18 224 308 EH53
Fosters Clo., Chis. 276 326 EM92
Fothergill Clo. E13 244 318 EG68
Fothergill Dr. N21 208 300 DM43
Fotheringham Rd., Enf. 204 300 DT42
Foubert's Pl. W1 45 316 DJ72
Foulden Rd. N16 117 306 DT63
Foulden Ter. N16 117 306 DT63
Foulis Ter. SW7 78 315 DD78
Foulser Rd. SW17 191 323 DF90
Foulsham Rd., Th.Hth. 273 324 DQ97
Founder Clo. E6 245 318 EP72
Founders Ct. EC2 50 316 DR72
Founders Gdns. SE19 273 324 DQ94
Foundry Clo. SE16 139 317 DY74
Foundry Ms. NW1 33 316 DJ70
Fount St. SW8 161 316 DK80
Fountain Clo., Uxb. 249 312 BQ71
Fountain Ct. EC4 60 316 DN73
Fountain Dr. SE19 273 324 DT91
Fountain Dr., Cars. 293 331 DF108
Fountain Grn. Sq. SE16 148 317 DU75
Fountain Ms. N5 116 306 DQ63
Fountain Pl. SW9 162 316 DN81
Fountain Rd. SW17 271 323 DD92
Fountain Rd., Th.Hth. 273 324 DQ96
Fountain Sq. SW1 80/1 316 DH77
Fountain St. E2 39 316 DT69
Fountains Ave., Felt. 258 321 BZ90
Fountains Clo., Felt. 258 321 BZ89
Fountains Cres. N14 208 300 DL45
Fountayne Rd. N15 222 307 DU56
Fountayne Rd. N16 102 307 DU61
Four Seasons Cres., Sutt. 284 331 CZ103
Four Seasons Ind. Est., Sthl. 251 321 CB76
Four Wents, The E4 211 301 ED47
Fouracres SW12 192 324 DH89
Fouracres, Enf. 203 301 DY39
Fourland Wk., Edg. 217 304 CQ51
Fournier St. E1 51 316 DT71
Fourth Ave. E12 234 308 EM63
Fourth Ave. W10 127 315 CY69
Fourth Ave., Hayes 249 312 BT74
Fourth Ave., Rom. 237 309 FC60
Fourth Cross Rd., Twick. 259 321 CD89
Fourth Way, Wem. 108 304 CQ63
Fowey Ave., Ilf. 224 308 EK57
Fowey Clo. E1 138 317 DV74
Fowler Clo. SW11 175 323 DD83
Fowler Rd. E7 234 308 EG63
Fowler Rd. N1 116 306 DP66
Fowler Rd., Ilf. 226 309 EV51
Fowler Rd., Mitch. 272 324 DG96
Fowlers Clo., Sid. 278 327 EY92
Fowlers Wk. W5 123 314 CK70
Fownes St. SW11 175 323 DE83
Fox and Knot St. EC1 48/9 316 DP71
Fox Clo. E1 128 317 DW70
Fox Clo. E16 244 318 EG71
Fox Clo., Borwd. 204 298 CK44
Fox Clo., Orp. 291 335 EU106
Fox Hill SE19 273 324 DT94
Fox Hill, Kes. 289 334 EH106
Fox Hill Gdns. SE19 273 324 DT94
Fox Hollow Dr., Bexh. 262 327 EX83
Fox Ho. Rd., Belv. 255 319 FB77
Fox La. N13 208 300 DL47
Fox La. W5 123 314 CL70
Fox La., Kes. 289 334 EH106
Fox Rd. E16 141 317 EF71
Foxberry Rd. SE4 183 325 DY83
Foxborough Gdns. SE4 182 325 EA86
Foxbourne Rd. SW17 192 324 DG89
Foxbury Ave., Chis. 277 326 ER93
Foxbury Clo., Brom. 276 326 EH93
Foxbury Clo., Orp. 291 335 EU106
Foxbury Rd., Brom. 276 326 EG93
Foxcombe Clo. E6 244 318 EK68
Foxcombe Rd. SW15 188 323 CU88
Foxcote SE5 86/7 316 DS78
Foxcroft Rd. SE18 253 318 EP81
Foxdell, Nthwd. 213 302 BR51
Foxearth Rd., S.Croy. 295 333 DV110
Foxes Dale SE3 252 326 EG83
Foxes Dale, Brom. 275 325 ED97
Foxfield Clo., Nthwd. 213 302 BT51
Foxfield Rd., Orp. 291 334 ER103
Foxglove Clo., Sthl. 242 313 BY73
Foxglove Clo., Stai. 264 320 BK88
Foxglove Gdns. E11 224 308 EJ56
Foxglove Gdns., Pur. 294 332 DL111
Foxglove La., Chess. 282 330 CN105
Foxglove St. W12 135 314 CT73
Foxglove Way, Wall. 285 332 DH102
Foxgrove N14 208 300 DL48
Foxgrove Ave., Beck. 275 325 EB94
Foxgrove Rd., Beck. 275 325 EB94
Foxhall Rd., Upmin. 239 311 FQ64
Foxham Rd. N19 99 306 DK62
Foxhole Rd. SE9 260 326 EL85
Foxholt Gdns. NW10 108 304 CQ66
Foxhome Clo., Chis. 277 326 EN93
Foxlands Cres., Dag. 237 309 FC64
Foxlands La., Dag. 237 309 FC64
Foxlands Rd., Dag. 237 309 FC64
Foxlees, Wem. 106 304 CG63
Foxley Clo. E8 118 307 DU64
Foxley Gdns., Pur. 294 332 DP113
Foxley Hill Rd., Pur. 294 332 DN112
Foxley La., Pur. 294 332 DJ111
Foxley Rd. SW9 162 316 DN80
Foxley Rd., Ken. 294 332 DP114
Foxley Rd., Th.Hth. 273 324 DP98
Foxley Sq. SW9 162 316 DP80
Foxmoor Ct., Uxb. 230 302 BG58
Foxmore St. SW11 159 315 DF81
Fox's Path, Mitch. 271 323 DE96
Foxton Gro., Mitch. 271 323 DD96
Foxwell Clo. SE4 181 325 DY83
Foxwell Ms. SE4 181 325 DY83
Foxwell St. SE4 181 325 DY83
Foxwood Clo. NW7 205 298 CS49
Foxwood Clo., Felt. 258 321 BV90
Foxwood Grn. Clo., Enf. 209 300 DS44
Foxwood Rd. SE3 183 325 EF84
Foyle Rd. N17 222 307 DU53
Foyle Rd. SE3 167 317 EF79
Framfield Clo. N12 207 299 DA48
Framfield Ct., Enf. 209 300 DS44
Framfield Rd. N5 116 306 DP64
Framfield Rd. W7 243 313 CF72
Framfield Rd., Mitch. 272 324 DG94
Framlingham Clo. E5 102 307 DW61
Framlingham Cres. SE9 276 326 EL91
Frampton Clo., Sutt. 292 331 DA108
Frampton Pk. Est. E9 118 307 DW66
Frampton Pk. Rd. E9 118 307 DW65
Frampton Rd., Houns. 258 321 BY85
Frampton St. NW8 30 315 DD70
Francemary Rd. SE4 182 325 EA85
Frances Rd. E4 223 307 EA51
Frances St. SE18 252 318 EM77
Franche Ct. Rd. SW17 190 323 DC90
Francis Ave., Bexh. 255 319 FA82
Francis Ave., Felt. 258 321 BU90
Francis Ave., Ilf. 235 308 ER61
Francis Barber Clo. SW16 272 324 DM91
Francis Chichester Way SW11 160 316 DG81
Francis Clo. E14 151 317 ED77
Francis Clo., Epsom 283 330 CR105
Francis Clo., Shep. 281 328 BN98
Francis Gro. SW19 270 323 CZ93
Francis Rd. E10 104 307 EC60
Francis Rd. N2 219 305 DF56
Francis Rd., Croy. 286 332 DP101
Francis Rd., Grnf. 122 314 CH68
Francis Rd., Har. 216 304 CG57
Francis Rd., Houns. 250 321 BX82
Francis Rd., Ilf. 235 308 ER61
Francis Rd., Orp. 278 327 EX97
Francis Rd., Pnr. 214 303 BW57
Francis Rd., Wall. 294 332 DJ107
Francis St. E15 121 307 EE64
Francis St. SW1 81 316 DJ77
Francis St., Ilf. 235 308 ER61
Francis Ter. N19 98 306 DJ62
Francis Wk. N1 23 316 DM67
Franciscan Rd. SW17 271 323 DF92
Francklyn Gdns., Edg. 205 298 CN48
Francombe Gdns., Rom. 228 310 FG58
Franconia Rd. SW4 177 324 DK85
Frank Bailey Wk. E12 235 308 EN64
Frank Burton Clo. SE7 252 318 EH78
Frank Dixon Clo. SE21 195 324 DS88
Frank Dixon Way SE21 195 324 DS88
Frank St. E13 244 318 EG70
Frank Trowell Ct., Felt. 258 321 BU88
Frankfurt Rd. SE24 178 324 DQ85
Frankham St. SE8 166 317 EA80
Frankland Clo. SE16 148 317 DW77
Frankland Rd. E4 211 301 EA50
Frankland Rd. SW7 66 315 DD76
Franklin Clo. N20 207 299 DC45
Franklin Clo. SE13 166 317 EB81
Franklin Clo. SE27 194 324 DP90
Franklin Clo., Kings.T. 269 322 CN97
Franklin Cres., Mitch. 272 324 DJ98
Franklin Ho. NW9 93 304 CT59
Franklin Pas. SE9 260 326 EL83
Franklin Rd. SE20 274 325 DW94
Franklin Rd., Bexh. 254 319 EY81
Franklin Rd., Horn. 238 310 FJ65
Franklin Sq. W14 147 315 CZ78
Franklin St. E3 130 317 EB69
Franklin St. N15 221 306 DS58
Franklin Way, Croy. 286 332 DL102
Franklins Ms., Har. 233 313 CC61
Franklin's Row SW3 79 315 DF78
Franklyn Gdns., Ilf. 225 308 ER51
Franklyn Rd. NW10 109 304 CT66
Franks Ave., N.Mal. 282 322 CQ98
Frankswood Ave., Orp. 290 334 EP99
Frankswood Ave., West Dr. 248 312 BM72
Franlaw Cres. N13 209 300 DQ49
Franmil Rd., Horn. 238 310 FG60
Fransfield Gro. SE26 196 325 DV90
Frant Clo. SE20 274 325 DW94
Frant Rd., Th.Hth. 286 332 DP99
Franthorne Way SE6 198 325 EB89
Fraser Clo. E6 244 318 EL72
Fraser Clo., Bex. 263 327 FC88
Fraser Ho., Brent. 143 314 CM78
Fraser Rd. E17 223 307 EB57
Fraser Rd. N9 210 301 DV48
Fraser Rd., Erith 255 319 FC78
Fraser Rd., Grnf. 122 314 CH67
Fraser St. W4 145 314 CS78
Frating Cres., Wdf.Grn. 224 308 EH51
Frays Ave., West Dr. 248 320 BK75
Frays Clo., West Dr. 248 320 BK76
Frays Lea, Uxb. 240 312 BJ68
Frays Waye, Uxb. 240 312 BJ67
Frazer Ave., Ruis. 232 313 BW64
Frazer Clo., Rom. 237 309 FF59
Frazier St. SE1 72 316 DN75
Frean St. SE16 148 317 DU76
Fred Wigg Twr. E11 105 307 EF61
Freda Corbett Clo. SE15 164 317 DU80
Frederic Ms. SW1 67 315 DF75
Frederic St. E17 222 307 DY57
Frederica Rd. E4 211 301 ED45
Frederica St. N7 115 306 DM66
Frederick Clo. W2 54/5 315 DE73
Frederick Clo., Sutt. 284 331 CZ105
Frederick Ct. NW2 95 305 CY62
Frederick Cres. SW9 162 316 DP80
Frederick Cres., Enf. 203 301 DW40
Frederick Gdns., Sutt. 284 331 CZ106
Frederick Pl. SE18 253 318 EP78
Frederick Rd. SE17 84/5 316 DP78
Frederick Rd., Rain. 247 319 FD68
Frederick Rd., Sutt. 284 331 CZ106
Frederick Sq. SE16 139 317 DY73
Frederick St. WC1 35 316 DM69
Frederick Ter. E8 27 316 DT67
Frederick's Pl. EC2 50 316 DR72
Fredericks Pl. N12 207 299 DC49
Frederick's Row EC1 36/7 316 DP69
Fredora Ave., Hayes 241 312 BT70
Free Prae Rd., Cher. 280 328 BG102
Freeborne Gdns., Rain. 238 310 FG65
Freedom Clo. E17 222 307 DY56
Freedom Rd. N17 221 306 DR54
Freedom St. SW11 159 315 DF82
Freedown La., Sutt. 292 331 DB113
Freegrove Rd. N7 115 306 DL64
Freeland Pk. NW4 218 305 CY54
Freeland Rd. W5 133 314 CM73
Freelands Gro., Brom. 276 326 EH95
Freelands Rd., Brom. 276 326 EH95
Freeling St. N1 115 306 DM66
Freeman Clo., Nthlt. 232 313 BY66
Freeman Dr., W.Mol. 266 329 BZ97
Freeman Rd., Mord. 285 331 DD99
Freeman Way, Horn. 228 311 FL58
Freemans Clo., Shep. 281 328 BS98
Freemans La., Hayes 249 312 BS73
Freemantle Ave., Enf. 210 301 DX43
Freemasons Rd. E16 244 318 EH71
Freemasons Rd., Croy. 287 332 DS102
Freesia Clo., Orp. 291 334 ET106
Freethorpe Clo. SE19 273 324 DS95
Freezeland Way, Uxb. 241 312 BN65
Freke Rd. SW11 176 324 DG83
Fremantle Rd., Belv. 255 319 FA77
Fremantle Rd., Ilf. 225 308 EQ54
Fremantle St. SE17 86/7 316 DS78
Fremont St. E9 128 317 DW67
French Ordinary Ct. EC3 62/3 316 DS73
French Pl. E1 38/9 316 DS70
French St., Sun. 266 329 BW96
Frendsbury Rd. SE4 181 325 DY84
Frensham Clo., Sthl. 242 313 BZ70
Frensham Ct., Mitch. 271 323 DD97
Frensham Dr. SW15 187 322 CT90
Frensham Rd. SE9 261 326 ER89
Frensham Rd., Ken. 294 332 DP114
Frensham St. SE15 164 317 DU79
Frere St. SW11 159 315 DE82
Fresh Wf. Rd., Bark. 245 318 EP67
Freshfield Ave. E8 117 306 DT66
Freshfield Clo. SE13 183 325 ED84
Freshfield Dr. N14 208 300 DH45
Freshfields, Croy. 288 333 DZ101
Freshfields Ave., Upmin. 239 311 FP64
Freshford St. SW18 190 323 DC90
Freshwater Clo. SW17 272 324 DG93
Freshwater Rd. SW17 272 324 DG93
Freshwater Rd., Dag. 236 309 EX60
Freshwell Ave., Rom. 226 309 EW56
Freshwood Clo., Beck. 275 325 EB95
Freshwood Way, Wall. 293 332 DH109
Freston Gdns., Barn. 207 299 DF43
Freston Pk. N3 218 305 CZ54
Freston Rd. W10 137 315 CX73
Freston Rd. W11 137 315 CX73
Freta Rd., Bexh. 262 327 EZ85
Frewin Rd. SW18 191 323 DD88
Friar Ms. SE27 194 324 DP90
Friar Rd., Hayes 242 313 BX70
Friar Rd., Orp. 291 335 EU99
Friar St. EC4 48/9 316 DP72
Friars Ave. N20 207 299 DE48
Friars Ave. SW15 187 322 CT90
Friars Clo. E4 211 301 EC48
Friars Clo. N2 219 305 DD56
Friars Clo., Nthlt. 242 313 BX69
Friars Gdns. W3 135 314 CR72
Friars La., Rich. 169 322 CK85
Friars Mead E14 150 317 EC76
Friars Ms. SE9 261 326 EN85
Friars Pl. La. W3 135 314 CR73
Friars Rd. E6 244 318 EK67
Friars Stile Pl., Rich. 169 322 CL86
Friars Stile Rd., Rich. 169 322 CL86
Friars Wk. N14 208 300 DH45
Friars Wk. SE2 254 319 EX78
Friars Way W3 135 314 CR72
Friars Way, Cher. 280 328 BG99
Friary Clo. N12 207 299 DE50
Friary Ct. SW1 57 316 DJ74
Friary Est. SE15 164 317 DU79
Friary Rd. N12 207 299 DD49
Friary Rd. SE15 164 317 DU80
Friary Rd. W3 134 314 CQ72
Friary Way N12 207 299 DE49
Friday Hill E4 211 301 EE47
Friday Hill E. E4 211 301 EE48
Friday Hill W. E4 211 301 EE47
Friday Rd., Erith 255 319 FD78
Friday Rd., Mitch. 271 323 DF94
Friday St. EC4 61 316 DQ73
Frideswide Pl. NW5 114 306 DJ64
Friend St. EC1 36/7 316 DP69
Friendly Pl. SE13 166 317 EB81
Friendly St. SE8 166 317 EA82
Friendly St. Ms. SE8 166 317 EA82
Friends Rd., Croy. 287 332 DR104
Friends Rd., Pur. 294 332 DP112
Friends Wk., Uxb. 240 312 BK66
Friendship Wk., Nthlt. 242 313 BX69
Friern Barnet La. N11 207 299 DF49
Friern Barnet La. N20 207 299 DC47
Friern Barnet Rd. N11 207 299 DF50
Friern Ct. N20 207 299 DD48
Friern Mt. Dr. N20 207 299 DC45
Friern Pk. N12 207 299 DC50
Friern Rd. SE22 196 325 DU87
Friern Watch Ave. N12 207 299 DC49
Frigate Ms. SE8 166 317 EA79
Frimley Ave., Horn. 239 311 FN60
Frimley Clo. SW19 189 323 CY89
Frimley Ct., Sid. 278 327 EW92
Frimley Gdns., Mitch. 271 323 DE97
Frimley Rd., Chess. 282 330 CK106
Frimley Rd., Ilf. 235 308 ES62
Frimley Way E1 129 317 DX70
Frimley Way, Wall. 286 332 DL106
Fringewood Clo., Nthwd. 213 302 BP53
Frinsted Clo., Orp. 278 327 EX98
Frinsted Rd., Erith 255 319 FD80
Frinton Dr., Wdf.Grn. 223 307 ED52
Frinton Ms., Ilf. 225 308 EN58
Frinton Rd. E6 244 318 EK69
Frinton Rd. N15 221 306 DS58
Frinton Rd. SW17 272 324 DG93
Frinton Rd., Rom. 226 309 EZ52
Frinton Rd., Sid. 262 327 EY89
Friston St. SW6 158 315 DB82
Friswell Pl., Bexh. 263 327 FA84
Frith Ct. NW7 218 305 CY52
Frith La. NW7 218 305 CY52
Frith Rd. E11 120 307 EC63
Frith Rd., Croy. 287 332 DQ103
Frith St. W1 46 316 DK72
Fritham Clo., N.Mal. 283 330 CS100
Frithville Gdns. W12 136 315 CW74
Frithwood Ave., Nthwd. 213 302 BS51
Frizlands La., Dag. 237 309 FB63
Frobisher Clo., Pnr. 232 313 BX59
Frobisher Cres., Stai. 264 320 BL87
Frobisher Gdns., Stai. 264 320 BL87
Frobisher Pas. E14 140 317 EA74
Frobisher Rd. E6 244 318 EM72
Frobisher Rd. N8 221 306 DN56
Frobisher Rd., Erith 255 319 FF80
Frobisher St. SE10 167 317 EE79
Frog La., Rain. 247 319 FD71
Frogley Rd. SE22 179 324 DT84
Frogmoor La., Rick. 212 302 BK47
Frogmore SW18 174 323 DA85
Frogmore Ave., Hayes 241 312 BS70
Frogmore Clo., Sutt. 284 331 CX104
Frogmore Gdns., Hayes 241 312 BS70
Frogmore Gdns., Sutt. 284 331 CY105
Frognal NW3 112 305 DC64
Frognal Ave., Har. 215 303 CF56
Frognal Ave., Sid. 278 327 EU92
Frognal Clo. NW3 112 305 DC64
Frognal Ct. NW3 112 305 DC65
Frognal Gdns. NW3 112 305 DC63
Frognal La. NW3 112 305 DB64
Frognal Par. NW3 112 305 DC65
Frognal Pl., Sid. 278 327 EU93
Frognal Ri. NW3 96 305 DC62
Frognal Way NW3 112 305 DC63
Froissart Rd. SE9 260 326 EK85
Frome Rd. N22 221 306 DP55
Frome St. N1 25 316 DQ68
Fromondes Rd., Sutt. 284 331 CY106
Front La., Upmin. 239 311 FS61
Frostic Wk. E1 138 317 DU71
Froude St. SW8 160 316 DH82
Fruen Rd., Felt. 265 320 BT87
Fry Rd. E6 234 308 EK66
Fry Rd. NW10 125 314 CT67
Fryatt Rd. N17 221 306 DR52
Fryatt St. E14 141 317 EE72
Fryent Clo. NW9 217 304 CN57
Fryent Cres. NW9 217 304 CS58
Fryent Flds. NW9 217 304 CS58
Fryent Gro. NW9 217 304 CS58
Fryent Way NW9 217 304 CN57
Frye's Bldgs. N1 24 316 DN68
Frying Pan All. E1 51 316 DT71
Fryston Ave., Couls. 293 332 DH114
Fryston Ave., Croy. 287 333 DU103
Fuchsia St. SE2 254 319 EV78
Fulbeck Dr. NW9 217 304 CS53
Fulbeck Way, Har. 215 303 CC54
Fulbourne Rd. E17 223 307 EC53
Fulbourne St. E1 138 317 DV71
Fulbrook Ms. N19 114 306 DJ63
Fulbrook Rd. N19 114 306 DJ63
Fulbrooks Ave., Wor.Pk. 283 330 CT102
Fulford St. SE16 148 317 DV75
Fulham Bdy. SW6 158 315 DA80
Fulham Clo., Uxb. 241 312 BQ70
Fulham Ct. SW6 158 315 DA80
Fulham High St. SW6 157 315 CY82
Fulham Palace Rd. SW6 157 315 CX79
Fulham Palace Rd. W6 146 315 CW78
Fulham Pk. Gdns. SW6 157 315 CZ82
Fulham Pk. Rd. SW6 157 315 CZ82
Fulham Rd. SW3 78 315 DD78
Fulham Rd. SW6 157 315 CY82
Fulham Rd. SW10 78 315 DD78
Fuller Clo. E2 128 317 DU70
Fuller Clo., Orp. 291 334 ET106
Fuller Rd., Dag. 236 309 EV62
Fuller St. NW4 218 305 CW56
Fuller Ter., Ilf. 235 308 EQ64
Fuller Way, Hayes 249 320 BT78
Fullers Ave., Surb. 282 330 CM103
Fullers Ave., Wdf.Grn. 223 307 EF52
Fullers Clo., Rom. 227 309 FC52
Fullers La., Rom. 227 309 FC52
Fullers Rd. E18 223 307 EF53
Fullers Way N., Surb. 282 330 CM104
Fullers Way S., Chess. 282 330 CL105
Fullers Wd., Croy. 288 333 EA106
Fullerton Rd. SW18 174 323 DC85
Fullerton Rd., Cars. 293 331 DE109
Fullerton Rd., Croy. 287 332 DT101
Fullwell Ave., Ilf. 224 308 EM53
Fullwoods Ms. N1 38 316 DR69
Fulmar Ct., Surb. 282 330 CM100
Fulmar Rd., Horn. 238 310 FG66
Fulmead St. SW6 158 315 DB81
Fulmer Clo., Hmptn. 266 329 BY92
Fulmer Rd. E16 244 318 EK71
Fulmer Way W13 142 314 CH76
Fulready Rd. E10 223 307 ED57
Fulstone Clo., Houns. 258 321 BZ84
Fulthorp Rd. SE3 167 317 EF82
Fulton Ms. W2 53 315 DC73
Fulton Rd., Wem. 92 304 CN62
Fulwell Cross Roundabout, Ilf. 225 308 ER54
Fulwell Pk. Ave., Twick. 259 321 CB89
Fulwell Rd., Tedd. 267 329 CD91
Fulwood Ave., Wem. 123 314 CM68
Fulwood Clo., Hayes 249 312 BT72
Fulwood Gdns., Twick. 259 321 CF86
Fulwood Pl. WC1 47 316 DM71
Fulwood Wk. SW19 189 323 CY88
Furber St. W6 146 315 CV76
Furham Feild, Pnr. 215 303 CA52
Furley Rd. SE15 164 317 DU80
Furlong Clo., Wall. 285 332 DG102
Furlong Rd. N7 116 306 DN65
Furmage St. SW18 190 323 DB87
Furneaux Ave. SE27 273 324 DP92
Furner Clo., Dart. 263 327 FF83
Furness Rd. NW10 126 315 CU68
Furness Rd. SW6 158 315 DB82
Furness Rd., Har. 233 313 CB59
Furness Rd., Mord. 284 331 DB101
Furness Way, Horn. 238 310 FG64
Furnival St. EC4 48 316 DN72
Furrow La. E9 118 307 DW64
Furrows, The, Uxb. 230 302 BJ57
Fursby Ave. N3 219 305 DA51
Further Acre NW9 217 304 CT54
Further Grn. Rd. SE6 199 325 EE87
Furtherfield Clo., Croy. 286 332 DN100
Furze Fm. Clo., Rom. 226 309 EY54
Furze Hill, Pur. 294 332 DL111
Furze La., Pur. 294 332 DL111
Furze Rd., Th.Hth. 273 324 DQ97
Furze St. E3 140 317 EA71
Furzedown Dr. SW17 272 324 DH92
Furzedown Rd. SW17 272 324 DH92
Furzedown Rd., Sutt. 293 331 DC111
Furzefield Clo., Chis. 277 326 EP93
Furzefield Rd. SE3 252 318 EH80
Furzeground Way, Uxb. 249 312 BQ74
Furzeham Rd., West Dr. 248 320 BL75
Furzewood, Sun. 266 329 BU95
Fuschia Ct., Wdf.Grn. 223 307 EE52
Fyfe Way, Brom. 276 326 EG96
Fyfield Clo., Brom. 275 325 ED98
Fyfield Ct. E7 234 308 EG65
Fyfield Rd. E17 223 307 ED55
Fyfield Rd. SW9 178 324 DN83
Fyfield Rd., Enf. 202 300 DS41
Fyfield Rd., Rain. 247 319 FF67
Fyfield Rd., Wdf.Grn. 224 308 EJ52
Fynes St. SW1 82 316 DK77

Gable Clo. SE26 274 325 DV91
Gable Clo., Pnr. 215 303 CA52
Gable Ct. SE26 274 325 DV92
Gables, The, Wem. 107 304 CM63
Gables Ave., Ashf. 264 328 BM92
Gables Clo. SE5 163 316 DS81
Gables Clo. SE12 260 326 EG88
Gabriel Clo., Felt. 266 329 BX91
Gabriel Clo., Rom. 227 309 FC52
Gabriel St. SE23 197 325 DX87
Gabrielle Clo., Wem. 91 304 CM62
Gabrielle Ct. NW3 113 305 DD65
Gad Clo. E13 244 318 EH69
Gaddesden Ave., Wem. 107 304 CM65
Gade Clo., Hayes 242 313 BV74
Gadsbury Clo. NW9 217 304 CT58
Gadsden Clo., Upmin. 229 311 FS58
Gadwall Clo. E16 244 318 EH72
Gadwall Way SE28 253 318 ER75
Gage Rd. E16 141 317 EE71
Gage St. WC1 46/7 316 DL71
Gainford St. N1 24 316 DN67
Gainsborough Ave. E12 235 308 EN64
Gainsborough Clo., Beck. 275 325 EA94
Gainsborough Ct. N12 207 299 DB50
Gainsborough Ct. W12 146 315 CW75
Gainsborough Dr., S.Croy. 295 333 DU113
Gainsborough Gdns. NW3 97 305 DD62
Gainsborough Gdns. NW11 95 305 CZ59
Gainsborough Gdns., Edg. 216 304 CM54
Gainsborough Gdns., Grnf. 233 313 CE64
Gainsborough Gdns., Islw. 259 321 CD85
Gainsborough Ms. SE26 196 325 DV90
Gainsborough Rd. E11 105 307 EE59
Gainsborough Rd. E15 131 317 EE69
Gainsborough Rd. N12 207 299 DB50
Gainsborough Rd. W4 145 314 CT77
Gainsborough Rd., Dag. 236 309 EV63
Gainsborough Rd., Hayes 241 312 BQ68
Gainsborough Rd., N.Mal. 283 330 CR100
Gainsborough Rd., Rich. 153 314 CM82
Gainsborough Rd., Wdf.Grn. 224 308 EL51
Gainsborough Sq., Bexh. 262 327 EX83
Gainsford Rd. E17 222 307 DZ56
Gainsford St. SE1 75 316 DT75
Gairloch Rd. SE5 163 316 DS82
Gaisford St. NW5 114 306 DJ65
Gaitskell Rd. SE9 261 326 EQ88
Galahad Rd., Brom. 260 326 EG90
Galata Rd. SW13 156 315 CU80
Galatea Sq. SE15 180 325 DV83
Galbraith St. E14 150 317 EC76
Gale Clo., Hmptn. 266 329 BY93
Gale Clo., Mitch. 271 323 DD97
Gale St. E3 140 317 EA71
Gale St., Dag. 236 309 EW64
Galeborough Ave., Wdf.Grn. 223 307 ED52
Galen Pl. WC1 46/7 316 DL71
Galena Rd. W6 146 315 CV77
Gales Gdns. E2 128 317 DV69
Gales Way, Wdf.Grn. 224 308 EL52
Galesbury Rd. SW18 174 323 DC86
Galgate Clo. SW19 189 323 CY88
Gallants Fm. Rd., Barn. 207 299 DE45
Galleon Clo. SE16 149 317 DX75
Gallery Gdns., Nthlt. 242 313 BX68
Gallery Rd. SE21 195 324 DR88
Galleywall Rd. SE16 148 317 DV77
Galleywood Cres., Rom. 227 309 FD51
Gallia Rd. N5 116 306 DP64
Galliard Clo. N9 210 301 DW44
Galliard Rd. N9 210 301 DU46
Gallions Clo., Bark. 246 319 EU69
Gallions Rd. E16 245 318 EP73
Gallions Rd. SE7 252 318 EH77
Gallions Roundabout E16 252 318 EK78
Gallon Clo. SE7 252 318 EJ77
Gallop, The, S.Croy. 295 333 DV108
Gallop, The, Sutt. 293 331 DD110
Gallosson Rd. SE18 253 318 ES77
Galloway Path, Croy. 287 332 DR105
Galloway Rd. W12 136 315 CU74
Gallows Cor., Rom. 228 310 FJ53
Gallus Clo. N21 208 300 DM44
Gallus Sq. SE3 260 326 EH83
Galpins Rd., Th.Hth. 286 332 DL99
Galsworthy Ave., Rom. 236 309 EV59
Galsworthy Clo. SE28 246 319 EV74
Galsworthy Cres. SE3 252 318 EJ81
Galsworthy Rd. NW2 111 305 CY63
Galsworthy Rd., Cher. 280 328 BG101
Galsworthy Rd., Kings.T. 269 322 CP94
Galsworthy Ter. N16 101 306 DS62
Galton St. W10 127 315 CY69
Galvani Way, Croy. 286 332 DM102
Galveston Rd. SW15 173 323 CZ85
Galway St. EC1 37 316 DQ69
Gambetta St. SW8 160 316 DH82
Gambia St. SE1 60/1 316 DP74
Gambole Rd. SW17 271 323 DE91
Gamlen Rd. SW15 173 323 CX84
Gamuel Clo. E17 223 307 EA58
Gander Grn. La., Sutt. 284 331 CY103
Gandhi Clo. E17 223 307 EA58
Gane Clo., Wall. 294 332 DL108
Ganton St. W1 57 316 DJ73
Gantshill Cres., Ilf. 225 308 EN57
Gantshill Cross, Ilf. 225 308 EN58
Gap Rd. SW19 271 323 DA92
Garage Rd. W3 134 314 CN72

Garbutt Pl. W1 44 316 DG71
Garbutt Rd., Upmin. 239 311 FQ61
Gard St. EC1 36/7 316 DP69
Garden Ave., Bexh. 263 327 FA83
Garden Ave., Mitch. 272 324 DH94
Garden City, Edg. 217 304 CN51
Garden Clo. E4 211 301 EA50
Garden Clo. SE12 260 326 EH90
Garden Clo. SW15 188 323 CV87
Garden Clo., Ashf. 265 328 BQ93
Garden Clo., Hmptn. 266 329 BZ92
Garden Clo., Nthlt. 242 313 BY67
Garden Clo., Ruis. 231 312 BS61
Garden Clo., Wall. 286 332 DL106
Garden Cotts., Orp. 278 327 EW96
Garden Ct. EC4 60 316 DN73
Garden Ct. SE15 163 316 DT81
Garden Ct., Rich. 153 314 CM81
Garden Ct., W.Mol. 267 329 CB98
Garden La. SW2 193 324 DM88
Garden La., Brom. 276 326 EH93
Garden Ms. W2 52 315 DA73
Garden Rd. NW8 29 315 DC69
Garden Rd. SE20 274 325 DW95
Garden Rd., Brom. 276 326 EH94
Garden Rd., Rich. 170 322 CN83
Garden Row SE1 72/3 316 DP76
Garden St. E1 139 317 DX71
Garden Ter. SW1 82 316 DK78
Garden Wk. EC2 38/9 316 DS69
Garden Wk., Beck. 274 325 DZ95
Garden Way NW10 108 304 CQ65
Gardeners Clo. N11 208 300 DG49
Gardeners Rd., Croy. 286 332 DP102
Gardenia Rd., Enf. 209 300 DS44
Gardens, The SE22 180 325 DU84
Gardens, The, Beck. 275 325 EC95
Gardens, The, Felt. 257 320 BR86
Gardens, The, Har. 215 303 CC58
Gardens, The, Pnr. 214 303 BZ58
Gardiner Ave. NW2 110 305 CW64
Gardiner Clo., Dag. 236 309 EX63
Gardiner Clo., Orp. 278 327 EW96
Gardner Clo. E11 224 308 EH58
Gardner Gro., Felt. 258 321 BZ89
Gardner Rd. E13 244 318 EH70
Gardners La. EC4 61 316 DQ73
Gardnor Rd. NW3 113 305 DD63
Garendon Gdns., Mord. 284 331 DB101
Garendon Rd., Mord. 284 331 DA101
Gareth Clo., Wor.Pk. 284 331 CX103
Gareth Gro., Brom. 276 326 EG91
Garfield Rd. E4 211 301 ED46
Garfield Rd. E13 131 317 EF70
Garfield Rd. SW11 176 324 DG83
Garfield Rd. SW19 271 323 DC92
Garfield Rd., Enf. 203 301 DW42
Garfield Rd., Twick. 184 322 CG88
Garford St. E14 140 317 EA73
Garganey Wk. SE28 246 319 EW73
Garibaldi St. SE18 253 318 ES77
Garland Rd. SE18 253 318 ER80
Garland Rd., Stan. 216 304 CL53
Garland Way, Horn. 228 311 FL56
Garlands Ct., Croy. 287 332 DR105
Garlick Hill EC4 61 316 DQ73
Garlies Rd. SE23 197 325 DY90
Garlinge Rd. NW2 111 305 CZ65
Garman Clo. N18 209 300 DR50
Garman Rd. N17 222 307 DW52
Garnault Ms. EC1 36 316 DN69
Garnault Pl. EC1 36 316 DN69
Garnault Rd., Enf. 202 300 DT38
Garner Rd. E17 223 307 EC53
Garner St. E2 128 317 DU68
Garnet Rd. NW10 109 304 CS65
Garnet Rd., Th.Hth. 273 324 DQ98
Garnet St. E1 138 317 DW73
Garnet Wk. E6 244 318 EL71
Garnett Clo. SE9 260 326 EM83
Garnett Rd. NW3 113 305 DF64
Garnett Way E17 222 307 DY53
Garnham Clo. N16 101 306 DT61
Garnham St. N16 101 306 DT61
Garnies Clo. SE15 163 316 DT80
Garrad's Rd. SW16 193 324 DK90
Garrard Clo., Bexh. 263 327 FA83
Garrard Clo., Chis. 277 326 EP92
Garrard Wk. NW10 109 304 CS65
Garratt Clo., Croy. 286 332 DL105
Garratt La. SW17 271 323 DD91
Garratt La. SW18 174 323 DB85
Garratt Rd., Edg. 217 304 CN52
Garratt Ter. SW17 271 323 DE91
Garrett Clo. W3 135 314 CR71
Garrett St. EC1 37 316 DQ70
Garrick Ave. NW11 218 305 CY58
Garrick Clo. SW18 174 323 DC84
Garrick Clo. W5 123 314 CL70
Garrick Clo., Rich. 169 322 CK85
Garrick Clo., Stai. 264 328 BG94
Garrick Cres., Croy. 287 332 DS103
Garrick Dr. NW4 218 305 CW54
Garrick Dr. SE28 253 318 ER76
Garrick Gdns., W.Mol. 267 329 CA97
Garrick Pk. NW4 218 305 CX54
Garrick Rd. NW9 217 304 CT58
Garrick Rd., Grnf. 243 313 CB70
Garrick Rd., Rich. 154 314 CN82
Garrick St. WC2 58/9 316 DL73
Garrick Way NW4 218 305 CX56
Garrison Clo. SE18 253 318 EN80
Garrolds Clo., Swan. 279 327 FD96
Garry Clo., Rom. 227 309 FE52
Garry Way, Rom. 227 309 FE52
Garside Clo. SE28 253 318 ER76
Garside Clo., Hmptn. 267 329 CB93
Garsington Ms. SE4 181 325 DZ83
Garston La., Ken. 295 332 DR114
Garter Way SE16 149 317 DX75
Garth, The, Hmptn. 267 329 CB93
Garth, The, Har. 216 304 CM58
Garth Clo. W4 145 314 CR78
Garth Clo., Kings.T. 268 322 CM92
Garth Clo., Mord. 284 331 CX101
Garth Clo., Ruis. 232 313 BX60
Garth Ct. W4 145 314 CR78
Garth Ms. W5 123 314 CL70
Garth Rd. NW2 95 305 CZ61
Garth Rd. W4 155 314 CR79
Garth Rd., Kings.T. 268 322 CM92
Garth Rd., Mord. 284 331 CW100
Garth Rd. Ind. Est., Mord. 284 331 CX101
Garthland Dr., Barn. 206 299 CV43
Garthorne Rd. SE23 197 325 DX87
Garthside, Rich. 268 322 CL92
Garthway N12 219 305 DE51
Gartmoor Gdns. SW19 189 323 CZ88
Gartmore Rd., Ilf. 235 308 ET61
Garton Pl. SW18 174 323 DC86
Gartons Clo., Enf. 203 301 DW42
Gartons Way SW11 174 323 DC83
Garvary Rd. E16 244 318 EH72
Garway Rd. W2 40/1 315 DB72
Gascoigne Gdns., Wdf.Grn. 223 307 EE52
Gascoigne Pl. E2 39 316 DT69
Gascoigne Rd., Bark. 245 318 EQ67
Gascony Ave. NW6 112 305 DA66
Gascoyne Clo., Rom. 228 310 FK52
Gascoyne Dr., Dart. 255 319 FF82
Gascoyne Rd. E9 119 307 DX66
Gaselee St. E14 140 317 EC73
Gasholder Pl. SE11 83 316 DM78
Gaskarth Rd. SW12 176 324 DH86
Gaskarth Rd., Edg. 217 304 CQ53
Gaskell Rd. N6 219 305 DF58
Gaskell St. SW4 161 316 DL82
Gaskin St. N1 24/5 316 DP67
Gaspar Clo. SW5 76/7 315 DB77
Gaspar Ms. SW5 76/7 315 DB77
Gassiot Rd. SW17 271 323 DF91
Gassiot Way, Sutt. 285 331 DD104
Gastein Rd. W6 157 315 CX79
Gaston Bell Clo., Rich. 169 322 CM83
Gaston Bri. Rd., Shep. 281 328 BR100
Gaston Rd., Mitch. 272 324 DG97
Gaston Way, Shep. 281 328 BQ99
Gataker St. SE16 148 317 DV76
Gatcombe Rd. E16 141 317 EE72
Gatcombe Rd. N19 99 306 DK62
Gate End, Nthwd. 214 303 BU52
Gate Ho. Sq. SE1 61 316 DQ74
Gate Ms. SW7 66/7 315 DE75
Gate St. WC2 47 316 DM72
Gateforth St. NW8 30/1 315 DE70
Gatehill Rd., Nthwd. 213 302 BT52
Gatehouse Clo., Kings.T. 269 322 CQ94
Gateley Rd. SW9 177 324 DM83
Gater Dr., Enf. 202 300 DR39
Gates Grn. Rd., Kes. 289 334 EH105
Gates Grn. Rd., W.Wick. 289 333 EF104
Gatesborough St. EC2 38/9 316 DS70
Gateside Rd. SW17 191 323 DF90
Gatestone Rd. SE19 273 324 DS93
Gateway SE17 162 316 DQ79
Gateway Arc. N1 24/5 316 DP68
Gateway Clo., Nthwd. 213 302 BQ51
Gateway Ind. Est. NW10 125 314 CT69
Gateway Ms. E8 117 306 DT64
Gateways, The SW3 78/9 315 DE77
Gatfield Gro., Felt. 259 321 CA89
Gathorne Rd. N22 221 306 DN54
Gathorne St. E2 129 317 DX68
Gatley Ave., Epsom 282 330 CP106
Gatliff Rd. SW1 80/1 316 DH78
Gatling Rd. SE2 254 319 EU78
Gatting Clo., Edg. 217 304 CQ52
Gatting Way, Uxb. 240 312 BL65
Gatton Clo., Sutt. 292 331 DB109
Gatton Rd. SW17 271 323 DE91
Gattons Way, Sid. 278 327 EZ91
Gatward Clo. N21 209 300 DP44
Gatward Grn. N9 209 300 DT47
Gatwick Rd. SW18 189 323 CZ87
Gatwick Way, Horn. 238 311 FM63
Gauden Clo. SW4 177 324 DK83
Gauden Rd. SW4 161 316 DK82
Gaumont Ter. W12 146 315 CW75
Gaunt St. SE1 73 316 DQ76
Gauntlet Clo., Nthlt. 232 313 BY66
Gauntlett Ct., Wem. 106 304 CH64
Gauntlett Rd., Sutt. 285 331 DD106
Gautrey Rd. SE15 164 317 DW82
Gautrey Sq. E6 244 318 EM72
Gavel St. SE17 86 316 DR77
Gaverick St. E14 150 317 EA77
Gavestone Cres. SE12 260 326 EH87
Gavestone Rd. SE12 260 326 EH87
Gaviller Pl. E5 118 307 DV63
Gavin St. SE18 253 318 ES77
Gavina Clo., Mord. 285 331 DD99
Gawber St. E2 128 317 DW69
Gawsworth Clo. E15 121 307 EE64
Gawthorne Ave. NW7 206 299 CY50
Gawthorne Ct. E3 130 317 EA68
Gay Clo. NW2 110 305 CV64
Gay Gdns., Dag. 237 309 FC63
Gay Rd. E15 131 317 ED68
Gay St. SW15 173 323 CX83
Gaydon Ho. W2 40/1 315 DB71
Gaydon La. NW9 217 304 CS53
Gayfere Rd., Epsom 283 331 CU106
Gayfere Rd., Ilf. 224 308 EM55
Gayfere St. SW1 70/1 316 DL76
Gayford Rd. W12 145 314 CT75
Gayhurst SE17 163 316 DR79
Gayhurst Rd. E8 118 307 DU66
Gaylor Rd., Nthlt. 232 313 BZ64
Gaynes Ct., Upmin. 239 311 FP63
Gaynes Hill Rd., Wdf.Grn. 224 308 EL51
Gaynes Pk. Rd., Upmin. 239 311 FN63
Gaynes Rd., Upmin. 239 311 FP61
Gaynesford Rd. SE23 197 325 DX89
Gaynesford Rd., Cars. 293 331 DF108
Gaysham Ave., Ilf. 225 308 EN57
Gaysham Hall, Ilf. 225 308 EP55
Gayton Ct., Har. 215 303 CF58
Gayton Cres. NW3 113 305 DD63
Gayton Rd. NW3 113 305 DD63
Gayton Rd. SE2 254 319 EW76
Gayton Rd., Har. 215 303 CF58
Gayville Rd. SW11 175 323 DF86
Gaywood Clo. SW2 193 324 DM88
Gaywood Est. SE1 72/3 316 DP76
Gaywood Rd. E17 223 307 EA55
Gaywood St. SE1 72/3 316 DP76
Gaza St. SE17 84/5 316 DP78
Geariesville Gdns., Ilf. 225 308 EP56
Geary Rd. NW10 110 305 CU64
Geary St. N7 115 306 DM64
GEC Est., Wem. 91 304 CK62
Geddes Pl., Bexh. 263 327 FA84
Gedeney Rd. N17 221 306 DQ53
Gedling Pl. SE1 75 316 DT76
Gee St. EC1 37 316 DQ70
Geere Rd. E15 131 317 EF67
Gees Ct. W1 44 316 DG72
Geffrye Ct. N1 26/7 316 DS68
Geffrye Est. N1 26/7 316 DS68
Geffrye St. E2 27 316 DT68
Geldart Rd. SE15 164 317 DV80
Geldeston Rd. E5 102 307 DU61
Gell Clo., Uxb. 230 312 BM62
Gellatly Rd. SE14 164 317 DW82
Gelsthorpe Rd., Rom. 227 309 FB52
Gemini Gro., Nthlt. 242 313 BY69
General Gordon Pl. SE18 253 318 EP77
General Wolfe Rd. SE10 167 317 ED81
Generals Wk., The, Enf. 203 301 DY37
Genesta Rd. SE18 253 318 EP79
Geneva Clo., Shep. 281 328 BS96
Geneva Dr. SW9 178 324 DN84
Geneva Gdns., Rom. 226 309 EY57
Geneva Rd., Kings.T. 268 322 CL98
Geneva Rd., Th.Hth. 287 332 DQ99
Genever Clo. E4 211 301 EA50
Genista Rd. N18 210 301 DV50
Genoa Ave. SW15 172 323 CW85
Genoa Rd. SE20 274 325 DW95
Genotin Rd., Enf. 202 300 DR41
Genotin Ter., Enf. 202 300 DR41
Gentian Row SE13 166 317 EC81
Gentlemans Row, Enf. 202 300 DQ41
Gentry Gdns. E13 244 318 EG70
Geoffrey Ave., Rom. 229 311 FN51
Geoffrey Clo. SE5 162 316 DQ82
Geoffrey Gdns. E6 244 318 EL68
Geoffrey Rd. SE4 181 325 DZ83
George Beard Rd. SE8 149 317 DZ77
George Comberton Wk. E12 235 308 EN64
George Ct. WC2 58/9 316 DL73
George Cres. N10 220 306 DG52
George Downing Est. N16 101 306 DT61
George V Ave., Pnr. 214 303 BZ53
George V Clo., Pnr. 215 303 CA55
George V Way, Grnf. 122 314 CH67
George Gange Way, Har. 215 303 CE55
George Gro. Rd. SE20 274 325 DU95
George Inn Yd. SE1 62 316 DR74
George La. E18 224 308 EG54
George La. SE13 182 325 EC86
George La., Brom. 289 334 EH102
George Lansbury Ho. N22 221 306 DN53
George Loveless Ho. E2 39 316 DT69
George Lowe Ct. W2 40/1 315 DB71
George Ms. NW1 33 316 DJ69
George Ms., Enf. 202 300 DR41
George Pl. N17 221 306 DS55
George Rd. E4 223 307 EA51
George Rd., Kings.T. 269 322 CP94
George Rd., N.Mal. 269 322 CT98
George Row SE16 148 317 DU75
George Sq. SW19 270 323 CZ97
George St. E16 141 317 EF72
George St. W1 43 315 DF72
George St. W7 243 313 CE74
George St., Bark. 235 308 EQ66
George St., Croy. 287 332 DQ103
George St., Houns. 250 321 BZ82
George St., Rich. 169 322 CK85
George St., Rom. 227 309 FF58
George St., Sthl. 250 321 BY77
George St., Sutt. 284 331 DB106
George St., Uxb. 240 312 BK66
George Wyver Clo. SW19 189 323 CY87
George Yd. EC3 50 316 DR72
George Yd. W1 56 316 DG73
Georges Clo., Orp. 278 327 EW97
Georges Mead, Borwd. 204 298 CK44
George's Rd. N7 115 306 DM64
Georges Rd., Brom. 276 326 EM97
Georges Sq. SW6 157 315 CZ79
Georgetown Clo. SE19 273 324 DR92
Georgette Pl. SE10 166 317 EC80
Georgeville Gdns., Ilf. 225 308 EP56
Georgia Rd., N.Mal. 269 322 CQ98
Georgia Rd., Th.Hth. 273 324 DP95
Georgian Clo., Brom. 289 334 EH101
Georgian Clo., Stai. 264 328 BH91
Georgian Clo., Stan. 216 304 CG52
Georgian Clo., Uxb. 240 312 BL63
Georgian Ct. SW16 272 324 DL91
Georgian Ct., Wem. 108 304 CN65
Georgian Way, Har. 233 313 CD61
Georgiana St. NW1 21 316 DJ67
Georgina Gdns. E2 39 316 DT69
Geraint Rd., Brom. 276 326 EG91
Gerald Ms. SW1 80 316 DG77
Gerald Rd. E16 131 317 EF70
Gerald Rd. SW1 80 316 DG77
Gerald Rd., Dag. 236 309 EZ61
Gerald Sq. SW1 80 316 DG77
Geraldine Rd. SW18 174 323 DC85
Geraldine Rd. W4 154 314 CN79
Geraldine St. SE11 72/3 316 DP76
Geralds Gro., Bans. 292 331 CX114
Gerard Ave., Houns. 259 321 CA87
Gerard Gdns., Rain. 247 319 FE68
Gerard Rd. SW13 155 314 CT81
Gerard Rd., Har. 216 304 CG58
Gerards Clo. SE16 148 317 DW78
Gerda Rd. SE9 261 326 EQ89
Germander Way E15 131 317 EE69
Gernon Rd. E3 129 317 DY68
Geron Way NW2 94 305 CV61
Gerrard Gdns., Pnr. 214 303 BU57
Gerrard Pl. W1 58 316 DK73
Gerrard Rd. N1 24/5 316 DP68
Gerrard St. W1 58 316 DK73
Gerrards Clo. N14 208 300 DJ43
Gerridge St. SE1 72 316 DN76
Gerry Raffles Sq. E15 121 307 ED65
Gertrude Rd., Belv. 255 319 FA77
Gertrude St. SW10 158 315 DC79
Gervase Clo., Wem. 92 304 CQ62
Gervase Rd., Edg. 217 304 CQ53
Gervase St. SE15 164 317 DV80
Ghent St. SE6 198 325 EA89
Ghent Way E8 117 306 DT65
Giant Arches Rd. SE24 194 324 DQ87
Gibbard Ms. SW19 270 323 CX92
Gibbfield Clo., Rom. 226 309 EY55
Gibbins Rd. E15 120 307 EC66
Gibbon Rd. SE15 164 317 DW82
Gibbon Rd. W3 135 314 CS73
Gibbon Rd., Kings.T. 268 322 CL95
Gibbon Wk. SW15 172 323 CU84
Gibbons Rd. NW10 109 304 CS65
Gibbs Ave. SE19 273 324 DR92
Gibbs Clo. SE19 273 324 DR92
Gibbs Grn. W14 147 315 CZ78
Gibbs Grn., Edg. 205 298 CQ50
Gibbs Rd. N18 210 301 DW49
Gibbs Sq. SE19 273 324 DR92
Gibraltar Wk. E2 39 316 DT69
Gibson Clo. E1 128 317 DW70
Gibson Clo. N21 209 300 DN44
Gibson Clo., Islw. 259 321 CD83
Gibson Gdns. N16 101 306 DT61
Gibson Pl., Stai. 256 320 BJ86
Gibson Rd. SE11 83 316 DM77
Gibson Rd., Dag. 236 309 EW60
Gibson Rd., Sutt. 284 331 DB106
Gibson Rd., Uxb. 240 312 BM63
Gibson Sq. N1 24 316 DN67
Gibson St. SE10 151 317 EE78
Gibson's Hill SW16 273 324 DN94
Gidea Ave., Rom. 228 310 FG55
Gidea Clo., Rom. 228 310 FG55
Gideon Clo., Belv. 255 319 FB77
Gideon Rd. SW11 176 324 DG83
Giesbach Rd. N19 98 306 DJ61
Giffard Rd. N18 209 300 DS50
Giffin St. SE8 166 317 EA80
Gifford Gdns. W7 243 313 CD71
Gifford St. N1 115 306 DL66
Gift La. E15 131 317 EF67
Giggs Hill, Orp. 278 327 EU96
Gilbert Clo. SE18 252 318 EM81
Gilbert Gro., Edg. 217 304 CR53
Gilbert Ho. EC2 49 316 DQ71
Gilbert Ho. SE8 166 317 EA79
Gilbert Pl. WC1 46/7 316 DL71
Gilbert Rd. SE11 84 316 DN77
Gilbert Rd. SW19 271 323 DC94
Gilbert Rd., Belv. 255 319 FA76
Gilbert Rd., Brom. 276 326 EG94
Gilbert Rd., Pnr. 214 303 BX56
Gilbert Rd., Rom. 227 309 FF56
Gilbert Rd., Uxb. 212 302 BK54
Gilbert St. E15 121 307 EE63
Gilbert St. W1 44 316 DG72
Gilbert St., Enf. 203 301 DW37
Gilbert St., Houns. 259 321 CC83
Gilbey Clo., Uxb. 241 312 BP63
Gilbey Rd. SW17 271 323 DE91
Gilbeys Yd. NW1 20/1 316 DH67
Gilbourne Rd. SE18 253 318 ET79
Gilda Ave., Enf. 210 301 DY43
Gilda Cres. N16 102 307 DU60
Gildea St. W1 44/5 316 DH71
Gilden Cres. NW5 114 306 DG64
Gildersome St. SE18 253 318 EN79
Giles Coppice SE19 273 324 DT91
Gilfrid Clo., Uxb. 249 312 BP72
Gilhams Ave., Bans. 292 331 CX112
Gilkes Cres. SE21 179 324 DS86
Gilkes Pl. SE21 179 324 DS86
Gill Ave. E16 244 318 EG72
Gill St. E14 139 317 DZ73
Gillam Way, Rain. 238 310 FG65
Gillards Ms. E17 223 307 EA56
Gillards Way E17 223 307 EA56
Gillender St. E3 130 317 EC70
Gillender St. E14 130 317 EC70
Gillespie Rd. N5 100 306 DN62
Gillett Ave. E6 244 318 EL68
Gillett Pl. N16 117 306 DS64
Gillett Rd., Th.Hth. 273 324 DR98
Gillett St. N16 117 306 DS64
Gillfoot NW1 21 316 DJ68
Gillham Ter. N17 222 307 DU51
Gilliam Gro., Pur. 294 332 DN110
Gillian Cres., Rom. 228 310 FJ54
Gillian Pk. Rd., Sutt. 284 331 CZ102
Gillian St. SE13 182 325 EB85
Gillies St. NW5 114 306 DG64
Gilling Ct. NW3 113 305 DE65
Gillingham Ms. SW1 81 316 DJ77
Gillingham Rd. NW2 95 305 CY62
Gillingham Row SW1 81 316 DJ77
Gillingham St. SW1 81 316 DJ77
Gillison Wk. SE16 148 317 DU76
Gillman Dr. E15 131 317 EF67
Gillmans Rd., Orp. 291 335 EV102
Gillum Clo., Barn. 207 299 DF46
Gilmore Clo., Uxb. 231 312 BN62
Gilmore Cres., Ashf. 265 328 BN92
Gilmore Rd. SE13 183 325 ED84
Gilmour Clo., Wal.Cr. 203 301 DU35
Gilpin Ave. SW14 171 322 CR84
Gilpin Clo., Mitch. 271 323 DE96
Gilpin Cres. N18 209 300 DT50
Gilpin Cres., Twick. 259 321 CB87
Gilpin Rd. E5 119 307 DY63
Gilpin Way, Hayes 257 320 BR80
Gilroy Clo., Rain. 237 309 FF65
Gilroy Way, Orp. 291 335 EV101
Gilsland Rd., Th.Hth. 273 324 DR98
Gilstead Ho., Bark. 246 319 EV68
Gilstead Rd. SW6 158 315 DB82
Gilston Rd. SW10 77 315 DC78
Gilton Rd. SE6 199 325 EE90
Giltspur St. EC1 48/9 316 DP72
Gippeswyck Clo., Pnr. 214 303 BX53
Gipsy Hill SE19 273 324 DS92
Gipsy La. SW15 172 323 CU83
Gipsy Rd. SE27 273 324 DQ91
Gipsy Rd., Well. 254 319 EX81
Gipsy Rd. Gdns. SE27 273 324 DQ91
Giralda Clo. E16 244 318 EK71
Giraud St. E14 140 317 EB72
Girdlers Rd. W14 147 315 CX77
Girdlestone Wk. N19 98 306 DJ61
Girdwood Rd. SW18 189 323 CY87
Girling Way, Felt. 258 321 BU83
Gironde Rd. SW6 157 315 CZ80
Girton Ave. NW9 217 304 CN55
Girton Clo., Nthlt. 233 313 CC65
Girton Gdns., Croy. 288 333 EA104
Girton Rd. SE26 274 325 DX92
Girton Rd., Nthlt. 233 313 CC65
Girton Vil. W10 137 315 CX72
Gisborne Gdns., Rain. 247 319 FF69
Gisbourne Clo., Wall. 286 332 DK104
Gisburn Rd. N8 220 306 DM56
Gissing Wk. N1 116 306 DN66
Gittens Clo., Brom. 275 325 EF91
Given Wilson Wk. E13 131 317 EF68
Glacier Way, Wem. 123 314 CK68
Gladbeck Way, Enf. 209 300 DP43
Gladding Rd. E12 234 308 EK63
Glade, The N21 208 300 DM44
Glade, The SE7 252 318 EJ80
Glade, The, Brom. 276 326 EK96
Glade, The, Croy. 288 333 DX99
Glade, The, Enf. 202 300 DN41
Glade, The, Epsom 283 331 CU106
Glade, The, Ilf. 224 308 EM53
Glade, The, Stai. 264 328 BH94
Glade, The, Sutt. 292 331 CY109
Glade, The, Upmin. 239 311 FQ64
Glade, The, W.Wick. 288 333 EB104
Glade Clo., Surb. 282 330 CK103
Glade Ct., Ilf. 224 308 EM53
Glade Gdns., Croy. 288 333 DY101
Glade La., Sthl. 251 321 CB75
Glades Pl., Brom. 276 326 EG96
Glades Shop. Cen., The, Brom. 276 326 EG96
Gladeside N21 208 300 DM45
Gladeside, Croy. 288 333 DX101
Gladesmore Rd. N15 221 306 DT58
Gladeswood Rd., Belv. 255 319 FB77
Gladiator St. SE23 197 325 DY87
Glading Ter. N16 101 306 DT62
Gladioli Clo., Hmptn. 267 329 CA93
Gladsdale Dr., Pnr. 214 303 BV56
Gladsmuir Rd. N19 98 306 DJ60
Gladstone Ave. E12 234 308 EL66
Gladstone Ave. N22 221 306 DN54
Gladstone Ave., Felt. 258 321 BU86
Gladstone Ave., Twick. 259 321 CD87
Gladstone Ms. NW6 111 305 CZ66
Gladstone Ms. SE20 274 325 DW94
Gladstone Pk. Gdns. NW2 110 305 CV63
Gladstone Pl. E3 129 317 DZ68
Gladstone Rd. SW19 271 323 DA94
Gladstone Rd. W4 145 314 CR76
Gladstone Rd., Croy. 287 332 DR101
Gladstone Rd., Kings.T. 269 322 CN97
Gladstone Rd., Orp. 291 334 EQ106
Gladstone Rd., Sthl. 250 321 BY75
Gladstone Rd., Surb. 282 330 CK103
Gladstone St. SE1 72/3 316 DP76
Gladstone Ter. SE27 273 324 DQ91
Gladstone Ter. SW8 160 316 DH81
Gladstone Way, Har. 215 303 CE55
Gladwell Rd. N8 220 306 DM58
Gladwell Rd., Brom. 276 326 EG93
Gladwyn Rd. SW15 173 323 CX83
Gladys Rd. NW6 112 305 DA66
Glaisher St. SE10 166 317 EC80
Glamis Cres., Hayes 249 320 BQ76
Glamis Dr., Horn. 238 311 FL60
Glamis Pl. E1 138 317 DW73
Glamis Rd. E1 138 317 DW73
Glamis Way, Nthlt. 233 313 CC65
Glamorgan Clo., Mitch. 272 324 DL97
Glamorgan Rd., Kings.T. 268 322 CJ94
Glanfield Rd., Beck. 274 325 DZ98
Glanleam Rd., Stan. 204 298 CK49
Glanville Dr., Horn. 238 311 FM60
Glanville Rd. SW2 177 324 DL85
Glanville Rd., Brom. 276 326 EH97
Glasbrook Ave., Twick. 258 321 BZ88
Glasbrook Rd. SE9 260 326 EK87
Glaserton Rd. N16 101 306 DS59
Glasford St. SW17 271 323 DF93
Glasgow Ho. W9 16/7 315 DB68
Glasgow Rd. E13 244 318 EH68
Glasgow Rd. N18 210 301 DV50
Glasgow Ter. SW1 81 316 DJ78
Glass St. E2 128 317 DV70
Glass Yd. SE18 253 318 EN76
Glasse Clo. W13 132 314 CG73
Glasshill St. SE1 72/3 316 DP75
Glasshouse All. EC4 48 316 DN72
Glasshouse Flds. E1 139 317 DX73
Glasshouse St. W1 57 316 DJ73
Glasshouse Wk. SE11 82/3 316 DL78
Glasshouse Yd. EC1 37 316 DQ70
Glasslyn Rd. N8 220 306 DK57
Glassmill La., Brom. 275 325 EF96
Glastonbury Ave., Wdf.Grn. 224 308 EK52
Glastonbury Rd. N9 209 300 DT46
Glastonbury Rd., Mord. 284 331 DA101
Glastonbury St. NW6 111 305 CZ64
Glaucus St. E3 140 317 EB71
Glazbury Rd. W14 147 315 CY77
Glazebrook Clo. SE21 195 324 DR89
Glazebrook Rd., Tedd. 267 329 CF94
Glebe, The SE3 183 325 EE83
Glebe, The SW16 272 324 DK91
Glebe, The, Chis. 277 326 EQ95
Glebe, The, West Dr. 248 320 BM77
Glebe, The, Wor.Pk. 283 330 CT102
Glebe Ave., Enf. 202 300 DP41
Glebe Ave., Har. 216 304 CL55
Glebe Ave., Mitch. 271 323 DE96
Glebe Ave., Ruis. 232 313 BV65
Glebe Ave., Uxb. 231 312 BQ62
Glebe Ave., Wdf.Grn. 224 308 EG51
Glebe Clo. W4 145 314 CS78
Glebe Clo., S.Croy. 295 332 DT111
Glebe Clo., Uxb. 241 312 BQ63
Glebe Cotts., Sutt. 284 331 DB105
Glebe Ct. W7 243 313 CD73
Glebe Ct., Mitch. 271 323 DF97
Glebe Ct., Stan. 204 298 CJ50
Glebe Cres. NW4 218 305 CW56
Glebe Cres., Har. 216 304 CL55
Glebe Gdns., N.Mal. 283 330 CS101
Glebe Ho. Dr., Brom. 289 334 EH102
Glebe Hyrst SE19 273 324 DT91
Glebe Hyrst, S.Croy. 295 332 DT112
Glebe La., Barn. 206 299 CU43
Glebe La., Har. 216 304 CL56
Glebe Path, Mitch. 271 323 DE97
Glebe Pl. SW3 159 315 DE79
Glebe Rd. E8 117 306 DT66
Glebe Rd. N3 219 305 DC53
Glebe Rd. N8 220 306 DM56
Glebe Rd. NW10 109 304 CT65
Glebe Rd. SW13 156 315 CU82
Glebe Rd., Brom. 276 326 EG95
Glebe Rd., Cars. 293 331 DF107
Glebe Rd., Dag. 237 309 FB65
Glebe Rd., Hayes 249 312 BT74
Glebe Rd., Stai. 264 328 BH92
Glebe Rd., Stan. 204 298 CJ50
Glebe Rd., Sutt. 292 331 CY109
Glebe Rd., Uxb. 240 312 BJ68
Glebe Side, Twick. 259 321 CF87
Glebe St. W4 145 314 CS78
Glebe Ter. E3 130 317 EA69
Glebe Way, Erith 255 319 FE79
Glebe Way, Felt. 259 321 CA90
Glebe Way, Horn. 238 311 FL59
Glebe Way, S.Croy. 295 332 DT112
Glebe Way, W.Wick. 289 333 EC103
Glebeland Gdns., Shep. 281 328 BQ100
Glebelands, Dart. 263 327 FF84
Glebelands Ave. E18 224 308 EG54
Glebelands Ave., Ilf. 235 308 ER59
Glebelands Clo. SE5 179 324 DS83
Glebelands Rd., Felt. 258 321 BU87
Gledhow Gdns. SW5 77 315 DC77
Gledstanes Rd. W14 147 315 CY78
Gledwood Ave., Hayes 249 312 BT71
Gledwood Cres., Hayes 249 312 BT71
Gledwood Dr., Hayes 249 312 BT71
Gledwood Gdns., Hayes 249 312 BT71
Gleeson Dr., Orp. 291 334 ET106
Glegg Pl. SW15 173 323 CX84
Glen, The, Brom. 275 325 EE96
Glen, The, Croy. 288 333 DX104
Glen, The, Enf. 202 300 DP42
Glen, The, Nthwd. 213 302 BR52
Glen, The, Orp. 290 334 EM104
Glen, The, Pnr. 232 313 BY59
Glen, The (Eastcote), Pnr. 214 303 BV57
Glen, The, Sthl. 250 321 BZ78
Glen, The, Wem. 107 304 CK63
Glen Albyn Rd. SW19 189 323 CX89
Glen Ave., Ashf. 265 328 BN91
Glen Clo., Shep. 281 328 BN98
Glen Cres., Wdf.Grn. 224 308 EH51
Glen Gdns., Croy. 286 332 DP104
Glen Ri., Wdf.Grn. 224 308 EH51
Glen Rd. E13 244 318 EJ70
Glen Rd. E17 222 307 DZ57
Glen Rd., Chess. 282 330 CL104
Glen Rd. End, Wall. 293 332 DH109
Glen Ter. E14 150 317 EC75
Glen Wk., Islw. 259 321 CD85
Glena Mt., Sutt. 285 331 DC105
Glenaffric Ave. E14 151 317 ED77
Glenalla Rd., Ruis. 231 312 BT59
Glenalmond Rd., Har. 216 304 CL56
Glenalvon Way SE18 252 318 EL77
Glenarm Rd. E5 118 307 DW64
Glenavon Rd. E15 121 307 EE66
Glenbarr Clo. SE9 261 326 EP83
Glenbow Rd., Brom. 275 325 EE93
Glenbrook Rd. NW6 112 305 DA64
Glenbuck Ct., Surb. 282 330 CK100
Glenbuck Rd., Surb. 282 330 CK100
Glenburnie Rd. SW17 191 323 DE90
Glencairn Dr. W5 122 314 CJ70
Glencairn Rd. SW16 272 324 DL94
Glencairne Clo. E16 244 318 EK71
Glencoe Ave., Ilf. 235 308 ER59
Glencoe Dr., Dag. 237 309 FA63
Glencoe Rd., Hayes 242 313 BX70
Glendale Ave. N22 221 306 DN52
Glendale Ave., Edg. 205 298 CN49
Glendale Ave., Rom. 236 309 EW59
Glendale Clo. SE9 261 326 EN83
Glendale Dr. SW19 270 323 CZ92
Glendale Gdns., Wem. 91 304 CK60
Glendale Ms., Beck. 275 325 EB95
Glendale Rd., Erith 255 319 FC77
Glendale Way SE28 246 319 EW73
Glendall St. SW9 177 324 DM84
Glendarvon St. SW15 173 323 CX83
Glendevon Clo., Edg. 205 298 CP48
Glendish Rd. N17 222 307 DU53
Glendor Gdns. NW7 205 298 CR49
Glendower Cres., Orp. 291 335 EU100
Glendower Gdns. SW14 171 322 CR83
Glendower Pl. SW7 78 315 DD77
Glendower Rd. E4 211 301 ED46
Glendower Rd. SW14 171 322 CR83
Glendown Rd. SE2 254 319 EU78
Glendun Rd. W3 135 314 CS73
Gleneagle Ms. SW16 272 324 DK92
Gleneagle Rd. SW16 272 324 DK93
Gleneagles, Stan. 216 304 CH51
Gleneagles Clo. SE16 148 317 DV78
Gleneagles Clo., Orp. 291 334 ER102
Gleneagles Clo., Rom. 228 311 FM52
Gleneagles Clo., Stai. 256 320 BK86
Gleneagles Clo., Stan. 216 304 CH51
Gleneagles Grn., Orp. 291 334 ER102
Gleneagles Twr., Sthl. 243 313 CC72
Gleneldon Ms. SW16 272 324 DL91
Gleneldon Rd. SW16 272 324 DL91
Glenelg Rd. SW2 177 324 DL85
Glenesk Rd. SE9 261 326 EN83
Glenfarg Rd. SE6 199 325 ED88
Glenfield Cres., Ruis. 231 312 BR59
Glenfield Rd. SW12 192 324 DJ88
Glenfield Rd. W13 142 314 CH75
Glenfield Rd., Ashf. 265 328 BP93
Glenfield Ter. W13 132 314 CH74
Glenfinlas Way SE5 162 316 DP80
Glenforth St. SE10 151 317 EF78
Glengall Causeway E14 150 317 EA76
Glengall Gro. E14 150 317 EC76
Glengall Rd. NW6 127 315 CZ67
Glengall Rd. SE15 87 316 DT78
Glengall Rd., Bexh. 262 327 EY83
Glengall Rd., Edg. 205 298 CP48
Glengall Rd., Wdf.Grn. 224 308 EG51
Glengall Ter. SE15 163 316 DT79
Glengarnock Ave. E14 150 317 EC77
Glengarry Rd. SE22 179 324 DS85
Glenham Dr., Ilf. 225 308 EP57
Glenhead Clo. SE9 261 326 EP83
Glenhill Clo. N3 219 305 DA54
Glenhouse Rd. SE9 261 326 EN85
Glenhurst Ave. NW5 114 306 DG63
Glenhurst Ave., Bex. 262 327 EZ88
Glenhurst Ave., Ruis. 231 312 BQ59
Glenhurst Ct. SE19 273 324 DT92
Glenhurst Ri. SE19 273 324 DQ94
Glenhurst Rd. N12 207 299 DD50
Glenhurst Rd., Brent. 152 314 CJ79
Glenilla Rd. NW3 113 305 DE65
Glenister Ho., Hayes 242 313 BV74
Glenister Pk. Rd. SW16 272 324 DK94
Glenister Rd. SE10 151 317 EF78
Glenister St. E16 245 318 EN74
Glenlea Rd. SE9 261 326 EN85
Glenloch Rd. NW3 113 305 DE65
Glenloch Rd., Enf. 203 301 DW40
Glenluce Rd. SE3 252 318 EG79
Glenlyon Rd. SE9 261 326 EN85
Glenmere Ave. NW7 218 305 CU52
Glenmill, Hmptn. 266 329 BZ92
Glenmore Rd. NW3 113 305 DE65
Glenmore Rd., Well. 253 318 ET80
Glenmore Way, Bark. 246 319 EU69
Glenmount Path SE18 253 318 EQ78
Glenn Ave., Pur. 294 332 DP111
Glennie Rd. SE27 194 324 DN90
Glenny Rd., Bark. 235 308 EQ65
Glenorchy Clo., Hayes 242 313 BY71
Glenparke Rd. E7 234 308 EH65
Glenrosa St. SW6 158 315 DC82
Glenrose Ct., Sid. 278 327 EV92
Glenroy St. W12 136 315 CW72
Glensdale Rd. SE4 181 325 DZ83
Glenshee Clo., Nthwd. 213 302 BQ51
Glenshiel Rd. SE9 261 326 EN85
Glenside, Chig. 225 308 EP51
Glentanner Way SW17 191 323 DD90
Glentham Gdns. SW13 156 315 CV79
Glentham Rd. SW13 156 315 CU79
Glenthorne Ave., Croy. 287 333 DV102
Glenthorne Clo., Sutt. 284 331 DA102
Glenthorne Clo., Uxb. 241 312 BN69
Glenthorne Gdns., Ilf. 225 308 EN55
Glenthorne Gdns., Sutt. 284 331 DA102
Glenthorne Ms. W6 146 315 CV77
Glenthorne Rd. E17 222 307 DY57
Glenthorne Rd. N11 207 299 DF50
Glenthorne Rd. W6 146 315 CV77
Glenthorne Rd., Kings.T. 268 322 CM98
Glenthorpe Rd., Mord. 284 331 CX99
Glenton Clo., Rom. 227 309 FE51
Glenton Rd. SE13 183 325 EE84
Glenton Way, Rom. 227 309 FE52
Glentrammon Clo., Orp. 291 334 ET106
Glentworth St. NW1 31 315 DF70
Glenure Rd. SE9 261 326 EN85
Glenview SE2 254 319 EX79
Glenview Rd., Brom. 276 326 EK96
Glenville Ave., Enf. 202 300 DQ38
Glenville Gro. SE8 165 317 DZ80

Glenville Ms. SW18 190 323 DB87
Glenville Rd., Kings.T. 269 322 CN95
Glenwood Ave. NW9 93 304 CS60
Glenwood Clo., Har. 215 303 CF57
Glenwood Dr., Rom. 228 310 FG57
Glenwood Gdns., Ilf. 225 308 EN57
Glenwood Gro. NW9 92 304 CQ60
Glenwood Rd. N15 221 306 DP57
Glenwood Rd. NW7 205 298 CS48
Glenwood Rd. SE6 197 325 DZ88
Glenwood Rd., Houns. 259 321 CD83
Glenwood Way, Croy. 288 333 DX100
Glenworth Ave. E14 151 317 ED77
Gliddon Rd. W14 147 315 CY77
Glimpsing Grn., Erith 254 319 EY76
Glisson Rd., Uxb. 241 312 BN68
Global App. E3 130 317 EB68
Globe Pond Rd. SE16 139 317 DY74
Globe Rd. E1 129 317 DX70
Globe Rd. E2 128 317 DW69
Globe Rd. E15 121 307 EF64
Globe Rd., Horn. 228 310 FG58
Globe Rd., Wdf.Grn. 224 308 EJ51
Globe Rope Wk. E14 150 317 EC77
Globe St. SE1 74 316 DR75
Globe Ter. E2 128 317 DW69
Globe Yd. W1 44/5 316 DH72
Glossop Rd., S.Croy. 295 332 DR109
Gloster Rd., N.Mal. 269 322 CS98
Gloucester Ave. NW1 114 306 DG66
Gloucester Ave., Horn. 229 311 FN56
Gloucester Ave., Sid. 261 326 ES89
Gloucester Ave., Well. 261 326 ET84
Gloucester Circ. SE10 166 317 EC80
Gloucester Clo. NW10 109 304 CR66
Gloucester Ct. EC3 62/3 316 DS73
Gloucester Ct., Rich. 154 314 CN80
Gloucester Ct., Uxb. 230 302 BG58
Gloucester Cres. NW1 20/1 316 DH67
Gloucester Cres., Stai. 264 328 BK93
Gloucester Dr. N4 100 306 DP61
Gloucester Dr. NW11 219 305 DA56
Gloucester Gdns. NW11 95 305 CZ59
Gloucester Gdns. W2 41 315 DC72
Gloucester Gdns., Ilf. 234 308 EL59
Gloucester Gdns., Sutt. 284 331 DB103
Gloucester Gate NW1 20/1 316 DH68
Gloucester Gate Ms. NW1 20/1 316 DH68
Gloucester Gro., Edg. 217 304 CR53
Gloucester Gro. Est. SE15 163 316 DS79
Gloucester Ho. N7 99 306 DL62
Gloucester Ho. NW6 16 315 DA68
Gloucester Ms. E10 104 307 EA59
Gloucester Ms. W2 41 315 DC72
Gloucester Ms. W. W2 41 315 DC72
Gloucester Par., Sid. 262 327 EU85
Gloucester Pl. NW1 31 315 DF70
Gloucester Pl. W1 43 315 DF71
Gloucester Pl. Ms. W1 43 315 DF71
Gloucester Rd. E10 104 307 EA59
Gloucester Rd. E11 224 308 EH57
Gloucester Rd. E12 234 308 EM62
Gloucester Rd. E17 222 307 DX54
Gloucester Rd. N17 221 306 DR55
Gloucester Rd. N18 209 300 DT50
Gloucester Rd. SW7 65 315 DC76
Gloucester Rd. W3 144 314 CQ75
Gloucester Rd. W5 142 314 CJ75
Gloucester Rd., Barn. 207 299 DB43
Gloucester Rd., Belv. 254 319 EZ78
Gloucester Rd., Croy. 287 332 DR102
Gloucester Rd., Enf. 202 300 DQ38
Gloucester Rd., Felt. 258 321 BW88
Gloucester Rd., Hmptn. 267 329 CB94
Gloucester Rd., Har. 215 303 CB57
Gloucester Rd., Houns. 258 321 BY84
Gloucester Rd., Kings.T. 269 322 CN96
Gloucester Rd., Rich. 154 314 CN80
Gloucester Rd., Rom. 227 309 FE58
Gloucester Rd., Tedd. 267 329 CE92
Gloucester Rd., Twick. 259 321 CC88
Gloucester Sq. E2 128 317 DU67
Gloucester Sq. W2 42 315 DD72
Gloucester St. SW1 81 316 DJ78
Gloucester Ter. W2 40/1 315 DB72
Gloucester Wk. W8 64 315 DA75
Gloucester Way EC1 36 316 DN69
Glover Clo. SE2 254 319 EW77
Glover Dr. N18 222 307 DW51
Glover Rd., Pnr. 214 303 BX58
Glovers Gro., Ruis. 231 312 BP59
Gloxinia Wk., Hmptn. 267 329 CA93
Glycena Rd. SW11 175 323 DF83
Glyn Clo. SE25 273 324 DS96
Glyn Ct. SW16 194 324 DN90
Glyn Dr., Sid. 278 327 EV91
Glyn Rd. E5 119 307 DX63
Glyn Rd., Enf. 203 301 DW42
Glyn Rd., Wor.Pk. 284 331 CX103
Glyn St. SE11 83 316 DM78
Glynde Ms. SW3 66/7 315 DE76
Glynde Rd., Bexh. 262 327 EX83
Glynde St. SE4 181 325 DZ86
Glyndebourne Pk., Orp. 290 334 EP103
Glyndon Rd. SE18 253 318 EQ77
Glynfield Rd. NW10 109 304 CS66
Glynne Rd. N22 221 306 DN54
Glynwood Ct. SE23 196 325 DW90
Goat La., Enf. 202 300 DT38
Goat Rd., Mitch. 285 331 DF101
Goat St. SE1 75 316 DT75
Goat Wf., Brent. 153 314 CL79
Goaters All. SW6 157 315 CZ80
Gobions Ave., Rom. 227 309 FD52
Godalming Ave., Wall. 286 332 DL106
Godalming Rd. E14 140 317 EB71
Godbold Rd. E15 131 317 EE69
Goddard Clo., Shep. 280 328 BM97
Goddard Rd., Beck. 274 325 DX98
Goddards Way, Ilf. 235 308 ER60
Goddington Chase, Orp. 291 335 EV105
Goddington La., Orp. 291 335 EU104
Godfrey Ave., Nthlt. 242 313 BY67
Godfrey Ave., Twick. 259 321 CD87
Godfrey Hill SE18 252 318 EL77
Godfrey Rd. SE18 252 318 EM77
Godfrey St. E15 130 317 EC68
Godfrey St. SW3 78/9 315 DE78
Godfrey Way, Houns. 258 321 BZ87
Goding St. SE11 82/3 316 DL78
Godley Rd. SW18 191 323 DD88
Godliman St. EC4 49 316 DQ72
Godman Rd. SE15 164 317 DV82
Godolphin Clo. N13 221 306 DP51
Godolphin Clo., Sutt. 292 331 CZ110
Godolphin Pl. W3 135 314 CR73
Godolphin Rd. W12 136 315 CV74
Godson Rd., Croy. 286 332 DN104
Godson St. N1 24 316 DN68
Godstone Rd., Ken. 294 332 DN112
Godstone Rd., Pur. 294 332 DN112
Godstone Rd., Sutt. 285 331 DC105
Godstone Rd., Twick. 168 322 CG86
Godstow Rd. SE2 254 319 EV75
Godwin Clo. N1 25 316 DQ68
Godwin Ct. NW1 21 316 DJ68
Godwin Rd. E7 234 308 EH63
Godwin Rd., Brom. 276 326 EJ97
Goffers Rd. SE3 167 317 EE82
Goffs Rd., Ashf. 265 328 BR93
Goidel Clo., Wall. 286 332 DK105
Golborne Gdns. W10 127 315 CZ70
Golborne Ms. W10 137 315 CY71
Golborne Rd. W10 137 315 CY71
Gold Hill, Edg. 217 304 CR51
Gold La., Edg. 217 304 CR51
Golda Clo., Barn. 206 299 CX44
Goldbeaters Gro., Edg. 217 304 CS51
Goldcliff Clo., Mord. 284 331 DA101
Goldcrest Clo. E16 244 318 EK71
Goldcrest Clo. SE28 246 319 EW73
Goldcrest Ms. W5 133 314 CK71
Goldcrest Way, Pur. 294 332 DK110
Golden Ct., Rich. 169 322 CK85
Golden Cres., Hayes 249 312 BS74
Golden Cross Ms. W11 137 315 CZ72
Golden La. EC1 37 316 DQ70
Golden La. Est. EC1 37 316 DQ70
Golden Manor W7 243 313 CE73
Golden Plover Clo. E16 244 318 EH72
Golden Sq. W1 57 316 DJ73
Golden Yd. NW3 112 305 DC63
Golders Clo., Edg. 205 298 CP50
Golders Gdns. NW11 95 305 CY59
Golders Grn. Cres. NW11 95 305 CZ59
Golders Grn. Rd. NW11 218 305 CY58
Golders Manor Dr. NW11 218 305 CX58
Golders Pk. Clo. NW11 96 305 DA60
Golders Ri. NW4 218 305 CX57
Golders Way NW11 95 305 CZ59
Goldfinch Clo., Orp. 291 335 EU106
Goldfinch Rd. SE28 253 318 ER76
Goldhawk Ms. W12 146 315 CV75
Goldhawk Rd. W6 145 314 CT77
Goldhawk Rd. W12 146 315 CU76
Goldhaze Clo., Wdf.Grn. 224 308 EK52
Goldhurst Ter. NW6 112 305 DB66
Golding St. E1 138 317 DU72
Goldington Cres. NW1 22 316 DK68
Goldington Cres. Gdns. NW1 22 316 DK68
Goldington St. NW1 22 316 DK68
Goldman Clo. E2 128 317 DU70
Goldney Rd. W9 28 315 DA70
Goldsborough Cres. E4 211 301 EB47
Goldsborough Rd. SW8 161 316 DK81
Goldsdown Clo., Enf. 203 301 DY40
Goldsdown Rd., Enf. 203 301 DX40
Goldsel Rd. Ind. Est., Swan. 279 327 FE98
Goldsmid St. SE18 253 318 ES78
Goldsmith Ave. E12 234 308 EL65
Goldsmith Ave. NW9 217 304 CS57
Goldsmith Ave. W3 135 314 CR73
Goldsmith Ave., Rom. 237 309 FA59
Goldsmith Clo. W3 135 314 CS74
Goldsmith Clo., Har. 233 313 CB60
Goldsmith La. NW9 217 304 CP56
Goldsmith Rd. E10 104 307 EA60
Goldsmith Rd. E17 222 307 DX54
Goldsmith Rd. N11 207 299 DF50
Goldsmith Rd. SE15 164 317 DU81
Goldsmith Rd. W3 135 314 CR74
Goldsmith St. EC2 49 316 DQ72
Goldsmith's Row E2 128 317 DU68
Goldsmith's Sq. E2 128 317 DU68
Goldsworthy Gdns. SE16 148 317 DW77
Goldwell Rd., Th.Hth. 272 324 DM98
Goldwin Clo. SE14 164 317 DW81
Goldwing Clo. E16 244 318 EG72
Golf Clo., Stan. 216 304 CJ52
Golf Club Dr., Kings.T. 269 322 CR94
Golf Ride, Enf. 202 300 DN35
Golf Rd. W5 133 314 CM72
Golf Rd., Brom. 277 326 EN97
Golf Side, Sutt. 292 331 CY111
Golf Side, Twick. 259 321 CD90
Golfe Rd., Ilf. 235 308 ER62
Golfside Clo. N20 207 299 DE48
Golfside Clo., N.Mal. 269 322 CS96
Goliath Clo., Wall. 294 332 DL108
Gollogly Ter. SE7 252 318 EJ78
Gomer Gdns., Tedd. 268 322 CG93
Gomer Pl., Tedd. 268 322 CG93
Gomm Rd. SE16 148 317 DW76
Gomshall Ave., Wall. 286 332 DL106
Gomshall Rd., Sutt. 292 331 CW110
Gondar Gdns. NW6 111 305 CZ64
Gonson Pl. SE8 166 317 EA79
Gonson St. SE8 166 317 EB79
Gonston Clo. SW19 189 323 CY89
Gonville Cres., Nthlt. 233 313 CB65
Gonville Rd., Th.Hth. 286 332 DM99
Gonville St. SW6 173 323 CY83
Goodall Rd. E11 104 307 EC62
Gooden Ct., Har. 233 313 CE62
Goodenough Rd. SW19 270 323 CZ94
Goodge Pl. W1 45 316 DJ71
Goodge St. W1 45 316 DJ71
Goodhall St. NW10 125 314 CS69
Goodhart Pl. E14 139 317 DY73
Goodhart Way, W.Wick. 289 333 EE101
Goodhew Rd., Croy. 287 333 DU100
Gooding Clo., N.Mal. 269 322 CQ98
Goodinge Clo. N7 115 306 DL65
Goodman Cres. SW2 193 324 DK89
Goodman Rd. E10 104 307 EC59
Goodmans Ct., Wem. 107 304 CK63
Goodman's Flds. E1 138 317 DU72
Goodman's Stile E1 138 317 DU72
Goodmans Yd. E1 63 316 DT73
Goodmayes Ave., Ilf. 236 309 EU60
Goodmayes La., Ilf. 236 309 EU61
Goodmayes Rd., Ilf. 236 309 EU60
Goodmead Rd., Orp. 291 335 EU101
Goodrich Rd. SE22 179 324 DT86
Goods Way NW1 22/3 316 DL68
Goodson Rd. NW10 109 304 CS66
Goodway Gdns. E14 141 317 ED72
Goodwin Clo. SE16 148 317 DU76
Goodwin Clo., Mitch. 271 323 DD97
Goodwin Dr., Sid. 262 327 EX90
Goodwin Gdns., Croy. 294 332 DP107
Goodwin Rd. N9 210 301 DW46
Goodwin Rd. W12 146 315 CU75
Goodwin Rd., Croy. 286 332 DP106
Goodwin St. N4 100 306 DN61
Goodwins Ct. WC2 58/9 316 DL73
Goodwood Ave., Enf. 203 301 DW37
Goodwood Ave., Horn. 238 311 FL63
Goodwood Clo., Mord. 271 323 DA98
Goodwood Clo., Stan. 204 298 CJ50
Goodwood Dr., Nthlt. 233 313 CA65
Goodwood Rd. SE14 165 317 DY80
Goodwyn Ave. NW7 205 298 CS50
Goodwyns Vale N10 220 306 DG53
Goodyers Gdns. NW4 218 305 CX57
Goosander Way SE28 253 318 ER76
Goose Grn. Clo., Orp. 278 327 EU96
Goose Sq. E6 244 318 EM72
Gooseacre La., Har. 216 304 CK57
Gooseley La. E6 245 318 EN69
Gooshays Gdns., Rom. 228 311 FL51
Goossens Clo., Sutt. 285 331 DC106
Gophir La. EC4 62 316 DR73
Gopsall St. N1 26 316 DR67
Gordon Ave. E4 223 307 EE51
Gordon Ave. SW14 171 322 CS84
Gordon Ave., Horn. 237 309 FF61
Gordon Ave., S.Croy. 295 332 DQ110
Gordon Ave., Stan. 215 303 CF52
Gordon Ave., Twick. 168 322 CG85
Gordon Clo. E17 223 307 EA58
Gordon Clo. N19 98 306 DJ60
Gordon Clo., Stai. 264 328 BH93
Gordon Ct. W12 136 315 CV72
Gordon Cres., Croy. 287 332 DS102
Gordon Cres., Hayes 250 321 BU76
Gordon Dr., Shep. 281 328 BR100
Gordon Gdns., Edg. 217 304 CP54
Gordon Gro. SE5 162 316 DP82
Gordon Hill, Enf. 202 300 DQ39
Gordon Ho. Rd. NW5 114 306 DG63
Gordon Pl. W8 64 315 DA75
Gordon Rd. E4 211 301 EE45
Gordon Rd. E11 224 308 EG58
Gordon Rd. E15 120 307 EC63
Gordon Rd. E18 224 308 EH53
Gordon Rd. N3 218 305 CZ52
Gordon Rd. N9 210 301 DV47
Gordon Rd. N11 220 306 DK52
Gordon Rd. SE15 164 317 DV82
Gordon Rd. W4 154 314 CP79
Gordon Rd. W5 132 314 CJ73
Gordon Rd. W13 132 314 CH73
Gordon Rd., Ashf. 264 320 BL90
Gordon Rd., Bark. 245 318 ES67
Gordon Rd., Beck. 274 325 DZ97
Gordon Rd., Belv. 255 319 FC77
Gordon Rd., Cars. 293 331 DF107
Gordon Rd., Enf. 202 300 DR39
Gordon Rd., Har. 215 303 CE55
Gordon Rd., Houns. 259 321 CC84
Gordon Rd., Ilf. 235 308 ER62
Gordon Rd., Kings.T. 268 322 CM95
Gordon Rd., Rich. 153 314 CM82
Gordon Rd., Rom. 226 309 EZ58
Gordon Rd., Shep. 281 328 BR100
Gordon Rd., Sid. 261 326 ES85
Gordon Rd., Sthl. 250 321 BY77
Gordon Rd., Surb. 282 330 CM101
Gordon Rd., West Dr. 248 312 BL73
Gordon Sq. WC1 34 316 DK70
Gordon St. E13 244 318 EG69
Gordon St. WC1 34 316 DK70
Gordon Way, Brom. 276 326 EG95
Gordonbrock Rd. SE4 182 325 EA85
Gordondale Rd. SW19 190 323 DA89
Gore Ct. NW9 217 304 CN57
Gore Rd. E9 128 317 DW67
Gore Rd. SW20 270 323 CW96
Gore St. SW7 65 315 DC76
Gorefield Pl. NW6 16 315 DA68
Goresbrook Rd., Dag. 246 319 EV67
Goresbrook Village, Dag. 246 319 EV67
Gorham Pl. W11 137 315 CY73
Goring Clo., Rom. 227 309 FC53
Goring Gdns., Dag. 236 309 EW63
Goring Rd. N11 220 306 DL51
Goring Rd., Dag. 237 309 FD65
Goring St. EC3 50/1 316 DS72
Goring Way, Grnf. 243 313 CC68
Gorleston Rd. N15 221 306 DR57
Gorleston St. W14 147 315 CY77
Gorman Rd. SE18 252 318 EM77
Gorringe Pk. Ave., Mitch. 271 323 DF94
Gorse Clo. E16 244 318 EG72
Gorse Ri. SW17 272 324 DG92
Gorse Rd., Croy. 288 333 EA104
Gorse Wk., West Dr. 248 312 BL72
Gorseway, Rom. 237 309 FD61
Gorst Rd. NW10 124 314 CQ70
Gorst Rd. SW11 175 323 DF86
Gorsuch Pl. E2 39 316 DT69
Gorsuch St. E2 39 316 DT69
Gosberton Rd. SW12 191 323 DF88
Gosbury Hill, Chess. 282 330 CL105
Gosfield Rd., Dag. 237 309 FA61
Gosfield St. W1 45 316 DJ71
Gosford Gdns., Ilf. 224 308 EM57
Goshawk Gdns., Hayes 241 312 BS69
Goslett Yd. WC2 46 316 DK72
Gosling Clo., Grnf. 243 313 CA69
Gosling Way SW9 162 316 DN81
Gospatrick Rd. N17 221 306 DQ52
Gospel Oak Est. NW5 113 305 DF64
Gosport Dr., Horn. 238 310 FJ65
Gosport Rd. E17 222 307 DZ57
Gosport Wk. N17 222 307 DV57
Gosport Way SE15 163 316 DT80
Gossage Rd. SE18 253 318 ER78
Gossage Rd., Uxb. 240 312 BM66
Gosset St. E2 39 316 DT69
Gosshill Rd., Chis. 277 326 EN96
Gossington Clo., Chis. 277 326 EP91
Gosterwood St. SE8 165 317 DY79
Gostling Rd., Twick. 259 321 CA88
Goston Gdns., Th.Hth. 273 324 DN97
Goswell Rd. EC1 24/5 316 DP68
Gothic Ct., Hayes 257 320 BR79
Gothic Rd., Twick. 259 321 CD89
Gottfried Ms. NW5 114 306 DJ63
Goudhurst Rd., Brom. 275 325 EE92
Gough Rd. E15 121 307 EF63
Gough Rd., Enf. 203 301 DV40
Gough Sq. EC4 48 316 DN72
Gough St. WC1 35 316 DM70
Gough Wk. E14 140 317 EA72
Gould Ct. SE19 273 324 DS92
Gould Rd., Felt. 265 320 BS87
Gould Rd., Twick. 259 321 CE88
Gould Ter. E8 118 307 DV64
Goulds Grn., Uxb. 249 312 BP72
Goulston St. E1 51 316 DT72
Goulton Rd. E5 118 307 DV63
Gourley Pl. N15 221 306 DS57
Gourley St. N15 221 306 DS57
Gourock Rd. SE9 261 326 EN85
Govan St. E2 128 317 DU67
Govett Ave., Shep. 281 328 BQ99
Govier Clo. E15 121 307 EE66
Gowan Ave. SW6 157 315 CY81
Gowan Rd. NW10 110 305 CV65
Gower Clo. SW4 176 324 DJ86
Gower Ct. WC1 34 316 DK70
Gower Ms. WC1 46 316 DK71
Gower Pl. WC1 33 316 DJ70
Gower Rd. E7 234 308 EG65
Gower Rd., Islw. 251 321 CF79
Gower St. WC1 33 316 DJ70
Gower's Wk. E1 138 317 DU72
Gowland Pl., Beck. 274 325 DZ96
Gowlett Rd. SE15 180 325 DU83
Gowrie Rd. SW11 176 324 DG83
Graburn Way, E.Mol. 267 329 CD97
Grace Ave., Bexh. 254 319 EZ82
Grace Clo. SE9 260 326 EK90
Grace Clo., Edg. 217 304 CQ52
Grace Clo., Ilf. 225 308 ET51
Grace Jones Clo. E8 118 307 DU65
Grace Path SE26 274 325 DW91
Grace Rd., Croy. 287 332 DQ100
Grace St. E3 130 317 EB69
Gracechurch St. EC3 62 316 DR73
Gracedale Rd. SW16 272 324 DH92
Gracefield Gdns. SW16 193 324 DL90
Grace's All. E1 138 317 DU73
Graces Ms. SE5 163 316 DR82
Graces Rd. SE5 163 316 DS82
Gradient, The SE26 274 325 DU91
Graeme Rd., Enf. 202 300 DR40
Graemesdyke Ave. SW14 170 322 CP83
Grafton Clo. W13 132 314 CG72
Grafton Clo., Houns. 258 321 BY88
Grafton Clo., Wor.Pk. 283 330 CS104
Grafton Ct., Felt. 265 320 BR88
Grafton Cres. NW1 114 306 DH65
Grafton Gdns. N4 221 306 DQ58
Grafton Gdns., Dag. 236 309 EY61
Grafton Ho. E3 130 317 EA69
Grafton Ms. N1 25 316 DQ68
Grafton Ms. W1 33 316 DJ70
Grafton Pk. Rd., Wor.Pk. 283 330 CS103
Grafton Pl. NW1 34 316 DK69
Grafton Rd. NW5 114 306 DG64
Grafton Rd. W3 134 314 CQ73
Grafton Rd., Croy. 286 332 DN102
Grafton Rd., Dag. 236 309 EY60
Grafton Rd., Har. 215 303 CC57
Grafton Rd., N.Mal. 269 322 CS97
Grafton Rd., Wor.Pk. 283 330 CR105
Grafton Sq. SW4 176 324 DJ83
Grafton St. W1 56/7 316 DH73
Grafton Ter. NW5 113 305 DF64
Grafton Way W1 33 316 DJ70
Grafton Way WC1 33 316 DJ70
Grafton Way, W.Mol. 266 329 BZ98
Grafton Yd. NW5 114 306 DH65
Graftons, The NW2 96 305 DA62
Graham Ave. W13 142 314 CH75
Graham Ave., Mitch. 272 324 DG95
Graham Clo., Croy. 288 333 EA103
Graham Gdns., Surb. 282 330 CL102
Graham Rd. E8 118 307 DU65
Graham Rd. E13 244 318 EG69
Graham Rd. N15 221 306 DP55
Graham Rd. NW4 218 305 CV58
Graham Rd. SW19 270 323 CZ94
Graham Rd. W4 145 314 CR76
Graham Rd., Bexh. 263 327 FA84
Graham Rd., Hmptn. 267 329 CA91
Graham Rd., Har. 215 303 CE55
Graham Rd., Mitch. 272 324 DG95
Graham Rd., Pur. 294 332 DN113
Graham St. N1 24/5 316 DP68
Graham Ter. SW1 80 316 DG77
Grahame Pk. Est. NW9 217 304 CT52
Grahame Pk. Way NW7 217 304 CT52
Grahame Pk. Way NW9 217 304 CT54
Grainger Clo., Nthlt. 233 313 CC64
Grainger Rd. N22 221 306 DQ53
Grainger Rd., Islw. 251 321 CF82
Grainge's Yd., Uxb. 240 312 BJ66
Gramer Clo. E11 105 307 ED61
Grampian Clo., Orp. 291 334 ET100
Grampian Gdns. NW2 95 305 CY60
Grampian Way, Hayes 257 320 BR80
Granard Ave. SW15 172 323 CV85
Granard Rd. SW12 191 323 DF87
Granary Clo. N9 210 301 DW45
Granary Rd. E1 128 317 DV70
Granary St. NW1 22 316 DK67
Granby Bldgs. SE11 83 316 DM77
Granby Rd. SE9 252 318 EM82
Granby St. E2 39 316 DT70
Granby Ter. NW1 21 316 DJ68
Grand Ave. EC1 48/9 316 DP71
Grand Ave. N10 220 306 DG56
Grand Ave., Surb. 282 330 CP99
Grand Ave., Wem. 108 304 CN64
Grand Ave. E., Wem. 108 304 CN65
Grand Depot Rd. SE18 253 318 EN78
Grand Dr. SW20 270 323 CW96
Grand Dr., Sthl. 251 321 CC75
Grand Par. Ms. SW15 173 323 CY85
Grand Union Cres. E8 128 317 DU67
Grand Union Ind. Est. NW10 124 314 CP68
Grand Union Wk. NW1 114 306 DH66
Grand Wk. E1 129 317 DY70
Granden Rd. SW16 272 324 DL96
Grandison Rd. SW11 175 323 DF85
Grandison Rd., Wor.Pk. 284 331 CW103
Granfield St. SW11 159 315 DD81
Grange, The N2 219 305 DD54
Grange, The N20 207 299 DC46
Grange, The SE1 75 316 DT76
Grange, The SW19 270 323 CX93
Grange, The, Croy. 288 333 DZ103
Grange, The, Wem. 108 304 CN66
Grange, The, Wor.Pk. 283 330 CR104
Grange Ave. N12 207 299 DC50
Grange Ave. N20 206 299 CY45
Grange Ave. SE25 273 324 DS96
Grange Ave., Barn. 207 299 DE46
Grange Ave., Stan. 216 304 CH54
Grange Ave., Twick. 259 321 CE89
Grange Ave., Wdf.Grn. 224 308 EG51
Grange Clo., Edg. 205 298 CQ50
Grange Clo., Hayes 249 312 BS71
Grange Clo., Houns. 250 321 BZ79
Grange Clo., Sid. 262 327 EU90
Grange Clo., W.Mol. 267 329 CB98
Grange Clo., Wdf.Grn. 224 308 EG52
Grange Ct. E8 117 306 DT66
Grange Ct. WC2 47 316 DM72
Grange Ct., Nthlt. 242 313 BW68
Grange Ct., Stai. 264 328 BG92
Grange Cres. SE28 246 319 EW72
Grange Dr., Chis. 276 326 EL93
Grange Fm. Clo., Har. 233 313 CC61
Grange Gdns. N14 208 300 DK46
Grange Gdns. NW3 96 305 DB62
Grange Gdns. SE25 273 324 DS96
Grange Gdns., Bans. 292 331 DB113
Grange Gdns., Pnr. 214 303 BY55
Grange Gro. N1 116 306 DQ65
Grange Hill SE25 273 324 DS96
Grange Hill, Edg. 205 298 CQ50
Grange Ho., Bark. 245 318 ER67
Grange La. SE21 195 324 DT89
Grange Meadow, Bans. 292 331 DB113
Grange Ms. SE10 167 317 ED80
Grange Par., Hayes 249 312 BT71
Grange Pk. W5 133 314 CL74
Grange Pk. Ave. N21 209 300 DQ44
Grange Pk. Pl. SW20 270 323 CV94
Grange Pk. Rd. E10 104 307 EB60
Grange Pk. Rd., Th.Hth. 273 324 DR98
Grange Pl. NW6 112 305 DA66
Grange Pl., Stai. 280 328 BJ96
Grange Rd. E10 104 307 EA60
Grange Rd. E13 131 317 EF69
Grange Rd. E17 222 307 DY57
Grange Rd. N6 220 306 DG58
Grange Rd. N17 222 307 DU51
Grange Rd. N18 222 307 DU51
Grange Rd. NW10 110 305 CV65
Grange Rd. SE1 74/5 316 DS76
Grange Rd. SE19 273 324 DR96
Grange Rd. SE25 273 324 DR97
Grange Rd. SW13 156 315 CU81
Grange Rd. W4 144 314 CP78
Grange Rd. W5 133 314 CK74
Grange Rd., Borwd. 204 298 CM43
Grange Rd., Chess. 282 330 CL104
Grange Rd., Edg. 217 304 CR51
Grange Rd., Har. 216 304 CG58
Grange Rd.
(South Harrow), Har. 233 313 CD61
Grange Rd., Hayes 249 312 BS72
Grange Rd., Ilf. 235 308 EP63
Grange Rd., Kings.T. 268 322 CL97
Grange Rd., Orp. 291 334 EQ103
Grange Rd., Rom. 228 310 FH52
Grange Rd., S.Croy. 295 332 DQ110
Grange Rd., Sthl. 250 321 BY75
Grange Rd., Sutt. 292 331 DA108
Grange Rd., Th.Hth. 273 324 DR98
Grange Rd., W.Mol. 267 329 CB98
Grange St. N1 26 316 DR68
Grange Vale, Sutt. 292 331 DB108
Grange Wk. SE1 74/5 316 DS76
Grange Way N12 207 299 DB49
Grange Yd. SE1 75 316 DT76
Grangecliffe Gdns. SE25 273 324 DS96
Grangecourt Rd. N16 101 306 DS60
Grangedale Clo., Nthwd. 213 302 BS53
Grangehill Pl. SE9 260 326 EM83
Grangehill Rd. SE9 260 326 EM84
Grangemill Rd. SE6 198 325 EA90
Grangemill Way SE6 198 325 EA89
Granger Way, Rom. 228 310 FG58
Grangeview Rd. N20 207 299 DC46
Grangeway NW6 112 305 DA66
Grangeway, The N21 209 300 DP44
Grangeway Gdns., Ilf. 224 308 EL57
Grangewood, Bex. 262 327 EZ88
Grangewood Clo., Pnr. 214 303 BU57
Grangewood Dr., Sun. 265 328 BT94
Grangewood La., Beck. 274 325 DZ93
Grangewood St. E6 244 318 EK67
Granham Gdns. N9 209 300 DT47
Granite St. SE18 253 318 ET78
Granleigh Rd. E11 105 307 EE61
Gransden Ave. E8 118 307 DV66
Gransden Rd. W12 145 314 CT75
Grant Clo. N14 208 300 DJ45
Grant Clo., Shep. 281 328 BP100
Grant Pl., Croy. 287 332 DT102
Grant Rd. SW11 175 323 DD84
Grant Rd., Croy. 287 332 DT102
Grant Rd., Har. 215 303 CE55
Grant St. E13 244 318 EG69
Grant St. N1 24 316 DN68
Grant Way, Islw. 152 314 CG80
Grantbridge St. N1 24/5 316 DP68
Grantchester Clo., Har. 233 313 CF62
Grantham Clo., Edg. 204 298 CL48
Grantham Gdns., Rom. 226 309 EZ58
Grantham Grn., Borwd. 205 298 CQ43
Grantham Pl. W1 56/7 316 DH74
Grantham Rd. E12 235 308 EN63
Grantham Rd. SW9 177 324 DL83
Grantham Rd. W4 155 314 CS80
Grantley Rd., Houns. 250 321 BW82
Grantley St. E1 129 317 DX69
Grantock Rd. E17 223 307 ED53
Granton Ave., Upmin. 238 311 FM61
Granton Rd. SW16 272 324 DJ95
Granton Rd., Ilf. 236 309 EU60
Granton Rd., Sid. 278 327 EW93
Grants Clo. NW7 218 305 CW52
Grantully Rd. W9 28/9 315 DB69
Granville Ave. N9 210 301 DW48
Granville Ave., Felt. 258 321 BU89
Granville Ave., Houns. 259 321 CA85
Granville Clo., Croy. 287 332 DS103
Granville Ct. N1 26 316 DR67
Granville Gdns. SW16 272 324 DM95
Granville Gdns. W5 133 314 CM74
Granville Gro. SE13 182 325 EC83
Granville Ms., Sid. 278 327 EU91
Granville Pk. SE13 182 325 EC83
Granville Pl. (N. Finchley) N12 219 305 DC52
Granville Pl. W1 44 316 DG72
Granville Pl., Pnr. 214 303 BX54
Granville Rd. E17 223 307 EB58
Granville Rd. E18 224 308 EH54
Granville Rd. N4 220 306 DM58
Granville Rd. N12 219 305 DB51
Granville Rd. N13 220 306 DM51
Granville Rd. N22 221 306 DP53
Granville Rd. NW2 95 305 CZ61
Granville Rd. NW6 16 315 DA68
Granville Rd. SW18 189 323 CZ87
Granville Rd. SW19 271 323 DA94
Granville Rd., Hayes 249 320 BT77
Granville Rd., Ilf. 235 308 EP60
Granville Rd., Sid. 278 327 EU91
Granville Rd., Uxb. 241 312 BP65
Granville Rd., Well. 262 327 EW83
Granville Sq. SE15 163 316 DS80
Granville Sq. WC1 35 316 DM69
Granville St. WC1 35 316 DM69
Grape St. WC2 46/7 316 DL72
Graphite Sq. SE11 83 316 DM78
Grasdene Rd. SE18 254 319 EU80
Grasmere Ave. SW15 269 322 CR91
Grasmere Ave. SW19 271 323 DA97
Grasmere Ave. W3 135 314 CR73
Grasmere Ave., Houns. 259 321 CB86
Grasmere Ave., Orp. 290 334 EP104
Grasmere Ave., Ruis. 231 312 BQ59
Grasmere Ave., Wem. 90 304 CJ59
Grasmere Clo., Felt. 265 320 BT88
Grasmere Ct. N22 220 306 DM51
Grasmere Gdns., Har. 216 304 CG54
Grasmere Gdns., Ilf. 224 308 EM57
Grasmere Gdns., Orp. 290 334 EP104
Grasmere Rd. E13 244 318 EG68
Grasmere Rd. N10 220 306 DH53
Grasmere Rd. N17 222 307 DU51
Grasmere Rd. SE25 287 333 DV100
Grasmere Rd. SW16 272 324 DM92
Grasmere Rd., Bexh. 255 319 FC81
Grasmere Rd., Brom. 275 325 EF95
Grasmere Rd., Orp. 290 334 EP104
Grasmere Rd., Pur. 294 332 DP111
Grass Pk. N3 218 305 CZ53
Grassington Rd., Sid. 278 327 EU91
Grassmere Rd., Horn. 228 311 FM56
Grassmount SE23 196 325 DV89
Grassmount, Pur. 294 332 DJ110
Grassway, Wall. 286 332 DJ105
Grasvenor Ave., Barn. 207 299 DB44
Grately Way SE15 163 316 DT80
Gratton Rd. W14 147 315 CY76
Gratton Ter. NW2 95 305 CX62
Gravel Hill N3 218 305 CZ54
Gravel Hill, Bexh. 263 327 FB85
Gravel Hill, Uxb. 240 312 BK64
Gravel Hill Clo., Bexh. 263 327 FB85
Gravel La. E1 51 316 DT72
Gravel Pit La. SE9 261 326 EQ85
Gravel Pit Way, Orp. 291 335 EU103
Gravel Rd., Brom. 290 334 EL104
Gravel Rd., Twick. 259 321 CE88
Gravelly Ride SW19 269 322 CT91
Gravelwood Clo., Chis. 261 326 EQ90
Graveney Gro. SE20 274 325 DW94
Graveney Rd. SW17 271 323 DE91
Gravesend Rd. W12 136 315 CU73
Gray Ave., Dag. 236 309 EZ60
Gray Gdns., Rain. 238 310 FG64
Gray St. SE1 72 316 DN75
Grayham Cres., N.Mal. 269 322 CR98
Grayham Rd., N.Mal. 269 322 CR98
Grayland Clo., Brom. 276 326 EK95
Grayling Clo. E16 131 317 EE70
Grayling Rd. N16 101 306 DR61
Grayling Sq. E2 128 317 DU69
Grays Fm. Rd., Orp. 278 327 EV95
Gray's Inn WC1 47 316 DM71
Gray's Inn Pl. WC1 47 316 DM71
Gray's Inn Rd. WC1 34/5 316 DL69
Gray's Inn Sq. WC1 48 316 DN71
Grays La., Ashf. 265 328 BP91
Grays Rd., Uxb. 240 312 BL67
Gray's Yd. W1 44 316 DG72
Grayscroft Rd. SW16 272 324 DK94
Grayshott Rd. SW11 160 316 DG82
Grayswood Gdns. SW20 270 323 CV96
Graywood Ct. N12 219 305 DC52
Grazebrook Rd. N16 101 306 DR61
Grazeley Clo., Bexh. 263 327 FC85
Grazeley Ct. SE19 273 324 DS91
Great Acre Ct. SW4 177 324 DK84
Great Bell All. EC2 50 316 DR72
Great Benty, West Dr. 248 320 BL77
Great Brownings SE21 273 324 DT91
Great Bushey Dr. N20 207 299 DB46
Great Cambridge Rd. N9 209 300 DR48
Great Cambridge Rd. N17 221 306 DR52
Great Cambridge Rd. N18 209 300 DR49
Great Cambridge Rd., Enf. 203 301 DU41
Great Castle St. W1 44/5 316 DH72
Great Cen. Ave., Ruis. 232 313 BW64
Great Cen. St. NW1 43 315 DF71
Great Cen. Way NW10 108 304 CQ63
Great Chapel St. W1 46 316 DK72
Great Chertsey Rd. W4 154 314 CQ82
Great Chertsey Rd., Felt. 259 321 CA90
Great Ch. La. W6 147 315 CX78
Great College St. SW1 70/1 316 DL76
Great Cross Ave. SE10 167 317 EE80
Great Cullings, Rom. 237 309 FE61
Great Cumberland Ms. W1 43 315 DF72
Great Cumberland Pl. W1 43 315 DF72
Great Dover St. SE1 74 316 DR75
Great Eastern Rd. E15 121 307 ED66
Great Eastern St. EC2 38/9 316 DS69
Great Eastern Wk. EC2 50/1 316 DS71
Great Elms Rd., Brom. 276 326 EJ98
Great Fld. NW9 217 304 CS53
Great Fleete Way, Bark. 246 319 EW68
Great Galley Clo., Bark. 246 319 EV69
Great Gdns. Rd., Horn. 228 310 FH58
Great George St. SW1 70 316 DK75
Great Guildford St. SE1 61 316 DQ74
Great Harry Dr. SE9 261 326 EN90
Great James St. WC1 47 316 DM71
Great Marlborough St. W1 45 316 DJ72
Great Maze Pond SE1 62 316 DR74
Great Nelmes Chase, Horn. 228 311 FM57
Great New St. EC4 48 316 DN72
Great Newport St. WC2 58 316 DK73
Great N. Rd. N2 219 305 DE56
Great N. Rd. N6 219 305 DF57
Great N. Rd.
(New Barnet), Barn. 207 299 DB43
Great N. Way NW4 218 305 CV53
Great Ormond St. WC1 46/7 316 DL71
Great Percy St. WC1 35 316 DM69
Great Peter St. SW1 70 316 DK76
Great Portland St. W1 32/3 316 DH70
Great Pulteney St. W1 57 316 DJ73
Great Queen St. WC2 46/7 316 DL72
Great Russell St. WC1 46 316 DK72
Great St. Helens EC3 50/1 316 DS72
Great St. Thomas Apostle EC4 61 316 DQ73
Great Scotland Yd. SW1 58/9 316 DL74
Great Smith St. SW1 70 316 DK76
Great South-West Rd., Felt. 265 320 BQ87
Great South-West Rd., Houns. 258 321 BV83
Great Spilmans SE22 179 324 DS85
Great Strand NW9 217 304 CT53
Great Suffolk St. SE1 60/1 316 DP74
Great Sutton St. EC1 36/7 316 DP70
Great Swan All. EC2 50 316 DR72
Great Thrift, Orp. 277 326 EQ98
Great Titchfield St. W1 45 316 DJ71
Great Twr. St. EC3 62/3 316 DS73
Great Trinity La. EC4 61 316 DQ73
Great Turnstile WC1 47 316 DM71
Great W. Rd. W4 144 314 CP78
Great W. Rd. W6 146 315 CU78
Great W. Rd., Brent. 144 314 CP78
Great W. Rd., Houns. 250 321 BY82
Great W. Rd., Islw. 251 321 CD80
Great Western Ind. Pk., Sthl. 251 321 CB75
Great Western Rd. W9 137 315 CZ71
Great Western Rd. W11 137 315 CZ71

Great Wf. Rd. E14	140	317	EB74
Great Winchester St. EC2	50	316	DR72
Great Windmill St. W1	58	316	DK73
Great Woodcote Dr., Pur.	294	332	DK110
Great Woodcote Pk., Pur.	294	332	DK110
Great Yd. SE1	74/5	316	DS75
Greatdown Rd. W7	243	313	CF70
Greatfield Ave. E6	244	318	EM70
Greatfield Clo. N19	114	306	DJ63
Greatfield Clo. SE4	182	325	EA84
Greatfields Dr., Uxb.	249	312	BN71
Greatfields Rd., Bark.	245	318	ER67
Greatham Wk. SW15	188	323	CU88
Greatorex St. E1	138	317	DU71
Greatwood, Chis.	277	326	EN94
Greaves Clo., Bark.	235	308	ES66
Greaves Pl. SW17	271	323	DE91
Grebe Ave., Hayes	242	313	BX72
Grebe Clo. E7	121	307	EF64
Grebe Clo. E17	222	307	DY52
Grecian Cres. SE19	273	324	DP93
Gredo Ho., Bark.	246	319	EV69
Greek Ct. W1	46	316	DK72
Greek St. W1	46	316	DK72
Greek Yd. WC2	58/9	316	DL73
Green, The E4	211	301	EC46
Green, The E11	224	308	EH58
Green, The E15	121	307	EE65
Green, The N9	210	301	DU47
Green, The N14	208	300	DK48
Green, The N21	209	300	DN45
Green, The SW14	170	322	CQ83
Green, The SW19	270	323	CX92
Green, The W3	135	314	CS72
Green, The W5	133	314	CK74
Green, The, Bexh.	255	319	FA81
Green, The, Brom.	289	334	EG101
Green, The, Cars.	285	332	DG105
Green, The, Felt.	258	321	BV89
Green, The, Hayes	249	312	BS72
Green, The, Houns.	251	321	CA79
Green, The, Mord.	270	323	CY98
Green, The, N.Mal.	269	322	CQ97
Green, The (St. Paul's Cray), Orp.	278	327	EV94
Green, The, Rich.	169	322	CK85
Green, The, Shep.	281	328	BS98
Green, The, Sid.	278	327	EU91
Green, The, Sthl.	250	321	BY76
Green, The, Sutt.	284	331	DB104
Green, The, Twick.	259	321	CE89
Green, The, Uxb.	231	312	BQ61
Green, The, Well.	261	326	ES84
Green, The, Wem.	90	304	CG61
Green, The, West Dr.	248	320	BK76
Green Acres, Croy.	287	332	DT104
Green Arbour Ct. EC1	48/9	316	DP72
Green Ave. NW7	205	298	CR49
Green Ave. W13	142	314	CH76
Green Bank E1	138	317	DV74
Green Bank N12	207	299	DB49
Green Banks, Upmin.	239	311	FS60
Green Clo. NW9	217	304	CQ58
Green Clo. NW11	96	305	DC59
Green Clo., Brom.	275	325	EE97
Green Clo., Cars.	285	331	DF103
Green Clo., Felt.	266	329	BY92
Green Cft., Edg.	205	298	CQ50
Green Curve, Bans.	292	331	CZ114
Green Dale SE5	179	324	DR84
Green Dale SE22	179	324	DS85
Green Dale Clo. SE22	179	324	DS85
Green Dragon Ct. SE1	62	316	DR74
Green Dragon La. N21	209	300	DN43
Green Dragon La., Brent.	143	314	CL78
Green Dragon Yd. E1	138	317	DU71
Green Dr., Sthl.	243	313	CA74
Green End N21	209	300	DP47
Green End, Chess.	282	330	CL105
Green Gdns., Orp.	291	334	EQ106
Green Glades, Horn.	228	311	FM58
Green Hill Ter. SE18	252	318	EM78
Green Hundred Rd. SE15	164	317	DU79
Green La. NW4	218	305	CX56
Green La. SE9	261	326	EP88
Green La. SE20	274	325	DX94
Green La. SW16	272	324	DM94
Green La. W7	251	321	CE75
Green La., Chis.	261	326	EP90
Green La., Dag.	236	309	EX61
Green La., Edg.	204	298	CM49
Green La., Felt.	266	329	BY92
Green La., Har.	233	313	CE62
Green La., Houns.	258	321	BV83
Green La., Ilf.	235	308	EQ61
Green La., Mord.	284	331	DA100
Green La., N.Mal.	283	330	CQ99
Green La., Nthwd.	213	302	BR52
Green La., Pur.	294	332	DJ111
Green La., Shep.	281	328	BQ100
Green La., Stan.	204	298	CH49
Green La., Sun.	265	328	BT94
Green La., Th.Hth.	273	324	DP95
Green La., Uxb.	249	312	BQ71
Green La., Wor.Pk.	283	331	CU102
Green La. Gdns., Th.Hth.	273	324	DP96
Green Las. N4	100	306	DP59
Green Las. N8	221	306	DP55
Green Las. N13	220	306	DM51
Green Las. N15	221	306	DP55
Green Las. N16	100	306	DQ62
Green Las. N21	209	300	DP47
Green Lawns, Ruis.	232	313	BW60
Green Leaf Ave., Wall.	286	332	DK105
Green Leas, Sun.	265	328	BT94
Green Leas Clo., Sun.	265	328	BT93
Green Man Gdns. W13	132	314	CG73
Green Man La. W13	132	314	CG73
Green Man La., Felt.	258	321	BU84
Green Moor Link N21	209	300	DP45
Green Pl., Dart.	263	327	FE85
Green Pt. E15	121	307	EE65
Green Pond Clo. E17	222	307	DY55
Green Pond Rd. E17	222	307	DY55
Green Rd. N14	208	300	DH44
Green Rd. N20	207	299	DC48
Green Shield Ind. Est. E16	244	318	EG74
Green St. E7	234	308	EH65
Green St. E13	234	308	EJ66
Green St. W1	55	315	DF73
Green St., Enf.	203	301	DW40
Green St., Sun.	266	329	BU95
Green Vale W5	133	314	CM72
Green Vale, Bexh.	262	327	EX85
Green Verges, Stan.	216	304	CK52
Green Wk. NW4	218	305	CX57
Green Wk. SE1	74/5	316	DS76
Green Wk., Dart.	263	327	FF85
Green Wk., Hmptn.	266	329	BZ93
Green Wk., Ruis.	231	312	BT60
Green Wk., Sthl.	251	321	CA78
Green Wk., Wdf.Grn.	224	308	EL51
Green Wk., The E4	211	301	EC46
Green Way SE9	260	326	EK85
Green Way, Brom.	290	334	EL100
Green Way, Sun.	266	329	BU98
Green Wrythe Cres., Cars.	285	331	DE102
Green Wrythe La., Cars.	285	331	DD100
Greenacre Clo., Swan.	279	327	FE98
Greenacre Gdns. E17	223	307	EC56
Greenacre Sq. SE16	149	317	DX75
Greenacre Wk. N14	208	300	DL48
Greenacres SE9	261	326	EN86
Greenacres Ave., Uxb.	230	312	BM62
Greenacres Clo., Nthlt.	232	313	BZ64
Greenacres Clo., Orp.	291	334	EQ105
Greenacres Dr., Stan.	216	304	CH51
Greenaway Gdns. NW3	112	305	DB63
Greenbank Ave., Wem.	106	304	CG64
Greenbank Clo. E4	211	301	EC47
Greenbank Cres. NW4	218	305	CY56
Greenbay Rd. SE7	252	318	EK80
Greenberry St. NW8	18/9	315	DE68
Greencoat Pl. SW1	81	316	DJ77
Greencoat Row SW1	69	316	DJ76
Greencourt Ave., Croy.	287	333	DV103
Greencourt Ave., Edg.	217	304	CP53
Greencourt Gdns., Croy.	287	333	DV102
Greencourt Rd., Orp.	291	334	ER99
Greencrest Pl. NW2	94	305	CV62
Greencroft Ave., Ruis.	232	313	BW61
Greencroft Clo. E6	244	318	EL71
Greencroft Gdns. NW6	112	305	DB66
Greencroft Gdns., Enf.	202	300	DS41
Greencroft Rd., Houns.	250	321	BZ81
Greene Fielde End, Stai.	264	328	BK94
Greenend Rd. W4	145	314	CS75
Greenfarm Clo., Orp.	291	334	ET106
Greenfell St. SE10	151	317	EE76
Greenfield Ave., Surb.	282	330	CP101
Greenfield Gdns. NW2	95	305	CY61
Greenfield Gdns., Dag.	246	319	EX67
Greenfield Gdns., Orp.	291	334	ER101
Greenfield Rd. E1	138	317	DU71
Greenfield Rd. N15	221	306	DS57
Greenfield Rd., Dag.	236	309	EW66
Greenfield Rd., Dart.	279	327	FD92
Greenfield Way, Har.	215	303	CB55
Greenford Ave. W7	243	313	CE70
Greenford Ave., Sthl.	242	313	BZ73
Greenford Gdns., Grnf.	243	313	CB69
Greenford Rd., Grnf.	243	313	CC72
Greenford Rd., Har.	233	313	CF63
Greenford Rd., Sthl.	243	313	CC72
Greenford Rd., Sutt.	284	331	DB105
Greengate, Grnf.	106	304	CH65
Greengate St. E13	244	318	EH68
Greenhalgh Wk. N2	219	305	DC56
Greenham Clo. SE1	72	316	DN75
Greenham Cres. E4	222	307	DZ51
Greenham Rd. N10	220	306	DG54
Greenhayes Ave., Bans.	292	331	DA114
Greenheys Clo., Nthwd.	213	302	BS53
Greenheys Dr. E18	223	307	EF55
Greenhill NW3	113	305	DD63
Greenhill SE18	252	318	EM78
Greenhill, Sutt.	285	331	DC103
Greenhill, Wem.	92	304	CP61
Greenhill Gdns., Nthlt.	242	313	BZ68
Greenhill Gro. E12	234	308	EL63
Greenhill Pk. NW10	125	314	CS67
Greenhill Pk., Barn.	207	299	DB43
Greenhill Rd. NW10	125	314	CS67
Greenhill Rd., Har.	215	303	CE58
Greenhill Ter., Nthlt.	242	313	BZ68
Greenhill Way, Har.	215	303	CE58
Greenhill Way, Wem.	92	304	CP61
Greenhill's Rents EC1	48/9	316	DP71
Greenhills Ter. N1	117	306	DR65
Greenhithe Clo., Sid.	261	326	ES87
Greenholm Rd. SE9	261	326	EP85
Greenhurst Rd. SE27	273	324	DN92
Greening St. SE2	254	319	EW77
Greenland Cres., Sthl.	250	321	BW76
Greenland Ms. SE8	149	317	DX78
Greenland Pl. NW1	20/1	316	DH67
Greenland Quay SE16	149	317	DX77
Greenland Rd. NW1	20/1	316	DH67
Greenland Rd., Barn.	206	299	CW44
Greenland St. NW1	20/1	316	DH67
Greenlands Rd., Stai.	264	328	BG91
Greenlaw Gdns., N.Mal.	283	330	CT101
Greenlaw St. SE18	253	318	EN76
Greenlea Trd. Pk. SW19	271	323	DD95
Greenleaf Clo. SW2	194	324	DN87
Greenleaf Rd. E6	244	318	EJ67
Greenleaf Rd. E17	222	307	DZ55
Greenleafe Dr., Ilf.	225	308	EP55
Greenleaves Ct., Ashf.	265	328	BP93
Greenleigh Ave., Orp.	278	327	EV98
Greenman St. N1	116	306	DQ66
Greenmoor Rd., Enf.	203	301	DW40
Greeno Cres., Shep.	281	328	BN99
Greenoak Way SW19	270	323	CX91
Greenock Rd. SW16	272	324	DK95
Greenock Rd. W3	144	314	CP76
Greenock Way, Rom.	227	309	FE52
Greenpark Ct., Wem.	106	304	CJ66
Green's Ct. W1	58	316	DK73
Green's End SE18	253	318	EP77
Greenshank Clo. E17	222	307	DY52
Greenside, Bex.	262	327	EY88
Greenside, Dag.	236	309	EW60
Greenside, Swan.	279	327	FD96
Greenside Clo. N20	207	299	DD47
Greenside Clo. SE6	199	325	ED89
Greenside Rd. W12	146	315	CU76
Greenside Rd., Croy.	286	332	DN101
Greenslade Rd., Bark.	235	308	ER66
Greenstead Ave., Wdf.Grn.	224	308	EJ52
Greenstead Clo., Wdf.Grn.	224	308	EJ51
Greenstead Gdns. SW15	172	323	CU85
Greenstead Gdns., Wdf.Grn.	224	308	EJ51
Greenstone Ms. E11	224	308	EG58
Greenvale Rd. SE9	260	326	EM84
Greenview Ave., Beck.	288	333	DY100
Greenview Ave., Croy.	288	333	DY100
Greenview Ct., Ashf.	264	328	BM91
Greenway N14	208	300	DL47
Greenway N20	207	299	DA47
Greenway SW20	270	323	CW98
Greenway, Chis.	277	326	EN92
Greenway, Dag.	236	309	EW61
Greenway, Har.	216	304	CL57
Greenway, Hayes	242	313	BU69
Greenway, Pnr.	214	303	BV54
Greenway, Rom.	229	311	FP51
Greenway, Wall.	286	332	DJ105
Greenway, The NW9	217	304	CR54
Greenway, The, Enf.	203	301	DX35
Greenway, The, Har.	215	303	CE53
Greenway, The, Houns.	258	321	BZ84
Greenway, The, Orp.	291	335	EV100
Greenway, The, Pnr.	214	303	BZ58
Greenway, The, Uxb.	240	312	BK68
Greenway, The (Ickenham), Uxb.	231	312	BP61
Greenway Ave. E17	223	307	ED56
Greenway Clo. N4	100	306	DQ61
Greenway Clo. N11	220	306	DG51
Greenway Clo. N15	221	306	DT56
Greenway Clo. N20	207	299	DA47
Greenway Clo. NW9	217	304	CR54
Greenway Dr., Stai.	280	328	BK95
Greenway Gdns. NW9	217	304	CR54
Greenway Gdns., Croy.	288	333	DZ104
Greenway Gdns., Grnf.	243	313	CA69
Greenway Gdns., Har.	215	303	CE54
Greenways, Beck.	275	325	EA96
Greenways, The, Twick.	168	322	CG86
Greenwell St. W1	32/3	316	DH70
Greenwich Ch. St. SE10	166	317	EC79
Greenwich Cres. E6	244	318	EL71
Greenwich High Rd. SE10	166	317	EB81
Greenwich Ind. Est. SE7	252	318	EH77
Greenwich Mkt. SE10	166	317	EC79
Greenwich Pk. SE10	167	317	ED80
Greenwich Pk. St. SE10	151	317	ED78
Greenwich S. St. SE10	166	317	EB81
Greenwich Vw. Pl. E14	150	317	EB76
Greenwood Ave., Dag.	237	309	FB63
Greenwood Ave., Enf.	203	301	DY40
Greenwood Clo., Mord.	270	323	CY98
Greenwood Clo., Orp.	291	334	ES100
Greenwood Clo., Sid.	262	327	EU89
Greenwood Ct. SW1	81	316	DJ78
Greenwood Dr. E4	211	301	EC50
Greenwood Gdns. N13	209	300	DP48
Greenwood Gdns., Ilf.	225	308	EQ52
Greenwood La., Hmptn.	267	329	CB92
Greenwood Pk., Kings.T.	269	322	CS94
Greenwood Pl. NW5	114	306	DH64
Greenwood Rd. E8	118	307	DU65
Greenwood Rd. E13	131	317	EF68
Greenwood Rd., Bex.	279	327	FD91
Greenwood Rd., Croy.	286	332	DP101
Greenwood Rd., Islw.	259	321	CF83
Greenwood Rd., Mitch.	272	324	DK97
Greenwood Ter. NW10	125	314	CR67
Greenwoods, The, Har.	233	313	CC61
Greer Rd., Har.	215	303	CC53
Greet St. SE1	60	316	DN74
Greg Clo. E10	223	307	EC58
Gregor Ms. SE3	252	318	EG80
Gregory Cres. SE9	260	326	EK87
Gregory Pl. W8	64/5	315	DB75
Gregory Rd., Rom.	226	309	EX56
Gregory Rd., Sthl.	251	321	CA76
Greig Clo. N8	220	306	DL57
Greig Ter. SE17	162	316	DP79
Grena Gdns., Rich.	169	322	CM84
Grena Rd., Rich.	169	322	CM84
Grenaby Ave., Croy.	287	332	DR101
Grenaby Rd., Croy.	287	332	DR101
Grenada Rd. SE7	252	318	EJ80
Grenade St. E14	139	317	DZ73
Grenadier St. E16	245	318	EN74
Grendon Gdns., Wem.	92	304	CN61
Grendon St. NW8	30/1	315	DE70
Grenfell Ave., Horn.	237	309	FF60
Grenfell Gdns., Har.	91	304	CL59
Grenfell Rd. W11	137	315	CX73
Grenfell Rd., Mitch.	271	323	DF93
Grenfell Twr. W11	137	315	CX73
Grenfell Wk. W11	137	315	CX73
Grennell Clo., Sutt.	285	331	DD103
Grennell Rd., Sutt.	285	331	DC104
Grenoble Gdns. N13	221	306	DN51
Grenville Clo. N3	218	305	CZ53
Grenville Clo., Surb.	283	330	CQ102
Grenville Gdns., Wdf.Grn.	224	308	EJ53
Grenville Ms. SW7	77	315	DC77
Grenville Ms., Hmptn.	267	329	CB92
Grenville Pl. NW7	205	298	CR50
Grenville Pl. SW7	65	315	DC76
Grenville Rd. N19	99	306	DL60
Grenville St. WC1	34/5	316	DL70
Gresham Ave. N20	207	299	DF49
Gresham Clo., Bex.	262	327	EY86
Gresham Clo., Enf.	202	300	DQ41
Gresham Dr., Rom.	226	309	EV57
Gresham Gdns. NW11	95	305	CY60
Gresham Rd. E6	244	318	EM68
Gresham Rd. E16	244	318	EH72
Gresham Rd. NW10	109	304	CR64
Gresham Rd. SE25	274	325	DU98
Gresham Rd. SW9	178	324	DN83
Gresham Rd., Beck.	274	325	DY96
Gresham Rd., Edg.	216	304	CM51
Gresham Rd., Hmptn.	267	329	CA93
Gresham Rd., Houns.	251	321	CC81
Gresham Rd., Uxb.	241	312	BN68
Gresham St. EC2	49	316	DQ72
Gresham Way SW19	190	323	DA90
Gresley Clo. E17	222	307	DY58
Gresley Clo. N15	221	306	DR56
Gresley Rd. N19	98	306	DJ60
Gresse St. W1	46	316	DK71
Gressenhall Rd. SW18	173	323	CZ86
Gresswell Clo., Sid.	262	327	EU90
Greswell St. SW6	157	315	CX81
Gretton Rd. N17	221	306	DS52
Greville Clo., Twick.	184	322	CH87
Greville Hall NW6	16/7	315	DB68
Greville Ms. NW6	16/7	315	DB68
Greville Pl. NW6	16/7	315	DB68
Greville Rd. E17	223	307	EC56
Greville Rd. NW6	16/7	315	DB68
Greville Rd., Rich.	169	322	CM86
Greville St. EC1	48	316	DN71
Grey Alders, Bans.	292	331	CW114
Grey Clo. NW11	219	305	DC58
Grey Eagle St. E1	51	316	DT71
Grey Twrs. Ave., Horn.	238	310	FK60
Grey Twrs. Gdns., Horn.	238	310	FK60
Greycoat Pl. SW1	70	316	DK76
Greycoat St. SW1	70	316	DK76
Greycot Rd., Beck.	275	325	EA92
Greyfell Clo., Stan.	204	298	CH50
Greyfields Clo., Pur.	294	332	DP113
Greyfriars Pas. EC1	48/9	316	DP72
Greyhound Hill NW4	218	305	CU55
Greyhound La. SW16	272	324	DK93
Greyhound Rd. N17	221	306	DS55
Greyhound Rd. NW10	126	315	CV69
Greyhound Rd. W6	157	315	CX79
Greyhound Rd. W14	157	315	CY79
Greyhound Rd., Sutt.	285	331	DC106
Greyhound Ter. SW16	272	324	DJ95
Greyhound Way, Dart.	263	327	FE86
Greys Pk. Clo., Kes.	290	334	EK106
Greystead Rd. SE23	196	325	DW87
Greystoke Ave., Pnr.	215	303	CA55
Greystoke Dr., Ruis.	231	302	BP58
Greystoke Gdns. W5	123	314	CL70
Greystoke Pk. Ter. W5	123	314	CK69
Greystoke Pl. EC4	48	316	DN72
Greystone Gdns., Har.	216	304	CJ58
Greystone Gdns., Ilf.	225	308	EQ54
Greystone Path E11	105	307	EF59
Greyswood St. SW16	272	324	DH93
Gridiron Pl., Upmin.	239	311	FP61
Grierson Rd. SE23	181	325	DY86
Griffin Ave., Upmin.	229	311	FS58
Griffin Clo. NW10	110	305	CV64
Griffin Manorway SE28	253	318	ER76
Griffin Rd. N17	221	306	DS54
Griffin Rd. SE18	253	318	ER78
Griffin Way, Sun.	266	329	BU96
Griffith Clo., Dag.	236	309	EW60
Griffiths Clo., Wor.Pk.	283	331	CV103
Griffiths Rd. SW19	271	323	DA94
Griggs App., Ilf.	235	308	EQ61
Griggs Pl. SE1	74/5	316	DS76
Griggs Rd. E10	223	307	EC58
Grilse Clo. N9	210	301	DV49
Grimsby St. E2	128	317	DU70
Grimsdyke Rd., Pnr.	214	303	BY52
Grimsel Path SE5	162	316	DP80
Grimshaw Clo. N6	98	306	DG59
Grimshaw Way, Rom.	227	309	FF57
Grimston Rd. SW6	157	315	CZ82
Grimstone Clo., Rom.	227	309	FB51
Grimwade Ave., Croy.	287	333	DU104
Grimwade Clo. SE15	180	325	DW83
Grimwade Cres. SE15	180	325	DW83
Grimwood Rd., Twick.	259	321	CF87
Grindal St. SE1	72	316	DN75
Grindall Clo., Croy.	286	332	DP105
Grindley Gdns., Croy.	287	332	DT100
Grinling Pl. SE8	166	317	EA79
Grinstead Rd. SE8	149	317	DY78
Grisedale Clo., Pur.	295	332	DR114
Grisedale Gdns., Pur.	295	332	DS114
Grittleton Ave., Wem.	108	304	CP65
Grittleton Rd. W9	28	315	DA70
Grizedale Ter. SE23	196	325	DV89
Grocer's Hall Ct. EC2	50	316	DR72
Grogan Clo., Hmptn.	266	329	BZ93
Groom Cres. SW18	191	323	DD87
Groom Pl. SW1	68	316	DG76
Groombridge Clo., Well.	262	327	EU85
Groombridge Rd. E9	119	307	DX66
Groomfield Clo. SW17	272	324	DG91
Grooms Dr., Pnr.	214	303	BU57
Grosmont Rd. SE18	253	318	ET79
Grosse Way SW15	172	323	CV86
Grosvenor Ave. N5	116	306	DQ64
Grosvenor Ave. SW14	171	322	CS83
Grosvenor Ave., Cars.	293	331	DF107
Grosvenor Ave., Har.	215	303	CB58
Grosvenor Ave., Hayes	241	312	BS68
Grosvenor Ave., Rich.	169	322	CL85
Grosvenor Cotts. SW1	80	316	DG77
Grosvenor Ct. N14	208	300	DJ45
Grosvenor Cres. NW9	217	304	CN56
Grosvenor Cres. SW1	68	316	DG75
Grosvenor Cres., Uxb.	241	312	BP66
Grosvenor Cres. Ms. SW1	68	316	DG75
Grosvenor Dr., Horn.	238	310	FJ60
Grosvenor Est. SW1	82	316	DK77
Grosvenor Gdns. E6	244	318	EK69
Grosvenor Gdns. N10	220	306	DJ55
Grosvenor Gdns. NW2	110	305	CW64
Grosvenor Gdns. NW11	218	305	CZ58
Grosvenor Gdns. SW1	68/9	316	DH76
Grosvenor Gdns. SW14	171	322	CS83
Grosvenor Gdns., Kings.T.	268	322	CK93
Grosvenor Gdns., Upmin.	239	311	FR60
Grosvenor Gdns., Wall.	294	332	DJ108
Grosvenor Gdns., Wdf.Grn.	224	308	EG51
Grosvenor Gdns. Ms. E. SW1	68/9	316	DH76
Grosvenor Gdns. Ms. N. SW1	68/9	316	DH76
Grosvenor Gdns. Ms. S. SW1	68/9	316	DH76
Grosvenor Gate W1	55	315	DF73
Grosvenor Hill SW19	270	323	CY93
Grosvenor Hill W1	56/7	316	DH73
Grosvenor Pk. SE5	162	316	DQ80
Grosvenor Pk. Rd. E17	223	307	EA57
Grosvenor Pl. SW1	68	316	DG75
Grosvenor Ri. E. E17	223	307	EB57
Grosvenor Rd. E6	244	318	EK67
Grosvenor Rd. E7	234	308	EH65
Grosvenor Rd. E10	104	307	EC60
Grosvenor Rd. E11	224	308	EG57
Grosvenor Rd. N3	218	305	CZ52
Grosvenor Rd. N9	210	301	DV46
Grosvenor Rd. N10	220	306	DH53
Grosvenor Rd. SE25	274	325	DU98
Grosvenor Rd. SW1	160	316	DH79
Grosvenor Rd. W4	144	314	CP78
Grosvenor Rd. W7	132	314	CG74
Grosvenor Rd., Belv.	255	319	FA79
Grosvenor Rd., Bexh.	262	327	EX85
Grosvenor Rd., Brent.	153	314	CK79
Grosvenor Rd., Dag.	236	309	EZ60
Grosvenor Rd., Houns.	258	321	BZ83
Grosvenor Rd., Ilf.	235	308	EQ62
Grosvenor Rd., Nthwd.	213	302	BT50
Grosvenor Rd., Orp.	291	334	ES100
Grosvenor Rd., Rich.	169	322	CL85
Grosvenor Rd., Rom.	237	309	FD59
Grosvenor Rd., Sthl.	250	321	BZ76
Grosvenor Rd., Stai.	264	328	BG94
Grosvenor Rd., Twick.	184	322	CG87
Grosvenor Rd., Wall.	293	332	DH107
Grosvenor Rd., W.Wick.	288	333	EB102
Grosvenor Sq. W1	56	316	DG73
Grosvenor St. W1	56/7	316	DH73
Grosvenor Ter. SE5	162	316	DQ79
Grosvenor Vale, Ruis.	231	312	BT61
Grosvenor Way E5	102	307	DW61
Grosvenor Wf. Rd. E14	151	317	ED77
Grote's Bldgs. SE3	167	317	EE82
Grote's Pl. SE3	167	317	EE82
Groton Rd. SW18	190	323	DB89
Grotto Pas. W1	44	316	DG71
Grotto Rd., Twick.	259	321	CF89
Grove, The E15	121	307	EE65
Grove, The N3	219	305	DA53
Grove, The N4	99	306	DM59
Grove, The N6	98	306	DG60
Grove, The N8	220	306	DK57
Grove, The N13	209	300	DN50
Grove, The N14	208	300	DJ43
Grove, The NW9	217	304	CR57
Grove, The NW11	95	305	CY59
Grove, The W5	133	314	CK74
Grove, The, Bexh.	262	327	EX84
Grove, The, Edg.	205	298	CP49
Grove, The, Enf.	202	300	DN40
Grove, The, Grnf.	243	313	CC72
Grove, The, Islw.	251	321	CE81
Grove, The, Sid.	278	327	EY92
Grove, The, Swan.	279	327	FF97
Grove, The, Tedd.	268	322	CG91
Grove, The, Twick.	168	322	CH86
Grove, The, Upmin.	239	311	FP63
Grove, The, Uxb.	241	312	BN64
Grove, The, W.Wick.	288	333	EB104
Grove Ave. N3	219	305	DA52
Grove Ave. N10	220	306	DJ54
Grove Ave. W7	243	313	CE72
Grove Ave., Pnr.	214	303	BY57
Grove Ave., Sutt.	292	331	DA107
Grove Ave., Twick.	259	321	CF88
Grove Clo. N14	208	300	DH45
Grove Clo. SE23	197	325	DY88
Grove Clo., Brom.	289	334	EG103
Grove Clo., Felt.	266	329	BY91
Grove Clo., Kings.T.	268	322	CM98
Grove Clo., Uxb.	241	312	BN64
Grove Cotts. SW3	159	315	DE79
Grove Ct. SE3	252	318	EG81
Grove Cres. E18	223	307	EF54
Grove Cres. NW9	217	304	CQ56
Grove Cres. SE5	163	316	DS82
Grove Cres., Felt.	266	329	BY91
Grove Cres., Kings.T.	268	322	CL97
Grove Cres. Rd. E15	121	307	ED65
Grove End E18	223	307	EF54
Grove End Rd. NW8	18	315	DD68
Grove Fm. Ind. Est., Mitch.	285	331	DF99
Grove Fm. Pk., Nthwd.	213	302	BR50
Grove Footpath, Surb.	268	322	CL98
Grove Gdns. E15	121	307	EE65
Grove Gdns. NW4	218	305	CU57
Grove Gdns. NW8	30/1	315	DE69
Grove Gdns., Dag.	237	309	FC62
Grove Gdns., Enf.	203	301	DX38
Grove Gdns., Tedd.	268	322	CG91
Grove Grn. Rd. E11	104	307	EC62
Grove Hall Ct. NW8	29	315	DC69
Grove Hill E18	223	307	EF54
Grove Hill, Har.	233	313	CE59
Grove Hill Rd. SE5	179	324	DS83
Grove Hill Rd., Har.	233	313	CE59
Grove Ho. Rd. N8	220	306	DL56
Grove La. SE5	163	316	DS82
Grove La., Couls.	293	332	DH114
Grove La., Kings.T.	268	322	CL98
Grove La., Uxb.	240	312	BM70
Grove Mkt. Pl. SE9	260	326	EM86
Grove Ms. W6	146	315	CW76
Grove Ms. W11	137	315	CZ72
Grove Pk. E11	224	308	EH58
Grove Pk. NW9	217	304	CQ56
Grove Pk. SE5	163	316	DS82
Grove Pk. Ave. E4	223	307	EB52
Grove Pk. Bri. W4	154	314	CQ80
Grove Pk. Gdns. W4	154	314	CQ80
Grove Pk. Ms. W4	154	314	CQ80
Grove Pk. Rd. N15	221	306	DS56
Grove Pk. Rd. SE9	260	326	EJ90
Grove Pk. Rd. W4	154	314	CP80
Grove Pk. Ter. W4	154	314	CP80
Grove Pas. E2	128	317	DV68
Grove Pas., Tedd.	268	322	CG92
Grove Pl. NW3	113	305	DD63
Grove Pl. W3	134	314	CQ74
Grove Pl. W5	133	314	CK74
Grove Pl., Bark.	245	318	EQ67
Grove Rd. E3	129	317	DX67
Grove Rd. E4	211	301	EC49
Grove Rd. E11	105	307	EF59
Grove Rd. E17	223	307	EB58
Grove Rd. E18	223	307	EF54
Grove Rd. N11	208	300	DH50
Grove Rd. N12	207	299	DD50
Grove Rd. N15	221	306	DS57
Grove Rd. NW2	110	305	CW65
Grove Rd. SW13	155	314	CT82
Grove Rd. SW19	271	323	DC94
Grove Rd. W3	134	314	CQ74
Grove Rd. W5	133	314	CK73
Grove Rd., Belv.	254	319	EZ79
Grove Rd., Bexh.	263	327	FC84
Grove Rd., Brent.	142	314	CJ78
Grove Rd., E.Mol.	267	329	CD98
Grove Rd., Edg.	217	304	CN51
Grove Rd., Houns.	259	321	CA84
Grove Rd., Islw.	251	321	CE81
Grove Rd., Mitch.	272	324	DG97
Grove Rd., Nthwd.	213	302	BR50
Grove Rd., Pnr.	214	303	BZ57
Grove Rd., Rich.	169	322	CM86
Grove Rd., Rick.	212	302	BG47
Grove Rd., Rom.	236	309	EV59
Grove Rd., Shep.	281	328	BQ100
Grove Rd., Surb.	282	330	CK99
Grove Rd., Sutt.	292	331	DA107
Grove Rd., Th.Hth.	273	324	DN98
Grove Rd., Twick.	259	321	CD90
Grove Rd., Uxb.	240	312	BK66
Grove Rd. W., Enf.	203	301	DW37
Grove St. N18	209	300	DT50
Grove St. SE8	149	317	DZ77
Grove Ter. NW5	98	306	DH62
Grove Ter., Tedd.	268	322	CG91
Grove Vale SE22	179	324	DS84
Grove Vale, Chis.	277	326	EN93
Grove Vil. E14	140	317	EB73
Grove Way, Uxb.	240	312	BK66
Grove Wd. Hill, Couls.	294	332	DJ114
Grovebarns, Stai.	264	328	BG93
Grovebury Clo., Erith	255	319	FD79
Grovebury Rd. SE2	254	319	EV75
Grovedale Rd. N19	99	306	DK61
Groveland Ave. SW16	272	324	DM94
Groveland Ct. EC4	49	316	DQ72
Groveland Rd., Beck.	274	325	DZ97
Groveland Way, N.Mal.	283	330	CQ99
Grovelands, W.Mol.	267	329	CA98
Grovelands Clo. SE5	163	316	DS82
Grovelands Clo., Har.	233	313	CB62
Grovelands Ct. N14	208	300	DK45
Grovelands Rd. N13	208	300	DM49
Grovelands Rd. N15	222	307	DU58
Grovelands Rd., Orp.	278	327	EU94
Grovelands Rd., Pur.	294	332	DL112
Groveley Rd., Sun.	265	328	BS92
Groveside Clo. W3	134	314	CP72
Groveside Clo., Cars.	285	331	DE103
Groveside Rd. E4	211	301	EE47
Grovestile Waye, Felt.	265	320	BR87
Groveway SW9	161	316	DM81
Groveway, Dag.	236	309	EX63
Groveway, Wem.	108	304	CQ64
Grovewood, Rich.	154	314	CN81
Grovewood Pl., Wdf.Grn.	224	308	EM51
Grummant Rd. SE15	163	316	DT81
Grundy St. E14	140	317	EB72
Gruneisen Rd. N3	219	305	DB52
Guardian Clo., Horn.	238	310	FH60
Gubbins La., Rom.	228	311	FM52
Gubyon Ave. SE24	178	324	DP85
Guerin Sq. E3	129	317	DZ69
Guernsey Clo., Houns.	251	321	CA81
Guernsey Gro. SE24	194	324	DQ87
Guernsey Rd. E11	105	307	ED60
Guibal Rd. SE12	260	326	EH87
Guild Rd. SE7	252	318	EK78
Guild Rd., Erith	255	319	FF80
Guildersfield Rd. SW16	272	324	DL94
Guildford Ave., Felt.	265	320	BT89
Guildford Gdns., Rom.	228	311	FL51
Guildford Gro. SE10	166	317	EB81
Guildford Rd. E6	244	318	EM72
Guildford Rd. E17	223	307	EC53
Guildford Rd. SW8	161	316	DL81
Guildford Rd., Croy.	287	332	DR100
Guildford Rd., Ilf.	235	308	ES61
Guildford Rd., Rom.	228	311	FL51
Guildford St., Stai.	264	328	BG93
Guildford Way, Wall.	286	332	DL106
Guildhall Bldgs. EC2	50	316	DR72
Guildhall Yd. EC2	50	316	DR72
Guildhouse St. SW1	81	316	DJ77
Guildown Ave. N12	207	299	DB49
Guildsway E17	222	307	DZ53
Guilford Ave., Surb.	282	330	CM99
Guilford Pl. WC1	35	316	DM70
Guilford St. WC1	34/5	316	DL70
Guilford Vil., Surb.	282	330	CM100
Guilsborough Clo. NW10	109	304	CS66
Guinness Bldgs. SE1	86/7	316	DS77
Guinness Clo. E9	119	307	DY66
Guinness Clo., Hayes	249	320	BR76
Guinness Sq. SE1	86/7	316	DS77
Guinness Trust Bldgs. SE11	84/5	316	DP78
Guinness Trust Bldgs. SW3	79	315	DF77
Guinness Trust Est. N16	101	306	DS60
Guinness Trust Est. SW9	178	324	DP84
Guion Rd. SW6	157	315	CZ82
Gull Clo., Wall.	294	332	DL108
Gull Wk., Horn.	238	310	FH66
Gulland Wk. N1	116	306	DQ65
Gulliver Clo., Nthlt.	242	313	BZ67
Gulliver Rd., Sid.	261	326	ES89
Gulliver St. SE16	149	317	DZ76
Gulston Wk. SW3	79	315	DF77
Gumleigh Rd. W5	142	314	CJ77
Gumley Gdns., Islw.	168	322	CG83
Gumping Rd., Orp.	291	334	EQ102
Gun St. E1	51	316	DT71
Gundulph Rd., Brom.	276	326	EJ97
Gunmakers La. E3	129	317	DY67
Gunnell Clo. SE26	274	325	DU91
Gunnell Clo., Croy.	287	333	DU100
Gunner La. SE18	253	318	EN78
Gunners Gro. E4	211	301	EC48
Gunners Rd. SW18	191	323	DD89
Gunnersbury Ave. W3	133	314	CM74
Gunnersbury Ave. W4	133	314	CM74
Gunnersbury Ave. W5	133	314	CM74
Gunnersbury Clo. W4	144	314	CP78
Gunnersbury Ct. W3	144	314	CP75
Gunnersbury Cres. W3	144	314	CN75
Gunnersbury Dr. W5	143	314	CM75
Gunnersbury Gdns. W3	144	314	CN75
Gunnersbury La. W3	144	314	CN76
Gunnersbury Ms. W4	144	314	CP78
Gunnersbury Pk. W3	143	314	CM77
Gunnersbury Pk. W5	143	314	CM77
Gunning St. SE18	253	318	ES77
Gunpowder Sq. EC4	48	316	DN72
Gunstor Rd. N16	117	306	DS63
Gunter Gro. SW10	158	315	DC79
Gunter Gro., Edg.	217	304	CR53
Gunterstone Rd. W14	147	315	CY77
Gunthorpe St. E1	51	316	DT71
Gunton Rd. E5	102	307	DV61
Gunton Rd. SW17	272	324	DG93
Gunwhale Clo. SE16	139	317	DX74
Gurdon Rd. SE7	252	318	EG78
Gurnard Clo., West Dr.	248	312	BK73
Gurnell Gro. W13	243	313	CF70
Gurney Clo. E15	121	307	EE64
Gurney Clo. E17	222	307	DX53
Gurney Clo., Bark.	235	308	EP65
Gurney Cres., Croy.	286	332	DM102
Gurney Dr. N2	219	305	DC56
Gurney Rd. E15	121	307	EE64
Gurney Rd., Cars.	285	332	DG104
Gurney Rd., Nthlt.	242	313	BV69
Guthrie St. SW3	78/9	315	DE78
Gutter La. EC2	49	316	DQ72
Guy Barnett Clo. SE3	260	326	EG83
Guy Rd., Wall.	286	332	DK104
Guy St. SE1	74	316	DR75
Guyatt Gdns., Mitch.	272	324	DG96
Guyscliff Rd. SE13	182	325	EC85
Gwalior Rd. SW15	173	323	CX83
Gwendolen Ave. SW15	173	323	CX84
Gwendolen Clo. SW15	173	323	CX85
Gwendoline Ave. E13	244	318	EH67
Gwendwr Rd. W14	147	315	CY78
Gwillim Clo., Sid.	262	327	EU85
Gwydor Rd., Beck.	274	325	DX98
Gwydyr Rd., Brom.	275	325	EF97
Gwyn Clo. SW6	158	315	DC80
Gwynne Ave., Croy.	288	333	DX101
Gwynne Clo. W4	155	314	CT79
Gwynne Pk. Ave., Wdf.Grn.	224	308	EM51
Gwynne Pl. WC1	35	316	DM69
Gwynne Rd. SW11	159	315	DD82
Gylcote Clo. SE5	179	324	DR84
Gyles Pk., Stan.	216	304	CJ52
Gyllyngdune Gdns., Ilf.	235	308	ET62
Ha-Ha Rd. SE18	252	318	EM79
Haarlem Rd. W14	147	315	CX76
Haberdasher Pl. N1	38	316	DR69
Haberdasher St. N1	38	316	DR69
Haccombe Rd. SW19	271	323	DC93
Hackbridge Grn., Wall.	285	332	DG103
Hackbridge Pk. Gdns., Cars.	285	332	DG103
Hackbridge Rd., Wall.	285	332	DG103
Hackford Rd. SW9	161	316	DM81
Hackforth Clo., Barn.	206	299	CV43
Hackington Cres., Beck.	275	325	EA93
Hackney Clo., Borwd.	205	298	CR43
Hackney Gro. E8	118	307	DV65
Hackney Rd. E2	39	316	DT69
Hacton Dr., Horn.	238	310	FK63
Hacton La., Horn.	238	311	FM61
Hacton La., Upmin.	238	311	FM64
Hadden Rd. SE28	253	318	ES76
Hadden Way, Grnf.	233	313	CD65
Haddington Rd., Brom.	275	325	ED91
Haddo St. SE10	166	317	EC79

Haddon Clo., Enf.	210	301	DU44
Haddon Clo., N.Mal.	283	330	CT99
Haddon Gro., Sid.	261	326	ET87
Haddon Rd., Sutt.	284	331	DB105
Haddonfield SE8	149	317	DX77
Hadfield Clo., Sthl.	242	313	BZ69
Hadfield Rd., Stai.	256	320	BK86
Hadleigh Clo. E1	128	317	DW70
Hadleigh Clo. SW20	270	323	CZ96
Hadleigh Dr., Sutt.	292	331	DA109
Hadleigh Rd. N9	210	301	DV45
Hadleigh St. E2	128	317	DW69
Hadleigh Wk. E6	244	318	EL72
Hadley Clo. N21	209	300	DN44
Hadley Clo., Borwd.	204	298	CM43
Hadley Gdns. W4	145	314	CR78
Hadley Gdns., Sthl.	250	321	BZ78
Hadley Rd., Belv.	254	319	EZ77
Hadley Rd., Mitch.	272	324	DK98
Hadley St. NW1	114	306	DH65
Hadley Way N21	209	300	DN44
Hadlow Pl. SE19	274	325	DU94
Hadlow Rd., Sid.	278	327	EU91
Hadlow Rd., Well.	254	319	EW80
Hadrian Clo., Stai.	264	320	BL88
Hadrian Clo., Wall.	294	332	DL108
Hadrian Est. E2	128	317	DU68
Hadrian St. SE10	151	317	EE78
Hadrian Way, Stai.	264	320	BK87
Hadrians Ride, Enf.	209	300	DT43
Hadyn Pk. Rd. W12	146	315	CU75
Hafer Rd. SW11	175	323	DF84
Hafton Rd. SE6	199	325	EE88
Haggard Rd., Twick.	184	322	CG87
Haggerston Rd. E8	117	306	DT66
Hague St. E2	128	317	DU69
Haig Rd., Stan.	204	298	CJ50
Haig Rd., Uxb.	249	312	BP71
Haig Rd. E. E13	244	318	EJ69
Haig Rd. W. E13	244	318	EJ69
Haigville Gdns., Ilf.	225	308	EP56
Hailes Clo. SW19	271	323	DC93
Hailey Rd., Erith	255	319	FA75
Haileybury Ave., Enf.	209	300	DT44
Haileybury Rd., Orp.	291	335	EU105
Hailsham Ave. SW2	193	324	DM89
Hailsham Clo., Surb.	282	330	CK101
Hailsham Dr., Har.	215	303	CD55
Hailsham Rd. SW17	272	324	DG93
Hailsham Ter. N18	209	300	DQ50
Haimo Rd. SE9	260	326	EK85
Hainault Ct. E17	223	307	ED56
Hainault Gore, Rom.	226	309	EY57
Hainault Rd. E11	104	307	EC60
Hainault Rd., Rom.	227	309	FC54
Hainault Rd. (Chadwell Heath), Rom.	226	309	EZ58
Hainault Rd. (Hainault), Rom.	226	309	EV55
Hainault St. SE9	261	326	EP88
Hainault St., Ilf.	235	308	EQ61
Hainford Clo. SE4	181	325	DX84
Haining Clo. W4	144	314	CN78
Hainthorpe Rd. SE27	194	324	DP90
Hainton Clo. E1	138	317	DV72
Halberd Ms. E5	102	307	DV61
Halbutt Gdns., Dag.	236	309	EZ62
Halbutt St., Dag.	236	309	EZ63
Halcomb St. N1	26/7	316	DS67
Halcot Ave., Bexh.	263	327	FB85
Halcrow St. E1	138	317	DV71
Halcyon Way, Horn.	238	311	FM60
Haldan Rd. E4	223	307	EC51
Haldane Clo. N10	220	306	DH52
Haldane Pl. SW18	190	323	DB88
Haldane Rd. E6	244	318	EK69
Haldane Rd. SE28	246	319	EX73
Haldane Rd. SW6	157	315	CZ80
Haldane Rd., Sthl.	243	313	CC73
Haldon Rd. SW18	173	323	CZ85
Hale, The E4	223	307	ED52
Hale, The N17	222	307	DU55
Hale Clo. E4	211	301	EC48
Hale Clo., Edg.	205	298	CQ50
Hale Clo., Orp.	291	334	EQ105
Hale Dr. NW7	217	304	CQ51
Hale End, Rom.	228	310	FH51
Hale End Clo., Ruis.	214	303	BU58
Hale End Rd. E4	223	307	ED51
Hale End Rd. E17	223	307	ED53
Hale End Rd., Wdf.Grn.	223	307	ED52
Hale Gdns. N17	222	307	DU55
Hale Gdns. W3	134	314	CN74
Hale Gro. Gdns. NW7	205	298	CR50
Hale La. NW7	205	298	CR50
Hale La., Edg.	205	298	CP50
Hale Path SE27	273	324	DP91
Hale Rd. E6	244	318	EL70
Hale Rd. N17	222	307	DU55
Hale St. E14	140	317	EB73
Hale Wk. W7	243	313	CE71
Halefield Rd. N17	222	307	DU53
Hales St. SE8	166	317	EA80
Halesowen Rd., Mord.	284	331	DB101
Halesworth Clo. E5	102	307	DW61
Halesworth Clo., Rom.	228	311	FL52
Halesworth Rd. SE13	182	325	EB83
Halesworth Rd., Rom.	228	311	FL51
Haley Rd. NW4	218	305	CW58
Half Acre, Brent.	153	314	CK79
Half Acre Rd. W7	243	313	CE74
Half Moon Ct. EC1	49	316	DQ71
Half Moon Cres. N1	23	316	DM68
Half Moon La. SE24	178	324	DQ86
Half Moon Pas. E1	51	316	DT72
Half Moon St. W1	56/7	316	DH74
Halford Rd. E10	223	307	ED57
Halford Rd. SW6	158	315	DA79
Halford Rd., Rich.	169	322	CL85
Halford Rd., Uxb.	241	312	BN64
Halfway St., Sid.	261	326	ER87
Haliburton Rd., Twick.	168	322	CG85
Haliday Wk. N1	117	306	DR65
Halidon Clo. E9	118	307	DW64
Halidon Ri., Rom.	229	311	FP51
Halifax Rd., Enf.	202	300	DQ40
Halifax Rd., Grnf.	243	313	CB67
Halifax St. SE26	274	325	DV91
Halifield Dr., Belv.	254	319	EY76
Haling Down Pas., S.Croy.	295	332	DQ109
Haling Gro., S.Croy.	295	332	DQ108
Haling Pk. Gdns., S.Croy.	294	332	DP107
Haling Pk. Rd., S.Croy.	294	332	DP107
Haling Rd., S.Croy.	295	332	DR107
Halkin Arc. SW1	68	316	DG76
Halkin Ms. SW1	68	316	DG76
Halkin Pl. SW1	68	316	DG76
Halkin St. SW1	68	316	DG75
Hall, The SE3	260	326	EG83
Hall Ave. N18	221	306	DR51
Hall Clo. W5	133	314	CL71
Hall Ct., Tedd.	267	329	CF92
Hall Dr. SE26	274	325	DW92
Hall Dr. W7	243	313	CE72
Hall Dr., Uxb.	212	302	BJ53
Hall Fm. Clo., Stan.	204	298	CH49
Hall Fm. Dr., Twick.	259	321	CD87
Hall Gdns. E4	210	301	DZ49
Hall Gate NW8	29	315	DC69
Hall La. E4	210	301	DY50
Hall La. NW4	218	305	CU53
Hall La., Hayes	257	320	BR80
Hall La., Upmin.	229	311	FQ54
Hall Oak Wk. NW6	111	305	CZ65
Hall Pk. Rd., Upmin.	239	311	FQ64
Hall Pl. W2	30	315	DD70
Hall Pl. Cres., Bex.	263	327	FC85
Hall Rd. E6	244	318	EM67
Hall Rd. E15	121	307	ED63
Hall Rd. NW8	29	315	DC69
Hall Rd., Islw.	259	321	CD85
Hall Rd., Rom.	226	309	EW58
Hall Rd. (Gidea Pk.), Rom.	228	310	FH55
Hall Rd., Wall.	293	332	DH109
Hall St. EC1	36/7	316	DP69
Hall St. N12	207	299	DC50
Hall Ter., Rom.	229	311	FN52
Hall Vw. SE9	260	326	EK89
Hall Way, Pur.	294	332	DP113
Hallam Clo., Chis.	276	326	EM92
Hallam Gdns., Pnr.	214	303	BY52
Hallam Ms. W1	44/5	316	DH71
Hallam Rd. N15	221	306	DP56
Hallam Rd. SW13	172	323	CV83
Hallam St. W1	44/5	316	DH71
Halland Way, Nthwd.	213	302	BR51
Halley Gdns. SE13	183	325	ED84
Halley Rd. E7	234	308	EJ65
Halley Rd. E12	234	308	EK65
Halley St. E14	139	317	DY71
Hallfield Est. W2	41	315	DC72
Halliday Sq., Sthl.	243	313	CD74
Halliford Clo., Shep.	281	328	BR98
Halliford Rd., Shep.	281	328	BS99
Halliford Rd., Sun.	281	328	BT99
Halliford St. N1	116	306	DQ66
Hallingbury Ct. E17	223	307	EB55
Halliwell Rd. SW2	177	324	DM86
Halliwick Rd. N10	220	306	DG53
Hallmark Trd. Est. NW10	108	304	CQ63
Hallmead Rd., Sutt.	284	331	DB104
Hallowell Ave., Croy.	286	332	DL105
Hallowell Clo., Mitch.	272	324	DG97
Hallowell Rd., Nthwd.	213	302	BS52
Hallowfield Way, Mitch.	271	323	DD97
Hallside Rd., Enf.	202	300	DT38
Hallsville Rd. E16	141	317	EF72
Hallswelle Rd. NW11	218	305	CZ57
Hallywell Cres. E6	244	318	EM71
Halons Rd. SE9	261	326	EN87
Halpin Pl. SE17	86	316	DR77
Halsbrook Rd. SE3	260	326	EJ83
Halsbury Clo., Stan.	204	298	CH49
Halsbury Rd. W12	136	315	CU74
Halsbury Rd. E., Nthlt.	233	313	CC63
Halsbury Rd. W., Nthlt.	233	313	CB64
Halsend, Hayes	242	313	BV74
Halsey Ms. SW3	79	315	DF77
Halsey St. SW3	79	315	DF77
Halsham Cres., Bark.	235	308	ET65
Halsmere Rd. SE5	162	316	DP81
Halstead Clo., Croy.	287	332	DQ104
Halstead Ct. N1	26	316	DR68
Halstead Gdns. N21	209	300	DR46
Halstead Rd. E11	224	308	EG57
Halstead Rd. N21	209	300	DR46
Halstead Rd., Enf.	202	300	DS42
Halstead Rd., Erith	255	319	FE81
Halston Clo. SW11	175	323	DF86
Halstow Rd. NW10	127	315	CX69
Halstow Rd. SE10	252	318	EG78
Halsway, Hayes	242	313	BU74
Halt Robin La., Belv.	255	319	FB77
Halt Robin Rd., Belv.	255	319	FA77
Halter Clo., Borwd.	205	298	CR43
Halton Cross St. N1	24/5	316	DP67
Halton Rd. N1	116	306	DP66
Ham, The, Brent.	152	314	CJ80
Ham Clo., Rich.	184	322	CJ90
Ham Common, Rich.	185	322	CK90
Ham Fm. Rd., Rich.	268	322	CK91
Ham Gate Ave., Rich.	268	322	CL91
Ham Pk. Rd. E7	234	308	EG66
Ham Pk. Rd. E15	121	307	EF66
Ham Ridings, Rich.	268	322	CM92
Ham St., Rich.	184	322	CH88
Ham Vw., Croy.	288	333	DY100
Ham Yd. W1	58	316	DK73
Hambalt Rd. SW4	176	324	DJ85
Hamble Clo., Ruis.	231	312	BS61
Hamble Ct., Kings.T.	268	322	CK94
Hamble St. SW6	174	323	DB83
Hamble Wk., Nthlt.	243	313	CA68
Hambledon Clo., Uxb.	249	312	BP71
Hambledon Gdns. SE25	273	324	DT97
Hambledon Pl. SE21	195	324	DS88
Hambledon Rd. SW18	189	323	CZ87
Hambledown Rd., Sid.	261	326	ER87
Hambleton Clo., Wor.Pk.	284	331	CW103
Hambridge Way SW2	194	324	DN87
Hambro Ave., Brom.	289	334	EG102
Hambro Rd. SW16	272	324	DK93
Hambrook Rd. SE25	274	325	DV97
Hambrough Rd., Sthl.	242	313	BY74
Hamden Cres., Dag.	237	309	FB62
Hamel Clo., Har.	216	304	CK55
Hamelin St. E14	140	317	EC72
Hameway E6	245	318	EN70
Hamfrith Rd. E15	121	307	EF65
Hamilton Ave. N9	210	301	DU45
Hamilton Ave., Ilf.	225	308	EP56
Hamilton Ave., Rom.	227	309	FD54
Hamilton Ave., Surb.	282	330	CN103
Hamilton Ave., Sutt.	284	331	CY102
Hamilton Clo. N17	221	306	DT55
Hamilton Clo. NW8	30	315	DD69
Hamilton Clo. SE16	149	317	DY75
Hamilton Clo., Felt.	265	328	BT92
Hamilton Clo., Pur.	294	332	DP112
Hamilton Ct. W5	133	314	CM73
Hamilton Ct. W9	29	315	DC69
Hamilton Cres. N13	209	300	DN49
Hamilton Cres., Har.	232	313	BZ62
Hamilton Cres., Houns.	259	321	CB85
Hamilton Dr., Rom.	228	311	FL54
Hamilton Gdns. NW8	29	315	DC69
Hamilton La. N5	116	306	DP63
Hamilton Ms. W1	68/9	316	DH75
Hamilton Pk. N5	116	306	DP63
Hamilton Pk. W. N5	116	306	DP63
Hamilton Pl. W1	56	316	DG74
Hamilton Pl., Sun.	266	329	BV94
Hamilton Rd. E15	131	317	EE69
Hamilton Rd. E17	222	307	DY54
Hamilton Rd. N2	219	305	DC55
Hamilton Rd. N9	210	301	DU45
Hamilton Rd. NW10	110	305	CU64
Hamilton Rd. NW11	95	305	CX59
Hamilton Rd. SE27	273	324	DR91
Hamilton Rd. SW19	271	323	DB94
Hamilton Rd. W4	145	314	CS75
Hamilton Rd. W5	133	314	CL73
Hamilton Rd., Bexh.	254	319	EY82
Hamilton Rd., Brent.	153	314	CK79
Hamilton Rd., Felt.	265	328	BT91
Hamilton Rd., Har.	215	303	CE57
Hamilton Rd., Hayes	242	313	BV73
Hamilton Rd., Ilf.	235	308	EP63
Hamilton Rd., Rom.	228	310	FH57
Hamilton Rd., Sid.	278	327	EU91
Hamilton Rd., Sthl.	242	313	BZ74
Hamilton Rd., Th.Hth.	273	324	DR97
Hamilton Rd., Twick.	259	321	CE88
Hamilton Rd., Uxb.	240	312	BK70
Hamilton Sq. SE1	74	316	DR75
Hamilton St. SE8	166	317	EA79
Hamilton Ter. NW8	16/7	315	DB68
Hamilton Wk., Erith	255	319	FF80
Hamilton Way N3	219	305	DA51
Hamilton Way N13	209	300	DP49
Hamilton Way, Wall.	294	332	DK109
Hamlea Clo. SE12	260	326	EG85
Hamlet, The SE5	179	324	DR83
Hamlet Clo. SE13	183	325	EE84
Hamlet Clo., Rom.	227	309	FA52
Hamlet Gdns. W6	146	315	CU77
Hamlet Rd. SE19	273	324	DT94
Hamlet Rd., Rom.	227	309	FA52
Hamlet Sq. NW2	95	305	CY62
Hamlet Sq. NW11	95	305	CY62
Hamlet Way SE1	74	316	DR75
Hamlets Way E3	129	317	DZ70
Hamlin Cres., Pnr.	214	303	BW57
Hamlyn Clo., Edg.	204	298	CL48
Hamlyn Gdns. SE19	273	324	DS94
Hammelton Grn. SW9	162	316	DP81
Hammelton Rd., Brom.	275	325	EF95
Hammers La. NW7	206	299	CU50
Hammersmith Bri. SW13	146	315	CV78
Hammersmith Bri. Rd. W6	146	315	CW78
Hammersmith Bdy. W6	146	315	CW77
Hammersmith Flyover W6	146	315	CW78
Hammersmith Gro. W6	146	315	CW75
Hammersmith Rd. W6	147	315	CX77
Hammersmith Rd. W14	147	315	CX77
Hammersmith Ter. W6	146	315	CU78
Hammet Clo., Hayes	242	313	BX71
Hammett St. EC3	63	316	DT73
Hammond Ave., Mitch.	272	324	DH96
Hammond Clo., Barn.	206	299	CY43
Hammond Clo., Grnf.	233	313	CD64
Hammond Clo., Hmptn.	267	329	CA95
Hammond Rd., Enf.	203	301	DV40
Hammond Rd., Sthl.	250	321	BY76
Hammond St. NW5	114	306	DJ65
Hammond Way SE28	246	319	EV73
Hammonds Clo., Dag.	236	309	EW62
Hamond Clo., S.Croy.	294	332	DP109
Hamonde Clo., Edg.	205	298	CP47
Hampden Ave., Beck.	274	325	DY96
Hampden Clo. NW1	22	316	DK68
Hampden Gurney St. W1	43	315	DF72
Hampden La. N17	221	306	DT53
Hampden Rd. N8	221	306	DN56
Hampden Rd. N10	220	306	DG52
Hampden Rd. N17	222	307	DU53
Hampden Rd. N19	99	306	DK61
Hampden Rd., Beck.	274	325	DY96
Hampden Rd., Har.	215	303	CC53
Hampden Rd., Kings.T.	269	322	CN97
Hampden Rd., Rom.	227	309	FB52
Hampden Sq. N14	208	300	DH46
Hampden Way N14	208	300	DH47
Hampermill La., Wat.	213	302	BT47
Hampshire Clo. N18	210	301	DV50
Hampshire Hog La. W6	146	315	CV77
Hampshire Rd. N22	220	306	DM52
Hampshire Rd., Horn.	229	311	FN56
Hampshire St. NW5	115	306	DK65
Hampson Way SW8	161	316	DM81
Hampstead Clo. SE28	246	319	EV74
Hampstead Gdns. NW11	219	305	DA58
Hampstead Gdns., Rom.	226	309	EV57
Hampstead Grn. NW3	113	305	DE64
Hampstead Gro. NW3	96	305	DC62
Hampstead High St. NW3	112	305	DC63
Hampstead Hill Gdns. NW3	113	305	DD63
Hampstead La. N6	97	305	DD59
Hampstead La. NW3	97	305	DD60
Hampstead Rd. NW1	21	316	DJ68
Hampstead Sq. NW3	96	305	DC62
Hampstead Wk. E3	129	317	DZ67
Hampstead Way NW11	218	305	CZ57
Hampton Clo. N11	208	300	DH50
Hampton Clo. NW6	28	315	DA69
Hampton Clo. SW20	270	323	CW94
Hampton Ct. N1	116	306	DP65
Hampton Ct. Cres., E.Mol.	267	329	CD97
Hampton Ct. Palace, E.Mol.	267	329	CE97
Hampton Ct. Par., E.Mol.	267	329	CE98
Hampton Ct. Rd., E.Mol.	267	329	CF97
Hampton Ct. Rd., Hmptn.	267	329	CC96
Hampton Ct. Rd., Kings.T.	268	322	CJ96
Hampton Fm. Ind. Est., Felt.	258	321	BY90
Hampton La., Felt.	266	329	BY91
Hampton Ri., Har.	216	304	CL58
Hampton Rd. E4	210	301	DZ50
Hampton Rd. E7	234	308	EH64
Hampton Rd. E11	105	307	ED60
Hampton Rd., Croy.	287	332	DQ100
Hampton Rd., Hmptn.	267	329	CD92
Hampton Rd., Ilf.	235	308	EP63
Hampton Rd., Tedd.	267	329	CD92
Hampton Rd., Twick.	259	321	CD90
Hampton Rd., Wor.Pk.	283	331	CU103
Hampton Rd. E., Felt.	258	321	BZ90
Hampton Rd. W., Felt.	258	321	BY89
Hampton St. SE1	85	316	DQ77
Hampton St. SE17	84/5	316	DP77
Hamshades Clo., Sid.	261	326	ET90
Hanah Ct. SW19	270	323	CX94
Hanameel St. E16	244	318	EH74
Hanbury Dr. N21	208	300	DM43
Hanbury Ms. N1	25	316	DQ67
Hanbury Rd. N17	222	307	DV54
Hanbury Rd. W3	144	314	CP75
Hanbury St. E1	51	316	DT71
Hanbury Wk., Bex.	263	327	FE90
Hancock Rd. E3	130	317	EC69
Hancock Rd. SE19	273	324	DR93
Hand Ct. WC1	47	316	DM71
Handa Wk. N1	117	306	DR65
Handcroft Rd., Croy.	286	332	DP101
Handel Clo., Edg.	216	304	CM51
Handel Pl. NW10	109	304	CR65
Handel St. WC1	34/5	316	DL70
Handel Way, Edg.	217	304	CN52
Handen Rd. SE12	183	325	EE85
Handforth Rd. SW9	162	316	DN80
Handforth Rd., Ilf.	235	308	EP62
Handley Rd. E9	128	317	DW67
Handowe Clo. NW4	218	305	CU56
Hands Wk. E16	244	318	EG72
Handside Clo., Wor.Pk.	284	331	CX102
Handsworth Ave. E4	223	307	ED51
Handsworth Rd. N17	221	306	DR55
Handtrough Way, Bark.	245	318	EP68
Hanford Clo. SW18	190	323	DA88
Hanford Row SW19	270	323	CW93
Hanger Grn. W5	124	314	CN70
Hanger La. W5	123	314	CL68
Hanger Vale La. W3	133	314	CM72
Hanger Vale La. W5	133	314	CM72
Hanger Vw. Way W3	134	314	CN72
Hankey Pl. SE1	74	316	DR75
Hankins La. NW7	205	298	CS47
Hanley Pl., Beck.	275	325	EA94
Hanley Rd. N4	99	306	DL60
Hanmer Wk. N7	99	306	DM62
Hannah Clo. NW10	108	304	CQ63
Hannah Clo., Beck.	275	325	EC97
Hannah Mary Way SE1	148	317	DU77
Hannah Ms., Wall.	294	332	DJ108
Hannay La. N8	99	306	DK59
Hannay Wk. SW16	193	324	DK89
Hannell Rd. SW6	157	315	CY80
Hannen Rd. SE27	194	324	DP90
Hannibal Rd. E1	138	317	DW71
Hannibal Rd., Stai.	264	320	BK87
Hannibal Way, Croy.	286	332	DM106
Hannington Rd. SW4	176	324	DH83
Hanover Ave. E16	141	317	EE72
Hanover Ave., Felt.	258	321	BU88
Hanover Circle, Hayes	249	312	BQ72
Hanover Clo., Rich.	154	314	CN80
Hanover Clo., Sutt.	284	331	CY105
Hanover Ct. W12	136	315	CU74
Hanover Dr., Chis.	277	326	EQ91
Hanover Gdns. SE11	162	316	DN79
Hanover Gdns., Ilf.	225	308	EQ52
Hanover Gate NW1	30/1	315	DE69
Hanover Pk. SE15	164	317	DU81
Hanover Pl. WC2	46/7	316	DL72
Hanover Rd. N15	221	306	DT56
Hanover Rd. NW10	110	305	CW66
Hanover Rd. SW19	271	323	DC94
Hanover Sq. W1	44/5	316	DH72
Hanover St. W1	44/5	316	DH72
Hanover St., Croy.	286	332	DP104
Hanover Ter. NW1	30/1	315	DE69
Hanover Ter., Islw.	152	314	CG81
Hanover Ter. Ms. NW1	30/1	315	DE69
Hanover Way, Bexh.	262	327	EX83
Hanover W. Ind. Est. NW10	125	314	CR69
Hanover Yd. N1	24/5	316	DP68
Hans Cres. SW1	67	315	DF76
Hans Pl. SW1	67	315	DF76
Hans Rd. SW3	67	315	DF76
Hans St. SW1	67	315	DF76
Hansard Ms. W14	147	315	CX75
Hansart Way, Enf.	202	300	DN39
Hansen Dr. N21	208	300	DM43
Hansha Dr., Edg.	217	304	CR53
Hansler Rd. SE22	179	324	DT85
Hansol Rd., Bexh.	262	327	EY85
Hanson Clo. SW12	192	324	DH87
Hanson Clo. SW14	170	322	CQ83
Hanson Clo., Beck.	275	325	EB93
Hanson Clo., West Dr.	248	320	BM76
Hanson Gdns., Sthl.	250	321	BY75
Hanson St. W1	45	316	DJ71
Hanway Pl. W1	46	316	DK72
Hanway Rd. W7	243	313	CD72
Hanway St. W1	46	316	DK72
Hanworth Rd., Felt.	258	321	BV88
Hanworth Rd., Hmptn.	266	329	BZ91
Hanworth Rd., Houns.	258	321	BY88
Hanworth Rd., Sun.	266	329	BU94
Hanworth Ter., Houns.	259	321	CB84
Hanworth Trd. Est., Felt.	258	321	BY90
Hapgood Clo., Grnf.	233	313	CD64
Harads Pl. E1	138	317	DU73
Harben Rd. NW6	112	305	DC66
Harberson Rd. E15	131	317	EF67
Harberson Rd. SW12	192	324	DH88
Harberton Rd. N19	98	306	DJ60
Harbet Rd. N18	210	301	DX50
Harbet Rd. W2	42	315	DD71
Harbex Clo., Bex.	263	327	FB87
Harbinger Rd. E14	150	317	EB77
Harbledown Pl., Orp.	278	327	EW98
Harbledown Rd. SW6	158	315	DA81
Harbledown Rd., S.Croy.	295	333	DU111
Harbord Clo. SE5	163	316	DR82
Harbord St. SW6	157	315	CX81
Harborough Ave., Sid.	261	326	ES87
Harborough Rd. SW16	272	324	DM91
Harbour Ave. SW10	158	315	DC81
Harbour Ex. Sq. E14	150	317	EB75
Harbour Rd. SE5	178	324	DQ83
Harbridge Ave. SW15	187	322	CT87
Harbury Rd., Cars.	293	331	DE109
Harbut Rd. SW11	175	323	DD84
Harcombe Rd. N16	101	306	DS62
Harcourt Ave. E12	234	308	EM63
Harcourt Ave., Edg.	205	298	CQ48
Harcourt Ave., Sid.	262	327	EW86
Harcourt Ave., Wall.	285	332	DH105
Harcourt Clo., Islw.	168	322	CG83
Harcourt Fld., Wall.	285	332	DH105
Harcourt Rd. E15	131	317	EF68
Harcourt Rd. N22	220	306	DK53
Harcourt Rd. SE4	181	325	DY84
Harcourt Rd. SW19	271	323	DA94
Harcourt Rd., Bexh.	262	327	EY84
Harcourt Rd., Th.Hth.	286	332	DM100
Harcourt Rd., Wall.	285	332	DH105
Harcourt St. W1	42/3	315	DE71
Harcourt Ter. SW10	76/7	315	DB78
Hardcastle Clo., Croy.	287	332	DT100
Hardcourts Clo., W.Wick.	288	333	EB104
Hardel Ri. SW2	194	324	DP88
Hardel Wk. SW2	194	324	DN87
Hardens Manorway SE7	252	318	EK76
Harders Rd. SE15	164	317	DV82
Hardess St. SE24	178	324	DQ83
Hardie Clo. NW10	109	304	CR64
Hardie Rd., Dag.	237	309	FC62
Harding Clo. SE17	162	316	DQ79
Harding Ho., Hayes	242	313	BU72
Harding Rd., Bexh.	254	319	EZ82
Hardinge Clo., Uxb.	249	312	BP72
Hardinge La. E1	138	317	DW72
Hardinge Rd. N18	209	300	DS50
Hardinge Rd. NW10	126	315	CV67
Hardinge St. E1	138	317	DW72
Hardings La. SE20	274	325	DX93
Hardley Cres., Horn.	228	310	FK55
Hardman Rd. SE7	252	318	EH78
Hardman Rd., Kings.T.	268	322	CL96
Hardwick Clo., Stan.	204	298	CJ50
Hardwick Grn. W13	132	314	CH71
Hardwick St. EC1	36	316	DN69
Hardwicke Ave., Houns.	251	321	CA81
Hardwicke Rd. N13	220	306	DL51
Hardwicke Rd. W4	144	314	CQ77
Hardwicke Rd., Rich.	268	322	CJ91
Hardwicke St., Bark.	245	318	EQ67
Hardwicks Way SW18	174	323	DA85
Hardwidge St. SE1	74/5	316	DS75
Hardy Ave. E16	141	317	EE72
Hardy Ave., Ruis.	232	313	BV64
Hardy Clo. SE16	149	317	DX75
Hardy Clo., Barn.	206	299	CY43
Hardy Clo., Pnr.	232	313	BX59
Hardy Rd. E4	222	307	DZ51
Hardy Rd. SE3	167	317	EF79
Hardy Rd. SW19	271	323	DB94
Hardy Way, Enf.	202	300	DN39
Hare & Billet Rd. SE3	167	317	ED81
Hare Ct. EC4	48	316	DN72
Hare Hall La., Rom.	228	310	FH56
Hare Marsh E2	128	317	DU70
Hare Pl. EC4	48	316	DN72
Hare Row E2	128	317	DV68
Hare St. SE18	253	318	EN76
Hare Wk. N1	26/7	316	DS68
Harebell Dr. E6	245	318	EN71
Harebell Way, Rom.	228	310	FK52
Harecastle Clo., Hayes	242	313	BY70
Harecourt Rd. N1	116	306	DQ65
Haredale Rd. SE24	178	324	DQ84
Haredon Clo. SE23	196	325	DW87
Harefield Ave., Sutt.	292	331	CY109
Harefield Clo., Enf.	202	300	DN39
Harefield Ms. SE4	181	325	DZ83
Harefield Rd. N8	220	306	DK57
Harefield Rd. SE4	181	325	DZ83
Harefield Rd. SW16	272	324	DM94
Harefield Rd., Rick.	212	302	BK47
Harefield Rd., Sid.	262	327	EX89
Harefield Rd., Uxb.	240	312	BJ66
Haresfield Rd., Dag.	237	309	FA65
Harewood Ave. NW1	30/1	315	DE70
Harewood Ave., Nthlt.	232	313	BY66
Harewood Clo., Nthlt.	232	313	BZ66
Harewood Dr., Ilf.	224	308	EM54
Harewood Pl. W1	44/5	316	DH72
Harewood Rd. SW19	271	323	DE93
Harewood Rd., Islw.	251	321	CF80
Harewood Rd., S.Croy.	295	332	DS107
Harewood Row NW1	42/3	315	DE71
Harewood Ter., Sthl.	250	321	BZ77
Harfield Gdns. SE5	179	324	DS83
Harfield Rd., Sun.	266	329	BX96
Harford Clo. E4	211	301	EB45
Harford Rd. E4	211	301	EB45
Harford St. E1	129	317	DY70
Harford Wk. N2	219	305	DD56
Harfst Way, Swan.	279	327	FC95
Hargood Clo., Har.	216	304	CL58
Hargood Rd. SE3	252	318	EJ81
Hargrave Pk. N19	98	306	DJ61
Hargrave Pl. N7	115	306	DK64
Hargrave Rd. N19	98	306	DJ61
Hargwyne St. SW9	177	324	DM83
Haringey Pk. N8	220	306	DL58
Haringey Pas. N4	221	306	DP57
Haringey Pas. N8	221	306	DP56
Haringey Rd. N8	220	306	DL56
Harington Ter. N9	209	300	DR48
Harington Ter. N18	209	300	DR48
Harkett Clo., Har.	215	303	CF54
Harkett Ct., Har.	215	303	CF54
Harland Ave., Croy.	287	332	DT104
Harland Ave., Sid.	261	326	ER90
Harland Clo. SW19	271	323	DB97
Harland Rd. SE12	260	326	EG88
Harlands Gro., Orp.	290	334	EP105
Harlech Gdns., Houns.	250	321	BW79
Harlech Rd. N14	208	300	DL48
Harlech Twr. W3	144	314	CQ75
Harlequin Ave., Brent.	152	314	CG79
Harlequin Clo., Hayes	242	313	BX71
Harlequin Clo., Islw.	259	321	CE85
Harlequin Rd., Tedd.	268	322	CH94
Harlescott Rd. SE15	181	325	DX84
Harlesden Clo., Rom.	228	311	FM52
Harlesden Gdns. NW10	125	314	CT67
Harlesden La. NW10	126	315	CU67
Harlesden Rd. NW10	126	315	CU67
Harlesden Rd., Rom.	228	311	FM51
Harlesden Wk., Rom.	228	311	FM52
Harleston Clo. E5	102	307	DW61
Harley Clo., Wem.	107	304	CK65
Harley Ct. E11	234	308	EG59
Harley Cres., Har.	215	303	CD56
Harley Gdns. SW10	77	315	DC78
Harley Gdns., Orp.	291	334	ES105
Harley Gro. E3	129	317	DZ69
Harley Pl. W1	44/5	316	DH71
Harley Rd. NW3	113	305	DD66
Harley Rd. NW10	125	314	CS68
Harley Rd., Har.	215	303	CD56
Harley St. W1	44/5	316	DH71
Harleyford, Brom.	276	326	EJ95
Harleyford Rd. SE11	161	316	DM79
Harleyford St. SE11	162	316	DN79
Harlington Clo., Hayes	257	320	BQ80
Harlington Rd., Bexh.	262	327	EY83
Harlington Rd., Houns.	257	320	BT84
Harlington Rd., Uxb.	241	312	BN69
Harlington Rd. E., Felt.	258	321	BV87
Harlington Rd. W., Felt.	258	321	BV86
Harlow Gdns., Rom.	227	309	FC51
Harlow Rd. N13	209	300	DR48
Harlow Rd., Rain.	247	319	FF67
Harlyn Dr., Pnr.	214	303	BV55
Harman Ave., Wdf.Grn.	223	307	EF51
Harman Clo. E4	211	301	ED49
Harman Clo. NW2	95	305	CY62
Harman Dr. NW2	95	305	CY62
Harman Dr., Sid.	261	326	ET86
Harman Pl., Pur.	294	332	DP111
Harman Rd., Enf.	209	300	DT43
Harmondsworth La., West Dr.	256	320	BL79
Harmondsworth Rd., West Dr.	248	320	BL78
Harmony Clo. NW11	218	305	CY57
Harmony Clo., Wall.	294	332	DK109
Harmony Way NW4	218	305	CW56
Harmood Gro. NW1	114	306	DH66
Harmood Pl. NW1	114	306	DH66
Harmood St. NW1	114	306	DH65
Harmsworth St. SE17	84/5	316	DP78
Harmsworth Way N20	206	299	CZ46
Harnage Rd., Brent.	152	314	CH80
Harness Rd. SE28	254	319	EU75
Harold Ave., Belv.	254	319	EZ78
Harold Ave., Hayes	249	320	BT76
Harold Ct. Rd., Rom.	229	311	FP51
Harold Est. SE1	74/5	316	DS76
Harold Gibbons Ct. SE7	252	318	EJ79
Harold Pl. SE11	84	316	DN78
Harold Rd. E4	211	301	EC49
Harold Rd. E11	105	307	EE60
Harold Rd. E13	244	318	EH67
Harold Rd. N8	220	306	DM57
Harold Rd. N15	221	306	DT57
Harold Rd. NW10	125	314	CR69
Harold Rd. SE19	273	324	DR94
Harold Rd., Sutt.	285	331	DD105
Harold Rd., Wdf.Grn.	224	308	EG53
Harold Vw., Rom.	228	311	FM54
Haroldstone Rd. E17	222	307	DX57
Harp All. EC4	48/9	316	DP72
Harp Island Clo. NW10	93	304	CR61
Harp La. EC3	62/3	316	DS73
Harp Rd. W7	243	313	CE70
Harpenden Rd. E12	234	308	EJ61
Harpenden Rd. SE27	194	324	DP89
Harper Clo. N14	208	300	DJ43
Harper Rd. E6	244	318	EM72
Harper Rd. SE1	73	316	DQ76
Harpers Yd. N17	221	306	DT53
Harpley Sq. E1	128	317	DW69
Harpour Rd., Bark.	235	308	EQ65
Harpsden St. SW11	160	316	DG81
Harpur Ms. WC1	47	316	DM71
Harpur St. WC1	47	316	DM71
Harraden Rd. SE3	252	318	EJ81
Harrap St. E14	140	317	EC73
Harrier Clo., Horn.	238	310	FH65
Harrier Ms. SE28	253	318	ER76
Harrier Rd. NW9	217	304	CS54
Harrier Way E6	244	318	EM71
Harriers Clo. W5	133	314	CL73
Harries Rd., Hayes	242	313	BW70
Harriet Clo. E8	128	317	DU67
Harriet Gdns., Croy.	287	333	DU103
Harriet St. SW1	67	315	DF75
Harriet Wk. SW1	67	315	DF75
Harringay Gdns. N8	221	306	DP56
Harringay Rd. N15	221	306	DP57
Harrington Clo. NW10	93	304	CR62
Harrington Clo., Croy.	286	332	DL103
Harrington Gdns. SW7	77	315	DC77
Harrington Hill E5	102	307	DV60
Harrington Rd. E11	105	307	EE60
Harrington Rd. SE25	274	325	DU98
Harrington Rd. SW7	78	315	DD77
Harrington Sq. NW1	21	316	DJ68
Harrington St. NW1	33	316	DJ69
Harrington Way SE18	252	318	EK76
Harriott Clo. SE10	151	317	EF77
Harris Clo., Enf.	202	300	DP39
Harris Clo., Houns.	251	321	CA81
Harris Rd., Bexh.	254	319	EY81
Harris Rd., Dag.	236	309	EZ64
Harris St. E17	103	307	DZ59
Harris St. SE5	163	316	DR80
Harris Way, Sun.	281	328	BS95
Harrison Clo., Nthwd.	213	302	BQ51
Harrison Ct., Shep.	281	328	BP99
Harrison Rd., Dag.	237	309	FB65
Harrison St. WC1	34/5	316	DL69
Harrisons Ri., Croy.	286	332	DP104
Harrold Rd., Dag.	236	309	EV64
Harrow Ave., Enf.	209	300	DT44
Harrow Cres., Rom.	228	310	FH52
Harrow Dr. N9	209	300	DT46
Harrow Dr., Horn.	228	310	FH58
Harrow Flds. Gdns., Har.	233	313	CE62
Harrow Gdns., Orp.	291	335	EV105
Harrow Grn. E11	105	307	EE62
Harrow La. E14	140	317	EC73
Harrow Manorway SE2	254	319	EW76
Harrow Pk., Har.	233	313	CE61
Harrow Pas., Kings.T.	268	322	CK96
Harrow Pl. E1	50/1	316	DS72
Harrow Rd. E6	244	318	EL67
Harrow Rd. E11	105	307	EE62
Harrow Rd. NW10	126	315	CV69
Harrow Rd. W2	127	315	CX69
Harrow Rd. W9	127	315	CX69
Harrow Rd. W10	127	315	CX69
Harrow Rd., Bark.	245	318	ES67
Harrow Rd., Cars.	285	331	DE106
Harrow Rd., Felt.	265	320	BN88
Harrow Rd., Ilf.	235	308	EQ63
Harrow Rd., Wem.	233	313	CF63
Harrow Rd. (Tokyngton), Wem.	108	304	CN64
Harrow Vw., Har.	215	303	CC53
Harrow Vw., Hayes	242	313	BU72
Harrow Vw., Uxb.	241	312	BQ69
Harrow Vw. Rd. W5	122	314	CH70
Harrow Way, Shep.	281	328	BQ96
Harrow Weald Pk., Har.	215	303	CD51
Harroway Rd. SW11	159	315	DD82
Harrowby St. W1	42/3	315	DE72
Harrowdene Clo., Wem.	107	304	CK63
Harrowdene Gdns., Tedd.	268	322	CG93
Harrowdene Rd., Wem.	107	304	CK64
Harrowes Meade, Edg.	205	298	CN48
Harrowgate Rd. E9	119	307	DY65
Hart Dyke Cres., Swan.	279	327	FD97
Hart Dyke Rd., Swan.	279	327	FD96
Hart Gro. W5	134	314	CN74
Hart Gro., Sthl.	243	313	CA71
Hart St. EC3	62/3	316	DS73
Harte Rd., Houns.	250	321	BZ82
Hartfield Ave., Borwd.	205	298	CN43
Hartfield Ave., Nthlt.	242	313	BV68
Hartfield Clo., Borwd.	205	298	CN43
Hartfield Cres. SW19	270	323	CZ94
Hartfield Cres., W.Wick.	289	334	EG104
Hartfield Gro. SE20	274	325	DW95
Hartfield Rd. SW19	270	323	CZ93
Hartfield Rd., Chess.	282	330	CK106
Hartfield Rd., W.Wick.	289	334	EG105
Hartfield Ter. E3	130	317	EA68
Hartford Ave., Har.	216	304	CG55
Hartford Rd., Bex.	263	327	FA86
Hartham Clo. N7	115	306	DL64
Hartham Clo., Islw.	152	314	CG81
Hartham Rd. N7	115	306	DL64
Hartham Rd. N17	221	306	DT54
Hartham Rd., Islw.	251	321	CF81
Harting Rd. SE9	276	326	EL91
Hartington Clo., Har.	233	313	CE63
Hartington Ct. W4	154	314	CP80
Hartington Rd. E16	244	318	EH72

Hartington Rd. E17 222 307 DY58
Hartington Rd. SW8 161 316 DL81
Hartington Rd. W4 154 314 CP80
Hartington Rd. W13 132 314 CH73
Hartington Rd., Sthl. 250 321 BY76
Hartington Rd., Twick. 184 322 CH87
Hartismere Rd. SW6 157 315 CZ80
Hartlake Rd. E9 119 307 DX65
Hartland Clo. N21 209 300 DQ44
Hartland Clo., Edg. 205 298 CN47
Hartland Dr., Edg. 205 298 CN47
Hartland Dr., Ruis. 232 313 BV62
Hartland Rd. E15 121 307 EF66
Hartland Rd. N11 207 299 DF50
Hartland Rd. NW1 114 306 DH66
Hartland Rd. NW6 127 315 CZ68
Hartland Rd., Hmptn. 267 329 CB91
Hartland Rd., Horn. 238 310 FG61
Hartland Rd., Islw. 168 322 CG83
Hartland Rd., Mord. 284 331 DA101
Hartland Way, Croy. 288 333 DY103
Hartland Way, Mord. 284 331 CZ101
Hartlands Clo., Bex. 262 327 EZ86
Hartley Ave. E6 244 318 EL67
Hartley Ave. NW7 205 298 CT50
Hartley Clo. NW7 205 298 CT50
Hartley Clo., Brom. 276 326 EM96
Hartley Rd. E11 105 307 EF60
Hartley Rd., Croy. 286 332 DP101
Hartley Rd., Well. 254 319 EW80
Hartley St. E2 128 317 DW69
Hartmann Rd. E16 244 318 EK74
Hartmoor Ms., Enf. 203 301 DX37
Hartnoll St. N7 115 306 DM64
Harton Clo., Brom. 276 326 EK95
Harton Rd. N9 210 301 DV47
Harton St. SE8 166 317 EA81
Harts Hill Clo., Uxb. 241 312 BN65
Harts La. SE14 165 317 DY80
Harts La., Bark. 235 308 EP65
Hartshorn All. EC3 50/1 316 DS72
Hartshorn Gdns. E6 245 318 EN70
Hartslock Dr. SE2 254 319 EX75
Hartsmead Rd. SE9 260 326 EM89
Hartsmoor Ms., Enf. 203 301 DX37
Hartsway, Enf. 203 301 DW42
Hartswood Rd. W12 145 314 CT75
Hartsworth Clo. E13 131 317 EF68
Hartville Rd. SE18 253 318 ES77
Hartwell Dr. E4 223 307 EC51
Hartwell St. E8 117 306 DT65
Harvard Hill W4 154 314 CP79
Harvard La. W4 144 314 CP78
Harvard Rd. SE13 182 325 EC85
Harvard Rd. W4 144 314 CP78
Harvard Rd., Islw. 251 321 CE81
Harvard Wk., Horn. 238 310 FG63
Harvel Clo., Orp. 278 327 EU97
Harvel Cres. SE2 254 319 EX78
Harvest Bank Rd., W.Wick. 289 333 EF104
Harvest Ct., Shep. 281 328 BN98
Harvest Rd., Felt. 266 329 BU91
Harvesters Clo., Islw. 259 321 CD85
Harvey Gdns. E11 105 307 EF60
Harvey Gdns. SE7 252 318 EJ78
Harvey Ho., Brent. 143 314 CL78
Harvey Pt. E16 244 318 EH71
Harvey Rd. E11 105 307 EE60
Harvey Rd. N8 220 306 DM57
Harvey Rd. SE5 163 316 DR81
Harvey Rd., Houns. 258 321 BZ87
Harvey Rd., Ilf. 235 308 EP64
Harvey Rd., Nthlt. 232 313 BW66
Harvey Rd., Uxb. 241 312 BN68
Harvey St. N1 26 316 DR67
Harveys La., Rom. 237 309 FD61
Harvil Rd. (Harefield), Uxb. 230 302 BJ56
Harvil Rd. (Ickenham), Uxb. 230 312 BL60
Harvill Rd., Sid. 278 327 EX92
Harvington Wk. E8 118 307 DU66
Harvist Est. N7 116 306 DN63
Harvist Rd. NW6 127 315 CX68
Harwell Clo., Ruis. 231 312 BR60
Harwell Pas. N2 219 305 DF56
Harwich La. EC2 50/1 316 DS71
Harwood Ave., Brom. 276 326 EH96
Harwood Ave., Horn. 228 311 FL55
Harwood Ave., Mitch. 271 323 DE97
Harwood Clo. N12 219 305 DE51
Harwood Clo., Wem. 107 304 CK63
Harwood Dr., Uxb. 240 312 BM67
Harwood Hall La., Upmin. 239 311 FP65
Harwood Rd. SW6 158 315 DA80
Harwood Ter. SW6 158 315 DB81
Harwoods Yd. N21 209 300 DN45
Hascombe Ter. SE5 163 316 DR82
Haselbury Rd. N9 209 300 DS48
Haselbury Rd. N18 209 300 DS49
Haseley End SE23 196 325 DW87
Haselrigge Rd. SW4 177 324 DK84
Haseltine Rd. SE26 274 325 DZ91
Haselwood Dr., Enf. 202 300 DP42
Haskard Rd., Dag. 236 309 EX63
Haskell Ho. NW10 125 314 CR67
Hasker St. SW3 78/9 315 DE77
Haslam Ave., Sutt. 284 331 CY102
Haslam Clo. N1 116 306 DN66
Haslam Clo., Uxb. 231 312 BQ61
Haslemere Ave. NW4 218 305 CX58
Haslemere Ave. SW18 190 323 DB89
Haslemere Ave. W7 142 314 CG76
Haslemere Ave. W13 142 314 CG76
Haslemere Ave., Barn. 207 299 DF46
Haslemere Ave., Houns. 250 321 BW82
Haslemere Ave., Mitch. 271 323 DD96
Haslemere Clo., Hmptn. 266 329 BZ92
Haslemere Clo., Wall. 286 332 DL106
Haslemere Gdns. N3 218 305 CZ55
Haslemere Heathrow Est., Houns. 250 321 BV82
Haslemere Rd. N8 99 306 DK59
Haslemere Rd. N21 209 300 DP47
Haslemere Rd., Bexh. 254 319 EZ82
Haslemere Rd., Ilf. 235 308 ET61
Haslemere Rd., Th.Hth. 286 332 DP99
Hasler Clo. SE28 246 319 EV73
Haslett Rd., Shep. 281 328 BS96
Hasluck Gdns., Barn. 207 299 DB44
Hassard St. E2 27 316 DT68
Hassendean Rd. SE3 252 318 EH79
Hassett Rd. E9 119 307 DX65
Hassock Wd., Kes. 290 334 EK105
Hassocks Clo. SE26 196 325 DV90
Hassocks Rd. SW16 272 324 DJ95
Hassop Rd. NW2 111 305 CX63
Hassop Wk. SE9 276 326 EL91
Hasted Rd. SE7 252 318 EK78
Hastings Ave., Ilf. 225 308 EQ56
Hastings Clo. SE15 164 317 DU80
Hastings Dr., Surb. 282 330 CJ100
Hastings Ho. SE18 252 318 EM77
Hastings Rd. N11 208 300 DJ50
Hastings Rd. N17 221 306 DR55
Hastings Rd. W13 132 314 CH73
Hastings Rd., Brom. 290 334 EL102
Hastings Rd., Croy. 287 332 DT102
Hastings Rd., Rom. 228 310 FH57
Hastings St. WC1 34/5 316 DL69
Hastoe Clo., Hayes 242 313 BY70
Hat and Mitre Ct. EC1 36/7 316 DP70
Hatch, The, Enf. 203 301 DX39
Hatch Gro., Rom. 226 309 EY56
Hatch La. E4 211 301 ED49
Hatch La., West Dr. 256 320 BK80
Hatch Pl., Kings.T. 268 322 CM92
Hatch Rd. SW16 272 324 DL96
Hatcham Pk. Ms. SE14 165 317 DX81
Hatcham Pk. Rd. SE14 165 317 DX81
Hatcham Rd. SE15 164 317 DW79
Hatchard Rd. N19 99 306 DK61
Hatchcroft NW4 218 305 CV55
Hatchett Rd., Felt. 265 320 BQ88
Hatchwood Clo., Wdf.Grn. 211 301 EF49
Hatcliffe Clo. SE3 183 325 EF83
Hatcliffe St. SE10 151 317 EF78
Hatfield Clo. SE14 165 317 DX80
Hatfield Clo., Horn. 238 310 FK64
Hatfield Clo., Ilf. 225 308 EP55
Hatfield Clo., Mitch. 271 323 DD98
Hatfield Clo., Sutt. 292 331 DB109
Hatfield Mead, Mord. 284 331 DA99
Hatfield Rd. E15 121 307 EE64
Hatfield Rd. W4 145 314 CR75
Hatfield Rd. W13 132 314 CG74
Hatfield Rd., Dag. 236 309 EY65
Hatfields SE1 60 316 DN74
Hathaway Clo., Brom. 290 334 EM102
Hathaway Clo., Ruis. 241 312 BT63
Hathaway Clo., Stan. 204 298 CG50
Hathaway Cres. E12 234 308 EM65
Hathaway Gdns. W13 243 313 CF71
Hathaway Gdns., Rom. 226 309 EX57
Hathaway Rd., Croy. 286 332 DP101
Hatherleigh Clo., Chess. 282 330 CK106
Hatherleigh Clo., Mord. 271 323 DA98
Hatherleigh Rd., Ruis. 232 313 BU61
Hatherleigh Way, Rom. 228 310 FK53
Hatherley Cres., Sid. 262 327 EU89
Hatherley Gdns. E6 244 318 EK68
Hatherley Gdns. N8 220 306 DL58
Hatherley Gro. W2 40/1 315 DB72
Hatherley Ms. E17 223 307 EA56
Hatherley Rd. E17 222 307 DZ56
Hatherley Rd., Rich. 153 314 CM81
Hatherley Rd., Sid. 278 327 EU91
Hatherley St. SW1 81 316 DJ77
Hathern Gdns. SE9 277 326 EN91
Hatherop Rd., Hmptn. 266 329 BZ94
Hathorne Clo. SE15 164 317 DV82
Hathway St. SE15 164 317 DW82
Hathway Ter. SE14 164 317 DW82
Hatley Ave., Ilf. 225 308 EQ56
Hatley Clo. N11 207 299 DF50
Hatley Rd. N4 99 306 DM61
Hatteraick St. SE16 148 317 DW75
Hattersfield Clo., Belv. 254 319 EZ77
Hatton Clo. SE18 253 318 ER80
Hatton Ct. E5 119 307 DY63
Hatton Gdn. EC1 36 316 DN70
Hatton Gdns., Mitch. 285 331 DF99
Hatton Grn., Felt. 258 321 BU84
Hatton Gro., West Dr. 248 320 BK75
Hatton Ho. E1 138 317 DU73
Hatton Pl. EC1 36 316 DN70
Hatton Rd., Croy. 286 332 DN102
Hatton Rd., Felt. 265 320 BQ87
Hatton Row NW8 30 315 DD70
Hatton St. NW8 30 315 DD70
Hatton Wall EC1 48 316 DN71
Haunch of Venison Yd. W1 44/5 316 DH72
Havana Clo., Rom. 227 309 FE57
Havana Rd. SW19 190 323 DA89
Havannah St. E14 150 317 EA75
Havant Rd. E17 223 307 EC55
Havant Way SE15 163 316 DT80
Havelock Pl., Har. 215 303 CE58
Havelock Rd. N17 222 307 DU54
Havelock Rd. SW19 271 323 DC92
Havelock Rd., Belv. 254 319 EZ77
Havelock Rd., Brom. 276 326 EJ98
Havelock Rd., Croy. 287 332 DT103
Havelock Rd., Har. 215 303 CE55
Havelock Rd., Sthl. 250 321 BY76
Havelock St. N1 22/3 316 DL67
Havelock St., Ilf. 235 308 EP61
Havelock Ter. SW8 160 316 DH80
Havelock Wk. SE23 196 325 DW88
Haven, The SE26 274 325 DV92
Haven, The, Rich. 170 322 CN83
Haven Clo. SE9 260 326 EM90
Haven Clo. SW19 189 323 CX90
Haven Clo., Hayes 249 312 BS71
Haven Clo., Sid. 278 327 EW93
Haven Clo., Swan. 279 327 FF96
Haven Grn. W5 133 314 CK72
Haven Grn. Ct. W5 133 314 CK72
Haven La. W5 133 314 CL72
Haven Pl. W5 133 314 CK73
Haven Rd., Ashf. 265 328 BP91
Haven St. NW1 114 306 DH66
Haven Ter. W5 133 314 CM73
Havenhurst Ri., Enf. 202 300 DN40
Havenwood, Wem. 92 304 CP62
Haverfield Gdns., Rich. 154 314 CN80
Haverfield Rd. E3 129 317 DY69
Haverford Way, Edg. 216 304 CM53
Haverhill Rd. E4 211 301 EC46
Haverhill Rd. SW12 192 324 DJ88
Havering Dr., Rom. 227 309 FE56
Havering Gdns., Rom. 226 309 EW57
Havering Rd., Rom. 227 309 FD55
Havering St. E1 139 317 DX72
Havering Way, Bark. 246 319 EV69
Haversfield Est., Brent. 143 314 CL78
Haversham Clo., Twick. 169 322 CK86
Haversham Pl. N6 97 305 DF61
Haverstock Hill NW3 113 305 DF65
Haverstock Rd. NW5 114 306 DG64
Haverstock St. N1 24/5 316 DP68
Haverthwaite Rd., Orp. 291 334 ER103
Havil St. SE5 163 316 DS80
Havisham Pl. SE19 273 324 DP93
Hawarden Gro. SE24 194 324 DQ87
Hawarden Hill NW2 94 305 CU62
Hawarden Rd. E17 222 307 DX56
Hawbridge Rd. E11 105 307 ED60
Hawes Clo., Nthwd. 213 302 BT52
Hawes La., W.Wick. 289 333 EC102
Hawes Rd. N18 222 307 DV51
Hawes Rd., Brom. 276 326 EH95
Hawes St. N1 116 306 DP66
Haweswater Ho., Islw. 259 321 CF85
Hawgood St. E3 140 317 EA71
Hawkdene E4 211 301 EB44
Hawke Pk. Rd. N22 221 306 DP55
Hawke Pl. SE16 149 317 DX75
Hawke Rd. SE19 273 324 DS93
Hawker Clo., Wall. 294 332 DL108
Hawkes Rd., Mitch. 271 323 DE95
Hawkesbury Rd. SW15 172 323 CV85
Hawkesfield Rd. SE23 197 325 DY89
Hawkesley Clo., Twick. 268 322 CG91
Hawkesworth Clo., Nthwd. 213 302 BS52
Hawkewood Rd., Sun. 266 329 BU97
Hawkhurst Gdns., Chess. 282 330 CL105
Hawkhurst Gdns., Rom. 227 309 FD51
Hawkhurst Rd. SW16 272 324 DK95
Hawkhurst Way, N.Mal. 283 330 CR99
Hawkhurst Way, W.Wick. 288 333 EB103
Hawkinge Wk., Orp. 278 327 EV97
Hawkinge Way, Horn. 238 310 FJ65
Hawkins Clo. NW7 205 298 CR50
Hawkins Clo., Har. 233 313 CD59
Hawkins Rd., Tedd. 268 322 CH93
Hawkins Way SE6 275 325 EA91
Hawkley Gdns. SE27 194 324 DP89
Hawkridge Clo., Rom. 226 309 EW58
Hawks Ms. SE10 166 317 EC80
Hawks Rd., Kings.T. 268 322 CM96
Hawksbrook La., Beck. 288 333 EB100
Hawkshaw Clo. SW2 193 324 DL87
Hawkshead Clo., Brom. 275 325 EE94
Hawkshead Rd. NW10 109 304 CT66
Hawkshead Rd. W4 145 314 CS75
Hawkslade Rd. SE15 181 325 DX85
Hawksley Rd. N16 101 306 DR62
Hawksmead Clo., Enf. 203 301 DX35
Hawksmoor Clo. E6 244 318 EL72
Hawksmoor Clo. SE18 253 318 ES78
Hawksmoor Ms. E1 138 317 DV73
Hawksmoor St. W6 157 315 CX79
Hawksmouth E4 211 301 EB45
Hawkstone Rd. SE16 148 317 DW77
Hawkwell Ct. E4 211 301 EC48
Hawkwell Wk. N1 25 316 DQ67
Hawkwood Cres. E4 211 301 EB44
Hawkwood La., Chis. 277 326 EQ95
Hawkwood Mt. E5 102 307 DV60
Hawlands Dr., Pnr. 232 313 BY59
Hawley Clo., Hmptn. 266 329 BZ93
Hawley Cres. NW1 114 306 DH66
Hawley Ms. NW1 114 306 DH66
Hawley Rd. N18 210 301 DX50
Hawley Rd. NW1 114 306 DH66
Hawley St. NW1 114 306 DH66
Hawley Way, Ashf. 265 328 BN92
Haws La., Stai. 256 320 BG86
Hawstead Rd. SE6 182 325 EB86
Hawthorn Ave. N13 208 300 DL50
Hawthorn Ave., Cars. 293 332 DG108
Hawthorn Ave., Rich. 153 314 CL82
Hawthorn Ave., Th.Hth. 273 324 DP95
Hawthorn Cen., Har. 215 303 CF56
Hawthorn Clo., Bans. 292 331 CY114
Hawthorn Clo., Hmptn. 267 329 CA92
Hawthorn Clo., Houns. 250 321 BV80
Hawthorn Clo., Orp. 291 334 ER100
Hawthorn Cotts., Well. 262 327 EU83
Hawthorn Ct., Rich. 154 314 CP81
Hawthorn Cres. SW17 272 324 DG92
Hawthorn Dr., Har. 215 303 CA58
Hawthorn Dr., Uxb. 240 312 BJ65
Hawthorn Dr., W.Wick. 289 333 EE105
Hawthorn Gdns. W5 143 314 CK76
Hawthorn Gro. SE20 274 325 DV94
Hawthorn Gro., Barn. 205 298 CT44
Hawthorn Gro., Enf. 202 300 DR38
Hawthorn Hatch, Brent. 152 314 CH80
Hawthorn Ms. NW7 218 305 CY53
Hawthorn Pl., Erith 255 319 FC78
Hawthorn Pl., Hayes 249 312 BT73
Hawthorn Rd. N8 220 306 DK55
Hawthorn Rd. N18 221 306 DT51
Hawthorn Rd. NW10 110 305 CU66
Hawthorn Rd., Bexh. 262 327 EZ84
Hawthorn Rd., Brent. 152 314 CH80
Hawthorn Rd., Sutt. 285 331 DE106
Hawthorn Rd., Wall. 293 332 DH108
Hawthorn Wk. W10 127 315 CY70
Hawthorn Way N9 209 300 DS47
Hawthorn Way, Stai. 264 320 BK87
Hawthornden Clo. N12 219 305 DE51
Hawthorndene Clo., Brom. 289 333 EF103
Hawthorndene Rd., Brom. 289 333 EF103
Hawthorne Ave., Har. 216 304 CG58
Hawthorne Ave., Mitch. 271 323 DD96
Hawthorne Ave., Ruis. 232 313 BV59
Hawthorne Clo. N1 117 306 DS65
Hawthorne Clo., Brom. 276 326 EM97
Hawthorne Clo., Sutt. 284 331 DB103
Hawthorne Cres., West Dr. 248 320 BM75
Hawthorne Fm. Ave., Nthlt. 242 313 BY67
Hawthorne Gro. NW9 92 304 CQ59
Hawthorne Ms., Grnf. 243 313 CC72
Hawthorne Rd. E17 223 307 EA55
Hawthorne Rd., Brom. 276 326 EM97
Hawthorne Way, Shep. 281 328 BR98
Hawthornes Cen., Har. 215 303 CF56
Hawtrey Ave., Nthlt. 242 313 BX68
Hawtrey Dr., Ruis. 232 313 BU59
Hawtrey Rd. NW3 113 305 DE66
Haxted Rd., Brom. 276 326 EH95
Hay Clo. E15 121 307 EE66
Hay Currie St. E14 140 317 EB72
Hay Hill W1 56/7 316 DH73
Hay La. NW9 217 304 CQ56
Hay St. E2 128 317 DU67
Hayburn Way, Horn. 237 309 FF60
Haycroft Gdns. NW10 126 315 CU67
Haycroft Rd. SW2 177 324 DL85
Haycroft Rd., Surb. 282 330 CK104
Hayday Rd. E16 244 318 EG71
Hayden Way, Rom. 227 309 FC54
Haydens Pl. W11 137 315 CZ72
Haydn Ave., Pur. 294 332 DN114
Haydns Ms. W3 134 314 CQ72
Haydock Ave., Nthlt. 233 313 CA65
Haydock Clo., Horn. 238 311 FM63
Haydock Grn., Nthlt. 233 313 CA65
Haydon Clo. NW9 217 304 CQ56
Haydon Clo., Enf. 209 300 DS44
Haydon Dr., Pnr. 214 303 BV56
Haydon Pk. Rd. SW19 271 323 DA92
Haydon Rd., Dag. 236 309 EW61
Haydon St. EC3 63 316 DT73
Haydon Wk. E1 63 316 DT73
Haydon Way SW11 175 323 DD84
Haydons Rd. SW19 271 323 DB92
Hayes Chase, W.Wick. 289 333 ED100
Hayes Clo., Brom. 289 334 EG103
Hayes Ct. SW2 193 324 DL88
Hayes Cres. NW11 218 305 CZ57
Hayes Cres., Sutt. 284 331 CX105
Hayes Dr., Rain. 238 310 FH66
Hayes End Clo., Hayes 241 312 BR70
Hayes End Dr., Hayes 241 312 BR70
Hayes End Rd., Hayes 241 312 BR70
Hayes Gdn., Brom. 289 334 EG103
Hayes Hill, Brom. 289 333 EE102
Hayes Hill Rd., Brom. 289 333 EF102
Hayes La., Beck. 275 325 EC97
Hayes La., Brom. 289 334 EG99
Hayes Mead Rd., Brom. 289 333 EE102
Hayes Pl. NW1 30/1 315 DE70
Hayes Rd., Brom. 276 326 EG98
Hayes Rd., Sthl. 250 321 BV77
Hayes St., Brom. 289 334 EH102
Hayes Way, Beck. 275 325 EC98
Hayes Wd. Ave., Brom. 289 334 EH102
Hayesford Pk. Dr., Brom. 289 333 EF99
Hayfield Pas. E1 128 317 DW70
Hayfield Rd., Orp. 291 335 EU99
Hayfield Yd. E1 128 317 DW70
Haygarth Pl. SW19 270 323 CX92
Haygreen Clo., Kings.T. 269 322 CP93
Hayland Clo. NW9 217 304 CR56
Hayles St. SE11 84/5 316 DP77
Haylett Gdns., Kings.T. 268 322 CK98
Hayling Ave., Felt. 258 321 BU90
Hayling Clo. N16 117 306 DS64
Hayling Rd., Wat. 213 302 BT48
Haymaker Clo., Uxb. 240 312 BM66
Hayman Cres., Hayes 241 312 BR68
Hayman St. N1 116 306 DP66
Haymarket SW1 58 316 DK73
Haymarket Arc. SW1 58 316 DK73
Haymer Gdns., Wor.Pk. 283 331 CU104
Haymerle Rd. SE15 164 317 DU79
Haymill Clo., Grnf. 243 313 CF69
Hayne Rd., Beck. 274 325 DZ96
Hayne St. EC1 48/9 316 DP71
Haynes Clo. N11 208 300 DG48
Haynes Clo. N17 222 307 DV52
Haynes Clo. SE3 183 325 EE83
Haynes La. SE19 273 324 DS93
Haynes Rd., Horn. 228 310 FK57
Haynes Rd., Wem. 107 304 CL66
Haynt Wk. SW20 270 323 CY97
Hay's La. SE1 62/3 316 DS74
Hay's Ms. W1 56/7 316 DH74
Hays Wk., Sutt. 292 331 CX110
Haysleigh Gdns. SE20 274 325 DU96
Haysoms Clo., Rom. 227 309 FE56
Haystall Clo., Hayes 241 312 BS68
Hayter Rd. SW2 177 324 DL85
Hayton Clo. E8 117 306 DT65
Hayward Clo. SW19 271 323 DB94
Hayward Clo., Bex. 263 327 FD85
Hayward Clo., Dart. 263 327 FD85
Hayward Gdns. SW15 172 323 CW86
Hayward Rd. N20 207 299 DC47
Hayward's Pl. EC1 36/7 316 DP70
Haywood Clo., Pnr. 214 303 BX54
Haywood Ri., Orp. 291 334 ES105
Haywood Rd., Brom. 276 326 EK98
Hayworth Clo., Enf. 203 301 DY40
Hazel Ave., West Dr. 249 320 BN76
Hazel Bank, Surb. 283 330 CQ102
Hazel Clo. N13 209 300 DR48
Hazel Clo. N19 98 306 DJ61
Hazel Clo. SE15 164 317 DU82
Hazel Clo., Brent. 152 314 CH80
Hazel Clo., Croy. 288 333 DX101
Hazel Clo., Horn. 238 310 FH62
Hazel Clo., Mitch. 272 324 DK98
Hazel Clo., Twick. 259 321 CC87
Hazel Gdns., Edg. 205 298 CP49
Hazel Gro. SE26 274 325 DX91
Hazel Gro., Enf. 210 301 DU44
Hazel Gro., Orp. 290 334 EP103
Hazel Gro., Rom. 226 309 EY55
Hazel Gro., Stai. 264 328 BH93
Hazel Gro., Wem. 123 314 CL67
Hazel Gro. Est. SE26 274 325 DX91
Hazel La., Rich. 185 322 CL89
Hazel Mead, Barn. 206 299 CV43
Hazel Ri., Horn. 228 310 FJ58
Hazel Rd. E15 121 307 EE64
Hazel Rd. NW10 126 315 CV69
Hazel Wk., Brom. 290 334 EN100
Hazel Way E4 222 307 DZ51
Hazel Way SE1 87 316 DT77
Hazelbank Ct., Cher. 280 328 BJ102
Hazelbank Rd. SE6 199 325 ED89
Hazelbank Rd., Cher. 280 328 BJ101
Hazelbourne Rd. SW12 176 324 DH86
Hazelbrouck Gdns., Ilf. 225 308 ER52
Hazelbury Clo. SW19 271 323 DA96
Hazelbury Grn. N9 209 300 DS48
Hazelbury La. N9 209 300 DS48
Hazelcroft, Pnr. 215 303 CB51
Hazelcroft Clo., Uxb. 240 312 BM66
Hazeldean Rd. NW10 109 304 CR66
Hazeldene Dr., Pnr. 214 303 BW55
Hazeldene Gdns., Uxb. 241 312 BQ67
Hazeldene Rd., Ilf. 236 309 EV61
Hazeldene Rd., Well. 254 319 EW82
Hazeldon Rd. SE4 181 325 DY85
Hazelgreen Clo. N21 209 300 DP46
Hazelhurst, Beck. 275 325 ED95
Hazelhurst Rd. SW17 271 323 DC91
Hazell Cres., Rom. 227 309 FB53
Hazellville Rd. N19 99 306 DK59
Hazelmere Clo., Felt. 257 320 BR86
Hazelmere Clo., Nthlt. 242 313 BZ68
Hazelmere Dr., Nthlt. 242 313 BZ68
Hazelmere Gdns., Horn. 228 310 FH57
Hazelmere Rd. NW6 127 315 CZ67
Hazelmere Rd., Nthlt. 242 313 BZ68
Hazelmere Rd., Orp. 277 326 EQ98
Hazelmere Wk., Nthlt. 242 313 BZ68
Hazelmere Way, Brom. 289 334 EG100
Hazeltree La., Nthlt. 242 313 BY69
Hazelwood Ave., Mord. 271 323 DB98
Hazelwood Clo. W5 143 314 CL75
Hazelwood Clo., Har. 215 303 CB56
Hazelwood Ct. NW10 93 304 CS62
Hazelwood Cres. N13 209 300 DN49
Hazelwood Cft., Surb. 282 330 CL100
Hazelwood Dr., Pnr. 214 303 BV54
Hazelwood Gro., S.Croy. 295 333 DV113
Hazelwood La. N13 209 300 DN49
Hazelwood Rd. E17 222 307 DY57
Hazelwood Rd., Enf. 209 300 DT44
Hazlebury Rd. SW6 158 315 DB82
Hazledean Rd., Croy. 287 332 DR103
Hazledene Rd. W4 154 314 CQ79
Hazlemere Gdns., Wor.Pk. 283 331 CU102
Hazlewell Rd. SW15 172 323 CV85
Hazlewood Clo. E5 103 307 DY62
Hazlewood Cres. W10 127 315 CY70
Hazlitt Ms. W14 147 315 CY76
Hazlitt Rd. W14 147 315 CY76
Heacham Ave., Uxb. 231 312 BQ62
Head St. E1 139 317 DX72
Headcorn Pl., Th.Hth. 272 324 DM98
Headcorn Rd. N17 221 306 DT52
Headcorn Rd., Brom. 276 326 EG92
Headcorn Rd., Th.Hth. 272 324 DM98
Headfort Pl. SW1 68 316 DG75
Headingley Clo., Ilf. 225 308 ET51
Headington Rd. SW18 190 323 DC89
Headlam Rd. SW4 177 324 DK86
Headlam St. E1 128 317 DV70
Headley App., Ilf. 225 308 EP57
Headley Ave., Wall. 286 332 DM106
Headley Ct. SE26 274 325 DW92
Headley Dr., Ilf. 225 308 EP58
Head's Ms. W11 40 315 DA72
Headstone Dr., Har. 215 303 CD55
Headstone Gdns., Har. 215 303 CC56
Headstone La., Har. 215 303 CB52
Headstone Rd., Har. 215 303 CE57
Headway Clo., Rich. 268 322 CJ91
Heald St. SE14 165 317 DZ81
Healey Dr., Orp. 291 334 ET105
Healey St. NW1 114 306 DH65
Heanor Ct. E5 103 307 DX62
Hearn Ri., Nthlt. 242 313 BX67
Hearn Rd., Rom. 227 309 FF58
Hearn St. EC2 38/9 316 DS70
Hearne Rd. W4 154 314 CN79
Hearn's Bldgs. SE17 86 316 DR77
Hearn's Ri., Orp. 278 327 EX98
Hearn's Rd., Orp. 278 327 EW98
Hearnville Rd. SW12 192 324 DG88
Heath, The W7 243 313 CE74
Heath Ave., Bexh. 254 319 EX79
Heath Brow NW3 96 305 DC62
Heath Clo. NW11 96 305 DB59
Heath Clo. W5 123 314 CM70
Heath Clo., Bans. 292 331 DB114
Heath Clo., Hayes 257 320 BR80
Heath Clo., Rom. 228 310 FG55
Heath Clo., Stai. 256 320 BJ86
Heath Ct., Houns. 258 321 BZ84
Heath Ct., Uxb. 240 312 BL66
Heath Dr. NW3 112 305 DB63
Heath Dr. SW20 270 323 CW98
Heath Dr., Rom. 228 310 FG53
Heath Dr., Sutt. 293 331 DC109
Heath End Rd., Bex. 263 327 FE88
Heath Gdns., Twick. 259 321 CF88
Heath Gro. SE20 274 325 DW94
Heath Gro., Sun. 265 328 BT94
Heath Hurst Rd. NW3 113 305 DE63
Heath La. SE3 167 317 ED82
Heath Mead SW19 189 323 CX90
Heath Pk. Ct., Rom. 228 310 FG57
Heath Pk. Dr., Brom. 276 326 EL97
Heath Pk. Rd., Rom. 228 310 FG57
Heath Ri. SW15 173 323 CX86
Heath Ri., Brom. 289 333 EF100
Heath Rd. SW8 160 316 DH82
Heath Rd., Bex. 263 327 FC88
Heath Rd., Dart. 263 327 FF86
Heath Rd., Har. 233 313 CC59
Heath Rd., Houns. 259 321 CB84
Heath Rd., Rom. 236 309 EX59
Heath Rd., Th.Hth. 273 324 DQ97
Heath Rd., Twick. 259 321 CF88
Heath Rd., Uxb. 241 312 BQ70
Heath Side NW3 113 305 DD63
Heath Side, Orp. 291 334 EQ102
Heath St. NW3 96 305 DC62
Heath Vw. N2 219 305 DC56
Heath Vw. Clo. N2 219 305 DC56
Heath Vil. SE18 253 318 ET78
Heath Vil. SW18 190 323 DC88
Heath Way, Erith 255 319 FC81
Heatham Pk., Twick. 259 321 CF87
Heathcock Ct. WC2 58/9 316 DL73
Heathcote Ave., Ilf. 224 308 EM54
Heathcote Gro. E4 211 301 EC48
Heathcote Rd., Twick. 168 322 CH86
Heathcote St. WC1 35 316 DM70
Heathcote Way, West Dr. 248 312 BK74
Heathcroft NW11 96 305 DB60
Heathcroft W5 123 314 CM70
Heathcroft Ave., Sun. 265 328 BT94
Heathdale Ave., Houns. 258 321 BY83
Heathdene Dr., Belv. 255 319 FB77
Heathdene Rd. SW16 272 324 DM94
Heathdene Rd., Wall. 293 332 DG108
Heathedge SE26 196 325 DV89
Heathend Rd., Bex. 263 327 FE88
Heather Ave., Rom. 227 309 FD54
Heather Clo. E6 245 318 EP72
Heather Clo. SE13 199 325 ED87
Heather Clo. SW8 176 324 DH83
Heather Clo., Hmptn. 266 329 BZ95
Heather Clo., Islw. 259 321 CD85
Heather Clo., Rom. 227 309 FD53
Heather Clo., Uxb. 248 312 BM71
Heather Dr., Enf. 202 300 DP40
Heather Dr., Rom. 227 309 FD54
Heather End, Swan. 279 327 FD98
Heather Gdns. NW11 218 305 CY58
Heather Gdns., Rom. 227 309 FD54
Heather Gdns., Sutt. 292 331 DA107
Heather Glen, Rom. 227 309 FD54
Heather La., West Dr. 248 312 BL72
Heather Pk. Dr., Wem. 108 304 CN66
Heather Rd. E4 222 307 DZ51
Heather Rd. NW2 93 304 CT61
Heather Rd. SE12 260 326 EG89
Heather Wk. W10 127 315 CY70
Heather Wk., Edg. 205 298 CP50
Heather Wk., Twick. 259 321 CA87
Heather Way, Rom. 227 309 FD54
Heather Way, Stan. 215 303 CF51
Heatherbank SE9 252 318 EM82
Heatherbank, Chis. 277 326 EN96
Heatherbank Clo., Dart. 263 327 FE86
Heatherdale Clo., Kings.T. 269 322 CP94
Heatherdene Clo. N12 219 305 DC53
Heatherdene Clo., Mitch. 271 323 DE98
Heatherlands, Sun. 266 329 BU93
Heatherley Dr., Ilf. 224 308 EL55
Heathers, The, Stai. 264 320 BM87
Heatherset Gdns. SW16 272 324 DM94
Heatherside Rd., Sid. 262 327 EX90
Heatherwood Clo. E12 234 308 EJ61
Heatherwood Dr., Hayes 241 312 BR68
Heathfield E4 211 301 EC48
Heathfield, Chis. 277 326 EQ93
Heathfield Ave. SW18 191 323 DD87
Heathfield Clo. E16 244 318 EK71
Heathfield Clo., Kes. 290 334 EJ106
Heathfield Dr., Mitch. 271 323 DE95
Heathfield Gdns. NW11 218 305 CX58
Heathfield Gdns. SW18 175 323 DD86
Heathfield Gdns. W4 144 314 CQ78
Heathfield Gdns., Croy. 287 332 DR105
Heathfield La., Chis. 277 326 EP93
Heathfield N., Twick. 259 321 CF87
Heathfield Pk. NW2 110 305 CW65
Heathfield Pk. Dr., Rom. 226 309 EV57
Heathfield Ri., Ruis. 231 312 BQ59
Heathfield Rd. SW18 174 323 DC86
Heathfield Rd. W3 144 314 CP75
Heathfield Rd., Bexh. 262 327 EZ84
Heathfield Rd., Brom. 275 325 EF94
Heathfield Rd., Croy. 287 332 DR105
Heathfield Rd., Kes. 290 334 EJ106
Heathfield S., Twick. 259 321 CF87
Heathfield Sq. SW18 191 323 DD87
Heathfield St. W11 137 315 CY73
Heathfield Ter. SE18 253 318 ES79
Heathfield Ter. W4 144 314 CQ78
Heathfields Ct., Houns. 258 321 BY85
Heathgate NW11 219 305 DB58
Heathland Rd. N16 101 306 DS60
Heathlands Clo., Sun. 281 328 BT96
Heathlands Clo., Twick. 259 321 CF88
Heathlands Way, Houns. 258 321 BY85
Heathlee Rd. SE3 183 325 EF84
Heathlee Rd., Dart. 263 327 FE86
Heathley End, Chis. 277 326 EQ93
Heathmans Rd. SW6 157 315 CZ81
Heathrow Clo., West Dr. 256 320 BH81
Heathrow Int. Trd. Est., Houns. 258 321 BV83
Heaths Clo., Enf. 202 300 DS40
Heathside, Houns. 258 321 BZ87
Heathside Ave., Bexh. 254 319 EY82
Heathside Clo., Nthwd. 213 302 BR50
Heathside Rd., Nthwd. 213 302 BR49
Heathstan Rd. W12 136 315 CU72
Heathurst Rd., S.Croy. 295 332 DS109
Heathview Ave., Dart. 263 327 FE86
Heathview Ct. SW19 189 323 CX89
Heathview Dr. SE2 254 319 EX79
Heathview Gdns. SW15 188 323 CW87
Heathview Rd., Th.Hth. 273 324 DN98
Heathville Rd. N19 99 306 DL59
Heathwall St. SW11 175 323 DF83
Heathway SE3 252 318 EG80
Heathway, Croy. 288 333 DZ104
Heathway, Dag. 236 309 EZ62
Heathwood Gdns. SE7 252 318 EL77
Heathwood Gdns., Swan. 279 327 FC96
Heathwood Wk., Bex. 263 327 FE88
Heaton Ave., Rom. 228 310 FH52
Heaton Clo. E4 211 301 EC48
Heaton Clo., Rom. 228 310 FJ52
Heaton Gra. Rd., Rom. 227 309 FF54
Heaton Rd. SE15 180 325 DU83
Heaton Rd., Mitch. 272 324 DG94
Heaton Way, Rom. 228 310 FJ52
Heaver Rd. SW11 175 323 DD83
Heavitree Clo. SE18 253 318 ER78
Heavitree Rd. SE18 253 318 ER78
Hebden Ct. E2 27 316 DT67
Hebden Ter. N17 221 306 DS51
Hebdon Rd. SW17 191 323 DE90
Heber Rd. NW2 111 305 CX64
Heber Rd. SE22 179 324 DT86
Hebron Rd. W6 146 315 CV76
Hecham Clo. E17 222 307 DY54
Heckfield Pl. SW6 158 315 DA80
Heckford St. E1 139 317 DX73
Hector St. SE18 253 318 ES77
Heddington Gro. N7 115 306 DM64
Heddon Clo., Islw. 168 322 CG84
Heddon Ct. Ave., Barn. 207 299 DF43
Heddon Rd., Barn. 207 299 DF43
Heddon St. W1 57 316 DJ73
Hedge Hill, Enf. 202 300 DP39
Hedge La. N13 209 300 DP48
Hedge Wk. SE6 275 325 EB92
Hedgeley, Ilf. 224 308 EM56
Hedgemans Rd., Dag. 236 309 EX66
Hedgemans Way, Dag. 236 309 EY65
Hedgerley Gdns., Grnf. 243 313 CC68
Hedgers Gro. E9 119 307 DY65
Hedgeside Rd., Nthwd. 213 302 BQ50
Hedgewood Gdns., Ilf. 225 308 EN56
Hedgley St. SE12 183 325 EF85
Hedingham Clo. N1 116 306 DQ66
Hedingham Rd., Dag. 236 309 EV64
Hedingham Rd., Horn. 239 311 FN60
Hedley Rd., Twick. 259 321 CA87
Hedley Row N5 117 306 DR64
Heenan Clo., Bark. 235 308 EQ65
Heene Rd., Enf. 202 300 DR39
Heidegger Cres. SW13 156 315 CV79
Heigham Rd. E6 234 308 EL66
Heighton Gdns., Croy. 286 332 DP106
Heights, The SE7 252 318 EJ78
Heights, The, Beck. 275 325 EC94
Heights, The, Nthlt. 232 313 BZ64
Heights Clo. SW20 270 323 CV94
Heiron St. SE17 162 316 DP79
Helby Rd. SW4 177 324 DK86
Helder Gro. SE12 199 325 EF87
Helder St., S.Croy. 295 332 DR107
Heldmann Clo., Houns. 259 321 CD84
Helen Ave., Felt. 258 321 BV87
Helen Clo. N2 219 305 DC55
Helen Clo., W.Mol. 267 329 CB98
Helen Rd., Horn. 228 310 FK55
Helen St. SE18 253 318 EP77
Helena Clo., Wall. 294 332 DL108
Helena Pl. E9 128 317 DW67
Helena Rd. E13 131 317 EF68
Helena Rd. E17 223 307 EA57
Helena Rd. NW10 110 305 CV64
Helena Rd. W5 133 314 CK71
Helena Sq. SE16 139 317 DY73
Helen's Pl. E2 128 317 DW69
Helenslea Ave. NW11 95 305 CZ60
Helford Clo., Ruis. 231 312 BS61
Helford Way, Upmin. 229 311 FR58
Helgiford Gdns., Sun. 265 328 BS94
Helix Gdns. SW2 177 324 DM86
Helix Rd. SW2 177 324 DM86
Hellings St. E1 138 317 DU74
Helme Clo. SW19 270 323 CZ92
Helmet Row EC1 37 316 DQ70
Helmsdale Clo., Hayes 242 313 BY70
Helmsdale Clo., Rom. 227 309 FE52
Helmsdale Rd. SW16 272 324 DK95
Helmsdale Rd., Rom. 227 309 FE52
Helmsley Pl. E8 118 307 DV66
Helsinki Sq. SE16 149 317 DY76
Helston Clo., Pnr. 214 303 BZ52
Helvetia St. SE6 197 325 DZ89
Hemans St. SW8 161 316 DK80
Hemberton Rd. SW9 177 324 DL83
Hemery Rd., Grnf. 233 313 CD64
Heming Rd., Edg. 217 304 CP52

Hemingford Clo. N12 207 299 DD50
Hemingford Rd. N1 23 316 DM67
Hemingford Rd., Sutt. 284 331 CW105
Hemington Ave. N11 207 299 DF50
Hemlock Rd. W12 135 314 CT73
Hemmen La., Hayes 249 312 BT72
Hemming Clo., Hmptn. 267 329 CA95
Hemming St. E1 128 317 DU70
Hemmings Clo., Sid. 262 327 EV89
Hemp Wk. SE17 86 316 DR77
Hempstead Rd. E17 223 307 ED54
Hemstal Rd. NW6 112 305 DA66
Hemsted Rd., Erith 255 319 FE80
Hemswell Dr. NW9 217 304 CS53
Hemsworth Ct. N1 26/7 316 DS68
Hemsworth St. N1 26/7 316 DS68
Hemus Pl. SW3 78/9 315 DE78
Hen & Chicken Ct. EC4 48 316 DN72
Henbane Path, Rom. 228 310 FK52
Henchman St. W12 135 314 CT72
Hendale Ave. NW4 218 305 CU55
Henderson Clo. NW10 108 304 CQ65
Henderson Clo., Horn. 238 310 FH61
Henderson Dr. NW8 30 315 DD70
Henderson Rd. E7 234 308 EJ65
Henderson Rd. N9 210 301 DV46
Henderson Rd. SW18 191 323 DE87
Henderson Rd., Croy. 287 332 DR100
Henderson Rd., Hayes 242 313 BU69
Hendham Rd. SW17 191 323 DE89
Hendon Ave. N3 218 305 CY53
Hendon Gdns., Rom. 227 309 FC51
Hendon La. N3 218 305 CY55
Hendon Pk. Row NW11 218 305 CZ58
Hendon Rd. N9 210 301 DU47
Hendon Way NW2 95 305 CX59
Hendon Way NW4 218 305 CV58
Hendon Way, Stai. 256 320 BK86
Hendon Wd. La. NW7 205 298 CT45
Hendre Rd. SE1 86/7 316 DS77
Hendren Clo., Grnf. 233 313 CD64
Hendrick Ave. SW12 191 323 DF87
Heneage La. EC3 50/1 316 DS72
Heneage St. E1 51 316 DT71
Henfield Clo. N19 98 306 DJ60
Henfield Clo., Bex. 263 327 FA86
Henfield Rd. SW19 270 323 CZ95
Hengelo Gdns., Mitch. 271 323 DD98
Hengist Rd. SE12 260 326 EH87
Hengist Rd., Erith 255 319 FB80
Hengist Way, Brom. 275 325 ED98
Hengrave Rd. SE23 196 325 DW87
Hengrove Ct., Bex. 262 327 EY88
Hengrove Cres., Ashf. 264 320 BK90
Henley Ave., Sutt. 284 331 CY104
Henley Clo., Grnf. 243 313 CC68
Henley Clo., Islw. 251 321 CF81
Henley Ct. N14 208 300 DJ45
Henley Dr. SE1 87 316 DT77
Henley Dr., Kings.T. 269 322 CT94
Henley Gdns., Pnr. 214 303 BV55
Henley Gdns., Rom. 226 309 EY57
Henley Rd. E16 252 318 EM75
Henley Rd. N18 209 300 DS49
Henley Rd. NW10 126 315 CW67
Henley Rd., Ilf. 235 308 EQ63
Henley St. SW11 160 316 DG82
Henley Way, Felt. 266 329 BX92
Henlow Pl., Rich. 267 322 CK89
Hennel Clo. SE23 196 325 DW90
Henniker Gdns. E6 244 318 EK69
Henniker Ms. SW3 159 315 DD79
Henniker Pt. E15 121 307 EE64
Henniker Rd. E15 121 307 ED64
Henning St. SW11 159 315 DE81
Henningham Rd. N17 221 306 DR53
Henrietta Ms. WC1 34/5 316 DL70
Henrietta Pl. W1 44/5 316 DH72
Henrietta St. E15 120 307 EC64
Henrietta St. WC2 58/9 316 DL73
Henriques St. E1 138 317 DU72
Henry Clo., Enf. 202 300 DS38
Henry Cooper Way SE9 260 326 EK90
Henry Darlot Dr. NW7 206 299 CX50
Henry Dickens Ct. W11 137 315 CX73
Henry Jackson Rd. SW15 173 323 CX83
Henry Rd. E6 244 318 EL68
Henry Rd. N4 100 306 DQ60
Henry Rd., Barn. 207 299 DD43
Henry St., Brom. 276 326 EH95
Henry's Ave., Wdf.Grn. 211 301 EF50
Henry's Wk., Ilf. 225 308 ER52
Henryson Rd. SE4 182 325 EA85
Hensford Gdns. SE26 274 325 DV91
Henshall St. N1 117 306 DR65
Henshaw St. SE17 86 316 DR77
Henshawe Rd., Dag. 236 309 EX62
Henshill Pt. E3 130 317 EB69
Henslowe Rd. SE22 180 325 DU85
Henson Ave. NW2 110 305 CW64
Henson Clo., Orp. 290 334 EP103
Henson Path, Har. 216 304 CK55
Henson Pl., Nthlt. 242 313 BW67
Henstridge Pl. NW8 18/9 315 DE68
Hensworth Rd., Ashf. 264 328 BK92
Henty Clo. SW11 159 315 DE80
Henty Wk. SW15 172 323 CV85
Henville Rd., Brom. 276 326 EJ95
Henwick Rd. SE9 260 326 EK83
Henwood Rd. SE16 148 317 DW76
Henwood Side, Wdf.Grn. 224 308 EM51
Hepburn Gdns., Brom. 289 333 EE102
Hepburn Ms. SW11 175 323 DF85
Hepple Clo., Islw. 152 314 CH82
Hepplestone Clo. SW15 172 323 CV86
Hepscott Rd. E9 120 307 EA65
Hepworth Ct., Bark. 236 309 EU64
Hepworth Gdns., Bark. 236 309 EU64
Hepworth Rd. SW16 272 324 DL94
Hepworth Wk. NW3 113 305 DE64
Hepworth Way, Walt. 281 328 BT102
Heracles Clo., Wall. 294 332 DL108
Herald Gdns., Wall. 285 332 DH104
Herald St. E2 128 317 DV70
Herald's Ct. SE11 84/5 316 DP77
Herald's Pl. SE11 84 316 DN77
Herbal Hill EC1 36 316 DN70
Herbert Cres. SW1 67 315 DF76
Herbert Gdns. NW10 126 315 CV67
Herbert Gdns. W4 154 314 CP79
Herbert Gdns., Rom. 236 309 EX59
Herbert Pl. SE18 253 318 EP79
Herbert Rd. E12 234 308 EL63
Herbert Rd. E17 103 307 DZ59
Herbert Rd. N11 220 306 DL52
Herbert Rd. N15 221 306 DT57
Herbert Rd. NW9 218 305 CU58
Herbert Rd. SE18 253 318 EN80
Herbert Rd. SW19 270 323 CZ94
Herbert Rd., Bexh. 254 319 EY82
Herbert Rd., Brom. 290 334 EK99
Herbert Rd., Horn. 238 311 FL59
Herbert Rd., Ilf. 235 308 ES61
Herbert Rd., Kings.T. 268 322 CM97
Herbert Rd., Sthl. 242 313 BZ74
Herbert St. E13 244 318 EG68
Herbert St. NW5 114 306 DG65
Herbert Ter. SE18 253 318 EP79
Herbrand St. WC1 34/5 316 DL70
Hercies Rd., Uxb. 240 312 BM66
Hercules Pl. N7 99 306 DL62
Hercules Rd. SE1 71 316 DM76
Hercules St. N7 99 306 DL62
Hercules Twr. SE14 165 317 DY79
Hereford Ave., Barn. 207 299 DF46
Hereford Clo., Stai. 280 328 BH95
Hereford Gdns. SE13 183 325 EE85
Hereford Gdns., Ilf. 234 308 EL59
Hereford Gdns., Pnr. 214 303 BY57
Hereford Gdns., Twick. 259 321 CC88
Hereford Ho. NW6 16 315 DA68
Hereford Ms. W2 40 315 DA72
Hereford Pl. SE14 165 317 DZ80
Hereford Retreat SE15 164 317 DU80
Hereford Rd. E11 224 308 EH57
Hereford Rd. W2 40 315 DA72
Hereford Rd. W3 134 314 CP73
Hereford Rd. W5 142 314 CJ76
Hereford Rd., Felt. 258 321 BW88
Hereford Sq. SW7 77 315 DC77
Hereford St. E2 128 317 DU70
Hereford Way, Chess. 282 330 CJ106
Hereward Ave., Pur. 294 332 DN111
Hereward Gdns. N13 209 300 DN50
Hereward Rd. SW17 271 323 DE91
Herga Ct., Har. 233 313 CE62
Herga Rd., Har. 215 303 CF56
Heriot Ave. E4 211 301 EA47
Heriot Rd. NW4 218 305 CW57
Heriot Rd., Cher. 280 328 BG101
Heriots Clo., Stan. 204 298 CG49
Heritage Clo., Uxb. 240 312 BJ70
Heritage Hill, Kes. 290 334 EJ106
Heritage Vw., Har. 233 313 CF62
Herlwyn Ave., Ruis. 231 312 BS61
Herlwyn Gdns. SW17 271 323 DF91
Hermes Pt. W9 28 315 DA70
Hermes St. N1 24 316 DN68
Hermes Wk., Nthlt. 243 313 CA68
Hermes Way, Wall. 294 332 DK108
Hermiston Ave. N8 220 306 DL57
Hermit Pl. NW6 16/7 315 DB67
Hermit Rd. E16 131 317 EF70
Hermit St. EC1 36/7 316 DP69
Hermitage, The SE23 196 325 DW88
Hermitage, The SW13 155 314 CT81
Hermitage, The, Felt. 265 320 BT90
Hermitage, The, Rich. 169 322 CL85
Hermitage, The, Uxb. 231 312 BK65
Hermitage Clo. E18 223 307 EF56
Hermitage Clo., Enf. 202 300 DP40
Hermitage Clo., Shep. 281 328 BN98
Hermitage Ct. E18 224 308 EG56
Hermitage Ct. NW2 96 305 DA62
Hermitage Gdns. NW2 96 305 DA62
Hermitage Gdns. SE19 273 324 DQ94
Hermitage La. N18 209 300 DR50
Hermitage La. NW2 96 305 DA62
Hermitage La. SE25 287 333 DU100
Hermitage La. SW16 272 324 DM94
Hermitage La., Croy. 287 333 DU100
Hermitage Path SW16 272 324 DL95
Hermitage Rd. N4 100 306 DP59
Hermitage Rd. N15 100 306 DQ59
Hermitage Rd. SE19 273 324 DQ94
Hermitage Row E8 118 307 DU64
Hermitage St. W2 42 315 DD71
Hermitage Wk. E18 223 307 EF56
Hermitage Wall E1 138 317 DU74
Hermitage Way, Stan. 216 304 CG53
Hermon Gro., Hayes 242 313 BU74
Hermon Hill E11 224 308 EG57
Hermon Hill E18 224 308 EH55
Herndon Rd. SW18 175 323 DC85
Herne Clo. NW10 109 304 CR64
Herne Hill SE24 178 324 DQ85
Herne Hill Rd. SE24 178 324 DQ83
Herne Ms. N18 210 301 DU49
Herne Pl. SE24 178 324 DP85
Herne Rd., Surb. 282 330 CK103
Heron Clo. E17 222 307 DZ54
Heron Clo. NW10 109 304 CS65
Heron Clo., Rick. 212 302 BK47
Heron Clo., Uxb. 240 312 BK65
Heron Ct., Brom. 276 326 EJ98
Heron Cres., Sid. 261 326 ES90
Heron Flight Ave., Horn. 238 310 FH66
Heron Hill, Belv. 254 319 EZ78
Heron Ms., Ilf. 235 308 EP61
Heron Pl. SE16 139 317 DY74
Heron Quay E14 140 317 EA74
Heron Rd. SE24 178 324 DQ84
Heron Rd., Croy. 287 332 DS103
Heron Rd., Twick. 168 322 CG84
Heron Sq., Rich. 167 322 CK85
Heron Wk., Nthwd. 213 302 BS49
Heron Way, Upmin. 239 311 FS60
Herondale Ave. SW18 191 323 DD88
Herongate Rd. E12 234 308 EJ61
Herongate Rd., Swan. 279 327 FE93
Herons, The E11 223 307 EF58
Heron's Pl., Islw. 168 322 CH83
Heronsforde W13 132 314 CJ72
Heronsgate, Edg. 205 298 CN50
Heronslea Dr., Stan. 204 298 CL50
Herrick Rd. N5 100 306 DQ62
Herrick St. SW1 82 316 DK77
Herries St. W10 127 315 CY68
Herringham Rd. SE7 252 318 EJ76
Herrings La., Cher. 280 328 BG100
Herrongate Clo., Enf. 202 300 DT40
Hersant Clo. NW10 126 315 CU67
Herschell Rd. SE23 197 325 DY87
Hersham Clo. SW15 188 323 CU87
Hertford Ave. SW14 171 322 CR85
Hertford Pl. W1 33 316 DJ70
Hertford Rd. N1 26/7 316 DS67
Hertford Rd. N2 219 305 DE55
Hertford Rd. N9 210 301 DW47
Hertford Rd., Bark. 235 308 EP66
Hertford Rd., Enf. 203 301 DW40
Hertford Rd., Ilf. 235 308 ES58
Hertford Rd., Wal.Cr. 203 301 DX35
Hertford Sq., Mitch. 272 324 DL98
Hertford St. W1 56 316 DG74
Hertford Wk., Belv. 255 319 FA78
Hertford Way, Mitch. 272 324 DL98
Hertslet Rd. N7 99 306 DM62
Hertsmere Rd. E14 140 317 EA73
Hervey Clo. N3 219 305 DA53
Hervey Pk. Rd. E17 222 307 DY56
Hervey Rd. SE3 252 318 EH81
Hesa Rd., Hayes 242 313 BU72
Hesketh Pl. W11 137 315 CY73
Hesketh Rd. E7 234 308 EG62
Heslop Rd. SW12 193 323 DF88
Hesper Ms. SW5 76/7 315 DB78
Hesperus Cres. E14 150 317 EB77
Hessel Rd. W13 142 314 CG75
Hessel St. E1 138 317 DV72
Hesselyn Dr., Rain. 238 310 FH66
Hester Rd. N18 210 301 DU50
Hester Rd. SW11 159 315 DE80
Hester Ter., Rich. 170 322 CN83
Hestercombe Ave. SW6 157 315 CY82
Hesterman Way, Croy. 286 332 DL102
Heston Ave., Houns. 250 321 BY79
Heston Gra. La., Houns. 250 321 BZ79
Heston Ind. Cen., Houns. 250 321 BW79
Heston Ind. Mall, Houns. 250 321 BZ80
Heston Rd., Houns. 251 321 CA79
Heston St. SE14 166 317 EA81
Hetherington Rd. SW4 177 324 DL84
Hetherington Rd., Shep. 281 328 BQ96
Hetherington Way, Uxb. 240 312 BL63
Hetley Gdns. SE19 273 324 DT94
Hetley Rd. W12 136 315 CV74
Heton Gdns. NW4 218 305 CU56
Hevelius Clo. SE10 151 317 EF78
Hever Cft. SE9 277 326 EN91
Hever Gdns., Brom. 277 326 EN96
Heverham Rd. SE18 253 318 ES77
Heversham Rd., Bexh. 255 319 FA82
Hewens Rd., Hayes 241 312 BQ70
Hewens Rd., Uxb. 241 312 BQ70
Hewer St. W10 137 315 CX71
Hewett Clo., Stan. 204 298 CH49
Hewett Pl., Swan. 279 327 FD98
Hewett Rd., Dag. 236 309 EW64
Hewett St. EC2 38/9 316 DS70
Hewish Rd. N18 209 300 DS49
Hewison St. E3 129 317 DZ68
Hewitt Ave. N22 221 306 DP54
Hewitt Clo., Croy. 288 333 EA104
Hewitt Rd. N8 221 306 DN57
Hewlett Rd. E3 129 317 DY68
Hexagon, The N6 97 305 DF60
Hexal Rd. SE6 199 325 EE90
Hexham Gdns., Islw. 152 314 CG80
Hexham Rd. SE27 194 324 DQ89
Hexham Rd., Mord. 285 331 DB102
Heybourne Rd. N17 222 307 DV52
Heybridge Ave. SW16 272 324 DL94
Heybridge Dr., Ilf. 225 308 ER54
Heybridge Way E10 103 307 DY59
Heyford Ave. SW8 161 316 DL80
Heyford Ave. SW20 270 323 CZ97
Heyford Rd., Mitch. 271 323 DE96
Heygate St. SE17 85 316 DQ77
Heylyn Sq. E3 129 317 DZ69
Heynes Rd., Dag. 236 309 EW63
Heysham La. NW3 96 305 DB62
Heysham Rd. N15 221 306 DR58
Heythorp St. SW18 189 323 CZ88
Heythrop Dr., Uxb. 240 312 BM63
Heywood Ave. NW9 217 304 CS53
Heyworth Rd. E5 118 307 DV63
Heyworth Rd. E15 121 307 EF63
Hibbert Rd. E17 103 307 DZ59
Hibbert Rd., Har. 215 303 CF54
Hibbert St. SW11 174 323 DC83
Hibbs Clo., Swan. 279 327 FD96
Hibernia Gdns., Houns. 259 321 CA84
Hibernia Rd., Houns. 259 321 CA84
Hichisson Rd. SE15 180 325 DW85
Hickin Clo. SE7 252 318 EK77
Hickin St. E14 150 317 EC76
Hickling Rd., Ilf. 235 308 EP64
Hickman Ave. E4 223 307 EC51
Hickman Clo. E16 244 318 EK71
Hickman Rd., Rom. 236 309 EW59
Hickmore Wk. SW4 176 324 DJ83
Hickory Clo. N9 210 301 DU45
Hicks Ave., Grnf. 243 313 CD68
Hicks Clo. SW11 175 323 DE83
Hicks St. SE8 149 317 DY78
Hidcote Gdns. SW20 270 323 CV97
Hide E6 245 318 EN72
Hide Pl. SW1 82 316 DK77
Hide Rd., Har. 215 303 CC56
Hides St. N7 115 306 DM65
Higgins Wk., Hmptn. 266 329 BY93
High Beech, S.Croy. 295 332 DS108
High Beeches, Bans. 292 331 CW114
High Beeches, Sid. 278 327 EY92
High Beeches Clo., Pur. 294 332 DK110
High Bri. SE10 151 317 ED78
High Bri. Wf. SE10 151 317 ED78
High Broom Cres., W.Wick. 288 333 EB101
High Cedar Dr. SW20 270 323 CV94
High Coombe Pl., Kings.T. 269 322 CR94
High Cross Cen. N15 222 307 DU56
High Cross Rd. N17 222 307 DU55
High Dr., N.Mal. 269 322 CQ95
High Elms, Upmin. 239 311 FS60
High Elms Clo., Nthwd. 213 302 BR51
High Firs, Swan. 279 327 FE98
High Gro. SE18 253 318 ER80
High Gro., Brom. 276 326 EJ95
High Hill Est. E5 102 307 DV60
High Hill Ferry E5 102 307 DV60
High Holborn WC1 46/7 316 DL72
High La. W7 243 313 CD71
High Lawns, Har. 233 313 CE62
High Level Dr. SE26 274 325 DU91
High Mead, Har. 215 303 CE57
High Mead, W.Wick. 289 333 ED103
High Meadow Clo., Pnr. 214 303 BV56
High Meadow Cres. NW9 217 304 CR57
High Meads Rd. E16 244 318 EK72
High Mt. NW4 218 305 CU58
High Pk. Ave., Rich. 154 314 CN81
High Pk. Rd., Rich. 154 314 CN81
High Path SW19 271 323 DB95
High Pt. N6 98 306 DG59
High Pt., SE9 261 326 EP90
High Rd. N2 219 305 DD53
High Rd. N11 208 300 DH50
High Rd. N12 207 299 DC49
High Rd. N15 221 306 DT58
High Rd. N17 221 306 DT55
High Rd. N20 207 299 DC47
High Rd. N22 220 306 DM51
High Rd. (Willesden) NW10 109 304 CT65
High Rd. (Harrow Weald), Har. 215 303 CE52
High Rd., Ilf. 235 308 EQ61
High Rd. (Goodmayes), Ilf. 236 309 EU60
High Rd. (Seven Kings), Ilf. 235 308 ET60
High Rd., Pnr. 214 303 BV57
High Rd.
(Chadwell Heath), Rom. 236 309 EU60
High Rd., Uxb. 248 312 BJ71
High Rd. (Ickenham), Uxb. 231 312 BP62
High Rd., Wem. 107 304 CL64
High Rd. Leyton E10 223 307 EB58
High Rd. Leyton E15 120 307 EC63
High Rd. Leytonstone E11 121 307 EE63
High Rd. Leytonstone E15 121 307 EE63
High Rd. Woodford Grn. E18 223 307 EF53
High Rd.
Woodford Grn., Wdf.Grn. 223 307 EF51
High St. E11 224 308 EG57
High St. E13 244 318 EG68
High St. E15 130 317 EC68
High St. E17 222 307 DY57
High St. N8 220 306 DL56
High St. N14 208 300 DK47
High St. NW7 206 299 CV50
High St. (Harlesden) NW10 125 314 CT68
High St. SE20 274 325 DW94
High St. (South Norwood) SE25 273 324 DT98
High St. SW6 173 323 CY83
High St. W3 134 314 CP74
High St. W5 133 314 CK73
High St., Beck. 275 325 EA96
High St. (Elstree), Borwd. 204 298 CK44
High St., Brent. 153 314 CL79
High St., Brom. 276 326 EG96
High St., Cars. 285 331 DF105
High St., Chis. 277 326 EP93
High St., Croy. 287 332 DQ104
High St., Edg. 217 304 CN51
High St. (Ponders End), Enf. 203 301 DW42
High St., Felt. 265 320 BT90
High St., Hmptn. 267 329 CB95
High St., Har. 233 313 CE60
High St. (Wealdstone), Har. 215 303 CE54
High St., Hayes 257 320 BR79
High St., Horn. 238 310 FK60
High St., Houns. 259 321 CB83
High St. (Cranford), Houns. 250 321 BU80
High St., Ilf. 225 308 EQ55
High St., Kings.T. 268 322 CK97
High St.
(Hampton Wick), Kings.T. 268 322 CJ95
High St., N.Mal. 269 322 CS98
High St., Nthwd. 213 302 BT53
High St., Orp. 291 335 EU103
High St. (Farnborough), Orp. 290 334 EP106
High St., Pnr. 214 303 BY55
High St., Pur. 294 332 DN111
High St., Rom. 227 309 FE57
High St., Ruis. 231 312 BS59
High St., Shep. 281 328 BP101
High St., Sthl. 242 313 BZ74
High St. (Stanwell), Stai. 256 320 BK86
High St., Sutt. 284 331 DB105
High St. (Cheam), Sutt. 292 331 CY107
High St., Swan. 279 327 FF97
High St., Tedd. 267 329 CF92
High St., Th.Hth. 273 324 DQ98
High St. (Whitton), Twick. 259 321 CC87
High St., Uxb. 240 312 BJ66
High St. (Cowley), Uxb. 240 312 BJ69
High St. (Harefield), Uxb. 212 302 BJ54
High St., Wem. 107 304 CM63
High St., West Dr. 256 320 BK79
High St. (Yiewsley), West Dr. 248 312 BK73
High St., W.Mol. 267 329 CA98
High St., W.Wick. 288 333 EB102
High St. Colliers Wd. SW19 271 323 DD94
High St. Ms. SW19 270 323 CY92
High St. N. E6 234 308 EL66
High St. N. E12 234 308 EL64
High St. S. E6 234 318 EM68
High St. Wimbledon SW19 270 323 CX92
High Timber St. EC4 61 316 DQ73
High Tor Clo., Brom. 276 326 EH94
High Tree Ct. W7 243 313 CE73
High Trees SW2 194 324 DN88
High Trees, Barn. 207 299 DE43
High Trees, Croy. 288 333 DY102
High Vw., Pnr. 214 303 BW55
High Vw., Sutt. 292 331 CZ111
High Vw. Clo. SE19 273 324 DT96
High Vw. Rd. E18 223 307 EF55
High Vw. Rd., Sid. 278 327 EV91
High Worple, Har. 232 313 BY59
Higham Hill Rd. E17 222 307 DY53
Higham Pl. E17 222 307 DY55
Higham Rd. N17 221 306 DR55
Higham Rd., Wdf.Grn. 224 308 EG51
Higham Sta. Ave. E4 223 307 EA51
Higham St. E17 222 307 DY55
Highams Lo. Business Cen. E17 222 307 DX55
Highams Pk. Ind. Est. E4 223 307 EC51
Highbank Way N8 221 306 DN58
Highbanks Clo., Well. 254 319 EV80
Highbanks Rd., Pnr. 215 303 CA51
Highbarrow Rd., Croy. 287 333 DU101
Highbridge SE10 151 317 ED78
Highbridge Rd., Bark. 245 318 EP67
Highbrook Rd. SE3 260 326 EK83
Highbury Ave., Th.Hth. 273 324 DN96
Highbury Clo., N.Mal. 269 322 CQ98
Highbury Clo., W.Wick. 288 333 EB103
Highbury Cor. N5 116 306 DP65
Highbury Cres. N5 116 306 DP64
Highbury Est. N5 116 306 DQ64
Highbury Gdns., Ilf. 235 308 ES61
Highbury Gra. N5 116 306 DQ63
Highbury Gro. N5 116 306 DP63
Highbury Hill N5 100 306 DN62
Highbury Ms. N7 116 306 DN65
Highbury New Pk. N5 116 306 DQ64
Highbury Pk. N5 116 306 DP63
Highbury Pk. Ms. N5 116 306 DQ63
Highbury Pl. N5 116 306 DP65
Highbury Quad. N5 100 306 DQ62
Highbury Rd. SW19 270 323 CY92
Highbury Sta. Rd. N1 116 306 DN65
Highbury Ter. N5 116 306 DP64
Highbury Ter. Ms. N5 116 306 DP64
Highclere Rd., N.Mal. 269 322 CR97
Highclere St. SE26 274 325 DY91
Highcliffe Dr. SW15 171 322 CT86
Highcliffe Gdns., Ilf. 224 308 EL57
Highcombe SE7 252 318 EH79
Highcombe Clo. SE9 260 326 EK88
Highcroft NW9 217 304 CS57
Highcroft Ave., Wem. 124 314 CN67
Highcroft Gdns. NW11 218 305 CZ58
Highcroft Rd. N19 99 306 DL59
Highcross Way SW15 188 323 CU88
Highdaun Dr. SW16 272 324 DM98
Highdown, Wor.Pk. 283 330 CS103
Highdown La., Sutt. 292 331 DB111
Highdown Rd. SW15 172 323 CV86
Higher Dr., Bans. 292 331 CX112
Higher Dr., Pur. 294 332 DN113
Highfield, Felt. 258 321 BU88
Highfield Ave. NW9 217 304 CQ57
Highfield Ave. NW11 95 305 CX59
Highfield Ave., Erith 255 319 FB79
Highfield Ave., Grnf. 233 313 CE64
Highfield Ave., Orp. 291 334 ET106
Highfield Ave., Pnr. 214 303 BZ57
Highfield Ave., Wem. 91 304 CL62
Highfield Clo. N22 221 306 DN53
Highfield Clo. NW9 217 304 CQ57
Highfield Clo. SE13 199 325 ED87
Highfield Clo., Nthwd. 213 302 BS53
Highfield Clo., Rom. 227 309 FC51
Highfield Clo., Surb. 282 330 CJ102
Highfield Ct. N14 208 300 DJ44
Highfield Cres., Horn. 238 311 FM61
Highfield Cres., Nthwd. 213 302 BS53
Highfield Dr., Brom. 275 325 EE98
Highfield Dr., Uxb. 231 312 BL62
Highfield Dr., W.Wick. 288 333 EB103
Highfield Gdns. NW11 218 305 CY58
Highfield Hill SE19 273 324 DR94
Highfield Link, Rom. 227 309 FD51
Highfield Rd. N21 209 300 DP47
Highfield Rd. NW11 218 305 CY58
Highfield Rd. W3 134 314 CP71
Highfield Rd., Bexh. 262 327 EZ85
Highfield Rd., Brom. 276 326 EM98
Highfield Rd., Cher. 280 328 BG102
Highfield Rd., Chis. 277 326 ET97
Highfield Rd., Felt. 258 321 BU89
Highfield Rd., Horn. 238 311 FM61
Highfield Rd., Islw. 251 321 CF81
Highfield Rd., Nthwd. 213 302 BS53
Highfield Rd., Pur. 294 332 DM110
Highfield Rd., Rom. 227 309 FC52
Highfield Rd., Sun. 281 328 BT98
Highfield Rd., Surb. 283 330 CQ101
Highfield Rd., Sutt. 285 331 DE106
Highfield Rd., Wdf.Grn. 224 308 EL52
Highfield Way, Horn. 238 311 FM61
Highfields Gro. N6 97 305 DF60
Highgate Ave. N6 98 306 DH59
Highgate Clo. N6 98 306 DG59
Highgate High St. N6 98 306 DG60
Highgate Hill N6 98 306 DH60
Highgate Hill N19 98 306 DH60
Highgate Rd. NW5 114 306 DH63
Highgate Wk. SE23 196 325 DW89
Highgate W. Hill N6 98 306 DG60
Highgrove Clo. N11 208 300 DJ50
Highgrove Clo., Chis. 276 326 EL95
Highgrove Ct., Beck. 275 325 EA94
Highgrove Ms., Cars. 285 331 DF104
Highgrove Rd., Dag. 236 309 EW64
Highgrove Way, Ruis. 214 303 BU58
Highland Ave. W7 243 313 CE72
Highland Ave., Dag. 237 309 FC62
Highland Cotts., Wall. 285 332 DH105
Highland Ct. E18 224 308 EH53
Highland Cft., Beck. 275 325 EB92
Highland Pk., Felt. 265 328 BT91
Highland Rd. SE19 273 324 DS93
Highland Rd., Bexh. 263 327 FA85
Highland Rd., Brom. 275 325 EF95
Highland Rd., Nthwd. 213 302 BT54
Highland Rd., Pur. 294 332 DN114
Highlands, The, Edg. 217 304 CP54
Highlands Ave. W3 134 314 CQ73
Highlands Clo. N4 99 306 DL59
Highlands Clo., Houns. 251 321 CB81
Highlands Gdns., Ilf. 234 308 EM60
Highlands Heath SW15 188 323 CW87
Highlands Rd., Barn. 207 299 DA43
Highlands Rd., Orp. 291 335 EV101
Highlea Clo. NW9 217 304 CS53
Highlever Rd. W10 136 315 CW71
Highmead SE18 253 318 ET80
Highmead Cres., Wem. 107 304 CM66
Highmore Rd. SE3 167 317 EE80
Highshore Rd. SE15 163 316 DT82
Highstead Cres., Erith 255 319 FE80
Highstone Ave. E11 224 308 EG58
Highview Ave., Edg. 205 298 CQ49
Highview Ave., Wall. 286 332 DM106
Highview Gdns. N3 218 305 CY56
Highview Gdns. N11 208 300 DJ50
Highview Gdns., Edg. 205 298 CQ50
Highview Gdns., Upmin. 239 311 FP61
Highview Ho., Rom. 226 309 EY56
Highview Rd. SE19 273 324 DR93
Highview Rd. W13 132 314 CG71
Highway, The E1 138 317 DU73
Highway, The E14 139 317 DX73
Highway, The, Orp. 291 335 EV106
Highway, The, Stan. 215 303 CF53
Highway, The, Sutt. 293 331 DC109
Highwood, Brom. 275 325 ED97
Highwood Ave. N12 207 299 DC49
Highwood Clo., Orp. 291 334 EQ103
Highwood Dr., Orp. 291 334 EQ103
Highwood Gdns., Ilf. 224 308 EM57
Highwood Gro. NW7 205 298 CR50
Highwood Hill NW7 205 298 CT47
Highwood Rd. N19 99 306 DL62
Highworth Rd. N11 220 306 DK51
Hilary Ave., Mitch. 272 324 DG97
Hilary Clo. SW6 158 315 DB80
Hilary Clo., Erith 255 319 FB81
Hilary Clo., Horn. 238 310 FK64
Hilary Rd. W12 135 314 CT72
Hilbert Rd., Sutt. 284 331 CX104
Hilborough Way, Orp. 291 334 ER106
Hilda May Ave., Swan. 279 327 FD97
Hilda Rd. E6 234 308 EK66
Hilda Rd. E16 131 317 EE70
Hilda Ter. SW9 162 316 DN82
Hilda Vale Clo., Orp. 290 334 EP105
Hilda Vale Rd., Orp. 290 334 EN105
Hildenborough Gdns., Brom. 275 325 EE93
Hildenlea Pl., Brom. 275 325 EE96
Hildreth St. SW12 192 324 DH88
Hildyard Rd. SW6 158 315 DA79
Hiley Rd. NW10 126 315 CW69
Hilgrove Rd. NW6 112 305 DC66
Hiliary Gdns., Stan. 216 304 CJ54
Hill Barn, S.Croy. 295 332 DS111
Hill Brow, Brom. 276 326 EK95
Hill Brow, Dart. 263 327 FF86
Hill Brow Clo., Bex. 279 327 FD91
Hill Clo. NW2 94 305 CV62
Hill Clo. NW11 219 305 DA58
Hill Clo., Barn. 206 299 CW43
Hill Clo., Chis. 277 326 EP92
Hill Clo., Har. 233 313 CE62
Hill Clo., Pur. 295 332 DQ112
Hill Clo., Stan. 204 298 CH49
Hill Ct., Nthlt. 233 313 CA64
Hill Cres. N20 207 299 DB47
Hill Cres., Bex. 263 327 FC88
Hill Cres., Har. 216 304 CG57
Hill Cres., Horn. 238 310 FJ58
Hill Cres., Surb. 282 330 CM99
Hill Cres., Wor.Pk. 284 331 CW103
Hill Crest, Sid. 262 327 EU87
Hill Crest Gdns. N3 218 305 CY56
Hill Dr. NW9 92 304 CQ60
Hill Dr. SW16 272 324 DM97
Hill End, Orp. 291 334 ET103
Hill End Rd., Uxb. 212 302 BJ52
Hill Fm. Rd. W10 136 315 CW71
Hill Gro., Rom. 227 309 FE55
Hill Ho. Ave., Stan. 215 303 CF52
Hill Ho. Clo. N21 209 300 DN45
Hill Ho. Rd. SW16 272 324 DM92
Hill La., Ruis. 231 312 BQ60
Hill Path SW16 272 324 DM92
Hill Ri. N9 210 301 DV44
Hill Ri. NW11 219 305 DB56
Hill Ri. SE23 196 325 DV88
Hill Ri., Grnf. 233 313 CC66
Hill Ri., Rich. 169 322 CK85
Hill Ri., Ruis. 231 312 BQ60
Hill Ri., Upmin. 239 311 FN61
Hill Ri., Walt. 281 328 BT101
Hill Rd. N10 219 305 DF53
Hill Rd. NW8 17 315 DC68
Hill Rd., Cars. 293 331 DE107
Hill Rd., Har. 216 304 CG57
Hill Rd., Mitch. 272 324 DH95
Hill Rd., Nthwd. 213 302 BR51
Hill Rd., Pnr. 214 303 BY58
Hill Rd., Pur. 294 332 DM112
Hill Rd., Sutt. 284 331 DB106
Hill Rd., Wem. 90 304 CH62
Hill St. W1 56 316 DG74
Hill St., Rich. 169 322 CK85
Hill Top NW11 219 305 DB56
Hill Top, Mord. 284 331 DB100
Hill Top Vw., Wdf.Grn. 224 308 EM51
Hill Vw. Cres., Orp. 291 334 ET102
Hill Vw. Dr., Well. 253 318 ES82
Hill Vw. Gdns. NW9 217 304 CR57
Hill Vw. Rd., Orp. 291 334 ET102
Hill Vw. Rd., Twick. 168 322 CG86
Hillary Rd., Sthl. 251 321 CA76
Hillbeck Clo. SE15 164 317 DW80
Hillbeck Way, Grnf. 243 313 CD67
Hillborne Clo., Hayes 250 321 BU78
Hillborough Clo. SW19 271 323 DC94
Hillbrook Rd. SW17 191 323 DF90
Hillbrow, N.Mal. 269 322 CT97
Hillbrow Rd., Brom. 275 325 EE94
Hillbury Ave., Har. 216 304 CH57
Hillbury Rd. SW17 192 324 DH90
Hillcote Ave. SW16 273 324 DN94
Hillcourt Ave. N12 219 305 DB51
Hillcourt Est. N16 101 306 DR60
Hillcourt Rd. SE22 180 325 DV86
Hillcrest N6 98 306 DG59
Hillcrest N21 209 300 DN45
Hillcrest Ave. NW11 218 305 CY57
Hillcrest Ave., Edg. 205 298 CP49
Hillcrest Ave., Pnr. 180 303 BX56
Hillcrest Clo. SE26 274 325 DU91
Hillcrest Clo., Beck. 288 333 DZ99
Hillcrest Gdns. NW2 94 305 CU62
Hillcrest Par., Couls. 293 332 DH114
Hillcrest Rd. E17 223 307 ED54
Hillcrest Rd. E18 223 307 EF54
Hillcrest Rd. W3 134 314 CN74
Hillcrest Rd. W5 133 314 CL71
Hillcrest Rd., Brom. 276 326 EG91
Hillcrest Rd., Dart. 263 327 FF87
Hillcrest Rd., Horn. 238 310 FG59
Hillcrest Rd., Orp. 291 335 EU103
Hillcrest Rd., Pur. 294 332 DM110
Hillcrest Vw., Beck. 288 333 DZ100
Hillcroft Ave., Pnr. 214 303 BZ58
Hillcroft Ave., Pur. 294 332 DJ113
Hillcroft Cres. W5 133 314 CK72
Hillcroft Cres., Ruis. 232 313 BX62
Hillcroft Cres., Wem. 107 304 CM63
Hillcroft Rd. E6 245 318 EP71
Hillcroome Rd., Sutt. 293 331 DD107
Hillcross Ave., Mord. 284 331 CX100
Hilldale Rd., Sutt. 284 331 CZ105
Hilldeane Rd., Pur. 294 332 DN109
Hilldene Ave., Rom. 228 310 FJ51
Hilldown Rd. SW16 272 324 DL94
Hilldown Rd., Brom. 289 333 EE102
Hilldrop Cres. N7 115 306 DK64
Hilldrop Est. N7 115 306 DK64
Hilldrop La. N7 115 306 DK64
Hilldrop Rd. N7 115 306 DK64
Hilldrop Rd., Brom. 276 326 EG93
Hillend SE18 253 318 EP81
Hillersdon Ave. SW13 156 315 CU82
Hillersdon Ave., Edg. 204 298 CM50
Hillery Clo. SE17 86 316 DR77
Hillfield Ave. N8 220 306 DL57
Hillfield Ave. NW9 217 304 CS57
Hillfield Ave., Mord. 285 331 DE100
Hillfield Ave., Wem. 107 304 CL66
Hillfield Clo., Har. 215 303 CC56
Hillfield Ct. NW3 113 305 DE64
Hillfield Pk. N10 220 306 DH56
Hillfield Pk. N21 209 300 DN47
Hillfield Pk. Ms. N10 220 306 DH56
Hillfield Rd. NW6 111 305 CZ64
Hillfield Rd., Hmptn. 266 329 BZ94
Hillfoot Ave., Rom. 227 309 FC53
Hillfoot Rd., Rom. 227 309 FC53
Hillgate Pl. SW12 192 324 DH87
Hillgate Pl. W8 52 315 DA74
Hillgate St. W8 52 315 DA74
Hilliard Rd., Nthwd. 213 302 BT53
Hilliards Ct. E1 138 317 DV74
Hilliards Rd., Uxb. 248 312 BK72
Hilliards St. E1 138 317 DW74
Hillier Clo., Barn. 207 299 DB44
Hillier Gdns., Croy. 286 332 DN106
Hillier Rd. SW11 175 323 DF86
Hilliers Ave., Uxb. 241 312 BN69
Hilliers La., Croy. 286 332 DL104
Hillingdon Ave., Stai. 264 320 BL88
Hillingdon Hill, Uxb. 240 312 BL69
Hillingdon Rd., Bexh. 255 319 FC82
Hillingdon Rd., Uxb. 240 312 BJ67
Hillingdon St. SE5 162 316 DP79
Hillingdon St. SE17 162 316 DP79
Hillington Gdns., Wdf.Grn. 224 308 EK54
Hillman Clo., Horn. 228 310 FK55
Hillman Clo., Uxb. 240 312 BL64
Hillman Dr. W10 126 315 CW70
Hillman St. E8 118 307 DV65
Hillmarton Rd. N7 115 306 DL64
Hillmead Dr. SW9 178 324 DP84
Hillmore Gro. SE26 274 325 DX92

Hillreach SE18	252	318	EM78
Hillrise Rd. N19	99	306	DL59
Hillrise Rd., Rom.	227	309	FC51
Hills La., Nthwd.	213	302	BS53
Hills Ms. W5	133	314	CL73
Hills Pl. W1	45	316	DJ72
Hillsboro Rd. SE22	179	324	DS85
Hillsgrove Clo., Well.	254	319	EW80
Hillside NW9	217	304	CR56
Hillside NW10	108	304	CQ66
Hillside SW19	270	323	CX93
Hillside, Barn.	207	299	DC43
Hillside, Erith	255	319	FD77
Hillside, Uxb.	230	302	BJ57
Hillside Ave. N11	219	305	DF51
Hillside Ave., Pur.	294	332	DP113
Hillside Ave., Wem.	107	304	CM63
Hillside Clo. NW8	16/7	315	DB68
Hillside Clo., Mord.	270	323	CY98
Hillside Cres., Enf.	202	300	DR38
Hillside Cres., Har.	233	313	CC60
Hillside Cres., Nthwd.	214	303	BU53
Hillside Dr., Edg.	217	304	CN51
Hillside Est. N15	221	306	DT58
Hillside Gdns. E17	223	307	ED55
Hillside Gdns. N6	220	306	DG58
Hillside Gdns. SW2	194	324	DN89
Hillside Gdns., Edg.	204	298	CM49
Hillside Gdns., Har.	91	304	CL59
Hillside Gdns., Nthwd.	214	303	BU52
Hillside Gdns., Wall.	294	332	DJ108
Hillside Gro. N14	208	300	DK45
Hillside Gro. NW7	218	305	CU52
Hillside La., Brom.	289	334	EG103
Hillside Pas. SW2	193	324	DM89
Hillside Ri., Nthwd.	214	303	BU52
Hillside Rd. N15	221	306	DS58
Hillside Rd. SW2	193	324	DM89
Hillside Rd. W5	133	314	CL71
Hillside Rd., Brom.	275	325	EF97
Hillside Rd., Croy.	286	332	DP106
Hillside Rd., Nthwd.	214	303	BU52
Hillside Rd., Sthl.	243	313	CA70
Hillside Rd., Surb.	268	322	CM98
Hillside Rd., Sutt.	292	331	CZ108
Hillsleigh Rd. W8	137	315	CZ74
Hillsmead Way, S.Croy.	295	333	DU113
Hillstowe St. E5	102	307	DW62
Hilltop, Sutt.	284	331	CZ101
Hilltop Gdns. NW4	218	305	CV53
Hilltop Gdns., Orp.	291	334	ES103
Hilltop Rd. NW6	112	305	DA66
Hilltop Way, Stan.	204	298	CG48
Hillview SW20	270	323	CV94
Hillview, Mitch.	272	324	DL98
Hillview Ave., Har.	216	304	CL57
Hillview Ave., Horn.	228	310	FJ58
Hillview Clo., Pnr.	214	303	BZ51
Hillview Clo., Pur.	294	332	DP111
Hillview Cres., Ilf.	224	308	EM58
Hillview Gdns. NW4	218	305	CX56
Hillview Gdns., Har.	215	303	CA55
Hillview Rd. NW7	206	299	CX49
Hillview Rd., Chis.	277	326	EN92
Hillview Rd., Pnr.	214	303	BZ52
Hillview Rd., Sutt.	285	331	DC104
Hillway N6	98	306	DG60
Hillway NW9	93	304	CS59
Hillworth Rd. SW2	194	324	DN87
Hilly Flds. Cres. SE4	182	325	EA83
Hillyard Rd. W7	243	313	CE71
Hillyard St. SW9	162	316	DN81
Hillyfield E17	222	307	DY55
Hilsea St. E5	118	307	DW63
Hilton Ave. N12	207	299	DD50
Hilton Clo., Uxb.	240	312	BH68
Hilversum Cres. SE22	179	324	DS85
Himley Rd. SW17	271	323	DE92
Hinchcliffe Clo., Wall.	294	332	DM108
Hinckler Clo., Wall.	294	332	DL108
Hinckley Rd. SE15	180	325	DU84
Hind Ct. EC4	48	316	DN72
Hind Cres., Erith	255	319	FD79
Hind Gro. E14	140	317	EA72
Hinde Ms. W1	44	316	DG72
Hinde St. W1	44	316	DG72
Hindes Rd., Har.	215	303	CD57
Hindhead Clo. N16	101	306	DS60
Hindhead Clo., Uxb.	249	312	BP71
Hindhead Gdns., Nthlt.	242	313	BY67
Hindhead Way, Wall.	286	332	DL106
Hindmans Rd. SE22	180	325	DU85
Hindmans Way, Dag.	246	319	EZ70
Hindmarsh Clo. E1	138	317	DU73
Hindrey Rd. E5	118	307	DV64
Hindsley's Pl. SE23	196	325	DW89
Hinkler Rd., Har.	216	304	CK55
Hinkley Clo., Uxb.	230	302	BJ56
Hinksey Path SE2	254	319	EX75
Hinstock Rd. SE18	253	318	EQ79
Hinton Ave., Houns.	258	321	BX84
Hinton Clo. SE9	260	326	EL88
Hinton Rd. N18	209	300	DS49
Hinton Rd. SE24	178	324	DP83
Hinton Rd., Uxb.	240	312	BJ67
Hinton Rd., Wall.	294	332	DJ107
Hippodrome Ms. W11	137	315	CY73
Hippodrome Pl. W11	137	315	CY73
Hiroshima Wk. SE7	252	318	EH76
Hiscocks Ho. NW10	108	304	CQ66
Hitcham Rd. E17	103	307	DZ59
Hitchcock Clo., Shep.	280	328	BM97
Hitchin Sq. E3	129	317	DY68
Hither Grn. La. SE13	182	325	EC85
Hitherbroom Rd., Hayes	242	313	BU74
Hitherfield Rd. SW16	193	324	DM89
Hitherfield Rd., Dag.	236	309	EY61
Hitherlands SW12	192	324	DH89
Hithermoor Rd., Stai.	256	320	BG86
Hitherwell Dr., Har.	215	303	CD53
Hitherwood Clo., Horn.	238	310	FK63
Hitherwood Dr. SE19	273	324	DT91
Hoadly Rd. SW16	193	324	DK90
Hobart Clo. N20	207	299	DE47
Hobart Clo., Hayes	242	313	BX70
Hobart Dr., Hayes	242	313	BX70
Hobart Gdns., Th.Hth.	273	324	DR97
Hobart La., Hayes	242	313	BX70
Hobart Pl. SW1	68/9	316	DH76
Hobart Pl., Rich.	169	322	CM86
Hobart Rd., Dag.	236	309	EX63
Hobart Rd., Hayes	242	313	BX70
Hobart Rd., Ilf.	225	308	EQ54
Hobart Rd., Wor.Pk.	283	331	CV104
Hobbayne Rd. W7	243	313	CD72
Hobbes Wk. SW15	172	323	CV85
Hobbs Grn. N2	219	305	DC55
Hobbs Ms., Ilf.	235	308	ET61
Hobbs Pl. Est. N1	26/7	316	DS67
Hobbs Rd. SE27	273	324	DQ91
Hobday St. E14	140	317	EB71
Hobill Wk., Surb.	282	330	CM100
Hoblands End, Chis.	277	326	ES93
Hobsons Pl. E1	138	317	DU71
Hobury St. SW10	158	315	DC79
Hockenden La., Swan.	279	327	FA97
Hocker St. E2	39	316	DT69
Hockett Clo. SE8	149	317	DY77
Hockley Ave. E6	244	318	EL68
Hockley Dr., Rom.	228	310	FH54
Hocroft Ave. NW2	95	305	CZ62
Hocroft Rd. NW2	111	305	CZ63
Hocroft Wk. NW2	95	305	CZ62
Hodder Dr., Grnf.	243	313	CF68
Hoddesdon Rd., Belv.	255	319	FA78
Hodford Rd. NW11	95	305	CZ60
Hodgkin Clo. SE28	246	319	EX73
Hodnet Gro. SE16	149	317	DX77
Hodson Clo., Har.	232	313	BZ62
Hoe La., Enf.	203	301	DU38
Hoe St. E17	223	307	EA57
Hofland Rd. W14	147	315	CX76
Hog Hill Rd., Rom.	226	309	EZ52
Hogan Ms. W2	42	315	DD71
Hogan Way E5	102	307	DU61
Hogarth Ave., Ashf.	265	328	BQ93
Hogarth Clo. E16	244	318	EK71
Hogarth Clo. W5	133	314	CL71
Hogarth Ct. EC3	62/3	316	DS73
Hogarth Ct. SE19	273	324	DT91
Hogarth Cres. SW19	271	323	DD95
Hogarth Cres., Croy.	287	332	DQ101
Hogarth Gdns., Houns.	251	321	CA80
Hogarth Hill NW11	218	305	CZ56
Hogarth La. W4	155	314	CS79
Hogarth Pl. SW5	76/7	315	DB77
Hogarth Rd. SW5	76/7	315	DB77
Hogarth Rd., Dag.	236	309	EV64
Hogarth Rd., Edg.	217	304	CN54
Hogarth Roundabout W4	155	314	CS79
Hogarth Way, Hmptn.	267	329	CC95
Hogshead Pas. E1	138	317	DV73
Hogsmill Way, Epsom	283	330	CQ106
Holbeach Gdns., Sid.	261	326	ES86
Holbeach Ms. SW12	192	324	DH88
Holbeach Rd. SE6	198	325	EA87
Holbeck Row SE15	164	317	DU80
Holbein Gate, Nthwd.	213	302	BS50
Holbein Ms. SW1	80	316	DG78
Holbein Pl. SW1	80	316	DG77
Holbein Ter., Dag.	236	309	EV63
Holberton Gdns. NW10	126	315	CV69
Holborn EC1	48	316	DN71
Holborn Circ. EC1	48	316	DN71
Holborn Pl. WC1	47	316	DM71
Holborn Rd. E13	244	318	EH70
Holborn Viaduct EC1	48	316	DN71
Holborn Way, Mitch.	271	323	DF96
Holbrook Clo. N19	98	306	DH60
Holbrook Clo., Enf.	202	300	DT39
Holbrook La., Chis.	277	326	ER94
Holbrook Rd. E15	131	317	EF68
Holbrook Way, Brom.	290	334	EM100
Holbrooke Ct. N7	99	306	DL62
Holbrooke Pl., Rich.	169	322	CK85
Holburne Clo. SE3	252	318	EJ81
Holburne Gdns. SE3	252	318	EK81
Holburne Rd. SE3	252	318	EJ81
Holcombe Hill NW7	206	299	CU48
Holcombe Rd. N17	221	306	DT55
Holcombe Rd., Ilf.	235	308	EN59
Holcombe St. W6	146	315	CV78
Holcote Clo., Belv.	254	319	EY76
Holcroft Rd. E9	118	307	DW66
Holdbrook Way, Rom.	228	311	FM54
Holden Ave. N12	207	299	DB50
Holden Ave. NW9	92	304	CQ60
Holden Clo., Dag.	236	309	EV62
Holden Pt. E15	121	307	ED65
Holden Rd. N12	207	299	DB50
Holden St. SW11	160	316	DG82
Holden Way, Upmin.	239	311	FR60
Holdenby Rd. SE4	181	325	DY85
Holdenhurst Ave. N12	219	305	DB52
Holder Clo. N3	219	305	DB52
Holderness Way SE27	273	324	DP92
Holdernesse Clo., Islw.	152	314	CG81
Holdernesse Rd. SW17	191	323	DF90
Holders Hill Ave. NW4	218	305	CX54
Holders Hill Circ. NW7	218	305	CY52
Holders Hill Cres. NW4	218	305	CX54
Holders Hill Dr. NW4	218	305	CX55
Holders Hill Gdns. NW4	218	305	CY54
Holders Hill Rd. NW4	218	305	CX54
Holders Hill Rd. NW7	218	305	CY53
Holdgate St. SE7	252	318	EK76
Holford Pl. WC1	35	316	DM69
Holford Rd. NW3	96	305	DC62
Holford St. WC1	36	316	DN69
Holgate Ave. SW11	175	323	DD83
Holgate Gdns., Dag.	237	309	FA65
Holgate Rd., Dag.	237	309	FA64
Holland Ave. SW20	269	322	CT95
Holland Ave., Sutt.	292	331	DA108
Holland Clo., Barn.	207	299	DD45
Holland Clo., Brom.	289	333	EF103
Holland Clo., Rom.	227	309	FC57
Holland Clo., Stan.	204	298	CH50
Holland Dr. SE23	197	325	DY90
Holland Gdns. W14	147	315	CY76
Holland Gro. SW9	162	316	DN80
Holland Pk. W8	147	315	CZ75
Holland Pk. W11	137	315	CY74
Holland Pk. Ave. W11	137	315	CY74
Holland Pk. Ave., Ilf.	225	308	ES58
Holland Pk. Gdns. W14	147	315	CY75
Holland Pk. Ms. W11	137	315	CZ74
Holland Pk. Rd. W14	147	315	CZ76
Holland Pas. N1	25	316	DQ67
Holland Pl. W8	64/5	315	DB75
Holland Rd. E6	244	318	EM67
Holland Rd. E15	131	317	EE69
Holland Rd. NW10	126	315	CU67
Holland Rd. SE25	287	333	DU99
Holland Rd. W14	147	315	CX75
Holland Rd., Wem.	107	304	CK65
Holland St. SE1	60/1	316	DP74
Holland St. W8	64	315	DA75
Holland Vil. Rd. W14	147	315	CY75
Holland Wk. N19	99	306	DK60
Holland Wk. W8	147	315	CZ75
Holland Wk., Stan.	204	298	CG50
Holland Way, Brom.	289	333	EF103
Hollands, The, Felt.	266	329	BX91
Hollands, The, Wor.Pk.	283	330	CT102
Hollar Rd. N16	101	306	DT62
Hollen St. W1	46	316	DK72
Holles Clo., Hmptn.	267	329	CA93
Holles St. W1	44/5	316	DH72
Holley Rd. W3	145	314	CS75
Hollickwood Ave. N12	219	305	DF51
Holliday Sq. SW11	175	323	DD83
Hollidge Way, Dag.	237	309	FB65
Hollies, The E11	224	308	EG57
Hollies, The N20	207	299	DD46
Hollies, The, Har.	216	304	CG56
Hollies Ave., Sid.	261	326	ET89
Hollies Clo. SW16	273	324	DN93
Hollies Clo., Twick.	259	321	CF89
Hollies End NW7	206	299	CV50
Hollies Rd. W5	142	314	CJ77
Hollies Way SW12	192	324	DG87
Holligrave Rd., Brom.	276	326	EG95
Hollingbourne Ave., Bexh.	254	319	EZ80
Hollingbourne Gdns. W13	132	314	CH71
Hollingbourne Rd. SE24	178	324	DQ85
Hollingsworth Rd., Croy.	295	333	DV107
Hollington Cres., N.Mal.	283	330	CT100
Hollington Rd. E6	244	318	EM69
Hollington Rd. N17	222	307	DU54
Hollingworth Clo., W.Mol.	266	329	BZ98
Hollingworth Rd., Orp.	290	334	EP101
Hollman Gdns. SW16	273	324	DP93
Hollow, The, Wdf.Grn.	211	301	EF49
Hollow Wk., Rich.	153	314	CL80
Holloway La., West Dr.	256	320	BK79
Holloway Rd. E6	244	318	EM69
Holloway Rd. E11	105	307	EE62
Holloway Rd. N7	99	306	DL62
Holloway Rd. N19	98	306	DJ61
Holloway St., Houns.	259	321	CB83
Hollowfield Wk., Nthlt.	232	313	BY65
Hollows, The, Brent.	153	314	CM79
Holly Ave., Stan.	216	304	CL54
Holly Bush Hill NW3	112	305	DC63
Holly Bush La., Hmptn.	266	329	BZ94
Holly Bush Steps NW3	112	305	DC63
Holly Bush Vale NW3	112	305	DC63
Holly Clo. NW10	109	304	CS66
Holly Clo., Felt.	266	329	BY92
Holly Clo., Wall.	293	332	DH108
Holly Cres., Beck.	288	333	DZ99
Holly Cres., Wdf.Grn.	223	307	ED52
Holly Dr. E4	211	301	EB45
Holly Dr., Brent.	152	314	CG79
Holly Fm. Rd., Sthl.	250	321	BY78
Holly Gdns., West Dr.	248	320	BM75
Holly Gro. NW9	92	304	CQ59
Holly Gro. SE15	163	316	DT82
Holly Gro., Pnr.	214	303	BY53
Holly Hedge Ter. SE13	183	325	ED85
Holly Hill N21	208	300	DM44
Holly Hill NW3	112	305	DC63
Holly Hill Rd., Belv.	255	319	FB78
Holly Hill Rd., Erith	255	319	FC78
Holly Lo. Gdns. N6	98	306	DG60
Holly Ms. SW10	77	315	DC78
Holly Mt. NW3	112	305	DC63
Holly Pk. N3	218	305	CZ55
Holly Pk. N4	99	306	DL59
Holly Pk. Est. N4	99	306	DM59
Holly Pk. Gdns. N3	219	305	DA55
Holly Pk. Rd. N11	208	300	DG50
Holly Pk. Rd. W7	243	313	CF74
Holly Rd. E11	105	307	EF59
Holly Rd. W4	145	314	CR77
Holly Rd., Enf.	203	301	DX36
Holly Rd., Hmptn.	267	329	CC93
Holly Rd., Houns.	259	321	CB84
Holly Rd., Twick.	184	322	CG88
Holly St. E8	117	306	DT65
Holly St. Est. E8	117	306	DT66
Holly Ter. N20	207	299	DC47
Holly Tree Ave., Swan.	279	327	FE96
Holly Vw. Clo. NW4	218	305	CU58
Holly Wk. NW3	112	305	DC63
Holly Wk., Enf.	202	300	DQ41
Holly Wk., Rich.	153	314	CL82
Holly Way, Mitch.	272	324	DK98
Hollybank Clo., Hmptn.	267	329	CA92
Hollyberry La. NW3	112	305	DC63
Hollybrake Clo., Chis.	277	326	ER94
Hollybush Clo. E11	224	308	EG57
Hollybush Clo., Har.	215	303	CE53
Hollybush Gdns. E2	128	317	DV69
Hollybush Hill E11	105	307	EF59
Hollybush Pl. E2	128	317	DV69
Hollybush Rd., Kings.T.	268	322	CL92
Hollybush St. E13	244	318	EH69
Hollybush Wk. SW9	178	324	DP84
Hollycroft Ave. NW3	96	305	DA62
Hollycroft Ave., Wem.	91	304	CM61
Hollycroft Clo., West Dr.	257	320	BN79
Hollycroft Gdns., West Dr.	257	320	BN79
Hollydale Dr., Brom.	290	334	EM104
Hollydale Rd. SE15	164	317	DW81
Hollydene SE15	164	317	DV81
Hollydown Way E11	105	307	ED62
Hollyfield Ave. N11	207	299	DF50
Hollyfield Rd., Surb.	282	330	CM101
Hollymead, Cars.	285	331	DF104
Hollymount Clo. SE10	166	317	EC81
Hollytree Clo. SW19	189	323	CX88
Hollywood Gdns., Hayes	242	313	BV72
Hollywood Ms. SW10	158	315	DC79
Hollywood Rd. E4	210	301	DY50
Hollywood Rd. SW10	158	315	DC79
Hollywood Way, Wdf.Grn.	223	307	ED52
Holm Gro., Uxb.	241	312	BN66
Holm Oak Clo. SW15	173	323	CZ86
Holm Oak Ms. SW4	177	324	DL85
Holm Wk. SE3	252	318	EG82
Holman Rd. SW11	159	315	DD82
Holman Rd., Epsom	283	330	CQ106
Holmbank Dr., Shep.	281	328	BS98
Holmbridge Gdns., Enf.	203	301	DX42
Holmbrook Dr. NW4	218	305	CX57
Holmbury Ct. SW17	191	323	DF90
Holmbury Ct. SW19	271	323	DE94
Holmbury Gdns., Hayes	249	312	BT74
Holmbury Pk., Brom.	276	326	EL94
Holmbury Vw. E5	102	307	DV60
Holmbush Rd. SW15	173	323	CY86
Holmcote Gdns. N5	116	306	DQ64
Holmcroft Way, Brom.	290	334	EM99
Holmdale Gdns. NW4	218	305	CX57
Holmdale Rd. NW6	112	305	DA64
Holmdale Rd., Chis.	277	326	EQ92
Holmdale Ter. N15	101	306	DS59
Holmdene Ave. NW7	218	305	CU51
Holmdene Ave. SE24	178	324	DQ85
Holmdene Ave., Har.	215	303	CB55
Holmdene Clo., Beck.	275	325	EC96
Holme Lacey Rd. SE12	183	325	EF86
Holme Rd. E6	244	318	EL67
Holme Rd., Horn.	239	311	FN60
Holme Way, Stan.	215	303	CF51
Holmead Rd. SW6	158	315	DB80
Holmefield Ct. NW3	113	305	DE65
Holmes Ave. E17	222	307	DZ55
Holmes Ave. NW7	206	299	CY50
Holmes Pl. SW10	158	315	DC79
Holmes Rd. NW5	114	306	DH65
Holmes Rd. SW19	271	323	DC94
Holmes Rd., Twick.	259	321	CF89
Holmes Ter. SE1	72	316	DN75
Holmesdale, Wal.Cr.	203	301	DW35
Holmesdale Ave. SW14	170	322	CP83
Holmesdale Clo. SE25	273	324	DT97
Holmesdale Rd. N6	98	306	DH59
Holmesdale Rd. SE25	287	332	DR99
Holmesdale Rd., Bexh.	254	319	EX82
Holmesdale Rd., Croy.	287	332	DR99
Holmesdale Rd., Rich.	153	314	CM81
Holmesdale Rd., Tedd.	268	322	CJ94
Holmesley Rd. SE23	181	325	DY86
Holmewood Gdns. SW2	193	324	DM87
Holmewood Rd. SE25	273	324	DS97
Holmewood Rd. SW2	193	324	DL87
Holmfield Ave. NW4	218	305	CX57
Holmhurst Rd., Belv.	255	319	FB78
Holmleigh Rd. N16	101	306	DS60
Holmleigh Rd. Est. N16	101	306	DT60
Holms St. E2	128	317	DU68
Holmsdale Gro., Bexh.	255	319	FE82
Holmshaw Clo. SE26	274	325	DY91
Holmside Rd. SW12	176	324	DG86
Holmsley Clo., N.Mal.	283	330	CT100
Holmstall Ave., Edg.	217	304	CQ55
Holmwood Ave., S.Croy.	295	332	DT113
Holmwood Clo., Har.	215	303	CC55
Holmwood Clo., Nthlt.	233	313	CB65
Holmwood Clo., Sutt.	292	331	CX109
Holmwood Gdns. N3	219	305	DA54
Holmwood Gdns., Wall.	293	332	DH107
Holmwood Gro. NW7	205	298	CR50
Holmwood Rd., Chess.	282	330	CK106
Holmwood Rd., Enf.	203	301	DX36
Holmwood Rd., Ilf.	235	308	ES61
Holmwood Rd., Sutt.	292	331	CW110
Holmwood Vil. SE7	252	318	EG78
Holne Chase N2	219	305	DC58
Holne Chase, Mord.	284	331	CZ100
Holness Rd. E15	121	307	EF65
Holroyd Rd. SW15	172	323	CW84
Holstein Way, Erith	254	319	EX76
Holstock Rd., Ilf.	235	308	EQ61
Holsworth Clo., Har.	215	303	CC57
Holsworthy Sq. WC1	35	316	DM70
Holsworthy Way, Chess.	282	330	CJ106
Holt, The, Ilf.	225	308	EQ51
Holt, The, Wall.	286	332	DJ105
Holt Clo. N10	220	306	DG56
Holt Clo. SE28	246	319	EV73
Holt Ct. E15	120	307	EC64
Holt Rd. E16	244	318	EL74
Holt Rd., Wem.	90	304	CH62
Holton St. E1	129	317	DX70
Holtwhite Ave., Enf.	202	300	DQ40
Holtwhites Hill, Enf.	202	300	DP39
Holwell Pl., Pnr.	214	303	BY56
Holwood Pk. Ave., Orp.	290	334	EM105
Holwood Pl. SW4	177	324	DK84
Holybourne Ave. SW15	188	323	CU87
Holyhead Clo. E3	130	317	EA69
Holyhead Clo. E6	244	318	EM71
Holyoak Rd. SE11	84/5	316	DP77
Holyoake Ct. SE16	149	317	DZ75
Holyoake Wk. N2	219	305	DC55
Holyoake Wk. W5	122	314	CJ70
Holyport Rd. SW6	156	315	CW80
Holyrood Ave., Har.	232	313	BY63
Holyrood Gdns., Edg.	217	304	CP55
Holyrood Rd., Barn.	207	299	DC44
Holyrood St. SE1	62/3	316	DS74
Holywell Clo. SE3	252	318	EG79
Holywell Clo., Stai.	264	320	BL88
Holywell La. EC2	38/9	316	DS70
Holywell Row EC2	38/9	316	DS70
Holywell Way, Stai.	264	320	BL88
Home Clo., Cars.	285	331	DF103
Home Clo., Nthlt.	242	313	BZ69
Home Ct., Felt.	258	321	BU88
Home Fm. Clo., Shep.	281	328	BS98
Home Fm. Rd., Rick.	212	302	BM49
Home Gdns., Dag.	237	309	FC62
Home Hill, Swan.	279	327	FF94
Home Lea, Orp.	291	334	ET106
Home Mead, Stan.	216	304	CJ53
Home Pk. Rd. SW19	270	323	CZ91
Home Pk. Wk., Kings.T.	268	322	CK98
Home Rd. SW11	159	315	DE82
Homecroft Rd. N22	221	306	DP53
Homecroft Rd. SE26	274	325	DW92
Homefarm Rd. W7	243	313	CE72
Homefield Ave., Ilf.	225	308	ES57
Homefield Clo. NW10	108	304	CQ65
Homefield Clo., Hayes	242	313	BX70
Homefield Clo., Orp.	278	327	EV98
Homefield Clo., Swan.	279	327	FF97
Homefield Gdns. N2	219	305	DD55
Homefield Gdns., Mitch.	271	323	DC96
Homefield Ms., Beck.	275	325	EA95
Homefield Pk., Sutt.	292	331	DB107
Homefield Ri., Orp.	291	335	EU102
Homefield Rd. SW19	270	323	CX93
Homefield Rd. W4	145	314	CT78
Homefield Rd., Brom.	276	326	EJ95
Homefield Rd., Edg.	217	304	CR51
Homefield Rd., Wem.	106	304	CG63
Homefield St. N1	26/7	316	DS68
Homeland Dr., Sutt.	292	331	DB109
Homelands Dr. SE19	273	324	DS94
Homeleigh Rd. SE15	181	325	DX85
Homemead SW12	192	324	DH89
Homemead Rd., Brom.	290	334	EM99
Homemead Rd., Croy.	288	333	DW100
Homer Clo., Bexh.	255	319	FC81
Homer Dr. E14	150	317	EA77
Homer Rd. E9	119	307	DY65
Homer Rd., Croy.	288	333	DX100
Homer Row W1	42/3	315	DE71
Homer St. W1	42/3	315	DE71
Homersham Rd., Kings.T.	269	322	CN96
Homerton Gro. E9	119	307	DX64
Homerton High St. E9	118	307	DW64
Homerton Rd. E9	119	307	DY64
Homerton Row E9	118	307	DW64
Homerton Ter. E9	118	307	DW65
Homesdale Clo. E11	224	308	EG57
Homesdale Rd., Brom.	276	326	EJ98
Homesdale Rd., Orp.	291	334	ES101
Homesfield NW11	219	305	DA57
Homestall Rd. SE22	180	325	DW85
Homestead, The N11	208	300	DH49
Homestead Paddock N14	208	300	DH43
Homestead Pk. NW2	93	304	CT62
Homestead Rd. SW6	157	315	CZ80
Homestead Rd., Dag.	236	309	EZ61
Homestead Rd., Stai.	264	328	BH93
Homewaters Ave., Sun.	281	328	BT95
Homeway, Rom.	229	311	FP51
Homewillow Clo. N21	209	300	DP44
Homewood Clo., Hmptn.	266	329	BZ93
Homewood Cres., Chis.	277	326	ES93
Honduras St. EC1	37	316	DQ70
Honey Clo., Dag.	237	309	FB65
Honey Hill, Uxb.	240	312	BM66
Honey La. EC2	49	316	DQ72
Honeybourne Rd. NW6	112	305	DB64
Honeybourne Way, Orp.	291	334	ER102
Honeybrook Rd. SW12	192	324	DJ87
Honeycroft Hill, Uxb.	240	312	BL66
Honeyden Rd., Sid.	278	327	EY93
Honeyman Clo. NW6	111	305	CX66
Honeypot Clo. NW9	216	304	CM56
Honeypot La. NW9	216	304	CL55
Honeypot La., Stan.	216	304	CL55
Honeysett Rd. N17	221	306	DT54
Honeysuckle Clo., Rom.	228	310	FK51
Honeysuckle Clo., Sthl.	242	313	BY73
Honeysuckle Gdns., Croy.	288	333	DX102
Honeywell Rd. SW11	175	323	DE86
Honeywood Rd. NW10	125	314	CT68
Honeywood Rd., Islw.	168	322	CG84
Honeywood Wk., Cars.	285	331	DF105
Honister Clo., Stan.	216	304	CH53
Honister Gdns., Stan.	216	304	CH53
Honister Hts., Pur.	295	332	DR114
Honister Pl., Stan.	216	304	CH53
Honiton Rd. NW6	127	315	CZ68
Honiton Rd., Rom.	227	309	FD58
Honiton Rd., Well.	253	318	ET82
Honley Rd. SE6	198	325	EB87
Honnor Rd., Stai.	264	328	BK94
Honor Oak Pk. SE23	181	325	DX86
Honor Oak Ri. SE23	180	325	DW86
Honor Oak Rd. SE23	196	325	DW88
Hood Ave. N14	208	300	DH44
Hood Ave. SW14	170	322	CQ85
Hood Ave., Orp.	291	335	EV99
Hood Clo., Croy.	286	332	DP102
Hood Ct. EC4	48	316	DN72
Hood Rd. SW20	269	322	CT94
Hood Rd., Rain.	247	319	FE68
Hood Wk., Rom.	227	309	FB53
Hoodcote Gdns. N21	209	300	DP45
Hook, The, Barn.	207	299	DD44
Hook Fm. Rd., Brom.	290	334	EK99
Hook Gate, Enf.	203	301	DV36
Hook Grn. La., Dart.	263	327	FF90
Hook Hill, S.Croy.	295	332	DS110
Hook La., Well.	261	326	ET84
Hook Ri. N., Surb.	282	330	CN104
Hook Ri. S., Surb.	282	330	CN104
Hook Rd., Chess.	282	330	CK106
Hook Rd., Surb.	282	330	CL104
Hook Wk., Edg.	217	304	CQ51
Hookers Rd. E17	222	307	DX55
Hooking Grn., Har.	215	303	CB57
Hooks Clo. SE15	164	317	DV81
Hooks Hall Dr., Dag.	237	309	FC62
Hooks Way SE22	196	325	DU88
Hookstone Way, Wdf.Grn.	224	308	EK52
Hoop La. NW11	95	305	CZ59
Hooper Rd. E16	244	318	EG72
Hooper Sq. E1	138	317	DU73
Hooper St. E1	138	317	DU73
Hooper's Ct. SW3	67	315	DF75
Hop Gdns. WC2	58/9	316	DL73
Hope Clo. N1	116	306	DQ65
Hope Clo. SE12	260	326	EH90
Hope Clo., Sutt.	285	331	DC106
Hope Clo., Wdf.Grn.	224	308	EJ51
Hope Pk., Brom.	275	325	EF94
Hope St. SW11	175	323	DD83
Hopedale Rd. SE7	252	318	EH79
Hopefield Ave. NW6	127	315	CY68
Hopes Clo., Houns.	251	321	CA79
Hopetown St. E1	51	316	DT71
Hopewell St. SE5	163	316	DR80
Hopewell Yd. SE5	163	316	DR80
Hopgood St. W12	136	315	CW74
Hopkins Clo. N10	220	306	DG52
Hopkins Clo., Rom.	228	310	FJ55
Hopkins Ms. E15	131	317	EF67
Hopkins St. W1	45	316	DJ72
Hopkinsons Pl. NW1	20	316	DG67
Hoppers Rd. N13	209	300	DN47
Hoppers Rd. N21	209	300	DN47
Hoppett Rd. E4	211	301	EE47
Hopping La. N1	116	306	DP65
Hoppingwood Ave., N.Mal.	269	322	CS97
Hoppner Rd., Hayes	241	312	BQ68
Hopton Gdns. SE1	60/1	316	DP74
Hopton Gdns., N.Mal.	283	331	CU100
Hopton Rd. SW16	272	324	DL92
Hopton St. SE1	60/1	316	DP74
Hopwood Clo. SW17	190	323	DC90
Hopwood Rd. SE17	163	316	DR79
Hopwood Wk. E8	118	307	DU66
Horace Ave., Rom.	237	309	FC60
Horace Rd. E7	234	308	EH63
Horace Rd., Ilf.	225	308	EQ55
Horace Rd., Kings.T.	268	322	CM97
Horatio Ct. SE16	138	317	DW74
Horatio Pl. E14	150	317	EC75
Horatio Pl. SW19	271	323	DA94
Horatio St. E2	128	317	DU68
Horatius Way, Croy.	286	332	DM106
Horbury Cres. W11	52	315	DA73
Horbury Ms. W11	137	315	CZ73
Horder Rd. SW6	157	315	CY81
Hordle Prom. E. SE15	163	316	DT80
Hordle Prom. N. SE15	163	316	DT80
Hordle Prom. S. SE15	163	316	DT80
Hordle Prom. W. SE15	163	316	DS80
Horizon Way SE7	252	318	EH77
Horley Clo., Bexh.	263	327	FA85
Horley Rd. SE9	276	326	EL91
Hormead Rd. W9	127	315	CZ70
Horn La. SE10	252	318	EG77
Horn La. W3	134	314	CQ74
Horn La., Bexh.	255	319	FC82
Horn La., Wdf.Grn.	224	308	EG51
Horn Pk. Clo. SE12	260	326	EH85
Horn Pk. La. SE12	260	326	EH85
Hornbeam Ave., Upmin.	239	311	FN63
Hornbeam Clo. SE11	84	316	DN77
Hornbeam Clo., Nthlt.	232	313	BZ64
Hornbeam Cres., Brent.	152	314	CH80
Hornbeam Gro. E4	211	301	EE48
Hornbeam La. E4	211	301	EE43
Hornbeam La., Bexh.	255	319	FC82
Hornbeam Rd., Hayes	242	313	BW71
Hornbeam Ter., Cars.	285	331	DE102
Hornbeam Twr. E11	105	307	ED62
Hornbeam Wk., Rich.	185	322	CM89
Hornbeam Way, Brom.	290	334	EN100
Hornbeams Ave., Enf.	203	301	DW35
Hornbeams Ri. N11	220	306	DG51
Hornbill Clo., Uxb.	248	312	BK72
Hornblower Clo. SE16	149	317	DY77
Hornbuckle Clo., Har.	233	313	CD61
Hornby Clo. NW3	113	305	DD66
Horncastle Clo. SE12	260	326	EG87
Horncastle Rd. SE12	260	326	EG87
Hornchurch Clo., Kings.T.	268	322	CK91
Hornchurch Rd., Horn.	237	309	FF60
Horndean Clo. SW15	188	323	CU88
Horndon Clo., Rom.	227	309	FC53
Horndon Grn., Rom.	227	309	FC53
Horndon Rd., Rom.	227	309	FC53
Horne Rd., Shep.	280	328	BM98
Horne Way SW15	156	315	CW82
Horner La., Mitch.	271	323	DD96
Hornfair Rd. SE7	252	318	EJ79
Hornford Way, Rom.	237	309	FE59
Horniman Dr. SE23	196	325	DV88
Horning Clo. SE9	276	326	EL91
Hornminster Glen, Horn.	239	311	FN61
Horns End, Pnr.	214	303	BW56
Horns Rd., Ilf.	225	308	ER58
Hornsey La. N6	98	306	DH60
Hornsey La. N19	98	306	DH60
Hornsey La. Est. N19	99	306	DK59
Hornsey La. Gdns. N6	98	306	DJ59
Hornsey Pk. Rd. N8	220	306	DM55
Hornsey Ri. N19	99	306	DK59
Hornsey Ri. Gdns. N19	99	306	DK59
Hornsey Rd. N7	99	306	DM62
Hornsey Rd. N19	99	306	DL60
Hornsey St. N7	115	306	DM64
Hornshay St. SE15	164	317	DW79
Hornton Pl. W8	64/5	315	DB75
Hornton St. W8	64	315	DA75
Horsa Clo., Wall.	294	332	DL108
Horsa Rd. SE12	260	326	EJ87
Horsa Rd., Erith	255	319	FB80
Horse and Dolphin Yd. W1	58	316	DK73
Horse Fair, Kings.T.	268	322	CK96
Horse Guards Ave. SW1	58/9	316	DL74
Horse Guards Rd. SW1	58	316	DK74
Horse Leaze E6	245	318	EN72
Horse Ride SW1	58	316	DK74
Horse Ride, Cars.	293	331	DF112
Horse Rd. E7	234	308	EH62
Horse Shoe Cres., Nthlt.	243	313	CA68
Horse Shoe Yd. W1	56/7	316	DH73
Horse Yd. N1	24/5	316	DP67
Horsebridges Clo., Dag.	246	319	EY67
Horsecroft Clo., Orp.	291	335	EV102
Horsecroft Rd., Edg.	217	304	CR52
Horseferry Pl. SE10	166	317	EC79
Horseferry Rd. E14	139	317	DX73
Horseferry Rd. SW1	82	316	DK77
Horsell Ct., Cher.	280	328	BH101
Horsell Rd. N5	116	306	DN64
Horsell Rd., Orp.	278	327	EV95
Horselydown La. SE1	75	316	DT75
Horsenden Ave., Grnf.	233	313	CE64
Horsenden Cres., Grnf.	233	313	CF64
Horsenden La. N., Grnf.	233	313	CF65
Horsenden La. S., Grnf.	122	314	CG67
Horseshoe, The, Couls.	294	332	DK113
Horseshoe Clo. E14	150	317	EC78
Horseshoe Clo. NW2	94	305	CV61
Horseshoe Grn., Sutt.	284	331	DB103
Horseshoe La. N20	206	299	CX46
Horseshoe La., Enf.	202	300	DQ41
Horsfeld Gdns. SE9	260	326	EL85
Horsfeld Rd. SE9	260	326	EK85
Horsford Rd. SW2	177	324	DM85
Horsham Ave. N12	207	299	DE50
Horsham Rd., Bexh.	263	327	FA86
Horsham Rd., Felt.	257	320	BQ86
Horsley Dr., Kings.T.	268	322	CK92
Horsley Rd. E4	211	301	EC47
Horsley Rd., Brom.	276	326	EH95
Horsley St. SE17	163	316	DR79
Horsmonden Clo., Orp.	291	334	ET101
Horsmonden Rd. SE4	181	325	DZ85
Hortensia Rd. SW10	158	315	DC80
Horticultural Pl. W4	145	314	CR78
Horton Ave. NW2	111	305	CY63
Horton Bri. Rd., West Dr.	248	312	BM74
Horton Clo., West Dr.	248	312	BM74
Horton Ind. Pk., West Dr.	248	312	BM74
Horton Rd. E8	118	307	DV65
Horton Rd., Stai.	256	320	BG85
Horton Rd., West Dr.	248	312	BL74
Horton St. SE13	182	325	EB83
Horton Way, Croy.	288	333	DX99
Hortus Rd. E4	211	301	EC47
Hortus Rd., Sthl.	250	321	BZ75
Hosack Rd. SW17	191	323	DF88
Hoser Ave. SE12	260	326	EG89
Hosier La. EC1	48/9	316	DP71
Hoskins Clo. E16	244	318	EJ72
Hoskins Clo., Hayes	249	320	BT78
Hoskins St. SE10	151	317	ED78
Hospital Bri. Rd., Twick.	259	321	CB87
Hospital La., Islw.	259	321	CF85
Hospital Rd. E9	119	307	DX64
Hospital Rd., Houns.	259	321	CA83
Hotham Clo., W.Mol.	267	329	CA97
Hotham Rd. SW15	172	323	CW83
Hotham Rd. SW19	271	323	DC94
Hotham Rd. Ms. SW19	271	323	DC94
Hotham St. E15	131	317	EE67
Hothfield Pl. SE16	148	317	DW76
Hotspur Rd., Nthlt.	243	313	CA68
Hotspur St. SE11	84	316	DN78
Houblon Rd., Rich.	169	322	CL85
Houghton Clo. E8	117	306	DT65
Houghton Clo., Hmptn.	266	329	BY93
Houghton Rd. N15	221	306	DT57
Houghton St. WC2	47	316	DM72
Houlder Cres., Croy.	294	332	DP107
Houndsden Rd. N21	208	300	DM44
Houndsditch EC3	50/1	316	DS72
Houndsfield Rd. N9	210	301	DV45
Hounslow Ave., Houns.	259	321	CB85
Hounslow Gdns., Houns.	259	321	CB85
Hounslow Rd. (Feltham), Felt.	258	321	BV88
Hounslow Rd. (Hanworth), Felt.	266	329	BX91
Hounslow Rd., Twick.	259	321	CB86
Houseman Way SE5	163	316	DR80
Houston Rd. SE23	197	325	DY89
Hove Ave. E17	222	307	DZ57
Hove Gdns., Sutt.	284	331	DB102
Hoveden Rd. NW2	111	305	CY64
Hoveton Rd. SE28	246	319	EW72
Howard Ave., Bex.	262	327	EW88
Howard Clo. N11	208	300	DG47
Howard Clo. NW2	111	305	CY63
Howard Clo. W3	134	314	CP72
Howard Clo., Hmptn.	267	329	CC93
Howard Clo., Sun.	265	328	BT93
Howard Ms. N5	116	306	DP63

Howard Pl. SW1	69	316	DJ76
Howard Rd. E6	244	318	EM68
Howard Rd. E11	105	307	EE62
Howard Rd. E17	223	307	EA55
Howard Rd. N15	221	306	DS58
Howard Rd. N16	117	306	DR63
Howard Rd. NW2	111	305	CX63
Howard Rd. SE20	274	325	DW95
Howard Rd. SE25	287	333	DU99
Howard Rd., Bark.	245	318	ER67
Howard Rd., Brom.	276	326	EG94
Howard Rd., Ilf.	235	308	EP63
Howard Rd., Islw.	259	321	CF83
Howard Rd., N.Mal.	269	322	CS97
Howard Rd., Sthl.	243	313	CB72
Howard Rd., Surb.	282	330	CM100
Howard Rd., Upmin.	239	311	FQ61
Howard Wk. N2	219	305	DC56
Howard Way, Barn.	206	299	CX43
Howards Clo., Pnr.	214	303	BV54
Howards Crest Clo., Beck.	275	325	EC96
Howards La. SW15	172	323	CV85
Howards Rd. E13	244	318	EG69
Howarth Ct. E15	120	307	EC64
Howarth Rd. SE2	254	319	EU78
Howberry Clo., Edg.	216	304	CK51
Howberry Rd., Edg.	216	304	CK51
Howberry Rd., Stan.	216	304	CK51
Howberry Rd., Th.Hth.	273	324	DR95
Howbury Rd. SE15	180	325	DW83
Howcroft Cres. N3	219	305	DA52
Howcroft La., Grnf.	243	313	CD69
Howden Clo. SE28	246	319	EX73
Howden Rd. SE25	273	324	DT96
Howden St. SE15	180	325	DU83
Howe Clo., Rom.	227	309	FA53
Howell Clo., Rom.	226	309	EX57
Howell Hill Clo., Epsom	292	331	CW111
Howell Hill Gro., Epsom	292	331	CW110
Howell Wk. SE1	84/5	316	DP77
Howes Clo. N3	219	305	DA55
Howgate Rd. SW14	171	322	CR83
Howick Pl. SW1	69	316	DJ76
Howie St. SW11	159	315	DE80
Howitt Rd. NW3	113	305	DE65
Howland Est. SE16	148	317	DW76
Howland Ms. E. W1	45	316	DJ71
Howland St. W1	45	316	DJ71
Howland Way SE16	149	317	DY75
Howletts La., Ruis.	231	302	BQ57
Howletts Rd. SE24	178	324	DQ86
Howley Pl. W2	41	315	DC71
Howley Rd., Croy.	286	332	DP104
Hows Clo., Uxb.	240	312	BJ67
Hows Rd., Uxb.	240	312	BJ67
Hows St. E2	27	316	DT68
Howsman Rd. SW13	156	315	CU79
Howson Rd. SE4	181	325	DY84
Howson Ter., Rich.	169	322	CL86
Hoxton Mkt. N1	38/9	316	DS69
Hoxton Sq. N1	38/9	316	DS69
Hoxton St. N1	26/7	316	DS67
Hoy St. E16	141	317	EF72
Hoylake Cres., Uxb.	231	312	BN61
Hoylake Gdns., Mitch.	272	324	DJ97
Hoylake Gdns., Rom.	229	311	FN52
Hoylake Gdns., Ruis.	232	313	BV60
Hoylake Rd. W3	135	314	CS72
Hoyland Clo. SE15	164	317	DV80
Hoyle Rd. SW17	271	323	DE92
Hubbard Rd. SE27	273	324	DQ91
Hubbard St. E15	131	317	EE67
Hubbards Chase, Horn.	229	311	FN57
Hubbards Clo., Horn.	229	311	FN57
Hubbinet Ind. Est., Rom.	227	309	FC55
Hubert Gro. SW9	177	324	DL83
Hubert Rd. E6	244	318	EK69
Hubert Rd., Rain.	247	319	FF69
Hucknall Clo., Rom.	228	311	FM51
Huddart St. E3	139	317	DZ71
Huddleston Clo. E2	128	317	DW68
Huddleston Rd. N7	98	306	DJ62
Huddlestone Rd. E7	121	307	EF63
Huddlestone Rd. NW2	110	305	CV65
Hudson Ct. SW19	271	323	DB94
Hudson Pl. SE18	253	318	EQ78
Hudson Rd., Bexh.	254	319	EZ82
Hudson Rd., Hayes	257	320	BR79
Hudson's Pl. SW1	81	316	DJ77
Huggin Ct. EC4	61	316	DQ73
Huggin Hill EC4	61	316	DQ73
Huggins Pl. SW2	193	324	DM88
Hugh Dalton Ave. SW6	157	315	CZ79
Hugh Gaitskell Clo. SW6	157	315	CZ79
Hugh Ms. SW1	80/1	316	DH77
Hugh Pl. SW1	82	316	DK77
Hugh St. SW1	80/1	316	DH77
Hughan Rd. E15	121	307	ED64
Hughenden Ave., Har.	216	304	CH57
Hughenden Gdns., Nthlt.	242	313	BW69
Hughenden Rd., Wor.Pk.	283	331	CU101
Hughendon Ter. E15	120	307	EC63
Hughes Rd., Ashf.	265	328	BQ94
Hughes Rd., Hayes	242	313	BU73
Hughes Wk., Croy.	287	332	DQ101
Hugo Gdns., Rain.	237	309	FF65
Hugo Rd. N19	114	306	DJ63
Hugon Rd. SW6	174	323	DB83
Huguenot Pl. E1	51	316	DT71
Huguenot Pl. SW18	174	323	DC85
Huguenot Sq. SE15	180	325	DV83
Hull Clo. SE16	149	317	DX75
Hull Clo., Sutt.	292	331	DB110
Hull St. EC1	37	316	DQ69
Hullbridge Ms. N1	26	316	DR67
Hulse Ave., Bark.	235	308	ER65
Hulse Ave., Rom.	227	309	FB53
Hulse Ter., Ilf.	235	308	EQ64
Hulverston Clo., Sutt.	292	331	DB110
Humber Dr. W10	127	315	CX70
Humber Dr., Upmin.	229	311	FR58
Humber Rd. NW2	94	305	CV61
Humber Rd. SE3	167	317	EF79
Humberstone Rd. E13	244	318	EJ69
Humberton Clo. E9	119	307	DY64
Humbolt Rd. W6	157	315	CY79
Hume Ter. E16	244	318	EJ72
Hume Way, Ruis.	214	303	BU58
Humes Ave. W7	251	321	CE76
Humphrey Clo., Ilf.	224	308	EM53
Humphrey St. SE1	87	316	DT78
Humphries Clo., Dag.	236	309	EZ63
Hundred Acre NW9	217	304	CT54
Hungerdown E4	211	301	EC46
Hungerford Bri. SE1	59	316	DM74
Hungerford Bri. WC2	59	316	DM74
Hungerford La. WC2	58/9	316	DL74
Hungerford Rd. N7	115	306	DK65
Hungerford St. E1	138	317	DV72
Hunsdon Clo., Dag.	236	309	EY65
Hunsdon Rd. SE14	165	317	DX80
Hunslett St. E2	128	317	DW68
Hunston Rd., Mord.	284	331	DB102
Hunt Rd., Sthl.	251	321	CA76
Hunt St. W11	137	315	CX74
Hunt Way SE22	196	325	DU88
Hunter Clo. SE1	74	316	DR76
Hunter Clo. SW12	192	324	DG88
Hunter Clo., Borwd.	205	298	CQ43
Hunter Dr., Horn.	238	310	FJ63
Hunter Ho., Felt.	258	321	BU88
Hunter Rd. SW20	270	323	CW95
Hunter Rd., Ilf.	235	308	EP64
Hunter Rd., Th.Hth.	273	324	DR97
Hunter St. WC1	34/5	316	DL70
Hunter Wk. E13	244	318	EG67
Hunter Wk., Borwd.	205	298	CQ43
Hunters, The, Beck.	275	325	EC95
Hunters Clo., Bex.	263	327	FE90
Hunters Ct., Rich.	169	322	CK85
Hunters Gro., Har.	216	304	CJ56
Hunters Gro., Hayes	242	313	BU74
Hunters Gro., Orp.	290	334	EP105
Hunters Hall Rd., Dag.	237	309	FA63
Hunters Hill, Ruis.	232	313	BW62
Hunters Meadow SE19	273	324	DS91
Hunters Rd., Chess.	282	330	CL104
Hunters Sq., Dag.	237	309	FA63

Hunters Way, Croy.	287	332	DS105
Hunters Way, Enf.	202	300	DN39
Hunting Gate Clo., Enf.	202	300	DN41
Hunting Gate Ms., Sutt.	284	331	DB104
Hunting Gate Ms., Twick.	259	321	CE88
Huntingdon Clo., Mitch.	272	324	DL98
Huntingdon Gdns. W4	154	314	CQ80
Huntingdon Gdns., Wor.Pk.	284	331	CW104
Huntingdon Rd. N2	219	305	DE55
Huntingdon Rd. N9	210	301	DW46
Huntingdon St. E16	141	317	EF72
Huntingdon St. N1	115	306	DM66
Huntingfield Rd. SW15	172	323	CU84
Huntings Rd., Dag.	237	309	FA65
Huntley Dr. N3	219	305	DA51
Huntley St. WC1	33	316	DJ70
Huntley Way SW20	270	323	CU96
Huntly Rd. SE25	273	324	DS98
Hunton St. E1	138	317	DU71
Hunt's Clo. SE3	252	318	EG82
Hunt's Ct. WC2	58	316	DK73
Hunts La. E15	130	317	EC68
Hunts Mead, Enf.	203	301	DX41
Hunts Mead Clo., Chis.	276	326	EM94
Hunts Slip Rd. SE21	195	324	DS90
Huntsman Rd., Ilf.	226	309	EU51
Huntsman St. SE17	86/7	316	DS77
Huntsmans Clo., Felt.	266	329	BV91
Huntsmans Dr., Upmin.	239	311	FQ64
Huntsmoor Rd., Epsom	283	330	CR106
Huntspill St. SW17	190	323	DC90
Huntsworth Ms. NW1	31	315	DF70
Hurley Cres. SE16	149	317	DX75
Hurley Rd., Grnf.	243	313	CB72
Hurlingham Ct. SW6	173	323	CZ83
Hurlingham Gdns. SW6	173	323	CZ83
Hurlingham Rd. SW6	157	315	CZ82
Hurlingham Rd., Bexh.	254	319	EZ80
Hurlingham Sq. SW6	174	323	DB83
Hurlock St. N5	100	306	DP62
Hurlstone Rd. SE25	287	332	DR99
Hurn Ct. Rd., Houns.	258	321	BX82
Hurnford Clo., S.Croy.	295	332	DS110
Huron Rd. SW17	192	324	DG89
Hurren Clo. SE3	183	325	EE83
Hurry Clo. E15	121	307	EE66
Hurst Ave. E4	211	301	EA49
Hurst Ave. N6	220	306	DJ58
Hurst Clo. E4	211	301	EA48
Hurst Clo. NW11	219	305	DB58
Hurst Clo., Brom.	289	333	EF102
Hurst Clo., Chess.	282	330	CN106
Hurst Clo., Nthlt.	232	313	BZ65
Hurst Est. SE2	254	319	EX78
Hurst Gro., Walt.	281	328	BT102
Hurst La. SE2	254	319	EX78
Hurst La., E.Mol.	267	329	CC98
Hurst Pk. Ave., Horn.	238	311	FL63
Hurst Pl., Nthwd.	213	302	BP53
Hurst Rd. E17	223	307	EB55
Hurst Rd. N21	209	300	DN46
Hurst Rd., Bex.	262	327	EW88
Hurst Rd., Croy.	287	332	DR106
Hurst Rd., E.Mol.	267	329	CA97
Hurst Rd., Erith	255	319	FC81
Hurst Rd., Sid.	262	327	EU89
Hurst Rd., W.Mol.	267	329	CA97
Hurst Springs, Bex.	262	327	EY88
Hurst St. SE24	178	324	DP86
Hurst Vw. Rd., S.Croy.	295	332	DS108
Hurst Way, S.Croy.	295	332	DS107
Hurstbourne Gdns., Bark.	235	308	ES65
Hurstbourne Rd. SE23	197	325	DY88
Hurstcourt Rd., Sutt.	284	331	DB102
Hurstdene Ave., Brom.	289	333	EF102
Hurstdene Ave., Stai.	264	328	BH93
Hurstdene Gdns. N15	101	306	DS59
Hurstfield, Brom.	289	334	EG99
Hurstfield Cres., Hayes	241	312	BS70
Hurstfield Rd., W.Mol.	267	329	CA97
Hurstlands Clo., Horn.	238	310	FJ59
Hurstleigh Gdns., Ilf.	224	308	EM53
Hurstmead Ct., Edg.	205	298	CP49
Hurstway Wk. W11	137	315	CX73
Hurstwood Ave. E18	224	308	EH56
Hurstwood Ave., Bex.	262	327	EY88
Hurstwood Ave., Bexh.	255	319	FB83
Hurstwood Ave., Erith	255	319	FE81
Hurstwood Ct., Upmin.	239	311	FP60
Hurstwood Dr., Brom.	276	326	EM97
Hurstwood Rd. NW11	218	305	CY56
Huson Clo. NW3	113	305	DE66
Hussars Clo., Houns.	258	321	BY83
Husseywell Cres., Brom.	289	334	EG102
Hutchings Clo., Horn.	238	311	FL62
Hutchings St. E14	150	317	EA75
Hutchings Wk. NW11	219	305	DB56
Hutchins Clo. E15	120	307	EC66
Hutchinson Ter., Wem.	91	304	CK62
Hutton Clo., Grnf.	233	313	CD64
Hutton Clo., Wdf.Grn.	224	308	EH51
Hutton Gdns., Har.	215	303	CC52
Hutton Gro. N12	207	299	DB50
Hutton La., Har.	215	303	CC52
Hutton Row, Edg.	217	304	CQ52
Hutton St. EC4	48	316	DN72
Hutton Wk., Har.	215	303	CC52
Huxbear St. SE4	181	325	DZ85
Huxley Clo., Nthlt.	242	313	BY67
Huxley Clo., Uxb.	240	312	BK70
Huxley Dr., Rom.	236	309	EV59
Huxley Gdns. NW10	123	314	CM69
Huxley Par. N18	209	300	DQ50
Huxley Pl. N13	209	300	DP48
Huxley Rd. E10	104	307	EC61
Huxley Rd. N18	209	300	DR49
Huxley Rd., Well.	261	326	ET83
Huxley Sayze N18	209	300	DQ50
Huxley St. W10	127	315	CY69
Hyacinth Clo., Hmptn.	267	329	CA93
Hyacinth Ct., Pnr.	214	303	BW55
Hyacinth Dr., Uxb.	240	312	BL66
Hyacinth Rd. SW15	188	323	CU88
Hyde, The NW9	217	304	CS56
Hyde Clo. E13	244	318	EG68
Hyde Clo., Ashf.	265	328	BS93
Hyde Ct. N20	207	299	DD48
Hyde Cres. NW9	217	304	CS57
Hyde Dr., Orp.	278	327	EV98
Hyde Ho. NW9	217	304	CS57
Hyde La. SW11	159	315	DE81
Hyde Pk. SW7	54/5	315	DE74
Hyde Pk. W1	54/5	315	DE74
Hyde Pk. W2	54/5	315	DE74
Hyde Pk. Ave. N21	209	300	DQ47
Hyde Pk. Cor. W1	68	316	DG75
Hyde Pk. Cres. W2	42/3	315	DE72
Hyde Pk. Gdns. N21	209	300	DQ46
Hyde Pk. Gdns. W2	54	315	DD73
Hyde Pk. Gdns. Ms. W2	54	315	DD73
Hyde Pk. Gate SW7	65	315	DC75
Hyde Pk. Gate Ms. SW7	65	315	DC75
Hyde Pk. Pl. W2	54/5	315	DE73
Hyde Pk. Sq. W2	42/3	315	DE72
Hyde Pk. Sq. Ms. W2	42/3	315	DE72
Hyde Pk. St. W2	42/3	315	DE72
Hyde Rd. N1	26/7	316	DS67
Hyde Rd., Bexh.	254	319	EZ82
Hyde Rd., Rich.	169	322	CM85
Hyde Rd., S.Croy.	295	332	DR113
Hyde St. SE8	166	317	EA79
Hyde Ter., Ashf.	265	328	BS93
Hyde Vale SE10	167	317	ED81
Hyde Wk., Mord.	284	331	DA101
Hyde Way N9	209	300	DT47
Hyde Way, Hayes	249	320	BT77
Hydefield Clo. N21	209	300	DR46
Hydefield Ct. N9	209	300	DS47
Hyderabad Way E15	121	307	EE66
Hydes Pl. N1	116	306	DP66
Hydeside Gdns. N9	209	300	DT47
Hydethorpe Ave. N9	209	300	DT47
Hydethorpe Rd. SW12	192	324	DJ88
Hyland Clo., Horn.	238	310	FH59
Hyland Way, Horn.	238	310	FH59
Hylands Rd. E17	223	307	ED54
Hylton St. SE18	253	318	ET77
Hyndewood SE23	197	325	DX90

Hyndman St. SE15	164	317	DV79
Hynton Rd., Dag.	236	309	EW61
Hyrstdene, S.Croy.	286	332	DP105
Hyson Rd. SE16	148	317	DV77
Hythe Ave., Bexh.	254	319	EY80
Hythe Clo. N18	210	301	DU49
Hythe Clo., Orp.	278	327	EW98
Hythe Path, Th.Hth.	273	324	DR97
Hythe Rd. NW10	126	315	CU70
Hythe Rd., Th.Hth.	273	324	DR96
Hyver Hill NW7	205	298	CR44
Ian Sq., Enf.	203	301	DX39
Ibbotson Ave. E16	141	317	EF72
Ibbott St. E1	128	317	DW70
Iberian Ave., Wall.	286	332	DK105
Ibis La. W4	154	314	CQ81
Ibis Way, Hayes	242	313	BX72
Ibscott Clo., Dag.	237	309	FC65
Ibsley Gdns. SW15	188	323	CU88
Ibsley Way, Barn.	207	299	DE43
Iceland Rd. E3	130	317	EA67
Ickburgh Est. E5	102	307	DV62
Ickburgh Rd. E5	102	307	DV62
Ickenham Clo., Ruis.	231	312	BR61
Ickenham Rd., Ruis.	231	312	BQ61
Ickenham Rd., Uxb.	231	312	BQ61
Ickleton Rd. SE9	276	326	EL91
Icknield Dr., Ilf.	225	308	EP57
Ickworth Pk. Rd. E17	222	307	DY56
Ida Rd. N15	221	306	DR57
Ida St. E14	140	317	EC72
Iden Clo., Brom.	275	325	EE97
Idlecombe Rd. SW17	272	324	DG93
Idmiston Rd. E15	121	307	EF64
Idmiston Rd. SE27	194	324	DQ90
Idmiston Rd., Wor.Pk.	283	330	CT101
Idmiston Sq., Wor.Pk.	283	330	CT102
Idol La. EC3	62/3	316	DS73
Idonia St. SE8	166	317	EA80
Iffley Clo., Uxb.	240	312	BK66
Iffley Rd. W6	146	315	CV76
Ifield Rd. SW10	158	315	DB79
Ifor Evans Pl. E1	129	317	DX70
Ightham Rd., Erith	255	319	FA80
Ikea Twr. NW10	109	304	CR64
Ilbert St. W10	127	315	CY69
Ilchester Gdns. W2	52/3	315	DB73
Ilchester Pl. W14	147	315	CZ76
Ilchester Rd., Dag.	236	309	EV64
Ildersly Gro. SE21	195	324	DR89
Ilderton Rd. SE15	164	317	DW80
Ilderton Rd. SE16	148	317	DV78
Ilex Clo., Sun.	266	329	BW96
Ilex Ho. N4	99	306	DM59
Ilex Rd. NW10	110	305	CT65
Ilex Way SW16	273	324	DN92
Ilford Hill, Ilf.	235	308	EN62
Ilford La., Ilf.	235	308	EP62
Ilfracombe Cres., Horn.	238	310	FJ63
Ilfracombe Gdns., Rom.	236	309	EV59
Ilfracombe Rd., Brom.	199	325	EF90
Iliffe St. SE17	84/5	316	DP78
Iliffe Yd. SE17	84/5	316	DP78
Ilkeston Ct. E5	119	307	DX63
Ilkley Clo. SE19	273	324	DR93
Ilkley Rd. E16	244	318	EJ71
Illingworth Clo., Mitch.	271	323	DD97
Illingworth Way, Enf.	202	300	DS42
Ilmington Rd., Har.	216	304	CK58
Ilminster Gdns. SW11	175	323	DE84
Imber Clo. N14	208	300	DJ45
Imber St. N1	26	316	DR67
Imperial Ave. N16	101	306	DT62
Imperial Clo., Har.	215	303	CA58
Imperial College Rd. SW7	66	315	DD76
Imperial Dr., Har.	233	313	CA59
Imperial Gdns., Mitch.	272	324	DH97
Imperial Ms. E6	244	318	EJ68
Imperial Rd. N22	220	306	DL53
Imperial Rd. SW6	158	315	DB81
Imperial Rd., Felt.	265	320	BS87
Imperial Sq. SW6	158	315	DB81
Imperial St. E3	130	317	EC69
Imperial Way, Chis.	261	326	EQ90
Imperial Way, Croy.	294	332	DN107
Imperial Way, Har.	216	304	CL58
Inca Dr. SE9	261	326	EP87
Inchmery Rd. SE6	198	325	EB89
Inchwood, Croy.	288	333	EB105
Independent Pl. E8	117	306	DT64
Independents Rd. SE3	183	325	EF83
Inderwick Rd. N8	220	306	DM57
Indescon Ct. E14	150	317	EA75
India Pl. WC2	59	316	DM73
India St. EC3	51	316	DT72
India Way W12	136	315	CV73
Indus Rd. SE7	252	318	EJ80
Industry Ter. SW9	178	324	DN83
Ingal Rd. E13	244	318	EG70
Ingate Pl. SW8	160	316	DH81
Ingatestone Rd. E12	234	308	EJ60
Ingatestone Rd. SE25	287	333	DV99
Ingatestone Rd., Wdf.Grn.	224	308	EH52
Ingelow Rd. SW8	160	316	DH82
Ingersoll Rd. W12	136	315	CV74
Ingersoll Rd., Enf.	203	301	DW38
Ingestre Pl. W1	45	316	DJ72
Ingestre Rd. E7	234	308	EG63
Ingestre Rd. NW5	114	306	DH63
Ingham Rd. NW6	112	305	DA63
Ingle Clo., Pnr.	214	303	BZ55
Inglebert St. EC1	36	316	DN69
Ingleboro Dr., Pur.	295	332	DQ113
Ingleborough St. SW9	162	316	DN82
Ingleby Clo., Dag.	237	309	FB65
Ingleby Dr., Har.	233	313	CD62
Ingleby Rd. N7	99	306	DL62
Ingleby Rd., Dag.	237	309	FB65
Ingleby Rd., Ilf.	235	308	EP60
Ingleby Way, Chis.	277	326	EN92
Ingleby Way, Wall.	294	332	DJ109
Ingledew Rd. SE18	253	318	ER78
Ingleglen, Horn.	239	311	FN59
Inglehurst Gdns., Ilf.	224	308	EM57
Inglemere Rd. SE23	197	325	DX90
Inglemere Rd., Mitch.	271	323	DF94
Inglesham Wk. E9	119	307	DZ65
Ingleside Clo., Beck.	275	325	EA94
Ingleside Gro. SE3	167	317	EF79
Inglethorpe St. SW6	157	315	CX81
Ingleton Ave., Well.	262	327	EU85
Ingleton Rd. N18	222	307	DU51
Ingleton Rd., Cars.	293	331	DE109
Ingleton St. SW9	162	316	DN82
Ingleway N12	219	305	DD51
Inglewood Clo. E14	150	317	EA77
Inglewood Clo., Horn.	238	310	FK63
Inglewood Clo., Ilf.	225	308	ET51
Inglewood Copse, Brom.	276	326	EL96
Inglewood Rd. NW6	112	305	DA64
Inglewood Rd., Bexh.	263	327	FD84
Inglis Barracks NW7	206	299	CY50
Inglis Rd. W5	133	314	CM73
Inglis Rd., Croy.	287	332	DT102
Inglis St. SE5	162	316	DP81
Ingram Ave. NW11	96	305	DC59
Ingram Clo. SE11	83	316	DM77
Ingram Clo., Stan.	204	298	CJ50
Ingram Rd. N2	219	305	DE56
Ingram Rd., Th.Hth.	273	324	DQ95
Ingram Way, Grnf.	243	313	CD67
Ingrave Ho., Dag.	246	319	EV67
Ingrave Rd., Rom.	227	309	FD56
Ingrave St. SW11	175	323	DD83
Ingrebourne Gdns., Upmin.	239	311	FQ60
Ingress St. W4	145	314	CS78
Ingreway, Rom.	229	311	FP51
Inigo Jones Rd. SE7	252	318	EL80
Inigo Pl. WC2	58/9	316	DL73
Inkerman Rd. NW5	114	306	DH65
Inks Grn. E4	211	301	EB50
Inman Rd. NW10	125	314	CS67
Inman Rd. SW18	190	323	DC87
Inner Circle NW1	32	316	DG69
Inner Pk. Rd. SW19	189	323	CX88
Inner Ring E., Houns.	257	320	BP83
Inner Ring W., Houns.	257	320	BN83

Inner Temple La. EC4	48	316	DN72
Innes Clo. SW20	270	323	CY96
Innes Gdns. SW15	172	323	CV86
Innes Yd., Croy.	287	332	DQ104
Inniskilling Rd. E13	244	318	EJ68
Inskip Clo. E10	104	307	EB61
Inskip Dr., Horn.	238	311	FL60
Inskip Rd., Dag.	236	309	EX60
Institute Pl. E8	118	307	DV64
Instone Clo., Wall.	294	332	DL108
Integer Gdns. E11	105	307	ED59
Interchange E. Ind. Est. E5	102	307	DW60
International Ave., Houns.	250	321	BW78
International Trd. Est., Sthl.	250	321	BV76
Inver Clo. E5	102	307	DW61
Inver Ct. W2	40/1	315	DB72
Inveraray Pl. SE18	253	318	ER79
Inverclyde Gdns., Rom.	226	309	EX56
Inveresk Gdns., Wor.Pk.	283	330	CT104
Inverforth Clo. NW3	96	305	DC61
Inverforth Rd. N11	208	300	DH50
Inverine Rd. SE7	252	318	EH78
Invermore Pl. SE18	253	318	EQ77
Inverness Ave., Enf.	202	300	DS39
Inverness Dr., Ilf.	225	308	ES51
Inverness Gdns. W8	52/3	315	DB74
Inverness Ms. W2	52/3	315	DB73
Inverness Pl. W2	52/3	315	DB73
Inverness Rd. N18	210	301	DV50
Inverness Rd., Houns.	258	321	BZ84
Inverness Rd., Sthl.	250	321	BY77
Inverness Rd., Wor.Pk.	284	331	CX102
Inverness St. NW1	20/1	316	DH67
Inverness Ter. W2	40/1	315	DB72
Inverton Rd. SE15	181	325	DX84
Invicta Clo., Chis.	277	326	EN92
Invicta Gro., Nthlt.	242	313	BZ69
Invicta Plaza SE1	60/1	316	DP74
Invicta Rd. SE3	252	318	EG80
Inville Rd. SE17	86	316	DR78
Inwen Ct. SE8	149	317	DY78
Inwood Ave., Houns.	259	321	CC83
Inwood Clo., Croy.	288	333	DY103
Inwood Rd., Houns.	259	321	CB84
Inworth St. SW11	159	315	DE82
Inworth Wk. N1	25	316	DQ67
Ion Sq. E2	128	317	DU68
Iona Clo. SE6	198	325	EA87
Ipswich Rd. SW17	272	324	DG93
Ireland Clo. E6	244	318	EM71
Ireland Pl. N22	220	306	DL52
Ireland Row E14	139	317	DZ72
Ireland Yd. EC4	48/9	316	DP72
Irene Rd. SW6	158	315	DA81
Irene Rd., Orp.	291	334	ET101
Ireton Clo. N10	220	306	DG52
Ireton St. E3	130	317	EA70
Iris Ave., Bex.	262	327	EY86
Iris Clo. E6	244	318	EL71
Iris Clo., Croy.	288	333	DX102
Iris Clo., Surb.	282	330	CM101
Iris Ct., Pnr.	214	303	BW55
Iris Cres., Bexh.	254	319	EZ79
Iris Path, Rom.	228	310	FJ52
Iris Rd., Epsom	282	330	CP106
Iris Way E4	222	307	DZ51
Irkdale Ave., Enf.	202	300	DT39
Iron Bri. Clo. NW10	109	304	CS64
Iron Bri. Clo., Sthl.	243	313	CC74
Iron Bri. Rd., Uxb.	249	320	BN75
Iron Bri. Rd., West Dr.	249	320	BN75
Iron Mill La., Dart.	263	327	FE84
Iron Mill Pl. SW18	174	323	DB86
Iron Mill Pl., Dart.	263	327	FF84
Iron Mill Rd. SW18	174	323	DB86
Ironmonger La. EC2	50	316	DR72
Ironmonger Pas. EC1	37	316	DQ69
Ironmonger Row EC1	37	316	DQ69
Ironmongers Pl. E14	150	317	EA77
Irons Way, Rom.	227	309	FC52
Ironside Clo. SE16	149	317	DX75
Irvine Ave., Har.	216	304	CG55
Irvine Clo. N20	207	299	DE47
Irvine Way, Orp.	291	334	ET101
Irving Ave., Nthlt.	242	313	BX67
Irving Gro. SW9	161	316	DM82
Irving Rd. W14	147	315	CX76
Irving St. WC2	58	316	DK73
Irving Way NW9	217	304	CT57
Irving Way, Swan.	279	327	FD96
Irwin Ave. SE18	253	318	ES80
Irwin Gdns. NW10	126	315	CV67
Isabel St. SW9	161	316	DM81
Isabella Clo. N14	208	300	DJ45
Isabella Dr., Orp.	291	334	EQ105
Isabella Rd. E9	118	307	DW64
Isabella St. SE1	60/1	316	DP74
Isambard Clo., Uxb.	240	312	BK70
Isambard Ms. E14	150	317	EC76
Isambard Pl. SE16	138	317	DW74
Isbell Gdns., Rom.	227	309	FE52
Isel Way SE22	179	324	DS85
Isham Rd. SW16	272	324	DL96
Isis Clo. SW15	172	323	DW84
Isis Clo., Ruis.	231	302	BQ58
Isis Dr., Upmin.	229	311	FS58
Isis St. SW18	190	323	DC89
Isla Rd. SE18	253	318	EQ79
Island Rd., Mitch.	271	323	DF94
Island Row E14	139	317	DY72
Islay Gdns., Houns.	258	321	BX85
Islay Wk. N1	116	306	DQ66
Isledon Rd. N7	100	306	DN62
Islehurst Clo., Chis.	277	326	EN95
Islington Grn. N1	24/5	316	DP67
Islington High St. N1	24	316	DN68
Islington Pk. Ms. N1	116	306	DN66
Islington Pk. St. N1	116	306	DN66
Islip Gdns., Edg.	217	304	CR52
Islip Gdns., Nthlt.	232	313	BY66
Islip Manor Rd., Nthlt.	232	313	BY66
Islip St. NW5	114	306	DJ64
Ismailia Rd. E7	234	308	EH66
Isom Clo. E13	244	318	EJ70
Ivanhoe Clo., Uxb.	248	312	BK71
Ivanhoe Dr., Har.	216	304	CG55
Ivanhoe Rd. SE5	179	324	DT83
Ivanhoe Rd., Houns.	258	321	BX83
Ivatt Pl. W14	147	315	CZ78
Ivatt Way N17	221	306	DP55
Ive Fm. Clo. E10	104	307	EA61
Ive Fm. La. E10	104	307	EA61
Iveagh Ave. NW10	124	314	CN68
Iveagh Clo. E9	129	317	DX67
Iveagh Clo. NW10	124	314	CN68
Iveagh Clo., Nthwd.	213	302	BP53
Iveagh Ter. NW10	124	314	CN68
Ivedon Rd., Well.	254	319	EW82
Iveley Rd. SW4	160	316	DJ82
Iver La., Iver	248	312	BG72
Iver La., Uxb.	240	312	BH70
Iver Rd., Iver	248	312	BG72
Ivere Dr., Barn.	207	299	DB44
Iverhurst Clo., Bexh.	262	327	EX85
Iverna Ct. W8	64	315	DA76
Iverna Gdns. W8	64	315	DA76
Iverna Gdns., Felt.	257	320	BR85
Iverson Rd. NW6	111	305	CZ65
Ives Gdns., Rom.	227	309	FF56
Ives Rd. E16	141	317	EE71
Ives St. SW3	78/9	315	DE77
Ivestor Ter. SE23	196	325	DW87
Ivimey St. E2	128	317	DU69
Ivinghoe Clo., Enf.	202	300	DS39
Ivinghoe Rd., Dag.	236	309	EV64
Ivor Gro. SE9	261	326	EP88
Ivor Pl. NW1	31	315	DF70
Ivor St. NW1	114	306	DJ66
Ivory Sq. SW11	174	323	DC83
Ivorydown, Brom.	276	326	EG91
Ivy Clo., Har.	232	313	BZ63
Ivy Clo., Pnr.	214	303	BW59
Ivy Clo., Sun.	266	329	BW96
Ivy Cotts. E14	140	317	EB73
Ivy Ct. SE16	148	317	DU78
Ivy Cres. W4	144	314	CQ77
Ivy Gdns. N8	220	306	DL58
Ivy Gdns., Mitch.	272	324	DK97

Ivy La., Houns.	258	321	BZ84
Ivy Pl., Surb.	282	330	CM100
Ivy Rd. E16	244	318	EG72
Ivy Rd. E17	223	307	EA58
Ivy Rd. N14	208	300	DJ45
Ivy Rd. NW2	110	305	CW63
Ivy Rd. SE4	181	325	DZ84
Ivy Rd. SW17	271	323	DE92
Ivy Rd., Houns.	259	321	CB84
Ivy Rd., Surb.	282	330	CN103
Ivy St. N1	26/7	316	DS68
Ivy Wk., Dag.	236	309	EY65
Ivybridge Clo., Twick.	184	322	CG87
Ivybridge Clo., Uxb.	240	312	BL69
Ivybridge Est., Islw.	259	321	CF85
Ivybridge La. WC2	58/9	316	DL73
Ivychurch Clo. SE20	274	325	DW94
Ivychurch La. SE17	86/7	316	DS78
Ivydale Rd. SE15	181	325	DX83
Ivydale Rd., Cars.	285	331	DF103
Ivyday Gro. SW16	193	324	DM90
Ivydene Clo., Sutt.	285	331	DC105
Ivyhouse Rd., Dag.	236	309	EX65
Ivyhouse Rd., Uxb.	241	312	BP63
Ivymount Rd. SE27	194	324	DN90
Ixworth Pl. SW3	78/9	315	DE78
Izane Rd., Bexh.	262	327	EZ84
Jacaranda Clo., N.Mal.	269	322	CS97
Jack Barnett Way N22	220	306	DM54
Jack Clow Rd. E15	131	317	EE68
Jack Cornwell St. E12	235	308	EN63
Jack Dash Way E6	244	318	EL70
Jack Walker Ct. N5	116	306	DP63
Jackass La., Kes.	289	334	EH106
Jackets La., Nthwd.	213	302	BP53
Jackman Ms. NW10	93	304	CS62
Jackman St. E8	128	317	DV67
Jacks La., Uxb.	212	302	BG52
Jackson Clo., Uxb.	240	312	BL66
Jackson Rd. N7	115	306	DM63
Jackson Rd., Bark.	245	318	ER67
Jackson Rd., Barn.	207	299	DD44
Jackson Rd., Brom.	290	334	EL103
Jackson Rd., Uxb.	240	312	BL66
Jackson St. SE18	253	318	EN79
Jackson Way, Sthl.	251	321	CB75
Jacksons La. N6	98	306	DG59
Jacksons Pl., Croy.	287	332	DR102
Jacksons Way, Croy.	288	333	EA104
Jacob St. SE1	75	316	DT75
Jacobs Ave., Rom.	228	311	FL54
Jacobs Clo., Dag.	237	309	FB63
Jacobs Ho. E13	244	318	EJ69
Jacob's Well Ms. W1	44	316	DG72
Jacqueline Clo., Nthlt.	242	313	BZ67
Jade Clo. E16	244	318	EK72
Jade Clo. NW2	95	305	CX59
Jade Clo., Dag.	236	309	EW60
Jaffe Rd., Ilf.	235	308	ER60
Jaffray Pl. SE27	273	324	DP91
Jaffray Rd., Brom.	276	326	EK98
Jaggard Way SW12	191	323	DF87
Jago Clo. SE18	253	318	EQ79
Jago Wk. SE5	163	316	DR80
Jamaica Rd. SE1	75	316	DT75
Jamaica Rd. SE16	148	317	DU76
Jamaica Rd., Th.Hth.	286	332	DP100
Jamaica St. E1	138	317	DW71
James Ave. NW2	110	305	CW64
James Ave., Dag.	236	309	EZ60
James Bedford Clo., Pnr.	214	303	BW54
James Boswell Clo. SW16	273	324	DN91
James Clo. E13	244	318	EG68
James Clo. NW11	218	305	CY58
James Clo., Rom.	228	310	FG57
James Collins Clo. W9	127	315	CZ70
James Ct. N1	116	306	DQ66
James Dudson Ct. NW10	108	304	CQ66
James Gdns. N22	221	306	DP52
James Hammett Ho. E2	39	316	DT69
James Joyce Wk. SE24	178	324	DP84
James La. E10	105	307	ED59
James La. E11	223	307	ED58
James Martin Clo., Uxb.	230	302	BG58
James Newman Ct. SE9	261	326	EN90
James Pl. N17	221	306	DT53
James Rd., Dart.	263	327	FF87
James Sinclair Pt. E13	244	318	EJ67
James St. W1	44	316	DG72
James St. WC2	58/9	316	DL73
James St., Bark.	235	308	EQ66
James St., Enf.	209	300	DT43
James St., Houns.	259	321	CD83
James Ter. SW14	171	322	CR83
James Yd. E4	223	307	ED51
Jameson Clo. W3	144	314	CQ75
Jameson St. W8	52	315	DA74
James's Cotts., Rich.	154	314	CN80
Jamestown Rd. NW1	20/1	316	DH67
Jamieson Ho., Houns.	258	321	BZ86
Jane St. E1	138	317	DV72
Janet St. E14	150	317	EA76
Janeway Pl. SE16	148	317	DV75
Janeway St. SE16	148	317	DU75
Janice Ms., Ilf.	235	308	EP62
Jansen Wk. SW11	175	323	DD84
Janson Clo. E15	121	307	EE64
Janson Clo. NW10	93	304	CS62
Janson Rd. E15	121	307	EE64
Jansons Rd. N15	221	306	DS55
Japan Cres. N4	99	306	DM59
Japan Rd., Rom.	226	309	EX58
Jardine Rd. E1	139	317	DX73
Jarrett Clo. SW2	194	324	DP88
Jarrow Clo., Mord.	284	331	DB99
Jarrow Rd. N17	222	307	DV56
Jarrow Rd. SE16	148	317	DW77
Jarrow Rd., Rom.	226	309	EW58
Jarrow Way E9	119	307	DY63
Jarvis Clo., Barn.	206	299	CX43
Jarvis Rd. SE22	179	324	DS84
Jarvis Rd., S.Croy.	295	332	DR107
Jarvis Way, Rom.	228	311	FL54
Jasmin Clo., Nthwd.	213	302	BT53
Jasmine Clo., Ilf.	235	308	EP64
Jasmine Clo., Orp.	290	334	EP103
Jasmine Clo., Sthl.	242	313	BY73
Jasmine Gdns., Croy.	288	333	EA104
Jasmine Gdns., Har.	233	313	CA61
Jasmine Gro. SE20	274	325	DV95
Jasmine Ter., West Dr.	249	320	BN75
Jasmine Way, E.Mol.	267	329	CE98
Jason Ct. W1	44	316	DG72
Jason Wk. SE9	277	326	EN91
Jasper Clo., Enf.	203	301	DW38
Jasper Pas. SE19	273	324	DT93
Jasper Rd. E16	244	318	EK72
Jasper Rd. SE19	273	324	DT93
Jasper Wk. N1	38	316	DR69
Javelin Way, Nthlt.	242	313	BX69
Jay Gdns., Chis.	276	326	EM91
Jay Ms. SW7	65	315	DC75
Jaycroft, Enf.	202	300	DN39
Jebb Ave. SW2	177	324	DL86
Jebb St. E3	130	317	EA68
Jedburgh Rd. E13	244	318	EJ69
Jedburgh St. SW11	176	324	DG84
Jeddo Rd. W12	145	314	CT75
Jefferies Ho. NW10	109	304	CR66
Jefferson Clo. W13	142	314	CH76
Jefferson Clo., Ilf.	225	308	EP57
Jefferson Wk. SE18	253	318	EN79
Jeffreys Pl. NW1	114	306	DJ66
Jeffreys Rd. SW4	161	316	DL82
Jeffreys Rd., Enf.	203	301	DZ41
Jeffreys St. NW1	114	306	DJ66
Jeffreys Wk. SW4	161	316	DL82
Jeffs Clo., Hmptn.	267	329	CB93
Jeffs Rd., Sutt.	284	331	CZ105
Jeger Ave. E2	27	316	DT67
Jeken Rd. SE9	260	326	EJ84
Jelf Rd. SW2	178	324	DN85
Jellicoe Gdns., Stan.	215	303	CF51
Jellicoe Rd. E13	244	318	EG70
Jellicoe Rd. N17	221	306	DR52
Jengar Clo., Sutt.	331	DB105	
Jenkins La. E6	245	318	EN68

Jenkins La., Bark.	245	318	EP68
Jenkins Rd. E13	244	318	EH70
Jenner Ave. W3	135	314	CR71
Jenner Ho. SE3	167	317	EE79
Jenner Pl. SW13	156	315	CV79
Jenner Rd. N16	101	306	DT62
Jennett Rd., Croy.	286	332	DN104
Jennifer Rd., Brom.	199	325	EF90
Jennings Rd. SE22	179	324	DT86
Jenningtree Way, Belv.	255	319	FC75
Jenny Hammond Clo. E11	105	307	EF62
Jenny Path, Rom.	228	310	FK52
Jenson Way SE19	273	324	DT94
Jenton Ave., Bexh.	254	319	EY81
Jephson Rd. E7	234	308	EJ66
Jephson St. SE5	163	316	DR81
Jephtha Rd. SW18	174	323	DA86
Jeppos La., Mitch.	271	323	DF98
Jerdan Pl. SW6	158	315	DA80
Jeremiah St. E14	140	317	EB72
Jeremys Grn. N18	210	301	DV49
Jermyn St. SW1	57	316	DJ74
Jerningham Ave., Ilf.	225	308	EP54
Jerningham Rd. SE14	165	317	DY82
Jerome Cres. NW8	30/1	315	DE70
Jerome St. E1	39	316	DT70
Jerrard St. N1	26/7	316	DS68
Jerrard St. SE13	182	325	EB83
Jersey Ave., Stan.	216	304	CH54
Jersey Dr., Orp.	291	334	ER100
Jersey Par., Houns.	251	321	CB81
Jersey Rd. E11	105	307	ED60
Jersey Rd. E16	244	318	EJ72
Jersey Rd. SW17	272	324	
DH93Jersey Rd. W7	142	314	CG75
Jersey Rd., Houns.	251	321	CB81
Jersey Rd., Ilf.	235	308	EP63
Jersey Rd., Islw.	251	321	CD80
Jersey Rd., Rain.	238	310	FG66
Jersey St. E2	128	317	DV69
Jerusalem Pas. EC1	36/7	316	DP70
Jervis Ave., Enf.	203	301	DY36
Jervis Ct. W1	44/5	316	DH72
Jerviston Gdns. SW16	273	324	DN92
Jesmond Ave., Wem.	107	304	CM65
Jesmond Clo., Mitch.	272	324	DG97
Jesmond Rd., Croy.	287	332	DT101
Jesmond Way, Stan.	204	298	CL50
Jessam Ave. E5	102	307	DV60
Jessamine Rd. W7	243	313	CE74
Jessamine Ter., Swan.	279	327	FC95
Jesse Rd. E10	104	307	EC60
Jessett Clo., Erith	255	319	FD77
Jessica Rd. SW18	174	323	DC86
Jessie Blythe La. N19	99	306	DL59
Jessiman Ter., Shep.	281	328	BN99
Jessop Ave., Sthl.	250	321	BZ77
Jessop Rd. SE24	178	324	DP84
Jessops Way, Croy.	286	332	DJ100
Jessup Clo. SE18	253	318	EQ77
Jetstar Way, Nthlt.	242	313	BY69
Jevington Way SE12	260	326	EH88
Jewel Rd. E17	223	307	EA55
Jewry St. EC3	51	316	DT72
Jew's Row SW18	174	323	DB84
Jews Wk. SE26	274	325	DV91
Jeymer Ave. NW2	110	305	CV64
Jeymer Dr., Grnf.	243	313	CC67
Jeypore Rd. SW18	190	323	DC87
Jillian Clo., Hmptn.	267	329	CA94
Jim Bradley Clo. SE18	253	318	EN77
Joan Cres. SE9	260	326	EK87
Joan Gdns., Dag.	236	309	EY61
Joan Rd., Dag.	236	309	EY60
Joan St. SE1	60/1	316	DP74
Jocelyn Rd., Rich.	169	322	CL83
Jocelyn St. SE15	164	317	DU81
Jockey's Flds. WC1	47	316	DM71
Jodane St. SE8	149	317	DZ77
Jodrell Clo., Islw.	152	314	CG81
Jodrell Rd. E3	129	317	DZ67
Joel St., Nthwd.	214	303	BU55
Joel St., Pnr.	214	303	BU55
Johanna St. SE1	72	316	DN75
John Adam St. WC2	58/9	316	DL73
John Aird Ct. W2	41	315	DC71
John Ashby Clo. SW2	177	324	DL86
John Barnes Wk. E15	121	307	EF65
John Bradshaw Rd. N14	208	300	DK46
John Burns Dr., Bark.	235	308	ES66
John Campbell Rd. N16	117	306	DS64
John Carpenter St. EC4	60/1	316	DP73
John Cornwall VC Ho. E12	235	308	EN63
John Deed Ind. Est., Mitch.	285	331	DF100
John Felton Rd. SE16	148	317	DU75
John Fisher St. E1	138	317	DU73
John Gooch Dr., Enf.	202	300	DP39
John Groom's Est., Edg.	205	298	CQ49
John Islip St. SW1	82	316	DK78
John Keats Ho. N22	220	306	DM52
John Maurice Clo. SE17	86	316	DR77
John McKenna Wk. SE16	148	317	DV76
John Newton Ct., Well.	262	327	EV83
John Parker Clo., Dag.	237	309	FB66
John Parker Sq. SW11	175	323	DD83
John Penn St. SE13	166	317	EB81
John Perrin Pl., Har.	91	304	CL59
John Princes St. W1	44/5	316	DH72
John Rennie Wk. E1	138	317	DV74
John Roll Way SE16	148	317	DU76
John Ruskin St. SE5	162	316	DP80
John Silkin La. SE8	149	317	DX78
John Smith Ave. SW6	157	315	CZ80
John Spencer Sq. N1	116	306	DP65
John St. E15	131	317	EF67
John St. SE25	274	325	DU98
John St. WC1	35	316	DM70
John St., Enf.	209	300	DT43
John St., Houns.	250	321	BY82
John Trundle Ct. EC2	49	316	DQ71
John Walsh Twr. E11	105	307	EF61
John Williams Clo. SE14	165	317	DX79
John Wilson St. SE18	253	318	EN76
John Woolley Clo. SE13	183	325	ED84
Johnby Clo., Enf.	203	301	DY37
Johns Ave. NW4	218	305	CW56
Johns Clo., Ashf.	265	328	BQ91
Johns La., Mord.	285	331	DC99
John's Ms. WC1	35	316	DM70
John's Pl. E1	138	317	DV72
John's Ter., Croy.	287	332	DS102
John's Ter., Rom.	229	311	FP51
Johnson Clo. E8	128	317	DU67
Johnson Rd., Brom.	290	334	EK99
Johnson Rd., Croy.	287	332	DR101
Johnson Rd., Houns.	250	321	BW80
Johnson St. E1	138	317	DW73
Johnson St., Sthl.	250	321	BW76
Johnsons Clo., Cars.	285	331	DE104
Johnson's Ct. EC4	48	316	DN72
Johnsons Dr., Hmptn.	267	329	CC95
Johnson's Pl. SW1	81	316	DJ78
Johnsons Way NW10	124	314	CP70
Johnsons Yd., Uxb.	240	312	BJ66
Johnston Clo. SW9	161	316	DM81
Johnston Ter. NW2	95	305	CX62
Johnstone Rd. E6	244	318	EM69
Joiner St. SE1	62	316	DR74
Joiner's Arms Yd. SE5	163	316	DR81
Jollys La., Har.	233	313	CD60
Jollys La., Hayes	242	313	BX71
Jonathan St. SE11	83	316	DM78
Jones Rd. E13	244	318	EH70
Jones St. W1	56/7	316	DH73
Jones Wk., Rich.	169	322	CM86
Jonquil Gdns., Hmptn.	266	329	BZ93
Jonson Clo., Hayes	242	313	BU71
Jonson Clo., Mitch.	272	324	DH98
Joram Way SE16	148	317	DV78
Jordan Clo., Dag.	237	309	FB63
Jordan Clo., Har.	232	313	BZ62
Jordan Clo., S.Croy.	295	332	DT111
Jordan Rd., Grnf.	122	314	CH67
Jordans Clo., Islw.	251	321	CE81
Jordans Clo., Stai.	264	320	BJ87
Joseph Ave. W3	135	314	CR72
Joseph Powell Clo. SW12	176	324	DH86
Joseph Ray Rd. E11	105	307	EE61
Joseph St. E3	129	317	DZ70
Josephine Ave. SW2	177	324	DM85
Joshua St. E14	140	317	EC72
Joubert St. SW11	159	315	DF82
Jowett St. SE15	163	316	DT80
Joyce Ave. N18	209	300	DT50
Joyce Dawson Way SE28	246	319	EU73
Joyce Page Clo. SE7	252	318	EK79
Joyce Wk. SW2	178	324	DN86
Joydens Wd. Rd., Bex.	279	327	FD91
Joydon Dr., Rom.	226	309	EV58
Joyners Clo., Dag.	236	309	EZ63
Jubb Powell Ho. N15	221	306	DS58
Jubilee Ave. E4	223	307	EC51
Jubilee Ave., Rom.	227	309	FB57
Jubilee Ave., Twick.	259	321	CC87
Jubilee Clo. NW9	217	304	CR58
Jubilee Clo., Pnr.	214	303	BW54
Jubilee Clo., Rom.	227	309	FB57
Jubilee Clo., Stai.	264	320	BJ87
Jubilee Ct., Stai.	264	328	BG92
Jubilee Cres. E14	150	317	EC76
Jubilee Cres. N9	210	301	DU46
Jubilee Dr., Ruis.	232	313	BX63
Jubilee Gdns., Sthl.	243	313	CA72
Jubilee Pl. SW3	78/9	315	DE78
Jubilee Rd., Grnf.	122	314	CH67
Jubilee Rd., Sutt.	292	331	CX108
Jubilee St. E1	138	317	DW72
Jubilee Way SW19	271	323	DB95
Jubilee Way, Chess.	282	330	CN105
Jubilee Way, Felt.	265	320	BT88
Jubilee Way, Sid.	262	327	EU89
Judd St. WC1	34/5	316	DL69
Jude St. E16	141	317	EF72
Judge Heath La., Hayes	249	312	BQ72
Judith Ave., Rom.	227	309	FB51
Juer St. SW11	159	315	DE80
Juglans Rd., Orp.	291	335	EU102
Julia Gdns., Bark.	246	319	EX68
Julia St. NW5	114	306	DG63
Julian Ave. W3	134	314	CP73
Julian Hill, Har.	233	313	CE61
Julian Pl. E14	150	317	EB78
Juliana Clo. N2	219	305	DC55
Julien Rd. W5	142	314	CJ77
Juliette Rd. E13	131	317	EF68
Junction App. SE13	182	325	EC83
Junction App. SW11	175	323	DE83
Junction Ave. W10	126	315	CW69
Junction Ms. W2	42/3	315	DE72
Junction Pl. W2	42	315	DD72
Junction Rd. E13	244	318	EH68
Junction Rd. N9	210	301	DU46
Junction Rd. N17	222	307	DU55
Junction Rd. N19	114	306	DJ63
Junction Rd. W5	143	314	CK77
Junction Rd., Ashf.	265	328	BQ92
Junction Rd., Har.	215	303	CE58
Junction Rd., Rom.	227	309	FF56
Junction Rd., S.Croy.	287	332	DR106
Junction Rd. E., Rom.	236	309	EY59
Junction Rd. W., Rom.	236	309	EY59
Junction Wf. N1	25	316	DQ68
June Clo., Couls.	293	332	DH114
Juniper Clo., Barn.	206	299	CX43
Juniper Clo., Rick.	212	302	BK48
Juniper Clo., Wem.	108	304	CM64
Juniper Cres. NW1	114	306	DG66
Juniper Gdns. SW16	272	324	DJ95
Juniper Gdns., Sun.	265	328	BT93
Juniper Gate, Rick.	212	302	BK47
Juniper La. E6	244	318	EL71
Juniper Rd., Ilf.	235	308	EP63
Juniper St. E1	138	317	DW73
Juniper Wk., Swan.	279	327	FD96
Juniper Way, Hayes	241	312	BR73
Juniper Way, Rom.	228	311	FL53
Juno Way SE14	165	317	DX79
Jupiter Way N7	115	306	DM65
Jupp Rd. E15	121	307	ED66
Jupp Rd. W. E15	130	317	EC67
Justice Wk. SW3	159	315	DE79
Justin Clo., Brent.	153	314	CK80
Justin Rd. E4	222	307	DZ51
Jute La., Enf.	203	301	DY40
Jutland Clo. N19	99	306	DL60
Jutland Rd. E13	244	318	EG70
Jutland Rd. SE6	198	325	EC87
Jutsums Ave., Rom.	227	309	FB58
Jutsums La., Rom.	227	309	FB58
Juxon Clo., Har.	215	303	CB53
Juxon St. SE11	83	316	DM77
Kaduna Clo., Pnr.	214	303	BV57
Kale Rd., Erith	254	319	EY75
Kambala Rd. SW11	175	323	DD83
Kangley Bri. Rd. SE26	274	325	DZ91
Karen Clo., Rain.	247	319	FE68
Karen Ct. SE4	165	317	DZ82
Karen Ct., Brom.	275	325	EF95
Karen Ter. E11	105	307	EF61
Karoline Gdns., Grnf.	243	313	CD68
Kashgar Rd. SE18	253	318	ET77
Kashmir Rd. SE7	252	318	EK80
Kassala Rd. SW11	159	315	DF81
Katella Trd. Est., Bark.	245	318	ES69
Kates Clo., Barn.	206	299	CU43
Katharine St., Croy.	287	332	DQ104
Katherine Gdns. SE9	184	326	EK84
Katherine Gdns., Ilf.	225	308	EQ52
Katherine Rd. E6	234	308	EK66
Katherine Rd. E7	234	308	EJ65
Katherine Rd., Twick.	184	322	CG88
Katherine Sq. W11	137	315	CY74
Kathleen Ave. W3	134	314	CQ71
Kathleen Ave., Wem.	107	304	CL66
Kathleen Rd. SW11	175	323	DF83
Kay Rd. SW9	161	316	DL82
Kay St. E2	128	317	DU68
Kay St. E15	121	307	ED66
Kay St., Well.	254	319	EV81
Kayemoor Rd., Sutt.	293	331	DE108
Kean St. WC2	47	316	DM72
Keatley Grn. E4	222	307	DZ51
Keats Ave., Rom.	228	310	FH52
Keats Clo. E11	224	308	EH57
Keats Clo. NW3	113	305	DE63
Keats Clo. SE1	87	316	DT77
Keats Clo. SW19	271	323	DD93
Keats Clo., Chig.	225	308	EQ51
Keats Clo., Enf.	210	301	DX43
Keats Clo., Hayes	242	313	BU71
Keats Gro. NW3	113	305	DE63
Keats Ho., Beck.	275	325	EA93
Keats Pl. EC2	50	316	DR71
Keats Rd., Belv.	255	319	FC76
Keats Rd., Well.	253	318	ES81
Keats Way, Croy.	288	333	DW100
Keats Way, Grnf.	243	313	CB71
Keats Way, West Dr.	248	320	BM77
Keble Clo., Nthlt.	233	313	CC64
Keble Clo., Wor.Pk.	283	330	CT102
Keble St. SW17	271	323	DC91
Kechill Gdns., Brom.	289	334	EG101
Kedelston Ct. E5	119	307	DX63
Kedleston Dr., Orp.	291	334	ET100
Kedleston Wk. E2	128	317	DV69
Keedonwood Rd., Brom.	275	325	EE92
Keel Clo. SE16	139	317	DX74
Keel Clo., Bark.	246	319	EY69
Keeley Rd., Croy.	287	332	DQ103
Keeley St. WC2	47	316	DM72
Keeling Rd. SE9	260	326	EK85
Keely Clo., Barn.	207	299	DE43
Keemor Clo. SE18	253	318	EN80
Keens Clo. SW16	272	324	DK92
Keens Rd., Croy.	287	332	DQ105
Keens Yd. N1	116	306	DP65
Keep, The SE3	252	318	EG82
Keep, The, Kings.T.	268	322	CM93
Keep La. N11	208	300	DG49
Keepers Ms., Tedd.	268	322	CJ93
Keesey St. SE17	163	316	DR79
Keetons Rd. SE16	148	317	DV76
Keevil Dr. SW19	189	323	CX87
Keighley Clo. N7	115	306	DL64
Keighley Rd., Rom.	228	311	FL52
Keightley Dr. SE9	261	326	EQ88
Keilder Clo., Uxb.	241	312	BN68
Keildon Rd. SW11	175	323	DF84
Keir, The SW19	270	323	CW92
Keir Hardie Est. E5	102	307	DV60
Keir Hardie Ho. W6	156	315	CW79
Keir Hardie Way, Bark.	236	309	EU66
Keir Hardie Way, Hayes	242	313	BU69
Keith Connor Clo. SW8	176	324	DH83
Keith Gro. W12	146	315	CU75
Keith Pk. Rd., Uxb.	240	312	BM66
Keith Rd. E17	222	307	DZ53
Keith Rd., Bark.	245	318	ER68
Keith Rd., Hayes	249	320	BS76
Keith Way, Horn.	238	311	FL59
Kelbrook Rd. SE3	252	318	EL82
Kelby Path SE9	261	326	EP90
Kelceda Clo. NW2	94	305	CU61
Kelf Gro., Hayes	249	312	BT72
Kelfield Gdns. W10	136	315	CW72
Kelfield Ms. W10	137	315	CX72
Kell St. SE1	72/3	316	DP76
Kelland Clo. N8	220	306	DK57
Kelland Rd. E13	244	318	EG70
Kellaway Rd. SE3	252	318	EJ82
Keller Cres. E12	234	308	EK63
Kellerton Rd. SE13	183	325	EE85
Kellett Rd. SW2	178	324	DN84
Kelling Gdns., Croy.	286	332	DP101
Kellino St. SW17	271	323	DF91
Kellner Rd. SE28	253	318	ET76
Kelly Clo., Shep.	281	328	BS96
Kelly Rd. NW7	218	305	CY51
Kelly St. NW1	114	306	DH65
Kelly Way, Rom.	226	309	EY57
Kelman Clo. SW4	161	316	DK82
Kelmore Gro. SE22	180	325	DU84
Kelmscott Clo. E17	222	307	DZ54
Kelmscott Gdns. W12	146	315	CU76
Kelmscott Rd. SW11	175	323	DE85
Kelross Pas. N5	116	306	DQ63
Kelross Rd. N5	116	306	DQ63
Kelsall Clo. SE3	252	318	EH82
Kelsey La., Beck.	275	325	EA97
Kelsey Pk. Ave., Beck.	275	325	EB96
Kelsey Pk. Rd., Beck.	275	325	EA96
Kelsey Rd., Orp.	278	327	EV96
Kelsey Sq., Beck.	275	325	EA96
Kelsey St. E2	128	317	DU70
Kelsey Way, Beck.	275	325	EA97
Kelshall Ct. N4	100	306	DQ61
Kelsie Way, Ilf.	225	308	ES51
Kelso Pl. W8	64/5	315	DB76
Kelso Rd., Cars.	285	331	DC101
Kelson Ho. E14	150	317	EC76
Kelston Rd., Ilf.	225	308	EP54
Kelvedon Clo., Kings.T.	269	322	CN93
Kelvedon Rd. SW6	157	315	CZ80
Kelvedon Wk., Rain.	247	319	FE67
Kelvedon Way, Wdf.Grn.	224	308	EM51
Kelvin Ave. N13	220	306	DM51
Kelvin Ave., Tedd.	267	329	CE93
Kelvin Cres., Har.	215	303	CE52
Kelvin Dr., Twick.	168	322	CH86
Kelvin Gdns., Croy.	286	332	DL101
Kelvin Gdns., Sthl.	243	313	CA72
Kelvin Gro. SE26	196	325	DV90
Kelvin Gro., Chess.	282	330	CL104
Kelvin Ind. Est., Grnf.	233	313	CB66
Kelvin Par., Orp.	291	334	ES102
Kelvin Rd. N5	116	306	DP63
Kelvin Rd., Well.	262	327	EU83
Kelvinbrook, W.Mol.	267	329	CB97
Kelvington Clo., Croy.	288	333	DY101
Kelvington Rd. SE15	181	325	DX85
Kember St. N1	115	306	DM66
Kemble Dr., Brom.	290	334	EL104
Kemble Rd. N17	222	307	DU53
Kemble Rd. SE23	197	325	DX88
Kemble Rd., Croy.	286	332	DN104
Kemble St. WC2	47	316	DM72
Kemerton Rd. SE5	178	324	DQ83
Kemerton Rd., Beck.	275	325	EB96
Kemerton Rd., Croy.	287	332	DT101
Kemeys St. E9	119	307	DY64
Kemnal Rd., Chis.	277	326	EQ94
Kemp Gdns., Croy.	287	332	DQ100
Kemp Rd., Dag.	236	309	EX60
Kempe Rd. NW6	127	315	CX68
Kempe Rd., Enf.	203	301	DV36
Kempis Way SE22	179	324	DS85
Kemplay Rd. NW3	113	305	DD63
Kemp's Ct. W1	45	316	DJ72
Kemps Dr. E14	140	317	EA73
Kemps Dr., Nthwd.	213	302	BT52
Kemps Gdns. SE13	182	325	EC85
Kempsford Gdns. SW5	76	315	DA78
Kempsford Rd. SE11	84	316	DN77
Kempshott Rd. SW16	272	324	DK94
Kempson Rd. SW6	158	315	DA81
Kempt St. SE18	253	318	EN79
Kempthorne Rd. SE8	149	317	DY77
Kempton Ave., Horn.	238	311	FM63
Kempton Ave., Nthlt.	233	313	CA65
Kempton Ave., Sun.	266	329	BV95
Kempton Clo., Erith	255	319	FC79
Kempton Clo., Uxb.	241	312	BQ63
Kempton Ct., Sun.	266	329	BV95
Kempton Rd. E6	244	318	EM67
Kempton Rd., Hmptn.	266	329	BZ96
Kempton Wk., Croy.	288	333	DY100
Kemsing Clo., Bex.	262	327	EY87
Kemsing Clo., Brom.	289	333	EF103
Kemsing Clo., Th.Hth.	273	324	DQ98
Kemsing Rd. SE10	252	318	EG78
Ken Way, Wem.	92	304	CQ61
Kenbury Clo., Uxb.	231	312	BN62
Kenbury Gdns. SE5	162	316	DQ82
Kenbury St. SE5	162	316	DQ82
Kenchester Clo. SW8	161	316	DL80
Kencot Way, Erith	254	319	EZ75
Kendal Ave. N18	209	300	DR49
Kendal Ave. W3	124	314	CN70
Kendal Ave., Bark.	235	308	ES66
Kendal Clo. SW9	162	316	DP80
Kendal Clo., Felt.	265	320	BT88
Kendal Clo., Hayes	241	312	BS68
Kendal Clo., Wdf.Grn.	211	301	EF47
Kendal Cft., Horn.	238	310	FG64
Kendal Gdns. N18	209	300	DR49
Kendal Gdns., Sutt.	285	331	DC103
Kendal Par. N18	209	300	DR49
Kendal Pl. SW15	173	323	CZ85
Kendal Rd. NW10	110	305	CU63
Kendal St. W2	42/3	315	DE72
Kendale Rd., Brom.	275	325	EE92
Kendall Ave., Beck.	274	325	DY96
Kendall Ave., S.Croy.	295	332	DR109
Kendall Ave. S., S.Croy.	295	332	DQ110
Kendall Ct. SW19	271	323	DD93
Kendall Pl. W1	44	316	DG71
Kendall Rd., Beck.	274	325	DY96
Kendall Rd., Islw.	152	314	CG82
Kendalmere Clo. N10	220	306	DH53
Kender St. SE14	164	317	DW81
Kendoa Rd. SW4	177	324	DK84
Kendon Clo. E11	224	308	EH57
Kendra Hall Rd., S.Croy.	294	332	DP108
Kendrey Gdns., Twick.	259	321	CE86
Kendrick Ms. SW7	78	315	DD77
Kendrick Pl. SW7	78	315	DD77
Kenelm Clo., Har.	90	304	CG62
Kenerne Dr., Barn.	206	299	CY43
Kenilford Rd. SW12	192	324	DH87
Kenilworth Ave. E17	223	307	EA54
Kenilworth Ave. SW19	271	323	DA92
Kenilworth Ave., Har.	232	313	BZ63
Kenilworth Ave., Rom.	229	311	FP51
Kenilworth Ct. SW15	173	323	CX83
Kenilworth Cres., Enf.	202	300	DS39
Kenilworth Gdns. SE18	253	318	EP82
Kenilworth Gdns., Hayes	249	312	BT71
Kenilworth Gdns., Horn.	238	310	FJ62
Kenilworth Gdns., Ilf.	235	308	ET61
Kenilworth Gdns., Sthl.	242	313	BZ69
Kenilworth Gdns., Stai.	264	328	BJ92
Kenilworth Rd. E3	129	317	DY68
Kenilworth Rd. NW6	127	315	CZ67
Kenilworth Rd. SE20	274	325	DX95
Kenilworth Rd. W5	133	314	CL74
Kenilworth Rd., Ashf.	264	320	BK90
Kenilworth Rd., Edg.	205	298	CQ48
Kenilworth Rd., Epsom	283	331	CU106
Kenilworth Rd., Orp.	291	334	EQ100
Kenley Ave. NW9	217	304	CS53
Kenley Clo., Bex.	263	327	FA87
Kenley Clo., Chis.	277	326	ES97
Kenley Gdns., Horn.	238	311	FM61
Kenley Gdns., Th.Hth.	273	324	DP98
Kenley La., Ken.	295	332	DQ114
Kenley Rd. SW19	270	323	CZ96
Kenley Rd., Kings.T.	269	322	CP96
Kenley Rd., Twick.	168	322	CG86
Kenley Wk. W11	137	315	CY73
Kenley Wk., Sutt.	284	331	CX105
Kenlor Rd. SW17	271	323	DD92
Kenmare Dr., Mitch.	271	323	DF94
Kenmare Gdns. N13	209	300	DQ49
Kenmare Rd., Th.Hth.	286	332	DN100
Kenmere Gdns., Wem.	124	314	CN67
Kenmere Rd., Well.	254	319	EW82
Kenmont Gdns. NW10	126	315	CV69
Kenmore Ave., Har.	216	304	CG56
Kenmore Clo., Rich.	154	314	CN80
Kenmore Cres., Hayes	241	312	BT69
Kenmore Gdns., Edg.	217	304	CP54
Kenmore Rd., Har.	216	304	CL57
Kenmore Rd., Ken.	294	332	DP114
Kenmure Rd. E8	118	307	DV64
Kenmure Yd. E8	118	307	DV64
Kennard Rd. E15	121	307	ED66
Kennard Rd. N11	207	299	DF50
Kennard St. E16	244	318	EM74
Kennard St. SW11	160	316	DG81
Kennedy Ave., Enf.	210	301	DW44
Kennedy Clo. E13	244	318	EG68
Kennedy Clo., Mitch.	272	324	DG95
Kennedy Clo., Orp.	291	334	ER102
Kennedy Clo., Pnr.	214	303	BZ51
Kennedy Path W7	243	313	CF70
Kennedy Rd. W7	243	313	CE71
Kennedy Rd., Bark.	245	318	ES67
Kennedy Wk. SE17	86	316	DR77
Kennel Hill SE22	179	324	DS83
Kennet Clo. SW11	175	323	DD84
Kennet Clo., Upmin.	229	311	FS58
Kennet Rd. W9	127	315	CZ70
Kennet Rd., Islw.	259	321	CF83
Kennet Sq., Mitch.	271	323	DE95
Kennet St. E1	138	317	DU74
Kennet Wf. La. EC4	61	316	DQ73
Kenneth Ave., Ilf.	235	308	EP63
Kenneth Cres. NW2	110	305	CV64
Kenneth Gdns., Stan.	216	304	CG51
Kenneth More Rd., Ilf.	235	308	EP62
Kenneth Rd., Rom.	236	309	EX59
Kenneth Robbins Ho. N17	222	307	DV52
Kennet Ct., Swan.	279	327	FE97
Kenninghall Rd. E15	242	313	BY71
Kenning St. SE16	148	317	DW75
Kenning Ter. N1	26/7	316	DS67
Kenninghall Rd. E5	102	307	DU62
Kenninghall Rd. N18	210	301	DW50
Kennings Way SE11	84	316	DN78
Kennington Grn. SE11	84	316	DN78
Kennington Gro. SE11	161	316	DM79
Kennington La. SE11	82/3	316	DL78
Kennington Oval SE11	161	316	DM79
Kennington Pk. Est. SE11	162	316	DN79
Kennington Pk. Gdns. SE11	162	316	DN79
Kennington Pk. Pl. SE11	162	316	DN79
Kennington Pk. Rd. SE11	162	316	DN79
Kennington Rd. SE1	72	316	DN76
Kennington Rd. SE11	72	316	DN76
Kenny Rd. NW7	206	299	CY50
Kenmylands Rd., Ilf.	226	309	EU52
Kenrick Pl. W1	44	316	DG71
Kensal Rd. W10	127	315	CX70
Kensington Ave. E12	234	308	EL65
Kensington Ave., Th.Hth.	273	324	DN95
Kensington Ch. Ct. W8	64/5	315	DB75
Kensington Ch. St. W8	52	315	DA74
Kensington Ch. Wk. W8	64/5	315	DB75
Kensington Clo. N11	220	306	DG51
Kensington Ct. W8	64/5	315	DB75
Kensington Ct. Gdns. W8	64/5	315	DB76
Kensington Ct. Ms. W8	64/5	315	DB75
Kensington Ct. Pl. W8	64/5	315	DB76
Kensington Dr., Wdf.Grn.	224	308	EK54
Kensington Gdns. W2	52/3	315	DB75
Kensington Gdns., Ilf.	234	308	EM60
Kensington Gdns., Kings.T.	268	322	CK97
Kensington Gdns. Sq. W2	40/1	315	DB72
Kensington Gate W8	65	315	DC76
Kensington Gore SW7	65	315	DC75
Kensington Hall Gdns. W14	147	315	CZ78
Kensington High St. W8	64	315	DA76
Kensington High St. W14	147	315	CZ76
Kensington Mall W8	52	315	DA74
Kensington Palace Gdns. W8	52/3	315	DB74
Kensington Pk. Gdns. W11	137	315	CZ73
Kensington Pk. Ms. W11	137	315	CZ72
Kensington Pk. Rd. W11	137	315	CZ72
Kensington Pl. W8	52	315	DA74
Kensington Rd. SW7	65	315	DC75
Kensington Rd. W8	64/5	315	DB75
Kensington Rd., Nthlt.	243	313	CA69
Kensington Rd., Rom.	227	309	FC58
Kensington Sq. W8	64/5	315	DB75
Kensington Ter., S.Croy.	295	332	DR108
Kent Ave. W13	132	314	CH71
Kent Ave., Dag.	247	319	FA70
Kent Ave., Well.	261	326	ET85
Kent Clo., Mitch.	286	332	DL98
Kent Clo., Stai.	264	328	BK93
Kent Clo., Uxb.	240	312	BJ65
Kent Dr., Horn.	238	310	FK63
Kent Dr., Tedd.	267	329	CE92
Kent Gdns. W13	132	314	CH71
Kent Gdns., Ruis.	214	303	BV58
Kent Ho. La., Beck.	274	325	DY92
Kent Ho. Rd. SE20	274	325	DX94
Kent Ho. Rd. SE26	274	325	DY92
Kent Ho. Rd., Beck.	274	325	DX94
Kent Pas. NW1	31	315	DF70
Kent Rd. N21	209	300	DR46
Kent Rd. W4	144	314	CQ76
Kent Rd., Dag.	237	309	FB64
Kent Rd., E.Mol.	267	329	CC98
Kent Rd., Kings.T.	268	322	CK97
Kent Rd., Orp.	291	335	EV100
Kent Rd., Rich.	154	314	CN80
Kent Rd., W.Wick.	288	333	EB102
Kent St. E2	27	316	DT68
Kent St. E13	244	318	EH69
Kent Ter. NW1	30/1	315	DE69
Kent Twrs. SE20	274	325	DV94
Kent Vw. Gdns., Ilf.	235	308	ES61
Kent Wk. SW9	178	324	DP84
Kent Way SE15	163	316	DT81
Kent Way, Surb.	282	330	CL104
Kent Yd. SW7	66/7	315	DE75
Kentford Way, Nthlt.	242	313	BY67
Kentish Bldgs. SE1	74	316	DR75
Kentish Rd., Belv.	255	319	FA77
Kentish Town Rd. NW1	114	306	DH66
Kentish Town Rd. NW5	114	306	DH65
Kentish Way, Brom.	276	326	EG96
Kentmere Rd. SE18	253	318	ES77
Kenton Ave., Har.	233	313	CF59
Kenton Ave., Sthl.	243	313	CA73
Kenton Ave., Sun.	266	329	BX96
Kenton Ct. W14	147	315	CZ76
Kenton Gdns., Har.	216	304	CJ57
Kenton La., Har.	215	303	CF51
Kenton Pk. Ave., Har.	216	304	CK56
Kenton Pk. Clo., Har.	216	304	CJ56
Kenton Pk. Cres., Har.	216	304	CK56
Kenton Pk. Rd., Har.	216	304	CJ56
Kenton Rd. E9	119	307	DX65
Kenton Rd., Har.	233	313	CF59
Kenton St. WC1	34/5	316	DL70
Kenton Way, Hayes	241	312	BS69
Kents Pas., Hmptn.	266	329	BZ95
Kentwode Grn. SW13	156	315	CU80
Kenver Ave. N12	219	305	DD51
Kenward Rd. SE9	260	326	EJ85
Kenway, Rom.	227	309	FC54
Kenway Rd. SW5	76/7	315	DB77
Kenwood Ave. N14	208	300	DK43
Kenwood Ave. SE14	165	317	DX81
Kenwood Clo. NW3	97	305	DD60
Kenwood Clo., West Dr.	257	320	BN79
Kenwood Dr., Beck.	275	325	EC97
Kenwood Gdns. E18	224	308	EH55
Kenwood Gdns., Ilf.	225	308	EN56
Kenwood Rd. N6	219	305	DF58
Kenwood Rd. N9	210	301	DU46
Kenworthy Rd. E9	119	307	DY64
Kenwyn Dr. NW2	93	304	CS62
Kenwyn Rd. SW4	177	324	DK84
Kenwyn Rd. SW20	270	323	CW95
Kenya Rd. SE7	252	318	EK80
Kenyngton Dr., Sun.	266	329	BU92
Kenyngton Pl., Har.	216	304	CJ57
Kenyon St. SW6	157	315	CX81
Keogh Rd. E15	121	307	EE65
Kepler Rd. SW4	177	324	DL84
Keppel Rd. E6	234	308	EM66
Keppel Rd., Dag.	236	309	EY63
Keppel Row SE1	61	316	DQ74
Keppel St. WC1	46	316	DK71
Kerbela St. E2	128	317	DU70
Kerbey St. E14	140	317	EB72
Kerfield Cres. SE5	163	316	DR81
Kerfield Pl. SE5	163	316	DR81
Kernow Clo., Horn.	238	311	FL61
Kerridge Ct. N1	117	306	DS65
Kerrison Pl. W5	133	314	CK74
Kerrison Rd. E15	131	317	ED67
Kerrison Rd. SW11	175	323	DE83
Kerrison Rd. W5	133	314	CK74
Kerrison Vil. W5	133	314	CK74
Kerry Ave., Stan.	204	298	CK49
Kerry Clo. E16	244	318	EH72
Kerry Clo. N13	208	300	DM47
Kerry Clo., Upmin.	239	311	FT59
Kerry Ct., Stan.	204	298	CK49
Kerry Dr., Upmin.	239	311	FT59
Kerry Path SE14	165	317	DZ79
Kerry Rd. SE14	165	317	DZ79
Kersey Gdns. SE9	276	326	EL91
Kersey Gdns., Rom.	228	311	FL53
Kersfield Rd. SW15	173	323	CX86
Kershaw Clo. SW18	175	323	DD86
Kershaw Rd., Dag.	237	309	FA62
Kersley Ms. SW11	159	315	DF82
Kersley Rd. N16	101	306	DS61
Kersley St. SW11	159	315	DF82
Kerstin Clo., Hayes	241	312	BT73
Kerswell Clo. N15	221	306	DS57
Kerwick Clo. N7	115	306	DM66
Keslake Rd. NW6	127	315	CX68
Kessock Clo. N17	222	307	DV57
Kesteven Clo., Ilf.	225	308	ET51
Kestlake Rd., Bex.	262	327	EW86
Keston Ave., Kes.	290	334	EJ106
Keston Clo. N18	209	300	DR48
Keston Clo., Well.	254	319	EW80
Keston Gdns., Kes.	290	334	EJ105
Keston Pk. Clo., Kes.	290	334	EM104
Keston Rd. N17	221	306	DR55
Keston Rd. SE15	180	325	DU83
Keston Rd., Th.Hth.	286	332	DM100
Kestrel Ave. E6	244	318	EL71
Kestrel Ave. SE24	178	324	DP85
Kestrel Clo. NW9	217	304	CS54
Kestrel Clo. NW10	109	304	CR64
Kestrel Clo., Horn.	238	310	FH66
Kestrel Ho. EC1	37	316	DQ69
Kestrel Ho. W13	243	313	CF70
Kestrel La., Kings.T.	268	322	CK92
Kestrel Pl. SE14	165	317	DY79
Kestrel Way, Croy.	269	322	CS92
Keswick Ave. SW15	269	322	CS92
Keswick Ave. SW19	271	323	DA96
Keswick Ave., Horn.	238	310	FK60
Keswick Bdy. SW15	173	323	CY85
Keswick Clo., Sutt.	285	331	DC105
Keswick Dr., Enf.	203	301	DW36
Keswick Gdns., Ilf.	224	308	EL57
Keswick Gdns., Ruis.	231	302	BR58
Keswick Gdns., Wem.	107	304	CL63
Keswick Ms. W5	133	314	CL74
Keswick Rd. SW15	173	323	CY85
Keswick Rd., Bexh.	255	319	FA82
Keswick Rd., Orp.	291	334	ET102
Keswick Rd., Twick.	259	321	CC86
Keswick Rd., W.Wick.	289	333	EE103
Kett Gdns. SW2	177	324	DM85
Kettering Rd., Enf.	203	301	DX37
Kettering Rd., Rom.	228	311	FL52
Kettering St. SW16	272	324	DJ93
Kettlebaston Rd. E10	103	307	DZ60
Kettlewell Ct., Swan.	279	327	FF96
Kevan Ho. SE5	162	316	DQ80
Kevelioc Rd. N17	221	306	DQ53
Kevin Clo., Houns.	250	321	BW82
Kevington Clo., Orp.	277	326	ET98
Kevington Dr., Chis.	277	326	ES98
Kevington Dr., Orp.	278	327	EU98
Kew Bri., Brent.	153	314	CM79
Kew Bri., Rich.	153	314	CM79
Kew Bri. Arches, Rich.	153	314	CM79
Kew Bri. Ct. W4	144	314	CN78
Kew Bri. Rd., Brent.	153	314	CM79
Kew Cres., Sutt.	284	331	CY104
Kew Foot Rd., Rich.	169	322	CL84
Kew Gdns. Rd., Rich.	153	314	CM80
Kew Grn., Rich.	153	314	CM79
Kew Meadow Path, Rich.	154	314	CP81
Kew Palace, Rich.	153	314	CL80
Kew Rd., Rich.	169	322	CL84
Kewferry Dr., Nthwd.	213	302	BP50
Kewferry Rd., Nthwd.	213	302	BQ51
Key Clo. E1	128	317	DV70
Keybridge Ho. SW8	161	316	DL79
Keyes Rd. NW2	111	305	CX64
Keymer Rd. SW2	193	324	DM89
Keynes Clo. N2	219	305	DF56
Keynsham Ave., Wdf.Grn.	211	301	EE49
Keynsham Gdns. SE9	260	326	EL85
Keynsham Rd. SE9	260	326	EK85
Keynsham Rd., Mord.	284	331	DB102
Keynsham Wk., Mord.	284	331	DB102
Keyse Rd. SE1	75	316	DT76
Keysham Ave., Houns.	250	321	BU81
Keystone Cres. N1	22/3	316	DL68
Keywood Dr., Sun.	266	329	BU93
Keyworth Clo. E5	119	307	DY63
Keyworth St. SE1	72/3	316	DP76
Kezia St. SE8	149	317	DY78
Khama Rd. SW17	271	323	DE91
Khartoum Rd. E13	244	318	EH69
Khartoum Rd. SW17	271	323	DD91
Khartoum Rd., Ilf.	235	308	EP64
Khyber Rd. SW11	159	315	DE82
Kibworth St. SW8	161	316	DM80
Kidbrooke Gdns. SE3	252	318	EG82
Kidbrooke Gro. SE3	252	318	EG81
Kidbrooke La. SE9	260	326	EL84
Kidbrooke Pk. Clo. SE3	252	318	EH81
Kidbrooke Pk. Rd. SE3	252	318	EH81
Kidbrooke Way SE3	252	318	EH82
Kidd Pl. SE7	252	318	EL78
Kidderminster Pl., Croy.	286	332	DP102
Kidderminster Rd., Croy.	286	332	DP102
Kidderpore Ave. NW3	112	305	DA63
Kidderpore Gdns. NW3	112	305	DA63
Kidlington Way NW9	217	304	CS54
Kidron Way E9	128	317	DW67
Kielder Clo., Ilf.	225	308	ET51
Kiffen St. EC2	38	316	DR70
Kilberry Clo., Islw.	251	321	CD81
Kilburn Bri. NW6	111	305	CZ66
Kilburn Bldgs. NW6	16/7	315	DB67
Kilburn Gate NW6	16/7	315	DB68
Kilburn High Rd. NW6	111	305	CZ66
Kilburn La. W9	127	315	CX69
Kilburn La. W10	127	315	CX69
Kilburn Pk. Rd. NW6	28	315	DA69
Kilburn Pl. NW6	16	315	DA67
Kilburn Priory NW6	16/7	315	DB67
Kilburn Sq. NW6	16	315	DA67
Kilburn Vale NW6	16/7	315	DB67

Kildare Clo., Ruis. 232 313 BW60
Kildare Gdns. W2 40 315 DA72
Kildare Rd. E16 244 318 EG71
Kildare Ter. W2 40 315 DA72
Kildare Wk. E14 140 317 EA72
Kildoran Rd. SW2 177 324 DL85
Kildowan Rd., Ilf. 236 309 EU60
Kilgour Rd. SE23 181 325 DY86
Kilkie St. SW6 158 315 DC82
Killarney Rd. SW18 174 323 DC86
Killearn Rd. SE6 199 325 ED88
Killester Gdns., Wor.Pk. 283 331 CV105
Killick St. N1 23 316 DM68
Killieser Ave. SW2 193 324 DL88
Killip Clo. E16 141 317 EF72
Killowen Ave., Nthlt. 233 313 CC64
Killowen Rd. E9 119 307 DX65
Killyon Rd. SW8 160 316 DJ82
Killyon Ter. SW8 160 316 DJ82
Kilmaine Rd. SW6 157 315 CY80
Kilmarnock Gdns., Dag. 236 309 EW62
Kilmarsh Rd. W6 146 315 CW77
Kilmartin Ave. SW16 272 324 DM97
Kilmartin Rd., Ilf. 236 309 EU61
Kilmartin Way, Horn. 238 310 FH64
Kilmeston Way SE15 163 316 DT80
Kilmington Rd. SW13 156 315 CU79
Kilmiston Ave., Shep. 281 328 BQ100
Kilmorey Gdns., Twick. 168 322 CH84
Kilmorey Rd., Twick. 168 322 CH84
Kilmorie Rd. SE23 197 325 DY88
Kiln Clo., Hayes 257 320 BR79
Kiln Ms. SW17 271 323 DD92
Kiln Pl. NW5 114 306 DG63
Kiln Way, Nthwd. 213 302 BS51
Kilner St. E14 140 317 EA71
Kilpatrick Way, Hayes 242 313 BY71
Kilravock St. W10 127 315 CY69
Kilross Rd., Felt. 265 320 BR88
Kilsby Wk., Dag. 236 309 EV65
Kilvinton Dr., Enf. 202 300 DR38
Kimbell Gdns. SW6 157 315 CY81
Kimber Rd. SW18 190 323 DA87
Kimberley Ave. E6 244 318 EL68
Kimberley Ave. SE15 164 317 DV82
Kimberley Ave., Ilf. 235 308 ER59
Kimberley Ave., Rom. 227 309 FC58
Kimberley Dr., Sid. 262 327 EX89
Kimberley Gdns. N4 221 306 DP57
Kimberley Gdns., Enf. 202 300 DT41
Kimberley Gate, Brom. 275 325 EF94
Kimberley Pl., Pur. 294 332 DN111
Kimberley Rd. E4 211 301 EE46
Kimberley Rd. E11 105 307 ED61
Kimberley Rd. E16 131 317 EF70
Kimberley Rd. E17 222 307 DZ53
Kimberley Rd. N17 222 307 DU54
Kimberley Rd. N18 222 307 DV51
Kimberley Rd. NW6 127 315 CY67
Kimberley Rd. SW9 161 316 DL82
Kimberley Rd., Beck. 274 325 DX96
Kimberley Rd., Croy. 286 332 DP100
Kimberley Way E4 211 301 EE46
Kimble Rd. SW19 271 323 DD93
Kimbolton Clo. SE12 183 325 EF86
Kimbolton Row SW3 78/9 315 DE77
Kimmeridge Gdns. SE9 276 326 EL91
Kimmeridge Rd. SE9 276 326 EL91
Kimpton Ind. Est., Sutt. 284 331 CZ103
Kimpton Rd. SE5 163 316 DR81
Kimpton Rd., Sutt. 284 331 CZ104
Kinburn St. SE16 149 317 DX75
Kincaid Rd. SE15 164 317 DV80
Kincardine Gdns. W9 127 315 CZ70
Kinch Gro., Har. 91 304 CM59
Kinder Clo. SE28 246 319 EX73
Kinder St. E1 138 317 DV72
Kinfauns Ave., Horn. 228 310 FJ58
Kinfauns Rd. SW2 194 324 DN89
Kinfauns Rd., Ilf. 236 309 EU60
King Alfred Ave. SE6 275 325 EA91
King Alfred Rd., Rom. 228 311 FM54
King & Queen Clo. SE9 276 326 EL91
King & Queen St. SE17 85 316 DQ78
King Arthur Clo. SE15 164 317 DW80
King Charles Cres., Surb. 282 330 CM101
King Charles Rd., Surb. 282 330 CM99
King Charles St. SW1 70 316 DK75
King Charles Ter. E1 138 317 DV73
King Charles Wk. SW19 189 323 CY88
King David La. E1 138 317 DW73
King Edward Dr., Chess. 282 330 CL104
King Edward Ms. SW13 156 315 CU81
King Edward Rd. E10 104 307 EC60
King Edward Rd. E17 222 307 DY55
King Edward Rd., Rom. 227 309 FF58
King Edward St. EC1 49 316 DQ72
King Edward Wk. SE1 72 316 DN76
King Edward's Gdns. W3 134 314 CN74
King Edwards Gro., Tedd. 268 322 CH93
King Edward's Pl. W3 134 314 CN74
King Edwards Rd. E9 128 317 DV67
King Edwards Rd. N9 210 301 DV45
King Edwards Rd., Bark. 245 318 ER67
King Edward's Rd., Enf. 203 301 DX42
King Edwards Rd., Ruis. 231 312 BR60
King Gdns., Croy. 286 332 DP106
King George Ave. E16 244 318 EK72
King George Ave., Ilf. 225 308 ER57
King George Clo., Rom. 227 309 FC55
King George Clo., Sun. 265 328 BT92
King George VI Ave., Mitch. 271 323 DF98
King George Sq., Rich. 169 322 CM86
King George St. SE10 166 317 EC80
King Georges Dr., Sthl. 242 313 BZ71
King Harolds Way, Bexh. 254 319 EX80
King Henry Ms., Orp. 291 334 ET106
King Henry St. N16 117 306 DS64
King Henry Ter. E1 138 317 DV73
King Henry's Rd. NW3 113 305 DE66
King Henrys Rd., Kings.T. 269 322 CP97
King Henry's Wk. N1 117 306 DS65
King James St. SE1 72/3 316 DP75
King John Ct. EC2 38/9 316 DS70
King John St. E1 139 317 DX71
King John's Wk. SE9 260 326 EK88
King Sq. EC1 37 316 DQ69
King Stairs Clo. SE16 148 317 DV75
King St. E13 244 318 EG70
King St. EC2 49 316 DQ72
King St. N2 219 305 DD55
King St. N17 221 306 DT53
King St. SW1 57 316 DJ74
King St. W3 134 314 CP74
King St. W6 146 315 CU77
King St. WC2 58/9 316 DL73
King St., Cher. 280 328 BG102
King St., Rich. 169 322 CK85
King St., Sthl. 250 321 BY76
King St., Twick. 184 322 CG88
King William IV Gdns. SE20 274 325 DW93
King William La. SE10 151 317 EE78
King William St. EC4 62 316 DR73
King William Wk. SE10 166 317 EC79
Kingaby Gdns., Rain. 238 310 FG66
Kingcup Clo., Croy. 288 333 DX102
Kingdon Rd. NW6 112 305 DA65
Kingfield Rd. W5 123 314 CK70
Kingfield St. E14 150 317 EC77
Kingfisher Clo. SE28 246 319 EW73
Kingfisher Clo., Har. 215 303 CF52
Kingfisher Clo., Nthwd. 213 302 BP53
Kingfisher Clo., Orp. 278 327 EX98
Kingfisher Ct. SW19 189 323 CY89
Kingfisher Dr., Rich. 268 322 CH91
Kingfisher Rd., Upmin. 239 311 FT60
Kingfisher Sq. SE8 165 317 DZ79
Kingfisher St. E6 244 318 EL71
Kingfisher Wk. NW9 217 304 CS54
Kingfisher Way NW10 109 304 CR65
Kingfisher Way, Beck. 288 333 DX99
Kingham Clo. SW18 190 323 DC87
Kingham Clo. W11 147 315 CY75
Kinghorn St. EC1 49 316 DQ71
Kinglake Est. SE17 86/7 316 DS78
Kinglake St. SE17 86/7 316 DS78
Kingly Ct. W1 57 316 DJ73
Kingly St. W1 57 316 DJ73
Kings Arbour, Sthl. 250 321 BY78
Kings Arms Ct. E1 138 317 DU71
Kings Arms Yd. EC2 50 316 DR72
Kings Ave. N10 220 306 DG55
Kings Ave. N21 209 300 DP46
King's Ave. SW4 177 324 DL85
King's Ave. SW12 193 324 DK88
Kings Ave. W5 133 314 CK72
Kings Ave., Brom. 275 325 EF93
Kings Ave., Cars. 293 331 DE108
Kings Ave., Grnf. 243 313 CB72
Kings Ave., Houns. 251 321 CB81
Kings Ave., N.Mal. 269 322 CS98
Kings Ave., Rom. 226 309 EZ58
Kings Ave., Sun. 265 328 BT92
Kings Ave., Wdf.Grn. 224 308 EH51
Kings Bench St. SE1 72/3 316 DP75
Kings Bench Wk. EC4 48 316 DN72
Kings Chase, E.Mol. 267 329 CC97
Kings Clo. E10 104 307 EB59
Kings Clo. NW4 218 305 CX56
Kings Clo., Dart. 263 327 FE84
Kings Clo., Nthwd. 213 302 BT51
Kings Clo., Stai. 264 328 BK94
Kings College Rd. NW3 113 305 DE66
Kings College Rd., Ruis. 231 302 BT58
Kings Ct. E13 244 318 EH67
Kings Ct. W6 146 315 CU77
Kings Ct., Wem. 92 304 CP61
Kings Cres. N4 100 306 DQ62
Kings Cres. Est. N4 100 306 DQ61
King's Cross Bri. WC1 34/5 316 DL69
King's Cross Rd. WC1 35 316 DM69
Kings Dr., Edg. 204 298 CM49
Kings Dr., Surb. 282 330 CN101
Kings Dr., Tedd. 267 329 CD92
Kings Dr., Wem. 92 304 CP61
Kings Fm. Ave., Rich. 170 322 CN84
Kings Gdns. NW6 112 305 DA66
Kings Gdns., Ilf. 235 308 ER60
Kings Gdns., Upmin. 239 311 FS59
King's Garth Ms. SE23 196 325 DW89
Kings Gro. SE15 164 317 DV81
Kings Gro., Rom. 228 310 FG57
Kings Hall Rd., Beck. 274 325 DY94
Kings Head Hill E4 211 301 EB45
Kings Head Yd. SE1 62 316 DR74
Kings Highway SE18 253 318 ES79
Kings Keep, Kings.T. 268 322 CL98
Kings La., Sutt. 293 331 DD107
Kings Lynn Clo., Rom. 228 310 FK51
Kings Lynn Dr., Rom. 228 310 FK51
Kings Lynn Path, Rom. 228 310 FK51
Kings Ms. SW4 177 324 DL85
King's Ms. WC1 35 316 DM70
King's Orchard SE9 260 326 EL86
Kings Paddock, Hmptn. 267 329 CC95
Kings Par., Cars. 285 331 DE104
King's Pas. E11 105 307 EE59
Kings Pas., Kings.T. 268 322 CK96
Kings Pl. SE1 73 316 DQ75
Kings Pl. W4 144 314 CQ77
King's Reach Twr. SE1 60 316 DN74
Kings Ride Gate, Rich. 170 322 CN84
Kings Rd. E4 211 301 ED46
Kings Rd. E6 244 318 EJ67
Kings Rd. E11 105 307 EE59
King's Rd. N17 221 306 DT53
Kings Rd. N18 210 301 DU50
Kings Rd. N22 220 306 DM53
Kings Rd. NW10 110 305 CV66
Kings Rd. SE25 274 325 DU97
King's Rd. SW1 159 315 DD79
King's Rd. SW3 159 315 DD79
King's Rd. SW6 158 315 DB80
King's Rd. SW10 158 315 DC80
Kings Rd. SW14 171 322 CR83
Kings Rd. SW19 271 323 DA93
Kings Rd. W5 133 314 CK71
Kings Rd., Bark. 235 308 EQ66
Kings Rd., Felt. 258 321 BW88
Kings Rd., Har. 232 313 BZ61
Kings Rd., Kings.T. 268 322 CL94
Kings Rd., Mitch. 272 324 DG97
Kings Rd., Orp. 291 334 ET105
Kings Rd., Rich. 169 322 CM86
Kings Rd., Rom. 228 310 FG57
Kings Rd., Surb. 282 330 CJ102
Kings Rd., Sutt. 292 331 DA110
Kings Rd., Tedd. 267 329 CD92
Kings Rd., Twick. 168 322 CH86
Kings Rd., Uxb. 240 312 BK68
Kings Rd., West Dr. 248 320 BM75
King's Scholars' Pas. SW1 69 316 DJ76
King's Ter. NW1 21 316 DJ67
Kings Ter., Islw. 168 322 CG83
Kings Wk., Kings.T. 268 322 CK95
Kings Wk., S.Croy. 295 333 DV114
Kings Way, Har. 215 303 CE56
Kingsand Rd. SE12 260 326 EG89
Kingsash Dr., Hayes 242 313 BY70
Kingsbridge Ave. W3 143 314 CM75
Kingsbridge Circ., Rom. 228 311 FL52
Kingsbridge Clo., Rom. 228 311 FL51
Kingsbridge Cres., Sthl. 242 313 BZ71
Kingsbridge Rd. W10 136 315 CW72
Kingsbridge Rd., Bark. 245 318 ER68
Kingsbridge Rd., Mord. 284 331 CX101
Kingsbridge Rd., Rom. 228 311 FL51
Kingsbridge Rd., Sthl. 250 321 BZ77
Kingsbridge Way, Hayes 241 312 BS69
Kingsbury Circle NW9 217 304 CN57
Kingsbury Rd. N1 117 306 DS65
Kingsbury Rd. NW9 217 304 CN57
Kingsbury Ter. N1 117 306 DS65
Kingsbury Trd. Est. NW9 217 304 CR58
Kingsclere Clo. SW15 188 323 CU87
Kingscliffe Gdns. SW19 189 323 CZ88
Kingscote Rd. W4 145 314 CR76
Kingscote Rd., Croy. 287 333 DV101
Kingscote Rd., N.Mal. 269 322 CR97
Kingscote St. EC4 60/1 316 DP73
Kingscourt Rd. SW16 193 324 DK90
Kingscroft Rd. NW2 111 305 CZ65
Kingsdale Gdns. W11 137 315 CX74
Kingsdale Rd. SE18 253 318 ET79
Kingsdale Rd. SE20 274 325 DX94
Kingsdown Ave. W3 135 314 CS73
Kingsdown Ave. W13 142 314 CH75
Kingsdown Ave., S.Croy. 294 332 DP109
Kingsdown Clo. W10 137 315 CX72
Kingsdown Rd. E11 105 307 EE62
Kingsdown Rd. N19 99 306 DL62
Kingsdown Rd., Sutt. 284 331 CY106
Kingsdown Way, Brom. 289 334 EG101
Kingsdowne Rd., Surb. 282 330 CL101
Kingsend, Ruis. 231 312 BR60
Kingsfield Ave., Har. 215 303 CB56
Kingsfield Dr., Enf. 203 301 DX35
Kingsfield Ho. SE9 260 326 EK90
Kingsfield Rd., Har. 233 313 CD59
Kingsfield Way, Enf. 203 301 DX35
Kingsford Ave., Wall. 294 332 DL108
Kingsford St. NW5 113 305 DF64
Kingsford Way E6 244 318 EM71
Kingsgate, Wem. 92 304 CQ62
Kingsgate Ave. N3 219 305 DA55
Kingsgate Clo., Bexh. 254 319 EY81
Kingsgate Clo., Orp. 278 327 EW97
Kingsgate Pl. NW6 112 305 DA66
Kingsgate Rd. NW6 112 305 DA66
Kingsgate Rd., Kings.T. 268 322 CL95
Kingsground SE9 260 326 EL87
Kingshall Ms. SE13 182 325 EC83
Kingshill Ave., Har. 216 304 CH56
Kingshill Ave., Hayes 241 312 BS69
Kingshill Ave., Nthlt. 242 313 BU69
Kingshill Ave., Rom. 227 309 FC51
Kingshill Ave., Wor.Pk. 283 331 CU101
Kingshill Dr., Har. 216 304 CH54
Kingshold Rd. E9 118 307 DW66
Kingsholm Gdns. SE9 260 326 EK84
Kingshurst Rd. SE12 260 326 EG87
Kingsland NW8 18/9 315 DE67
Kingsland Grn. E8 117 306 DS65
Kingsland High St. E8 117 306 DT65
Kingsland Pas. E8 117 306 DS65
Kingsland Rd. E2 38/9 316 DS69
Kingsland Rd. E8 26/7 316 DS67
Kingsland Rd. E13 244 318 EJ69
Kingslawn Clo. SW15 172 323 CV85
Kingsleigh Pl., Mitch. 271 323 DF97
Kingsleigh Wk., Brom. 275 325 EF98
Kingsley Ave. W13 132 314 CG72
Kingsley Ave., Houns. 251 321 CC82
Kingsley Ave., Sthl. 243 313 CA73
Kingsley Ave., Sutt. 285 331 DD105
Kingsley Clo. N2 219 305 DC57
Kingsley Clo., Dag. 237 309 FB63
Kingsley Ct., Edg. 205 298 CP47
Kingsley Dr., Wor.Pk. 283 330 CT103
Kingsley Flats SE1 86/7 316 DS77
Kingsley Gdns. E4 211 301 EA50
Kingsley Gdns., Horn. 228 310 FK56
Kingsley Ms. E1 138 317 DV73
Kingsley Ms. W8 64/5 315 DB76
Kingsley Ms., Chis. 277 326 EP93
Kingsley Pl. N6 98 306 DG59
Kingsley Rd. E7 234 308 EG66
Kingsley Rd. E17 223 307 EC54
Kingsley Rd. N13 209 300 DN49
Kingsley Rd. NW6 127 315 CZ67
Kingsley Rd. SW19 271 323 DB92
Kingsley Rd., Croy. 286 332 DN102
Kingsley Rd., Har. 233 313 CC63
Kingsley Rd., Houns. 251 321 CB81
Kingsley Rd., Ilf. 225 308 EQ53
Kingsley Rd., Pnr. 214 303 BZ56
Kingsley St. SW11 175 323 DF83
Kingsley Way N2 219 305 DC57
Kingsley Wd. Dr. SE9 260 326 EM90
Kingslyn Cres. SE19 273 324 DS95
Kingsman Par. SE18 252 318 EM76
Kingsman St. SE18 252 318 EM76
Kingsmead, Rich. 169 322 CM86
Kingsmead Ave. N9 210 301 DV46
Kingsmead Ave. NW9 93 304 CR59
Kingsmead Ave., Mitch. 272 324 DJ97
Kingsmead Ave., Rom. 227 309 FE58
Kingsmead Ave., Sun. 266 329 BW96
Kingsmead Ave., Surb. 282 330 CN103
Kingsmead Ave., Wor.Pk. 283 331 CV103
Kingsmead Clo., Sid. 262 327 EU89
Kingsmead Clo., Tedd. 268 322 CH93
Kingsmead Dr., Nthlt. 232 313 BZ66
Kingsmead Est. E9 119 307 DY63
Kingsmead Rd. SW2 194 324 DN89
Kingsmead Way E9 119 307 DY63
Kingsmere Clo. SW15 173 323 CY83
Kingsmere Pk. NW9 92 304 CP60
Kingsmere Rd. SW19 189 323 CX89
Kingsmill Gdns., Dag. 236 309 EZ64
Kingsmill Rd., Dag. 236 309 EZ64
Kingsmill Ter. NW8 18 315 DD68
Kingsnympton Pk., Kings.T. 269 322 CP94
Kingspark Ct. E18 224 308 EG55
Kingsridge SW19 189 323 CY89
Kingsthorpe Rd. SE26 274 325 DX91
Kingston Ave., Felt. 257 320 BS86
Kingston Ave., Sutt. 284 331 CY104
Kingston Ave., West Dr. 248 312 BM73
Kingston Bri., Kings.T. 268 322 CK96
Kingston Bypass SW15 269 322 CS91
Kingston Bypass SW20 269 322 CS93
Kingston Bypass, N.Mal. 270 323 CU98
Kingston Clo., Nthlt. 232 313 BZ66
Kingston Clo., Rom. 226 309 EY55
Kingston Clo., Tedd. 268 322 CH93
Kingston Ct. N4 221 306 DQ58
Kingston Cres., Ashf. 264 328 BJ92
Kingston Cres., Beck. 274 325 DZ95
Kingston Gdns., Croy. 286 332 DL104
Kingston Hall Rd., Kings.T. 268 322 CK97
Kingston Hill, Kings.T. 269 322 CN95
Kingston Hill Ave., Rom. 226 309 EY55
Kingston Hill Pl., Kings.T. 269 322 CQ91
Kingston La., Tedd. 268 322 CG92
Kingston La., Uxb. 240 312 BL69
Kingston La., West Dr. 248 320 BM75
Kingston Pk. Est., Kings.T. 269 322 CP93
Kingston Pl., Har. 215 303 CF52
Kingston Rd. N9 210 301 DU47
Kingston Rd. SW15 188 323 CU89
Kingston Rd. SW19 270 323 CY96
Kingston Rd. SW20 270 323 CW96
Kingston Rd., Ashf. 264 328 BL93
Kingston Rd., Barn. 207 299 DD43
Kingston Rd., Epsom 283 330 CS105
Kingston Rd., Ilf. 235 308 EP63
Kingston Rd., Kings.T. 269 322 CP97
Kingston Rd., N.Mal. 269 322 CR98
Kingston Rd., Rom. 227 309 FF56
Kingston Rd., Sthl. 250 321 BZ75
Kingston Rd., Surb. 282 330 CP103
Kingston Rd., Tedd. 268 322 CH92
Kingston Rd., Wor.Pk. 283 330 CQ104
Kingston Sq. SE19 273 324 DR92
Kingston Vale SW15 269 322 CR91
Kingstown St. NW1 20 316 DG67
Kingswater Pl. SW11 159 315 DE80
Kingsway N12 219 305 DC51
Kingsway SW14 170 322 CP83
Kingsway WC2 47 316 DM72
Kingsway, Croy. 286 332 DM106
Kingsway, Enf. 210 301 DV43
Kingsway, Hayes 249 312 BQ71
Kingsway, N.Mal. 270 323 CW98
Kingsway, Orp. 291 334 EQ99
Kingsway, Stai. 264 320 BK88
Kingsway, Wem. 107 304 CL63
Kingsway, W.Wick. 289 333 EE104
Kingsway Bus. Pk., Hmptn. 266 329 BZ95
Kingsway Cres., Har. 215 303 CC56
Kingsway Ind. Est. N18 222 307 DX51
Kingsway Rd., Sutt. 292 331 CY107
Kingswear Rd. NW5 98 306 DH62
Kingswear Rd., Ruis. 232 313 BU61
Kingswood Ave. NW6 127 315 CY67
Kingswood Ave., Belv. 254 319 EZ77
Kingswood Ave., Brom. 275 325 EE97
Kingswood Ave., Hmptn. 267 329 CB93
Kingswood Ave., Houns. 250 321 BZ81
Kingswood Ave., Swan. 279 327 FF98
Kingswood Ave., Th.Hth. 286 332 DN99
Kingswood Clo. N20 207 299 DC45
Kingswood Clo. SW8 161 316 DL80
Kingswood Clo., Enf. 209 300 DS43
Kingswood Clo., N.Mal. 283 330 CT100
Kingswood Clo., Orp. 291 334 ER101
Kingswood Clo., Surb. 282 330 CL101
Kingswood Dr. SE19 273 324 DS91
Kingswood Dr., Cars. 285 331 DF102
Kingswood Dr., Sutt. 292 331 DB109
Kingswood Est. SE21 273 324 DS91
Kingswood Pk. N3 218 305 CZ54
Kingswood Pl. SE13 183 325 EE84
Kingswood Rd. SE20 274 325 DW93
Kingswood Rd. SW2 177 324 DL86
Kingswood Rd. SW19 270 323 CZ94
Kingswood Rd. W4 144 314 CQ76
Kingswood Rd., Brom. 275 325 ED98
Kingswood Rd., Ilf. 236 309 EU60
Kingswood Rd., Wem. 92 304 CN62
Kingswood Ter. W4 144 314 CQ76
Kingswood Way, Wall. 286 332 DL106
Kingsworth Clo., Beck. 288 333 DY99
Kingsworthy Clo., Kings.T. 268 322 CM97
Kingthorpe Rd. NW10 109 304 CR66
Kingthorpe Ter. NW10 109 304 CR65
Kingwood Rd. SW6 157 315 CY80
Kinlet Rd. SE18 253 318 EQ81
Kinloch Dr. NW9 93 304 CR59
Kinloch St. N7 99 306 DM62
Kinloss Gdns. N3 218 305 CZ55
Kinloss Rd., Cars. 285 331 DC101
Kinnaird Ave. W4 154 314 CQ80
Kinnaird Ave., Brom. 275 325 EF93
Kinnaird Clo., Brom. 275 325 EF93
Kinnaird Way, Wdf.Grn. 224 308 EM51
Kinnear Rd. W12 145 314 CT75
Kinnerton Pl. N. SW1 67 315 DF75
Kinnerton Pl. S. SW1 67 315 DF75
Kinnerton St. SW1 68 316 DG75
Kinnerton Yd. SW1 67 315 DF75
Kinnoul Rd. W6 157 315 CY79
Kinross Ave., Wor.Pk. 283 331 CU103
Kinross Clo., Edg. 205 298 CP47
Kinross Clo., Har. 216 304 CL57
Kinross Clo., Sun. 265 328 BT92
Kinross Dr., Sun. 265 328 BT92
Kinsale Rd. SE15 180 325 DU83
Kintore Way SE1 87 316 DT77
Kintyre Clo. SW16 272 324 DM96
Kinveachy Gdns. SE7 252 318 EL78
Kinver Rd. SE26 274 325 DW91
Kipling Dr. SW19 271 323 DD93
Kipling Est. SE1 74 316 DR75
Kipling Pl., Stan. 215 303 CF51
Kipling Rd., Bexh. 254 319 EY81
Kipling St. SE1 74 316 DR75
Kipling Ter. N9 209 300 DR48
Kipling Twrs., Rom. 228 310 FH52
Kippington Dr. SE9 260 326 EK88
Kirby Clo., Epsom 283 330 CT106
Kirby Clo., Ilf. 225 308 ES51
Kirby Clo., Nthwd. 213 302 BT51
Kirby Est. SE16 148 317 DV76
Kirby Gro. SE1 74/5 316 DS75
Kirby St. EC1 48 316 DN71
Kirchen Rd. W13 132 314 CH73
Kirk La. SE18 253 318 EQ79
Kirk Ri., Sutt. 284 331 DB104
Kirk Rd. E17 222 307 DZ58
Kirkdale SE26 274 325 DW91
Kirkdale Rd. E11 105 307 EE60
Kirkfield Clo. W13 132 314 CH74
Kirkham Rd. E6 244 318 EL72
Kirkham St. SE18 253 318 ES79
Kirkland Ave., Ilf. 225 308 EN54
Kirkland Clo., Sid. 261 326 ES86
Kirkland Wk. E8 117 306 DT65
Kirkleas Rd., Surb. 282 330 CL102
Kirklees Rd., Dag. 236 309 EW64
Kirklees Rd., Th.Hth. 286 332 DN99
Kirkley Rd. SW19 271 323 DA95
Kirkly Clo., S.Croy. 295 332 DS109
Kirkman Pl. W1 46 316 DK71
Kirkmichael Rd. E14 140 317 EC72
Kirks Pl. E14 139 317 DZ71
Kirkside Rd. SE3 252 318 EG79
Kirkstall Ave. N17 221 306 DR56
Kirkstall Gdns. SW2 193 324 DK88
Kirkstall Rd. SW2 193 324 DK88
Kirkstead Ct. E5 103 307 DY62
Kirksted Rd., Mord. 284 331 DB102
Kirkstone Way, Brom. 275 325 EE93
Kirkton Rd. N15 221 306 DS56
Kirkwall Pl. E2 128 317 DW69
Kirkwood Rd. SE15 164 317 DV82
Kirn Rd. W13 132 314 CH73
Kirrane Clo., N.Mal. 283 330 CT99
Kirtley Rd. SE26 274 325 DY91
Kirtling St. SW8 160 316 DJ80
Kirton Clo. W4 145 314 CR77
Kirton Clo., Horn. 238 310 FJ65
Kirton Gdns. E2 39 316 DT69
Kirton Rd. E13 244 318 EJ68
Kirton Wk., Edg. 217 304 CQ52
Kirwyn Way SE5 162 316 DP80
Kitcat Ter. E3 130 317 EA69
Kitchener Rd. E7 234 308 EH65
Kitchener Rd. E17 223 307 EB53
Kitchener Rd. N2 219 305 DE55
Kitchener Rd. N17 221 306 DR55
Kitchener Rd., Dag. 237 309 FB65
Kitchener Rd., Th.Hth. 273 324 DR97
Kite Yd. SW11 159 315 DF81
Kitley Gdns. SE19 273 324 DT95
Kitson Rd. SE5 163 316 DR80
Kitson Rd. SW13 156 315 CU81
Kittiwake Rd., Nthlt. 242 313 BX69
Kittiwake Way, Hayes 242 313 BX71
Kitto Rd. SE14 165 317 DX82
Kiver Rd. N19 99 306 DK61
Kiwi Clo., Twick. 168 322 CH86
Klea Ave. SW4 176 324 DJ86
Knapdale Clo. SE23 196 325 DV89
Knapmill Rd. SE6 198 325 EA89
Knapmill Way SE6 198 325 EB89
Knapp Clo. NW10 109 304 CS65
Knapp Rd. E3 130 317 EA70
Knapp Rd., Ashf. 264 328 BM91
Knapton Ms. SW17 272 324 DG93
Knaresborough Dr. SW18 190 323 DB88
Knaresborough Pl. SW5 76/7 315 DB77
Knatchbull Rd. NW10 125 314 CR67
Knatchbull Rd. SE5 162 316 DP82
Knebworth Ave. E17 223 307 EA53
Knebworth Rd. N16 117 306 DS63
Knee Hill SE2 254 319 EW77
Knee Hill Cres. SE2 254 319 EW77
Kneller Gdns., Islw. 259 321 CD86
Kneller Rd. SE4 181 325 DY84
Kneller Rd., N.Mal. 283 330 CS101
Kneller Rd., Twick. 259 321 CC86
Knighten St. E1 138 317 DU74
Knightland Rd. E5 102 307 DV61
Knighton Clo., Rom. 227 309 FD58
Knighton Clo., S.Croy. 294 332 DP108
Knighton Pk. Rd. SE26 274 325 DX92
Knighton Rd. E7 234 308 EG62
Knighton Rd., Rom. 227 309 FC58
Knighton St. E1 138 317 DU74
Knighton Way La., Uxb. 240 312 BH65
Knightrider Ct. EC4 61 316 DQ73
Knightrider St. EC4 61 316 DQ73
Knights Arc. SW1 67 315 DF75
Knights Ave. W5 143 314 CL75
Knights Clo. E9 118 307 DW64
Knights Ct., Kings.T. 268 322 CL97
Knights Ct., Rom. 226 309 EY58
Knights Hill SE27 273 324 DP92
Knights Hill Sq. SE27 273 324 DP91
Knights La. N9 210 301 DU48
Knights Pk., Kings.T. 268 322 CL97
Knights Ridge, Orp. 291 335 EV106
Knights Rd. E16 252 318 EG75
Knights Rd., Stan. 204 298 CJ49
Knights Wk. SE11 84/5 316 DP77
Knights Way, Ilf. 225 308 EQ51
Knightsbridge SW1 67 315 DF75
Knightsbridge SW7 66/7 315 DE75
Knightsbridge Cres., Stai. 264 328 BH93
Knightsbridge Gdns., Rom. 227 309 FD57
Knightsbridge Grn. SW1 67 315 DF75
Knightswood Clo., Edg. 205 298 CQ47
Knightwood Cres., N.Mal. 283 330 CS100
Knivet Rd. SW6 158 315 DA79
Knobs Hill Rd. E15 130 317 EB67
Knockholt Clo., Sutt. 292 331 DB110
Knockholt Rd. SE9 260 326 EK85
Knole, The SE9 277 326 EN91
Knole Clo., Croy. 288 333 DW100
Knole Gate, Sid. 261 326 ES90
Knoll, The W13 132 314 CJ71
Knoll, The, Beck. 275 325 EB95
Knoll, The, Brom. 289 334 EG102
Knoll Ct. SE19 273 324 DT92
Knoll Cres., Nthwd. 213 302 BS54
Knoll Dr. N14 208 300 DG45
Knoll Ri., Orp. 291 334 ET102
Knoll Rd. SW18 174 323 DC85
Knoll Rd., Bex. 263 327 FA87
Knoll Rd., Sid. 278 327 EV92
Knollmead, Surb. 283 330 CQ102
Knolls Clo., Wor.Pk. 283 331 CV104
Knollys Clo. SW16 194 324 DN90
Knollys Rd. SW16 193 324 DM90
Knottisford St. E2 128 317 DW69
Knotts Grn. Ms. E10 223 307 EB58
Knotts Grn. Rd. E10 223 307 EB58
Knowl Pk., Borwd. 204 298 CL43
Knowl Way, Borwd. 204 298 CM43
Knowle Ave., Bexh. 254 319 EY80
Knowle Clo. SW9 178 324 DN83
Knowle Grn., Stai. 264 328 BG92
Knowle Pk. Ave., Stai. 264 328 BH93
Knowle Rd., Brom. 290 334 EL103
Knowle Rd., Twick. 259 321 CE88
Knowles Clo., West Dr. 248 312 BL74
Knowles Hill Cres. SE13 183 325 ED85
Knowles Wk. SW4 176 324 DJ83
Knowlton Grn., Brom. 289 333 EF99
Knowsley Ave., Sthl. 243 313 CB74
Knowsley Rd. SW11 159 315 DF82
Knox Rd. E7 121 307 EF65
Knox St. W1 43 315 DF71
Knoyle St. SE14 165 317 DY79
Kohat Rd. SW19 271 323 DB92
Korda Clo., Shep. 280 328 BM97
Kossuth St. SE10 151 317 EE78
Kotree Way SE1 148 317 DU77
Kramer Ms. SW5 76 315 DA78
Kreedman Wk. E8 118 307 DU64
Kreisel Wk., Rich. 153 314 CM79
Kuala Gdns. SW16 272 324 DM95
Kuhn Way E7 234 308 EG64
Kydbrook Clo., Orp. 291 334 EQ101
Kylemore Clo. E6 244 318 EK68
Kylemore Rd. NW6 112 305 DA66
Kymberley Rd., Har. 215 303 CE58
Kyme Rd., Horn. 227 309 FF58
Kynance Gdns., Stan. 216 304 CJ53
Kynance Ms. SW7 65 315 DC76
Kynance Pl. SW7 65 315 DC76
Kynaston Ave. N16 101 306 DT62
Kynaston Ave., Th.Hth. 287 332 DQ99
Kynaston Clo., Har. 215 303 CD52
Kynaston Cres., Th.Hth. 287 332 DQ99
Kynaston Rd. N16 101 306 DS62
Kynaston Rd., Brom. 276 326 EG92
Kynaston Rd., Enf. 202 300 DR39
Kynaston Rd., Orp. 291 335 EV101
Kynaston Rd., Th.Hth. 287 332 DQ99
Kynaston Wd., Har. 215 303 CD52
Kynock Rd. N18 210 301 DW49
Kyrle Rd. SW11 175 323 DF86
Kyverdale Rd. N16 101 306 DT59

La Tourne Gdns., Orp. 291 334 EQ104
Laburnham Ave., West Dr. 248 312 BM73
Laburnham Gdns., Upmin. 239 311 FT59
Laburnum Ave. N9 209 300 DS47
Laburnum Ave. N17 221 306 DR52
Laburnum Ave., Horn. 237 309 FF62
Laburnum Ave., Sutt. 285 331 DE104
Laburnum Ave., Swan. 279 327 FC97
Laburnum Clo. E4 222 307 DZ51
Laburnum Clo. N11 220 306 DG51
Laburnum Clo. SE15 164 317 DW80
Laburnum Ct. E2 27 316 DT67
Laburnum Ct., Stan. 204 298 CJ49
Laburnum Cres., Sun. 266 329 BV95
Laburnum Gdns. N21 209 300 DQ47
Laburnum Gdns., Croy. 288 333 DX101
Laburnum Gro. N21 209 300 DQ47
Laburnum Gro. NW9 92 304 CQ59
Laburnum Gro., Houns. 258 321 BZ84
Laburnum Gro., N.Mal. 269 322 CR96
Laburnum Gro., Ruis. 231 302 BR58
Laburnum Gro., Sthl. 242 313 BZ70
Laburnum Ho., Dag. 237 309 FA61
Laburnum Rd. SW19 271 323 DC94
Laburnum Rd., Cher. 280 328 BG102
Laburnum Rd., Hayes 249 320 BT77
Laburnum Rd., Mitch. 272 324 DG96
Laburnum St. E2 27 316 DT67
Laburnum Wk., Horn. 238 310 FJ64
Laburnum Way, Brom. 290 334 EN101
Laburnum Way, Stai. 264 320 BM88
Lacebark Clo., Sid. 261 326 ET87
Lacey Clo. N9 210 301 DU47
Lacey Dr., Dag. 236 309 EV63
Lacey Dr., Edg. 204 298 CL49
Lacey Dr., Hmptn. 266 329 BZ95
Lacey Wk. E3 130 317 EA68
Lackington St. EC2 50 316 DR71
Lackmore Rd., Enf. 203 301 DW35
Lacock Clo. SW19 271 323 DC93
Lacon Rd. SE22 180 325 DU84
Lacy Rd. SW15 173 323 CX84
Ladas Rd. SE27 273 324 DQ91
Ladbroke Cres. W11 137 315 CY72
Ladbroke Gdns. W11 137 315 CZ73
Ladbroke Gro. W10 127 315 CX70
Ladbroke Gro. W11 137 315 CY72
Ladbroke Ms. W11 137 315 CY74
Ladbroke Rd. W11 137 315 CZ74
Ladbroke Rd., Enf. 209 300 DT44
Ladbroke Sq. W11 137 315 CZ73
Ladbroke Ter. W11 137 315 CZ73
Ladbroke Wk. W11 137 315 CZ74
Ladbrook Clo., Pnr. 214 303 BZ57
Ladbrook Rd. SE25 273 324 DR97
Ladbrooke Cres., Sid. 262 327 EX90
Ladderstile Ride, Kings.T. 269 322 CQ92
Ladderswood Way N11 208 300 DJ50
Ladds Way, Swan. 279 327 FD98
Lady Booth Rd., Kings.T. 268 322 CL96
Lady Hay, Wor.Pk. 283 330 CT103
Lady Margaret Rd. N19 114 306 DJ63
Lady Margaret Rd. NW5 114 306 DJ64
Lady Margaret Rd., Sthl. 242 313 BZ71
Lady Somerset Rd. NW5 114 306 DH63
Ladybower Ct. E5 119 307 DY63
Ladycroft Gdns., Orp. 291 334 EQ106
Ladycroft Rd. SE13 182 325 EB83
Ladycroft Wk., Stan. 216 304 CK53
Ladycroft Way, Orp. 291 334 EQ106
Ladygate La., Ruis. 231 302 BP58
Ladysmith Ave. E6 244 318 EL68
Ladysmith Ave., Ilf. 235 308 ER59
Ladysmith Rd. E16 131 317 EF69
Ladysmith Rd. N17 222 307 DU54
Ladysmith Rd. N18 210 301 DV50
Ladysmith Rd. SE9 261 326 EN86
Ladysmith Rd., Enf. 202 300 DS41
Ladysmith Rd., Har. 215 303 CE54
Ladywell Clo. SE4 181 325 DZ84
Ladywell Hts. SE4 181 325 DZ86
Ladywell Rd. SE13 182 325 EB85
Ladywell St. E15 131 317 EF67
Ladywood Ave., Orp. 291 334 ES99
Ladywood Rd., Surb. 282 330 CN103
Lafone Ave., Felt. 258 321 BW88
Lafone St. SE1 75 316 DT75
Lagado Ms. SE16 139 317 DX74
Lagonda Ave., Ilf. 225 308 ET51
Lagoon Rd., Orp. 291 335 EV99
Laing Clo., Ilf. 225 308 ER51
Laing Dean, Nthlt. 242 313 BW67
Laings Ave., Mitch. 271 323 DF96
Lainlock Pl., Houns. 251 321 CB81
Lainson St. SW18 190 323 DA87
Laird Ho. SE5 162 316 DQ80
Lairdale Clo. SE21 194 324 DQ88
Lairs Clo. N7 115 306 DL65
Laitwood Rd. SW12 192 324 DH88
Lake Ave., Brom. 276 326 EG93
Lake Clo. SW19 270 323 CZ92
Lake Gdns., Dag. 237 309 FA64
Lake Gdns., Rich. 184 322 CH89
Lake Gdns., Wall. 285 332 DH104
Lake Ho. Rd. E11 234 308 EG62
Lake Ri., Rom. 227 309 FF54
Lake Rd. SW19 270 323 CZ92
Lake Rd., Croy. 288 333 DZ103
Lake Rd., Rom. 226 309 EX56
Lake Vw., Edg. 204 298 CM50
Lakedale Rd. SE18 253 318 ES78
Lakefield Rd. N22 221 306 DP54
Lakehall Gdns., Th.Hth. 286 332 DP99
Lakehall Rd., Th.Hth. 286 332 DP99
Lakehurst Rd., Epsom 283 330 CS106
Lakeland Clo., Har. 215 303 CD51
Lakenheath N14 208 300 DJ43
Laker Pl. SW15 173 323 CY86
Lakes Rd., Kes. 290 334 EJ106
Lakeside N3 219 305 DB54
Lakeside W13 132 314 CJ72
Lakeside, Beck. 275 325 EB97
Lakeside, Wall. 285 332 DH104
Lakeside Ave. SE28 246 319 EU74
Lakeside Ave., Ilf. 224 308 EK56
Lakeside Clo. SE25 274 325 DU96
Lakeside Clo., Ruis. 231 302 BR56
Lakeside Clo., Sid. 262 327 EW85
Lakeside Ct. N4 100 306 DP61
Lakeside Ct., Borwd. 205 298 CN43
Lakeside Cres., Barn. 207 299 DF43
Lakeside Dr., Brom. 290 334 EL104
Lakeside Rd. N13 208 300 DM49

Lakeside Rd. W14	147	315	CX76
Lakeside Way, Wem.	108	304	CN63
Lakeswood Rd., Orp.	290	334	EP99
Lakeview Ct. SW19	189	323	CY89
Lakeview Rd. SE27	273	324	DN92
Lakeview Rd., Well.	262	327	EV84
Lakis Clo. NW3	112	305	DC63
Laleham Ave. NW7	205	298	CR48
Laleham Pk., Stai.	280	328	BJ99
Laleham Reach, Cher.	280	328	BH96
Laleham Rd. SE6	198	325	EC87
Laleham Rd., Shep.	280	328	BL98
Lalor St. SW6	157	315	CY82
Lamb La. E8	118	307	DV66
Lamb St. E1	51	316	DT71
Lamb Wk. SE1	74/5	316	DS75
Lambarde Ave. SE9	277	326	EN91
Lamberhurst Rd. SE27	273	324	DN91
Lamberhurst Rd., Dag.	236	309	EY60
Lambert Ave., Rich.	170	322	CN83
Lambert Jones Ms. EC2	49	316	DQ71
Lambert Rd. E16	244	318	EH72
Lambert Rd. N12	207	299	DC50
Lambert Rd. SW2	177	324	DL85
Lambert Rd., Bans.	292	331	DA114
Lambert St. N1	116	306	DN66
Lambert Wk., Wem.	91	304	CK62
Lambert Way N12	207	299	DC50
Lamberts Pl., Croy.	287	332	DR102
Lamberts Rd., Surb.	282	330	CL99
Lambeth Bri. SE1	82/3	316	DL77
Lambeth Bri. SW1	82/3	316	DL77
Lambeth High St. SE1	83	316	DM77
Lambeth Hill EC4	61	316	DQ73
Lambeth Palace Rd. SE1	71	316	DM76
Lambeth Rd. SE1	71	316	DM76
Lambeth Rd. SE11	71	316	DM76
Lambeth Rd., Croy.	286	332	DN101
Lambeth Wk. SE11	83	316	DM77
Lamble St. NW5	114	306	DG64
Lambley Rd., Dag.	236	309	EV65
Lambolle Pl. NW3	113	305	DE65
Lambolle Rd. NW3	113	305	DE65
Lambourn Clo. W7	251	321	CF75
Lambourn Rd. SW4	176	324	DH83
Lambourne Ave. SW19	270	323	CZ91
Lambourne Gdns. E4	211	301	EA47
Lambourne Gdns., Bark.	235	308	ET66
Lambourne Gdns., Enf.	202	300	DT40
Lambourne Gdns., Horn.	238	310	FK61
Lambourne Gro., Kings.T.	269	322	CP96
Lambourne Pl. SE3	252	318	EH81
Lambourne Rd. E11	105	307	ED59
Lambourne Rd., Bark.	235	308	ES66
Lambourne Rd., Ilf.	235	308	ES61
Lambrook Ter. SW6	157	315	CY81
Lamb's Bldgs. EC1	38	316	DR70
Lambs Conduit Pas. WC1	47	316	DM71
Lamb's Conduit St. WC1	35	316	DM70
Lambs Meadow, Wdf.Grn.	224	308	EK54
Lambs Ms. N1	24/5	316	DP67
Lamb's Pas. EC1	50	316	DR71
Lambs Ter. N9	209	300	DR47
Lambs Wk., Enf.	202	300	DQ40
Lambscroft Ave. SE9	260	326	EJ90
Lambton Pl. W11	137	315	CZ72
Lambton Rd. N19	99	306	DL60
Lambton Rd. SW20	270	323	CW95
Lamerock Rd., Brom.	275	325	EF91
Lamerton Rd., Ilf.	225	308	EP54
Lamerton St. SE8	166	317	EA79
Lamford Clo. N17	221	306	DR52
Lamington St. W6	146	315	CV77
Lamlash St. SE11	84/5	316	DP77
Lammas Ave., Mitch.	272	324	DG96
Lammas Grn. SE26	196	325	DV90
Lammas Pk. W5	142	314	CJ75
Lammas Pk. Gdns. W5	132	314	CJ74
Lammas Pk. Rd. W5	132	314	CJ74
Lammas Rd. E9	119	307	DX66
Lammas Rd. E10	103	307	DY61
Lammas Rd., Rich.	268	322	CJ91
Lammermoor Rd. SW12	192	324	DH87
Lamont Rd. SW10	158	315	DC79
Lamont Rd. Pas. SW10	159	315	DD79
Lamorbey Clo., Sid.	261	326	ET88
Lamorna Clo. E17	223	307	EC54
Lamorna Clo., Orp.	291	335	EU101
Lamorna Gro., Stan.	216	304	CK53
Lampard Gro. N16	101	306	DT60
Lampern Sq. E2	128	317	DU69
Lampeter Sq. W6	157	315	CY79
Lamplighter Clo. E1	128	317	DW70
Lampmead Rd. SE12	183	325	EF85
Lamport Clo. SE18	252	318	EM77
Lampton Ave., Houns.	251	321	CB81
Lampton Ho. Clo. SW19	270	323	CX91
Lampton Pk. Rd., Houns.	251	321	CB82
Lampton Rd., Houns.	251	321	CB82
Lamson Rd., Rain.	247	319	FF70
Lanacre Ave. NW9	217	304	CR53
Lanark Clo. W5	132	314	CJ71
Lanark Pl. W9	29	315	DC70
Lanark Rd. W9	16/7	315	DB68
Lanark Sq. E14	150	317	EB76
Lanata Wk., Hayes	242	313	BX70
Lanbury Rd. SE15	181	325	DX84
Lancashire Ct. W1	56/7	316	DH73
Lancaster Ave. E18	224	308	EH56
Lancaster Ave. SE27	194	324	DP89
Lancaster Ave. SW19	270	323	CX92
Lancaster Ave., Bark.	235	308	ES66
Lancaster Ave., Mitch.	286	332	DL99
Lancaster Clo. N1	117	306	DS66
Lancaster Clo. N17	222	307	DU52
Lancaster Clo. NW9	217	304	CT52
Lancaster Clo., Brom.	275	325	EF98
Lancaster Clo., Kings.T.	268	322	CK92
Lancaster Cotts., Rich.	169	322	CL86
Lancaster Ct. SE27	194	324	DP89
Lancaster Ct. SW6	157	315	CZ80
Lancaster Ct. W2	53	315	DC73
Lancaster Ct., Bans.	292	331	CZ114
Lancaster Dr. E14	140	317	EC74
Lancaster Dr. NW3	113	305	DE65
Lancaster Dr., Horn.	238	310	FH64
Lancaster Gdns. SW19	270	323	CY92
Lancaster Gdns. W13	142	314	CH75
Lancaster Gdns., Kings.T.	268	322	CK92
Lancaster Gate W2	53	315	DC73
Lancaster Gro. NW3	113	305	DD65
Lancaster Ms. SW18	174	323	DB85
Lancaster Ms. W2	53	315	DC73
Lancaster Ms., Rich.	169	322	CL86
Lancaster Pk., Rich.	169	322	CL85
Lancaster Pl. SW19	270	323	CX92
Lancaster Pl. WC2	59	316	DM73
Lancaster Pl., Houns.	250	321	BW82
Lancaster Pl., Ilf.	235	308	EQ64
Lancaster Pl., Twick.	168	322	CG86
Lancaster Rd. E7	234	308	EG66
Lancaster Rd. E11	105	307	EE61
Lancaster Rd. E17	222	307	DX54
Lancaster Rd. N4	99	306	DM59
Lancaster Rd. N11	220	306	DK51
Lancaster Rd. N18	209	300	DT50
Lancaster Rd. NW10	110	305	CU64
Lancaster Rd. SE25	273	324	DT96
Lancaster Rd. SW19	270	323	CX92
Lancaster Rd. W11	137	315	CY72
Lancaster Rd., Barn.	207	299	DD43
Lancaster Rd., Enf.	202	300	DR39
Lancaster Rd., Har.	215	303	CA57
Lancaster Rd., Nthlt.	233	313	CC65
Lancaster Rd., Sthl.	242	313	BY73
Lancaster Rd., Uxb.	240	312	BK65
Lancaster St. SE1	72/3	316	DP75
Lancaster Ter. W2	54	315	DD73
Lancaster Wk. W2	54	315	DD74
Lancaster Wk., Hayes	249	312	BQ72
Lance Rd., Har.	233	313	CC59
Lancefield St. W10	127	315	CZ69
Lancell St. N16	101	306	DS61
Lancelot Ave., Wem.	107	304	CK63
Lancelot Cres., Wem.	107	304	CK63
Lancelot Gdns., Barn.	208	300	DG45
Lancelot Pl. SW7	67	315	DF75
Lancelot Rd., Ilf.	225	308	ES51
Lancelot Rd., Well.	262	327	EU84
Lancelot Rd., Wem.	107	304	CK63
Lancer Sq. W8	64/5	315	DB75
Lancey Clo. SE7	252	318	EK77
Lanchester Rd. N6	219	305	DF57
Lancing Gdns. N9	209	300	DT46
Lancing Rd. W13	132	314	CH73
Lancing Rd., Croy.	286	332	DM100
Lancing Rd., Felt.	265	320	BT89
Lancing Rd., Ilf.	225	308	ER58
Lancing Rd., Orp.	291	335	EU103
Lancing Rd., Rom.	228	311	FL52
Lancing St. NW1	34	316	DK69
Lancresse Clo., Uxb.	240	312	BK65
Lancresse Ct. N1	26/7	316	DS67
Landcroft Rd. SE22	179	324	DT85
Landells Rd. SE22	179	324	DT86
Landford Clo., Rick.	212	302	BL47
Landford Rd. SW15	172	323	CW83
Landgrove Rd. SW19	271	323	DA92
Landmann Way SE14	165	317	DX79
Landon Pl. SW1	67	315	DF76
Landon Wk. E14	140	317	EB73
Landon Way, Ashf.	265	328	BP93
Landons Clo. E14	140	317	EC74
Landor Rd. SW9	177	324	DL83
Landor Wk. W12	146	315	CU75
Landport Way SE15	163	316	DT80
Landra Gdns. N21	209	300	DP44
Landridge Rd. SW6	157	315	CZ82
Landrock Rd. N8	220	306	DL58
Lands End, Borwd.	204	298	CK44
Landscape Rd., Wdf.Grn.	224	308	EH52
Landseer Ave. E12	235	308	EN64
Landseer Clo. SW19	271	323	DC95
Landseer Clo., Edg.	217	304	CN54
Landseer Clo., Horn.	238	310	FH60
Landseer Rd. N19	99	306	DL62
Landseer Rd., Enf.	210	301	DU43
Landseer Rd., N.Mal.	283	330	CR101
Landseer Rd., Sutt.	292	331	DA107
Landstead Rd. SE18	253	318	ER80
Landway, The, Orp.	278	327	EW97
Lane, The NW8	17	315	DC68
Lane, The SE3	260	326	EG83
Lane, The, Cher.	280	328	BG97
Lane App. NW7	206	299	CY50
Lane Clo. NW2	94	305	CV62
Lane End, Bexh.	263	327	FB83
Lane Ms. E12	234	308	EM62
Lanercost Clo. SW2	194	324	DN89
Lanercost Gdns. N14	208	300	DL45
Lanercost Rd. SW2	194	324	DN89
Lanesborough Pl. SW1	68	316	DG75
Laneside, Chis.	277	326	EP92
Laneside, Edg.	205	298	CQ50
Laneside Ave., Dag.	236	309	EZ59
Laneway SW15	172	323	CV85
Lanfranc Rd. E3	129	317	DY68
Lanfrey Pl. W14	147	315	CZ78
Lang St. E1	128	317	DW70
Langbourne Ave. N6	98	306	DG61
Langbrook Rd. SE3	260	326	EK83
Langcroft Clo., Cars.	285	331	DF104
Langdale Ave., Mitch.	271	323	DF97
Langdale Clo. SE17	162	316	DQ79
Langdale Clo. SW14	170	322	CP84
Langdale Clo., Dag.	236	309	EW60
Langdale Clo., Orp.	290	334	EP104
Langdale Cres., Bexh.	255	319	FA80
Langdale Dr., Hayes	241	312	BS68
Langdale Gdns., Grnf.	122	314	CH69
Langdale Gdns., Horn.	238	310	FG64
Langdale Gdns., Wal.Cr.	203	301	DX35
Langdale Rd. SE10	166	317	EC80
Langdale Rd., Th.Hth.	273	324	DN98
Langdale St. E1	138	317	DV72
Langdon Ct. NW10	125	314	CS67
Langdon Cres. E6	245	318	EN68
Langdon Dr. NW9	92	304	CQ60
Langdon Pk. Rd. N6	98	306	DJ59
Langdon Pl. SW14	170	322	CQ83
Langdon Rd. E6	245	318	EN67
Langdon Rd., Brom.	276	326	EH97
Langdon Rd., Mord.	285	331	DC99
Langdon Shaw, Sid.	277	326	ET92
Langdon Wk., Mord.	285	331	DC99
Langdon Way SE1	148	317	DU77
Langford Clo. E8	118	307	DU64
Langford Clo. N15	221	306	DS58
Langford Clo. NW8	17	315	DC68
Langford Ct. NW8	17	315	DC68
Langford Grn. SE5	179	324	DS83
Langford Pl. NW8	17	315	DC68
Langford Pl., Sid.	262	327	EU90
Langford Rd. SW6	158	315	DB82
Langford Rd., Wdf.Grn.	224	308	EJ51
Langham Clo. N15	221	306	DP55
Langham Ct., Horn.	238	310	FK59
Langham Dr., Rom.	226	309	EV58
Langham Gdns. N21	209	300	DN43
Langham Gdns. W13	132	314	CH73
Langham Gdns., Edg.	217	304	CQ52
Langham Gdns., Rich.	268	322	CJ91
Langham Gdns., Wem.	90	304	CJ61
Langham Ho. Clo., Rich.	268	322	CK91
Langham Pl. N15	221	306	DP55
Langham Pl. W1	44/5	316	DH71
Langham Pl. W4	155	314	CS79
Langham Rd. N15	221	306	DP55
Langham Rd. SW20	270	323	CW95
Langham Rd., Edg.	217	304	CQ51
Langham Rd., Tedd.	268	322	CH92
Langham St. W1	44/5	316	DH71
Langhedge Clo. N18	221	306	DT51
Langhedge La. N18	221	306	DT51
Langhedge La. Ind. Est. N18	221	306	DT51
Langholm Clo. SW12	193	324	DK87
Langhorne Rd., Dag.	237	309	FA66
Langland Ct., Nthwd.	213	302	BQ52
Langland Cres., Stan.	216	304	CK54
Langland Dr., Pnr.	214	303	BY52
Langland Gdns. NW3	112	305	DB64
Langland Gdns., Croy.	288	333	DZ103
Langler Rd. NW10	126	315	CW68
Langley Ave., Ruis.	232	313	BV61
Langley Ave., Surb.	282	330	CK102
Langley Ave., Wor.Pk.	284	331	CX102
Langley Clo., Rom.	228	310	FK52
Langley Ct. SE9	261	326	EN86
Langley Ct. WC2	58/9	316	DL73
Langley Ct., Beck.	288	333	EB99
Langley Cres. E11	234	308	EH59
Langley Cres., Dag.	236	309	EW66
Langley Cres., Edg.	205	298	CQ48
Langley Cres., Hayes	257	320	BT80
Langley Dr. E11	234	308	EH59
Langley Dr. W3	144	314	CP75
Langley Gdns., Brom.	276	326	EJ98
Langley Gdns., Dag.	236	309	EX66
Langley Gdns., Orp.	290	334	EP100
Langley Gro., N.Mal.	269	322	CS96
Langley La. SW8	161	316	DL79
Langley Oaks Ave., S.Croy.	295	333	DU110
Langley Pk. NW7	217	304	CS51
Langley Pk. Rd., Sutt.	285	331	DC106
Langley Rd. SW19	270	323	CZ95
Langley Rd., Beck.	274	325	DY98
Langley Rd., Islw.	251	321	CF82
Langley Rd., Surb.	282	330	CL101
Langley Rd., Well.	254	319	EW79
Langley St. WC2	46/7	316	DL72
Langley Way, W.Wick.	289	333	ED102
Langmead St. SE27	273	324	DP91
Langmore Ct., Bexh.	262	327	EX83
Langridge Ms., Hmptn.	266	329	BZ93
Langroyd Rd. SW17	191	323	DF89
Langside Ave. SW15	172	323	CU84
Langside Cres. N14	208	300	DK48
Langston Hughes Clo. SE24	178	324	DP84
Langthorn Ct. EC2	50	316	DR72
Langthorne Rd. E11	104	307	EC62
Langthorne St. SW6	157	315	CX81
Langton Ave. E6	245	318	EN69
Langton Ave. N20	207	299	DC45
Langton Clo. WC1	35	316	DM70
Langton Gro., Nthwd.	213	302	BQ50
Langton Ri. SE23	196	325	DV87
Langton Rd. NW2	94	305	CW62
Langton Rd. SW9	162	316	DP80
Langton Rd., Har.	215	303	CC52
Langton St. SW10	158	315	DC79
Langton Way SE3	167	317	EF81
Langton Way, Croy.	287	332	DS104
Langtry Rd. NW8	16/7	315	DB67
Langtry Rd., Nthlt.	242	313	BX68
Langtry Wk. NW8	112	305	DC66
Langwood Chase, Tedd.	268	322	CJ93
Langworth Dr., Hayes	242	313	BU72
Lanhill Rd. W9	28	315	DA70
Lanier Rd. SE13	182	325	EC86
Lanigan Dr., Houns.	259	321	CB85
Lankaster Gdns. N2	219	305	DD53
Lankers Dr., Har.	214	303	BZ58
Lankton Clo., Beck.	275	325	EC95
Lannock Rd., Hayes	249	312	BS74
Lannoy Rd. SE9	261	326	EQ88
Lanrick Rd. E14	141	317	ED72
Lanridge Rd. SE2	254	319	EX76
Lansbury Ave. N18	209	300	DR50
Lansbury Ave., Bark.	236	309	EU66
Lansbury Ave., Felt.	258	321	BV86
Lansbury Ave., Rom.	226	309	EY57
Lansbury Clo. NW10	108	304	CQ64
Lansbury Dr., Hayes	241	312	BS68
Lansbury Est. E14	140	317	EB72
Lansbury Gdns. E14	140	317	EC72
Lansbury Rd., Enf.	203	301	DX39
Lansbury Way N18	209	300	DS50
Lansdell Rd., Mitch.	272	324	DG96
Lansdown Rd. E7	234	308	EJ66
Lansdown Rd., Sid.	262	327	EV90
Lansdowne Ave., Bexh.	254	319	EW80
Lansdowne Ave., Orp.	290	334	EP102
Lansdowne Clo. SW20	270	323	CX94
Lansdowne Clo., Surb.	282	330	CP103
Lansdowne Clo., Twick.	259	321	CF88
Lansdowne Ct., Wor.Pk.	283	331	CU103
Lansdowne Cres. W11	137	315	CZ73
Lansdowne Dr. E8	118	307	DU65
Lansdowne Gdns. SW8	161	316	DL81
Lansdowne Grn. SW8	161	316	DL81
Lansdowne Gro. NW10	109	304	CS63
Lansdowne Hill SE27	194	324	DP90
Lansdowne La. SE7	252	318	EK78
Lansdowne Ms. SE7	252	318	EK78
Lansdowne Ms. W11	137	315	CZ74
Lansdowne Pl. SE1	74	316	DR76
Lansdowne Pl. SE19	273	324	DT94
Lansdowne Ri. W11	137	315	CY73
Lansdowne Rd. E4	211	301	EA47
Lansdowne Rd. E11	105	307	EF61
Lansdowne Rd. E17	223	307	EA58
Lansdowne Rd. E18	224	308	EG55
Lansdowne Rd. N3	218	305	CZ52
Lansdowne Rd. N10	220	306	DJ54
Lansdowne Rd. N17	222	307	DU53
Lansdowne Rd. SW20	270	323	CW94
Lansdowne Rd. W11	137	315	CY73
Lansdowne Rd., Brom.	276	326	EG94
Lansdowne Rd., Croy.	287	332	DQ103
Lansdowne Rd., Har.	233	313	CE59
Lansdowne Rd., Houns.	259	321	CB83
Lansdowne Rd., Ilf.	235	308	ET60
Lansdowne Rd., Pur.	294	332	DN112
Lansdowne Rd., Stai.	264	328	BH94
Lansdowne Rd., Stan.	216	304	CJ51
Lansdowne Rd., Uxb.	249	312	BP72
Lansdowne Row W1	56/7	316	DH74
Lansdowne Ter. WC1	34/5	316	DL70
Lansdowne Wk. W11	137	315	CZ74
Lansdowne Way SW8	161	316	DK81
Lansdowne Wd. Clo. SE27	194	324	DP90
Lansfield Ave. N18	210	301	DU49
Lant St. SE1	73	316	DQ75
Lantern Clo. SW15	172	323	CU84
Lantern Clo., Wem.	107	304	CK64
Lanterns Ct. E14	150	317	EA75
Lanvanor Rd. SE15	164	317	DW82
Lapford Clo. W9	127	315	CZ70
Lapponum Wk., Hayes	242	313	BX71
Lapse Wd. Wk. SE23	196	325	DV89
Lapstone Gdns., Har.	216	304	CJ58
Lapwing Ct., Surb.	282	330	CN104
Lapwing Way, Hayes	242	313	BX72
Lara Clo. SE13	182	325	EC86
Larbert Rd. SW16	272	324	DJ94
Larch Ave. W3	135	314	CS74
Larch Clo. E13	244	318	EH70
Larch Clo. N11	220	306	DG52
Larch Clo. N19	98	306	DJ61
Larch Clo. SE8	165	317	DZ79
Larch Clo. SW12	192	324	DH88
Larch Cres., Hayes	242	313	BW70
Larch Dr. W4	144	314	CN78
Larch Grn. NW9	217	304	CS53
Larch Gro., Sid.	261	326	ET88
Larch Ms. N19	98	306	DJ61
Larch Rd. E10	104	307	EA61
Larch Rd. NW2	110	305	CW63
Larch Tree Way, Croy.	288	333	EA104
Larch Wk., Swan.	279	327	FD96
Larch Way, Brom.	290	334	EN101
Larchdene, Orp.	290	334	EN103
Larches, The N13	209	300	DQ48
Larches, The, Nthwd.	213	302	BQ51
Larches, The, Uxb.	241	312	BP68
Larches Ave. SW14	171	322	CR84
Larches Ave., Enf.	203	301	DW35
Larchwood Ave., Rom.	227	309	FB51
Larchwood Clo., Rom.	227	309	FC51
Larchwood Rd. SE9	261	326	EP89
Larcom St. SE17	85	316	DQ77
Larcombe Clo., Croy.	287	332	DT105
Larden Rd. W3	135	314	CS74
Largewood Ave., Surb.	282	330	CM103
Largo Wk., Erith	255	319	FE81
Larissa St. SE17	86	316	DR78
Lark Row E2	128	317	DW67
Lark Way, Cars.	285	331	DE101
Larkbere Rd. SE26	274	325	DY91
Larkfield Ave., Har.	216	304	CH55
Larkfield Clo., Brom.	289	333	EF103
Larkfield Rd., Rich.	169	322	CL84
Larkfield Rd., Sid.	261	326	ET90
Larkhall Ct., Rom.	227	309	FC54
Larkhall La. SW4	161	316	DK82
Larkhall Ri. SW4	176	324	DJ83
Larkham Clo., Felt.	265	320	BS90
Larkhill Ter. SE18	253	318	EN80
Larks Gro., Bark.	235	308	ES66
Larksfield Gro., Enf.	203	301	DV39
Larkshall Cres. E4	211	301	EC49
Larkshall Rd. E4	211	301	EC50
Larkspur Clo. E6	244	318	EL71
Larkspur Clo. N17	221	306	DR52
Larkspur Clo. NW9	217	304	CP57
Larkspur Clo., Ruis.	231	312	BQ59
Larkspur Way, Epsom	282	330	CP106
Larkswood Ct. E4	211	301	ED50
Larkswood Ri., Pnr.	214	303	BW56
Larkswood Rd. E4	211	301	EA49
Larkway Clo. NW9	217	304	CR56
Larmans Rd., Enf.	203	301	DW36
Larnach Rd. W6	157	315	CX79
Larne Rd., Ruis.	231	312	BT59
Larner Rd., Erith	255	319	FE80
Larpent Ave. SW15	172	323	CW85
Larwood Clo., Grnf.	233	313	CD64
Las Palmas Est., Shep.	281	328	BQ101
Lascelles Ave., Har.	233	313	CD59
Lascelles Clo. E11	105	307	ED61
Lascotts Rd. N22	220	306	DM51
Lassa Rd. SE9	260	326	EL85
Lassell St. SE10	151	317	ED78
Lasseter Pl. SE3	167	317	EF79
Lasterton St. E8	118	307	DV65
Latchett Rd. E18	224	308	EH53
Latchingdon Ct. E17	222	307	DX56
Latchingdon Gdns., Wdf.Grn.	224	308	EL51
Latchmere Clo., Rich.	268	322	CL92
Latchmere La., Kings.T.	268	322	CM93
Latchmere Pas. SW11	159	315	DE82
Latchmere Rd. SW11	159	315	DF82
Latchmere Rd., Kings.T.	268	322	CL94
Latchmere St. SW11	159	315	DF82
Lateward Rd., Brent.	153	314	CK79
Latham Clo. E6	244	318	EL72
Latham Clo., Twick.	184	322	CG87
Latham Ho. E1	139	317	DX72
Latham Rd., Bexh.	263	327	FA85
Latham Rd., Twick.	259	321	CF87
Lathams Way, Croy.	286	332	DM102
Lathkill Clo., Enf.	209	300	DT45
Lathom Rd. E6	234	308	EL66
Latimer SE17	86/7	316	DS78
Latimer Ave. E6	244	318	EM67
Latimer Clo., Pnr.	214	303	BW53
Latimer Clo., Wor.Pk.	283	331	CV105
Latimer Dr., Horn.	238	310	FK62
Latimer Gdns., Pnr.	214	303	BW53
Latimer Pl. W10	136	315	CW72
Latimer Rd. E7	234	308	EH63
Latimer Rd. N15	221	306	DS58
Latimer Rd. SW19	271	323	DB93
Latimer Rd. W10	136	315	CW71
Latimer Rd., Croy.	286	332	DP104
Latimer Rd., Tedd.	267	329	CF92
Latimer St. E1	139	317	DX71
Latona Rd. SE15	164	317	DU79
Lattimer Pl. W4	155	314	CT80
Latymer Ct. W6	147	315	CX77
Latymer Rd. N9	209	300	DT47
Latymer Way N9	209	300	DR47
Laud St. SE11	83	316	DM78
Laud St., Croy.	287	332	DQ104
Lauder Clo., Nthlt.	242	313	BX68
Lauderdale Dr., Rich.	185	322	CK90
Lauderdale Pl. EC2	49	316	DQ71
Lauderdale Rd. W9	28/9	315	DB69
Lauderdale Twr. EC2	49	316	DQ71
Laughton Rd., Nthlt.	242	313	BX67
Launcelot Rd., Brom.	276	326	EG91
Launcelot St. SE1	72	316	DN75
Launceston Clo., Rom.	228	310	FJ53
Launceston Gdns., Grnf.	122	314	CJ67
Launceston Pl. W8	65	315	DC76
Launceston Rd., Grnf.	122	314	CJ67
Launch St. E14	150	317	EC76
Laundress La. N16	102	307	DU62
Laundry La. N1	25	316	DQ67
Laundry Rd. W6	157	315	CY79
Laura Clo. E11	224	308	EJ57
Laura Clo., Enf.	209	300	DS43
Laura Pl. E5	118	307	DW63
Lauradale Rd. N2	219	305	DF56
Laurel Ave., Twick.	259	321	CF88
Laurel Bank Gdns. SW6	157	315	CZ82
Laurel Bank Rd., Enf.	202	300	DQ39
Laurel Bank Vil. W7	243	313	CE74
Laurel Clo. N19	98	306	DJ61
Laurel Clo. SW17	271	323	DE92
Laurel Clo., Ilf.	225	308	EQ51
Laurel Clo., Sid.	262	327	EU90
Laurel Cres., Croy.	288	333	EA104
Laurel Cres., Rom.	237	309	FE60
Laurel Dr. N21	209	300	DN45
Laurel Gdns. E4	211	301	EB45
Laurel Gdns. NW7	205	298	CR48
Laurel Gdns. W7	243	313	CE74
Laurel Gdns., Houns.	258	321	BY84
Laurel Gro. SE20	274	325	DV94
Laurel Gro. SE26	274	325	DX91
Laurel La., West Dr.	248	320	BL77
Laurel Pk., Har.	215	303	CF52
Laurel Rd. SW13	156	315	CU82
Laurel Rd. SW20	270	323	CV95
Laurel Rd., Hmptn.	267	329	CD92
Laurel St. E8	117	306	DT65
Laurel Vw. N12	207	299	DB48
Laurel Way E18	223	307	EF56
Laurel Way N20	207	299	DA48
Laurence Ms. W12	146	315	CU75
Laurence Pountney Hill EC4	62	316	DR73
Laurence Pountney La. EC4	62	316	DR73
Laurie Gro. SE14	165	317	DY81
Laurie Rd. W7	243	313	CE71
Laurie Wk., Rom.	227	309	FE56
Laurier Rd. NW5	98	306	DH62
Laurier Rd., Croy.	287	332	DT101
Laurimel Clo., Stan.	216	304	CH51
Lauriston Rd. E9	129	317	DX67
Lauriston Rd. SW19	270	323	CX93
Lausanne Rd. N8	221	306	DN56
Lausanne Rd. SE15	164	317	DW81
Lauser Rd., Stai.	264	320	BJ87
Lavell St. N16	117	306	DR63
Lavender Ave. NW9	92	304	CQ60
Lavender Ave., Mitch.	271	323	DE95
Lavender Ave., Wor.Pk.	284	331	CW104
Lavender Clo. SW3	159	315	DD79
Lavender Clo., Brom.	290	334	EL100
Lavender Clo., Cars.	285	332	DH105
Lavender Clo., Rom.	228	310	FK52
Lavender Ct., W.Mol.	267	329	CB97
Lavender Gdns. SW11	175	323	DF84
Lavender Gdns., Enf.	202	300	DP39
Lavender Gdns., Har.	215	303	CE51
Lavender Gro. E8	118	307	DU66
Lavender Gro., Mitch.	271	323	DE95
Lavender Hill SW11	175	323	DF84
Lavender Hill, Enf.	202	300	DN39
Lavender Hill, Swan.	279	327	FD97
Lavender Ms., Wall.	294	332	DL107
Lavender Pl., Ilf.	235	308	EP64
Lavender Ri., West Dr.	249	320	BN75
Lavender Rd. SE16	139	317	DY74
Lavender Rd. SW11	175	323	DD83
Lavender Rd., Cars.	285	332	DG105
Lavender Rd., Croy.	286	332	DM100
Lavender Rd., Enf.	202	300	DR39
Lavender Rd., Epsom	282	330	CP106
Lavender Rd., Sutt.	285	331	DD105
Lavender Rd., Uxb.	248	312	BM71
Lavender Sq. E11	105	307	ED62
Lavender St. E15	121	307	EE65
Lavender Sweep SW11	175	323	DF84
Lavender Ter. SW11	175	323	DE83
Lavender Vale, Wall.	294	332	DK107
Lavender Wk. SW11	175	323	DF84
Lavender Wk., Mitch.	272	324	DG97
Lavender Way, Croy.	288	333	DX100
Lavengro Rd. SE27	194	324	DQ89
Lavenham Rd. SW18	189	323	CZ89
Lavernock Rd., Bexh.	255	319	FA82
Lavers Rd. N16	101	306	DS62
Laverstoke Gdns. SW15	187	322	CT87
Laverton Ms. SW5	76/7	315	DB77
Laverton Pl. SW5	76/7	315	DB77
Lavidge Rd. SE9	260	326	EL89
Lavina Gro. N1	23	316	DM68
Lavington Rd. W13	132	314	CH74
Lavington Rd., Croy.	286	332	DM104
Lavington St. SE1	60/1	316	DP74
Law Ho., Bark.	246	319	EU68
Law St. SE1	74	316	DR76
Lawdons Gdns., Croy.	286	332	DP105
Lawford Clo., Horn.	238	310	FJ63
Lawford Clo., Wall.	294	332	DL109
Lawford Rd. N1	117	306	DS66
Lawford Rd. NW5	114	306	DJ65
Lawford Rd. W4	154	314	CQ80
Lawless St. E14	140	317	EB73
Lawley Rd. N14	208	300	DH45
Lawley St. E5	118	307	DW63
Lawn, The, Sthl.	251	321	CA78
Lawn Ave., West Dr.	248	320	BJ75
Lawn Clo. N9	209	300	DT45
Lawn Clo., Brom.	276	326	EH93
Lawn Clo., N.Mal.	269	322	CS96
Lawn Clo., Ruis.	231	312	BT62
Lawn Clo., Swan.	279	327	FC96
Lawn Cres., Rich.	154	314	CN82
Lawn Fm. Gro., Rom.	226	309	EY56
Lawn Gdns. W7	243	313	CE74
Lawn Ho. Clo. E14	150	317	EC75
Lawn La. SW8	161	316	DL79
Lawn Pl. SE15	163	316	DT81
Lawn Rd. NW3	113	305	DF64
Lawn Rd., Beck.	274	325	DZ94
Lawn Rd., Uxb.	240	312	BJ66
Lawn Ter. SE3	183	325	EE83
Lawn Vale, Pnr.	214	303	BY54
Lawnfield NW2	111	305	CX66
Lawns, The E4	211	301	EA50
Lawns, The SE3	183	325	EE83
Lawns, The SE19	273	324	DR95
Lawns, The, Pnr.	215	303	CB52
Lawns, The, Sid.	278	327	EV91
Lawns, The, Sutt.	292	331	CY108
Lawnside SE3	183	325	EF84
Lawnsway, Rom.	227	309	FC52
Lawrence Ave. E12	235	308	EN63
Lawrence Ave. E17	222	307	DX53
Lawrence Ave. N13	209	300	DP49
Lawrence Ave. NW7	205	298	CS49
Lawrence Ave., N.Mal.	283	330	CR100
Lawrence Bldgs. N16	101	306	DT62
Lawrence Campe Clo. N20	207	299	DD48
Lawrence Clo. E3	130	317	EA69
Lawrence Clo. N15	221	306	DS55
Lawrence Ct. NW7	205	298	CS50
Lawrence Cres., Dag.	237	309	FB62
Lawrence Cres., Edg.	217	304	CN54
Lawrence Dr., Uxb.	241	312	BQ63
Lawrence Est., Houns.	258	321	BW84
Lawrence Gdns. NW7	205	298	CT48
Lawrence Hill E4	211	301	EA47
Lawrence La. EC2	49	316	DQ72
Lawrence Pl. N1	22/3	316	DL67
Lawrence Rd. E6	244	318	EL67
Lawrence Rd. E13	244	318	EH67
Lawrence Rd. N15	221	306	DS56
Lawrence Rd. N18	210	301	DV49
Lawrence Rd. SE25	273	324	DT98
Lawrence Rd. W5	143	314	CK77
Lawrence Rd., Erith	255	319	FB80
Lawrence Rd., Hmptn.	266	329	BZ94
Lawrence Rd., Hayes	241	312	BQ68
Lawrence Rd., Houns.	258	321	BW84
Lawrence Rd., Pnr.	214	303	BX58
Lawrence Rd., Rich.	268	322	CJ91
Lawrence Rd., Rom.	228	310	FH57
Lawrence Rd., W.Wick.	289	334	EG105
Lawrence St. E16	141	317	EF71
Lawrence St. NW7	205	298	CT50
Lawrence St. SW3	159	315	DE79
Lawrence Way NW10	108	304	CQ63
Lawrence Weaver Clo., Mord.	284	331	DB100
Lawrie Pk. Ave. SE26	274	325	DV92
Lawrie Pk. Cres. SE26	274	325	DV92
Lawrie Pk. Gdns. SE26	274	325	DV91
Lawrie Pk. Rd. SE26	274	325	DV93
Lawson Clo. E16	244	318	EJ71
Lawson Clo. SW19	189	323	CX90
Lawson Est. SE1	74	316	DR76
Lawson Gdns., Pnr.	214	303	BV55
Lawson Rd., Enf.	203	301	DW39
Lawson Rd., Sthl.	242	313	BZ70
Lawton Rd. E3	129	317	DY69
Lawton Rd. E10	105	307	ED60
Laxcon Clo. NW10	108	304	CQ64
Laxley Clo. SE5	162	316	DP80
Laxton Pl. NW1	32/3	316	DH70
Layard Rd. SE16	148	317	DV77
Layard Rd., Enf.	202	300	DT39
Layard Rd., Th.Hth.	273	324	DR96
Layard Sq. SE16	148	317	DV77
Laycock St. N1	116	306	DN65
Layer Gdns. W3	134	314	CN73
Layfield Clo. NW4	94	305	CV59
Layfield Cres. NW4	94	305	CV59
Layfield Rd. NW4	94	305	CV59
Layhams Rd., Kes.	289	333	EF106
Layhams Rd., W.Wick.	289	333	ED104
Laymarsh Clo., Belv.	254	319	EZ76
Laymead Clo., Nthlt.	232	313	BY65
Laystall St. EC1	36	316	DN70
Layton Cres., Croy.	286	332	DN106
Layton Rd. N1	24	316	DN68
Layton Rd., Brent.	143	314	CK78
Layton Rd., Houns.	259	321	CB84
Laytons Bldgs. SE1	74	316	DR75
Laytons La., Sun.	281	328	BT96
Layzell Wk. SE9	260	326	EK88
Lazar Wk. N7	99	306	DM61
Le May Ave. SE12	260	326	EH90
Lea Bri. Rd. E5	102	307	DV62
Lea Bri. Rd. E10	104	307	EA59
Lea Bri. Rd. E17	223	307	ED57
Lea Cres., Ruis.	241	312	BT63
Lea Gdns., Wem.	107	304	CM63
Lea Hall Rd. E10	104	307	EA60
Lea Rd., Beck.	275	325	EA96
Lea Rd., Enf.	202	300	DR39
Lea Rd., Sthl.	250	321	BY77
Lea Side Ind. Est., Enf.	203	301	DZ41
Lea Vale, Dart.	263	327	FD84
Lea Valley Rd. E4	210	301	DX43
Lea Valley Rd., Enf.	210	301	DX43
Lea Valley Viaduct E4	210	301	DX50
Lea Valley Viaduct N18	210	301	DX50
Lea Vw. Hos. E5	102	307	DV60
Leabank Clo., Har.	233	313	CE62
Leabank Sq. E9	120	307	EA65
Leabank Vw. N15	222	307	DU58
Leabourne Rd. N16	222	307	DU58
Leacroft, Stai.	264	328	BG92
Leacroft Ave. SW12	191	323	DF87
Leacroft Clo., Stai.	264	328	BH91
Leacroft Clo., West Dr.	248	312	BL72
Leadale Ave. E4	210	301	DZ47
Leadale Rd. N15	222	307	DU58
Leadale Rd. N16	222	307	DU58
Leadbeaters Clo. N11	207	299	DF50
Leadenhall Mkt. EC3	50/1	316	DS72
Leadenhall Pl. EC3	50/1	316	DS72
Leadenhall St. EC3	50/1	316	DS72
Leader Ave. E12	235	308	EN64
Leadings, The, Wem.	92	304	CQ62
Leaf Clo., Nthwd.	213	302	BR52
Leaf Gro. SE27	273	324	DN92
Leafield Clo. SW16	273	324	DP93
Leafield La., Sid.	278	327	EZ91
Leafield Rd. SW20	270	323	CZ97
Leafield Rd., Sutt.	284	331	DA103
Leafy Gro., Kes.	290	334	EJ106
Leafy Oak Rd. SE12	276	326	EJ91
Leafy Way, Croy.	287	332	DT103
Leagrave St. E5	102	307	DW62
Leaholme Way, Ruis.	231	302	BQ58
Leahurst Rd. SE13	183	325	ED85
Leake Ct. SE1	71	316	DM75
Leake St. SE1	71	316	DM75
Lealand Rd. N15	221	306	DT58
Leamington Ave. E17	223	307	EA57
Leamington Ave., Brom.	276	326	EJ92
Leamington Ave., Mord.	270	323	CY98
Leamington Ave., Orp.	291	334	ES105
Leamington Clo. E12	234	308	EM64
Leamington Clo., Brom.	276	326	EJ92
Leamington Clo., Houns.	259	321	CC85
Leamington Clo., Rom.	229	311	FN51
Leamington Cres., Har.	232	313	BY62
Leamington Gdns., Ilf.	235	308	ET61
Leamington Pk. W3	135	314	CR71
Leamington Pl., Hayes	241	312	BT70
Leamington Rd., Sthl.	250	321	BX77
Leamington Rd. Vil. W11	137	315	CZ71
Leamore St. W6	146	315	CV77
Leamouth Rd. E6	244	318	EL72
Leamouth Rd. E14	141	317	ED72
Leander Ct. SE8	166	317	EA81
Leander Rd. SW2	193	324	DM87
Leander Rd., Nthlt.	243	313	CA68
Leander Rd., Th.Hth.	272	324	DM98
Learoyd Gdns. E6	245	318	EN73
Leas, The, Stai.	264	328	BG91
Leas, The, Upmin.	239	311	FR59
Leas Dale SE9	261	326	EN90
Leas Grn., Chis.	277	326	ET93
Leaside Ave. N10	220	306	DG55
Leaside Ct., Uxb.	241	312	BP69
Leaside Rd. E5	102	307	DW60
Leasowes Rd. E10	104	307	EA60
Leasway, Upmin.	239	311	FQ62
Leathart Clo., Horn.	238	310	FH66
Leather Bottle La., Belv.	254	319	EZ77
Leather Clo., Mitch.	272	324	DG96
Leather Gdns. E15	131	317	EE67
Leather La. EC1	36	316	DN70
Leather La., Horn.	238	310	FK60

Leatherbottle Grn., Erith 254 319 EZ76
Leatherdale St. E1 128 317 DW70
Leatherhead Clo. N16 101 306 DS60
Leathermarket Ct. SE1 74/5 316 DS75
Leathermarket St. SE1 74/5 316 DS75
Leathsail Rd., Har. 233 313 CB62
Leathwaite Rd. SW11 175 323 DF84
Leathwell Rd. SE8 166 317 EB82
Leaveland Clo., Beck. 275 325 EA98
Leaver Gdns., Grnf. 243 313 CD68
Leavesden Rd., Stan. 216 304 CG51
Leaway E10 103 307 DX60
Lebanon Ave., Felt. 266 329 BX92
Lebanon Ct., Twick. 184 322 CH87
Lebanon Gdns. SW18 174 323 DA85
Lebanon Pk., Twick. 184 322 CH87
Lebanon Rd. SW18 174 323 DA85
Lebanon Rd., Croy. 287 332 DS102
Lebrun Sq. SE3 260 326 EH83
Lechmere App., Wdf.Grn. 224 308 EJ54
Lechmere Ave., Wdf.Grn. 224 308 EK54
Lechmere Rd. NW2 110 305 CV65
Leckford Rd. SW18 190 323 DC89
Leckwith Ave., Bexh. 254 319 EY79
Lecky St. SW7 78 315 DD78
Leconfield Ave. SW13 171 322 CT83
Leconfield Rd. N5 117 306 DR63
Leconfield Wk., Horn. 238 310 FJ65
Leda Ave., Enf. 203 301 DX38
Leda Rd. SE18 252 318 EM76
Ledbury Est. SE15 164 317 DV80
Ledbury Ms. N. W11 52 315 DA73
Ledbury Ms. W. W11 52 315 DA73
Ledbury Pl., Croy. 287 332 DQ105
Ledbury Rd. W11 137 315 CZ72
Ledbury Rd., Croy. 287 332 DQ105
Ledbury St. SE15 164 317 DU80
Ledrington Rd. SE19 274 325 DU93
Ledway Dr., Wem. 91 304 CM59
Lee Ave., Rom. 226 309 EY58
Lee Bri. SE13 182 325 EC83
Lee Ch. St. SE13 183 325 EE84
Lee Clo. E17 222 307 DX53
Lee Conservancy Rd. E9 119 307 DZ64
Lee Gdns. Ave., Horn. 239 311 FN60
Lee Grn. SE12 183 325 EF85
Lee Grn., Orp. 291 335 EU99
Lee High Rd. SE12 183 325 EF84
Lee High Rd. SE13 183 325 ED84
Lee Pk. SE3 183 325 EF84
Lee Pk. Way N9 210 301 DY48
Lee Pk. Way N18 210 301 DX50
Lee Rd. NW7 218 305 CX52
Lee Rd. SE3 183 325 EF83
Lee Rd. SW19 271 323 DB95
Lee Rd., Enf. 210 301 DU44
Lee Rd., Grnf. 122 314 CJ67
Lee St. E8 27 316 DT67
Lee Ter. SE3 183 325 EE83
Lee Ter. SE13 183 325 EE83
Lee Valley Trd. Est. N18 210 301 DX50
Lee Vw., Enf. 202 300 DP39
Leechcroft Ave., Sid. 261 326 ET85
Leechcroft Ave., Swan. 279 327 FF97
Leechcroft Rd., Wall. 285 332 DG104
Leecroft Rd., Barn. 206 299 CY43
Leeds Pl. N4 99 306 DM61
Leeds Rd., Ilf. 235 308 ER60
Leeds St. N18 210 301 DU50
Leefern Rd. W12 146 315 CU75
Leegate SE12 183 325 EF85
Leeke St. WC1 35 316 DM69
Leeland Rd. W13 132 314 CG74
Leeland Ter. W13 132 314 CG74
Leeland Way NW10 109 304 CT63
Leerdam Dr. E14 150 317 EC76
Lees, The, Croy. 288 333 DZ103
Lees Ave., Nthwd. 213 302 BT54
Lees Pl. W1 56 316 DG73
Lees Rd., Uxb. 241 312 BP70
Leeside, Barn. 206 299 CY43
Leeside Cres. NW11 218 305 CY58
Leeside Rd. N17 222 307 DV51
Leeson Rd. SE24 178 324 DN84
Leesons Hill, Chis. 277 326 ES97
Leesons Hill, Orp. 278 327 EU97
Leesons Way, Orp. 277 326 ET96
Leeward Gdns. SW19 270 323 CZ92
Leeway SE8 149 317 DZ78
Leeway Clo., Pnr. 214 303 BZ52
Leewood Clo. SE12 183 325 EF86
Leewood Pl., Swan. 279 327 FD98
Lefevre Wk. E3 129 317 DZ67
Lefroy Rd. W12 145 314 CT75
Legard Rd. N5 100 306 DP62
Legatt Rd. SE9 260 326 EK85
Leggatt Rd. E15 130 317 EC68
Legge St. SE13 182 325 EC85
Leghorn Rd. NW10 125 314 CT68
Leghorn Rd. SE18 253 318 ER78
Legion Clo. N1 116 306 DN66
Legion Ct., Mord. 284 331 DA100
Legion Rd., Grnf. 243 313 CC67
Legion Way N12 219 305 DE52
Legon Ave., Rom. 237 309 FC60
Legrace Ave., Houns. 250 321 BX82
Leicester Ave., Mitch. 272 324 DL98
Leicester Clo., Wor.Pk. 284 331 CW105
Leicester Ct. WC2 58 316 DK73
Leicester Gdns., Ilf. 235 308 ES59
Leicester Pl. WC2 58 316 DK73
Leicester Rd. E11 224 308 EH57
Leicester Rd. N2 219 305 DE55
Leicester Rd. NW10 109 304 CR66
Leicester Rd., Barn. 207 299 DB43
Leicester Rd., Croy. 287 332 DS101
Leicester Sq. WC2 58 316 DK73
Leicester St. WC2 58 316 DK73
Leigh Ave., Ilf. 224 308 EK56
Leigh Clo., N.Mal. 269 322 CR98
Leigh Ct., Har. 233 313 CE60
Leigh Gdns. NW10 126 315 CW68
Leigh Hunt Dr. N14 208 300 DK46
Leigh Hunt St. SE1 73 316 DQ75
Leigh Orchard Clo. SW16 193 324 DM90
Leigh Pl. EC1 48 316 DN71
Leigh Pl., Well. 254 319 EU82
Leigh Rd. E6 235 308 EN65
Leigh Rd. E10 104 307 EC59
Leigh Rd. N5 116 306 DP63
Leigh Rd., Houns. 259 321 CD84
Leigh St. WC1 34/5 316 DL70
Leigh Ter., Orp. 278 327 EV97
Leigham Ave. SW16 193 324 DL90
Leigham Ct. Rd. SW16 193 324 DL89
Leigham Dr., Islw. 251 321 CE80
Leigham Vale SW2 194 324 DN89
Leigham Vale SW16 193 324 DM90
Leighton Ave. E12 235 308 EN64
Leighton Ave., Pnr. 214 303 BY55
Leighton Clo., Edg. 217 304 CN54
Leighton Cres. NW5 114 306 DJ64
Leighton Gdns. NW10 126 315 CV68
Leighton Gdns., S.Croy. 295 333 DV113
Leighton Gro. NW5 114 306 DJ64
Leighton Pl. NW5 114 306 DJ64
Leighton Rd. NW5 114 306 DJ64
Leighton Rd. W13 142 314 CG75
Leighton Rd., Enf. 209 300 DT43
Leighton Rd., Har. 215 303 CD54
Leighton St., Croy. 286 332 DP102
Leila Parnell Pl. SE7 252 318 EJ79
Leinster Ave. SW14 170 322 CQ83
Leinster Gdns. W2 41 315 DC72
Leinster Ms. W2 53 315 DC73
Leinster Pl. W2 41 315 DC72
Leinster Rd. N10 220 306 DH56
Leinster Rd. NW6 28 315 DA69
Leinster Sq. W2 40 315 DA72
Leinster Ter. W2 53 315 DC73
Leith Clo. NW9 93 304 CR60
Leith Hill, Orp. 278 327 EU95
Leith Hill Grn., Orp. 278 327 EU95
Leith Rd. N22 221 306 DP53
Leith Yd. NW6 16 315 DA67
Leithcote Gdns. SW16 272 324 DM91
Leithcote Path SW16 193 324 DM90
Lela Ave., Houns. 250 321 BW82
Lelitia Clo. E8 128 317 DU67
Leman St. E1 51 316 DT72
Lemark Clo., Stan. 204 298 CJ50
Lemmon Rd. SE10 167 317 EE79
Lemna Rd. E11 105 307 EE59
Lemonwell Ct. SE9 261 326 EQ85
Lemonwell Dr. SE9 261 326 EQ85
Lemsford Clo. N15 222 307 DU57
Lemsford Ct. N4 100 306 DQ61
Lemuel St. SW18 174 323 DB86
Len Freeman Pl. SW6 157 315 CZ80
Lena Gdns. W6 146 315 CW76
Lena Kennedy Clo. E4 223 307 EC51
Lenanton Steps E14 150 317 EA75
Lendal Ter. SW4 177 324 DK83
Lenelby Rd., Surb. 282 330 CN102
Lenham Rd. SE12 183 325 EF84
Lenham Rd., Bexh. 254 319 EZ79
Lenham Rd., Sutt. 284 331 DB105
Lenham Rd., Th.Hth. 273 324 DR96
Lennard Ave., W.Wick. 289 333 EE103
Lennard Clo., W.Wick. 289 333 EE103
Lennard Rd. SE20 274 325 DX93
Lennard Rd., Beck. 274 325 DY94
Lennard Rd., Brom. 290 334 EM102
Lennard Rd., Croy. 287 332 DQ102
Lennon Rd. NW2 110 305 CW65
Lennox Clo., Rom. 227 309 FF58
Lennox Gdns. NW10 109 304 CT63
Lennox Gdns. SW1 67 315 DF76
Lennox Gdns., Croy. 286 332 DP105
Lennox Gdns., Ilf. 234 308 EM60
Lennox Gdns. Ms. SW1 67 315 DF76
Lennox Rd. E17 222 307 DZ58
Lennox Rd. N4 99 306 DM61
Lenor Clo., Bexh. 262 327 EY84
Lens Rd. E7 234 308 EJ66
Lensbury Way SE2 254 319 EW76
Lenthall Pl. SW7 77 315 DC77
Lenthall Rd. E8 117 306 DT66
Lenthorp Rd. SE10 151 317 EF77
Lentmead Rd., Brom. 199 325 EF90
Lenton Ri., Rich. 169 322 CL83
Lenton St. SE18 253 318 ER77
Lenville Way SE16 148 317 DU78
Leo St. SE15 164 317 DV80
Leo Yd. EC1 36/7 316 DP70
Leof Cres. SE6 275 325 EB92
Leominster Rd., Mord. 285 331 DC100
Leominster Wk., Mord. 285 331 DC100
Leonard Ave., Mord. 285 331 DC99
Leonard Ave., Rom. 237 309 FD60
Leonard Rd. E4 223 307 EA51
Leonard Rd. E7 234 308 EG63
Leonard Rd. N9 209 300 DT48
Leonard Rd. SW16 272 324 DJ95
Leonard Rd., Sthl. 250 321 BX76
Leonard Robbins Path SE28 246 319 EV73
Leonard St. E16 244 318 EL74
Leonard St. EC2 38 316 DR70
Leontine Clo. SE15 164 317 DU80
Leopards Ct. EC1 48 316 DN71
Leopold Ave. SW19 270 323 CZ92
Leopold Ms. E9 128 317 DW67
Leopold Rd. E17 223 307 EA57
Leopold Rd. N2 219 305 DD55
Leopold Rd. N18 210 301 DV50
Leopold Rd. NW10 109 304 CS66
Leopold Rd. SW19 270 323 CZ91
Leopold Rd. W5 133 314 CM74
Leopold St. E3 139 317 DZ71
Leopold Ter. SW19 271 323 DA92
Lepe Clo., Brom. 275 325 EE91
Leppoc Rd. SW4 177 324 DK85
Leroy St. SE1 86/7 316 DS77
Lescombe Clo. SE23 197 325 DY90
Lescombe Rd. SE23 197 325 DY90
Lesley Clo., Bex. 263 327 FB87
Lesley Clo., Swan. 279 327 FD97
Leslie Gdns., Sutt. 292 331 DA107
Leslie Gro., Croy. 287 332 DR102
Leslie Gro. Pl., Croy. 287 332 DR102
Leslie Pk. Rd., Croy. 287 332 DS102
Leslie Rd. E11 120 307 EC63
Leslie Rd. E16 244 318 EH72
Leslie Rd. N2 219 305 DD55
Leslie Smith Sq. SE18 253 318 EN79
Lesney Fm. Est., Erith 255 319 FD80
Lesney Pk., Erith 255 319 FD79
Lesney Pk. Rd., Erith 255 319 FD79
Lessar Ave. SW4 176 324 DH85
Lessing St. SE23 197 325 DY87
Lessingham Ave. SW17 271 323 DF91
Lessingham Ave., Ilf. 225 308 EN55
Lessington Ave., Rom. 227 309 FC58
Lessness Ave., Bexh. 254 319 EX80
Lessness Pk., Belv. 254 319 EZ78
Lessness Rd., Belv. 255 319 FA78
Lessness Rd., Mord. 285 331 DC100
Lester Ave. E15 131 317 EE70
Leswin Pl. N16 101 306 DT62
Leswin Rd. N16 101 306 DT62
Letchford Gdns. NW10 126 315 CU69
Letchford Ms. NW10 126 315 CU69
Letchford Ter., Har. 215 303 CB53
Letchworth Ave., Felt. 265 320 BT87
Letchworth Clo., Brom. 289 334 EG99
Letchworth Dr., Brom. 289 334 EG99
Letchworth St. SW17 271 323 DF91
Lethbridge Clo. SE13 166 317 EC81
Lett Rd. E15 121 307 ED66
Letterstone Rd. SW6 157 315 CZ80
Lettice St. SW6 157 315 CZ81
Lettsom St. SE5 163 316 DS82
Lettsom Wk. E13 244 318 EG68
Leucha Rd. E17 222 307 DY57
Levana Clo. SW19 189 323 CY88
Levehurst Way SW4 161 316 DL82
Leven Rd. E14 140 317 EC71
Leven Way, Hayes 249 312 BS72
Levendale Rd. SE23 197 325 DY89
Lever St. EC1 36/7 316 DP69
Leverett St. SW3 78/9 315 DE77
Leverholme Gdns. SE9 261 326 EN90
Leverson St. SW16 272 324 DJ93
Leverton Pl. NW5 114 306 DJ64
Leverton St. NW5 114 306 DJ64
Levett Gdns., Ilf. 235 308 ET63
Levett Rd., Bark. 235 308 ES65
Levine Gdns., Bark. 246 319 EX68
Levison Way N19 99 306 DK61
Lewes Clo., Nthlt. 233 313 CA65
Lewes Rd. N12 207 299 DE50
Lewes Rd., Brom. 276 326 EK96
Lewesdon Clo. SW19 189 323 CX88
Leweston Pl. N16 101 306 DT59
Lewey Ho. E3 129 317 DZ70
Lewgars Ave. NW9 217 304 CQ58
Lewin Rd. SW14 171 322 CR83
Lewin Rd. SW16 272 324 DK93
Lewin Rd., Bexh. 262 327 EY85
Lewis Ave. E17 223 307 EA53
Lewis Clo. N14 208 300 DJ45
Lewis Clo., Uxb. 212 302 BJ54
Lewis Cres. NW10 108 304 CQ64
Lewis Gdns. N2 219 305 DD54
Lewis Gro. SE13 182 325 EC83
Lewis Rd., Horn. 228 310 FJ58
Lewis Rd., Mitch. 271 323 DD96
Lewis Rd., Rich. 169 322 CK85
Lewis Rd., Sid. 262 327 EW90
Lewis Rd., Sthl. 250 321 BY75
Lewis Rd., Sutt. 284 331 DB105
Lewis Rd., Well. 262 327 EW83
Lewis St. NW1 114 306 DH65
Lewis Way, Dag. 237 309 FB65
Lewisham High St. SE13 182 325 EB86
Lewisham Hill SE13 166 317 EC82
Lewisham Pk. SE13 182 325 EC85
Lewisham Rd. SE13 166 317 EB81
Lewisham St. SW1 70 316 DK75
Lewisham Way SE4 166 317 EA82
Lewisham Way SE14 165 317 DZ81
Lexden Dr., Rom. 226 309 EV58
Lexden Rd. W3 134 314 CP74
Lexden Rd., Mitch. 272 324 DK98
Lexham Gdns. W8 76 315 DA77
Lexham Gdns. Ms. W8 64/5 315 DB76
Lexham Ho., Bark. 245 318 ER67
Lexham Ms. W8 76 315 DA77
Lexham Wk. W8 64/5 315 DB76
Lexington Ct., Pur. 295 332 DQ110
Lexington St. W1 57 316 DJ73
Lexington Way, Upmin. 229 311 FT58
Lexton Gdns. SW12 193 324 DK88
Ley St., Ilf. 235 308 EP61
Leyborne Ave. W13 142 314 CH75
Leyborne Pk., Rich. 154 314 CN81
Leybourne Clo., Brom. 289 334 EG100
Leybourne Rd. E11 105 307 EF60
Leybourne Rd. NW1 114 306 DH66
Leybourne Rd. NW9 217 304 CN57
Leybourne Rd., Uxb. 241 312 BQ67
Leybourne St. NW1 114 306 DH66
Leybridge Ct. SE12 260 326 EG85
Leyburn Clo. E17 223 307 EC56
Leyburn Cres., Rom. 228 311 FL52
Leyburn Gdns., Croy. 287 332 DT103
Leyburn Gro. N18 222 307 DU51
Leyburn Rd. N18 222 307 DU51
Leyburn Rd., Rom. 228 311 FL52
Leyden St. E1 51 316 DT71
Leydenhatch La., Swan. 279 327 FC95
Leydon Clo. SE16 139 317 DX74
Leyes Rd. E16 244 318 EJ72
Leyfield, Wor.Pk. 283 330 CS102
Leyland Ave., Enf. 203 301 DY40
Leyland Rd. SE12 183 325 EF85
Leylang Rd. SE14 165 317 DX80
Leys, The N2 219 305 DC56
Leys, The, Har. 216 304 CL58
Leys Ave., Dag. 247 319 FC67
Leys Clo., Dag. 237 309 FC66
Leys Clo., Har. 215 303 CD57
Leys Clo., Uxb. 212 302 BK53
Leys Gdns., Barn. 208 300 DG43
Leys Rd. E., Enf. 203 301 DY39
Leys Rd. W., Enf. 203 301 DY39
Leysdown Ave., Bexh. 263 327 FC84
Leysdown Rd. SE9 260 326 EL89
Leysfield Rd. W12 146 315 CU76
Leyspring Rd. E11 105 307 EF60
Leyswood Dr., Ilf. 225 308 ES57
Leythe Rd. W3 144 314 CQ75
Leyton Business Cen. E10 104 307 EA61
Leyton Cross Rd., Dart. 263 327 FF90
Leyton Gra. E10 104 307 EB60
Leyton Gra. Est. E10 104 307 EA60
Leyton Grn. Rd. E10 223 307 EC58
Leyton Ind. Village E10 103 307 DX59
Leyton Pk. Rd. E10 104 307 EC62
Leyton Rd. E15 121 307 ED64
Leyton Rd. SW19 271 323 DC94
Leyton Way E11 105 307 EE59
Leytonstone Rd. E15 121 307 EE65
Leywick St. E15 131 317 EE68
Liardet St. SE14 165 317 DY79
Liberia Rd. N5 116 306 DP65
Liberty, The, Rom. 227 309 FE57
Liberty Ave. SW19 271 323 DC95
Liberty Ms. SW12 176 324 DH86
Liberty St. SW9 161 316 DM81
Libra Rd. E3 129 317 DZ67
Libra Rd. E13 244 318 EG68
Library Pl. E1 138 317 DV73
Library St. SE1 72/3 316 DP75
Library Way, Twick. 259 321 CC87
Lichfield Gdns., Rich. 169 322 CL84
Lichfield Gro. N3 219 305 DA53
Lichfield Rd. E3 129 317 DY69
Lichfield Rd. E6 244 318 EK69
Lichfield Rd. N9 210 301 DU47
Lichfield Rd. NW2 111 305 CY63
Lichfield Rd., Dag. 236 309 EV63
Lichfield Rd., Houns. 258 321 BW83
Lichfield Rd., Nthwd. 214 303 BU55
Lichfield Rd., Rich. 153 314 CM81
Lichfield Rd., Wdf.Grn. 211 301 EE49
Lichfield Sq., Rich. 169 322 CL84
Lichfield Ter., Upmin. 239 311 FS61
Lichlade Clo., Orp. 291 334 ET105
Lidbury Rd. NW7 218 305 CY51
Lidcote Gdns. SW9 162 316 DN82
Liddall Way, West Dr. 248 312 BM74
Liddell Clo., Har. 216 304 CK55
Liddell Gdns. NW10 126 315 CW68
Liddell Rd. NW6 112 305 DA65
Lidding Rd., Har. 216 304 CK57
Liddington Rd. E15 131 317 EF67
Liddon Rd. E13 244 318 EH69
Liddon Rd., Brom. 276 326 EJ97
Liden Clo. E17 103 307 DZ60
Lidfield Rd. N16 117 306 DR63
Lidgate Rd. SE15 163 316 DT80
Lidiard Rd. SW18 190 323 DC89
Lidlington Pl. NW1 21 316 DJ68
Lido Sq. N17 221 306 DR53
Lidyard Rd. N19 98 306 DJ60
Liffler Rd. SE18 253 318 ES78
Lifford St. SW15 173 323 CX84
Liffords Pl. SW13 155 314 CT82
Lightcliffe Rd. N13 209 300 DN49
Lighter Clo. SE16 149 317 DY77
Lighterman Ms. E1 139 317 DX72
Lightermans Rd. E14 150 317 EA75
Lightermans Wk. SW18 174 323 DA84
Lightfoot Rd. N8 220 306 DL57
Lightley Clo., Wem. 107 304 CM66
Ligonier St. E2 39 316 DT70
Lila Pl., Swan. 279 327 FE98
Lilac Clo. E4 222 307 DZ51
Lilac Gdns. W5 143 314 CK76
Lilac Gdns., Croy. 288 333 EA104
Lilac Gdns., Hayes 249 312 BS72
Lilac Gdns., Rom. 237 309 FE60
Lilac Gdns., Swan. 279 327 FD97
Lilac Pl. SE11 83 316 DM77
Lilac Pl., West Dr. 248 312 BM73
Lilac St. W12 136 315 CU73
Lilacs Ave., Enf. 203 301 DW36
Lilburne Gdns. SE9 260 326 EL85
Lilburne Rd. SE9 260 326 EL85
Lilburne Wk. NW10 108 304 CQ65
Lile Cres. W7 243 313 CE71
Lilestone Est. NW8 30 315 DD70
Lilestone St. NW8 30/1 315 DE70
Lilford Rd. SE5 162 316 DP82
Lilian Barker Clo. SE12 260 326 EG85
Lilian Board Way, Grnf. 233 313 CD64
Lilian Clo. N16 101 306 DS62
Lilian Gdns., Wdf.Grn. 224 308 EH53
Lilian Rd. SW16 272 324 DJ95
Lillechurch Rd., Dag. 236 309 EV65
Lilleshall Rd., Mord. 285 331 DD99
Lilley Clo. E1 138 317 DU74
Lilley La. NW7 205 298 CR50
Lillian Ave. W3 144 314 CN75
Lillian Rd. SW13 156 315 CU79
Lillie Rd. SW6 157 315 CX79
Lillie Yd. SW6 158 315 DA79
Lillieshall Rd. SW4 176 324 DH83
Lillington Gdns. Est. SW1 81 316 DJ77
Lilliput Ave., Nthlt. 242 313 BY67
Lilliput Rd., Rom. 237 309 FD59
Lily Clo. W14 147 315 CX77
Lily Gdns., Wem. 122 314 CJ68
Lily Pl. EC1 48 316 DN71
Lily Rd. E17 223 307 EA58
Lilyville Rd. SW6 157 315 CZ81
Limbourne Ave., Dag. 236 309 EZ59
Limburg Rd. SW11 175 323 DF84
Lime Ave., Upmin. 239 311 FN63
Lime Ave., West Dr. 248 312 BM73
Lime Clo. E1 138 317 DU74
Lime Clo., Brom. 276 326 EL98
Lime Clo., Cars. 285 331 DF103
Lime Clo., Har. 216 304 CG54
Lime Clo., Pnr. 231 302 BT55
Lime Clo., Rom. 227 309 FC56
Lime Ct., Mitch. 271 323 DD96
Lime Cres., Sun. 266 329 BW96
Lime Gro. N20 206 299 CZ46
Lime Gro. W12 146 315 CW75
Lime Gro., Hayes 249 312 BR73
Lime Gro., Ilf. 225 308 ET51
Lime Gro., N.Mal. 269 322 CR97
Lime Gro., Orp. 290 334 EP103
Lime Gro., Ruis. 214 303 BV58
Lime Gro., Sid. 261 326 ET86
Lime Gro., Twick. 259 321 CF86
Lime Meadow Ave., S.Croy. 295 333 DU113
Lime Rd., Rich. 169 322 CM84
Lime Rd., Swan. 279 327 FD97
Lime Row, Erith 254 319 EZ76
Lime St. E17 222 307 DY56
Lime St. EC3 62/3 316 DS73
Lime St. Pas. EC3 62/3 316 DS73
Lime Ter. W7 243 313 CE73
Lime Tree Gro., Croy. 288 333 DZ104
Lime Tree Pl., Mitch. 272 324 DH95
Lime Tree Rd., Houns. 251 321 CB81
Lime Tree Ter. SE6 197 325 DZ88
Lime Tree Wk., Enf. 202 300 DQ38
Lime Tree Wk., W.Wick. 289 333 EF105
Lime Wk. E15 131 317 EE67
Lime Wk., Uxb. 240 312 BJ64
Limeburner La. EC4 48/9 316 DP72
Limedene Clo., Pnr. 214 303 BX53
Limeharbour E14 150 317 EB76
Limehouse Causeway E14 139 317 DZ73
Limehouse Flds. Est. E14 139 317 DY71
Limekiln Dr. SE7 252 318 EH79
Limerick Clo. SW12 192 324 DJ87
Limerick Gdns., Upmin. 239 311 FT59
Limerston St. SW10 158 315 DC79
Limes, The W2 52 315 DA73
Limes, The, Brom. 290 334 EL103
Limes Ave. E11 224 308 EH56
Limes Ave. N12 207 299 DC49
Limes Ave. NW7 217 304 CS51
Limes Ave. NW11 95 305 CY59
Limes Ave. SE20 274 325 DV94
Limes Ave. SW13 155 314 CT82
Limes Ave., Cars. 285 331 DF102
Limes Ave., Croy. 286 332 DN104
Limes Ave., The N11 208 300 DH50
Limes Clo., Ashf. 265 328 BN92
Limes Fld. Rd. SW14 171 322 CS83
Limes Gdns. SW18 174 323 DA86
Limes Gro. SE13 182 325 EC84
Limes Pl., Croy. 287 332 DR101
Limes Rd., Beck. 275 325 EB96
Limes Rd., Croy. 287 332 DR100
Limes Row, Orp. 290 334 EP106
Limes Wk. SE15 180 325 DV84
Limes Wk. W5 143 314 CK75
Limesdale Gdns., Edg. 217 304 CQ54
Limesford Rd. SE15 181 325 DX84
Limestone Wk., Erith 254 319 EX76
Limetree Clo. SW2 193 324 DM88
Limetree Ter., Well. 262 327 EU83
Limetree Wk. SW17 272 324 DG92
Limewood Clo. W13 132 314 CH72
Limewood Ct., Ilf. 224 308 EM57
Limewood Rd., Erith 255 319 FC80
Limpsfield Ave. SW19 189 323 CX89
Limpsfield Ave., Th.Hth. 286 332 DM99
Limpsfield Rd., S.Croy. 295 333 DU112
Linacre Ct. W6 147 315 CX78
Linacre Rd. NW2 110 305 CV65
Linberry Wk. SE8 149 317 DY77
Linchmere Rd. SE12 199 325 EF87
Lincoln Ave. N14 208 300 DJ48
Lincoln Ave. SW19 189 323 CX90
Lincoln Ave., Rom. 237 309 FD60
Lincoln Ave., Twick. 259 321 CB89
Lincoln Clo. SE25 287 333 DU100
Lincoln Clo., Erith 255 319 FF82
Lincoln Clo., Grnf. 243 313 CC67
Lincoln Clo., Har. 214 303 BZ57
Lincoln Clo., Horn. 229 311 FN57
Lincoln Ct. N16 101 306 DR59
Lincoln Ct., Borwd. 205 298 CR43
Lincoln Cres., Enf. 209 300 DS43
Lincoln Gdns., Ilf. 234 308 EL59
Lincoln Grn. Rd., Orp. 291 334 ET99
Lincoln Ms. NW6 127 315 CZ67
Lincoln Ms. SE21 195 324 DR88
Lincoln Rd. E7 234 308 EK65
Lincoln Rd. E13 244 318 EH70
Lincoln Rd. E18 224 308 EG53
Lincoln Rd. N2 219 305 DE55
Lincoln Rd. SE25 274 325 DV97
Lincoln Rd., Enf. 202 300 DS42
Lincoln Rd., Erith 255 319 FF82
Lincoln Rd., Felt. 258 321 BZ90
Lincoln Rd., Har. 214 303 BZ57
Lincoln Rd., Mitch. 286 332 DL99
Lincoln Rd., N.Mal. 269 322 CQ97
Lincoln Rd., Nthwd. 213 302 BT54
Lincoln Rd., Sid. 278 327 EV92
Lincoln Rd., Wem. 107 304 CK65
Lincoln Rd., Wor.Pk. 283 331 CV102
Lincoln St. E11 105 307 EE61
Lincoln St. SW3 79 315 DF77
Lincoln Way, Enf. 210 301 DV43
Lincoln Way, Sun. 281 328 BS95
Lincolns, The NW7 205 298 CT48
Lincoln's Inn WC2 47 316 DM72
Lincoln's Inn Flds. WC2 47 316 DM72
Lincombe Rd., Brom. 199 325 EF90
Lind Rd., Sutt. 285 331 DC106
Lind St. SE8 166 317 EA82
Lindal Cres., Enf. 208 300 DL43
Lindal Rd. SE4 181 325 DZ85
Lindales, The N17 221 306 DT51
Lindbergh Rd., Wall. 294 332 DL108
Linden Ave. NW10 127 315 CX68
Linden Ave., Enf. 203 301 DU39
Linden Ave., Houns. 259 321 CB85
Linden Ave., Ruis. 232 313 BU60
Linden Ave., Th.Hth. 273 324 DP98
Linden Ave., Wem. 107 304 CM64
Linden Clo. N14 208 300 DJ44
Linden Clo., Orp. 291 335 EU106
Linden Clo., Ruis. 232 313 BU60
Linden Clo., Stan. 204 298 CH50
Linden Ct. W12 136 315 CW74
Linden Cres., Grnf. 233 313 CF65
Linden Cres., Kings.T. 268 322 CM96
Linden Cres., Wdf.Grn. 224 308 EH51
Linden Gdns. W2 52 315 DA73
Linden Gdns. W4 145 314 CS78
Linden Gdns., Enf. 203 301 DU39
Linden Gro. SE15 180 325 DV83
Linden Gro. SE26 274 325 DW93
Linden Gro., N.Mal. 269 322 CS97
Linden Gro., Tedd. 267 329 CF92
Linden Lawns, Wem. 107 304 CM63
Linden Lea N2 219 305 DC57
Linden Leas, W.Wick. 289 333 ED103
Linden Ms. N1 117 306 DR64
Linden Ms. W2 52 315 DA73
Linden Pl., Mitch. 271 323 DE98
Linden Rd. E17 222 307 DZ57
Linden Rd. N10 220 306 DH56
Linden Rd. N11 207 299 DF47
Linden Rd. N15 221 306 DQ56
Linden Rd., Hmptn. 267 329 CA94
Linden St., Rom. 227 309 FD56
Linden Wk. N19 98 306 DJ61
Linden Way N14 208 300 DJ44
Linden Way, Pur. 294 332 DJ110
Linden Way, Shep. 281 328 BQ99
Lindenfield, Chis. 277 326 EP96
Lindens, The N12 207 299 DD50
Lindens, The W4 154 314 CQ81
Lindeth Clo., Stan. 216 304 CJ51
Lindfield Gdns. NW3 112 305 DC64
Lindfield Rd. W5 122 314 CJ70
Lindfield Rd., Croy. 287 332 DT100
Lindfield St. E14 140 317 EA72
Lindisfarne Rd. SW20 270 323 CU94
Lindisfarne Rd., Dag. 236 309 EW62
Lindisfarne Way E9 119 307 DY63
Lindley Est. SE15 164 317 DU80
Lindley Rd. E10 104 307 EB61
Lindley St. E1 138 317 DW71
Lindo St. SE15 164 317 DW82
Lindore Rd. SW11 175 323 DF84
Lindores Rd., Cars. 285 331 DC101
Lindrop St. SW6 158 315 DC82
Lindsay Clo., Stai. 256 320 BK85
Lindsay Dr., Har. 216 304 CL58
Lindsay Dr., Shep. 281 328 BR100
Lindsay Rd., Hmptn. 267 329 CB91
Lindsay Rd., Wor.Pk. 283 331 CV103
Lindsay Sq. SW1 82 316 DK78
Lindsell St. SE10 166 317 EC81
Lindsey Clo., Brom. 276 326 EK97
Lindsey Clo., Mitch. 272 324 DL98
Lindsey Gdns., Felt. 265 320 BR87
Lindsey Ms. N1 116 306 DQ66
Lindsey Rd., Dag. 236 309 EW63
Lindsey Rd., Uxb. 230 312 BG62
Lindsey St. EC1 48/9 316 DP71
Lindsey Way, Horn. 228 310 FJ57
Lindum Rd., Tedd. 268 322 CJ94
Lindway SE27 273 324 DP92
Lindwood Clo. E6 244 318 EL71
Linfield Clo. NW4 218 305 CW55
Linford Rd. E17 223 307 EC55
Linford St. SW8 160 316 DJ81
Ling Rd. E16 244 318 EG71
Ling Rd., Erith 255 319 FC79
Lingards Rd. SE13 182 325 EC84
Lingey Clo., Sid. 261 326 ET89
Lingfield Ave., Kings.T. 268 322 CL98
Lingfield Ave., Upmin. 238 311 FM62
Lingfield Clo., Enf. 209 300 DS44
Lingfield Clo., Nthwd. 213 302 BS52
Lingfield Cres. SE9 261 326 ER84
Lingfield Gdns. N9 210 301 DV45
Lingfield Rd. SW19 270 323 CX93
Lingfield Rd., Wor.Pk. 284 331 CW104
Lingham St. SW9 161 316 DL82
Lings Coppice SE21 195 324 DR89
Lingwell Rd. SW17 191 323 DE90
Lingwood Gdns., Islw. 251 321 CE80
Lingwood Rd. E5 102 307 DU59
Linhope St. NW1 31 315 DF70
Link, The SE9 261 326 EN90
Link, The W3 134 314 CP72
Link, The, Enf. 203 301 DY39
Link, The, Nthlt. 232 313 BZ64
Link, The, Pnr. 232 313 BW59
Link, The, Wem. 90 304 CJ60
Link La., Wall. 294 332 DK107
Link Rd. N11 208 300 DG49
Link Rd., Dag. 247 319 FB68
Link Rd., Felt. 265 320 BT87
Link Rd., Wall. 285 332 DG102
Link St. E9 118 307 DW64
Link Way, Brom. 290 334 EL101
Link Way, Dag. 236 309 EW63
Link Way, Horn. 238 311 FL60
Link Way, Pnr. 214 303 BX53
Link Way, Stai. 264 328 BH93
Link Way, Uxb. 230 302 BG58
Linkfield, Brom. 289 334 EG100
Linkfield, W.Mol. 267 329 CB97
Linkfield Rd., Islw. 251 321 CF82
Linklea Clo. NW9 217 304 CS52
Links, The E17 222 307 DY56
Links Ave., Mord. 271 323 DA98
Links Ave., Rom. 228 310 FH55
Links Dr. N20 207 299 DA46
Links Gdns. SW16 273 324 DN94
Links Rd. NW2 93 304 CT61
Links Rd. SW17 272 324 DG93
Links Rd. W3 134 314 CN72
Links Rd., Ashf. 264 328 BL92
Links Rd., W.Wick. 289 333 EC102
Links Vw. N3 218 305 CZ52
Links Vw. Clo., Stan. 216 304 CG51
Links Vw. Rd., Croy. 288 333 EA104
Links Vw. Rd., Hmptn. 267 329 CC92
Links Way, Beck. 288 333 EA100
Links Way, Nthwd. 213 302 BQ52
Links Yd. E1 138 317 DU71
Linkscroft Ave., Ashf. 265 328 BP93
Linkside N12 218 305 CZ51
Linkside, N.Mal. 269 322 CS96
Linksway NW4 218 305 CX54
Linkway N4 100 306 DQ59
Linkway SW20 270 323 CV97
Linkway, Rich. 184 322 CH90
Linkway, The, Barn. 207 299 DB44
Linkway, The, Sutt. 293 331 DC109
Linkwood Wk. NW1 115 306 DK66
Linley Cres., Rom. 227 309 FB55
Linley Rd. N17 221 306 DS54
Linnell Clo. NW11 219 305 DB58
Linnell Dr. NW11 219 305 DB58
Linnell Rd. N18 210 301 DU50
Linnell Rd. SE5 163 316 DS82
Linnet Clo. N9 210 301 DX46
Linnet Clo. SE28 246 319 EW73
Linnet Ms. SW12 192 324 DG87
Linnett Clo. E4 211 301 EC49
Linom Rd. SW4 177 324 DL84
Linscott Rd. E5 118 307 DW63
Linsdell Rd., Bark. 245 318 EQ67
Linsey St. SE16 148 317 DU77
Linslade Clo., Houns. 258 321 BY85
Linslade Clo., Pnr. 214 303 BV55
Linstead Ct. SE9 261 326 ES86
Linstead St. NW6 112 305 DA66
Linstead Way SW18 189 323 CY87
Linster Gro., Borwd. 205 298 CQ43
Lintaine Clo. W6 157 315 CY79
Linthorpe Ave., Wem. 106 304 CJ65
Linthorpe Rd. N16 101 306 DS59
Linton Clo., Mitch. 285 331 DF101
Linton Clo., Well. 254 319 EV81
Linton Gdns. E6 244 318 EL72
Linton Gro. SE27 273 324 DP92
Linton Rd., Bark. 235 308 EQ66
Linton St. N1 25 316 DQ67
Lintons, The, Bark. 235 308 EQ66
Lintott Ct., Stai. 256 320 BK86
Linver Rd. SW6 157 315 CZ82
Linwood Clo. E6 244 318 EL71
Linwood Clo. SE5 163 316 DT82
Linwood Cres., Enf. 203 301 DU39
Linwood Way SE15 163 316 DT80
Linzee Rd. N8 220 306 DL56
Lion Ave., Twick. 259 321 CF88
Lion Clo. SE4 182 325 EA86
Lion Clo., Shep. 280 328 BL97
Lion Gate Gdns., Rich. 169 322 CM83
Lion Pk. Ave., Chess. 282 330 CN105
Lion Rd. E6 244 318 EM71
Lion Rd. N9 210 301 DU47
Lion Rd., Bexh. 262 327 EZ84
Lion Rd., Croy. 287 332 DQ99
Lion Rd., Twick. 259 321 CF88
Lion Way, Brent. 153 314 CK80
Lion Wf. Rd., Islw. 168 322 CH83
Lion Yd. SW4 177 324 DK84
Lionel Gdns. SE9 260 326 EK85
Lionel Ms. W10 137 315 CY71
Lionel Rd. SE9 260 326 EK85
Lionel Rd., Brent. 143 314 CL76
Lions Clo. SE9 260 326 EJ90
Liphook Clo., Horn. 237 309 FF63
Liphook Cres. SE23 196 325 DW87
Lipsham Clo., Bans. 293 331 DD113
Lipton Clo. SE28 246 319 EW73
Lipton Rd. E1 139 317 DX72
Lisbon Ave., Twick. 259 321 CC89
Lisburne Rd. NW3 113 305 DF63
Lisford St. SE15 163 316 DT81
Lisgar Ter. W14 147 315 CZ77
Liskeard Clo., Chis. 277 326 EQ93
Liskeard Gdns. SE3 252 318 EG81
Lisle St. WC2 58 316 DK73
Lismore Circ. NW5 114 306 DG64
Lismore Clo., Islw. 152 314 CG82
Lismore Rd. N17 221 306 DR55
Lismore Rd., S.Croy. 295 332 DS107
Lismore Wk. N1 116 306 DQ65
Liss Way SE15 163 316 DT80
Lissenden Gdns. NW5 114 306 DG63
Lisson Grn. Est. NW8 30/1 315 DE69
Lisson Gro. NW1 30/1 315 DE70
Lisson Gro. NW8 30 315 DD70
Lisson St. NW1 42/3 315 DE71
Lister Ave., Rom. 228 310 FK54
Lister Clo. W3 135 314 CR71
Lister Clo., Mitch. 271 323 DE95
Lister Gdns. N18 209 300 DQ50

Lister Ho. SE3 167 317 EE79
Lister Rd. E11 105 307 EE60
Lister St. E13 244 318 EG69
Lister Wk. SE28 246 319 EX73
Liston Rd. N17 222 307 DU53
Liston Rd. SW4 176 324 DJ83
Liston Way, Wdf.Grn. 224 308 EJ52
Listowel Clo. SW9 162 316 DN80
Listowel Rd., Dag. 237 309 FA62
Listria Pk. N16 101 306 DS61
Litchfield Ave. E15 121 307 EE65
Litchfield Ave., Mord. 284 331 CZ101
Litchfield Gdns. NW10 110 305 CU65
Litchfield Rd., Sutt. 285 331 DC105
Litchfield St. WC2 58 316 DK73
Litchfield Way NW11 219 305 DB57
Lithos Rd. NW3 112 305 DC65
Little Acre, Beck. 275 325 EA97
Little Albany St. NW1 32/3 316 DH69
Little Argyll St. W1 45 316 DJ72
Little Aston Rd., Rom. 229 311 FN52
Little Benty, West Dr. 248 320 BK77
Little Birches, Sid. 261 326 ES89
Little Boltons, The SW5 76/7 315 DB78
Little Boltons, The SW10 76/7 315 DB78
Little Bornes SE21 273 324 DS91
Little Britain EC1 48/9 316 DP71
Little Brownings SE23 196 325 DV89
Little Bury St. N9 209 300 DR46
Little Cedars N12 207 299 DC49
Little Chester St. SW1 68/9 316 DH76
Little College La. EC4 62 316 DR73
Little College St. SW1 70/1 316 DL76
Little Ct., W.Wick. 289 333 EE103
Little Dean's Yd. SW1 70/1 316 DL76
Little Dimocks SW12 192 324 DH89
Little Dorrit Ct. SE1 74 316 DQ75
Little Ealing La. W5 142 314 CJ77
Little Edward St. NW1 32/3 316 DH69
Little Elms, Hayes 257 320 BR80
Little Essex St. WC2 60 316 DN73
Little Ferry Rd., Twick. 184 322 CH88
Little Friday Rd. E4 211 301 EE47
Little Gaynes Gdns., Upmin. 239 311 FP63
Little Gaynes La., Upmin. 238 311 FM63
Little Gearies, Ilf. 225 308 EP56
Little George St. SW1 70/1 316 DL75
Little Gra., Grnf. 122 314 CG69
Little Grn., Rich. 169 322 CK84
Little Grn. St. NW5 114 306 DH63
Little Heath SE7 252 318 EL78
Little Heath, Rom. 226 309 EV56
Little Heath Rd., Bexh. 254 319 EY81
Little Ilford La. E12 234 308 EM63
Little Marlborough St. W1 45 316 DJ72
Little Moss La., Pnr. 214 303 BY54
Little New St. EC4 48 316 DN72
Little Newport St. WC2 58 316 DK73
Little Orchard Clo., Pnr. 214 303 BY54
Little Pk. Dr., Felt. 258 321 BX89
Little Pk. Gdns., Enf. 202 300 DQ41
Little Portland St. W1 45 316 DJ72
Little Queens Rd., Tedd. 267 329 CF93
Little Redlands, Brom. 276 326 EL96
Little Rd., Croy. 287 332 DS102
Little Rd., Hayes 249 320 BT75
Little Roke Ave., Ken. 294 332 DP113
Little Roke Rd., Ken. 295 332 DQ114
Little Russell St. WC1 46/7 316 DL71
Little St. James's St. SW1 57 316 DJ74
Little St. Leonards SW14 170 322 CQ83
Little Sanctuary SW1 70 316 DK75
Little Smith St. SW1 70 316 DK76
Little Somerset St. E1 51 316 DT72
Little Strand NW9 217 304 CT54
Little Stream Clo., Nthwd. 213 302 BS50
Little Thrift, Orp. 277 326 EQ98
Little Titchfield St. W1 45 316 DJ71
Little Trinity La. EC4 61 316 DQ73
Little Turnstile WC1 47 316 DM71
Little Wd. Clo., Orp. 278 327 EU95
Little Woodcote La., Cars. 293 332 DG112
Little Woodcote La., Pur. 293 332 DG112
Little Woodcote La., Wall. 293 332 DG112
Littlebrook Clo., Croy. 288 333 DX100
Littlebury Rd. SW4 177 324 DK83
Littlecombe SE7 252 318 EH79
Littlecombe Clo. SW15 173 323 CX86
Littlecote Clo. SW19 189 323 CX87
Littlecote Pl., Pnr. 214 303 BZ53
Littlecroft SE9 261 326 EN83
Littledale SE2 254 319 EU79
Littlefield Clo. N19 114 306 DJ63
Littlefield Clo., Kings.T. 183 322 CL96
Littlefield Rd., Edg. 217 304 CQ52
Littlegrove, Barn. 207 299 DE44
Littleheath Rd., S.Croy. 295 333 DV108
Littlejohn Rd. W7 243 313 CF72
Littlejohn Rd., Orp. 291 335 EU100
Littlemede SE9 260 326 EM90
Littlemoor Rd., Ilf. 235 308 ER62
Littlemore Rd. SE2 254 319 EU75
Littlers Clo. SW19 271 323 DD95
Littlestone Clo., Beck. 275 325 EA93
Littleton Ave. E4 211 301 EF46
Littleton Cres., Har. 233 313 CF61
Littleton La., Shep. 280 328 BK101
Littleton Rd., Ashf. 265 328 BQ94
Littleton Rd., Har. 233 313 CF61
Littleton St. SW18 190 323 DC89
Littlewood SE13 182 325 EC85
Littlewood Clo. W13 142 314 CH76
Livermere Rd. E8 27 316 DT67
Liverpool Gro. SE17 86 316 DR78
Liverpool Rd. E10 223 307 EC58
Liverpool Rd. E16 141 317 EE71
Liverpool Rd. N1 116 306 DN66
Liverpool Rd. N7 116 306 DN64
Liverpool Rd. W5 143 314 CK75
Liverpool Rd., Kings.T. 269 322 CN94
Liverpool Rd., Th.Hth. 273 324 DQ97
Liverpool St. EC2 50/1 316 DS71
Livesey Clo., Kings.T. 268 322 CM97
Livesey Pl. SE15 164 317 DU79
Livingston College Twrs. E10 223 307 EC58
Livingstone Pl. E14 150 317 EC78
Livingstone Rd. E15 130 317 EC67
Livingstone Rd. E17 223 307 EB58
Livingstone Rd. N13 220 306 DL51
Livingstone Rd. SW11 175 323 DD83
Livingstone Rd., Houns. 259 321 CC84
Livingstone Rd., Sthl. 242 313 BX73
Livingstone Rd., Th.Hth. 273 324 DQ96
Livingstone Ter., Rain. 247 319 FE67
Livingstone Wk. SW11 175 323 DD83
Livonia St. W1 45 316 DJ72
Lizard St. EC1 37 316 DQ69
Lizban St. SE3 252 318 EH80
Llanelly Rd. NW2 95 305 CZ61
Llanover Rd. SE18 253 318 EN79
Llanover Rd., Wem. 91 304 CK62
Llanthony Rd., Mord. 285 331 DD100
Llanvanor Rd. NW2 95 305 CZ61
Llewellyn St. SE16 148 317 DU75
Lloyd Ave. SW16 272 324 DL95
Lloyd Ave., Couls. 293 332 DG114
Lloyd Baker St. WC1 35 316 DM69
Lloyd Ct., Pnr. 214 303 BX57
Lloyd Pk. Ave., Croy. 287 332 DT105
Lloyd Rd. E6 244 318 EM67
Lloyd Rd. E17 223 307 DX56
Lloyd Rd., Dag. 236 309 EZ65
Lloyd Rd., Wor.Pk. 284 331 CW104
Lloyd Sq. WC1 36 316 DN69
Lloyd St. WC1 35 316 DN69
Lloyd's Ave. EC3 50/1 316 DS72
Lloyds Pl. SE3 167 317 EE82
Lloyd's Row EC1 36/7 316 DP69
Lloyds Way, Beck. 288 333 DY99
Loampit Hill SE13 166 317 EA82
Loampit Vale SE13 182 325 EB83
Loanda Clo. E8 27 316 DT67
Loats Rd. SW2 177 324 DL86
Lobelia Clo. E6 244 318 EL71
Locarno Rd. W3 134 314 CQ74
Locarno Rd., Grnf. 243 313 CC70
Lochaber Rd. SE13 183 325 EE84
Lochaline St. W6 156 315 CW79
Lochan Clo., Hayes 242 313 BY70
Lochinvar St. SW12 192 324 DH87
Lochmere Clo., Erith 255 319 FB79
Lochnagar St. E14 140 317 EC71
Lock Chase SE3 183 325 EE83
Lock Clo., Sthl. 251 321 CC75
Lock Rd., Rich. 268 322 CJ91
Locke Clo., Rain. 237 309 FF65
Lockesfield Pl. E14 150 317 EB78
Lockesley Dr., Orp. 291 334 ET100
Lockesley Sq., Surb. 282 330 CK100
Locket Rd., Har. 215 303 CE55
Lockfield Ave., Enf. 203 301 DY40
Lockgate Clo. E9 119 307 DZ64
Lockhart Clo. N7 115 306 DM65
Lockhart Clo., Enf. 210 301 DV43
Lockhart St. E3 129 317 DZ70
Lockhurst St. E5 119 307 DX63
Lockie Pl. SE25 274 325 DU97
Lockier Wk., Wem. 91 304 CK62
Lockington Rd. SW8 160 316 DH81
Lockmead Rd. N15 222 307 DU58
Lockmead Rd. SE13 182 325 EC83
Locks La., Mitch. 271 323 DF95
Lockside E14 139 317 DY73
Locksley Est. E14 139 317 DZ72
Locksley St. E14 139 317 DZ71
Locksmeade Rd., Rich. 268 322 CJ91
Lockwood Clo. SE26 274 325 DX91
Lockwood Ind. Pk. N17 222 307 DV55
Lockwood Sq. SE16 148 317 DV76
Lockwood Wk., Rom. 227 309 FE57
Lockwood Way E17 222 307 DX54
Lockwood Way, Chess. 282 330 CN106
Lockyer Est. SE1 74 316 DR75
Lockyer St. SE1 74 316 DR75
Loddiges Rd. E9 118 307 DW66
Loder St. SE15 164 317 DW80
Lodge Ave. SW14 171 322 CS83
Lodge Ave., Borwd. 204 298 CM43
Lodge Ave., Croy. 286 332 DN104
Lodge Ave., Dag. 246 319 EU67
Lodge Ave., Har. 216 304 CL56
Lodge Ave., Rom. 228 310 FG57
Lodge Clo. N18 209 300 DQ50
Lodge Clo., Edg. 216 304 CM51
Lodge Clo., Epsom 292 331 CW110
Lodge Clo., Islw. 152 314 CH81
Lodge Clo., Orp. 291 335 EV102
Lodge Clo., Uxb. 240 312 BJ70
Lodge Clo., Wall. 285 332 DG102
Lodge Ct., Horn. 238 311 FL61
Lodge Cres., Orp. 291 335 EV102
Lodge Dr. N13 209 300 DN49
Lodge Gdns., Beck. 288 333 DZ99
Lodge Hill SE2 254 319 EV80
Lodge Hill, Ilf. 224 308 EL56
Lodge Hill, Well. 254 319 EV80
Lodge La. N12 207 299 DC50
Lodge La., Bex. 262 327 EX86
Lodge La., Rom. 227 309 FA52
Lodge Pl., Sutt. 284 331 DB106
Lodge Rd. NW4 218 305 CW56
Lodge Rd. NW8 30 316 DD69
Lodge Rd., Brom. 276 326 EH94
Lodge Rd., Croy. 286 332 DP100
Lodge Rd., Sutt. 284 331 DB106
Lodge Rd., Wall. 285 332 DH106
Lodge Vil., Wdf.Grn. 223 307 EF52
Lodge Way, Ashf. 264 320 BL89
Lodge Way, Shep. 281 328 BQ96
Lodgehill Pk. Clo., Har. 233 313 CB61
Lodore Gdns. NW9 217 304 CS57
Lodore Grn., Uxb. 230 312 BL62
Lodore St. E14 140 317 EC72
Loftie St. SE16 148 317 DU75
Lofting Rd. N1 115 306 DM66
Loftus Rd. W12 136 315 CV74
Logan Clo., Enf. 203 301 DX39
Logan Clo., Houns. 258 321 BZ83
Logan Ms. W8 76 315 DA77
Logan Pl. W8 76 315 DA77
Logan Rd. N9 210 301 DV47
Logan Rd., Wem. 91 304 CL61
Loggetts, The SE21 195 324 DR90
Logs Hill, Chis. 276 326 EL94
Logs Hill Clo., Chis. 276 326 EL95
Lois Dr., Shep. 281 328 BP99
Lolesworth Clo. E1 51 316 DT71
Lollard St. SE11 84 316 DN77
Loman St. SE1 72/3 316 DP75
Lomas Ct. E8 117 306 DT66
Lomas St. E1 138 317 DU71
Lombard Ave., Enf. 203 301 DX39
Lombard Ave., Ilf. 235 308 ES60
Lombard Business Pk. SW19 271 323 DB96
Lombard Ct. EC3 62 316 DR73
Lombard La. EC4 48 316 DN72
Lombard Rd. N11 208 300 DH50
Lombard Rd. SW11 159 315 DD82
Lombard Rd. SW19 271 323 DB96
Lombard St. EC3 62 316 DR72
Lombard Wall SE7 252 318 EH76
Lombards, The, Horn. 238 311 FM59
Lombardy Pl. W2 52/3 315 DB73
Lomond Clo. N15 221 306 DS57
Lomond Clo., Wem. 107 304 CM66
Lomond Gro. SE5 163 316 DR80
Lomond Ho. SE5 163 316 DR81
Loncroft Rd. SE5 163 316 DS79
Londesborough Rd. N16 117 306 DS63
London Bri. EC4 62 316 DR73
London Bri. SE1 62 316 DR74
London Bri. St. SE1 62 316 DR74
London Bri. Wk. SE1 62 316 DR74
London City Airport E16 244 318 EL74
London Flds. E8 118 307 DV66
London Flds. E. Side E8 118 307 DV66
London Flds. W. Side E8 118 307 DU66
London Ind. Pk. E6 245 318 EP71
London La. E8 118 307 DV66
London La., Brom. 275 325 EF94
London Ms. W2 42 315 DD72
London Rd. E13 244 318 EG68
London Rd. SE1 72/3 316 DP76
London Rd. SE23 196 325 DV88
London Rd. SW16 272 324 DM95
London Rd. SW17 271 323 DF96
London Rd., Ashf. 264 320 BJ90
London Rd., Bark. 235 308 EP66
London Rd., Brent. 251 321 CF82
London Rd., Brom. 275 325 EF94
London Rd., Croy. 286 332 DP102
London Rd. (Crayford), Dart. 263 327 FD85
London Rd., Enf. 202 300 DR42
London Rd., Felt. 264 320 BH90
London Rd., Har. 233 313 CE61
London Rd., Houns. 259 321 CC83
London Rd., Islw. 251 321 CF82
London Rd., Kings.T. 268 322 CM96
London Rd., Mitch. 271 323 DE98
London Rd. (Bedd. Cor.), Mitch. 285 332 DG101
London Rd., Mord. 284 331 DA99
London Rd., Rick. 212 302 BM47
London Rd., Rom. 227 309 FA58
London Rd., Stan. 204 298 CJ50
London Rd., Sutt. 284 331 CW104
London Rd., Swan. 279 327 FC95
London Rd., Th.Hth. 286 332 DN99
London Rd., Twick. 184 322 CG87
London Rd., Wall. 285 332 DH105
London Rd., Wem. 107 304 CL64
London Stile W4 144 314 CN78
London St. EC3 62/3 316 DS73
London St. W2 42 315 DD72
London St., Cher. 280 328 BG101
London Wall EC2 49 316 DQ71
London Wall Bldgs. EC2 50 316 DR71
Londons Clo., Upmin. 239 311 FQ64
Lonesome Way SW16 272 324 DH95
Long Acre WC2 58/9 316 DL73
Long Ct. WC2 58 316 DK73
Long Deacon Rd. E4 211 301 EE46
Long Dr. W3 135 314 CS72
Long Dr., Grnf. 243 313 CB67
Long Dr., Ruis. 232 313 BX63
Long Elmes, Har. 215 303 CB53
Long Fld. NW9 217 304 CS52
Long Gro., Rom. 228 311 FL54
Long Hedges, Houns. 251 321 CA81
Long La. EC1 48/9 316 DP71
Long La. N2 219 305 DC54
Long La. N3 219 305 DB52
Long La. SE1 74 316 DR75
Long La., Bexh. 254 319 EX80
Long La., Croy. 287 333 DV100
Long La., Stai. 264 320 BM89
Long La., Uxb. 241 312 BP67
Long Leys E4 223 307 EB51
Long Mark Rd. E16 244 318 EK71
Long Mead NW9 217 304 CT53
Long Meadow NW5 115 306 DK64
Long Meadow Clo., W.Wick. 289 333 EC101
Long Pond Rd. SE3 167 317 EE81
Long Reach Ct., Bark. 245 318 ER68
Long Reach Rd., Bark. 245 318 ET70
Long Rd. SW4 176 324 DH84
Long St. E2 39 316 DT69
Long Wk. SE1 74/5 316 DS76
Long Wk. SE18 253 318 EP79
Long Wk. SW13 155 314 CS82
Long Wk., N.Mal. 269 322 CQ97
Long Wk. Rd., Uxb. 249 312 BP74
Long Yd. WC1 35 316 DM70
Longacre Pl., Cars. 293 332 DG107
Longacre Rd. E17 223 307 ED53
Longbeach Rd. SW11 175 323 DF83
Longberrys NW2 95 305 CZ62
Longboat Row, Sthl. 242 313 BZ72
Longbridge Rd., Bark. 235 308 ER65
Longbridge Rd., Dag. 236 309 EU63
Longbridge Way SE13 182 325 EC85
Longbridge Way, Uxb. 240 312 BH68
Longbury Clo., Orp. 278 327 EV97
Longbury Dr., Orp. 278 327 EV97
Longcroft SE9 260 326 EM90
Longcroft Ave., Bans. 293 331 DC114
Longcrofte Rd., Edg. 216 304 CK52
Longdon Wd., Kes. 290 334 EL104
Longdown Rd. SE6 275 325 EA91
Longfellow Rd. E17 222 307 DZ58
Longfellow Rd., Wor.Pk. 283 331 CU102
Longfellow Way SE1 87 316 DT77
Longfield, Brom. 275 325 EF95
Longfield Ave. E17 222 307 DY56
Longfield Ave. NW7 218 305 CU52
Longfield Ave. W5 132 314 CJ73
Longfield Ave., Enf. 203 301 DW37
Longfield Ave., Horn. 237 309 FF59
Longfield Ave., Wall. 285 332 DG102
Longfield Ave., Wem. 91 304 CL60
Longfield Cres. SE26 196 325 DW90
Longfield Dr. SW14 170 322 CP85
Longfield Dr., Mitch. 271 323 DE94
Longfield Est. SE1 87 316 DT77
Longfield Rd. W5 132 314 CJ72
Longfield St. SW18 190 323 DA87
Longfield Wk. W5 132 314 CJ72
Longford Ave., Felt. 257 320 BS86
Longford Ave., Sthl. 243 313 CA73
Longford Ave., Stai. 264 320 BL88
Longford Clo., Hmptn. 267 329 CA91
Longford Clo., Hayes 242 313 BX73
Longford Ct. E5 119 307 DX63
Longford Ct. NW4 218 305 CX56
Longford Ct., Epsom 283 330 CQ105
Longford Gdns., Hayes 242 313 BX73
Longford Gdns., Sutt. 285 331 DC104
Longford Rd., Twick. 259 321 CA88
Longford St. NW1 32/3 316 DH70
Longford Wk. SW2 194 324 DN87
Longford Way, Stai. 264 320 BL88
Longhayes Ave., Rom. 226 309 EX56
Longheath Gdns., Croy. 288 333 DW99
Longhedge Ho. SE26 273 324 DT91
Longhedge St. SW11 160 316 DG82
Longhill Rd. SE6 199 325 ED89
Longhook Gdns., Nthlt. 242 313 BU68
Longhope Clo. SE15 163 316 DS79
Longhurst Rd. SE13 183 325 ED85
Longhurst Rd., Croy. 287 333 DV100
Longland Ct. SE1 148 317 DU78
Longland Dr. N20 207 299 DB48
Longlands Ave., Couls. 293 332 DG114
Longlands Ct. W11 137 315 CZ73
Longlands Ct., Mitch. 272 324 DG95
Longlands Pk. Cres., Sid. 261 326 ES90
Longlands Rd., Sid. 261 326 ES90
Longleat Ms., Orp. 278 327 EW98
Longleat Rd., Enf. 209 300 DS43
Longleat Way, Felt. 265 320 BR87
Longleigh La. SE2 254 319 EW79
Longleigh La., Bexh. 254 319 EW79
Longlents Ho. NW10 125 314 CR67
Longley Ave., Wem. 123 314 CM67
Longley Rd. SW17 271 323 DE93
Longley Rd., Croy. 286 332 DP101
Longley Rd., Har. 215 303 CC57
Longley St. SE1 148 317 DU77
Longley Way NW2 94 305 CW62
Longmead, Chis. 277 326 EN96
Longmead Dr., Sid. 262 327 EX89
Longmead Rd. SW17 271 323 DF92
Longmead Rd., Hayes 249 312 BT73
Longmeadow Rd., Sid. 261 326 ES88
Longmoor Pt. SW15 188 323 CV88
Longmoore St. SW1 81 316 DJ77
Longmore Ave., Barn. 207 299 DC44
Longnor Rd. E1 129 317 DX69
Longport Clo., Ilf. 226 309 EU51
Longridge La., Sthl. 243 313 CB72
Longridge Rd. SW5 76 315 DA77
Longs Ct., Rich. 169 322 CM84
Longshaw Rd. E4 211 301 ED48
Longshore SE8 149 317 DZ77
Longstaff Cres. SW18 174 323 DA86
Longstaff Rd. SW18 174 323 DA86
Longstone Ave. NW10 109 304 CT66
Longstone Rd. SW17 272 324 DH92
Longthornton Rd. SW16 272 324 DJ96
Longton Ave. SE26 274 325 DU91
Longton Gro. SE26 274 325 DV91
Longview Way, Rom. 227 309 FD53
Longville Rd. SE11 84/5 316 DP77
Longwalk Rd., Uxb. 249 312 BP74
Longwood Clo., Upmin. 239 311 FQ64
Longwood Dr. SW15 172 323 CU86
Longwood Gdns., Ilf. 224 308 EM56
Longworth Clo. SE28 246 319 EX72
Loning, The NW9 217 304 CS56
Loning, The, Enf. 203 301 DW38
Lonsdale Ave. E6 244 318 EK69
Lonsdale Ave., Rom. 227 309 FC58
Lonsdale Ave., Wem. 107 304 CL64
Lonsdale Clo. E6 244 318 EL70
Lonsdale Clo. SE9 260 326 EK90
Lonsdale Clo., Edg. 204 298 CM50
Lonsdale Clo., Pnr. 214 303 BY52
Lonsdale Clo., Uxb. 249 312 BQ71
Lonsdale Cres., Ilf. 225 308 EP58
Lonsdale Gdns., Th.Hth. 272 324 DM98
Lonsdale Ms., Rich. 154 314 CN81
Lonsdale Pl. N1 116 306 DN66
Lonsdale Rd. E11 105 307 EF59
Lonsdale Rd. NW6 127 315 CZ67
Lonsdale Rd. SE25 274 325 DV98
Lonsdale Rd. SW13 156 315 CU79
Lonsdale Rd. W4 145 314 CT77
Lonsdale Rd. W11 137 315 CZ72
Lonsdale Rd., Bexh. 254 319 EZ82
Lonsdale Rd., Sthl. 250 321 BX76
Lonsdale Sq. N1 24 316 DN67
Loobert Rd. N15 221 306 DS55
Looe Gdns., Ilf. 225 308 EP55
Loop Rd., Chis. 277 326 EQ93
Lopen Rd. N18 209 300 DS49
Loraine Clo., Enf. 210 301 DW43
Loraine Rd. N7 115 306 DM63
Loraine Rd. W4 154 314 CP79
Lord Ave., Ilf. 224 308 EM56
Lord Chancellor Wk., Kings.T. 269 322 CQ95
Lord Gdns., Ilf. 224 308 EL56
Lord Hills Bri. W2 40/1 315 DB71
Lord Hills Rd. W2 40/1 315 DB71
Lord Holland La. SW9 162 316 DN81
Lord Knyvett Clo., Stai. 256 320 BK86
Lord Napier Pl. W6 146 315 CU78
Lord N. St. SW1 70/1 316 DL76
Lord Roberts Ms. SW6 158 315 DB80
Lord Roberts Ter. SE18 253 318 EN78
Lord St. E16 244 318 EL74
Lord Warwick St. SE18 252 318 EM76
Lordell Pl. SW19 270 323 CW93
Lorden Wk. E2 128 317 DU69
Lord's Clo. SE21 194 324 DQ89
Lords Clo., Felt. 258 321 BY89
Lord's Vw. NW8 30 316 DD69
Lordsbury Fld., Wall. 294 332 DJ110
Lordship Gro. N16 221 306 DR61
Lordship La. N17 221 306 DQ53
Lordship La. N22 221 306 DN54
Lordship La. SE22 179 324 DT86
Lordship La. Est. SE22 196 325 DU88
Lordship Pk. N16 100 306 DQ61
Lordship Pk. Ms. N16 100 306 DQ61
Lordship Pl. SW3 159 315 DE79
Lordship Rd. N16 101 306 DR60
Lordship Rd., Nthlt. 232 313 BY66
Lordship Ter. N16 101 306 DR61
Lordsmead Rd. N17 221 306 DS53
Lorenzo St. WC1 35 316 DM69
Loretto Gdns., Har. 216 304 CL56
Lorian Clo. N12 207 299 DB49
Loring Rd. N20 207 299 DE47
Loring Rd., Islw. 251 321 CF82
Loris Rd. W6 146 315 CW76
Lorn Ct. SW9 162 316 DN82
Lorn Rd. SW9 161 316 DM82
Lorne Ave., Croy. 288 333 DX101
Lorne Clo. NW8 30/1 315 DE69
Lorne Gdns. E11 224 308 EJ56
Lorne Gdns. W11 147 315 CX75
Lorne Gdns., Croy. 288 333 DX101
Lorne Rd. E7 234 308 EH63
Lorne Rd. E17 223 307 EA57
Lorne Rd. N4 99 306 DM60
Lorne Rd., Har. 215 303 CF54
Lorne Rd., Rich. 169 322 CM85
Lorraine Pk., Har. 215 303 CE52
Lorrimore Rd. SE17 162 316 DP79
Lorrimore Sq. SE17 162 316 DP79
Losberne Way SE16 148 317 DU78
Lothair Rd. W5 143 314 CK75
Lothair Rd. N. N4 221 306 DP58
Lothair Rd. S. N4 100 306 DN59
Lothbury EC2 50 316 DR72
Lothian Ave., Hayes 242 313 BV71
Lothian Clo., Wem. 106 304 CG63
Lothian Rd. SW9 162 316 DP81
Lothrop St. W10 127 315 CY69
Lots Rd. SW10 158 315 DC80
Lotus Clo. SE21 194 324 DQ90
Loubet St. SW17 271 323 DF93
Loudoun Ave., Ilf. 225 308 EP57
Loudoun Rd. NW8 112 305 DC66
Loudoun Rd. Ms. NW8 17 315 DC67
Loudwater Clo., Sun. 266 329 BU98
Loudwater Rd., Sun. 266 329 BU98
Lough Rd. N7 115 306 DM64
Loughborough Est. SW9 162 316 DP82
Loughborough Pk. SW9 178 324 DP84
Loughborough Rd. SW9 162 316 DN82
Loughborough St. SE11 83 316 DM78
Louis Ms. N10 220 306 DH53
Louisa Gdns. E1 129 317 DX70
Louisa Ho. SW15 171 322 CT84
Louisa St. E1 129 317 DX70
Louise Aumonier Wk. N19 99 306 DL59
Louise Bennett Clo. SE24 178 324 DP84
Louise Gdns., Rain. 247 319 FE69
Louise Rd. E15 121 307 EE65
Louisville Rd. SW17 192 324 DG90
Louvaine Rd. SW11 175 323 DD84
Lovage App. E6 244 318 EL71
Lovat Clo. NW2 93 304 CT62
Lovat La. EC3 62/3 316 DS73
Lovat Wk., Houns. 250 321 BY80
Lovatt Clo., Edg. 217 304 CP51
Lovatt Dr., Ruis. 231 302 BT57
Love La. EC2 49 316 DQ72
Love La. N17 221 306 DT52
Love La. SE18 253 318 EP77
Love La. SE25 274 325 DV97
Love La., Bex. 262 327 EZ86
Love La., Mitch. 271 323 DE97
Love La., Mord. 284 331 DA101
Love La., Pnr. 214 303 BY55
Love La., Surb. 282 330 CJ103
Love La., Sutt. 292 331 CY107
Love La., Wdf.Grn. 224 308 EM51
Love Wk. SE5 163 316 DR82
Loveday Rd. W13 132 314 CH74
Lovegrove St. SE1 148 317 DU78
Lovegrove Wk. E14 140 317 EC74
Lovekyn Clo., Kings.T. 268 322 CM96
Lovel Ave., Well. 254 319 EU82
Lovelace Ave., Brom. 290 334 EN100
Lovelace Gdns., Bark. 236 309 EU63
Lovelace Gdns., Surb. 282 330 CK101
Lovelace Grn. SE9 260 326 EM83
Lovelace Rd. SE21 194 324 DQ89
Lovelace Rd., Barn. 207 299 DE45
Lovelace Rd., Surb. 282 330 CJ101
Lovelinch Clo. SE15 164 317 DW79
Lovell Ho. E8 128 317 DU67
Lovell Pl. SE16 149 317 DY76
Lovell Rd., Enf. 203 301 DV35
Lovell Rd., Rich. 184 322 CJ90
Lovell Rd., Sthl. 243 313 CB72
Lovell Wk., Rain. 238 310 FG65
Loveridge Ms. NW6 111 305 CZ65
Loveridge Rd. NW6 111 305 CZ65
Lovers Wk. N3 219 305 DA52
Lovers Wk. NW7 218 305 CY51
Lovers Wk. SE10 167 317 EE80
Lover's Wk. W1 56 316 DG74
Lovett Dr., Cars. 285 331 DC101
Lovett Rd., Uxb. 230 302 BJ55
Lovett Way NW10 108 304 CQ64
Lovett's Pl. SW18 174 323 DB84
Lovibonds Ave., Orp. 290 334 EP105
Lovibonds Ave., West Dr. 248 312 BM72
Low Cross Wd. La. SE21 195 324 DT90
Low Hall Clo. E4 211 301 EA45
Low Hall La. E17 222 307 DY58
Lowbrook Rd., Ilf. 235 308 EP63
Lowdell Clo., West Dr. 248 312 BL72
Lowden Rd. N9 210 301 DV46
Lowden Rd. SE24 178 324 DQ84
Lowden Rd., Sthl. 242 313 BY73
Lowe Ave. E16 244 318 EG71
Lowell St. E14 139 317 DY72
Lowen Rd., Rain. 247 319 FD68
Lower Aberdeen Wf. E14 139 317 DZ74
Lower Addiscombe Rd., Croy. 287 332 DS102
Lower Addison Gdns. W14 147 315 CY75
Lower Barn Rd., Pur. 295 332 DR113
Lower Bedfords Rd., Rom. 227 309 FE51
Lower Belgrave St. SW1 68/9 316 DH76
Lower Boston Rd. W7 243 313 CE74
Lower Broad St., Dag. 247 319 FA67
Lower Camden, Chis. 276 326 EM94
Lower Ch. St., Croy. 286 332 DP103
Lower Clapton Rd. E5 118 307 DW64
Lower Clarendon Wk. W11 137 315 CY72
Lower Common S. SW15 172 323 CV83
Lower Coombe St., Croy. 287 332 DQ105
Lower Cft., Swan. 279 327 FF98
Lower Downs Rd. SW20 270 323 CX95
Lower Drayton Pl., Croy. 286 332 DP103
Lower Dunnymans, Bans. 292 331 CZ114
Lower George St., Rich. 169 322 CK85
Lower Gravel Rd., Brom. 290 334 EL102
Lower Grn. W., Mitch. 271 323 DE97
Lower Grosvenor Pl. SW1 68/9 316 DH76
Lower Gro. Rd., Rich. 169 322 CM86
Lower Hall La. E4 210 301 DY50
Lower Ham Rd., Kings.T. 268 322 CK93
Lower Hampton Rd., Sun. 266 329 BW97
Lower James St. W1 57 316 DJ73
Lower John St. W1 57 316 DJ73
Lower Kenwood Ave., Enf. 208 300 DK43
Lower Lea Crossing E14 141 317 EE73
Lower Maidstone Rd. N11 220 306 DJ51
Lower Mall W6 146 315 CV78
Lower Mardyke Ave., Rain. 247 319 FC68
Lower Marsh SE1 71 316 DM75
Lower Marsh La., Kings.T. 268 322 CM98
Lower Merton Ri. NW3 113 305 DE66
Lower Morden La., Mord. 284 331 CX100
Lower Mortlake Rd., Rich. 169 322 CL84
Lower Northfield, Bans. 292 331 CZ114
Lower Pk. Rd. N11 208 300 DJ50
Lower Pk. Rd., Belv. 255 319 FA76
Lower Richmond Rd. SW14 170 322 CP83
Lower Richmond Rd. SW15 172 323 CV83
Lower Richmond Rd., Rich. 170 322 CN83
Lower Rd. SE8 149 317 DX77
Lower Rd. SE16 148 317 DW76
Lower Rd., Belv. 255 319 FB76
Lower Rd., Erith 255 319 FD77
Lower Rd., Har. 233 313 CD60
Lower Rd., Ken. 294 332 DP113
Lower Rd., Orp. 291 335 EV100
Lower Rd., Sutt. 285 331 DC105
Lower Rd., Swan. 279 327 FF94
Lower Robert St. WC2 58/9 316 DL73
Lower Sawley Wd., Bans. 292 331 CZ114
Lower Sloane St. SW1 80 316 DG77
Lower Sq., Islw. 168 322 CH83
Lower Sta. Rd. (Crayford), Dart. 263 327 FE86
Lower Strand NW9 217 304 CT54
Lower Sunbury Rd., Hmptn. 266 329 BZ96
Lower Sydenham Ind. Est. SE26 274 325 DZ92
Lower Talbot Wk. W11 137 315 CY72
Lower Teddington Rd., Kings.T. 268 322 CK94
Lower Ter. NW3 96 305 DC62
Lower Thames St. EC3 62 316 DR73
Lowestoft Clo. E5 102 307 DW61
Loweswater Clo., Wem. 91 304 CK61
Lowfield Rd. NW6 112 305 DA66
Lowfield Rd. W3 134 314 CQ72
Lowick Rd., Har. 215 303 CE56
Lowlands Dr., Stai. 256 320 BK85
Lowlands Gdns., Rom. 227 309 FB58
Lowlands Rd., Har. 215 303 CE58
Lowlands Rd., Pnr. 214 303 BW58
Lowman Rd. N7 115 306 DM63
Lowndes Clo. SW1 68 316 DG76
Lowndes Pl. SW1 68 316 DG76
Lowndes Sq. SW1 67 315 DF75
Lowndes St. SW1 67 315 DF76
Lowood Ct. SE19 273 324 DT92
Lowood St. E1 138 317 DV73
Lowry Cres., Mitch. 271 323 DE96
Lowry Rd., Dag. 236 309 EV64
Lowshoe La., Rom. 227 309 FA53
Lowswood Clo., Nthwd. 213 302 BQ53
Lowth Rd. SE5 162 316 DQ82
Lowther Clo., Borwd. 204 298 CM43
Lowther Gdns. SW7 66 315 DD75
Lowther Hill SE23 197 325 DY87
Lowther Rd. E17 222 307 DY54
Lowther Rd. N7 116 306 DN64
Lowther Rd. SW13 155 314 CT81
Lowther Rd., Kings.T. 268 322 CM95
Lowther Rd., Stan. 216 304 CM55
Loxford Ave. E6 244 318 EK68
Loxford La., Ilf. 235 308 EQ64
Loxford Rd., Bark. 235 308 EP65
Loxham Rd. E4 223 307 EA52
Loxham St. WC1 34/5 316 DL69
Loxley Clo. SE26 274 325 DX92
Loxley Rd. SW18 191 323 DD88
Loxley Rd., Hmptn. 266 329 BZ91
Loxton Rd. SE23 197 325 DX88
Loxwood Clo., Felt. 265 320 BR88
Loxwood Rd. N17 221 306 DS55
Lubbock Rd., Chis. 276 326 EM94
Lubbock St. SE14 164 317 DW80
Lucan Dr., Stai. 264 328 BK94
Lucan Pl. SW3 78/9 315 DE77
Lucas Ave. E13 244 318 EH67
Lucas Ave., Har. 233 313 CA61
Lucas Ct., Har. 233 313 CA60
Lucas Rd. SE20 274 325 DW93
Lucas Sq. NW11 219 305 DA58
Lucas St. SE8 166 317 EA81
Lucerne Clo. N13 208 300 DL48
Lucerne Ct., Erith 254 319 EY76
Lucerne Gro. E17 223 307 ED56
Lucerne Ms. W8 52 315 DA74
Lucerne Rd. N5 116 306 DP63
Lucerne Rd., Orp. 291 334 ET102
Lucerne Rd., Th.Hth. 286 332 DP99
Lucerne Way, Rom. 228 310 FK51
Lucey Rd. SE16 148 317 DU76
Lucey Way SE16 148 317 DU76
Lucie Ave., Ashf. 265 328 BP93
Lucien Rd. SW17 272 324 DG91
Lucien Rd. SW19 190 323 DB89
Lucknow St. SE18 253 318 ES80
Lucorn Clo. SE12 183 325 EF86
Lucy Cres. W3 134 314 CQ71
Lucy Gdns., Dag. 236 309 EY62
Luddesdon Rd., Erith 255 319 FA79
Ludford Clo. NW9 217 304 CS54
Ludford Clo., Croy. 286 332 DP105
Ludgate Bdy. EC4 48/9 316 DP72
Ludgate Circ. EC4 48/9 316 DP72
Ludgate Hill EC4 48/9 316 DP72
Ludgate Sq. EC4 48/9 316 DP72
Ludham Clo. SE28 246 319 EW72
Ludlow Clo., Brom. 276 326 EG97
Ludlow Clo., Har. 232 313 BZ63
Ludlow Rd. W5 122 314 CJ70
Ludlow Rd., Felt. 266 329 BU91
Ludlow St. EC1 37 316 DQ70
Ludlow Way N2 219 305 DC56
Ludovick Wk. SW15 171 322 CS84
Ludwick Ms. SE14 165 317 DY80
Luffield Rd. SE2 254 319 EV76
Luffman Rd. SE12 260 326 EH90
Lugard Rd. SE15 164 317 DV82
Lugg App. E12 235 308 EN62
Luke Ho. E1 138 317 DV72
Luke St. EC2 38/9 316 DS70
Lukin Cres. E4 211 301 ED48
Lukin St. E1 138 317 DW72
Lullingstone Ave., Swan. 279 327 FF97
Lullingstone Clo., Orp. 278 327 EV94
Lullingstone Cres., Orp. 278 327 EU94
Lullingstone La. SE13 183 325 ED86
Lullingstone Rd., Belv. 254 319 EZ79
Lullington Garth N12 206 299 CZ50
Lullington Garth, Borwd. 205 298 CP43
Lullington Garth, Brom. 275 325 EE94
Lullington Rd. SE20 274 325 DU94
Lullington Rd., Dag. 236 309 EY66
Lulot Gdns. N19 98 306 DH61
Lulworth SE17 86 316 DR78
Lulworth Ave., Houns. 251 321 CB80
Lulworth Ave., Wem. 90 304 CJ59
Lulworth Clo., Har. 232 313 BZ62
Lulworth Cres., Mitch. 271 323 DE96
Lulworth Dr., Pnr. 232 313 BX59
Lulworth Gdns., Har. 232 313 BY61
Lulworth Rd. SE9 260 326 EL89
Lulworth Rd. SE15 164 317 DV82
Lulworth Rd., Well. 253 318 ET82
Lulworth Waye, Hayes 242 313 BV72
Lumen Rd., Wem. 91 304 CK61
Lumley Clo., Belv. 255 319 FA79
Lumley Ct. WC2 58/9 316 DL73
Lumley Gdns., Sutt. 284 331 CY106
Lumley Rd., Sutt. 292 331 CY107
Lumley St. W1 44 316 DG72
Luna Rd., Th.Hth. 273 324 DQ97
Lunar Ho., Croy. 287 332 DQ102
Lundy Dr., Hayes 249 320 BS77
Lundy Wk. N1 116 306 DQ65
Lunham Rd. SE19 273 324 DS93
Lupin Clo. SW2 194 324 DP89
Lupin Clo., Croy. 288 333 DX102
Lupin Clo., West Dr. 248 320 BK78
Lupin Cres., Ilf. 235 308 EP62
Lupton Clo. SE12 276 326 EH91
Lupton St. NW5 114 306 DJ63
Lupus St. SW1 80/1 316 DH78
Luralda Gdns. E14 150 317 EC78
Lurgan Ave. W6 157 315 CX79
Lurline Gdns. SW11 160 316 DG81

Luscombe Ct., Brom.	275	325	EE96
Luscombe Way SW8	161	316	DL80
Lushington Rd. NW10	126	315	CV68
Lushington Rd. SE6	275	325	EB92
Lushington Ter. E8	118	307	DU64
Luther Clo., Edg.	205	298	CQ47
Luther King Clo. E17	222	307	DY58
Luther Rd., Tedd.	267	329	CF92
Luton Pl. SE10	166	317	EC80
Luton Rd. E17	222	307	DZ55
Luton Rd., Sid.	262	327	EW90
Luton St. NW8	30	315	DD70
Lutton Ter. NW3	113	305	DD63
Luttrell Ave. SW15	172	323	CV85
Lutwyche Rd. SE6	197	325	DZ89
Luxborough St. W1	44	316	DG71
Luxemburg Gdns. W6	147	315	CX77
Luxfield Rd. SE9	260	326	EL88
Luxford St. SE16	149	317	DX77
Luxmore Gdns. SE4	165	317	DZ81
Luxmore St. SE4	165	317	DZ81
Luxor St. SE5	178	324	DQ83
Lyal Rd. E3	129	317	DY68
Lyall Ave. SE21	195	324	DS90
Lyall Ms. SW1	68	316	DG76
Lyall Ms. W. SW1	68	316	DG76
Lyall St. SW1	68	316	DG76
Lycett Pl. W12	146	315	CU75
Lych Gate Rd., Orp.	291	335	EU102
Lych Gate Wk., Hayes	249	312	BT73
Lyconby Gdns., Croy.	288	333	DY101
Lydd Clo., Sid.	261	326	ES90
Lydd Rd., Bexh.	254	319	EZ80
Lydden Ct. SE9	261	326	ES86
Lydden Gro. SW18	190	323	DB87
Lydden Rd. SW18	190	323	DB87
Lydeard Rd. E6	234	308	EM66
Lydford Clo. N16	117	306	DS64
Lydford Rd. N15	221	306	DR57
Lydford Rd. NW2	110	305	CW65
Lydford Rd. W9	127	315	CZ70
Lydhurst Ave. SW2	193	324	DM89
Lydia Rd., Erith	255	319	FF79
Lydney Clo. SE15	163	316	DS80
Lydney Clo. SW19	189	323	CY89
Lydon Rd. SW4	176	324	DJ83
Lydstep Rd., Chis.	277	326	EN91
Lyford Rd. SW18	191	323	DD87
Lygon Pl. SW1	68/9	316	DH76
Lyham Clo. SW2	177	324	DL86
Lyham Rd. SW2	177	324	DL85
Lyle Clo., Mitch.	285	332	DG101
Lymbourne Clo., Sutt.	292	331	DA110
Lyme Fm. Rd. SE12	260	326	EG84
Lyme Gro. E9	118	307	DW66
Lyme Rd., Well.	254	319	EV81
Lyme St. NW1	114	306	DJ66
Lyme Ter. NW1	114	306	DJ66
Lymer Ave. SE19	273	324	DT92
Lymescote Gdns., Sutt.	284	331	DA103
Lyminge Clo., Sid.	277	326	ET91
Lyminge Gdns. SW18	191	323	DE88
Lymington Ave. N22	221	306	DN54
Lymington Clo. E6	244	318	EM71
Lymington Clo. SW16	272	324	DK96
Lymington Dr., Ruis.	231	312	BR61
Lymington Gdns., Epsom	283	330	CT106
Lymington Rd. NW6	112	305	DB65
Lymington Rd., Dag.	236	309	EX60
Lympstone Gdns. SE15	164	317	DU80
Lyn Ms. E3	129	317	DZ69
Lynbridge Gdns. N13	209	300	DP49
Lynbrook Clo. SE15	163	316	DS80
Lynbrook Clo., Rain.	247	319	FD68
Lynch, The, Uxb.	240	312	BJ67
Lynch Clo., Uxb.	240	312	BJ66
Lynch Wk. SE8	165	317	DZ79
Lynchen Clo., Houns.	250	321	BU81
Lyncott Cres. SW4	176	324	DH84
Lyncroft Ave., Pnr.	214	303	BY57
Lyncroft Gdns. NW6	112	305	DA64
Lyncroft Gdns. W13	142	314	CJ75
Lyncroft Gdns., Houns.	259	321	CC85
Lyndale NW2	111	305	CZ63
Lyndale Ave. NW2	95	305	CZ62
Lyndale Clo. SE3	167	317	EF79
Lynden Way, Swan.	279	327	FC97
Lyndhurst Ave. N12	219	305	DF51
Lyndhurst Ave. NW7	217	304	CS51
Lyndhurst Ave. SW16	272	324	DK96
Lyndhurst Ave., Pnr.	214	303	BV53
Lyndhurst Ave., Sthl.	243	313	CB74
Lyndhurst Ave., Sun.	266	329	BU97
Lyndhurst Ave., Surb.	282	330	CP102
Lyndhurst Ave., Twick.	258	321	BZ88
Lyndhurst Clo. NW10	93	304	CR62
Lyndhurst Clo., Bexh.	263	327	FB83
Lyndhurst Clo., Croy.	287	332	DT104
Lyndhurst Clo., Orp.	290	334	EP105
Lyndhurst Dr. E10	104	307	EC59
Lyndhurst Dr., Horn.	238	310	FJ60
Lyndhurst Dr., N.Mal.	283	330	CS100
Lyndhurst Gdns. N3	218	305	CY53
Lyndhurst Gdns. NW3	113	305	DD64
Lyndhurst Gdns., Bark.	235	308	ES65
Lyndhurst Gdns., Enf.	202	300	DS42
Lyndhurst Gdns., Ilf.	225	308	ER58
Lyndhurst Gdns., Pnr.	214	303	BV53
Lyndhurst Gro. SE15	163	316	DS82
Lyndhurst Rd. E4	223	307	EC52
Lyndhurst Rd. N18	210	301	DU49
Lyndhurst Rd. N22	220	306	DM51
Lyndhurst Rd. NW3	113	305	DD64
Lyndhurst Rd., Bexh.	263	327	FB83
Lyndhurst Rd., Grnf.	243	313	CB70
Lyndhurst Rd., Th.Hth.	273	324	DN98
Lyndhurst Sq. SE15	163	316	DT81
Lyndhurst Ter. NW3	113	305	DD64
Lyndhurst Way SE15	163	316	DT81
Lyndhurst Way, Sutt.	292	331	DA108
Lyndon Ave., Pnr.	214	303	BY51
Lyndon Ave., Sid.	261	326	ET85
Lyndon Ave., Wall.	285	332	DG104
Lyndon Rd., Belv.	255	319	FA77
Lyne Cres. E17	222	307	DZ53
Lynegrove Ave., Ashf.	265	328	BQ92
Lyneham Wk. E5	119	307	DY64
Lyneham Wk., Pnr.	231	302	BT55
Lynett Rd., Dag.	236	309	EX61
Lynette Ave. SW4	176	324	DH86
Lynford Clo., Edg.	217	304	CQ53
Lynford Gdns., Edg.	205	298	CP48
Lynford Gdns., Ilf.	235	308	ET61
Lynhurst Cres., Uxb.	241	312	BQ66
Lynhurst Rd., Uxb.	241	312	BQ66
Lynmere Rd., Well.	254	319	EV82
Lynmouth Ave., Enf.	209	300	DT44
Lynmouth Ave., Mord.	284	331	CX101
Lynmouth Dr., Ruis.	232	313	BV61
Lynmouth Gdns., Grnf.	122	314	CH67
Lynmouth Gdns., Houns.	250	321	BX81
Lynmouth Ri., Orp.	278	327	EV98
Lynmouth Rd. E17	222	307	DY58
Lynmouth Rd. N2	219	305	DF56
Lynmouth Rd. N16	101	306	DT60
Lynmouth Rd., Grnf.	122	314	CH67
Lynn Clo., Ashf.	265	328	BR92
Lynn Clo., Har.	215	303	CD54
Lynn Ms. E11	105	307	EE61
Lynn Rd. E11	105	307	EE61
Lynn Rd. SW12	192	324	DH87
Lynn Rd., Ilf.	235	308	ER59
Lynn St., Enf.	202	300	DR39
Lynne Way NW10	109	304	CS65
Lynne Way, Nthlt.	242	313	BX68
Lynross Clo., Rom.	228	311	FM54
Lynscott Way, S.Croy.	294	332	DP109
Lynsted Clo., Bexh.	263	327	FB85
Lynsted Clo., Brom.	276	326	EJ96
Lynsted Ct., Beck.	274	325	DY96
Lynsted Gdns. SE9	260	326	EK83
Lynton Ave. N12	[illegible]	299	DD49
Lynton Ave. NW9	217	304	CT56
Lynton Ave. W13	132	314	CG72
Lynton Ave., Orp.	278	327	EV98
Lynton Ave., Rom.	227	309	FA53
Lynton Clo. NW10	109	304	CS64
Lynton Clo., Chess.	282	330	CL105
Lynton Clo., Islw.	259	321	CF84
Lynton Cres., Ilf.	225	308	EP58
Lynton Est. SE1	148	317	DU77
Lynton Gdns. N11	220	306	DK51
Lynton Gdns., Enf.	209	300	DS45
Lynton Mead N20	207	299	DA48
Lynton Rd. E4	211	301	EB50
Lynton Rd. N8	220	306	DK57
Lynton Rd. NW6	127	315	CZ67
Lynton Rd. SE1	87	316	DT77
Lynton Rd. W3	134	314	CN73
Lynton Rd., Croy.	286	332	DN100
Lynton Rd., Har.	232	313	BY61
Lynton Rd., N.Mal.	283	330	CR99
Lynton Wk., Hayes	231	312	BS69
Lynwood Clo. E18	224	308	EJ53
Lynwood Clo., Har.	232	313	BY62
Lynwood Clo., Rom.	227	309	FB51
Lynwood Dr., Nthwd.	213	302	BS53
Lynwood Dr., Rom.	227	309	FB51
Lynwood Dr., Wor.Pk.	283	331	CU103
Lynwood Gdns., Croy.	286	332	DM105
Lynwood Gdns., Sthl.	242	313	BZ71
Lynwood Gro. N21	209	300	DN46
Lynwood Gro., Orp.	291	334	ES101
Lynwood Rd. SW17	191	323	DF90
Lynwood Rd. W5	123	314	CL70
Lyon Business Pk., Bark.	245	318	ES68
Lyon Meade, Stan.	216	304	CJ53
Lyon Pk. Ave., Wem.	107	304	CL65
Lyon Rd. SW19	271	323	DC95
Lyon Rd., Har.	215	303	CF58
Lyon Rd., Rom.	237	309	FF59
Lyon St. N1	115	306	DM66
Lyon Way, Grnf.	243	313	CE67
Lyons Pl. NW8	30	315	DD70
Lyons Wk. W14	147	315	CY77
Lyonsdown Ave., Barn.	207	299	DC44
Lyonsdown Rd., Barn.	207	299	DB44
Lyoth Rd., Orp.	291	334	EQ103
Lyric Dr., Grnf.	243	313	CB70
Lyric Rd. SW13	155	314	CT81
Lysander Gdns., Surb.	282	330	CM100
Lysander Gro. N19	99	306	DK60
Lysander Rd., Croy.	294	332	DM107
Lysander Rd., Ruis.	231	312	BR61
Lysander Way, Orp.	291	334	EQ104
Lysia St. SW6	157	315	CX80
Lysias Rd. SW12	176	324	DH86
Lysons Wk. SW15	172	323	CU85
Lytchet Rd., Brom.	276	326	EH94
Lytchet Way, Enf.	203	301	DW39
Lytchgate Clo., S.Croy.	295	332	DS108
Lytcott Dr., W.Mol.	266	329	BZ97
Lytcott Gro. SE22	179	324	DT85
Lyte St. E2	128	317	DW68
Lytham Gro. W5	123	314	CM69
Lytham St. SE17	86	316	DR78
Lyttelton Clo. NW3	113	305	DE66
Lyttelton Rd. E10	104	307	EB62
Lyttelton Rd. N2	219	305	DC57
Lyttleton Rd. N8	221	306	DN55
Lytton Ave. N13	209	300	DN47
Lytton Ave., Enf.	203	301	DY38
Lytton Clo. N2	219	305	DC58
Lytton Clo., Nthlt.	232	313	BZ66
Lytton Gdns., Wall.	286	332	DK105
Lytton Gro. SW15	173	323	CX85
Lytton Rd. E11	105	307	EE59
Lytton Rd., Pnr.	214	303	BY52
Lytton Rd., Rom.	228	310	FH57
Lytton Strachey Path SE28	246	319	EV73
Lyveden Rd. SE3	252	318	EH80
Lyveden Rd. SW17	271	323	DE93
Maberley Cres. SE19	274	325	DU94
Maberley Rd. SE19	273	324	DT95
Maberley Rd., Beck.	274	325	DX97
Mabledon Pl. WC1	34	316	DK69
Mablethorpe Rd. SW6	157	315	CY80
Mabley St. E9	119	307	DY64
Macaret Clo. N20	207	299	DC45
MacArthur Clo. E7	234	308	EG65
Macarthur Ter. SE7	252	318	EK79
Macaulay Ct. SW4	176	324	DH83
Macaulay Rd. E6	244	318	EK68
Macaulay Rd. SW4	176	324	DH83
Macaulay Sq. SW4	176	324	DH84
Macaulay Way SE28	246	319	EV73
Macauley Ms. SE13	166	317	EC81
Macbean St. SE18	253	318	EP76
Macbeth St. W6	146	315	CV78
Macclesfield Bri. NW1	18/9	315	DE68
Macclesfield Rd. EC1	37	316	DQ69
Macclesfield Rd. SE25	287	333	DV99
Macclesfield St. W1	53	316	DK73
Macdonald Ave., Dag.	237	309	FB62
Macdonald Ave., Horn.	228	311	FL55
Macdonald Rd. E7	234	308	EG63
Macdonald Rd. E17	223	307	EC54
Macdonald Rd. N11	207	299	DF50
Macdonald Rd. N19	98	306	DJ61
Macdonald Way, Horn.	228	311	FL56
Macduff Rd. SW11	160	316	DG81
Mace Clo. E1	138	317	DV74
Mace St. E2	129	317	DX68
MacFarlane La., Islw.	251	321	CF79
Macfarlane Rd. W12	136	315	CW74
Macfarren Pl. NW1	32	316	DG70
Macgregor Rd. E16	244	318	EJ71
Machell Rd. SE15	180	325	DW83
Mackay Rd. SW4	176	324	DH84
Mackennal St. NW8	18/9	315	DE68
Mackenzie Rd. N7	115	306	DM65
Mackenzie Rd., Beck.	274	325	DW96
Mackenzie Wk. E14	140	317	EA74
Mackeson Rd. NW3	113	305	DF63
Mackie Rd. SW2	194	324	DN87
Mackintosh La. E9	119	307	DX64
Macklin St. WC2	46/7	316	DL72
Mackrow Wk. E14	140	317	EC73
Macks Rd. SE16	148	317	DU77
Mackworth St. NW1	33	316	DJ69
Maclaren Ms. SW15	172	323	CW84
Maclean Rd. SE23	181	325	DY86
Macleod Rd. N21	208	300	DL43
Macleod St. SE17	85	316	DQ78
Maclise Rd. W14	147	315	CY76
Macoma Rd. SE18	253	318	ER79
Macoma Ter. SE18	253	318	ER79
Macon Way, Upmin.	239	311	FS59
Maconochies Rd. E14	150	317	EB78
Macquarie Way E14	150	317	EB77
Macready Pl. N7	115	306	DL63
Macroom Rd. W9	127	315	CZ69
Mada Rd., Orp.	290	334	EP103
Maddams St. E3	130	317	EB70
Maddison Clo., Tedd.	267	329	CF93
Maddock Way SE17	162	316	DP79
Maddocks Clo., Sid.	278	327	EX92
Maddox St. W1	56/7	316	DH73
Madeira Ave., Brom.	275	325	EE94
Madeira Gro., Wdf.Grn.	224	308	EJ51
Madeira Rd. E11	105	307	ED60
Madeira Rd. N13	209	300	DP49
Madeira Rd. SW16	272	324	DL92
Madeira Rd., Mitch.	271	323	DF98
Madeley Rd. W5	133	314	CL72
Madeline Gro., Ilf.	235	308	ER64
Madeline Rd. SE20	274	325	DU94
Madge Gill Way E6	244	318	EL67
Madinah Rd. E8	118	307	DU65
Madison Cres., Bexh.	254	319	EW80
Madison Gdns., Bexh.	254	319	EW80
Madison Gdns., Brom.	275	325	EF97
Madras Pl. N7	116	306	DN65
Madras Rd., Ilf.	235	308	EP63
Madrid Rd. SW13	156	315	CU81
Madrigal La. SE5	162	316	DP80
Madron St. SE17	86/7	316	DS78
Mafeking Ave. E6	244	318	EL68
Mafeking Ave., Brent.	153	314	CL79
Mafeking Ave., Ilf.	235	308	ER59
Mafeking Rd. E16	131	317	EF70
Mafeking Rd. N17	222	307	DU54
Mafeking Rd., Enf.	202	300	DT41
Magdala Ave. N19	98	306	DH61
Magdala Rd., Islw.	168	322	CG83
Magdala Rd., S.Croy.	295	332	DR108
Magdalen Gro., Orp.	291	335	EV105
Magdalen Pas. E1	63	316	DT73
Magdalen Rd. SW18	190	323	DC88
Magdalen St. SE1	62/3	316	DS74
Magdalene Clo. SE15	164	317	DV82
Magdalene Gdns. E6	245	318	EN70
Magdalene Rd., Shep.	280	328	BM97
Magee St. SE11	162	316	DN79
Maggie Blake's Cause SE1	63	316	DT74
Magnet Rd., Wem.	91	304	CK61
Magnin Clo. E8	128	317	DU67
Magnolia Clo., Kings.T.	269	322	CP93
Magnolia Ct., Har.	91	304	CM59
Magnolia Ct., Rich.	154	314	CP81
Magnolia Gdns. E10	104	307	EB61
Magnolia Pl. SW4	177	324	DL85
Magnolia Pl. W5	133	314	CL71
Magnolia Rd. W4	154	314	CP79
Magnolia St., West Dr.	248	320	BK77
Magnolia Way, Epsom	283	330	CQ106
Magpie All. EC4	48	316	DN72
Magpie Clo. E7	121	307	EF64
Magpie Clo. NW9	217	304	CS54
Magpie Clo., Enf.	203	301	DU39
Magpie Hall Clo., Brom.	290	334	EL100
Magpie Hall La., Brom.	290	334	EL101
Magpie Pl. SE14	165	317	DY79
Magri Wk. E1	138	317	DW71
Maguire Dr., Rich.	268	322	CJ91
Maguire St. SE1	75	316	DT75
Mahatma Gandhi Ho., Wem.	107	304	CM64
Mahlon Ave., Ruis.	232	313	BV64
Mahogany Clo. SE16	139	317	DY74
Mahon Clo., Enf.	202	300	DT39
Maida Ave. E4	211	301	EB45
Maida Ave. W2	41	315	DC71
Maida Rd., Belv.	255	319	FA76
Maida Vale W9	16/7	315	DB68
Maida Way E4	211	301	EB45
Maiden Erlegh Ave., Bex.	262	327	EY88
Maiden La. NW1	115	306	DK66
Maiden La. SE1	61	316	DQ74
Maiden La. WC2	58/9	316	DL73
Maiden Rd. E15	121	307	EE66
Maidenstone Hill SE10	166	317	EC81
Maids of Honour Row, Rich.	169	322	CK85
Maidstone Ave., Rom.	227	309	FC54
Maidstone Bldgs. SE1	62	316	DR74
Maidstone Ho. E14	140	317	EB72
Maidstone Rd. N11	220	306	DJ51
Maidstone Rd., Sid.	278	327	EX93
Maidstone Rd., Swan.	279	327	FC95
Maidstone St. E2	128	317	DU68
Main Ave., Enf.	209	300	DT43
Main Ave., Nthwd.	213	302	BQ48
Main Dr., Wem.	91	304	CK62
Main Rd., Orp.	278	327	EW98
Main Rd., Rom.	227	309	FF56
Main Rd., Sid.	261	326	ES90
Main Rd., Swan.	279	327	FF94
Main St., Felt.	266	329	BX92
Mainridge Rd., Chis.	277	326	EN91
Maisemore St. SE15	164	317	DU80
Maisie Webster Clo., Stai.	264	320	BK87
Maitland Clo. SE10	166	317	EB80
Maitland Clo., Houns.	258	321	BZ83
Maitland Pk. Est. NW3	113	305	DF65
Maitland Pk. Rd. NW3	113	305	DF65
Maitland Pk. Vil. NW3	113	305	DF65
Maitland Pl. E5	118	307	DV63
Maitland Rd. E15	121	307	EF65
Maitland Rd. SE26	274	325	DX93
Maize Row E14	139	317	DZ73
Majendie Rd. SE18	253	318	ER78
Majestic Way, Mitch.	271	323	DF96
Major Rd. E15	121	307	ED64
Major Rd. SE16	148	317	DU76
Makepeace Ave. N6	98	306	DG61
Makepeace Rd. E11	224	308	EG56
Makepeace Rd., Nthlt.	242	313	BY67
Makins St. SW3	78/9	315	DE77
Malabar St. E14	150	317	EA75
Malam Gdns. E14	140	317	EB73
Malan Sq., Rain.	238	310	FH65
Malbrook Rd. SW15	172	323	CV84
Malcolm Ct., Stan.	204	298	CJ50
Malcolm Cres. NW4	218	305	CU58
Malcolm Dr., Surb.	282	330	CK102
Malcolm Pl. E2	128	317	DW70
Malcolm Rd. E1	128	317	DW70
Malcolm Rd. SE20	274	325	DW94
Malcolm Rd. SE25	287	333	DU100
Malcolm Rd. SW19	270	323	CY93
Malcolm Rd., Uxb.	240	312	BM63
Malcolm Way E11	224	308	EG57
Malcolms Way N14	208	300	DJ43
Malden Ave. SE25	274	325	DV97
Malden Ave., Grnf.	233	313	CE64
Malden Cres. NW1	114	306	DG65
Malden Grn. Ave., Wor.Pk.	283	330	CT102
Malden Hill, N.Mal.	269	322	CT97
Malden Hill Gdns., N.Mal.	269	322	CT97
Malden Pk., N.Mal.	283	330	CT100
Malden Pl. NW5	114	306	DG64
Malden Rd. NW5	113	305	DF64
Malden Rd., N.Mal.	283	330	CS99
Malden Rd., Sutt.	284	331	CW104
Malden Rd., Wor.Pk.	283	330	CT101
Malden Way, N.Mal.	283	330	CR100
Maldon Clo. E15	121	307	ED64
Maldon Clo. N1	25	316	DQ67
Maldon Clo. SE5	179	324	DS83
Maldon Rd. N9	209	300	DT48
Maldon Rd. W3	134	314	CQ73
Maldon Rd., Rom.	237	309	FC59
Maldon Rd., Wall.	285	332	DH106
Maldon Wk., Wdf.Grn.	224	308	EJ51
Malet Pl. WC1	34	316	DK70
Malet St. WC1	34	316	DK70
Maley Ave. SE27	194	324	DP89
Malford Ct. E18	224	308	EG54
Malford Gro. E18	223	307	EF56
Malfort Rd. SE5	179	324	DS83
Malham Rd. SE23	197	325	DX88
Malins Clo., Barn.	206	299	CV43
Mall, The E15	121	307	ED66
Mall, The N14	208	300	DL48
Mall, The SW1	69	316	DJ75
Mall, The SW14	170	322	CQ85
Mall, The W5	133	314	CL73
Mall, The, Brom.	276	326	EG97
Mall, The, Croy.	287	332	DQ102
Mall, The, Har.	216	304	CM58
Mall, The, Horn.	238	310	FH60
Mall, The, Surb.	282	330	CK99
Mall Rd. W6	146	315	CV78
Mallams Ms. SW9	178	324	DP83
Mallard Clo. E9	119	307	DZ65
Mallard Clo. W7	251	321	CE75
Mallard Clo., Barn.	207	299	DD44
Mallard Clo., Twick.	259	321	CA87
Mallard Clo., Upmin.	239	311	FT59
Mallard Path SE28	253	318	ER76
Mallard Pl., Twick.	184	322	CH90
Mallard Wk. SE28	253	318	ER76
Mallard Wk., Beck.	288	333	DX99
Mallard Wk., Sid.	278	327	EW93
Mallard Way NW9	92	304	CQ59
Mallard Way, Nthwd.	213	302	BQ52
Mallard Way, Wall.	294	332	DJ109
Mallards, The, Stai.	280	328	BH96
Mallards Rd., Wdf.Grn.	224	308	EH52
Mallet Dr., Nthlt.	232	313	BZ64
Mallet Rd. SE13	183	325	ED86
Malling Clo., Croy.	288	333	DW100
Malling Gdns., Mord.	285	331	DC100
Malling Way, Brom.	289	333	EF101
Mallinson Clo., Horn.	238	310	FJ64
Mallinson Rd. SW11	175	323	DE85
Mallinson Rd., Croy.	286	332	DK104
Mallord St. SW3	159	315	DD79
Mallory Clo. SE4	181	325	DY84
Mallory Gdns., Barn.	208	300	DG45
Mallory St. NW8	30/1	315	DE70
Mallow Clo., Croy.	288	333	DX102
Mallow Mead NW7	218	305	CY52
Mallow St. EC1	38	316	DR70
Mallows, The, Uxb.	231	312	BP62
Malm Clo., Rick.	212	302	BK47
Malmains Clo., Beck.	275	325	ED98
Malmains Way, Beck.	275	325	EC98
Malmesbury Clo., Pnr.	231	302	BT56
Malmesbury Rd. E3	129	317	DZ69
Malmesbury Rd. E16	141	317	EE71
Malmesbury Rd. E18	223	307	EF53
Malmesbury Rd., Mord.	285	331	DC101
Malmesbury Ter. E16	141	317	EF71
Malpas Dr., Pnr.	214	303	BX57
Malpas Rd. E8	118	307	DV65
Malpas Rd. SE4	165	317	DZ82
Malpas Rd., Dag.	236	309	EX65
Malt St. SE1	164	317	DU79
Malta Rd. E10	104	307	EA60
Malta St. EC1	36/7	316	DP70
Maltby Clo., Orp.	291	335	EU102
Maltby Dr., Enf.	203	301	DV38
Maltby St. SE1	75	316	DT76
Malthouse Dr. W4	155	314	CS79
Malthouse Dr., Felt.	266	329	BX92
Malthouse Pas. SW13	155	314	CS82
Malthus Path SE28	246	319	EW74
Malting Ho. E14	139	317	DZ73
Malting Way, Islw.	259	321	CF83
Maltings, The, Orp.	291	334	ET102
Maltings Clo. SW13	155	314	CS82
Maltings Ms., Sid.	262	327	EU90
Maltings Pl. SW6	158	315	DB81
Malton Ms. SE18	253	318	ES79
Malton Ms. W10	137	315	CY72
Malton Rd. W10	137	315	CY72
Malton St. SE18	253	318	ES79
Maltravers St. WC2	59	316	DM73
Malva Clo. SW18	174	323	DB85
Malvern Ave. E4	223	307	ED52
Malvern Ave., Bexh.	254	319	EY80
Malvern Ave., Har.	232	313	BY62
Malvern Clo. SE20	274	325	DU96
Malvern Clo. W10	137	315	CZ71
Malvern Clo., Mitch.	272	324	DJ97
Malvern Clo., Surb.	282	330	CL102
Malvern Clo., Uxb.	231	312	BN61
Malvern Ct. SE14	164	317	DW80
Malvern Ct. SW7	78	315	DD77
Malvern Dr., Felt.	266	329	BX92
Malvern Dr., Ilf.	235	308	ET63
Malvern Gdns. NW2	95	305	CY61
Malvern Gdns. NW6	127	315	CZ68
Malvern Gdns., Har.	216	304	CL56
Malvern Ms. NW6	28	315	DA69
Malvern Pl. NW6	127	315	CZ69
Malvern Rd. E6	244	318	EL67
Malvern Rd. E8	118	307	DU66
Malvern Rd. E11	105	307	EE61
Malvern Rd. N8	220	306	DM55
Malvern Rd. N17	222	307	DU55
Malvern Rd. NW6	28	315	DA69
Malvern Rd., Enf.	203	301	DY36
Malvern Rd., Hmptn.	267	329	CA94
Malvern Rd., Hayes	257	320	BS80
Malvern Rd., Horn.	228	310	FG58
Malvern Rd., Orp.	291	335	EV105
Malvern Rd., Surb.	282	330	CL103
Malvern Rd., Th.Hth.	273	324	DN98
Malvern Ter. N1	24	316	DN67
Malvern Ter. N9	209	300	DT46
Malvern Way W13	132	314	CH71
Malwood Rd. SW12	176	324	DH86
Malyons, The, Shep.	281	328	BR100
Malyons Rd. SE13	182	325	EB85
Malyons Rd., Swan.	279	327	FF94
Malyons Ter. SE13	182	325	EB85
Managers St. E14	140	317	EC74
Manatee Pl., Wall.	286	332	DK104
Manaton Clo. SE15	180	325	DV83
Manaton Cres., Sthl.	243	313	CA72
Manbey Gro. E15	121	307	EE65
Manbey Pk. Rd. E15	121	307	EE65
Manbey Rd. E15	121	307	EE65
Manbey St. E15	121	307	EE65
Manborough Ave. E6	244	318	EM69
Manbre Rd. W6	156	315	CW79
Manchester Dr. W10	127	315	CY70
Manchester Gro. E14	150	317	EC78
Manchester Ms. W1	44	316	DG71
Manchester Rd. E14	150	317	EC78
Manchester Rd. N15	221	306	DR58
Manchester Rd., Th.Hth.	273	324	DQ97
Manchester Row, Dart.	263	327	FE85
Manchester Sq. W1	44	316	DG72
Manchester St. W1	44	316	DG71
Manchester Way, Dag.	237	309	FB63
Manchuria Rd. SW11	176	324	DG86
Manciple St. SE1	74	316	DR75
Mandalay Rd. SW4	176	324	DJ85
Mandarin St. E14	140	317	EA73
Mandarin Way, Hayes	242	313	BX72
Mandela Clo. NW10	108	304	CQ66
Mandela Rd. E16	244	318	EG72
Mandela St. NW1	21	316	DJ67
Mandela St. SW9	162	316	DN80
Mandela Way SE1	86/7	316	DS77
Mandeville Clo. SE3	167	317	EF80
Mandeville Clo. SW20	270	323	CY95
Mandeville Ct. E4	210	301	DY49
Mandeville Dr., Surb.	282	330	CK102
Mandeville Pl. W1	44	316	DG72
Mandeville Rd. N14	208	300	DH47
Mandeville Rd., Enf.	203	301	DY36
Mandeville Rd., Islw.	152	314	CG82
Mandeville Rd., Nthlt.	232	313	BZ66
Mandeville Rd., Shep.	281	328	BN99
Mandeville St. E5	103	307	DY62
Mandrake Rd. SW17	191	323	DF89
Mandrake Way E15	121	307	EE66
Mandrell Rd. SW2	177	324	DL85
Manette St. W1	46	316	DK72
Manfred Rd. SW15	173	323	CZ85
Manger Rd. N7	115	306	DL65
Mangold Way, Erith	254	319	EY76
Manhattan Ct., Nthlt.	242	313	BX69
Manhattan Wf. E16	252	318	EG75
Manilla St. E14	150	317	EA75
Manister Rd. SE2	254	319	EU76
Manitoba Ct. SE16	148	317	DW75
Manley Ct. N16	101	306	DT62
Manley St. NW1	20	316	DG67
Manly Dixon Dr., Enf.	203	301	DY37
Mann Clo., Croy.	287	332	DQ104
Mannin Rd., Rom.	236	309	EV59
Manning Gdns., Har.	91	304	CK59
Manning Pl., Rich.	169	322	CM86
Manning Rd. E17	222	307	DY57
Manning Rd., Dag.	237	309	FA65
Manningford Clo. EC1	36/7	316	DP69
Manningtree Clo. SW19	189	323	CY88
Manningtree Rd., Ruis.	232	313	BV63
Manningtree St. E1	138	317	DU72
Mannock Rd. N22	221	306	DP55
Manns Clo., Islw.	259	321	CF85
Manns Rd., Edg.	217	304	CN51
Manoel Rd., Twick.	259	321	CC89
Manor Ave. SE4	165	317	DZ82
Manor Ave., Horn.	228	310	FJ57
Manor Ave., Houns.	258	321	BX83
Manor Ave., Nthlt.	232	313	BZ66
Manor Clo. E17	222	307	DY54
Manor Clo. NW7	205	298	CR50
Manor Clo. NW9	217	304	CP57
Manor Clo. SE28	246	319	EW73
Manor Clo., Dag.	237	309	FD65
Manor Clo. (Crayford), Dart.	263	327	FD84
Manor Clo., Rom.	228	310	FG57
Manor Clo., Ruis.	231	312	BT60
Manor Clo., Wor.Pk.	283	330	CS102
Manor Cotts., Nthwd.	213	302	BT53
Manor Cotts. App. N2	219	305	DC54
Manor Ct. E10	104	307	EB60
Manor Ct. N2	219	305	DF57
Manor Ct. SW6	158	315	DB81
Manor Ct., Enf.	203	301	DV36
Manor Ct., Twick.	259	321	CC89
Manor Ct., Wem.	107	304	CL64
Manor Ct. Rd. W7	243	313	CE73
Manor Cres., Horn.	228	310	FJ57
Manor Cres., Surb.	282	330	CN100
Manor Dr. N14	208	300	DH45
Manor Dr. N20	207	299	DE48
Manor Dr. NW7	205	298	CR50
Manor Dr., Felt.	266	329	BX92
Manor Dr., Sun.	266	329	BU96
Manor Dr., Surb.	282	330	CM100
Manor Dr., Wem.	107	304	CM63
Manor Dr., The, Wor.Pk.	283	330	CS102
Manor Dr. N., N.Mal.	283	330	CR100
Manor Dr. N., Wor.Pk.	283	330	CS102
Manor Est. SE16	148	317	DV77
Manor Fm. Ave., Shep.	281	328	BP100
Manor Fm. Clo., Wor.Pk.	283	330	CS102
Manor Fm. Dr. E4	211	301	EE48
Manor Fm. Rd., Enf.	203	301	DV36
Manor Fm. Rd., Th.Hth.	273	324	DN96
Manor Fm. Rd., Wem.	123	314	CK67
Manor Flds. SW15	173	323	CX86
Manor Gdns. N7	99	306	DL62
Manor Gdns. SW20	270	323	CZ96
Manor Gdns. W3	144	314	CN77
Manor Gdns., Hmptn.	267	329	CB94
Manor Gdns., Rich.	169	322	CM84
Manor Gdns., Ruis.	232	313	BW64
Manor Gdns., S.Croy.	295	332	DT107
Manor Gdns., Sun.	266	329	BU95
Manor Gate, Nthlt.	232	313	BY66
Manor Gro. SE15	164	317	DW79
Manor Gro., Beck.	275	325	EB96
Manor Gro., Rich.	170	322	CN84
Manor Hall Ave. NW4	218	305	CW54
Manor Hall Dr. NW4	218	305	CX54
Manor Ho. Ct., Shep.	281	328	BP101
Manor Ho. Dr. NW6	111	305	CX66
Manor Ho. Dr., Nthwd.	213	302	BP52
Manor Ho. Way, Islw.	168	322	CH83
Manor La. SE12	183	325	EE86
Manor La. SE13	183	325	EE85
Manor La., Felt.	258	321	BU89
Manor La., Hayes	257	320	BR79
Manor La., Sun.	266	329	BU96
Manor La., Sutt.	285	331	DC106
Manor La. Ter. SE13	183	325	EE84
Manor Ms. NW6	16	315	DA68
Manor Ms. SE4	165	317	DZ82
Manor Mt. SE23	196	325	DW88
Manor Par. NW10	125	314	CT68
Manor Pk. SE13	183	325	ED85
Manor Pk., Chis.	277	326	ER96
Manor Pk., Rich.	169	322	CM84
Manor Pk. Clo., W.Wick.	288	333	EB102
Manor Pk. Cres., Edg.	217	304	CN51
Manor Pk. Dr., Har.	215	303	CB55
Manor Pk. Gdns., Edg.	205	298	CN50
Manor Pk. Par. SE13	183	325	ED84
Manor Pk. Rd. E12	234	308	EK63
Manor Pk. Rd. N2	219	305	DC55
Manor Pk. Rd. NW10	125	314	CT67
Manor Pk. Rd., Chis.	277	326	EQ95
Manor Pk. Rd., Sutt.	285	331	DC106
Manor Pk. Rd., W.Wick.	288	333	EB102
Manor Pl. SE17	84/5	316	DP78
Manor Pl., Chis.	277	326	ER96
Manor Pl., Felt.	258	321	BU88
Manor Pl., Mitch.	272	324	DJ97
Manor Pl., Stai.	264	328	BH92
Manor Pl., Sutt.	284	331	DB106
Manor Pl., Walt.	281	328	BT101
Manor Rd. E10	104	307	EA59
Manor Rd. E15	131	317	EE68
Manor Rd. E16	131	317	EE70
Manor Rd. E17	222	307	DY54
Manor Rd. N16	101	306	DR61
Manor Rd. N17	222	307	DU53
Manor Rd. N22	220	306	DL51
Manor Rd. SE25	274	325	DU98
Manor Rd. SW20	270	323	CZ96
Manor Rd. W13	132	314	CG73
Manor Rd., Ashf.	264	328	BM92
Manor Rd., Bark.	235	308	ET65
Manor Rd., Barn.	206	299	CY43
Manor Rd., Beck.	275	325	EA96
Manor Rd., Bex.	263	327	FB88
Manor Rd., Chig.	225	308	EN51
Manor Rd., Dag.	237	309	FC65
Manor Rd., Dart.	263	327	FE84
Manor Rd., E.Mol.	267	329	CD98
Manor Rd., Enf.	202	300	DQ40
Manor Rd., Erith	255	319	FF79
Manor Rd., Har.	216	304	CG58
Manor Rd., Hayes	242	313	BU72
Manor Rd., Mitch.	272	324	DJ98
Manor Rd., Rich.	169	322	CM83
Manor Rd., Rom.	228	310	FG57
Manor Rd. (Chadwell Heath), Rom.	226	309	EX58
Manor Rd., Ruis.	231	312	BR60
Manor Rd., Sid.	262	327	EU90
Manor Rd., Sutt.	292	331	CZ108
Manor Rd., Tedd.	268	322	CG92
Manor Rd., Twick.	259	321	CC89
Manor Rd., Wall.	285	332	DH105
Manor Rd., Walt.	281	328	BT101
Manor Rd., W.Wick.	288	333	EB103
Manor Rd., Wdf.Grn.	224	308	EM51
Manor Rd. N., Wall.	285	332	DH105
Manor Sq., Dag.	236	309	EW61
Manor Vale, Brent.	142	314	CJ78
Manor Vw. N3	219	305	DB54
Manor Way E4	211	301	ED49
Manor Way NW9	217	304	CS56
Manor Way SE3	183	325	EF84
Manor Way, Beck.	275	325	EA96
Manor Way, Bex.	263	327	FA88
Manor Way, Bexh.	263	327	FD83
Manor Way, Brom.	290	334	EL100
Manor Way, Har.	215	303	CB56
Manor Way, Mitch.	272	324	DJ97
Manor Way, Orp.	291	334	EQ99
Manor Way, Pur.	294	332	DL112
Manor Way, Rain.	247	319	FE72
Manor Way, Ruis.	231	312	BS59
Manor Way, S.Croy.	295	332	DS107
Manor Way, Sthl.	250	321	BX77
Manor Way, Wor.Pk.	283	330	CS102
Manor Way, The, Wall.	285	332	DH105
Manor Waye, Uxb.	240	312	BK67
Manor Wd. Rd., Pur.	294	332	DL113
Manorbrook SE3	260	326	EG84
Manordene Rd. SE28	246	319	EW72
Manorfield Clo. N19	114	306	DJ63
Manorfields Clo., Chis.	277	326	ET97
Manorgate Rd., Kings.T.	269	322	CN95
Manorhall Gdns. E10	104	307	EA60
Manorside Clo. SE2	254	319	EW77
Manorway, Enf.	209	300	DS45
Manpreet Ct. E12	234	308	EM64
Manresa Rd. SW3	78/9	315	DE78
Mansard Beeches SW17	272	324	DG92
Mansard Clo., Horn.	238	310	FG61
Mansard Clo., Pnr.	214	303	BX55
Manse Clo., Hayes	257	320	BR79
Manse Rd. N16	101	306	DT62
Mansel Gro. E17	223	307	EA53
Mansel Rd. SW19	270	323	CY93
Mansell Rd. W3	145	314	CR75
Mansell Rd., Grnf.	243	313	CB71
Mansell St. E1	51	316	DT72
Manser Rd., Rain.	247	319	FE69
Mansergh Clo. SE18	252	318	EL80
Mansfield Ave. N15	221	306	DR56
Mansfield Ave., Barn.	207	299	DF44
Mansfield Ave., Ruis.	232	313	BV60
Mansfield Clo. N9	210	301	DU44
Mansfield Dr., Hayes	241	312	BS70
Mansfield Gdns., Horn.	238	310	FK61
Mansfield Hill E4	211	301	EB46
Mansfield Ms. W1	44/5	316	DH71
Mansfield Pl. NW3	112	305	DC63
Mansfield Rd. E11	224	308	EH58
Mansfield Rd. E17	222	307	DZ56
Mansfield Rd. NW3	113	305	DF64
Mansfield Rd. W3	124	314	CP70
Mansfield Rd., Chess.	282	330	CJ106
Mansfield Rd., Ilf.	235	308	EN61
Mansfield Rd., S.Croy.	295	332	DR107
Mansfield Rd., Swan.	279	327	FE93
Mansfield St. W1	44/5	316	DH71

Mansford St. E2 128 317 DU68
Manship Rd., Mitch. 272 324 DG94
Mansion Gdns. NW3 96 305 DB62
Mansion Ho. EC4 50 316 DR72
Mansion Ho. Pl. EC4 50 316 DR72
Manson Ms. SW7 77 315 DC77
Manson Pl. SW7 78 315 DD77
Mansted Gdns., Rom. 236 309 EW59
Manston Ave., Sthl. 251 321 CA77
Manston Clo. SE20 274 325 DW95
Manston Gro., Kings.T. 268 322 CK92
Manston Way, Horn. 238 310 FH65
Manstone Rd. NW2 111 305 CY64
Manthorp Rd. SE18 253 318 EQ78
Mantilla Rd. SW17 272 324 DG91
Mantle Rd. SE4 181 325 DY83
Mantle Way E15 121 307 EE66
Mantlet Clo. SW16 272 324 DJ94
Manton Ave. W7 251 321 CF75
Manton Clo., Hayes 249 312 BS73
Manton Rd. SE2 254 319 EU77
Mantua St. SW11 175 323 DD83
Mantus Clo. E1 128 317 DW70
Mantus Rd. E1 128 317 DW70
Manus Way N20 207 299 DC47
Manville Gdns. SW17 192 324 DH89
Manville Rd. SW17 192 324 DG89
Manwood Rd. SE4 181 325 DZ85
Manwood St. E16 244 318 EM74
Manygate La., Shep. 281 328 BQ101
Manygates SW12 192 324 DH89
Mape St. E2 128 317 DV70
Mapesbury Rd. NW2 111 305 CY66
Mapeshill Pl. NW2 110 305 CW65
Maple Ave. E4 210 301 DZ50
Maple Ave. W3 135 314 CS74
Maple Ave., Har. 233 313 CB61
Maple Ave., Upmin. 239 311 FP62
Maple Ave., West Dr. 248 312 BL73
Maple Clo. N16 222 307 DU58
Maple Clo. SW4 177 324 DK86
Maple Clo., Hmptn. 266 329 BZ93
Maple Clo., Hayes 242 313 BX69
Maple Clo., Horn. 238 310 FH62
Maple Clo., Mitch. 272 324 DH95
Maple Clo., Orp. 291 334 ER99
Maple Clo., Ruis. 214 303 BV58
Maple Clo., Swan. 279 327 FE96
Maple Ct., N.Mal. 269 322 CR97
Maple Cres., Sid. 262 327 EU86
Maple Gdns., Edg. 217 304 CS52
Maple Gdns., Stai. 264 320 BL89
Maple Gro. NW9 92 304 CQ59
Maple Gro. W5 142 314 CJ76
Maple Gro., Brent. 152 314 CH80
Maple Gro., Sthl. 242 313 BZ71
Maple Ind. Est., Felt. 258 321 BU90
Maple Leaf Dr., Sid. 261 326 ET88
Maple Leaf Sq. SE16 149 317 DX75
Maple Ms. NW6 16/7 315 DB68
Maple Ms. SW16 272 324 DM92
Maple Pl. W1 33 316 DJ70
Maple Pl., West Dr. 248 312 BM73
Maple Rd. E11 223 307 EE58
Maple Rd. SE20 274 325 DV95
Maple Rd., Hayes 242 313 BW69
Maple Rd., Surb. 282 330 CK100
Maple St. W1 45 316 DJ71
Maple St., Rom. 227 309 FC56
Maple Wk. W10 127 315 CX70
Maple Wk., Sutt. 292 331 DB110
Maple Way, Felt. 258 321 BU90
Maplecroft Clo. E6 244 318 EL72
Mapledale Ave., Croy. 287 333 DU103
Mapledene, Chis. 277 326 EQ92
Mapledene Rd. E8 118 307 DU66
Maplehurst Clo., Kings.T. 268 322 CL98
Mapleleafe Gdns., Ilf. 225 308 EP55
Maples, The, Bans. 292 331 DB114
Maples Pl. E1 138 317 DV71
Maplestead Rd. SW2 193 324 DM87
Maplestead Rd., Dag. 246 319 EV67
Maplethorpe Rd., Th.Hth. 273 324 DN98
Mapleton Clo., Brom. 289 334 EG100
Mapleton Cres. SW18 174 323 DB86
Mapleton Cres., Enf. 203 301 DW38
Mapleton Rd. E4 211 301 EC48
Mapleton Rd. SW18 174 323 DA86
Mapleton Rd., Enf. 203 301 DV40
Maplin Clo. N21 208 300 DM44
Maplin Rd. E16 244 318 EG72
Maplin St. E3 129 317 DZ69
Mapperley Dr., Wdf.Grn. 223 307 EE52
Maran Way, Erith 254 319 EX75
Marban Rd. W9 127 315 CZ69
Marble Arch W1 55 315 DF73
Marble Clo. W3 134 314 CP74
Marble Dr. NW2 95 305 CX60
Marble Hill Clo., Twick. 184 322 CH87
Marble Hill Gdns., Twick. 184 322 CH87
Marble Quay E1 138 317 DU74
Marbrook Ct. SE12 260 326 EJ90
Marcellina Way, Orp. 291 334 ES104
March Rd., Twick. 184 322 CG87
Marchant Rd. E11 105 307 ED61
Marchant St. SE14 165 317 DY79
Marchbank Rd. W14 157 315 CZ79
Marchmant Clo., Horn. 238 310 FJ62
Marchmont Gdns., Rich. 169 322 CM85
Marchmont Rd., Rich. 169 322 CM85
Marchmont Rd., Wall. 294 332 DJ108
Marchmont St. WC1 34/5 316 DL70
Marchside Clo., Houns. 250 321 BX81
Marchwood Clo. SE5 163 316 DS80
Marchwood Cres. W5 132 314 CJ72
Marcia Rd. SE1 86/7 316 DS77
Marcilly Rd. SW18 175 323 DD85
Marco Rd. W6 146 315 CV76
Marcon Pl. E8 118 307 DV64
Marconi Rd. E10 104 307 EA60
Marconi Way, Sthl. 243 313 CB72
Marcourt Lawns W5 123 314 CL70
Marcus Ct. E15 131 317 EE67
Marcus Garvey Way SE24 178 324 DN84
Marcus St. E15 131 317 EE67
Marcus St. SW18 174 323 DB86
Marcus Ter. SW18 174 323 DB86
Mardale Dr. NW9 217 304 CR57
Mardell Rd., Croy. 288 333 DX99
Marden Ave., Brom. 289 333 EF100
Marden Cres., Bex. 263 327 FC85
Marden Cres., Croy. 286 332 DM100
Marden Rd. N17 221 306 DS55
Marden Rd., Croy. 286 332 DM100
Marden Rd., Rom. 227 309 FE58
Marden Sq. SE16 148 317 DV76
Marder Rd. W13 142 314 CG75
Mardon St. E14 139 317 DY71
Mare St. E8 128 317 DV67
Marechal Niel Ave., Sid. 261 326 ER90
Mares Fld., Croy. 287 332 DS104
Maresfield Gdns. NW3 112 305 DC64
Marfleet Clo., Cars. 285 331 DE103
Margaret Ave. E4 211 301 EB44
Margaret Bondfield Ave., Bark. 236 309 EU66
Margaret Bldgs. N16 101 306 DT60
Margaret Clo., Rom. 228 310 FH57
Margaret Clo., Stai. 264 328 BK93
Margaret Ct. W1 45 316 DJ72
Margaret Dr., Horn. 238 311 FM60
Margaret Gardner Dr. SE9 260 326 EM89
Margaret Ingram Clo. SW6 157 315 CZ79
Margaret Rd. N16 101 306 DT60
Margaret Rd., Bex. 262 327 EX86
Margaret Rd., Rom. 228 310 FH57
Margaret Sq., Uxb. 240 312 BJ67
Margaret St. W1 44/5 316 DH72
Margaret Way, Ilf. 224 308 EL58
Margaretta Ter. SW3 159 315 DE79
Margaretting Rd. E12 234 308 EJ60
Margate Rd. SW2 177 324 DL85
Margery Pk. Rd. E7 234 308 EG65
Margery Rd., Dag. 236 309 EX62
Margery St. WC1 36 316 DN69
Margin Dr. SW19 270 323 CX92
Margravine Gdns. W6 147 315 CX78
Margravine Rd. W6 147 315 CX78
Marham Gdns. SW18 191 323 DE88

Marham Gdns., Mord. 285 331 DC100
Maria Clo. SE1 148 317 DU77
Maria Ter. E1 129 317 DX70
Maria Theresa Clo., N.Mal. 283 330 CR99
Mariam Gdns., Horn. 238 311 FM61
Marian Clo., Hayes 242 313 BX70
Marian Ct., Sutt. 284 331 DB106
Marian Pl. E2 128 317 DV68
Marian Rd. SW16 272 324 DJ95
Marian Sq. E2 128 317 DU68
Marian St. E2 128 317 DV68
Marian Way NW10 109 304 CT66
Maricas Ave., Har. 215 303 CD52
Marie Lloyd Gdns. N19 99 306 DL59
Marie Lloyd Wk. E8 118 307 DU65
Mariette Way, Wall. 294 332 DL109
Marigold All. SE1 60/1 316 DP73
Marigold Clo., Sthl. 242 313 BY73
Marigold Rd. N17 222 307 DW52
Marigold St. SE16 148 317 DV75
Marigold Way E4 222 307 DZ51
Marigold Way, Croy. 288 333 DX102
Marina App., Hayes 242 313 BY71
Marina Ave., N.Mal. 283 331 CV99
Marina Clo., Brom. 276 326 EG97
Marina Clo., Cher. 280 328 BH102
Marina Dr., Well. 253 318 ES82
Marina Gdns., Rom. 227 309 FB57
Marina Way, Tedd. 268 322 CK94
Marine Dr. SE18 252 318 EM77
Marine St. SE16 148 317 DU76
Marinefield Rd. SW6 158 315 DB82
Mariner Gdns., Rich. 184 322 CJ90
Mariner Rd. E12 234 308 EM63
Mariners Ms. E14 151 317 ED77
Mariners Wk., Erith 255 319 FF79
Marion Ave., Shep. 281 328 BP99
Marion Clo., Ilf. 225 308 ER52
Marion Cres., Orp. 291 335 EU99
Marion Gro., Wdf.Grn. 211 301 EE50
Marion Rd. NW7 206 299 CU50
Marion Rd., Th.Hth. 287 332 DQ99
Marischal Rd. SE13 183 325 ED83
Maritime St. E3 129 317 DZ70
Marius Pas. SW17 192 324 DG89
Marius Rd. SW17 192 324 DG89
Marjorie Gro. SW11 175 323 DF84
Marjorie Ms. E1 139 317 DX72
Mark Ave. E4 211 301 EB44
Mark Clo., Bexh. 254 319 EY81
Mark Clo., Sthl. 243 313 CB74
Mark La. EC3 62/3 316 DS73
Mark Rd. N22 221 306 DP54
Mark St. E15 121 307 EE66
Mark St. EC2 38/9 316 DS70
Markab Rd., Nthwd. 213 302 BT50
Marke Clo., Kes. 290 334 EL105
Market Ct. W1 45 316 DJ72
Market Est. N7 115 306 DL65
Market Hill SE18 253 318 EN76
Market La., Edg. 217 304 CQ53
Market Link, Rom. 227 309 FE56
Market Meadow, Orp. 278 327 EW98
Market Ms. W1 56/7 316 DH74
Market Par. SE15 164 317 DU82
Market Pl. N2 219 305 DE55
Market Pl. NW11 219 305 DC56
Market Pl. SE16 148 317 DU77
Market Pl. W1 45 316 DJ72
Market Pl. W3 134 314 CQ74
Market Pl., Bexh. 263 327 FA84
Market Pl., Brent. 153 314 CK80
Market Pl., Enf. 202 300 DR41
Market Pl., Kings.T. 268 322 CK96
Market Pl., Rom. 227 309 FE57
Market Rd. N7 115 306 DL65
Market Rd., Rich. 170 322 CN83
Market Row SW9 178 324 DN84
Market Sq. E14 140 317 EB72
Market Sq. N9 210 301 DU47
Market Sq., Brom. 276 326 EG96
Market Sq., Uxb. 240 312 BJ66
Market St. E6 244 318 EM68
Market St. SE18 253 318 EN77
Market Way E14 140 317 EB72
Markfield Gdns. E4 211 301 EB45
Markfield Rd. N15 222 307 DU56
Markham Pl. SW3 79 315 DF78
Markham Sq. SW3 79 315 DF78
Markham St. SW3 78/9 315 DE78
Markhole Clo., Hmptn. 266 329 BZ94
Markhouse Ave. E17 222 307 DY58
Markhouse Rd. E17 222 307 DZ57
Markmanor Ave. E17 103 307 DY59
Marks Rd., Rom. 227 309 FC57
Marksbury Ave., Rich. 170 322 CN83
Markway, The, Sun. 266 329 BW96
Markwell Clo. SE26 274 325 DV91
Markwell Clo., W.Wick. 289 333 EE103
Markyate Rd., Dag. 236 309 EV64
Marl Rd. SW18 174 323 DB84
Marl St. SW18 174 323 DC84
Marlands Rd., Ilf. 224 308 EL55
Marlborough Ave. E8 128 317 DU67
Marlborough Ave. N14 208 300 DJ48
Marlborough Ave., Edg. 205 298 CP48
Marlborough Ave., Ruis. 231 302 BQ58
Marlborough Bldgs. SW3 78/9 315 DE77
Marlborough Clo. N20 207 299 DF48
Marlborough Clo. SE17 85 316 DQ77
Marlborough Clo. SW19 271 323 DE94
Marlborough Clo., Orp. 291 334 ET101
Marlborough Clo., Upmin. 239 311 FS60
Marlborough Ct. W8 76 315 DA77
Marlborough Cres. W4 145 314 CR76
Marlborough Dr., Ilf. 224 308 EL55
Marlborough Gdns. N20 207 299 DF48
Marlborough Gdns., Upmin. 239 311 FR60
Marlborough Gate Ho. W2 54 315 DD73
Marlborough Gro. SE1 148 317 DU78
Marlborough Hill NW8 17 315 DC67
Marlborough Hill, Har. 215 303 CD56
Marlborough La. SE7 252 318 EJ79
Marlborough Pk. Ave., Sid. 262 327 EU88
Marlborough Pl. NW8 17 315 DC68
Marlborough Rd. E4 223 307 EA51
Marlborough Rd. E7 234 308 EJ66
Marlborough Rd. E15 121 307 EE63
Marlborough Rd. E18 224 308 EG55
Marlborough Rd. N9 209 300 DT46
Marlborough Rd. N19 99 306 DK61
Marlborough Rd. N22 220 306 DL52
Marlborough Rd. SW1 57 316 DJ74
Marlborough Rd. SW19 271 323 DE93
Marlborough Rd. W4 144 314 CQ78
Marlborough Rd. W5 143 314 CK75
Marlborough Rd., Ashf. 264 328 BK92
Marlborough Rd., Bexh. 262 327 EX83
Marlborough Rd., Brom. 276 326 EJ98
Marlborough Rd., Dag. 236 309 EV63
Marlborough Rd., Felt. 258 321 BX89
Marlborough Rd., Hmptn. 267 329 CA93
Marlborough Rd., Islw. 152 314 CH81
Marlborough Rd., Rich. 169 322 CL86
Marlborough Rd., Rom. 227 309 FA56
Marlborough Rd., S.Croy. 295 332 DQ108
Marlborough Rd., Sthl. 250 321 BW76
Marlborough Rd., Sutt. 284 331 DA104
Marlborough Rd., Uxb. 241 312 BP70
Marlborough St. SW3 78/9 315 DE77
Marlborough Yd. N19 99 306 DK61
Marler Rd. SE23 197 325 DY88
Marley Ave., Bexh. 254 319 EX79
Marley Clo. N15 221 306 DP56
Marley Clo., Grnf. 243 313 CA69
Marley Wk. NW2 110 305 CW64
Marlin Clo., Sun. 265 328 BS93
Marlingdene Clo., Hmptn. 267 329 CA93
Marlings Clo., Chis. 277 326 ES98
Marlings Pk. Ave., Chis. 277 326 ES98
Marlins, The, Nthwd. 213 302 BT50
Marlins Clo., Sutt. 285 331 DC106
Marloes Clo., Wem. 107 304 CK63
Marloes Rd. W8 64/5 315 DB76
Marlow Clo. SE20 274 325 DV97
Marlow Ct. NW6 111 305 CX66
Marlow Ct. NW9 217 304 CS55
Marlow Cres., Twick. 259 321 CF86

Marlow Dr., Sutt. 284 331 CX103
Marlow Gdns., Hayes 249 320 BR76
Marlow Rd. E6 244 318 EM69
Marlow Rd. SE20 274 325 DV97
Marlow Rd., Sthl. 250 321 BZ76
Marlow Way SE16 149 317 DX75
Marlowe Clo., Chis. 277 326 ER93
Marlowe Clo., Ilf. 225 308 EQ53
Marlowe Gdns. SE9 261 326 EN86
Marlowe Gdns., Rom. 228 310 FJ53
Marlowe Rd. E17 223 307 EC56
Marlowe Sq., Mitch. 272 324 DJ98
Marlowe Way, Croy. 286 332 DL103
Marlowes, The NW8 18 315 DD67
Marlowes, The, Dart. 263 327 FD84
Marlton St. SE10 151 317 EF78
Marlwood Clo., Sid. 261 326 ES89
Marmadon Rd. SE18 253 318 ET77
Marmion App. E4 211 301 EA49
Marmion Ave. E4 210 301 DZ49
Marmion Clo. E4 210 301 DZ49
Marmion Ms. SW11 176 324 DG83
Marmion Rd. SW11 176 324 DG84
Marmont Rd. SE15 164 317 DU81
Marmora Rd. SE22 180 325 DW86
Marmot Rd., Houns. 258 321 BX83
Marne Ave. N11 208 300 DH49
Marne Ave., Well. 262 327 EU83
Marne St. W10 127 315 CY69
Marnell Way, Houns. 258 321 BX83
Marney Rd. SW11 176 324 DG84
Marnham Ave. NW2 111 305 CY63
Marnham Cres., Grnf. 243 313 CB69
Marnock Rd. SE4 181 325 DZ85
Maroon St. E14 139 317 DY71
Maroons Way SE6 275 325 EA92
Marquess Rd. N1 117 306 DR65
Marquis Clo., Wem. 107 304 CM66
Marquis Rd. N4 99 306 DM60
Marquis Rd. N22 220 306 DM51
Marquis Rd. NW1 115 306 DK65
Marrabon Clo., Sid. 262 327 EU88
Marrick Clo. SW15 172 323 CU84
Marrilyne Ave., Enf. 203 301 DZ38
Marriots Clo. NW9 217 304 CT58
Marriott Clo., Felt. 257 320 BR86
Marriott Rd. E15 131 317 EE67
Marriott Rd. N4 99 306 DM60
Marriott Rd. N10 219 305 DF53
Marryat Pl. SW19 270 323 CY91
Marryat Rd. SW19 270 323 CX92
Marryat Rd., Enf. 203 301 DV35
Marryat Sq. SW6 157 315 CY81
Marsala Rd. SE13 182 325 EB84
Marsden Rd. N9 210 301 DV47
Marsden Rd. SE15 179 324 DT83
Marsden St. NW5 114 306 DG65
Marsden Way, Orp. 291 334 ES104
Marsh Ave., Mitch. 271 323 DF96
Marsh Clo. NW7 205 298 CT48
Marsh Ct. SW19 271 323 DC95
Marsh Dr. NW9 217 304 CT58
Marsh Fm. Rd., Twick. 259 321 CF88
Marsh Grn. Rd., Dag. 247 319 FA67
Marsh Hill E9 119 307 DY64
Marsh La. E10 104 307 EA61
Marsh La. N17 222 307 DV53
Marsh La. NW7 205 298 CR49
Marsh La., Stan. 204 298 CJ50
Marsh Rd., Pnr. 214 303 BY56
Marsh Rd., Wem. 123 314 CK69
Marsh St. E14 150 317 EB77
Marsh Ter., Orp. 278 327 EX98
Marsh Wall E14 140 317 EA74
Marsh Way, Rain. 247 319 FD72
Marshall Clo. SW18 174 323 DC86
Marshall Clo., Har. 233 313 CD59
Marshall Clo., Houns. 258 321 BZ85
Marshall Clo., S.Croy. 295 333 DU113
Marshall Dr., Hayes 249 312 BT71
Marshall Path SE28 246 319 EV73
Marshall Rd. N17 221 306 DR53
Marshall St. W1 45 316 DJ72
Marshalls Clo. N11 208 300 DH49
Marshalls Dr., Rom. 227 309 FE55
Marshall's Gro. SE18 252 318 EL77
Marshalls Pl. SE16 75 316 DT76
Marshalls Rd., Rom. 227 309 FD56
Marshall's Rd., Sutt. 284 331 DB105
Marshalsea Rd. SE1 73 316 DQ75
Marsham Clo., Chis. 277 326 EP92
Marsham St. SW1 70 316 DK76
Marshbrook Clo. SE3 260 326 EK83
Marshfield St. E14 150 317 EC76
Marshgate La. E15 120 307 EB66
Marshgate Path SE28 253 318 EQ77
Marshgate Sidings E15 120 307 EB66
Marshside Clo. N9 210 301 DW46
Marsland Clo. SE17 84/5 316 DP78
Marston Ave., Dag. 237 309 FA61
Marston Clo. NW6 112 305 DC66
Marston Clo., Dag. 237 309 FA62
Marston Rd., Ilf. 224 308 EL53
Marston Rd., Tedd. 268 322 CH92
Marston Way SE19 273 324 DP94
Marsworth Ave., Pnr. 214 303 BX53
Marsworth Clo., Hayes 242 313 BY71
Mart St. WC2 58/9 316 DL73
Martaban Rd. N16 101 306 DT61
Martel Pl. E8 117 306 DT65
Martell Rd. SE21 195 324 DR90
Martello St. E8 118 307 DV66
Martello Ter. E8 118 307 DV66
Marten Rd. E17 223 307 EA54
Martens Ave., Bexh. 263 327 FB84
Martens Clo., Bexh. 263 327 FC84
Martha Ct. E2 128 317 DV68
Martha Rd. E4 222 307 DZ51
Martha Rd. E15 121 307 EE65
Martha St. E1 138 317 DV72
Martham Clo. SE28 246 319 EX73
Marthorne Cres., Har. 215 303 CD54
Martin Bowes Rd. SE9 260 326 EM83
Martin Clo. N9 210 301 DX46
Martin Clo., Uxb. 240 312 BL68
Martin Cres., Croy. 286 332 DN102
Martin Dale Ind. Est., Enf. 203 301 DV41
Martin Dene, Bexh. 262 327 EZ85
Martin Dr., Nthlt. 232 313 BZ64
Martin Gdns., Dag. 236 309 EW63
Martin Gro., Mord. 271 323 DA97
Martin La. EC4 62 316 DR73
Martin Ri., Bexh. 262 327 EZ85
Martin Rd., Dag. 236 309 EW63
Martin Way SW20 270 323 CX96
Martin Way, Mord. 271 323 DA97
Martinbridge Trd. Est., Enf. 203 301 DU42
Martindale SW14 170 322 CQ85
Martindale Ave. E16 244 318 EG73
Martindale Ave., Orp. 291 335 EU106
Martindale Rd. SW12 192 324 DH87
Martindale Rd., Houns. 258 321 BY84
Martineau Est. E1 138 317 DW73
Martineau Ms. N5 116 306 DP63
Martineau Rd. N5 116 306 DP63
Martineau St. E1 138 317 DW73
Martingale Clo., Sun. 266 329 BU98
Martingales Clo., Rich. 185 322 CK90
Martins Clo., Orp. 278 327 EX97
Martins Clo., W.Wick. 289 333 ED103
Martins Rd., Brom. 275 325 EE96
Martins Wk. N10 220 306 DG53
Martinstown Clo., Horn. 229 311 FN58
Martlesham Clo., Horn. 238 310 FJ64
Martlet Gro., Nthlt. 242 313 BX69
Martlett Ct. WC2 46/7 316 DL72
Martley Dr., Ilf. 225 308 EP57
Martock Clo., Har. 216 304 CG56
Marton Clo. SE6 198 325 EA90
Marton Rd. N16 101 306 DS61
Martys Yd. NW3 113 305 DD63
Marvell Ave., Hayes 242 313 BU71
Marvels Clo. SE12 260 326 EH89
Marvels La. SE12 260 326 EH89
Marville Rd. SW6 157 315 CZ80
Marvin St. E8 118 307 DV65
Marwell Clo., Rom. 228 310 FG58
Marwell Clo., W.Wick. 289 333 EF103

Marwood Clo., Well. 262 327 EV83
Marwood Way SE16 148 317 DV78
Mary Adelaide Clo. SW15 269 322 CS91
Mary Ann Gdns. SE8 166 317 EA79
Mary Clo., Stan. 216 304 CM56
Mary Datchelor Clo. SE5 163 316 DR81
Mary Gardener Dr. SE9 260 326 EM89
Mary Grn. NW8 16/7 315 DB67
Mary Kingsley Ct. N19 99 306 DL59
Mary Lawrenson Pl. SE3 252 318 EG80
Mary Macarthur Ho. W6 157 315 CY79
Mary Peters Dr., Grnf. 233 313 CD64
Mary Pl. W11 137 315 CY73
Mary Rose Clo., Hmptn. 267 329 CA95
Mary Rose Mall E6 245 318 EN71
Mary Rose Way N20 207 299 DD46
Mary Seacole Clo. E8 27 316 DT67
Mary St. E16 141 317 EF71
Mary St. N1 25 316 DQ67
Mary Ter. NW1 20/1 316 DH67
Maryatt Ave., Har. 233 313 CB61
Marybank SE18 252 318 EM77
Maryfield Clo., Bex. 263 327 FE90
Maryland Pk. E15 121 307 EE64
Maryland Pt. E15 121 307 EE65
Maryland Rd. E15 121 307 ED64
Maryland Rd. N22 220 306 DM51
Maryland Rd., Th.Hth. 273 324 DP95
Maryland Sq. E15 121 307 EE64
Maryland St. E15 121 307 ED64
Maryland Wk. N1 25 316 DQ67
Maryland Way, Sun. 266 329 BU96
Marylands Rd. W9 28 315 DA70
Marylebone Flyover NW1 42/3 315 DE71
Marylebone Flyover W2 42 315 DD71
Marylebone High St. W1 44 316 DG71
Marylebone La. W1 44 316 DG72
Marylebone Ms. W1 44/5 316 DH71
Marylebone Pas. W1 45 316 DJ72
Marylebone Rd. NW1 42/3 315 DE71
Marylebone St. W1 44 316 DG71
Marylee Way SE11 83 316 DM77
Maryon Gro. SE7 252 318 EL77
Maryon Ms. NW3 113 305 DE63
Maryon Rd. SE7 252 318 EL77
Maryon Rd. SE18 252 318 EL77
Mary's Clo. N17 221 306 DT53
Mary's Ter., Twick. 184 322 CG87
Masbro Rd. W14 147 315 CX76
Mascalls Ct. SE7 252 318 EJ79
Mascalls Rd. SE7 252 318 EJ79
Mascotte Rd. SW15 173 323 CX84
Mascotts Clo. NW2 94 305 CV62
Masefield Ave., Borwd. 205 298 CP43
Masefield Ave., Sthl. 243 313 CA73
Masefield Clo., Erith 255 319 FF81
Masefield Clo., Rom. 228 310 FJ53
Masefield Cres. N14 208 300 DJ43
Masefield Cres., Rom. 228 310 FJ53
Masefield Dr., Upmin. 239 311 FQ59
Masefield Gdns. E6 245 318 EN70
Masefield La., Hayes 242 313 BV70
Masefield Rd., Hmptn. 266 329 BZ91
Masefield Vw., Orp. 291 334 EQ104
Masefield Way, Stai. 264 320 BM88
Mashie Rd. W3 135 314 CS72
Mashiters Hill, Rom. 227 309 FD54
Mashiters Wk., Rom. 227 309 FE55
Maskall Clo. SW2 194 324 DN88
Maskani Wk. SW16 272 324 DJ94
Maskell Rd. SW17 190 323 DC90
Maskelyne Clo. SW11 159 315 DE81
Mason Bradbear Ct. N1 117 306 DR65
Mason Clo. E16 244 318 EG73
Mason Clo. SE16 148 317 DU78
Mason Clo. SW20 270 323 CX95
Mason Clo., Bexh. 263 327 FB83
Mason Clo., Hmptn. 266 329 BZ95
Mason Dr., Rom. 228 311 FL54
Mason Rd., Wdf.Grn. 211 301 EE49
Mason St. SE17 86 316 DR77
Masons Arms Ms. W1 56/7 316 DH73
Masons Ave. EC2 50 316 DR72
Masons Ave., Croy. 287 332 DQ104
Masons Ave., Har. 215 303 CF56
Masons Ct., Wem. 92 304 CN61
Masons Grn. La. W3 124 314 CN70
Masons Hill SE18 253 318 EP77
Masons Hill, Brom. 276 326 EG97
Mason's Pl. EC1 37 316 DQ69
Masons Pl., Mitch. 271 323 DF95
Masons Rd., Enf. 203 301 DV36
Mason's Yd. SW1 57 316 DJ74
Mason's Yd. SW19 270 323 CX92
Massey Clo. N11 208 300 DH50
Massie Rd. E8 118 307 DU65
Massinger St. SE17 86/7 316 DS77
Massingham St. E1 129 317 DX70
Masson Ave., Ruis. 232 313 BW65
Mast Ho. Ter. E14 150 317 EA77
Master Gunner Pl. SE18 252 318 EL80
Masterman Ho. SE5 163 316 DR80
Masterman Rd. E6 244 318 EL69
Masters St. E1 139 317 DX71
Mastmaker Rd. E14 150 317 EA75
Maswell Pk. Cres., Houns. 259 321 CC85
Maswell Pk. Rd., Houns. 259 321 CB85
Matcham Rd. E11 105 307 EE62
Matchless Dr. SE18 253 318 EN80
Matfield Clo., Brom. 289 334 EG99
Matfield Rd., Belv. 255 319 FA79
Matham Gro. SE22 179 324 DT84
Matheson Rd. W14 147 315 CZ77
Mathews Pk. Ave. E15 121 307 EF65
Matilda St. N1 23 316 DM67
Matlock Clo. SE24 178 324 DQ84
Matlock Clo., Barn. 206 299 CX44
Matlock Ct. SE5 179 324 DR84
Matlock Cres., Sutt. 284 331 CY105
Matlock Gdns., Horn. 238 311 FL62
Matlock Gdns., Sutt. 284 331 CY105
Matlock Pl., Sutt. 284 331 CY105
Matlock Rd. E10 223 307 EC58
Matlock St. E14 139 317 DY72
Matlock Way, N.Mal. 269 322 CR95
Matrimony Pl. SW8 160 316 DJ82
Matson Ct., Wdf.Grn. 223 307 EE52
Matthew Arnold Clo., Stai. 264 328 BJ93
Matthew Clo. W10 127 315 CX70
Matthew Ct., Mitch. 286 332 DK99
Matthew Parker St. SW1 70 316 DK75
Matthews Ave. E6 245 318 EN68
Matthews Clo.
(Havering-atte-Bower), Rom. 228 311 FM53
Matthews Rd., Grnf. 233 313 CD64
Matthews St. SW11 159 315 DF82
Matthews Yd. WC2 46/7 316 DL72
Matthias Rd. N16 117 306 DR64
Mattingley Way SE15 163 316 DT80
Mattison Rd. N4 221 306 DN58
Mattock La. W5 132 314 CJ74
Mattock La. W13 132 314 CH74
Maud Cashmore Way SE18 252 318 EM76
Maud Gdns. E13 131 317 EF67
Maud Gdns., Bark. 245 318 ET68
Maud Rd. E10 104 307 EC62
Maud Rd. E13 131 317 EF68
Maud St. E16 141 317 EF71
Maude Rd. E17 222 307 DY57
Maude Rd. SE5 163 316 DS81
Maude Ter. E17 222 307 DY56
Maudlin's Grn. E1 138 317 DU74
Maudslay Rd. SE9 260 326 EM83
Maudsley Ho., Brent. 143 314 CL78
Mauleverer Rd. SW2 177 324 DL85
Maundeby Wk. NW10 109 304 CS65
Maunder Rd. W7 243 313 CE74
Maunsel St. SW1 82 316 DK77
Maurice Ave. N22 221 306 DP54
Maurice Brown Clo. NW7 206 299 CX50
Maurice St. W12 136 315 CV72
Maurice Wk. NW11 219 305 DC56
Maurier Clo., Nthlt. 242 313 BW67
Mauritius Rd. SE10 151 317 EE77
Maury Rd. N16 102 307 DU61
Mavelstone Clo., Brom. 276 326 EL95
Mavelstone Rd., Brom. 276 326 EK95
Maverton Rd. E3 130 317 EA67

Mavis Ave., Epsom 283 330 CS106
Mavis Clo., Epsom 283 330 CS106
Mavis Gro., Horn. 238 311 FL61
Mavis Wk. E6 244 318 EL71
Mawbey Est. SE1 87 316 DT78
Mawbey Pl. SE1 87 316 DT78
Mawbey Rd. SE1 87 316 DT78
Mawbey St. SW8 161 316 DL80
Mawney Clo., Rom. 227 309 FB54
Mawney Rd., Rom. 227 309 FB54
Mawson Clo. SW20 270 323 CY96
Mawson La. W4 155 314 CT79
Maxey Gdns., Dag. 236 309 EY63
Maxey Rd. SE18 253 318 EQ77
Maxey Rd., Dag. 236 309 EY64
Maxfield Clo. N20 207 299 DC45
Maxilla Gdns. W10 137 315 CX72
Maxilla Wk. W10 137 315 CX72
Maxim Rd. N21 209 300 DN44
Maxim Rd., Dart. 263 327 FE85
Maxim Rd., Erith 255 319 FE77
Maximfeldt Rd., Erith 255 319 FE78
Maxted Pk., Har. 233 313 CE59
Maxted Rd. SE15 179 324 DT83
Maxwell Clo., Croy. 286 332 DL101
Maxwell Clo., Rick. 212 302 BG47
Maxwell Gdns., Orp. 291 334 ET104
Maxwell Rd. SW6 158 315 DB80
Maxwell Rd., Ashf. 265 328 BQ93
Maxwell Rd., Nthwd. 213 302 BR52
Maxwell Rd., Well. 262 327 EU83
Maxwell Rd., West Dr. 248 320 BM77
Maxwelton Ave. NW7 205 298 CR50
Maxwelton Clo. NW7 205 298 CR50
May Ave., Orp. 291 335 EV99
May Ct. SW19 271 323 DB95
May Gdns., Wem. 122 314 CJ69
May Rd. E4 223 307 EA51
May Rd. E13 244 318 EG68
May Rd., Twick. 259 321 CE88
May St. W14 147 315 CZ78
May Tree La., Stan. 215 303 CF52
May Wk. E13 244 318 EH68
Maya Rd. N2 219 305 DC56
Mayall Rd. SE24 178 324 DP85
Maybank Ave. E18 224 308 EH54
Maybank Ave., Horn. 238 310 FJ64
Maybank Ave., Wem. 233 313 CF64
Maybank Gdns., Pnr. 214 303 BU57
Maybank Lo., Horn. 238 310 FJ64
Maybank Rd. E18 224 308 EH53
Maybells Commercial Est.,
Bark. 246 319 EX68
Mayberry Pl., Surb. 282 330 CM101
Maybourne Clo. SE26 274 325 DV92
Maybrick Rd., Horn. 228 310 FJ57
Maybrook Meadow Est., Bark. 236 309 EU64
Maybury Clo., Orp. 290 334 EP99
Maybury Gdns. NW10 110 305 CV65
Maybury Ms. N6 98 306 DJ59
Maybury Rd. E13 244 318 EJ70
Maybury Rd., Bark. 245 318 ET68
Maybury St. SW17 271 323 DE92
Maybush Rd., Horn. 238 311 FL59
Maychurch Clo., Stan. 216 304 CK52
Maycock Gro., Nthwd. 213 302 BT51
Maycroft, Pnr. 214 303 BV54
Maycross Ave., Mord. 270 323 CZ97
Mayday Gdns. SE3 252 318 EL82
Mayday Rd., Th.Hth. 286 332 DP100
Mayerne Rd. SE9 260 326 EK85
Mayes Rd. N22 220 306 DM54
Mayesbrook Rd., Bark. 245 318 ET67
Mayesbrook Rd., Dag. 236 309 EV62
Mayesbrook Rd., Ilf. 236 309 EU62
Mayesford Rd., Rom. 236 309 EW59
Mayeswood Rd. SE12 260 326 EJ90
Mayfair Ave., Bexh. 254 319 EX81
Mayfair Ave., Ilf. 234 308 EM61
Mayfair Ave., Rom. 226 309 EX58
Mayfair Ave., Twick. 259 321 CC87
Mayfair Ave., Wor.Pk. 283 330 CT102
Mayfair Clo., Beck. 275 325 EB95
Mayfair Clo., Surb. 282 330 CL102
Mayfair Gdns. N17 221 306 DQ51
Mayfair Gdns., Wdf.Grn. 224 308 EG52
Mayfair Ms. NW1 113 305 DF66
Mayfair Pl. W1 56/7 316 DH74
Mayfair Ter. N14 208 300 DK45
Mayfield, Bexh. 262 327 EZ83
Mayfield Ave. N12 207 299 DC49
Mayfield Ave. N14 208 300 DJ47
Mayfield Ave. W4 145 314 CS77
Mayfield Ave. W13 142 314 CH76
Mayfield Ave., Har. 216 304 CH57
Mayfield Ave., Orp. 291 334 ET101
Mayfield Ave., Wdf.Grn. 224 308 EG51
Mayfield Clo. E8 117 306 DT65
Mayfield Clo. SW4 177 324 DK85
Mayfield Clo., Ashf. 265 328 BP93
Mayfield Clo., Uxb. 241 312 BP69
Mayfield Cres. N9 210 301 DV44
Mayfield Cres., Th.Hth. 272 324 DM98
Mayfield Dr., Pnr. 214 303 BZ56
Mayfield Gdns. NW4 218 305 CX58
Mayfield Gdns. W7 243 313 CD72
Mayfield Rd. E4 211 301 EC47
Mayfield Rd. E8 117 306 DT66
Mayfield Rd. E13 131 317 EF70
Mayfield Rd. E17 222 307 DY54
Mayfield Rd. N8 220 306 DM57
Mayfield Rd. SW19 270 323 CZ95
Mayfield Rd. W3 134 314 CP73
Mayfield Rd. W12 145 314 CS75
Mayfield Rd., Belv. 255 319 FC77
Mayfield Rd., Brom. 290 334 EL99
Mayfield Rd., Dag. 236 309 EW60
Mayfield Rd., Enf. 203 301 DX40
Mayfield Rd., S.Croy. 295 332 DR109
Mayfield Rd., Sutt. 293 331 DD107
Mayfield Rd., Th.Hth. 272 324 DM98
Mayfields, Wem. 92 304 CN61
Mayfields Clo., Wem. 92 304 CN61
Mayflower Clo. SE16 149 317 DX77
Mayflower Ct. SE16 148 317 DW75
Mayflower Rd. SW9 177 324 DL83
Mayflower St. SE16 148 317 DW75
Mayfly Clo., Pnr. 232 313 BW59
Mayfly Gdns., Nthlt. 242 313 BX69
Mayford Clo. SW12 191 323 DF87
Mayford Clo., Beck. 274 325 DX97
Mayford Rd. SW12 191 323 DF87
Maygood St. N1 23 316 DM68
Maygoods Clo., Uxb. 248 312 BK71
Maygoods Grn., Uxb. 248 312 BK71
Maygoods La., Uxb. 248 312 BK71
Maygoods Vw., Uxb. 248 312 BJ71
Maygreen Cres., Horn. 238 310 FG59
Maygrove Rd. NW6 111 305 CZ65
Mayhew Clo. E4 211 301 EA48
Mayhill Rd. SE7 252 318 EH79
Mayhill Rd., Barn. 206 299 CY43
Maylands Ave., Horn. 238 310 FH63
Maylands Dr., Sid. 262 327 EX90
Maylands Dr., Uxb. 240 312 BK65
Maylands Way, Rom. 229 311 FQ51
Maynard Clo. N15 221 306 DS56
Maynard Clo. SW6 158 315 DB80
Maynard Clo., Erith 255 319 FF80
Maynard Path E17 223 307 EC57
Maynard Rd. E17 223 307 EC57
Maynards, Horn. 238 311 FL59
Maynards Quay E1 138 317 DW73
Maynooth Gdns., Cars. 285 331 DF101
Mayo Rd. NW10 109 304 CS65
Mayo Rd., Croy. 287 332 DR99
Mayo Rd., Walt. 281 328 BT101
Mayola Rd. E5 118 307 DW63
Mayow Rd. SE23 197 325 DX90
Mayow Rd. SE26 274 325 DX91
Mayplace Clo., Bexh. 263 327 FB83
Mayplace La. SE18 253 318 EP80
Mayplace Rd. E., Bexh. 263 327 FB83
Mayplace Rd. E., Dart. 263 327 FE84
Mayplace Rd. W., Bexh. 263 327 FA84
Maypole Cres., Ilf. 225 308 ER52
Mayroyd Ave., Surb. 282 330 CN103
Mays Ct. WC2 58/9 316 DL73

Mays Hill Rd., Brom. 275 325 EE96
Mays La. E4 211 301 ED47
Mays La., Barn. 206 299 CU45
Mays Rd., Tedd. 267 329 CD92
Maysoule Rd. SW11 175 323 DD84
Mayswood Gdns., Dag. 237 309 FC65
Mayton St. N7 99 306 DM62
Maytree Clo., Edg. 205 298 CQ48
Maytree Clo., Rain. 247 319 FE68
Maytree Wk. SW2 194 324 DN89
Mayville Est. N16 117 306 DS64
Mayville Rd. E11 105 307 EE61
Mayville Rd., Ilf. 235 308 EP64
Maywater Clo., S.Croy. 295 332 DR111
Maywin Dr., Horn. 238 311 FM60
Maywood Clo., Beck. 275 325 EB94
Maze Hill SE3 167 317 EE80
Maze Hill SE10 167 317 EE79
Maze Rd., Rich. 154 314 CN80
Mazenod Ave. NW6 112 305 DA66
McAdam Dr., Enf. 202 300 DP40
McAuley Clo. SE1 72 316 DN76
McAuley Clo. SE9 261 326 EP85
McCall Clo. SW4 161 316 DL82
McCall Cres. SE7 252 318 EL78
McCarthy Rd., Felt. 266 329 BX92
McCoid Way SE1 73 316 DQ75
McCrone Ms. NW3 113 305 DD65
McCullum Rd. E3 129 317 DZ67
McDermott Clo. SW11 175 323 DE83
McDermott Rd. SE15 180 325 DU83
McDonough Clo., Chess. 282 330 CL105
McDowall Rd. SE5 162 316 DQ81
McDowell Clo. E16 141 317 EF71
McEntee Ave. E17 222 307 DY53
McEwan Way E15 131 317 ED67
McGrath Rd. E15 121 307 EF64
McGregor Rd. W11 137 315 CZ71
McIntosh Clo., Rom. 227 309 FE55
McIntosh Clo., Wall. 294 332 DL108
McIntosh Rd., Rom. 227 309 FE55
McKay Rd. SW20 270 323 CV94
McKerrell Rd. SE15 164 317 DU81
McLeod Rd. SE2 254 319 EU77
McLeod's Ms. SW7 76/7 315 DB77
McMillan St. SE8 166 317 EA79
McNeil Rd. SE5 163 316 DS82
McNicol Dr. NW10 124 314 CQ68
McRae La., Mitch. 285 331 DF101
Mead, The N2 219 305 DC54
Mead, The W13 132 314 CH71
Mead, The, Beck. 275 325 EC95
Mead, The, Stan. 216 304 CJ53
Mead, The, Uxb. 231 312 BN61
Mead, The, Wall. 294 332 DK107
Mead, The, W.Wick. 289 333 ED102
Mead Clo., Har. 215 303 CD53
Mead Clo., Rom. 228 310 FG54
Mead Clo., Uxb. 230 312 BG61
Mead Ct. NW9 217 304 CQ57
Mead Cres. E4 211 301 EC49
Mead Cres., Sutt. 285 331 DE105
Mead Gro., Rom. 226 309 EX55
Mead Ho. Rd., Hayes 241 312 BR70
Mead La., Cher. 280 328 BJ102
Mead La. Caravan Pk., Cher. 280 328 BJ102
Mead Path SW17 271 323 DC91
Mead Pl. E9 118 307 DW65
Mead Pl., Croy. 286 332 DP102
Mead Plat NW10 108 304 CQ65
Mead Rd., Chis. 277 326 EQ93
Mead Rd., Edg. 217 304 CN51
Mead Rd., Rich. 184 322 CJ90
Mead Rd., Uxb. 240 312 BK65
Mead Row SE1 72 316 DN76
Mead Way, Brom. 289 333 EE100
Mead Way, Croy. 288 333 DY103
Meadcroft Rd. SE11 162 316 DP79
Meade Clo. W4 154 314 CN79
Meadfield, Edg. 205 298 CP47
Meadfield Grn., Edg. 205 298 CP47
Meadfoot Rd. SW16 272 324 DJ94
Meadhurst Rd., Cher. 280 328 BH102
Meadlands Dr., Rich. 185 322 CK89
Meadow, The, Chis. 277 326 EQ93
Meadow Ave., Croy. 288 333 DX100
Meadow Bank N21 208 300 DM44
Meadow Clo. E4 211 301 EB46
Meadow Clo. E9 119 307 DZ64
Meadow Clo. SE6 275 325 EA92
Meadow Clo. SW20 270 323 CW98
Meadow Clo., Barn. 206 299 CZ44
Meadow Clo., Bexh. 262 327 EZ85
Meadow Clo., Chis. 277 326 EP92
Meadow Clo., Enf. 203 301 DY38
Meadow Clo., Houns. 259 321 CA86
Meadow Clo., Nthlt. 243 313 CA68
Meadow Clo., Pur. 294 332 DK113
Meadow Clo., Rich. 185 322 CL88
Meadow Clo., Ruis. 231 302 BT58
Meadow Clo., Sutt. 284 331 DB103
Meadow Dr. N10 220 306 DG55
Meadow Dr. NW4 218 305 CW54
Meadow Gdns., Edg. 217 304 CP51
Meadow Garth NW10 108 304 CQ65
Meadow Hill, N.Mal. 283 330 CS100
Meadow Hill, Pur. 294 332 DJ113
Meadow La., Cars. 285 331 DE103
Meadow Ms. SW8 161 316 DM79
Meadow Pl. SW8 161 316 DL80
Meadow Pl. W4 155 314 CS80
Meadow Ri., Couls. 294 332 DK113
Meadow Rd. SW8 161 316 DM80
Meadow Rd. SW19 271 323 DC94
Meadow Rd., Ashf. 265 328 BR92
Meadow Rd., Bark. 235 308 ET66
Meadow Rd., Brom. 275 325 EE95
Meadow Rd., Dag. 236 309 EZ65
Meadow Rd., Felt. 258 321 BY89
Meadow Rd., Pnr. 214 303 BX56
Meadow Rd., Rom. 237 309 FC60
Meadow Rd., Sthl. 242 313 BZ73
Meadow Rd., Sutt. 285 331 DE106
Meadow Row SE1 73 316 DQ76
Meadow Stile, Croy. 287 332 DQ104
Meadow Vw., Har. 233 313 CE60
Meadow Vw., Sid. 262 327 EV87
Meadow Vw. Rd., Hayes 241 312 BQ70
Meadow Vw. Rd., Th.Hth. 286 332 DP99
Meadow Wk. E18 224 308 EG56
Meadow Wk., Dag. 236 309 EZ65
Meadow Wk., Wall. 285 332 DH104
Meadow Way NW9 217 304 CR57
Meadow Way, Chess. 282 330 CL106
Meadow Way, Orp. 290 334 EN104
Meadow Way, Ruis. 214 303 BV58
Meadow Way, Upmin. 239 311 FQ62
Meadow Way, Wem. 107 304 CK63
Meadow Way, The, Har. 215 303 CE53
Meadow Waye, Houns. 250 321 BY79
Meadowbank NW3 113 305 DF66
Meadowbank SE3 183 325 EF83
Meadowbank, Surb. 282 330 CM100
Meadowbank Clo. SW6 156 315 CW80
Meadowbank Clo., Barn. 205 298 CT43
Meadowbank Gdns., Houns. 250 321 BU81
Meadowbank Rd. NW9 93 304 CR59
Meadowbanks, Barn. 206 299 CU43
Meadowcourt Rd. SE3 183 325 EF84
Meadowcroft, Brom. 276 326 EM97
Meadowcroft Rd. N13 209 300 DN47
Meadowlands, Horn. 238 311 FL59
Meadowlea Clo., West Dr. 256 320 BK79
Meadows Clo. E10 104 307 EA61
Meadows End, Sun. 266 329 BU95
Meadowside SE9 260 326 EJ84
Meadowside Rd., Sutt. 292 331 CY109
Meadowside Rd., Upmin. 239 311 FQ64
Meadowsweet Clo. E16 244 318 EK71
Meadowview, Orp. 278 327 EW97
Meadowview Rd. SE6 275 325 EA91
Meadowview Rd., Bex. 262 327 EY86
Meads, The, Edg. 217 304 CR51
Meads, The, Sutt. 284 331 CY104
Meads, The, Upmin. 239 311 FS61
Meads, The, Uxb. 240 312 BL70
Meads La., Ilf. 235 308 ES59
Meads Rd. N22 221 306 DP54
Meads Rd., Enf. 203 301 DY39
Meadvale Rd. W5 122 314 CH70
Meadvale Rd., Croy. 287 332 DT101
Meadway N14 208 300 DK47
Meadway NW11 219 305 DB58
Meadway SW20 270 323 CW98
Meadway, Ashf. 265 328 BN91
Meadway, Beck. 275 325 EC95
Meadway, Enf. 203 301 DW37
Meadway, Ilf. 235 308 ES63
Meadway, Rom. 228 310 FG54
Meadway, Ruis. 231 302 BR58
Meadway, Stai. 264 328 BG94
Meadway, Surb. 283 330 CQ102
Meadway, Twick. 259 321 CD88
Meadway, The SE3 167 317 ED82
Meadway, The, Orp. 291 335 EV106
Meadway Clo. NW11 219 305 DB58
Meadway Clo., Pnr. 215 303 CB51
Meadway Ct. NW11 219 305 DB58
Meadway Gdns., Ruis. 231 302 BR58
Meadway Gate NW11 219 305 DA58
Meaford Way SE20 274 325 DV94
Meakin Est. SE1 74/5 316 DS76
Meanley Rd. E12 234 308 EL63
Meard St. W1 46 316 DK72
Meath Clo., Orp. 291 335 EV99
Meath Rd. E15 131 317 EF68
Meath Rd., Ilf. 235 308 EQ62
Meath St. SW11 160 316 DH81
Mechanics Path SE8 166 317 EA80
Mecklenburgh Pl. WC1 35 316 DM70
Mecklenburgh Sq. WC1 35 316 DM70
Mecklenburgh St. WC1 35 316 DM69
Medburn St. NW1 22 316 DK68
Medcalf Rd., Enf. 203 301 DZ37
Medcroft Gdns. SW14 170 322 CQ84
Medebourne Clo. SE3 260 326 EG83
Medesenge Way N13 221 306 DP51
Medfield St. SW15 188 323 CU87
Medhurst Clo. E3 129 317 DY68
Medhurst Rd. E3 129 317 DY68
Median Rd. E5 118 307 DW64
Medina Gro. N7 100 306 DN62
Medina Rd. N7 100 306 DN62
Medland Clo., Wall. 285 332 DG102
Medlar Clo., Nthlt. 242 313 BY68
Medlar St. SE5 162 316 DQ81
Medley Rd. NW6 112 305 DA65
Medman Clo., Uxb. 240 312 BJ68
Medora Rd. SW2 193 324 DM87
Medora Rd., Rom. 227 309 FD56
Medusa Rd. SE6 182 325 EB86
Medway Bldgs. E3 129 317 DY68
Medway Clo., Croy. 288 333 DW100
Medway Clo., Ilf. 235 308 EQ64
Medway Dr., Grnf. 243 313 CF68
Medway Gdns., Wem. 106 304 CG63
Medway Ms. E3 129 317 DY68
Medway Par., Grnf. 243 313 CF68
Medway Rd. E3 129 317 DY68
Medway St. SW1 70 316 DK76
Medwin St. SW4 177 324 DM84
Meerbrook Rd. SE3 260 326 EJ83
Meeson Rd. E15 131 317 EF67
Meeson St. E5 119 307 DY63
Meeting Flds. Path E9 118 307 DW65
Meeting Ho. La. SE15 164 317 DV81
Meetinghouse All. E1 138 317 DV74
Mehetabel Rd. E9 118 307 DW65
Meister Clo., Ilf. 235 308 ER60
Melancholy Wk., Rich. 184 322 CJ89
Melanda Clo., Chis. 276 326 EM92
Melanie Clo., Bexh. 254 319 EY81
Melba Way SE13 166 317 EB81
Melbourne Ave. N13 220 306 DM51
Melbourne Ave. W13 132 314 CG74
Melbourne Ave., Pnr. 215 303 CB55
Melbourne Clo., Orp. 291 334 ES101
Melbourne Clo., Uxb. 241 312 BN63
Melbourne Clo., Wall. 286 332 DJ106
Melbourne Ct. E5 119 307 DY63
Melbourne Ct. N10 220 306 DH52
Melbourne Ct. SE20 274 325 DU94
Melbourne Gdns., Rom. 226 309 EY57
Melbourne Gro. SE22 179 324 DS84
Melbourne Ho., Hayes 242 313 BW70
Melbourne Ms. SE6 198 325 EC87
Melbourne Ms. SW9 162 316 DN81
Melbourne Pl. WC2 59 316 DM73
Melbourne Rd. E6 244 318 EM67
Melbourne Rd. E10 104 307 EB59
Melbourne Rd. E17 222 307 DY56
Melbourne Rd. SW19 271 323 DA95
Melbourne Rd., Ilf. 235 308 EP60
Melbourne Rd., Tedd. 268 322 CJ93
Melbourne Rd., Wall. 285 332 DH106
Melbourne Sq. SW9 162 316 DN81
Melbourne Ter. SW6 158 315 DB80
Melbourne Way, Enf. 209 300 DT44
Melbury Ave., Sthl. 251 321 CB76
Melbury Clo., Cher. 280 328 BG101
Melbury Clo., Chis. 276 326 EL93
Melbury Ct. W8 147 315 CZ76
Melbury Dr. SE5 163 316 DS80
Melbury Gdns. SW20 270 323 CV95
Melbury Rd. W14 147 315 CZ76
Melbury Rd., Har. 216 304 CM57
Melbury Ter. NW1 30/1 315 DE70
Melcombe Gdns., Har. 216 304 CM58
Melcombe Pl. NW1 43 315 DF71
Melcombe St. NW1 31 315 DF70
Meldex Clo. NW7 218 305 CW51
Meldon Clo. SW6 158 315 DB81
Meldone Clo., Surb. 282 330 CP100
Meldrum Rd., Ilf. 236 309 EU61
Melfield Gdns. SE6 275 325 EB91
Melford Ave., Bark. 235 308 ES65
Melford Clo., Chess. 282 330 CM106
Melford Rd. E6 244 318 EM70
Melford Rd. E11 105 307 EE61
Melford Rd. E17 222 307 DY56
Melford Rd. SE22 196 325 DU87
Melford Rd., Ilf. 235 308 ER61
Melfort Ave., Th.Hth. 273 324 DP97
Melfort Rd., Th.Hth. 273 324 DP97
Melgund Rd. N5 116 306 DN64
Melina Clo., Hayes 249 312 BR71
Melina Pl. NW8 30 315 DD69
Melina Rd. W12 146 315 CV75
Melior Pl. SE1 74/5 316 DS75
Melior St. SE1 74 316 DR75
Meliot Rd. SE6 199 325 ED89
Melksham Clo., Rom. 228 311 FM52
Melksham Dr., Rom. 228 311 FM52
Melksham Gdns., Rom. 228 311 FL52
Melksham Grn., Rom. 228 311 FM52
Mell St. SE10 151 317 EE78
Meller Clo., Croy. 286 332 DL104
Melling Dr., Enf. 203 301 DU39
Melling St. SE18 253 318 ES79
Mellish Clo., Bark. 245 318 ET67
Mellish St. E14 150 317 EA76
Mellison Rd. SW17 271 323 DE92
Mellitus St. W12 135 314 CT72
Mellow Clo., Bans. 292 331 DB114
Mellow La. E., Hayes 241 312 BQ69
Mellow La. W., Uxb. 241 312 BQ69
Mellows Rd., Ilf. 224 308 EM55
Mellows Rd., Wall. 286 332 DK106
Mells Cres. SE9 276 326 EM91
Melody La. N5 116 306 DP64
Melody Rd. SW18 174 323 DC85
Melon Pl. W8 64/5 315 DB75
Melon Rd. E11 105 307 EE62
Melon Rd. SE15 164 317 DU81
Melrose Ave. N22 221 306 DP53
Melrose Ave. NW2 110 305 CV64
Melrose Ave. SW16 272 324 DM97
Melrose Ave. SW19 189 323 CZ89
Melrose Ave., Borwd. 205 298 CP43
Melrose Ave., Grnf. 243 313 CB68
Melrose Ave., Mitch. 272 324 DH94
Melrose Ave., Twick. 259 321 CB87
Melrose Clo. SE12 260 326 EG88
Melrose Clo., Grnf. 243 313 CB68
Melrose Clo., Hayes 242 313 BU71
Melrose Cres., Orp. 291 334 ER105
Melrose Dr., Sthl. 243 313 CA74
Melrose Gdns. W6 146 315 CW76
Melrose Gdns., Edg. 217 304 CP54
Melrose Gdns., N.Mal. 269 322 CR97
Melrose Rd. SW13 155 314 CT82
Melrose Rd. SW18 173 323 CZ86
Melrose Rd. SW19 271 323 DA96
Melrose Rd. W3 144 314 CQ76
Melrose Rd., Pnr. 214 303 BZ56
Melrose Ter. W6 146 315 CW75
Melsa Rd., Mord. 285 331 DC100
Melstock Ave., Upmin. 239 311 FQ63
Meltham Way SE16 148 317 DV78
Melthorne Dr., Ruis. 232 313 BW62
Melthorpe Gdns. SE3 252 318 EK81
Melton Clo., Ruis. 232 313 BW60
Melton Ct. SW7 78 315 DD77
Melton Gdns., Rom. 237 309 FF59
Melton St. NW1 33 316 DJ69
Melville Ave. SW20 270 323 CU94
Melville Ave., Grnf. 233 313 CF64
Melville Ave., S.Croy. 287 332 DT106
Melville Clo., Uxb. 231 312 BR62
Melville Gdns. N13 209 300 DN50
Melville Rd. E17 222 307 DZ55
Melville Rd. NW10 109 304 CR66
Melville Rd. SW13 156 315 CU81
Melville Rd., Rom. 227 309 FB52
Melville Rd., Sid. 262 327 EW89
Melville Vil. Rd. W3 135 314 CR74
Melvin Rd. SE20 274 325 DW95
Melyn Clo. N7 114 306 DJ63
Memel Ct. EC1 37 316 DQ70
Memel St. EC1 37 316 DQ70
Memess Path SE18 253 318 EN79
Memorial Ave. E15 131 317 EE69
Memorial Clo., Houns. 250 321 BZ79
Mendip Clo. SE26 274 325 DW91
Mendip Clo. SW19 189 323 CY89
Mendip Clo., Hayes 257 320 BR80
Mendip Clo., Wor.Pk. 284 331 CW103
Mendip Dr. NW2 95 305 CY61
Mendip Rd. SW11 174 323 DC83
Mendip Rd., Bexh. 255 319 FE81
Mendip Rd., Horn. 238 310 FG59
Mendip Rd., Ilf. 225 308 ES57
Mendora Rd. SW6 157 315 CY80
Mendoza Clo., Horn. 228 311 FL57
Menelik Rd. NW2 111 305 CY63
Menlo Gdns. SE19 273 324 DR94
Menotti St. E2 128 317 DU70
Menthone Pl., Horn. 238 310 FK59
Mentmore Clo., Har. 216 304 CJ58
Mentmore Ter. E8 118 307 DV66
Meon Ct., Islw. 251 321 CE82
Meon Rd. W3 144 314 CQ75
Meopham Rd., Mitch. 272 324 DJ95
Mepham Cres., Har. 215 303 CC52
Mepham Gdns., Har. 215 303 CC52
Mepham St. SE1 59 316 DM74
Mera Dr., Bexh. 263 327 FA84
Merantun Way SW19 271 323 DC95
Merbury Clo. SE13 183 325 ED85
Merbury Rd. SE28 253 318 ES75
Mercator Rd. SE13 183 325 ED84
Mercer Pl., Pnr. 214 303 BW54
Mercer St. WC2 46/7 316 DL72
Mercer Wk., Uxb. 240 312 BJ66
Merceron St. E1 128 317 DV70
Mercers Clo. SE10 151 317 EF77
Mercers Pl. W6 146 315 CW77
Mercers Rd. N19 99 306 DK62
Merchant St. E3 129 317 DZ69
Merchiston Rd. SE6 199 325 ED89
Merchland Rd. SE9 261 326 EQ88
Mercia Gro. SE13 182 325 EC84
Mercier Rd. SW15 173 323 CY85
Mercury Cen. Ind. Est., Felt. 258 321 BU85
Mercury Gdns., Rom. 227 309 FE56
Mercury Way SE14 165 317 DX79
Mercy Ter. SE13 182 325 EB84
Mere Clo. SW15 189 323 CX87
Mere Clo., Orp. 290 334 EN103
Mere End, Croy. 288 333 DX101
Mere Rd., Shep. 281 328 BP100
Mere Side, Orp. 290 334 EN103
Merebank La., Croy. 286 332 DM106
Meredith Ave. NW2 110 305 CW64
Meredith Clo., Pnr. 214 303 BX52
Meredith St. E13 244 318 EG69
Meredith St. EC1 36/7 316 DP69
Meredyth Rd. SW13 156 315 CU82
Meretone Clo. SE4 181 325 DY84
Merevale Cres., Mord. 285 331 DC100
Mereway Rd., Twick. 259 321 CD88
Merewood Clo., Brom. 277 326 EN96
Merewood Rd., Bexh. 255 319 FC82
Mereworth Clo., Brom. 289 333 EF99
Mereworth Dr. SE18 253 318 EP80
Merganser Gdns. SE28 253 318 ER76
Meriden Clo., Brom. 276 326 EK94
Meriden Clo., Ilf. 225 308 EQ53
Meridian Gate E14 150 317 EC75
Meridian Rd. SE7 252 318 EK80
Meridian Trd. Est. SE7 252 318 EH77
Meridian Wk. N17 221 306 DS51
Meridian Way N9 210 301 DX47
Meridian Way N18 222 307 DW51
Meridian Way, Enf. 210 301 DX44
Merifield Rd. SE9 260 326 EJ84
Merino Clo. E11 224 308 EJ56
Merino Pl., Sid. 262 327 EU86
Merivale Rd. SW15 173 323 CY84
Merivale Rd., Har. 233 313 CC59
Merle Ave., Uxb. 212 302 BH54
Merlewood Dr., Chis. 276 326 EM95
Merley Ct. NW9 92 304 CQ60
Merlin Clo., Croy. 287 332 DS105
Merlin Clo., Mitch. 271 323 DE97
Merlin Clo., Nthlt. 242 313 BW69
Merlin Clo., Rom. 227 309 FD51
Merlin Cres., Edg. 216 304 CM53
Merlin Gdns., Brom. 260 326 EG90
Merlin Gdns., Rom. 227 309 FD51
Merlin Gro., Beck. 274 325 DZ98
Merlin Gro., Ilf. 225 308 EP51
Merlin Rd. E12 234 308 EK61
Merlin Rd., Rom. 227 309 FD51
Merlin Rd., Well. 262 327 EU84
Merlin Rd. N., Well. 262 327 EU84
Merlin St. WC1 36 316 DN69
Merling Clo., Chess. 282 330 CK106
Merlins Ave., Har. 232 313 BZ62
Mermagen Dr., Rain. 238 310 FH66
Mermaid Ct. SE1 74 316 DR75
Mermaid Ct. SE16 139 317 DZ74
Merredene St. SW2 177 324 DM86
Merriam Clo. E4 211 301 EC50
Merrick Rd., Sthl. 250 321 BZ75
Merrick Sq. SE1 73 316 DQ76
Merridene N21 209 300 DP44
Merrielands Cres., Dag. 246 319 EZ67
Merrilands Rd., Wor.Pk. 284 331 CW102
Merrilees Rd., Sid. 261 326 ES88
Merriman Rd. SE3 252 318 EJ81
Merrington Rd. SW6 158 315 DA79
Merrion Ave., Stan. 204 298 CK50
Merrion Wk. SE17 86 316 DR78
Merritt Rd. SE4 181 325 DZ85
Merrivale N14 208 300 DK44
Merrivale Ave., Ilf. 224 308 EK56
Merrow Rd., Sutt. 292 331 CX109
Merrow St. SE17 162 316 DQ79
Merrow Wk. SE17 86 316 DR78
Merrows Clo., Nthwd. 213 302 BQ51
Merry Meet, Bans. 293 331 DF114
Merrydown Way, Chis. 276 326 EL95
Merryfield SE3 167 317 EF82
Merryfield Gdns., Stan. 204 298 CJ50
Merryfields, Uxb. 240 312 BL68
Merryfields Way SE6 198 325 EB87
Merryhill Clo. E4 211 301 EB45
Merryhills Ct. N14 208 300 DJ43
Mersea Ho., Bark. 235 308 EP65
Mersey Ave., Upmin. 229 311 FR58
Mersey Rd. E17 222 307 DZ55
Mersey Wk., Nthlt. 243 313 CA68
Mersham Dr. NW9 217 304 CN57
Mersham Pl. SE20 274 325 DV95
Mersham Rd., Th.Hth. 273 324 DR97
Merten Rd., Rom. 236 309 EY59
Merthyr Ter. SW13 156 315 CV79
Merton Ave. W4 145 314 CT77
Merton Ave., Nthlt. 233 313 CC64
Merton Ave., Uxb. 241 312 BP66
Merton Gdns., Orp. 290 334 EP99
Merton Hall Gdns. SW20 270 323 CY95
Merton Hall Rd. SW19 270 323 CY94
Merton High St. SW19 271 323 DC94
Merton Ind. Pk. SW19 271 323 DC95
Merton La. N6 97 305 DF61
Merton Mans. SW20 270 323 CX96
Merton Pk. Par. SW19 270 323 CZ95
Merton Ri. NW3 113 305 DE66
Merton Rd. E17 223 307 EC57
Merton Rd. SE25 287 333 DU99
Merton Rd. SW18 174 323 DA85
Merton Rd. SW19 271 323 DB94
Merton Rd., Bark. 235 308 ET66
Merton Rd., Enf. 202 300 DR38
Merton Rd., Har. 233 313 CC60
Merton Rd., Ilf. 235 308 ET59
Merton Way, Uxb. 241 312 BP66
Merton Way, W.Mol. 267 329 CB98
Merttins Rd. SE15 181 325 DX85
Meru Clo. NW5 114 306 DG63
Mervan Rd. SW2 178 324 DN84
Mervyn Ave. SE9 261 326 EQ90
Mervyn Rd. W13 142 314 CG76
Mervyn Rd., Shep. 281 328 BQ101
Messaline Ave. W3 134 314 CQ72
Messant Clo., Rom. 228 310 FK54
Messent Rd. SE9 260 326 EJ85
Messeter Pl. SE9 261 326 EN86
Messina Ave. NW6 112 305 DA66
Metcalf Rd., Ashf. 265 328 BP92
Metcalfe Wk., Felt. 266 329 BY91
Meteor St. SW11 176 324 DG84
Meteor Way, Wall. 294 332 DL108
Metheringham Way NW9 217 304 CS53
Methley St. SE11 84 316 DN78
Methuen Clo., Edg. 217 304 CN52
Methuen Pk. N10 220 306 DH54
Methuen Rd., Belv. 255 319 FB77
Methuen Rd., Bexh. 262 327 EZ84
Methuen Rd., Edg. 217 304 CN52
Methwold Rd. W10 137 315 CX71
Metro Ind. Cen., Islw. 251 321 CE82
Metropolitan Cen., The, Grnf. 243 313 CB67
Mews, The N1 25 316 DQ67
Mews, The, Ilf. 224 308 EK57
Mews, The, Rom. 227 309 FE56
Mews, The, Twick. 168 322 CH86
Mews Deck E1 138 317 DV73
Mews St. E1 138 317 DU74
Mexfield Rd. SW15 173 323 CZ85
Meyer Gro., Enf. 203 301 DU38
Meyer Rd., Erith 255 319 FC79
Meymott St. SE1 60/1 316 DP74
Meynell Cres. E9 119 307 DX66
Meynell Gdns. E9 119 307 DX66
Meynell Rd. E9 119 307 DX66
Meynell Rd., Rom. 228 310 FH52
Meyrick Rd. NW10 110 305 CU65
Meyrick Rd. SW11 175 323 DD83
Mezen Clo., Nthwd. 213 302 BR50
Miah Ter. E1 138 317 DU74
Miall Wk. SE26 274 325 DY91
Micawber Ave., Uxb. 241 312 BN70
Micawber St. N1 37 316 DQ69
Michael Faraday Ho. SE17 86/7 316 DS78
Michael Gdns., Horn. 228 310 FK56
Michael Gaynor Clo. W7 243 313 CF74
Michael Rd. E11 105 307 EE60
Michael Rd. SE25 273 324 DS97
Michael Rd. SW6 158 315 DB81
Michaelmas Clo. SW20 270 323 CW97
Michaels Clo. SE13 183 325 EE84
Micheldever Rd. SE12 183 325 EE86
Michelham Gdns., Twick. 184 322 CG90
Michels Row, Rich. 169 322 CL84
Michigan Ave. E12 234 308 EM63
Michleham Down N12 206 299 CZ49
Mickleham Clo., Orp. 277 326 ET96
Mickleham Gdns., Sutt. 292 331 CY107
Mickleham Rd., Orp. 277 326 ET95
Micklethwaite Rd. SW6 158 315 DA79
Midas Met. Ind. Est., The, Mord. 284 331 CX102
Midcroft, Ruis. 231 312 BS60
Middle Dene NW7 205 298 CR48
Middle Fld. NW8 18 315 DD67
Middle Grn., Stai. 264 328 BK94
Middle Grn. Clo., Surb. 282 330 CM100
Middle La. N8 220 306 DL57
Middle La., Tedd. 267 329 CF93
Middle La. Ms. N8 220 306 DL57
Middle Pk. Ave. SE9 260 326 EK86
Middle Path, Har. 233 313 CD60
Middle Rd. E13 244 318 EG68
Middle Rd. SW16 272 324 DJ96
Middle Rd., Barn. 207 299 DE44
Middle Rd., Har. 233 313 CD61
Middle Row W10 127 315 CY70
Middle St. EC1 49 316 DQ71
Middle St., Croy. 287 332 DQ104
Middle Temple EC4 60 316 DN73
Middle Temple La. EC4 48 316 DN72
Middle Way SW16 272 324 DK96
Middle Way, Erith 254 319 EY76
Middle Way, Hayes 242 313 BX70
Middle Way, The, Har. 215 303 CF54
Middle Yd. SE1 62/3 316 DS74
Middlefield Gdns., Ilf. 225 308 EP58
Middlefielde W13 132 314 CH71
Middleham Gdns. N18 222 307 DU51
Middleham Rd. N18 222 307 DU51
Middlesborough Rd. N18 222 307 DU51
Middlesex Bus. Cen., The, Sthl. 250 321 BZ75
Middlesex Ct. W4 145 314 CT77
Middlesex Pas. EC1 48/9 316 DP71
Middlesex Rd., Mitch. 272 324 DL98
Middlesex St. E1 50/1 316 DS71
Middlesex Wf. E5 102 307 DW61
Middleton Ave. E4 210 301 DZ49
Middleton Ave., Grnf. 243 313 CD68
Middleton Ave., Sid. 278 327 EW93
Middleton Bldgs. W1 45 316 DJ71
Middleton Clo. E4 210 301 DZ48
Middleton Dr. SE16 149 317 DX75
Middleton Dr., Pnr. 214 303 BU55
Middleton Gdns., Ilf. 225 308 EP58
Middleton Gro. N7 115 306 DL64
Middleton Ms. N7 115 306 DL64
Middleton Rd. E8 117 306 DT66
Middleton Rd. NW11 96 305 DA59
Middleton Rd., Cars. 285 331 DD101
Middleton Rd., Hayes 249 312 BR71
Middleton Rd., Mord. 284 331 DB100
Middleton St. E2 128 317 DV69
Middleton Way SE13 183 325 ED84
Middleway NW11 219 305 DB57
Midfield Ave., Bexh. 263 327 FC83
Midfield Way, Orp. 278 327 EU95
Midford Pl. W1 33 316 DJ70
Midholm NW11 219 305 DB56
Midholm, Wem. 92 304 CN60
Midholm Clo. NW11 219 305 DB56
Midholm Rd., Croy. 288 333 DY103
Midhope St. WC1 34/5 316 DL69
Midhurst Ave. N10 220 306 DG55
Midhurst Ave., Croy. 286 332 DN101
Midhurst Clo., Horn. 238 310 FG63
Midhurst Gdns., Uxb. 241 312 BQ66
Midhurst Hill, Bexh. 263 327 FA86
Midhurst Rd. W13 142 314 CG75
Midland Pl. E14 150 317 EC78
Midland Rd. E10 104 307 EC59
Midland Rd. NW1 22 316 DK68
Midland Ter. NW2 95 305 CX62
Midland Ter. NW10 125 314 CS70
Midleton Rd., N.Mal. 269 322 CQ96
Midlothian Rd. E3 139 317 DY71
Midmoor Rd. SW12 192 324 DJ88
Midmoor Rd. SW19 270 323 CX95
Midship Clo. SE16 139 317 DX74
Midstrath Rd. NW10 109 304 CS63
Midsummer Ave., Houns. 258 321 BZ84
Midway, Sutt. 284 331 CZ101
Midway Ave., Cher. 280 328 BG97
Midwinter Clo., Well. 262 327 EU83
Midwood Clo. NW2 94 305 CV62
Miers Clo. E6 245 318 EN67
Mighell Ave., Ilf. 224 308 EK57
Milborne Gro. SW10 77 315 DC78
Milborne St. E9 118 307 DW65
Milborough Cres. SE12 183 325 EE86
Milburn Dr., West Dr. 248 312 BL73
Milcote St. SE1 72/3 316 DP75
Mildenhall Rd. E5 118 307 DW63
Mildmay Ave. N1 117 306 DR65
Mildmay Gro. N. N1 117 306 DR64
Mildmay Gro. S. N1 117 306 DR64
Mildmay Pk. N1 117 306 DR64
Mildmay Rd. N1 117 306 DR64
Mildmay Rd., Ilf. 235 308 EP62
Mildmay Rd., Rom. 227 309 FC57
Mildmay St. N1 117 306 DR65
Mildred Ave., Hayes 249 320 BR77
Mildred Ave., Nthlt. 233 313 CB64
Mildred Rd., Erith 255 319 FE78
Mile End, The E17 222 307 DX53
Mile End Pl. E1 129 317 DX70
Mile End Rd. E1 138 317 DW71
Mile End Rd. E3 129 317 DY70
Mile Rd., Wall. 285 332 DH102
Miles Pl. NW1 42/3 315 DE71
Miles Pl., Surb. 268 322 CM98
Miles Rd. N8 220 306 DL55
Miles Rd., Mitch. 271 323 DD97
Miles St. SW8 161 316 DL79
Miles Way N20 207 299 DE47
Milespit Hill NW7 206 299 CV50
Milestone Clo. N9 210 301 DU47
Milestone Clo., Sutt. 293 331 DD107
Milestone Rd. SE19 273 324 DT93
Milfoil St. W12 136 315 CU73
Milford Clo. SE2 254 319 EY79
Milford Gdns., Croy. 288 333 DX99
Milford Gdns., Edg. 217 304 CN52
Milford Gdns., Wem. 107 304 CK63
Milford Gro., Sutt. 285 331 DC105
Milford La. WC2 59 316 DM73
Milford Ms. SW16 193 324 DM90
Milford Rd. W13 132 314 CH74
Milford Rd., Sthl. 243 313 CA73
Milford Way SE15 163 316 DT81
Milk St. E16 245 318 EP74
Milk St. EC2 49 316 DQ72
Milk St., Brom. 276 326 EH93
Milk Yd. E1 138 317 DW73
Milkwell Gdns., Wdf.Grn. 224 308 EH52
Milkwell Yd. SE5 162 316 DQ81
Milkwood Rd. SE24 178 324 DP85
Mill Ave., Uxb. 240 312 BJ68
Mill Brook Rd., Orp. 278 327 EW98
Mill Clo., Cars. 285 332 DG103
Mill Clo., West Dr. 248 320 BK76
Mill Ct. E10 104 307 EC62
Mill Fm. Ave., Sun. 265 328 BS94
Mill Fm. Clo., Pnr. 214 303 BW54
Mill Fm. Cres., Houns. 258 321 BY88
Mill Gdns. SE26 274 325 DV91
Mill Grn. Rd., Mitch. 285 331 DF101
Mill Hill SW13 156 315 CU82
Mill Hill Circ. NW7 205 298 CT50
Mill Hill Gro. W3 134 314 CP74
Mill Hill Rd. SW13 156 315 CU82
Mill Hill Rd. W3 144 314 CP75
Mill La. NW6 111 305 CY64
Mill La. SE18 253 318 EN78
Mill La., Cars. 285 331 DF105
Mill La., Croy. 286 332 DM104
Mill La. (Chadwell Heath), Rom. 226 309 EY58
Mill La., Wdf.Grn. 211 301 EF50
Mill Mead Ind. Cen. N17 222 307 DV54
Mill Mead Rd. N17 222 307 DV55
Mill Pk. Ave., Horn. 238 311 FL61
Mill Pl. E14 139 317 DZ72
Mill Pl., Chis. 277 326 EP95
Mill Pl., Kings.T. 268 322 CM97
Mill Plat, Islw. 152 314 CG82
Mill Plat Ave., Islw. 152 314 CG82
Mill Ridge, Edg. 204 298 CM50
Mill Rd. E16 244 318 EH74
Mill Rd. SE13 182 325 EC83
Mill Rd. SW19 271 323 DC94
Mill Rd., Erith 255 319 FC80
Mill Rd., Ilf. 235 308 EN62
Mill Rd., Twick. 259 321 CC89
Mill Rd., West Dr. 248 320 BJ76
Mill Row N1 26/7 316 DS67
Mill Shot Clo. SW6 156 315 CW81
Mill St. SE1 75 316 DT75
Mill St. W1 57 316 DJ73
Mill St., Kings.T. 268 322 CL97
Mill Trd. Est., The NW10 124 314 CQ69
Mill Vale, Brom. 275 325 EF96
Mill Vw. Gdns., Croy. 288 333 DX104
Mill Way, Felt. 258 321 BV85
Mill Yd. E1 138 317 DU73
Millais Ave. E12 235 308 EN64
Millais Gdns., Edg. 217 304 CN54
Millais Rd. E11 120 307 EC63
Millais Rd., Enf. 209 300 DT43
Millais Rd., N.Mal. 283 330 CS101
Millais Way, Epsom 283 330 CQ105
Millard Clo. N16 117 306 DS64
Millard Ter., Dag. 237 309 FA65
Millbank SW1 82/3 316 DL77
Millbank, Stai. 264 328 BH92
Millbank Twr. SW1 82/3 316 DL77
Millbank Way SE12 260 326 EG85
Millbourne Rd., Felt. 266 329 BY91
Millbrook Ave., Well. 261 326 ER84
Millbrook Gdns., Rom. 227 309 FE54
Millbrook Gdns.
(Chadwell Heath), Rom. 226 309 EZ58
Millbrook Rd. N9 210 301 DV46
Millbrook Rd. SW9 178 324 DP83
Millender Wk. SE16 148 317 DW77
Millennium Pl. E2 128 317 DV68
Millennium Sq. SE1 75 316 DT75
Miller Clo., Mitch. 285 331 DF101
Miller Clo., Pnr. 214 303 BW54
Miller Rd. SW19 271 323 DD93
Miller Rd., Croy. 286 332 DM102
Miller St. NW1 21 316 DJ68
Miller Wk. SE1 60 316 DN74
Miller's Ave. E8 117 306 DT64
Millers Clo. NW7 206 299 CU49
Millers Clo., Stai. 264 328 BH92
Millers Ct. W4 145 314 CT78
Millers Grn. Clo., Enf. 202 300 DP41
Millers Meadow Clo. SE3 183 325 EF85
Miller's Ter. E8 117 306 DT64
Millers Way W6 146 315 CW75
Millet Rd., Grnf. 243 313 CB69
Millfield, Sun. 281 328 BR95
Millfield Ave. E17 222 307 DY53
Millfield La. N6 97 305 DF61
Millfield Pl. N6 98 306 DG61
Millfield Rd., Edg. 217 304 CQ54
Millfield Rd., Houns. 258 321 BY88
Millfields Clo., Orp. 278 327 EV98
Millfields Est. E5 103 307 DX62
Millfields Rd. E5 118 307 DW63
Millgrove St. SW11 160 316 DG81
Millharbour E14 150 317 EB76
Millhaven Clo., Rom. 226 309 EV58
Millhouse Pl. SE27 273 324 DP91
Millicent Rd. E10 103 307 DZ60
Milligan St. E14 139 317 DZ73
Milling Rd., Edg. 217 304 CR52
Millington Rd., Hayes 249 320 BS76
Millman Ms. WC1 35 316 DM70
Millman Pl. WC1 35 316 DM70
Millman St. WC1 35 316 DM70
Millmark Gro. SE14 165 317 DY82
Millmarsh La., Enf. 203 301 DY40
Millpond Est. SE16 148 317 DV75
Mills Clo., Uxb. 241 312 BN68
Mills Ct. EC2 38/9 316 DS70
Mills Gro. E14 140 317 EC71
Mills Gro. NW4 218 305 CX55

Mills Row W4	145	314	CR77
Millside, Cars.	285	331	DF103
Millside Pl., Islw.	152	314	CH82
Millson Clo. N20	207	299	DD47
Millstream Clo. N13	209	300	DN50
Millstream Rd. SE1	75	316	DT75
Millwall Dock Rd. E14	150	317	EA76
Millway NW7	205	298	CS50
Millway Gdns., Nthlt.	232	313	BZ65
Millwood Rd., Houns.	259	321	CC85
Millwood Rd., Orp.	278	327	EW97
Millwood St. W10	137	315	CY71
Milman Clo., Pnr.	214	303	BX55
Milman Rd. NW6	127	315	CX68
Milman's St. SW10	159	315	DD79
Milne Feild, Pnr.	215	303	CA52
Milne Gdns. SE9	260	326	EL85
Milne Way, Uxb.	212	302	BH53
Milner Dr., Twick.	259	321	CD87
Milner Pl. N1	24	316	DN67
Milner Pl., Cars.	285	332	DG105
Milner Rd. E15	131	317	EE69
Milner Rd. SW19	271	323	DB95
Milner Rd., Dag.	236	309	EW61
Milner Rd., Kings.T.	268	322	CK97
Milner Rd., Mord.	285	331	DD99
Milner Rd., Th.Hth.	273	324	DR97
Milner Sq. N1	116	306	DP66
Milner St. SW3	79	315	DF77
Milnthorpe Rd. W4	155	314	CR79
Milo Rd. SE22	179	324	DT86
Milroy Wk. SE1	60/1	316	DP74
Milson Rd. W14	147	315	CX76
Milton Ave. E6	234	308	EK66
Milton Ave. N6	98	306	DJ59
Milton Ave. NW9	217	304	CQ55
Milton Ave. NW10	124	314	CQ67
Milton Ave., Barn.	206	299	CZ43
Milton Ave., Croy.	287	332	DR101
Milton Ave., Horn.	237	309	FF61
Milton Ave., Sutt.	285	331	DD104
Milton Clo. N2	219	305	DC57
Milton Clo. SE1	87	316	DT77
Milton Clo., Hayes	242	313	BU72
Milton Clo., Sutt.	285	331	DD104
Milton Ct. EC2	50	316	DR71
Milton Ct., Uxb.	231	312	BP62
Milton Ct. Rd. SE14	165	317	DY79
Milton Cres., Ilf.	235	308	EQ59
Milton Dr., Borwd.	205	298	CP43
Milton Dr., Shep.	280	328	BL98
Milton Gdn. Est. N16	117	306	DS63
Milton Gdns., Stai.	264	320	BM88
Milton Gro. N11	208	300	DJ50
Milton Gro. N16	117	306	DR63
Milton Pk. N6	98	306	DJ59
Milton Pl. N7	116	306	DN64
Milton Rd. E17	223	307	EA56
Milton Rd. N6	98	306	DJ59
Milton Rd. N15	221	306	DP56
Milton Rd. NW7	206	299	CU50
Milton Rd. NW9	94	305	CU59
Milton Rd. SE24	178	324	DP86
Milton Rd. SW14	171	322	CR83
Milton Rd. SW19	271	323	DC93
Milton Rd. W3	135	314	CR74
Milton Rd. W7	243	313	CF73
Milton Rd., Belv.	255	319	FA77
Milton Rd., Croy.	287	332	DR102
Milton Rd., Hmptn.	267	329	CA94
Milton Rd., Har.	215	303	CE56
Milton Rd., Mitch.	272	324	DG94
Milton Rd., Rom.	228	310	FG58
Milton Rd., Sutt.	284	331	DA104
Milton Rd., Uxb.	241	312	BN63
Milton Rd., Wall.	294	332	DJ107
Milton Rd., Well.	253	318	ET81
Milton St. EC2	50	316	DR71
Milton Way, West Dr.	248	320	BM77
Milverton Dr., Uxb.	241	312	BQ63
Milverton Gdns., Ilf.	235	308	ET61
Milverton Rd. NW6	110	305	CW66
Milverton St. SE11	84	316	DN78
Milverton Way SE9	277	326	EN91
Milward St. E1	138	317	DV71
Milward Wk. SE18	253	318	EN79
Mimosa Clo., Rom.	228	310	FJ52
Mimosa Rd., Hayes	242	313	BW71
Mimosa St. SW6	157	315	CZ81
Mina Rd. SE17	86/7	316	DS78
Mina Rd. SW19	271	323	DA95
Minard Rd. SE6	199	325	EE87
Minchenden Cres. N14	208	300	DJ48
Mincing La. EC3	62/3	316	DS73
Minden Rd. SE20	274	325	DV95
Minden Rd., Sutt.	284	331	CZ103
Minehead Rd. SW16	272	324	DM92
Minehead Rd., Har.	233	313	CA62
Minera Ms. SW1	80	316	DG77
Mineral St. SE18	253	318	ES77
Minerva Clo. SW9	162	316	DN80
Minerva Clo., Sid.	261	326	ES90
Minerva Rd. E4	223	307	EB52
Minerva Rd. NW10	124	314	CQ69
Minerva Rd., Kings.T.	268	322	CM96
Minerva St. E2	128	317	DV68
Minet Ave. NW10	125	314	CS68
Minet Dr., Hayes	242	313	BU74
Minet Gdns. NW10	125	314	CS68
Minet Gdns., Hayes	242	313	BU74
Minet Rd. SW9	162	316	DP82
Minford Gdns. W14	147	315	CX75
Ming St. E14	140	317	EA73
Mingard Wk. N7	99	306	DM61
Ministry Way SE9	260	326	EM89
Miniver Pl. EC4	61	316	DQ73
Mink Ct., Houns.	250	321	BW82
Minniedale, Surb.	282	330	CM99
Minnow St. SE17	86/7	316	DS77
Minnow Wk. SE17	86/7	316	DS77
Minories EC3	51	316	DT72
Minshull Pl., Beck.	275	325	EA94
Minshull St. SW8	161	316	DK81
Minson Rd. E9	129	317	DX67
Minstead Gdns. SW15	187	322	CT87
Minstead Way, N.Mal.	283	330	CS100
Minster Ave., Sutt.	284	331	DA103
Minster Ct. EC3	62	316	DR73
Minster Dr., Croy.	287	332	DS105
Minster Pavement EC3	62	316	DR73
Minster Rd. NW2	111	305	CY64
Minster Rd., Brom.	276	326	EH94
Minster Wk. N8	220	306	DL56
Minster Way, Horn.	238	311	FM60
Minsterley Ave., Shep.	281	328	BS98
Minstrel Gdns., Surb.	282	330	CM99
Mint Clo., Uxb.	241	312	BP69
Mint Rd., Wall.	285	332	DH105
Mint St. SE1	73	316	DQ75
Mint Wk., Croy.	287	332	DQ104
Mintern Clo. N13	209	300	DP48
Mintern St. N1	26	316	DR68
Minterne Ave., Sthl.	251	321	CA77
Minterne Rd., Har.	216	304	CM57
Minterne Waye, Hayes	242	313	BW72
Minton Ms. NW6	112	305	DB65
Mirabel Rd. SW6	157	315	CZ80
Miramar Way, Horn.	238	310	FK64
Miranda Clo. E1	138	317	DW71
Miranda Ct. W3	133	314	CM72
Miranda Rd. N19	98	306	DJ60
Mirfield St. SE7	252	318	EK76
Miriam Rd. SE18	253	318	ES78
Mirror Path SE9	260	326	EJ90
Misbourne Rd., Uxb.	241	312	BN67
Missenden Clo., Felt.	265	320	BT88
Missenden Gdns., Mord.	285	331	DC100
Mission Gro. E17	222	307	DY57
Mission Pl. SE15	164	317	DU81
Mission Sq., Brent.	153	314	CL79
Mistletoe Clo., Croy.	288	333	DX102
Mitali Pas. E1	138	317	DU72
Mitcham Gdn. Village, Mitch.	285	332	DG99
Mitcham Ind. Est., Mitch.	272	324	DG95
Mitcham La. SW16	272	324	DH93
Mitcham Pk., Mitch.	271	323	DE98
Mitcham Rd. E6	244	318	EL69
Mitcham Rd. SW17	271	323	DF92
Mitcham Rd., Croy.	286	332	DL100
Mitcham Rd., Ilf.	235	308	ET59
Mitchell Clo. SE2	254	319	EW77
Mitchell Clo., Belv.	255	319	FC76
Mitchell Rd. N13	209	300	DP50
Mitchell Rd., Orp.	291	334	ET105
Mitchell St. EC1	37	316	DQ70
Mitchell Wk. E6	244	318	EL71
Mitchell Way NW10	108	304	CQ65
Mitchell Way, Brom.	276	326	EG95
Mitchellbrook Way NW10	109	304	CR65
Mitchison Rd. N1	117	306	DR65
Mitchley Ave., Pur.	295	332	DQ113
Mitchley Ave., S.Croy.	295	332	DS113
Mitchley Gro., S.Croy.	295	333	DU113
Mitchley Hill, S.Croy.	295	332	DS113
Mitchley Rd. N17	222	307	DU55
Mitchley Vw., S.Croy.	295	333	DU113
Mitford Rd. N19	99	306	DL61
Mitre, The E14	139	317	DZ73
Mitre Ave. E17	222	307	DZ55
Mitre Clo., Brom.	275	325	EF96
Mitre Clo., Shep.	281	328	BR100
Mitre Clo., Sutt.	293	331	DC108
Mitre Ct. EC2	49	316	DQ72
Mitre Ct. EC4	48	316	DN72
Mitre Rd. E15	131	317	EE68
Mitre Rd. SE1	72	316	DN75
Mitre Sq. EC3	50/1	316	DS72
Mitre St. EC3	50/1	316	DS72
Mitre Way NW10	126	315	CV70
Moat, The, N.Mal.	269	322	CS95
Moat Cres. N3	219	305	DB55
Moat Cft., Well.	262	327	EW83
Moat Dr. E13	244	318	EJ68
Moat Dr., Har.	215	303	CC56
Moat Dr., Ruis.	231	312	BS59
Moat Fm. Rd., Nthlt.	232	313	BZ65
Moat Pl. SW9	177	324	DM83
Moat Pl. W3	134	314	CP72
Moat Pl., Uxb.	240	312	BH63
Moatside, Enf.	203	301	DW42
Moatside, Felt.	266	329	BW91
Moberley Rd. SW4	193	324	DK87
Modbury Gdns. NW5	114	306	DG65
Modder Pl. SW15	173	323	CX84
Model Cotts. SW14	170	322	CQ84
Model Fm. Clo. SE9	260	326	EL90
Modling Ho. E2	129	317	DX69
Moelwyn Hughes Ct. N7	115	306	DK64
Moelyn Ms., Har.	216	304	CG57
Moffat Rd. N13	220	306	DL51
Moffat Rd. SW17	271	323	DE91
Moffat Rd., Th.Hth.	273	324	DQ96
Mogden La., Islw.	259	321	CE85
Mohmmad Khan Rd. E11	105	307	EF60
Moiety Rd. E14	150	317	EA75
Moir Clo., S.Croy.	295	333	DU109
Moira Clo. N17	221	306	DS54
Moira Rd. SE9	260	326	EM84
Moland Mead SE16	149	317	DX78
Molash Rd., Orp.	278	327	EX98
Molasses Row SW11	174	323	DC83
Mole Abbey Gdns., W.Mol.	267	329	CA97
Mole Ct., Epsom	283	330	CQ105
Molescroft SE9	261	326	EQ90
Molesey Dr., Sutt.	284	331	CY103
Molesford Rd. SW6	158	315	DA81
Molesham Clo., W.Mol.	267	329	CB97
Molesham Way, W.Mol.	267	329	CB97
Molesworth St. SE13	182	325	EC84
Molineaux Pl., Tedd.	268	322	CG92
Mollison Ave., Enf.	210	301	DY43
Mollison Dr., Wall.	294	332	DK108
Mollison Way, Edg.	216	304	CM54
Molly Huggins Clo. SW12	192	324	DJ87
Molyneux St. W1	42/3	315	DE71
Mona Rd. SE15	164	317	DW82
Mona St. E16	141	317	EF71
Monahan Ave., Pur.	294	332	DM112
Monarch Clo., Felt.	265	320	BS87
Monarch Clo., W.Wick.	289	333	EF105
Monarch Dr. E16	244	318	EK71
Monarch Ms. E17	223	307	EB57
Monarch Ms. SW16	273	324	DN92
Monarch Rd., Belv.	255	319	FA76
Monarchs Way, Ruis.	231	312	BR60
Monastery Gdns., Enf.	202	300	DR40
Monaveen Gdns., W.Mol.	267	329	CA97
Monck St. SW1	70	316	DK76
Monclar Rd. SE5	179	324	DR84
Moncorvo Clo. SW7	66/7	315	DE75
Moncrieff Clo. E6	244	318	EL72
Moncrieff Pl. SE15	164	317	DU82
Moncrieff St. SE15	164	317	DU82
Mondial Way, Hayes	257	320	BQ80
Monega Rd. E7	234	308	EJ65
Monega Rd. E12	234	308	EK65
Money La., West Dr.	248	320	BK76
Monier Rd. E3	120	307	EA66
Monivea Rd., Beck.	274	325	DZ94
Monk Dr. E16	244	318	EG72
Monk Pas. E16	244	318	EG73
Monk St. SE18	253	318	EN77
Monkfrith Ave. N14	208	300	DH44
Monkfrith Clo. N14	208	300	DH45
Monkfrith Way N14	208	300	DG45
Monkleigh Rd., Mord.	270	323	CY97
Monks Ave., Barn.	207	299	DC44
Monks Clo. SE2	254	319	EX77
Monks Clo., Enf.	202	300	DQ40
Monks Clo., Har.	233	313	CB61
Monks Clo., Ruis.	232	313	BX63
Monks Dr. W3	134	314	CN71
Monks Orchard Rd., Beck.	288	333	EA102
Monks Pk., Wem.	108	304	CP65
Monks Pk. Gdns., Wem.	108	304	CP66
Monks Rd., Enf.	202	300	DQ40
Monks Way NW11	218	305	CZ56
Monks Way, Beck.	288	333	EA100
Monks Way, Orp.	291	334	EQ102
Monks Way, Stai.	264	328	BK94
Monks Way, West Dr.	256	320	BL79
Monksdene Gdns., Sutt.	284	331	DB104
Monkswell Ct. N10	220	306	DG53
Monkswood Gdns., Borwd.	205	298	CR43
Monkswood Gdns., Ilf.	225	308	EN55
Monkton Rd., Well.	253	318	ET82
Monkton St. SE11	84	316	DN77
Monkville Ave. NW11	218	305	CZ56
Monkwell Sq. EC2	49	316	DQ71
Monmouth Ave. E18	224	308	EH55
Monmouth Ave., Kings.T.	268	322	CJ94
Monmouth Clo. W4	145	314	CR76
Monmouth Clo., Mitch.	272	324	DL98
Monmouth Clo., Well.	262	327	EU84
Monmouth Gro. W5	143	314	CL77
Monmouth Pl. W2	40	315	DA72
Monmouth Rd. E6	244	318	EM69
Monmouth Rd. N9	210	301	DV47
Monmouth Rd. W2	40	315	DA72
Monmouth Rd., Dag.	236	309	EZ64
Monmouth Rd., Hayes	249	320	BS77
Monmouth St. WC2	46/7	316	DL72
Monnery Rd. N19	98	306	DJ62
Monnow Rd. SE1	148	317	DU78
Mono La., Felt.	258	321	BV89
Monoux Gro. E17	223	307	EA53
Monro Gdns., Har.	215	303	CE52
Monroe Cres., Enf.	203	301	DV39
Monroe Dr. SW14	170	322	CP85
Mons Way, Brom.	290	334	EL100
Monsal Ct. E5	119	307	DX63
Monsell Rd. N4	100	306	DP62
Monson Rd. NW10	126	315	CU68
Monson Rd. SE14	165	317	DX80
Montacute Rd. SE6	197	325	DZ87
Montacute Rd., Mord.	285	331	DC100
Montagu Cres. N18	210	301	DV49
Montagu Gdns. N18	210	301	DV49
Montagu Gdns., Wall.	286	332	DJ105
Montagu Mans. W1	43	315	DF71
Montagu Ms. N. W1	43	315	DF71
Montagu Ms. S. W1	43	315	DF72
Montagu Ms. W. W1	43	315	DF72
Montagu Pl. W1	43	315	DF71
Montagu Rd. N9	210	301	DW48
Montagu Rd. N18	210	301	DV50
Montagu Rd. NW4	218	305	CU58
Montagu Rd. Ind. Est. N18	210	301	DW49
Montagu Row W1	43	315	DF71
Montagu Sq. W1	43	315	DF71
Montagu St. W1	43	315	DF72
Montague Ave. SE4	181	325	DZ84
Montague Ave. W7	243	313	CF74
Montague Ave., S.Croy.	295	332	DS112
Montague Clo. SE1	62	316	DR74
Montague Gdns. W3	134	314	CN73
Montague Pl. WC1	46	316	DK71
Montague Rd. E8	118	307	DU64
Montague Rd. E11	105	307	EF62
Montague Rd. N8	220	306	DM57
Montague Rd. N15	222	307	DU56
Montague Rd. SW19	271	323	DB94
Montague Rd. W7	251	321	CF75
Montague Rd. W13	132	314	CH72
Montague Rd., Croy.	286	332	DP102
Montague Rd., Houns.	259	321	CB83
Montague Rd., Rich.	169	322	CL86
Montague Rd., Sthl.	250	321	BY77
Montague Rd., Uxb.	240	312	BK66
Montague Sq. SE15	164	317	DW80
Montague St. EC1	49	316	DQ71
Montague St. WC1	46/7	316	DL71
Montague Waye, Sthl.	250	321	BY76
Montalt Rd., Wdf.Grn.	211	301	EF50
Montana Clo., S.Croy.	295	332	DQ110
Montana Gdns., Sutt.	285	331	DC106
Montana Rd. SW17	272	324	DG91
Montana Rd. SW20	270	323	CW95
Montbelle Rd. SE9	261	326	EP90
Montbretia Clo., Orp.	278	327	EW98
Montcalm Clo., Brom.	289	334	EG100
Montcalm Clo., Hayes	242	313	BV69
Montcalm Rd. SE7	252	318	EK80
Montclare St. E2	39	316	DT70
Monteagle Ave., Bark.	235	308	EQ65
Monteagle Way E5	102	307	DU62
Monteagle Way SE15	180	325	DV83
Montefiore St. SW8	160	316	DH82
Montego Clo. SE24	178	324	DN84
Monteith Rd. E3	129	317	DZ67
Montem Rd. SE23	197	325	DZ87
Montem Rd., N.Mal.	269	322	CS98
Montem St. N4	99	306	DM60
Montenotte Rd. N8	220	306	DJ57
Monterey Clo., Bex.	263	327	FC89
Montesole Ct., Pnr.	214	303	BW54
Montford Pl. SE11	84	316	DN78
Montford Rd., Sun.	266	329	BU98
Montfort Gdns., Ilf.	225	308	EQ51
Montfort Pl. SW19	189	323	CX88
Montgolfier Wk., Nthlt.	242	313	BY69
Montgomery Clo., Mitch.	272	324	DL98
Montgomery Clo., Sid.	261	326	ET86
Montgomery Rd. W4	144	314	CQ77
Montgomery Rd., Edg.	216	304	CM51
Montholme Rd. SW11	175	323	DF86
Monthope Rd. E1	138	317	DU71
Montolieu Gdns. SW15	172	323	CV85
Montpelier Ave. W5	132	314	CJ71
Montpelier Ave., Bex.	262	327	EX87
Montpelier Clo., Uxb.	241	312	BN67
Montpelier Gdns. E6	244	318	EK69
Montpelier Gdns., Rom.	236	309	EW59
Montpelier Gro. NW5	114	306	DJ64
Montpelier Ms. SW7	66/7	315	DE76
Montpelier Pl. E1	138	317	DW72
Montpelier Pl. SW7	66/7	315	DE76
Montpelier Ri. NW11	95	305	CY59
Montpelier Ri., Wem.	91	304	CK60
Montpelier Rd. N3	219	305	DC53
Montpelier Rd. SE15	164	317	DV81
Montpelier Rd. W5	133	314	CK71
Montpelier Rd., Pur.	294	332	DP110
Montpelier Rd., Sutt.	285	331	DC105
Montpelier Row SE3	167	317	EF82
Montpelier Row, Twick.	184	322	CH87
Montpelier Sq. SW7	66/7	315	DE75
Montpelier St. SW7	66/7	315	DE76
Montpelier Ter. SW7	66/7	315	DE75
Montpelier Vale SE3	167	317	EF82
Montpelier Wk. SW7	66/7	315	DE76
Montpelier Way NW11	95	305	CY59
Montrave Rd. SE20	274	325	DW94
Montreal Pl. WC2	59	316	DM73
Montreal Rd., Ilf.	235	308	EQ59
Montrell Rd. SW2	193	324	DL88
Montrose Ave. NW6	127	315	CY68
Montrose Ave., Edg.	217	304	CQ54
Montrose Ave., Rom.	228	310	FJ54
Montrose Ave., Sid.	262	327	EU87
Montrose Ave., Twick.	259	321	CB87
Montrose Ave., Well.	261	326	ER83
Montrose Clo., Ashf.	265	328	BQ93
Montrose Clo., Well.	261	326	ET83
Montrose Ct. SW7	66	315	DD75
Montrose Cres. N12	219	305	DC51
Montrose Cres., Wem.	107	304	CL65
Montrose Gdns., Mitch.	271	323	DF97
Montrose Gdns., Sutt.	284	331	DA103
Montrose Pl. SW1	68	316	DG75
Montrose Rd., Felt.	265	320	BR87
Montrose Rd., Har.	215	303	CE54
Montrose Way SE23	197	325	DX88
Montserrat Ave., Wdf.Grn.	223	307	ED52
Montserrat Clo. SE19	273	324	DR92
Montserrat Rd. SW15	173	323	CY84
Monument Gdns. SE13	182	325	EC85
Monument St. EC3	62	316	DR73
Monument Way N17	221	306	DT55
Monza St. E1	138	317	DW73
Moodkee St. SE16	148	317	DW76
Moody St. E1	129	317	DX69
Moon St. N1	24/5	316	DP67
Moor La. EC2	50	316	DR71
Moor La., Chess.	282	330	CL105
Moor La., Upmin.	239	311	FS60
Moor La., West Dr.	256	320	BJ79
Moor Mead Rd., Twick.	168	322	CG86
Moor Pk. Est., Nthwd.	213	302	BQ49
Moor Pk. Gdns., Kings.T.	269	322	CS94
Moor Pk. Rd., Nthwd.	213	302	BQ50
Moor Pl. EC2	50	316	DR71
Moor St. W1	46	316	DK72
Moorcroft Gdns., Brom.	290	334	EL99
Moorcroft La., Uxb.	249	312	BN71
Moorcroft Rd. SW16	193	324	DL90
Moorcroft Way, Pnr.	214	303	BY57
Moordown SE18	253	318	EN81
Moore Clo. SW14	170	322	CQ83
Moore Clo., Mitch.	272	324	DH96
Moore Clo., Wall.	294	332	DL109
Moore Cres., Dag.	246	319	EV67
Moore Pk. Rd. SW6	158	315	DB80
Moore Rd. SE19	273	324	DQ93
Moore St. SW3	79	315	DF77
Moore Wk. E7	234	308	EG63
Moore Way SE22	196	325	DU88
Moore Way, Sutt.	292	331	DA109
Moorefield Rd. N17	221	306	DT55
Mooreland Rd., Brom.	275	325	EF94
Moorey Clo. E15	131	317	EF67
Moorfield Ave. W5	123	314	CK70
Moorfield Rd., Chess.	282	330	CL106
Moorfield Rd., Enf.	203	301	DW39
Moorfield Rd., Orp.	291	335	EU101
Moorfield Rd., Uxb.	248	312	BK72
Moorfield Rd. (Harefield), Uxb.	230	312	BG59
Moorfields EC2	50	316	DR71
Moorfields Highwalk EC2	50	316	DR71
Moorgate EC2	50	316	DR71
Moorgate Pl. EC2	50	316	DR72
Moorhall Rd., Uxb.	230	302	BH58
Moorhayes Dr., Stai.	280	328	BJ97
Moorhead Way SE3	260	326	EH83
Moorhouse Rd. W2	40	315	DA72
Moorhouse Rd., Har.	216	304	CK55
Moorings, The SE28	246	319	EV73
Moorland Clo., Rom.	227	309	FB53
Moorland Clo., Twick.	259	321	CA87
Moorland Rd. SW9	178	324	DP84
Moorland Rd., West Dr.	256	320	BJ79
Moorlands Ave. NW7	218	305	CV51
Moorlands Est. SW9	178	324	DN84
Moormead Dr., Epsom	283	330	CS106
Moorside Rd., Brom.	199	325	EE90
Moot Ct. NW9	217	304	CN57
Mora Rd. NW2	110	305	CW63
Mora St. EC1	37	316	DQ69
Morant Pl. N22	220	306	DM53
Morant St. E14	140	317	EA73
Morat St. SW9	161	316	DM81
Moravian Pl. SW10	159	315	DD79
Moravian St. E2	128	317	DW69
Moray Ave., Hayes	249	312	BT74
Moray Clo., Rom.	227	309	FE52
Moray Ms. N7	99	306	DM61
Moray Rd. N4	99	306	DM61
Moray Way, Rom.	227	309	FD52
Mordaunt Gdns., Dag.	236	309	EY66
Mordaunt Ho. NW10	125	314	CR67
Mordaunt Rd. NW10	125	314	CR67
Mordaunt St. SW9	177	324	DM83
Morden Clo. SE13	166	317	EC82
Morden Ct., Mord.	271	323	DB98
Morden Gdns., Grnf.	233	313	CF64
Morden Gdns., Mitch.	271	323	DD98
Morden Hall Rd., Mord.	271	323	DB97
Morden Hill SE13	166	317	EC82
Morden La. SE13	166	317	EC81
Morden Rd. SE3	252	318	EG82
Morden Rd. SW19	271	323	DB95
Morden Rd., Mitch.	271	323	DC98
Morden Rd., Rom.	236	309	EY59
Morden Rd. Ms. SE3	252	318	EG82
Morden St. SE13	166	317	EB81
Morden Way, Sutt.	284	331	DA101
Morden Wf. Rd. SE10	151	317	EE76
Mordon Rd., Ilf.	235	308	ET59
Mordred Rd. SE6	199	325	EE89
More Clo. E16	141	317	EF72
More Clo. W14	147	315	CX77
More Clo., Pur.	294	332	DN111
Morecambe Clo. E1	139	317	DX71
Morecambe Clo., Horn.	238	310	FH64
Morecambe Gdns., Stan.	204	298	CK49
Morecambe St. SE17	85	316	DQ77
Morecambe Ter. N18	209	300	DR49
Morecoombe Clo., Kings.T.	269	322	CP94
Moree Way N18	210	301	DU49
Moreland St. EC1	36/7	316	DP69
Moreland Way E4	211	301	EB48
Morella Rd. SW12	191	323	DF87
Morello Ave., Uxb.	249	312	BP71
Morello Clo., Swan.	279	327	FD98
Moremead Rd. SE6	274	325	DZ91
Morena St. SE6	198	325	EB87
Moresby Ave., Surb.	282	330	CP101
Moresby Rd. E5	102	307	DV60
Moresby Wk. SW8	160	316	DH82
Moretaine Rd., Ashf.	264	320	BK90
Moreton Ave., Islw.	251	321	CE81
Moreton Clo. E5	102	307	DW61
Moreton Clo. N15	221	306	DR58
Moreton Clo. NW7	218	305	CW51
Moreton Clo., Swan.	279	327	FE96
Moreton Pl. SW1	81	316	DJ78
Moreton Rd. N15	221	306	DR58
Moreton Rd., S.Croy.	287	332	DR106
Moreton Rd., Wor.Pk.	283	331	CU103
Moreton St. SW1	81	316	DJ78
Moreton Ter. SW1	81	316	DJ78
Moreton Ter. Ms. N. SW1	81	316	DJ78
Moreton Ter. Ms. S. SW1	81	316	DJ78
Moreton Twr. W3	134	314	CP74
Morford Clo., Ruis.	232	313	BV59
Morford Way, Ruis.	232	313	BV59
Morgan Ave. E17	223	307	ED56
Morgan Clo., Dag.	237	309	FA66
Morgan Clo., Nthwd.	213	302	BT50
Morgan Rd. N7	116	306	DN64
Morgan Rd. W10	137	315	CZ71
Morgan Rd., Brom.	276	326	EG94
Morgan St. E3	129	317	DY69
Morgan St. E16	141	317	EF71
Morgan Way, Wdf.Grn.	224	308	EL51
Morgans La. SE1	62/3	316	DS74
Morgans La., Hayes	249	312	BR71
Moriatry Clo. N7	115	306	DL63
Morie St. SW18	174	323	DB84
Morieux Rd. E10	103	307	DZ60
Moring Rd. SW17	272	324	DG91
Morkyns Wk. SE21	195	324	DS90
Morland Ave., Croy.	287	332	DS102
Morland Clo. NW11	96	305	DB60
Morland Clo., Hmptn.	266	329	BZ92
Morland Clo., Mitch.	271	323	DE97
Morland Gdns. NW10	109	304	CR66
Morland Gdns., Sthl.	243	313	CB74
Morland Ms. N1	116	306	DN66
Morland Rd. E17	222	307	DX57
Morland Rd. SE20	274	325	DX93
Morland Rd., Croy.	287	332	DS102
Morland Rd., Dag.	237	309	FA66
Morland Rd., Har.	216	304	CL57
Morland Rd., Ilf.	235	308	EP61
Morland Rd., Sutt.	285	331	DC106
Morley Ave. E4	223	307	ED52
Morley Ave. N18	210	301	DU49
Morley Ave. N22	221	306	DN54
Morley Clo., Orp.	290	334	EP103
Morley Clo., Ruis.	232	313	BW61
Morley Cres., Edg.	205	298	CQ47
Morley Cres. E., Stan.	216	304	CJ54
Morley Cres. W., Stan.	216	304	CJ55
Morley Hill, Enf.	202	300	DR38
Morley Rd. E10	104	307	EC60
Morley Rd. E15	131	317	EF68
Morley Rd. SE13	182	325	EC84
Morley Rd., Bark.	245	318	ER67
Morley Rd., Chis.	277	326	EQ95
Morley Rd., Rom.	226	309	EY57
Morley Rd., S.Croy.	295	332	DT110
Morley Rd., Sutt.	284	331	CZ102
Morley Rd., Twick.	169	322	CK86
Morley St. SE1	72	316	DN76
Morna Rd. SE5	162	316	DQ82
Morning La. E9	118	307	DW65
Morningside Rd., Wor.Pk.	283	331	CV103
Mornington Ave. W14	147	315	CZ77
Mornington Ave., Brom.	276	326	EJ97
Mornington Ave., Ilf.	235	308	EN59
Mornington Ct., Bex.	263	327	FC88
Mornington Cres. NW1	21	316	DJ68
Mornington Cres., Houns.	250	321	BV81
Mornington Gro. E3	130	317	EA69
Mornington Ms. SE5	162	316	DQ81
Mornington Pl. NW1	20/1	316	DH68
Mornington Rd. E4	211	301	ED45
Mornington Rd. E11	105	307	EF60
Mornington Rd. SE8	165	317	DZ80
Mornington Rd., Ashf.	265	328	BQ92
Mornington Rd., Grnf.	243	313	CB71
Mornington Rd., Wdf.Grn.	211	301	EF49
Mornington St. NW1	20/1	316	DH68
Mornington Ter. NW1	20/1	316	DH68
Mornington Wk., Rich.	268	322	CJ91
Morocco St. SE1	74/5	316	DS75
Morpeth Gro. E9	129	317	DX67
Morpeth Rd. E9	128	317	DW67
Morpeth St. E2	129	317	DX69
Morpeth Ter. SW1	69	316	DJ76
Morpeth Wk. N17	222	307	DV52
Morrab Gdns., Ilf.	235	308	ET62
Morris Ave. E12	234	308	EM64
Morris Clo., Croy.	288	333	DY100
Morris Clo., Orp.	291	334	ES104
Morris Ct. E4	211	301	EB48
Morris Gdns. SW18	190	323	DA87
Morris Pl. N4	100	306	DN61
Morris Rd. E14	140	317	EB71
Morris Rd. E15	121	307	ED63
Morris Rd., Dag.	236	309	EZ61
Morris Rd., Islw.	259	321	CF83
Morris Rd., Rom.	228	310	FH52
Morris St. E1	138	317	DV72
Morrish Rd. SW2	193	324	DL87
Morrison Ave. N17	221	306	DS55
Morrison Rd., Bark.	246	319	EY68
Morrison Rd., Hayes	242	313	BV69
Morrison St. SW11	176	324	DG83
Morse Clo. E13	244	318	EG69
Morse Clo., Uxb.	212	302	BJ54
Morshead Rd. W9	28	315	DA69
Morson Rd., Enf.	210	301	DY44
Morston Gdns. SE9	276	326	EM91
Morten Clo. SW4	177	324	DK86
Morten Gdns., Uxb.	230	312	BG59
Morteyne Rd. N17	221	306	DR53
Mortgramit Sq. SE18	253	318	EN76
Mortham St. E15	131	317	EE67
Mortimer Clo. NW2	95	305	CZ62
Mortimer Clo. SW16	193	324	DK89
Mortimer Cres. NW6	16/7	315	DB67
Mortimer Cres., Wor.Pk.	283	330	CR104
Mortimer Dr., Enf.	209	300	DS43
Mortimer Est. NW6	16/7	315	DB67
Mortimer Mkt. WC1	33	316	DJ70
Mortimer Pl. NW6	16/7	315	DB67
Mortimer Rd. E6	244	318	EM69
Mortimer Rd. N1	117	306	DS66
Mortimer Rd. NW10	126	315	CW69
Mortimer Rd. W13	132	314	CJ72
Mortimer Rd., Erith	255	319	FD79
Mortimer Rd., Mitch.	271	323	DF95
Mortimer Rd., Orp.	291	335	EU102
Mortimer Sq. W11	137	315	CX73
Mortimer St. W1	45	316	DJ72
Mortimer Ter. NW5	114	306	DH63
Mortlake Clo., Croy.	286	332	DL104
Mortlake Dr., Mitch.	271	323	DE95
Mortlake High St. SW14	171	322	CR83
Mortlake Rd. E16	244	318	EH72
Mortlake Rd., Ilf.	235	308	EQ63
Mortlake Rd., Rich.	154	314	CN80
Mortlake Ter., Rich.	154	314	CN80
Mortlock Clo. SE15	164	317	DV81
Morton Cres. N14	208	300	DK49
Morton Gdns., Wall.	286	332	DJ106
Morton Ms. SW5	76/7	315	DB77
Morton Pl. SE1	72	316	DN76
Morton Rd. E15	121	307	EF66
Morton Rd. N1	116	306	DQ66
Morton Rd., Mord.	285	331	DD99
Morton Way N14	208	300	DJ48
Morval Rd. SW2	178	324	DN85
Morvale Clo., Belv.	254	319	EZ77
Morven Rd. SW17	191	323	DF90
Morville St. E3	130	317	EA68
Morwell St. WC1	46	316	DK71
Moscow Pl. W2	52/3	315	DB73
Moscow Rd. W2	52/3	315	DB73
Moselle Ave. N22	221	306	DN54
Moselle Clo. N8	220	306	DM55
Moselle Ho. N17	221	306	DT52
Moselle Pl. N17	221	306	DT52
Moselle St. N17	221	306	DT52
Moss Clo. E1	138	317	DU71
Moss Clo., Pnr.	214	303	BZ54
Moss Clo., Rick.	212	302	BK47
Moss Gdns., Felt.	258	321	BU89
Moss Hall Cres. N12	219	305	DB51
Moss Hall Gro. N12	219	305	DB51
Moss La., Pnr.	214	303	BY53
Moss La., Rom.	227	309	FF58
Moss Rd., Dag.	237	309	FA66
Mossborough Clo. N12	219	305	DB51
Mossbury Rd. SW11	175	323	DE83
Mossdown Clo., Belv.	255	319	FA77
Mossendew Clo., Uxb.	212	302	BK53
Mossford Ct., Ilf.	225	308	EP55
Mossford Grn., Ilf.	225	308	EP55
Mossford La., Ilf.	225	308	EP54
Mossford St. E3	129	317	DZ70
Mossington Gdns. SE16	148	317	DW77
Mosslea Rd. SE20	274	325	DW93
Mosslea Rd., Brom.	290	334	EK99
Mosslea Rd., Orp.	291	334	EQ104
Mossop St. SW3	78/9	315	DE77
Mossville Gdns., Mord.	270	323	CZ97
Moston Clo., Hayes	249	320	BT78
Mostyn Ave., Wem.	107	304	CM64
Mostyn Gdns. NW10	127	315	CX69
Mostyn Gro. E3	130	317	EA68
Mostyn Rd. SW9	162	316	DN81
Mostyn Rd. SW19	270	323	CZ95
Mostyn Rd., Edg.	217	304	CR52
Mosul Way, Brom.	290	334	EL100
Motcomb St. SW1	68	316	DG76
Mothers Sq., The E5	118	307	DV63
Motley Ave. EC2	38/9	316	DS70
Motley St. SW8	160	316	DJ82
Motspur Pk., N.Mal.	283	330	CT100
Mottingham Gdns. SE9	260	326	EK88
Mottingham La. SE9	260	326	EJ88
Mottingham La. SE12	260	326	EJ88
Mottingham Rd. N9	210	301	DX44
Mottingham Rd. SE9	260	326	EL89
Mottisfont Rd. SE2	254	319	EU76
Moulins Rd. E9	118	307	DW66
Moulton Ave., Houns.	250	321	BY82
Moultrie Way, Upmin.	239	311	FS59
Mound, The SE9	261	326	EN90
Moundfield Rd. N16	222	307	DU58
Mount, The N20	207	299	DC47
Mount, The NW3	112	305	DC63
Mount, The, N.Mal.	269	322	CT97
Mount, The, Wem.	92	304	CP61
Mount, The, Wor.Pk.	283	331	CV105
Mount Adon Pk. SE22	196	325	DU87
Mount Angelus Rd. SW15	187	322	CT87
Mount Ararat Rd., Rich.	169	322	CL85
Mount Ash Rd. SE26	196	325	DV90
Mount Ave. E4	211	301	EA48
Mount Ave. W5	132	314	CJ71
Mount Ave., Rom.	229	311	FQ51
Mount Ave., Sthl.	243	313	CA72
Mount Clo. W5	132	314	CJ71
Mount Clo., Brom.	276	326	EL95
Mount Clo., Cars.	293	332	DG109
Mount Cor., Felt.	258	321	BX89
Mount Ct. SW15	173	323	CY83
Mount Ct., W.Wick.	289	333	EE103
Mount Culver Ave., Sid.	278	327	EX93
Mount Dr., Bexh.	262	327	EY85
Mount Dr., Har.	214	303	BZ57
Mount Dr., Wem.	92	304	CQ61
Mount Echo Ave. E4	211	301	EB47
Mount Echo Dr. E4	211	301	EB46
Mount Ephraim La. SW16	193	324	DK90
Mount Ephraim Rd. SW16	193	324	DK90
Mount Est., The E5	102	307	DV61
Mount Felix, Walt.	281	328	BT102
Mount Gdns. SE26	196	325	DV90
Mount Gro., Edg.	205	298	CQ48
Mount Ms., Hmptn.	267	329	CB95
Mount Mills EC1	36/7	316	DP69
Mount Nod Rd. SW16	193	324	DM90
Mount Pk., Cars.	293	332	DG109
Mount Pk. Ave., Har.	233	313	CD61
Mount Pk. Ave., S.Croy.	294	332	DP109
Mount Pk. Cres. W5	133	314	CK72
Mount Pk. Rd. W5	133	314	CK71
Mount Pk. Rd., Har.	233	313	CD62
Mount Pk. Rd., Pnr.	214	303	BU57
Mount Pleasant SE27	273	324	DQ92
Mount Pleasant WC1	36	316	DN70
Mount Pleasant, Ruis.	232	313	BW61
Mount Pleasant, Uxb.	212	302	BG53
Mount Pleasant, Wem.	123	314	CL67
Mount Pleasant Cres. N4	99	306	DM59
Mount Pleasant Hill E5	102	307	DV61
Mount Pleasant La. E5	102	307	DV61
Mount Pleasant Pl. SE18	253	318	ER77
Mount Pleasant Rd. E17	222	307	DY54
Mount Pleasant Rd. N17	221	306	DS53
Mount Pleasant Rd. NW10	110	305	CW66
Mount Pleasant Rd. SE13	182	325	EC86
Mount Pleasant Rd. W5	122	314	CJ70
Mount Pleasant Rd., N.Mal.	269	322	CQ97
Mount Pleasant Rd., Rom.	227	309	FD51
Mount Pleasant Vil. N4	99	306	DM59
Mount Pleasant Wk., Bex.	263	327	FC85
Mount Rd. NW2	94	305	CV62
Mount Rd. NW4	218	305	CU58
Mount Rd. SE19	273	324	DR93
Mount Rd. SW19	190	323	DA89
Mount Rd., Barn.	207	299	DE43
Mount Rd., Bexh.	262	327	EX85
Mount Rd., Chess.	282	330	CM106
Mount Rd., Dag.	236	309	EZ60

Mount Rd., Dart. 263 327 FF86
Mount Rd., Felt. 258 321 BY90
Mount Rd., Hayes 249 320 BT75
Mount Rd., Ilf. 235 308 EP64
Mount Rd., Mitch. 271 323 DD96
Mount Rd., N.Mal. 269 322 CR97
Mount Row W1 56/7 316 DH73
Mount Sq., The NW3 96 305 DC62
Mount Stewart Ave., Har. 216 304 CK58
Mount St. W1 56 316 DG73
Mount Ter. E1 138 317 DV71
Mount Vernon NW3 112 305 DC63
Mount Vw. NW7 205 298 CR48
Mount Vw. W5 123 314 CK70
Mount Vw. Rd. E4 211 301 EC45
Mount Vw. Rd. N4 99 306 DL59
Mount Vw. Rd. NW9 217 306 CR57
Mount Vil. SE27 194 324 DP90
Mount Way, Cars. 293 332 DG109
Mountacre Clo. SE26 273 324 DT91
Montague Pl. E14 140 317 EC73
Mountbatten Clo. SE18 253 318 ES79
Mountbatten Clo. SE19 273 324 DS92
Mountbatten Ct. SE16 138 317 DW74
Mountbatten Gdns., Beck. 274 325 DY98
Mountbatten Ms. SW18 190 323 DC88
Mountbel Rd., Stan. 216 304 CG53
Mountcombe Clo., Surb. 282 330 CL101
Mountearl Gdns. SW16 193 324 DM90
Mountfield Clo. SE6 199 325 ED87
Mountfield Rd. E6 218 318 EN68
Mountfield Rd. N3 218 305 CZ55
Mountfield Rd. W5 133 314 CK72
Mountfield Way, Orp. 278 327 EW98
Mountford St. E1 138 317 DU72
Mountfort Cres. N1 116 306 DN66
Mountfort Ter. N1 116 306 DN66
Mountgrove Rd. N5 100 306 DP62
Mounthurst Rd., Brom. 289 333 EF101
Mountington Pk. Clo., Har. 216 304 CK58
Mountjoy Clo. SE2 254 319 EV75
Mountjoy Ho. EC2 49 316 DQ71
Mounts Pond Rd. SE3 167 317 ED82
Mountsfield Clo., Stai. 256 320 BG85
Mountsfield Ct. SE13 183 325 ED86
Mountside, Felt. 258 321 BY90
Mountside, Stan. 215 303 CF53
Mountview, Nthwd. 213 302 BT51
Mountview Ct. N8 221 306 DP56
Mountview Rd., Orp. 291 335 EU101
Mountwood, W.Mol. 267 329 CA97
Mountwood Clo., S.Croy. 295 333 DV110
Movers La., Bark. 245 318 ER67
Mowatt Clo. N19 99 306 DK60
Mowbray Rd. NW6 111 305 CY66
Mowbray Rd. SE19 273 324 DT95
Mowbray Rd., Edg. 205 298 CN49
Mowbray Rd., Rich. 184 322 CJ90
Mowbrays Clo., Rom. 227 309 FC53
Mowbrays Rd., Rom. 227 309 FC54
Mowlem St. E2 128 317 DV68
Mowlem Trd. Est. N17 222 307 DW52
Mowll St. SW9 162 316 DN80
Moxon Clo. E13 131 317 EF68
Moxon St. W1 44 316 DG71
Moye Clo. E2 128 317 DU67
Moyers Rd. E10 104 307 EC59
Moylan Rd. W6 157 315 CY79
Moyne Pl. NW10 124 314 CN68
Moynihan Dr. N21 208 300 DL43
Moys Clo., Croy. 286 332 DL100
Moyser Rd. SW16 272 324 DH92
Mozart St. W10 127 315 CZ69
Mozart Ter. SW1 80 316 DG77
Muchelney Rd., Mord. 285 331 DC100
Mud La. W5 133 314 CK71
Mudlarks Way SE7 252 318 EH76
Mudlarks Way SE10 151 317 EF76
Muggeridge Rd., Dag. 237 309 FB63
Muir Rd. E5 118 307 DU63
Muir St. E16 244 318 EM74
Muirdown Ave. SW14 171 322 CR84
Muirfield W3 135 314 CS72
Muirfield Clo. SE16 148 317 DV78
Muirfield Cres. E14 150 317 EB76
Muirkirk Rd. SE6 198 325 EC88
Mulberry Ave., Stai. 264 320 BL88
Mulberry Clo. E4 211 301 EA47
Mulberry Clo. N8 220 306 DL57
Mulberry Clo. NW3 113 305 DD63
Mulberry Clo. NW4 218 305 CW55
Mulberry Clo. SE7 252 318 EK79
Mulberry Clo. SE22 180 325 DU86
Mulberry Clo. SW3 159 315 DD79
Mulberry Clo. SW16 272 324 DJ91
Mulberry Clo., Nthlt. 242 313 BY68
Mulberry Clo., Rom. 228 310 FH56
Mulberry Ct., Bark. 235 308 ET66
Mulberry Cres., Brent. 152 314 CH80
Mulberry Cres., West Dr. 249 320 BN75
Mulberry La., Croy. 287 332 DT102
Mulberry Ms., Wall. 294 332 DJ107
Mulberry Par., West Dr. 249 320 BN76
Mulberry Pl. W6 146 315 CU78
Mulberry Rd. E8 117 306 DT66
Mulberry St. E1 138 317 DU72
Mulberry Trees, Shep. 281 328 BR101
Mulberry Wk. SW3 159 315 DD79
Mulberry Way E18 224 308 EH54
Mulberry Way, Belv. 255 319 FC75
Mulberry Way, Ilf. 225 308 EQ56
Mulgrave Rd. NW10 109 304 CT63
Mulgrave Rd. SW6 157 315 CZ79
Mulgrave Rd. W5 123 314 CK70
Mulgrave Rd., Croy. 287 332 DR104
Mulgrave Rd., Har. 216 304 CG61
Mulgrave Rd., Sutt. 292 331 CZ108
Mulholland Clo., Mitch. 272 324 DH96
Mulkern Rd. N19 99 306 DK60
Mull Wk. N1 116 306 DQ65
Mullards Clo., Mitch. 285 331 DF102
Muller Rd. SW4 177 324 DK86
Mullet Gdns. E2 128 317 DU68
Mullins Path SW14 171 322 CR83
Mullion Clo., Har. 215 303 CB53
Mulready St. NW8 30/1 315 DE70
Multi Way W3 145 314 CS75
Multon Rd. SW18 191 323 DD87
Mulvaney Way SE1 74 316 DR75
Mumford Ct. EC2 49 316 DQ72
Mumford Rd. SE24 178 324 DP85
Muncaster Clo., Ashf. 265 328 BN91
Muncaster Rd. SW11 175 323 DF85
Muncaster Rd., Ashf. 265 328 BP92
Muncies Ms. SE6 198 325 EC89
Mund St. W14 147 315 CZ78
Mundania Rd. SE22 180 325 DV86
Munday Rd. E16 244 318 EG72
Munden St. W14 147 315 CY77
Mundford Rd. E5 102 307 DW61
Mundon Gdns., Ilf. 235 308 ER60
Mundy St. N1 38/9 316 DS69
Mungo Pk. Rd., Rain. 238 310 FG65
Munnery Way, Orp. 290 334 EN103
Munnings Gdns., Islw. 259 321 CD85
Munro Dr. N11 220 306 DJ51
Munro Ms. W10 137 315 CY71
Munro Ter. SW10 159 315 DD79
Munslow Gdns., Sutt. 285 331 DC105
Munster Ave., Houns. 258 321 BY84
Munster Ct., Tedd. 268 322 CJ93
Munster Gdns. N13 209 300 DP49
Munster Ms. SW6 157 315 CY80
Munster Rd. SW6 157 315 CY80
Munster Rd., Tedd. 268 322 CH93
Munster Sq. NW1 32/3 316 DH69
Munton Rd. SE17 85 316 DQ77
Murchison Ave., Bex. 262 327 EX88
Murchison Rd. E10 104 307 EC61
Murdoch Clo., Stai. 264 328 BG92
Murdock Clo. E16 141 317 EF72
Murdock St. SE15 164 317 DV79
Murfett Clo. SW19 189 323 CY89
Murfitt Way, Upmin. 239 311 FN63
Muriel St. N1 23 316 DM67
Murillo Rd. SE13 183 325 ED84
Murphy St. SE1 72 316 DN75
Murray Ave., Brom. 276 326 EH97

Murray Ave., Houns. 259 321 CB85
Murray Cres., Pnr. 214 303 BX53
Murray Gro. N1 25 316 DQ68
Murray Ms. NW1 115 306 DK66
Murray Rd. SW19 270 323 CX93
Murray Rd. W5 143 314 CK77
Murray Rd., Nthwd. 213 302 BS53
Murray Rd., Orp. 278 327 EV97
Murray Rd., Rich. 184 322 CH89
Murray Sq. E16 244 318 EG72
Murray St. NW1 115 306 DK66
Murray Ter. NW3 113 305 DD63
Murray Ter. W5 143 314 CK77
Mursell Est. SW8 161 316 DM81
Murtwell Dr., Chig. 225 308 EQ51
Musard Rd. W6 157 315 CY79
Musbury St. E1 138 317 DW72
Muscal W6 157 315 CY79
Muscatel Pl. SE5 163 316 DS81
Muschamp Rd. SE15 179 324 DT83
Muschamp Rd., Cars. 285 331 DE103
Muscovy St. EC3 62/3 316 DS73
Museum La. SW7 66 315 DD76
Museum Pas. E2 128 317 DV69
Museum St. WC1 46/7 316 DL71
Musgrave Cres. SW6 158 315 DA80
Musgrave Rd., Islw. 153 321 CF81
Musgrove Rd. SE14 165 317 DX81
Musjid Rd. SW11 159 315 DD82
Musquash Way, Houns. 250 321 BW82
Muston Rd. E5 102 307 DV61
Mustow Pl. SW6 157 315 CZ82
Muswell Ave. N10 220 306 DH53
Muswell Hill N10 220 306 DH55
Muswell Hill Bdy. N10 220 306 DH55
Muswell Hill Pl. N10 220 306 DH56
Muswell Hill Rd. N6 220 306 DG58
Muswell Hill Rd. N10 220 306 DG58
Muswell Ms. N10 220 306 DH55
Muswell Rd. N10 220 306 DH55
Mutrix Rd. NW6 16 315 DA67
Mutton Pl. NW1 114 306 DH65
Muybridge Rd., N.Mal. 269 322 CQ96
Myatt Rd. SW9 162 316 DP81
Myatt's Flds. N. SW9 162 316 DN81
Myatt's Flds. S. SW9 162 316 DN82
Mycenae Rd. SE3 252 318 EG80
Myddelton Ave., Enf. 202 300 DS38
Myddelton Clo., Enf. 202 300 DT39
Myddelton Gdns. N21 209 300 DP45
Myddelton Pk. N20 207 299 DD48
Myddelton Pas. EC1 36 316 DN69
Myddelton Rd. N8 220 306 DL56
Myddelton Sq. EC1 36 316 DN69
Myddelton St. EC1 36 316 DN69
Myddleton Ms. N22 220 306 DL52
Myddleton Rd. N22 220 306 DL52
Myddleton Rd., Uxb. 240 312 BJ67
Myers La. SE14 165 317 DX79
Mylis Clo. SE26 274 325 DV91
Mylius Clo. SE14 164 317 DW81
Mylne St. EC1 24 316 DN68
Myra St. SE2 254 319 EU77
Myrdle St. E1 138 317 DU71
Myrna Clo. SW19 271 323 DE94
Myron Pl. SE13 182 325 EC83
Myrtle Ave., Felt. 257 320 BS84
Myrtle Ave., Ruis. 232 313 BU59
Myrtle Clo., Barn. 207 299 DF46
Myrtle Clo., Erith 255 319 FE81
Myrtle Clo., Uxb. 248 312 BM71
Myrtle Clo., West Dr. 248 320 BM76
Myrtle Gdns. W7 243 313 CE74
Myrtle Gro., Enf. 202 300 DR38
Myrtle Gro., N.Mal. 269 322 CQ96
Myrtle Rd. E6 244 318 EL67
Myrtle Rd. E17 222 307 DY58
Myrtle Rd. N13 209 300 DQ48
Myrtle Rd. W3 134 314 CQ74
Myrtle Rd., Croy. 288 333 EA104
Myrtle Rd., Hmptn. 267 329 CC93
Myrtle Rd., Houns. 251 321 CC82
Myrtle Rd., Ilf. 235 308 EP61
Myrtle Rd., Rom. 228 310 FJ51
Myrtle Rd., Sutt. 285 331 DC106
Myrtle Wk. N1 26/7 316 DS68
Myrtleberry Clo. E8 117 306 DT65
Myrtledene Rd. SE2 254 319 EU78
Myrtleside Clo., Nthwd. 213 302 BR52
Mysore Rd. SW11 175 323 DF83
Myth Clo., Upmin. 229 311 FR58
Myton Rd. SE21 195 324 DR90

Nadine St. SE7 252 318 EJ78
Nagasaki Wk. SE7 252 318 EJ76
Nagle Clo. E17 223 307 ED54
Nag's Head Ct. EC1 37 316 DQ70
Nags Head La., Brwd. 229 311 FS51
Nags Head La., Upmin. 229 311 FQ54
Nags Head La., Well. 262 327 EV83
Nags Head Rd., Enf. 203 301 DW42
Nairn Rd., Ruis. 232 313 BW65
Nairn St. E14 140 317 EC71
Nairne Gro. SE24 179 324 DR85
Naish Ct. N1 22/3 316 DL67
Nallhead Rd., Felt. 266 329 BW92
Namton Dr., Th.Hth. 272 324 DM98
Nan Clark's La. NW7 205 298 CT47
Nankin St. E14 140 317 EA72
Nansen Rd. SW11 176 324 DG84
Nant Rd. NW2 95 305 CZ61
Nant St. E2 128 317 DV69
Nantes Clo. SW18 174 323 DC84
Nantes Pas. E1 51 316 DT71
Naoroji St. WC1 36 316 DN69
Napier Ave. E14 150 317 EA78
Napier Ave. SW6 173 323 CZ83
Napier Clo. SE8 165 317 DZ80
Napier Clo. W14 147 315 CZ76
Napier Clo., Horn. 238 310 FH60
Napier Clo., West Dr. 248 320 BM76
Napier Ct. SW6 173 323 CZ83
Napier Gro. N1 25 316 DQ68
Napier Ho., Rain. 247 319 FF69
Napier Pl. W14 147 315 CZ76
Napier Rd. E6 245 318 EN67
Napier Rd. E11 121 307 EE63
Napier Rd. E15 131 317 EE68
Napier Rd. N17 221 306 DS55
Napier Rd. NW10 126 315 CV69
Napier Rd. SE25 274 325 DV98
Napier Rd. W14 147 315 CY76
Napier Rd., Ashf. 265 328 BR94
Napier Rd., Belv. 254 319 EZ77
Napier Rd., Brom. 276 326 EH98
Napier Rd., Enf. 210 301 DX43
Napier Rd., Houns. 256 320 BK81
Napier Rd., Islw. 168 322 CG84
Napier Rd., S.Croy. 295 332 DR108
Napier Rd., Wem. 107 304 CK64
Napier Ter. N1 116 306 DP66
Napoleon Rd. E5 102 307 DV62
Napoleon Rd., Twick. 184 322 CH87
Napton Clo., Hayes 242 313 BY70
Narbonne Ave. SW4 176 324 DJ85
Narboro Ct., Rom. 228 310 FG57
Narborough Clo., Uxb. 231 312 BQ61
Narborough St. SW6 158 315 DB82
Narcissus Rd. NW6 112 305 DA64
Naresby Fold, Stan. 216 304 CJ51
Narford Rd. E5 102 307 DU62
Narrow St. E14 139 317 DY73
Narrow Way, Brom. 290 334 EL100
Nascot St. W12 136 315 CW72
Naseby Clo. NW6 112 305 DC66
Naseby Clo., Islw. 251 321 CE81
Naseby Rd. SE19 273 324 DR93
Naseby Rd., Dag. 237 309 FA62
Naseby Rd., Ilf. 224 308 EM53
Nash Grn., Brom. 276 326 EG93
Nash Pl. E14 140 317 EB74
Nash Rd. N9 210 301 DW47
Nash Rd. SE4 181 325 DY84
Nash Rd., Rom. 226 309 EX56
Nash St. NW1 32/3 316 DH69
Nash's Yd., Uxb. 240 312 BK66
Nasmyth St. W6 146 315 CV76
Nassau Path SE28 246 319 EW74

Nassau Rd. SW13 155 314 CT81
Nassau St. W1 45 316 DJ71
Nassington Rd. NW3 113 305 DE63
Natal Rd. N11 220 306 DL51
Natal Rd. SW16 272 324 DK93
Natal Rd., Ilf. 235 308 EP63
Natal Rd., Th.Hth. 273 324 DR97
Natalie Clo., Felt. 265 320 BR87
Natalie Ms., Twick. 259 321 CD90
Nathan Clo., Upmin. 239 311 FS60
Nathan Way SE28 253 318 ES76
Nathaniel Clo. E1 51 316 DT71
Nathans Rd., Wem. 90 304 CJ60
Nation Way E4 211 301 EC46
Naunton Way, Horn. 238 310 FK62
Naval Row E14 140 317 EC73
Naval Wk., Brom. 276 326 EG97
Navarino Gro. E8 118 307 DU65
Navarino Rd. E8 118 307 DU65
Navarre Rd. E6 244 318 EL68
Navarre St. E2 39 316 DT70
Navenby Wk. E3 130 317 EA70
Navestock Clo. E4 211 301 EC48
Navestock Cres., Wdf.Grn. 224 308 EJ53
Navestock Ho., Bark. 246 319 EV68
Navigator Dr., Sthl. 251 321 CC75
Navy St. SW4 177 324 DK83
Naylor Gro., Enf. 210 301 DX43
Naylor Rd. N20 207 299 DC47
Naylor Rd. SE15 164 317 DV80
Nazareth Gdns. SE15 164 317 DV82
Nazeing Wk., Rain. 247 319 FE67
Nazrul St. E2 39 316 DT69
Neal Ave., Sthl. 242 313 BZ69
Neal Clo., Nthwd. 214 303 BU53
Neal St. WC2 46/7 316 DL72
Nealden St. SW9 177 324 DM83
Neale Clo. N2 219 305 DC55
Neal's Yd. WC2 46/7 316 DL72
Near Acre NW9 217 304 CT53
Neasden Clo. NW10 109 304 CS64
Neasden La. NW10 93 304 CS62
Neasden La. N. NW10 93 304 CR62
Neasden Underpass NW10 93 304 CR62
Neasham Rd., Dag. 236 309 EV64
Neate St. SE5 163 316 DS79
Neath Gdns., Mord. 285 331 DC100
Neathouse Pl. SW1 81 316 DJ77
Neats Acre, Ruis. 231 312 BR59
Neatscourt Rd. E6 244 318 EK71
Neave Cres., Rom. 228 310 FJ53
Nebraska St. SE1 74 316 DR75
Neckinger SE16 75 316 DT76
Neckinger Est. SE16 75 316 DT76
Neckinger St. SE1 75 316 DT75
Nectarine Way SE13 166 317 EB82
Needham Rd. W11 40 315 DA72
Needham Ter. NW2 95 305 CX62
Needleman St. SE16 149 317 DX75
Neela Clo., Uxb. 241 312 BP63
Neeld Cres. NW4 218 305 CV57
Neeld Cres., Wem. 108 304 CN64
Neil Clo., Ashf. 265 328 BQ92
Neil Wates Cres. SW2 194 324 DN88
Nelgarde Rd. SE6 198 325 EA87
Nell Gwynne Ave., Shep. 281 328 BR100
Nella Rd. W6 157 315 CX79
Nelldale Rd. SE16 148 317 DW77
Nellgrove Rd., Uxb. 241 312 BP70
Nello James Gdns. SE27 273 324 DR91
Nelmes Clo., Horn. 228 311 FM57
Nelmes Cres., Horn. 228 311 FL57
Nelmes Rd., Horn. 238 311 FL59
Nelmes Way, Horn. 228 310 FK56
Nelson Clo., Croy. 286 332 DP102
Nelson Clo., Felt. 265 320 BT88
Nelson Clo., Rom. 227 309 FB53
Nelson Clo., Uxb. 241 312 BP69
Nelson Ct. SE16 138 317 DW74
Nelson Gdns. E2 128 317 DU69
Nelson Gdns., Houns. 259 321 CA86
Nelson Gro. Rd. SW19 271 323 DB95
Nelson La., Uxb. 241 312 BP69
Nelson Mandela Clo. N10 220 306 DG54
Nelson Mandela Rd. SE3 252 326 EJ83
Nelson Pas. EC1 37 316 DQ69
Nelson Pl. N1 24/5 316 DP68
Nelson Pl., Sid. 278 327 EU91
Nelson Rd. E4 223 307 EA51
Nelson Rd. E11 224 308 EG56
Nelson Rd. N8 220 306 DM57
Nelson Rd. N9 210 301 DV47
Nelson Rd. N15 221 306 DS56
Nelson Rd. SE10 166 317 EC79
Nelson Rd. SW19 271 323 DB94
Nelson Rd., Ashf. 264 328 BL92
Nelson Rd., Belv. 254 319 EZ78
Nelson Rd., Brom. 276 326 EJ98
Nelson Rd., Enf. 210 301 DX44
Nelson Rd., Har. 233 313 CD60
Nelson Rd., Houns. 259 321 CA86
Nelson Rd.
(Heathrow Airport), Houns. 256 320 BM81
Nelson Rd., N.Mal. 283 330 CR99
Nelson Rd., Rain. 247 319 FF68
Nelson Rd., Sid. 278 327 EU91
Nelson Rd., Stan. 216 304 CJ51
Nelson Rd., Twick. 259 321 CB87
Nelson Rd., Uxb. 241 312 BP69
Nelson Sq. SE1 72/3 316 DP75
Nelson St. E1 138 317 DV72
Nelson St. E6 244 318 EM68
Nelson St. E16 141 317 EF73
Nelson Ter. N1 24/5 316 DP68
Nelson Trd. Est. SW19 271 323 DB95
Nelson Wk. SE16 139 317 DY74
Nelson's Row SW4 177 324 DK84
Nelsons Yd. NW1 21 316 DJ68
Nelwyn Ave., Horn. 228 311 FM57
Nemoure Rd. W3 134 314 CQ73
Nene Gdns., Felt. 258 321 BZ89
Nene Rd., Houns. 257 320 BP81
Nepaul Rd. SW11 159 315 DE82
Nepean St. SW15 172 323 CU86
Neptune Rd., Har. 215 303 CD58
Neptune Rd.
(Heathrow Airport), Houns. 257 320 BR81
Neptune St. SE16 148 317 DW76
Nesbit Rd. SE9 260 326 EK84
Nesbitt Clo. SE3 183 325 EE83
Nesbitt Sq. SE19 273 324 DS94
Nesham St. E1 138 317 DU74
Ness St. SE16 148 317 DU76
Nesta Rd., Wdf.Grn. 223 307 EE51
Nestles Ave., Hayes 249 320 BT76
Nestor Ave. N21 209 300 DP44
Nether Clo. N3 219 305 DA52
Nether St. N3 219 305 DA53
Nether St. N12 219 305 DB51
Netheravon Rd. W7 243 313 CF74
Netheravon Rd. N. W4 145 314 CT77
Netheravon Rd. S. W4 145 314 CT78
Netherbury Rd. W5 143 314 CK76
Netherby Rd. SE23 196 325 DW87
Nethercourt Ave. N3 219 305 DA51
Netherfield Gdns., Bark. 235 308 ER65
Netherfield Rd. N12 207 299 DB50
Netherfield Rd. SW17 192 324 DG90
Netherford Rd. SW4 160 316 DJ82
Netherhall Gdns. NW3 112 305 DC65
Netherhall Way NW3 112 305 DC64
Netherlands Rd., Barn. 207 299 DD44
Netherleigh Clo. N6 98 306 DH60
Netherpark Dr., Rom. 227 309 FF54
Netherton Gro. SW10 158 315 DC79
Netherton Rd. N15 221 306 DR58
Netherton Rd., Twick. 168 322 CG85
Netherwood N2 219 305 DD54
Netherwood Pl. W14 147 315 CX76
Netherwood Rd. W14 147 315 CX76
Netherwood St. NW6 111 305 CZ66
Netley Clo., Sutt. 284 331 CX106
Netley Gdns., Mord. 285 331 DC101
Netley Rd. E17 222 307 DZ57
Netley Rd., Brent. 153 314 CL79
Netley Rd.
(Heathrow Airport), Houns. 257 320 BR81
Netley Rd., Ilf. 225 308 ER57

Netley Rd., Mord. 285 331 DC101
Netley St. NW1 33 316 DJ69
Nettlecombe Clo., Sutt. 292 331 DB109
Nettleden Ave., Wem. 108 304 CN65
Nettlefold Pl. SE27 194 324 DP90
Nettlestead Clo., Beck. 274 325 DZ94
Nettleton Rd. SE14 165 317 DX81
Nettleton Rd., Houns. 257 320 BP81
Nettleton Rd., Uxb. 240 312 BM63
Nettlewood Rd. SW16 272 324 DK94
Neuchatel Rd. SE6 197 325 DZ89
Nevada Clo., N.Mal. 269 322 CQ98
Nevada St. SE10 166 317 EC79
Nevern Pl. SW5 76 315 DA77
Nevern Rd. SW5 76 315 DA77
Nevern Sq. SW5 76 315 DA77
Nevil Clo., Nthwd. 213 302 BR50
Nevill Clo. W3 144 314 CQ75
Nevill Rd. N16 117 306 DS63
Neville Ave., N.Mal. 269 322 CR95
Neville Clo. E11 105 307 EF62
Neville Clo. NW1 22 316 DK68
Neville Clo. NW6 127 315 CZ68
Neville Clo. SE15 164 317 DU80
Neville Clo., Bans. 292 331 DB114
Neville Clo., Houns. 251 321 CB82
Neville Clo., Sid. 277 326 ET91
Neville Dr. N2 219 305 DC58
Neville Gdns., Dag. 236 309 EX62
Neville Gill Clo. SW18 174 323 DB86
Neville Pl. N22 220 306 DM53
Neville Rd. E7 234 308 EG66
Neville Rd. NW6 127 315 CZ68
Neville Rd. W5 123 314 CK70
Neville Rd., Croy. 287 332 DR101
Neville Rd., Dag. 236 309 EX61
Neville Rd., Ilf. 225 308 EQ53
Neville Rd., Kings.T. 269 322 CN96
Neville Rd., Rich. 184 322 CJ89
Neville St. SW7 78 315 DD78
Neville Ter. SW7 78 315 DD78
Neville Wk., Cars. 285 331 DE101
Nevilles Ct. NW2 94 305 CU62
Nevin Dr. E4 211 301 EB46
Nevis Clo., Rom. 227 309 FE51
Nevis Rd. SW17 192 324 DG89
New Ash Clo. N2 219 305 DD55
New Barn Rd., Swan. 279 327 FE95
New Barn St. E13 244 318 EG70
New Barns Ave., Mitch. 272 324 DK98
New Bond St. W1 44/5 316 DH72
New Brent St. NW4 218 305 CW57
New Bri. St. EC4 48/9 316 DP72
New Broad St. EC2 50/1 316 DS71
New Bdy. W5 132 314 CJ73
New Bdy., Hmptn. 267 329 CD92
New Burlington Ms. W1 57 316 DJ73
New Burlington Pl. W1 57 316 DJ73
New Burlington St. W1 57 316 DJ73
New Butt La. SE8 166 317 EA80
New Butt La. N. SE8 166 317 EA80
New Cavendish St. W1 44 316 DG71
New Change EC4 49 316 DQ72
New Chapel Sq., Felt. 258 321 BV88
New Charles St. EC1 36/7 316 DP69
New Ch. Rd. SE5 163 316 DR80
New City Rd. E13 244 318 EJ69
New Clo. SW19 271 323 DC97
New Clo., Felt. 266 329 BY92
New College Ms. N1 116 306 DN66
New Compton St. WC2 46 316 DK72
New Ct. EC4 60 316 DN73
New Covent Gdn. Mkt. SW8 161 316 DK80
New Coventry St. W1 58 316 DK73
New Crane Pl. E1 138 317 DW74
New Cross SE14 164 317 DW80
New Cross Rd. SE14 164 317 DW80
New End NW3 112 305 DC63
New End Sq. NW3 113 305 DD63
New Era Est. N1 26/7 316 DS67
New Fm. Ave., Brom. 276 326 EG98
New Fm. La., Nthwd. 213 302 BS53
New Ferry App. SE18 253 318 EN76
New Fetter La. EC4 48 316 DN72
New Forest La., Chig. 225 308 EN51
New Gdn. Dr., West Dr. 248 320 BL75
New Globe Wk. SE1 61 316 DQ74
New Goulston St. E1 51 316 DT72
New Hall Dr., Rom. 228 311 FL53
New Heston Rd., Houns. 250 321 BZ80
New Horizon Ct., Brent. 152 314 CG79
New Inn Bdy. EC2 38/9 316 DS70
New Inn Pas. WC2 47 316 DM72
New Inn St. EC2 38/9 316 DS70
New Inn Yd. EC2 38/9 316 DS70
New James Ct. SE15 180 325 DV83
New Kent Rd. SE1 73 316 DQ76
New King St. SE8 166 317 EA79
New Kings Rd. SW6 157 315 CZ82
New London St. EC3 62/3 316 DS73
New Lydenburgh St. SE7 252 318 EJ76
New Mill Rd., Orp. 278 327 EW95
New Mt. St. E15 121 307 ED66
New N. Pl. EC2 38/9 316 DS70
New N. Rd. N1 116 306 DQ66
New N. Rd., Ilf. 225 308 ER52
New N. St. WC1 47 316 DM71
New Oak Rd. N2 219 305 DC54
New Orleans Wk. N19 99 306 DK59
New Oxford St. WC1 46 316 DK72
New Par., Ashf. 264 328 BM91
New Pk. Ave. N13 209 300 DQ48
New Pk. Clo., Nthlt. 232 313 BY65
New Pk. Ct. SW2 193 324 DL87
New Pk. Par. SW2 177 324 DL86
New Pk. Rd. SW2 193 324 DK88
New Pk. Rd., Ashf. 265 328 BQ92
New Pk. Rd., Uxb. 212 302 BJ53
New Peachey La., Uxb. 248 312 BK72
New Pl. Gdns., Upmin. 239 311 FR61
New Pl. Sq. SE16 148 317 DV76
New Plaistow Rd. E15 131 317 EE67
New Printing Ho. Sq. WC1 35 316 DM70
New Priory Ct. NW6 112 305 DA66
New Quebec St. W1 43 315 DF72
New Ride SW7 66/7 315 DE75
New River Cres. N13 209 300 DP49
New River Wk. N1 116 306 DQ65
New Rd. E1 138 317 DV71
New Rd. E4 211 301 EB49
New Rd. N8 220 306 DL57
New Rd. N9 210 301 DU48
New Rd. N17 221 306 DT53
New Rd. N22 221 306 DQ53
New Rd. NW7 219 305 CY52
New Rd. (Barnet Gate) NW7 205 298 CT45
New Rd. SE2 254 319 EX77
New Rd., Borwd. 204 298 CK44
New Rd., Brent. 143 314 CK78
New Rd., Dag. 247 319 FA67
New Rd., Felt. 257 320 BR86
New Rd. (East Bedfont), Felt. 258 321 BV88
New Rd. (Hanworth), Felt. 266 329 BY92
New Rd., Har. 233 313 CF63
New Rd., Hayes 257 320 BQ80
New Rd., Houns. 259 321 CB84
New Rd., Ilf. 235 308 ES61
New Rd., Kings.T. 269 322 CN94
New Rd., Mitch. 285 331 DF102
New Rd., Orp. 291 335 EU101
New Rd., Rain. 247 319 FC68
New Rd., Rich. 268 322 CJ91
New Rd., Shep. 281 328 BN97
New Rd., Swan. 279 327 FF97
New Rd. (Hextable), Swan. 279 327 FF94
New Rd., Uxb. 241 312 BQ70
New Rd., Well. 254 319 EV82
New Rd., W.Mol. 267 329 CA97
New Row WC2 58/9 316 DL73
New Spring Gdns. Wk. SE11 82/3 316 DL78
New Sq. E6 244 318 EM72
New Sq. WC2 47 316 DM72
New Sq., Felt. 265 320 BQ88
New Sq. Pas. WC2 47 316 DM72
New St. EC2 50/1 316 DS71
New St., Stai. 264 328 BG91
New St. Hill, Brom. 276 326 EH92
New St. Sq. EC4 48 316 DN72
New Trinity Rd. N2 219 305 DD55

New Turnstile WC1 47 316 DM71
New Union Clo. E14 150 317 EC76
New Union St. EC2 50 316 DR71
New Wanstead E11 223 307 EF58
New Way Rd. NW9 217 304 CS56
New Wf. Rd. N1 22/3 316 DL68
New Windsor St., Uxb. 240 312 BJ66
New Years Grn. La., Uxb. 230 302 BL58
New Zealand Ave., Walt. 281 328 BT102
New Zealand Way W12 136 315 CV73
New Zealand Way, Rain. 247 319 FF69
Newall Rd., Houns. 257 320 BQ81
Newark Cres. NW10 125 314 CR69
Newark Knok E6 245 318 EN72
Newark Rd., S.Croy. 295 332 DR107
Newark St. E1 138 317 DV71
Newark Way NW4 218 305 CU56
Newbery Rd., Erith 255 319 FF81
Newbolt Ave., Sutt. 284 331 CW106
Newborough Grn., N.Mal. 269 322 CR98
Newburgh Rd. W3 134 314 CQ74
Newburgh St. W1 45 316 DJ72
Newburn St. SE11 83 316 DM78
Newbury Ave., Enf. 203 301 DZ38
Newbury Clo., Nthlt. 232 313 BZ65
Newbury Clo., Rom. 228 310 FK51
Newbury Gdns., Epsom 283 330 CT105
Newbury Gdns., Rom. 228 310 FK51
Newbury Gdns., Upmin. 238 311 FM62
Newbury Ho. N22 220 306 DL53
Newbury Ms. NW5 114 306 DG65
Newbury Rd. E4 223 307 EC51
Newbury Rd., Brom. 276 326 EG97
Newbury Rd., Houns. 256 320 BM81
Newbury Rd., Ilf. 225 308 ES58
Newbury St. EC1 49 316 DQ71
Newbury Way, Nthlt. 232 313 BZ65
Newby Clo., Enf. 202 300 DS40
Newby Pl. E14 140 317 EC73
Newby St. SW8 176 324 DH83
Newcastle Ave., Ilf. 226 309 EU51
Newcastle Clo. EC4 48/9 316 DP72
Newcastle Pl. W2 42 315 DD71
Newcastle Row EC1 36 316 DN70
Newcombe Gdns. SW16 272 324 DL91
Newcombe Pk. NW7 205 298 CS50
Newcombe Pk., Wem. 123 314 CM67
Newcombe Ri., West Dr. 248 312 BL72
Newcombe St. W8 52 315 DA74
Newcomen Rd. E11 105 307 EF62
Newcomen Rd. SW11 175 323 DD83
Newcomen St. SE1 74 316 DR75
Newcourt, Uxb. 248 312 BJ71
Newcourt St. NW8 18/9 315 DE68
Newcroft Clo., Uxb. 248 312 BM71
Newdales Clo. N9 210 301 DU47
Newdene Ave., Nthlt. 242 313 BX68
Newdigate Grn., Uxb. 212 302 BK53
Newdigate Rd., Uxb. 212 302 BJ53
Newdigate Rd. E., Uxb. 212 302 BK53
Newell St. E14 139 317 DZ72
Newent Clo. SE15 163 316 DS80
Newent Clo., Cars. 285 331 DF102
Newfield Clo., Hmptn. 267 329 CA95
Newfield Ri. NW2 94 305 CV62
Newgale Gdns., Edg. 216 304 CM53
Newgate, Croy. 287 332 DQ102
Newgate Clo., Felt. 258 321 BY89
Newgate St. E4 211 301 EF48
Newgate St. EC1 48/9 316 DP72
Newham Way E6 245 318 EN70
Newham Way E16 141 317 EF71
Newhams Clo., Brom. 276 326 EM97
Newhams Row SE1 74/5 316 DS75
Newhaven Clo., Hayes 249 320 BT77
Newhaven Cres., Ashf. 265 328 BR92
Newhaven Gdns. SE9 260 326 EK84
Newhaven La. E16 131 317 EF70
Newhaven Rd. SE25 287 332 DR99
Newhouse Ave., Rom. 226 309 EX55
Newhouse Clo., N.Mal. 283 330 CS101
Newhouse Wk., Mord. 285 331 DC101
Newick Clo., Bex. 263 327 FB86
Newick Rd. E5 102 307 DV62
Newing Grn., Brom. 276 326 EK94
Newington Barrow Way N7 99 306 DM62
Newington Butts SE1 84/5 316 DP77
Newington Butts SE11 84/5 316 DP77
Newington Causeway SE1 72/3 316 DP76
Newington Grn. N1 117 306 DR64
Newington Grn. N16 117 306 DR64
Newington Grn. Rd. N1 117 306 DR65
Newington Way N7 99 306 DM61
Newland Clo., Pnr. 214 303 BY51
Newland Ct., Wem. 92 304 CN61
Newland Dr., Enf. 203 301 DV39
Newland Gdns. W13 142 314 CG75
Newland Rd. N8 220 306 DL55
Newland St. E16 244 318 EL74
Newlands, The, Wall. 294 332 DJ108
Newlands Clo., Edg. 204 298 CL48
Newlands Clo., Sthl. 250 321 BY78
Newlands Clo., Wem. 106 304 CJ65
Newlands Ct. SE9 261 326 EN86
Newlands Pk. SE26 274 325 DX92
Newlands Pl., Barn. 206 299 CX43
Newlands Quay E1 138 317 DW73
Newlands Rd. SW16 272 324 DL96
Newlands Rd., Wdf.Grn. 211 301 EF47
Newlands Way, Chess. 282 330 CJ106
Newling Clo. E6 244 318 EM72
Newlyn Clo., Uxb. 249 312 BN71
Newlyn Gdns., Har. 232 313 BZ59
Newlyn Rd. N17 221 306 DT53
Newlyn Rd. NW2 94 305 CW60
Newlyn Rd., Well. 253 318 ET82
Newman Clo., Horn. 228 311 FL57
Newman Pas. W1 45 316 DJ71
Newman Rd. E13 131 318 EH69
Newman Rd. E17 222 307 DX57
Newman Rd., Brom. 276 326 EG95
Newman Rd., Croy. 286 332 DM102
Newman Rd., Hayes 242 313 BV73
Newman St. W1 45 316 DJ71
Newman Yd. W1 45 316 DJ72
Newman's Ct. EC3 50 316 DR72
Newmans La., Surb. 282 330 CK100
Newman's Row WC2 47 316 DM71
Newmarket Ave., Nthlt. 233 313 CB64
Newmarket Grn. SE9 260 326 EK87
Newmarket Way, Horn. 238 311 FL63
Newminster Rd., Mord. 285 331 DC100
Newnes Path SW15 172 323 CV84
Newnham Ave., Ruis. 232 313 BW60
Newnham Clo., Nthlt. 233 313 CC64
Newnham Clo., Th.Hth. 273 324 DQ96
Newnham Gdns., Nthlt. 233 313 CC65
Newnham Ms. N22 220 306 DM53
Newnham Rd. N22 220 306 DM53
Newnham Ter. SE1 72 316 DN76
Newnham Way, Har. 216 304 CL57
Newnhams Clo., Brom. 276 326 EM97
Newnton Clo. N4 101 306 DR59
Newport Ave. E13 244 318 EH70
Newport Ave. E14 140 317 ED73
Newport Clo., Enf. 203 301 DY37
Newport Ct. WC2 58 316 DK73
Newport Pl. WC2 58 316 DK73
Newport Rd. E10 104 307 EC61
Newport Rd. E17 222 307 DY56
Newport Rd. SW13 156 315 CU81
Newport Rd., Hayes 249 312 BR71
Newport Rd., Houns. 257 320 BN81
Newport St. SE11 83 316 DM77
Newquay Cres., Har. 232 313 BY61
Newquay Rd. SE6 198 325 EB89
Newry Rd., Twick. 168 322 CG85
Newsam Ave. N15 221 306 DR57
Newstead Ave., Orp. 291 334 ER104
Newstead Clo. N12 219 305 DE51
Newstead Rd. SE12 199 325 EF87
Newstead Wk., Cars. 285 331 DC101
Newstead Way SW19 270 323 CX91
Newton Ave. N10 220 306 DG53
Newton Ave. W3 144 314 CQ75
Newton Clo. E17 222 307 DY58
Newton Gro. W4 145 314 CS77
Newton Rd. E15 121 307 ED64
Newton Rd. N15 221 306 DT57

Newton Rd. NW2	94	305	CW62
Newton Rd. SW19	270	323	CY94
Newton Rd. W2	40/1	315	DB72
Newton Rd., Har.	215	303	CE54
Newton Rd., Islw.	251	321	CF82
Newton Rd., Pur.	294	332	DJ112
Newton Rd., Well.	262	327	EU83
Newton Rd., Wem.	107	304	CM66
Newton St. WC2	46/7	316	DL72
Newton Wk., Edg.	217	304	CP53
Newton Way N18	209	300	DQ50
Newtons Clo., Rain.	237	309	FF66
Newtons Yd. SW18	174	323	DB85
Newtown Rd., Uxb.	240	312	BH65
Newtown St. SW11	160	316	DH81
Niagara Ave. W5	142	314	CJ77
Niagara Clo. N1	26	316	DR68
Nibthwaite Rd., Har.	215	303	CE57
Nichol Clo. N14	208	300	DK46
Nichol La., Brom.	276	326	EG94
Nicholas Clo., Grnf.	243	313	CB68
Nicholas Ct. E13	244	318	EH69
Nicholas Gdns. W5	143	314	CK75
Nicholas La. EC4	62	316	DR73
Nicholas Pas. EC4	50	316	DR72
Nicholas Rd. E1	128	317	DW70
Nicholas Rd., Borwd.	204	298	CM44
Nicholas Rd., Croy.	286	332	DL105
Nicholas Rd., Dag.	236	309	EZ61
Nicholas Way, Nthwd.	213	302	BQ53
Nicholay Rd. N19	99	306	DK61
Nicholes Rd., Houns.	259	321	CA84
Nicholl St. E2	128	317	DU67
Nicholls Ave., Uxb.	241	312	BN70
Nichollsfield Wk. N7	115	306	DM64
Nichols Clo. N4	99	306	DM60
Nichols Grn. W5	133	314	CL71
Nicholson Rd., Croy.	287	332	DT102
Nicholson St. SE1	60/1	316	DP74
Nickelby Clo. SE28	246	319	EW72
Nickelby Clo., Uxb.	249	312	BP72
Nicol Clo., Twick.	168	322	CH86
Nicola Clo., Har.	215	303	CD54
Nicola Clo., S.Croy.	295	332	DQ107
Nicola Ms., Ilf.	225	308	EP52
Nicoll Pl. NW4	218	305	CV58
Nicoll Rd. NW10	125	314	CS67
Nicoll Way, Borwd.	205	298	CR43
Nicosia Rd. SW18	191	323	DE87
Niederwald Rd. SE26	274	325	DY91
Nield Rd., Hayes	249	320	BT75
Nigel Clo., Nthlt.	242	313	BY67
Nigel Ms., Ilf.	235	308	EP63
Nigel Playfair Ave. W6	146	315	CV77
Nigel Rd. E7	234	308	EJ64
Nigel Rd. SE15	180	325	DU83
Nigeria Rd. SE7	252	318	EJ80
Nightingale Ave. E4	211	301	EE50
Nightingale Ave., Upmin.	239	311	FT60
Nightingale Clo. E4	211	301	EE49
Nightingale Clo. W4	154	314	CQ79
Nightingale Clo., Cars.	285	332	DG103
Nightingale Clo., Pnr.	214	303	BW57
Nightingale Est. E5	102	307	DU62
Nightingale Gro. SE13	183	325	ED85
Nightingale La. E11	224	308	EH57
Nightingale La. N6	97	305	DE59
Nightingale La. N8	220	306	DL56
Nightingale La. SW4	176	324	DH86
Nightingale La. SW12	191	323	DF87
Nightingale La., Brom.	276	326	EJ96
Nightingale La., Rich.	185	322	CL87
Nightingale Ms. E3	129	317	DY68
Nightingale Ms., Kings.T.	268	322	CK97
Nightingale Pl. SE18	253	318	EN79
Nightingale Pl. SW10	158	315	DC79
Nightingale Rd. E5	102	307	DV62
Nightingale Rd. N9	210	301	DW44
Nightingale Rd. N22	220	306	DL53
Nightingale Rd. NW10	125	314	CT68
Nightingale Rd. W7	243	313	CF74
Nightingale Rd., Cars.	285	331	DF104
Nightingale Rd., Hmptn.	267	329	CA92
Nightingale Rd., Orp.	291	334	EQ100
Nightingale Sq. SW12	192	324	DG87
Nightingale Vale SE18	253	318	EN79
Nightingale Wk. SW4	176	324	DH86
Nightingale Way E6	244	318	EL71
Nightingale Way, Swan.	279	327	FE97
Nightingales, The, Stai.	264	320	BM87
Nile Path SE18	253	318	EN79
Nile Rd. E13	244	318	EJ68
Nile St. N1	38	316	DR69
Nile Ter. SE15	87	316	DT78
Nimegen Way SE22	179	324	DS85
Nimrod Clo., Nthlt.	242	313	BX69
Nimrod Pas. N1	117	306	DS65
Nimrod Rd. SW16	272	324	DH93
Nimrod Rd., Houns.	257	320	BN81
Nine Acres Clo. E12	234	308	EL64
Nine Elms Ave., Uxb.	248	312	BK71
Nine Elms Clo., Felt.	265	320	BT88
Nine Elms Clo., Uxb.	248	312	BK72
Nine Elms La. SW8	160	316	DJ80
Nine Stiles Clo., Uxb.	240	312	BH65
Nineteenth Rd., Mitch.	272	324	DL98
Ninhams Wd., Orp.	290	334	EN105
Ninth Ave., Hayes	242	313	BU73
Nisbet Ho. E9	119	307	DX64
Nithdale Rd. SE18	253	318	EP80
Nithsdale Gro., Uxb.	231	312	BQ62
Niton Clo., Barn.	206	299	CX44
Niton Rd., Rich.	170	322	CN83
Niton St. SW6	157	315	CX80
Nobel Dr., Hayes	257	320	BR80
Nobel Rd. N18	210	301	DW49
Noble St. EC2	49	316	DQ72
Noel Pk. Rd. N22	221	306	DN54
Noel Rd. E6	244	318	EL70
Noel Rd. N1	24/5	316	DP68
Noel Rd. W3	134	314	CN72
Noel Sq., Dag.	236	309	EW63
Noel St. W1	45	316	DJ72
Noel Ter. SE23	196	325	DW89
Nolan Way E5	118	307	DU63
Nolton Pl., Edg.	216	304	CM53
Nonsuch Clo., Ilf.	225	308	EP51
Nonsuch Wk., Sutt.	292	331	CW110
Nora Gdns. NW4	218	305	CX56
Norbiton Ave., Kings.T.	269	322	CN95
Norbiton Common Rd., Kings.T.	269	322	CP97
Norbiton Rd. E14	139	317	DZ72
Norbreck Gdns. NW10	123	314	CM69
Norbreck Par. NW10	123	314	CM69
Norbroke St. W12	135	314	CT73
Norburn St. W10	137	315	CY71
Norbury Ave. SW16	272	324	DM95
Norbury Ave., Houns.	259	321	CD84
Norbury Ave., Th.Hth.	273	324	DN96
Norbury Clo. SW16	273	324	DN95
Norbury Ct. Rd. SW16	272	324	DL97
Norbury Cres. SW16	272	324	DM95
Norbury Cross SW16	272	324	DL97
Norbury Gdns., Rom.	226	309	EX57
Norbury Gro. NW7	205	298	CS48
Norbury Hill SW16	273	324	DN94
Norbury Ri. SW16	272	324	DL97
Norbury Rd. E4	211	301	EA50
Norbury Rd., Th.Hth.	273	324	DQ96
Norcombe Gdns., Har.	216	304	CJ58
Norcott Clo., Hayes	242	313	BW70
Norcott Rd. N16	102	307	DU61
Norcroft Gdns. SE22	196	325	DU87
Norcutt Rd., Twick.	259	321	CE88
Nordenfeldt Rd., Erith	255	319	FD78
Norfield Rd., Dart.	279	327	FC91
Norfolk Ave. N13	221	306	DP51
Norfolk Ave. N15	221	306	DT58
Norfolk Ave., S.Croy.	295	332	DT110
Norfolk Clo. N2	219	305	DE55
Norfolk Clo. N13	221	306	DP51
Norfolk Clo., Twick.	168	322	CH86
Norfolk Cres. W2	42/3	315	DE72
Norfolk Cres., Sid.	261	326	ES87
Norfolk Gdns., Bexh.	254	319	EZ81
Norfolk Ho. SE3	167	317	EE79
Norfolk Ho. Rd. SW16	193	324	DK90
Norfolk Pl. W2	42	315	DD72
Norfolk Pl., Well.	254	319	EU82
Norfolk Rd. E6	244	318	EM67
Norfolk Rd. E17	222	307	DX54
Norfolk Rd. NW8	18	315	DD67
Norfolk Rd. NW10	109	304	CS66
Norfolk Rd. SW19	271	323	DE94
Norfolk Rd., Bark.	235	308	ES66
Norfolk Rd., Dag.	237	309	FB64
Norfolk Rd., Enf.	210	301	DV44
Norfolk Rd., Felt.	258	321	BW88
Norfolk Rd., Har.	215	303	CB57
Norfolk Rd., Ilf.	235	308	ES60
Norfolk Rd., Rom.	227	309	FC58
Norfolk Rd., Th.Hth.	273	324	DQ97
Norfolk Rd., Upmin.	239	311	FN62
Norfolk Rd., Uxb.	240	312	BK65
Norfolk Row SE1	71	316	DM76
Norfolk Sq. W2	42	315	DD72
Norfolk Sq. Ms. W2	42	315	DD72
Norfolk St. E7	234	308	EG64
Norfolk Ter. W6	147	315	CY78
Norgrove St. SW12	192	324	DG88
Norhyrst Ave. SE25	273	324	DT97
Nork Gdns., Bans.	292	331	CY114
Nork Way, Bans.	292	331	CY114
Norland Pl. W11	137	315	CY74
Norland Rd. W11	137	315	CX74
Norland Sq. W11	137	315	CY74
Norlands Cres., Chis.	277	326	EP95
Norlands Gate, Chis.	277	326	EP95
Norley Vale SW15	188	323	CU88
Norlington Rd. E10	104	307	EC60
Norlington Rd. E11	105	307	ED60
Norman Ave. N22	221	306	DP53
Norman Ave., Felt.	258	321	BY89
Norman Ave., S.Croy.	295	332	DQ110
Norman Ave., Sthl.	242	313	BY73
Norman Ave., Twick.	184	322	CH87
Norman Clo., Orp.	291	334	EQ104
Norman Clo., Rom.	227	309	FB54
Norman Ct., Ilf.	235	308	ER59
Norman Cres., Houns.	250	321	BX80
Norman Cres., Pnr.	214	303	BW53
Norman Gro. E3	129	317	DY68
Norman Rd. E6	244	318	EM70
Norman Rd. E11	105	307	ED61
Norman Rd. N15	221	306	DT57
Norman Rd. SE10	166	317	EB80
Norman Rd. SW19	271	323	DC94
Norman Rd., Ashf.	265	328	BR93
Norman Rd., Belv.	255	319	FB76
Norman Rd., Horn.	238	310	FG59
Norman Rd., Ilf.	235	308	EP64
Norman Rd., Sutt.	284	331	DA106
Norman Rd., Th.Hth.	286	332	DP99
Norman St. EC1	37	316	DQ69
Norman Way N14	208	300	DL47
Norman Way W3	134	314	CP71
Normanby Clo. SW15	173	323	CZ85
Normanby Rd. NW10	109	304	CT63
Normand Gdns. W14	157	315	CY79
Normand Ms. W14	157	315	CY79
Normand Rd. W14	157	315	CZ79
Normandy Ave., Barn.	206	299	CZ43
Normandy Dr., Hayes	249	312	BQ72
Normandy Rd. SW9	162	316	DN81
Normandy Ter. E16	244	318	EH72
Normandy Way, Erith	255	319	FE81
Normanhurst, Ashf.	265	328	BN92
Normanhurst Ave., Bexh.	254	319	EX81
Normanhurst Dr., Twick.	168	322	CH85
Normanhurst Rd. SW2	193	324	DM89
Normanhurst Rd., Orp.	278	327	EV96
Norman's Bldgs. EC1	37	316	DQ69
Normans Clo. NW10	109	304	CR65
Normans Clo., Uxb.	248	312	BM71
Normans Mead NW10	109	304	CR65
Normansfield Ave., Tedd.	268	322	CJ94
Normanshire Ave. E4	211	301	EC49
Normanshire Dr. E4	211	301	EA49
Normanton Ave. SW19	190	323	DA89
Normanton Pk. E4	211	301	EE48
Normanton Rd., S.Croy.	287	332	DS106
Normanton St. SE23	197	325	DX89
Normington Clo. SW16	273	324	DN92
Norrice Lea N2	219	305	DD57
Norris St. SW1	58	316	DK73
Norris Way, Dart.	263	327	FF83
Norroy Rd. SW15	173	323	CX84
Norseman Clo., Ilf.	236	309	EV60
Norseman Way, Grnf.	243	313	CB67
Norstead Pl. SW15	188	323	CU89
North Access Rd. E17	222	307	DX58
North Acre NW9	217	304	CS53
North Acton Rd. NW10	125	314	CR68
North App., Nthwd.	213	302	BQ47
North Audley St. W1	56	316	DG73
North Ave. N18	210	301	DU49
North Ave. W13	132	314	CH71
North Ave., Cars.	293	332	DG108
North Ave., Har.	215	303	CB58
North Ave., Hayes	242	313	BU73
North Ave., Rich.	154	314	CN81
North Ave., Sthl.	242	313	BZ73
North Bank NW8	30/1	315	DE69
North Birkbeck Rd. E11	105	307	ED62
North Branch Ave. W10	126	315	CW69
North Carriage Dr. W2	54/5	315	DE73
North Circular Rd. E4	222	307	DZ52
North Circular Rd. E18	224	308	EH53
North Circular Rd. N3	218	305	CZ56
North Circular Rd. N12	219	305	DD53
North Circular Rd. N13	209	300	DN50
North Circular Rd. NW2	93	304	CS62
North Circular Rd. NW10	109	304	CS63
North Circular Rd. NW11	218	305	CX58
North Clo., Barn.	206	299	CW43
North Clo., Bexh.	262	327	EX84
North Clo., Dag.	247	319	FA67
North Clo., Felt.	257	320	BR86
North Clo., Mord.	270	323	CY98
North Colonnade E14	140	317	EA74
North Common Rd. W5	133	314	CL73
North Common Rd., Uxb.	240	312	BK64
North Countess Rd. E17	222	307	DZ54
North Ct. W1	45	316	DJ71
North Cray Rd., Bex.	263	327	FA89
North Cray Rd., Sid.	278	327	EY93
North Cres. E16	131	317	ED70
North Cres. N3	218	305	CZ54
North Cres. WC1	46	316	DK71
North Cross Rd. SE22	179	324	DT85
North Cross Rd., Ilf.	225	308	EQ56
North Dene NW7	205	298	CR48
North Dene, Houns.	251	321	CB81
North Down, S.Croy.	295	332	DS111
North Dr. SW16	272	324	DJ91
North Dr., Houns.	251	321	CC82
North Dr., Orp.	291	334	ES105
North Dr., Rom.	228	310	FJ55
North Dr., Ruis.	231	312	BS59
North End NW3	96	305	DC61
North End, Croy.	287	332	DQ103
North End Ave. NW3	96	305	DC61
North End Cres. W14	147	315	CZ77
North End Ho. W14	147	315	CY77
North End Par. W14	147	315	CY77
North End Rd. NW11	96	305	DA60
North End Rd. SW6	157	315	CZ79
North End Rd. W14	147	315	CY77
North End Rd., Wem.	92	304	CN62
North End Way NW3	96	305	DC61
North Eyot Gdns. W6	145	314	CT78
North Feltham Trd. Est., Felt.	258	321	BV85
North Flockton St. SE16	148	317	DU75
North Gdn. E14	139	317	DZ74
North Gdns. SW19	271	323	DD94
North Glade, The, Bex.	262	327	EZ87
North Gower St. NW1	33	316	DJ69
North Grn. NW9	217	304	CS52
North Gro. N6	98	306	DG59
North Gro. N15	221	306	DR57
North Hatton Rd. (Heathrow Airport), Houns.	257	320	BR81
North Hill N6	219	305	DF58
North Hill Ave. N6	219	305	DF58
North Hyde Gdns., Hayes	250	321	BU77
North Hyde La., Houns.	250	321	BY79
North Hyde La., Sthl.	250	321	BX78
North Hyde Rd., Hayes	249	320	BS76
North La., Tedd.	267	329	CF93
North Lo. Clo. SW15	173	323	CX85
North Mall N9	210	301	DV47
North Ms. WC1	35	316	DM70
North Par., Chess.	282	330	CL106
North Pk. SE9	261	326	EN86
North Pas. SW18	174	323	DA85
North Peckham Est. SE15	163	316	DS80
North Perimeter Rd., Uxb.	240	312	BL69
North Pl., Mitch.	271	323	DF94
North Pl., Tedd.	267	329	CF93
North Pole Rd. W10	136	315	CW71
North Ride W2	54/5	315	DE74
North Rd. N6	98	306	DG59
North Rd. N7	115	306	DL65
North Rd. N9	210	301	DV46
North Rd. SE18	253	318	ES77
North Rd. SW19	271	323	DC93
North Rd. W5	143	314	CK76
North Rd., Belv.	255	319	FB76
North Rd., Brent.	153	314	CL79
North Rd., Brom.	276	326	EH95
North Rd., Dart.	263	327	FF87
North Rd., Edg.	217	304	CP53
North Rd., Felt.	257	320	BR86
North Rd., Hayes	249	312	BR71
North Rd., Ilf.	235	308	ES61
North Rd., Rich.	170	322	CN83
North Rd., Rom.	226	309	EY57
North Rd., Sthl.	243	313	CA72
North Rd., Surb.	282	330	CK100
North Rd., West Dr.	248	320	BM76
North Rd., W.Wick.	288	333	EB102
North Row W1	55	315	DF73
North Several SE3	167	317	ED82
North Sq. N9	210	301	DV47
North Sq. NW11	219	305	DA57
North St. E13	244	318	EH68
North St. NW4	218	305	CW57
North St. SW4	176	324	DJ83
North St., Bark.	235	308	EP65
North St., Bexh.	263	327	FA84
North St., Brom.	276	326	EG95
North St., Cars.	285	331	DF104
North St., Horn.	238	310	FK59
North St., Islw.	168	322	CG83
North St., Rom.	227	309	FD55
North St. Pas. E13	244	318	EH68
North Tenter St. E1	51	316	DT72
North Ter. SW3	66/7	315	DE76
North Verbena Gdns. W6	146	315	CU78
North Vw. SW19	270	323	CW92
North Vw. W5	122	314	CJ70
North Vw., Ilf.	226	309	EU52
North Vw., Pnr.	232	313	BW59
North Vw. Cres. NW10	109	304	CT63
North Vw. Dr., Wdf.Grn.	224	308	EK54
North Vw. Rd. N8	220	306	DK55
North Vil. NW1	115	306	DK65
North Wk. W2	53	315	DC73
North Way N9	210	301	DX47
North Way N11	220	306	DJ51
North Way NW9	217	304	CP55
North Way, Mord.	270	323	CY97
North Way, Pnr.	214	303	BW55
North Way, Uxb.	240	312	BL66
North Wf. Rd. W2	42	315	DD71
North Woolwich Rd. E16	244	318	EG74
North Woolwich R'bout E16	244	318	EK74
North Worple Way SW14	171	322	CR83
Northall Rd., Bexh.	255	319	FC82
Northampton Gro. N1	117	306	DR65
Northampton Pk. N1	116	306	DQ65
Northampton Rd. EC1	36	316	DN70
Northampton Rd., Croy.	287	333	DU103
Northampton Rd., Enf.	203	301	DY42
Northampton Sq. EC1	36/7	316	DP69
Northampton St. N1	116	306	DQ66
Northanger Rd. SW16	272	324	DL93
Northbank Rd. E17	223	307	EC54
Northborough Rd. SW16	272	324	DK97
Northbourne, Brom.	289	334	EG101
Northbourne Rd. SW4	177	324	DK84
Northbrook Dr., Nthwd.	213	302	BS53
Northbrook Rd. N22	220	306	DL52
Northbrook Rd. SE13	183	325	ED85
Northbrook Rd., Barn.	206	299	CY44
Northbrook Rd., Croy.	287	332	DR99
Northbrook Rd., Ilf.	235	308	EN61
Northburgh St. EC1	36/7	316	DP70
Northchurch SE17	86	316	DR78
Northchurch Rd. N1	117	306	DR66
Northchurch Rd., Wem.	108	304	CN65
Northchurch Ter. N1	117	306	DS66
Northcliffe Clo., Wor.Pk.	283	330	CS104
Northcliffe Dr. N20	206	299	CZ46
Northcote Ave. W5	133	314	CL73
Northcote Ave., Islw.	168	322	CG85
Northcote Ave., Sthl.	242	313	BY73
Northcote Ave., Surb.	282	330	CN101
Northcote Rd. E17	222	307	DY56
Northcote Rd. NW10	109	304	CS66
Northcote Rd. SW11	175	323	DE85
Northcote Rd., Croy.	287	332	DR100
Northcote Rd., N.Mal.	269	322	CR97
Northcote Rd., Sid.	277	326	ES91
Northcote Rd., Twick.	168	322	CG85
Northcott Ave. N22	220	306	DL53
Northcroft Rd. W13	142	314	CH75
Northcroft Ter. W13	142	314	CH75
Northdene Gdns. N15	221	306	DT58
Northdown Clo., Ruis.	231	312	BT62
Northdown Gdns., Ilf.	225	308	ES57
Northdown Rd., Horn.	238	310	FH59
Northdown Rd., Sutt.	292	331	DA110
Northdown Rd., Well.	254	319	EV82
Northdown St. N1	22/3	316	DL68
Northend Rd., Dart.	255	319	FF81
Northend Rd., Erith	255	319	FF81
Northern Ave. N9	209	300	DS47
Northern Perimeter Rd., Houns.	257	320	BP81
Northern Perimeter Rd. W., Houns.	256	320	BK81
Northern Relief Rd., Bark.	235	308	EP66
Northern Rd. E13	244	318	EH68
Northernhay Wk., Mord.	270	323	CY98
Northey Ave., Sutt.	292	331	CX110
Northey St. E14	139	317	DY73
Northfield Ave. W5	132	314	CH74
Northfield Ave. W13	132	314	CH74
Northfield Ave., Pnr.	214	303	BX56
Northfield Clo., Brom.	276	326	EL95
Northfield Clo., Hayes	249	320	BT76
Northfield Ct., Stai.	280	328	BH95
Northfield Cres., Sutt.	284	331	CY105
Northfield Gdns., Dag.	236	309	EZ63
Northfield Pk., Hayes	249	320	BS76
Northfield Path, Dag.	236	309	EZ63
Northfield Rd. E6	234	308	EM66
Northfield Rd. N16	101	306	DS59
Northfield Rd. W13	142	314	CH75
Northfield Rd., Dag.	236	309	EZ63
Northfield Rd., Enf.	210	301	DV43
Northfield Rd., Houns.	250	321	BX80
Northfield Rd., Stai.	280	328	BH95
Northfields SW18	174	323	DA84
Northfields Ind. Est., Wem.	124	314	CN67
Northfields Rd. W3	134	314	CP71
Northgate, Nthwd.	213	302	BQ52
Northgate Dr. NW9	217	304	CS58
Northiam N12	207	299	DA49
Northiam St. E9	128	317	DV67
Northington St. WC1	35	316	DM70
Northlands Ave., Orp.	291	334	ES105
Northlands St. SE5	162	316	DQ82
Northolm, Edg.	205	298	CR49
Northolme Gdns., Edg.	217	304	CN53
Northolme Ri., Orp.	291	334	ES103
Northolme Rd. N5	116	306	DQ63
Northolt Ave., Ruis.	232	313	BV64
Northolt Gdns., Grnf.	233	313	CF64
Northolt Ind. Est., Nthlt.	233	313	CB66
Northolt Rd., Har.	233	313	CB63
Northolt Rd., Houns.	256	320	BK81
Northolt Way, Horn.	238	310	FJ64
Northover, Brom.	199	325	EF90
Northport St. N1	26	316	DR67
Northrop Rd., Houns.	257	320	BS82
Northside Rd., Brom.	276	326	EG95
Northspur Rd., Sutt.	284	331	DA104
Northstead Rd. SW2	194	324	DN89
Northumberland All. EC3	50/1	316	DS72
Northumberland Ave. E12	234	308	EJ60
Northumberland Ave. WC2	58/9	316	DL74
Northumberland Ave., Enf.	203	301	DV39
Northumberland Ave., Horn.	228	310	FJ57
Northumberland Ave., Islw.	251	321	CF81
Northumberland Ave., Well.	261	326	ER84
Northumberland Clo., Erith	255	319	FC80
Northumberland Clo., Stai.	256	320	BL86
Northumberland Cres., Felt.	257	320	BS86
Northumberland Gdns. N9	209	300	DT48
Northumberland Gdns., Brom.	277	326	EN98
Northumberland Gdns., Islw.	152	314	CG80
Northumberland Gdns., Mitch.	286	332	DK99
Northumberland Gro. N17	222	307	DV52
Northumberland Pk. N17	221	306	DT52
Northumberland Pk., Erith	255	319	FC80
Northumberland Pl. W2	40	315	DA72
Northumberland Pl., Rich.	169	322	CK86
Northumberland Rd. E6	244	318	EL72
Northumberland Rd. E17	104	307	EA59
Northumberland Rd., Barn.	207	299	DC44
Northumberland Rd., Har.	214	303	BZ57
Northumberland Row, Twick.	259	321	CE88
Northumberland St. WC2	58/9	316	DL74
Northumberland Way, Erith	255	319	FC81
Northumbria St. E14	140	317	EA72
Northview, Swan.	279	327	FE96
Northway NW7	218	305	CU52
Northway NW11	219	305	DB57
Northway, Wall.	286	332	DJ105
Northway Circ. NW7	205	298	CR49
Northway Cres. NW7	205	298	CR49
Northway Rd. SE5	178	324	DQ83
Northway Rd., Croy.	287	332	DT100
Northweald La., Kings.T.	268	322	CK92
Northwest Pl. N1	24	316	DN68
Northwick Ave., Har.	216	304	CG58
Northwick Circle, Har.	216	304	CJ58
Northwick Clo. NW8	30	315	DD70
Northwick Pk. Rd., Har.	215	303	CF58
Northwick Rd., Wem.	123	314	CK67
Northwick Ter. NW8	30	315	DD70
Northwick Wk., Har.	233	313	CF59
Northwold Dr., Pnr.	214	303	BW55
Northwold Est. E5	102	307	DU61
Northwold Rd. E5	102	307	DU61
Northwold Rd. N16	101	306	DT61
Northwood Ave., Horn.	238	310	FG63
Northwood Ave., Pur.	294	332	DN112
Northwood Gdns. N12	207	299	DD50
Northwood Gdns., Grnf.	233	313	CF64
Northwood Gdns., Ilf.	225	308	EN56
Northwood Hall N6	98	306	DJ59
Northwood Ho. SE27	273	324	DR91
Northwood Pl., Erith	254	319	EZ76
Northwood Rd. N6	98	306	DH59
Northwood Rd. SE23	197	325	DZ88
Northwood Rd., Cars.	293	332	DG107
Northwood Rd., Houns.	256	320	BK81
Northwood Rd., Th.Hth.	273	324	DP96
Northwood Rd., Uxb.	212	302	BJ53
Northwood Way SE19	273	324	DR93
Northwood Way, Nthwd.	214	303	BU53
Northwood Way, Uxb.	212	302	BK53
Norton Ave., Surb.	282	330	CP101
Norton Clo. E4	211	301	EA50
Norton Clo., Enf.	203	301	DV40
Norton Folgate E1	50/1	316	DS71
Norton Gdns. SW16	272	324	DL96
Norton Rd. E10	103	307	DZ60
Norton Rd., Dag.	237	309	FD65
Norton Rd., Uxb.	240	312	BK69
Norton Rd., Wem.	107	304	CK65
Norval Rd., Wem.	90	304	CH61
Norway Gate SE16	149	317	DY76
Norway Pl. E14	139	317	DZ72
Norway St. SE10	166	317	EB79
Norwich Ho. E14	140	317	EB72
Norwich Ms., Ilf.	236	309	EU60
Norwich Pl., Bexh.	263	327	FA84
Norwich Rd. E7	234	308	EG64
Norwich Rd., Dag.	247	319	FA68
Norwich Rd., Grnf.	243	313	CB67
Norwich Rd., Nthwd.	231	302	BT55
Norwich Rd., Th.Hth.	273	324	DQ97
Norwich St. EC4	48	316	DN72
Norwich Wk., Edg.	217	304	CQ52
Norwood Ave., Rom.	237	309	FD59
Norwood Ave., Wem.	123	314	CM67
Norwood Clo., Sthl.	251	321	CA77
Norwood Clo., Twick.	259	321	CD89
Norwood Cres., Houns.	257	320	BQ81
Norwood Dr., Har.	214	303	BZ58
Norwood Gdns., Hayes	242	313	BW70
Norwood Gdns., Sthl.	250	321	BZ77
Norwood Grn. Rd., Sthl.	251	321	CA77
Norwood High St. SE27	194	324	DP90
Norwood Pk. Rd. SE27	273	324	DQ92
Norwood Rd. SE24	194	324	DP88
Norwood Rd. SE27	194	324	DP89
Norwood Rd., Sthl.	250	321	BZ77
Norwood Ter., Sthl.	251	321	CB77
Nota Ms. N3	219	305	DA53
Notley St. SE5	163	316	DR80
Notre Dame Est. SW4	176	324	DJ84
Notson Rd. SE25	274	325	DV98
Notting Barn Rd. W10	127	315	CX70
Notting Hill Gate W11	52	315	DA74
Nottingdale Sq. W11	137	315	CY74
Nottingham Ave. E16	244	318	EJ71
Nottingham Ct. WC2	46/7	316	DL72
Nottingham Pl. W1	44	316	DG71
Nottingham Rd. E10	223	307	EC58
Nottingham Rd. SW17	191	323	DF88
Nottingham Rd., Islw.	251	321	CF82
Nottingham Rd., S.Croy.	287	332	DQ105
Nottingham St. W1	44	316	DG71
Nottingham Ter. NW1	32	316	DG70
Nova Ms., Sutt.	284	331	CY101
Nova Rd., Croy.	286	332	DP102
Novar Clo., Orp.	291	334	ET101
Novar Rd. SE9	261	326	EQ88
Novello St. SW6	158	315	DA81
Nowell Rd. SW13	156	315	CU79
Nower Hill, Pnr.	214	303	BZ56
Noyna Rd. SW17	191	323	DF90
Nuding Clo. SE13	182	325	EA83
Nugent Rd. N19	99	306	DL60
Nugent Rd. SE25	273	324	DT97
Nugent Ter. NW8	17	315	DC68
Nugents Ct., Pnr.	214	303	BY53
Nugents Pk., Pnr.	214	303	BY53
Nun Ct. EC2	50	316	DR72
Nuneaton Rd., Dag.	236	309	EX66
Nunhead Cres. SE15	180	325	DV83
Nunhead Est. SE15	180	325	DV84
Nunhead Grn. SE15	180	325	DV83
Nunhead Gro. SE15	180	325	DV83
Nunhead La. SE15	180	325	DV83
Nunhead Pas. SE15	180	325	DU83
Nunnington Clo. SE9	260	326	EL90
Nunns Rd., Enf.	202	300	DQ40
Nupton Dr., Barn.	206	299	CW44
Nursery, The, Erith	255	319	FF80
Nursery Ave. N3	219	305	DC54
Nursery Ave., Bexh.	262	327	EZ83
Nursery Ave., Croy.	288	333	DX103
Nursery Clo. SE4	165	317	DZ82
Nursery Clo. SW15	173	323	CX84
Nursery Clo., Croy.	288	333	DX103
Nursery Clo., Enf.	203	301	DX39
Nursery Clo., Felt.	258	321	BV87
Nursery Clo., Orp.	291	334	ET101
Nursery Clo., Rom.	226	309	EX58
Nursery Clo., Swan.	279	327	FC96
Nursery Ct. N17	221	306	DT52
Nursery Gdns., Chis.	277	326	EP93
Nursery Gdns., Enf.	203	301	DX39
Nursery Gdns., Stai.	264	328	BH94
Nursery Gdns., Sun.	281	328	BT96
Nursery La. E2	27	316	DT67
Nursery La. E7	234	308	EG65
Nursery La. W10	136	315	CW71
Nursery Rd. E9	118	307	DW65
Nursery Rd. N2	219	305	DD53
Nursery Rd. N14	208	300	DJ45
Nursery Rd. SW9	177	324	DM84
Nursery Rd., Pnr.	214	303	BW55
Nursery Rd., Sun.	281	328	BS96
Nursery Rd., Sutt.	285	331	DC105
Nursery Rd., Th.Hth.	273	324	DR98
Nursery Rd. Merton SW19	271	323	DB96
Nursery Rd. Mitcham, Mitch.	271	323	DE97
Nursery Rd. Wimbledon SW19	270	323	CY94
Nursery Row SE17	86	316	DR77
Nursery St. N17	221	306	DT52
Nursery Wk. NW4	218	305	CV55
Nursery Wk., Rom.	237	309	FD59
Nursery Waye, Uxb.	240	312	BK67
Nurserymans Rd. N11	208	300	DG49
Nurstead Rd., Erith	255	319	FA80
Nutbourne St. W10	127	315	CY69
Nutbrook St. SE15	180	325	DU83
Nutbrowne Rd., Dag.	246	319	EZ67
Nutcroft Rd. SE15	164	317	DV80
Nutfield Clo. N18	222	307	DU51
Nutfield Clo., Cars.	285	331	DE104
Nutfield Gdns., Ilf.	235	308	ET61
Nutfield Gdns., Nthlt.	242	313	BW68
Nutfield Rd. E15	120	307	EC63
Nutfield Rd. NW2	94	305	CU61
Nutfield Rd. SE22	179	324	DT85
Nutfield Rd., Th.Hth.	273	324	DP98
Nutfield Way, Orp.	290	334	EN103
Nutford Pl. W1	42/3	315	DE72
Nuthatch Clo., Stai.	264	320	BM88
Nuthatch Gdns. SE28	253	318	ER75
Nuthurst Ave. SW2	193	324	DM89
Nutley Clo., Swan.	279	327	FF95
Nutley Ter. NW3	112	305	DC65
Nutmead Clo., Bex.	263	327	FC88
Nutmeg Clo. E16	131	317	EE70
Nutmeg La. E14	141	317	ED72
Nutt Gro., Edg.	204	298	CK47
Nutt St. SE15	163	316	DT80
Nuttall St. N1	26/7	316	DS68
Nutter La. E11	224	308	EJ58
Nutty La., Shep.	281	328	BQ97
Nutwell St. SW17	271	323	DE92
Nuxley Rd., Belv.	254	319	EZ79
Nyanza St. SE18	253	318	ER79
Nye Bevan Est. E5	103	307	DX62
Nylands Ave., Rich.	154	314	CN81
Nymans Gdns. SW20	270	323	CV97
Nynehead St. SE14	165	317	DY80
Nyon Gro. SE6	197	325	DZ89
Nyssa Clo., Wdf.Grn.	224	308	EM51
Nyth Clo., Upmin.	229	311	FR58
Nyton Clo. N19	99	306	DL60
Oak Apple Ct. SE12	260	326	EG89
Oak Ave. N8	220	306	DL56
Oak Ave. N10	220	306	DH52
Oak Ave. N17	221	306	DR52
Oak Ave., Croy.	288	333	EA102
Oak Ave., Hmptn.	266	329	BY92
Oak Ave., Houns.	250	321	BY80
Oak Ave., Upmin.	239	311	FP62
Oak Ave., Uxb.	231	312	BP61
Oak Ave., West Dr.	249	320	BN76
Oak Clo. N14	208	300	DH45
Oak Clo., Dart.	263	327	FE84
Oak Clo., Sutt.	285	331	DC103
Oak Cottage Clo. SE6	199	325	EF88
Oak Cres. E16	141	317	EE71
Oak Dene W13	132	314	CH71
Oak Gdns., Croy.	288	333	EA103
Oak Gdns., Edg.	217	304	CQ54
Oak Glade, Nthwd.	213	302	BP53
Oak Glen, Horn.	228	311	FL55
Oak Gro. NW2	111	305	CX63
Oak Gro., Ruis.	232	313	BV59
Oak Gro., Sun.	266	329	BV94
Oak Gro., W.Wick.	289	333	EC103
Oak Gro. Rd. SE20	274	325	DW96
Oak Hill, Wdf.Grn.	223	307	ED52
Oak Hill Clo., Wdf.Grn.	223	307	ED52
Oak Hill Ct. SW19	270	323	CX94
Oak Hill Cres., Wdf.Grn.	223	307	ED52
Oak Hill Gdns., Wdf.Grn.	223	307	EE53
Oak Hill Pk. NW3	112	305	DB63
Oak Hill Pk. Ms. NW3	112	305	DC63
Oak Hill Way NW3	112	305	DC63
Oak La. E14	139	317	DZ73
Oak La. N2	219	305	DD54
Oak La. N11	220	306	DK51
Oak La., Islw.	259	321	CE84
Oak La., Twick.	184	322	CG87
Oak La., Wdf.Grn.	211	301	EF49
Oak Lo. Clo., Stan.	204	298	CJ50
Oak Lo. Dr., W.Wick.	288	333	EB101
Oak Manor Dr., Wem.	107	304	CM64
Oak Pk. Gdns. SW19	189	323	CX87
Oak Pl. SW18	174	323	DB85
Oak Rd. W5	133	314	CK73
Oak Rd. (Northumberland Heath), Erith	255	319	FC80
Oak Rd., N.Mal.	269	322	CR96
Oak Rd., Rom.	228	311	FM53
Oak Row SW16	272	324	DJ96
Oak Side, Uxb.	240	312	BH65
Oak St., Rom.	227	309	FC57
Oak Tree Clo. W5	132	314	CJ72
Oak Tree Clo., Stan.	216	304	CH52
Oak Tree Ct., Borwd.	204	298	CK44
Oak Tree Dell NW9	217	304	CQ57
Oak Tree Dr. N20	207	299	DB46
Oak Tree Gdns., Brom.	276	326	EH92
Oak Tree Rd. NW8	30/1	315	DE69
Oak Village NW5	114	306	DG63
Oak Way N14	208	300	DH45
Oak Way W3	135	314	CS74
Oak Way, Croy.	288	333	DX100
Oak Way, Felt.	265	320	BS88
Oakapple Clo., S.Croy.	295	333	DV114
Oakbank Gro. SE24	178	324	DQ84
Oakbrook Clo., Brom.	276	326	EH91
Oakbury Rd. SW6	158	315	DB82
Oakcombe Clo., N.Mal.	269	322	CS95
Oakcroft Clo., Pnr.	214	303	BV54
Oakcroft Rd. SE13	167	317	ED82
Oakcroft Rd., Chess.	282	330	CM105
Oakcroft Vil., Chess.	282	330	CM105
Oakdale N14	208	300	DH46
Oakdale Ave., Har.	216	304	CL57
Oakdale Ave., Nthwd.	214	303	BU54
Oakdale Ct. E4	211	301	EC50
Oakdale Gdns. E4	211	301	EC50
Oakdale Rd. E7	234	308	EH66
Oakdale Rd. E11	105	307	ED61
Oakdale Rd. E18	224	308	EH54
Oakdale Rd. N4	221	306	DQ58
Oakdale Rd. SE15	180	325	DW83
Oakdale Rd. SW16	272	324	DL92
Oakdale Way, Mitch.	285	332	DG101
Oakden St. SE11	84	316	DN77
Oakdene SE15	164	317	DV81
Oakdene Ave., Chis.	277	326	EN92
Oakdene Ave., Erith	255	319	FC79
Oakdene Clo., Horn.	228	310	FH58
Oakdene Clo., Pnr.	214	303	BZ52
Oakdene Dr., Surb.	283	330	CQ101
Oakdene Ms., Sutt.	284	331	CZ102
Oakdene Pk. N3	218	305	CZ52
Oakdene Rd., Orp.	291	334	ET99
Oakdene Rd., Uxb.	241	312	BP68
Oake Ct. SW15	173	323	CY85
Oakenshaw Clo., Surb.	282	330	CL101
Oakes Clo. E6	244	318	EM72
Oakeshott Ave. N6	98	306	DG61
Oakey La. SE1	72	316	DN76
Oakfield E4	211	301	EB50
Oakfield Ave., Har.	216	304	CH55
Oakfield Clo., N.Mal.	283	330	CT99
Oakfield Clo., Ruis.	231	302	BT58
Oakfield Ct. N8	99	306	DL59
Oakfield Ct. NW2	95	305	CX59
Oakfield Gdns. N18	209	300	DS49
Oakfield Gdns. SE19	273	324	DT92

Oakfield Gdns., Beck. 288 333 EA99
Oakfield Gdns., Cars. 285 331 DE102
Oakfield Gdns., Grnf. 243 313 CD70
Oakfield La., Bex. 263 327 FE89
Oakfield La., Kes. 290 334 EJ105
Oakfield Rd. E6 244 318 EL67
Oakfield Rd. E17 222 307 DY54
Oakfield Rd. N3 219 305 DB53
Oakfield Rd. N4 221 306 DN58
Oakfield Rd. N14 208 300 DL48
Oakfield Rd. SE20 274 325 DV95
Oakfield Rd. SW19 189 323 CX90
Oakfield Rd., Ashf. 265 328 BP91
Oakfield Rd., Croy. 287 332 DQ102
Oakfield Rd., Ilf. 235 308 EP61
Oakfield Rd., Orp. 291 335 EU101
Oakfield St. SW10 158 315 DC79
Oakfields Rd. NW11 218 305 CY58
Oakford Rd. NW5 114 306 DJ63
Oakhall Ct. E11 224 308 EH58
Oakhall Dr., Sun. 265 328 BT92
Oakhall Rd. E11 224 308 EH58
Oakham Clo. SE6 197 325 DZ89
Oakham Dr., Brom. 275 325 EF98
Oakhampton Rd. NW7 218 305 CX52
Oakhill, Surb. 282 330 CL101
Oakhill Ave. NW3 112 305 DB63
Oakhill Ave., Pnr. 214 303 BY54
Oakhill Ct. E11 224 308 EH58
Oakhill Ct. SW19 270 323 CX94
Oakhill Cres., Surb. 282 330 CL101
Oakhill Dr., Surb. 282 330 CL101
Oakhill Gro., Surb. 282 330 CL100
Oakhill Path, Surb. 282 330 CL100
Oakhill Pl. SW15 174 323 DA85
Oakhill Rd. SW15 173 323 CZ85
Oakhill Rd. SW16 272 324 DL95
Oakhill Rd., Beck. 275 325 EC96
Oakhill Rd., Orp. 291 334 ET102
Oakhill Rd., Surb. 282 330 CL100
Oakhill Rd., Sutt. 284 331 DB104
Oakhouse Rd., Bexh. 263 327 FA85
Oakhurst Ave., Barn. 207 299 DE45
Oakhurst Ave., Bexh. 254 319 EY80
Oakhurst Clo. E17 223 307 EE56
Oakhurst Clo., Chis. 225 308 EQ53
Oakhurst Clo., Tedd. 267 329 CE92
Oakhurst Gdns. E4 211 301 EF46
Oakhurst Gdns. E17 223 307 EE56
Oakhurst Gdns., Bexh. 254 319 EY80
Oakhurst Gro. SE22 180 325 DU84
Oakhurst Ri., Cars. 293 331 DE110
Oakhurst Rd., Enf. 203 301 DX36
Oakington Ave., Har. 233 313 CA59
Oakington Ave., Hayes 249 320 BR77
Oakington Ave., Wem. 91 304 CM62
Oakington Dr., Sun. 266 329 BW96
Oakington Manor Dr., Wem. 108 304 CN64
Oakington Rd. W9 28 315 DA70
Oakington Way N8 220 306 DL58
Oakland Rd. E15 121 307 EE63
Oaklands N21 208 300 DM47
Oaklands, Ken. 295 332 DQ114
Oaklands, Twick. 259 321 CC87
Oaklands Ave. N9 210 301 DV44
Oaklands Ave., Islw. 251 321 CF79
Oaklands Ave., Rom. 227 309 FE55
Oaklands Ave., Sid. 261 326 ET87
Oaklands Ave., Th.Hth. 273 324 DN98
Oaklands Ave., W.Wick. 288 333 EB104
Oaklands Clo., Bexh. 262 327 EZ85
Oaklands Clo., Chess. 282 330 CJ105
Oaklands Clo., Orp. 291 334 ES100
Oaklands Ct., Wem. 107 304 CK64
Oaklands Est. SW4 176 324 DJ86
Oaklands Gdns., Ken. 295 332 DQ114
Oaklands Gate, Nthwd. 213 302 BS51
Oaklands Gro. W12 136 315 CU74
Oaklands Pk. Ave., Ilf. 235 308 ER61
Oaklands Pl. SW4 176 324 DJ84
Oaklands Rd. N20 206 299 CZ45
Oaklands Rd. NW2 111 305 CX63
Oaklands Rd. SW14 171 322 CR83
Oaklands Rd. W7 251 321 CF75
Oaklands Rd., Bexh. 262 327 EZ84
Oaklands Rd., Brom. 275 325 EE94
Oaklands Way, Wall. 294 332 DK108
Oaklea Pas., Kings.T. 268 322 CK97
Oakleafe Gdns., Ilf. 225 308 EP55
Oakleigh Ave. N20 207 299 DD47
Oakleigh Ave., Edg. 217 304 CP54
Oakleigh Ave., Surb. 282 330 CN102
Oakleigh Clo. N20 207 299 DF48
Oakleigh Clo., Swan. 279 327 FE97
Oakleigh Ct., Barn. 207 299 DE44
Oakleigh Ct., Edg. 217 304 CQ54
Oakleigh Cres. N20 207 299 DE47
Oakleigh Gdns. N20 207 299 DC46
Oakleigh Gdns., Edg. 204 298 CM50
Oakleigh Gdns., Orp. 291 334 ES105
Oakleigh Ms. N20 207 299 DC47
Oakleigh Pk. Ave., Chis. 277 326 EN96
Oakleigh Pk. N. N20 207 299 DD46
Oakleigh Pk. S. N20 207 299 DE45
Oakleigh Rd., Pnr. 214 303 BZ51
Oakleigh Rd., Uxb. 241 312 BQ66
Oakleigh Rd. N. N20 207 299 DE47
Oakleigh Rd. S. N11 208 300 DG48
Oakleigh Way, Mitch. 272 324 DH95
Oakleigh Way, Surb. 282 330 CN102
Oakley Ave. W5 134 314 CN73
Oakley Ave., Bark. 235 308 ET66
Oakley Ave., Croy. 286 332 DM105
Oakley Clo. E4 211 301 EC48
Oakley Clo. E6 244 318 EL72
Oakley Clo. W7 243 313 CE73
Oakley Clo., Islw. 251 321 CD81
Oakley Ct., Mitch. 285 332 DG102
Oakley Cres. EC1 24/5 316 DP68
Oakley Dr. SE9 261 326 ER88
Oakley Dr. SE13 182 325 EC85
Oakley Dr., Brom. 290 334 EL104
Oakley Gdns. N8 220 306 DM57
Oakley Gdns. SW3 159 315 DE79
Oakley Pk., Bex. 262 327 EW87
Oakley Pl. SE1 87 316 DT78
Oakley Rd. N1 117 306 DR66
Oakley Rd. SE25 287 333 DV99
Oakley Rd., Brom. 290 334 EL104
Oakley Rd., Har. 215 303 CE58
Oakley Sq. NW1 21 316 DJ68
Oakley St. SW3 159 315 DE79
Oakley Wk. W6 157 315 CX79
Oakley Yd. E2 39 316 DT70
Oaklodge Way NW7 217 304 CT51
Oakmead Ave., Brom. 289 334 EG100
Oakmead Gdns., Edg. 205 298 CR49
Oakmead Pl., Mitch. 271 323 DE95
Oakmead Rd. SW12 192 324 DG88
Oakmead Rd., Croy. 286 332 DK100
Oakmeade, Pnr. 215 303 CA51
Oakmere Rd. SE2 254 319 EU79
Oakmount Pl., Orp. 291 334 ER102
Oakridge Dr. N2 219 305 DD55
Oakridge La., Brom. 275 325 ED92
Oakridge Rd., Brom. 275 325 ED91
Oaks, The N12 207 299 DB49
Oaks, The SE18 253 318 EQ78
Oaks, The, Hayes 241 312 BQ68
Oaks, The, Ruis. 231 312 BS59
Oaks, The, Swan. 279 327 FE96
Oaks, The, Wdf.Grn. 223 307 EE52
Oaks Ave. SE19 273 324 DS92
Oaks Ave., Felt. 258 321 BY89
Oaks Ave., Rom. 227 309 FC54
Oaks Ave., Wor.Pk. 283 331 CV104
Oaks Gro. E4 211 301 EE47
Oaks La., Croy. 288 333 DW104
Oaks La., Ilf. 225 308 ES57
Oaks Rd., Croy. 287 333 DV106
Oaks Rd., Ken. 294 332 DP114
Oaks Rd., Stai. 256 320 BK86
Oaks Track, Cars. 293 331 DF111
Oaks Track, Wall. 293 332 DH110
Oaks Way, Cars. 293 331 DF108
Oaks Way, Ken. 295 332 DQ114
Oaks Way, Surb. 282 330 CK103
Oaksford Ave. SE26 196 325 DV90
Oakshade Rd., Brom. 275 325 ED91
Oakshaw Rd. SW18 190 323 DB87
Oakside, Uxb. 240 312 BH65
Oakthorpe Rd. N13 209 300 DN50
Oaktree Ave. N13 209 300 DP48
Oaktree Gro., Ilf. 235 308 ER64
Oakview Gdns. N2 219 305 DD56
Oakview Gro., Croy. 288 333 DY102
Oakview Rd. SE6 275 325 EB92
Oakway SW20 270 323 CW98
Oakway, Brom. 275 325 ED96
Oakway Clo., Bex. 262 327 EY86
Oakways SE9 261 326 EP86
Oakwood, Wall. 293 332 DH109
Oakwood Ave. N14 208 300 DK45
Oakwood Ave., Beck. 275 325 EC96
Oakwood Ave., Brom. 276 326 EH97
Oakwood Ave., Mitch. 271 323 DD96
Oakwood Ave., Pur. 294 332 DP112
Oakwood Ave., Sthl. 243 313 CA73
Oakwood Chase, Horn. 228 311 FM58
Oakwood Clo. N14 208 300 DJ44
Oakwood Clo., Chis. 276 326 EM93
Oakwood Clo., Wdf.Grn. 224 308 EL51
Oakwood Ct. W14 147 315 CZ76
Oakwood Cres. N21 208 300 DL44
Oakwood Cres., Grnf. 106 304 CG65
Oakwood Dr. SE19 273 324 DR93
Oakwood Dr., Bexh. 263 327 FD84
Oakwood Dr., Edg. 217 304 CQ51
Oakwood Gdns., Ilf. 235 308 ET61
Oakwood Gdns., Orp. 291 334 EQ103
Oakwood Gdns., Sutt. 284 331 DA103
Oakwood La. W14 147 315 CZ76
Oakwood Pk. Rd. N14 208 300 DK45
Oakwood Pl., Croy. 286 332 DN100
Oakwood Rd. NW11 219 305 DA56
Oakwood Rd. SW20 270 323 CU95
Oakwood Rd., Croy. 286 332 DN100
Oakwood Rd., Orp. 291 334 EQ103
Oakwood Rd., Pnr. 214 303 BV54
Oakwood Vw. N14 208 300 DK43
Oakworth Rd. W10 136 315 CW71
Oasthouse Way, Orp. 278 327 EV98
Oat La. EC2 49 316 DQ72
Oates Clo., Brom. 275 325 ED97
Oatfield Rd., Orp. 291 334 ET102
Oatland Ri. E17 222 307 DY54
Oatlands Rd., Enf. 203 301 DW39
Oban Clo. E13 244 318 EJ70
Oban Ho., Bark. 245 318 ER68
Oban Rd. E13 244 318 EJ69
Oban Rd. SE25 273 324 DR98
Oban St. E14 141 317 ED72
Oberon Way, Shep. 280 328 BL97
Oberstein Rd. SW11 175 323 DD84
Oborne Clo. SE24 178 324 DP85
Observatory Gdns. W8 64 315 DA75
Observatory Rd. SW14 170 322 CQ84
Occupation La. SE18 253 318 EP81
Occupation La. W5 143 314 CK77
Occupation Rd. SE17 85 316 DQ78
Occupation Rd. W13 142 314 CH75
Ocean Est. E1 129 317 DX70
Ocean St. E1 139 317 DX71
Ockendon Rd. N1 117 306 DR65
Ockendon Rd., Upmin. 239 311 FQ64
Ockham Dr., Orp. 278 327 EU94
Ockley Rd. SW16 272 324 DL91
Ockley Rd., Croy. 286 332 DM101
Octagon Arc. EC2 50/1 316 DS71
Octavia Clo., Mitch. 285 331 DE99
Octavia Rd., Islw. 259 321 CF83
Octavia St. SW11 159 315 DE81
Octavia Way SE28 246 319 EV73
Octavia Way, Stai. 264 328 BG93
Octavius St. SE8 166 317 EA80
Odard Rd., W.Mol. 267 329 CA98
Odessa Rd. E7 121 307 EF63
Odessa Rd. NW10 126 315 CU68
Odessa St. SE16 149 317 DZ75
Odger St. SW11 159 315 DF82
Odhams Wk. WC2 46/7 316 DL72
Odyssey Business Pk., Ruis. 232 313 BV64
Offas Mead E9 119 307 DY63
Offenbach Ho. E2 129 317 DX68
Offenham Rd. SE9 276 326 EM91
Offerton Rd. SW4 176 324 DJ83
Offham Slope N12 206 299 CZ50
Offley Rd. SW9 160 316 DN80
Offord Clo. N17 222 307 DU52
Offord Rd. N1 115 306 DM66
Offord St. N1 115 306 DM66
Ogilby St. SE18 252 318 EM77
Oglander Rd. SE15 179 324 DT84
Ogle St. W1 45 316 DJ71
Oglethorpe Rd., Dag. 236 309 EZ62
Ohio Rd. E13 131 317 EF70
Oil Mill La. W6 146 315 CU78
Okeburn Rd. SW17 272 324 DG92
Okehampton Clo. N12 207 299 DD50
Okehampton Cres., Well. 254 319 EV81
Okehampton Rd. NW10 126 315 CW67
Okehampton Rd., Rom. 228 310 FJ51
Okehampton Sq., Rom. 228 310 FJ51
Okemore Gdns., Orp. 278 327 EW98
Olaf St. W11 137 315 CX73
Old Bailey EC4 48/9 316 DP72
Old Barn Clo., Sutt. 292 331 CY108
Old Barn Way, Bexh. 263 327 FD83
Old Barrack Yd. SW1 68 316 DG75
Old Barrowfield E15 131 317 EE67
Old Bethnal Grn. Rd. E2 128 317 DU69
Old Bexley La., Bex. 263 327 FD89
Old Bexley La., Dart. 263 327 FF88
Old Bond St. W1 57 316 DJ73
Old Brewers Yd. WC2 46/7 316 DL72
Old Brewery Ms. NW3 113 305 DD63
Old Bri. Clo., Nthlt. 243 313 CA68
Old Bri. St., Kings.T. 268 322 CK96
Old Broad St. EC2 50 316 DR72
Old Bromley Rd., Brom. 275 325 ED92
Old Brompton Rd. SW5 76/7 315 DB78
Old Brompton Rd. SW7 76/7 315 DB78
Old Bldgs. WC2 48 316 DN72
Old Burlington St. W1 57 316 DJ73
Old Castle St. E1 51 316 DT72
Old Cavendish St. W1 44/5 316 DH72
Old Change Ct. EC4 49 316 DQ72
Old Charlton Rd., Shep. 281 328 BQ99
Old Chelsea Ms. SW3 159 315 DD79
Old Ch. La. NW9 93 304 CR61
Old Ch. La., Grnf. 122 314 CG69
Old Ch. La., Stan. 204 298 CH50
Old Ch. Rd. E1 139 317 DX72
Old Ch. Rd. E4 211 301 EA49
Old Ch. St. SW3 159 315 DD78
Old Clem Sq. SE18 253 318 EN79
Old Compton St. W1 58 316 DK73
Old Cote Dr., Houns. 251 321 CA79
Old Ct. Pl. W8 64/5 315 DB75
Old Deer Pk. Gdns., Rich. 169 322 CL83
Old Devonshire Rd. SW12 192 324 DH87
Old Dock Clo., Rich. 154 314 CN79
Old Dover Rd. SE3 252 318 EG80
Old Fm. Ave. N14 208 300 DJ45
Old Fm. Ave., Sid. 261 326 ER88
Old Fm. Clo., Houns. 258 321 BZ84
Old Fm. Gdns., Swan. 279 327 FF97
Old Fm. Pas., Hmptn. 267 329 CC95
Old Fm. Rd. N2 219 305 DD53
Old Fm. Rd., Hmptn. 266 329 BZ93
Old Fm. Rd., West Dr. 248 320 BK75
Old Fm. Rd. E., Sid. 262 327 EU89
Old Fm. Rd. W., Sid. 261 326 ET89
Old Fish St. Hill EC4 61 316 DQ73
Old Fleet La. EC4 48/9 316 DP72
Old Ford Rd. E2 128 317 DW68
Old Ford Rd. E3 129 317 DX68
Old Forge Clo., Stan. 204 298 CG49
Old Forge Cres., Shep. 281 328 BP100
Old Forge Ms. W12 146 315 CV75
Old Forge Rd., Enf. 202 300 DT38
Old Forge Way, Sid. 262 327 EV91
Old Fox Footpath, S.Croy. 295 332 DS108
Old Gannon Clo., Nthwd. 213 302 BQ50
Old Gloucester St. WC1 46/7 316 DL71
Old Hall Clo., Pnr. 214 303 BY53
Old Hall Dr., Pnr. 214 303 BY53
Old Hatch Manor, Ruis. 231 312 BT59
Old Hill, Chis. 277 326 EN95
Old Homesdale Rd., Brom. 276 326 EJ98
Old Hospital Clo. SW12 191 323 DF88
Old Ho. Clo. SW19 270 323 CY92
Old Ho. Gdns., Twick. 168 322 CJ86
Old Howlett's La., Ruis. 231 302 BR58
Old Jamaica Rd. SE16 148 317 DU76
Old James St. SE15 180 325 DV83
Old Jewry EC2 50 316 DR72
Old Kent Rd. SE1 86/7 316 DS77
Old Kent Rd. SE15 164 317 DV79
Old Kenton La. NW9 217 304 CP57
Old Kingston Rd., Wor.Pk. 283 330 CQ104
Old Lo. La., Pur. 294 332 DM113
Old Lo. Pl., Twick. 168 322 CH86
Old Lo. Way, Stan. 204 298 CG50
Old Maidstone Rd., Sid. 278 327 EZ94
Old Malden La., Wor.Pk. 283 330 CR104
Old Manor Dr., Islw. 259 321 CC86
Old Manor Ho. Ms., Shep. 281 328 BN97
Old Manor Way, Bexh. 255 319 FD82
Old Manor Way, Chis. 276 326 EM92
Old Manor Yd. SW5 76/7 315 DB77
Old Marylebone Rd. NW1 42/3 315 DE71
Old Ms., Har. 215 303 CE57
Old Mill Ct. E18 224 308 EJ55
Old Mill La. W6 146 315 CU78
Old Mill La., Uxb. 248 312 BH71
Old Mill Pl., Rom. 227 309 FD58
Old Mill Rd. SE18 253 318 ER79
Old Mill Rd., Uxb. 248 312 BG62
Old Mitre Ct. EC4 48 316 DN72
Old Montague St. E1 138 317 DU71
Old Nichol St. E2 39 316 DT70
Old N. St. WC1 47 316 DM71
Old Oak Common La. NW10 125 314 CS70
Old Oak Common La. W3 135 314 CS71
Old Oak La. NW10 125 314 CT69
Old Oak Rd. W3 135 314 CT73
Old Orchard, Sun. 266 329 BW96
Old Orchard, The NW3 113 305 DF63
Old Orchard Clo., Uxb. 249 312 BN72
Old Palace La., Rich. 168 322 CJ85
Old Palace Rd., Croy. 286 332 DP104
Old Palace Ter., Rich. 169 322 CK85
Old Palace Yd. SW1 70/1 316 DL76
Old Palace Yd., Rich. 169 322 CK85
Old Paradise St. SE11 83 316 DM77
Old Pk. Ave. SW12 176 324 DG86
Old Pk. Ave., Enf. 202 300 DQ42
Old Pk. Gro., Enf. 202 300 DQ42
Old Pk. La. W1 56 316 DG74
Old Pk. Ms., Houns. 250 321 BZ80
Old Pk. Ridings N21 209 300 DP44
Old Pk. Rd. N13 208 300 DM49
Old Pk. Rd. SE2 254 319 EU78
Old Pk. Rd., Enf. 202 300 DP41
Old Pk. Rd. S., Enf. 202 300 DP42
Old Pk. Vw., Enf. 202 300 DN41
Old Perry St., Chis. 277 326 ES93
Old Pound Clo., Islw. 152 314 CG81
Old Pye St. SW1 70 316 DK76
Old Quebec St. W1 43 315 DF72
Old Queen St. SW1 70 316 DK75
Old Rectory Gdns., Edg. 217 304 CN51
Old Rd. SE13 183 325 EE84
Old Rd., Dart. 263 327 FD85
Old Rd., Enf. 203 301 DW39
Old Rope Wk., Sun. 266 329 BV97
Old Royal Free Pl. N1 24 316 DN67
Old Royal Free Sq. N1 24 316 DN67
Old Ruislip Rd., Nthlt. 242 313 BW68
Old Sch. Clo. SW19 271 323 DA96
Old Sch. Clo., Beck. 274 325 DX96
Old Seacoal La. EC4 48/9 316 DP72
Old S. Clo., Pnr. 214 303 BX53
Old S. Lambeth Rd. SW8 161 316 DL80
Old Sq. WC2 47 316 DM72
Old Sta. Rd., Hayes 249 320 BT76
Old Stockley Rd., West Dr. 249 320 BP75
Old St. E13 244 318 EH68
Old St. EC1 37 316 DQ70
Old Swan Yd., Cars. 285 331 DF105
Old Town SW4 176 324 DJ83
Old Town, Croy. 286 332 DP104
Old Tram Yd. SE18 253 318 ES77
Old Woolwich Rd. SE10 151 317 ED78
Old York Rd. SW18 174 323 DB85
Oldacre Ms. SW12 192 324 DH87
Oldberry Rd., Edg. 217 304 CR51
Oldborough Rd., Wem. 90 304 CJ61
Oldbury Clo., Orp. 278 327 EX98
Oldbury Pl. W1 44 316 DG71
Oldbury Rd., Enf. 203 301 DU40
Oldchurch Gdns., Rom. 237 309 FD59
Oldchurch Ri., Rom. 237 309 FD59
Oldchurch Rd., Rom. 227 309 FE58
Olden La., Pur. 294 332 DN112
Oldfield Circ., Nthlt. 233 313 CC65
Oldfield Clo., Brom. 276 326 EM98
Oldfield Clo., Grnf. 233 313 CE64
Oldfield Clo., Stan. 204 298 CG50
Oldfield Fm. Gdns., Grnf. 243 313 CD67
Oldfield Gro. SE16 149 317 DX77
Oldfield La. N., Grnf. 243 313 CD68
Oldfield La. S., Grnf. 243 313 CC69
Oldfield Ms. N6 98 306 DJ59
Oldfield Rd. N16 101 306 DS62
Oldfield Rd. NW10 109 304 CT66
Oldfield Rd. SW19 270 323 CY93
Oldfield Rd. W3 145 314 CT75
Oldfield Rd., Bexh. 254 319 EY82
Oldfield Rd., Brom. 276 326 EL98
Oldfield Rd., Hmptn. 266 329 BZ95
Oldfields Rd., Sutt. 284 331 CZ104
Oldham Ter. W3 134 314 CQ74
Oldhill St. N16 102 307 DU60
Oldridge Rd. SW12 192 324 DG87
Oldstead Rd., Brom. 275 325 ED91
Oleander Clo., Orp. 291 334 ER106
O'Leary Sq. E1 138 317 DW71
Oley Pl. E1 139 317 DX71
Olinda Rd. N16 221 306 DT58
Oliphant St. W10 127 315 CX69
Olive Rd. E13 244 318 EJ69
Olive Rd. NW2 110 305 CW63
Olive Rd. SW19 271 323 DC94
Olive Rd. W5 143 314 CK76
Olive St., Rom. 227 309 FD57
Oliver Ave. SE25 273 324 DT97
Oliver Clo. W4 154 314 CP79
Oliver Gdns. E6 244 318 EL72
Oliver Goldsmith Est. SE15 164 317 DU81
Oliver Gro. SE25 273 324 DT98
Oliver Rd. E10 104 307 EB61
Oliver Rd. E17 223 307 EC57
Oliver Rd., N.Mal. 269 322 CQ96
Oliver Rd., Rain. 247 319 FF67
Oliver Rd., Sutt. 285 331 DD105
Oliver Rd., Swan. 279 327 FD97
Olivers Yd. EC1 38 316 DR70
Olivette St. SW15 173 323 CX83
Olivia Gdns., Uxb. 212 302 BJ53
Ollerton Grn. E3 129 317 DZ67
Ollerton Rd. N11 208 300 DK50
Olley Clo., Wall. 294 332 DL107
Ollgar Clo. W12 135 314 CT74
Olliffe St. E14 150 317 EC76
Olmar St. SE1 164 317 DU79
Olney Rd. SE17 162 316 DP79
Olron Cres., Bexh. 262 327 EX85
Olven Rd. SE18 253 318 EQ79
Olveston Wk., Cars. 285 331 DD100
Olwen Ms., Pnr. 214 303 BX54
Olyffe Ave., Well. 254 319 EU81
Olyffe Dr., Beck. 275 325 EC95
Olympia Ms. W2 52/3 315 DB73
Olympia Way W14 147 315 CY76
Olympic Way, Grnf. 243 313 CB67
Olympic Way, Wem. 92 304 CN62
Olympus Sq. E5 118 307 DU62
Oman Ave. NW2 110 305 CW63
O'Meara St. SE1 61 316 DQ74
Omega Clo. E14 150 317 EB76
Omega Pl. N1 22/3 316 DL68
Omega St. SE14 166 317 EA81
Ommaney Rd. SE14 165 317 DX81
Omnibus Way E17 223 307 EA54
Ondine Rd. SE15 179 324 DT84
One Tree Clo. SE23 180 325 DW86
Onega Gate SE16 149 317 DY76
O'Neill Path SE18 253 318 EN79
Ongar Clo., Rom. 226 309 EW57
Ongar Rd. SW6 158 315 DA79
Ongar Way, Rain. 247 319 FE67
Onra Rd. E17 104 307 EA59
Onslow Ave., Rich. 169 322 CL85
Onslow Ave., Sutt. 292 331 CZ110
Onslow Clo. E4 211 301 ED47
Onslow Cres., Chis. 277 326 EP95
Onslow Dr., Sid. 262 327 EX90
Onslow Gdns. E18 224 308 EH55
Onslow Gdns. N10 220 306 DH57
Onslow Gdns. N21 209 300 DN43
Onslow Gdns. SW7 78 315 DD78
Onslow Gdns., S.Croy. 295 333 DU112
Onslow Gdns., Wall. 294 332 DJ107
Onslow Ms., Cher. 280 328 BG100
Onslow Ms. E. SW7 78 315 DD77
Onslow Ms. W. SW7 78 315 DD77
Onslow Rd., Croy. 286 332 DN102
Onslow Rd., N.Mal. 270 323 CU98
Onslow Rd., Rich. 169 322 CL85
Onslow Sq. SW7 78 315 DD77
Onslow St. EC1 36 316 DN70
Ontario St. SE1 72/3 316 DP76
Ontario Way E14 140 317 EA73
Opal Clo. E16 244 318 EK72
Opal Ms. NW6 127 315 CZ67
Opal Ms., Ilf. 235 308 EP61
Opal St. SE11 84/5 316 DP77
Openshaw Rd. SE2 254 319 EV77
Openview SW18 190 323 DC88
Ophelia Gdns. NW2 95 305 CY62
Ophir Ter. SE15 164 317 DU81
Opossum Way, Houns. 250 321 BW82
Oppenheim Rd. SE13 166 317 EC82
Oppidans Ms. NW3 113 305 DF66
Oppidans Rd. NW3 113 305 DF66
Orange Ct. E1 138 317 DU74
Orange Gro. E11 105 307 EE62
Orange Hill Rd., Edg. 217 304 CQ52
Orange Pl. SE16 148 317 DW76
Orange St. WC2 58 316 DK73
Orange Yd. W1 46 316 DK72
Orangery, The, Rich. 184 322 CJ89
Orangery La. SE9 260 326 EM85
Oratory La. SW3 78 315 DD78
Orb St. SE17 86 316 DR77
Orbain Rd. SW6 157 315 CY80
Orbel St. SW11 159 315 DE81
Orchard, The N14 208 300 DH43
Orchard, The N21 209 300 DR44
Orchard, The NW11 219 305 DA57
Orchard, The SE3 167 317 ED82
Orchard, The W4 145 314 CR77
Orchard, The W5 133 314 CK71
Orchard, The, Houns. 251 321 CB84
Orchard, The, Swan. 279 327 FD96
Orchard Ave. N3 219 305 DA55
Orchard Ave. N14 208 300 DJ44
Orchard Ave. N20 207 299 DD47
Orchard Ave., Ashf. 265 328 BQ93
Orchard Ave., Belv. 254 319 EY79
Orchard Ave., Croy. 288 333 DY103
Orchard Ave., Felt. 257 320 BR85
Orchard Ave., Houns. 250 321 BY80
Orchard Ave., Mitch. 285 332 DG102
Orchard Ave., N.Mal. 269 322 CS96
Orchard Ave., Sthl. 242 313 BY74
Orchard Clo. E4 211 301 EA49
Orchard Clo. E11 224 308 EH56
Orchard Clo. N1 116 306 DQ66
Orchard Clo. NW2 94 305 CU62
Orchard Clo. SE23 180 325 DW86
Orchard Clo. SW20 270 323 CW98
Orchard Clo. W10 137 315 CY71
Orchard Clo., Ashf. 265 328 BQ93
Orchard Clo., Bans. 292 331 DB114
Orchard Clo., Bexh. 254 319 EY81
Orchard Clo., Edg. 216 304 CL51
Orchard Clo., Nthlt. 233 313 CC64
Orchard Clo., Ruis. 231 312 BQ59
Orchard Clo., Uxb. 240 312 BH65
Orchard Clo., Wem. 123 314 CL67
Orchard Ct., Islw. 240 321 CD81
Orchard Ct., Twick. 259 321 CD89
Orchard Ct., Wor.Pk. 283 331 CU102
Orchard Cres., Edg. 205 298 CQ50
Orchard Cres., Enf. 202 300 DT39
Orchard Dr. SE3 167 317 EE82
Orchard Dr., Edg. 204 298 CM50
Orchard Dr., Uxb. 240 312 BK70
Orchard Gdns., Chess. 282 330 CL105
Orchard Gdns., Sutt. 284 331 DA106
Orchard Gate NW9 217 304 CS56
Orchard Gate, Grnf. 106 304 CH64
Orchard Grn., Orp. 291 334 ES103
Orchard Gro. SE20 274 325 DU94
Orchard Gro., Croy. 288 333 DY101
Orchard Gro., Edg. 217 304 CN53
Orchard Gro., Har. 216 304 CM57
Orchard Gro., Orp. 291 334 ET103
Orchard Hill SE13 166 317 EB82
Orchard Hill, Cars. 285 331 DF106
Orchard Hill, Dart. 263 327 FE85
Orchard La. SW20 270 323 CV95
Orchard Ms. N1 117 306 DR66
Orchard Pl. E14 141 317 EE73
Orchard Pl. N17 221 306 DT52
Orchard Ri., Croy. 288 333 DY102
Orchard Ri., Kings.T. 269 322 CQ95
Orchard Ri., Pnr. 231 302 BT55
Orchard Ri., Rich. 170 322 CP84
Orchard Ri. E., Sid. 261 326 ES85
Orchard Ri. W., Sid. 261 326 ES85
Orchard Rd. N6 98 306 DH59
Orchard Rd. SE3 167 317 EE82
Orchard Rd. SE18 253 318 ER77
Orchard Rd., Belv. 255 319 FA77
Orchard Rd., Brent. 152 314 CJ79
Orchard Rd., Brom. 276 326 EJ95
Orchard Rd., Chess. 282 330 CL105
Orchard Rd., Dag. 247 319 FA67
Orchard Rd., Enf. 203 301 DW43
Orchard Rd., Hmptn. 266 329 BZ94
Orchard Rd., Hayes 249 312 BT73
Orchard Rd., Houns. 258 321 BZ85
Orchard Rd., Kings.T. 268 322 CL96
Orchard Rd., Mitch. 285 332 DG102
Orchard Rd.
(Farnborough), Orp. 290 334 EP106
Orchard Rd., Rich. 170 322 CN83
Orchard Rd., Rom. 227 309 FB54
Orchard Rd., Sid. 277 326 ES91
Orchard Rd., S.Croy. 295 333 DV114
Orchard Rd., Sun. 266 329 BV94
Orchard Rd., Sutt. 284 331 DA105
Orchard Rd., Twick. 168 322 CG85
Orchard Rd., Well. 262 327 EV83
Orchard Sq. W14 147 315 CZ78
Orchard St. E17 222 307 DY56
Orchard St. W1 44 316 DG72
Orchard Ter., Enf. 210 301 DU44
Orchard Vw., Uxb. 240 312 BK70
Orchard Way, Ashf. 248 320 BM89
Orchard Way, Beck. 288 333 DY99
Orchard Way, Croy. 288 333 DY102
Orchard Way, Enf. 202 300 DS41
Orchard Way, Sutt. 285 331 DD105
Orchard Waye, Uxb. 240 312 BK68
Orchardleigh Ave., Enf. 203 301 DW40
Orchardmede N21 209 300 DR44
Orchardson St. NW8 30 315 DD70
Orchid Clo. E6 244 318 EL71
Orchid Clo., Sthl. 242 313 BY72
Orchid Rd. N14 208 300 DJ45
Orchid St. W12 136 315 CU73
Orchis Way, Rom. 228 311 FM51
Orde Hall St. WC1 47 316 DM71
Ordell Rd. E3 129 317 DZ68
Ordnance Clo., Felt. 258 321 BU90
Ordnance Cres. SE10 151 317 EE75
Ordnance Hill NW8 18 315 DD67
Ordnance Ms. NW8 18 315 DD68
Ordnance Rd. E16 141 317 EF71
Ordnance Rd. SE18 253 318 EN79
Ordnance Rd., Enf. 203 301 DX37
Oregano Dr. E14 141 317 ED72
Oregon Ave. E12 234 308 EM63
Oregon Clo., N.Mal. 269 322 CQ98
Oregon Sq., Orp. 291 334 ER102
Orestes Ms. NW6 112 305 DA64
Orford Ct. SE27 194 324 DP89
Orford Gdns., Twick. 259 321 CF89
Orford Rd. E17 223 307 EA57
Orford Rd. E18 224 308 EH55
Orford Rd. SE6 198 325 EB90
Organ La. E4 211 301 EC47
Oriel Clo., Mitch. 272 324 DK98
Oriel Ct. NW3 112 305 DC63
Oriel Gdns., Ilf. 224 308 EM55
Oriel Pl. NW3 112 305 DC63
Oriel Rd. E9 119 307 DX65
Oriel Way, Nthlt. 233 313 CB66
Orient Ind. Pk. E10 104 307 EA61
Orient St. SE11 84/5 316 DP77
Orient Way E5 103 307 DX62
Oriental Rd. E16 244 318 EK74
Oriental St. E14 140 317 EA73
Oriole Way SE28 246 319 EV73
Orion Way, Nthwd. 213 302 BT49
Orissa Rd. SE18 253 318 ES78
Orkney St. SW11 160 316 DG82
Orlando Rd. SW4 176 324 DJ83
Orleans Rd. SE19 273 324 DR93
Orleans Rd., Twick. 184 322 CH87
Orleston Ms. N7 116 306 DN65
Orleston Rd. N7 116 306 DN65
Orley Fm. Rd., Har. 233 313 CE62
Orlop St. SE10 151 317 EE78
Ormanton Rd. SE26 274 325 DU91
Orme Ct. W2 52/3 315 DB73
Orme Ct. Ms. W2 52/3 315 DB73
Orme La. W2 52/3 315 DB73
Orme Rd., Kings.T. 269 322 CP96
Orme Sq. W2 52/3 315 DB73
Ormeley Rd. SW12 192 324 DH87
Ormerod Gdns., Mitch. 272 324 DG96
Ormesby Clo. SE28 246 319 EX73
Ormesby Way, Har. 216 304 CM58
Ormiston Gro. W12 136 315 CV74
Ormiston Rd. SE10 252 318 EG78
Ormond Ave., Hmptn. 267 329 CB95
Ormond Ave., Rich. 169 322 CK85
Ormond Clo. WC1 46/7 316 DL71
Ormond Clo., Rom. 228 310 FK54
Ormond Cres., Hmptn. 267 329 CB95
Ormond Dr., Hmptn. 267 329 CB94
Ormond Ms. WC1 34/5 316 DL70
Ormond Rd. N19 99 306 DL60
Ormond Rd., Rich. 169 322 CK85
Ormond Yd. SW1 57 316 DJ74
Ormonde Ave., Orp. 291 334 EQ103
Ormonde Gate SW3 79 315 DF78
Ormonde Pl. SW1 80 316 DG77
Ormonde Rd. SW14 170 322 CQ83
Ormonde Rd., Nthwd. 213 302 BR49
Ormonde Ter. NW8 19 315 DF67
Ormsby Gdns., Grnf. 243 313 CC68
Ormsby Pl. N16 101 306 DT62
Ormsby Pt. SE18 253 318 EP77
Ormsby St. E2 27 316 DT68
Ormside St. SE15 164 317 DW79
Ornan Rd. NW3 113 305 DE64
Oronsay Wk. N1 116 306 DQ65
Orpen Wk. N16 101 306 DS62
Orpheus St. SE5 163 316 DR81
Orpington Gdns. N18 209 300 DS48
Orpington Rd. N21 209 300 DN46
Orpington Rd., Chis. 277 326 ES97
Orpwood Clo., Hmptn. 266 329 BZ93
Orsett St. SE11 83 316 DM78
Orsett Ter. W2 40/1 315 DB72
Orsett Ter., Wdf.Grn. 224 308 EJ52
Orsman Rd. N1 26/7 316 DS67
Orton St. E1 138 317 DU74
Orville Rd. SW11 159 315 DD82
Orwell Clo., Rain. 247 319 FD71
Orwell Ct. N5 116 306 DQ63
Orwell Rd. E13 244 318 EJ67
Osbaldeston Rd. N16 102 307 DU61
Osbert St. SW1 82 316 DK77
Osberton Rd. SE12 260 326 EG85
Osborn Clo. E8 128 317 DU67
Osborn Gdns. NW7 218 305 CX52
Osborn La. SE23 197 325 DY87
Osborn St. E1 51 316 DT71
Osborn Ter. SE3 183 325 EF84
Osborne Ave., Stai. 264 320 BL87
Osborne Clo., Beck. 274 325 DY98
Osborne Clo., Felt. 266 329 BX92
Osborne Clo., Horn. 228 310 FH58
Osborne Gdns., Th.Hth. 273 324 DQ96
Osborne Gro. E17 222 307 DZ56
Osborne Gro. N4 100 306 DN60
Osborne Ms. E17 222 307 DZ56
Osborne Pl., Sutt. 285 331 DD106
Osborne Rd. E7 244 318 EH64
Osborne Rd. E9 119 307 DZ65
Osborne Rd. E10 104 307 EB62
Osborne Rd. N4 100 306 DN60
Osborne Rd. N13 209 300 DN48
Osborne Rd. NW2 110 305 CV65
Osborne Rd. W3 144 314 CP75
Osborne Rd., Belv. 254 319 EZ78
Osborne Rd., Dag. 236 309 EZ64
Osborne Rd., Enf. 203 301 DY40
Osborne Rd., Horn. 228 310 FH58
Osborne Rd., Houns. 258 321 BZ83
Osborne Rd., Kings.T. 268 322 CL94
Osborne Rd., Sthl. 243 313 CC72
Osborne Rd., Th.Hth. 273 324 DQ96
Osborne Rd., Uxb. 240 312 BJ66
Osborne Sq., Dag. 236 309 EZ63
Osborne Ter. SW17 272 324 DG92
Oscar St. SE8 166 317 EA81
Oseney Cres. NW5 114 306 DJ65
Osgood Ave., Orp. 291 334 ET106
Osgood Gdns., Orp. 291 334 ET106
O'Shea Gro. E3 129 317 DZ67
Osidge La. N14 208 300 DG46
Osier Ms. W4 155 314 CT79
Osier St. E1 129 317 DW70
Osier Way E10 104 307 EB62
Osier Way, Bans. 292 331 CY114
Osier Way, Mitch. 285 332 DE99
Osiers Rd. SW18 174 323 DA84
Oslac Rd. SE6 275 325 EB92
Oslo Ct. NW8 18/9 315 DE68
Oslo Sq. SE16 149 317 DY76
Osman Clo. N15 221 306 DR58
Osman Rd. N9 210 301 DU48
Osman Rd. W6 146 315 CW76
Osmond Clo., Har. 233 313 CC61
Osmond Gdns., Wall. 286 332 DJ106
Osmund St. W12 135 314 CT72
Osnaburgh St. NW1 32/3 316 DH70
Osnaburgh Ter. NW1 32/3 316 DH70
Osney Wk., Cars. 285 331 DD100
Osprey Clo. E6 244 318 EL71
Osprey Clo. E11 224 308 EG56
Osprey Clo. E17 222 307 DY52
Osprey Clo., West Dr. 248 320 BK75
Osprey Ms., Enf. 210 301 DX43
Ospringe Clo. SE20 274 325 DW94
Ospringe Ct. SE9 261 326 ER86
Ospringe Rd. NW5 114 306 DJ63
Osram Rd., Wem. 91 304 CK62
Osric Path N1 26/7 316 DS68
Ossian Ms. N4 99 306 DM59
Ossian Rd. N4 99 306 DM59
Ossington Bldgs. W1 44 316 DG71
Ossington Clo. W2 52/3 315 DB73
Ossington St. W2 52/3 315 DB73
Ossory Rd. SE1 164 317 DU79
Ossulston St. NW1 22 316 DK68
Ossulton Pl. N2 219 305 DC55
Ossulton Way N2 219 305 DC56
Ostade Rd. SW2 193 324 DM87
Osten Ms. SW7 64/5 315 DB76
Oster Ter. E17 222 307 DX57

Osterley Ave., Islw. 251 321 CD80
Osterley Clo., Orp. 278 327 EU95
Osterley Ct., Islw. 251 321 CD81
Osterley Cres., Islw. 251 321 CE81
Osterley Gdns., Th.Hth. 273 324 DQ96
Osterley Ho. E14 140 317 EB72
Osterley La., Islw. 251 321 CC78
Osterley La., Sthl. 251 321 CA78
Osterley Pk., Islw. 251 321 CD78
Osterley Pk. Rd., Sthl. 250 321 BZ76
Osterley Pk. Vw. Rd. W7 251 321 CE75
Osterley Rd. N16 117 306 DS63
Osterley Rd., Islw. 251 321 CE80
Osterley Views, Sthl. 243 313 CC74
Ostliffe Rd. N13 209 300 DP50
Oswald Rd., Sthl. 242 313 BY74
Oswald St. E5 103 307 DX62
Oswald Ter. NW2 94 305 CW62
Oswalds Mead E9 119 307 DY63
Osward Pl. N9 210 301 DV47
Osward Rd. SW17 191 323 DF89
Oswell Ho. E1 138 317 DV74
Oswin St. SE11 84/5 316 DP77
Oswyth Rd. SE5 163 316 DS82
Otford Clo. SE20 274 325 DW95
Otford Clo., Bex. 263 327 FB86
Otford Clo., Brom. 277 326 EN97
Otford Cres. SE4 181 325 DZ86
Othello Clo. SE11 84/5 316 DP78
Otis St. E3 130 317 EC69
Otley App., Ilf. 225 308 EP58
Otley Dr., Ilf. 225 308 EP58
Otley Rd. E16 244 318 EJ72
Otley Ter. E5 103 307 DX62
Otlinge Clo., Orp. 278 327 EX98
Ottawa Gdns., Dag. 237 309 FD66
Ottaway St. E5 102 307 DU62
Ottenden Clo., Orp. 291 334 ES105
Otter Rd., Grnf. 243 313 CC70
Otterbourne Rd. E4 211 301 ED48
Otterbourne Rd., Croy. 286 332 DP103
Otterburn Gdns., Islw. 152 314 CG80
Otterburn Ho. SE5 162 316 DQ80
Otterburn St. SW17 271 323 DF93
Otterden St. SE6 275 325 EA91
Otterfield Rd., West Dr. 248 312 BL73
Otters Clo., Orp. 278 327 EX98
Otto Clo. SE26 196 325 DV90
Otto St. SE17 162 316 DP79
Oulton Clo. E5 102 307 DW61
Oulton Clo. SE28 246 319 EW72
Oulton Cres., Bark. 235 308 ET65
Oulton Rd. N15 221 306 DR57
Ouseley Rd. SW12 191 323 DF88
Outer Circle NW1 32 316 DG70
Outgate Rd. NW10 109 304 CT66
Outram Pl. N1 22/3 316 DL67
Outram Rd. E6 244 318 EL67
Outram Rd. N22 220 306 DK53
Outram Rd., Croy. 287 332 DT103
Outwich St. EC3 50/1 316 DS72
Oval, The E2 128 317 DV68
Oval, The, Bans. 292 331 DA114
Oval, The, Sid. 262 327 EU87
Oval Pl. SW8 161 316 DM80
Oval Rd. NW1 20/1 316 DH67
Oval Rd., Croy. 287 332 DR103
Oval Rd. N., Dag. 247 319 FB67
Oval Rd. S., Dag. 247 319 FB68
Oval Way SE11 83 316 DM78
Overbrae, Beck. 275 325 EA93
Overbrook Wk., Edg. 217 304 CN52
Overbury Ave., Beck. 275 325 EB97
Overbury Rd. N15 221 306 DR58
Overbury St. E5 119 307 DX63
Overcliff Rd. SE13 182 325 EA83
Overcourt Clo., Sid. 262 327 EV86
Overdale Ave., N.Mal. 269 322 CQ96
Overdale Rd. W5 142 314 CJ76
Overdown Rd. SE6 275 325 EA91
Overhill Rd. SE22 196 325 DU87
Overhill Rd., Pur. 294 332 DN109
Overhill Way, Beck. 289 333 EC99
Overlea Rd. E5 102 307 DU59
Overmead, Sid. 261 326 ER87
Oversley Ho. W2 40 315 DA71
Overstand Clo., Beck. 288 333 EA99
Overstone Gdns., Croy. 288 333 DZ101
Overstone Rd. W6 146 315 CW76
Overton Clo. NW10 108 304 CQ65
Overton Clo., Islw. 251 321 CF81
Overton Ct. E11 234 308 EG59
Overton Dr. E11 234 308 EG59
Overton Dr., Rom. 236 309 EW59
Overton Rd. E10 103 307 DY60
Overton Rd. N14 208 300 DL43
Overton Rd. SE2 254 319 EW76
Overton Rd. SW9 162 316 DN82
Overton Rd., Sutt. 292 331 DA107
Overton Rd. E. SE2 254 319 EX76
Overtons Yd., Croy. 287 332 DQ104
Ovesdon Ave., Har. 232 313 BZ60
Ovett Clo. SE19 273 324 DS93
Ovex Clo. E14 150 317 EC75
Ovington Gdns. SW3 66/7 315 DE76
Ovington Ms. SW3 66/7 315 DE76
Ovington Sq. SW3 66/7 315 DE76
Ovington St. SW3 78/9 315 DE77
Owen Clo. SE28 246 319 EW74
Owen Clo., Hayes 242 313 BV69
Owen Gdns., Wdf.Grn. 224 308 EL51
Owen Rd. N13 209 300 DQ49
Owen Rd., Hayes 242 313 BV69
Owen St. EC1 24 316 DN68
Owen Wk. SE20 274 325 DU94
Owen Waters Ho., Ilf. 225 308 EN53
Owen Way NW10 108 304 CQ64
Owenite St. SE2 254 319 EV77
Owen's Ct. EC1 36/7 316 DP69
Owen's Row EC1 36/7 316 DP69
Owens Way SE23 197 325 DY87
Owgan Clo. SE5 163 316 DR80
Owlets Hall Clo., Horn. 228 311 FM55
Ownstead Gdns., S.Croy. 295 332 DT111
Oxberry Ave. SW6 157 315 CY82
Oxendon St. SW1 58 316 DK73
Oxenford St. SE15 179 324 DT83
Oxenholme NW1 21 316 DJ68
Oxenpark Ave., Wem. 91 304 CL59
Oxestalls Rd. SE8 149 317 DY78
Oxford Ave. SW20 270 323 CY96
Oxford Ave., Hayes 257 320 BT80
Oxford Ave., Horn. 229 311 FN56
Oxford Ave., Houns. 251 321 CA78
Oxford Circ. Ave. W1 45 316 DJ72
Oxford Clo. N9 210 301 DV47
Oxford Clo., Ashf. 265 328 BQ94
Oxford Clo., Mitch. 272 324 DJ97
Oxford Clo., Nthwd. 213 302 BQ49
Oxford Ct. EC4 62 316 DR73
Oxford Ct. W3 134 314 CN72
Oxford Ct., Felt. 266 329 BX91
Oxford Cres., N.Mal. 283 330 CR100
Oxford Dr., Ruis. 232 313 BW61
Oxford Gdns. N20 207 299 DD46
Oxford Gdns. N21 209 300 DQ45
Oxford Gdns. W4 144 314 CN78
Oxford Gdns. W10 137 315 CX72
Oxford Gdns., Uxb. 230 312 BG62
Oxford Gate W6 147 315 CX77
Oxford Ms., Bex. 263 327 FA87
Oxford Pl. NW10 93 304 CR62
Oxford Rd. E15 121 307 ED65
Oxford Rd. N4 100 306 DN60
Oxford Rd. N9 210 301 DV47
Oxford Rd. NW6 16 315 DA68
Oxford Rd. SE19 273 324 DR93
Oxford Rd. SW15 173 323 CY84
Oxford Rd. W5 133 314 CK73
Oxford Rd., Cars. 293 331 DE107
Oxford Rd., Enf. 210 301 DV43
Oxford Rd., Har. 215 303 CC58
Oxford Rd. (Wealdstone), Har. 215 303 CF55
Oxford Rd., Ilf. 235 308 EQ64
Oxford Rd., Rom. 228 311 FM51
Oxford Rd., Sid. 278 327 EV92
Oxford Rd., Tedd. 267 329 CD92
Oxford Rd., Uxb. 240 312 BJ65
Oxford Rd., Wall. 286 332 DJ106
Oxford Rd. N. W4 144 314 CP78
Oxford Rd. S. W4 144 314 CN78
Oxford Sq. W2 42/3 315 DE72
Oxford St. W1 44 316 DG72
Oxford Wk., Sthl. 242 313 BZ74
Oxford Way, Felt. 266 329 BX91
Oxgate Gdns. NW2 94 305 CV62
Oxgate La. NW2 94 305 CV61
Oxhawth Cres., Brom. 290 334 EN99
Oxleas E6 245 318 EP72
Oxleas Clo., Well. 253 318 ER82
Oxleay Ct., Har. 233 313 CA60
Oxleay Rd., Har. 233 313 CA60
Oxleigh Clo., N.Mal. 283 330 CS99
Oxley Clo. SE1 87 316 DT78
Oxley Clo., Rom. 228 310 FJ54
Oxleys Rd. NW2 94 305 CV62
Oxlip Clo., Croy. 288 333 DX102
Oxlow La., Dag. 236 309 EZ63
Oxonian St. SE22 179 324 DT84
Oxted Clo., Mitch. 271 323 DD97
Oxtoby Way SW16 272 324 DK95
Oyster Catchers Clo. E16 244 318 EH72
Oyster Row E1 138 317 DW72
Ozolins Way E16 244 318 EG72

Pablo Neruda Clo. SE24 178 324 DP84
Pace Pl. E1 138 317 DV72
Paceheath Clo., Rom. 227 309 FD51
Pacific Clo., Felt. 265 320 BT88
Pacific Rd. E16 244 318 EG72
Packet Boat La., Uxb. 248 312 BH72
Packington Rd. W3 144 314 CQ76
Packington Sq. N1 25 316 DQ67
Packington St. N1 24/5 316 DP67
Packmores Rd. SE9 261 326 ER85
Padbury SE17 86/7 316 DS78
Padbury Clo., Felt. 265 320 BR88
Padbury Ct. E2 39 316 DT69
Padcroft Rd., West Dr. 248 312 BK74
Paddenswick Rd. W6 146 315 CU76
Paddington Clo., Hayes 242 313 BX70
Paddington Grn. W2 42 315 DD71
Paddington St. W1 44 316 DG71
Paddock, The, Uxb. 241 312 BP63
Paddock Clo. SE3 260 326 EG83
Paddock Clo. SE26 274 325 DX91
Paddock Clo., Nthlt. 243 313 CA68
Paddock Clo., Orp. 290 334 EP105
Paddock Clo., Wor.Pk. 283 330 CS102
Paddock Gdns. SE19 273 324 DS93
Paddock Rd. NW2 94 305 CU62
Paddock Rd., Bexh. 262 327 EY84
Paddock Rd., Ruis. 232 313 BX62
Paddock Way, Chis. 277 326 ER94
Paddocks, The, Wem. 92 304 CP61
Paddocks Clo., Har. 233 313 CB63
Paddocks Way, Cher. 280 328 BH102
Padfield Rd. SE5 178 324 DQ83
Padnall Rd., Rom. 226 309 EX55
Padstow Rd., Enf. 202 300 DP40
Padstow Wk., Felt. 265 320 BT88
Padua Rd. SE20 274 325 DW95
Pagden St. SW8 160 316 DH81
Page Clo., Dag. 236 309 EY64
Page Clo., Hmptn. 266 329 BY93
Page Clo., Har. 216 304 CM58
Page Cres., Croy. 286 332 DN106
Page Cres., Erith 255 319 FF80
Page Grn. Rd. N15 222 307 DU57
Page Grn. Ter. N15 221 306 DT57
Page Heath La., Brom. 276 326 EK97
Page Heath Vil., Brom. 276 326 EK97
Page Meadow NW7 218 305 CU52
Page Rd., Felt. 257 320 BR86
Page St. NW7 218 305 CU51
Page St. SW1 82 316 DK77
Pageant Ave. NW9 217 304 CR53
Pageant Wk., Croy. 287 332 DS104
Pageantmaster Ct. EC4 48/9 316 DP72
Pagehurst Rd., Croy. 287 333 DV101
Pages Hill N10 220 306 DG54
Pages La. N10 220 306 DG54
Pages La., Rom. 229 311 FP54
Pages La., Uxb. 240 312 BJ65
Pages Wk. SE1 86/7 316 DS77
Pages Yd. W4 155 314 CS79
Paget Ave., Sutt. 285 331 DD104
Paget Clo., Hmptn. 267 329 CD91
Paget Gdns., Chis. 277 326 EP95
Paget La., Islw. 251 321 CD83
Paget Pl., Kings.T. 269 322 CQ93
Paget Ri. SE18 253 318 EN79
Paget Rd. N16 101 306 DR60
Paget Rd., Ilf. 235 308 EP63
Paget Rd., Uxb. 241 312 BQ70
Paget St. EC1 36/7 316 DP69
Paget Ter. SE18 253 318 EN79
Pagnell St. SE14 165 317 DZ80
Pagoda Ave., Rich. 169 322 CM83
Pagoda Gdns. SE3 167 317 ED82
Paignton Rd. N15 221 306 DS58
Paignton Rd., Ruis. 232 313 BU62
Paines Brook Rd., Rom. 228 311 FM51
Paines Brook Way, Rom. 228 311 FM51
Paines Clo., Pnr. 214 303 BY54
Paines La., Pnr. 214 303 BY53
Pains Clo., Mitch. 272 324 DH96
Painsthorpe Rd. N16 101 306 DS62
Painters La., Enf. 203 301 DY35
Painters Rd., Ilf. 225 308 ET55
Paisley Rd. N22 221 306 DP53
Paisley Rd., Cars. 285 331 DD102
Pakeman St. N7 99 306 DM62
Pakenham Clo. SW12 192 324 DG88
Pakenham St. WC1 35 316 DM69
Palace Ave. W8 52/3 315 DB74
Palace Ct. NW3 112 305 DB64
Palace Ct. W2 52/3 315 DB73
Palace Ct., Brom. 277 326 EH95
Palace Ct., Har. 216 304 CL58
Palace Ct. Gdns. N10 220 306 DJ55
Palace Gdns., Enf. 202 300 DR42
Palace Gdns. Ms. W8 52 315 DA74
Palace Gdns. Ter. W8 52 315 DA74
Palace Gate W8 65 315 DC75
Palace Gates Rd. N22 220 306 DK54
Palace Grn. W8 64/5 315 DB75
Palace Gro. SE19 273 324 DT94
Palace Gro., Brom. 277 326 EH95
Palace Ms. E17 222 307 DZ56
Palace Ms. SW1 80 316 DG77
Palace Ms. SW6 157 315 CZ80
Palace Pl. SW1 69 316 DJ76
Palace Rd. N8 220 306 DK57
Palace Rd. N11 220 306 DK52
Palace Rd. SE19 273 324 DT94
Palace Rd. SW2 193 324 DM88
Palace Rd., Brom. 277 326 EH95
Palace Rd., E.Mol. 267 329 CD97
Palace Rd., Kings.T. 268 322 CK98
Palace Rd., Ruis. 232 313 BY63
Palace Rd. Est. SW2 193 324 DM88
Palace Sq. SE19 273 324 DT94
Palace St. SW1 69 316 DJ76
Palace Vw. SE12 260 326 EG89
Palace Vw., Brom. 277 326 EH97
Palace Vw., Croy. 288 333 DZ105
Palace Vw. Rd. E4 211 301 EB50
Palamos Rd. E10 104 307 EA60
Palatine Ave. N16 117 306 DT63
Palatine Rd. N16 117 306 DS63
Palermo Rd. NW10 126 315 CU68
Palestine Gro. SW19 271 323 DD95
Palewell Clo., Orp. 278 327 EV96
Palewell Common Dr. SW14 171 322 CR85
Palewell Pk. SW14 171 322 CR85
Palfrey Pl. SW8 161 316 DM80
Palgrave Ave., Sthl. 243 313 CA73
Palgrave Rd. W12 145 314 CT76
Palissy St. E2 39 316 DT69
Pall Mall SW1 57 316 DJ74
Pall Mall E. SW1 58 316 DK74
Pall Mall Pl. SW1 57 316 DJ74
Pallant Way, Orp. 290 334 EN104
Pallet Way SE18 252 318 EL81
Palliser Rd. W14 147 315 CY78
Palm Ave., Sid. 278 327 EX93
Palm Clo. E10 104 307 EB62
Palm Gro. W5 143 314 CL76
Palm Rd., Rom. 227 309 FC57
Palmar Cres., Bexh. 263 327 FA83
Palmar Rd., Bexh. 255 319 FA82
Palmarsh Clo., Orp. 278 327 EX98
Palmeira Rd., Bexh. 262 327 EX83
Palmer Ave., Sutt. 284 331 CW105
Palmer Clo., Houns. 251 321 CA81
Palmer Clo., W.Wick. 289 333 ED104
Palmer Cres., Kings.T. 268 322 CL97
Palmer Gdns., Barn. 206 299 CX43
Palmer Pl. N7 116 306 DN64
Palmer Rd. E13 244 318 EH70
Palmer Rd., Dag. 236 309 EX60
Palmer St. SW1 70 316 DK76
Palmers Gro., W.Mol. 267 329 CA98
Palmers La., Enf. 203 301 DW39
Palmers Moor La., Iver 240 312 BG70
Palmers Pas. SW14 170 322 CQ83
Palmers Rd. E2 129 317 DX68
Palmers Rd. N11 208 300 DJ50
Palmers Rd. SW14 170 322 CQ83
Palmers Rd. SW16 272 324 DM96
Palmersfield Rd., Bans. 292 331 DA114
Palmerston Cres. N13 208 300 DM50
Palmerston Cres. SE18 253 318 EQ79
Palmerston Gro. SW19 271 323 DA94
Palmerston Rd. E7 234 308 EH64
Palmerston Rd. E17 222 307 DZ55
Palmerston Rd. N22 220 306 DM52
Palmerston Rd. NW6 111 305 CZ66
Palmerston Rd. SW14 170 322 CQ84
Palmerston Rd. SW19 271 323 DA94
Palmerston Rd. W3 144 314 CQ76
Palmerston Rd., Cars. 285 331 DF105
Palmerston Rd., Har. 215 303 CE55
Palmerston Rd., Orp. 291 334 EQ105
Palmerston Rd., Sutt. 285 331 DC105
Palmerston Rd., Th.Hth. 287 332 DR99
Palmerston Rd., Twick. 259 321 CE86
Palmerston Way SW8 160 316 DH80
Pamela Gdns., Pnr. 214 303 BV57
Pamela Wk. E8 128 317 DU67
Pampisford Rd., Pur. 294 332 DN111
Pampisford Rd., S.Croy. 295 332 DQ107
Pams Way, Epsom 283 330 CR106
Pancras La. EC4 49 316 DQ72
Pancras Rd. NW1 22 316 DK68
Pandora Rd. NW6 112 305 DA65
Panfield Ms., Ilf. 225 308 EN58
Panfield Rd. SE2 254 319 EU76
Pangbourne Ave. W10 136 315 CW71
Pangbourne Dr., Stan. 204 298 CK50
Pankhurst Clo. SE14 165 317 DX80
Pankhurst Clo., Islw. 259 321 CF83
Panmuir Rd. SW20 270 323 CV95
Panmure Clo. N5 116 306 DP63
Panmure Rd. SE26 196 325 DV90
Pannard Pl., Sthl. 243 313 CB73
Pansy Gdns. W12 136 315 CU73
Panters, Swan. 279 327 FF94
Pantile Wk., Uxb. 240 312 BJ66
Pantiles, The NW11 218 305 CZ57
Pantiles, The, Bexh. 254 319 EZ80
Pantiles, The, Brom. 276 326 EL97
Pantiles Clo. N13 209 300 DP50
Panton St. SW1 58 316 DK73
Panyer All. EC4 49 316 DQ72
Papermill Clo., Cars. 285 332 DG105
Papillons Wk. SE3 260 326 EG83
Papworth Gdns. N7 115 306 DM64
Papworth Way SW2 194 324 DN87
Parade, The SW11 159 315 DF80
Parade, The, Dart. 263 327 FF85
Parade, The, Rom. 229 311 FP51
Parade, The, Sun. 265 328 BT94
Parade Ms. SE27 194 324 DP89
Paradise Pas. N7 116 306 DN65
Paradise Pl. SE18 252 318 EL77
Paradise Rd. SW4 161 316 DL82
Paradise Rd., Rich. 169 322 CL85
Paradise Row E2 128 317 DV69
Paradise St. SE16 148 317 DV75
Paradise Wk. SW3 159 315 DF79
Paragon, The SE3 167 317 EF82
Paragon Clo. E16 244 318 EG72
Paragon Gro., Surb. 282 330 CM100
Paragon Ms. SE1 86 316 DR77
Paragon Pl. SE3 167 317 EF82
Paragon Pl., Surb. 282 330 CM100
Paragon Rd. E9 118 307 DW65
Parbury Rd. SE23 181 325 DY86
Parchmore Rd., Th.Hth. 273 324 DP96
Parchmore Way, Th.Hth. 273 324 DP96
Pardon St. EC1 36/7 316 DP70
Pardoner St. SE1 74 316 DR76
Parfett St. E1 138 317 DU71
Parfitt Clo. NW3 96 305 DC61
Parfrey St. W6 156 315 CW79
Parham Dr., Ilf. 225 308 EP58
Parham Way N10 220 306 DJ54
Paris Gdns. SE1 60/1 316 DP74
Parish Clo., Horn. 238 310 FH61
Parish Gate Dr., Sid. 261 326 ES86
Parish La. SE20 274 325 DX93
Parish Ms. SE20 274 325 DX94
Parish Wf. Pl. SE18 252 318 EL77
Park, The N6 220 306 DG58
Park, The NW11 96 305 DB60
Park, The SE19 273 324 DS94
Park, The SE23 196 325 DV88
Park, The W5 133 314 CK74
Park, The, Cars. 285 331 DF106
Park, The, Sid. 278 327 EU91
Park App., Well. 262 327 EV84
Park Ave. E6 245 318 EN67
Park Ave. E15 121 307 EE65
Park Ave. N3 219 305 DB53
Park Ave. N13 209 300 DN48
Park Ave. N18 210 301 DU49
Park Ave. N22 220 306 DL54
Park Ave. NW2 110 305 CV65
Park Ave. NW10 123 314 CM69
Park Ave. NW11 96 305 DB60
Park Ave. SW14 171 322 CR84
Park Ave., Bark. 235 308 EQ65
Park Ave., Barn. 207 299 DC43
Park Ave., Brom. 275 325 EF94
Park Ave., Cars. 293 332 DG107
Park Ave., Chis. 277 326 ES97
Park Ave., Enf. 209 300 DR43
Park Ave., Houns. 259 321 CB86
Park Ave., Ilf. 235 308 EN60
Park Ave., Mitch. 272 324 DH94
Park Ave., Orp. 291 335 EU103
Park Ave. (Farnborough), Orp. 290 334 EM104
Park Ave., Ruis. 231 302 BR58
Park Ave., Sthl. 250 321 BZ75
Park Ave., Upmin. 239 311 FS59
Park Ave., W.Wick. 289 333 EC103
Park Ave. Ms., Mitch. 272 324 DH94
Park Ave. N. N8 220 306 DK55
Park Ave. N. NW10 110 305 CV64
Park Ave. Rd. N17 222 307 DV52
Park Ave. S. N8 220 306 DK56
Park Boul., Rom. 227 309 FF53
Park Chase, Wem. 107 304 CM63
Park Clo. E9 128 317 DW67
Park Clo. NW2 94 305 CV62
Park Clo. NW10 123 314 CM69
Park Clo. SW1 67 315 DF75
Park Clo. W4 145 314 CR78
Park Clo. W14 147 315 CZ76
Park Clo., Cars. 293 331 DF107
Park Clo., Hmptn. 267 329 CC95
Park Clo., Har. 215 303 CE53
Park Clo., Houns. 259 321 CC85
Park Clo., Kings.T. 269 322 CN95
Park Clo., Rick. 213 302 BP49
Park Ct. SE26 274 325 DV93
Park Ct., Kings.T. 268 322 CJ95
Park Ct., N.Mal. 269 322 CR98
Park Ct., Wem. 107 304 CL64
Park Cres. N3 219 305 DB52
Park Cres. W1 32/3 316 DH70
Park Cres., Enf. 202 300 DR42
Park Cres., Erith 255 319 FC79
Park Cres., Har. 215 303 CE53
Park Cres., Horn. 238 310 FG59
Park Cres., Twick. 259 321 CD88
Park Cres. Ms. E. W1 32/3 316 DH70
Park Cres. Ms. W. W1 32/3 316 DH70
Park Cres. Rd., Erith 255 319 FD79
Park Cft., Edg. 217 304 CQ53
Park Dale N11 220 306 DK51
Park Dr. N21 209 300 DQ44
Park Dr. NW11 96 305 DB60
Park Dr. SE7 252 318 EL79
Park Dr. SW14 171 322 CR84
Park Dr. W3 144 314 CN76
Park Dr., Dag. 237 309 FC62
Park Dr., Har. 233 313 CA59
Park Dr. (Harrow Weald), Har. 215 303 CE51
Park Dr., Rom. 227 309 FD56
Park Dr., Upmin. 239 311 FP63
Park Dr. Clo. SE7 252 318 EL78
Park End NW3 113 305 DE63
Park End, Brom. 275 325 EF95
Park End Rd., Rom. 227 309 FE56
Park Fm. Clo. N2 219 305 DC55
Park Fm. Clo., Pnr. 214 303 BV57
Park Fm. Rd., Brom. 276 326 EK95
Park Fm. Rd., Kings.T. 268 322 CL94
Park Fm. Rd., Upmin. 238 311 FM64
Park Gdn. Pl. W2 42 315 DD72
Park Gdns. NW9 217 304 CP55
Park Gdns., Erith 255 319 FD77
Park Gdns., Kings.T. 268 322 CM92
Park Gate N2 219 305 DD55
Park Gate N21 208 300 DM45
Park Gate W5 133 314 CK71
Park Gro. E15 244 318 EG67
Park Gro. N11 220 306 DK52
Park Gro., Bexh. 263 327 FC84
Park Gro., Brom. 276 326 EH95
Park Gro., Edg. 204 298 CM50
Park Gro. Rd. E11 105 307 EE61
Park Hall Rd. N2 219 305 DE56
Park Hall Rd. SE21 195 324 DR90
Park Hill SE23 196 325 DV89
Park Hill SW4 177 324 DK85
Park Hill W5 133 314 CK71
Park Hill, Brom. 276 326 EL98
Park Hill, Cars. 293 331 DE107
Park Hill, Rich. 169 322 CM86
Park Hill Clo., Cars. 285 331 DE106
Park Hill Ct. SW17 191 323 DF90
Park Hill Ri., Croy. 287 332 DS103
Park Hill Rd., Brom. 275 325 EE96
Park Hill Rd., Croy. 287 332 DS103
Park Hill Rd., Sid. 261 326 ES90
Park Hill Rd., Wall. 293 332 DH107
Park Ho. N21 208 300 DM45
Park Ho. Gdns., Twick. 168 322 CJ86
Park La. E15 131 317 ED67
Park La. N9 209 300 DS48
Park La. N17 221 306 DT52
Park La. N18 209 300 DS49
Park La. W1 55 315 DF73
Park La., Cars. 285 332 DG105
Park La., Croy. 287 332 DR104
Park La., Har. 233 313 CB62
Park La., Hayes 249 312 BS71
Park La., Horn. 227 309 FF58
Park La. (Elm Pk.), Horn. 238 310 FH65
Park La., Houns. 250 321 BU80
Park La., Rich. 169 322 CK84
Park La. (Chadwell Heath), Rom. 226 309 EX58
Park La., Stan. 204 298 CG48
Park La., Sutt. 292 331 CY107
Park La., Tedd. 267 329 CF93
Park La., Uxb. 212 302 BG53
Park La., Wem. 107 304 CL64
Park La. Clo. N17 222 307 DU52
Park Lawns, Wem. 107 304 CM63
Park Mead, Har. 233 313 CB62
Park Mead, Sid. 262 327 EV85
Park Ms. SE24 178 324 DQ86
Park Ms., Chis. 277 326 EP93
Park Ms., E.Mol. 267 329 CC98
Park Ms., Hmptn. 267 329 CC92
Park Nook Gdns., Enf. 202 300 DR37
Park Par. NW10 125 314 CT68
Park Pl. E14 140 317 EA74
Park Pl. SW1 57 316 DJ74
Park Pl. W3 144 314 CN77
Park Pl. W5 133 314 CK74
Park Pl., Hmptn. 267 329 CC93
Park Pl., Wem. 107 304 CM63
Park Pl. Vil. W2 41 315 DC71
Park Ridings N8 221 306 DN55
Park Ri. SE23 197 325 DY88
Park Ri., Har. 215 303 CE53
Park Ri. Rd. SE23 197 325 DY88
Park Rd. E6 244 318 EJ67
Park Rd. E10 104 307 EA60
Park Rd. E12 234 308 EH60
Park Rd. E15 244 318 EG67
Park Rd. E17 222 307 DZ57
Park Rd. N2 219 305 DD55
Park Rd. N8 220 306 DJ56
Park Rd. N11 220 306 DK52
Park Rd. N14 208 300 DK45
Park Rd. N15 221 306 DP56
Park Rd. N18 209 300 DT49
Park Rd. NW1 31 315 DF70
Park Rd. NW4 94 305 CU59
Park Rd. NW8 30/1 315 DE69
Park Rd. NW9 93 304 CR59
Park Rd. NW10 125 314 CS67
Park Rd. SE25 273 324 DS98
Park Rd. SW19 271 323 DD94
Park Rd. W4 154 314 CQ80
Park Rd. W7 243 313 CF73
Park Rd., Ashf. 265 328 BP92
Park Rd., Beck. 274 325 DZ94
Park Rd., Brom. 276 326 EH95
Park Rd., Chis. 277 326 EP93
Park Rd., E.Mol. 267 329 CC98
Park Rd., Enf. 203 301 DY36
Park Rd., Felt. 266 329 BX91
Park Rd., Hmptn. 267 329 CB91
Park Rd., Hayes 249 312 BS71
Park Rd., Houns. 259 321 CB85
Park Rd., Ilf. 235 308 ER62
Park Rd., Islw. 152 314 CH81
Park Rd., Kings.T. 268 322 CM92
Park Rd. (Hmptn Wick), Kings.T. 268 322 CJ95
Park Rd., N.Mal. 269 322 CR98
Park Rd., Rich. 169 322 CM86
Park Rd., Shep. 281 328 BN102
Park Rd., Stai. 256 320 BH86
Park Rd., Sun. 266 329 BV94
Park Rd., Surb. 282 330 CM100
Park Rd., Sutt. 292 331 CY107
Park Rd., Swan. 279 327 FF98
Park Rd., Tedd. 267 329 CF94
Park Rd., Twick. 169 322 CJ86
Park Rd., Uxb. 240 312 BL66
Park Rd., Wall. 285 332 DH106
Park Rd. (Hackbridge), Wall. 285 332 DH103
Park Rd., Wem. 107 304 CL65
Park Rd. E. W3 144 314 CP75
Park Rd. E., Uxb. 240 312 BK68
Park Rd. N. W3 144 314 CP75
Park Rd. N. W4 145 314 CR78
Park Rd. W., Kings.T. 268 322 CJ95
Park Row SE10 167 317 ED79
Park Royal Rd. NW10 124 314 CQ70
Park Royal Rd. W3 124 314 CQ70
Park Side, Sutt. 292 331 CY107
Park Sq. E. NW1 32/3 316 DH70
Park Sq. Ms. NW1 32/3 316 DH70
Park Sq. W. NW1 32/3 316 DH70
Park St. SE1 61 316 DQ74
Park St. W1 56 316 DG73
Park St., Croy. 287 332 DQ103
Park St., Tedd. 267 329 CE93
Park Ter., Wor.Pk. 283 331 CU102
Park Vw. N21 208 300 DM45
Park Vw. W3 134 314 CQ71
Park Vw., N.Mal. 269 322 CT97
Park Vw., Pnr. 214 303 BZ53
Park Vw., Wem. 108 304 CP64
Park Vw. Ct., Ilf. 225 308 ES58
Park Vw. Cres. N11 208 300 DH49
Park Vw. Est. E2 129 317 DX68
Park Vw. Gdns. NW4 218 305 CX58
Park Vw. Gdns., Bark. 245 318 ES68
Park Vw. Gdns., Ilf. 224 308 EM56
Park Vw. Rd. N3 219 305 DB53
Park Vw. Rd. N17 222 307 DU55
Park Vw. Rd. NW10 109 304 CT63
Park Vw. Rd. W5 133 314 CL71
Park Vw. Rd., Pnr. 214 303 BV52
Park Vw. Rd., Sthl. 243 313 CA74
Park Vw. Rd., Uxb. 248 312 BM72
Park Vw. Rd., Well. 262 327 EV83
Park Village E. NW1 20/1 316 DH68
Park Village W. NW1 20/1 316 DH68
Park Vil., Rom. 226 309 EX58
Park Vista SE10 167 317 ED79
Park Wk. N6 98 306 DG59
Park Wk. SW10 158 315 DC79
Park Way N20 207 299 DF49
Park Way NW11 218 305 CY57
Park Way, Bex. 263 327 FE90
Park Way, Edg. 217 304 CP53
Park Way, Enf. 202 300 DN40
Park Way, Felt. 258 321 BV87
Park Way, Ilf. 235 308 ET62
Park Way, Ruis. 232 313 BU60
Park Way, W.Mol. 267 329 CB97
Park W. W2 42 315 DD72
Park W. Pl. W2 42/3 315 DE72
Parkcroft Rd. SE12 199 325 EF87
Parkdale Cres., Wor.Pk. 283 330 CR104
Parkdale Rd. SE18 253 318 ES78
Parke Rd. SW13 156 315 CU81
Parke Rd., Sun. 266 329 BU98
Parker Clo. E16 244 318 EL74
Parker Ms. WC2 46/7 316 DL72
Parker Rd., Croy. 287 332 DQ105
Parker St. E16 244 318 EL74
Parker St. WC2 46/7 316 DL72
Parkers Row SE1 75 316 DT75
Parkfield Ave. SW14 171 322 CS84
Parkfield Ave., Felt. 258 321 BU90
Parkfield Ave., Har. 215 303 CC54
Parkfield Ave., Nthlt. 242 313 BX68
Parkfield Ave., Uxb. 241 312 BP69
Parkfield Clo., Edg. 217 304 CP51
Parkfield Clo., Nthlt. 242 313 BY68
Parkfield Cres., Felt. 258 321 BU90
Parkfield Cres., Har. 215 303 CC54
Parkfield Cres., Ruis. 232 313 BY62
Parkfield Dr., Nthlt. 242 313 BX68
Parkfield Gdns., Har. 215 303 CB55
Parkfield Rd. NW10 110 305 CU66
Parkfield Rd. SE14 165 317 DZ81
Parkfield Rd., Felt. 258 321 BU90
Parkfield Rd., Har. 233 313 CC62
Parkfield Rd., Nthlt. 233 313 BY68
Parkfield Rd., Uxb. 231 312 BP61
Parkfield St. N1 24 316 DN68
Parkfield Way, Brom. 290 334 EM100
Parkfields SW15 172 323 CW84
Parkfields, Croy. 288 333 DZ102
Parkfields Ave. NW9 93 304 CR60
Parkfields Ave. SW20 270 323 CV96
Parkfields Clo., Cars. 285 332 DG105
Parkfields Rd., Kings.T. 268 322 CM92
Parkgate SE3 260 326 EF83
Parkgate Clo., Kings.T. 269 322 CP93
Parkgate Gdns. SW14 171 322 CR85
Parkgate Rd. SW11 159 315 DE80
Parkgate Rd., Wall. 285 332 DG106
Parkham Ct., Brom. 275 325 EE96
Parkham St. SW11 159 315 DD81
Parkhill Clo., Horn. 238 310 FJ62
Parkhill Rd. E4 211 301 EC46
Parkhill Rd. NW3 113 305 DF64
Parkhill Rd., Bex. 262 327 EZ87
Parkhill Wk. NW3 113 305 DF64
Parkholme Rd. E8 118 307 DU65
Parkhouse St. SE5 163 316 DR80
Parkhurst Gdns., Bex. 263 327 FA87
Parkhurst Rd. E12 235 308 EN63
Parkhurst Rd. E17 222 307 DY56
Parkhurst Rd. N7 115 306 DL63
Parkhurst Rd. N11 208 300 DG49
Parkhurst Rd. N17 222 307 DU54
Parkhurst Rd. N22 220 306 DM51
Parkhurst Rd., Bex. 263 327 FA87
Parkhurst Rd., Sutt. 285 331 DD105
Parkland Ave., Rom. 227 309 FE55
Parkland Ave., Upmin. 239 311 FP64
Parkland Gdns. SW19 189 323 CX88
Parkland Gro., Ashf. 265 328 BN91
Parkland Rd. N22 220 306 DM54
Parkland Rd., Ashf. 265 328 BN91
Parkland Rd., Wdf.Grn. 224 308 EG52
Parkland Wk. N4 100 306 DN59
Parkland Wk. N6 98 306 DJ59
Parkland Wk. N10 220 306 DH56
Parklands N6 98 306 DH59
Parklands, Surb. 282 330 CM99
Parklands Clo. SW14 170 322 CQ85
Parklands Ct., Houns. 250 321 BX82
Parklands Dr. N3 218 305 CY55
Parklands Rd. SW16 272 324 DH92
Parklands Way, Wor.Pk. 283 330 CS103
Parklea Clo. NW9 217 304 CS53
Parkleigh Rd. SW19 271 323 DB96
Parkleys, Rich. 268 322 CK91
Parkmead SW15 172 323 CV86
Parkmead Gdns. NW7 217 304 CT51
Parkshot, Rich. 169 322 CL84
Parkside N3 219 305 DB53
Parkside NW2 94 305 CU62
Parkside NW7 218 305 CU51
Parkside SE3 167 317 EF80
Parkside SW19 270 323 CX91
Parkside, Hmptn. 267 329 CD92
Parkside, Sid. 262 327 EV89
Parkside Ave. SW19 270 323 CX92
Parkside Ave., Bexh. 255 319 FD82
Parkside Ave., Brom. 276 326 EL98
Parkside Ave., Rom. 227 309 FD55
Parkside Clo. SE20 274 325 DW94
Parkside Cres. N7 100 306 DN62
Parkside Cres., Surb. 283 330 CQ100
Parkside Cross, Bexh. 255 319 FE82
Parkside Dr., Edg. 205 298 CN48
Parkside Est. E9 128 317 DW67
Parkside Gdns. SW19 270 323 CX91
Parkside Gdns., Barn. 207 299 DF46
Parkside Ho., Dag. 237 309 FC62
Parkside Rd. SW11 160 316 DG81
Parkside Rd., Belv. 255 319 FB77
Parkside Rd., Houns. 259 321 CB85
Parkside Rd., Nthwd. 213 302 BT50
Parkside Ter. N18 209 300 DR49
Parkside Way, Har. 215 303 CB56
Parkstead Rd. SW15 172 323 CU85
Parkstone Ave. N18 209 300 DT50
Parkstone Ave., Horn. 228 310 FK58
Parkstone Rd. E17 223 307 EC55
Parkstone Rd. SE15 164 317 DU82
Parkthorne Clo., Har. 215 303 CB58
Parkthorne Dr., Har. 215 303 CA58
Parkthorne Rd. SW12 193 324 DK87
Parkview Ct. SW18 174 323 DA86
Parkview Dr. SW19 271 323 DD96
Parkview Rd. SE9 261 326 EP88
Parkview Rd., Croy. 287 333 DU102
Parkville Rd. SW6 157 315 CZ80
Parkway N14 208 300 DL47
Parkway NW1 20/1 316 DH67
Parkway SW20 270 323 CX98
Parkway, Erith 254 319 EY76
Parkway, Rom. 227 309 FF54
Parkway, Uxb. 241 312 BN66
Parkway, The, Hayes 242 313 BW72
Parkway, The (Cranford), Houns. 250 321 BU79
Parkway Ms., Mitch. 272 324 DH94
Parkway Trd. Est., Houns. 250 321 BW79
Parkwood N20 207 299 DF48
Parkwood, Beck. 275 325 EA95
Parkwood Gro., Sun. 266 329 BU97

Parkwood Ms. N6 220 306 DH58
Parkwood Rd. SW19 270 323 CZ92
Parkwood Rd., Bex. 262 327 EZ87
Parkwood Rd., Islw. 251 321 CF81
Parliament Ct. E1 50/1 316 DS71
Parliament Hill NW3 113 305 DE63
Parliament Ms. SW14 154 314 CQ82
Parliament Sq. SW1 70/1 316 DL75
Parliament St. SW1 70/1 316 DL75
Parma Cres. SW11 175 323 DF84
Parmiter St. E2 128 317 DV68
Parnell Clo., Edg. 205 298 CP49
Parnell Rd. E3 129 317 DZ67
Parnham St. E14 139 317 DY72
Parolles Rd. N19 98 306 DJ60
Paroma Rd., Belv. 255 319 FA76
Parr Clo. N9 210 301 DV49
Parr Ct., Felt. 266 329 BW91
Parr Rd. E6 244 318 EK67
Parr Rd., Stan. 216 304 CK53
Parr St. N1 26 316 DR68
Parrs Clo., S.Croy. 295 332 DR109
Parrs Pl., Hmptn. 267 329 CA94
Parry Ave. E6 244 318 EM72
Parry Pl. SE18 253 318 EP77
Parry Rd. SE25 273 324 DS97
Parry Rd. W10 127 315 CY69
Parry St. SW8 161 316 DL79
Parsifal Rd. NW6 112 305 DA64
Parsley Gdns., Croy. 288 333 DX102
Parsloes Ave., Dag. 236 309 EX63
Parson St. NW4 218 305 CW56
Parsonage Clo., Hayes 249 312 BT72
Parsonage Gdns., Enf. 202 300 DQ40
Parsonage La., Enf. 202 300 DR40
Parsonage La., Sid. 278 327 EZ91
Parsonage Manorway, Belv. 255 319 FA79
Parsonage St. E14 150 317 EC77
Parsons Cres., Edg. 205 298 CN48
Parsons Grn. SW6 158 315 DA82
Parsons Grn. La. SW6 158 315 DA81
Parsons Gro., Edg. 205 298 CN48
Parsons Hill SE18 253 318 EN76
Parson's Ho. W2 30 315 DD70
Parson's Mead, Croy. 286 332 DP102
Parsons Mead, E.Mol. 267 329 CC97
Parsons Rd. E13 244 318 EJ68
Parthenia Rd. SW6 158 315 DA81
Partingdale La. NW7 206 299 CX50
Partington Clo. N19 99 306 DK60
Partridge Clo. E16 244 318 EK71
Partridge Clo., Barn. 206 299 CW44
Partridge Ct. EC1 36/7 316 DP70
Partridge Dr., Orp. 291 334 EQ104
Partridge Grn. SE9 261 326 EN90
Partridge Knoll, Pur. 294 332 DP112
Partridge Rd., Hmptn. 266 329 BZ93
Partridge Rd., Sid. 261 326 ES90
Partridge Sq. E6 244 318 EL71
Partridge Way N22 220 306 DL53
Parvin St. SW8 161 316 DK81
Pasadena Clo., Hayes 250 321 BU75
Pascal St. SW8 161 316 DK80
Pascoe Rd. SE13 183 325 ED85
Pasley Clo. SE17 85 316 DQ78
Pasquier Rd. E17 222 307 DY55
Passey Pl. SE9 260 326 EM86
Passfield Dr. E14 140 317 EB71
Passfield Path SE28 246 319 EV73
Passing All. EC1 36/7 316 DP70
Passmore Gdns. N11 220 306 DK51
Passmore St. SW1 80 316 DG78
Pasteur Clo. NW9 217 304 CS54
Pasteur Dr., Rom. 228 310 FK54
Pasteur Gdns. N18 209 300 DP50
Paston Clo. E5 103 307 DX62
Paston Cres. SE12 260 326 EH87
Pastor St. SE11 84/5 316 DP77
Pasture Clo., Wem. 90 304 CH62
Pasture Rd. SE6 199 325 EE88
Pasture Rd., Dag. 236 309 EZ63
Pasture Rd., Wem. 90 304 CH61
Pastures, The N20 206 299 CZ46
Pastures Mead, Uxb. 241 312 BN65
Patcham Ct., Sutt. 293 331 DC109
Patcham Ter. SW8 160 316 DH81
Pater St. W8 64 315 DA76
Paternoster Row EC4 49 316 DQ72
Paternoster Sq. EC4 48/9 316 DP72
Paterson Rd., Ashf. 264 328 BK92
Pates Manor Dr., Felt. 265 320 BR87
Path, The SW19 271 323 DB95
Pathfield Rd. SW16 272 324 DK93
Patience Rd. SW11 159 315 DE82
Patio Clo. SW4 177 324 DK86
Patmore Est. SW8 160 316 DJ81
Patmore St. SW8 160 316 DJ81
Patmos Rd. SW9 162 316 DP80
Paton Clo. E3 130 317 EA69
Paton St. EC1 37 316 DQ69
Patricia Ct., Chis. 277 326 ER95
Patricia Ct., Well. 254 319 EV80
Patricia Dr., Horn. 238 311 FL60
Patricia Gdns., Sutt. 292 331 DA111
Patrick Connolly Gdns. E3 130 317 EB69
Patrick Pas. SW11 159 315 DE82
Patrick Rd. E13 244 318 EJ69
Patrington Clo., Uxb. 240 312 BJ69
Patriot Sq. E2 128 317 DV68
Patrol Pl. SE6 182 325 EB86
Patshull Pl. NW5 114 306 DJ65
Patshull Rd. NW5 114 306 DJ65
Patten All., Rich. 169 322 CK85
Patten Rd. SW18 191 323 DE87
Pattenden Rd. SE6 197 325 DZ88
Patterdale Clo., Brom. 275 325 EF93
Patterdale Rd. SE15 164 317 DW80
Patterson Ct. SE19 273 324 DT94
Patterson Rd. SE19 273 324 DT93
Pattinson Pt. E16 244 318 EG71
Pattison Rd. NW2 96 305 DA62
Pattison Wk. SE18 253 318 EQ78
Paul Clo. E15 121 307 EE66
Paul Gdns., Croy. 287 332 DT103
Paul Robeson Clo. E6 245 318 EN69
Paul St. E15 131 317 EE67
Paul St. EC2 38 316 DR70
Paulet Rd. SE5 162 316 DP82
Paulhan Rd., Har. 216 304 CJ56
Paulin Dr. N21 209 300 DN45
Pauline Cres., Twick. 259 321 CC88
Paulinus Clo., Orp. 278 327 EW96
Pauls Wk. EC4 61 316 DQ73
Paultons Sq. SW3 159 315 DD79
Paultons St. SW3 159 315 DD79
Pauntley St. N19 98 306 DJ60
Paved Ct., Rich. 169 322 CK85
Paveley Dr. SW11 159 315 DE80
Paveley St. NW8 30/1 315 DE70
Pavement, The SW4 176 324 DJ84
Pavement, The W5 143 314 CL76
Pavement Ms., Rom. 236 309 EX59
Pavement Sq., Croy. 287 333 DU102
Pavet Clo., Dag. 237 309 FB65
Pavilion Gdns., Stai. 264 328 BH94
Pavilion Ms. N3 219 305 DA54
Pavilion Rd. SW1 67 315 DF76
Pavilion Rd., Ilf. 234 308 EM59
Pavilion St. SW1 67 315 DF76
Pavilion Ter., E.Mol. 267 329 CF98
Pavilion Ter., Ilf. 225 308 ES57
Pavilion Way, Edg. 217 304 CP52
Pavilion Way, Ruis. 232 313 BW61
Pawleyne Clo. SE20 274 325 DW94
Pawsey Clo. E13 244 318 EG67
Pawson's Rd., Croy. 287 332 DQ100
Paxford Rd., Wem. 90 304 CH61
Paxton Clo., Rich. 153 314 CM82
Paxton Pl. SE27 273 324 DS91
Paxton Rd. N17 221 306 DT52
Paxton Rd. SE23 197 325 DY90
Paxton Rd. W4 155 314 CS79
Paxton Rd., Brom. 276 326 EG94
Paxton Ter. SW1 160 316 DH79
Payne Rd. E3 130 317 EB68
Payne St. SE8 165 317 DZ79
Paynell Ct. SE3 183 325 EE83
Paynes Wk. W6 157 315 CY79
Paynesfield Ave. SW14 171 322 CR83
Peabody Ave. SW1 80/1 316 DH78
Peabody Clo. SE10 166 317 EB81
Peabody Dws. WC1 34/5 316 DL70
Peabody Est. EC1 37 316 DQ70
Peabody Est. N17 221 306 DS53
Peabody Est. SE1 60 316 DN74
Peabody Est. SE24 194 324 DQ87
Peabody Est. SW3 159 315 DE79
Peabody Est. W6 146 315 CW78
Peabody Est. W10 126 315 CW70
Peabody Hill SE21 194 324 DP88
Peabody Hill Est. SE21 194 324 DP88
Peabody Sq. N1 24/5 316 DP67
Peabody Sq. SE1 72/3 316 DP75
Peabody Trust SE1 61 316 DQ74
Peabody Yd. N1 25 316 DQ67
Peace Clo. N14 208 300 DH43
Peace Clo. SE25 273 324 DS98
Peace Gro., Wem. 92 304 CP61
Peace St. SE18 253 318 EP79
Peach Rd. W10 127 315 CX69
Peach Tree Ave., West Dr. 248 312 BM72
Peaches Clo., Sutt. 292 331 CY108
Peachey La., Uxb. 248 312 BK71
Peachum Rd. SE3 167 317 EF79
Peacock Ave., Felt. 265 320 BR88
Peacock Clo., Horn. 228 311 FL56
Peacock St. SE17 84/5 316 DP77
Peacock Wk. E16 244 318 EH72
Peacock Yd. SE17 84/5 316 DP77
Peak, The SE26 196 325 DW90
Peak Hill SE26 274 325 DW91
Peak Hill Ave. SE26 274 325 DW91
Peak Hill Gdns. SE26 274 325 DW91
Peaketon Ave., Ilf. 224 308 EK56
Peaks Hill, Pur. 294 332 DK110
Peaks Hill Ri., Pur. 294 332 DL110
Peal Gdns. W13 122 314 CG70
Peall Rd., Croy. 286 332 DM100
Pear Clo. NW9 217 304 CR56
Pear Clo. SE14 165 317 DY80
Pear Pl. SE1 72 316 DN75
Pear Rd. E11 105 307 ED62
Pear Tree Ave., West Dr. 248 312 BM72
Pear Tree Clo. E2 27 316 DT67
Pear Tree Clo., Swan. 279 327 FD96
Pear Tree Ct. EC1 36 316 DN70
Pear Tree Rd., Ashf. 265 328 BQ92
Pearce Clo., Mitch. 272 324 DG96
Pearce Rd., W.Mol. 267 329 CB97
Pearcefield Ave. SE23 196 325 DW88
Pearcroft Rd. E11 105 307 ED61
Peardon St. SW8 160 316 DH82
Peareswood Gdns., Stan. 216 304 CK53
Peareswood Rd., Erith 255 319 FF81
Pearfield Rd. SE23 197 325 DY90
Pearl Clo. E6 245 318 EN72
Pearl Clo. NW2 95 305 CX59
Pearl Rd. E17 223 307 EA55
Pearl St. E1 138 317 DV74
Pearmain Clo., Shep. 281 328 BP99
Pearman St. SE1 72 316 DN76
Pears Rd., Houns. 259 321 CC83
Pearscroft Ct. SW6 158 315 DB81
Pearscroft Rd. SW6 158 315 DB81
Pearson St. E2 27 316 DT68
Pearsons Ave. SE14 166 317 EA81
Peartree Ave. SW17 190 323 DC90
Peartree Clo., Erith 255 319 FD81
Peartree Clo., Mitch. 271 323 DE96
Peartree Clo., S.Croy. 295 333 DV114
Peartree Gdns., Dag. 236 309 EV63
Peartree Gdns., Rom. 227 309 FB54
Peartree La. E1 138 317 DW73
Peartree Rd., Enf. 202 300 DS41
Peartree St. EC1 36/7 316 DP70
Peary Pl. E2 128 317 DW69
Pease Clo., Horn. 238 310 FH66
Peatfield Clo., Sid. 261 326 ES90
Pebworth Rd., Har. 90 304 CG61
Peckarmans Wd. SE26 195 324 DT90
Peckett Sq. N5 116 306 DQ63
Peckford Pl. SW9 162 316 DN82
Peckham Gro. SE15 163 316 DS80
Peckham High St. SE15 164 317 DU81
Peckham Hill St. SE15 164 317 DU80
Peckham Pk. Rd. SE15 164 317 DU80
Peckham Rd. SE5 163 316 DS81
Peckham Rd. SE15 163 316 DT81
Peckham Rye SE15 180 325 DU83
Peckham Rye SE22 180 325 DU84
Peckwater St. NW5 114 306 DJ64
Pedlars Wk. N7 115 306 DL65
Pedley Rd., Dag. 236 309 EW60
Pedley St. E1 128 317 DU70
Pedro St. E5 103 307 DX62
Pedworth Gdns. SE16 148 317 DW77
Peek Cres. SW19 270 323 CX92
Peel Clo. E4 211 301 EB47
Peel Clo. N9 210 301 DU48
Peel Dr. NW9 217 304 CT55
Peel Dr., Ilf. 224 308 EL55
Peel Gro. E2 128 317 DW68
Peel Pas. W8 52 315 DA74
Peel Pl., Ilf. 224 308 EL54
Peel Prec. NW6 16 315 DA68
Peel Rd. E18 223 307 EF53
Peel Rd. NW6 127 315 CZ69
Peel Rd., Har. 215 303 CF55
Peel Rd., Orp. 291 334 EQ106
Peel Rd., Wem. 91 304 CK62
Peel St. W8 52 315 DA74
Peel Way, Rom. 228 311 FM54
Peel Way, Uxb. 240 312 BL70
Peerage Way, Horn. 238 311 FL59
Peerless Dr., Uxb. 230 302 BJ56
Peerless St. EC1 38 316 DR69
Pegamoid Rd. N18 210 301 DW48
Pegasus Pl. SE11 162 316 DN79
Pegelm Gdns., Horn. 238 311 FM59
Pegg Rd., Houns. 250 321 BX80
Peggotty Way, Uxb. 249 312 BP72
Pegley Gdns. SE12 260 326 EG89
Pegwell St. SE18 253 318 ES80
Pekin Clo. E14 140 317 EA72
Pekin St. E14 140 317 EA72
Peldon Ct., Rich. 169 322 CM84
Peldon Wk. N1 24/5 316 DP67
Pelham Ave., Bark. 245 318 ET67
Pelham Clo. SE5 179 324 DS83
Pelham Cres. SW7 78/9 315 DE77
Pelham Pl. SW7 78/9 315 DE77
Pelham Rd. E18 224 308 EH55
Pelham Rd. N15 221 306 DT56
Pelham Rd. N22 221 306 DN54
Pelham Rd. SW19 271 323 DA94
Pelham Rd., Beck. 274 325 DW96
Pelham Rd., Bexh. 263 327 FA83
Pelham Rd., Ilf. 235 308 ER61
Pelham St. SW7 78 315 DD77
Pelican Est. SE15 163 316 DT81
Pelican Pas. E1 128 317 DW70
Pelican Wk. SW9 178 324 DP84
Pelier St. SE17 162 316 DQ79
Pelinore Rd. SE6 199 325 EE89
Pellant Rd. SW6 157 315 CY80
Pellatt Gro. N22 221 306 DN53
Pellatt Rd. SE22 179 324 DT85
Pellatt Rd., Wem. 91 304 CK61
Pellerin Rd. N16 117 306 DS64
Pelling St. E14 140 317 EA72
Pellipar Clo. N13 209 300 DN48
Pellipar Gdns. SE18 252 318 EM78
Pelly Rd. E13 244 318 EG67
Pelter St. E2 39 316 DT69
Pelton Ave., Sutt. 292 331 DB110
Pelton Rd. SE10 151 317 EE78
Pembar Ave. E17 222 307 DY55
Pember Rd. NW10 127 315 CX69
Pemberton Ave., Rom. 228 310 FJ55
Pemberton Gdns. N19 98 306 DJ62
Pemberton Gdns., Rom. 226 309 EY57
Pemberton Gdns., Swan. 279 327 FE97
Pemberton Ho. SE26 274 325 DU91
Pemberton Pl. E8 118 307 DV66
Pemberton Rd. N4 221 306 DN57
Pemberton Rd., E.Mol. 267 329 CC98
Pemberton Row EC4 48 316 DN72
Pemberton Ter. N19 98 306 DJ62
Pembrey Way, Horn. 238 310 FJ65
Pembridge Ave., Twick. 258 321 BZ88
Pembridge Cres. W11 52 315 DA73
Pembridge Gdns. W2 52 315 DA73
Pembridge Ms. W11 52 315 DA73
Pembridge Pl. W2 52 315 DA73
Pembridge Rd. W11 52 315 DA73
Pembridge Sq. W2 52 315 DA73
Pembridge Vil. W11 52 315 DA73
Pembroke Ave., Enf. 203 301 DV38
Pembroke Ave., Har. 216 304 CG55
Pembroke Ave., Surb. 282 330 CP99
Pembroke Clo. SW1 68 316 DG75
Pembroke Clo., Erith 255 319 FD77
Pembroke Clo., Horn. 228 311 FM56
Pembroke Gdns. W8 147 315 CZ77
Pembroke Gdns., Dag. 237 309 FB62
Pembroke Gdns. Clo. W8 147 315 CZ76
Pembroke Ms. E3 129 317 DY69
Pembroke Ms. N10 220 306 DG53
Pembroke Ms. W8 64 315 DA76
Pembroke Pl. W8 64 315 DA76
Pembroke Pl., Edg. 217 304 CN52
Pembroke Rd. E6 244 318 EM71
Pembroke Rd. E17 223 307 EB57
Pembroke Rd. N8 220 306 DL56
Pembroke Rd. N10 220 306 DG53
Pembroke Rd. N13 209 300 DQ48
Pembroke Rd. N15 221 306 DT57
Pembroke Rd. SE25 273 324 DS98
Pembroke Rd. W8 76 315 DA77
Pembroke Rd., Brom. 276 326 EJ96
Pembroke Rd., Erith 255 319 FC78
Pembroke Rd., Grnf. 243 313 CB69
Pembroke Rd., Ilf. 235 308 ET60
Pembroke Rd., Mitch. 272 324 DG96
Pembroke Rd., Nthwd. 213 302 BQ48
Pembroke Rd., Ruis. 231 312 BS60
Pembroke Rd., Wem. 91 304 CK62
Pembroke Sq. W8 64 315 DA76
Pembroke St. N1 115 306 DL66
Pembroke Studios W8 147 315 CZ76
Pembroke Vil. W8 76 315 DA77
Pembroke Vil., Rich. 169 322 CK84
Pembroke Wk. W8 76 315 DA77
Pembroke Way, Hayes 249 320 BQ76
Pembury Ave., Wor.Pk. 283 331 CU102
Pembury Clo., Brom. 289 333 EF101
Pembury Clo., Couls. 293 332 DG114
Pembury Ct., Hayes 257 320 BR79
Pembury Cres., Sid. 262 327 EY90
Pembury Pl. E5 118 307 DV64
Pembury Rd. E5 118 307 DV64
Pembury Rd. N17 221 306 DT53
Pembury Rd. SE25 274 325 DU98
Pembury Rd., Bexh. 254 319 EY80
Pemdevon Rd., Croy. 286 332 DN101
Pemell Clo. E1 128 317 DW70
Pemerich Clo., Hayes 249 320 BT78
Pempath Pl., Wem. 91 304 CK61
Penally Pl. N1 26 316 DR67
Penang St. E1 138 317 DV74
Penarth St. SE15 164 317 DW79
Penberth Rd. SE6 198 325 EC88
Penbury Rd., Sthl. 250 321 BZ77
Pencombe Ms. W11 137 315 CZ73
Pencraig Way SE15 164 317 DV79
Penda Rd., Erith 255 319 FB80
Pendarves Rd. SW20 270 323 CW95
Penda's Mead E9 119 307 DY63
Pendell Ave., Hayes 257 320 BT80
Pendennis Rd. N17 221 306 DR55
Pendennis Rd. SW16 272 324 DL91
Penderel Rd., Houns. 259 321 CA85
Penderry Ri. SE6 199 325 ED89
Penderyn Way N7 115 306 DK63
Pendle Rd. SW16 272 324 DH93
Pendlestone Rd. E17 223 307 EB57
Pendragon Rd., Brom. 199 325 EF90
Pendragon Wk. NW9 217 304 CS58
Pendrell Rd. SE4 165 317 DY82
Pendrell St. SE18 253 318 ER79
Pendula Dr., Hayes 242 313 BX70
Pendulum Ms. E8 117 306 DT64
Penerley Rd. SE6 198 325 EB88
Penfold Clo., Croy. 286 332 DN104
Penfold La., Bex. 262 327 EX88
Penfold Pl. NW1 42/3 315 DE71
Penfold Rd. N9 210 301 DX46
Penfold St. NW1 30 315 DD70
Penfold St. NW8 30 315 DD70
Penford Gdns. SE9 260 326 EK83
Penford St. SE5 162 316 DP82
Pengarth Rd., Bex. 262 327 EX85
Penge Ho. SW11 175 323 DD83
Penge La. SE20 274 325 DW94
Penge Rd. E13 244 318 EJ67
Penge Rd. SE20 274 325 DU97
Penge Rd. SE25 274 325 DU97
Penhall Rd. SE7 252 318 EK77
Penhill Rd., Bex. 262 327 EW86
Penhurst Rd., Ilf. 225 308 EP52
Penifather La., Grnf. 243 313 CD69
Peninsular Clo., Felt. 257 320 BR86
Penistone Rd. SW16 272 324 DL94
Penistone Wk., Rom. 228 310 FJ51
Penketh Dr., Har. 233 313 CD62
Penmon Rd. SE2 254 319 EU76
Penn Clo., Grnf. 243 313 CB68
Penn Clo., Har. 216 304 CJ56
Penn Clo., Uxb. 240 312 BK70
Penn Gdns., Chis. 277 326 EP96
Penn Gdns., Rom. 227 309 FA52
Penn La., Bex. 262 327 EX86
Penn Rd. N7 115 306 DL64
Penn St. N1 26 316 DR67
Pennack Rd. SE15 163 316 DT79
Pennant Ms. W8 76/7 315 DB77
Pennant Ter. E17 222 307 DZ54
Pennard Rd. W12 146 315 CW75
Pennards, The, Sun. 266 329 BW96
Penner Clo. SW19 189 323 CY89
Pennethorne Clo. E9 128 317 DW67
Pennethorne Rd. SE15 164 317 DV80
Pennine Dr. NW2 95 305 CX61
Pennine La. NW2 95 305 CY61
Pennine Way, Bexh. 255 319 FE81
Pennine Way, Hayes 257 320 BR80
Pennington Clo. SE27 273 324 DR91
Pennington Clo., Rom. 227 309 FA51
Pennington Dr. N21 208 300 DL43
Pennington St. E1 138 317 DU73
Pennington Way SE12 260 326 EJ89
Penniston Clo. N17 221 306 DQ54
Penny La., Shep. 281 328 BS101
Penny Ms. SW12 192 324 DH87
Penny Rd. NW10 124 314 CP69
Pennyfields E14 140 317 EA73
Pennymoor Wk. W9 127 315 CZ69
Pennyroyal Ave. E6 245 318 EN72
Penpoll Rd. E8 118 307 DV65
Penpool La., Well. 262 327 EV83
Penrhyn Ave. E17 222 307 DZ53
Penrhyn Cres. E17 223 307 EA53
Penrhyn Cres. SW14 170 322 CQ84
Penrhyn Gro. E17 223 307 EA53
Penrhyn Rd., Kings.T. 268 322 CL98
Penrith Clo. SW15 173 323 CY85
Penrith Clo., Beck. 275 325 EB95
Penrith Clo., Uxb. 240 312 BK66
Penrith Cres., Rain. 238 310 FG64
Penrith Pl. SE27 194 324 DP89
Penrith Rd. N15 221 306 DR57
Penrith Rd., Ilf. 225 308 ET51
Penrith Rd., N.Mal. 269 322 CR98
Penrith Rd., Rom. 229 311 FN51
Penrith Rd., Th.Hth. 273 324 DQ96
Penrith St. SW16 272 324 DJ93
Penrose Gro. SE17 85 316 DQ78
Penrose Ho. SE17 85 316 DQ78
Penrose St. SE17 85 316 DQ78
Penry St. SE1 86/7 316 DS77
Penryn St. NW1 22 316 DK68
Pensbury Pl. SW8 160 316 DJ82
Pensbury St. SW8 160 316 DJ82
Pensford Ave., Rich. 154 314 CN82
Penshurst Ave., Sid. 262 327 EU86
Penshurst Gdns., Edg. 205 298 CP50
Penshurst Grn., Brom. 289 333 EF99
Penshurst Rd. E9 119 307 DX66
Penshurst Rd. N17 221 306 DT52
Penshurst Rd., Bexh. 254 319 EZ81
Penshurst Rd., Th.Hth. 286 332 DP99
Penshurst Wk., Brom. 289 333 EF99
Penshurst Way, Orp. 278 327 EW98
Penshurst Way, Sutt. 292 331 DA108
Penstemon Clo. N3 219 305 DA51
Penstock Footpath N22 220 306 DL55
Pentavia Retail Pk. NW7 217 304 CT52
Pentelowe Gdns., Felt. 258 321 BU86
Pentire Clo., Upmin. 229 311 FS58
Pentire Rd. E17 223 307 ED53
Pentland Ave., Edg. 205 298 CP47
Pentland Ave., Shep. 281 328 BN99
Pentland Clo. NW11 95 305 CY61
Pentland Gdns. SW18 174 323 DC86
Pentland Pl., Nthlt. 242 313 BY67
Pentland St. SW18 174 323 DC86
Pentland Way, Uxb. 231 312 BQ62
Pentlands Clo., Mitch. 272 324 DH97
Pentlow St. SW15 172 323 CW83
Pentney Rd. E4 211 301 ED46
Pentney Rd. SW12 192 324 DJ88
Pentney Rd. SW19 270 323 CY95
Penton Gro. N1 24 316 DN68
Penton Hall Dr., Stai. 280 328 BG95
Penton Hook Rd., Stai. 264 328 BG94
Penton Pk. Est., Cher. 280 328 BH97
Penton Pl. SE17 84/5 316 DP78
Penton Ri. WC1 35 316 DM69
Penton St. N1 24 316 DN68
Pentonville Rd. N1 23 316 DM68
Pentrich Ave., Enf. 203 301 DU38
Pentridge St. SE15 163 316 DT80
Pentyre Ave. N18 209 300 DR50
Penwerris Ave., Islw. 251 321 CC80
Penwith Rd. SW18 190 323 DA89
Penwortham Rd. SW16 272 324 DH93
Penwortham Rd., S.Croy. 295 332 DQ110
Penylan Pl., Edg. 217 304 CN52
Penywern Rd. SW5 76 315 DA78
Penzance Clo., Uxb. 212 302 BK53
Penzance Gdns., Rom. 229 311 FN51
Penzance Pl. W11 137 315 CY74
Penzance Rd., Rom. 229 311 FN51
Penzance St. W11 137 315 CY74
Peony Ct., Wdf.Grn. 223 307 EE52
Peony Gdns. W12 136 315 CU73
Peploe Rd. NW6 127 315 CX68
Peplow Clo., West Dr. 248 312 BK74
Pepper Clo. E6 244 318 EM71
Pepper St. E14 150 317 EB76
Pepper St. SE1 73 316 DQ75
Peppermead Sq. SE13 182 325 EA85
Peppermint Clo., Croy. 286 332 DL101
Peppermint Pl. E11 105 307 EE62
Peppie Clo. N16 101 306 DS61
Pepys Clo., Uxb. 241 312 BP63
Pepys Cres. E16 141 317 EE72
Pepys Cres., Barn. 206 299 CW43
Pepys Ri., Orp. 291 334 ET102
Pepys Rd. SE14 165 317 DX81
Pepys Rd. SW20 270 323 CW96
Pepys St. EC3 62/3 316 DS73
Perceval Ave. NW3 113 305 DE64
Perch St. E8 117 306 DT63
Percheron Clo., Islw. 168 322 CG83
Percheron Rd., Borwd. 205 298 CR44
Percival Ct. N17 221 306 DT52
Percival Ct., Nthlt. 233 313 CA64
Percival Gdns., Rom. 226 309 EW58
Percival Rd. SW14 170 322 CQ84
Percival Rd., Enf. 202 300 DT42
Percival Rd., Felt. 265 320 BT89
Percival Rd., Horn. 228 310 FJ58
Percival Rd., Orp. 290 334 EP103
Percival St. EC1 36/7 316 DP70
Percival Way, Epsom 283 330 CQ105
Percy Ave., Ashf. 265 328 BN92
Percy Bryant Rd., Sun. 265 328 BS94
Percy Bush Rd., West Dr. 248 320 BM76
Percy Circ. WC1 35 316 DM69
Percy Gdns., Enf. 210 301 DX43
Percy Gdns., Hayes 241 312 BS69
Percy Gdns., Islw. 168 322 CG83
Percy Gdns., Wor.Pk. 283 330 CS102
Percy Ms. W1 46 316 DK71
Percy Pas. W1 45 316 DJ71
Percy Rd. E11 105 307 EE59
Percy Rd. E16 141 317 EE71
Percy Rd. N12 207 299 DC50
Percy Rd. N21 209 300 DQ45
Percy Rd. NW6 28 315 DA69
Percy Rd. SE20 274 325 DX95
Percy Rd. SE25 287 333 DU99
Percy Rd. W12 146 315 CU75
Percy Rd., Bexh. 254 319 EY82
Percy Rd., Hmptn. 267 329 CA94
Percy Rd., Ilf. 236 309 EU59
Percy Rd., Islw. 168 322 CG84
Percy Rd., Mitch. 285 332 DG101
Percy Rd., Rom. 227 309 FB55
Percy Rd., Twick. 259 321 CB88
Percy St. W1 46 316 DK71
Percy Way, Twick. 259 321 CC88
Percy Yd. WC1 35 316 DM69
Peregrine Clo. NW10 109 304 CR64
Peregrine Ct. SW16 272 324 DM91
Peregrine Ct., Well. 253 318 ET81
Peregrine Gdns., Croy. 288 333 DY103
Peregrine Ho. EC1 36/7 316 DP69
Peregrine Rd., Sun. 281 328 BT96
Peregrine Wk., Horn. 238 310 FH65
Peregrine Way SW19 270 323 CW94
Perham Rd. W14 147 315 CY78
Peridot St. E6 244 318 EL71
Perifield SE21 194 324 DQ88
Perimeade Rd., Grnf. 122 314 CJ68
Periton Rd. SE9 260 326 EK84
Perivale Gdns. W13 122 314 CH70
Perivale Gra., Grnf. 122 314 CG69
Perivale Ind. Pk., Grnf. 122 314 CG67
Perivale La., Grnf. 122 314 CG69
Perivale New Bus. Cen., Grnf. 122 314 CH68
Perkins Clo., Wem. 106 304 CH64
Perkins Ct., Ashf. 264 328 BM92
Perkin's Rents SW1 70 316 DK76
Perkins Rd., Ilf. 225 308 ER57
Perkins Sq. SE1 61 316 DQ74
Perks Clo. SE3 183 325 EE83
Perpins Rd. SE9 261 326 ER86
Perran Rd. SW2 194 324 DP89
Perran Wk., Brent. 143 314 CL78
Perren St. NW5 114 306 DH65
Perrers Rd. W6 146 315 CV77
Perrin Clo., Ashf. 264 328 BM92
Perrin Rd., Wem. 106 304 CG63
Perrins Ct. NW3 112 305 DC63
Perrins La. NW3 112 305 DC63
Perrin's Wk. NW3 112 305 DC63
Perrott St. SE18 253 318 EQ77
Perry Ave. W3 135 314 CR72
Perry Clo., Rain. 247 319 FD68
Perry Clo., Uxb. 249 312 BQ72
Perry Ct. N15 221 306 DS58
Perry Gdns. N9 209 300 DS48
Perry Garth, Nthlt. 242 313 BW67
Perry Hall Clo., Orp. 291 335 EU101
Perry Hall Rd., Orp. 291 334 ET100
Perry Hill SE6 197 325 DZ90
Perry How, Wor.Pk. 283 330 CT102
Perry Mead, Enf. 202 300 DP40
Perry Oaks Dr.
(Heathrow Airport), Houns. 256 320 BH82
Perry Ri. SE23 197 325 DY90
Perry Rd., Dag. 246 319 EZ70
Perry St., Chis. 277 326 ER93
Perry St., Dart. 263 327 FE84
Perry St. Gdns., Chis. 277 326 ES93
Perry Vale SE23 196 325 DW89
Perryfield Way NW9 217 304 CT58
Perryfield Way, Rich. 184 322 CH89
Perryman Ho., Bark. 245 318 EQ67
Perrymans Fm. Rd., Ilf. 225 308 ER58
Perrymead St. SW6 158 315 DA81
Perryn Rd. SE16 148 317 DV76
Perryn Rd. W3 135 314 CR74
Perrys Pl. W1 46 316 DK72
Persant Rd. SE6 199 325 EE90
Perseverance Pl. SW9 162 316 DN80
Perseverance Pl., Rich. 169 322 CL83
Pershore Clo., Ilf. 225 308 EP57
Pershore Gro., Cars. 285 331 DD100
Pert Clo. N10 220 306 DH51
Perth Ave. NW9 93 304 CR59
Perth Ave., Hayes 242 313 BW70
Perth Clo. SW20 270 323 CU96
Perth Rd. E10 103 307 DY60
Perth Rd. E13 244 318 EH68
Perth Rd. N4 100 306 DN60
Perth Rd. N22 221 306 DP53
Perth Rd., Bark. 245 318 ER67
Perth Rd., Beck. 275 325 EC96
Perth Rd., Ilf. 225 308 EN58
Perth Ter., Ilf. 235 308 EQ59
Perwell Ave., Har. 232 313 BZ60
Perwell Ct., Har. 232 313 BZ60
Peter Ave. NW10 110 305 CV66
Peter St. W1 58 316 DK73
Peterboat Clo. SE10 151 317 EE77
Peterborough Ave., Upmin. 239 311 FS60
Peterborough Gdns., Ilf. 234 308 EL59
Peterborough Ms. SW6 158 315 DA82
Peterborough Rd. E10 223 307 EC57
Peterborough Rd. SW6 158 315 DA82
Peterborough Rd., Cars. 285 331 DE100
Peterborough Rd., Har. 233 313 CE60
Peterborough Vil. SW6 158 315 DB81
Peterchurch Ho. SE15 164 317 DV79
Petergate SW11 174 323 DC84
Peters Clo., Dag. 236 309 EX60
Peters Clo., Stan. 216 304 CK51
Peters Clo., Well. 253 318 ES82
Peters Hill EC4 49 316 DQ72
Peter's La. EC1 48/9 316 DP71
Peters Path SE26 274 325 DV91
Petersfield Ave., Rom. 228 311 FL51
Petersfield Ave., Stai. 264 328 BJ92
Petersfield Clo. N18 209 300 DQ50
Petersfield Clo., Rom. 229 311 FN51
Petersfield Ri. SW15 188 323 CV88
Petersfield Rd. W3 144 314 CQ75
Petersfield Rd., Stai. 264 328 BJ92
Petersham Clo., Rich. 185 322 CK89
Petersham Clo., Sutt. 284 331 CZ106
Petersham Dr., Orp. 277 326 ET96
Petersham Gdns., Orp. 277 326 ET96
Petersham La. SW7 65 315 DC76
Petersham Ms. SW7 65 315 DC76
Petersham Pl. SW7 65 315 DC76
Petersham Rd., Rich. 169 322 CK86
Petersham Ter., Croy. 286 332 DL104
Peterstone Rd. SE2 254 319 EV76
Peterstow Clo. SW19 189 323 CY89
Peterwood Way, Croy. 286 332 DM103
Petherton Rd. N5 116 306 DQ64
Petley Rd. W6 156 315 CW79
Peto Pl. NW1 32/3 316 DH70
Peto St. N. E16 141 317 EF73
Petrie Clo. NW2 111 305 CY65
Pett Clo., Horn. 238 310 FH61
Pett St. SE18 252 318 EL77
Petticoat Sq. E1 51 316 DT72
Pettits Boul., Rom. 227 309 FE53
Pettits Clo., Rom. 227 309 FE54
Pettits La., Rom. 227 309 FE54
Pettits La. N., Rom. 227 309 FD53
Pettits Pl., Dag. 237 309 FA64
Pettits Rd., Dag. 237 309 FA64
Pettiward Clo. SW15 172 323 CW84
Pettley Gdns., Rom. 227 309 FD57
Pettman Cres. SE28 253 318 ER76
Petts Hill, Nthlt. 233 313 CB64
Petts La., Shep. 281 328 BN98
Petts Wd. Rd., Orp. 291 334 EQ99
Pettsgrove Ave., Wem. 106 304 CJ64
Petty France SW1 69 316 DJ76
Petworth Clo., Nthlt. 232 313 BZ66
Petworth Gdns. SW20 270 323 CV97
Petworth Gdns., Uxb. 241 312 BQ67
Petworth Rd. N12 207 299 DE50
Petworth Rd., Bexh. 263 327 FA85
Petworth St. SW11 159 315 DE81
Petworth Way, Horn. 237 309 FF63
Petyt Pl. SW3 159 315 DE79
Petyward SW3 78/9 315 DE77
Pevel Ho., Dag. 237 309 FA61
Pevensey Ave. N11 208 300 DK50
Pevensey Ave., Enf. 202 300 DR40
Pevensey Clo., Islw. 251 321 CC80
Pevensey Rd. E7 121 307 EF63
Pevensey Rd. SW17 271 323 DD91
Pevensey Rd., Felt. 258 321 BY88
Peverel E6 245 318 EN72
Peveret Clo. N11 208 300 DH50
Peveril Dr., Tedd. 267 329 CD92
Pewsey Clo. E4 211 301 EA50
Peyton Pl. SE10 166 317 EC80
Pharaoh Clo., Mitch. 285 331 DF101
Pheasant Clo. E16 244 318 EG72
Pheasant Clo., Pur. 294 332 DP113
Phelp St. SE17 163 316 DR79
Phelps Way, Hayes 249 320 BT77
Phene St. SW3 159 315 DE79
Phil Brown Pl. SW8 160 316 DH82
Philan Way, Rom. 227 309 FD51
Philbeach Gdns. SW5 76 315 DA78
Philchurch Pl. E1 138 317 DU72
Philip Ave., Rom. 237 309 FD60
Philip Ave., Swan. 279 327 FD98
Philip Clo., Rom. 237 309 FD60
Philip Gdns., Croy. 288 333 DZ103
Philip La. N15 221 306 DR56
Philip Rd. SE15 180 325 DU83
Philip Rd., Rain. 247 319 FE69
Philip Rd., Stai. 264 328 BK93
Philip St. E13 244 318 EG70
Philip Wk. SE15 180 325 DV83
Philipot Path SE9 260 326 EM86
Philippa Gdns. SE9 260 326 EK85
Philips Clo., Cars. 285 332 DG102
Phillida Rd., Rom. 229 311 FN54
Phillimore Gdns. NW10 126 315 CW67
Phillimore Gdns. W8 64 315 DA75
Phillimore Gdns. Clo. W8 64 315 DA76
Phillimore Pl. W8 64 315 DA75
Phillimore Wk. W8 64 315 DA76
Phillipp St. N1 26/7 316 DS67
Philpot La. EC3 62/3 316 DS73
Philpot Path, Ilf. 235 308 EQ62
Philpot Sq. SW6 174 323 DB83
Philpot St. E1 138 317 DV72
Philpots Clo., West Dr. 248 312 BK73
Phineas Pett Rd. SE9 260 326 EL83
Phipp St. EC2 38/9 316 DS70
Phipps Bri. Rd. SW19 271 323 DC96
Phipps Bri. Rd., Mitch. 271 323 DC96
Phipps Hatch La., Enf. 202 300 DQ38
Phipp's Ms. SW1 68/9 316 DH76
Phoebeth Rd. SE4 182 325 EA85
Phoenix Clo. E8 27 316 DT67
Phoenix Clo., Nthwd. 213 302 BT49
Phoenix Clo., W.Wick. 289 333 ED103
Phoenix Dr., Kes. 290 334 EK104
Phoenix Pk., Brent. 143 314 CK78
Phoenix Pl. WC1 35 316 DM70
Phoenix Rd. NW1 34 316 DK69
Phoenix Rd. SE20 274 325 DW93
Phoenix St. WC2 46 316 DK72
Phoenix Way, Houns. 250 321 BW79
Phoenix Wf. SE10 151 317 EF75
Phyllis Ave., N.Mal. 283 331 CV99
Physic Pl. SW3 159 315 DF79
Piazza, The WC2 58/9 316 DL73
Picardy Manorway, Belv. 255 319 FB76
Picardy Rd., Belv. 255 319 FA78
Picardy St., Belv. 255 319 FA76
Piccadilly W1 56/7 316 DH74
Piccadilly Arc. SW1 57 316 DJ74
Piccadilly Circ. W1 57 316 DJ73
Piccadilly Pl. W1 57 316 DJ73
Pickard St. EC1 36/7 316 DP69

Pickering Ave. E6 245 318 EN68
Pickering Gdns., Croy. 287 332 DT100
Pickering Ms. W2 40/1 315 DB72
Pickering Pl. SW1 57 316 DJ74
Pickering St. N1 24/5 316 DP67
Pickets St. SW12 192 324 DH87
Pickett Cft., Stan. 216 304 CK53
Picketts Lock La. N9 210 301 DW47
Pickford Clo., Bexh. 254 319 EY82
Pickford La., Bexh. 254 319 EY82
Pickford Rd., Bexh. 262 327 EY84
Pickford Wf. N1 25 316 DQ68
Pickhurst Grn., Brom. 289 333 EF101
Pickhurst La., Brom. 289 333 EF101
Pickhurst La., W.Wick. 289 333 EE99
Pickhurst Mead, Brom. 289 333 EF101
Pickhurst Pk., Brom. 289 333 EE99
Pickhurst Ri., W.Wick. 289 333 EC101
Pickle Herring St. SE1 62/3 316 DS74
Pickwick Clo., Houns. 258 321 BY85
Pickwick Ct. SE9 260 326 EL88
Pickwick Ms. N18 209 300 DS50
Pickwick Pl., Har. 233 313 CE59
Pickwick Rd. SE21 195 324 DR87
Pickwick St. SE1 73 316 DQ75
Pickwick Way, Chis. 277 326 EQ93
Pickworth Clo. SW8 161 316 DL80
Picton Pl. W1 44 316 DG72
Picton St. SE5 163 316 DR80
Piedmont Rd. SE18 253 318 ER78
Pield Heath Ave., Uxb. 241 312 BN70
Pield Heath Rd., Uxb. 240 312 BL70
Pier Head E1 138 317 DV74
Pier Par. E16 253 318 EN75
Pier Rd. E16 253 318 EN75
Pier Rd., Erith 255 319 FE79
Pier Rd., Felt. 258 321 BV85
Pier St. E14 150 317 EC77
Pier Ter. SW18 174 323 DC84
Pier Way SE28 253 318 ER76
Piermont Grn. SE22 180 325 DV85
Piermont Pl., Brom. 276 326 EL96
Piermont Rd. SE22 180 325 DV85
Pierrepoint Arc. N1 24/5 316 DP68
Pierrepoint Rd. W3 134 314 CP73
Pierrepoint Row N1 24/5 316 DP68
Pigeon La., Hmptn. 267 329 CA91
Pigott St. E14 140 317 EA72
Pike Clo., Brom. 276 326 EH92
Pike La., Upmin. 239 311 FT64
Pike Rd. NW7 205 298 CR49
Pikes End, Pnr. 214 303 BV56
Pikestone Clo., Hayes 242 313 BY70
Pilgrim Clo., Mord. 284 331 DB101
Pilgrim Hill SE27 273 324 DQ91
Pilgrim Hill, Orp. 278 327 EX96
Pilgrim St. EC4 48/9 316 DP72
Pilgrimage St. SE1 74 316 DR75
Pilgrims Clo. N13 208 300 DM49
Pilgrims Clo., Nthlt. 233 313 CC64
Pilgrims Ct. SE3 252 318 EG81
Pilgrim's La. NW3 113 305 DD63
Pilgrims Pl. NW3 113 305 DD63
Pilgrims Ri., Barn. 207 299 DE43
Pilgrims Way E6 244 318 EL67
Pilgrims Way N19 99 306 DK60
Pilgrims Way, S.Croy. 295 332 DT107
Pilgrim's Way, Wem. 92 304 CP60
Pilkington Rd. SE15 164 317 DV82
Pilkington Rd., Orp. 291 334 EQ103
Pilot Ind. Est. NW10 125 314 CR70
Pilsdon Clo. SW19 189 323 CX88
Pimlico Rd. SW1 80 316 DG78
Pimlico Wk. N1 38/9 316 DS69
Pimpernel Way, Rom. 228 310 FK51
Pinchin St. E1 138 317 DU73
Pincott Pl. SE4 181 325 DX83
Pincott Rd. SW19 271 323 DC94
Pincott Rd., Bexh. 263 327 FA85
Pindar St. EC2 50/1 316 DS71
Pindock Ms. W9 28/9 315 DB70
Pine Ave. E15 121 307 ED64
Pine Ave., W.Wick. 288 333 EB102
Pine Clo. E10 104 307 EB61
Pine Clo. N14 208 300 DJ45
Pine Clo. N19 98 306 DJ61
Pine Clo. SE20 274 325 DW94
Pine Clo., Stan. 204 298 CH49
Pine Clo., Swan. 279 327 FF98
Pine Coombe, Croy. 288 333 DX105
Pine Ct., Upmin. 239 311 FN63
Pine Cres., Cars. 293 331 DD111
Pine Gdns., Ruis. 232 313 BV60
Pine Gdns., Surb. 282 330 CN100
Pine Glade, Orp. 290 334 EM105
Pine Gro. N4 99 306 DL61
Pine Gro. N20 206 299 CZ46
Pine Gro. SW19 270 323 CZ92
Pine Pl., Bans. 292 331 CX114
Pine Pl., Hayes 241 312 BT70
Pine Ridge, Cars. 293 332 DG109
Pine Rd. N11 208 300 DG47
Pine Rd. NW2 110 305 CW63
Pine St. EC1 36 316 DN70
Pine Tree Clo., Houns. 250 321 BV81
Pine Trees Dr., Uxb. 240 312 BL63
Pine Wk., Cars. 293 331 DD110
Pine Wk., Surb. 282 330 CN100
Pine Wk. E., Cars. 293 331 DD111
Pine Wk. W., Cars. 293 331 DD111
Pine Wd., Sun. 266 329 BU95
Pineapple Ct. SW1 69 316 DJ76
Pinecrest Gdns., Orp. 290 334 EP105
Pinecroft, Rom. 228 310 FJ56
Pinedene SE15 164 317 DV81
Pinefield Clo. E14 140 317 EA73
Pinehurst Wk., Orp. 291 334 ES102
Pinelands Clo. SE3 167 317 EF80
Pinemartin Clo. NW2 94 305 CW62
Pines, The N14 208 300 DJ43
Pines, The, Pur. 295 332 DQ113
Pines, The, Sun. 266 329 BU97
Pines Ave., Enf. 203 301 DV36
Pines Clo., Nthwd. 213 302 BS51
Pines Rd., Brom. 276 326 EL96
Pinewood Ave., Pnr. 215 303 CB51
Pinewood Ave., Sid. 261 326 ES88
Pinewood Ave., Uxb. 248 312 BM72
Pinewood Clo., Croy. 288 333 DY104
Pinewood Clo., Orp. 291 334 ER102
Pinewood Clo., Pnr. 215 303 CB51
Pinewood Dr., Orp. 291 334 ES106
Pinewood Dr., Stai. 264 328 BG92
Pinewood Gro. W5 132 314 CJ72
Pinewood Rd. SE2 254 319 EX79
Pinewood Rd., Brom. 276 326 EG98
Pinewood Rd., Felt. 258 321 BV90
Pinfold Rd. SW16 272 324 DL91
Pinglestone Clo., West Dr. 256 320 BL80
Pinkcoat Clo., Felt. 258 321 BV90
Pinkerton Pl. SW16 272 324 DK91
Pinkham Way N11 220 306 DG52
Pinkwell Ave., Hayes 249 320 BR77
Pinkwell La., Hayes 249 320 BQ77
Pinley Gdns., Dag. 246 319 EV67
Pinn Clo., Uxb. 248 312 BK72
Pinn Way, Ruis. 231 312 BR59
Pinnacle Hill, Bexh. 263 327 FB84
Pinnacle Hill N., Bexh. 263 327 FB83
Pinnell Pl. SE9 260 326 EK84
Pinnell Rd. SE9 260 326 EK84
Pinner Ct., Pnr. 215 303 CA56
Pinner Grn., Pnr. 214 303 BW54
Pinner Gro., Pnr. 214 303 BY56
Pinner Hill, Pnr. 214 303 BV52
Pinner Hill Rd., Pnr. 214 303 BW53
Pinner Pk. Ave., Har. 215 303 CB55
Pinner Pk. Gdns., Har. 215 303 CC54
Pinner Rd., Har. 215 303 CB57
Pinner Rd., Nthwd. 213 302 BT53
Pinner Rd., Pnr. 214 303 BZ56
Pinner Vw., Har. 215 303 CC56
Pintail Clo. E6 244 318 EL71
Pintail Rd., Wdf.Grn. 224 308 EH52
Pintail Way, Hayes 242 313 BX71
Pinto Clo., Borwd. 205 298 CR44
Pinto Way SE3 260 326 EH84
Pioneer St. SE15 164 317 DU81
Pioneer Way W12 136 315 CV72
Pioneer Way, Swan. 279 327 FE97
Piper Clo. N7 115 306 DM64
Piper Rd., Kings.T. 269 322 CN97
Piper's Gdns., Croy. 288 333 DY101
Pipers Grn. NW9 217 304 CQ57
Pipers Grn. La., Edg. 204 298 CL48
Pipewell Rd., Cars. 285 331 DE100
Pippin Clo. NW2 94 305 CV62
Pippin Clo., Croy. 288 333 DZ102
Pippins Clo., West Dr. 248 320 BK76
Pippins Ct., Ashf. 265 328 BP93
Piquet Rd. SE20 274 325 DW96
Pirbright Rd. SW18 189 323 CZ88
Pirie Clo. SE5 179 324 DR83
Pirie St. E16 244 318 EH74
Pitcairn Clo., Rom. 227 309 FA56
Pitcairn Rd., Mitch. 271 323 DF94
Pitchford St. E15 121 307 ED66
Pitfield Cres. SE28 246 319 EU74
Pitfield Est. N1 38/9 316 DS69
Pitfield St. N1 38/9 316 DS69
Pitfield Way NW10 108 304 CQ65
Pitfield Way, Enf. 203 301 DW39
Pitfold Clo. SE12 260 326 EG86
Pitfold Rd. SE12 260 326 EG86
Pitlake, Croy. 286 332 DP103
Pitman St. SE5 162 316 DQ80
Pitsea Pl. E1 139 317 DX72
Pitsea St. E1 139 317 DX72
Pitshanger La. W5 122 314 CH70
Pitshanger Pk. W13 122 314 CG70
Pitt Cres. SW19 271 323 DB91
Pitt Rd., Orp. 291 334 EQ105
Pitt Rd., Th.Hth. 287 332 DQ99
Pitt St. SE15 163 316 DT80
Pitt St. W8 64 315 DA75
Pittman Gdns., Ilf. 235 308 EQ64
Pitt's Head Ms. W1 56 316 DG74
Pittsmead Ave., Brom. 289 334 EG101
Pittville Gdns. SE25 274 325 DU97
Pixfield Ct., Brom. 275 325 EF96
Pixley St. E14 139 317 DZ72
Place Fm. Ave., Orp. 291 334 ER102
Plaistow Gro. E15 131 317 EF67
Plaistow Gro., Brom. 276 326 EH94
Plaistow La., Brom. 276 326 EG94
Plaistow Pk. Rd. E13 244 318 EH68
Plaistow Rd. E13 131 317 EF67
Plaistow Rd. E15 131 317 EF67
Plaitford Clo., Rick. 212 302 BL47
Plane St. SE26 196 325 DV90
Plane Tree Cres., Felt. 258 321 BV90
Plane Tree Wk. SE19 273 324 DS93
Planes, The, Cher. 280 328 BJ101
Plantagenet Clo., Wor.Pk. 283 330 CR105
Plantagenet Gdns., Rom. 236 309 EX59
Plantagenet Pl., Rom. 236 309 EX59
Plantain Gdns. E11 105 307 ED62
Plantain Pl. SE1 74 316 DR75
Plantation, The SE3 252 318 EG82
Plantation Wf. SW11 174 323 DC83
Plasel Ct. E13 244 318 EG67
Plashet Gro. E6 244 318 EJ67
Plashet Rd. E13 244 318 EG67
Plassy Rd. SE6 198 325 EB87
Platford Grn., Horn. 228 311 FL55
Platina St. EC2 38 316 DR70
Plato Rd. SW2 177 324 DL84
Platt, The SW15 173 323 CX83
Platt St. NW1 22 316 DK68
Platt's Eyot, Hmptn. 267 329 CA96
Platt's La. NW3 112 305 DA63
Platts Rd., Enf. 203 301 DW39
Plawsfield Rd., Beck. 274 325 DX95
Plaxtol Clo., Brom. 276 326 EJ95
Plaxtol Rd., Erith 255 319 FA79
Playfair St. W6 146 315 CW78
Playfield Ave., Rom. 227 309 FC53
Playfield Cres. SE22 179 324 DT85
Playfield Rd., Edg. 217 304 CQ54
Playford Rd. N4 99 306 DM61
Playgreen Way SE6 198 325 EA90
Playground Clo., Beck. 274 325 DX96
Playhouse Yd. EC4 48/9 316 DP72
Plaza W., Houns. 251 321 CB81
Pleasance, The SW15 172 323 CV84
Pleasance Rd. SW15 172 323 CV85
Pleasance Rd., Orp. 278 327 EV96
Pleasant Gro., Croy. 288 333 DZ104
Pleasant Pl. N1 116 306 DP66
Pleasant Rd., Kings.T. 269 322 CQ97
Pleasant Row NW1 20/1 316 DH67
Pleasant Vw., Erith 255 319 FE78
Pleasant Vw. Pl., Orp. 290 334 EP106
Pleasant Way, Wem. 122 314 CJ68
Plender St. NW1 21 316 DJ67
Plender St. Est. NW1 21 316 DJ67
Pleshey Rd. N7 115 306 DK63
Plesman Way, Wall. 294 332 DL109
Plevna Cres. N15 221 306 DS58
Plevna Rd. N9 210 301 DU48
Plevna Rd., Hmptn. 267 329 CB95
Plevna St. E14 150 317 EC76
Pleydell Ave. SE19 273 324 DT94
Pleydell Ave. W6 145 314 CT77
Pleydell Ct. EC4 48 316 DN72
Pleydell Est. EC1 37 316 DQ69
Pleydell St. EC4 48 316 DN72
Plimsoll Clo. E14 140 317 EB72
Plimsoll Rd. N4 100 306 DN62
Plough Ct. EC3 62 316 DR73
Plough Fm. Clo., Ruis. 231 302 BR58
Plough La. SE22 179 324 DT86
Plough La. SW17 271 323 DC91
Plough La. SW19 271 323 DB92
Plough La., Pur. 294 332 DM109
Plough La., Tedd. 268 322 CG92
Plough La., Uxb. 212 302 BJ51
Plough La., Wall. 286 332 DL105
Plough La. Clo., Wall. 286 332 DL106
Plough Ms. SW11 175 323 DD84
Plough Pl. EC4 48 316 DN72
Plough Ri., Upmin. 239 311 FS59
Plough Rd. SW11 175 323 DD83
Plough St. E1 51 316 DT72
Plough Ter. SW11 175 323 DD84
Plough Way SE16 149 317 DX77
Plough Yd. EC2 38/9 316 DS70
Ploughmans Clo. NW1 22 316 DK67
Ploughmans End, Islw. 259 321 CD85
Plover Gdns., Upmin. 239 311 FT60
Plover Way SE16 149 317 DY76
Plover Way, Hayes 242 313 BX72
Plowden Bldgs. EC4 48 316 DN72
Plowman Clo. N18 209 300 DR50
Plowman Way, Dag. 236 309 EW60
Plum Garth, Brent. 143 314 CK77
Plum La. SE18 253 318 EP80
Plumbers Row E1 138 317 DU71
Plumbridge St. SE10 166 317 EC81
Plummer La., Mitch. 271 323 DF96
Plummer Rd. SW4 193 324 DK87
Plumpton Ave., Horn. 238 311 FL63
Plumpton Clo., Nthlt. 233 313 CA65
Plumpton Way, Cars. 285 331 DE104
Plumstead Common Rd. SE18 253 318 EP79
Plumstead High St. SE18 253 318 ER77
Plumstead Rd. SE18 253 318 EP77
Plumtree Clo., Dag. 237 309 FC65
Plumtree Clo., Wall. 294 332 DK108
Plumtree Ct. EC4 48/9 316 DP72
Plymouth Ho., Rain. 247 319 FF69
Plymouth Rd. E16 244 318 EG71
Plymouth Rd., Brom. 276 326 EH95
Plymouth Wf. E14 151 317 ED77
Plympton Ave. NW6 111 305 CZ66
Plympton Clo., Belv. 254 319 EY76
Plympton Pl. NW8 30/1 315 DE70
Plympton Rd. NW6 111 305 CZ66
Plympton St. NW8 30/1 315 DE70
Plymstock Rd., Well. 254 319 EW80
Pocklington Clo. NW9 217 304 CS54
Pocock Ave., West Dr. 248 320 BM76
Pocock St. SE1 72/3 316 DP75
Podmore Rd. SW18 174 323 DC84
Poets Rd. N5 117 306 DR64
Poets Way, Har. 215 303 CE56
Point, The, Ruis. 232 313 BU63
Point Clo. SE10 166 317 EC81
Point Hill SE10 166 317 EC80
Point of Thomas Path E1 138 317 DW73
Point Pl., Wem. 108 304 CP66
Point Pleasant SW18 174 323 DA84
Pointalls Clo. N3 219 305 DC54
Pointer Clo. SE28 246 319 EX72
Pointers Clo. E14 150 317 EB78
Poland St. W1 45 316 DJ72
Pole Cat All., Brom. 289 333 EF103
Pole Hill Rd. E4 211 301 EC45
Pole Hill Rd., Uxb. 241 312 BP70
Polebrook Rd. SE3 260 326 EJ83
Polecroft La. SE6 197 325 DZ89
Polehamptons, The, Hmptn. 267 329 CC94
Polesden Gdns. SW20 270 323 CV96
Polesworth Ho. W2 40 315 DA71
Polesworth Rd., Dag. 236 309 EX66
Pollard Clo. E16 244 318 EG73
Pollard Clo. N7 115 306 DM63
Pollard Rd. N20 207 299 DE47
Pollard Rd., Mord. 285 331 DD99
Pollard Row E2 128 317 DU69
Pollard St. E2 128 317 DU69
Pollard Wk., Sid. 278 327 EW93
Pollards Cres. SW16 272 324 DL97
Pollards Hill E. SW16 272 324 DM97
Pollards Hill N. SW16 272 324 DL97
Pollards Hill S. SW16 272 324 DL97
Pollards Hill W. SW16 272 324 DL97
Pollards Wd. Rd. SW16 272 324 DL96
Pollen St. W1 45 316 DJ72
Pollitt Dr. NW8 30 315 DD70
Polperro Clo., Orp. 291 334 ET100
Polsted Rd. SE6 197 325 DZ87
Polthorne Est. SE18 253 318 EQ77
Polthorne Gro. SE18 253 318 EQ77
Polworth Rd. SW16 272 324 DL92
Polygon, The SW4 176 324 DJ84
Polygon Rd. NW1 22 316 DK68
Polytechnic St. SE18 253 318 EN77
Pomell Way E1 51 316 DT72
Pomeroy St. SE14 164 317 DW81
Pomfret Rd. SE5 178 324 DP83
Pomoja La. N19 99 306 DK61
Pond Clo. SE3 167 317 EF82
Pond Clo., Uxb. 212 302 BJ54
Pond Cottage La., W.Wick. 288 333 EA102
Pond Cotts. SE21 195 324 DS88
Pond Grn., Ruis. 231 312 BS61
Pond Hill Gdns., Sutt. 292 331 CY107
Pond Mead SE21 179 324 DR86
Pond Path, Chis. 277 326 EP93
Pond Pl. SW3 78/9 315 DE77
Pond Rd. E15 131 317 EE68
Pond Rd. SE3 167 317 EF82
Pond Sq. N6 98 306 DG60
Pond St. NW3 113 305 DE64
Pond Wk., Upmin. 239 311 FS61
Pond Way, Tedd. 268 322 CJ93
Ponder St. N7 115 306 DM66
Ponders End Ind. Est., Enf. 203 301 DZ42
Pondfield Rd., Brom. 289 333 EE102
Pondfield Rd., Dag. 237 309 FB64
Pondfield Rd., Orp. 290 334 EP104
Pondside Clo., Hayes 257 320 BR80
Pondwood Ri., Orp. 291 334 ES101
Ponler St. E1 138 317 DV72
Ponsard Rd. NW10 126 315 CV69
Ponsford St. E9 118 307 DW64
Ponsonby Pl. SW1 82 316 DK78
Ponsonby Rd. SW15 188 323 CV87
Ponsonby Ter. SW1 82 316 DK78
Pont St. SW1 67 315 DF76
Pont St. Ms. SW1 67 315 DF76
Pontefract Rd., Brom. 275 325 EF92
Ponton Rd. SW8 161 316 DK79
Pontypool Pl. SE1 72/3 316 DP75
Pontypool Wk., Rom. 228 310 FJ51
Pool Clo., Beck. 275 325 EA92
Pool Ct. SE6 198 325 EA89
Pool End Clo., Shep. 281 328 BN99
Pool Rd., Har. 233 313 CD59
Poole Clo., Ruis. 231 312 BS61
Poole Ct. Rd., Houns. 250 321 BY82
Poole Rd. E9 119 307 DX65
Poole Rd., Horn. 238 311 FM59
Poole St. N1 26 316 DR67
Poole Way, Hayes 241 312 BR69
Pooles Bldgs. EC1 36 316 DN70
Pooles La. SW10 158 315 DC80
Pooles La., Dag. 246 319 EY68
Pooles Pk. N4 100 306 DN61
Poolmans St. SE16 149 317 DX75
Poolsford Rd. NW9 217 304 CS56
Poonah St. E1 138 317 DW72
Pope Clo. SW19 271 323 DD93
Pope Clo., Felt. 265 320 BT88
Pope Rd., Brom. 290 334 EK99
Pope St. SE1 74/5 316 DS75
Popes Ave., Twick. 259 321 CE89
Popes Dr. N3 219 305 DA53
Popes Gro., Croy. 288 333 DZ104
Popes Gro., Twick. 259 321 CE89
Pope's Head All. EC3 50 316 DR72
Popes La. W5 143 314 CK76
Popes Rd. SW9 178 324 DN83
Popham Clo., Felt. 258 321 BZ90
Popham Rd. N1 25 316 DQ67
Popham St. N1 25 316 DQ67
Poplar Ave., Mitch. 271 323 DF95
Poplar Ave., Orp. 290 334 EP103
Poplar Ave., Sthl. 251 321 CB76
Poplar Ave., West Dr. 248 312 BM73
Poplar Bath St. E14 140 317 EB73
Poplar Clo. E9 119 307 DZ64
Poplar Clo., Pnr. 214 303 BX53
Poplar Ct. SW19 271 323 DA92
Poplar Dr., Bans. 292 331 CY114
Poplar Gdns., N.Mal. 269 322 CR96
Poplar Gro. N11 220 306 DG51
Poplar Gro. W6 146 315 CW75
Poplar Gro., N.Mal. 269 322 CR97
Poplar Gro., Wem. 92 304 CQ62
Poplar High St. E14 140 317 EB73
Poplar Mt., Belv. 255 319 FB77
Poplar Pl. SE28 246 319 EW73
Poplar Pl. W2 52/3 315 DB73
Poplar Pl., Hayes 242 313 BU73
Poplar Rd. SE24 178 324 DQ84
Poplar Rd. SW19 271 323 DA96
Poplar Rd., Ashf. 265 328 BQ93
Poplar Rd., Sutt. 284 331 CZ102
Poplar Rd., Uxb. 240 312 BJ64
Poplar Rd. S. SW19 271 323 DA97
Poplar St., Rom. 227 309 FC56
Poplar Vw., Wem. 91 304 CK61
Poplar Wk. SE24 178 324 DQ84
Poplar Wk., Croy. 287 332 DQ103
Poplar Way, Felt. 258 321 BU90
Poplar Way, Ilf. 225 308 EQ56
Poplars, The N14 208 300 DH43
Poplars Ave. NW10 110 305 CW65
Poplars Clo., Ruis. 231 312 BS60
Poplars Rd. E17 223 307 EB58
Poppins Ct. EC4 48/9 316 DP72
Poppleton Rd. E11 223 307 EE58
Poppy Clo., Wall. 285 332 DG102
Poppy La., Croy. 288 333 DW101
Porch Way N20 207 299 DF48
Porchester Clo., Horn. 228 311 FL58
Porchester Gdns. W2 52/3 315 DB73
Porchester Gdns. Ms. W2 40/1 315 DB72
Porchester Mead, Beck. 275 325 EA93
Porchester Ms. W2 40/1 315 DB72
Porchester Pl. W2 42/3 315 DE72
Porchester Rd. W2 40/1 315 DB71
Porchester Rd., Kings.T. 269 322 CP96
Porchester Sq. W2 40/1 315 DB72
Porchester Ter. W2 53 315 DC73
Porchester Ter. N. W2 40/1 315 DB72
Porchfield Clo., Sutt. 292 331 DB110
Porcupine Clo. SE9 260 326 EL89
Porden Rd. SW2 177 324 DM84
Porlock Ave., Har. 233 313 CC60
Porlock Rd. W10 127 315 CX70
Porlock Rd., Enf. 209 300 DT45
Porlock St. SE1 74 316 DR75
Porrington Clo., Chis. 277 326 EN95
Port Cres. E13 244 318 EH70
Portal Clo. SE27 194 324 DN90
Portal Clo., Ruis. 232 313 BU63
Portal Clo., Uxb. 240 312 BL66
Portbury Clo. SE15 164 317 DU81
Portchester Clo. SE5 179 324 DR84
Portcullis Lo. Rd., Enf. 202 300 DR41
Portelet Rd. E1 129 317 DX69
Porten Rd. W14 147 315 CY76
Porter Rd. E6 244 318 EM72
Porter Sq. N19 99 306 DL60
Porter St. SE1 61 316 DQ74
Porter St. W1 43 315 DF71
Porters Ave., Dag. 236 309 EV65
Porters Wk. E1 138 317 DV73
Porters Way, West Dr. 248 320 BM76
Portersfield Rd., Enf. 202 300 DS42
Porteus Rd. W2 41 315 DC71
Portgate Clo. W9 127 315 CZ70
Porthcawe Rd. SE26 274 325 DY91
Porthkerry Ave., Well. 262 327 EU84
Portia Way E3 129 317 DZ70
Portinscale Rd. SW15 173 323 CY85
Portland Ave. N16 101 306 DT59
Portland Ave., N.Mal. 283 330 CT101
Portland Ave., Sid. 262 327 EU86
Portland Clo., Rom. 226 309 EY57
Portland Cres. SE9 260 326 EL89
Portland Cres., Felt. 265 328 BR91
Portland Cres., Grnf. 243 313 CB70
Portland Cres., Stan. 216 304 CK54
Portland Dr., Enf. 202 300 DS38
Portland Gdns. N4 221 306 DP58
Portland Gdns., Rom. 226 309 EX57
Portland Gro. SW8 161 316 DM81
Portland Hts., Nthwd. 213 302 BT49
Portland Ms. W1 45 316 DJ72
Portland Pl. W1 44/5 316 DH71
Portland Ri. N4 100 306 DP60
Portland Ri. Est. N4 100 306 DQ60
Portland Rd. N15 221 306 DT56
Portland Rd. SE9 260 326 EL89
Portland Rd. SE25 274 325 DU98
Portland Rd. W11 137 315 CY73
Portland Rd., Ashf. 264 320 BL90
Portland Rd., Brom. 276 326 EJ91
Portland Rd., Hayes 241 312 BS69
Portland Rd., Kings.T. 268 322 CL97
Portland Rd., Mitch. 271 323 DE96
Portland Rd., Sthl. 250 321 BZ76
Portland Sq. E1 138 317 DV74
Portland St. SE17 86 316 DR78
Portland Ter., Rich. 169 322 CK84
Portland Wk. SE17 163 316 DR79
Portman Ave. SW14 171 322 CR83
Portman Clo. W1 43 315 DF72
Portman Clo., Bex. 263 327 FE88
Portman Clo., Bexh. 262 327 EX83
Portman Dr., Wdf.Grn. 224 308 EK54
Portman Gdns. NW9 217 304 CR54
Portman Gdns., Uxb. 241 312 BN66
Portman Gate NW1 30/1 315 DE70
Portman Ms. S. W1 44 316 DG72
Portman Pl. E2 128 317 DW69
Portman Rd., Kings.T. 268 322 CM96
Portman Sq. W1 44 316 DG72
Portman St. W1 44 316 DG72
Portmeadow Wk. SE2 254 319 EX75
Portmeers Clo. E17 222 307 DZ58
Portnall Rd. W9 127 315 CZ68
Portnoi Clo., Rom. 227 309 FD54
Portobello Ct. W11 137 315 CZ73
Portobello Ms. W11 52 315 DA73
Portobello Rd. W10 137 315 CY71
Portobello Rd. W11 137 315 CZ72
Porton Ct., Surb. 282 330 CJ100
Portpool La. EC1 48 316 DN71
Portree Clo. N22 220 306 DM52
Portree St. E14 141 317 ED72
Portsdown, Edg. 205 298 CN50
Portsdown Ave. NW11 218 305 CZ58
Portsdown Ms. NW11 218 305 CZ58
Portsea Ms. W2 42/3 315 DE72
Portsea Pl. W2 42/3 315 DE72
Portslade Rd. SW8 160 316 DJ82
Portsmouth Rd. SW15 188 323 CV87
Portsmouth Rd., Kings.T. 268 322 CK98
Portsmouth Rd., Surb. 282 330 CJ100
Portsmouth St. WC2 47 316 DM72
Portsoken St. E1 63 316 DT73
Portswood Pl. SW15 187 322 CT87
Portugal Gdns., Twick. 259 321 CC89
Portugal St. WC2 47 316 DM72
Portway E15 131 317 EF67
Portway Gdns. SE18 252 318 EK80
Post La., Twick. 259 321 CD88
Post Office App. E7 234 308 EH64
Post Office Ct. EC3 50 316 DR72
Post Office Way SW8 161 316 DK80
Postern Grn., Enf. 202 300 DN40
Postmill Clo., Croy. 288 333 DX104
Postway Ms., Ilf. 235 308 EP62
Potier St. SE1 74 316 DR76
Pott St. E2 128 317 DV69
Potter Clo., Mitch. 272 324 DH96
Potter St., Nthwd. 214 303 BU53
Potter St., Pnr. 214 303 BV53
Potter St. Hill, Pnr. 214 303 BV51
Potterne Clo. SW19 189 323 CX87
Potters Clo., Croy. 288 333 DY102
Potters Flds. SE1 62/3 316 DS74
Potters Gro., N.Mal. 269 322 CQ98
Potters Hts. Clo., Pnr. 214 303 BV52
Potters La. SW16 272 324 DK93
Potters Rd. SW6 158 315 DC82
Pottery La. W11 137 315 CY73
Pottery Rd., Bex. 263 327 FC89
Pottery Rd., Brent. 153 314 CL79
Pottery St. SE16 148 317 DV75
Poulett Gdns., Twick. 259 321 CF88
Poulett Rd. E6 244 318 EM68
Poulner Way SE15 163 316 DT80
Poulters Wd., Kes. 290 334 EK106
Poulton Ave., Sutt. 285 331 DD104
Poulton Clo. E8 118 307 DV64
Poultry EC2 50 316 DR72
Pound Clo., Orp. 291 334 ER103
Pound Clo., Surb. 282 330 CJ102
Pound Ct. Dr., Orp. 291 334 ER103
Pound La. NW10 110 305 CU65
Pound Pk. Rd. SE7 252 318 EK77
Pound Pl. SE9 261 326 EN86
Pound Rd., Cher. 280 328 BH101
Pound St., Cars. 285 331 DF106
Pound Way, Chis. 277 326 EQ94
Pountney Rd. SW11 176 324 DG83
Poverest Rd., Orp. 291 334 ET99
Powder Mill La., Twick. 258 321 BZ87
Powell Clo., Chess. 282 330 CK106
Powell Clo., Edg. 216 304 CM51
Powell Clo., Wall. 294 332 DK108
Powell Gdns., Dag. 237 309 FA63
Powell Rd. E5 102 307 DV62
Powell's Wk. W4 155 314 CS79
Power Rd. W4 144 314 CN77
Powers Ct., Twick. 185 322 CK87
Powerscroft Rd. E5 118 307 DW63
Powerscroft Rd., Sid. 278 327 EW93
Powis Gdns. NW11 95 305 CZ59
Powis Gdns. W11 137 315 CZ72
Powis Ms. W11 137 315 CZ72
Powis Pl. WC1 34/5 316 DL70
Powis Rd. E3 130 317 EB69
Powis Sq. W11 137 315 CZ72
Powis St. SE18 253 318 EN76
Powis Ter. W11 137 315 CZ72
Powle Ter., Ilf. 235 308 EQ64
Powlett Pl. NW1 114 306 DH65
Pownall Gdns., Houns. 259 321 CB84
Pownall Rd. E8 128 317 DU67
Pownall Rd., Houns. 259 321 CB84
Pownsett Ter., Ilf. 235 308 EQ64
Powster Rd., Brom. 276 326 EH92
Powys Clo., Bexh. 254 319 EX79
Powys La. N13 208 300 DL49
Powys La. N14 208 300 DL49
Poynders Ct. SW4 176 324 DJ86
Poynders Gdns. SW4 192 324 DJ87
Poynders Rd. SW4 176 324 DJ86
Poynings Rd. N19 98 306 DJ62
Poynings Way N12 207 299 DA50
Poynings Way, Rom. 228 311 FL53
Poyntell Cres., Chis. 277 326 ER95
Poynter Rd., Enf. 210 301 DU43
Poynton Rd. N17 222 307 DU54
Poyntz Rd. SW11 159 315 DF82
Poyser St. E2 128 317 DV68
Praed Ms. W2 42 315 DD72
Praed St. W2 42 315 DD72
Pragel St. E13 244 318 EH68
Pragnell Rd. SE12 260 326 EH89
Prague Pl. SW2 177 324 DL85
Prah Rd. N4 100 306 DN61
Prairie St. SW8 160 316 DG82
Pratt Ms. NW1 21 316 DJ67
Pratt St. NW1 21 316 DJ67
Pratt Wk. SE11 83 316 DM77
Pratts Pas., Kings.T. 268 322 CL96
Prayle Gro. NW2 95 305 CX60
Prebend Gdns. W4 145 314 CT77
Prebend Gdns. W6 145 314 CT77
Prebend St. N1 25 316 DQ67
Precinct, The, W.Mol. 267 329 CB97
Precinct Rd., Hayes 242 313 BU73
Precincts, The, Mord. 284 331 DB100
Premier Cor. W9 127 315 CZ68
Premier Pl. SW15 173 323 CY84
Premiere Pl. E14 140 317 EA73
Prendergast Rd. SE3 183 325 EE83
Prentis Rd. SW16 272 324 DK91
Prentiss Ct. SE7 252 318 EK77
Presburg Rd., N.Mal. 283 330 CS99
Presburg St. E5 103 307 DX62
Prescelly Pl., Edg. 216 304 CM53
Prescot St. E1 63 316 DT73
Prescott Ave., Orp. 290 334 EP100
Prescott Clo. SW16 272 324 DL94
Prescott Clo., Horn. 238 310 FH60
Prescott Ho. SE17 162 316 DP79
Prescott Pl. SW4 177 324 DK83
Presentation Ms. SW2 193 324 DM88
President Dr. E1 138 317 DV74
President St. EC1 37 316 DQ69
Press Rd. NW10 93 304 CR62
Press Rd., Uxb. 240 312 BK65
Prestage Way E14 140 317 EC73
Prestbury Rd. E7 234 308 EJ66
Prestbury Sq. SE9 276 326 EM91
Prested Rd. SW11 175 323 DE84
Preston Ave. E4 223 307 ED51
Preston Clo. SE1 86/7 316 DS77
Preston Clo., Twick. 259 321 CE90
Preston Dr. E11 224 308 EJ57
Preston Dr., Bexh. 254 319 EX81
Preston Gdns. NW10 109 304 CS65
Preston Gdns., Enf. 203 301 DY37
Preston Gdns., Ilf. 224 308 EL58
Preston Hill, Har. 91 304 CL59
Preston Pl. NW2 110 305 CU65
Preston Pl., Rich. 169 322 CL85
Preston Rd. E11 223 307 EE58
Preston Rd. SE19 273 324 DP93
Preston Rd. SW20 269 322 CT94
Preston Rd., Har. 91 304 CL59
Preston Rd., Shep. 281 328 BN99
Preston Rd., Wem. 91 304 CL61
Preston Waye, Har. 91 304 CL60
Prestons Rd. E14 150 317 EC75
Prestons Rd., Brom. 289 334 EG104
Prestwick Clo., Sthl. 250 321 BY78
Prestwood Ave., Har. 216 304 CH56
Prestwood Clo. SE18 254 319 EU80
Prestwood Clo., Har. 216 304 CH56
Prestwood Gdns., Croy. 287 332 DQ101
Prestwood St. N1 25 316 DQ68
Pretoria Ave. E17 222 307 DY56
Pretoria Clo. N17 221 306 DT52
Pretoria Cres. E4 211 301 EC46
Pretoria Rd. E4 211 301 EC46
Pretoria Rd. E11 105 307 ED60
Pretoria Rd. E16 131 317 EF70
Pretoria Rd. N17 221 306 DT52
Pretoria Rd. SW16 272 324 DH93
Pretoria Rd., Ilf. 235 308 EP64
Pretoria Rd., Rom. 227 309 FC56
Pretoria Rd. N. N18 221 306 DT51
Prevost Rd. N11 208 300 DG47
Price Clo. NW7 218 305 CY51
Price Clo. SW17 191 323 DF90
Price Rd., Croy. 286 332 DP105
Price Way, Hmptn. 266 329 BY93
Price's Yd. N1 23 316 DM67
Pricklers Hill, Barn. 207 299 DB44
Prickley Wd., Brom. 289 333 EF102
Priddy's Yd., Croy. 287 332 DQ103
Prideaux Pl. W3 135 314 CR73
Prideaux Pl. WC1 35 316 DM69
Prideaux Rd. SW9 177 324 DL83
Pridham Rd., Th.Hth. 273 324 DR98
Priest Ct. EC2 49 316 DQ72
Priest Pk. Ave., Har. 233 313 CA61
Priestfield Rd. SE23 197 325 DY90
Priestlands Pk. Rd., Sid. 261 326 ET90
Priestley Clo. N16 101 306 DT59
Priestley Gdns., Rom. 226 309 EV58
Priestley Rd., Mitch. 272 324 DG96
Priestley Way E17 222 307 DX55
Priestley Way NW2 94 305 CU60
Priests Ave., Rom. 227 309 FD54
Priests Bri. SW14 171 322 CS83
Priests Bri. SW15 171 322 CS83
Prima Rd. SW9 162 316 DN80
Primrose Ave., Enf. 202 300 DR39
Primrose Ave., Rom. 236 309 EU59
Primrose Clo. SE6 275 325 EC92
Primrose Clo., Har. 232 313 BZ62
Primrose Clo., Wall. 285 332 DH101
Primrose Gdns. NW3 113 305 DE65
Primrose Gdns., Ruis. 232 313 BW64
Primrose Glen, Horn. 228 311 FL56
Primrose Hill EC4 48 316 DN72
Primrose Hill Ct. NW3 113 305 DF66
Primrose Hill Rd. NW3 113 305 DF66
Primrose Hill Studios NW1 20 316 DG67
Primrose La., Croy. 288 333 DW102
Primrose Ms. NW1 113 305 DF66
Primrose Ms. SE3 252 318 EH80
Primrose Rd. E10 104 307 EB60
Primrose Rd. E18 224 308 EH54
Primrose St. EC2 50/1 316 DS71
Primrose Way, Wem. 123 314 CK68
Primula St. W12 136 315 CU72
Prince Albert Rd. NW1 19 315 DF68
Prince Albert Rd. NW8 30/1 315 DE69
Prince Arthur Ms. NW3 112 305 DC63
Prince Arthur Rd. NW3 112 305 DC64
Prince Charles Dr. NW4 94 305 CW59
Prince Charles Rd. SE3 167 317 EF82
Prince Charles Way, Wall. 285 332 DH104
Prince Consort Dr., Chis. 277 326 ER95
Prince Consort Rd. SW7 65 315 DC76
Prince Edward Rd. E9 119 307 DZ65
Prince George Duke of Kent Ct., Chis. 277 326 ER94
Prince George Rd. N16 117 306 DS63
Prince George's Ave. SW20 270 323 CW96
Prince George's Rd. SW19 271 323 DD95
Prince Henry Rd. SE7 252 318 EK80
Prince Imperial Rd. SE18 252 318 EM81
Prince Imperial Rd., Chis. 277 326 EP94
Prince John Rd. SE9 260 326 EL85
Prince of Orange La. SE10 166 317 EC80
Prince of Wales Clo. NW4 218 305 CV56
Prince of Wales Dr. SW8 160 316 DH80
Prince of Wales Dr. SW11 159 315 DE81
Prince of Wales Footpath, Enf. 203 301 DX37
Prince of Wales Gate SW7 66/7 315 DE75
Prince of Wales Pas. NW1 33 316 DJ69
Prince of Wales Rd. E16 244 318 EJ72
Prince of Wales Rd. NW5 114 306 DG65
Prince of Wales Rd. SE3 167 317 EF81
Prince of Wales Rd., Sutt. 285 331 DD103
Prince of Wales Ter. W4 145 314 CS78
Prince of Wales Ter. W8 64/5 315 DB75

Prince Regent Ct. SE16	139	317	DY74
Prince Regent La. E13	244	318	EH69
Prince Regent La. E16	244	318	EJ71
Prince Regent Rd., Houns.	259	321	CC83
Prince Rd. SE25	287	332	DS99
Prince Rupert Rd. SE9	260	326	EM84
Prince St. SE8	165	317	DZ79
Princedale Rd. W11	137	315	CY74
Princelet St. E1	51	316	DT71
Prince's Arc. SW1	57	316	DJ74
Princes Ave. N3	219	305	DA53
Princes Ave. N10	220	306	DH55
Princes Ave. N13	209	300	DN50
Princes Ave. N22	220	306	DK53
Princes Ave. NW9	217	304	CN56
Princes Ave. W3	144	314	CN76
Princes Ave., Cars.	293	331	DF108
Princes Ave., Enf.	203	301	DY36
Princes Ave., Grnf.	243	313	CB72
Princes Ave., Orp.	291	334	ES99
Princes Ave., Surb.	282	330	CN102
Princes Clo. N4	100	306	DP60
Princes Clo. NW9	217	304	CN56
Princes Clo. SW4	176	324	DJ83
Princes Clo., Edg.	205	298	CN50
Princes Clo., Sid.	262	327	EX90
Princes Clo., Tedd.	267	329	CD91
Princes Ct. E1	138	317	DV73
Princes Ct., Wem.	107	304	CL64
Princes Dr., Har.	215	303	CE55
Princes Gdns. SW7	66	315	DD76
Princes Gdns. W3	134	314	CN71
Princes Gdns. W5	122	314	CJ70
Princes Gate SW7	66/7	315	DE75
Princes Gate Ct. SW7	66	315	DD75
Princes Gate Ms. SW7	66	315	DD76
Princes La. N10	220	306	DH55
Princes Ms. W2	52	315	DA73
Princes Pk., Rain.	238	310	FG66
Princes Pk. Ave. NW11	218	305	CY58
Princes Pk. Ave., Hayes	249	312	BR73
Princes Pk. Circle, Hayes	249	312	BR73
Princes Pk. Clo., Hayes	249	312	BR73
Princes Pk. La., Hayes	249	312	BR73
Princes Pk. Par., Hayes	249	312	BR73
Princes Pl. SW1	57	316	DJ74
Princes Pl. W11	137	315	CY74
Princes Plain, Brom.	290	334	EL101
Princes Ri. SE13	166	317	EC82
Princes Riverside Rd. SE16	139	317	DX74
Princes Rd. N18	210	301	DW49
Princes Rd. SE20	274	325	DX93
Princes Rd. SW14	171	322	CR83
Princes Rd. SW19	271	323	DA93
Princes Rd. W13	132	314	CH74
Princes Rd., Ashf.	264	328	BM92
Princes Rd., Felt.	265	320	BT89
Princes Rd., Ilf.	225	308	ER56
Princes Rd., Kings.T.	269	322	CN95
Princes Rd., Rich.	169	322	CM85
Princes Rd. (Kew), Rich.	153	314	CM81
Princes Rd., Rom.	228	310	FG57
Princes Rd., Tedd.	267	329	CD91
Princes Sq. W2	52/3	315	DB73
Princes St. EC2	50	316	DR72
Princes St. N17	221	306	DS51
Princes St. W1	44/5	316	DH72
Princes St., Bexh.	262	327	EZ84
Princes St., Rich.	169	322	CL85
Princes St., Sutt.	285	331	DD105
Princes Ter. E13	244	318	EH67
Princes Way SW19	189	323	CX87
Princes Way, Croy.	286	332	DM106
Princes Way, Ruis.	232	313	BY63
Princes Way, W.Wick.	289	333	EF105
Princes Yd. W11	137	315	CY74
Princess Ave., Wem.	91	304	CL61
Princess Ct. SE16	149	317	DZ76
Princess Cres. N4	100	306	DP61
Princess La., Ruis.	231	312	BS60
Princess May Rd. N16	117	306	DS63
Princess Ms. NW3	113	305	DD65
Princess Par., Orp.	290	334	EN104
Princess Rd. NW1	20	316	DG67
Princess Rd. NW6	16	315	DA68
Princess Rd., Croy.	287	332	DQ100
Princess St. SE1	72/3	316	DP76
Princesses Wk., Rich.	153	314	CL80
Princethorpe Ho. W2	40/1	315	DB71
Princethorpe Rd. SE26	274	325	DX91
Princeton Ct. SW15	173	323	CX83
Princeton St. WC1	47	316	DM71
Pringle Gdns. SW16	272	324	DJ91
Print Village SE15	163	316	DT82
Printer St. EC4	48	316	DN72
Printers Inn Ct. EC4	48	316	DN72
Printing Ho. Yd. E2	38/9	316	DS69
Printinghouse La., Hayes	249	320	BS75
Priolo Rd. SE7	252	318	EJ78
Prior Ave., Sutt.	293	331	DE108
Prior Bolton St. N1	116	306	DP65
Prior Rd., Ilf.	235	308	EN62
Prior St. SE10	166	317	EC80
Prioress Rd. SE27	194	324	DP90
Prioress St. SE1	74	316	DR76
Priors Cft. E17	222	307	DY54
Priors Fld., Nthlt.	232	313	BY65
Priors Gdns., Ruis.	232	313	BW64
Priors Mead, Enf.	202	300	DS39
Priors Pk., Horn.	238	310	FJ62
Priorsford Ave., Orp.	278	327	EU98
Priory, The SE3	183	325	EF84
Priory Ave. E4	210	301	DZ48
Priory Ave. E17	223	307	EA57
Priory Ave. N8	220	306	DK56
Priory Ave. W4	145	314	CS77
Priory Ave., Orp.	291	334	ER100
Priory Ave., Sutt.	284	331	CX105
Priory Ave., Uxb.	230	302	BJ56
Priory Ave., Wem.	233	313	CF63
Priory Clo. E4	210	301	DZ48
Priory Clo. E18	224	308	EG53
Priory Clo. N3	218	305	CZ53
Priory Clo. N14	208	300	DH43
Priory Clo. N20	206	299	CZ45
Priory Clo. SW19	271	323	DB95
Priory Clo., Beck.	274	325	DY97
Priory Clo., Chis.	276	326	EM95
Priory Clo., Hmptn.	266	329	BZ95
Priory Clo., Hayes	242	313	BV73
Priory Clo., Ruis.	231	312	BT60
Priory Clo., Sun.	266	329	BU94
Priory Clo. (Denham), Uxb.	230	312	BG62
Priory Clo. (Harefield), Uxb.	230	302	BH56
Priory Clo. (Sudbury), Wem.	233	313	CF63
Priory Ct. E17	222	307	DZ54
Priory Ct. EC4	48/9	316	DP72
Priory Ct. SW8	161	316	DK81
Priory Ct. Est. E17	222	307	DZ54
Priory Cres. SE19	273	324	DQ94
Priory Cres., Sutt.	284	331	CX105
Priory Cres., Wem.	90	304	CG62
Priory Dr. SE2	254	319	EX78
Priory Fld. Dr., Edg.	205	298	CP49
Priory Gdns. N6	220	306	DH58
Priory Gdns. SE25	273	324	DT98
Priory Gdns. SW13	171	322	CT83
Priory Gdns. W4	145	314	CS77
Priory Gdns. W5	123	314	CL69
Priory Gdns., Ashf.	265	328	BR92
Priory Gdns., Hmptn.	266	329	BZ94
Priory Gdns., Uxb.	230	302	BJ56
Priory Gdns., Wem.	106	304	CG63
Priory Grn., Stai.	264	328	BH92
Priory Grn. Est. N1	23	316	DM68
Priory Gro. SW8	161	316	DL81
Priory Hill, Wem.	106	304	CG63
Priory La. SW15	171	322	CS86
Priory La., Rich.	154	314	CN80
Priory La., W.Mol.	267	329	CA98
Priory Ms. SW8	161	316	DL81
Priory Ms., Stai.	264	328	BH92
Priory Pk. SE3	183	325	EF83
Priory Pk. Rd. NW6	127	315	CZ67
Priory Pk. Rd., Wem.	106	304	CG63
Priory Rd. E6	244	318	EK67
Priory Rd. N8	220	306	DJ56
Priory Rd. NW6	16/7	315	DB67
Priory Rd. SW19	271	323	DD94
Priory Rd. W4	145	314	CR76
Priory Rd., Bark.	235	308	ER66
Priory Rd., Chess.	282	330	CL104
Priory Rd., Croy.	286	332	DN101
Priory Rd., Hmptn.	266	329	BZ94
Priory Rd., Houns.	259	321	CC85
Priory Rd., Rich.	154	314	CN80
Priory Rd., Sutt.	284	331	CX105
Priory St. E3	130	317	EB69
Priory Ter. NW6	16/7	315	DB67
Priory Ter., Sun.	266	329	BU94
Priory Wk. SW10	77	315	DC78
Priory Way, Har.	215	303	CB56
Priory Way, Sthl.	250	321	BX76
Priory Way, West Dr.	256	320	BL79
Pritchard's Rd. E2	128	317	DU68
Priter Rd. SE16	148	317	DU76
Priter Way SE16	148	317	DU76
Private Rd., Enf.	209	300	DR43
Probert Rd. SW2	178	324	DN85
Probyn Rd. SW2	194	324	DP89
Procter St. WC1	47	316	DM71
Proctor Clo., Mitch.	272	324	DG95
Proctors Clo., Felt.	258	321	BU88
Progress Bus. Pk., The, Croy.	286	332	DM103
Progress Way N22	221	306	DN53
Progress Way, Croy.	286	332	DM103
Progress Way, Enf.	210	301	DU43
Promenade, The W4	155	314	CS81
Promenade App. Rd. W4	155	314	CS80
Promenade de Verdun, Pur.	294	332	DK111
Prospect Clo. SE26	274	325	DV91
Prospect Clo., Belv.	255	319	FA77
Prospect Clo., Houns.	250	321	BZ81
Prospect Clo., Ruis.	232	313	BX59
Prospect Cotts. SW18	174	323	DA84
Prospect Cres., Twick.	259	321	CC86
Prospect Hill E17	223	307	EB56
Prospect Pl. E1	138	317	DW74
Prospect Pl. N2	219	305	DD56
Prospect Pl. N17	221	306	DS53
Prospect Pl. NW2	95	305	CZ62
Prospect Pl. NW3	112	305	DC63
Prospect Pl., Brom.	276	326	EH97
Prospect Pl., Rom.	227	309	FC54
Prospect Ring N2	219	305	DD55
Prospect Rd. NW2	95	305	CZ62
Prospect Rd., Barn.	207	299	DA43
Prospect Rd., Horn.	228	311	FM55
Prospect Rd., Surb.	282	330	CJ100
Prospect Rd., Wdf.Grn.	224	308	EJ51
Prospect St. SE16	148	317	DV75
Prospect Vale SE18	252	318	EL77
Prospero Rd. N19	98	306	DJ60
Prothero Gdns. NW4	218	305	CV57
Prothero Ho. NW10	109	304	CR66
Prothero Rd. SW6	157	315	CY80
Prout Gro. NW10	109	304	CS63
Prout Rd. E5	102	307	DV62
Provence St. N1	25	316	DQ68
Providence Ct. W1	56	316	DG73
Providence La., Hayes	257	320	BR80
Providence Pl. N1	24/5	316	DP67
Providence Pl., Rom.	226	309	EZ54
Providence Rd., West Dr.	248	312	BL74
Providence Row N1	23	316	DM68
Providence Sq. SE1	75	316	DT75
Providence St. N1	25	316	DQ68
Providence Yd. E2	128	317	DU69
Provident Ind. Est., Hayes	250	321	BU75
Provost Est. N1	26	316	DR68
Provost Rd. NW3	113	305	DF66
Provost St. N1	26	316	DR68
Prowse Pl. NW1	114	306	DH66
Pruden Clo. N14	208	300	DJ47
Prudent Pas. EC2	50	316	DR72
Prusom St. E1	138	317	DV74
Pryors, The NW3	97	305	DD62
Pudding La. EC3	62	316	DR73
Pudding Mill La. E15	130	317	EB67
Puddle Dock EC4	60/1	316	DP73
Puddledock La., Dart.	279	327	FE92
Puffin Clo., Beck.	288	333	DX99
Pulborough Rd. SW18	189	323	CZ87
Pulborough Way, Houns.	258	321	BW84
Pulford Rd. N15	221	306	DR58
Pulham Ave. N2	219	305	DC56
Pulleyns Ave. E6	244	318	EL69
Pullman Ct. SW2	193	324	DL88
Pullman Gdns. SW15	172	323	CW86
Pullman Pl. SE9	260	326	EL85
Pulross Rd. SW9	177	324	DM83
Pulteney Clo. E3	129	317	DZ67
Pulteney Rd. E18	224	308	EH55
Pulteney Ter. N1	23	316	DM67
Pulton Pl. SW6	158	315	DA80
Puma Ct. E1	51	316	DT71
Pump All., Brent.	153	314	CK80
Pump Clo., Nthlt.	243	313	CA68
Pump Ct. EC4	48	316	DN72
Pump La. SE14	164	317	DW80
Pump La., Hayes	249	320	BT75
Pump Pail N., Croy.	287	332	DQ104
Pump Pail S., Croy.	287	332	DQ104
Pumping Sta. Rd. W4	155	314	CS80
Pundersons Gdns. E2	128	317	DV69
Punjab La., Sthl.	242	313	BZ74
Purbeck Ave., N.Mal.	283	330	CT100
Purbeck Dr. NW2	95	305	CX61
Purbeck Rd., Horn.	238	310	FG59
Purbrook Est. SE1	74/5	316	DS75
Purbrook St. SE1	74/5	316	DS76
Purcell Clo., Ken.	295	332	DR114
Purcell Cres. SW6	157	315	CX80
Purcell Ms. NW10	109	304	CS66
Purcell Rd., Grnf.	243	313	CB71
Purcell St. N1	26/7	316	DS68
Purcells Ave., Edg.	205	298	CN50
Purchese St. NW1	22	316	DK68
Purdy St. E3	130	317	EB70
Purelake Ms. SE13	183	325	ED83
Purland Clo., Dag.	236	309	EZ60
Purland Rd. SE28	253	318	ET75
Purleigh Ave., Wdf.Grn.	224	308	EL51
Purley Ave. NW2	95	305	CY61
Purley Bury Ave., Pur.	295	332	DQ111
Purley Bury Clo., Pur.	295	332	DQ111
Purley Clo., Ilf.	225	308	EN54
Purley Downs Rd., Pur.	295	332	DQ110
Purley Downs Rd., S.Croy.	295	332	DQ110
Purley Hill, Pur.	294	332	DP112
Purley Knoll, Pur.	294	332	DM111
Purley Oaks Rd., S.Croy.	295	332	DR109
Purley Pk. Rd., Pur.	294	332	DP110
Purley Pl. N1	116	306	DP66
Purley Ri., Pur.	294	332	DM112
Purley Rd. N9	209	300	DR48
Purley Rd., Pur.	294	332	DN111
Purley Rd., S.Croy.	295	332	DR108
Purley Vale, Pur.	294	332	DP113
Purley Way, Croy.	286	332	DM101
Purley Way, Pur.	294	332	DN111
Purneys Rd. SE9	260	326	EK84
Purrett Rd. SE18	253	318	ET78
Purser's Cross Rd. SW6	157	315	CZ81
Pursewardens Clo. W13	132	314	CJ74
Pursley Rd. NW7	218	305	CV52
Purves Rd. NW10	126	315	CV68
Puteaux Ho. E2	129	317	DX68
Putney Bri. SW6	173	323	CY83
Putney Bri. SW15	173	323	CY83
Putney Bri. App. SW6	173	323	CY83
Putney Bri. Rd. SW15	173	323	CY84
Putney Bri. Rd. SW18	174	323	DA85
Putney Common SW15	172	323	CW83
Putney Heath SW15	188	323	CV87
Putney Heath La. SW15	173	323	CX86
Putney High St. SW15	173	323	CX84
Putney Hill SW15	173	323	CX86
Putney Pk. Ave. SW15	172	323	CU84
Putney Pk. La. SW15	172	323	CV84
Putney Rd., Enf.	203	301	DX36
Pycroft Way N9	210	301	DU48
Pyecombe Cor. N12	206	299	CZ49
Pyghtle, The, Uxb.	230	312	BG59
Pylbrook Rd., Sutt.	284	331	DA104
Pylon Way, Croy.	286	332	DL102
Pym Clo., Barn.	207	299	DD43
Pymers Mead SE21	194	324	DQ88
Pymmes Clo. N13	208	300	DM50
Pymmes Clo. N17	222	307	DV53
Pymmes Gdns. N. N9	209	300	DT48
Pymmes Gdns. S. N9	209	300	DT48
Pymmes Grn. Rd. N11	208	300	DH49
Pymmes Rd. N13	220	306	DL51
Pynchester Clo., Uxb.	231	312	BN61
Pyne Rd., Surb.	282	330	CN102
Pyne Ter. SW19	189	323	CX88
Pynham Clo. SE2	254	319	EV76
Pynnacles Clo., Stan.	204	298	CH50
Pyrland Rd. N5	117	306	DR64
Pyrland Rd., Rich.	169	322	CM86
Pyrmont Gro. SE27	194	324	DP90
Pyrmont Rd. W4	154	314	CN79
Pyrmont Rd., Ilf.	235	308	EQ61
Pytchley Cres. SE19	273	324	DQ93
Pytchley Rd. SE22	179	324	DS83
Quadrangle, The W2	42/3	315	DE72
Quadrant, The SE24	178	324	DQ85
Quadrant, The SW20	270	323	CY95
Quadrant, The, Bexh.	254	319	EX80
Quadrant, The, Rich.	169	322	CL84
Quadrant, The, Sutt.	293	331	DC107
Quadrant Arc. W1	57	316	DJ73
Quadrant Arc., Rom.	227	309	FE57
Quadrant Gro. NW5	113	305	DF64
Quadrant Rd., Rich.	169	322	CK84
Quadrant Rd., Th.Hth.	273	324	DP98
Quaggy Wk. SE3	260	326	EG84
Quainton St. NW10	93	304	CR62
Quaker La., Sthl.	251	321	CA76
Quaker St. E1	39	316	DT70
Quakers Course NW9	217	304	CT53
Quakers La., Islw.	152	314	CG81
Quakers Wk. N21	209	300	DR44
Quality Ct. WC2	48	316	DN72
Quantock Clo., Hayes	257	320	BR80
Quantock Dr., Wor.Pk.	284	331	CW103
Quantock Gdns. NW2	95	305	CX61
Quantock Rd., Bexh.	255	319	FE82
Quarles Clo., Rom.	227	309	FA52
Quarley Way SE15	163	316	DT80
Quarr Rd., Cars.	285	331	DD100
Quarrendon St. SW6	158	315	DA82
Quarry Pk. Rd., Sutt.	292	331	CZ107
Quarry Ri., Sutt.	292	331	CZ107
Quarry Rd. SW18	174	323	DC86
Quarter Mile La. E10	120	307	EB63
Quarterdeck, The E14	150	317	EA75
Quay W., Tedd.	268	322	CH92
Quebec Ms. W1	43	315	DF72
Quebec Rd., Hayes	242	313	BW73
Quebec Rd., Ilf.	235	308	EP59
Quebec Way SE16	149	317	DX75
Queen Adelaide Rd. SE20	274	325	DW93
Queen Alexandra's Ct. SW19	270	323	CZ92
Queen Anne Ave. N15	221	306	DT57
Queen Anne Ave., Brom.	275	325	EF97
Queen Anne Ms. W1	44/5	316	DH71
Queen Anne Rd. E9	119	307	DX65
Queen Anne St. W1	44/5	316	DH71
Queen Anne Ter. E1	138	317	DV73
Queen Anne's Clo., Twick.	259	321	CD90
Queen Anne's Gdns. W4	145	314	CS76
Queen Annes Gdns. W5	143	314	CL75
Queen Annes Gdns., Enf.	209	300	DS44
Queen Anne's Gdns., Mitch.	271	323	DF97
Queen Anne's Gate SW1	70	316	DK75
Queen Anne's Gate, Bexh.	262	327	EX83
Queen Anne's Gro. W4	145	314	CS76
Queen Annes Gro. W5	143	314	CL75
Queen Annes Gro., Enf.	209	300	DR45
Queen Annes Pl., Enf.	209	300	DS44
Queen Anne's Wk. WC1	34/5	316	DL70
Queen Caroline Est. W6	146	315	CW78
Queen Caroline St. W6	146	315	CW78
Queen Elizabeth Gdns., Mord.	271	323	DA98
Queen Elizabeth Rd. E17	222	307	DY55
Queen Elizabeth Rd., Kings.T.	268	322	CM96
Queen Elizabeth St. SE1	75	316	DT75
Queen Elizabeth Wk. SW13	156	315	CU81
Queen Elizabeth Wk., Wall.	286	332	DK105
Queen Elizabeths Clo. N16	101	306	DR61
Queen Elizabeths Dr. N14	208	300	DK46
Queen Elizabeths Wk. N16	101	306	DR61
Queen Margaret's Gro. N1	117	306	DS64
Queen Mary Ave., Mord.	284	331	CX99
Queen Mary Clo., Rom.	227	309	FF58
Queen Mary Clo., Surb.	282	330	CN104
Queen Mary Rd. SE19	273	324	DP93
Queen Mary Rd., Shep.	281	328	BQ96
Queen Mary's Ave., Cars.	293	331	DF108
Queen of Denmark Ct. SE16	149	317	DZ76
Queen Sq. WC1	34/5	316	DL70
Queen Sq. Pl. WC1	34/5	316	DL70
Queen St. EC4	61	316	DQ73
Queen St. N17	221	306	DS51
Queen St. W1	56/7	316	DH74
Queen St., Bexh.	262	327	EZ83
Queen St., Cher.	280	328	BG102
Queen St., Croy.	287	332	DQ104
Queen St., Erith	255	319	FE79
Queen St., Rom.	227	309	FD58
Queen St. Pl. EC4	61	316	DQ73
Queen Victoria Ave., Wem.	107	304	CK66
Queen Victoria St. EC4	60/1	316	DP73
Queen Victoria Ter. E1	138	317	DV73
Queenborough Gdns., Chis.	277	326	ER93
Queenborough Gdns., Ilf.	225	308	EN56
Queenhill Rd., S.Croy.	295	333	DV110
Queenhithe EC4	61	316	DQ73
Queens Acre, Sutt.	292	331	CX108
Queens Ave. N3	219	305	DC52
Queens Ave. N10	220	306	DG55
Queens Ave. N20	207	299	DD47
Queen's Ave. N21	209	300	DP46
Queens Ave., Felt.	266	329	BW91
Queens Ave., Grnf.	243	313	CB72
Queens Ave., Stan.	216	304	CH55
Queen's Circ. SW8	160	316	DH80
Queens Clo., Edg.	205	298	CN50
Queens Clo., Wall.	285	332	DH106
Queens Club Gdns. W14	157	315	CY79
Queens Ct. SE23	196	325	DW89
Queens Ct., Rich.	169	322	CM86
Queens Cres. NW5	114	306	DG65
Queens Cres., Rich.	169	322	CM85
Queens Dr. E10	104	307	EA59
Queens Dr. N4	100	306	DP61
Queens Dr. W3	133	314	CM72
Queens Dr., Surb.	282	330	CN101
Queen's Elm Sq. SW3	78	315	DD78
Queens Gdns. NW4	218	305	CW57
Queens Gdns. W2	41	315	DC72
Queens Gdns. W5	132	314	CJ71
Queen's Gdns., Houns.	250	321	BY81
Queens Gdns., Rain.	247	319	FD68
Queens Gdns., Upmin.	229	311	FT58
Queen's Gate SW7	65	315	DC76
Queen's Gate Gdns. SW7	65	315	DC76
Queens Gate Gdns. SW15	172	323	CV84
Queen's Gate Ms. SW7	65	315	DC76
Queen's Gate Pl. SW7	65	315	DC76
Queen's Gate Pl. Ms. SW7	65	315	DC76
Queen's Gate Ter. SW7	65	315	DC76
Queen's Gro. NW8	18	315	DD67
Queen's Gro. Ms. NW8	18	315	DD67
Queens Gro. Rd. E4	211	301	ED46
Queen's Head St. N1	24/5	316	DP67
Queens Head Yd. SE1	62	316	DR74
Queens Ho., Tedd.	267	329	CF93
Queens La. N10	220	306	DH55
Queens La., Ashf.	264	328	BM91
Queens Mkt. E13	244	318	EJ67
Queens Ms. W2	52/3	315	DB73
Queens Par. N11	207	299	DF50
Queens Par. W5	133	314	CM72
Queens Pk. Ct. W10	127	315	CX69
Queens Pk. Gdns., Felt.	258	321	BU90
Queens Pk. Rd., Rom.	228	311	FM53
Queens Pas., Chis.	277	326	EP93
Queens Pl., Mord.	271	323	DA98
Queen's Prom., Kings.T.	268	322	CK97
Queens Reach, E.Mol.	267	329	CE98
Queens Ride SW13	172	323	CU83
Queens Ride SW15	172	323	CW83
Queen's Ride, Rich.	186	322	CP88
Queens Ri., Rich.	169	322	CM86
Queens Rd. E11	105	307	ED59
Queens Rd. E13	244	318	EH67
Queen's Rd. E17	222	307	DZ58
Queens Rd. N3	219	305	DC53
Queens Rd. N9	210	301	DV48
Queen's Rd. N11	220	306	DL52
Queens Rd. NW4	218	305	CW57
Queens Rd. SE14	164	317	DV81
Queens Rd. SE15	164	317	DV81
Queens Rd. SW14	171	322	CR83
Queens Rd. SW19	270	323	CZ93
Queens Rd. W5	133	314	CL72
Queens Rd., Bark.	235	308	EQ65
Queens Rd., Beck.	274	325	DY96
Queens Rd., Brom.	276	326	EG96
Queens Rd., Chis.	277	326	EP93
Queen's Rd., Croy.	286	332	DP100
Queens Rd., Enf.	202	300	DS42
Queen's Rd., Erith	255	319	FE79
Queens Rd., Felt.	258	321	BV88
Queens Rd., Hmptn.	267	329	CB91
Queens Rd., Hayes	249	312	BS72
Queen's Rd., Houns.	259	321	CB83
Queens Rd., Ilf.	235	308	EQ65
Queens Rd., Kings.T.	269	322	CN94
Queens Rd., Mitch.	271	323	DD96
Queens Rd., Mord.	271	323	DA98
Queens Rd., N.Mal.	269	322	CT98
Queens Rd., Rich.	169	322	CM86
Queens Rd., Sthl.	250	321	BX75
Queens Rd., Sutt.	292	331	DA110
Queen's Rd., Tedd.	267	329	CE93
Queens Rd., Twick.	259	321	CF87
Queens Rd., Uxb.	240	312	BJ69
Queens Rd., Wall.	285	332	DH106
Queen's Rd., Well.	254	319	EV82
Queens Rd., West Dr.	248	320	BM75
Queens Rd. W. E13	244	318	EG68
Queen's Row SE17	163	316	DR79
Queens Ter. E13	244	318	EH67
Queen's Ter. NW8	18	315	DD67
Queens Ter., Islw.	168	322	CG84
Queens Ter. Cotts. W7	251	321	CE75
Queens Wk. E4	211	301	ED46
Queens Wk. NW9	92	304	CQ61
Queen's Wk. SW1	57	316	DJ74
Queens Wk. W5	122	314	CJ70
Queens Wk., Ashf.	264	328	BK91
Queens Wk., Har.	215	303	CE56
Queens Wk., Ruis.	232	313	BX62
Queen's Wk., The SE1	62	316	DR74
Queens Way NW4	218	305	CW57
Queens Way, Felt.	266	329	BW91
Queens Well Ave. N20	207	299	DE49
Queen's Wd. Rd. N10	220	306	DH58
Queens Yd. WC1	33	316	DJ70
Queensberry Ms. W. SW7	78	315	DD77
Queensberry Pl. SW7	78	315	DD77
Queensberry Way SW7	78	315	DD77
Queensborough Ms. W2	53	315	DC73
Queensborough Pas. W2	53	315	DC73
Queensborough S. Bldgs. W2	53	315	DC73
Queensborough Studios W2	53	315	DC73
Queensborough Ter. W2	52/3	315	DB73
Queensbridge Pk., Islw.	259	321	CE85
Queensbridge Rd. E2	27	316	DT67
Queensbridge Rd. E8	117	306	DT66
Queensbury Circle Par., Har.	216	304	CL55
Queensbury Pl., Rich.	169	322	CK85
Queensbury Rd. NW9	93	304	CR59
Queensbury Rd., Wem.	123	314	CM68
Queensbury Sta. Par., Edg.	216	304	CM55
Queensbury St. N1	116	306	DQ66
Queenscourt, Wem.	107	304	CL63
Queenscroft Rd. SE9	260	326	EK86
Queensdale Cres. W11	137	315	CX74
Queensdale Pl. W11	137	315	CY74
Queensdale Rd. W11	137	315	CX74
Queensdale Wk. W11	137	315	CY74
Queensdown Rd. E5	118	307	DV63
Queensferry Wk. N17	222	307	DV56
Queensgate Gdns., Chis.	277	326	ER95
Queensgate Pl. NW6	112	305	DA66
Queensland Ave. N18	221	306	DQ51
Queensland Ave. SW19	271	323	DB95
Queensland Pl. N7	116	306	DN63
Queensland Rd. N7	116	306	DN63
Queensmead NW8	18	315	DD67
Queensmead Rd., Brom.	275	325	EF96
Queensmere Clo. SW19	189	323	CX89
Queensmere Rd. SW19	189	323	CX89
Queensmill Rd. SW6	157	315	CX80
Queensthorpe Rd. SE26	274	325	DX91
Queenstown Gdns., Rain.	247	319	FF69
Queenstown Ms. SW8	160	316	DH82
Queenstown Rd. SW8	160	316	DH79
Queensville Rd. SW12	193	324	DK87
Queensway W2	40/1	315	DB72
Queensway, Croy.	294	332	DM107
Queensway, Enf.	203	301	DV42
Queensway, Orp.	291	334	EQ99
Queensway, Sun.	266	329	BV96
Queensway, W.Wick.	289	333	EE104
Queenswood Ave. E17	223	307	EC53
Queenswood Ave., Hmptn.	267	329	CB93
Queenswood Ave., Houns.	250	321	BZ82
Queenswood Ave., Th.Hth.	286	332	DN99
Queenswood Ave., Wall.	286	332	DK105
Queenswood Gdns. E11	234	308	EH60
Queenswood Pk. N3	218	305	CY54
Queenswood Rd. SE23	197	325	DX90
Queenswood Rd., Sid.	261	326	ET85
Quemerford Rd. N7	115	306	DM64
Quentin Pl. SE13	183	325	EE83
Quentin Rd. SE13	183	325	EE83
Quernmore Clo., Brom.	276	326	EG93
Quernmore Rd. N4	221	306	DN58
Quernmore Rd., Brom.	276	326	EG93
Querrin St. SW6	158	315	DC82
Quex Ms. NW6	16	315	DA67
Quex Rd. NW6	16	315	DA67
Quick Pl. N1	24/5	316	DP67
Quick Rd. W4	145	314	CS78
Quick St. N1	24/5	316	DP68
Quick St. Ms. N1	24/5	316	DP68
Quicks Rd. SW19	271	323	DB94
Quickswood NW3	113	305	DE66
Quiet Nook, Kes.	290	334	EK104
Quill La. SW15	173	323	CX84
Quill St. N4	100	306	DN62
Quill St. W5	123	314	CL69
Quilp St. SE1	73	316	DQ75
Quilter St. E2	128	317	DU69
Quilter St. SE18	253	318	ET78
Quinta Dr., Barn.	206	299	CV43
Quintin Ave. SW20	270	323	CZ95
Quintin Clo., Pnr.	214	303	BV57
Quinton Clo., Beck.	275	325	EC97
Quinton Clo., Houns.	250	321	BV80
Quinton Clo., Wall.	285	332	DH105
Quinton St. SW18	190	323	DC89
Quixley St. E14	141	317	ED73
Quorn Rd. SE22	179	324	DS84
Rabbit Row W8	52	315	DA74
Rabbits Rd. E12	234	308	EL63
Rabournmead Dr., Nthlt.	232	313	BY64
Raby Rd., N.Mal.	269	322	CR98
Raby St. E14	139	317	DY72
Raccoon Way, Houns.	250	321	BW82
Rachel Pt. E5	118	307	DU63
Rackham Ms. SW16	272	324	DJ93
Racton Rd. SW6	158	315	DA79
Radbourne Ave. W5	142	314	CJ77
Radbourne Clo. E5	119	307	DX63
Radbourne Cres. E17	223	307	ED54
Radbourne Rd. SW12	192	324	DJ87
Radcliffe Ave. NW10	126	315	CU68
Radcliffe Ave., Enf.	202	300	DQ39
Radcliffe Gdns., Cars.	293	331	DE108
Radcliffe Ms., Hmptn.	267	329	CC92
Radcliffe Path SW8	160	316	DJ82
Radcliffe Rd. N21	209	300	DP46
Radcliffe Rd., Croy.	287	332	DT103
Radcliffe Rd., Har.	216	304	CG54
Radcliffe Sq. SW15	173	323	CX86
Radcliffe Way, Nthlt.	242	313	BX69
Radcot Pt. SE23	197	325	DX90
Radcot St. SE11	84	316	DN78
Raddington Rd. W10	137	315	CY71
Radfield Way, Sid.	261	326	ER87
Radford Rd. SE13	182	325	EC85
Radford Way, Bark.	245	318	ET69
Radipole Rd. SW6	157	315	CZ81
Radland Rd. E16	141	317	EF72
Radlet Ave. SE26	196	325	DV90
Radlett Clo. E7	121	307	EF65
Radlett Pl. NW8	18/9	315	DE67
Radley Ave., Ilf.	235	308	ET63
Radley Clo., Felt.	265	320	BT88
Radley Ct. SE16	149	317	DX75
Radley Gdns., Har.	216	304	CL56
Radley Ms. W8	64	315	DA76
Radley Rd. N17	221	306	DS54
Radley's La. E18	224	308	EG54
Radleys Mead, Dag.	237	309	FB65
Radlix Rd. E10	104	307	EA60
Radnor Ave., Har.	215	303	CE57
Radnor Ave., Well.	262	327	EV85
Radnor Clo., Chis.	277	326	ES93
Radnor Clo., Mitch.	272	324	DL98
Radnor Cres. SE18	254	319	EU80
Radnor Cres., Ilf.	224	308	EM57
Radnor Gdns., Enf.	202	300	DS39
Radnor Gdns., Twick.	259	321	CF89
Radnor Gro., Uxb.	241	312	BN68
Radnor Ms. W2	42	315	DD72
Radnor Pl. W2	42/3	315	DE72
Radnor Rd. NW6	127	315	CY67
Radnor Rd. SE15	164	317	DU80
Radnor Rd., Har.	215	303	CD57
Radnor Rd., Twick.	259	321	CF88
Radnor St. EC1	37	316	DQ69
Radnor Ter. W14	147	315	CZ77
Radnor Wk. E14	150	317	EA77
Radnor Wk. SW3	78/9	315	DE78
Radnor Wk., Croy.	288	333	DY100
Radnor Way NW10	124	314	CP70
Radstock Ave., Har.	216	304	CG55
Radstock St. SW11	159	315	DE80
Raebarn Gdns., Barn.	206	299	CV43
Raeburn Ave., Surb.	282	330	CP102
Raeburn Clo. NW11	219	305	DC58
Raeburn Clo., Kings.T.	268	322	CK94
Raeburn Rd., Edg.	217	304	CN54
Raeburn Rd., Hayes	241	312	BR68
Raeburn Rd., Sid.	261	326	ES86
Raeburn St. SW2	177	324	DL84
Rafford Way, Brom.	276	326	EH96
Raft Rd. SW18	174	323	DA84
Raggleswood, Chis.	277	326	EN95
Raglan Clo., Houns.	258	321	BY85
Raglan Ct. SE12	260	326	EG85
Raglan Ct., S.Croy.	286	332	DP106
Raglan Ct., Wem.	107	304	CM63
Raglan Rd. E17	223	307	EC57
Raglan Rd. SE18	253	318	EQ78
Raglan Rd., Belv.	254	319	EZ78
Raglan Rd., Brom.	276	326	EJ98
Raglan Rd., Enf.	209	300	DS45
Raglan St. NW5	114	306	DH65
Raglan Ter., Har.	233	313	CB63
Raglan Way, Nthlt.	233	313	CC65
Ragley Clo. W3	144	314	CQ75
Raider Clo., Rom.	227	309	FA53
Railey Ms. NW5	114	306	DJ64
Railshead Rd., Islw.	168	322	CH84
Railton Rd. SE24	178	324	DN84
Railway App. N4	221	306	DN58
Railway App. SE1	62	316	DR74
Railway App., Har.	215	303	CF56
Railway App., Twick.	184	322	CG87
Railway App., Wall.	293	332	DH107
Railway Ave. SE16	148	317	DW75
Railway Ms. E3	130	317	EA69
Railway Ms. W10	137	315	CY72
Railway Pas., Tedd.	268	322	CG93
Railway Pl. SW19	270	323	CZ93
Railway Pl., Belv.	255	319	FA76
Railway Ri. SE22	179	324	DS84
Railway Rd., Tedd.	267	329	CF91
Railway Side SW13	171	322	CS83
Railway St. N1	22/3	316	DL68
Railway St., Rom.	236	309	EW60
Railway Ter. SE13	182	325	EB85
Railway Ter., Felt.	258	321	BU88
Rainborough Clo. NW10	108	304	CQ65
Rainbow Ave. E14	150	317	EB78
Rainbow Ind. Est., West Dr.	248	312	BK73
Rainbow Quay SE16	149	317	DY76
Rainbow St. SE5	163	316	DS80
Raine St. E1	138	317	DV74
Rainham Clo. SE9	261	326	ER86
Rainham Clo. SW11	175	323	DE86
Rainham Rd. NW10	126	315	CW69
Rainham Rd. N., Dag.	237	309	FA61
Rainham Rd. S., Dag.	237	309	FB63
Rainhill Way E3	130	317	EA69
Rainsborough Ave. SE8	149	317	DY77
Rainsford Clo., Stan.	204	298	CJ50
Rainsford Rd. NW10	124	314	CP68
Rainsford St. W2	42/3	315	DE72
Rainsford Way, Horn.	238	310	FG60
Rainton Rd. SE7	252	318	EG78
Rainville Rd. W6	156	315	CW79
Raisins Hill, Pnr.	214	303	BW55
Raith Ave. N14	208	300	DK48
Raleana Rd. E14	140	317	EC74
Raleigh Ave., Hayes	242	313	BV71
Raleigh Ave., Wall.	286	332	DK105
Raleigh Clo. NW4	218	305	CW57
Raleigh Clo., Erith	255	319	FF79
Raleigh Clo., Pnr.	232	313	BX59
Raleigh Clo., Ruis.	231	312	BT61
Raleigh Ct. SE16	139	317	DX74
Raleigh Ct., Stai.	264	328	BG91
Raleigh Ct., Wall.	293	332	DH107
Raleigh Dr. N20	207	299	DE48
Raleigh Dr., Surb.	283	330	CQ102
Raleigh Gdns. SW2	177	324	DM86
Raleigh Gdns., Mitch.	271	323	DF97
Raleigh Ms. N1	24/5	316	DP67
Raleigh Ms., Orp.	291	334	ET106
Raleigh Rd. N8	221	306	DN56
Raleigh Rd. SE20	274	325	DX94
Raleigh Rd., Enf.	202	300	DR42
Raleigh Rd., Felt.	265	320	BT90
Raleigh Rd., Rich.	169	322	CM83
Raleigh Rd., Sthl.	250	321	BY78
Raleigh St. N1	24/5	316	DP67
Raleigh Way N14	208	300	DK46
Raleigh Way, Felt.	266	329	BW91
Ralph Ct. W2	40/1	315	DB72
Ralph Perring Ct., Beck.	275	325	EA98
Ralston St. SW3	79	315	DF78
Ram Pas., Kings.T.	268	322	CK96
Ram Pl. E9	118	307	DW65
Ram St. SW18	174	323	DB85
Rama Clo. SW16	272	324	DL94
Rama Ct., Har.	233	313	CE61
Ramac Ind. Est. SE7	252	318	EG77
Ramac Way SE7	252	318	EH78
Rambler Clo. SW16	272	324	DJ91
Rame Clo. SW17	272	324	DG92
Ramilles Clo. SW2	177	324	DL86
Ramillies Pl. W1	45	316	DJ72
Ramillies Rd. NW7	205	298	CS47
Ramillies Rd. W4	145	314	CR77
Ramillies Rd., Sid.	262	327	EV86
Ramillies St. W1	45	316	DJ72
Ramney Dr., Enf.	203	301	DY36
Rampart St. E1	138	317	DV72
Rampayne St. SW1	82	316	DK78
Rampton Clo. E4	211	301	EA48
Rams Gro., Rom.	226	309	EY56
Ramsay Gdns., Rom.	228	310	FJ53
Ramsay Pl., Har.	233	313	CE60
Ramsay Rd. E7	121	307	EE63
Ramsay Rd. W3	144	314	CQ76
Ramscroft Clo. N9	209	300	DS45
Ramsdale Rd. SW17	272	324	DG92
Ramsden Dr., Rom.	227	309	FA52

Ramsden Rd. N11	207	299	DF50
Ramsden Rd. SW12	176	324	DG86
Ramsden Rd., Erith	255	319	FD80
Ramsden Rd., Orp.	291	335	EV101
Ramsey Clo. NW9	217	304	CT58
Ramsey Clo., Grnf.	233	313	CD64
Ramsey Ho., Wem.	107	304	CL65
Ramsey Ms. SW3	159	315	DE79
Ramsey Rd., Th.Hth.	286	332	DM100
Ramsey St. E2	128	317	DU70
Ramsey Wk. N1	117	306	DR65
Ramsey Way N14	208	300	DJ45
Ramsgate St. E8	117	306	DT65
Ramsgill App., Ilf.	225	308	ET56
Ramsgill Dr., Ilf.	225	308	ET57
Ramulis Dr., Hayes	242	313	BX70
Ramus Wd. Ave., Orp.	291	334	ES106
Rancliffe Gdns. SE9	260	326	EL84
Rancliffe Rd. E6	244	318	EL68
Randall Ave. NW2	93	304	CS61
Randall Clo. SW11	159	315	DE81
Randall Clo., Erith	255	319	FC79
Randall Dr., Horn.	238	310	FJ63
Randall Pl. SE10	166	317	EC80
Randall Rd. SE11	83	316	DM78
Randall Row SE11	83	316	DM77
Randell's Rd. N1	22/3	316	DL67
Randle Rd., Rich.	268	322	CJ91
Randlesdown Rd. SE6	275	325	EA91
Randolph App. E16	244	318	EJ72
Randolph Ave. W9	16/7	315	DB68
Randolph Clo., Bexh.	263	327	FC83
Randolph Clo., Kings.T.	269	322	CQ92
Randolph Cres. W9	29	315	DC70
Randolph Gdns. NW6	16/7	315	DB68
Randolph Gro., Rom.	226	309	EW57
Randolph Ho., Croy.	287	332	DQ102
Randolph Ms. W9	29	315	DC70
Randolph Rd. E17	223	307	EB57
Randolph Rd. W9	29	315	DC70
Randolph Rd., Sthl.	250	321	BZ75
Randolph St. NW1	114	306	DJ66
Randon Clo., Har.	215	303	CB54
Ranelagh Ave. SW6	173	323	CZ83
Ranelagh Ave. SW13	156	315	CU82
Ranelagh Bri. W2	40/1	315	DB71
Ranelagh Clo., Edg.	205	298	CN49
Ranelagh Dr., Edg.	205	298	CN49
Ranelagh Dr., Twick.	168	322	CH84
Ranelagh Gdns. E11	224	308	EJ57
Ranelagh Gdns. SW6	173	323	CZ83
Ranelagh Gdns. W4	154	314	CQ80
Ranelagh Gdns. W6	145	314	CT76
Ranelagh Gdns., Ilf.	234	308	EM60
Ranelagh Gro. SW1	80	316	DG78
Ranelagh Ms. W5	143	314	CK75
Ranelagh Pl., N.Mal.	283	330	CS99
Ranelagh Rd. E6	245	318	EN67
Ranelagh Rd. E11	121	307	EE63
Ranelagh Rd. E15	131	317	EE67
Ranelagh Rd. N17	221	306	DS55
Ranelagh Rd. N22	220	306	DM53
Ranelagh Rd. NW10	125	314	CT68
Ranelagh Rd. SW1	81	316	DJ78
Ranelagh Rd. W5	143	314	CK75
Ranelagh Rd., Sthl.	242	313	BX74
Ranelagh Rd., Wem.	107	304	CK65
Ranfurly Rd., Sutt.	284	331	DA103
Range Way, Shep.	281	328	BN101
Rangefield Rd., Brom.	275	325	EE92
Rangemoor Rd. N15	221	306	DT57
Rangers Rd. E4	211	301	EE45
Rangers Sq. SE10	167	317	ED81
Rangeworth Pl., Sid.	261	326	ET90
Rangoon St. EC3	51	316	DT72
Rankin Clo. NW9	217	304	CS55
Ranleigh Gdns., Bexh.	254	319	EZ80
Ranmere St. SW12	192	324	DH88
Ranmoor Clo., Har.	215	303	CD56
Ranmoor Gdns., Har.	215	303	CD56
Ranmore Ave., Croy.	287	332	DT104
Ranmore Path, Orp.	278	327	EU98
Ranmore Rd., Sutt.	292	331	CX109
Rannoch Clo., Edg.	205	298	CP47
Rannoch Rd. W6	156	315	CW79
Rannock Ave. NW9	93	304	CR59
Ransom Rd. SE7	252	318	EJ78
Ransom Wk. SE7	252	318	EJ78
Ranston St. NW1	42/3	315	DE71
Ranulf Rd. NW2	111	305	CZ63
Ranwell Clo. E3	129	317	DZ67
Ranwell St. E3	129	317	DZ67
Ranworth Clo., Erith	255	319	FE82
Ranworth Rd. N9	210	301	DW47
Ranyard Clo., Chess.	282	330	CM104
Raphael Ave., Rom.	227	309	FF54
Raphael St. SW7	67	315	DF75
Rashleigh St. SW8	160	316	DH82
Rasper Rd. N20	207	299	DC47
Rastell Ave. SW2	193	324	DK89
Ratcliff Rd. E7	234	308	EJ64
Ratcliffe Clo. SE12	260	326	EG87
Ratcliffe Clo., Uxb.	240	312	BK69
Ratcliffe Cross St. E1	139	317	DX72
Ratcliffe La. E14	139	317	DY72
Ratcliffe Orchard E1	139	317	DX73
Rathbone Mkt. E16	141	317	EF71
Rathbone Pl. W1	46	316	DK71
Rathbone Pt. E5	118	307	DU63
Rathbone St. E16	141	317	EF71
Rathbone St. W1	45	316	DJ71
Rathcoole Ave. N8	220	306	DM57
Rathcoole Gdns. N8	220	306	DM57
Rathfern Rd. SE6	197	325	DZ88
Rathgar Ave. W13	132	314	CH74
Rathgar Clo. N3	218	305	CZ54
Rathgar Rd. SW9	178	324	DP83
Rathlin Wk. N1	116	306	DQ65
Rathmell Dr. SW4	177	324	DK86
Rathmore Rd. SE7	252	318	EH78
Rattray Rd. SW2	178	324	DN84
Raul Rd. SE15	164	317	DU81
Raveley St. NW5	114	306	DJ63
Raven Clo. NW9	217	304	CS54
Raven Ct. E5	102	307	DU62
Raven Rd. E18	224	308	EJ54
Raven Row E1	138	317	DV71
Ravendale Rd., Sun.	281	328	BT96
Ravenet St. SW11	160	316	DH81
Ravenfield Rd. SW17	191	323	DF90
Ravenhill Rd. E13	244	318	EJ68
Ravenna Rd. SW15	173	323	CX85
Ravenor Pk. Rd., Grnf.	243	313	CB69
Ravens Clo., Brom.	275	325	EF96
Ravens Clo., Enf.	202	300	DS40
Ravens Ms. SE12	260	326	EG85
Ravens Way SE12	260	326	EG85
Ravensbourne Ave., Brom.	275	325	ED94
Ravensbourne Ave., Stai.	264	320	BL88
Ravensbourne Cres., Rom.	228	311	FM55
Ravensbourne Gdns. W13	132	314	CH71
Ravensbourne Gdns., Ilf.	225	308	EN53
Ravensbourne Pk. SE6	198	325	EA87
Ravensbourne Pk. Cres. SE6	197	325	DZ87
Ravensbourne Pl. SE13	166	317	EB82
Ravensbourne Rd. SE6	197	325	DZ88
Ravensbourne Rd., Brom.	276	326	EG97
Ravensbourne Rd., Twick.	168	322	CJ86
Ravensbury Ave., Mord.	285	331	DC99
Ravensbury Gro., Mitch.	271	323	DD98
Ravensbury La., Mitch.	271	323	DD98
Ravensbury Path, Mitch.	271	323	DD98
Ravensbury Rd. SW18	190	323	DA89
Ravensbury Rd., Orp.	277	326	ET97
Ravensbury Ter. SW18	190	323	DB88
Ravenscar Rd., Brom.	275	325	EE91
Ravenscar Rd., Surb.	282	330	CM103
Ravenscourt, Sun.	281	328	BT95
Ravenscourt Ave. W6	146	315	CU77
Ravenscourt Clo., Horn.	238	311	FL62
Ravenscourt Clo., Ruis.	231	312	BQ59
Ravenscourt Dr., Horn.	238	311	FL62
Ravenscourt Gdns. W6	146	315	CU77
Ravenscourt Gro., Horn.	238	311	FL61
Ravenscourt Pk. W6	146	315	CU76
Ravenscourt Pl. W6	146	315	CV77
Ravenscourt Rd. W6	146	315	CV77
Ravenscourt Rd., Orp.	278	327	EU97
Ravenscourt Sq. W6	146	315	CU76
Ravenscraig Rd. N11	208	300	DH49
Ravenscroft Ave. NW11	95	305	CZ59
Ravenscroft Ave., Wem.	91	304	CL60
Ravenscroft Clo. E16	244	318	EG71
Ravenscroft Cres. SE9	260	326	EM90
Ravenscroft Rd. E16	244	318	EG71
Ravenscroft Rd. W4	144	314	CQ77
Ravenscroft Rd., Beck.	274	325	DW96
Ravenscroft St. E2	27	316	DT68
Ravensdale Ave. N12	207	299	DC49
Ravensdale Gdns. SE19	273	324	DR94
Ravensdale Ms., Stai.	264	328	BH93
Ravensdale Rd. N16	101	306	DT59
Ravensdale Rd., Houns.	258	321	BY83
Ravensdon St. SE11	84	316	DN78
Ravensfield Clo., Dag.	236	309	EX63
Ravensfield Gdns., Epsom	283	330	CS106
Ravenshaw St. NW6	111	305	CZ64
Ravenshill, Chis.	277	326	EP95
Ravenshurst Ave. NW4	218	305	CW56
Ravenside Clo. N18	210	301	DX50
Ravenside Retail Pk. N18	210	301	DX50
Ravenslea Rd. SW12	191	323	DF87
Ravensmead Rd., Brom.	275	325	ED94
Ravensmede Way W4	145	314	CT77
Ravenstone SE17	86/7	316	DS78
Ravenstone Rd. N8	221	306	DN55
Ravenstone Rd. NW9	217	304	CT58
Ravenstone St. SW12	192	324	DG88
Ravenswood, Bex.	262	327	EY88
Ravenswood Ave., Surb.	282	330	CM103
Ravenswood Ave., W.Wick.	289	333	EC102
Ravenswood Ct., Kings.T.	269	322	CP93
Ravenswood Cres., Har.	232	313	BZ61
Ravenswood Cres., W.Wick.	289	333	EC102
Ravenswood Gdns., Islw.	251	321	CE81
Ravenswood Pk., Nthwd.	214	303	BU51
Ravenswood Rd. E17	223	307	EC56
Ravenswood Rd. SW12	192	324	DH87
Ravenswood Rd., Croy.	286	332	DP104
Ravensworth Rd. NW10	126	315	CV69
Ravensworth Rd. SE9	260	326	EM90
Ravent Rd. SE11	83	316	DM77
Ravey St. EC2	38/9	316	DS70
Ravine Gro. SE18	253	318	ES79
Rawlings Clo., Orp.	291	334	ET106
Rawlings St. SW3	79	315	DF77
Rawlins Clo. N3	218	305	CY55
Rawnsley Ave., Mitch.	285	331	DD99
Rawreth Wk. N1	25	316	DQ67
Rawson St. SW11	160	316	DG81
Rawsthorne Clo. E16	244	318	EM74
Rawstone Wk. E13	244	318	EG68
Rawstorne Pl. EC1	36/7	316	DP69
Rawstorne St. EC1	36/7	316	DP69
Ray Gdns., Bark.	246	319	EU68
Ray Gdns., Stan.	204	298	CH50
Ray Lo. Rd., Wdf.Grn.	224	308	EJ51
Ray Massey Way E6	244	318	EL67
Ray St. EC1	36	316	DN70
Ray St. Bri. EC1	36	316	DN70
Ray Wk. N7	99	306	DM61
Rayburn Rd., Horn.	239	311	FN59
Raydean Rd., Barn.	207	299	DB43
Raydon St. N19	98	306	DH61
Raydons Gdns., Dag.	236	309	EY64
Raydons Rd., Dag.	236	309	EY64
Rayfield Clo., Brom.	290	334	EL100
Rayford Ave. SE12	199	325	EF87
Rayleas Clo. SE18	253	318	EP81
Rayleigh Ave., Tedd.	267	329	CE93
Rayleigh Clo. N13	209	300	DR48
Rayleigh Ct., Kings.T.	268	322	CM96
Rayleigh Ri., S.Croy.	295	332	DS107
Rayleigh Rd. N13	209	300	DQ48
Rayleigh Rd. SW19	270	323	CZ95
Rayleigh Rd., Wdf.Grn.	224	308	EJ51
Raymead Ave., Th.Hth.	286	332	DN99
Raymere Gdns. SE18	253	318	ER80
Raymond Ave. E18	223	307	EF55
Raymond Ave. W13	142	314	CG76
Raymond Bldgs. WC1	47	316	DM71
Raymond Clo. SE26	274	325	DW92
Raymond Ct. N10	220	306	DG52
Raymond Rd. E13	234	308	EJ66
Raymond Rd. SW19	270	323	CY93
Raymond Rd., Beck.	274	325	DY98
Raymond Rd., Ilf.	235	308	ER59
Raymouth Rd. SE16	148	317	DV77
Rayne Ct. E18	223	307	EF56
Rayner Twr. E10	104	307	EA59
Rayners Clo., Wem.	107	304	CK64
Rayners Ct., Har.	233	313	CA60
Rayners Cres., Nthlt.	242	313	BV69
Rayners Gdns., Nthlt.	242	313	BV68
Rayners La., Har.	233	313	CA60
Rayners La., Pnr.	214	303	BZ57
Rayners Rd. SW15	173	323	CY85
Raynes Ave. E11	234	308	EJ59
Raynham Ave. N18	222	307	DU51
Raynham Rd. N18	210	301	DU50
Raynham Rd. W6	146	315	CV77
Raynham Ter. N18	210	301	DU50
Raynor Clo., Sthl.	242	313	BZ74
Raynor Pl. N1	25	316	DQ67
Raynton Clo., Har.	232	313	BY60
Raynton Clo., Hayes	241	312	BT70
Raynton Dr., Hayes	241	312	BT70
Raynton Rd., Enf.	203	301	DX37
Rays Ave. N18	210	301	DW49
Rays Rd. N18	210	301	DW49
Rays Rd., W.Wick.	289	333	EC101
Raywood Clo., Hayes	257	320	BQ80
Raywood St. SW8	160	316	DH81
Reachview Clo. NW1	114	306	DJ66
Reade Wk. NW10	109	304	CS66
Reading La. E8	118	307	DV65
Reading Rd., Nthlt.	233	313	CB64
Reading Rd., Sutt.	285	331	DC106
Reading Way NW7	206	299	CX50
Reads Clo., Ilf.	235	308	EP62
Reapers Clo. NW1	22	316	DK67
Reapers Way, Islw.	259	321	CD85
Reardon Path E1	138	317	DV74
Reardon St. E1	138	317	DV74
Reaston St. SE14	165	317	DX80
Rebecca Ter. SE16	148	317	DW76
Reckitt Rd. W4	145	314	CS78
Record St. SE15	164	317	DW79
Recovery St. SW17	271	323	DE92
Recreation Ave., Rom.	227	309	FC57
Recreation Ave. (Harold Wd.), Rom.	228	311	FM54
Recreation Rd. SE26	274	325	DX91
Recreation Rd., Brom.	275	325	EF96
Recreation Rd., Sid.	261	326	ET90
Recreation Rd., Sthl.	250	321	BY77
Recreation Way, Mitch.	272	324	DL97
Rector St. N1	25	316	DQ67
Rectory Clo. E4	211	301	EA48
Rectory Clo. N3	218	305	CZ54
Rectory Clo. SW20	270	323	CW97
Rectory Clo., Dart.	263	327	FE84
Rectory Clo., Shep.	281	328	BN97
Rectory Clo., Sid.	278	327	EV91
Rectory Clo., Stan.	204	298	CH50
Rectory Clo., Surb.	282	330	CJ102
Rectory Cres. E11	224	308	EJ58
Rectory Fld. Cres. SE7	252	318	EJ80
Rectory Gdns. N8	220	306	DL56
Rectory Gdns. SW4	176	324	DJ83
Rectory Gdns., Nthlt.	242	313	BZ67
Rectory Gdns., Upmin.	239	311	FR61
Rectory Grn., Beck.	274	325	DZ95
Rectory Gro. SW4	176	324	DJ83
Rectory Gro., Croy.	286	332	DP103
Rectory Gro., Hmptn.	266	329	BZ91
Rectory La. SW17	272	324	DG93
Rectory La., Bans.	293	331	DF114
Rectory La., Edg.	217	304	CN51
Rectory La., Sid.	278	327	EV91
Rectory La., Stan.	204	298	CH50
Rectory La., Wall.	286	332	DJ104
Rectory Orchard SW19	270	323	CY91
Rectory Pk., S.Croy.	295	332	DS113
Rectory Pk. Ave., Nthlt.	242	313	BY69
Rectory Pl. SE18	253	318	EN77
Rectory Rd. E12	234	308	EM64
Rectory Rd. E17	223	307	EB55
Rectory Rd. N16	101	306	DT61
Rectory Rd. SW13	156	315	CU82
Rectory Rd. W3	134	314	CP74
Rectory Rd., Beck.	275	325	EA95
Rectory Rd., Dag.	237	309	FA65
Rectory Rd., Hayes	242	313	BU72
Rectory Rd., Houns.	250	321	BV81
Rectory Rd., Sthl.	250	321	BZ76
Rectory Rd., Sutt.	284	331	DA104
Rectory Sq. E1	139	317	DX71
Rectory Way, Uxb.	231	312	BP61
Reculver Ms. N18	210	301	DU49
Reculver Rd. SE16	149	317	DX78
Red Anchor Clo. SW3	159	315	DE79
Red Barracks Rd. SE18	252	318	EM77
Red Cedars Rd., Orp.	291	334	ES101
Red Hill, Chis.	277	326	EP92
Red Ho. La., Bexh.	262	327	EX84
Red Ho. Rd., Croy.	286	332	DK100
Red Ho. Sq. N1	116	306	DQ65
Red Lion Clo. SE17	162	316	DQ79
Red Lion Ct. EC4	48	316	DN72
Red Lion Hill N2	219	305	DD54
Red Lion La. SE18	253	318	EN81
Red Lion Pl. SE18	253	318	EN81
Red Lion Rd., Surb.	282	330	CM103
Red Lion Row SE17	162	316	DQ79
Red Lion Sq. SW18	174	323	DA85
Red Lion Sq. WC1	47	316	DM71
Red Lion St. WC1	47	316	DM71
Red Lion St., Rich.	169	322	CK85
Red Lion Yd. W1	56	316	DG74
Red Lo. Cres., Bex.	263	327	FD90
Red Lo. Rd., Bex.	263	327	FD90
Red Lo. Rd., W.Wick.	289	333	EC102
Red Oak Clo., Orp.	290	334	EP104
Red Path E9	119	307	DZ65
Red Pl. W1	56	316	DG73
Red Post Hill SE21	179	324	DR85
Red Post Hill SE24	179	324	DR84
Redan Pl. W2	40/1	315	DB72
Redan St. W14	147	315	CX76
Redan Ter. SE5	162	316	DQ82
Redbarn Clo., Pur.	294	332	DP111
Redberry Gro. SE26	196	325	DW90
Redbourne Ave. N3	219	305	DA53
Redbridge Gdns. SE5	163	316	DS80
Redbridge La. E., Ilf.	224	308	EK58
Redbridge La. W. E11	224	308	EH58
Redburn St. SW3	159	315	DF79
Redcar Clo., Nthlt.	233	313	CB65
Redcar St. SE5	162	316	DQ80
Redcastle Clo. E1	138	317	DW73
Redchurch St. E2	39	316	DT70
Redcliffe Clo. SW5	76/7	315	DB78
Redcliffe Gdns. SW5	76/7	315	DB78
Redcliffe Gdns. SW10	76/7	315	DB78
Redcliffe Gdns., Ilf.	235	308	EN60
Redcliffe Ms. SW10	76/7	315	DB78
Redcliffe Pl. SW10	158	315	DC79
Redcliffe Rd. SW10	77	315	DC78
Redcliffe Sq. SW10	76/7	315	DB78
Redcliffe St. SW10	158	315	DB79
Redclose Ave., Mord.	284	331	DA99
Redclyffe Rd. E6	244	318	EJ67
Redcroft Rd., Sthl.	243	313	CC73
Redcross Way SE1	73	316	DQ75
Redden Ct. Rd., Rom.	228	311	FL55
Reddings, The NW7	205	298	CT48
Reddings Clo. NW7	205	298	CT49
Reddington Clo., S.Croy.	295	332	DS109
Reddins Rd. SE15	164	317	DU79
Reddons Rd., Beck.	274	325	DY94
Reddy Rd., Erith	255	319	FF79
Rede Pl. W2	40	315	DA72
Redesdale Gdns., Islw.	152	314	CG80
Redesdale St. SW3	159	315	DE79
Redfern Ave., Houns.	259	321	CA87
Redfern Clo., Uxb.	240	312	BJ67
Redfern Gdns., Rom.	228	310	FK54
Redfern Rd. NW10	109	304	CS66
Redfern Rd. SE6	198	325	EC87
Redfield La. SW5	76	315	DA77
Redford Ave., Couls.	293	332	DH114
Redford Ave., Th.Hth.	272	324	DM98
Redford Ave., Wall.	294	332	DL107
Redford Clo., Felt.	265	320	BT90
Redford Wk. N1	24/5	316	DP67
Redford Way, Uxb.	240	312	BJ66
Redgate Dr., Brom.	289	334	EH103
Redgate Ter. SW15	173	323	CX86
Redgrave Clo., Croy.	287	332	DT100
Redgrave Rd. SW15	173	323	CX83
Redhill Dr., Edg.	217	304	CQ54
Redhill St. NW1	20/1	316	DH68
Redington Gdns. NW3	112	305	DB63
Redington Rd. NW3	112	305	DB63
Redlands Ct., Brom.	275	325	EF94
Redlands Gdns., W.Mol.	266	329	BZ98
Redlands Rd., Enf.	203	301	DY39
Redlands Way SW2	193	324	DM87
Redlaw Way SE16	148	317	DU78
Redleaf Clo., Belv.	255	319	FA79
Redleaves Ave., Ashf.	265	328	BP92
Redlees Clo., Islw.	168	322	CG84
Redman Clo., Nthlt.	242	313	BW68
Redman's Rd. E1	138	317	DW71
Redmead La. E1	138	317	DU74
Redmead Rd., Hayes	249	320	BS77
Redmore Rd. W6	146	315	CV77
Redpoll Way, Erith	254	319	EX75
Redriff Est. SE16	149	317	DY76
Redriff Rd. SE16	149	317	DX76
Redriff Rd., Rom.	227	309	FB54
Redriffe Rd. E13	131	317	EF67
Redroofs Clo., Beck.	275	325	EB95
Redruth Clo. N22	220	306	DM52
Redruth Rd. E9	128	317	DW67
Redstart Clo. E6	244	318	EL71
Redstart Clo. SE14	165	317	DY80
Redston Rd. N8	220	306	DJ56
Redvers Rd. N22	221	306	DN54
Redvers St. N1	38/9	316	DS69
Redwald Rd. E5	119	307	DX63
Redway Dr., Twick.	259	321	CC87
Redwing Path SE28	253	318	ER75
Redwood Clo. N14	208	300	DK45
Redwood Clo. SE16	139	317	DY74
Redwood Clo., Ken.	295	332	DQ114
Redwood Clo., Uxb.	241	312	BP68
Redwood Est., Houns.	250	321	BV79
Redwood Gdns. E4	211	301	EB44
Redwood Twr. E11	105	307	ED62
Redwood Wk., Surb.	282	330	CK102
Redwood Way, Barn.	206	299	CX43
Redwoods SW15	188	323	CU88
Reece Ms. SW7	78	315	DD77
Reed Ave., Orp.	291	334	ES104
Reed Clo. E16	244	318	EG71
Reed Clo. SE12	260	326	EG85
Reed Pl., Shep.	280	328	BM102
Reed Pond Wk., Rom.	227	309	FF54
Reed Rd. N17	221	306	DT54
Reede Gdns., Dag.	237	309	FB64
Reede Rd., Dag.	237	309	FA65
Reede Way, Dag.	237	309	FB65
Reedham Clo. N17	222	307	DV56
Reedham Dr., Pur.	294	332	DM113
Reedham St. SE15	164	317	DU82
Reedholm Vil. N16	117	306	DR63
Reeds Pl. NW1	114	306	DJ66
Reedsfield Clo., Ashf.	265	328	BP91
Reedsfield Rd., Ashf.	265	328	BP91
Reedworth St. SE11	84	316	DN77
Reenglass Rd., Stan.	204	298	CK49
Rees Gdns., Croy.	287	332	DT100
Rees St. N1	25	316	DQ67
Reesland Clo. E12	235	308	EN65
Reets Fm. Clo. NW9	217	304	CS58
Reeves Ave. NW9	93	304	CR59
Reeves Cor., Croy.	286	332	DP103
Reeves Cres., Swan.	279	327	FD97
Reeves Ms. W1	56	316	DG73
Reeves Rd. E3	130	317	EB70
Reeves Rd. SE18	253	318	EP79
Reform Row N17	221	306	DT54
Reform St. SW11	159	315	DF82
Regal Clo. E1	138	317	DU71
Regal Clo. W5	133	314	CK71
Regal Ct. N18	209	300	DT50
Regal Cres., Wall.	285	332	DH104
Regal Dr. N11	208	300	DH50
Regal La. NW1	20	316	DG67
Regal Row SE15	164	317	DW81
Regal Way, Har.	216	304	CL58
Regan Way N1	26/7	316	DS68
Regarth Ave., Rom.	227	309	FE58
Regency Clo. W5	133	314	CL72
Regency Clo., Hmptn.	266	329	BZ92
Regency Cres. NW4	218	305	CX54
Regency Dr., Ruis.	231	312	BS60
Regency Gdns., Horn.	238	310	FJ59
Regency Ms. NW10	110	305	CU65
Regency Ms., Beck.	275	325	EC95
Regency Ms., Islw.	259	321	CE85
Regency Pl. SW1	82	316	DK77
Regency St. SW1	82	316	DK77
Regency Ter. SW3	78	315	DD78
Regency Wk., Croy.	288	333	DY100
Regency Wk., Rich.	169	322	CL86
Regency Way, Bexh.	262	327	EX83
Regent Ave., Uxb.	241	312	BP66
Regent Clo. N12	207	299	DC50
Regent Clo., Har.	216	304	CL58
Regent Clo., Houns.	250	321	BV81
Regent Gdns., Ilf.	226	309	EU58
Regent Pl. SW19	271	323	DB92
Regent Pl. W1	57	316	DJ73
Regent Pl., Croy.	287	332	DT102
Regent Rd. SE24	178	324	DP86
Regent Rd., Surb.	282	330	CM99
Regent Sq. E3	130	317	EB69
Regent Sq. WC1	34/5	316	DL69
Regent Sq., Belv.	255	319	FB77
Regent St. NW10	127	315	CX69
Regent St. SW1	58	316	DK73
Regent St. W1	44/5	316	DH72
Regent St. W4	144	314	CN78
Regents Ave. N13	209	300	DN50
Regents Bri. Gdns. SW8	161	316	DL80
Regents Clo., Hayes	249	312	BS71
Regents Clo., S.Croy.	295	332	DS107
Regents Dr., Kes.	290	334	EK106
Regents Ms. NW8	17	315	DC68
Regent's Pk. NW1	19	315	DF68
Regent's Pk. Est. NW1	33	316	DJ69
Regents Pk. Rd. N3	218	305	CZ56
Regents Pk. Rd. NW1	19	315	DF67
Regents Pk. Ter. NW1	20/1	316	DH67
Regent's Pl. NW1	33	316	DJ70
Regent's Pl. SE3	252	318	EG82
Regents Row E8	128	317	DU67
Regina Rd. N4	99	306	DM60
Regina Rd. SE25	274	325	DU97
Regina Rd. W13	132	314	CG74
Regina Rd., Sthl.	250	321	BY77
Regina Ter. W13	132	314	CH74
Reginald Rd. E7	234	308	EG65
Reginald Rd. SE8	166	317	EA80
Reginald Rd., Nthwd.	213	302	BT53
Reginald Rd., Rom.	229	311	FN53
Reginald Sq. SE8	166	317	EA80
Regis Rd. NW5	114	306	DH64
Regnart Bldgs. NW1	33	316	DJ70
Reid Clo., Pnr.	214	303	BU56
Reidhaven Rd. SE18	253	318	ES77
Reigate Ave., Sutt.	284	331	DA103
Reigate Rd., Brom.	199	325	EF90
Reigate Rd., Ilf.	235	308	ET61
Reigate Way, Wall.	286	332	DL106
Reighton Rd. E5	102	307	DU62
Relay Rd. W12	136	315	CW74
Relf Rd. SE15	180	325	DU83
Relko Gdns., Sutt.	285	331	DD106
Relton Ms. SW7	66/7	315	DE76
Rembrandt Clo. E14	151	317	ED76
Rembrandt Clo. SW1	80	316	DG77
Rembrandt Rd. SE13	183	325	EE84
Rembrandt Rd., Edg.	217	304	CN54
Remington Rd. E6	244	318	EL72
Remington Rd. N15	221	306	DR58
Remington St. N1	24/5	316	DP68
Remnant St. WC2	47	316	DM72
Rempstone Ms. N1	26	316	DR68
Remus Rd. E3	120	307	EA66
Rendle Clo., Croy.	287	332	DT99
Rendlesham Rd. E5	118	307	DU63
Rendlesham Rd., Enf.	202	300	DP39
Renforth St. SE16	148	317	DW75
Renfree Way, Shep.	280	328	BM101
Renfrew Clo. E6	245	318	EN73
Renfrew Rd. SE11	84/5	316	DP77
Renfrew Rd., Houns.	250	321	BX82
Renfrew Rd., Kings.T.	269	322	CP94
Renmuir St. SW17	271	323	DF93
Rennell St. SE13	182	325	EC83
Rennels Way, Islw.	251	321	CE82
Renness Rd. E17	222	307	DY55
Rennets Clo. SE9	261	326	ES85
Rennets Wd. Rd. SE9	261	326	ER85
Rennie Clo., Ashf.	264	320	BK90
Rennie Est. SE16	148	317	DV77
Rennie St. SE1	60/1	316	DP74
Renown Clo., Croy.	286	332	DP102
Renown Clo., Rom.	227	309	FA53
Rensburg Rd. E17	222	307	DX57
Renshaw Clo., Belv.	254	319	EZ79
Renters Ave. NW4	218	305	CW58
Renwick Ind. Est., Bark.	246	319	EV67
Renwick Rd., Bark.	246	319	EV70
Repens Way, Hayes	242	313	BX70
Rephidim St. SE1	74	316	DR76
Replingham Rd. SW18	189	323	CZ88
Reporton Rd. SW6	157	315	CY81
Repository Rd. SE18	252	318	EM79
Repton Ave., Hayes	249	320	BR77
Repton Ave., Rom.	228	310	FG55
Repton Ave., Wem.	106	304	CJ63
Repton Clo., Cars.	285	331	DE106
Repton Ct., Beck.	275	325	EB95
Repton Dr., Rom.	228	310	FG56
Repton Gdns., Rom.	228	310	FG55
Repton Gro., Ilf.	224	308	EM53
Repton Rd., Har.	216	304	CM56
Repton Rd., Orp.	291	335	EU104
Repton St. E14	139	317	DY72
Repulse Clo., Rom.	227	309	FB53
Reservoir Rd. N14	208	300	DJ43
Reservoir Rd. SE4	165	317	DY82
Reservoir Rd., Ruis.	231	302	BQ57
Resolution Wk. SE18	252	318	EM76
Restell Clo. SE3	167	317	EE79
Reston Pl. SW7	65	315	DC75
Restons Cres. SE9	261	326	ER86
Restormel Clo., Houns.	259	321	CA85
Retcar Clo. N19	98	306	DH61
Retcar Pl. N19	98	306	DH61
Retford Clo., Rom.	229	311	FN51
Retford Path, Rom.	229	311	FN51
Retford Rd., Rom.	228	311	FM51
Retingham Way E4	211	301	EB47
Retreat, The NW9	217	304	CR57
Retreat, The SW14	171	322	CS83
Retreat, The, Har.	233	313	CA59
Retreat, The, Surb.	282	330	CM100
Retreat, The, Th.Hth.	273	324	DR98
Retreat, The, Wor.Pk.	283	331	CV103
Retreat Clo., Har.	216	304	CJ57
Retreat Pl. E9	118	307	DW65
Retreat Rd., Rich.	169	322	CK85
Reunion Row E1	138	317	DV73
Reveley Sq. SE16	149	317	DY75
Revell Ri. SE18	253	318	ET79
Revell Rd., Kings.T.	269	322	CP96
Revell Rd., Sutt.	292	331	CZ107
Revelon Rd. SE4	181	325	DY83
Revelstoke Rd. SW18	189	323	CZ89
Reventlow Rd. SE9	261	326	EQ88
Reverdy Rd. SE1	148	317	DU77
Reverend Clo., Har.	233	313	CB62
Revesby Rd., Cars.	285	331	DD100
Review Rd. NW2	93	304	CT61
Review Rd., Dag.	247	319	FB67
Rewell St. SW6	158	315	DC80
Rewley Rd., Cars.	285	331	DD100
Rex Ave., Ashf.	265	328	BN93
Rex Clo., Rom.	227	309	FB52
Rex Pl. W1	56	316	DG73
Reydon Ave. E11	224	308	EJ58
Reynard Clo. SE4	181	325	DY83
Reynard Clo., Brom.	276	326	EM97
Reynard Dr. SE19	273	324	DT94
Reynard Pl. SE14	165	317	DY79
Reynardson Rd. N17	221	306	DQ52
Reynolds Ave. E12	235	308	EN64
Reynolds Ave., Rom.	236	309	EW59
Reynolds Clo. NW11	96	305	DB59
Reynolds Clo. SW19	271	323	DD95
Reynolds Clo., Cars.	285	331	DF102
Reynolds Ct. E11	105	307	EF62
Reynolds Dr., Edg.	216	304	CM55
Reynolds Pl. SE3	252	318	EH80
Reynolds Pl., Rich.	169	322	CM86
Reynolds Rd. SE15	180	325	DW85
Reynolds Rd. W4	144	314	CQ76
Reynolds Rd., Hayes	242	313	BW70
Reynolds Rd., N.Mal.	283	330	CR101
Reynolds Way, Croy.	287	332	DS105
Rheidol Ms. N1	25	316	DQ68
Rheidol Ter. N1	25	316	DQ67
Rheingold Way, Wall.	294	332	DL109
Rheola Clo. N17	221	306	DT53
Rhoda St. E2	39	316	DT70
Rhodes Ave. N22	220	306	DJ53
Rhodes Moorhouse Ct., Mord.	284	331	DA100
Rhodes St. N7	115	306	DM64
Rhodesia Rd. E11	105	307	ED61
Rhodesia Rd. SW9	161	316	DL82
Rhodeswell Rd. E14	139	317	DY71
Rhodrons Ave., Chess.	282	330	CL106
Rhondda Gro. E3	129	317	DY69
Rhyl Rd., Grnf.	243	313	CF68
Rhyl St. NW5	114	306	DG65
Rhys Ave. N11	220	306	DK52
Rialto Rd., Mitch.	272	324	DG96
Ribble Clo., Wdf.Grn.	224	308	EJ51
Ribblesdale Ave., Nthlt.	233	313	CB65
Ribblesdale Rd. N8	220	306	DM56
Ribblesdale Rd. SW16	272	324	DH93
Ribbon Dance Ms. SE5	163	316	DR81
Ribchester Ave., Grnf.	243	313	CF69
Ribston Clo., Brom.	290	334	EM102
Ricardo Path SE28	246	319	EW74
Ricardo St. E14	140	317	EB72
Ricards Rd. SW19	270	323	CZ92
Rich La. SW5	76/7	315	DB78
Rich St. E14	139	317	DZ73
Richard Clo. SE18	252	318	EL77
Richard Foster Clo. E17	103	307	DZ59
Richard St. E1	138	317	DV72
Richards Ave., Rom.	227	309	FC57
Richards Clo., Har.	216	304	CG57
Richards Clo., Hayes	257	320	BR79
Richards Clo., Uxb.	241	312	BN67
Richards Pl. E17	223	307	EA55
Richards Pl. SW3	78/9	315	DE77
Richardson Clo. E8	27	316	DT67
Richardson Rd. E15	131	317	EE68
Richardson's Ms. W1	33	316	DJ70
Richbell Pl. WC1	47	316	DM71
Richborne Ter. SW8	161	316	DM80
Richborough Clo., Orp.	278	327	EX98
Richborough Rd. NW2	111	305	CY63
Riches Rd., Ilf.	235	308	EQ61
Richford Rd. E15	131	317	EF67
Richford St. W6	146	315	CW75
Richland Ave., Couls.	293	332	DG114
Richlands Ave., Epsom	283	331	CU105
Richmond Ave. E4	211	301	ED50
Richmond Ave. N1	23	316	DM67
Richmond Ave. NW10	110	305	CW65
Richmond Ave. SW20	270	323	CY95
Richmond Ave., Felt.	257	320	BS86
Richmond Ave., Uxb.	241	312	BP65
Richmond Bri., Rich.	169	322	CK85
Richmond Bri., Twick.	169	322	CK86
Richmond Bldgs. W1	46	316	DK72
Richmond Clo. E17	222	307	DZ58
Richmond Clo., Borwd.	205	298	CQ43
Richmond Cres. E4	211	301	ED50
Richmond Cres. N1	23	316	DM67
Richmond Cres. N9	210	301	DU46
Richmond Dr., Shep.	281	328	BQ100
Richmond Gdns. NW4	218	305	CU57
Richmond Gdns., Har.	215	303	CF52
Richmond Grn., Croy.	286	332	DL104
Richmond Gro. N1	116	306	DP66
Richmond Gro., Surb.	282	330	CM100
Richmond Hill, Rich.	169	322	CL86
Richmond Hill Ct., Rich.	169	322	CL86
Richmond Ms. W1	46	316	DK72
Richmond Ms., Tedd.	267	329	CF93
Richmond Pk., Kings.T.	186	322	CN88
Richmond Pk., Rich.	186	322	CN88
Richmond Pk. Rd. SW14	170	322	CQ85
Richmond Pk. Rd., Kings.T.	268	322	CL95
Richmond Pl. SE18	253	318	EQ77
Richmond Retail Pk., Rich.	154	314	CP81
Richmond Rd. E4	211	301	ED46
Richmond Rd. E7	234	308	EH64
Richmond Rd. E8	117	306	DT66
Richmond Rd. E11	105	307	ED61
Richmond Rd. N2	219	305	DC54
Richmond Rd. N11	220	306	DL51
Richmond Rd. N15	221	306	DS58
Richmond Rd. SW20	270	323	CV95
Richmond Rd. W5	143	314	CL75
Richmond Rd., Barn.	207	299	DB43
Richmond Rd., Croy.	286	332	DL104
Richmond Rd., Ilf.	235	308	EQ62
Richmond Rd., Islw.	168	322	CG83
Richmond Rd., Kings.T.	268	322	CK92
Richmond Rd., Rom.	227	309	FF58
Richmond Rd., Th.Hth.	273	324	DP97
Richmond Rd., Twick.	184	322	CG88
Richmond St. E13	244	318	EG68
Richmond Ter. SW1	70/1	316	DL75
Richmond Ter. Ms. SW1	70/1	316	DL75
Richmond Way E11	234	308	EG61
Richmond Way W12	147	315	CX75
Richmond Way W14	147	315	CX75
Richmount Gdns. SE3	260	326	EG83
Rick Roberts Way E15	130	317	EC67
Rickard Clo. NW4	218	305	CU56
Rickard Clo. SW2	194	324	DN88
Rickard Clo., West Dr.	248	320	BK76
Rickards Clo., Surb.	282	330	CL102
Rickett St. SW6	158	315	DA79
Rickman St. E1	128	317	DW69
Rickmansworth Rd., Nthwd.	213	302	BP50
Rickmansworth Rd., Pnr.	214	303	BV54
Rickmansworth Rd., Uxb.	212	302	BJ53
Rickthorne Rd. N19	99	306	DL61
Rickyard Path SE9	260	326	EL84
Ridding La., Grnf.	233	313	CF64
Riddlesdown Ave., Pur.	295	332	DQ111
Riddlesdown Rd., Pur.	295	332	DQ110
Riddons Rd. SE12	260	326	EJ90
Ride, The, Brent.	142	314	CH78
Ride, The, Enf.	203	301	DW41
Rideout St. SE18	252	318	EM77
Rider Clo., Sid.	261	326	ES86
Ridgdale St. E3	130	317	EA68
Ridge, The, Bex.	262	327	EZ87
Ridge, The, Couls.	294	332	DL114
Ridge, The, Orp.	291	334	ER103
Ridge, The, Pur.	294	332	DJ110
Ridge, The, Surb.	282	330	CN99
Ridge, The, Twick.	259	321	CD87
Ridge Ave. N21	209	300	DQ45
Ridge Ave., Dart.	263	327	FF86
Ridge Clo. NW4	218	305	CX54
Ridge Clo. NW9	217	304	CR56
Ridge Hill NW11	95	305	CY60
Ridge Langley, S.Croy.	295	333	DU109
Ridge Pk., Pur.	294	332	DK110
Ridge Rd. N8	220	306	DM58
Ridge Rd. N21	209	300	DQ46
Ridge Rd. NW2	95	305	CZ62
Ridge Rd., Mitch.	272	324	DH94
Ridge Rd., Sutt.	284	331	CY102
Ridge Way SE19	273	324	DS93

Ridge Way, Dart. 263 327 FF86
Ridge Way, Felt. 258 321 BY90
Ridge Way, The, S.Croy. 295 332 DS109
Ridgebrook Rd. SE3 260 326 EJ83
Ridgecroft Clo., Bex. 263 327 FC88
Ridgemont Gdns., Edg. 205 298 CQ49
Ridgemount Ave., Croy. 288 333 DX103
Ridgemount Clo. SE20 274 325 DV94
Ridgemount Gdns., Enf. 202 300 DP41
Ridgeview Clo., Barn. 206 299 CX44
Ridgeview Rd. N20 207 299 DB48
Ridgeway, Brom. 289 334 EG103
Ridgeway, The E4 211 301 EB47
Ridgeway, The N3 219 305 DB52
Ridgeway, The N11 207 299 DF49
Ridgeway, The N14 208 300 DL47
Ridgeway, The NW7 206 299 CU48
Ridgeway, The NW9 217 304 CS56
Ridgeway, The NW11 95 305 CZ60
Ridgeway, The W3 144 314 CN76
Ridgeway, The, Croy. 286 332 DM104
Ridgeway, The, Enf. 202 300 DN39
Ridgeway, The, Har. 214 303 BZ57
Ridgeway, The (Kenton), Har. 216 304 CJ58
Ridgeway, The (Gidea Pk.), Rom. 228 310 FG56
Ridgeway, The (Harold Wd.), Rom. 228 311 FM53
Ridgeway, The, Ruis. 232 313 BU59
Ridgeway, The, Stan. 216 304 CJ51
Ridgeway, The, Sutt. 293 331 DD107
Ridgeway Ave., Barn. 207 299 DF44
Ridgeway Cres., Orp. 291 334 ES104
Ridgeway Cres. Gdns., Orp. 291 334 ES103
Ridgeway Dr., Brom. 276 326 EH92
Ridgeway E., Sid. 261 326 ET85
Ridgeway Gdns. N6 98 306 DJ59
Ridgeway Gdns., Ilf. 224 308 EL57
Ridgeway Rd. SW9 178 324 DP83
Ridgeway Rd., Islw. 251 321 CE80
Ridgeway Rd. N., Islw. 251 321 CE79
Ridgeway Wk., Nthlt. 232 313 BY65
Ridgeway W., Sid. 261 326 ES85
Ridgewell Clo. N1 25 316 DQ67
Ridgewell Clo. SE26 274 325 DZ91
Ridgewell Clo., Dag. 247 319 FB67
Ridgmount Gdns. WC1 46 316 DK71
Ridgmount Pl. WC1 46 316 DK71
Ridgmount Rd. SW18 174 323 DB85
Ridgmount St. WC1 46 316 DK71
Ridgway SW19 270 323 CW94
Ridgway Gdns. SW19 270 323 CX94
Ridgway Pl. SW19 270 323 CY93
Ridgwell Rd. E16 244 318 EJ71
Riding, The NW11 95 305 CZ59
Riding Hill, S.Croy. 295 333 DU113
Riding Ho. St. W1 45 316 DJ71
Ridings, The W5 123 314 CM70
Ridings, The, Sun. 266 329 BU95
Ridings, The, Surb. 282 330 CN99
Ridings Ave. N21 202 300 DP42
Ridings Clo. N6 98 306 DJ59
Ridler Rd., Enf. 202 300 DS38
Ridley Ave. W13 142 314 CH76
Ridley Clo., Rom. 228 310 FH53
Ridley Rd. E7 234 308 EJ63
Ridley Rd. E8 117 306 DT64
Ridley Rd. NW10 126 315 CU68
Ridley Rd. SW19 271 323 DB94
Ridley Rd., Brom. 275 325 EF97
Ridley Rd., Well. 254 319 EV81
Ridley Several SE3 252 318 EH82
Ridsdale Rd. SE20 274 325 DV95
Riefield Rd. SE9 261 326 EQ84
Riffel Rd. NW2 110 305 CW64
Rifle Pl. SE11 162 316 DN79
Rifle Pl. W11 137 315 CX74
Rifle St. E14 140 317 EB71
Rigault Rd. SW6 157 315 CY82
Rigby Clo., Croy. 286 332 DN104
Rigby La., Hayes 249 320 BQ75
Rigby Ms., Ilf. 235 308 EP61
Rigden St. E14 140 317 EB72
Rigeley Rd. NW10 126 315 CU69
Rigg App. E10 103 307 DX60
Rigge Pl. SW4 177 324 DK84
Rigger Row SW11 174 323 DC83
Riggindale Rd. SW16 272 324 DK91
Riley Rd. SE1 75 316 DT76
Riley Rd., Enf. 203 301 DW38
Riley St. SW10 159 315 DD80
Rinaldo Rd. SW12 192 324 DH87
Ring, The W2 54 315 DD73
Ring Clo., Brom. 276 326 EH94
Ring Rd. W12 136 315 CW73
Ringcroft St. N7 116 306 DN64
Ringers Rd., Brom. 276 326 EG97
Ringford Rd. SW18 173 323 CZ85
Ringlewell Clo., Enf. 203 301 DV40
Ringmer Ave. SW6 157 315 CY81
Ringmer Gdns. N19 99 306 DL61
Ringmer Pl. N21 209 300 DR43
Ringmer Way, Brom. 290 334 EM99
Ringmore Ri. SE23 196 325 DV87
Ringshall Rd., Orp. 278 327 EU97
Ringslade Rd. N22 220 306 DM54
Ringstead Rd. SE6 198 325 EB87
Ringstead Rd., Sutt. 285 331 DD105
Ringway N11 220 306 DJ51
Ringway, Sthl. 250 321 BX78
Ringwold Clo., Beck. 274 325 DY94
Ringwood Ave. N2 219 305 DF54
Ringwood Ave., Croy. 286 332 DL101
Ringwood Ave., Horn. 238 310 FK61
Ringwood Clo., Pnr. 214 303 BW55
Ringwood Gdns. E14 150 317 EA77
Ringwood Gdns. SW15 188 323 CU89
Ringwood Rd. E17 222 307 DZ58
Ringwood Way N21 209 300 DP46
Ringwood Way, Hmptn. 267 329 CA91
Ripley Clo., Brom. 290 334 EM99
Ripley Gdns. SW14 171 322 CR83
Ripley Gdns., Sutt. 285 331 DC105
Ripley Ms. E11 105 307 EE59
Ripley Rd. E16 244 318 EJ72
Ripley Rd., Belv. 255 319 FA77
Ripley Rd., Enf. 202 300 DQ39
Ripley Rd., Hmptn. 267 329 CA94
Ripley Rd., Ilf. 235 308 ET61
Ripley Vil. W5 132 314 CJ72
Riplington Ct. SW15 188 323 CU87
Ripon Clo., Nthlt. 233 313 CA64
Ripon Gdns., Chess. 282 330 CK106
Ripon Gdns., Ilf. 234 308 EL59
Ripon Rd. N9 210 301 DV45
Ripon Rd. N17 221 306 DR55
Ripon Rd. SE18 253 318 EP79
Ripon Way, Borwd. 205 298 CQ43
Rippersley Rd., Well. 254 319 EU81
Ripple Rd., Bark. 245 318 ER67
Ripple Rd., Dag. 246 319 EX67
Rippleside Commercial Est., Bark. 246 319 EW68
Ripplevale Gro. N1 115 306 DM66
Rippolson Rd. SE18 253 318 ET78
Ripston Rd., Ashf. 265 328 BR92
Risborough Dr., Wor.Pk. 283 331 CU101
Risborough St. SE1 72/3 316 DP75
Risdon St. SE16 148 317 DW75
Rise, The E11 224 308 EG57
Rise, The N13 209 300 DN49
Rise, The NW7 217 304 CT51
Rise, The NW10 109 304 CR63
Rise, The, Bex. 262 327 EW87
Rise, The, Borwd. 204 298 CM43
Rise, The, Dart. 263 327 FF84
Rise, The, Edg. 205 298 CP50
Rise, The, Grnf. 106 304 CG64
Rise, The, Sid. 262 327 EW87
Rise, The, Uxb. 240 312 BM68
Rise Pk. Boul., Rom. 227 309 FF53
Rise Pk. Par., Rom. 227 309 FE54
Risebridge Chase, Rom. 227 309 FF52
Risebridge Rd., Rom. 227 309 FF54
Risedale Rd., Bexh. 263 327 FB83
Riseldine Rd. SE23 181 325 DY86
Rising Hill Clo., Nthwd. 213 302 BQ51
Rising Sun Ct. EC1 48/9 316 DP71
Risinghill St. N1 23 316 DM68
Risingholme Clo., Har. 215 303 CE53
Risingholme Rd., Har. 215 303 CE54
Risings, The E17 223 307 ED56
Risley Ave. N17 221 306 DQ53
Rita Rd. SW8 161 316 DL79
Ritches Rd. N15 221 306 DQ57
Ritchie Rd., Croy. 287 333 DV100
Ritchie St. N1 24 316 DN68
Ritchings Ave. E17 222 307 DY56
Ritherdon Rd. SW17 192 324 DG89
Ritson Rd. E8 118 307 DU65
Ritter St. SE18 253 318 EN79
Rivaz Pl. E9 118 307 DW65
Rivenhall Gdns. E18 223 307 EF56
River Ave. N13 209 300 DP48
River Bank N21 209 300 DQ45
River Bank, E.Mol. 267 329 CE97
River Bank, W.Mol. 266 329 BZ97
River Barge Clo. E14 150 317 EC75
River Brent Business Pk. W7 251 321 CE76
River Clo. E11 224 308 EJ58
River Clo., Ruis. 231 302 BT58
River Clo., Surb. 282 330 CK99
River Crane Wk., Felt. 258 321 BX88
River Crane Wk., Twick. 168 322 CG86
River Dr., Upmin. 229 311 FQ58
River Front, Enf. 202 300 DR41
River Gdns., Cars. 285 332 DG104
River Gdns., Felt. 258 321 BV84
River Gro. Pk., Beck. 274 325 DZ95
River La., Rich. 185 322 CK88
River Meads Ave., Twick. 259 321 CA90
River Pk. Gdns., Brom. 275 325 ED94
River Pk. Rd. N22 220 306 DM54
River Pl. N1 116 306 DQ66
River Reach, Tedd. 268 322 CJ92
River Rd., Bark. 245 318 ES68
River Rd. Business Pk., Bark. 245 318 ET69
River St. EC1 36 316 DN69
River Ter. W6 146 315 CW78
River Vw., Enf. 202 300 DQ41
River Vw. Gdns., Twick. 259 321 CF89
River Wk., Uxb. 240 312 BJ64
River Way SE10 151 317 EF76
River Way, Twick. 259 321 CB89
Riverbank Way, Brent. 152 314 CJ79
Rivercourt Rd. W6 146 315 CV77
Riverdale SE13 182 325 EC83
Riverdale Dr. SW18 190 323 DB88
Riverdale Gdns., Twick. 168 322 CJ86
Riverdale Rd. SE18 253 318 ET78
Riverdale Rd., Bex. 262 327 EY87
Riverdale Rd., Erith 255 319 FB78
Riverdale Rd., Felt. 266 329 BZ91
Riverdale Rd., Twick. 168 322 CJ86
Riverdene, Edg. 205 298 CQ48
Riverdene Rd., Ilf. 235 308 EN62
Riverhead Clo. E17 222 307 DX54
Riverhead Dr., Sutt. 292 331 DB110
Rivermead, E.Mol. 267 329 CC97
Rivermead Clo., Tedd. 268 322 CH92
Rivermead Ct. SW6 173 323 CZ83
Rivermount, Walt. 281 328 BT101
Riversdale Rd. N5 100 306 DP62
Riversdale Rd., Rom. 227 309 FB52
Riversfield Rd., Enf. 202 300 DS41
Riverside NW4 94 305 CV59
Riverside SE7 252 318 EH76
Riverside, Cher. 280 328 BG97
Riverside, Twick. 184 322 CH88
Riverside, The, E.Mol. 267 329 CD97
Riverside Clo. E5 102 307 DW60
Riverside Clo. W7 243 313 CE70
Riverside Clo., Kings.T. 268 322 CK98
Riverside Clo., Orp. 278 327 EW96
Riverside Clo., Wall. 285 332 DH104
Riverside Ct. E4 211 301 EB44
Riverside Ct. SW8 161 316 DK79
Riverside Dr. NW11 218 305 CY58
Riverside Dr. W4 155 314 CR80
Riverside Dr., Mitch. 285 331 DE99
Riverside Dr., Rich. 184 322 CH89
Riverside Gdns. N3 218 305 CY55
Riverside Gdns. W6 146 315 CV78
Riverside Gdns., Enf. 202 300 DQ40
Riverside Gdns., Wem. 123 314 CL68
Riverside Ind. Est. SE10 151 317 EF76
Riverside Ind. Est., Bark. 246 319 EU69
Riverside Ind. Est., Enf. 210 301 DY44
Riverside Ms., Croy. 286 332 DL104
Riverside Pl., Stai. 256 320 BK86
Riverside Rd. E15 130 317 EC68
Riverside Rd. N15 222 307 DU58
Riverside Rd. SW17 271 323 DB91
Riverside Rd., Sid. 262 327 EY90
Riverside Rd. (Stanwell), Stai. 256 320 BK85
Riverside Wk. SE1 60 316 DN74
Riverside Wk., Bex. 262 327 EX87
Riverside Wk., Islw. 259 321 CE83
Riverside Wk., Kings.T. 268 322 CK96
Riverside Way, Uxb. 240 312 BH67
Riverton Clo. W9 127 315 CZ69
Riverview Gdns. SW13 156 315 CV79
Riverview Gro. W4 154 314 CP79
Riverview Pk. SE6 198 325 EA88
Riverview Rd. W4 154 314 CP79
Riverview Rd., Epsom 283 330 CR106
Riverway N13 209 300 DN49
Riverway, Stai. 280 328 BH95
Riverwood La., Chis. 277 326 ER95
Rivington Ave., Wdf.Grn. 224 308 EK54
Rivington Ct. NW10 126 315 CU67
Rivington Cres. NW7 217 304 CT52
Rivington Pl. EC2 38/9 316 DS69
Rivington St. EC2 38/9 316 DS69
Rivington Wk. E8 128 317 DU67
Rivulet Rd. N17 221 306 DQ52
Rixon Ho. SE18 253 318 EP79
Rixon St. N7 100 306 DN62
Rixsen Rd. E12 234 308 EL64
Roach Rd. E3 120 307 EA66
Roads Pl. N19 99 306 DL61
Roan St. SE10 166 317 EB80
Robarts Clo., Pnr. 214 303 BV57
Robb Rd., Stan. 216 304 CG51
Robert Adam St. W1 44 316 DG72
Robert Clo. W9 29 315 DC70
Robert Dashwood Way SE17 85 316 DQ77
Robert Gentry Ho. W14 147 315 CY78
Robert Keen Clo. SE15 164 317 DU81
Robert Lowe Clo. SE14 165 317 DX80
Robert Owen Ho. SW6 157 315 CX81
Robert St. E16 245 318 EP74
Robert St. NW1 32/3 316 DH69
Robert St. SE18 253 318 ER78
Robert St. WC2 58/9 316 DL73
Robert St., Croy. 287 332 DQ104
Roberta St. E2 128 317 DU69
Roberton Dr., Brom. 276 326 EJ95
Roberts Clo. SE9 261 326 ER88
Roberts Clo., Pnr. 214 303 BV57
Roberts Clo., Rom. 228 310 FH53
Roberts Clo., Stai. 256 320 BJ86
Roberts Clo., Sutt. 292 331 CX108
Roberts Clo., West Dr. 248 312 BL74
Roberts Ms. SW1 68 316 DG76
Robert's Pl. EC1 36 316 DN70
Roberts Rd. E17 223 307 EB53
Roberts Rd. NW7 218 305 CY51
Roberts Rd., Belv. 255 319 FA78
Robertsbridge Rd., Cars. 285 331 DC102
Robertson Rd. E15 130 317 EC67
Robertson St. SW8 176 324 DH83
Robeson St. E3 139 317 DZ71
Robin Clo. NW7 205 298 CS48
Robin Clo., Hmptn. 266 329 BY92
Robin Clo., Rom. 227 309 FD52
Robin Ct. SE16 148 317 DU77
Robin Cres. E6 244 318 EL71
Robin Gro. N6 98 306 DG61
Robin Gro., Brent. 152 314 CJ79
Robin Gro., Har. 216 304 CM58
Robin Hill Dr., Chis. 276 326 EL93
Robin Hood Dr., Har. 215 303 CF52
Robin Hood Grn., Orp. 291 335 EU99
Robin Hood La. E14 140 317 EC72
Robin Hood La. SW15 269 322 CS91
Robin Hood La., Bexh. 262 327 EY85
Robin Hood La., Sutt. 284 331 DA106
Robin Hood Rd. SW19 270 323 CV92
Robin Hood Way SW15 269 322 CS91
Robin Hood Way SW20 269 322 CS91
Robin Hood Way, Grnf. 233 313 CF65
Robin Way, Orp. 278 327 EV97
Robina Clo., Bexh. 262 327 EX84
Robina Clo., Nthwd. 213 302 BT53
Robinhood Clo., Mitch. 272 324 DJ98
Robinhood La., Mitch. 272 324 DJ97
Robinia Cres. E10 104 307 EA61
Robins Clo., Uxb. 248 312 BJ71
Robins Ct. SE12 260 326 EJ90
Robins Gro., W.Wick. 289 334 EG104
Robinscroft Ms. SE10 166 317 EB81
Robinson Clo., Horn. 238 310 FH66
Robinson Rd. E2 128 317 DW68
Robinson Rd. SW17 271 323 DE93
Robinson Rd., Dag. 237 309 FA63
Robinson St. SW3 159 315 DF79
Robinsons Clo. W13 132 314 CG71
Robinwood Gro., Uxb. 240 312 BM70
Robinwood Pl. SW15 269 322 CR91
Roborough Wk., Horn. 238 310 FJ65
Robsart St. SW9 161 316 DM82
Robson Ave. NW10 126 315 CU67
Robson Clo. E6 244 318 EL72
Robson Clo., Enf. 202 300 DP40
Robson Rd. SE27 194 324 DP90
Roch Ave., Edg. 216 304 CM54
Rochdale Rd. E17 104 307 EA59
Rochdale Rd. SE2 254 319 EV78
Rochdale Way SE8 166 317 EA80
Roche Rd. SW16 272 324 DL95
Roche Wk., Cars. 285 331 DD100
Rochelle Clo. SW11 175 323 DD84
Rochelle St. E2 39 316 DT69
Rochemont Wk. E8 27 316 DT67
Rochester Ave. E13 244 318 EJ67
Rochester Ave., Brom. 276 326 EH96
Rochester Ave., Felt. 265 320 BT89
Rochester Clo. SW16 272 324 DL94
Rochester Clo., Enf. 202 300 DS39
Rochester Clo., Sid. 262 327 EV86
Rochester Dr., Bex. 262 327 EZ86
Rochester Dr., Pnr. 214 303 BX57
Rochester Gdns., Croy. 287 332 DS104
Rochester Gdns., Ilf. 234 308 EM59
Rochester Ms. NW1 114 306 DJ66
Rochester Pl. NW1 114 306 DJ65
Rochester Rd. NW1 114 306 DJ65
Rochester Rd., Cars. 285 331 DF105
Rochester Rd., Nthwd. 231 302 BT55
Rochester Row SW1 81 316 DJ77
Rochester Sq. NW1 114 306 DJ66
Rochester St. SW1 70 316 DK76
Rochester Ter. NW1 114 306 DJ65
Rochester Wk. SE1 62 316 DR74
Rochester Way SE3 252 318 EJ82
Rochester Way SE9 260 326 EM83
Rochester Way, Dart. 263 327 FD87
Rochester Way Relief Rd. SE3 252 318 EH81
Rochester Way Relief Rd. SE9 260 326 EJ84
Rochford Ave., Rom. 226 309 EW57
Rochford Clo. E6 244 318 EK68
Rochford Clo., Horn. 238 310 FH65
Rochford St. NW5 113 305 DF64
Rochford Wk. E8 118 307 DU66
Rochford Way, Croy. 286 332 DL100
Rock Ave. SW14 171 322 CR83
Rock Gdns., Dag. 237 309 FB64
Rock Gro. Way SE16 148 317 DV77
Rock Hill SE26 273 324 DT91
Rock St. N4 100 306 DN61
Rockbourne Rd. SE23 197 325 DX88
Rockchase Gdns., Horn. 228 311 FL58
Rockells Pl. SE22 180 325 DV86
Rockford Ave., Grnf. 122 314 CG68
Rockhall Rd. NW2 111 305 CX63
Rockhampton Clo. SE27 273 324 DN91
Rockhampton Rd. SE27 273 324 DN91
Rockhampton Rd., S.Croy. 295 332 DS107
Rockingham Ave., Horn. 228 310 FH58
Rockingham Clo. SW15 171 322 CT84
Rockingham Clo., Uxb. 240 312 BJ67
Rockingham Est. SE1 73 316 DQ76
Rockingham Par., Uxb. 240 312 BJ66
Rockingham Rd., Uxb. 240 312 BH67
Rockingham St. SE1 73 316 DQ76
Rockland Rd. SW15 173 323 CY84
Rocklands Dr., Stan. 216 304 CH54
Rockley Rd. W14 147 315 CX75
Rockmount Rd. SE18 253 318 ET78
Rockmount Rd. SE19 273 324 DR93
Rocks La. SW13 172 323 CU83
Rockware Ave., Grnf. 243 313 CD67
Rockways, Barn. 205 298 CT44
Rockwell Gdns. SE19 273 324 DS91
Rockwell Rd., Dag. 237 309 FB64
Rockwood Pl. W12 146 315 CW75
Rocliffe St. N1 24/5 316 DP68
Rocmoale Way SE8 166 317 EA80
Rocombe Cres. SE23 196 325 DW87
Rocque La. SE3 183 325 EF83
Rodborough Rd. NW11 96 305 DA60
Roden Ct. N6 99 306 DK59
Roden Gdns., Croy. 287 332 DS100
Roden St. N7 99 306 DM62
Roden St., Ilf. 235 308 EN62
Rodenhurst Rd. SW4 176 324 DJ86
Roderick Rd. NW3 113 305 DF63
Rodgers Clo., Borwd. 204 298 CK44
Roding Ave., Wdf.Grn. 224 308 EL51
Roding La. N., Wdf.Grn. 224 308 EL51
Roding La. S., Ilf. 224 308 EK56
Roding La. S., Wdf.Grn. 224 308 EK55
Roding Ms. E1 138 317 DU74
Roding Rd. E5 119 307 DY63
Roding Rd. E6 245 318 EP71
Roding Trd. Est., Bark. 235 308 EP66
Rodings, The, Upmin. 229 311 FR58
Rodings, The, Wdf.Grn. 224 308 EJ51
Rodings Row, Barn. 206 299 CY43
Rodmarton St. W1 43 315 DF71
Rodmell Clo., Hayes 242 313 BY70
Rodmell Slope N12 206 299 CZ50
Rodmere St. SE10 151 317 EE78
Rodmill La. SW2 193 324 DL87
Rodney Clo., Croy. 286 332 DP102
Rodney Clo., N.Mal. 283 330 CS99
Rodney Clo., Pnr. 232 313 BY59
Rodney Ct. W9 29 315 DC70
Rodney Gdns., Pnr. 214 303 BV57
Rodney Gdns., W.Wick. 289 334 EG105
Rodney Pl. E17 222 307 DY54
Rodney Pl. SE17 85 316 DQ77
Rodney Pl. SW19 271 323 DC95
Rodney Rd. E11 224 308 EH56
Rodney Rd. SE17 85 316 DQ77
Rodney Rd., Mitch. 271 323 DE96
Rodney Rd., N.Mal. 283 330 CS99
Rodney Rd., Twick. 259 321 CA87
Rodney St. N1 23 316 DM68
Rodney Way, Rom. 227 309 FA53
Rodway Rd. SW15 188 323 CU87
Rodway Rd., Brom. 276 326 EH95
Rodwell Clo., Ruis. 232 313 BW60
Rodwell Pl., Edg. 217 304 CN51
Rodwell Rd. SE22 179 324 DT86
Roe End NW9 217 304 CQ56
Roe Grn. NW9 217 304 CQ57
Roe La. NW9 217 304 CP56
Roe Way, Wall. 294 332 DL108
Roebourne Way E16 253 318 EN75
Roebuck Clo., Felt. 266 329 BV91
Roebuck La. N17 221 306 DT51
Roebuck Rd., Chess. 282 330 CN106
Roedean Ave., Enf. 203 301 DW39
Roedean Clo., Enf. 203 301 DW39
Roedean Clo., Orp. 291 335 EV105
Roedean Cres. SW15 171 322 CS86
Roehampton Clo. SW15 172 323 CU84
Roehampton Dr., Chis. 277 326 EQ93
Roehampton Gate SW15 171 322 CS86
Roehampton High St. SW15 188 323 CU87
Roehampton La. SW15 172 323 CU84
Roehampton Vale SW15 187 322 CT90
Rofant Rd., Nthwd. 213 302 BS51
Roffey St. E14 150 317 EC75
Rogate Ho. E5 102 307 DU62
Roger St. WC1 35 316 DM70
Rogers Gdns., Dag. 237 309 FA64
Rogers Rd. E16 141 317 EF72
Rogers Rd. SW17 271 323 DD91
Rogers Rd., Dag. 237 309 FA64
Rogers Ruff, Nthwd. 213 302 BQ53
Rogers Wk. N12 207 299 DB48
Rojack Rd. SE23 197 325 DX88
Roke Clo., Ken. 295 332 DQ114
Roke Lo. Rd., Ken. 294 332 DP113
Rokeby Gdns., Wdf.Grn. 224 308 EG53
Rokeby Pl. SW20 270 323 CV94
Rokeby Rd. SE4 165 317 DZ82
Rokeby St. E15 131 317 ED67
Roker Pk. Ave., Uxb. 240 312 BL63
Rokesby Clo., Well. 253 318 ER82
Rokesby Pl., Wem. 107 304 CK64
Rokesly Ave. N8 220 306 DL57
Roland Gdns. SW7 77 315 DC78
Roland Gdns., Felt. 258 321 BZ90
Roland Ms. E1 139 317 DX71
Roland Rd. E17 223 307 ED56
Roland Way SE17 86 316 DR78
Roland Way SW7 77 315 DC78
Roland Way, Wor.Pk. 283 330 CT103
Roles Gro., Rom. 226 309 EX56
Rolinsden Way, Kes. 290 334 EK105
Roll Gdns., Ilf. 225 308 EN57
Rollesby Way SE28 246 319 EW73
Rolleston Ave., Orp. 290 334 EP100
Rolleston Clo., Orp. 290 334 EP101
Rolleston Rd., S.Croy. 295 332 DR108
Rollins St. SE15 164 317 DW79
Rollit Cres., Houns. 259 321 CA85
Rollit St. N7 115 306 DM64
Rollo Rd., Swan. 279 327 FF94
Rolls Bldgs. EC4 48 316 DN72
Rolls Pk. Ave. E4 223 307 EA51
Rolls Pk. Rd. E4 211 301 EB50
Rolls Pas. EC4 48 316 DN72
Rolls Rd. SE1 87 316 DT78
Rollscourt Ave. SE24 178 324 DQ85
Rolt St. SE8 165 317 DY79
Rolvenden Gdns., Brom. 276 326 EK94
Rolvenden Pl. N17 222 307 DU53
Rom Cres., Rom. 237 309 FF59
Rom Valley Way, Rom. 227 309 FE58
Roma Read Clo. SW15 188 323 CV87
Roma Rd. E17 222 307 DY55
Roman Clo. W3 144 314 CP75
Roman Clo., Felt. 258 321 BW85
Roman Clo., Rain. 247 319 FD68
Roman Clo., Uxb. 212 302 BG53
Roman Ri. SE19 273 324 DR93
Roman Rd. E2 128 317 DW69
Roman Rd. E3 129 317 DY68
Roman Rd. E6 244 318 EK70
Roman Rd. N10 220 306 DH52
Roman Rd. NW2 94 305 CW62
Roman Rd. W4 145 314 CT77
Roman Rd., Ilf. 235 308 EP65
Roman Sq. SE28 246 319 EU74
Roman Way N7 115 306 DM65
Roman Way SE15 164 317 DW80
Roman Way, Croy. 286 332 DP103
Roman Way, Dart. 263 327 FE85
Roman Way, Enf. 209 300 DT43
Roman Way Ind. Est. N1 115 306 DM66
Romanhurst Ave., Brom. 275 325 EE98
Romanhurst Gdns., Brom. 275 325 EE98
Romany Gdns. E17 222 307 DY53
Romany Gdns., Sutt. 284 331 DA101
Romany Ri., Orp. 291 334 EQ102
Romberg Rd. SW17 192 324 DG90
Romborough Gdns. SE13 182 325 EC85
Romborough Way SE13 182 325 EC85
Romeland, Borwd. 204 298 CK44
Romero Clo. SW9 177 324 DM83
Romero Sq. SE3 260 326 EJ84
Romeyn Rd. SW16 193 324 DM90
Romford Rd. E7 234 308 EH64
Romford Rd. E12 234 308 EL63
Romford Rd. E15 121 307 EE65
Romford Rd., Rom. 226 309 EY52
Romford St. E1 138 317 DU71
Romilly Rd. N4 100 306 DP61
Romilly St. W1 58 316 DK73
Rommany Rd. SE27 273 324 DR91
Romney Chase, Horn. 228 311 FM58
Romney Clo. N17 222 307 DV53
Romney Clo. NW11 96 305 DC60
Romney Clo. SE14 164 317 DW80
Romney Clo., Ashf. 265 328 BQ92
Romney Clo., Chess. 282 330 CL105
Romney Clo., Har. 233 313 CA59
Romney Dr., Brom. 276 326 EK94
Romney Dr., Har. 233 313 CA59
Romney Gdns., Bexh. 254 319 EZ81
Romney Ms. W1 44 316 DG71
Romney Par., Hayes 241 312 BR68
Romney Rd. SE10 166 317 EC79
Romney Rd., Hayes 241 312 BR68
Romney Rd., N.Mal. 283 330 CR100
Romney Row NW2 95 305 CX61
Romney St. SW1 70/1 316 DL76
Romola Rd. SE24 194 324 DP88
Romsey Clo., Orp. 290 334 EP105
Romsey Gdns., Dag. 246 319 EX67
Romsey Rd. W13 132 314 CG73
Romsey Rd., Dag. 246 319 EX67
Ron Leighton Way E6 244 318 EL67
Rona Rd. NW3 114 306 DG63
Rona Wk. N1 117 306 DR65
Ronald Ave. E15 131 317 EE69
Ronald Clo., Beck. 274 325 DZ98
Ronald Rd., Rom. 229 311 FN53
Ronald St. E1 138 317 DW72
Ronalds Rd. N5 116 306 DN64
Ronalds Rd., Brom. 276 326 EG95
Ronaldstone Rd., Sid. 261 326 ES86
Ronart St., Har. 215 303 CF55
Rondu Rd. NW2 111 305 CY64
Ronelean Rd., Surb. 282 330 CM104
Roneo Cor., Horn. 237 309 FF60
Roneo Link, Horn. 237 309 FF60
Ronver Rd. SE12 260 326 EG88
Rood La. EC3 62/3 316 DS73
Rook Clo., Horn. 238 310 FG66
Rook Wk. E6 244 318 EL72
Rooke Way SE10 151 317 EF78
Rookeries Clo., Felt. 258 321 BV90
Rookery Clo. NW9 217 304 CT57
Rookery Cres., Dag. 237 309 FB66
Rookery Dr., Chis. 277 326 EN95
Rookery La., Brom. 290 334 EK100
Rookery Rd. SW4 176 324 DJ84
Rookery Rd., Stai. 264 328 BH92
Rookery Way NW9 217 304 CT57
Rookfield Ave. N10 220 306 DJ56
Rookfield Clo. N10 220 306 DJ56
Rookley Clo., Sutt. 292 331 DB110
Rooksmead Rd., Sun. 281 328 BT96
Rookstone Rd. SW17 271 323 DF92
Rookwood Ave., N.Mal. 270 323 CU98
Rookwood Ave., Wall. 286 332 DK105
Rookwood Gdns. E4 211 301 EF46
Rookwood Ho., Bark. 245 318 ER68
Rookwood Rd. N16 101 306 DT59
Roosevelt Way, Dag. 237 309 FD65
Rootes Dr. W10 127 315 CX70
Rope St. SE16 149 317 DY76
Rope Wk., Sun. 266 329 BW97
Rope Wk. Gdns. E1 138 317 DU72
Rope Yd. Rails SE18 253 318 EP76
Ropemaker Rd. SE16 149 317 DY75
Ropemaker St. EC2 50 316 DR71
Ropemakers Flds. E14 139 317 DZ73
Roper La. SE1 74/5 316 DS75
Roper St. SE9 260 326 EM86
Roper Way, Mitch. 272 324 DG96
Ropers Ave. E4 211 301 EB50
Ropers Wk. SW2 194 324 DN87
Ropery St. E3 129 317 DZ70
Ropley St. E2 128 317 DU68
Rosa Alba Ms. N5 116 306 DQ63
Rosa Ave., Ashf. 265 328 BN91
Rosaline Rd. SW6 157 315 CY80
Rosamond St. SE26 196 325 DV90
Rosamund Clo., S.Croy. 287 332 DR105
Rosary Clo., Houns. 250 321 BY82
Rosary Gdns. SW7 77 315 DC77
Rosary Gdns., Ashf. 265 328 BP91
Rosaville Rd. SW6 157 315 CZ80
Roscoe St. EC1 37 316 DQ70
Roscoff Clo., Edg. 217 304 CQ53
Rose All. SE1 61 316 DQ74
Rose & Crown Ct. EC2 49 316 DQ72
Rose & Crown Yd. SW1 57 316 DJ74
Rose Ave. E18 224 308 EH54
Rose Ave., Mitch. 271 323 DF95
Rose Ave., Mord. 285 331 DC99
Rose Bates Dr. NW9 217 304 CN56
Rose Ct. E1 50/1 316 DS71
Rose Ct. SE26 196 325 DV89
Rose Ct., Pnr. 214 303 BW55
Rose Dale, Orp. 290 334 EP103
Rose End, Wor.Pk. 284 331 CX102
Rose Gdn. Clo., Edg. 216 304 CL51
Rose Gdns. W5 143 314 CK76
Rose Gdns., Felt. 258 321 BU89
Rose Gdns., Sthl. 243 313 CA70
Rose Gdns., Stai. 264 320 BK87
Rose Glen NW9 217 304 CR56
Rose Glen, Rom. 237 309 FE60
Rose Hill, Sutt. 284 331 DB104
Rose La., Rom. 226 309 EX55
Rose St. WC2 58/9 316 DL73
Rose Wk., Pur. 294 332 DK111
Rose Wk., Surb. 282 330 CP99
Rose Wk., W.Wick. 289 333 EC103
Rose Way SE12 260 326 EG85
Roseacre Clo. W13 132 314 CH71
Roseacre Clo., Horn. 238 311 FM60
Roseacre Clo., Shep. 281 328 BN99
Roseacre Rd., Well. 262 327 EV83
Roseary Clo., West Dr. 248 320 BK77
Rosebank SE20 274 325 DV94
Rosebank Ave., Horn. 238 310 FJ64
Rosebank Ave., Wem. 233 313 CF63
Rosebank Clo. N12 207 299 DE50
Rosebank Clo., Tedd. 268 322 CG93
Rosebank Gdns. E3 129 317 DZ68
Rosebank Gro. E17 222 307 DZ55
Rosebank Rd. E17 223 307 EB58
Rosebank Rd. W7 251 321 CE75
Rosebank Vil. E17 223 307 EA56
Rosebank Wk. NW1 115 306 DK66
Rosebank Wk. SE18 252 318 EL77
Rosebank Way W3 135 314 CR72
Roseberry Clo., Upmin. 229 311 FT58
Roseberry Gdns. N4 221 306 DP58
Roseberry Gdns., Orp. 291 334 ES104
Roseberry Gdns., Upmin. 229 311 FS58
Roseberry Pl. E8 117 306 DT65
Roseberry St. SE16 148 317 DV77
Rosebery Ave. E12 234 308 EL65
Rosebery Ave. EC1 36 316 DN70
Rosebery Ave. N17 222 307 DU54
Rosebery Ave., Har. 232 313 BY63
Rosebery Ave., N.Mal. 269 322 CT96
Rosebery Ave., Sid. 261 326 ES87
Rosebery Ave., Th.Hth. 273 324 DQ96
Rosebery Clo., Mord. 284 331 CX100
Rosebery Ct. EC1 36 316 DN70
Rosebery Gdns. N8 220 306 DL57
Rosebery Gdns. W13 132 314 CG72
Rosebery Gdns., Sutt. 284 331 DB105
Rosebery Ms. N10 220 306 DJ54
Rosebery Ms. SW2 177 324 DL86
Rosebery Rd. N9 210 301 DU48
Rosebery Rd. N10 220 306 DJ54
Rosebery Rd. SW2 177 324 DL86
Rosebery Rd., Houns. 259 321 CC85
Rosebery Rd., Kings.T. 269 322 CP96
Rosebery Rd., Sutt. 292 331 CZ107
Rosebery Sq. EC1 36 316 DN70
Rosebery Sq., Kings.T. 269 322 CP96
Rosebine Ave., Twick. 259 321 CD87
Rosebury Rd. SW6 158 315 DB82
Rosebury Vale, Ruis. 232 313 BU61
Rosecourt Rd., Croy. 286 332 DM100
Rosecroft Ave. NW3 96 305 DA62
Rosecroft Gdns. NW2 94 305 CU62
Rosecroft Gdns., Twick. 259 321 CD88
Rosecroft Rd., Sthl. 243 313 CA70
Rosecroft Wk., Pnr. 214 303 BX57
Rosecroft Wk., Wem. 107 304 CK64
Rosedale Ave., Hayes 249 312 BR71
Rosedale Clo. SE2 254 319 EV76
Rosedale Clo. W7 251 321 CF75
Rosedale Clo., Stan. 216 304 CH51
Rosedale Ct. N5 116 306 DP63
Rosedale Gdns., Dag. 236 309 EV66
Rosedale Rd. E7 234 308 EJ64
Rosedale Rd., Dag. 236 309 EV66
Rosedale Rd., Epsom 283 331 CU106
Rosedale Rd., Rich. 169 322 CL84
Rosedale Rd., Rom. 227 309 FC54
Rosedale Ter. W6 146 315 CV76
Rosedene NW6 127 315 CX67
Rosedene Ave. SW16 193 324 DM90
Rosedene Ave., Croy. 286 332 DL101
Rosedene Ave., Grnf. 243 313 CA69
Rosedene Ave., Mord. 284 331 DA99
Rosedene Ct., Ruis. 231 312 BS60
Rosedene Gdns., Ilf. 225 308 EN56
Rosedene Ter. E10 104 307 EB61
Rosedew Rd. W6 157 315 CX79
Rosefield Clo., Cars. 285 331 DE106
Rosefield Gdns. E14 140 317 EA73
Rosefield Rd., Stai. 264 328 BG91
Roseford Ct. W12 147 315 CX75
Rosehart Ms. W11 40 315 DA72
Rosehatch Ave., Rom. 226 309 EX55
Roseheath Rd., Houns. 258 321 BZ85
Rosehill, Hmptn. 267 329 CA95
Rosehill Ave., Sutt. 285 331 DC102
Rosehill Gdns., Grnf. 233 313 CF64
Rosehill Gdns., Sutt. 284 331 DB103
Rosehill Pk. W., Sutt. 284 331 DB102
Rosehill Rd. SW18 174 323 DC86
Roseland Clo. N17 221 306 DR52
Roseleigh Ave. N5 116 306 DP63
Roseleigh Clo., Twick. 169 322 CK86
Rosemary Ave. N3 219 305 DB54
Rosemary Ave. N9 210 301 DV46
Rosemary Ave., Enf. 202 300 DR39
Rosemary Ave., Houns. 250 321 BX82
Rosemary Ave., Rom. 227 309 FF55
Rosemary Ave., W.Mol. 267 329 CA97
Rosemary Clo., Croy. 286 332 DL101
Rosemary Clo., Uxb. 249 312 BN71
Rosemary Dr. E14 141 317 ED72
Rosemary Dr., Ilf. 224 308 EK57
Rosemary Gdns. SW14 170 322 CQ83
Rosemary Gdns., Chess. 282 330 CL105
Rosemary Gdns., Dag. 236 309 EZ60
Rosemary La. SW14 170 322 CQ83
Rosemary Pl. N1 26 316 DR67
Rosemary Rd. SE15 163 316 DT80
Rosemary Rd. SW17 190 323 DC90
Rosemary Rd., Well. 253 318 ET81
Rosemary St. N1 26 316 DR67
Rosemead NW9 93 304 CT59
Rosemead, Cher. 280 328 BH101
Rosemead Ave., Felt. 265 320 BT89
Rosemead Ave., Mitch. 272 324 DJ96
Rosemead Ave., Wem. 107 304 CL64
Rosemont Ave. N12 219 305 DC51
Rosemont Rd. NW3 112 305 DC65
Rosemont Rd. W3 134 314 CP73
Rosemont Rd., Kings.T. 269 322 CQ97
Rosemont Rd., N.Mal. 269 322 CQ97
Rosemont Rd., Rich. 169 322 CL86
Rosemont Rd., Wem. 123 314 CL67
Rosemoor St. SW3 79 315 DF77
Rosemount Clo., Wdf.Grn. 224 308 EM51
Rosemount Dr., Brom. 276 326 EM98
Rosemount Rd. W13 132 314 CG72
Rosenau Cres. SW11 159 315 DE81
Rosenau Rd. SW11 159 315 DE81
Rosendale Rd. SE21 194 324 DQ87
Rosendale Rd. SE24 194 324 DQ87

Roseneath Ave. N21	209	300	DP46
Roseneath Rd. SW11	176	324	DG86
Roseneath Wk., Enf.	202	300	DR42
Rosens Wk., Edg.	205	298	CP48
Rosenthal Rd. SE6	182	325	EB86
Rosenthorpe Rd. SE15	181	325	DX85
Roserton St. E14	150	317	EC75
Rosery, The, Croy.	288	333	DX100
Roses, The, Wdf.Grn.	223	307	EF52
Rosethorn Clo. SW12	193	324	DK87
Rosetta Clo. SW8	161	316	DL80
Rosetti Ter., Dag.	236	309	EV63
Roseveare Rd. SE12	276	326	EJ91
Roseville Ave., Houns.	259	321	CA85
Roseville Rd., Hayes	250	321	BU78
Rosevine Rd. SW20	270	323	CW95
Roseway SE21	179	324	DR86
Rosewell Clo. SE20	274	325	DV94
Rosewood, Dart.	279	327	FE91
Rosewood, Sutt.	293	331	DC110
Rosewood Ave., Grnf.	106	304	CG64
Rosewood Ave., Horn.	238	310	FG64
Rosewood Clo., Sid.	262	327	EW90
Rosewood Ct., Brom.	276	326	EJ95
Rosewood Ct., Rom.	226	309	EW57
Rosewood Dr., Enf.	202	300	DN35
Rosewood Dr., Shep.	280	328	BM99
Rosewood Gdns. SE13	166	317	EC82
Rosewood Gro., Sutt.	285	331	DC103
Rosewood Sq. W12	136	315	CU72
Rosewood Ter. SE20	274	325	DW94
Rosher Clo. E15	121	307	ED66
Rosina St. E9	119	307	DX64
Roskell Rd. SW15	173	323	CX83
Roslin Rd. W3	144	314	CP76
Roslin Way, Brom.	276	326	EG92
Roslyn Clo., Mitch.	271	323	DD96
Roslyn Gdns., Rom.	227	309	FE54
Roslyn Rd. N15	221	306	DR57
Rosmead Rd. W11	137	315	CY73
Rosoman Pl. EC1	36	316	DN70
Rosoman St. EC1	36	316	DN69
Ross Ave. NW7	206	299	CY50
Ross Ave., Dag.	236	309	EZ61
Ross Clo., Har.	215	303	CC52
Ross Clo., Hayes	249	320	BR76
Ross Ct. SW15	189	323	CX87
Ross Par., Wall.	293	332	DH107
Ross Rd. SE25	273	324	DR97
Ross Rd., Twick.	259	321	CB88
Ross Rd., Wall.	286	332	DJ106
Ross Way SE9	260	326	EL83
Ross Way, Nthwd.	213	302	BT49
Rossall Clo., Horn.	228	310	FG58
Rossall Cres. NW10	123	314	CM69
Rossdale, Sutt.	285	331	DE106
Rossdale Dr. N9	210	301	DW44
Rossdale Dr. NW9	92	304	CQ60
Rossdale Rd. SW15	172	323	CW84
Rosse Ms. SE3	252	318	EH81
Rossendale St. E5	102	307	DV61
Rossendale Way NW1	21	316	DJ67
Rossetti Rd. SE16	148	317	DV78
Rossignol Gdns., Cars.	285	332	DG103
Rossindel Rd., Houns.	259	321	CA85
Rossington St. E5	102	307	DU61
Rossiter Flds., Barn.	206	299	CY44
Rossiter Rd. SW12	192	324	DH88
Rossland Clo., Bexh.	263	327	FB85
Rosslyn Ave. E4	211	301	EF47
Rosslyn Ave. SW13	171	322	CS83
Rosslyn Ave., Barn.	207	299	DE44
Rosslyn Ave., Dag.	236	309	EZ59
Rosslyn Ave., Felt.	258	321	BU86
Rosslyn Ave., Rom.	228	311	FM54
Rosslyn Clo., Hayes	249	312	BR71
Rosslyn Clo., Sun.	265	328	BS93
Rosslyn Clo., W.Wick.	289	333	EF104
Rosslyn Cres., Har.	215	303	CF56
Rosslyn Cres., Wem.	107	304	CL63
Rosslyn Hill NW3	113	305	DD63
Rosslyn Ms. NW3	113	305	DD63
Rosslyn Pk. Ms. NW3	113	305	DD64
Rosslyn Rd. E17	223	307	EC56
Rosslyn Rd., Bark.	235	308	ER66
Rosslyn Rd., Twick.	168	322	CJ86
Rossmore Rd. NW1	30/1	315	DE70
Rosswood Gdns., Wall.	293	332	DH107
Rostella Rd. SW17	271	323	DD91
Rostrevor Ave. N15	221	306	DT58
Rostrevor Gdns., Hayes	249	312	BS74
Rostrevor Gdns., Sthl.	250	321	BY78
Rostrevor Ms. SW6	157	315	CZ81
Rostrevor Rd. SW6	157	315	CZ81
Rostrevor Rd. SW19	271	323	DA92
Rotary St. SE1	72/3	316	DP76
Roth Wk. N7	99	306	DM62
Rothbury Gdns., Islw.	152	314	CG80
Rothbury Rd. E9	119	307	DZ66
Rothbury Wk. N17	222	307	DU52
Rotherfield Rd., Cars.	285	332	DG105
Rotherfield Rd., Enf.	203	301	DX37
Rotherfield St. N1	116	306	DQ66
Rotherham Wk. SE1	60/1	316	DP74
Rotherhill Ave. SW16	272	324	DK93
Rotherhithe New Rd. SE16	148	317	DV78
Rotherhithe Old Rd. SE16	149	317	DX77
Rotherhithe St. SE16	148	317	DW75
Rotherhithe Tunnel E1	139	317	DX74
Rotherhithe Tunnel App. E14	139	317	DY73
Rotherhithe Tunnel App. SE16	148	317	DW75
Rothermere Rd., Croy.	286	332	DM106
Rotherwick Hill W5	123	314	CM70
Rotherwick Rd. NW11	96	305	DA59
Rotherwood Clo. SW20	270	323	CY95
Rotherwood Rd. SW15	173	323	CX83
Rothery St. N1	24/5	316	DP67
Rothery Ter. SW9	162	316	DP80
Rothesay Ave. SW20	270	323	CY96
Rothesay Ave., Grnf.	233	313	CD65
Rothesay Ave., Rich.	170	322	CP84
Rothesay Rd. SE25	273	324	DR98
Rothsay Rd. E7	234	308	EJ66
Rothsay St. SE1	74/5	316	DS76
Rothsay Wk. E14	150	317	EA77
Rothschild Rd. W4	144	314	CQ76
Rothschild St. SE27	273	324	DP91
Rothwell Gdns., Dag.	236	309	EW66
Rothwell Rd., Dag.	246	319	EW67
Rothwell St. NW1	19	315	DF67
Rotten Row SW1	67	315	DF75
Rotten Row SW7	66/7	315	DE75
Rotterdam Dr. E14	150	317	EC76
Rouel Rd. SE16	148	317	DU76
Rougemont Ave., Mord.	284	331	DA100
Roughs, The, Nthwd.	213	302	BS48
Round Gro., Croy.	288	333	DX101
Round Hill SE26	196	325	DW90
Roundacre SW19	189	323	CX89
Roundaway Rd., Ilf.	224	308	EM53
Roundel Clo. SE4	181	325	DZ84
Roundhay Clo. SE23	197	325	DX89
Roundtable Rd., Brom.	199	325	EF90
Roundtree Rd., Wem.	106	304	CH64
Roundway, The N17	221	306	DQ53
Roundways, The, Ruis.	231	312	BT62
Roundwood, Chis.	277	326	EP96
Roundwood Ave., Uxb.	249	312	BQ74
Roundwood Clo., Ruis.	231	312	BR59
Roundwood Rd. NW10	109	304	CT65
Rounton Rd. E3	130	317	EA70
Roupell Rd. SW2	193	324	DM88
Roupell St. SE1	60	316	DN74
Rousden St. NW1	114	306	DJ66
Rouse Gdns. SE21	273	324	DS91
Routemaster Clo. E13	244	318	EH69
Routh Ct., Felt.	265	320	BS88
Routh Rd. SW18	191	323	DE87
Routh St. E6	244	318	EM71
Routledge Clo. N19	99	306	DK60
Rover Ave., Ilf.	225	308	ET51
Rowallan Rd. SW6	157	315	CY80
Rowan Ave. E4	222	307	DZ51
Rowan Clo. SW16	272	324	DJ95
Rowan Clo. W5	143	314	CL75
Rowan Clo., N.Mal.	269	322	CS96
Rowan Clo., Stan.	215	303	CF51
Rowan Clo., Wem.	90	304	CG62
Rowan Cres. SW16	272	324	DJ95
Rowan Dr. NW9	218	305	CU55
Rowan Gdns., Croy.	287	332	DT104
Rowan Ind. Est., Croy.	287	332	DS101
Rowan Pl., Hayes	249	312	BT73
Rowan Rd. SW16	272	324	DJ96
Rowan Rd. W6	147	315	CX77
Rowan Rd., Bexh.	262	327	EY83
Rowan Rd., Brent.	152	314	CH80
Rowan Rd., Swan.	279	327	FD97
Rowan Rd., West Dr.	248	320	BK77
Rowan Ter. W6	147	315	CX77
Rowan Wk. N2	219	305	DC57
Rowan Wk. N19	98	306	DJ61
Rowan Wk. W10	127	315	CY70
Rowan Wk., Brom.	290	334	EM104
Rowan Wk., Horn.	228	310	FK56
Rowan Way, Rom.	226	309	EW55
Rowans, The N13	209	300	DP48
Rowans, The, Sun.	265	328	BT92
Rowantree Clo. N21	209	300	DR46
Rowantree Rd. N21	209	300	DR46
Rowantree Rd., Enf.	202	300	DP40
Rowanwood Ave., Sid.	262	327	EU88
Rowben Clo. N20	207	299	DB46
Rowberry Clo. SW6	156	315	CW80
Rowcross St. SE1	87	316	DT78
Rowdell Rd., Nthlt.	243	313	CA67
Rowden Pk. Gdns. E4	223	307	EA51
Rowden Rd. E4	223	307	EA51
Rowden Rd., Beck.	274	325	DY95
Rowden Rd., Epsom	282	330	CP105
Rowditch La. SW11	160	316	DG82
Rowdon Ave. NW10	110	305	CV66
Rowdowns Rd., Dag.	246	319	EZ67
Rowe Gdns., Bark.	245	318	ET68
Rowe La. E9	118	307	DW64
Rowe Wk., Har.	233	313	CA62
Rowena Cres. SW11	159	315	DE82
Rowfant Rd. SW17	192	324	DG88
Rowhill Rd. E5	118	307	DV63
Rowhill Rd., Dart.	279	327	FF93
Rowhill Rd., Swan.	279	327	FF93
Rowington Clo. W2	40/1	315	DB71
Rowland Ave., Har.	216	304	CJ55
Rowland Ct. E16	131	317	EF70
Rowland Gro. SE26	196	325	DV90
Rowland Hill Ave. N17	221	306	DQ52
Rowland Hill St. NW3	113	305	DE64
Rowland Way SW19	271	323	DB95
Rowland Way, Ashf.	265	328	BQ94
Rowlands Clo. N6	220	306	DG58
Rowlands Clo. NW7	218	305	CU52
Rowlands Rd., Dag.	236	309	EZ61
Rowley Ave., Sid.	262	327	EV87
Rowley Clo., Wem.	107	304	CM66
Rowley Gdns. N4	100	306	DQ59
Rowley Grn. Rd., Barn.	205	298	CT43
Rowley Ind. Est. W3	144	314	CP76
Rowley Rd. N15	221	306	DQ57
Rowley Way NW8	16/7	315	DB67
Rowlheys Pl., West Dr.	248	320	BL76
Rowlls Rd., Kings.T.	268	322	CM97
Rowney Gdns., Dag.	236	309	EW65
Rowney Rd., Dag.	236	309	EV65
Rowntree Clifford Clo. E13	244	318	EH69
Rowntree Path SE28	246	319	EV73
Rowntree Rd., Twick.	259	321	CE88
Rowse Clo. E15	130	317	EC67
Rowsley Ave. NW4	218	305	CW55
Rowstock Gdns. N7	115	306	DK64
Rowton Rd. SE18	253	318	EQ80
Rowzill Rd., Swan.	279	327	FF93
Roxborough Ave., Har.	233	313	CE59
Roxborough Ave., Islw.	251	321	CF80
Roxborough Pk., Har.	233	313	CE59
Roxborough Rd., Har.	215	303	CD57
Roxbourne Clo., Nthlt.	232	313	BX65
Roxburgh Ave., Upmin.	239	311	FQ62
Roxburgh Rd. SE27	273	324	DP92
Roxburn Way, Ruis.	231	312	BT62
Roxby Pl. SW6	158	315	DA79
Roxeth Ct., Ashf.	265	328	BN92
Roxeth Grn. Ave., Har.	233	313	CB62
Roxeth Gro., Har.	233	313	CB63
Roxeth Hill, Har.	233	313	CD61
Roxford Clo., Shep.	281	328	BS99
Roxley Rd. SE13	182	325	EB86
Roxton Gdns., Croy.	288	333	EA106
Roxwell Rd. W12	146	315	CU75
Roxwell Rd., Bark.	246	319	EU68
Roxwell Trd. Pk. E10	103	307	DY59
Roxwell Way, Wdf.Grn.	224	308	EJ52
Roxy Ave., Rom.	236	309	EW59
Roy Gdns., Ilf.	225	308	ES56
Roy Gro., Hmptn.	267	329	CB93
Roy Rd., Nthwd.	213	302	BT52
Roy Sq. E14	139	317	DY73
Royal Albert Dock E16	244	318	EL73
Royal Albert Roundabout E16	252	318	EK75
Royal Albert Way E16	244	318	EJ73
Royal Arc. W1	57	316	DJ73
Royal Ave. SW3	79	315	DF78
Royal Ave., Wor.Pk.	283	330	CS103
Royal Circ. SE27	194	324	DN90
Royal Clo. N16	101	306	DS60
Royal Clo., Ilf.	236	309	EU59
Royal Clo., Uxb.	248	312	BM72
Royal Clo., Wor.Pk.	283	330	CS103
Royal College St. NW1	114	306	DJ66
Royal Ct. EC3	50	316	DR72
Royal Ct. SE16	149	317	DZ76
Royal Cres. W11	137	315	CX74
Royal Cres., Ruis.	232	313	BY63
Royal Cres. Ms. W11	137	315	CX74
Royal Docks Rd. E6	245	318	EP72
Royal Docks Rd., Bark.	245	318	EP72
Royal Ex. EC3	50	316	DR72
Royal Ex. Ave. EC3	50	316	DR72
Royal Ex. Bldgs. EC3	50	316	DR72
Royal Ex. Steps EC3	50	316	DR72
Royal Hill SE10	166	317	EC80
Royal Hospital Rd. SW3	159	315	DF79
Royal La., Uxb.	248	312	BM71
Royal La., West Dr.	248	312	BM72
Royal London Est., The N17	222	307	DU51
Royal London Ind. Est. NW10	125	314	CR68
Royal Mint Ct. EC3	63	316	DT73
Royal Mint Pl. E1	63	316	DT73
Royal Mint St. E1	63	316	DT73
Royal Mt. Ct., Twick.	259	321	CE90
Royal Naval Pl. SE14	165	317	DZ80
Royal Oak Ct. N1	38/9	316	DS69
Royal Oak Pl. SE22	180	325	DV86
Royal Oak Rd. E8	118	307	DV65
Royal Oak Rd., Bexh.	262	327	EZ85
Royal Opera Arc. SW1	58	316	DK74
Royal Orchard Clo. SW18	189	323	CY87
Royal Par. SE3	167	317	EF82
Royal Par. SW6	157	315	CY80
Royal Par. W5	123	314	CL69
Royal Par., Chis.	277	326	EQ94
Royal Par. Ms. SE3	167	317	EF82
Royal Par. Ms., Chis.	277	326	EQ94
Royal Pl. SE10	166	317	EC80
Royal Rd. E16	244	318	EJ72
Royal Rd. SE17	162	316	DP79
Royal Rd., Sid.	262	327	EX90
Royal Rd., Tedd.	267	329	CD92
Royal Route, Wem.	108	304	CN63
Royal St. SE1	71	316	DM76
Royal Victor Pl. E3	129	317	DX68
Royal Victoria Dock E16	244	318	EG73
Royal Wk., Wall.	285	332	DH104
Royal Windsor Ct., Surb.	282	330	CN102
Royalty Ms. W1	46	316	DK72
Roycraft Ave., Bark.	245	318	ET68
Roycraft Clo., Bark.	245	318	ET68
Roycroft Clo. E18	224	308	EH53
Roycroft Clo. SW2	194	324	DN88
Roydene Rd. SE18	253	318	ES79
Roydon Clo. SW11	160	316	DH81
Roydon St. SW11	160	316	DH81
Royle Clo., Rom.	228	310	FH57
Royle Cres. W13	122	314	CG70
Royston Ave. E4	211	301	EA50
Royston Ave., Sutt.	285	331	DD104
Royston Ave., Wall.	286	332	DK105
Royston Clo., Houns.	250	321	BV81
Royston Ct. SE24	178	324	DQ86
Royston Ct., Rich.	153	314	CM81
Royston Ct., Surb.	282	330	CN104
Royston Gdns., Ilf.	224	308	EK58
Royston Gro., Pnr.	215	303	CA51
Royston Par., Ilf.	224	308	EK58
Royston Pk. Rd., Pnr.	214	303	BZ51
Royston Rd. SE20	274	325	DX95
Royston Rd., Dart.	263	327	FF86
Royston Rd., Rich.	169	322	CL85
Royston Rd., Rom.	229	311	FN52
Royston St. E2	128	317	DW68
Roystons, The, Surb.	282	330	CP99
Rozel Ct. N1	26/7	316	DS67
Rozel Rd. SW4	176	324	DJ83
Rubastic Rd., Sthl.	250	321	BW76
Rubens Rd., Nthlt.	242	313	BW68
Rubens St. SE6	197	325	DZ89
Ruberoid Rd., Enf.	203	301	DZ41
Ruby Ms. E17	223	307	EA55
Ruby Rd. E17	223	307	EA55
Ruby St. SE15	164	317	DV79
Ruby Triangle SE15	164	317	DV79
Ruckholt Clo. E10	104	307	EB62
Ruckholt Rd. E10	120	307	EB63
Rucklidge Ave. NW10	125	314	CT68
Rudall Cres. NW3	113	305	DD63
Ruddington Clo. E5	119	307	DY63
Ruddstreet Clo. SE18	253	318	EP77
Ruddy Way NW7	218	305	CU51
Rudland Rd., Bexh.	263	327	FB83
Rudloe Rd. SW12	192	324	DJ87
Rudolf Pl. SW8	161	316	DL79
Rudolph Ct. SE22	196	325	DU87
Rudolph Rd. E13	131	317	EF68
Rudolph Rd. NW6	16	315	DA68
Rudyard Gro. NW7	217	304	CQ51
Ruffetts, The, S.Croy.	295	333	DV108
Ruffetts Clo., S.Croy.	295	333	DV108
Rufford Clo., Har.	216	304	CG58
Rufford St. N1	22/3	316	DL67
Rufford Twr. W3	134	314	CP74
Rufus Clo., Ruis.	232	313	BY62
Rufus St. N1	38/9	316	DS69
Rugby Ave. N9	209	300	DT46
Rugby Ave., Grnf.	233	313	CD65
Rugby Ave., Wem.	106	304	CH64
Rugby Clo., Har.	215	303	CE56
Rugby Gdns., Dag.	236	309	EW65
Rugby La., Sutt.	292	331	CX109
Rugby Rd. NW9	217	304	CN56
Rugby Rd. W4	145	314	CS75
Rugby Rd., Dag.	236	309	EV65
Rugby Rd., Islw.	259	321	CE85
Rugby Rd., Twick.	259	321	CE85
Rugby St. WC1	35	316	DM70
Rugby Wk., Sutt.	292	331	CX109
Rugg St. E14	140	317	EA73
Ruggles-Brise Rd., Ashf.	264	328	BK92
Ruislip Clo., Grnf.	243	313	CB70
Ruislip Rd., Grnf.	243	313	CA69
Ruislip Rd., Nthlt.	242	313	BX69
Ruislip Rd. E. W7	243	313	CD70
Ruislip Rd. E. W13	243	313	CF70
Ruislip Rd. E., Grnf.	243	313	CD70
Ruislip St. SW17	271	323	DF91
Rum Clo. E1	138	317	DW73
Rumbold Rd. SW6	158	315	DB80
Rumsey Clo., Hmptn.	266	329	BZ93
Rumsey Ms. N4	100	306	DP62
Rumsey Rd. SW9	177	324	DM83
Runbury Circ. NW9	93	304	CR61
Runcorn Clo. N17	222	307	DV56
Runcorn Pl. W11	137	315	CY73
Rundell Cres. NW4	218	305	CV57
Runes Clo., Mitch.	271	323	DD98
Runnel Fld., Har.	233	313	CE62
Running Horse Yd., Brent.	153	314	CL79
Runnymede SW19	271	323	DC95
Runnymede Clo., Twick.	259	321	CB87
Runnymede Ct., Croy.	287	332	DT103
Runnymede Cres. SW16	272	324	DK95
Runnymede Gdns., Grnf.	243	313	CD68
Runnymede Gdns., Twick.	259	321	CB87
Runnymede Rd., Twick.	259	321	CB86
Runway, The, Ruis.	232	313	BV64
Rupack St. SE16	148	317	DW75
Rupert Ave., Wem.	107	304	CL64
Rupert Ct. W1	58	316	DK73
Rupert Gdns. SW9	162	316	DP82
Rupert Rd. N19	99	306	DK62
Rupert Rd. NW6	127	315	CZ68
Rupert Rd. W4	145	314	CS76
Rupert St. W1	58	316	DK73
Rural Clo., Horn.	238	310	FH60
Rural Way SW16	272	324	DH94
Ruscoe Rd. E16	141	317	EF72
Ruscombe Way, Felt.	265	320	BT87
Rush, The SW19	270	323	CZ95
Rush Grn. Gdns., Rom.	237	309	FC60
Rush Grn. Rd., Rom.	237	309	FC60
Rush Gro. St. SE18	252	318	EM77
Rush Hill Ms. SW11	176	324	DG83
Rush Hill Rd. SW11	176	324	DG83
Rusham Rd. SW12	175	323	DF86
Rushbrook Cres. E17	222	307	DZ53
Rushbrook Rd. SE9	261	326	EQ89
Rushcroft Rd. E4	223	307	EA52
Rushcroft Rd. SW2	178	324	DN84
Rushden Clo. SE19	273	324	DR94
Rushden Gdns. NW7	218	305	CW51
Rushden Gdns., Ilf.	225	308	EN54
Rushdene SE2	254	319	EW76
Rushdene Ave., Barn.	207	299	DE45
Rushdene Clo., Nthlt.	242	313	BW68
Rushdene Cres., Nthlt.	242	313	BW68
Rushdene Rd., Pnr.	214	303	BX58
Rushdon Clo., Rom.	228	310	FG57
Rushen Wk., Cars.	285	331	DD102
Rushes Mead, Uxb.	240	312	BJ67
Rushet Rd., Orp.	278	327	EU96
Rushey Clo., N.Mal.	269	322	CR98
Rushey Grn. SE6	198	325	EB87
Rushey Mead SE4	182	325	EA85
Rushford Rd. SE4	181	325	DZ86
Rushgrove Ave. NW9	217	304	CS57
Rushley Clo., Kes.	290	334	EK105
Rushmead E2	128	317	DV69
Rushmead, Rich.	184	322	CH90
Rushmead Clo., Croy.	287	332	DT105
Rushmere Ave., Upmin.	239	311	FQ62
Rushmere Ct., Wor.Pk.	283	331	CU103
Rushmere Pl. SW19	270	323	CX92
Rushmoor Clo., Pnr.	214	303	BV56
Rushmoor Clo., Rick.	212	302	BK47
Rushmore Clo., Brom.	276	326	EL97
Rushmore Cres. E5	119	307	DX63
Rushmore Rd. E5	118	307	DW63
Rusholme Ave., Dag.	237	309	FA62
Rusholme Gro. SE19	273	324	DS92
Rusholme Rd. SW15	173	323	CX86
Rushout Ave., Har.	216	304	CH58
Rushton St. N1	26	316	DR68
Rushworth Ave. NW4	218	305	CU55
Rushworth Gdns. NW4	218	305	CU55
Rushworth St. SE1	72/3	316	DP75
Rushy Meadow La., Cars.	285	331	DE103
Ruskin Ave. E12	234	308	EL65
Ruskin Ave., Felt.	257	320	BT86
Ruskin Ave., Rich.	154	314	CN80
Ruskin Ave., Upmin.	239	311	FQ59
Ruskin Ave., Well.	254	319	EU82
Ruskin Clo. NW11	219	305	DB58
Ruskin Dr., Orp.	291	334	ES104
Ruskin Dr., Well.	262	327	EU83
Ruskin Dr., Wor.Pk.	283	331	CV103
Ruskin Gdns. W5	123	314	CK70
Ruskin Gdns., Har.	216	304	CM56
Ruskin Gdns., Rom.	228	310	FH52
Ruskin Gro., Well.	254	319	EU82
Ruskin Pk. Ho. SE5	179	324	DR83
Ruskin Rd. N17	221	306	DT53
Ruskin Rd., Belv.	255	319	FA77
Ruskin Rd., Cars.	285	331	DF106
Ruskin Rd., Croy.	286	332	DP103
Ruskin Rd., Islw.	259	321	CF83
Ruskin Rd., Sthl.	242	313	BY73
Ruskin Wk. N9	210	301	DU47
Ruskin Wk. SE24	178	324	DQ85
Ruskin Wk., Brom.	290	334	EL100
Ruskin Way SW19	271	323	DD95
Rusland Ave., Orp.	291	334	ER104
Rusland Pk. Rd., Har.	215	303	CE56
Rusper Clo. NW2	94	305	CW62
Rusper Clo., Stan.	204	298	CJ49
Rusper Rd. N22	221	306	DP54
Rusper Rd., Dag.	236	309	EW65
Russell Ave. N22	221	306	DN54
Russell Clo. NW10	108	304	CQ66
Russell Clo. SE7	252	318	EJ80
Russell Clo. W4	155	314	CT79
Russell Clo., Beck.	275	325	EB97
Russell Clo., Bexh.	263	327	FA84
Russell Clo., Nthwd.	213	302	BQ50
Russell Clo., Ruis.	232	313	BW61
Russell Ct. SW1	57	316	DJ74
Russell Dr., Stai.	256	320	BK86
Russell Gdns. N20	207	299	DE47
Russell Gdns. NW11	218	305	CY58
Russell Gdns. W14	147	315	CY76
Russell Gdns., Rich.	184	322	CJ89
Russell Gdns., West Dr.	249	320	BN78
Russell Gdns. Ms. W14	147	315	CY75
Russell Grn. Clo., Pur.	294	332	DN110
Russell Gro. NW7	205	298	CS50
Russell Gro. SW9	162	316	DN81
Russell Hill, Pur.	294	332	DM110
Russell Hill Pl., Pur.	294	332	DN111
Russell Hill Rd., Pur.	294	332	DN110
Russell Kerr Clo. W4	154	314	CQ80
Russell La. N20	207	299	DE47
Russell Mead, Har.	215	303	CF52
Russell Pl. NW3	113	305	DE64
Russell Pl. SE16	149	317	DY76
Russell Rd. E4	210	301	DZ49
Russell Rd. E10	223	307	EB58
Russell Rd. E16	244	318	EG72
Russell Rd. E17	222	307	DZ55
Russell Rd. N8	220	306	DK58
Russell Rd. N13	220	306	DM51
Russell Rd. N15	221	306	DS57
Russell Rd. N20	207	299	DE47
Russell Rd. NW9	217	304	CT58
Russell Rd. SW19	271	323	DA94
Russell Rd. W14	147	315	CY76
Russell Rd., Enf.	202	300	DT38
Russell Rd., Mitch.	271	323	DE97
Russell Rd., Nthlt.	233	313	CC64
Russell Rd., Nthwd.	213	302	BQ48
Russell Rd., Shep.	281	328	BP101
Russell Rd., Twick.	259	321	CF86
Russell Sq. WC1	34/5	316	DL70
Russell St. WC2	58/9	316	DL73
Russell Wk., Rich.	169	322	CM86
Russell Way, Sutt.	284	331	DA106
Russell's Footpath SW16	272	324	DL92
Russet Clo., Uxb.	241	312	BQ70
Russet Cres. N7	115	306	DM64
Russet Dr., Croy.	288	333	DY102
Russets Clo. E4	211	301	ED49
Russett Clo., Orp.	291	335	EV106
Russett Way SE13	166	317	EB82
Russett Way, Swan.	279	327	FD96
Russetts, The, Horn.	228	311	FL56
Russia Ct. EC2	49	316	DQ72
Russia Dock Rd. SE16	139	317	DY74
Russia La. E2	128	317	DW68
Russia Row EC2	49	316	DQ72
Russia Wk. SE16	149	317	DX75
Russington Rd., Shep.	281	328	BR100
Rust Sq. SE5	163	316	DR80
Rusthall Ave. W4	145	314	CR77
Rusthall Clo., Croy.	288	333	DW100
Rustic Ave. SW16	272	324	DH94
Rustic Clo., Upmin.	239	311	FS60
Rustic Pl., Wem.	107	304	CK63
Rustic Wk. E16	244	318	EH72
Rustington Wk., Mord.	284	331	CZ101
Ruston Ave., Surb.	282	330	CP101
Ruston Gdns. N14	208	300	DG44
Ruston Ms. W11	137	315	CY72
Ruston St. E3	129	317	DZ67
Rutford Rd. SW16	272	324	DL92
Ruth Clo., Stan.	216	304	CM56
Rutherford Clo., Sutt.	293	331	DD107
Rutherford St. SW1	82	316	DK77
Rutherford Twr., Sthl.	243	313	CB72
Rutherford Way, Wem.	92	304	CN62
Rutherglen Rd. SE2	254	319	EU79
Ruthin Clo. NW9	217	304	CS58
Ruthin Rd. SE3	252	318	EG79
Ruthven St. E9	129	317	DX67
Rutland App., Horn.	229	311	FN57
Rutland Ave., Sid.	262	327	EU87
Rutland Clo. SW14	170	322	CP83
Rutland Clo. SW19	271	323	DE94
Rutland Clo., Bex.	262	327	EX88
Rutland Ct., Enf.	210	301	DV43
Rutland Dr., Horn.	229	311	FN57
Rutland Dr., Mord.	284	331	CZ100
Rutland Dr., Rich.	185	322	CK88
Rutland Gdns. N4	221	306	DP58
Rutland Gdns. SW7	66/7	315	DE75
Rutland Gdns. W13	132	314	CG71
Rutland Gdns., Croy.	287	332	DS105
Rutland Gdns., Dag.	236	309	EW64
Rutland Gdns. Ms. SW7	66/7	315	DE75
Rutland Gate SW7	66/7	315	DE75
Rutland Gate, Belv.	255	319	FB78
Rutland Gate, Brom.	275	325	EF98
Rutland Gate Ms. SW7	66/7	315	DE75
Rutland Gro. W6	146	315	CV78
Rutland Ms. NW8	16/7	315	DB67
Rutland Ms. E. SW7	66/7	315	DE76
Rutland Ms. S. SW7	66/7	315	DE76
Rutland Pk. NW2	110	305	CW65
Rutland Pk. SE6	197	325	DZ89
Rutland Pl. EC1	48/9	316	DP71
Rutland Rd. E7	234	308	EK66
Rutland Rd. E9	128	317	DW67
Rutland Rd. E11	224	308	EH57
Rutland Rd. E17	223	307	EA58
Rutland Rd. SW19	271	323	DE94
Rutland Rd., Har.	215	303	CC58
Rutland Rd., Hayes	249	320	BR77
Rutland Rd., Ilf.	235	308	EP63
Rutland Rd., Sthl.	243	313	CA70
Rutland Rd., Twick.	259	321	CD89
Rutland St. SW7	66/7	315	DE76
Rutland Wk. SE6	197	325	DZ89
Rutley Clo. SE17	162	316	DP79
Rutley Clo., Rom.	228	310	FK54
Rutlish Rd. SW19	271	323	DA95
Rutter Gdns., Mitch.	271	323	DD98
Rutters Clo., West Dr.	249	320	BN75
Rutts Ter. SE14	165	317	DX81
Ruvigny Gdns. SW15	173	323	CX83
Ruxley Clo., Epsom	282	330	CP106
Ruxley Clo., Sid.	278	327	EY93
Ruxley Cor. Ind. Est., Sid.	278	327	EX93
Ruxley Ms., Epsom	282	330	CP106
Ruxton Clo., Swan.	279	327	FE97
Ryalls Ct. N20	207	299	DF48
Ryan Clo. SE3	260	326	EJ84
Ryan Clo., Ruis.	232	313	BV60
Ryan Dr., Brent.	152	314	CG79
Ryarsh Cres., Orp.	291	334	ES105
Rycott Path SE22	196	325	DU87
Rycroft Way N17	221	306	DT55
Ryculff Sq. SE3	167	317	EF82
Rydal Clo. NW4	218	305	CX53
Rydal Clo., Pur.	295	332	DR113
Rydal Cres., Grnf.	122	314	CH69
Rydal Dr., Bexh.	254	319	EZ82
Rydal Dr., W.Wick.	289	333	EE103
Rydal Gdns. NW9	217	304	CS57
Rydal Gdns. SW15	269	322	CS92
Rydal Gdns., Houns.	259	321	CB86
Rydal Gdns., Wem.	90	304	CJ60
Rydal Rd. SW16	272	324	DK91
Rydal Way, Enf.	210	301	DW44
Rydal Way, Ruis.	232	313	BW63
Ryde, The, Stai.	280	328	BH95
Ryde Pl., Twick.	168	322	CJ86
Ryde Vale Rd. SW12	192	324	DH89
Ryder Clo., Brom.	276	326	EH92
Ryder Ct. SW1	57	316	DJ74
Ryder Dr. SE16	148	317	DV78
Ryder Gdns., Rain.	237	309	FF65
Ryder Ms. E9	118	307	DW64
Ryder St. SW1	57	316	DJ74
Ryder Yd. SW1	57	316	DJ74
Ryders Ter. NW8	17	315	DC68
Rydon St. N1	25	316	DQ67
Rydons Clo. SE9	260	326	EL83
Rydons Pk., Walt.	281	328	BT102
Rydston Clo. N7	115	306	DM66
Rye, The N14	208	300	DJ45
Rye Clo., Bex.	263	327	FB86
Rye Clo., Horn.	238	310	FJ64
Rye Hill Est. SE15	180	325	DW84
Rye Hill Pk. SE15	180	325	DW84
Rye La. SE15	164	317	DU82
Rye Pas. SE15	180	325	DU83
Rye Rd. SE15	181	325	DX84
Rye Wk. SW15	173	323	CX85
Rye Way, Edg.	216	304	CM51
Ryecotes Mead SE21	195	324	DS88
Ryecroft Ave., Ilf.	225	308	EP54
Ryecroft Ave., Twick.	259	321	CB87
Ryecroft Cres., Barn.	206	299	CV43
Ryecroft Rd. SE13	182	325	EC85
Ryecroft Rd. SW16	273	324	DN93
Ryecroft Rd., Orp.	291	334	ER100
Ryecroft St. SW6	158	315	DB81
Ryedale SE22	180	325	DV86
Ryefield Ave., Uxb.	241	312	BP66
Ryefield Path SW15	188	323	CU88
Ryefield Rd. SE19	273	324	DQ93
Ryeland Clo., West Dr.	248	312	BL72
Ryelands Cres. SE12	260	326	EJ86
Ryfold Rd. SW19	190	323	DA90
Ryhope Rd. N11	208	300	DH49
Ryland Clo., Felt.	265	328	BT91
Ryland Ho., Croy.	287	332	DQ104
Ryland Rd. NW5	114	306	DH65
Rylandes Rd. NW2	94	305	CU62
Rylandes Rd., S.Croy.	295	333	DV109
Rylett Cres. W12	145	314	CT75
Rylett Rd. W12	145	314	CT76
Rylston Rd. N13	209	300	DR48
Rylston Rd. SW6	157	315	CZ79
Rymer Rd., Croy.	287	332	DS101
Rymer St. SE24	178	324	DP86
Rymill St. E16	245	318	EN74
Rysbrack St. SW3	67	315	DF76
Sabah Ct., Ashf.	265	328	BN91
Sabbarton St. E16	141	317	EF72
Sabella Ct. E3	129	317	DZ68
Sabine Rd. SW11	175	323	DF83
Sable Clo., Houns.	258	321	BW83
Sable St. N1	116	306	DP66
Sach Rd. E5	102	307	DV61
Sackville Ave., Brom.	289	334	EG102
Sackville Clo., Har.	233	313	CD62
Sackville Ct., Rom.	228	311	FL53
Sackville Cres., Rom.	228	311	FL53
Sackville Est. SW16	193	324	DL90
Sackville Gdns., Ilf.	234	308	EM60
Sackville Rd., Sutt.	292	331	DA108
Sackville St. W1	57	316	DJ73
Sackville Way SE22	196	325	DU88
Saddle Yd. W1	56/7	316	DH74
Saddlebrook Pk., Sun.	265	328	BS94
Saddlers Clo., Borwd.	205	298	CR44
Saddlers Clo., Pnr.	215	303	CA51
Saddlers Ms., Wem.	233	313	CF63
Saddlescombe Way N12	207	299	DA50
Saddleworth Rd., Rom.	228	310	FJ51
Saddleworth Sq., Rom.	228	310	FJ51
Sadler Clo., Mitch.	271	323	DF96
Sadlers Ride, W.Mol.	267	329	CB97
Saffron Ave. E14	141	317	ED73
Saffron Clo. NW11	218	305	CZ57
Saffron Clo., Croy.	286	332	DL100
Saffron Ct., Felt.	265	320	BQ87
Saffron Hill EC1	36	316	DN70
Saffron Rd., Rom.	227	309	FC54
Saffron St. EC1	48	316	DN71
Saffron Way, Surb.	282	330	CK102
Sage Clo. E6	244	318	EM71
Sage St. E1	138	317	DW73
Sage Way WC1	35	316	DM69
Saigasso Clo. E16	244	318	EK72
Sail St. SE11	83	316	DM77
Sainfoin Rd. SW17	192	324	DG89
Sainsbury Rd. SE19	273	324	DS92
St. Agatha's Dr., Kings.T.	268	322	CM93
St. Agathas Gro., Cars.	285	331	DF102
St. Agnes Clo. E9	128	317	DW67
St. Agnes Pl. SE11	162	316	DP79
St. Agnes Well EC1	38	316	DR70
St. Aidans Ct., Bark.	246	319	EV69
St. Aidan's Rd. SE22	180	325	DV86
St. Aidans Rd. W13	142	314	CH75
St. Albans Ave. E6	244	318	EM69
St. Alban's Ave. W4	145	314	CR76
St. Albans Ave., Felt.	266	329	BX92
St. Albans Ave., Upmin.	239	311	FS60
St. Albans Clo. NW11	96	305	DA60
St. Albans Cres. N22	221	306	DN53
St. Alban's Cres., Wdf.Grn.	224	308	EG52
St. Alban's Gdns., Tedd.	268	322	CG92
St. Albans Gro. W8	64/5	315	DB76
St. Alban's Gro., Cars.	285	331	DE101
St. Albans La. NW11	96	305	DA60
St. Alban's Pl. N1	24/5	316	DP67
St. Albans Rd. NW5	98	306	DG62
St. Albans Rd. NW10	125	314	CS67
St. Albans Rd., Ilf.	235	308	ET60
St. Alban's Rd., Kings.T.	268	322	CL93
St. Alban's Rd., Sutt.	284	331	CZ105
St. Alban's Rd., Wdf.Grn.	224	308	EG52
St. Albans St. SW1	58	316	DK73
St. Albans Ter. W6	157	315	CY79
St. Albans Twr. E4	222	307	DZ51
St. Alfege Pas. SE10	166	317	EC79
St. Alfege Rd. SE7	252	318	EK79
St. Alphage Gdns. EC2	49	316	DQ71
St. Alphage Highwalk EC2	50	316	DR71
St. Alphage Wk., Edg.	217	304	CQ54
St. Alphege Rd. N9	210	301	DW45
St. Alphonsus Rd. SW4	177	324	DK84
St. Amunds Clo. SE6	275	325	EA91
St. Andrew St. EC4	48	316	DN71
St. Andrews Ave., Horn.	237	309	FF64
St. Andrews Ave., Wem.	106	304	CG63
St. Andrew's Clo. N12	207	299	DC49
St. Andrews Clo. NW2	94	305	CV62
St. Andrews Clo. SE16	148	317	DV78
St. Andrew's Clo., Islw.	251	321	CD81
St. Andrews Clo., Ruis.	232	313	BX61
St. Andrew's Clo., Shep.	281	328	BR98
St. Andrews Clo., Stan.	216	304	CJ54
St. Andrew's Ct. SW18	190	323	DC89
St. Andrews Dr., Orp.	291	335	EV100
St. Andrews Dr., Stan.	216	304	CJ53
St. Andrew's Gro. N16	101	306	DR60
St. Andrew's Hill EC4	60/1	316	DP73
St. Andrew's Ms. N16	101	306	DS60
St. Andrews Ms. SE3	252	318	EG80
St. Andrews Pl. NW1	32/3	316	DH70
St. Andrews Rd. E11	223	307	EE58
St. Andrews Rd. E13	244	318	EH69
St. Andrews Rd. E17	222	307	DX54
St. Andrews Rd. N9	210	301	DW45
St. Andrews Rd. NW9	93	304	CR60
St. Andrews Rd. NW10	110	305	CV65
St. Andrews Rd. NW11	218	305	CZ58
St. Andrews Rd. W3	135	314	CS72
St. Andrews Rd. W7	251	321	CE75
St. Andrews Rd. W14	157	315	CY79
St. Andrews Rd., Cars.	285	331	DE104
St. Andrews Rd., Croy.	287	332	DQ105
St. Andrews Rd., Enf.	202	300	DR41
St. Andrews Rd., Ilf.	234	308	EM59
St. Andrews Rd., Rom.	227	309	FD58
St. Andrews Rd., Sid.	262	327	EX90
St. Andrew's Rd., Surb.	282	330	CK100
St. Andrews Rd., Uxb.	240	312	BL67
St. Andrews Sq. W11	137	315	CY72
St. Andrew's Sq., Surb.	282	330	CK100

Salem Pl., Croy. 287 332 DQ104
Salem Rd. W2 52/3 315 DB73
Salford Rd. SW2 193 324 DK88
Salhouse Clo. SE28 246 319 EW72
Salisbury Ave. N3 218 305 CZ55
Salisbury Ave., Bark. 235 308 ER66
Salisbury Ave., Sutt. 292 331 CZ107
Salisbury Clo. SE17 86 316 DR77
Salisbury Clo., Upmin. 239 311 FT61
Salisbury Clo., Wor.Pk. 283 330 CT104
Salisbury Ct. EC4 48/9 316 DP72
Salisbury Gdns. SW19 270 323 CY94
Salisbury Hall Gdns. E4 223 307 EA51
Salisbury Ho. E14 140 317 EB72
Salisbury Ms. SW6 157 315 CZ80
Salisbury Pl. SW9 162 316 DP80
Salisbury Pl. W1 43 315 DF71
Salisbury Rd. E4 211 301 EA48
Salisbury Rd. E7 234 308 EG65
Salisbury Rd. E10 104 307 EC61
Salisbury Rd. E12 234 308 EK64
Salisbury Rd. E17 223 307 EC57
Salisbury Rd. N4 221 306 DP57
Salisbury Rd. N9 210 301 DU48
Salisbury Rd. N22 221 306 DP53
Salisbury Rd. SE25 287 333 DU100
Salisbury Rd. SW19 270 323 CY94
Salisbury Rd. W13 142 314 CG75
Salisbury Rd., Bans. 292 331 DB114
Salisbury Rd., Bex. 263 327 FA88
Salisbury Rd., Brom. 290 334 EL99
Salisbury Rd., Cars. 293 331 DF107
Salisbury Rd., Dag. 237 309 FB65
Salisbury Rd., Enf. 203 301 DZ37
Salisbury Rd., Felt. 258 321 BW88
Salisbury Rd., Har. 215 303 CD57
Salisbury Rd., Houns. 258 321 BW83
Salisbury Rd. (Heathrow Airport), Houns. 257 320 BQ85
Salisbury Rd., Ilf. 235 308 ES61
Salisbury Rd., N.Mal. 269 322 CR97
Salisbury Rd., Pnr. 214 303 BU56
Salisbury Rd., Rich. 169 322 CL84
Salisbury Rd., Rom. 228 310 FH57
Salisbury Rd., Sthl. 250 321 BY77
Salisbury Rd., Uxb. 240 312 BH68
Salisbury Rd., Wor.Pk. 283 330 CR105
Salisbury Sq. EC4 48 316 DN72
Salisbury St. NW8 30/1 315 DE70
Salisbury St. W3 144 314 CQ75
Salisbury Ter. SE15 180 325 DW83
Salisbury Wk. N19 98 306 DJ61
Salix Clo., Sun. 266 329 BV94
Salliesfield, Twick. 259 321 CD86
Salmen Rd. E13 131 317 EF68
Salmon La. E14 139 317 DY72
Salmon Rd., Belv. 255 319 FA78
Salmon St. E14 139 317 DZ72
Salmon St. NW9 92 304 CP60
Salmond Clo., Stan. 216 304 CG51
Salmons Rd. N9 210 301 DU46
Salomons Rd. E13 244 318 EJ71
Salop Rd. E17 222 307 DX58
Saltash Clo., Sutt. 284 331 CZ105
Saltash Rd., Ilf. 225 308 ER52
Saltash Rd., Well. 254 319 EW81
Saltcoats Rd. W4 145 314 CS75
Saltcroft Clo., Wem. 92 304 CP60
Salter Rd. SE16 139 317 DX74
Salter St. E14 140 317 EA73
Salter St. NW10 126 315 CU69
Salterford Rd. SW17 272 324 DG93
Salters Hall Ct. EC4 62 316 DR73
Salters Hill SE19 273 324 DR92
Salters Rd. E17 223 307 ED56
Salters Rd. W10 127 315 CX70
Salterton Rd. N7 99 306 DL62
Saltford Clo., Erith 255 319 FE78
Salthill Clo., Uxb. 240 312 BL64
Saltley Clo. E6 244 318 EL72
Saltoun Rd. SW2 178 324 DN84
Saltram Clo. N15 221 306 DT56
Saltram Cres. W9 127 315 CZ69
Saltwell St. E14 140 317 EA73
Saltwood Gro. SE17 86 316 DR78
Salusbury Rd. NW6 127 315 CY67
Salvia Gdns., Grnf. 122 314 CG68
Salvin Rd. SW15 173 323 CX83
Salway Clo., Wdf.Grn. 223 307 EF52
Salway Pl. E15 121 307 EE65
Salway Rd. E15 121 307 ED65
Sam Bartram Clo. SE7 252 318 EJ78
Samantha Clo. E17 103 307 DZ59
Sambruck Ms. SE6 198 325 EB89
Samels Ct. W6 146 315 CU78
Samford St. NW8 30/1 315 DE70
Samos Rd. SE20 274 325 DV96
Sampson Ave., Barn. 206 299 CX43
Sampson Clo., Belv. 254 319 EX76
Sampson St. E1 138 317 DU74
Sampsons Ct., Shep. 281 328 BQ99
Samson St. E13 244 318 EJ68
Samuel Clo. E8 27 316 DT67
Samuel Clo. SE14 165 317 DX79
Samuel Clo. SE18 252 318 EL77
Samuel Gray Gdns., Kings.T. 268 322 CK95
Samuel Johnson Clo. SW16 273 324 DN91
Samuel Lewis Trust Dws. E8 118 307 DU63
Samuel Lewis Trust Dws. N1 116 306 DN66
Samuel Lewis Trust Dws. SW3 78/9 315 DE77
Samuel Lewis Trust Dws. SW6 158 315 DA80
Samuel St. SE18 252 318 EM77
Samuels Clo. W6 146 315 CU78
Sancroft Clo. NW2 94 305 CV62
Sancroft Rd., Har. 215 303 CF54
Sancroft St. SE11 83 316 DM78
Sanctuary, The SW1 70 316 DK76
Sanctuary, The, Bex. 262 327 EX86
Sanctuary, The, Mord. 284 331 DB100
Sanctuary Clo., Uxb. 212 302 BJ52
Sanctuary Rd., Houns. 257 320 BN86
Sanctuary St. SE1 73 316 DQ75
Sandal Rd. N18 210 301 DU50
Sandal Rd., N.Mal. 283 330 CR99
Sandal St. E15 131 317 EE67
Sandale Clo. N16 101 306 DR62
Sandall Clo. W5 123 314 CL70
Sandall Rd. NW5 114 306 DJ65
Sandall Rd. W5 123 314 CL70
Sandalwood Clo. E1 129 317 DY70
Sandalwood Rd., Felt. 258 321 BV90
Sandbach Pl. SE18 253 318 EQ78
Sandbanks, Felt. 265 320 BS88
Sandbourne Ave. SW19 271 323 DB96
Sandbourne Rd. SE4 165 317 DY82
Sandbrook Clo. NW7 217 304 CR51
Sandbrook Rd. N16 101 306 DS62
Sandby Grn. SE9 260 326 EL83
Sandcliff Rd., Erith 255 319 FD77
Sandcroft Clo. N13 221 306 DP51
Sandell St. SE1 72 316 DN75
Sandells Ave., Ashf. 265 328 BQ91
Sanders Clo., Hmptn. 267 329 CC92
Sanders La. NW7 218 305 CW52
Sanders Way N19 99 306 DK60
Sanderson Clo. NW5 114 306 DH63
Sanderson Rd., Uxb. 240 312 BJ65
Sanderstead Ave. NW2 95 305 CY61
Sanderstead Clo. SW12 192 324 DJ87
Sanderstead Ct. Ave., S.Croy. 295 333 DU113
Sanderstead Hill, S.Croy. 295 332 DS111
Sanderstead Rd. E10 103 307 DY60
Sanderstead Rd., Orp. 295 335 EV100
Sanderstead Rd., S.Croy. 295 332 DR108
Sandfield Gdns., Th.Hth. 273 324 DP97
Sandfield Ind. Est., Hmptn. 266 329 BZ95
Sandfield Pas., Th.Hth. 273 324 DQ97
Sandfield Rd., Th.Hth. 273 324 DP97
Sandford Ave. N22 221 306 DQ53
Sandford Clo. E6 244 318 EM70
Sandford Ct. N16 101 306 DS60
Sandford La. N16 101 306 DT61
Sandford Rd. E6 244 318 EL69
Sandford Rd., Bexh. 262 327 EY84
Sandford Rd., Brom. 276 326 EG97
Sandford St. SW6 158 315 DB80
Sandgate Clo., Rom. 237 309 FC59
Sandgate La. SW18 191 323 DE88
Sandgate Rd., Well. 254 319 EW80
Sandgate St. SE15 164 317 DV79
Sandham Pt. SE18 253 318 EP77
Sandhills, Wall. 286 332 DK105
Sandhills Meadow, Shep. 281 328 BQ101
Sandhurst Ave., Har. 214 303 CB58
Sandhurst Ave., Surb. 282 330 CP101
Sandhurst Clo. NW9 217 304 CN55
Sandhurst Clo., S.Croy. 295 332 DS109
Sandhurst Dr., Ilf. 235 308 ET63
Sandhurst Rd. N9 210 301 DW44
Sandhurst Rd. NW9 217 304 CN55
Sandhurst Rd. SE6 199 325 ED88
Sandhurst Rd., Bex. 262 327 EX85
Sandhurst Rd., Orp. 291 335 EU104
Sandhurst Rd., Sid. 261 326 ET90
Sandhurst Way, S.Croy. 295 332 DS108
Sandiford Rd., Sutt. 284 331 CZ103
Sandiland Cres., Brom. 289 333 EF103
Sandilands, Croy. 287 333 DU103
Sandilands Rd. SW6 158 315 DB81
Sandison St. SE15 179 325 DT83
Sandland St. WC1 47 316 DM71
Sandling Ri. SE9 261 326 EN90
Sandlings, The N22 221 306 DN54
Sandmere Rd. SW4 177 324 DL84
Sandow Cres., Hayes 249 320 BT76
Sandown Ave., Dag. 237 309 FC65
Sandown Ave., Horn. 238 310 FK61
Sandown Clo., Houns. 250 321 BU81
Sandown Dr., Cars. 293 332 DG109
Sandown Rd. SE25 287 333 DV99
Sandown Way, Nthlt. 232 313 BY65
Sandpiper Clo. E17 222 307 DX53
Sandpiper Clo. SE16 147 317 DZ75
Sandpiper Way, Orp. 278 327 EX98
Sandpit Pl. SE7 252 318 EL78
Sandpit Rd., Brom. 275 325 EE92
Sandpits Rd., Croy. 288 333 DX105
Sandpits Rd., Rich. 185 322 CK89
Sandra Clo. N22 221 306 DQ53
Sandra Clo., Houns. 259 321 CB85
Sandridge Clo., Har. 215 303 CE56
Sandridge Ct. N4 100 306 DQ62
Sandridge St. N19 98 306 DJ61
Sandringham Ave. SW20 270 323 CY95
Sandringham Clo. SW19 189 323 CX88
Sandringham Clo., Enf. 202 300 DS40
Sandringham Clo., Ilf. 225 308 EQ55
Sandringham Ct. W9 29 315 DC69
Sandringham Cres., Har. 233 313 CA61
Sandringham Dr., Ashf. 264 328 BK91
Sandringham Dr., Well. 253 318 ES82
Sandringham Gdns. N8 220 306 DL58
Sandringham Gdns. N12 219 305 DC51
Sandringham Gdns., Houns. 250 321 BU81
Sandringham Gdns., Ilf. 225 308 EQ55
Sandringham Ms. W5 133 314 CK73
Sandringham Rd. E7 234 308 EJ64
Sandringham Rd. E8 117 306 DT64
Sandringham Rd. E10 223 307 ED58
Sandringham Rd. N22 221 306 DQ55
Sandringham Rd. NW2 110 305 CV65
Sandringham Rd. NW11 95 305 CY59
Sandringham Rd., Bark. 235 308 ET65
Sandringham Rd., Brom. 276 326 EG92
Sandringham Rd., Houns. 256 320 BK85
Sandringham Rd., Nthlt. 233 313 CA66
Sandringham Rd., Th.Hth. 287 332 DQ99
Sandringham Rd., Wor.Pk. 283 331 CU104
Sandrock Pl., Croy. 288 333 DX105
Sandrock Rd. SE13 182 325 EA83
Sand's End La. SW6 158 315 DB81
Sands Way, Wdf.Grn. 224 308 EM51
Sandstone Pl. N19 98 306 DH61
Sandstone Rd. SE12 260 326 EH89
Sandtoft Rd. SE7 252 318 EH79
Sandway Path, Orp. 278 327 EW98
Sandway Rd., Orp. 278 327 EW98
Sandwell Cres. NW6 112 305 DA65
Sandwich St. WC1 34/5 316 DL69
Sandy Bury, Orp. 291 334 ER104
Sandy Dr., Felt. 265 320 BS88
Sandy Hill Ave. SE18 253 318 EP78
Sandy Hill Rd. SE18 253 318 EP78
Sandy Hill Rd., Wall. 294 332 DJ109
Sandy La., Har. 216 304 CM58
Sandy La., Kings.T. 268 322 CH95
Sandy La., Mitch. 272 324 DG95
Sandy La., Nthwd. 213 302 BT47
Sandy La., Orp. 291 335 EU101
Sandy La. (St. Paul's Cray), Orp. 278 327 EW96
Sandy La., Rich. 184 322 CJ89
Sandy La., Sid. 278 327 EX94
Sandy La., Sutt. 292 331 CY108
Sandy La., Tedd. 268 322 CG94
Sandy La. Est., Rich. 185 322 CK89
Sandy La. N., Wall. 294 332 DK107
Sandy La. S., Wall. 294 332 DK107
Sandy Lo. La., Nthwd. 213 302 BR47
Sandy Lo. Rd., Rick. 213 302 BP47
Sandy Lo. Way, Nthwd. 213 302 BS50
Sandy Ridge, Chis. 277 326 EN93
Sandy Rd. NW3 96 305 DB61
Sandy Way, Croy. 288 333 DZ104
Sandy Way, Walt. 281 328 BT102
Sandycombe Rd., Felt. 258 321 BU88
Sandycombe Rd., Twick. 168 322 CJ86
Sandycoombe Rd., Rich. 170 322 CN83
Sandycroft SE2 254 319 EU79
Sandycroft, Epsom 292 331 CW110
Sandyhill Rd., Ilf. 235 308 EP63
Sandymount Ave., Stan. 204 298 CJ50
Sandy's Row E1 50/1 316 DS71
Sanford La. N16 101 306 DT61
Sanford St. SE14 165 317 DY79
Sanford Ter. N16 101 306 DT61
Sanford Wk. N16 101 306 DT61
Sanford Wk. SE14 165 317 DY79
Sanger Ave., Chess. 282 330 CL106
Sangley Rd. SE6 198 325 EB87
Sangley Rd. SE25 273 324 DS98
Sangora Rd. SW11 175 323 DD84
Sans Wk. EC1 36 316 DN70
Sansom Rd. E11 105 307 EF61
Sansom St. SE5 163 316 DR80
Santley St. SW4 177 324 DL84
Santos Rd. SW18 174 323 DA85
Saphora Clo., Orp. 291 334 ER106
Sapphire Clo. E6 245 318 EN72
Sapphire Clo., Dag. 236 309 EW60
Sapphire Rd. SE8 149 317 DY78
Sara Ct., Beck. 275 325 EB95
Saracen Clo., Croy. 287 332 DR100
Saracen St. E14 140 317 EA72
Saracen's Head Yd. EC3 51 316 DT72
Sarah Ho. SW15 171 322 CT84
Sarah St. N1 38/9 316 DS69
Saratoga Rd. E5 118 307 DW63
Sardinia St. WC2 47 316 DM72
Sargeant Clo., Uxb. 240 312 BK69
Sarita Clo., Har. 215 303 CD54
Sarjant Path SW19 189 323 CX89
Sark Clo., Houns. 251 321 CA80
Sark Wk. E16 244 318 EH72
Sarnesfield Ho. SE15 164 317 DV79
Sarnesfield Rd., Enf. 202 300 DR41
Sarre Ave., Horn. 238 310 FJ65
Sarre Rd. NW2 111 305 CZ64
Sarsen Ave., Houns. 250 321 BZ82
Sarsfeld Rd. SW12 191 323 DF89
Sarsfield Rd., Grnf. 122 314 CH68
Sartor Rd. SE15 181 325 DX84
Satanita Clo. E16 244 318 EK72
Satchell Mead NW9 217 304 CT53
Satchwell Rd. E2 128 317 DU69
Sauls Grn. E11 105 307 EE62
Saunders Clo. E14 139 317 DZ73
Saunders Ness Rd. E14 150 317 EC78
Saunders Rd. SE18 253 318 ET78
Saunders Rd., Uxb. 240 312 BM66
Saunders St. SE11 84 316 DN77
Saunders Way SE28 246 319 EV73
Saunderton Rd., Wem. 106 304 CH64
Saunton Ave., Hayes 257 320 BT80
Saunton Rd., Horn. 238 310 FG60
Savage Gdns. E6 244 318 EM72
Savage Gdns. EC3 62/3 316 DS73
Savay Clo., Uxb. 230 312 BG59
Savay La., Uxb. 230 302 BG58
Savernake Rd. N9 210 301 DU44
Savernake Rd. NW3 113 305 DF63
Savile Clo., N.Mal. 283 330 CS99
Savile Gdns., Croy. 287 332 DT103
Savile Row W1 57 316 DJ73
Savill Gdns. SW20 270 323 CU97
Savill Row, Wdf.Grn. 223 307 EF51
Saville Cres., Ashf. 265 328 BR93
Saville Rd. E16 244 318 EL74
Saville Rd. W4 145 314 CR76
Saville Rd., Rom. 226 309 EZ58
Saville Rd., Twick. 259 321 CF88
Saville Row, Brom. 289 333 EF102
Saville Row, Enf. 203 301 DX40
Savona Clo. SW19 270 323 CY94
Savona Est. SW8 160 316 DJ80
Savona St. SW8 160 316 DJ80
Savoy Ave., Hayes 249 320 BS77
Savoy Bldgs. WC2 59 316 DM73
Savoy Clo. E15 131 317 EE67
Savoy Clo., Edg. 205 298 CN50
Savoy Clo., Uxb. 212 302 BK54
Savoy Ct. WC2 58/9 316 DL73
Savoy Hill WC2 59 316 DM73
Savoy Pl. WC2 58/9 316 DL73
Savoy Row WC2 59 316 DM73
Savoy Steps WC2 59 316 DM73
Savoy St. WC2 59 316 DM73
Savoy Way WC2 59 316 DM73
Sawbill Clo., Hayes 242 313 BX71
Sawkins Clo. SW19 189 323 CY89
Sawley Rd. W12 135 314 CT74
Sawtry Clo., Cars. 285 331 DD101
Sawyer Clo. N9 210 301 DU47
Sawyer St. SE1 73 316 DQ75
Sawyers Clo., Dag. 237 309 FC65
Sawyer's Hill, Rich. 185 322 CM87
Sawyers Lawn W13 243 313 CF72
Saxby Rd. SW2 193 324 DL87
Saxham Rd., Bark. 245 318 ET68
Saxlingham Rd. E4 211 301 ED48
Saxon Ave., Felt. 258 321 BY89
Saxon Clo. E17 104 307 EA59
Saxon Clo., Rom. 228 311 FM54
Saxon Clo., Surb. 282 330 CK100
Saxon Clo., Uxb. 248 312 BL71
Saxon Dr. W3 134 314 CP72
Saxon Gdns., Sthl. 242 313 BY73
Saxon Rd. E3 129 317 DZ68
Saxon Rd. E6 244 318 EM70
Saxon Rd. N22 221 306 DP53
Saxon Rd. SE25 287 332 DR99
Saxon Rd., Ashf. 265 328 BR93
Saxon Rd., Brom. 275 325 EF94
Saxon Rd., Ilf. 235 308 EP65
Saxon Rd., Sthl. 242 313 BY74
Saxon Rd., Wem. 92 304 CQ62
Saxon Wk., Sid. 278 327 EW93
Saxon Way N14 208 300 DK44
Saxon Way, West Dr. 256 320 BJ79
Saxonbury Ave., Sun. 266 329 BV97
Saxonbury Clo., Mitch. 271 323 DD97
Saxonbury Gdns., Surb. 282 330 CJ102
Saxony Par., Hayes 249 312 BQ71
Saxton Clo. SE13 183 325 ED83
Saxville Rd., Orp. 278 327 EV97
Sayers Wk., Rich. 185 322 CM87
Sayes Ct. SE8 149 317 DZ78
Sayes Ct. Rd., Orp. 278 327 EU97
Sayes Ct. St. SE8 165 317 DZ79
Scads Hill Clo., Orp. 291 334 ET100
Scala St. W1 45 316 DJ71
Scales Rd. N17 221 306 DT55
Scampston Ms. W10 137 315 CX72
Scandrett St. E1 138 317 DV74
Scarba Wk. N1 117 306 DR65
Scarborough Clo., Sutt. 292 331 CZ111
Scarborough Rd. E11 105 307 ED60
Scarborough Rd. N4 100 306 DN59
Scarborough Rd. N9 210 301 DW45
Scarborough St. E1 51 316 DT72
Scarbrook Rd., Croy. 287 332 DQ104
Scarle Rd., Wem. 107 304 CK65
Scarlet Clo., Orp. 278 327 EV98
Scarlet Rd. SE6 199 325 EE90
Scarlette Manor Way SW2 194 324 DN87
Scarsbrook Rd. SE3 260 326 EK83
Scarsdale Pl. W8 64/5 315 DB76
Scarsdale Rd., Har. 233 313 CC62
Scarsdale Vil. W8 64 315 DA76
Scarth Rd. SW13 171 322 CT83
Scawen Rd. SE8 149 317 DY78
Scawfell St. E2 27 316 DT68
Scaynes Link N12 207 299 DA50
Sceaux Est. SE5 163 316 DS81
Sceaux Gdns. SE5 163 316 DT81
Sceptre Rd. E2 128 317 DW69
Schofield Wk. SE3 252 318 EH80
Scholars Rd. E4 211 301 EC46
Scholars Rd. SW12 192 324 DJ88
Scholefield Rd. N19 99 306 DK61
School Cres., Dart. 263 327 FF84
School Ho. La., Tedd. 268 322 CH94
School Ho. La. SE23 196 325 DV89
School La., Kings.T. 268 322 CJ95
School La., Pnr. 214 303 BY56
School La., Shep. 281 328 BP100
School La., Surb. 282 330 CM102
School La., Well. 262 327 EV83
School Pas., Kings.T. 268 322 CM96
School Pas., Sthl. 242 313 BZ74
School Rd. E12 234 308 EM63
School Rd. NW10 125 314 CR70
School Rd., Ashf. 265 328 BP93
School Rd., Chis. 277 326 EQ95
School Rd., Dag. 247 319 FA67
School Rd., E.Mol. 267 329 CD98
School Rd., Hmptn. 267 329 CC93
School Rd., Houns. 259 321 CC83
School Rd., Kings.T. 268 322 CJ95
School Rd., West Dr. 256 320 BK79
School Rd. Ave., Hmptn. 267 329 CC93
School Wk., Sun. 281 328 BT98
School Way N12 207 299 DC49
Schoolbell Ms. E3 129 317 DY68
Schoolhouse La. E1 139 317 DX73
Schoolway N12 219 305 DD51
Schoolway, Dag. 236 309 EW62
Schooner Clo. SE16 149 317 DX75
Schubert Rd. SW15 173 323 CZ85
Schubert Rd., Borwd. 204 298 CK44
Sclater St. E1 39 316 DT70
Scoble Pl. N16 117 306 DT63
Scoles Cres. SW2 194 324 DN88
Scoresby St. SE1 60/1 316 DP74
Scorton Ave., Grnf. 122 314 CG68
Scot Gro., Pnr. 214 303 BX52
Scotch Common W13 132 314 CG71
Scoter Clo., Wdf.Grn. 224 308 EH52
Scotland Grn. N17 221 306 DT54
Scotland Grn. Rd., Enf. 210 301 DX43
Scotland Grn. Rd. N., Enf. 203 301 DX42
Scotland Pl. SW1 58/9 316 DL74
Scotney Wk., Horn. 238 310 FK64
Scotsdale Clo., Orp. 277 326 ES98
Scotsdale Clo., Sutt. 292 331 CY108
Scotsdale Rd. SE12 260 326 EH85
Scotswood St. EC1 36 316 DN70
Scotswood Wk. N17 222 307 DU52
Scott Clo. SW16 272 324 DM95
Scott Clo., Epsom 283 330 CQ106
Scott Clo., West Dr. 248 320 BM77
Scott Ct. W3 144 314 CQ75
Scott Cres., Erith 255 319 FF81
Scott Cres., Har. 233 313 CB60
Scott Ellis Gdns. NW8 30 315 DD69
Scott Gdns., Houns. 250 321 BX80
Scott Ho. N18 210 301 DU50
Scott Lidgett Cres. SE16 148 317 DU75
Scott Russell Pl. E14 150 317 EB78
Scott St. E1 128 317 DV70
Scottes La., Dag. 236 309 EX60
Scotts Ave., Brom. 275 325 ED96
Scotts Ave., Sun. 265 328 BS94
Scotts Clo., Horn. 238 310 FJ64
Scotts Clo., Stai. 264 320 BK88
Scotts Dr., Hmptn. 267 329 CB94
Scotts La., Brom. 275 325 ED98
Scotts Rd. E10 104 307 EC60
Scotts Rd. W12 146 315 CV75
Scotts Rd., Brom. 276 326 EG94
Scotts Rd., Sthl. 250 321 BW76
Scotts Way, Sun. 265 328 BS93
Scott's Yd. EC4 62 316 DR73
Scottwell Dr. NW9 217 304 CT57
Scoulding Rd. E16 244 318 EG72
Scouler St. E14 141 317 ED73
Scout App. NW10 109 304 CS63
Scout La. SW4 176 324 DJ83
Scout Way NW7 205 298 CR49
Scovell Cres. SE1 73 316 DQ75
Scovell Rd. SE1 73 316 DQ75
Scrattons Ter., Bark. 246 319 EX67
Scriven St. E8 27 316 DT67
Scrooby St. SE6 182 325 EB86
Scrubs La. NW10 126 315 CU69
Scrubs La. W10 126 315 CU69
Scrutton Clo. SW12 193 324 DK87
Scrutton St. EC2 38/9 316 DS70
Scudamore La. NW9 217 304 CQ56
Scutari Rd. SE22 180 325 DW85
Scylla Cres., Houns. 265 320 BP87
Scylla Rd. SE15 180 325 DV83
Scylla Rd., Houns. 257 320 BP86
Seabright St. E2 128 317 DV69
Seabrook Dr., W.Wick. 289 333 EE103
Seabrook Gdns., Rom. 237 309 FA59
Seabrook Rd., Dag. 236 309 EX62
Seaburn Clo., Rain. 247 319 FE68
Seacole Clo. W3 135 314 CR71
Seacourt Rd. SE2 254 319 EX75
Seafield Rd. N11 208 300 DJ49
Seaford Clo., Ruis. 231 312 BR61
Seaford Rd. E17 223 307 EB55
Seaford Rd. N15 221 306 DR56
Seaford Rd. W13 132 314 CH74
Seaford Rd., Enf. 202 300 DS42
Seaford Rd., Houns. 256 320 BK85
Seaford St. WC1 35 316 DM69
Seaforth Ave., N.Mal. 283 331 CV99
Seaforth Clo., Rom. 227 309 FE52
Seaforth Cres. N5 116 306 DQ64
Seaforth Gdns. N21 208 300 DM45
Seaforth Gdns., Epsom 283 330 CT105
Seaforth Pl. SW1 69 316 DJ76
Seager Pl. E3 139 317 DZ71
Seagrave Rd. SW6 158 315 DA79
Seagry Rd. E11 224 308 EG58
Seal St. E8 117 306 DT63
Sealand Rd., Houns. 257 320 BN86
Sealand Wk., Nthlt. 242 313 BY69
Searle Pl. N4 99 306 DM60
Searles Clo. SW11 159 315 DE80
Searles Rd. SE1 86 316 DR77
Sears St. SE5 163 316 DR80
Seasprite Clo., Nthlt. 242 313 BX69
Seaton Ave., Ilf. 235 308 ES64
Seaton Clo. E13 244 318 EH70
Seaton Clo. SE11 84/5 316 DP78
Seaton Clo. SW15 188 323 CV88
Seaton Clo., Twick. 259 321 CD86
Seaton Dr., Ashf. 264 320 BL89
Seaton Gdns., Ruis. 232 313 BU62
Seaton Pl. NW1 33 316 DJ70
Seaton Pt. E5 118 307 DU63
Seaton Rd., Hayes 249 320 BR77
Seaton Rd., Mitch. 271 323 DE96
Seaton Rd., Twick. 259 321 CC86
Seaton Rd., Well. 254 319 EW80
Seaton Rd., Wem. 123 314 CL68
Seaton St. N18 210 301 DU50
Sebastian St. EC1 36/7 316 DP69
Sebastopol Rd. N9 210 301 DU49
Sebbon St. N1 116 306 DP66
Sebert Rd. E7 234 308 EH64
Sebright Pas. E2 128 317 DU68
Secker Cres., Har. 215 303 CC53
Secker St. SE1 60 316 DN74
Second Ave. E12 234 308 EL63
Second Ave. E13 244 318 EG69
Second Ave. E17 223 307 EA57
Second Ave. N18 210 301 DW49
Second Ave. NW4 218 305 CX56
Second Ave. SW14 171 322 CS83
Second Ave. W3 135 314 CT74
Second Ave. W10 127 315 CY70
Second Ave., Dag. 247 319 FB67
Second Ave., Enf. 209 300 DT43
Second Ave., Hayes 249 312 BT74
Second Ave., Rom. 226 309 EW57
Second Ave., Wem. 91 304 CK61
Second Clo., W.Mol. 267 329 CC98
Second Cross Rd., Twick. 259 321 CD89
Second Way, Wem. 108 304 CP63
Sedan Way SE17 86/7 316 DS78
Sedcombe Clo., Sid. 278 327 EV91
Sedcote Rd., Enf. 210 301 DW43
Sedding St. SW1 80 316 DG77
Seddon Ho. EC2 49 316 DQ71
Seddon Rd., Mord. 285 331 DD99
Seddon St. WC1 35 316 DM69
Sedge Rd. N17 222 307 DW52
Sedgebrook Rd. SE3 252 318 EK82
Sedgecombe Ave., Har. 216 304 CJ57
Sedgeford Rd. W12 135 314 CT74
Sedgehill Rd. SE6 275 325 EA91
Sedgemere Ave. N2 219 305 DC55
Sedgemere Rd. SE2 254 319 EW76
Sedgemoor Dr., Dag. 237 309 FA63
Sedgeway SE6 199 325 EE88
Sedgewick Ave., Uxb. 241 312 BP66
Sedgewood Clo., Brom. 289 333 EF101
Sedgmoor Pl. SE5 163 316 DS80
Sedgwick Rd. E10 104 307 EC61
Sedgwick St. E9 119 307 DX64
Sedleigh Rd. SW18 173 323 CZ86
Sedlescombe Rd. SW6 157 315 CZ79
Sedley Gro., Uxb. 230 312 BJ56
Sedley Pl. W1 44/5 316 DH72
Sedum Clo. NW9 217 304 CP57
Seeley Dr. SE21 273 324 DS91
Seelig Ave. NW9 94 305 CU59
Seely Rd. SW17 272 324 DG93
Seething La. EC3 62/3 316 DS73
Seething Wells La., Surb. 282 330 CJ100
Sefton Ave. NW7 205 298 CR50
Sefton Ave., Har. 215 303 CD53
Sefton Clo., Orp. 277 326 ET98
Sefton Rd., Croy. 287 333 DU102
Sefton Rd., Orp. 277 326 ET98
Sefton St. SW15 172 323 CW83
Sefton Way, Uxb. 248 312 BJ72
Segal Clo. SE23 197 325 DY87
Sekforde St. EC1 36/7 316 DP70
Sekhon Ter., Felt. 259 321 CA90
Selah Dr., Swan. 279 327 FC95
Selan Gdns., Hayes 242 313 BV71
Selbie Ave. NW10 109 304 CT64
Selborne Ave. E12 235 308 EN63
Selborne Ave. E17 222 307 DZ56
Selborne Ave., Bex. 262 327 EY88
Selborne Gdns. NW4 218 305 CU56
Selborne Gdns., Grnf. 122 314 CG68
Selborne Rd. E17 222 307 DZ57
Selborne Rd. N14 208 300 DL48
Selborne Rd. N22 220 306 DM53
Selborne Rd. SE5 163 316 DR82
Selborne Rd., Croy. 287 332 DS104
Selborne Rd., Ilf. 235 308 EN61
Selborne Rd., N.Mal. 269 322 CS96
Selborne Rd., Sid. 278 327 EV91
Selborne Wk. E17 222 307 DY57
Selbourne Ave., Surb. 282 330 CM103
Selby Chase, Ruis. 232 313 BV61
Selby Clo. E6 244 318 EL71
Selby Clo., Chis. 277 326 EN93
Selby Gdns., Sthl. 243 313 CA70
Selby Grn., Cars. 285 331 DE101
Selby Rd. E11 105 307 EE62
Selby Rd. E13 244 318 EH71
Selby Rd. N17 221 306 DS51
Selby Rd. SE20 274 325 DU96
Selby Rd. W5 122 314 CH70
Selby Rd., Ashf. 265 328 BQ93
Selby Rd., Cars. 285 331 DE101
Selby St. E1 128 317 DU70
Selcroft Rd., Pur. 294 332 DP112
Selden Rd. SE15 164 317 DW82
Selden Wk. N7 99 306 DM61
Selhurst Clo. SW19 189 323 CX88
Selhurst New Rd. SE25 287 332 DS100
Selhurst Pl. SE25 287 332 DS100
Selhurst Rd. N9 209 300 DR48
Selhurst Rd. SE25 287 332 DS99
Selinas La., Dag. 236 309 EY59
Selkirk Dr., Erith 255 319 FE81
Selkirk Rd. SW17 271 323 DE91
Selkirk Rd., Twick. 259 321 CC89
Sellers Hall Clo. N3 219 305 DA52
Sellincourt Rd. SW17 271 323 DE92
Sellindge Clo., Beck. 274 325 DZ94
Sellon Ms. SE11 83 316 DM77
Sellons Ave. NW10 125 314 CT67
Sellwood Dr., Barn. 206 299 CX43
Selsdon Ave., S.Croy. 295 332 DR107
Selsdon Clo., Rom. 227 309 FC53
Selsdon Clo., Surb. 282 330 CL99
Selsdon Rd. E11 234 308 EG59
Selsdon Rd. E13 244 318 EJ67
Selsdon Rd. NW2 93 304 CT61
Selsdon Rd. SE27 194 324 DP90
Selsdon Rd., S.Croy. 287 332 DR106
Selsdon Rd. Ind. Est., S.Croy. 295 332 DR107
Selsdon Way E14 150 317 EB76
Selsea Pl. N16 117 306 DS64
Selsey Cres., Well. 254 319 EX81
Selsey St. E14 140 317 EA71
Selvage La. NW7 205 298 CR50
Selway Clo., Pnr. 214 303 BV55
Selwood Clo., Stai. 256 320 BJ86
Selwood Gdns., Stai. 256 320 BJ86
Selwood Pl. SW7 78 315 DD78
Selwood Rd., Chess. 287 330 CK105
Selwood Rd., Croy. 287 333 DV103
Selwood Rd., Sutt. 284 331 CZ102
Selwood Ter. SW7 78 315 DD78
Selworthy Clo. E11 224 308 EG57
Selworthy Rd. SE6 197 325 DZ90
Selwyn Ave. E4 223 307 EC51
Selwyn Ave., Ilf. 225 308 ET58
Selwyn Ave., Rich. 169 322 CL83
Selwyn Clo., Houns. 258 321 BY84
Selwyn Ct. SE3 183 325 EF83
Selwyn Ct., Edg. 217 304 CP52
Selwyn Cres., Well. 262 327 EV83
Selwyn Pl., Orp. 278 327 EV97
Selwyn Rd. E3 129 317 DZ68
Selwyn Rd. E13 244 318 EH67
Selwyn Rd. NW10 109 304 CR66
Selwyn Rd., N.Mal. 283 330 CR99
Semley Gate E9 119 307 DZ65
Semley Pl. SW1 80 316 DG77
Semley Rd. SW16 272 324 DL96
Senate St. SE15 164 317 DW82
Senator Wk. SE28 253 318 ER76
Seneca Rd., Th.Hth. 273 324 DQ98
Senga Rd., Wall. 285 332 DG102
Senhouse Rd., Sutt. 284 331 CX104
Senior St. W2 40/1 315 DB71
Senlac Rd. SE12 260 326 EH88
Sennen Rd., Enf. 209 300 DT45
Sennen Wk. SE9 260 326 EL90
Senrab St. E1 139 317 DX72
Sentinel Clo., Nthlt. 242 313 BY70
Sentinel Sq. NW4 218 305 CW56
Sentis Ct., Nthwd. 213 302 BS51
September Way, Stan. 216 304 CH51
Sequoia Gdns., Orp. 291 334 ET101
Sequoia Pk., Pnr. 215 303 CB51
Serbin Clo. E10 104 307 EC59
Serjeants Inn EC4 48 316 DN72
Serle St. WC2 47 316 DM72
Sermon Dr., Swan. 279 327 FC97
Sermon La. EC4 49 316 DQ72
Serpentine Rd. W2 55 315 DF74
Servaden Dr., Brom. 276 326 EK95
Setchell Rd. SE1 87 316 DT77
Setchell Way SE1 87 316 DT77
Seth St. SE16 148 317 DW75
Seton Gdns., Dag. 236 309 EW66
Settle Pt. E13 244 318 EG68
Settle Rd. E13 244 318 EG68
Settles St. E1 138 317 DU71
Settrington Rd. SW6 158 315 DB82
Seven Acres, Cars. 285 331 DE103
Seven Acres, Nthwd. 214 303 BU51
Seven Clo., Cars. 285 331 DE103
Seven Kings Rd., Ilf. 235 308 ET60
Seven Sisters Rd. N4 100 306 DQ59
Seven Sisters Rd. N7 99 306 DM62
Seven Sisters Rd. N15 221 306 DR58
Seven Stars Cor. W12 146 315 CU76
Sevenoaks Clo., Bexh. 263 327 FB84
Sevenoaks Clo., Sutt. 292 331 DA110
Sevenoaks Ct., Nthwd. 213 302 BQ52
Sevenoaks Ho. SE25 274 325 DU97
Sevenoaks Rd. SE4 181 325 DY86
Sevenoaks Rd., Orp. 291 334 ET105
Sevenoaks Way, Orp. 278 327 EW98
Sevenoaks Way, Sid. 278 327 EW94
Seventh Ave. E12 235 308 EM63
Seventh Ave., Hayes 249 312 BT74
Severn Ave., Rom. 228 310 FH55
Severn Dr., Enf. 203 301 DU38
Severn Dr., Upmin. 229 311 FR58
Severn Way NW10 109 304 CT64
Severnake Clo. E14 150 317 EA77
Severus Rd. SW11 175 323 DE84
Seville Ms. N1 117 306 DS66
Seville St. SW1 67 315 DF75
Sevington Rd. NW4 218 305 CV58
Sevington St. W9 28/9 315 DB70
Seward Rd. W7 142 314 CG75
Seward Rd., Beck. 274 325 DX96
Seward St. EC1 36/7 316 DP70
Sewardstone Gdns. E4 211 301 EB43
Sewardstone Rd. E2 128 317 DW68
Sewardstone Rd. E4 211 301 EB45
Sewdley St. E5 119 307 DX63
Sewell Rd. SE2 254 319 EU75
Sewell St. E13 244 318 EG69
Sextant Ave. E14 151 317 ED77
Sexton Clo., Rain. 247 319 FF67
Seymer Rd., Rom. 227 309 FD55
Seymour Ave. N17 222 307 DU54
Seymour Ave., Mord. 284 331 CX101
Seymour Clo., Pnr. 214 303 BZ53
Seymour Ct. E4 211 301 EF47
Seymour Dr., Brom. 290 334 EM102
Seymour Gdns. SE4 181 325 DY83
Seymour Gdns., Felt. 266 329 BW91
Seymour Gdns., Ilf. 234 308 EM60
Seymour Gdns., Ruis. 213 313 BX60
Seymour Gdns., Surb. 282 330 CM99
Seymour Gdns., Twick. 184 322 CH87
Seymour Ms. W1 44 316 DG72
Seymour Pl. SE25 274 325 DV98
Seymour Pl. W1 42/3 315 DE71
Seymour Rd. E4 211 301 EB46
Seymour Rd. E6 244 318 EK68
Seymour Rd. E10 103 307 DZ60
Seymour Rd. N3 219 305 DB52
Seymour Rd. N8 221 306 DN57
Seymour Rd. N9 210 301 DV47
Seymour Rd. SW18 189 323 CZ87
Seymour Rd. SW19 189 323 CX90
Seymour Rd. W4 144 314 CQ77
Seymour Rd., Cars. 285 332 DG106
Seymour Rd., Hmptn. 267 329 CC92
Seymour Rd., Kings.T. 268 322 CK95
Seymour Rd., Mitch. 285 332 DG101
Seymour St. W1 43 315 DF72
Seymour St. W2 43 315 DF72
Seymour Ter. SE20 274 325 DV95
Seymour Vil. SE20 274 325 DV95
Seymour Wk. SW10 158 315 DC79
Seymour Way, Sun. 265 328 BS94
Seyssel St. E14 150 317 EC77
Shaa Rd. W3 135 314 CR73
Shacklegate La., Tedd. 267 329 CE91
Shackleton Clo. SE23 196 325 DV89
Shackleton Rd., Sthl. 242 313 BZ73

Smithfield St. EC1	48/9	316	DP71
Smithies Ct. E15	120	307	EC64
Smithies Rd. SE2	254	319	EV77
Smith's Ct. W1	57	316	DJ73
Smiths Fm. Est., Nthlt.	243	313	CA68
Smiths Yd. SW18	190	323	DC89
Smith's Yd., Croy.	287	332	DQ104
Smithson Rd. N17	221	306	DR53
Smithwood Clo. SW19	189	323	CY88
Smithy St. E1	138	317	DW71
Smock Wk., Croy.	287	332	DQ100
Smokehouse Yd. EC1	48/9	316	DP71
Smugglers Way SW18	174	323	DB84
Smyrks Rd. SE17	86/7	316	DS78
Smyrna Rd. NW6	112	305	DA66
Smythe St. E14	140	317	EB73
Snakes La. E., Wdf.Grn.	224	308	EJ51
Snakes La. W., Wdf.Grn.	224	308	EG51
Snaresbrook Dr., Stan.	204	298	CK49
Snaresbrook Rd. E11	223	307	EE56
Snarsgate St. W10	136	315	CW71
Sneath Ave. NW11	95	305	CZ59
Snells Pk. N18	221	306	DT51
Sneyd Rd. NW2	110	305	CW63
Snow Hill EC1	48/9	316	DP71
Snow Hill Ct. EC1	48/9	316	DP72
Snowbury Rd. SW6	158	315	DB82
Snowden Ave., Uxb.	241	312	BP68
Snowden St. EC2	38/9	316	DS70
Snowdon Cres., Hayes	249	320	BQ76
Snowdon Dr. NW9	217	304	CS58
Snowdown Clo. SE20	274	325	DX95
Snowdrop Clo., Hmptn.	267	329	CA93
Snowdrop Path, Rom.	228	310	FK52
Snowman Ho. NW6	112	305	DB66
Snowsfields SE1	74	316	DR75
Snowshill Rd. E12	234	308	EL64
Snowy Fielder Waye, Islw.	152	314	CH82
Soames St. SE15	179	324	DT83
Soames Wk., N.Mal.	269	322	CS95
Socket La., Brom.	289	334	EH100
Soham Rd., Enf.	203	301	DZ37
Soho Sq. W1	46	316	DK72
Soho St. W1	46	316	DK72
Sojourner Truth Clo. E8	118	307	DV65
Solander Gdns. E1	138	317	DV73
Solebay St. E1	129	317	DY70
Solent Ri. E13	244	318	EG69
Solent Rd. NW6	112	305	DA64
Solent Rd., Houns.	256	320	BM86
Soley Ms. WC1	36	316	DN69
Solna Ave. SW15	172	323	CW85
Solna Rd. N21	209	300	DR46
Solomon Ave. N9	210	301	DU49
Solomon's Pas. SE15	180	325	DV84
Solon New Rd. SW4	177	324	DL84
Solon New Rd. Est. SW4	177	324	DL84
Solon Rd. SW2	177	324	DL84
Solway Clo. E8	117	306	DT65
Solway Clo., Houns.	258	321	BY83
Solway Rd. N22	221	306	DP53
Solway Rd. SE22	180	325	DU84
Somaford Gro., Barn.	207	299	DD44
Somali Rd. NW2	111	305	CZ64
Somerby Rd., Bark.	235	308	ER66
Somerfield Rd. N4	100	306	DP61
Somerford Clo., Pnr.	214	303	BU56
Somerford Gro. N16	117	306	DT63
Somerford Gro. N17	222	307	DU52
Somerford Gro. Est. N16	117	306	DT63
Somerford St. E1	128	317	DV70
Somerford Way SE16	149	317	DY75
Somerhill Ave., Sid.	262	327	EV87
Somerhill Rd., Well.	254	319	EV82
Somerleyton Pas. SW9	178	324	DP84
Somerleyton Rd. SW9	178	324	DN84
Somers Clo. NW1	22	316	DK68
Somers Cres. W2	42/3	315	DE72
Somers Ms. W2	42/3	315	DE72
Somers Pl. SW2	193	324	DM87
Somers Rd. E17	222	307	DZ56
Somers Rd. SW2	177	324	DM86
Somersby Gdns., Ilf.	224	308	EM57
Somerset Ave. SW20	270	323	CV96
Somerset Ave., Chess.	282	330	CK105
Somerset Ave., Well.	261	326	ET85
Somerset Clo. N17	221	306	DR54
Somerset Clo., N.Mal.	283	330	CS100
Somerset Clo., Wdf.Grn.	224	308	EG53
Somerset Est. SW11	159	315	DD81
Somerset Gdns. N6	98	306	DG59
Somerset Gdns. SE13	166	317	EB82
Somerset Gdns. SW16	272	324	DM97
Somerset Gdns., Horn.	239	311	FN60
Somerset Gdns., Tedd.	267	329	CE92
Somerset Rd. E17	223	307	EA57
Somerset Rd. N17	221	306	DT55
Somerset Rd. N18	209	300	DT50
Somerset Rd. NW4	218	305	CW56
Somerset Rd. SW19	189	323	CX90
Somerset Rd. W4	145	314	CR76
Somerset Rd. W13	132	314	CH74
Somerset Rd., Barn.	207	299	DB43
Somerset Rd., Brent.	153	314	CK79
Somerset Rd., Har.	215	303	CC58
Somerset Rd., Kings.T.	268	322	CM96
Somerset Rd., Orp.	291	335	EU101
Somerset Rd., Sthl.	242	313	BZ72
Somerset Rd., Tedd.	267	329	CE92
Somerset Sq. W14	147	315	CY75
Somerset Waye, Houns.	250	321	BY80
Somersham Rd., Bexh.	254	319	EY82
Somerton Ave., Rich.	170	322	CP83
Somerton Rd. NW2	95	305	CX62
Somerton Rd. SE15	180	325	DV84
Somertrees Ave. SE12	260	326	EH89
Somervell Rd., Har.	232	313	BZ64
Somerville Rd. SE20	274	325	DX94
Somerville Rd., Rom.	226	309	EW58
Sonderburg Rd. N7	99	306	DM61
Sondes St. SE17	163	316	DR79
Sonia Ct., Har.	215	303	CF58
Sonia Gdns. N12	207	299	DC49
Sonia Gdns. NW10	109	304	CT63
Sonia Gdns., Houns.	251	321	CA80
Sonning Gdns., Hmptn.	266	329	BY93
Sonning Rd. SE25	287	333	DU100
Soper Clo. E4	210	301	DZ50
Sophia Clo. N7	115	306	DM65
Sophia Rd. E10	104	307	EB60
Sophia Rd. E16	244	318	EH72
Sophia Sq. SE16	139	317	DY73
Sopwith Ave., Chess.	282	330	CL106
Sopwith Clo., Kings.T.	268	322	CM92
Sopwith Rd., Houns.	250	321	BW80
Sopwith Way SW8	160	316	DH80
Sopwith Way, Kings.T.	268	322	CL95
Sorrel Clo. SE28	246	319	EU74
Sorrel Gdns. E6	244	318	EL71
Sorrel La. E14	141	317	ED72
Sorrel Wk., Rom.	227	309	FF55
Sorrell Clo. SE14	165	317	DY80
Sorrento Rd., Sutt.	284	331	DA104
Sotheby Rd. N5	100	306	DQ62
Sotheran Clo. E8	128	317	DU67
Sotheron Rd. SW6	158	315	DB80
Soudan Rd. SW11	159	315	DF81
Souldern Rd. W14	147	315	CX76
South Access Rd. E17	103	307	DY59
South Acre NW9	217	304	CT54
South Africa Rd. W12	136	315	CV74
South App., Nthwd.	213	302	BR48
South Audley St. W1	56	316	DG73
South Ave. E4	211	301	EB45
South Ave., Cars.	293	332	DG108
South Ave., Rich.	154	314	CN82
South Ave., Sthl.	242	313	BZ73
South Ave. Gdns., Sthl.	242	313	BZ73
South Bank, Chis.	261	326	EQ90
South Bank, Surb.	282	330	CL100
South Bank Ter., Surb.	282	330	CL100
South Birkbeck Rd. E11	105	307	ED62
South Black Lion La. W6	146	315	CU78
South Bolton Gdns. SW5	76/7	315	DB78
South Border, The, Pur.	294	332	DK111
South Carriage Dr. SW1	66/7	315	DE75
South Carriage Dr. SW7	66/7	315	DE75
South Clo. N6	220	306	DH58
South Clo., Bexh.	262	327	EX84
South Clo., Dag.	247	319	FA67
South Clo., Mord.	284	331	DB100
South Clo., Pnr.	232	313	BZ59
South Clo., Twick.	259	321	CA90
South Clo., West Dr.	248	320	BM76
South Colonnade E14	140	317	EA74
South Common Rd., Uxb.	240	312	BL65
South Countess Rd. E17	222	307	DZ55
South Cres. E16	131	317	ED70
South Cres. WC1	46	316	DK71
South Cross Rd., Ilf.	225	308	EQ57
South Croxted Rd. SE21	195	324	DR90
South Dene NW7	205	298	CR48
South Dr., Bans.	293	331	DE113
South Dr., Orp.	291	334	ES106
South Dr., Rom.	228	310	FJ55
South Dr., Ruis.	231	312	BS60
South Dr., Sutt.	292	331	CY110
South Ealing Rd. W5	143	314	CK75
South Eastern Ave. N9	209	300	DT48
South Eaton Pl. SW1	80	316	DG77
South Eden Pk. Rd., Beck.	288	333	EB100
South Edwardes Sq. W8	147	315	CZ76
South End W8	64/5	315	DB76
South End, Croy.	287	332	DQ105
South End Clo. NW3	113	305	DE63
South End Rd. NW3	113	305	DE63
South End Rd., Horn.	238	310	FH65
South End Row W8	64/5	315	DB76
South Esk Rd. E7	234	308	EJ65
South Gdns. SW19	271	323	DD94
South Gate Ave., Felt.	265	328	BR91
South Gipsy Rd., Well.	262	327	EX83
South Glade, The, Bex.	262	327	EZ88
South Grn. NW9	217	304	CS53
South Gro. E17	222	307	DZ57
South Gro. N6	98	306	DG60
South Gro. N15	221	306	DR57
South Gro. Ho. N6	98	306	DG60
South Hill, Chis.	276	326	EM93
South Hill Ave., Har.	233	313	CC62
South Hill Gro., Har.	233	313	CE63
South Hill Pk. NW3	113	305	DE63
South Hill Pk. Gdns. NW3	113	305	DE63
South Hill Rd., Brom.	275	325	EE97
South Huxley N18	209	300	DR50
South Island Pl. SW9	161	316	DM80
South Kensington Sta. Arc. SW7	78	315	DD77
South Lambeth Pl. SW8	161	316	DL79
South Lambeth Rd. SW8	161	316	DL79
South La., Kings.T.	268	322	CK97
South La., N.Mal.	269	322	CR98
South La. W., N.Mal.	269	322	CR98
South Lo. Ave., Mitch.	272	324	DL98
South Mall N9	210	301	DU48
South Mead NW9	217	304	CT53
South Meadows, Wem.	107	304	CM64
South Molton La. W1	44/5	316	DH72
South Molton Rd. E16	244	318	EG72
South Molton St. W1	44/5	316	DH72
South Norwood Hill SE25	273	324	DS95
South Oak Rd. SW16	272	324	DM91
South Par. SW3	78	315	DD78
South Par. W4	145	314	CR77
South Pk. SW6	158	315	DA82
South Pk. Cres. SE6	199	325	EF88
South Pk. Cres., Ilf.	235	308	ER62
South Pk. Dr., Bark.	235	308	ES62
South Pk. Dr., Ilf.	235	308	ES61
South Pk. Gro., N.Mal.	269	322	CQ98
South Pk. Hill Rd., S.Croy.	287	332	DR106
South Pk. Ms. SW6	174	323	DB83
South Pk. Rd. SW19	271	323	DA93
South Pk. Rd., Ilf.	235	308	ER62
South Pk. Ter., Ilf.	235	308	ES62
South Pk. Way, Ruis.	232	313	BW65
South Penge Pk. Est. SE20	274	325	DV96
South Perimeter Rd., Uxb.	240	312	BL69
South Pl. EC2	50	316	DR71
South Pl., Enf.	210	301	DW43
South Pl., Surb.	282	330	CM101
South Pl. Ms. EC2	50	316	DR71
South Ri., Cars.	293	331	DE109
South Ri. Way SE18	253	318	ER78
South Rd. N9	210	301	DU46
South Rd. SE23	197	325	DX89
South Rd. SW19	271	323	DC93
South Rd. W5	143	314	CK77
South Rd., Edg.	217	304	CP53
South Rd., Erith	255	319	FF80
South Rd., Felt.	266	329	BX92
South Rd., Hmptn.	266	329	BY93
South Rd. (Chadwell Heath), Rom.	226	309	EY58
South Rd. (Little Heath), Rom.	226	309	EW57
South Rd., Sthl.	250	321	BZ75
South Rd., Twick.	259	321	CD90
South Rd., West Dr.	249	320	BN76
South Row SE3	167	317	EF82
South Sea St. SE16	149	317	DZ76
South Side W6	145	314	CT76
South Sq. NW11	219	305	DB58
South Sq. WC1	48	316	DN71
South St. W1	56	316	DG74
South St., Brom.	276	326	EG96
South St., Enf.	210	301	DW43
South St., Islw.	168	322	CG83
South St., Rain.	247	319	FC68
South St., Rom.	227	309	FE57
South Tenter St. E1	63	316	DT73
South Ter. SW7	78/9	315	DE77
South Ter., Surb.	282	330	CL100
South Vale SE19	273	324	DS93
South Vale, Har.	233	313	CE63
South Vw., Brom.	276	326	EH96
South Vw. Dr. E18	224	308	EH55
South Vw. Dr., Upmin.	239	311	FN62
South Vw. Rd. N8	220	306	DK55
South Vw. Rd., Pnr.	214	303	BV51
South Vil. NW1	115	306	DK65
South Wk., Hayes	249	312	BR71
South Wk., W.Wick.	289	333	EE104
South Way N9	210	301	DW47
South Way N11	220	306	DJ51
South Way, Brom.	289	334	EG101
South Way, Cars.	293	331	DD110
South Way, Croy.	288	333	DY104
South Way, Har.	215	303	CA56
South Way, Wem.	108	304	CN64
South W. India Dock Entrance E14	150	317	EC75
South Western Rd., Twick.	168	322	CG86
South Wf. Rd. W2	42	315	DD72
South Woodford to Barking Relief Rd. E11	224	308	EJ55
South Woodford to Barking Relief Rd. E12	235	308	EN63
South Woodford to Barking Relief Rd. E18	224	308	EJ55
South Woodford to Barking Relief Rd., Bark.	235	308	EN63
South Woodford to Barking Relief Rd., Ilf.	224	308	EJ55
South Worple Ave. SW14	171	322	CS83
South Worple Way SW14	171	322	CR83
Southacre Way, Pnr.	214	303	BW53
Southall La., Houns.	250	321	BV79
Southall Pl. SE1	74	316	DR75
Southam St. W10	127	315	CY70
Southampton Bldgs. WC2	48	316	DN71
Southampton Gdns., Mitch.	286	332	DL99
Southampton Pl. WC1	46/7	316	DL71
Southampton Rd. NW5	113	305	DF64
Southampton Rd., Houns.	256	320	BL86
Southampton Row WC1	46/7	316	DL71
Southampton St. WC2	58/9	316	DL73
Southampton Way SE5	163	316	DR80
Southborough Clo., Surb.	282	330	CK102
Southborough La., Brom.	290	334	EL99
Southborough Rd. E9	119	307	DX66
Southborough Rd., Brom.	276	326	EL97
Southborough Rd., Surb.	282	330	CL102
Southbourne, Brom.	289	334	EG101
Southbourne Ave. NW9	217	304	CQ54
Southbourne Clo., Pnr.	232	313	BY59
Southbourne Cres. NW4	218	305	CY56
Southbourne Gdns. SE12	260	326	EH85
Southbourne Gdns., Ilf.	235	308	EQ64
Southbourne Gdns., Ruis.	232	313	BV60
Southbridge Pl., Croy.	287	332	DQ105
Southbridge Rd., Croy.	287	332	DQ105
Southbridge Way, Sthl.	250	321	BY75
Southbrook Ms. SE12	183	325	EF86
Southbrook Rd. SE12	183	325	EF86
Southbrook Rd. SW16	272	324	DL95
Southbury Ave., Enf.	210	301	DU43
Southbury Clo., Horn.	238	310	FK64
Southbury Rd., Enf.	202	300	DR41
Southchurch Rd. E6	244	318	EM68
Southcombe St. W14	147	315	CY77
Southcote Ave., Felt.	265	320	BT89
Southcote Ave., Surb.	282	330	CP101
Southcote Ri., Ruis.	231	312	BR59
Southcote Rd. E17	222	307	DX57
Southcote Rd. N19	114	306	DJ63
Southcote Rd. SE25	287	333	DV99
Southcote Rd., S.Croy.	295	332	DS110
Southcroft Ave., Well.	261	326	ES83
Southcroft Ave., W.Wick.	289	333	EC103
Southcroft Rd. SW16	272	324	DH93
Southcroft Rd. SW17	272	324	DG93
Southcroft Rd., Orp.	291	334	ES104
Southdale, Chig.	225	308	ER51
Southdean Gdns. SW19	189	323	CZ89
Southdown Ave. W7	142	314	CG76
Southdown Cres., Har.	233	313	CC60
Southdown Cres., Ilf.	225	308	ES57
Southdown Dr. SW20	270	323	CX94
Southdown Rd. SW20	270	323	CX95
Southdown Rd., Cars.	293	332	DG109
Southdown Rd., Horn.	238	310	FH59
Southend Arterial Rd., Horn.	228	311	FL55
Southend Arterial Rd., Rom.	228	310	FK54
Southend Arterial Rd., Upmin.	229	311	FP56
Southend Clo. SE9	261	326	EP86
Southend Cres. SE9	261	326	EP86
Southend La. SE6	275	325	EA91
Southend La. SE26	274	325	DZ91
Southend Rd. E4	222	307	DZ51
Southend Rd. E6	234	308	EM66
Southend Rd. E17	223	307	ED53
Southend Rd. E18	223	307	EF54
Southend Rd., Beck.	275	325	EA94
Southend Rd., Wdf.Grn.	224	308	EJ54
Southern Ave. SE25	273	324	DT97
Southern Ave., Felt.	258	321	BU88
Southern Gro. E3	129	317	DZ69
Southern Perimeter Rd., Houns.	256	320	BJ85
Southern Pl., Swan.	279	327	FD98
Southern Rd. E13	244	318	EH68
Southern Rd. N2	219	305	DF56
Southern Row W10	127	315	CY70
Southern St. N1	23	316	DM68
Southern Way, Rom.	227	309	FA58
Southerngate Way SE14	165	317	DY80
Southerton Rd. W6	146	315	CW76
Southey Rd. N15	221	306	DS57
Southey Rd. SW9	162	316	DN81
Southey Rd. SW19	271	323	DA94
Southey St. SE20	274	325	DX94
Southfield, Barn.	206	299	CX44
Southfield Clo., Uxb.	241	312	BN69
Southfield Cotts. W7	251	321	CF75
Southfield Gdns., Twick.	267	329	CF91
Southfield Pk., Har.	215	303	CB56
Southfield Rd. N17	221	306	DS54
Southfield Rd. W4	145	314	CR75
Southfield Rd., Chis.	277	326	ET97
Southfield Rd., Enf.	210	301	DV44
Southfields NW4	218	305	CV55
Southfields, Swan.	279	327	FE94
Southfields Ave., Ashf.	265	328	BP93
Southfields Ct. SW19	189	323	CY88
Southfields Pas. SW18	174	323	DA86
Southfields Rd. SW18	174	323	DA86
Southfleet Rd., Orp.	291	334	ES104
Southgate Ave., Felt.	265	328	BR91
Southgate Circ. N14	208	300	DK46
Southgate Gro. N1	117	306	DR66
Southgate Rd. N1	26	316	DR67
Southholme Clo. SE19	273	324	DT95
Southill La., Pnr.	214	303	BV56
Southill Rd., Chis.	276	326	EL93
Southill St. E14	140	317	EB72
Southland Rd. SE18	253	318	ET80
Southland Way, Houns.	259	321	CD85
Southlands Ave., Orp.	291	334	ER105
Southlands Gro., Brom.	276	326	EL97
Southlands Rd., Brom.	290	334	EJ99
Southly Clo., Sutt.	284	331	DA104
Southmead Rd. SW19	189	323	CY88
Southmoor Way E9	119	307	DZ65
Southold Ri. SE9	260	326	EM90
Southolm St. SW11	160	316	DH81
Southover N12	207	299	DA48
Southover, Brom.	276	326	EG92
Southport Rd. SE18	253	318	ER77
Southridge Pl. SW20	270	323	CX94
Southsea Rd., Kings.T.	268	322	CL98
Southside Common SW19	270	323	CW93
Southspring, Sid.	261	326	ER87
Southvale Rd. SE3	167	317	EE82
Southview Ave. NW10	109	304	CT64
Southview Clo. SW17	272	324	DG92
Southview Clo., Bex.	262	327	EZ86
Southview Cres., Ilf.	225	308	EP58
Southview Gdns., Wall.	294	332	DJ108
Southview Rd., Brom.	275	325	ED91
Southville SW8	161	316	DK81
Southville Clo., Felt.	265	320	BS88
Southville Cres., Felt.	265	320	BS88
Southville Rd., Felt.	265	320	BS88
Southwark Bri. EC4	61	316	DQ74
Southwark Bri. SE1	61	316	DQ74
Southwark Bri. Rd. SE1	72/3	316	DP76
Southwark Gro. SE1	61	316	DQ74
Southwark Pk. Est. SE16	148	317	DV77
Southwark Pk. Rd. SE16	87	316	DT77
Southwark Pl., Brom.	276	326	EM97
Southwark St. SE1	60/1	316	DP74
Southwater Clo. E14	139	317	DZ72
Southwater Clo., Beck.	275	325	EB94
Southway N20	207	299	DA47
Southway NW7	218	305	CU52
Southway NW11	219	305	DB57
Southway SW20	270	323	CW98
Southway, Wall.	286	332	DJ105
Southwell Ave., Nthlt.	233	313	CA65
Southwell Gdns. SW7	77	315	DC77
Southwell Gro. Rd. E11	105	307	EE61
Southwell Rd. SE5	178	324	DQ83
Southwell Rd., Croy.	286	332	DN100
Southwell Rd., Har.	216	304	CK58
Southwest Rd. E11	105	307	ED60
Southwick Ms. W2	42	315	DD72
Southwick Pl. W2	42/3	315	DE72
Southwick St. W2	42/3	315	DE72
Southwold Dr., Bark.	236	309	EU64
Southwold Rd. E5	102	307	DV61
Southwold Rd., Bex.	263	327	FB86
Southwood Ave. N6	98	306	DH59
Southwood Ave., Kings.T.	269	322	CQ95
Southwood Clo., Brom.	276	326	EM98
Southwood Clo., Wor.Pk.	284	331	CX102
Southwood Dr., Surb.	283	330	CQ101
Southwood Gdns., Ilf.	225	308	EP56
Southwood La. N6	98	306	DG59
Southwood Lawn Rd. N6	98	306	DG59
Southwood Rd. SE9	261	326	EP89
Southwood Rd. SE28	246	319	EV74
Southwood Smith St. N1	24	316	DN67
Soval Ct., Nthwd.	213	302	BR52
Sovereign Clo. E1	138	317	DV73
Sovereign Clo. W5	132	314	CJ71
Sovereign Clo., Ruis.	231	312	BS60
Sovereign Ct., Brom.	290	334	EM99
Sovereign Ct., W.Mol.	266	329	BZ98
Sovereign Cres. SE16	139	317	DY74
Sovereign Gro., Wem.	91	304	CK62
Sovereign Ms. E2	27	316	DT68
Sovereign Pk. NW10	124	314	CP70
Sovereign Rd., Bark.	246	319	EW69
Sowerby Clo. SE9	260	326	EL85
Sowrey Ave., Rain.	237	309	FF65
Spa Clo. SE25	273	324	DS95
Spa Grn. Est. EC1	36	316	DN69
Spa Hill SE19	273	324	DR95
Spa Rd. SE16	75	316	DT76
Space Waye, Felt.	258	321	BU85
Spafield St. EC1	36	316	DN70
Spalding Rd. NW4	218	305	CW58
Spalding Rd. SW17	272	324	DH92
Spanby Rd. E3	130	317	EA70
Spaniards Clo. NW11	97	305	DD60
Spaniards End NW3	96	305	DC60
Spaniards Rd. NW3	96	305	DC62
Spanish Pl. W1	44	316	DG72
Spanish Rd. SW18	174	323	DC85
Sparkbridge Rd., Har.	215	303	CE56
Sparks Clo. W3	135	314	CR72
Sparks Clo., Dag.	236	309	EX61
Sparks Clo., Hmptn.	266	329	BY93
Sparrow Clo., Hmptn.	266	329	BY93
Sparrow Dr., Orp.	291	334	EQ102
Sparrow Fm. Dr., Felt.	258	321	BW86
Sparrow Fm. Rd., Epsom	283	331	CU105
Sparrow Grn., Dag.	237	309	FB62
Sparrows La. SE9	261	326	EQ87
Sparsholt Rd. N19	99	306	DM60
Sparsholt Rd., Bark.	245	318	ES67
Sparta St. SE10	166	317	EC81
Spear Ms. SW5	76	315	DA77
Spearman St. SE18	253	318	EN79
Spearpoint Gdns., Ilf.	225	308	ET56
Spears Rd. N19	99	306	DL60
Speart La., Houns.	250	321	BY80
Spedan Clo. NW3	96	305	DB62
Speed Ho. EC2	50	316	DR71
Speedbird Way, West Dr.	256	320	BH80
Speedwell St. SE8	166	317	EA80
Speedy Pl. WC1	34/5	316	DL69
Speke Ho. SE5	162	316	DQ80
Speke Rd., Th.Hth.	273	324	DR96
Spekehill SE9	260	326	EM90
Speldhurst Clo., Brom.	289	334	EG99
Speldhurst Rd. E9	119	307	DX66
Speldhurst Rd. W4	145	314	CR76
Spellbrook Wk. N1	25	316	DQ67
Spelman St. E1	138	317	DU71
Spelthorne Gro., Sun.	265	328	BT94
Spelthorne La., Ashf.	281	328	BQ95
Spence Clo. SE16	149	317	DZ75
Spencer Ave. N13	220	306	DM51
Spencer Ave., Hayes	242	313	BU71
Spencer Clo. N3	219	305	DA54
Spencer Clo. NW10	123	314	CM69
Spencer Clo., Orp.	291	334	ES103
Spencer Clo., Uxb.	240	312	BJ69
Spencer Ct. NW8	17	315	DC68
Spencer Dr. N2	219	305	DC58
Spencer Gdns. SE9	260	326	EM85
Spencer Gdns. SW14	170	322	CQ85
Spencer Hill SW19	270	323	CY93
Spencer Hill Rd. SW19	270	323	CY94
Spencer Ms. W6	157	315	CY79
Spencer Pk. SW18	175	323	DD85
Spencer Pas. E2	128	317	DV68
Spencer Pl. N1	116	306	DP66
Spencer Pl., Croy.	287	332	DR101
Spencer Ri. NW5	114	306	DH63
Spencer Rd. E6	244	318	EK67
Spencer Rd. E17	223	307	EC54
Spencer Rd. N8	220	306	DM57
Spencer Rd. N11	208	300	DH49
Spencer Rd. N17	222	307	DU53
Spencer Rd. SW18	175	323	DD84
Spencer Rd. SW20	270	323	CV95
Spencer Rd. W3	134	314	CQ74
Spencer Rd. W4	154	314	CQ80
Spencer Rd., Brom.	275	325	EF94
Spencer Rd., E.Mol.	267	329	CD98
Spencer Rd., Har.	215	303	CE54
Spencer Rd., Ilf.	235	308	ET60
Spencer Rd., Islw.	251	321	CC81
Spencer Rd., Mitch.	272	324	DG97
Spencer Rd. (Beddington), Mitch.	285	332	DG101
Spencer Rd., Rain.	247	319	FD69
Spencer Rd., S.Croy.	287	332	DS106
Spencer Rd., Twick.	259	321	CE90
Spencer Rd., Wem.	90	304	CJ61
Spencer St. EC1	36/7	316	DP69
Spencer St., Sthl.	250	321	BX75
Spencer Wk. NW3	112	305	DC63
Spencer Wk. SW15	173	323	CX84
Spenser Cres., Upmin.	239	311	FQ59
Spenser Gro. N16	117	306	DS63
Spenser Rd. SE24	178	324	DN85
Spenser St. SW1	69	316	DJ76
Spensley Wk. N16	101	306	DR62
Speranza St. SE18	253	318	ET78
Sperling Rd. N17	221	306	DS54
Spert St. E14	139	317	DY73
Spey St. E14	140	317	EC71
Spey Way, Rom.	227	309	FE52
Speyside N14	208	300	DJ44
Spezia Rd. NW10	126	315	CU68
Spicer Clo. SW9	162	316	DP82
Spice's Yd., Croy.	287	332	DQ105
Spiers Clo., N.Mal.	283	330	CT100
Spigurnell Rd. N17	221	306	DR53
Spikes Bri. Rd., Sthl.	242	313	BY72
Spilsby Clo. NW9	217	304	CS54
Spilsby Rd., Rom.	228	310	FK52
Spindlewood Gdns., Croy.	287	332	DS105
Spindrift Ave. E14	150	317	EA77
Spinel Clo. SE18	253	318	ET78
Spingate Clo., Horn.	238	310	FK64
Spinnells Rd., Har.	232	313	BZ60
Spinney, The N21	209	300	DN45
Spinney, The SW16	192	324	DJ90
Spinney, The, Pur.	294	332	DP111
Spinney, The, Sid.	278	327	EY91
Spinney, The, Stan.	204	298	CL49
Spinney, The, Sun.	266	329	BU95
Spinney, The, Sutt.	284	331	CW105
Spinney, The, Swan.	279	327	FE96
Spinney, The, Wem.	90	304	CG62
Spinney Clo., N.Mal.	283	330	CS99
Spinney Clo., Rain.	247	319	FE68
Spinney Clo., West Dr.	248	312	BL73
Spinney Dr., Felt.	265	320	BQ87
Spinney Gdns. SE19	273	324	DT92
Spinney Gdns., Dag.	236	309	EY64
Spinney Oak, Brom.	276	326	EL96
Spinneys, The, Brom.	276	326	EM96
Spirit Quay E1	138	317	DU74
Spital Sq. E1	50/1	316	DS71
Spital St. E1	138	317	DU71
Spital Yd. E1	50/1	316	DS71
Spitalfields Mkt. E1	51	316	DT71
Spitfire Est., Houns.	250	321	BW78
Spitfire Way, Houns.	250	321	BW78
Splendour Wk. SE16	148	317	DW78
Spode Wk. NW6	112	305	DB65
Spondon Rd. N15	222	307	DU56
Spoonbill Way, Hayes	242	313	BX71
Spooner Wk., Wall.	286	332	DK106
Sportsbank St. SE6	198	325	EC87
Spottons Gro. N17	221	306	DQ53
Spout Hill, Croy.	288	333	EA106
Spout La., Stai.	256	320	BG85
Spout La. N., Stai.	256	320	BH84
Spratt Hall Rd. E11	224	308	EG58
Spray La., Twick.	259	321	CE86
Spray St. SE18	253	318	EP77
Spreighton Rd., W.Mol.	267	329	CB98
Sprimont Pl. SW3	79	315	DF77
Spring Bri. Ms. W5	133	314	CK73
Spring Bri. Rd. W5	133	314	CK73
Spring Clo., Barn.	206	299	CX43
Spring Clo., Dag.	236	309	EX60
Spring Clo., Uxb.	212	302	BK53
Spring Clo. La., Sutt.	292	331	CY107
Spring Cotts., Surb.	282	330	CK99
Spring Ct., Sid.	262	327	EU90
Spring Ct. Rd., Enf.	202	300	DN38
Spring Dr., Pnr.	214	303	BU58
Spring Gdns. N5	116	306	DQ64
Spring Gdns. SW1	58	316	DK74
Spring Gdns., Horn.	238	310	FH63
Spring Gdns., Rom.	227	309	FC57
Spring Gdns., Wall.	286	332	DJ106
Spring Gdns., Wdf.Grn.	224	308	EJ52
Spring Gdns. Ind. Est., Rom.	227	309	FC57
Spring Gro. SE19	273	324	DT94
Spring Gro. W4	144	314	CN78
Spring Gro., Hmptn.	267	329	CB95
Spring Gro., Mitch.	272	324	DG95
Spring Gro. Cres., Houns.	251	321	CC81
Spring Gro. Rd., Houns.	251	321	CB81
Spring Gro. Rd., Islw.	251	321	CD81
Spring Gro. Rd., Rich.	169	322	CM85
Spring Hill E5	102	307	DU59
Spring Hill SE26	274	325	DW91
Spring Lake, Stan.	204	298	CH49
Spring La. E5	102	307	DV59
Spring La. N10	220	306	DG55
Spring La. SE25	287	333	DV100
Spring Ms. W1	43	315	DF71
Spring Pk. Ave., Croy.	288	333	DX103
Spring Pk. Dr. N4	100	306	DQ60
Spring Pk. Rd., Croy.	288	333	DX103
Spring Pas. SW15	173	323	CX83
Spring Path NW3	113	305	DD64
Spring Pl. NW5	114	306	DH64
Spring Rd., Felt.	265	320	BT90
Spring Shaw Rd., Orp.	278	327	EU95
Spring St. W2	42	315	DD72
Spring Ter., Rich.	169	322	CL85
Spring Vale, Bexh.	263	327	FB84
Spring Vale Clo., Swan.	279	327	FF94
Spring Vil. Rd., Edg.	217	304	CN52
Spring Wk. E1	138	317	DU71
Springall St. SE15	164	317	DV80
Springbank N21	208	300	DM44
Springbank Ave., Horn.	238	310	FJ64
Springbank Rd. SE13	183	325	ED86
Springbank Wk. NW1	115	306	DK66
Springbourne Ct., Beck.	275	325	EC95
Springclose La., Sutt.	292	331	CY107
Springcroft Ave. N2	219	305	DF56
Springdale Ms. N16	117	306	DR63
Springdale Rd. N16	117	306	DR63
Springfield E5	102	307	DV60
Springfield Ave. N10	220	306	DJ55
Springfield Ave. SW20	270	323	CZ97
Springfield Ave., Hmptn.	267	329	CB93
Springfield Ave., Swan.	279	327	FF98
Springfield Clo. N12	207	299	DB50
Springfield Clo., Stan.	204	298	CG48
Springfield Dr., Ilf.	225	308	EQ58
Springfield Gdns. E5	102	307	DV60
Springfield Gdns. NW9	217	304	CR57
Springfield Gdns., Brom.	276	326	EM98
Springfield Gdns., Ruis.	232	313	BV60
Springfield Gdns., Upmin.	239	311	FP62
Springfield Gdns., W.Wick.	288	333	EB103
Springfield Gdns., Wdf.Grn.	224	308	EJ52
Springfield Gro. SE7	252	318	EJ79
Springfield Gro., Sun.	281	328	BT95
Springfield La. NW6	16/7	315	DB67
Springfield Mt. NW9	217	304	CR57
Springfield Pl., N.Mal.	269	322	CQ98
Springfield Ri. SE26	196	325	DV90
Springfield Rd. E4	211	301	EE46
Springfield Rd. E6	234	308	EM66
Springfield Rd. E15	131	317	EE69
Springfield Rd. E17	222	307	DZ58
Springfield Rd. N11	208	300	DH50
Springfield Rd. N15	222	307	DU56
Springfield Rd. NW8	17	315	DC67
Springfield Rd. SE26	274	325	DV92
Springfield Rd. SW19	270	323	CZ92
Springfield Rd. W7	243	313	CE74
Springfield Rd., Ashf.	264	328	BM92
Springfield Rd., Bexh.	263	327	FB83
Springfield Rd., Brom.	276	326	EM98
Springfield Rd., Epsom	292	331	CW110
Springfield Rd., Har.	215	303	CE58
Springfield Rd., Hayes	242	313	BW74
Springfield Rd., Kings.T.	268	322	CL97
Springfield Rd., Tedd.	268	322	CG92
Springfield Rd., Th.Hth.	273	324	DQ95
Springfield Rd., Twick.	259	321	CA88
Springfield Rd., Wall.	285	332	DG106
Springfield Rd., Well.	262	327	EV83
Springfield Wk. NW6	16/7	315	DB67
Springfield Wk., Orp.	291	334	ER102
Springfields Clo., Cher.	280	328	BH102
Springhead Rd., Erith	255	319	FF79
Springhill Clo. SE5	179	324	DR83
Springhurst Clo., Croy.	288	333	DZ105
Springpark Dr., Beck.	275	325	EC97
Springpond Rd., Dag.	236	309	EY64
Springrice Rd. SE13	183	325	ED86
Springvale Ave., Brent.	143	314	CL78
Springvale Est. W14	147	315	CY76
Springvale Ter. W14	147	315	CX76
Springvale Way, Orp.	278	327	EW97
Springwater Clo. SE18	253	318	EN81
Springwell Ave. NW10	125	314	CT67
Springwell Ave., Rick.	212	302	BG47
Springwell Clo. SW16	273	324	DN91
Springwell Ct., Houns.	250	321	BX82
Springwell La., Rick.	212	302	BG47
Springwell La., Uxb.	212	302	BH50
Springwell Rd. SW16	273	324	DN91
Springwell Rd., Houns.	250	321	BX82
Springwood Clo., Uxb.	212	302	BK53
Springwood Cres., Edg.	205	298	CP47
Springwood Way, Rom.	228	310	FG57
Sprowston Ms. E7	234	308	EG65
Sprowston Rd. E7	234	308	EG64
Spruce Ct. W5	143	314	CL76
Spruce Hills Rd. E17	223	307	EC54
Spruce Pk., Brom.	275	325	EF98
Sprucedale Clo., Swan.	279	327	FE96
Sprucedale Gdns., Croy.	288	333	DX105
Sprucedale Gdns., Wall.	294	332	DK109
Sprules Rd. SE4	165	317	DY82
Spur Rd. N15	221	306	DR56
Spur Rd. SE1	71	316	DM75
Spur Rd. SW1	69	316	DJ75
Spur Rd., Bark.	245	318	EQ69
Spur Rd., Edg.	204	298	CL49
Spur Rd., Felt.	258	321	BV85
Spur Rd., Islw.	152	314	CH80
Spur Rd., Orp.	291	335	EU103
Spur Rd. Est., Edg.	204	298	CM49
Spurfield, W.Mol.	267	329	CB97
Spurgeon Ave. SE19	273	324	DR95
Spurgeon Rd. SE19	273	324	DR95
Spurgeon St. SE1	74	316	DR76
Spurling Rd. SE22	179	324	DT84
Spurling Rd., Dag.	236	309	EZ65
Spurrell Ave., Bex.	279	327	FD91
Spurstowe Rd. E8	118	307	DV65
Spurstowe Ter. E8	118	307	DV64
Squadrons App., Horn.	238	310	FJ65
Square, The W6	146	315	CW78
Square, The, Cars.	285	332	DG106
Square, The, Hayes	249	312	BR74
Square, The, Ilf.	235	308	EN59
Square, The, Rich.	169	322	CK85
Square, The, Swan.	279	327	FD97
Square, The, West Dr.	256	320	BH81
Square Rigger Row SW11	174	323	DC83
Squarey St. SW17	190	323	DC90
Squires Bri. Rd., Shep.	280	328	BM98
Squires Ct. SW19	271	323	DA91
Squires Ct., Cher.	280	328	BH102
Squires Fld., Swan.	279	327	FF95
Squires La. N3	219	305	DB54
Squires Mt. NW3	97	305	DD62
Squires Rd., Shep.	280	328	BM98
Squires Wk., Ashf.	265	328	BR94
Squires Way, Dart.	279	327	FD91
Squires Wd. Dr., Chis.	276	326	EM94
Squirrel Clo., Houns.	258	321	BW83
Squirrels, The SE13	183	325	ED83
Squirrels, The, Pnr.	214	303	BZ55
Squirrels Clo. N12	207	299	DC49
Squirrels Clo., Uxb.	241	312	BN66
Squirrels Grn., Wor.Pk.	283	331	CU103
Squirrels Heath Ave., Rom.	228	310	FH55
Squirrels Heath La., Horn.	228	310	FK56
Squirrels Heath La., Rom.	228	310	FJ56
Squirrels Heath Rd., Rom.	228	311	FL55
Squirrels Ms. W13	132	314	CG73

Stour Rd. E3 120 307 EA66
Stour Rd., Dag. 237 309 FA61
Stour Way, Upmin. 229 311 FS58
Stourcliffe St. W1 43 315 DF72
Stourhead Clo. SW19 189 323 CX87
Stourhead Gdns. SW20 270 323 CU97
Stourton Ave., Felt. 266 329 BZ91
Stow Cres. E17 222 307 DY52
Stowage SE8 166 317 EA79
Stowe Cres., Ruis. 231 302 BP58
Stowe Gdns. N9 209 300 DT46
Stowe Pl. N15 221 306 DS55
Stowe Rd. W12 146 315 CV75
Stowe Rd., Orp. 291 335 EV105
Stowting Rd., Orp. 291 334 ES105
Stox Mead, Har. 215 303 CD53
Stracey Rd. E7 234 308 EG63
Stracey Rd. NW10 125 314 CR67
Strachan Pl. SW19 270 323 CW93
Stradbroke Dr., Chig. 225 308 EN51
Stradbroke Gro., Ilf. 224 308 EL55
Stradbroke Pk., Chig. 225 308 EP51
Stradbroke Rd. N5 116 306 DQ63
Stradella Rd. SE24 178 324 DQ86
Strafford Ave., Ilf. 225 308 EN54
Strafford Rd. W3 144 314 CQ75
Strafford Rd., Houns. 258 321 BZ83
Strafford Rd., Twick. 184 322 CG87
Strafford St. E14 150 317 EA75
Strahan Rd. E3 129 317 DY69
Straight, The, Sthl. 250 321 BX75
Straightsmouth SE10 166 317 EC80
Strait Rd. E6 244 318 EL73
Straker's Rd. SE15 180 325 DV84
Strand WC2 58/9 316 DL73
Strand La. WC2 59 316 DM73
Strand on the Grn. W4 154 314 CN79
Strand Pl. N18 209 300 DS49
Strand Sch. App. W4 154 314 CN79
Strandfield Clo. SE18 253 318 ES78
Strangways Ter. W14 147 315 CZ76
Stranraer Rd., Houns. 256 320 BL86
Stranraer Way N1 115 306 DL66
Strasburg Rd. SW11 160 316 DH81
Stratfield Pk. Clo. N21 209 300 DP45
Stratford Ave. W8 64 315 DA76
Stratford Ave., Uxb. 240 312 BM68
Stratford Cen., The E15 121 307 ED66
Stratford Clo., Bark. 236 309 EU66
Stratford Clo., Dag. 237 309 FC66
Stratford Ct., N.Mal. 269 322 CR98
Stratford Gro. SW15 173 323 CX84
Stratford Ho. Ave., Brom. 276 326 EL97
Stratford Mkt. E15 131 317 ED67
Stratford Pl. W1 44/5 316 DH72
Stratford Rd. E13 131 317 EF67
Stratford Rd. W3 144 314 CQ75
Stratford Rd. W8 64 315 DA76
Stratford Rd., Hayes 242 313 BV70
Stratford Rd., Houns. 257 320 BP86
Stratford Rd., Sthl. 250 321 BY77
Stratford Rd., Th.Hth. 273 324 DN98
Stratford Vil. NW1 114 306 DJ66
Strath Ter. SW11 175 323 DE84
Strathan Clo. SW18 173 323 CY86
Strathaven Rd. SE12 260 326 EH86
Strathblaine Rd. SW11 175 323 DD85
Strathbrook Rd. SW16 272 324 DM94
Strathcona Rd., Wem. 91 304 CK61
Strathdale SW16 272 324 DM92
Strathdon Dr. SW17 191 323 DD90
Strathearn Ave., Hayes 257 320 BT80
Strathearn Ave., Twick. 259 321 CB88
Strathearn Pl. W2 54/5 315 DE73
Strathearn Rd. SW19 271 323 DA92
Strathearn Rd., Sutt. 284 331 DA106
Stratheden Par. SE3 252 318 EG80
Stratheden Rd. SE3 252 318 EG81
Strathfield Gdns., Bark. 235 308 ER65
Strathleven Rd. SW2 177 324 DL84
Strathmore Gdns. N3 219 305 DB53
Strathmore Gdns. W8 52 315 DA74
Strathmore Gdns., Edg. 217 304 CP54
Strathmore Gdns., Horn. 237 309 FF60
Strathmore Rd. SW19 190 323 DA90
Strathmore Rd., Croy. 287 332 DQ101
Strathmore Rd., Tedd. 267 329 CE91
Strathnairn St. SE1 148 317 DU77
Strathray Gdns. NW3 113 305 DE65
Strathville Rd. SW18 190 323 DA89
Strathyre Ave. SW16 273 324 DN97
Stratton Ave., Enf. 202 300 DR37
Stratton Ave., Wall. 294 332 DK109
Stratton Clo. SW19 271 323 DA96
Stratton Clo., Bexh. 262 327 EY83
Stratton Clo., Edg. 216 304 CM51
Stratton Clo., Houns. 250 321 BZ81
Stratton Dr., Bark. 235 308 ET64
Stratton Gdns., Sthl. 242 313 BZ72
Stratton Rd. SW19 271 323 DA96
Stratton Rd., Bexh. 262 327 EY83
Stratton Rd., Sun. 281 328 BT96
Stratton St. W1 56/7 316 DH74
Strattondale St. E14 150 317 EC76
Strauss Rd. W4 145 314 CR75
Strawberry Flds., Swan. 279 327 FE95
Strawberry Hill, Twick. 259 321 CF90
Strawberry Hill Clo., Twick. 267 329 CF91
Strawberry Hill Rd., Twick. 259 321 CF90
Strawberry La., Cars. 285 331 DF104
Strawberry Vale N2 219 305 DD53
Strawberry Vale, Twick. 259 321 CF90
Strayfield Rd., Enf. 202 300 DP37
Streakes Fld. Rd. NW2 94 305 CU61
Stream La., Edg. 205 298 CP50
Stream Way, Belv. 254 319 EZ79
Streamdale SE2 254 319 EU79
Streamside Clo. N9 209 300 DT46
Streamside Clo., Brom. 276 326 EG98
Streatfield Ave. E6 244 318 EM67
Streatfield Rd., Har. 216 304 CL55
Streatham Clo. SW16 193 324 DL90
Streatham Common N. SW16 272 324 DL92
Streatham Common S. SW16 272 324 DL93
Streatham Ct. SW16 193 324 DL90
Streatham High Rd. SW16 272 324 DL92
Streatham Hill SW2 193 324 DL89
Streatham Pl. SW2 193 324 DL87
Streatham Rd. SW16 272 324 DG95
Streatham Rd., Mitch. 272 324 DG95
Streatham St. WC1 46/7 316 DL72
Streatham Vale SW16 272 324 DJ95
Streathbourne Rd. SW17 192 324 DG89
Streatley Pl. NW3 112 305 DC63
Streatley Rd. NW6 111 305 CZ66
Streeters La., Wall. 286 332 DK104
Streetfield Ms. SE3 260 326 EG83
Streimer Rd. E15 130 317 EC68
Strelley Way W3 135 314 CS73
Stretton Rd., Croy. 287 332 DS101
Stretton Rd., Rich. 184 322 CJ89
Strickland Rd., Belv. 255 319 FA77
Strickland Row SW18 191 323 DD87
Strickland St. SE8 166 317 EA81
Strickland Way, Orp. 291 334 ET105
Stride Rd. E13 131 317 EF68
Strode Clo. N10 220 306 DG52
Strode Rd. E7 234 308 EG63
Strode Rd. N17 221 306 DS54
Strode Rd. NW10 110 305 CU65
Strode Rd. SW6 157 315 CY80
Strodes Cres., Stai. 264 328 BJ92
Strone Rd. E7 234 308 EJ65
Strone Rd. E12 234 308 EK65
Strone Way, Hayes 242 313 BY70
Strongbow Cres. SE9 260 326 EM85
Strongbow Rd. SE9 260 326 EM85
Strongbridge Clo., Har. 233 313 CA60
Stronsa Rd. W12 145 314 CT75
Strood Ave., Rom. 237 309 FD60
Stroud Cres. SW15 188 323 CU90
Stroud Fld., Nthlt. 232 313 BY65
Stroud Gate, Har. 233 313 CB63
Stroud Grn. Gdns., Croy. 288 333 DW101
Stroud Grn. Rd. N4 99 306 DM60
Stroud Grn. Way, Croy. 287 333 DV101
Stroud Rd. SE25 287 333 DU100
Stroud Rd. SW19 190 323 DA90
Stroud Way, Ashf. 265 328 BP93
Stroudes Clo., Wor.Pk. 283 330 CS101
Stroudley Wk. E3 130 317 EB69
Strouts Pl. E2 39 316 DT69
Strutton Grd. SW1 70 316 DK76
Strype St. E1 51 316 DT71
Stuart Ave. NW9 94 305 CU59
Stuart Ave. W5 133 314 CM74
Stuart Ave., Brom. 289 334 EG102
Stuart Ave., Har. 232 313 BZ62
Stuart Clo., Swan. 279 327 FF94
Stuart Clo., Uxb. 241 312 BN65
Stuart Ct. (Elstree), Borwd. 204 298 CK44
Stuart Cres. N22 220 306 DM53
Stuart Cres., Croy. 288 333 DZ105
Stuart Cres., Hayes 249 312 BQ72
Stuart Evans Clo., Well. 262 327 EW83
Stuart Gro., Tedd. 267 329 CE92
Stuart Mantle Way, Erith 255 319 FD80
Stuart Pl., Mitch. 271 323 DF95
Stuart Rd. NW6 28 315 DA69
Stuart Rd. SE15 180 325 DW84
Stuart Rd. SW19 190 323 DA90
Stuart Rd. W3 134 314 CQ74
Stuart Rd., Bark. 235 308 ET66
Stuart Rd., Barn. 207 299 DE45
Stuart Rd., Har. 215 303 CF55
Stuart Rd., Rich. 184 322 CH89
Stuart Rd., Th.Hth. 273 324 DQ98
Stuart Rd., Well. 254 319 EV81
Stuart Twr. W9 29 315 DC69
Stuart Way, Stai. 264 328 BH93
Stubbers La., Upmin. 239 311 FR65
Stubbs Dr. SE16 148 317 DV78
Stubbs Ms., Dag. 236 309 EV63
Stubbs Pt. E13 244 318 EG70
Stubbs Way SW19 271 323 DD95
Stucley Pl. NW1 114 306 DH66
Stucley Rd., Houns. 251 321 CC80
Studd St. N1 24/5 316 DP67
Studdridge St. SW6 158 315 DA82
Studholme Ct. NW3 112 305 DA63
Studholme St. SE15 164 317 DV80
Studio Pl. SW1 67 315 DF75
Studios Rd., Shep. 280 328 BM97
Studland SE17 86 316 DR78
Studland Clo., Sid. 261 326 ET90
Studland Rd. SE26 274 325 DX92
Studland Rd. W7 243 313 CD72
Studland Rd., Kings.T. 268 322 CL93
Studland St. W6 146 315 CV77
Studley Ave. E4 223 307 ED52
Studley Clo. E5 119 307 DY64
Studley Ct., Sid. 278 327 EV92
Studley Dr., Ilf. 224 308 EK58
Studley Est. SW4 161 316 DL81
Studley Gra. Rd. W7 251 321 CE75
Studley Rd. E7 234 308 EH65
Studley Rd. SW4 161 316 DL81
Studley Rd., Dag. 236 309 EX66
Stukeley Rd. E7 234 308 EH66
Stukeley St. WC2 46/7 316 DL72
Stumps Hill La., Beck. 275 325 EA93
Sturdy Rd. SE15 164 317 DV82
Sturge Ave. E17 223 307 EB53
Sturge St. SE1 73 316 DQ75
Sturgeon Rd. SE17 84/5 316 DP78
Sturges Fld., Chis. 277 326 ER93
Sturgess Ave. NW4 94 305 CU59
Sturmer Way N7 115 306 DM64
Sturminster Clo., Hayes 242 313 BW72
Sturrock Clo. N15 221 306 DR56
Sturry St. E14 140 317 EB72
Sturt St. N1 25 316 DQ68
Stutfield St. E1 138 317 DU72
Styles Gdns. SW9 178 324 DP83
Styles Way, Beck. 275 325 EC98
Sudbourne Rd. SW2 177 324 DL85
Sudbrook Gdns., Rich. 185 322 CL90
Sudbrook La., Rich. 185 322 CL88
Sudbrooke Rd. SW12 175 323 DF86
Sudbury E6 245 318 EN72
Sudbury Ave., Wem. 106 304 CJ64
Sudbury Ct. E5 119 307 DY63
Sudbury Ct. Dr., Har. 233 313 CF62
Sudbury Ct. Rd., Har. 233 313 CF62
Sudbury Cres., Brom. 276 326 EG93
Sudbury Cres., Wem. 106 304 CH64
Sudbury Cft., Wem. 233 313 CF63
Sudbury Gdns., Croy. 287 332 DS105
Sudbury Hts. Ave., Grnf. 233 313 CF64
Sudbury Hill, Har. 233 313 CE61
Sudbury Hill Clo., Wem. 233 313 CF63
Sudbury Rd., Bark. 235 308 ET64
Sudeley St. N1 24/5 316 DP68
Sudlow Rd. SW18 174 323 DA85
Sudrey St. SE1 73 316 DQ75
Suez Ave., Grnf. 243 313 CF68
Suez Rd., Enf. 203 301 DY42
Suffield Rd. E4 211 301 EB48
Suffield Rd. N15 221 306 DT57
Suffield Rd. SE20 274 325 DW96
Suffolk Clo., Borwd. 205 298 CR43
Suffolk Ct. E10 104 307 EA59
Suffolk Ct., Ilf. 225 308 ES58
Suffolk La. EC4 62 316 DR73
Suffolk Pk. Rd. E17 222 307 DY56
Suffolk Pl. SW1 58 316 DK74
Suffolk Rd. E13 244 318 EG69
Suffolk Rd. N15 221 306 DR58
Suffolk Rd. NW10 109 304 CS66
Suffolk Rd. SE25 273 324 DT98
Suffolk Rd. SW13 155 314 CT80
Suffolk Rd., Bark. 235 308 ER66
Suffolk Rd., Dag. 237 309 FC64
Suffolk Rd., Enf. 210 301 DV43
Suffolk Rd., Har. 214 303 BZ58
Suffolk Rd., Ilf. 225 308 ES58
Suffolk Rd., Sid. 278 327 EW93
Suffolk Rd., Wor.Pk. 283 330 CT103
Suffolk St. E7 234 308 EG64
Suffolk St. SW1 58 316 DK73
Suffolk Way, Horn. 229 311 FN56
Sugar Bakers Ct. EC3 50/1 316 DS72
Sugar Ho. La. E15 130 317 EC68
Sugar Loaf Wk. E2 128 317 DW69
Sugar Quay Wk. EC3 62/3 316 DS73
Sugden Rd. SW11 176 324 DG83
Sugden Way, Bark. 245 318 ET68
Sulgrave Gdns. W6 146 315 CW75
Sulgrave Rd. W6 146 315 CW76
Sulina Rd. SW2 193 324 DL87
Sulivan Ct. SW6 158 315 DA82
Sulivan Rd. SW6 174 323 DA83
Sullivan Ave. E16 244 318 EK71
Sullivan Clo. SW11 175 323 DE83
Sullivan Clo., W.Mol. 267 329 CA97
Sullivan Cres., Uxb. 212 302 BK54
Sullivan Rd. SE11 84 316 DN77
Sullivan Way, Borwd. 204 298 CJ44
Sullivans Reach, Walt. 281 328 BT101
Sultan Rd. E11 224 308 EH56
Sultan St. SE5 162 316 DQ80
Sultan St., Beck. 274 325 DX96
Sumatra Rd. NW6 112 305 DA64
Sumburgh Rd. SW12 176 324 DG86
Summer Gro., Borwd. 204 298 CK44
Summer Hill, Borwd. 205 298 CN43
Summer Hill, Chis. 277 326 EN96
Summer Hill Vil., Chis. 277 326 EN95
Summer Ho. Rd. N16 101 306 DS61
Summer St. EC1 36 316 DN70
Summer Trees, Sun. 266 329 BV95
Summercourt Rd. E1 138 317 DW72
Summerdene Clo. SW16 272 324 DJ94
Summerfield Ave. NW6 127 315 CY68
Summerfield La., Surb. 282 330 CK103
Summerfield Rd. W5 122 314 CH70
Summerfield St. SE12 199 325 EF87
Summerfields Ave. N12 219 305 DE51
Summerhill Clo., Orp. 291 334 ES104
Summerhill Gro., Enf. 209 300 DS44
Summerhill Rd. N15 221 306 DR56
Summerhill Way, Mitch. 272 324 DG95
Summerhouse Ave., Houns. 250 321 BY81
Summerhouse Dr., Bex. 279 327 FD91
Summerhouse Dr., Dart. 279 327 FD92
Summerhouse La., Uxb. 212 302 BG52
Summerhouse La., West Dr. 256 320 BK79
Summerhouse La. Ind. Est., Uxb. 212 302 BG51
Summerland Gdns. N10 220 306 DH55
Summerlands Ave. W3 134 314 CQ73
Summerlee Ave. N2 219 305 DF56
Summerlee Gdns. N2 219 305 DF56
Summerley St. SW18 190 323 DB89
Summers Clo., Sutt. 292 331 DA108
Summers Clo., Wem. 92 304 CP60
Summers La. N12 219 305 DD52
Summers Row N12 219 305 DE51
Summersby Rd. N6 220 306 DH58
Summerstown SW17 190 323 DC90
Summerton Way SE28 246 319 EX73
Summerville Gdns., Sutt. 292 331 CZ107
Summerwood Rd., Islw. 259 321 CF85
Summit Ave. NW9 217 304 CR57
Summit Clo. N14 208 300 DJ47
Summit Clo. NW9 217 304 CR56
Summit Clo., Edg. 217 304 CN52
Summit Ct. NW2 111 305 CY64
Summit Dr., Wdf.Grn. 224 308 EK54
Summit Est. N16 102 307 DU59
Summit Rd. E17 223 307 EB56
Summit Rd., Nthlt. 233 313 CA66
Summit Way N14 208 300 DH47
Summit Way SE19 273 324 DS94
Sumner Ave. SE15 163 316 DT81
Sumner Clo., Orp. 291 334 EQ105
Sumner Est. SE15 163 316 DT80
Sumner Gdns., Croy. 286 332 DN102
Sumner Pl. SW7 78 315 DD77
Sumner Pl. Ms. SW7 78 315 DD77
Sumner Rd. SE15 163 316 DT80
Sumner Rd., Croy. 286 332 DN102
Sumner Rd., Har. 233 313 CC59
Sumner Rd. S., Croy. 286 332 DN102
Sumner St. SE1 60/1 316 DP74
Sumpter Clo. NW3 112 305 DC65
Sun Ct. EC3 50 316 DR72
Sun Ct., Erith 255 319 FF82
Sun La. SE3 252 318 EH80
Sun Pas. SE16 148 317 DU76
Sun Rd. W14 147 315 CZ78
Sun St. EC2 50 316 DR71
Sun St. Pas. EC2 50/1 316 DS71
Sun Wk. E1 138 317 DU74
Sunbeam Cres. W10 126 315 CW70
Sunbeam Rd. NW10 125 314 CR70
Sunbury Ave. NW7 205 298 CR50
Sunbury Ave. SW14 171 322 CR84
Sunbury Ct., Sun. 266 329 BX96
Sunbury Ct. Island, Sun. 266 329 BX96
Sunbury Ct. Ms., Sun. 266 329 BX96
Sunbury Ct. Rd., Sun. 266 329 BW96
Sunbury Cres., Felt. 265 328 BT91
Sunbury Gdns. NW7 205 298 CR50
Sunbury La. SW11 159 315 DD81
Sunbury Rd., Felt. 265 320 BT90
Sunbury Rd., Sutt. 284 331 CX104
Sunbury St. SE18 252 318 EM76
Sunbury Way, Felt. 266 329 BW92
Suncroft Pl. SE26 196 325 DW90
Sunderland Ct. SE22 196 325 DU87
Sunderland Mt. SE23 197 325 DX89
Sunderland Rd. SE23 197 325 DX88
Sunderland Rd. W5 143 314 CK76
Sunderland Ter. W2 40/1 315 DB72
Sunderland Way E12 234 308 EK61
Sundew Ave. W12 136 315 CU73
Sundial Ave. SE25 273 324 DT97
Sundorne Rd. SE7 252 318 EH78
Sundown Ave., S.Croy. 295 332 DT111
Sundown Rd., Ashf. 265 328 BQ92
Sundra Wk. E1 129 317 DX70
Sundridge Ave., Brom. 276 326 EK96
Sundridge Ave., Chis. 276 326 EL94
Sundridge Ave., Well. 253 318 ER82
Sundridge Ho., Brom. 276 326 EH92
Sundridge Pl., Croy. 287 333 DU102
Sundridge Rd., Croy. 287 332 DT101
Sunfields Pl. SE3 252 318 EH80
Sunflower Way, Rom. 228 310 FK53
Sunkist Way, Wall. 294 332 DL109
Sunland Ave., Bexh. 262 327 EY84
Sunleigh Rd., Wem. 123 314 CL67
Sunley Gdns., Grnf. 122 314 CG67
Sunmead Rd., Sun. 266 329 BU97
Sunna Gdns., Sun. 266 329 BV96
Sunningdale N14 208 300 DK50
Sunningdale Ave. W3 135 314 CS73
Sunningdale Ave., Bark. 245 318 ER67
Sunningdale Ave., Felt. 258 321 BY89
Sunningdale Ave., Ruis. 232 313 BW60
Sunningdale Clo. E6 244 318 EM69
Sunningdale Clo. SE16 148 317 DV78
Sunningdale Clo. SE28 246 319 EX72
Sunningdale Clo., Stan. 216 304 CG52
Sunningdale Clo., Surb. 282 330 CL103
Sunningdale Gdns. NW9 217 304 CQ57
Sunningdale Gdns. W8 64 315 DA76
Sunningdale Rd., Brom. 276 326 EL98
Sunningdale Rd., Rain. 238 310 FG66
Sunningdale Rd., Sutt. 284 331 CZ105
Sunningfields Cres. NW4 218 305 CV54
Sunningfields Rd. NW4 218 305 CV55
Sunninghill Rd. SE13 166 317 EB82
Sunnings La., Upmin. 239 311 FQ64
Sunny Bank SE25 274 325 DU97
Sunny Cres. NW10 108 304 CQ66
Sunny Gdns. Par. NW4 218 305 CW54
Sunny Gdns. Rd. NW4 218 305 CV54
Sunny Hill NW4 218 305 CV55
Sunny Nook Gdns., S.Croy. 295 332 DR107
Sunny Rd., The, Enf. 203 301 DX39
Sunny Vw. NW9 217 304 CR57
Sunny Way N12 219 305 DE52
Sunnycroft Gdns., Upmin. 239 311 FT59
Sunnycroft Rd. SE25 274 325 DU97
Sunnycroft Rd., Houns. 251 321 CB82
Sunnycroft Rd., Sthl. 243 313 CA71
Sunnydale, Orp. 290 334 EN103
Sunnydale Gdns. NW7 217 304 CR51
Sunnydale Rd. SE12 260 326 EH85
Sunnydene Ave. E4 211 301 ED50
Sunnydene Ave., Ruis. 232 313 BU60
Sunnydene Clo., Rom. 228 311 FM52
Sunnydene Gdns., Wem. 106 304 CJ65
Sunnydene Rd., Pur. 294 332 DP113
Sunnydene St. SE26 274 325 DY91
Sunnyfield NW7 205 298 CT49
Sunnyfield Rd., Chis. 278 327 EU97
Sunnyhill Clo. E5 119 307 DY63
Sunnyhill Rd. SW16 272 324 DL91
Sunnyhurst Clo., Sutt. 284 331 DA104
Sunnymead Ave., Mitch. 272 324 DJ97
Sunnymead Rd. NW9 93 304 CR59
Sunnymead Rd. SW15 172 323 CV85
Sunnymede Ave., Cars. 293 331 DD111
Sunnymede Dr., Ilf. 225 308 EP57
Sunnyside NW2 95 305 CZ62
Sunnyside SW19 270 323 CY93
Sunnyside Dr. E4 211 301 EC45
Sunnyside Gdns., Upmin. 239 311 FQ61
Sunnyside Pas. SW19 270 323 CY93
Sunnyside Pl. SW19 270 323 CY93
Sunnyside Rd. E10 104 307 EA60
Sunnyside Rd. N19 99 306 DK59
Sunnyside Rd. W5 133 314 CK74
Sunnyside Rd., Ilf. 235 308 EQ62
Sunnyside Rd., Tedd. 267 329 CD91
Sunnyside Rd. E. N9 210 301 DU48
Sunnyside Rd. N. N9 209 300 DT48
Sunnyside Rd. S. N9 209 300 DT48
Sunray Ave. SE24 179 324 DR84
Sunray Ave., Brom. 290 334 EL100
Sunray Ave., Surb. 282 330 CP103
Sunray Ave., West Dr. 248 320 BK75
Sunrise Ave., Horn. 238 310 FJ61
Sunrise Clo., Felt. 258 321 BZ90
Sunset Ave. E4 211 301 EB46
Sunset Ave., Wdf.Grn. 211 301 EF49
Sunset Gdns. SE25 273 324 DT96
Sunset Rd. SE5 178 324 DQ84
Sunset Rd. SE28 246 319 EU74
Sunshine Way, Mitch. 271 323 DF96
Sunwell Clo. SE15 164 317 DV81
Surbiton Ct., Surb. 282 330 CJ100
Surbiton Cres., Kings.T. 282 330 CL99
Surbiton Hall Clo., Kings.T. 268 322 CL98
Surbiton Hill Pk., Surb. 282 330 CM99
Surbiton Hill Rd., Surb. 268 322 CL98
Surbiton Par., Surb. 282 330 CL100
Surbiton Rd., Kings.T. 268 322 CK98
Surlingham Clo. SE28 246 319 EX73
Surma Clo. E1 128 317 DU70
Surr St. N7 115 306 DL64
Surrendale Pl. W9 28 315 DA70
Surrey Canal Rd. SE14 165 317 DX79
Surrey Canal Rd. SE15 164 317 DW79
Surrey Cres. W4 144 314 CN78
Surrey Dr., Horn. 229 311 FN56
Surrey Gdns. N4 221 306 DQ58
Surrey Gro. SE17 86/7 316 DS78
Surrey Gro., Sutt. 285 331 DD104
Surrey La. SW11 159 315 DE81
Surrey La. Est. SW11 159 315 DE81
Surrey Lo. SE1 72 316 DN76
Surrey Ms. SE27 273 324 DS91
Surrey Mt. SE23 196 325 DV88
Surrey Quays Rd. SE16 148 317 DW76
Surrey Rd. SE15 181 325 DX85
Surrey Rd., Bark. 235 308 ES66
Surrey Rd., Dag. 237 309 FB64
Surrey Rd., Har. 215 303 CC57
Surrey Rd., W.Wick. 288 333 EB102
Surrey Row SE1 72/3 316 DP75
Surrey Sq. SE17 86/7 316 DS78
Surrey St. E13 244 318 EH69
Surrey St. WC2 59 316 DM73
Surrey St., Croy. 287 332 DQ103
Surrey Ter. SE17 86/7 316 DS77
Surrey Water Rd. SE16 139 317 DX74
Surridge Gdns. SE19 273 324 DR93
Susan Clo., Rom. 227 309 FC55
Susan Rd. SE3 252 318 EH82
Susan Wd., Chis. 277 326 EN95
Susannah St. E14 140 317 EB72
Sussex Ave., Islw. 259 321 CE83
Sussex Ave., Rom. 228 311 FM52
Sussex Clo. N19 99 306 DL61
Sussex Clo., Ilf. 224 308 EM58
Sussex Clo., N.Mal. 269 322 CS98
Sussex Clo., Twick. 168 322 CH86
Sussex Cres., Nthlt. 233 313 CA65
Sussex Gdns. N4 221 306 DQ57
Sussex Gdns. N6 219 305 DF57
Sussex Gdns. W2 42 315 DD72
Sussex Ms. E. W2 42 315 DD72
Sussex Ms. W. W2 54 315 DD73
Sussex Pl. NW1 31 315 DF70
Sussex Pl. W2 42 315 DD72
Sussex Pl. W6 146 315 CW78
Sussex Pl., Erith 255 319 FB80
Sussex Pl., N.Mal. 269 322 CS98
Sussex Ring N12 207 299 DA50
Sussex Rd. E6 245 318 EN67
Sussex Rd., Cars. 293 331 DF107
Sussex Rd., Erith 255 319 FB80
Sussex Rd., Har. 215 303 CC57
Sussex Rd., Mitch. 286 332 DL99
Sussex Rd., N.Mal. 269 322 CS98
Sussex Rd., Sid. 278 327 EV92
Sussex Rd., S.Croy. 295 332 DR107
Sussex Rd., Sthl. 250 321 BX76
Sussex Rd., Uxb. 241 312 BQ63
Sussex Rd., W.Wick. 288 333 EB102
Sussex Sq. W2 54 315 DD73
Sussex St. E13 244 318 EH69
Sussex St. SW1 80/1 316 DH78
Sussex Wk. SW9 178 324 DP84
Sussex Way N7 99 306 DL61
Sussex Way N19 99 306 DL60
Sussex Way, Barn. 208 300 DH43
Sutcliffe Clo. NW11 219 305 DB57
Sutcliffe Ho., Hayes 242 313 BU72
Sutcliffe Rd. SE18 253 318 ES79
Sutcliffe Rd., Well. 254 319 EW82
Sutherland Ave. W9 28 315 DA70
Sutherland Ave. W13 132 314 CH72
Sutherland Ave., Hayes 250 321 BU77
Sutherland Ave., Orp. 291 334 ET100
Sutherland Ave., Sun. 281 328 BT96
Sutherland Ave., Well. 261 326 ES84
Sutherland Ct. NW9 217 304 CP56
Sutherland Dr. SW19 271 323 DD95
Sutherland Gdns. SW14 171 322 CS83
Sutherland Gdns., Sun. 281 328 BT96
Sutherland Gdns., Wor.Pk. 283 331 CV101
Sutherland Gro. SW18 173 323 CY86
Sutherland Gro., Tedd. 267 329 CE92
Sutherland Pl. W2 40 315 DA72
Sutherland Pt. E5 118 307 DV63
Sutherland Rd. E17 222 307 DX54
Sutherland Rd. N9 210 301 DU46
Sutherland Rd. N17 222 307 DU52
Sutherland Rd. W4 155 314 CS79
Sutherland Rd. W13 132 314 CG72
Sutherland Rd., Belv. 255 319 FA76
Sutherland Rd., Croy. 286 332 DN101
Sutherland Rd., Enf. 210 301 DX43
Sutherland Rd., Sthl. 242 313 BZ72
Sutherland Rd. Path E17 222 307 DX55
Sutherland Row SW1 80/1 316 DH78
Sutherland Sq. SE17 85 316 DQ78
Sutherland St. SW1 80/1 316 DH78
Sutherland Wk. SE17 85 316 DQ78
Sutlej Rd. SE7 252 318 EJ80
Sutterton St. N7 115 306 DM65
Sutton Clo., Beck. 275 325 EB95
Sutton Clo., Pnr. 214 303 BU57
Sutton Common Rd., Sutt. 284 331 CZ101
Sutton Ct. W4 154 314 CQ79
Sutton Ct. Rd. E13 244 318 EJ69
Sutton Ct. Rd. W4 154 314 CQ80
Sutton Ct. Rd., Sutt. 293 331 DC107
Sutton Ct. Rd., Uxb. 241 312 BP67
Sutton Cres., Barn. 206 299 CX43
Sutton Dene, Houns. 251 321 CB81
Sutton Est. SW3 78/9 315 DE78
Sutton Est. W10 136 315 CW71
Sutton Est., The N1 116 306 DP66
Sutton Gdns., Bark. 245 318 ES67
Sutton Gdns., Croy. 287 332 DT99
Sutton Grn., Bark. 245 318 ES67
Sutton Gro., Sutt. 285 331 DD105
Sutton Hall Rd., Houns. 251 321 CA80
Sutton La., Houns. 258 321 BZ83
Sutton La., Sutt. 292 331 DB111
Sutton La. N. W4 144 314 CQ78
Sutton La. S. W4 154 314 CQ79
Sutton Pk. Rd., Sutt. 292 331 DB107
Sutton Pl. E9 118 307 DW64
Sutton Rd. E13 131 317 EF70
Sutton Rd. E17 222 307 DX53
Sutton Rd. N10 220 306 DG53
Sutton Rd., Bark. 245 318 ES68
Sutton Rd., Houns. 251 321 CA81
Sutton Row W1 46 316 DK72
Sutton Sq. E9 118 307 DW64
Sutton Sq., Houns. 250 321 BZ81
Sutton St. E1 138 317 DW73
Sutton Way W10 136 315 CW71
Sutton Way, Houns. 250 321 BZ81
Suttons Ave., Horn. 238 310 FJ62
Suttons Gdns., Horn. 238 310 FK62
Suttons La., Horn. 238 310 FK64
Sutton's Way EC1 37 316 DQ70
Swaby Rd. SW18 190 323 DC88
Swaffham Way N22 221 306 DP52
Swaffield Rd. SW18 190 323 DB87
Swain Clo. SW16 272 324 DH93
Swain Rd., Th.Hth. 287 332 DQ99
Swains Clo., West Dr. 248 320 BL75
Swains La. N6 98 306 DG60
Swains Rd. SW17 271 323 DF94
Swainson Rd. W3 145 314 CT75
Swaisland Dr., Dart. 263 327 FF85
Swakeleys Dr., Uxb. 240 312 BM63
Swakeleys Rd., Uxb. 240 312 BL63
Swallands Rd. SE6 198 325 EA90
Swallow Clo. SE14 165 317 DX81
Swallow Clo., Erith 255 319 FE81
Swallow Dr. NW10 109 304 CR65
Swallow Dr., Nthlt. 243 313 CA68
Swallow Pas. W1 44/5 316 DH72
Swallow Pl. W1 44/5 316 DH72
Swallow St. E6 244 318 EL71
Swallow St. W1 57 316 DJ73
Swallow Wk., Horn. 238 310 FH65
Swallowfield Rd. SE7 252 318 EH78
Swallowfield Way, Hayes 249 320 BR75
Swan App. E6 244 318 EL71
Swan Ave., Upmin. 239 311 FT60
Swan Clo. E17 222 307 DY53
Swan Clo., Croy. 287 332 DS101
Swan Clo., Felt. 266 329 BY91
Swan Clo., Orp. 278 327 EU97
Swan Ct. SW3 78/9 315 DE78
Swan Dr. NW9 217 304 CS54
Swan La. EC4 62 316 DR73
Swan La. N20 207 299 DC48
Swan La., Dart. 263 327 FF87
Swan Mead SE1 74/5 316 DS76
Swan Pas. E1 63 316 DT73
Swan Pl. SW13 155 314 CT82
Swan Rd. SE16 148 317 DW75
Swan Rd. SE18 252 318 EK76
Swan Rd., Felt. 266 329 BY92
Swan Rd., Sthl. 243 313 CB72
Swan Rd., West Dr. 248 320 BK75
Swan St. SE1 73 316 DQ76
Swan St., Islw. 168 322 CH83
Swan Wk. SW3 159 315 DF79
Swan Wk., Rom. 227 309 FE57
Swan Wk., Shep. 281 328 BS101
Swan Way, Enf. 203 301 DX40
Swan Yd. N1 116 306 DP65
Swanage Rd. E4 223 307 EC52
Swanage Rd. SW18 174 323 DC86
Swanage Waye, Hayes 242 313 BW72
Swanbourne Dr., Horn. 238 310 FJ64
Swanbridge Rd., Bexh. 255 319 FA81
Swandon Way SW18 174 323 DB84
Swanfield St. E2 39 316 DT69
Swanley Bypass, Sid. 279 327 FC96
Swanley Bypass, Swan. 279 327 FC96
Swanley La., Swan. 279 327 FF97
Swanley Rd., Well. 254 319 EW81
Swanscombe Rd. W4 145 314 CS78
Swanscombe Rd. W11 137 315 CX74
Swansea Rd., Enf. 203 301 DW42
Swansland Gdns. E17 222 307 DY53
Swanton Gdns. SW19 189 323 CX88
Swanton Rd., Erith 255 319 FB80
Swanwick Clo. SW15 187 322 CT87
Sward Rd., Orp. 291 335 EU100
Swaton Rd. E3 130 317 EA70
Swaylands Rd., Belv. 255 319 FA79
Swaythling Clo. N18 210 301 DV49
Sweden Gate SE16 149 317 DY76
Swedenborg Gdns. E1 138 317 DU73
Sweeney Cres. SE1 75 316 DT75
Sweeps Ditch Clo., Stai. 264 328 BG94
Sweet Briar Grn. N9 209 300 DT48
Sweet Briar Gro. N9 209 300 DT48
Sweet Briar Wk. N18 209 300 DT49
Sweetcroft La., Uxb. 240 312 BM66
Sweetmans Ave., Pnr. 214 303 BX55
Sweets Way N20 207 299 DD47
Swete St. E13 244 318 EG68
Swetenham Wk. SE18 253 318 EQ78
Sweyn Pl. SE3 252 318 EG82
Swift Clo. E17 222 307 DY53
Swift Clo., Har. 233 313 CB61
Swift Clo., Hayes 249 312 BT72
Swift Clo., Upmin. 239 311 FS60
Swift Rd., Felt. 266 329 BX91
Swift Rd., Sthl. 250 321 BZ76
Swift St. SW6 157 315 CZ81
Swiftsden Way, Brom. 275 325 EE93
Swinbrook Rd. W10 137 315 CY71
Swinburne Ct. SE5 179 324 DR84
Swinburne Cres., Croy. 288 333 DW100
Swinburne Rd. SW15 172 323 CU84
Swinderby Rd., Wem. 107 304 CL65
Swindon Clo., Ilf. 235 308 ES61
Swindon Rd., Houns. 257 320 BQ86
Swindon St. W12 136 315 CV74
Swinfield Clo., Felt. 266 329 BY91
Swinford Gdns. SW9 178 324 DP83
Swingate La. SE18 253 318 ES80
Swinnerton St. E9 119 307 DY64
Swinton Clo., Wem. 92 304 CP60
Swinton Pl. WC1 35 316 DM69
Swinton St. WC1 35 316 DM69
Swires Shaw, Kes. 290 334 EK105
Swiss Ter. NW6 113 305 DD66
Swithland Gdns. SE9 277 326 EN91
Swyncombe Ave. W5 142 314 CH77
Swynford Gdns. NW4 218 305 CU56
Sybil Ms. N4 221 306 DP58
Sybil Phoenix Clo. SE8 149 317 DX78
Sybil Thorndike Ho. N1 116 306 DQ65
Sybourn St. E17 103 307 DZ59
Sycamore Ave. W5 143 314 CK76
Sycamore Ave., Hayes 249 312 BS73
Sycamore Ave., Sid. 261 326 ET86
Sycamore Ave., Upmin. 239 311 FN62
Sycamore Clo. E16 131 317 EE70
Sycamore Clo. N9 210 301 DU49
Sycamore Clo. SE9 260 326 EL89
Sycamore Clo. W3 135 314 CS74
Sycamore Clo., Barn. 207 299 DD44
Sycamore Clo., Cars. 285 331 DF105
Sycamore Clo., Felt. 258 321 BU90
Sycamore Clo., Nthlt. 242 313 BY67
Sycamore Clo., West Dr. 248 312 BM73
Sycamore Dr., Swan. 279 327 FE97
Sycamore Gdns. W6 146 315 CV75
Sycamore Gdns., Mitch. 271 323 DD96
Sycamore Gro. NW9 92 304 CQ59
Sycamore Gro. SE6 182 325 EC86
Sycamore Gro. SE20 274 325 DU94
Sycamore Gro., N.Mal. 269 322 CR97
Sycamore Hill N11 220 306 DG51
Sycamore Ms. SW4 176 324 DJ83
Sycamore Ri., Bans. 292 331 CX114
Sycamore Rd. SW19 270 323 CW93
Sycamore St. EC1 37 316 DQ70
Sycamore Wk. W10 127 315 CY70
Sycamore Wk., Ilf. 225 308 EQ56
Sycamore Way, Tedd. 268 322 CJ93
Sycamore Way, Th.Hth. 286 332 DN99
Sydenham Ave. SE26 274 325 DV92
Sydenham Clo., Rom. 227 309 FF56
Sydenham Cotts. SE12 260 326 EJ89
Sydenham Hill SE23 196 325 DV88
Sydenham Hill SE26 273 324 DT91
Sydenham Hill Est. SE26 196 325 DU90
Sydenham Pk. SE26 196 325 DW90
Sydenham Pk. Rd. SE26 196 325 DW90
Sydenham Ri. SE23 196 325 DV89
Sydenham Rd. SE26 274 325 DX92
Sydenham Rd., Croy. 287 332 DQ102
Sydmons Ct. SE23 196 325 DW87
Sydner Ms. N16 117 306 DT63
Sydner Rd. N16 117 306 DT63
Sydney Ave., Pur. 294 332 DM112
Sydney Clo. SW3 78 315 DD77
Sydney Cres., Ashf. 265 328 BP93
Sydney Gro. NW4 218 305 CW57
Sydney Ms. SW3 78 315 DD77
Sydney Pl. SW7 78 315 DD77
Sydney Rd. E11 224 308 EH58
Sydney Rd. N8 221 306 DN56
Sydney Rd. N10 220 306 DG53
Sydney Rd. SE2 254 319 EW76
Sydney Rd. SW20 270 323 CX96
Sydney Rd. W13 132 314 CG74
Sydney Rd., Bexh. 262 327 EX84
Sydney Rd., Enf. 202 300 DR41
Sydney Rd., Felt. 258 321 BU88
Sydney Rd., Ilf. 225 308 EQ54
Sydney Rd., Rich. 169 322 CL84
Sydney Rd., Sid. 277 326 ES91
Sydney Rd., Sutt. 284 331 DA105
Sydney Rd., Tedd. 267 329 CF92
Sydney St. SW3 78/9 315 DE78
Sykes Dr., Stai. 264 328 BH92
Sylvan Ave. N3 219 305 DA54
Sylvan Ave. N22 220 306 DM52
Sylvan Ave. NW7 217 304 CT51
Sylvan Ave., Horn. 228 311 FL58

Sylvan Ave., Rom. 226 309 EZ58
Sylvan Clo., S.Croy. 295 333 DV110
Sylvan Est. SE19 273 324 DT95
Sylvan Gdns., Surb. 282 330 CK101
Sylvan Gro. NW2 111 305 CX63
Sylvan Gro. SE15 164 317 DV79
Sylvan Hill SE19 273 324 DS95
Sylvan Rd. E7 234 308 EG65
Sylvan Rd. E11 224 308 EG57
Sylvan Rd. E17 223 307 EA57
Sylvan Rd. SE19 273 324 DT95
Sylvan Rd., Ilf. 235 308 EQ61
Sylvan Wk., Brom. 276 326 EM97
Sylvan Way, Dag. 236 309 EV62
Sylvan Way, W.Wick. 289 333 EE105
Sylvana Clo., Uxb. 240 312 BM67
Sylverdale Rd., Croy. 286 332 DP104
Sylverdale Rd., Pur. 294 332 DP113
Sylvester Ave., Chis. 276 326 EM93
Sylvester Path E8 118 307 DV65
Sylvester Rd. E8 118 307 DV65
Sylvester Rd. E17 103 307 DZ59
Sylvester Rd. N2 219 305 DC54
Sylvester Rd., Wem. 106 304 CJ64
Sylvestrus Clo., Kings.T. 269 322 CN95
Sylvia Ave., Pnr. 214 303 BY51
Sylvia Gdns., Wem. 108 304 CP66
Symes Ms. NW1 21 316 DJ68
Symons St. SW3 79 315 DF77
Syon Gate Way, Brent. 152 314 CG80
Syon La., Islw. 251 321 CF79
Syon Pk. Gdns., Islw. 251 321 CF80
Syon Vista, Rich. 153 314 CK81

Tabard Gdn. Est. SE1 74 316 DR75
Tabard St. SE1 74 316 DR75
Tabernacle Ave. E13 244 318 EG70
Tabernacle St. EC2 38 316 DR70
Tableer Ave. SW4 176 324 DJ85
Tabley Rd. N7 115 306 DL63
Tabor Gdns., Sutt. 292 331 CZ107
Tabor Gro. SW19 270 323 CY94
Tabor Rd. W6 146 315 CV76
Tabrums Way, Upmin. 239 311 FS59
Tachbrook Est. SW1 82 316 DK78
Tachbrook Ms. SW1 81 316 DJ77
Tachbrook Rd., Felt. 265 320 BT87
Tachbrook Rd., Sthl. 250 321 BX77
Tachbrook Rd., Uxb. 240 312 BJ68
Tachbrook St. SW1 81 316 DJ77
Tack Ms. SE4 182 325 EA83
Tadema Rd. SW10 158 315 DC80
Tadlows Clo., Upmin. 239 311 FP64
Tadmor Clo., Sun. 281 328 BT98
Tadmor St. W12 137 315 CX74
Tadworth Ave., N.Mal. 283 330 CT99
Tadworth Par., Horn. 238 310 FH63
Tadworth Rd. NW2 94 305 CU61
Taeping St. E14 150 317 EB77
Taffy's How, Mitch. 271 323 DE97
Taft Way E3 130 317 EB69
Tagg's Island, Hmptn. 267 329 CD96
Tailworth St. E1 138 317 DU71
Tait Rd., Croy. 287 332 DS101
Takeley Clo., Rom. 227 309 FD54
Talacre Rd. NW5 114 306 DG65
Talbot Ave. N2 219 305 DD55
Talbot Clo. N15 221 306 DT56
Talbot Ct. EC3 62 316 DR73
Talbot Cres. NW4 218 305 CU57
Talbot Gdns., Ilf. 236 309 EU61
Talbot Ho. E14 140 317 EB72
Talbot Pl. SE3 167 317 EE82
Talbot Rd. E6 245 318 EN68
Talbot Rd. E7 234 308 EG63
Talbot Rd. N6 220 306 DG58
Talbot Rd. N15 221 306 DT56
Talbot Rd. N22 220 306 DJ54
Talbot Rd. SE22 179 324 DS84
Talbot Rd. W2 40 315 DA72
Talbot Rd. W11 137 315 CZ72
Talbot Rd. W13 132 314 CG73
Talbot Rd., Ashf. 264 328 BK92
Talbot Rd., Brom. 276 326 EH98
Talbot Rd., Cars. 285 332 DG106
Talbot Rd., Dag. 236 309 EZ65
Talbot Rd., Har. 215 303 CF54
Talbot Rd., Islw. 168 322 CG84
Talbot Rd., Sthl. 250 321 BY77
Talbot Rd., Th.Hth. 273 324 DR98
Talbot Rd., Twick. 259 321 CE88
Talbot Rd., Wem. 107 304 CK64
Talbot Sq. W2 42 315 DD72
Talbot Wk. NW10 109 304 CS65
Talbot Wk. W11 137 315 CY72
Talbot Yd. SE1 62 316 DR74
Talfourd Pl. SE15 163 316 DT81
Talfourd Rd. SE15 163 316 DT81
Talgarth Rd. W6 147 315 CX78
Talgarth Rd. W14 147 315 CX78
Talgarth Wk. NW9 217 304 CS57
Talisman Clo., Ilf. 236 309 EV60
Talisman Sq. SE26 274 325 DU91
Talisman Way, Wem. 91 304 CM62
Tall Elms Clo., Brom. 289 333 EF99
Tall Trees SW16 272 324 DM97
Tall Trees Clo., Horn. 228 310 FK58
Tallack Clo., Har. 215 303 CE52
Tallack Rd. E10 103 307 DZ60
Tallis Clo. E16 244 318 EH72
Tallis Gro. SE7 252 318 EH79
Tallis St. EC4 60 316 DN73
Tallis Vw. NW10 109 304 CR65
Tally Ho Cor. N12 207 299 DC50
Talma Gdns., Twick. 259 321 CE86
Talma Rd. SW2 178 324 DN84
Talmage Clo. SE23 196 325 DW87
Talman Gro., Stan. 216 304 CK51
Talwin St. E3 130 317 EB69
Tamar Clo., Upmin. 229 311 FS58
Tamar Sq., Wdf.Grn. 224 308 EH51
Tamar St. SE7 252 318 EL76
Tamar Way N17 221 306 DT55
Tamarind Yd. E1 138 317 DU74
Tamarisk Sq. W12 135 314 CT73
Tamesis Gdns., Wor.Pk. 283 330 CS103
Tamian Est., Houns. 258 321 BW84
Tamian Way, Houns. 258 321 BW84
Tamworth Ave., Wdf.Grn. 223 307 EE51
Tamworth Gdns., Pnr. 214 303 BV54
Tamworth La., Mitch. 272 324 DG96
Tamworth Pk., Mitch. 272 324 DH98
Tamworth Pl., Croy. 287 332 DQ103
Tamworth Rd., Croy. 286 332 DP103
Tamworth St. SW6 158 315 DA79
Tancred Rd. N4 221 306 DP58
Tandridge Dr., Orp. 291 334 ER102
Tandridge Gdns., S.Croy. 295 332 DT113
Tandridge Pl., Orp. 291 334 ER101
Tanfield Ave. NW2 109 304 CT63
Tanfield Rd., Croy. 287 332 DQ105
Tangent Rd., Rom. 228 310 FK53
Tangier Rd., Rich. 170 322 CP84
Tangle Tree Clo. N3 219 305 DB55
Tanglebury Clo., Brom. 276 326 EL98
Tangles Clo., Uxb. 241 312 BN69
Tanglewood Clo., Croy. 288 333 DW104
Tanglewood Way, Felt. 258 321 BV90
Tangley Gro. SW15 187 322 CT87
Tangley Pk. Rd., Hmptn. 266 329 BZ92
Tanglyn Ave., Shep. 281 328 BN99
Tangmere Cres., Horn. 238 310 FH65
Tangmere Gdns., Nthlt. 242 313 BW68
Tangmere Gro., Kings.T. 268 322 CK92
Tangmere Way NW9 217 304 CS54
Tanhurst Wk. SE2 254 319 EX76
Tankerton Rd., Surb. 282 330 CM103
Tankerton St. WC1 34/5 316 DL69
Tankerville Rd. SW16 272 324 DK94
Tankridge Rd. NW2 94 305 CV61
Tanner St. SE1 74/5 316 DS75
Tanner St., Bark. 235 308 EQ65
Tanners End La. N18 209 300 DS49
Tanners Hill SE8 165 317 DZ81
Tanners La., Ilf. 225 308 EQ55
Tannery Clo., Beck. 288 333 DX99
Tannery Clo., Dag. 237 309 FB62
Tannington Ter. N5 100 306 DN62
Tannsfeld Rd. SE26 274 325 DX92
Tansley Clo. N7 115 306 DK64
Tanswell Est. SE1 72 316 DN75
Tanswell St. SE1 72 316 DN75
Tansy Clo. E6 245 318 EN72
Tansy Clo., Rom. 228 311 FL51
Tant Ave. E16 141 317 EF72
Tantallon Rd. SW12 192 324 DG88
Tantony Gro., Rom. 226 309 EX55
Tanworth Clo., Nthwd. 213 302 BQ51
Tanyard La., Bex. 263 327 FA87
Tanza Rd. NW3 113 305 DF63
Tapestry Clo., Sutt. 292 331 DB108
Taplow NW3 113 305 DD66
Taplow SE17 86 316 DR78
Taplow Rd. N13 209 300 DQ49
Taplow St. N1 25 316 DQ68
Tapp St. E1 128 317 DV70
Tappesfield Rd. SE15 180 325 DW83
Tarbert Rd. SE22 179 324 DS85
Tarbert Wk. E1 138 317 DW73
Target Clo., Felt. 257 320 BS86
Tariff Cres. SE8 149 317 DZ77
Tariff Rd. N17 222 307 DU51
Tarleton Gdns. SE23 196 325 DV88
Tarling Clo., Sid. 262 327 EV90
Tarling Rd. E16 141 317 EF72
Tarling Rd. N2 219 305 DC54
Tarling St. E1 138 317 DV72
Tarling St. Est. E1 138 317 DW72
Tarmac Way, West Dr. 256 320 BH80
Tarn St. SE1 73 316 DQ76
Tarnbank, Enf. 208 300 DL43
Tarnwood Pk. SE9 260 326 EM87
Tarquin Ho. SE26 274 325 DU91
Tarragon Clo. SE14 165 317 DY80
Tarragon Gdns. SE14 165 317 DY80
Tarragon Gro. SE26 274 325 DX93
Tarrant Pl. W1 43 315 DF71
Tarrington Clo. SW16 193 324 DK90
Tarry La. SE8 149 317 DY77
Tarver Rd. SE17 84/5 316 DP78
Tarves Way SE10 166 317 EB80
Tash Pl. N11 208 300 DH50
Tasker Clo., Hayes 257 320 BQ80
Tasker Ho., Bark. 245 318 ER68
Tasker Rd. NW3 113 305 DF64
Tasman Rd. SW9 177 324 DL83
Tasman Wk. E16 244 318 EK72
Tasmania Ter. N18 221 306 DQ51
Tasso Rd. W6 157 315 CY79
Tatam Rd. NW10 109 304 CR66
Tate & Lyle Jetty E16 252 318 EL75
Tate Rd. E16 244 318 EM74
Tate Rd., Sutt. 284 331 DA106
Tatnell Rd. SE23 181 325 DY86
Tattersall Clo. SE9 260 326 EL85
Tatton Cres. N16 101 306 DT59
Tatum St. SE17 86 316 DR77
Taunton Ave. SW20 270 323 CV96
Taunton Ave., Houns. 251 321 CC82
Taunton Clo., Bexh. 255 319 FD82
Taunton Clo., Ilf. 225 308 ET51
Taunton Clo., Sutt. 284 331 DA102
Taunton Ct. N17 221 306 DS52
Taunton Dr. N2 219 305 DC54
Taunton Dr., Enf. 202 300 DN41
Taunton Ms. NW1 31 315 DF70
Taunton Pl. NW1 31 315 DF70
Taunton Rd. SE12 183 325 EE85
Taunton Rd., Grnf. 243 313 CB67
Taunton Way, Stan. 216 304 CL54
Tavern Clo., Cars. 285 331 DE101
Tavern La. SW9 162 316 DN82
Taverner Sq. N5 116 306 DQ63
Taverners Clo. W11 137 315 CY74
Taverners Way E4 211 301 EE46
Tavistock Ave. E17 222 307 DX55
Tavistock Ave., Grnf. 122 314 CG68
Tavistock Clo. N16 117 306 DS64
Tavistock Clo., Rom. 228 310 FK53
Tavistock Clo., Stai. 264 328 BK94
Tavistock Cres. W11 137 315 CZ71
Tavistock Cres., Mitch. 272 324 DL98
Tavistock Gdns., Ilf. 235 308 ES63
Tavistock Gate, Croy. 287 332 DR102
Tavistock Gro., Croy. 287 332 DR101
Tavistock Ms. E18 224 308 EG56
Tavistock Ms. W11 137 315 CZ72
Tavistock Pl. E18 224 308 EG55
Tavistock Pl. N14 208 300 DH45
Tavistock Pl. WC1 34/5 316 DL70
Tavistock Rd. E7 121 307 EF63
Tavistock Rd. E15 121 307 EF65
Tavistock Rd. E18 224 308 EG55
Tavistock Rd. N4 221 306 DR58
Tavistock Rd. NW10 125 314 CT68
Tavistock Rd. W11 137 315 CZ72
Tavistock Rd., Brom. 275 325 EF98
Tavistock Rd., Cars. 285 331 DD102
Tavistock Rd., Croy. 287 332 DR102
Tavistock Rd., Edg. 217 304 CN53
Tavistock Rd., Uxb. 241 312 BQ64
Tavistock Rd., Well. 254 319 EW81
Tavistock Rd., West Dr. 248 312 BK74
Tavistock Sq. WC1 34 316 DK70
Tavistock St. WC2 58/9 316 DL73
Tavistock Ter. N19 99 306 DK62
Tavistock Wk., Cars. 285 331 DD102
Taviton St. WC1 34 316 DK70
Tavy Bri. SE2 254 319 EW76
Tavy Clo. SE11 84 316 DN78
Tawney Rd. SE28 246 319 EV73
Tawny Ave., Upmin. 239 311 FP64
Tawny Clo. W13 132 314 CH74
Tawny Clo., Felt. 258 321 BU90
Tawny Way SE16 149 317 DX77
Tay Way, Rom. 227 309 FF53
Tayben Ave., Twick. 259 321 CE86
Taybridge Rd. SW11 176 324 DG83
Tayburn Clo. E14 140 317 EC72
Tayfield Clo., Uxb. 231 312 BQ62
Taylor Ave., Rich. 154 314 CP82
Taylor Clo. N17 222 307 DU52
Taylor Clo., Hmptn. 267 329 CC92
Taylor Clo., Orp. 291 334 ET105
Taylor Clo., Rom. 227 309 FA52
Taylor Ct. E15 120 307 EC64
Taylor Rd., Mitch. 271 323 DE94
Taylor Rd., Wall. 285 332 DH106
Taylors Bldgs. SE18 253 318 EP77
Taylors Clo., Sid. 277 326 ET91
Taylors Grn. W3 135 314 CS72
Taylors La. NW10 109 304 CS66
Taylors La. SE26 274 325 DV91
Taymount Ri. SE23 196 325 DW89
Tayport Clo. N1 115 306 DL66
Tayside Dr., Edg. 205 298 CP48
Taywood Rd., Nthlt. 242 313 BZ69
Teak Clo. SE16 139 317 DY74
Teal Ave., Orp. 278 327 EX98
Teal Clo. E16 244 318 EK71
Teal Dr., Nthwd. 213 302 BQ52
Teale St. E2 128 317 DU68
Tealing Dr., Epsom 283 330 CR105
Teasel Clo., Croy. 288 333 DX102
Teasel Way E15 131 317 EE69
Tebworth Rd. N17 221 306 DT52
Teck Clo., Islw. 152 314 CG82
Tedder Clo., Ruis. 232 313 BV64
Tedder Clo., Uxb. 240 312 BM66
Teddington Lock, Tedd. 268 322 CG91
Teddington Pk., Tedd. 267 329 CF92
Teddington Pk. Rd., Tedd. 267 329 CF91
Tedworth Gdns. SW3 79 315 DF78
Tedworth Sq. SW3 79 315 DF78
Tee, The W3 135 314 CS72
Tees Ave., Grnf. 243 313 CE68
Tees Clo., Upmin. 229 311 FR58
Teesdale Ave., Islw. 152 314 CG81
Teesdale Clo. E2 128 317 DU68
Teesdale Gdns. SE25 273 324 DS96
Teesdale Gdns., Islw. 152 314 CG81
Teesdale Rd. E11 223 307 EF58
Teesdale St. E2 128 317 DV68
Teesdale Yd. E2 128 317 DV68
Teeswater Ct., Erith 254 319 EX76
Teevan Clo., Croy. 287 333 DU101
Teevan Rd., Croy. 287 333 DU102
Teignmouth Clo. SW4 177 324 DK84
Teignmouth Clo., Edg. 216 304 CM54
Teignmouth Gdns., Grnf. 243 313 CF68
Teignmouth Rd. NW2 111 305 CX64
Teignmouth Rd., Well. 254 319 EW82
Telcote Way, Ruis. 232 313 BW59
Telegraph Hill NW3 96 305 DB62
Telegraph Ms., Ilf. 236 309 EU60
Telegraph Rd. SW15 188 323 CV87
Telegraph St. EC2 50 316 DR72
Telegraph Track, Wall. 293 332 DH110
Telemann Sq. SE3 260 326 EH83
Telephone Pl. SW6 157 315 CZ79
Telfer Clo. W3 144 314 CQ75
Telferscot Rd. SW12 193 324 DK88
Telford Ave. SW2 193 324 DK88
Telford Clo. E17 103 307 DY59
Telford Clo. SE19 273 324 DT93
Telford Clo. W3 144 314 CQ75
Telford Rd. N11 220 306 DJ51
Telford Rd. NW9 218 305 CU58
Telford Rd. SE9 261 326 ER89
Telford Rd. W10 137 315 CY71
Telford Rd., Sthl. 243 313 CB73
Telford Rd., Twick. 259 321 CA87
Telford Ter. SW1 160 316 DJ79
Telford Way W3 135 314 CS71
Telford Way, Hayes 242 313 BY71
Telfords Yd. E1 138 317 DU73
Telham Rd. E6 245 318 EN68
Tell Gro. SE22 179 324 DT84
Tellson Ave. SE18 252 318 EK81
Telscombe Clo., Orp. 291 334 ES103
Temeraire St. SE16 148 317 DW75
Temperley Rd. SW12 192 324 DG87
Tempest Way, Rain. 238 310 FG65
Templar Dr. SE28 246 319 EX72
Templar Ho. NW2 111 305 CZ65
Templar Pl., Hmptn. 267 329 CA94
Templar St. SE5 162 316 DP82
Templars Ave. NW11 218 305 CZ58
Templars Cres. N3 219 305 DA54
Templars Dr., Har. 215 303 CD51
Temple EC4 60 316 DN73
Temple Ave. EC4 60 316 DN73
Temple Ave. N20 207 299 DD45
Temple Ave., Croy. 288 333 DZ103
Temple Ave., Dag. 237 309 FA60
Temple Clo. E11 105 307 EE59
Temple Clo. N3 218 305 CZ54
Temple Clo. SE28 253 318 EQ76
Temple Fortune Hill NW11 219 305 DA57
Temple Fortune La. NW11 218 305 CZ57
Temple Gdns. N21 209 300 DP47
Temple Gdns. NW11 218 305 CZ58
Temple Gdns., Dag. 236 309 EX62
Temple Gdns., Rick. 213 302 BP49
Temple Gro. NW11 219 305 DA58
Temple Gro., Enf. 202 300 DP41
Temple La. EC4 48 316 DN72
Temple Mead Clo., Stan. 216 304 CH51
Temple Mill La. E15 120 307 EA63
Temple Pk., Uxb. 241 312 BN69
Temple Pl. WC2 59 316 DM73
Temple Rd. E6 244 318 EL67
Temple Rd. N8 220 306 DM56
Temple Rd. NW2 110 305 CW63
Temple Rd. W4 144 314 CQ76
Temple Rd. W5 143 314 CK76
Temple Rd., Croy. 287 332 DR105
Temple Rd., Houns. 259 321 CB84
Temple Rd., Rich. 153 314 CM82
Temple Sheen SW14 170 322 CP84
Temple Sheen Rd. SW14 170 322 CP84
Temple St. E2 128 317 DV68
Temple Way, Sutt. 285 331 DD104
Temple W. Ms. SE11 72/3 316 DP76
Templecombe Rd. E9 128 317 DW67
Templecombe Way, Mord. 284 331 CY99
Templecroft, Ashf. 265 328 BR93
Templedene Ave., Stai. 264 328 BH94
Templehof Ave. NW2 94 305 CW59
Templeman Rd. W7 243 313 CF71
Templemead Clo. W3 135 314 CS72
Templeton Ave. E4 211 301 EA49
Templeton Clo. N16 117 306 DS64
Templeton Clo. SE19 273 324 DR95
Templeton Pl. SW5 76 315 DA77
Templeton Rd. N15 221 306 DR58
Templewood W13 132 314 CH71
Templewood Ave. NW3 96 305 DB62
Templewood Gdns. NW3 96 305 DB62
Tempsford Clo., Enf. 202 300 DQ41
Temsford Clo., Har. 215 303 CC54
Tenbury Clo. E7 234 308 EK64
Tenbury Ct. SW2 193 324 DK88
Tenby Ave., Har. 216 304 CH54
Tenby Clo. N15 221 306 DT56
Tenby Clo., Rom. 226 309 EY58
Tenby Gdns., Nthlt. 233 313 CA65
Tenby Rd. E17 222 307 DY57
Tenby Rd., Edg. 216 304 CM53
Tenby Rd., Enf. 203 301 DW41
Tenby Rd., Rom. 226 309 EY58
Tenby Rd., Well. 254 319 EX81
Tench St. E1 138 317 DV74
Tenda Rd. SE16 148 317 DV77
Tendring Way, Rom. 226 309 EW57
Tenham Ave. SW2 193 324 DK89
Tenison Ct. W1 57 316 DJ73
Tenison Way SE1 59 316 DM74
Tenniel Clo. W2 41 315 DC72
Tennis Ct. La., E.Mol. 267 329 CF97
Tennis St. SE1 74 316 DR75
Tennison Ave., Borwd. 205 298 CP43
Tennison Rd. SE25 273 324 DT98
Tenniswood Rd., Enf. 202 300 DS39
Tennyson Ave. E11 234 308 EG59
Tennyson Ave. E12 234 308 EL66
Tennyson Ave. NW9 217 304 CQ55
Tennyson Ave., N.Mal. 283 331 CV99
Tennyson Ave., Twick. 259 321 CF88
Tennyson Clo., Enf. 210 301 DX43
Tennyson Clo., Felt. 257 320 BT86
Tennyson Clo., Well. 253 318 ET81
Tennyson Rd. E10 104 307 EB60
Tennyson Rd. E15 121 307 EE66
Tennyson Rd. E17 222 307 DZ58
Tennyson Rd. NW6 127 315 CZ67
Tennyson Rd. NW7 206 299 CU50
Tennyson Rd. SE20 274 325 DX94
Tennyson Rd. SW19 271 323 DC93
Tennyson Rd. W7 243 313 CF73
Tennyson Rd., Ashf. 264 328 BL92
Tennyson Rd., Houns. 251 321 CC82
Tennyson Rd., Rom. 228 310 FJ52
Tennyson Rd., Well. 253 318 ET81
Tennyson St. SW8 160 316 DH82
Tennyson Way, Horn. 238 310 FG61
Tensing Rd., Sthl. 251 321 CA76
Tent Peg La., Orp. 291 334 EQ99
Tent St. E1 128 317 DV70
Tentelow La., Sthl. 251 321 CA78
Tenter Grd. E1 51 316 DT71
Tenter Pas. E1 51 316 DT72
Tenterden Clo. NW4 218 305 CX55
Tenterden Clo. SE9 276 326 EM91
Tenterden Dr. NW4 218 305 CX55
Tenterden Gdns. NW4 218 305 CX55
Tenterden Gdns., Croy. 287 333 DU101
Tenterden Gro. NW4 218 305 CX55
Tenterden Rd. N17 221 306 DT52
Tenterden Rd., Croy. 287 333 DU101
Tenterden Rd., Dag. 236 309 EZ61
Tenterden St. W1 44/5 316 DH72
Terborch Way SE22 179 324 DS85
Teresa Ms. E17 223 307 EA56
Teresa Wk. N10 220 306 DH57
Terling Clo. E11 105 307 EF62
Terling Rd., Dag. 237 309 FA61
Terling Wk. N1 25 316 DQ67
Terminus Pl. SW1 68/9 316 DH76
Tern Gdns., Upmin. 239 311 FS60
Terrace, The E4 211 301 EE48
Terrace, The N3 218 305 CZ54
Terrace, The NW6 16 315 DA67
Terrace, The SW13 155 314 CS82
Terrace, The, Har. 90 304 CH60
Terrace, The, Wdf.Grn. 224 308 EG51
Terrace Gdns. SW13 155 314 CT82
Terrace La., Rich. 169 322 CL86
Terrace Rd. E9 118 307 DW66
Terrace Rd. E13 244 318 EG67
Terrace Wk., Dag. 236 309 EY64
Terrapin Rd. SW17 192 324 DH90
Terretts Pl. N1 116 306 DP66
Terrick Rd. N22 220 306 DL53
Terrick St. W12 136 315 CV72
Terrilands, Pnr. 214 303 BZ55
Terront Rd. N15 221 306 DQ57
Tessa Sanderson Pl. SW8 176 324 DH83
Tessa Sanderson Way, Grnf. 233 313 CD64
Testerton Wk. W11 137 315 CX73
Tetbury Pl. N1 24/5 316 DP67
Tetcott Rd. SW10 158 315 DC80
Tetherdown N10 220 306 DG55
Tetterby Way SE16 148 317 DU78
Tetty Way, Brom. 276 326 EG96
Teversham La. SW8 161 316 DL81
Teviot Clo., Well. 254 319 EV81
Teviot St. E14 140 317 EC71
Tewkesbury Ave. SE23 196 325 DV87
Tewkesbury Ave., Pnr. 214 303 BY57
Tewkesbury Clo. N15 221 306 DR58
Tewkesbury Gdns. NW9 217 304 CP55
Tewkesbury Rd. N15 221 306 DR58
Tewkesbury Rd. W13 132 314 CG73
Tewkesbury Rd., Cars. 285 331 DD102
Tewkesbury Ter. N11 220 306 DJ51
Tewson Rd. SE18 253 318 ES77
Teynham Ave., Enf. 209 300 DR44
Teynham Grn., Brom. 289 334 EG99
Teynton Ter. N17 221 306 DQ53
Thackeray Ave. N17 222 307 DU54
Thackeray Clo. SW19 270 323 CX94
Thackeray Clo., Har. 233 313 CA60
Thackeray Clo., Islw. 152 314 CG82
Thackeray Clo., Uxb. 249 312 BP72
Thackeray Dr., Ilf. 236 309 EU59
Thackeray Dr., Rom. 236 309 EU59
Thackeray Rd. E6 244 318 EK68
Thackeray Rd. SW8 160 316 DH82
Thackeray St. W8 64/5 315 DB75
Thackrah Clo. N2 219 305 DC54
Thakeham Clo. SE26 274 325 DV92
Thalia Clo. SE10 167 317 ED79
Thame Rd. SE16 149 317 DX75
Thames Ave. SW10 158 315 DC81
Thames Ave., Cher. 280 328 BG97
Thames Ave., Dag. 247 319 FA70
Thames Ave., Grnf. 243 313 CF68
Thames Bank SW14 154 314 CQ82
Thames Circle E14 150 317 EA77
Thames Clo., Cher. 280 328 BH101
Thames Clo., Hmptn. 267 329 CB96
Thames Ct., W.Mol. 267 329 CB96
Thames Dr., Ruis. 231 302 BQ58
Thames Meadow, Shep. 281 328 BR102
Thames Meadow, W.Mol. 267 329 CA96
Thames Pl. SW15 173 323 CX83
Thames Rd. E16 244 318 EK74
Thames Rd. W4 154 314 CN79
Thames Rd., Bark. 245 318 ES69
Thames Rd., Dart. 255 319 FF82
Thames Rd. Ind. Est. E16 244 318 EK74
Thames Side, Cher. 280 328 BJ99
Thames Side, Kings.T. 268 322 CK95
Thames Side, Stai. 280 328 BH96
Thames Side, Tedd. 268 322 CK94
Thames St. SE10 166 317 EB79
Thames St., Hmptn. 267 329 CB95
Thames St., Kings.T. 268 322 CK96
Thames St., Sun. 266 329 BU98
Thames St., Walt. 281 328 BT101
Thames Village W4 154 314 CQ81
Thames Wf. E16 141 317 EF74
Thamesbank Pl. SE28 246 319 EW72
Thamesfield Ct., Shep. 281 328 BQ101
Thamesgate Clo., Rich. 268 322 CH91
Thameshill Ave., Rom. 227 309 FC54
Thameside, Tedd. 268 322 CJ94
Thameside Ind. Est. E16 252 318 EL75
Thameside Wk. SE28 246 319 EV72
Thamesmead Spine Rd., Belv. 255 319 FC75
Thamesmere Dr. SE28 246 319 EU73
Thamesvale Clo., Houns. 251 321 CA82
Thane Vil. N7 99 306 DM62
Thane Wks. N7 99 306 DM62
Thanescroft Gdns., Croy. 287 332 DS104
Thanet Dr., Kes. 290 334 EK104
Thanet Pl., Croy. 287 332 DQ105
Thanet Rd., Bex. 263 327 FA87
Thanet Rd., Erith 255 319 FE80
Thanet St. WC1 34/5 316 DL69
Thanington Ct. SE9 261 326 ES86
Thant Clo. E10 104 307 EB62
Tharp Rd., Wall. 286 332 DK106
Thatcham Gdns. N20 207 299 DC45
Thatcher Clo., West Dr. 248 320 BL75
Thatchers Way, Islw. 259 321 CD85
Thatches Gro., Rom. 226 309 EY56
Thavies Inn EC1 48 316 DN72
Thaxted Pl. SW20 270 323 CX94
Thaxted Rd. SE9 261 326 EQ89
Thaxted Wk., Rain. 247 319 FF67
Thaxton Rd. W14 157 315 CZ79
Thayer St. W1 44 316 DG71
Thayers Fm. Rd., Beck. 274 325 DY95
Theatre St. SW11 175 323 DF83
Theberton St. N1 24 316 DN67
Theed St. SE1 60 316 DN74
Thelma Gdns. SE3 252 318 EK81
Thelma Gdns., Felt. 258 321 BY90
Thelma Gro., Tedd. 268 322 CG93
Theobald Cres., Har. 215 303 CB53
Theobald Rd. E17 103 307 DZ59
Theobald Rd., Croy. 286 332 DP103
Theobald St. SE1 74 316 DR76
Theobalds Ave. N12 207 299 DC49
Theobalds Ct. N4 100 306 DQ61
Theobalds Pk. Rd., Enf. 202 300 DP35
Theobald's Rd. WC1 47 316 DM71
Theodore Rd. SE13 183 325 ED86
Therapia La., Croy. 286 332 DK101
Therapia Rd. SE22 180 325 DW86
Theresa Rd. W6 146 315 CU77
Theresas Wk., S.Croy. 295 332 DR110
Therfield Ct. N4 100 306 DQ61
Thermopylae Gate E14 150 317 EB77
Theseus Wk. N1 24/5 316 DP68
Thesiger Rd. SE20 274 325 DX94
Thessaly Rd. SW8 160 316 DJ80
Thetford Clo. N13 221 306 DP51
Thetford Gdns., Dag. 236 309 EX66
Thetford Rd., Ashf. 264 328 BL91
Thetford Rd., Dag. 236 309 EX66
Thetford Rd., N.Mal. 283 330 CR100
Thetis Ter., Rich. 154 314 CN79
Theydon Gdns., Rain. 237 309 FE66
Theydon Gro., Wdf.Grn. 224 308 EJ51
Theydon Rd. E5 102 307 DW61
Theydon St. E17 103 307 DZ59
Thicket, The, West Dr. 248 312 BL72
Thicket Cres., Sutt. 285 331 DC105
Thicket Gro. SE20 274 325 DU94
Thicket Gro., Dag. 236 309 EW65
Thicket Rd. SE20 274 325 DU94
Thicket Rd., Sutt. 285 331 DC105
Thickthorne La., Stai. 264 328 BJ94
Third Ave. E12 234 308 EL63
Third Ave. E13 244 318 EG69
Third Ave. E17 223 307 EA57
Third Ave. W3 135 314 CT74
Third Ave. W10 127 315 CY69
Third Ave., Dag. 247 319 FB67
Third Ave., Enf. 209 300 DT43
Third Ave., Hayes 249 312 BT74
Third Ave., Rom. 226 309 EW58
Third Ave., Wem. 91 304 CK61
Third Clo., W.Mol. 267 329 CB98
Third Cross Rd., Twick. 259 321 CD89
Third Way, Wem. 108 304 CP63
Thirleby Rd. SW1 69 316 DJ76
Thirleby Rd., Edg. 217 304 CR53
Thirlmere Ave., Grnf. 122 314 CJ69
Thirlmere Gdns., Nthwd. 213 302 BP50
Thirlmere Gdns., Wem. 90 304 CJ60
Thirlmere Ho., Islw. 259 321 CF85
Thirlmere Ri., Brom. 275 325 EF93
Thirlmere Rd. N10 220 306 DH53
Thirlmere Rd. SW16 272 324 DK91
Thirlmere Rd., Bexh. 255 319 FC82
Thirsk Clo., Nthlt. 233 313 CA65
Thirsk Rd. SE25 273 324 DR98
Thirsk Rd. SW11 176 324 DG83
Thirsk Rd., Mitch. 272 324 DG94
Thistle Gro. SW10 77 315 DC78
Thistlebrook SE2 254 319 EW76
Thistlecroft Gdns., Stan. 216 304 CK53
Thistledene Ave., Har. 232 313 BY62
Thistlemead, Chis. 277 326 EP96
Thistlewaite Rd. E5 102 307 DV62
Thistlewood Clo. N7 99 306 DM61
Thistleworth Clo., Islw. 251 321 CD80
Thistley Clo. N12 219 305 DE51
Thomas Baines Rd. SW11 175 323 DD83
Thomas Darby Ct. W11 137 315 CY72
Thomas Dean Rd. SE26 274 325 DZ91
Thomas Dinwiddy Rd. SE12 260 326 EJ89
Thomas Doyle St. SE1 72/3 316 DP76
Thomas Hardy Ho. N22 220 306 DM52
Thomas La. SE6 198 325 EA87
Thomas More Ho. EC2 49 316 DQ71
Thomas More St. E1 138 317 DU73
Thomas More Way N2 219 305 DC55
Thomas Pl. W8 64/5 315 DB76
Thomas Rd. E14 139 317 DZ72
Thomas Sims Ct., Horn. 238 310 FH64
Thomas St. SE18 253 318 EP77
Thomas Wall Clo., Sutt. 284 331 DB106
Thomas ‡ Beckett Clo., Wem. 233 313 CF63
Thompson Ave., Rich. 170 322 CN83
Thompson Clo., Ilf. 235 308 EQ61
Thompson Rd. SE22 179 324 DT86
Thompson Rd., Dag. 236 309 EZ62
Thompson Rd., Uxb. 240 312 BL66
Thompson's Ave. SE5 162 316 DQ80
Thomson Cres., Croy. 286 332 DN102
Thomson Rd., Har. 215 303 CE55
Thorburn Sq. SE1 148 317 DU77
Thorburn Way SW19 271 323 DD95
Thoresby St. N1 37 316 DQ69
Thorn Clo., Brom. 290 334 EN100
Thorn Clo., Nthlt. 242 313 BZ69
Thorn Ho., Beck. 274 325 DY95
Thorn Ter. SE15 180 325 DW83
Thornaby Gdns. N18 222 307 DU51
Thornbank Clo., Stai. 256 320 BG85
Thornbury Ave., Islw. 251 321 CD80
Thornbury Clo. N16 117 306 DS64
Thornbury Rd. SW2 177 324 DL86
Thornbury Rd., Islw. 251 321 CD80
Thornbury Sq. N6 98 306 DJ60
Thornby Rd. E5 102 307 DW62
Thorncliffe Rd. SW2 177 324 DL86
Thorncliffe Rd., Sthl. 250 321 BZ78
Thorncombe Rd. SE22 179 324 DS85
Thorncroft, Horn. 228 310 FH58
Thorncroft Rd., Sutt. 284 331 DB105
Thorncroft St. SW8 161 316 DL80
Thorndean St. SW18 190 323 DC89
Thorndene Ave. N11 208 300 DG46
Thorndike Ave., Nthlt. 242 313 BX67
Thorndike Clo. SW10 158 315 DC80
Thorndike St. SW1 82 316 DK77
Thorndon Clo., Orp. 277 326 ET96
Thorndon Gdns., Epsom 283 330 CS106
Thorndon Rd., Orp. 277 326 ET96
Thorndyke Ct., Pnr. 214 303 BZ52
Thorne Clo. E11 121 307 EE63
Thorne Clo. E16 141 317 EF72
Thorne Clo., Ashf. 265 328 BQ94
Thorne Clo., Erith 255 319 FC79
Thorne Pas. SW13 155 314 CS82
Thorne Rd. SW8 161 316 DL80
Thorne St. E16 141 317 EF72
Thorne St. SW13 171 322 CS83
Thorneloe Gdns., Croy. 286 332 DN106
Thornes Clo., Beck. 275 325 EC97
Thornet Wd. Rd., Brom. 277 326 EN97
Thorney Cres. SW11 159 315 DD80
Thorney Hedge Rd. W4 144 314 CP77
Thorney Mill Rd., Iver 248 320 BG76
Thorney St. SW1 82/3 316 DL77
Thornfield Ave. NW7 218 305 CY53
Thornfield Rd. W12 146 315 CV75
Thornford Rd. SE13 182 325 EC85
Thorngate Rd. W9 28 315 DA70
Thorngrove Rd. E13 244 318 EH67
Thornham Gro. E15 121 307 ED64
Thornham St. SE10 166 317 EB79
Thornhaugh Ms. WC1 34 316 DK70
Thornhaugh St. WC1 46 316 DK71
Thornhill Ave. SE18 253 318 ES80
Thornhill Ave., Surb. 282 330 CL103
Thornhill Bri. Wf. N1 23 316 DM67
Thornhill Cres. N1 115 306 DM66
Thornhill Gdns. E10 104 307 EB61
Thornhill Gdns., Bark. 235 308 ES66
Thornhill Gro. N1 115 306 DM66
Thornhill Ho. N1 116 306 DN66
Thornhill Rd. E10 104 307 EB61
Thornhill Rd. N1 116 306 DN66
Thornhill Rd., Croy. 287 332 DQ101
Thornhill Rd., Nthwd. 213 302 BQ49
Thornhill Rd., Surb. 282 330 CL103
Thornhill Rd., Uxb. 240 312 BM63
Thornhill Sq. N1 115 306 DM66
Thornhill Way, Shep. 281 328 BN99
Thornlaw Rd. SE27 273 324 DN91
Thornley Clo. N17 222 307 DU52
Thornley Dr., Har. 233 313 CB61
Thornley Pl. SE10 151 317 EE78
Thornsbeach Rd. SE6 198 325 EC88
Thornsett Pl. SE20 274 325 DV96
Thornsett Rd. SE20 274 325 DV96
Thornsett Rd. SW18 190 323 DB88
Thornside, Edg. 217 304 CN51
Thornton Ave. SW2 193 324 DK88
Thornton Ave. W4 145 314 CS77
Thornton Ave., Croy. 286 332 DM100
Thornton Ave., West Dr. 248 320 BM76
Thornton Clo., West Dr. 248 320 BM76
Thornton Ct. SW20 284 331 CX99
Thornton Dene, Beck. 275 325 EA96
Thornton Gdns. SW12 193 324 DK88
Thornton Gro., Pnr. 215 303 CA51
Thornton Hill SW19 270 323 CY94
Thornton Pl. W1 43 315 DF71
Thornton Rd. E11 105 307 ED61
Thornton Rd. N18 210 301 DW48
Thornton Rd. SW12 193 324 DK87
Thornton Rd. SW14 171 322 CR83
Thornton Rd. SW19 270 323 CX93
Thornton Rd., Belv. 255 319 FB77
Thornton Rd., Brom. 276 326 EG92
Thornton Rd., Cars. 285 331 DD102
Thornton Rd., Croy. 286 332 DM101
Thornton Rd., Ilf. 235 308 EP63
Thornton Rd., Th.Hth. 286 332 DN99
Thornton Rd. E. SW19 270 323 CX93
Thornton Row, Th.Hth. 286 332 DN99
Thornton St. SW9 162 316 DN82
Thornton Way NW11 219 305 DB57
Thorntons Fm. Ave., Rom. 237 309 FC60
Thorntree Rd. SE7 252 318 EK78
Thornville Gro. SW19 271 323 DC96
Thornville St. SE8 166 317 EA81
Thornwood Clo. E18 224 308 EH54
Thornwood Rd. SE13 183 325 EE85
Thorogood Gdns. E15 121 307 EE64
Thorogood Way, Rain. 247 319 FE67
Thorold Rd. N22 220 306 DL52
Thorold Rd., Ilf. 235 308 EP61
Thorparch Rd. SW8 161 316 DK81
Thorpe Clo. W10 137 315 CY72
Thorpe Clo., Orp. 291 334 ES103
Thorpe Cres. E17 222 307 DZ54
Thorpe Hall Rd. E17 223 307 EC53
Thorpe Lo., Horn. 228 310 FK58
Thorpe Rd. E6 244 318 EM67
Thorpe Rd. E7 121 307 EF63
Thorpe Rd. E17 223 307 EC54

Thorpe Rd. N15	221	306	DS58
Thorpe Rd., Bark.	235	308	ER66
Thorpe Rd., Kings.T.	268	322	CL94
Thorpebank Rd. W12	136	315	CU74
Thorpedale Gdns., Ilf.	225	308	EN56
Thorpedale Rd. N4	99	306	DL61
Thorpewood Ave. SE26	196	325	DV89
Thorpland Ave., Uxb.	231	312	BQ62
Thorsden Way SE19	273	324	DS91
Thorton Rd. Retail Pk., Croy.	286	332	DM100
Thorverton Rd. NW2	95	305	CY62
Thoydon Rd. E3	129	317	DY68
Thrale Rd. SW16	272	324	DJ91
Thrale St. SE1	61	316	DQ74
Thrasher Clo. E8	27	316	DT67
Thrawl St. E1	51	316	DT71
Threadneedle St. EC2	50	316	DR72
Three Colt St. E14	139	317	DZ72
Three Colts Cor. E2	128	317	DU70
Three Colts La. E2	128	317	DV70
Three Cors., Bexh.	255	319	FB82
Three Cups Yd. WC1	47	316	DM71
Three Kings Rd., Mitch.	272	324	DG97
Three Kings Yd. W1	56/7	316	DH73
Three Mill La. E3	130	317	EC69
Three Oak La. SE1	75	316	DT75
Three Oaks Clo., Uxb.	230	312	BM62
Threshers Pl. W11	137	315	CY73
Thriffwood SE26	196	325	DW90
Throckmorten Rd. E16	244	318	EH72
Throgmorton Ave. EC2	50	316	DR72
Throgmorton St. EC2	50	316	DR72
Throwley Clo. SE2	254	319	EW76
Throwley Rd., Sutt.	284	331	DB106
Throwley Way, Sutt.	284	331	DB105
Thrupp Clo., Mitch.	272	324	DH96
Thrush Grn., Har.	215	303	CA56
Thrush St. SE17	85	316	DQ78
Thruxton Way SE15	163	316	DT80
Thunderer Rd., Dag.	246	319	EY70
Thurbarn Rd. SE6	275	325	EB92
Thurland Rd. SE16	148	317	DU76
Thurlby Clo., Har.	216	304	CG58
Thurlby Rd. SE27	273	324	DN91
Thurlby Rd., Wem.	107	304	CK65
Thurleigh Ave. SW12	176	324	DG86
Thurleigh Rd. SW12	191	323	DF87
Thurleston Ave., Mord.	284	331	CY99
Thurlestone Ave. N12	219	305	DF51
Thurlestone Ave., Ilf.	235	308	ET63
Thurlestone Clo., Shep.	281	328	BQ100
Thurlestone Rd. SE27	194	324	DN90
Thurloe Clo. SW7	78/9	315	DE77
Thurloe Gdns., Rom.	227	309	FF58
Thurloe Pl. SW7	78	315	DD77
Thurloe Pl. Ms. SW7	78	315	DD77
Thurloe Sq. SW7	78/9	315	DE77
Thurloe St. SW7	78	315	DD77
Thurlow Clo. E4	223	307	EB51
Thurlow Gdns., Ilf.	225	308	ER51
Thurlow Gdns., Wem.	107	304	CK64
Thurlow Hill SE21	194	324	DQ88
Thurlow Pk. Rd. SE21	194	324	DP88
Thurlow Rd. NW3	113	305	DD64
Thurlow Rd. W7	142	314	CG75
Thurlow St. SE17	86	316	DR78
Thurlow Ter. NW5	114	306	DG64
Thurlston Rd., Ruis.	232	313	BU62
Thurnby Ct., Twick.	259	321	CE90
Thursland Rd., Sid.	278	327	EY92
Thursley Gdns. SW19	189	323	CX89
Thursley Rd. SE9	260	326	EM90
Thurso Clo., Rom.	229	311	FP51
Thurso St. SW17	271	323	DD91
Thurstan Rd. SW20	270	323	CV94
Thurston Rd. SE13	166	317	EB82
Thurston Rd., Sthl.	242	313	BZ72
Thurtle Rd. E2	27	316	DT67
Thwaite Clo., Erith	255	319	FC79
Thyer Clo., Orp.	291	334	EQ105
Thyra Gro. N12	219	305	DB51
Tibbatts Rd. E3	130	317	EB70
Tibbenham Wk. E13	131	317	EF68
Tibberton Sq. N1	116	306	DQ66
Tibbets Clo. SW19	189	323	CX88
Tibbets Cor. SW19	189	323	CX87
Tibbet's Ride SW15	189	323	CX87
Tiber Gdns. N1	23	316	DM67
Ticehurst Clo., Orp.	278	327	EU94
Ticehurst Rd. SE23	197	325	DY89
Tickford Clo. SE2	254	319	EW75
Tidal Basin Rd. E16	141	317	EF73
Tidenham Gdns., Croy.	287	332	DS104
Tideswell Rd. SW15	172	323	CW84
Tideswell Rd., Croy.	288	333	EA104
Tideway Clo., Rich.	268	322	CH91
Tidey St. E3	140	317	EA71
Tidford Rd., Well.	253	318	ET82
Tidworth Rd. E3	130	317	EA70
Tiepigs La., Brom.	289	333	EF102
Tiepigs La., W.Wick.	289	333	EE103
Tierney Rd. SW2	193	324	DL87
Tiger La., Brom.	276	326	EH98
Tiger Way E5	118	307	DV63
Tilbrook Rd. SE3	260	326	EJ83
Tilbury Clo. SE15	163	316	DT80
Tilbury Clo., Orp.	278	327	EV96
Tilbury Rd. E6	244	318	EM68
Tilbury Rd. E10	104	307	EC59
Tildesley Rd. SW15	172	323	CW86
Tile Fm. Rd., Orp.	291	334	ER104
Tile Kiln La. N6	98	306	DJ60
Tile Kiln La. N13	209	300	DQ50
Tile Kiln La., Bex.	263	327	FC89
Tile Kiln La., Uxb.	231	312	BP59
Tile Yd. E14	139	317	DZ72
Tilehurst Rd. SW18	191	323	DD88
Tilehurst Rd., Sutt.	284	331	CY106
Tileyard Rd. N7	115	306	DL66
Tilford Gdns. SW19	189	323	CX88
Tilia Rd. E5	118	307	DV63
Tilia Wk. SW9	178	324	DP84
Tiller Rd. E14	150	317	EA76
Tillett Clo. NW10	108	304	CQ65
Tillett Sq. SE16	149	317	DY75
Tillett Way E2	128	317	DU69
Tilling Rd. NW2	94	305	CW60
Tilling Way, Wem.	107	304	CK63
Tillingbourne Gdns. N3	218	305	CZ55
Tillingbourne Grn., Orp.	277	326	ET98
Tillingbourne Way N3	218	305	CZ55
Tillingham Way N12	207	299	DA49
Tillman St. E1	138	317	DV72
Tilloch St. N1	115	306	DM66
Tillotson Rd. N9	209	300	DT47
Tillotson Rd., Har.	215	303	CB52
Tillotson Rd., Ilf.	235	308	EN59
Tilney Ct. EC1	37	316	DQ70
Tilney Gdns. N1	117	306	DR65
Tilney Rd., Dag.	236	309	EZ65
Tilney Rd., Sthl.	250	321	BW77
Tilney St. W1	56	316	DG74
Tilson Gdns. SW2	193	324	DL87
Tilson Ho. SW2	193	324	DL87
Tilson Rd. N17	222	307	DU53
Tilt Yd. App. SE9	260	326	EM86
Tilton St. SW6	157	315	CY79
Tiltwood, The W3	134	314	CQ73
Timber Clo., Chis.	277	326	EN96
Timber Mill Way SW4	177	324	DK83
Timber Pond Rd. SE16	139	317	DX74
Timber Slip Dr., Wall.	294	332	DK109
Timber St. EC1	37	316	DQ70
Timbercroft, Epsom	283	330	CS105
Timbercroft La. SE18	253	318	ES79
Timberdene NW4	218	305	CX54
Timberdene Ave., Ilf.	225	308	EQ53
Timberland Rd. E1	138	317	DV72
Timberling Gdns., S.Croy.	295	332	DR109
Timberwharf Rd. N16	222	307	DU58
Time Sq. E8	117	306	DT64
Times Sq., Sutt.	284	331	DB106
Timothy Clo. SW4	176	324	DJ85
Timothy Clo., Bexh.	262	327	EY85
Timothy Rd. E3	139	317	DZ71
Timsbury Wk. SW15	188	323	CU88
Tindal St. SW9	162	316	DP81
Tindale Clo., S.Croy.	295	332	DR111
Tindall Clo., Rom.	228	311	FM54
Tinderbox All. SW14	171	322	CR83
Tinniswood Clo. N5	116	306	DN64
Tinsley Rd. E1	138	317	DW71
Tintagel Cres. SE22	179	324	DT84
Tintagel Dr., Stan.	204	298	CK49
Tintagel Gdns. SE22	179	324	DT84
Tintern Ave. NW9	217	304	CP55
Tintern Clo. SW15	173	323	CY85
Tintern Clo. SW19	271	323	DC94
Tintern Gdns. N14	208	300	DL45
Tintern Path NW9	217	304	CS58
Tintern Rd. N22	221	306	DQ53
Tintern Rd., Cars.	285	331	DD102
Tintern St. SW4	177	324	DL84
Tintern Way, Har.	233	313	CB60
Tinto Rd. E16	244	318	EG70
Tinwell Ms., Borwd.	205	298	CQ43
Tinworth St. SE11	82/3	316	DL78
Tippetts Clo., Enf.	202	300	DQ39
Tipthorpe Rd. SW11	176	324	DG83
Tipton Dr., Croy.	287	332	DS105
Tiptree Clo. E4	211	301	EC48
Tiptree Clo., Horn.	239	311	FN60
Tiptree Cres., Ilf.	225	308	EN55
Tiptree Dr., Enf.	202	300	DR42
Tiptree Est., Ilf.	225	308	EN55
Tiptree Rd., Ruis.	232	313	BV63
Tirlemont Rd., S.Croy.	295	332	DQ108
Tirrell Rd., Croy.	287	332	DQ100
Tisbury Ct. W1	58	316	DK73
Tisbury Rd. SW16	272	324	DL96
Tisdall Pl. SE17	86	316	DR77
Titchborne Row W2	42/3	315	DE72
Titchfield Rd. NW8	19	315	DF67
Titchfield Rd., Cars.	285	331	DD102
Titchfield Rd., Enf.	203	301	DY37
Titchfield Wk., Cars.	285	331	DD101
Titchwell Rd. SW18	191	323	DD87
Tite St. SW3	159	315	DF79
Tithe Barn Clo., Kings.T.	268	322	CM95
Tithe Barn Way, Nthlt.	242	313	BV68
Tithe Clo. NW7	218	305	CU53
Tithe Fm. Ave., Har.	233	313	CA62
Tithe Fm. Clo., Har.	233	313	CA62
Tithe Wk. NW7	218	305	CU53
Titley Clo. E4	211	301	EA50
Titmus Clo., Uxb.	249	312	BQ72
Titmuss Ave. SE28	246	319	EV73
Titmuss St. W12	146	315	CV75
Tiverton Ave., Ilf.	225	308	EN55
Tiverton Dr. SE9	261	326	EQ88
Tiverton Rd. N15	221	306	DR58
Tiverton Rd. N18	209	300	DS50
Tiverton Rd. NW10	127	315	CX67
Tiverton Rd., Edg.	216	304	CM54
Tiverton Rd., Houns.	251	321	CC82
Tiverton Rd., Ruis.	232	313	BU62
Tiverton Rd., Th.Hth.	286	332	DN99
Tiverton Rd., Wem.	123	314	CL68
Tiverton St. SE1	73	316	DQ76
Tiverton Way, Chess.	282	330	CJ106
Tivoli Ct. SE16	149	317	DZ75
Tivoli Gdns. SE18	252	318	EL77
Tivoli Rd. N8	220	306	DK57
Tivoli Rd. SE27	273	324	DQ92
Tivoli Rd., Houns.	258	321	BY84
Toad La., Houns.	258	321	BZ84
Tobacco Quay E1	138	317	DV73
Tobago St. E14	150	317	EA75
Tobin Clo. NW3	113	305	DE66
Toby La. E1	129	317	DY70
Toby Way, Surb.	282	330	CP103
Todds Wk. N7	99	306	DM61
Token Yd. SW15	173	323	CY84
Tokenhouse Yd. EC2	50	316	DR72
Tokyngton Ave., Wem.	108	304	CN65
Toland Sq. SW15	172	323	CU85
Tolcarne Dr., Pnr.	214	303	BU54
Toley Ave., Wem.	91	304	CL59
Tollbridge Clo. W10	127	315	CY70
Tollesbury Gdns., Ilf.	225	308	ER55
Tollet St. E1	129	317	DX70
Tollgate Dr. SE21	195	324	DS89
Tollgate Gdns. NW6	16/7	315	DB68
Tollgate Rd. E6	244	318	EK71
Tollgate Rd. E16	244	318	EJ71
Tollgate Rd., Wal.Cr.	203	301	DX35
Tollhouse La., Wall.	294	332	DJ109
Tollhouse Way N19	98	306	DJ61
Tollington Pk. N4	99	306	DM61
Tollington Pl. N4	99	306	DM61
Tollington Rd. N7	115	306	DM63
Tollington Way N7	99	306	DL62
Tolmers Sq. NW1	33	316	DJ70
Tolpuddle Ave. E13	244	318	EJ67
Tolpuddle St. N1	24	316	DN68
Tolsford Rd. E5	118	307	DV64
Tolson Rd., Islw.	168	322	CG83
Tolverne Rd. SW20	270	323	CW95
Tolworth Clo., Surb.	282	330	CP102
Tolworth Gdns., Rom.	226	309	EX57
Tolworth Pk. Rd., Surb.	282	330	CM103
Tolworth Ri. N., Surb.	283	330	CQ101
Tolworth Ri. S., Surb.	283	330	CQ102
Tolworth Rd., Surb.	282	330	CL103
Tom Coombs Clo. SE9	260	326	EL84
Tom Cribb Rd. SE28	253	318	EQ76
Tom Gros. Clo. E15	121	307	ED64
Tom Hood Clo. E15	121	307	ED64
Tom Mann Clo., Bark.	245	318	ES67
Tom Nolan Clo. E15	131	317	EE68
Tom Smith Clo. SE10	167	317	EE79
Tom Thumbs Arch E3	130	317	EA68
Tomahawk Gdns., Nthlt.	242	313	BX69
Tomkyns La., Upmin.	229	311	FR54
Tomlins Gro. E3	130	317	EA69
Tomlins Orchard, Bark.	245	318	EQ67
Tomlins Ter. E14	139	317	DZ71
Tomlins Wk. N7	99	306	DM61
Tomlinson Clo. E2	39	316	DT69
Tomlinson Clo. W4	144	314	CP78
Tompion St. EC1	36/7	316	DP69
Tomswood Ct., Ilf.	225	308	EQ53
Tomswood Hill, Ilf.	225	308	EP52
Tomswood Rd., Chig.	225	308	EN51
Tonbridge Clo., Bans.	293	331	DF114
Tonbridge Cres., Har.	216	304	CL56
Tonbridge Ho. SE25	274	325	DU97
Tonbridge Rd., Rom.	228	310	FK52
Tonbridge Rd., W.Mol.	266	329	BY98
Tonbridge St. WC1	34/5	316	DL69
Tonbridge Wk. WC1	34/5	316	DL69
Tonfield Rd., Sutt.	284	331	CZ102
Tonge Clo., Beck.	288	333	EA99
Tonsley Hill SW18	174	323	DB85
Tonsley Pl. SW18	174	323	DB85
Tonsley Rd. SW18	174	323	DB85
Tonsley St. SW18	174	323	DB85
Tonstall Rd., Mitch.	272	324	DG96
Tony Cannell Ms. E3	129	317	DZ69
Tooke Clo., Pnr.	214	303	BY53
Took's Ct. EC4	48	316	DN72
Tooley St. SE1	62/3	316	DS74
Toorack Rd., Har.	215	303	CD54
Tooting Bec Gdns. SW16	272	324	DK91
Tooting Bec Rd. SW16	272	324	DH91
Tooting Bec Rd. SW17	192	324	DG90
Tooting Gro. SW17	271	323	DE92
Tooting High St. SW17	271	323	DE93
Tootswood Rd., Brom.	289	333	EE99
Top Dartford Rd., Swan.	279	327	FF94
Top Ho. Ri. E4	211	301	EC45
Top Pk., Beck.	289	333	EE99
Topaz Wk. NW2	95	305	CX59
Topcliffe Dr., Orp.	291	334	ER106
Topham Sq. N17	221	306	DQ53
Topham St. EC1	36	316	DN70
Topiary Sq., Rich.	169	322	CM83
Topley St. SE9	260	326	EK84
Topp Wk. NW2	94	305	CW61
Topping La., Uxb.	240	312	BK69
Topsfield Clo. N8	220	306	DK57
Topsfield Par. N8	220	306	DL57
Topsfield Rd. N8	220	306	DL57
Topsham Rd. SW17	191	323	DF90
Tor Gdns. W8	64	315	DA75
Tor Rd., Well.	254	319	EW81
Torbay Rd. NW6	111	305	CZ66
Torbay Rd., Har.	232	313	BY61
Torbay St. NW1	114	306	DH66
Torbitt Way, Ilf.	225	308	ET57
Torbridge Clo., Edg.	216	304	CL52
Torbrook Clo., Bex.	262	327	EY86
Torcross Dr. SE23	196	325	DW89
Torcross Rd., Ruis.	232	313	BV62
Tormead Clo., Sutt.	292	331	DA107
Tormount Rd. SE18	253	318	ES79
Toronto Ave. E12	234	308	EM63
Toronto Rd. E11	121	307	ED63
Toronto Rd., Ilf.	235	308	EP60
Torquay Gdns., Ilf.	224	308	EK56
Torquay St. W2	40/1	315	DB71
Torr Rd. SE20	274	325	DX94
Torrance Clo., Horn.	238	310	FH60
Torre Wk., Cars.	285	331	DE102
Torrens Rd. E15	121	307	EF65
Torrens Rd. SW2	177	324	DM85
Torrens Sq. E15	121	307	EF65
Torrens St. EC1	24	316	DN68
Torriano Ave. NW5	115	306	DK64
Torriano Cotts. NW5	114	306	DJ64
Torriano Ms. NW5	115	306	DK64
Torridge Gdns. SE15	180	325	DW84
Torridge Rd., Th.Hth.	286	332	DP99
Torridon Rd. SE6	199	325	ED87
Torridon Rd. SE13	199	325	EE87
Torrington Ave. N12	207	299	DD50
Torrington Clo. N12	207	299	DD49
Torrington Dr., Har.	233	313	CB63
Torrington Gdns. N11	220	306	DJ51
Torrington Gdns., Grnf.	122	314	CJ67
Torrington Gro. N12	207	299	DE50
Torrington Pk. N12	207	299	DC50
Torrington Pl. E1	138	317	DU74
Torrington Pl. WC1	46	316	DK71
Torrington Rd. E18	224	308	EG55
Torrington Rd., Dag.	236	309	EZ60
Torrington Rd., Grnf.	122	314	CJ67
Torrington Rd., Ruis.	231	312	BT62
Torrington Sq. WC1	34	316	DK70
Torrington Sq., Croy.	287	332	DR101
Torrington Way, Mord.	284	331	DA101
Torver Rd., Har.	215	303	CE56
Torver Way, Orp.	291	334	ER103
Torwood Rd. SW15	172	323	CU85
Tothill St. SW1	70	316	DK75
Totnes Rd., Well.	254	319	EV80
Totnes Wk. N2	219	305	DD56
Tottan Ter. E1	139	317	DX72
Tottenhall Rd. N13	221	306	DN51
Tottenham Ct. Rd. W1	33	316	DJ70
Tottenham Grn. E. N15	221	306	DT56
Tottenham La. N8	220	306	DL57
Tottenham Ms. W1	45	316	DJ71
Tottenham Rd. N1	117	306	DS65
Tottenham St. W1	45	316	DJ71
Totterdown St. SW17	271	323	DF91
Totteridge Common N20	206	299	CU47
Totteridge Grn. N20	207	299	DA47
Totteridge La. N20	207	299	DA47
Totteridge Rd., Enf.	203	301	DX37
Totteridge Village N20	206	299	CY46
Totternhoe Clo., Har.	216	304	CJ57
Totton Rd., Th.Hth.	273	324	DN97
Toulmin St. SE1	73	316	DQ75
Toulon St. SE5	162	316	DQ80
Tournay Rd. SW6	157	315	CZ80
Toussaint Wk. SE16	148	317	DU76
Tovil Clo. SE20	274	325	DV96
Towcester Rd. E3	130	317	EB70
Tower Bri. E1	63	316	DT74
Tower Bri. SE1	63	316	DT74
Tower Bri. App. E1	63	316	DT74
Tower Bri. Piazza SE1	63	316	DT74
Tower Bri. Rd. SE1	74/5	316	DS76
Tower Clo. NW3	113	305	DD64
Tower Clo. SE20	274	325	DV94
Tower Clo., Ilf.	225	308	EP51
Tower Clo., Orp.	291	334	ET103
Tower Ct. WC2	46/7	316	DL72
Tower Gdns. Rd. N17	221	306	DQ53
Tower Hamlets Rd. E7	121	307	EF63
Tower Hamlets Rd. E17	223	307	EA55
Tower Hill EC3	62/3	316	DS73
Tower Hill Ter. EC3	62/3	316	DS73
Tower La., Wem.	91	304	CK62
Tower Ms. E17	223	307	EA56
Tower Pier EC3	62/3	316	DS73
Tower Pl. EC3	62/3	316	DS73
Tower Pt., Enf.	202	300	DR42
Tower Ri., Rich.	169	322	CL83
Tower Rd. NW10	110	305	CU66
Tower Rd., Belv.	255	319	FC77
Tower Rd., Bexh.	263	327	FA84
Tower Rd., Orp.	291	334	ET103
Tower Rd., Twick.	259	321	CF90
Tower Royal EC4	61	316	DQ73
Tower St. WC2	46	316	DK72
Tower Ter. N22	220	306	DM54
Tower Vw., Croy.	288	333	DX101
Towers Ave., Uxb.	241	312	BQ69
Towers Pl., Rich.	169	322	CL85
Towers Rd., Pnr.	214	303	BY52
Towers Rd., Sthl.	243	313	CA70
Towfield Rd., Felt.	258	321	BZ89
Towing Path Wk. N1	22	316	DK67
Town, The, Enf.	202	300	DR41
Town Ct. Path N4	100	306	DQ60
Town Fld. Way, Islw.	152	314	CG82
Town Hall App. N16	117	306	DS63
Town Hall App. Rd. N15	221	306	DT56
Town Hall Ave. W4	145	314	CR78
Town Hall Rd. SW11	175	323	DF83
Town La., Stai.	256	320	BK86
Town Meadow, Brent.	153	314	CK80
Town Quay, Bark.	245	318	EP67
Town Rd. N9	210	301	DV47
Town Sq., Erith	255	319	FE79
Town Tree Rd., Ashf.	265	328	BN92
Towncourt Cres., Orp.	291	334	EQ99
Towncourt La., Orp.	291	334	ER100
Towney Mead, Nthlt.	242	313	BZ68
Townfield Rd., Hayes	249	312	BT74
Townfield Sq., Hayes	249	312	BT73
Townholm Cres. W7	251	321	CF76
Townley Ct. E15	121	307	EF65
Townley Rd. SE22	179	324	DS85
Townley Rd., Bexh.	262	327	EZ86
Townley St. SE17	86	316	DR78
Townmead Rd. SW6	174	323	DB83
Townmead Rd., Rich.	154	314	CP82
Townsend Ave. N14	208	300	DK49
Townsend Ind. Est. NW10	124	314	CQ68
Townsend La. NW9	93	304	CR59
Townsend Rd. N15	221	306	DT57
Townsend Rd., Ashf.	264	328	BL92
Townsend Rd., Sthl.	242	313	BY74
Townsend St. SE17	86	316	DR77
Townsend Way, Nthwd.	213	302	BT52
Townsend Yd. N6	98	306	DG60
Townshend Clo., Sid.	278	327	EV93
Townshend Est. NW8	18/9	315	DE68
Townshend Rd. NW8	18/9	315	DE67
Townshend Rd., Chis.	277	326	EP92
Townshend Rd., Rich.	169	322	CM84
Townshend Ter., Rich.	169	322	CM84
Townson Ave., Nthlt.	242	313	BU69
Townson Way, Nthlt.	242	313	BU68
Towpath, Shep.	280	328	BM102
Towpath Way, Croy.	287	332	DT100
Towton Rd. SE27	194	324	DQ89
Toynbec Clo., Chis.	277	326	EP91
Toynbee Rd. SW20	270	323	CY95
Toynbee St. E1	51	316	DT71
Toyne Way N6	219	305	DF58
Tracey Ave. NW2	110	305	CW64
Tracy Ct., Stan.	216	304	CJ52
Trade Clo. N13	209	300	DN49
Trader Rd. E6	245	318	EP72
Tradescant Rd. SW8	161	316	DL80
Trading Est. Rd. NW10	124	314	CQ70
Trafalgar Ave. N17	221	306	DS51
Trafalgar Ave. SE15	87	316	DT78
Trafalgar Ave., Wor.Pk.	284	331	CX102
Trafalgar Business Cen., Bark.	245	318	ET70
Trafalgar Clo. SE16	149	317	DY77
Trafalgar Gdns. E1	139	317	DX71
Trafalgar Gdns. W8	64/5	315	DB76
Trafalgar Gro. SE10	167	317	ED79
Trafalgar Pl. E11	224	308	EG56
Trafalgar Pl. N18	210	301	DU50
Trafalgar Rd. SE10	167	317	ED79
Trafalgar Rd. SW19	271	323	DB94
Trafalgar Rd., Rain.	247	319	FF68
Trafalgar Rd., Twick.	259	321	CD89
Trafalgar Sq. SW1	58	316	DK74
Trafalgar Sq. WC2	58	316	DK74
Trafalgar St. SE17	86	316	DR78
Trafalgar Ter., Har.	233	313	CE60
Trafalgar Way E14	140	317	EC74
Trafalgar Way, Croy.	286	332	DM103
Trafford Clo. E15	120	307	EB64
Trafford Clo., Ilf.	225	308	ET51
Trafford Rd., Th.Hth.	286	332	DM99
Tramway Ave. E15	121	307	EE66
Tramway Ave. N9	210	301	DV45
Tramway Path, Mitch.	271	323	DE98
Tranby Pl. E9	119	307	DX64
Tranley Ms. NW3	113	305	DE63
Tranmere Rd. N9	209	300	DT45
Tranmere Rd. SW18	190	323	DC88
Tranmere Rd., Twick.	259	321	CB87
Tranquil Pas. SE3	167	317	EF82
Tranquil Ri., Erith	255	319	FE78
Tranquil Vale SE3	167	317	EE82
Transay Wk. N1	117	306	DR65
Transept St. NW1	42/3	315	DE71
Transmere Clo., Orp.	291	334	EQ100
Transmere Rd., Orp.	291	334	EQ100
Transom Clo. SE16	149	317	DY77
Transom Sq. E14	150	317	EB77
Transport Ave., Brent.	142	314	CG78
Tranton Rd. SE16	148	317	DU76
Traps La., N.Mal.	269	322	CS95
Travellers Way, Houns.	250	321	BW82
Travers Clo. E17	222	307	DX53
Travers Rd. N7	100	306	DN62
Treadgold St. W11	137	315	CX73
Treadway St. E2	128	317	DV68
Treaty Rd., Houns.	259	321	CB83
Treaty St. N1	23	316	DM67
Trebeck St. W1	56/7	316	DH74
Trebovir Rd. SW5	76	315	DA78
Treby St. E3	129	317	DZ70
Trecastle Way N7	115	306	DK63
Tredegar Ms. E3	129	317	DZ69
Tredegar Rd. E3	129	317	DZ68
Tredegar Rd. N11	220	306	DK52
Tredegar Sq. E3	129	317	DZ69
Tredegar Ter. E3	129	317	DZ69
Trederwen Rd. E8	128	317	DU67
Tredown Rd. SE26	274	325	DW92
Tredwell Clo., Brom.	276	326	EL98
Tredwell Rd. SE27	273	324	DP91
Tree Clo., Rich.	185	322	CK88
Tree Rd. E16	244	318	EJ72
Treen Ave. SW13	171	322	CS83
Treeside Clo., West Dr.	248	320	BK77
Treetops Clo. SE2	254	319	EY78
Treetops Clo., Nthwd.	213	302	BR50
Treeview Clo. SE19	273	324	DS95
Treewall Gdns., Brom.	276	326	EH91
Trefgarne Rd., Dag.	237	309	FA61
Trefil Wk. N7	115	306	DL63
Trefoil Rd. SW18	174	323	DC85
Tregaron Ave. N8	220	306	DL58
Tregaron Gdns., N.Mal.	269	322	CS98
Tregarvon Rd. SW11	176	324	DG84
Tregenna Ave., Har.	232	313	BZ63
Tregenna Clo. N14	208	300	DJ43
Tregenna Ct., Har.	233	313	CA63
Trego Rd. E9	120	307	EA66
Tregothnan Rd. SW9	177	324	DL83
Tregunter Rd. SW10	158	315	DC79
Trehearn Rd., Ilf.	225	308	ER52
Trehern Rd. SW14	171	322	CR83
Treherne Ct. SW9	162	316	DN81
Treherne Ct. SW17	272	324	DG91
Trehurst St. E5	119	307	DY64
Trelawn Rd. E10	104	307	EC62
Trelawn Rd. SW2	178	324	DN85
Trelawney Clo. E17	223	307	EB56
Trelawney Est. E9	118	307	DW65
Trelawney Rd., Ilf.	225	308	ER52
Trellick Twr. W10	127	315	CZ70
Trellis Sq. E3	129	317	DZ69
Treloar Gdns. SE19	273	324	DR93
Tremadoc Rd. SW4	177	324	DK84
Tremaine Clo. SE4	166	317	EA82
Tremaine Rd. SE20	274	325	DV96
Trematon Pl., Tedd.	268	322	CJ94
Tremlett Gro. N19	98	306	DJ62
Tremlett Ms. N19	98	306	DJ62
Trenance Gdns., Ilf.	236	309	EU62
Trench Yd. Ct., Mord.	284	331	DB100
Trenchard Ave., Ruis.	232	313	BV63
Trenchard Clo., Stan.	216	304	CG51
Trenchard Ct., Mord.	284	331	DB100
Trenchard St. SE10	151	317	ED78
Trenchold St. SW8	161	316	DL79
Trenholme Clo. SE20	274	325	DV94
Trenholme Rd. SE20	274	325	DV94
Trenholme Ter. SE20	274	325	DV94
Trenmar Gdns. NW10	126	315	CV69
Trent Ave. W5	142	314	CJ76
Trent Ave., Upmin.	229	311	FR58
Trent Gdns. N14	208	300	DH44
Trent Rd. SW2	177	324	DM85
Trent Way, Hayes	241	312	BS69
Trent Way, Wor.Pk.	284	331	CW104
Trentbridge Clo., Ilf.	225	308	ET51
Trentham Dr., Orp.	278	327	EU98
Trentham St. SW18	190	323	DA88
Treport St. SW18	190	323	DB87
Tresco Clo., Brom.	275	325	EE93
Tresco Gdns., Ilf.	236	309	EU61
Tresco Rd. SE15	180	325	DV84
Trescoe Gdns., Har.	232	313	BY59
Tresham Cres. NW8	30/1	315	DE70
Tresham Rd., Bark.	235	308	ET66
Tresham Wk. E9	118	307	DW64
Tresilian Ave. N21	208	300	DM43
Tressell Clo. N1	116	306	DP66
Tressillian Cres. SE4	182	325	EA83
Tressillian Rd. SE4	181	325	DZ84
Trestis Clo., Hayes	242	313	BY71
Treswell Rd., Dag.	246	319	EY67
Tretawn Gdns. NW7	205	298	CS49
Tretawn Pk. NW7	205	298	CS49
Trevanion Rd. W14	147	315	CY77
Treve Ave., Har.	233	313	CC59
Trevelyan Ave. E12	234	308	EM63
Trevelyan Cres., Har.	91	304	CK59
Trevelyan Gdns. NW10	126	315	CW67
Trevelyan Rd. E15	121	307	EF63
Trevelyan Rd. SW17	271	323	DE92
Treveris St. SE1	60/1	316	DP74
Treverton St. W10	127	315	CY70
Treville St. SW15	188	323	CV87
Treviso Rd. SE23	197	325	DX89
Trevithick Clo., Felt.	265	320	BT88
Trevithick St. SE8	166	317	EA79
Trevone Gdns., Pnr.	214	303	BY58
Trevor Clo., Barn.	207	299	DD44
Trevor Clo., Brom.	289	333	EF101
Trevor Clo., Har.	215	303	CF52
Trevor Clo., Islw.	259	321	CF85
Trevor Clo., Nthlt.	242	313	BW68
Trevor Cres., Ruis.	241	312	BT63
Trevor Gdns., Edg.	217	304	CR53
Trevor Gdns., Nthlt.	242	313	BW68
Trevor Gdns., Ruis.	232	313	BU63
Trevor Pl. SW7	66/7	315	DE75
Trevor Rd. SW19	270	323	CY94
Trevor Rd., Edg.	217	304	CR53
Trevor Rd., Hayes	249	320	BS75
Trevor Rd., Wdf.Grn.	224	308	EG52
Trevor Sq. SW7	66/7	315	DE76
Trevor St. SW7	66/7	315	DE75
Trevose Rd. E17	223	307	ED53
Trewenna Dr., Chess.	282	330	CK106
Trewince Rd. SW20	270	323	CW95
Trewint St. SW18	190	323	DC89
Trewsbury Rd. SE26	274	325	DX92
Triandra Way, Hayes	242	313	BX71
Triangle, The EC1	36/7	316	DP70
Triangle, The N13	209	300	DN49
Triangle, The, Bark.	235	308	EQ65
Triangle, The, Hmptn.	267	329	CC95
Triangle, The, Kings.T.	269	322	CQ96
Triangle Ct. E16	244	318	EK71
Triangle Pl. SW4	177	324	DK84
Triangle Rd. E8	128	317	DV67
Trident Gdns., Nthlt.	242	313	BX69
Trident St. SE16	149	317	DX77
Trident Wk. SE16	149	317	DX77
Trident Way, Sthl.	250	321	BV76
Trig La. EC4	61	316	DQ73
Trigon Rd. SW8	161	316	DM80
Trilby Rd. SE23	197	325	DX89
Trim St. SE14	165	317	DZ79
Trimmer Wk., Brent.	153	314	CL79
Trinder Gdns. N19	99	306	DL60
Trinder Rd. N19	99	306	DL60
Trinder Rd., Barn.	206	299	CW43
Tring Ave. W5	133	314	CM74
Tring Ave., Sthl.	242	313	BZ72
Tring Ave., Wem.	108	304	CN65
Tring Clo., Ilf.	225	308	ER57
Trinidad Gdns., Dag.	237	309	FD66
Trinidad St. E14	139	317	DZ73
Trinity Ave. N2	219	305	DD55
Trinity Ave., Enf.	209	300	DT44
Trinity Ch. Pas. SW13	156	315	CV79
Trinity Ch. Rd. SW13	156	315	CV79
Trinity Ch. Sq. SE1	73	316	DQ76
Trinity Clo. E8	117	306	DT65
Trinity Clo. E11	105	307	EE61
Trinity Clo. NW3	113	305	DD63
Trinity Clo. SE13	183	325	ED84
Trinity Clo., Brom.	290	334	EL102
Trinity Clo., Houns.	258	321	BY84
Trinity Clo., Nthwd.	213	302	BS51
Trinity Clo., S.Croy.	295	332	DS109
Trinity Clo., Stai.	256	320	BJ86
Trinity Cotts., Rich.	169	322	CM83
Trinity Ct. N1	117	306	DS66
Trinity Ct. SE7	252	318	EK77
Trinity Cres. SW17	191	323	DF89
Trinity Gdns. SW9	177	324	DM84
Trinity Gro. SE10	166	317	EC81
Trinity Ms. SE20	274	325	DV95
Trinity Ms. W10	137	315	CX72
Trinity Path SE26	196	325	DW90
Trinity Pl., Bexh.	262	327	EZ84
Trinity Ri. SW2	194	324	DN88
Trinity Rd. N2	219	305	DD55
Trinity Rd. N22	220	306	DL52
Trinity Rd. SW17	191	323	DF89
Trinity Rd. SW18	175	323	DD85
Trinity Rd. SW19	271	323	DA93
Trinity Rd., Ilf.	225	308	EQ55
Trinity Rd., Rich.	169	322	CM83
Trinity Rd., Sthl.	242	313	BY74
Trinity Sq. EC3	62/3	316	DS73
Trinity St. E16	244	318	EG71
Trinity St. SE1	73	316	DQ75
Trinity St., Enf.	202	300	DQ40
Trinity Wk. NW3	112	305	DC65
Trinity Way E4	222	307	DZ51
Trinity Way W3	135	314	CS73
Trio Pl. SE1	73	316	DQ75
Tristan Sq. SE3	183	325	EE83
Tristram Clo. E17	223	307	ED55
Tristram Rd., Brom.	275	325	EF91
Triton Sq. NW1	33	316	DJ70
Tritton Ave., Croy.	286	332	DL105
Tritton Rd. SE21	195	324	DR90
Triumph Clo., Hayes	257	320	BQ81
Triumph Ho., Bark.	246	319	EU69
Triumph Rd. E6	244	318	EM72
Trojan Ct. NW6	111	305	CY66
Trojan Way, Croy.	286	332	DM104
Troon St. E1	139	317	DY72
Trosley Rd., Belv.	255	319	FA79
Trossachs Rd. SE22	179	324	DS85
Trothy Rd. SE1	148	317	DU77
Trott Rd. N10	219	305	DF52
Trott St. SW11	159	315	DD81
Trotwood, Chig.	225	308	ER51
Troughton Rd. SE7	252	318	EH78
Trout La., West Dr.	248	312	BH73
Trout Rd., West Dr.	248	312	BK74
Troutbeck Rd. SE14	165	317	DY81
Trouville Rd. SW4	176	324	DJ86
Trowbridge Est. E9	119	307	DZ65
Trowbridge Rd. E9	119	307	DZ65
Trowbridge Rd., Rom.	228	310	FK51
Trowlock Ave., Tedd.	268	322	CJ93
Trowlock Island, Tedd.	268	322	CJ92
Trowlock Way, Tedd.	268	322	CK93
Troy Ct. SE18	253	318	EP77
Troy Rd. SE19	273	324	DR93
Troy Town SE15	180	325	DU83
Truesdale Dr., Uxb.	230	302	BJ56
Truesdale Rd. E6	244	318	EM72
Trulock Ct. N17	222	307	DU52
Trulock Rd. N17	222	307	DU52
Truman Clo., Edg.	217	304	CP52
Truman's Rd. N16	117	306	DS64
Trump St. EC2	49	316	DQ72
Trumper Way, Uxb.	240	312	BJ67
Trumpers Way W7	251	321	CE75
Trumpington Rd. E7	121	307	EF63
Trundle St. SE1	73	316	DQ75
Trundleys Rd. SE8	149	317	DX78
Trundleys Ter. SE8	149	317	DX77
Trunks All., Swan.	279	327	FB96
Truro Gdns., Ilf.	234	308	EL59
Truro Rd. E17	222	307	DZ56
Truro Rd. N22	220	306	DL52
Truro St. NW5	114	306	DG65
Truro Wk., Rom.	228	310	FJ51
Truro Way, Hayes	241	312	BS69
Truslove Rd. SE27	273	324	DN92
Trussley Rd. W6	146	315	CW76
Trust Wk. SE21	194	324	DP88
Trustons Gdns., Horn.	238	310	FG59
Tryfan Clo., Ilf.	224	308	EK57
Tryon St. SW3	79	315	DF78
Tuam Rd. SE18	253	318	ER79
Tubbenden Clo., Orp.	291	334	ES103
Tubbenden Dr., Orp.	291	334	ER105
Tubbenden La., Orp.	291	334	ER105
Tubbenden La. S., Orp.	291	334	ER106
Tubbs Rd. NW10	125	314	CT68
Tuck Rd., Rain.	238	310	FG65
Tudor Ave., Hmptn.	267	329	CA93
Tudor Ave., Rom.	228	310	FG55
Tudor Ave., Wor.Pk.	283	331	CV104
Tudor Clo. N6	98	306	DJ59
Tudor Clo. NW3	113	305	DE64
Tudor Clo. NW7	218	305	CU51
Tudor Clo. NW9	92	304	CQ61
Tudor Clo. SW2	177	324	DM86
Tudor Clo., Ashf.	264	328	BL91
Tudor Clo., Chess.	282	330	CL106
Tudor Clo., Chis.	276	326	EM95
Tudor Clo., Pnr.	214	303	BU57
Tudor Clo., Sutt.	292	331	CY107
Tudor Clo., Wall.	294	332	DJ108
Tudor Ct. E17	103	307	DZ59
Tudor Ct., Felt.	266	329	BW91
Tudor Ct. N., Wem.	108	304	CN64
Tudor Ct. S., Wem.	108	304	CN64
Tudor Cres., Enf.	202	300	DQ39
Tudor Cres., Ilf.	225	308	EP51
Tudor Dr., Kings.T.	268	322	CK92
Tudor Dr., Mord.	284	331	CX100
Tudor Dr., Rom.	228	310	FG56
Tudor Est. NW10	124	314	CP69
Tudor Gdns. NW9	92	304	CQ61
Tudor Gdns. SW13	171	322	CS83
Tudor Gdns. W3	134	314	CN71
Tudor Gdns., Rom.	228	310	FG56
Tudor Gdns., Twick.	259	321	CF88
Tudor Gdns., Upmin.	239	311	FQ61
Tudor Gdns., W.Wick.	289	333	EC104
Tudor Gro. E9	118	307	DW66
Tudor Gro. N20	207	299	DE48
Tudor Pl. W1	46	316	DK72

Tudor Pl., Mitch. 271 323 DE94
Tudor Rd. E4 223 307 EB51
Tudor Rd. E6 244 318 EJ67
Tudor Rd. E9 128 317 DV67
Tudor Rd. N9 210 301 DV45
Tudor Rd. SE19 273 324 DT94
Tudor Rd. SE25 287 333 DV99
Tudor Rd., Ashf. 265 328 BR93
Tudor Rd., Bark. 245 318 ET67
Tudor Rd., Beck. 275 325 EB97
Tudor Rd., Hmptn. 267 329 CA94
Tudor Rd., Har. 215 303 CD54
Tudor Rd., Hayes 249 312 BR72
Tudor Rd., Houns. 259 321 CD84
Tudor Rd., Kings.T. 269 322 CN94
Tudor Rd., Pnr. 214 303 BW54
Tudor Rd., Sthl. 242 313 BY73
Tudor Sq., Hayes 249 312 BR71
Tudor St. EC4 60 316 DN73
Tudor Wk., Bex. 262 327 EY86
Tudor Way N14 208 300 DK46
Tudor Way W3 144 314 CN75
Tudor Way, Orp. 291 334 ER100
Tudor Way, Uxb. 241 312 BN65
Tudor Well Clo., Stan. 204 298 CH50
Tudway Rd. SE3 260 326 EH83
Tufnell Pk. Rd. N7 115 306 DK63
Tufnell Pk. Rd. N19 114 306 DJ63
Tufton Gdns., W.Mol. 267 329 CB96
Tufton Rd. E4 211 301 EA49
Tufton St. SW1 70 316 DK76
Tugboat St. SE28 253 318 ES75
Tugela Rd., Croy. 287 332 DR100
Tugela St. SE6 197 325 DZ89
Tugmutton Clo., Orp. 290 334 EP105
Tuilerie St. E2 128 317 DU68
Tulip Clo. E6 244 318 EM71
Tulip Clo., Croy. 288 333 DX102
Tulip Clo., Hmptn. 266 329 BZ93
Tulip Clo., Rom. 228 310 FK51
Tulip Clo., Sthl. 251 321 CC75
Tulip Ct., Pnr. 214 303 BW55
Tulip Dr., Ilf. 235 308 EP64
Tulip Gdns., Ilf. 235 308 EP65
Tull St., Mitch. 285 331 DF101
Tulse Clo., Beck. 275 325 EC97
Tulse Hill SW2 178 324 DN86
Tulse Hill Est. SW2 178 324 DN86
Tulsemere Rd. SE27 194 324 DQ89
Tummons Gdns. SE25 273 324 DS96
Tun Yd. SW8 160 316 DH82
Tuncombe Rd. N18 209 300 DS49
Tunis Rd. W12 136 315 CV74
Tunley Grn. E14 139 317 DZ71
Tunley Rd. NW10 125 314 CS67
Tunley Rd. SW17 192 324 DG88
Tunmarsh La. E13 244 318 EH69
Tunnan Leys E6 245 318 EN72
Tunnel Ave. SE10 151 317 ED75
Tunnel Gdns. N11 220 306 DJ52
Tunnel Rd. SE16 148 317 DW75
Tunstall Ave., Ilf. 226 309 EU51
Tunstall Clo., Orp. 291 334 ES105
Tunstall Rd. SW9 177 324 DM84
Tunstall Rd., Croy. 287 332 DS102
Tunstall Wk., Brent. 153 314 CL79
Tunstock Way, Belv. 254 319 EY76
Tunworth Clo. NW9 217 304 CQ58
Tunworth Cres. SW15 171 322 CT86
Tupelo Rd. E10 104 307 EB61
Turenne Clo. SW18 174 323 DC84
Turin Rd. N9 210 301 DW45
Turin St. E2 128 317 DU69
Turkey Oak Clo. SE19 273 324 DS95
Turkey St., Enf. 203 301 DU36
Turks Clo., Uxb. 241 312 BN69
Turk's Head Yd. EC1 48/9 316 DP71
Turks Row SW3 79 315 DF78
Turle Rd. N4 99 306 DM60
Turle Rd. SW16 272 324 DL96
Turleway Clo. N4 99 306 DM60
Turley Clo. E15 131 317 EE67
Turnagain La. EC4 48/9 316 DP72
Turnage Rd., Dag. 236 309 EY60
Turnberry Clo. SE16 148 317 DV78
Turnberry Quay E14 150 317 EB76
Turnberry Way, Orp. 291 334 ER102
Turnbury Clo. SE28 246 319 EX72
Turnchapel Ms. SW4 176 324 DH83
Turner Ave. N15 221 306 DS56
Turner Ave., Mitch. 271 323 DF95
Turner Ave., Twick. 259 321 CC90
Turner Clo. NW11 219 305 DB58
Turner Clo., Hayes 241 312 BQ68
Turner Dr. NW11 219 305 DB58
Turner Rd. E17 223 307 EC55
Turner Rd., Edg. 216 304 CL54
Turner Rd., N.Mal. 283 330 CR101
Turner St. E1 138 317 DV71
Turner St. E16 141 317 EF72
Turners Clo., Stai. 264 328 BH92
Turners Meadow Way, Beck. 274 325 DZ95
Turners Rd. E3 139 317 DZ71
Turners Way, Croy. 286 332 DN103
Turners Wd. NW11 96 305 DC60
Turneville Rd. W14 157 315 CZ79
Turney Rd. SE21 194 324 DQ87
Turnham Grn. Ter. W4 145 314 CS77
Turnham Grn. Ter. Ms. W4 145 314 CS77
Turnham Rd. SE4 181 325 DY85
Turnmill St. EC1 36 316 DN70
Turnpike Clo. SE8 165 317 DZ80
Turnpike Ho. EC1 36/7 316 DP69
Turnpike La. N8 220 306 DM56
Turnpike La., Sutt. 285 331 DC106
Turnpike La., Uxb. 240 312 BL69
Turnpike Link, Croy. 287 332 DS103
Turnpike Way, Islw. 152 314 CG81
Turnpin La. SE10 166 317 EC79
Turnstone Clo. E13 244 318 EG69
Turnstone Clo. NW9 217 304 CS54
Turnstone Clo., Uxb. 241 312 BP64
Turpentine La. SW1 80/1 316 DH78
Turpin Ave., Rom. 227 309 FA51
Turpin Rd., Felt. 257 320 BT86
Turpin Way N19 99 306 DK61
Turpin Way, Wall. 293 332 DH108
Turpington Clo., Brom. 290 334 EL100
Turpington La., Brom. 290 334 EL101
Turquand St. SE17 85 316 DQ77
Turret Gro. SW4 176 324 DJ83
Turton Rd., Wem. 107 304 CL64
Turville St. E2 39 316 DT70
Tuscan Rd. SE18 253 318 ER78
Tuskar St. SE10 151 317 EE78
Tustin Est. SE15 164 317 DW79
Tweed Glen, Rom. 227 309 FD52
Tweed Grn., Rom. 227 309 FD52
Tweed Way, Rom. 227 309 FD52
Tweedale Ct. E15 120 307 EC64
Tweeddale Gro., Uxb. 231 312 BQ62
Tweeddale Rd., Cars. 285 331 DD102
Tweedmouth Rd. E13 244 318 EH68
Tweedy Rd., Brom. 276 326 EG95
Tweezer's All. WC2 60 316 DN73
Twelvetrees Cres. E3 130 317 EC70
Twickenham Bri., Rich. 168 322 CJ85
Twickenham Bri., Twick. 168 322 CJ85
Twickenham Clo., Croy. 286 332 DM104
Twickenham Gdns., Grnf. 106 304 CG64
Twickenham Gdns., Har. 215 303 CE52
Twickenham Rd. E11 105 307 ED61
Twickenham Rd., Felt. 258 321 BZ90
Twickenham Rd., Islw. 168 322 CG85
Twickenham Rd., Rich. 168 322 CJ85
Twickenham Rd., Tedd. 268 322 CG91
Twickenham Trd. Est., Twick. 259 321 CF86
Twig Folly Clo. E2 129 317 DX68
Twigg Clo., Erith 255 319 FE80
Twilley St. SW18 190 323 DB87
Twine Clo., Bark. 246 319 EV69
Twine Ct. E1 138 317 DW73
Twineham Grn. N12 207 299 DA49
Twining Ave., Twick. 259 321 CC90
Twinn Rd. NW7 218 305 CY51
Twisden Rd. NW5 114 306 DH63
Twybridge Way NW10 108 304 CQ66
Twyford Abbey Rd. NW10 123 314 CM69
Twyford Ave. N2 219 305 DF55
Twyford Ave. W3 134 314 CN73
Twyford Cres. W3 134 314 CN74
Twyford Pl. WC2 47 316 DM72
Twyford Rd., Cars. 285 331 DD102
Twyford Rd., Har. 233 313 CB60
Twyford Rd., Ilf. 235 308 EQ64
Twyford St. N1 23 316 DM67
Tyas Rd. E16 131 317 EF70
Tybenham Rd. SW19 270 323 CZ97
Tyberry Rd., Enf. 203 301 DV41
Tyburn La., Har. 233 313 CE59
Tyburn Way W1 55 315 DF73
Tye La., Orp. 291 334 EQ106
Tyers Est. SE1 74/5 316 DS75
Tyers Gate SE1 74/5 316 DS75
Tyers St. SE11 83 316 DM78
Tyers Ter. SE11 83 316 DM78
Tyeshurst Clo. SE2 254 319 EY78
Tyle Grn., Horn. 228 311 FL56
Tylecroft Rd. SW16 272 324 DL96
Tylehurst Gdns., Ilf. 235 308 EQ64
Tyler Clo. E2 27 316 DT68
Tyler St. SE10 151 317 EE78
Tyler's Ct. W1 46 316 DK72
Tylers Cres., Horn. 238 310 FJ64
Tylers Gate, Har. 216 304 CL58
Tylers Path, Cars. 285 331 DF105
Tylney Ave. SE19 273 324 DT92
Tylney Rd. E7 234 308 EJ63
Tylney Rd., Brom. 276 326 EK96
Tynan Clo., Felt. 258 321 BU88
Tyndale Ct. E14 150 317 EB78
Tyndale La. N1 116 306 DP66
Tyndale Ter. N1 116 306 DP66
Tyndall Rd. E10 104 307 EC61
Tyndall Rd., Well. 261 326 ET83
Tyne Clo., Upmin. 229 311 FR58
Tyne St. E1 51 316 DT72
Tyneham Rd. SW11 160 316 DG82
Tynemouth Clo. E6 245 318 EP72
Tynemouth Dr., Enf. 203 301 DU38
Tynemouth Rd. N15 221 306 DT56
Tynemouth Rd. SE18 253 318 ET78
Tynemouth Rd., Mitch. 272 324 DG94
Tynemouth St. SW6 158 315 DC82
Type St. E2 129 317 DX68
Tyrawley Rd. SW6 158 315 DB81
Tyrell Clo., Har. 233 313 CE62
Tyrell Ct., Cars. 285 331 DF105
Tyrell Sq., Mitch. 271 323 DE95
Tyrells Clo., Upmin. 239 311 FP61
Tyrols Rd. SE23 197 325 DX88
Tyron Way, Sid. 277 326 ES91
Tyrone Rd. E6 244 318 EM68
Tyrrel Way NW9 93 304 CT59
Tyrrell Ave., Well. 262 327 EU85
Tyrrell Rd. SE22 180 325 DU84
Tyrwhitt Rd. SE4 182 325 EA83
Tysoe Ave., Enf. 203 301 DZ36
Tysoe St. EC1 36 316 DN69
Tyson Rd. SE23 196 325 DW87
Tyssen Pas. E8 117 306 DT65
Tyssen Rd. N16 101 306 DT62
Tyssen St. E8 117 306 DT65
Tyssen St. N1 26/7 316 DS68
Tytherton Rd. N19 99 306 DK62

Uamvar St. E14 140 317 EB71
Uckfield Gro., Mitch. 272 324 DG95
Uckfield Rd., Enf. 203 301 DX37
Udall Gdns., Rom. 227 309 FA51
Udall St. SW1 81 316 DJ77
Udney Pk. Rd., Tedd. 268 322 CG92
Uffington Rd. NW10 126 315 CU67
Uffington Rd. SE27 273 324 DN91
Ufford Clo., Har. 215 303 CB52
Ufford Rd., Har. 215 303 CB52
Ufford St. SE1 72 316 DN75
Ufton Gro. N1 117 306 DR66
Ufton Rd. N1 117 306 DR66
Uhura Sq. N16 101 306 DS62
Ujima Ct. SW16 272 324 DL91
Ullathorne Rd. SW16 272 324 DJ91
Ulleswater Rd. N14 208 300 DL49
Ullin St. E14 140 317 EC71
Ullswater Clo. SW15 269 322 CR91
Ullswater Clo., Brom. 275 325 EE94
Ullswater Clo., Hayes 241 312 BS68
Ullswater Ct., Har. 233 313 CA59
Ullswater Cres. SW15 269 322 CR91
Ullswater Rd. SE27 194 324 DP89
Ullswater Rd. SW13 156 315 CU80
Ullswater Way, Horn. 238 310 FG64
Ulster Gdns. N13 209 300 DQ49
Ulster Pl. NW1 32/3 316 DH70
Ulster Ter. NW1 32/3 316 DH70
Ulundi Rd. SE3 167 317 EE79
Ulva Rd. SW15 173 323 CX85
Ulverscroft Rd. SE22 179 324 DT85
Ulverston Rd. E17 223 307 ED54
Ulverstone Rd. SE27 194 324 DP89
Ulysses Rd. NW6 111 305 CZ64
Umberston St. E1 138 317 DU72
Umbria St. SW15 172 323 CU86
Umfreville Rd. N4 221 306 DP58
Undercliff Rd. SE13 182 325 EA83
Underhill, Barn. 207 299 DA43
Underhill Pas. NW1 20/1 316 DH67
Underhill Rd. SE22 180 325 DU85
Underhill St. NW1 20/1 316 DH67
Underne Ave. N14 208 300 DH47
Undershaft EC3 50/1 316 DS72
Undershaw Rd., Brom. 199 325 EF90
Underwood, Croy. 289 333 EC106
Underwood, The SE9 260 326 EM89
Underwood Rd. E1 128 317 DU70
Underwood Rd. E4 211 301 EB50
Underwood Rd., Wdf.Grn. 224 308 EJ52
Underwood Row N1 37 316 DQ69
Underwood St. N1 37 316 DQ69
Undine Rd. E14 150 317 EB77
Undine St. SW17 271 323 DF92
Uneeda Dr., Grnf. 243 313 CD67
Union Cotts. E15 121 307 EE66
Union Ct. EC2 50/1 316 DS72
Union Ct., Rich. 169 322 CL85
Union Dr. E1 129 317 DY70
Union Gro. SW8 161 316 DK82
Union Rd. N11 220 306 DK51
Union Rd. SW4 161 316 DK82
Union Rd. SW8 161 316 DK82
Union Rd., Brom. 290 334 EK99
Union Rd., Croy. 287 332 DQ101
Union Rd., Nthlt. 243 313 CA68
Union Rd., Wem. 107 304 CL65
Union Sq. N1 25 316 DQ67
Union St. E15 130 317 EC67
Union St. SE1 61 316 DQ74
Union St., Kings.T. 268 322 CK96
Union Wk. E2 38/9 316 DS69
Unity Clo. NW10 110 305 CU65
Unity Clo. SE19 273 324 DQ92
Unity Rd., Enf. 203 301 DW37
Unity Way SE18 252 318 EK76
Unity Wf. SE1 75 316 DT75
University Clo. NW7 217 304 CT52
University Gdns., Bex. 262 327 EZ87
University Pl., Erith 255 319 FB80
University Rd. SW19 271 323 DD93
University St. WC1 33 316 DJ70
Unwin Ave., Felt. 257 320 BR85
Unwin Clo. SE15 164 317 DU79
Unwin Rd. SW7 66 315 DD76
Unwin Rd., Islw. 259 321 CE83
Upbrook Ms. W2 41 315 DC72
Upcerne Rd. SW10 158 315 DC80
Upchurch Clo. SE20 274 325 DV94
Upcroft Ave., Edg. 205 298 CQ50
Updale Rd., Sid. 277 326 ET91
Upfield, Croy. 287 333 DV103
Upfield Rd. W7 243 313 CF70
Upgrove Manor Way SW2 194 324 DN87
Uphall Rd., Ilf. 235 308 EP64
Upham Pk. Rd. W4 145 314 CS77
Uphill Dr. NW7 205 298 CS50
Uphill Dr. NW9 217 304 CQ57
Uphill Gro. NW7 205 298 CS49
Uphill Rd. NW7 205 298 CS49
Upland Ct. Rd., Rom. 228 311 FM54
Upland Ms. SE22 180 325 DU85
Upland Rd. E13 131 317 EF70
Upland Rd. SE22 180 325 DU85
Upland Rd., Bexh. 262 327 EZ83
Upland Rd., S.Croy. 287 332 DR106
Upland Rd., Sutt. 293 331 DD107
Uplands, Beck. 275 325 EA96
Uplands, The, Ruis. 232 313 BU60
Uplands Ave. E17 222 307 DX54
Uplands Business Pk. E17 222 307 DX55
Uplands Clo. SW14 170 322 CP85
Uplands End, Wdf.Grn. 224 308 EL52
Uplands Pk. Rd., Enf. 202 300 DN41
Uplands Rd. N8 220 306 DM57
Uplands Rd., Barn. 208 300 DG46
Uplands Rd., Orp. 291 335 EV102
Uplands Rd., Rom. 226 309 EX55
Uplands Rd., Wdf.Grn. 224 308 EL52
Uplands Way N21 209 300 DN43
Upminster Rd., Horn. 238 311 FM61
Upminster Rd., Upmin. 239 311 FN61
Upney Clo., Horn. 238 310 FJ64
Upney La., Bark. 235 308 ES65
Upnor Way SE17 86/7 316 DS78
Uppark Dr., Ilf. 225 308 EQ58
Upper Abbey Rd., Belv. 254 319 EZ77
Upper Addison Gdns. W14 147 315 CY75
Upper Bardsey Wk. N1 116 306 DQ65
Upper Belgrave St. SW1 68 316 DG76
Upper Berkeley St. W1 43 315 DF72
Upper Beulah Hill SE19 273 324 DS95
Upper Brentwood Rd., Rom. 228 310 FJ56
Upper Brighton Rd., Surb. 282 330 CK100
Upper Brockley Rd. SE4 165 317 DZ82
Upper Brook St. W1 56 316 DG73
Upper Butts, Brent. 152 314 CJ79
Upper Caldy Wk. N1 116 306 DQ65
Upper Camelford Wk. W11 137 315 CY72
Upper Cavendish Ave. N3 219 305 DA55
Upper Cheyne Row SW3 159 315 DE79
Upper Clapton Rd. E5 102 307 DV60
Upper Clarendon Wk. W11 137 315 CY72
Upper Dengie Wk. N1 25 316 DQ67
Upper Dunnymans, Bans. 292 331 CZ114
Upper Elmers End Rd., Beck. 274 325 DY98
Upper Fm. Rd., W.Mol. 266 329 BZ98
Upper Fosters NW4 218 305 CW57
Upper Grn. E., Mitch. 271 323 DF96
Upper Grn. W., Mitch. 271 323 DF97
Upper Grenfell Wk. W11 137 315 CX73
Upper Grosvenor St. W1 56 316 DG73
Upper Grotto Rd., Twick. 259 321 CF89
Upper Grd. SE1 60 316 DN74
Upper Gro. SE25 273 324 DS98
Upper Gro. Rd., Belv. 254 319 EZ79
Upper Gulland Wk. N1 116 306 DQ65
Upper Halliford Bypass, Shep. 281 328 BS99
Upper Halliford Grn., Shep. 281 328 BS98
Upper Halliford Rd., Shep. 281 328 BS98
Upper Ham Rd., Rich. 268 322 CK91
Upper Handa Wk. N1 117 306 DR65
Upper Harley St. NW1 32 316 DG70
Upper Hawkwell Wk. N1 25 316 DQ67
Upper Holly Hill Rd., Belv. 255 319 FB78
Upper James St. W1 57 316 DJ73
Upper John St. W1 57 316 DJ73
Upper Lismore Wk. N1 116 306 DQ65
Upper Mall W6 146 315 CU78
Upper Marsh SE1 71 316 DM75
Upper Montagu St. W1 43 315 DF71
Upper Mulgrave Rd., Sutt. 292 331 CY108
Upper N. St. E14 140 317 EA71
Upper Palace Rd., E.Mol. 267 329 CC97
Upper Pk. Rd. N11 208 300 DH50
Upper Pk. Rd. NW3 113 305 DF65
Upper Pk. Rd., Belv. 255 319 FB77
Upper Pk. Rd., Brom. 276 326 EH95
Upper Pk. Rd., Kings.T. 269 322 CN93
Upper Phillimore Gdns. W8 64 315 DA75
Upper Rainham Rd., Horn. 237 309 FF60
Upper Ramsey Wk. N1 117 306 DR65
Upper Rawreth Wk. N1 25 316 DQ67
Upper Richmond Rd. SW15 173 323 CY84
Upper Richmond Rd. W. SW14 171 322 CR84
Upper Richmond Rd. W., Rich. 170 322 CN84
Upper Rd. E13 244 318 EG69
Upper Rd., Wall. 286 332 DK106
Upper St. Martin's La. WC2 58/9 316 DL73
Upper Sawley Wd., Bans. 292 331 CZ114
Upper Selsdon Rd., S.Croy. 295 332 DS108
Upper Sheppey Wk. N1 116 306 DQ66
Upper Sheridan Rd., Belv. 255 319 FA77
Upper Shirley Rd., Croy. 288 333 DW103
Upper Sq., Islw. 168 322 CG83
Upper St. N1 24 316 DN68
Upper Sunbury Rd., Hmptn. 266 329 BY95
Upper Sutton La., Houns. 251 321 CA80
Upper Tachbrook St. SW1 81 316 DJ77
Upper Talbot Wk. W11 137 315 CY72
Upper Teddington Rd., Kings.T. 268 322 CJ94
Upper Ter. NW3 96 305 DC62
Upper Thames St. EC4 61 316 DQ73
Upper Tollington Pk. N4 100 306 DN59
Upper Tooting Pk. SW17 191 323 DF89
Upper Tooting Rd. SW17 271 323 DF91
Upper Town Rd., Grnf. 243 313 CB70
Upper Tulse Hill SW2 193 324 DM87
Upper Vernon Rd., Sutt. 285 331 DD106
Upper Walthamstow Rd. E17 223 307 ED56
Upper Wickham La., Well. 262 327 EV83
Upper Wimpole St. W1 44 316 DH71
Upper Woburn Pl. WC1 34 316 DK69
Upper Woodcote Village, Pur. 294 332 DK113
Upperton Rd., Sid. 277 326 ET92
Upperton Rd. E. E13 244 318 EJ69
Upperton Rd. W. E13 244 318 EJ69
Uppingham Ave., Stan. 216 304 CH53
Upsdell Ave. N13 221 306 DN51
Upstall St. SE5 162 316 DP81
Upton Ave. E7 234 308 EG66
Upton Clo., Bex. 262 327 EZ86
Upton Ct. SE20 274 325 DW94
Upton Dene, Sutt. 292 331 DB108
Upton Gdns., Har. 216 304 CH57
Upton La. E7 234 308 EH65
Upton Pk. Rd. E7 234 308 EH66
Upton Rd. N18 210 301 DU50
Upton Rd. SE18 253 318 EQ79
Upton Rd., Bex. 262 327 EZ86
Upton Rd., Bexh. 262 327 EY84
Upton Rd., Houns. 259 321 CA83
Upton Rd., Th.Hth. 273 324 DR96
Upton Rd. S., Bex. 262 327 EZ86
Upway N12 219 305 DE52
Upwood Rd. SE12 260 326 EG86
Upwood Rd. SW16 272 324 DL95
Urban Ave., Horn. 238 310 FJ62
Urlwin St. SE5 162 316 DQ79
Urlwin Wk. SW9 162 316 DN81
Urmston Dr. SW19 189 323 CY88
Ursula Ms. N4 100 306 DQ60
Ursula St. SW11 159 315 DE81
Urswick Gdns., Dag. 236 309 EY66
Urswick Rd. E9 118 307 DW64
Urswick Rd., Dag. 236 309 EX66
Usborne Ms. SW8 161 316 DM80
Usher Rd. E3 129 317 DZ68
Usk Rd. SW11 174 323 DC84
Usk St. E2 129 317 DX69
Utopia Village NW1 20 316 DG67
Uvedale Rd., Dag. 237 309 FA62
Uvedale Rd., Enf. 209 300 DR43
Uverdale Rd. SW10 158 315 DC80
Uxbridge Gdns., Felt. 258 321 BX89
Uxbridge Ind. Est., Uxb. 240 312 BH69
Uxbridge Rd. W3 134 314 CN74
Uxbridge Rd. W5 133 314 CM73
Uxbridge Rd. W7 243 313 CF74
Uxbridge Rd. W12 136 315 CU74
Uxbridge Rd. W13 132 314 CH74
Uxbridge Rd., Felt. 258 321 BW88
Uxbridge Rd., Hmptn. 267 329 CA91
Uxbridge Rd., Har. 215 303 CD52
Uxbridge Rd., Hayes 249 312 BT72
Uxbridge Rd., Kings.T. 268 322 CK98
Uxbridge Rd., Pnr. 214 303 BW54
Uxbridge Rd., Sthl. 243 313 CA74
Uxbridge Rd., Stan. 215 303 CF51
Uxbridge Rd., Uxb. 241 312 BP69
Uxbridge St. W8 52 315 DA74
Uxendon Cres., Wem. 91 304 CL60
Uxendon Hill, Wem. 91 304 CM60

Valan Leas, Brom. 275 325 EE97
Valance Ave. E4 211 301 EE46
Vale, The N10 220 306 DG53
Vale, The N14 208 300 DK45
Vale, The NW11 95 305 CX62
Vale, The SW3 159 315 DD79
Vale, The W3 135 314 CR74
Vale, The, Couls. 294 332 DK114
Vale, The, Croy. 288 333 DX103
Vale, The, Felt. 258 321 BV86
Vale, The, Houns. 251 321 BY79
Vale, The, Ruis. 232 313 BW63
Vale, The, Sun. 266 329 BU93
Vale, The, Wdf.Grn. 224 308 EG52
Vale Ave., Borwd. 205 298 CP43
Vale Clo. N2 219 305 DF55
Vale Clo. W9 29 315 DC69
Vale Clo., Orp. 290 334 EN105
Vale Cotts. SW15 269 322 CR91
Vale Ct. W9 29 315 DC69
Vale Cres. SW15 187 322 CS90
Vale Cft., Pnr. 214 303 BY57
Vale End SE22 179 324 DS84
Vale Gro. N4 100 306 DQ59
Vale Gro. W3 135 314 CR74
Vale La. W3 134 314 CN71
Vale of Health NW3 97 305 DD62
Vale Par. SW15 269 322 CR91
Vale Ri. NW11 95 305 CZ60
Vale Rd. E7 234 308 EH65
Vale Rd. N4 100 306 DQ59
Vale Rd., Brom. 277 326 EN96
Vale Rd., Epsom 283 330 CT105
Vale Rd., Mitch. 272 324 DK97
Vale Rd., Sutt. 284 331 DB105
Vale Rd., Wor.Pk. 283 330 CT104
Vale Rd. N., Surb. 282 330 CL103
Vale Rd. S., Surb. 282 330 CL103
Vale Row N5 100 306 DP62
Vale Royal N7 115 306 DL66
Vale St. SE27 195 324 DR90
Vale Ter. N4 221 306 DQ58
Valence Ave., Dag. 236 309 EX60
Valence Circ., Dag. 236 309 EX62
Valence Rd., Erith 255 319 FD80
Valence Wd. Rd., Dag. 236 309 EX62
Valencia Rd., Stan. 204 298 CJ49
Valency Clo., Nthwd. 213 302 BT49
Valentia Pl. SW9 178 324 DN84
Valentine Ave., Bex. 262 327 EY89
Valentine Ct. SE23 197 325 DX89
Valentine Pl. SE1 72/3 316 DP75
Valentine Rd. E9 119 307 DX65
Valentine Rd., Har. 233 313 CC62
Valentine Row SE1 72/3 316 DP75
Valentines Rd., Ilf. 235 308 EP60
Valentines Way, Rom. 237 309 FD61
Valerian Way E15 131 317 EE69
Valeswood Rd., Brom. 275 325 EF92
Valetta Gro. E13 244 318 EG68
Valetta Rd. W3 146 314 CS75
Valette St. E9 118 307 DV65
Valiant Clo., Nthlt. 242 313 BX69
Valiant Clo., Rom. 227 309 FA54
Valiant Ho. SE7 252 318 EJ78
Valiant Path NW9 217 304 CS52
Valiant Way E6 244 318 EM71
Vallance Rd. E1 128 317 DU70
Vallance Rd. E2 128 317 DU69
Vallance Rd. N22 220 306 DJ54
Vallentin Rd. E17 223 307 EC56
Valley Ave. N12 207 299 DD49
Valley Clo., Dart. 263 327 FF86
Valley Clo., Pnr. 214 303 BV54
Valley Ct., Ken. 295 332 DQ114
Valley Dr. NW9 217 304 CN58
Valley Flds. Cres., Enf. 202 300 DN40
Valley Gdns. SW19 271 323 DD94
Valley Gdns., Wem. 107 304 CM66
Valley Gro. SE7 252 318 EJ78
Valley Link Ind. Est., Enf. 210 301 DY44
Valley Ms., Twick. 184 322 CG89
Valley Rd. SW16 272 324 DM92
Valley Rd., Belv. 255 319 FB77
Valley Rd., Brom. 275 325 EE96
Valley Rd., Dart. 263 327 FF86
Valley Rd., Erith 255 319 FD77
Valley Rd., Ken. 295 332 DR114
Valley Rd., Orp. 278 327 EV95
Valley Rd., Uxb. 240 312 BL68
Valley Side E4 211 301 EA47
Valley Side Par. E4 211 301 EA47
Valley Vw., Barn. 206 299 CY44
Valley Wk., Croy. 288 333 DW103
Valleyfield Rd. SW16 272 324 DM92
Valliere Rd. NW10 126 315 CU69
Valliers Wd. Rd., Sid. 261 326 ER88
Vallis Way W13 132 314 CH71
Vallis Way, Chess. 282 330 CK105
Valmar Rd. SE5 162 316 DQ81
Valnay St. SW17 271 323 DF92
Valognes Ave. E17 222 307 DY53
Valonia Gdns. SW18 173 323 CZ86
Vambery Rd. SE18 253 318 EQ79
Van Dyck Ave., N.Mal. 283 330 CR101
Vanbrough Cres., Nthlt. 242 313 BW67
Vanbrugh Clo. E16 244 318 EK71
Vanbrugh Flds. SE3 167 317 EF79
Vanbrugh Hill SE3 167 317 EF79
Vanbrugh Hill SE10 167 317 EF79
Vanbrugh Pk. SE3 167 317 EF80
Vanbrugh Pk. Rd. SE3 167 317 EF80
Vanbrugh Pk. Rd. W. SE3 167 317 EF80
Vanbrugh Rd. W4 145 314 CR76
Vanbrugh Ter. SE3 167 317 EF81
Vanburgh Clo., Orp. 291 334 ES102
Vancouver Rd. SE23 197 325 DY89
Vancouver Rd., Edg. 217 304 CP53
Vancouver Rd., Hayes 242 313 BV70
Vancouver Rd., Rich. 268 322 CJ91
Vanderbilt Rd. SW18 190 323 DB88
Vandome Clo. E16 244 318 EH72
Vandon Pas. SW1 69 316 DJ76
Vandon St. SW1 69 316 DJ76
Vandy St. EC2 38/9 316 DS70
Vandyke Clo. SW15 173 323 CX86
Vandyke Cross SE9 260 326 EL85
Vane Clo. NW3 113 305 DD63
Vane Clo., Har. 216 304 CM58
Vane St. SW1 81 316 DJ77
Vanessa Clo., Belv. 255 319 FA78
Vanessa Way, Bex. 262 327 FD90
Vanguard Clo., Croy. 286 332 DP102
Vanguard Clo., Rom. 227 309 FB54
Vanguard St. SE8 166 317 EA81
Vanguard Way, Wall. 294 332 DL108
Vanoc Gdns., Brom. 276 326 EG91
Vansittart Rd. E7 121 307 EF63
Vansittart St. SE14 165 317 DY80
Vanston Pl. SW6 158 315 DA80
Vant Rd. SW17 271 323 DF92
Vantage Ms. E14 140 317 EC74
Varcoe Rd. SE16 148 317 DV78
Varden Clo. W3 135 314 CR72
Varden St. E1 137 317 DV72
Vardens Rd. SW11 175 323 DD84
Vardon Clo. N3 218 305 CY53
Varley Par. NW9 217 304 CS56
Varley Rd. E16 244 318 EH72
Varley Way, Mitch. 271 323 DD96
Varna Rd. SW6 157 315 CY80
Varna Rd., Hmptn. 267 329 CB95
Varndell St. NW1 33 316 DJ69
Varsity Dr., Twick. 259 321 CE85
Varsity Row SW14 154 314 CQ82
Vartry Rd. N15 221 306 DR58
Vassall Rd. SW9 162 316 DN80
Vauban Est. SE16 75 316 DT76
Vauban St. SE16 75 316 DT76
Vaughan Ave. NW4 218 305 CU57
Vaughan Ave. W6 145 314 CT77
Vaughan Ave., Horn. 238 310 FK63
Vaughan Clo., Hmptn. 266 329 BY93
Vaughan Gdns., Ilf. 234 308 EM59
Vaughan Rd. E15 121 307 EF65
Vaughan Rd. SE5 178 324 DQ83
Vaughan Rd., Har. 233 313 CC59
Vaughan Rd., Well. 253 318 ET82
Vaughan St. SE16 149 317 DZ75
Vaughan Way E1 138 317 DU73
Vaughan Williams Clo. SE8 166 317 EA80
Vauxhall Bri. SE1 82/3 316 DL78
Vauxhall Bri. SW1 82/3 316 DL78
Vauxhall Bri. Rd. SW1 69 316 DJ76
Vauxhall Gdns., S.Croy. 295 332 DQ107
Vauxhall Gdns. Est. SE11 83 316 DM78
Vauxhall Gro. SW8 161 316 DM79
Vauxhall St. SE11 83 316 DM78
Vauxhall Wk. SE11 83 316 DM78
Vawdrey Clo. E1 128 317 DW70
Veals Mead, Mitch. 271 323 DE95
Vectis Gdns. SW17 272 324 DH93
Vectis Rd. SW17 272 324 DH93
Veda Rd. SE13 182 325 EA84
Vega Cres., Nthwd. 213 302 BT50
Velde Way SE22 179 324 DS85
Velletri Ho. E2 129 317 DX68
Vellicoe Rd. E13 244 318 EG70
Vellum Dr., Cars. 285 332 DG104
Venables Clo., Dag. 237 309 FB63
Venables St. NW8 30 315 DD70
Vencourt Pl. W6 146 315 CU77
Venetia Rd. N4 221 306 DP58
Venetia Rd. W5 143 314 CK75
Venetian Rd. SE5 162 316 DQ82
Venn St. SW4 176 324 DJ84
Venner Rd. SE26 274 325 DW93
Venners Clo., Bexh. 255 319 FE82
Ventnor Ave., Stan. 216 304 CH53
Ventnor Dr. N20 207 299 DB48
Ventnor Gdns., Bark. 235 308 ES65
Ventnor Rd. SE14 165 317 DX80
Ventnor Rd., Sutt. 292 331 DB108
Venture Clo., Bex. 262 327 EY87
Venue St. E14 140 317 EC71
Venus Rd. SE18 252 318 EM76
Veny Cres., Horn. 238 310 FK64
Vera Ave. N21 209 300 DN43
Vera Lynn Clo. E7 234 308 EG63
Vera Rd. SW6 157 315 CY81
Verbena Clo. E16 131 317 EF70
Verbena Clo., West Dr. 248 320 BK78
Verbena Gdns. W6 146 315 CU78
Verdant La. SE6 199 325 EE88
Verdayne Ave., Croy. 288 333 DX102
Verdun Rd. SE18 254 319 EU79
Verdun Rd. SW13 156 315 CU79
Vere St. W1 44/5 316 DH72
Vereker Dr., Sun. 266 329 BU97
Vereker Rd. W14 157 315 CY78
Verity Clo. W11 137 315 CY72
Vermont Clo., Enf. 202 300 DP42
Vermont Rd. SE19 273 324 DR93
Vermont Rd. SW18 174 323 DB86
Vermont Rd., Sutt. 284 331 DB104
Verney Gdns., Dag. 236 309 EY63
Verney Rd. SE16 164 317 DU79
Verney Rd., Dag. 236 309 EY63
Verney St. NW10 93 304 CR62
Verney Way SE16 148 317 DV78
Vernham Rd. SE18 253 318 EQ79
Vernon Ave. E12 234 308 EM63
Vernon Ave. SW20 270 323 CX96
Vernon Ave., Enf. 203 301 DY36
Vernon Ave., Wdf.Grn. 224 308 EH52
Vernon Clo., Orp. 278 327 EV97
Vernon Ct., Stan. 216 304 CH53
Vernon Cres., Barn. 208 300 DG44
Vernon Dr., Stan. 216 304 CG53
Vernon Dr., Uxb. 212 302 BJ53
Vernon Ms. E17 222 307 DZ56
Vernon Ms. W14 147 315 CY77
Vernon Pl. WC1 46/7 316 DL71
Vernon Ri. WC1 35 316 DM69
Vernon Ri., Grnf. 233 313 CD64
Vernon Rd. E3 129 317 DZ68
Vernon Rd. E11 105 307 EE60
Vernon Rd. E15 121 307 EE66
Vernon Rd. E17 222 307 DZ56
Vernon Rd. N8 221 306 DN55
Vernon Rd. SW14 171 322 CR83
Vernon Rd., Felt. 258 321 BU90
Vernon Rd., Ilf. 235 308 ET60
Vernon Rd., Sutt. 285 331 DC106
Vernon Sq. WC1 35 316 DM69
Vernon St. W14 147 315 CY77
Vernon Yd. W11 138 315 CZ73
Veroan Rd., Bexh. 254 319 EY82
Verona Clo., Uxb. 248 312 BJ71
Verona Dr., Surb. 282 330 CL103
Verona Rd. E7 234 308 EG66
Veronica Clo., Rom. 228 310 FJ52
Veronica Gdns. SW16 272 324 DJ95
Veronica Rd. SW17 192 324 DH90
Veronique Gdns., Ilf. 225 308 EQ57
Verran Rd. SW12 192 324 DH87
Versailles Rd. SE20 274 325 DU94
Verulam Ave. E17 222 307 DZ58
Verulam Ave., Pur. 294 332 DJ112
Verulam Bldgs. WC1 47 316 DM71
Verulam Rd., Grnf. 243 313 CA70
Verulam St. WC1 48 316 DN71
Verwood Rd., Har. 215 303 CC54
Veryan Clo., Orp. 278 327 EW98
Vesey Path E14 140 317 EB72
Vespan Rd. W12 144 315 CU75
Vesta Rd. SE4 165 317 DY82
Vestris Rd. SE23 197 325 DX89
Vestry Ms. SE5 163 316 DS81
Vestry Rd. E17 223 307 EB56
Vestry Rd. SE5 163 316 DS81
Vestry St. N1 38 316 DR69
Vevey St. SE6 197 325 DZ89
Veysey Gdns., Dag. 237 309 FA62
Viaduct Pl. E2 128 317 DV69
Viaduct St. E2 128 317 DV69
Vian Ave., Enf. 203 301 DY35
Vian St. SE13 182 325 EB83
Vibart Gdns. SW2 193 324 DM87
Vibart Wk. N1 22/3 316 DL67
Vicarage Ave. SE3 252 318 EG80
Vicarage Clo., Erith 255 319 FC79
Vicarage Clo., Nthlt. 242 313 BZ67
Vicarage Clo., Ruis. 231 312 BR59
Vicarage Ct. W8 64/5 315 DB75
Vicarage Ct., Felt. 265 320 BQ87
Vicarage Cres. SW11 159 315 DD81
Vicarage Dr. SW14 171 322 CR85
Vicarage Dr., Bark. 235 308 EQ66
Vicarage Dr., Beck. 275 325 EA95
Vicarage Fm. Rd., Houns. 250 321 BY82
Vicarage Gdns. SW14 170 322 CQ85
Vicarage Gdns. W8 52 315 DA74
Vicarage Gdns., Mitch. 271 323 DE97
Vicarage Gate W8 52/3 315 DB74
Vicarage Gro. SE5 163 316 DR81
Vicarage La. E6 244 318 EM69
Vicarage La. E15 121 307 EE66
Vicarage La., Ilf. 235 308 ER60
Vicarage La. (Laleham), Stai. 280 328 BH97
Vicarage Pk. SE18 253 318 EQ78
Vicarage Path N8 99 306 DL59
Vicarage Rd. E10 104 307 EA59
Vicarage Rd. E15 121 307 EF66
Vicarage Rd. N17 222 307 DU52
Vicarage Rd. NW4 218 305 CU58
Vicarage Rd. SE18 253 318 EQ78
Vicarage Rd. SW14 171 322 CR85
Vicarage Rd., Bex. 263 327 FB88
Vicarage Rd., Croy. 286 332 DN104
Vicarage Rd., Dag. 237 309 FB66
Vicarage Rd., Horn. 238 310 FG60
Vicarage Rd., Kings.T. 268 322 CK96
Vicarage Rd.
(Hampton Wick), Kings.T. 268 322 CJ95
Vicarage Rd., Sun. 265 328 BT92
Vicarage Rd., Sutt. 284 331 DB105
Vicarage Rd., Tedd. 268 322 CG92
Vicarage Rd., Twick. 259 321 CE89

Vicarage Rd. (Whitton), Twick.	259	321	CC86
Vicarage Rd., Wdf.Grn.	224	308	EL52
Vicarage Way NW10	93	304	CR62
Vicarage Way, Har.	233	313	CA59
Vicars Bri. Clo., Wem.	123	314	CL68
Vicars Clo. E9	128	317	DW67
Vicars Clo. E15	244	318	EG67
Vicars Clo., Enf.	202	300	DS40
Vicars Hill SE13	182	325	EB84
Vicars Moor La. N21	209	300	DN45
Vicars Oak Rd. SE19	273	324	DS93
Vicars Rd. NW5	114	306	DG64
Vicars Wk., Dag.	236	309	EV62
Viceroy Clo. N2	219	305	DE56
Viceroy Ct. NW8	18/9	315	DE68
Viceroy Par. N2	219	305	DE55
Viceroy Rd. SW8	161	316	DL81
Vickers Rd., Erith	255	319	FD78
Vickers Way, Houns.	258	321	BY85
Victor App., Horn.	238	310	FK60
Victor Clo., Horn.	238	310	FK60
Victor Ct., Horn.	238	310	FK60
Victor Ct., Rain.	247	319	FD68
Victor Gdns., Horn.	238	310	FK60
Victor Gro., Wem.	107	304	CL66
Victor Rd. NW10	126	315	CV68
Victor Rd. SE20	274	325	DX94
Victor Rd., Har.	215	303	CC55
Victor Rd., Tedd.	267	329	CE91
Victor Vil. N9	209	300	DR48
Victor Wk. NW9	217	304	CS54
Victor Wk., Horn.	238	310	FK60
Victoria Ave. E6	244	318	EK67
Victoria Ave. EC2	50/1	316	DS71
Victoria Ave. N3	218	305	CZ53
Victoria Ave., Houns.	258	321	BZ85
Victoria Ave., Rom.	227	309	FB51
Victoria Ave., S.Croy.	295	332	DQ110
Victoria Ave., Surb.	282	330	CK100
Victoria Ave., Uxb.	241	312	BP65
Victoria Ave., Wall.	285	332	DG104
Victoria Ave., Wem.	108	304	CP65
Victoria Ave., W.Mol.	267	329	CA97
Victoria Clo., Hayes	249	312	BR72
Victoria Clo., W.Mol.	267	329	CA97
Victoria Cotts., Rich.	153	314	CM81
Victoria Ct., Wem.	108	304	CN65
Victoria Cres. N15	221	306	DS57
Victoria Cres. SE19	273	324	DS93
Victoria Cres. SW19	270	323	CZ94
Victoria Cres., Iver	248	312	BG73
Victoria Dock Rd. E16	244	318	EG73
Victoria Dr. SW19	189	323	CX87
Victoria Embk. EC4	60	316	DN73
Victoria Embk. SW1	70/1	316	DL75
Victoria Embk. WC2	59	316	DM73
Victoria Gdns. W11	52	315	DA74
Victoria Gdns., Houns.	250	321	BY81
Victoria Gro. N12	207	299	DD50
Victoria Gro. W8	65	315	DC76
Victoria Gro. Ms. W2	52/3	315	DB73
Victoria Hill Rd., Swan.	279	327	FF95
Victoria Ind. Est. NW10	125	314	CS69
Victoria La., Hayes	249	320	BQ78
Victoria Ms. NW6	16	315	DA67
Victoria Ms. SW4	176	324	DH84
Victoria Ms. SW18	190	323	DC88
Victoria Pk. E9	129	317	DY67
Victoria Pk. Rd. E9	128	317	DW67
Victoria Pk. Sq. E2	128	317	DW69
Victoria Pas. NW8	30	315	DD70
Victoria Pl., Rich.	169	322	CK85
Victoria Pt. E13	244	318	EG68
Victoria Ri. SW4	176	324	DH83
Victoria Rd. E4	211	301	EE46
Victoria Rd. E11	121	307	EE63
Victoria Rd. E13	244	318	EG68
Victoria Rd. E17	223	307	EC54
Victoria Rd. E18	224	308	EH54
Victoria Rd. N4	99	306	DM59
Victoria Rd. N9	209	300	DT48
Victoria Rd. N15	222	307	DU56
Victoria Rd. N18	209	300	DT49
Victoria Rd. N22	220	306	DJ53
Victoria Rd. NW4	218	305	CW56
Victoria Rd. NW6	127	315	CZ68
Victoria Rd. NW7	205	298	CT50
Victoria Rd. NW10	125	314	CS70
Victoria Rd. SW14	171	322	CR83
Victoria Rd. W3	135	314	CR71
Victoria Rd. W5	132	314	CH71
Victoria Rd. W8	65	315	DC75
Victoria Rd., Bark.	235	308	EP65
Victoria Rd., Bexh.	263	327	FA84
Victoria Rd., Brom.	290	334	EK99
Victoria Rd., Chis.	277	326	EN92
Victoria Rd., Dag.	237	309	FB64
Victoria Rd., Erith	255	319	FE79
Victoria Rd., Felt.	258	321	BV88
Victoria Rd., Kings.T.	268	322	CM96
Victoria Rd., Mitch.	271	323	DE94
Victoria Rd., Rom.	227	309	FE58
Victoria Rd., Ruis.	232	313	BU60
Victoria Rd., Sid.	261	326	ET90
Victoria Rd., Sthl.	250	321	BZ76
Victoria Rd., Surb.	282	330	CK100
Victoria Rd., Sutt.	285	331	DD106
Victoria Rd., Tedd.	268	322	CG93
Victoria Rd., Twick.	184	322	CH87
Victoria Rd., Uxb.	240	312	BJ66
Victoria Sq. SW1	68/9	316	DH76
Victoria Sta. SW1	80/1	316	DH77
Victoria Steps, Brent.	153	314	CM79
Victoria St. E15	121	307	EE66
Victoria St. SW1	69	316	DJ76
Victoria St., Belv.	254	319	EZ78
Victoria Ter. N4	100	306	DN60
Victoria Ter. NW10	125	314	CS69
Victoria Ter., Har.	233	313	CE60
Victoria Vil., Rich.	169	322	CM83
Victoria Way SE7	252	318	EH78
Victoria Wf. E14	139	317	DY73
Victorian Gro. N16	117	306	DS63
Victorian Rd. N16	101	306	DS62
Victors Dr., Hmptn.	266	329	BY93
Victory Ave., Mord.	285	331	DC99
Victory Business Cen., Islw.	259	321	CF84
Victory Pl. E14	139	317	DY73
Victory Pl. SE17	85	316	DQ77
Victory Pl. SE19	273	324	DS93
Victory Rd. E11	224	308	EH56
Victory Rd. SW19	271	323	DC94
Victory Rd., Cher.	280	328	BG102
Victory Rd. Ms. SW19	271	323	DC94
Victory Wk. SE8	166	317	EA81
Victory Way SE16	149	317	DY75
Victory Way, Houns.	250	321	BW78
Victory Way, Rom.	227	309	FB54
Vienna Clo., Ilf.	224	308	EL54
View, The SE2	254	319	EY78
View Clo. N6	97	305	DF59
View Clo., Har.	215	303	CD56
View Rd. N6	97	305	DF59
Viewfield Clo., Har.	91	304	CL59
Viewfield Rd. SW18	173	323	CZ86
Viewfield Rd., Bex.	262	327	EW88
Viewland Rd. SE18	253	318	ET78
Viga Rd. N21	209	300	DN44
Vigilant Clo. SE26	274	325	DU91
Vignoles Rd., Rom.	237	309	FA59
Vigo St. W1	57	316	DJ73
Viking Clo. E3	129	317	DY68
Viking Ct. SW6	158	315	DA79
Viking Gdns. E6	244	318	EL70
Viking Pl. E10	103	307	DZ60
Viking Rd., Sthl.	242	313	BY73
Viking Way, Erith	255	319	FC76
Villa Rd. SW9	178	324	DN83
Villa St. SE17	86	316	DR78
Villacourt Rd. SE18	254	319	EU80
Village, The SE7	252	318	EJ79
Village Arc. E4	211	301	ED46
Village Clo. E4	211	301	EC50
Village Clo. NW3	113	305	DE64
Village Hts., Wdf.Grn.	211	301	EF50
Village Ms. NW9	93	304	CR61
Village Pk. Clo., Enf.	209	300	DS44
Village Rd. N3	218	305	CY54
Village Rd., Enf.	209	300	DR45
Village Row, Sutt.	292	331	DA108
Village Way NW10	109	304	CR63
Village Way SE21	179	324	DR86
Village Way, Ashf.	264	328	BM91
Village Way, Beck.	275	325	EA97
Village Way, Pnr.	232	313	BY59
Village Way, S.Croy.	295	333	DU113
Village Way E., Har.	233	313	CA59
Villas Rd. SE18	253	318	EQ77
Villier St., Uxb.	240	312	BK68
Villiers Ave., Surb.	282	330	CM99
Villiers Ave., Twick.	258	321	BZ88
Villiers Clo. E10	104	307	EA61
Villiers Clo., Surb.	268	322	CM98
Villiers Ct. N20	207	299	DC45
Villiers Gro., Sutt.	292	331	CX109
Villiers Path, Surb.	282	330	CL99
Villiers Rd. NW2	110	305	CU65
Villiers Rd., Beck.	274	325	DX96
Villiers Rd., Islw.	251	321	CE82
Villiers Rd., Kings.T.	268	322	CM98
Villiers Rd., Sthl.	242	313	BZ74
Villiers St. WC2	58/9	316	DL74
Vincam Clo., Twick.	259	321	CA87
Vince St. EC1	38	316	DR69
Vincent Ave., Cars.	293	331	DD111
Vincent Ave., Surb.	282	330	CP102
Vincent Clo. SE16	149	317	DY75
Vincent Clo., Brom.	276	326	EH98
Vincent Clo., Ilf.	225	308	EQ51
Vincent Clo., Sid.	261	326	ES88
Vincent Clo., West Dr.	257	320	BN79
Vincent Dr., Shep.	281	328	BS97
Vincent Gdns. NW2	93	304	CT62
Vincent Ms. E3	130	317	EA68
Vincent Rd. E4	223	307	ED51
Vincent Rd. N15	221	306	DQ56
Vincent Rd. N22	221	306	DN54
Vincent Rd. SE18	253	318	EP77
Vincent Rd. W3	144	314	CQ76
Vincent Rd., Croy.	287	332	DS101
Vincent Rd., Dag.	236	309	EY66
Vincent Rd., Houns.	250	321	BX82
Vincent Rd., Islw.	251	321	CD81
Vincent Rd., Kings.T.	269	322	CN97
Vincent Rd., Wem.	107	304	CM66
Vincent Row, Hmptn.	267	329	CC93
Vincent Sq. SW1	81	316	DJ77
Vincent St. E16	141	317	EF71
Vincent St. SW1	82	316	DK77
Vincent Ter. N1	24/5	316	DP68
Vincents Path, Nthlt.	232	313	BY65
Vine Clo., Stai.	256	320	BG85
Vine Clo., Surb.	282	330	CM100
Vine Clo., Sutt.	285	331	DC104
Vine Clo., West Dr.	249	320	BN77
Vine Ct. E1	138	317	DU71
Vine Ct., Har.	216	304	CL58
Vine Gdns., Ilf.	235	308	EQ64
Vine Gro., Uxb.	241	312	BN66
Vine Hill EC1	36	316	DN70
Vine La. SE1	62/3	316	DS74
Vine La., Uxb.	240	312	BM67
Vine Pl. W5	133	314	CL74
Vine Pl., Houns.	259	321	CB84
Vine Rd. E15	121	307	EF66
Vine Rd. SW13	171	322	CT83
Vine Rd., E.Mol.	267	329	CC98
Vine Sq. W14	147	315	CZ78
Vine St. EC3	51	316	DT72
Vine St. W1	57	316	DJ73
Vine St., Rom.	227	309	FC56
Vine St., Uxb.	240	312	BK67
Vine St. Bri. EC1	36	316	DN70
Vine Yd. SE1	73	316	DQ75
Vinegar All. E17	223	307	EB56
Vinegar St. E1	138	317	DV74
Vinegar Yd. SE1	74/5	316	DS75
Vineries, The N14	208	300	DJ43
Vineries, The, Enf.	202	300	DS41
Vineries Bank NW7	206	299	CV50
Vineries Clo., Dag.	237	309	FA65
Vineries Clo., West Dr.	257	320	BN79
Vines Ave. N3	219	305	DB53
Viney Rd. SE13	182	325	EB83
Vineyard, The, Rich.	169	322	CL85
Vineyard Ave. NW7	218	305	CY52
Vineyard Clo. SE6	198	325	EA88
Vineyard Clo., Kings.T.	268	322	CM97
Vineyard Gro. N3	219	305	DB53
Vineyard Hill Rd. SW19	270	323	CZ91
Vineyard Pas., Rich.	169	322	CL85
Vineyard Path SW14	171	322	CR83
Vineyard Rd., Felt.	258	321	BU90
Vineyard Row, Kings.T.	268	322	CJ95
Vineyard Wk. EC1	36	316	DN70
Vining St. SW9	178	324	DN84
Vinlake Ave., Uxb.	230	312	BM62
Vinson Clo., Orp.	291	335	EU102
Vintry Ms. E17	223	307	EA56
Viola Ave. SE2	254	319	EV77
Viola Ave., Felt.	258	321	BW86
Viola Ave., Stai.	264	320	BL88
Viola Sq. W12	135	314	CT73
Violet Ave., Enf.	202	300	DR38
Violet Ave., Uxb.	248	312	BM71
Violet Clo., Wall.	285	332	DG102
Violet Gdns., Croy.	286	332	DP106
Violet Hill NW8	17	315	DC68
Violet La., Croy.	294	332	DP107
Violet Rd. E3	130	317	EB70
Violet Rd. E17	223	307	EA58
Violet Rd. E18	224	308	EH54
Violet St. E2	128	317	DV70
Virgil Pl. W1	43	315	DF71
Virgil St. SE1	71	316	DM76
Virginia Clo., N.Mal.	269	322	CQ98
Virginia Gdns., Ilf.	225	308	EQ54
Virginia Rd. E2	39	316	DT69
Virginia Rd., Th.Hth.	273	324	DP95
Virginia St. E1	138	317	DU73
Virginia Wk. SW2	177	324	DM86
Viscount Clo. N11	208	300	DH50
Viscount Dr. E6	244	318	EM71
Viscount Gro., Nthlt.	242	313	BX69
Viscount Rd., Stai.	264	320	BL88
Viscount St. EC1	49	316	DQ71
Viscount Way, Houns.	257	320	BS84
Vista, The SE9	260	326	EK86
Vista, The, Sid.	277	326	ET92
Vista Ave., Enf.	203	301	DX40
Vista Dr., Ilf.	224	308	EK57
Vista Way, Har.	216	304	CL58
Viveash Clo., Hayes	249	320	BT76
Vivian Ave. NW4	218	305	CU57
Vivian Ave., Wem.	108	304	CN64
Vivian Gdns., Wem.	108	304	CN64
Vivian Rd. E3	129	317	DY68
Vivian Sq. SE15	180	325	DV83
Vivian Way N2	219	305	DD57
Vivienne Clo., Twick.	169	322	CK86
Voce Rd. SE18	253	318	ER80
Voewood Clo., N.Mal.	283	330	CT100
Volta Way, Croy.	286	332	DM102
Voltaire Rd. SW4	177	324	DK83
Voltaire Way, Hayes	249	312	BS73
Voluntary Pl. E11	224	308	EG58
Vorley Rd. N19	98	306	DJ61
Voss Ct. SW16	272	324	DL93
Voss St. E2	128	317	DU69
Voyagers Clo. SE28	246	319	EW72
Vulcan Clo., Wall.	294	332	DM108
Vulcan Gate, Enf.	202	300	DN41
Vulcan Rd. SE4	165	317	DZ82
Vulcan Sq. E14	150	317	EA77
Vulcan Ter. SE4	165	317	DZ82
Vulcan Way N7	115	306	DM65
Vyne, The, Bexh.	263	327	FB83
Vyner Rd. W3	135	314	CR73
Vyner St. E2	128	317	DV67
Vyners Way, Uxb.	241	312	BN64
Wadding St. SE17	86	316	DR77
Waddington Clo., Enf.	202	300	DS42
Waddington Rd. E15	121	307	ED64
Waddington St. E15	121	307	ED65
Waddington Way SE19	273	324	DQ94
Waddon Clo., Croy.	286	332	DN104
Waddon Ct. Rd., Croy.	286	332	DN105
Waddon Marsh Way, Croy.	286	332	DM102
Waddon New Rd., Croy.	286	332	DP104
Waddon Pk. Ave., Croy.	286	332	DN104
Waddon Rd., Croy.	286	332	DN104
Waddon Way, Croy.	294	332	DN107
Wade Rd. E16	244	318	EJ72
Wades Gro. N21	209	300	DN45
Wades Hill N21	209	300	DN44
Wades La., Tedd.	268	322	CG92
Wades Ms. N21	209	300	DN45
Wades Pl. E14	140	317	EB73
Wadeson St. E2	128	317	DV68
Wadeville Ave., Rom.	226	309	EZ58
Wadeville Clo., Belv.	255	319	FA78
Wadham Ave. E17	223	307	EB52
Wadham Clo., Shep.	281	328	BQ101
Wadham Gdns. NW3	113	305	DE66
Wadham Gdns., Grnf.	233	313	CD65
Wadham Rd. E17	223	307	EB53
Wadham Rd. SW15	173	323	CY84
Wadhurst Clo. SE20	274	325	DV96
Wadhurst Rd. SW8	160	316	DJ81
Wadhurst Rd. W4	145	314	CR76
Wadley Rd. E11	105	307	EE59
Wadsworth Clo., Enf.	210	301	DX43
Wadsworth Clo., Grnf.	122	314	CJ68
Wadsworth Rd., Grnf.	122	314	CH68
Wager St. E3	129	317	DZ70
Waggon Ms. N14	208	300	DJ46
Waghorn Rd. E13	244	318	EJ67
Waghorn Rd., Har.	216	304	CK55
Waghorn St. SE15	180	325	DU83
Wagner St. SE15	164	317	DW80
Wagtail Clo. NW9	217	304	CS54
Wagtail Way, Orp.	278	327	EX98
Waights Ct., Kings.T.	268	322	CL95
Wainfleet Ave., Rom.	227	309	FC54
Wainford Clo. SW19	189	323	CX88
Wainwright Gro., Islw.	259	321	CD84
Waite Davies Rd. SE12	199	325	EF87
Waite St. SE15	163	316	DT79
Waithman St. EC4	48/9	316	DP72
Wakefield Gdns. SE19	273	324	DS94
Wakefield Gdns., Ilf.	224	308	EL58
Wakefield Ms. WC1	34/5	316	DL69
Wakefield Rd. N11	208	300	DK50
Wakefield Rd. N15	221	306	DT57
Wakefield Rd., Rich.	169	322	CK85
Wakefield St. E6	244	318	EK67
Wakefield St. N18	210	301	DU50
Wakefield St. WC1	34/5	316	DL69
Wakeham St. N1	117	306	DR65
Wakehams Hill, Pnr.	214	303	BZ55
Wakehurst Rd. SW11	175	323	DE85
Wakelin Rd. E15	131	317	EE68
Wakeling Rd. W7	243	313	CF71
Wakeling St. E14	139	317	DY72
Wakeman Rd. NW10	126	315	CW69
Wakemans Hill Ave. NW9	217	304	CR57
Wakerfield Clo., Horn.	228	311	FM57
Wakering Rd., Bark.	235	308	EQ65
Wakerley Clo. E6	244	318	EM72
Wakley St. EC1	36/7	316	DP69
Walberswick St. SW8	161	316	DL80
Walbrook EC4	62	316	DR73
Walbrook Ho. N9	210	301	DW47
Walbrook Wf. EC4	61	316	DQ73
Walburgh St. E1	138	317	DV72
Walburton Rd., Pur.	294	332	DJ113
Walcorde Ave. SE17	85	316	DQ77
Walcot Rd., Enf.	203	301	DZ40
Walcot Sq. SE11	84	316	DN77
Walcott St. SW1	81	316	DJ77
Waldair Ct. E16	253	318	EP75
Waldair Wf. E16	253	318	EP75
Waldeck Gro. SE27	194	324	DP90
Waldeck Rd. N15	221	306	DP56
Waldeck Rd. SW14	170	322	CQ83
Waldeck Rd. W4	154	314	CN79
Waldeck Rd. W13	132	314	CH72
Waldeck Ter. SW14	170	322	CQ83
Waldegrave Ave., Tedd.	267	329	CF92
Waldegrave Gdns., Twick.	259	321	CF89
Waldegrave Gdns., Upmin.	239	311	FP60
Waldegrave Pk., Twick.	267	329	CF91
Waldegrave Rd. N8	221	306	DN55
Waldegrave Rd. SE19	273	324	DT94
Waldegrave Rd. W5	133	314	CM73
Waldegrave Rd., Brom.	276	326	EL98
Waldegrave Rd., Dag.	236	309	EW61
Waldegrave Rd., Tedd.	267	329	CF91
Waldegrave Rd., Twick.	267	329	CF91
Waldegrove, Croy.	287	332	DT104
Waldemar Ave. SW6	157	315	CY81
Waldemar Ave. W13	132	314	CJ74
Waldemar Rd. SW19	271	323	DA92
Walden Ave. N13	209	300	DQ49
Walden Ave., Chis.	276	326	EM91
Walden Ave., Rain.	247	319	FD69
Walden Clo., Belv.	254	319	EZ78
Walden Gdns., Th.Hth.	272	324	DM98
Walden Rd. N17	221	306	DR53
Walden Rd., Chis.	276	326	EM93
Walden Rd., Horn.	228	310	FK58
Walden St. E1	138	317	DV72
Walden Way NW7	218	305	CX51
Walden Way, Horn.	228	310	FK58
Walden Way, Ilf.	225	308	ES52
Waldenshaw Rd. SE23	196	325	DW88
Waldo Clo. SW4	176	324	DJ85
Waldo Pl., Mitch.	271	323	DE94
Waldo Rd. NW10	126	315	CU69
Waldo Rd., Brom.	276	326	EK97
Waldorf Clo., S.Croy.	294	332	DP109
Waldram Cres. SE23	196	325	DW88
Waldram Pk. Rd. SE23	197	325	DX88
Waldram Pl. SE23	196	325	DW88
Waldrist Way, Erith	254	319	EZ75
Waldron Gdns., Brom.	275	325	ED97
Waldron Ms. SW3	159	315	DD79
Waldron Rd. SW18	190	323	DC90
Waldron Rd., Har.	233	313	CE60
Waldronhyrst, S.Croy.	286	332	DP105
Waldrons, The, Croy.	286	332	DP105
Waldrons Path, S.Croy.	287	332	DQ105
Waleran Clo., Stan.	215	303	CF51
Waleran Flats SE1	86/7	316	DS77
Walerand Rd. SE13	166	317	EC82
Wales Ave., Cars.	285	331	DE106
Wales Fm. Rd. W3	135	314	CR71
Waley St. E1	139	317	DY71
Walfield Ave. N20	207	299	DB45
Walford Rd. N16	117	306	DS63
Walford Rd., Uxb.	240	312	BJ68
Walfrey Gdns., Dag.	236	309	EY66
Walham Gro. SW6	158	315	DA80
Walham Ri. SW19	270	323	CY93
Walham Yd. SW6	158	315	DA80
Walk, The, Horn.	238	311	FM61
Walk, The, Sun.	265	328	BT94
Walkden Rd., Chis.	277	326	EN92
Walker Clo. N11	208	300	DJ49
Walker Clo. SE18	253	318	EQ77
Walker Clo. W7	243	313	CE74
Walker Clo., Dart.	263	327	FF83
Walker Clo., Hmptn.	266	329	BZ93
Walkers Ct. E8	118	307	DU65
Walkers Ct. W1	58	316	DK73
Walkers Pl. SW15	173	323	CY83
Walkerscroft Mead SE21	194	324	DQ88
Walkford Way SE15	163	316	DT80
Walks, The N2	219	305	DD55
Wall End Rd. E6	235	308	EN66
Wall St. N1	117	306	DR65
Wallace Clo. SE28	246	319	EX73
Wallace Clo., Horn.	238	310	FH60
Wallace Clo., Shep.	281	328	BR98
Wallace Clo., Uxb.	240	312	BL68
Wallace Cres., Cars.	285	331	DF106
Wallace Rd. N1	116	306	DQ65
Wallace Way N19	99	306	DK61
Wallasey Cres., Uxb.	231	312	BN61
Wallbutton Rd. SE4	165	317	DY82
Wallcote Ave. NW2	95	305	CX60
Wallenger Ave., Rom.	228	310	FH55
Waller Dr., Nthwd.	214	303	BU54
Waller Rd. SE14	165	317	DX81
Wallers Clo., Dag.	246	319	EY67
Wallers Clo., Wdf.Grn.	224	308	EM51
Wallflower St. W12	135	314	CT73
Wallgrave Rd. SW5	76/7	315	DB77
Wallingford Ave. W10	137	315	CX71
Wallingford Rd., Uxb.	240	312	BH68
Wallington Clo., Ruis.	231	302	BQ58
Wallington Rd., Ilf.	235	308	ET59
Wallington Sq., Wall.	293	332	DH107
Wallis All. SE1	73	316	DQ75
Wallis Clo. SW11	175	323	DD83
Wallis Ms. N22	221	306	DN55
Wallis Rd. E9	119	307	DZ65
Wallis Rd., Sthl.	243	313	CB72
Walliss Cotts. SW2	193	324	DL87
Wallorton Gdns. SW14	171	322	CR84
Wallside EC2	49	316	DQ71
Wallwood Rd. E11	105	307	ED60
Wallwood St. E14	139	317	DZ71
Walm La. NW2	110	305	CW65
Walmer Clo. E4	211	301	EB47
Walmer Clo., Orp.	291	334	ER105
Walmer Clo., Rom.	227	309	FB54
Walmer Gdns. W13	142	314	CG75
Walmer Ho. N9	209	300	DT46
Walmer Pl. W1	43	315	DF71
Walmer Rd. W10	136	315	CW72
Walmer Rd. W11	137	315	CY73
Walmer St. W1	43	315	DF71
Walmer Ter. SE18	253	318	EQ77
Walmgate Rd., Grnf.	122	314	CH67
Walmington Fold N12	219	305	DA51
Walney Wk. N1	116	306	DQ65
Walnut Ave., West Dr.	249	320	BN76
Walnut Clo. SE8	165	317	DZ79
Walnut Clo., Cars.	285	331	DF106
Walnut Clo., Hayes	249	312	BS73
Walnut Clo., Ilf.	225	308	EQ56
Walnut Ct. W5	143	314	CL75
Walnut Gdns. E15	121	307	EE63
Walnut Gro., Bans.	292	331	CX114
Walnut Gro., Enf.	209	300	DR43
Walnut Ms., Sutt.	293	331	DC108
Walnut Rd. E10	104	307	EA61
Walnut Tree Ave., Mitch.	271	323	DE97
Walnut Tree Clo. SW13	155	314	CT81
Walnut Tree Clo., Bans.	292	331	CY112
Walnut Tree Clo., Chis.	277	326	EQ95
Walnut Tree Cotts. SW19	270	323	CY91
Walnut Tree Rd. SE10	151	317	EE78
Walnut Tree Rd., Brent.	153	314	CL79
Walnut Tree Rd., Dag.	236	309	EX61
Walnut Tree Rd., Erith	255	319	FE78
Walnut Tree Rd., Houns.	250	321	BZ79
Walnut Tree Rd., Shep.	281	328	BQ96
Walnut Tree Wk. SE11	84	316	DN77
Walnut Way, Ruis.	232	313	BW65
Walnut Way, Swan.	279	327	FD96
Walnuts, The, Orp.	291	335	EU102
Walnuts Rd., Orp.	291	335	EU102
Walpole Ave., Rich.	153	314	CM82
Walpole Clo. W13	142	314	CJ75
Walpole Clo., Pnr.	215	303	CA51
Walpole Cres., Tedd.	267	329	CF92
Walpole Gdns. W4	144	314	CQ78
Walpole Gdns., Twick.	259	321	CE89
Walpole Ms. NW8	18	315	DD67
Walpole Ms. SW19	271	323	DD93
Walpole Pk. W5	132	314	CJ74
Walpole Pl. SE18	253	318	EP77
Walpole Pl., Tedd.	267	329	CF92
Walpole Rd. E6	234	308	EJ66
Walpole Rd. E17	222	307	DY56
Walpole Rd. E18	223	307	EF53
Walpole Rd. (Downhills Way) N17	221	306	DQ55
Walpole Rd. (Lordship La.) N17	221	306	DQ54
Walpole Rd. SW19	271	323	DD93
Walpole Rd., Brom.	290	334	EK99
Walpole Rd., Croy.	287	332	DR103
Walpole Rd., Surb.	282	330	CL101
Walpole Rd., Tedd.	267	329	CF92
Walpole Rd., Twick.	259	321	CE89
Walpole St. SW3	79	315	DF78
Walrond Ave., Wem.	107	304	CL64
Walsham Clo. N16	102	307	DU59
Walsham Clo. SE28	246	319	EX73
Walsham Rd. SE14	165	317	DX82
Walsham Rd., Felt.	258	321	BV87
Walsingham Gdns., Epsom	283	330	CS105
Walsingham Pk., Chis.	277	326	ER96
Walsingham Pl. SW4	175	323	DF84
Walsingham Rd. E5	102	307	DU62
Walsingham Rd. W13	132	314	CG74
Walsingham Rd., Enf.	202	300	DR42
Walsingham Rd., Mitch.	285	331	DF99
Walsingham Rd., Orp.	278	327	EV95
Walsingham Wk., Belv.	255	319	FA79
Walt Whitman Clo. SE24	178	324	DP84
Walter Rodney Clo. E6	234	308	EM65
Walter St. E2	129	317	DX69
Walter St., Kings.T.	268	322	CL95
Walter Ter. E1	139	317	DX72
Walter Wk., Edg.	217	304	CQ51
Walters Ho. SE17	162	316	DP79
Walters Rd. SE25	273	324	DS98
Walters Rd., Enf.	210	301	DW43
Walters Way SE23	181	325	DX86
Walters Yd., Brom.	276	326	EG96
Walterton Rd. W9	127	315	CZ70
Waltham Ave. NW9	217	304	CN58
Waltham Ave., Hayes	249	320	BQ76
Waltham Dr., Edg.	217	304	CN54
Waltham Gdns., Enf.	203	301	DW36
Waltham Pk. Way E17	223	307	EA53
Waltham Rd., Cars.	285	331	DD101
Waltham Rd., Sthl.	250	321	BY76
Waltham Rd., Wdf.Grn.	224	308	EL51
Waltham Way E4	210	301	DZ49
Walthamstow Ave. E4	210	301	DY50
Walthamstow Bus. Cen. E17	223	307	EC54
Waltheof Ave. N17	221	306	DR53
Waltheof Gdns. N17	221	306	DR53
Walton Ave., Har.	232	313	BZ64
Walton Ave., N.Mal.	269	322	CT98
Walton Ave., Sutt.	284	331	CY104
Walton Bri., Shep.	281	328	BS101
Walton Bri. Rd., Shep.	281	328	BR100
Walton Clo. E5	103	307	DX62
Walton Clo. NW2	94	305	CV61
Walton Clo. SW8	161	316	DL80
Walton Clo., Har.	215	303	CD56
Walton Cres., Har.	232	313	BZ63
Walton Dr. NW10	109	304	CR65
Walton Dr., Har.	215	303	CD56
Walton Gdns. W3	134	314	CP71
Walton Gdns., Felt.	265	328	BT91
Walton Gdns., Wem.	91	304	CL61
Walton La., Shep.	281	328	BR101
Walton Pl. SW3	67	315	DF76
Walton Rd. E12	235	308	EN63
Walton Rd. E13	244	318	EJ68
Walton Rd. N15	221	306	DT56
Walton Rd., E.Mol.	266	329	BY98
Walton Rd., Har.	215	303	CD56
Walton Rd., Rom.	226	309	EZ52
Walton Rd., Sid.	262	327	EW89
Walton Rd., W.Mol.	266	329	BY98
Walton St. SW3	78/9	315	DE77
Walton St., Enf.	202	300	DR39
Walton Way W3	134	314	CP71
Walton Way, Mitch.	272	324	DJ98
Walworth Pl. SE17	85	316	DQ78
Walworth Rd. SE1	85	316	DQ77
Walworth Rd. SE17	85	316	DQ77
Walwyn Ave., Brom.	276	326	EK97
Wanborough Dr. SW15	188	323	CV88
Wanderer Dr., Bark.	246	319	EV69
Wandle Bank SW19	271	323	DD94
Wandle Bank, Croy.	286	332	DL104
Wandle Ct., Epsom	283	330	CQ105
Wandle Ct. Gdns., Croy.	286	332	DL104
Wandle Rd. SW17	191	323	DE89
Wandle Rd., Croy.	287	332	DQ104
Wandle Rd. (Waddon), Croy.	286	332	DL104
Wandle Rd., Mord.	271	323	DC98
Wandle Rd., Wall.	285	332	DH103
Wandle Side, Croy.	286	332	DM104
Wandle Side, Wall.	285	332	DH104
Wandle Way SW18	190	323	DB88
Wandle Way, Mitch.	285	331	DF99
Wandon Rd. SW6	158	315	DB80
Wandsworth Bri. SW6	174	323	DB83
Wandsworth Bri. SW18	174	323	DB83
Wandsworth Bri. Rd. SW6	158	315	DB81
Wandsworth Bus. Cen., Grnf.	122	314	CJ68
Wandsworth Common SW12	191	323	DF87
Wandsworth Common N. Side SW18	174	323	DC85
Wandsworth Common W. Side SW18	174	323	DC85
Wandsworth High St. SW18	174	323	DA85
Wandsworth Plain SW18	174	323	DA85
Wandsworth Rd. SW8	176	324	DH83
Wangey Rd., Rom.	236	309	EX59
Wanless Rd. SE24	178	324	DQ83
Wanley Rd. SE5	179	324	DR84
Wanlip Rd. E13	244	318	EH70
Wannock Gdns., Ilf.	225	308	EP52
Wansbeck Rd. E9	119	307	DZ66
Wansdown Pl. SW6	158	315	DB80
Wansey St. SE17	85	316	DQ77
Wansford Rd., Wdf.Grn.	224	308	EJ53
Wanstead Clo., Brom.	276	326	EJ96
Wanstead La., Ilf.	224	308	EL58
Wanstead Pk. E11	234	308	EJ59
Wanstead Pk. Ave. E12	234	308	EK61
Wanstead Pk. Rd., Ilf.	224	308	EL58
Wanstead Pl. E11	224	308	EG58
Wanstead Rd., Brom.	276	326	EJ96
Wansunt Rd., Bex.	263	327	FC88
Wantage Rd. SE12	183	325	EF85
Wantz Rd., Dag.	237	309	FB63
Wapping Dock St. E1	138	317	DV74
Wapping High St. E1	138	317	DU74
Wapping La. E1	138	317	DV73
Wapping Wall E1	138	317	DW74
Warbank La., Kings.T.	269	322	CT94
Warbeck Rd. W12	146	315	CV75
Warberry Rd. N22	220	306	DM54
Warboys App., Kings.T.	269	322	CP93
Warboys Cres. E4	211	301	EC50
Warboys Rd., Kings.T.	269	322	CP93
Warburton Clo., Har.	215	303	CD51
Warburton Rd. E8	128	317	DV67
Warburton Rd., Twick.	259	321	CB88
Warburton St. E8	128	317	DV67
Warburton Ter. E17	223	307	EB54
Ward Clo., Erith	255	319	FD79
Ward Clo., S.Croy.	287	332	DS106
Ward Gdns., Rom.	228	310	FK54
Ward Rd. E15	131	317	ED67
Ward Rd. N19	98	306	DJ62
Wardalls Gro. SE14	164	317	DW80
Wardell Clo. NW7	217	304	CS52
Wardell Fld. NW9	217	304	CS53
Warden Ave., Har.	232	313	BZ60
Warden Rd. NW5	114	306	DG65
Wardens Gro. SE1	61	316	DQ74
Wardle St. E9	119	307	DX64
Wardley St. SW18	190	323	DB87
Wardo Ave. SW6	157	315	CY81
Wardour Ms. W1	45	316	DJ72
Wardour St. W1	45	316	DJ72
Wardrobe Pl. EC4	48/9	316	DP72
Wardrobe Ter. EC4	60/1	316	DP73
Wards Rd., Ilf.	235	308	ER59
Wareham Clo., Houns.	259	321	CB84
Waremead Rd., Ilf.	225	308	EP57
Warepoint Dr. SE28	253	318	ER75
Warfield Rd. NW10	127	315	CX69
Warfield Rd., Felt.	265	320	BS87
Warfield Rd., Hmptn.	267	329	CB95
Warfield Yd. NW10	127	315	CX69
Wargrave Ave. N15	221	306	DT58
Wargrave Rd., Har.	233	313	CC62
Warham Rd. N4	221	306	DN57
Warham Rd., Har.	215	303	CF54
Warham Rd., S.Croy.	286	332	DP106
Warham St. SE5	162	316	DP80
Waring Rd., Sid.	278	327	EW93
Waring St. SE27	273	324	DQ91
Warkworth Gdns., Islw.	152	314	CG80
Warkworth Rd. N17	221	306	DR52
Warland Rd. SE18	253	318	ER80
Warley Ave., Dag.	236	309	EZ59
Warley Ave., Hayes	242	313	BU72
Warley Clo. E10	103	307	DZ60
Warley Rd. N9	210	301	DW47
Warley Rd., Hayes	242	313	BU72
Warley Rd., Ilf.	225	308	EN53
Warley Rd., Upmin.	229	311	FQ54
Warley Rd., Wdf.Grn.	224	308	EH52
Warley St. E2	129	317	DX69
Warlingham Rd., Th.Hth.	273	324	DP98
Warlock Rd. W9	127	315	CZ70
Warlters Clo. N7	115	306	DL63
Warlters Rd. N7	115	306	DL63
Warltersville Rd. N19	99	306	DL59
Warmington Clo. E5	103	307	DX62
Warmington Rd. SE24	178	324	DQ86
Warmington St. E13	244	318	EG70
Warminster Gdns. SE25	274	325	DU96
Warminster Rd. SE25	274	325	DU97
Warminster Sq. SE25	274	325	DU96
Warminster Way, Mitch.	272	324	DH95
Warndon St. SE16	148	317	DW77
Warne Pl., Sid.	262	327	EV86
Warneford Rd., Har.	216	304	CK55
Warneford St. E9	128	317	DV67
Warner Ave., Sutt.	284	331	CY103
Warner Clo. E15	121	307	EE64
Warner Clo. NW9	93	304	CT59
Warner Clo., Hmptn.	266	329	BZ92
Warner Clo., Hayes	257	320	BR80
Warner Par., Hayes	257	320	BR80
Warner Pl. E2	128	317	DU68
Warner Rd. E17	222	307	DY56
Warner Rd. N8	220	306	DK56
Warner Rd. SE5	162	316	DQ81
Warner Rd., Brom.	275	325	EF94
Warner St. EC1	36	316	DN70
Warner Yd. EC1	36	316	DN70
Warners La., Kings.T.	268	322	CK92
Warnford Ind. Est., Hayes	249	320	BS75
Warnford Rd., Orp.	291	334	ET106
Warnham Ct. Rd., Cars.	293	331	DF108
Warnham Rd. N12	207	299	DD50
Warple Ms. W3	145	314	CS75
Warple Way W3	145	314	CS75
Warren, The E12	234	308	EL63
Warren, The, Cars.	293	331	DD109
Warren, The, Hayes	242	313	BU72
Warren, The, Houns.	250	321	BZ80
Warren, The, Wor.Pk.	283	330	CR105
Warren Ave. E10	104	307	EC62
Warren Ave., Brom.	275	325	EE94
Warren Ave., Orp.	291	334	ET106
Warren Ave., Rich.	170	322	CP84
Warren Ave., Sutt.	292	331	CZ110
Warren Clo. N9	210	301	DX45
Warren Clo. SE21	194	324	DQ87
Warren Clo., Bexh.	263	327	FA85
Warren Clo., Hayes	242	313	BV71
Warren Clo., Wem.	91	304	CK61
Warren Cres. N9	209	300	DT45
Warren Cutting, Kings.T.	269	322	CR94
Warren Dr., Grnf.	243	313	CB70
Warren Dr., Horn.	238	310	FG63
Warren Dr., Orp.	291	335	EV106
Warren Dr., Ruis.	232	313	BX59
Warren Dr., The E11	234	308	EJ59
Warren Dr. N., Surb.	282	330	CP102
Warren Dr. S., Surb.	283	330	CQ102
Warren Flds., Stan.	204	298	CJ49
Warren Footpath, Twick.	184	322	CJ88
Warren Gdns. E15	121	307	ED64
Warren Gdns., Orp.	291	335	EU106
Warren Ho. E3	130	317	EB69
Warren La. SE18	253	318	EP76
Warren Ms. W1	33	316	DJ70
Warren Pk., Kings.T.	269	322	CQ93
Warren Pk. Rd., Sutt.	293	331	DD107
Warren Pl. E1	139	317	DX72
Warren Pond Rd. E4	211	301	EF46

Warren Ri., N.Mal.	269	322	CR95
Warren Rd. E4	211	301	EC47
Warren Rd. E10	104	307	EC62
Warren Rd. E11	224	308	EJ58
Warren Rd. NW2	93	304	CT61
Warren Rd. SW19	271	323	DE93
Warren Rd., Ashf.	265	328	BS94
Warren Rd., Bans.	292	331	CW114
Warren Rd., Bexh.	263	327	FA85
Warren Rd., Brom.	289	334	EG103
Warren Rd., Croy.	287	332	DS102
Warren Rd., Ilf.	225	308	ER57
Warren Rd., Kings.T.	269	322	CQ93
Warren Rd., Orp.	291	334	ET106
Warren Rd., Pur.	294	332	DP112
Warren Rd., Sid.	262	327	EW90
Warren Rd., Twick.	259	321	CC86
Warren Rd., Uxb.	240	312	BL63
Warren St. W1	33	316	DJ70
Warren Ter., Rom.	226	309	EX56
Warren Wk. SE7	252	318	EJ79
Warren Way NW7	218	305	CY51
Warren Wd. Clo., Brom.	289	334	EG103
Warrender Rd. N19	98	306	DJ62
Warrender Way, Ruis.	232	313	BU59
Warrens Shawe La., Edg.	205	298	CP47
Warriner Ave., Horn.	238	310	FK61
Warriner Gdns. SW11	159	315	DF81
Warrington Cres. W9	29	315	DC70
Warrington Gdns. W9	29	315	DC70
Warrington Gdns., Horn.	228	310	FJ58
Warrington Pl. E14	140	317	EC74
Warrington Rd., Croy.	286	332	DP104
Warrington Rd., Dag.	236	309	EX61
Warrington Rd., Har.	215	303	CE57
Warrington Rd., Rich.	169	322	CK85
Warrington Sq., Dag.	236	309	EX61
Warrington St. E13	244	318	EG70
Warrior Sq. E12	235	308	EN63
Warsaw Clo., Ruis.	232	313	BV65
Warsdale Dr. NW9	217	304	CR57
Warspite Rd. SE18	252	318	EK76
Warton Rd. E15	120	307	EC66
Warwall E6	245	318	EP72
Warwick Ave. W2	41	315	DC71
Warwick Ave. W9	28/9	315	DB70
Warwick Ave., Edg.	205	298	CP48
Warwick Ave., Har.	232	313	BZ63
Warwick Ave., Stai.	264	328	BJ93
Warwick Clo., Barn.	207	299	DD43
Warwick Clo., Bex.	262	327	EZ87
Warwick Clo., Hmptn.	267	329	CC94
Warwick Clo., Orp.	291	335	EU104
Warwick Ct. SE15	164	317	DU82
Warwick Ct. WC1	47	316	DM71
Warwick Ct., Surb.	282	330	CL103
Warwick Cres. W2	41	315	DC71
Warwick Cres., Hayes	241	312	BT70
Warwick Dene W5	133	314	CL74
Warwick Dr. SW15	172	323	CV83
Warwick Est. W2	40/1	315	DB71
Warwick Gdns. N4	221	306	DQ57
Warwick Gdns. W14	147	315	CZ76
Warwick Gdns., Ilf.	235	308	EP60
Warwick Gdns., Rom.	228	310	FJ55
Warwick Gro. E5	102	307	DV60
Warwick Gro., Surb.	282	330	CM101
Warwick Ho. St. SW1	58	316	DK74
Warwick La. EC4	48/9	316	DP72
Warwick Pas. EC4	48/9	316	DP72
Warwick Pl. W5	143	314	CK75
Warwick Pl. W9	41	315	DC71
Warwick Pl., Uxb.	240	312	BJ66
Warwick Pl. N. SW1	81	316	DJ77
Warwick Rd. E4	211	301	EA50
Warwick Rd. E11	224	308	EH57
Warwick Rd. E12	234	308	EL64
Warwick Rd. E15	121	307	EF65
Warwick Rd. E17	222	307	DZ53
Warwick Rd. N11	220	306	DK51
Warwick Rd. N18	209	300	DS49
Warwick Rd. SE20	274	325	DV97
Warwick Rd. SW5	147	315	CZ77
Warwick Rd. W5	143	314	CK75
Warwick Rd. W14	147	315	CZ77
Warwick Rd., Ashf.	264	328	BL92
Warwick Rd., Couls.	294	332	DJ114
Warwick Rd., Enf.	203	301	DZ37
Warwick Rd., Houns.	258	321	BV83
Warwick Rd., Kings.T.	268	322	CJ95
Warwick Rd., N.Mal.	269	322	CQ97
Warwick Rd., Sid.	278	327	EV92
Warwick Rd., Sthl.	250	321	BZ76
Warwick Rd., Sutt.	285	331	DC105
Warwick Rd., Th.Hth.	273	324	DN97
Warwick Rd., Twick.	259	321	CE88
Warwick Rd., Well.	262	327	EW83
Warwick Rd., West Dr.	248	320	BL75
Warwick Row SW1	68/9	316	DH76
Warwick Sq. EC4	48/9	316	DP72
Warwick Sq. SW1	81	316	DJ78
Warwick Sq. Ms. SW1	82	316	DK77
Warwick St. W1	57	316	DJ73
Warwick Ter. SE18	253	318	ER79
Warwick Way SW1	80/1	316	DH78
Warwick Yd. EC1	37	316	DQ70
Warwickshire Path SE8	165	317	DZ80
Washington Ave. E12	234	308	EL63
Washington Clo. E3	130	317	EB69
Washington Rd. E6	234	308	EJ66
Washington Rd. E18	223	307	EF54
Washington Rd. SW13	156	315	CU80
Washington Rd., Kings.T.	269	322	CN96
Washington Rd., Wor.Pk.	283	331	CV103
Wastdale Rd. SE23	197	325	DX88
Wat Tyler Rd. SE3	166	317	EC82
Wat Tyler Rd. SE10	166	317	EC82
Watchfield Ct. W4	144	314	CQ78
Watcombe Cotts., Rich.	154	314	CN79
Watcombe Pl. SE25	287	333	DV99
Watcombe Rd. SE25	287	333	DV99
Water Gdns., Stan.	216	304	CH51
Water La. E15	121	307	EE65
Water La. EC3	62/3	316	DS73
Water La. NW1	114	306	DH66
Water La. SE14	164	317	DW80
Water La., Ilf.	235	308	ES62
Water La., Kings.T.	268	322	CK95
Water La., Rich.	169	322	CK85
Water La., Sid.	262	327	EZ90
Water La., Twick.	184	322	CG88
Water Lily Clo., Sthl.	251	321	CC75
Water Rd., Wem.	123	314	CM67
Water St. WC2	59	316	DM73
Water Twr. Clo., Uxb.	240	312	BL64
Water Twr. Hill, Croy.	287	332	DR105
Water Twr. Pl. N1	24	316	DN67
Waterbank Rd. SE6	198	325	EB90
Waterbeach Rd., Dag.	236	309	EW65
Waterbrook La. NW4	218	305	CW57
Watercress Pl. N1	117	306	DS66
Waterdale Rd. SE2	254	319	EU79
Waterdell Pl., Rick.	212	302	BG47
Waterden Rd. E15	120	307	EA64
Waterer Ri., Wall.	294	332	DK107
Waterfall Clo. N14	208	300	DJ48
Waterfall Cotts. SW19	271	323	DD93
Waterfall Rd. N11	208	300	DH49
Waterfall Rd. N14	208	300	DJ48
Waterfall Rd. SW19	271	323	DD93
Waterfall Ter. SW17	271	323	DE93
Waterfield Clo. SE28	246	319	EV74
Waterfield Clo., Belv.	255	319	FA76
Waterfield Gdns. SE25	273	324	DR98
Waterford Rd. SW6	158	315	DB80
Watergardens, The, Kings.T.	269	322	CQ93
Watergate EC4	60/1	316	DP73
Watergate St. SE8	166	317	EA79
Watergate Wk. WC2	58/9	316	DL73
Waterhall Ave. E4	211	301	EE49
Waterhall Clo. E17	222	307	DX53
Waterhead Clo., Erith	255	319	FE80
Waterhouse Clo. E16	244	318	EK71
Waterhouse Clo. NW3	113	305	DD64
Waterhouse Clo. W6	147	315	CX77
Waterhouse Sq. EC1	48	316	DN71
Wateridge Clo. E14	150	317	EA76
Wateringbury Clo., Orp.	278	327	EV97
Waterloo Bri. SE1	59	316	DM74
Waterloo Bri. WC2	59	316	DM73
Waterloo Clo. E9	118	307	DW64
Waterloo Clo., Felt.	265	320	BT88
Waterloo Est. E2	128	317	DW68
Waterloo Gdns. E2	128	317	DW68
Waterloo Gdns., Rom.	227	309	FD58
Waterloo Pas. NW6	111	305	CZ66
Waterloo Pl. SW1	58	316	DK74
Waterloo Pl., Rich.	169	322	CL85
Waterloo Pl. (Kew), Rich.	154	314	CN79
Waterloo Rd. E6	234	308	EJ66
Waterloo Rd. E7	121	307	EF64
Waterloo Rd. E10	104	307	EA59
Waterloo Rd. NW2	94	305	CU60
Waterloo Rd. SE1	60	316	DN74
Waterloo Rd., Ilf.	225	308	EQ54
Waterloo Rd., Rom.	227	309	FE58
Waterloo Rd., Sutt.	285	331	DD106
Waterloo Rd., Uxb.	240	312	BJ67
Waterloo Ter. N1	116	306	DP66
Waterlow Ct. NW11	96	305	DB59
Waterlow Rd. N19	98	306	DJ60
Waterman St. SW15	173	323	CX83
Waterman Way E1	138	317	DV74
Waterman's Clo., Kings.T.	268	322	CL94
Watermans Wk. SE16	139	317	DY74
Watermead, Felt.	265	320	BS88
Watermead La., Cars.	285	331	DF101
Watermead Rd. SE6	275	325	EB91
Watermead Way N17	222	307	DU55
Watermeadow La. SW6	158	315	DC82
Watermen's Sq. SE20	274	325	DW94
Watermill Clo., Rich.	184	322	CJ90
Watermill La. N18	209	300	DS50
Watermill Way SW19	271	323	DC95
Watermill Way, Felt.	258	321	BZ89
Watermint Clo., Orp.	278	327	EX98
Watermint Quay N16	222	307	DU58
Waters Gdns., Dag.	237	309	FA64
Waters Rd. SE6	199	325	EE90
Waters Rd., Kings.T.	269	322	CP96
Waters Sq., Kings.T.	269	322	CP97
Watersedge, Epsom	283	330	CQ105
Watersfield Way, Edg.	216	304	CK52
Waterside, Beck.	275	325	EA95
Waterside, Dart.	263	327	FE85
Waterside, Uxb.	248	312	BJ71
Waterside Clo. E3	129	317	DZ67
Waterside Clo. SE16	148	317	DU75
Waterside Clo., Bark.	236	309	EU63
Waterside Clo., Nthlt.	242	313	BZ69
Waterside Clo., Rom.	229	311	FN52
Waterside Clo., Surb.	282	330	CL103
Waterside Pl. NW1	20	316	DG67
Waterside Pt. SW11	159	315	DE80
Waterside Rd., Sthl.	251	321	CA76
Waterside Trd. Cen. W7	251	321	CE76
Waterside Way SW17	271	323	DC91
Watersmeet Way SE28	246	319	EW72
Waterson St. E2	38/9	316	DS69
Watersplash Clo., Kings.T.	268	322	CL97
Watersplash La., Hayes	250	321	BU77
Watersplash La., Houns.	250	321	BV78
Watersplash Rd., Shep.	281	328	BN99
Waterview Ho. E14	139	317	DY71
Waterworks La. E5	103	307	DX61
Waterworks Rd. SW2	177	324	DM86
Waterworks Yd., Croy.	287	332	DQ104
Watery La. SW20	270	323	CZ96
Watery La., Nthlt.	242	313	BW68
Watery La., Sid.	278	327	EV93
Wates Way, Mitch.	285	331	DF100
Wateville Rd. N17	221	306	DQ53
Watford Bypass, Borwd.	204	298	CG45
Watford Clo. SW11	159	315	DE81
Watford Rd. E16	244	318	EG71
Watford Rd., Borwd.	204	298	CJ44
Watford Rd., Har.	90	304	CG59
Watford Rd., Nthwd.	213	302	BT52
Watford Rd., Wem.	90	304	CG61
Watford Way NW4	218	305	CU56
Watford Way NW7	205	298	CS49
Watkin Rd., Wem.	92	304	CP62
Watkinson Rd. N7	115	306	DM65
Watling Ave., Edg.	217	304	CQ53
Watling Ct. EC4	49	316	DQ72
Watling Ct., Borwd.	204	298	CK44
Watling Fm. Clo., Stan.	204	298	CJ45
Watling Gdns. NW2	111	305	CY65
Watling St. EC4	49	316	DQ72
Watling St., Bexh.	263	327	FB84
Watlings Clo., Croy.	288	333	DY100
Watlington Gro. SE26	274	325	DY92
Watney Mkt. E1	138	317	DV72
Watney Rd. SW14	170	322	CQ83
Watney St. E1	138	317	DV72
Watneys Rd., Mitch.	286	332	DK99
Watson Ave. E6	235	308	EN66
Watson Ave., Sutt.	284	331	CY104
Watson Clo. N16	117	306	DR64
Watson Clo. SW19	271	323	DE93
Watson Gdns., Rom.	228	310	FK54
Watson St. E13	244	318	EH68
Watsons Ms. W1	42/3	315	DE71
Watsons Rd. N22	220	306	DM53
Watson's St. SE8	166	317	EA80
Watsons Yd. NW2	93	304	CT61
Wattisfield Rd. E5	102	307	DW62
Watts Bri. Rd., Erith	255	319	FF79
Watts Clo. N15	221	306	DS57
Watts Gro. E3	140	317	EB71
Watts La., Chis.	277	326	EP95
Watts La., Tedd.	268	322	CG92
Watts St. E1	138	317	DV74
Watts Way SW7	66	315	DD76
Wauthier Clo. N13	209	300	DP50
Wavel Ms. N8	220	306	DK56
Wavel Ms. NW6	112	305	DB66
Wavel Pl. SE26	273	324	DT91
Wavell Dr., Sid.	261	326	ES86
Wavendon Ave. W4	145	314	CR78
Waveney Ave. SE15	180	325	DV84
Waveney Clo. E1	138	317	DU74
Waverley Ave. E4	210	301	DZ49
Waverley Ave. E17	223	307	ED55
Waverley Ave., Surb.	282	330	CP100
Waverley Ave., Sutt.	284	331	DB103
Waverley Ave., Twick.	258	321	BZ88
Waverley Ave., Wem.	107	304	CM64
Waverley Clo. E18	224	308	EJ53
Waverley Clo., Brom.	290	334	EK99
Waverley Clo., Hayes	249	320	BR77
Waverley Cres. SE18	253	318	ER79
Waverley Cres., Rom.	228	310	FJ52
Waverley Gdns. E6	244	318	EL71
Waverley Gdns. NW10	123	314	CM68
Waverley Gdns., Bark.	245	318	ES68
Waverley Gdns., Ilf.	225	308	EQ54
Waverley Gdns., Nthwd.	214	303	BU53
Waverley Gro. N3	218	305	CX55
Waverley Ind. Pk., Har.	215	303	CD55
Waverley Pl. N4	100	306	DP61
Waverley Pl. NW8	18	315	DD68
Waverley Rd. E17	223	307	EC55
Waverley Rd. E18	224	308	EJ53
Waverley Rd. N8	220	306	DL58
Waverley Rd. N17	222	307	DV52
Waverley Rd. SE18	253	318	EQ78
Waverley Rd. SE25	274	325	DV98
Waverley Rd., Enf.	202	300	DP42
Waverley Rd., Har.	232	313	BY60
Waverley Rd., Sthl.	243	313	CA73
Waverley Vil. N17	221	306	DT54
Waverley Wk. W2	40	315	DA71
Waverley Way, Cars.	293	331	DE107
Waverton Ho. E3	129	317	DZ67
Waverton Rd. SW18	190	323	DC87
Waverton St. W1	56	316	DG74
Wavertree Ct. SW2	193	324	DM88
Wavertree Rd. E18	224	308	EG54
Wavertree Rd. SW2	193	324	DL88
Waxlow Cres., Sthl.	243	313	CA72
Waxlow Rd. NW10	124	314	CQ68
Waxwell Clo., Pnr.	214	303	BX54
Waxwell La., Pnr.	214	303	BX54
Waxwell Ter. SE1	71	316	DM75
Waybourne Gro., Ruis.	231	302	BQ58
Waycross Rd., Upmin.	239	311	FS59
Waye Ave., Houns.	250	321	BU81
Wayfarer Rd., Nthlt.	242	313	BX69
Wayfield Link SE9	261	326	ER86
Wayford St. SW11	159	315	DE82
Wayland Ave. E8	118	307	DU64
Waylands, Swan.	279	327	FF98
Waylands Mead, Beck.	275	325	EB95
Wayleave, The SE28	246	319	EV73
Waylett Pl. SE27	194	324	DP90
Waylett Pl., Wem.	91	304	CK62
Wayman Ct. E8	118	307	DV65
Wayne Clo., Orp.	291	334	ET104
Waynflete Ave., Croy.	286	332	DP104
Waynflete Sq. W10	137	315	CX72
Waynflete St. SW18	190	323	DC89
Wayside NW11	95	305	CY60
Wayside SW14	170	322	CQ85
Wayside Ave., Horn.	238	310	FK61
Wayside Clo. N14	208	300	DJ44
Wayside Clo., Rom.	227	309	FF55
Wayside Commercial Est., Bark.	246	319	EU68
Wayside Ct., Twick.	168	322	CJ86
Wayside Ct., Wem.	92	304	CN62
Wayside Gdns. SE9	276	326	EM91
Wayside Gdns., Dag.	237	309	FA64
Wayside Gro. SE9	276	326	EM91
Wayside Ms., Ilf.	225	308	EN57
Weald, The, Chis.	276	326	EM93
Weald Clo. SE16	148	317	DV78
Weald Clo., Brom.	290	334	EL103
Weald La., Har.	215	303	CD54
Weald Ri., Har.	215	303	CF52
Weald Rd., Uxb.	241	312	BN68
Weald Sq. E5	102	307	DV61
Weald Way, Hayes	241	312	BS69
Weald Way, Rom.	227	309	FB58
Wealdstone Rd., Sutt.	284	331	CZ103
Wealdwood Gdns., Pnr.	215	303	CB51
Weale Rd. E4	211	301	ED48
Wear Pl. E2	128	317	DV69
Weardale Gdns., Enf.	202	300	DR39
Weardale Rd. SE13	183	325	ED84
Wearside Rd. SE13	182	325	EB85
Weatherley Clo. E3	139	317	DZ71
Weaver Clo. E6	245	318	EP72
Weaver St. E1	128	317	DU70
Weaver Wk. SE27	273	324	DQ91
Weavers Clo., Islw.	259	321	CE84
Weavers Ter. SW6	158	315	DA79
Weavers Way NW1	115	306	DK66
Webb Est. E5	102	307	DU59
Webb Gdns. E13	244	318	EG70
Webb Pl. NW10	125	314	CT69
Webb Rd. SE3	167	317	EF79
Webb St. SE1	74/5	316	DS76
Webber Clo., Borwd.	204	298	CK44
Webber Row SE1	72	316	DN75
Webber St. SE1	72	316	DN75
Webbs Rd. SW11	175	323	DF84
Webbs Rd., Hayes	242	313	BV69
Webbscroft Rd., Dag.	237	309	FB63
Webster Clo., Horn.	238	310	FK62
Webster Gdns. W5	133	314	CK74
Webster Rd. E11	104	307	EC62
Webster Rd. SE16	148	317	DU76
Wedderburn Rd. NW3	113	305	DD64
Wedderburn Rd., Bark.	245	318	ER67
Wedgewood Clo., Nthwd.	213	302	BQ52
Wedgewood Wk. NW6	112	305	DB64
Wedgewood Way SE19	273	324	DQ94
Wedgwood Ms. W1	46	316	DK72
Wedlake Clo., Horn.	238	311	FL60
Wedlake St. W10	127	315	CY70
Wedmore Ave., Ilf.	225	308	EN53
Wedmore Gdns. N19	99	306	DK61
Wedmore Ms. N19	99	306	DK62
Wedmore Rd., Grnf.	243	313	CD69
Wedmore St. N19	99	306	DK62
Wednesbury Gdns., Rom.	228	311	FM52
Wednesbury Grn., Rom.	228	311	FM52
Wednesbury Rd., Rom.	228	311	FM52
Weech Rd. NW6	112	305	DA63
Weedington Rd. NW5	114	306	DG64
Weekley Sq. SW11	175	323	DD83
Weigall Rd. SE12	260	326	EG84
Weighouse St. W1	44	316	DG72
Weighton Rd. SE20	274	325	DV96
Weighton Rd., Har.	215	303	CD53
Weihurst Gdns., Sutt.	285	331	DD106
Weimar St. SW15	173	323	CY83
Weir Est. SW12	192	324	DJ87
Weir Hall Ave. N18	221	306	DR51
Weir Hall Gdns. N18	209	300	DR50
Weir Hall Rd. N17	221	306	DR51
Weir Hall Rd. N18	209	300	DR50
Weir Rd. SW12	192	324	DJ87
Weir Rd. SW19	190	323	DB90
Weir Rd., Bex.	263	327	FB87
Weir Rd., Cher.	280	328	BH101
Weirdale Ave. N20	207	299	DF47
Weir's Pas. NW1	34	316	DK69
Weiss Rd. SW15	173	323	CX83
Welbeck Ave., Brom.	276	326	EG91
Welbeck Ave., Hayes	242	313	BV70
Welbeck Ave., Sid.	262	327	EU88
Welbeck Clo. N12	207	299	DD50
Welbeck Clo., N.Mal.	283	330	CT99
Welbeck Rd. E6	244	318	EK69
Welbeck Rd., Barn.	207	299	DD44
Welbeck Rd., Cars.	285	331	DE102
Welbeck Rd., Har.	233	313	CB60
Welbeck Rd., Sutt.	285	331	DD103
Welbeck St. W1	44	316	DG71
Welbeck Wk., Cars.	285	331	DE102
Welbeck Way W1	44/5	316	DH72
Welby St. SE5	162	316	DP81
Welch Pl., Pnr.	214	303	BW53
Welcote Dr., Nthwd.	213	302	BR51
Weld Pl. N11	208	300	DH50
Weldon Clo., Ruis.	232	313	BV65
Weldon Dr., W.Mol.	266	329	BZ98
Welfare Rd. E15	121	307	EE66
Welford Clo. E5	103	307	DX62
Welford Pl. SW19	270	323	CY91
Welham Rd. SW16	272	324	DH93
Welham Rd. SW17	272	324	DG92
Welhouse Rd., Cars.	285	331	DE102
Well App., Barn.	206	299	CW43
Well Clo. SW16	272	324	DM91
Well Clo., Ruis.	232	313	BY62
Well Cottage Clo. E11	234	308	EJ59
Well Ct. EC4	49	316	DQ72
Well Ct. SW16	272	324	DM91
Well Gro. N20	207	299	DC45
Well Hall Par. SE9	260	326	EM84
Well Hall Rd. SE9	260	326	EL83
Well La. SW14	170	322	CQ85
Well Pas. NW3	97	305	DD62
Well Rd. NW3	97	305	DD62
Well Rd., Barn.	206	299	CW43
Well St. E9	118	307	DW66
Well St. E15	121	307	EE65
Well Wk. NW3	113	305	DD63
Wellacre Rd., Har.	216	304	CH58
Wellan Clo., Sid.	262	327	EV85
Welland Gdns., Grnf.	243	313	CF68
Welland Ms. E1	138	317	DU74
Welland St. SE10	166	317	EC79
Wellands Clo., Brom.	276	326	EM96
Wellbrook Rd., Orp.	290	334	EN105
Wellclose Sq. E1	138	317	DU73
Wellclose St. E1	138	317	DU73
Welldon Cres., Har.	215	303	CE58
Weller St. SE1	73	316	DQ75
Weller's Ct. N1	22/3	316	DL68
Wellesley Ave. W6	146	315	CV76
Wellesley Ave., Nthwd.	213	302	BT50
Wellesley Ct. W9	29	315	DC69
Wellesley Ct. Rd., Croy.	287	332	DR103
Wellesley Cres., Twick.	259	321	CE89
Wellesley Gro., Croy.	287	332	DR103
Wellesley Pk. Ms., Enf.	202	300	DP40
Wellesley Pl. NW1	34	316	DK69
Wellesley Rd. E11	224	308	EG57
Wellesley Rd. E17	223	307	EA58
Wellesley Rd. N22	221	306	DN54
Wellesley Rd. NW5	114	306	DG64
Wellesley Rd. W4	144	314	CN78
Wellesley Rd., Croy.	287	332	DQ102
Wellesley Rd., Har.	215	303	CE57
Wellesley Rd., Ilf.	235	308	EP61
Wellesley Rd., Sutt.	293	331	DC107
Wellesley Rd., Twick.	259	321	CD90
Wellesley St. E1	139	317	DX71
Wellesley Ter. N1	37	316	DQ69
Wellfield Ave. N10	220	306	DH55
Wellfield Gdns., Cars.	293	331	DE109
Wellfield Rd. SW16	272	324	DL91
Wellfield Wk. SW16	272	324	DM92
Wellfit St. SE24	178	324	DP83
Wellgarth, Grnf.	106	304	CH65
Wellgarth Rd. NW11	96	305	DB60
Wellhouse Rd., Beck.	274	325	DZ98
Welling High St., Well.	262	327	EU83
Welling Way SE9	261	326	ER83
Welling Way, Well.	261	326	ES83
Wellings Ho., Hayes	242	313	BV74
Wellington Ave. E4	211	301	EA47
Wellington Ave. N9	210	301	DV48
Wellington Ave. N15	221	306	DT58
Wellington Ave., Houns.	259	321	CA85
Wellington Ave., Pnr.	214	303	BZ53
Wellington Ave., Sid.	262	327	EU86
Wellington Ave., Wor.Pk.	284	331	CW104
Wellington Bldgs. SW1	80/1	316	DH78
Wellington Clo. SE14	165	317	DX81
Wellington Clo. W11	40	315	DA72
Wellington Clo., Dag.	237	309	FC66
Wellington Clo., Walt.	281	328	BT102
Wellington Ct. NW8	18	315	DD68
Wellington Ct., Stai.	264	320	BL87
Wellington Cres., N.Mal.	269	322	CQ97
Wellington Dr., Dag.	237	309	FC66
Wellington Dr., Pur.	294	332	DM110
Wellington Gdns. SE7	252	318	EJ78
Wellington Gdns., Twick.	267	329	CD91
Wellington Ms. SE7	252	318	EJ79
Wellington Ms. SE22	180	325	DU84
Wellington Pk. Ind. Est. NW2	94	305	CU60
Wellington Pas. E11	224	308	EG57
Wellington Pl. N2	219	305	DE57
Wellington Pl. NW8	30	315	DD69
Wellington Rd. E6	244	318	EM67
Wellington Rd. E7	121	307	EF63
Wellington Rd. E10	103	307	DY60
Wellington Rd. E11	224	308	EG57
Wellington Rd. E17	222	307	DY55
Wellington Rd. NW8	18	315	DD68
Wellington Rd. NW10	127	315	CX69
Wellington Rd. SW19	190	323	DA89
Wellington Rd. W5	142	314	CJ76
Wellington Rd., Ashf.	264	328	BL92
Wellington Rd., Belv.	254	319	EZ78
Wellington Rd., Bex.	262	327	EX85
Wellington Rd., Brom.	276	326	EJ98
Wellington Rd., Croy.	286	332	DP101
Wellington Rd., Enf.	202	300	DS42
Wellington Rd., Felt.	257	320	BS85
Wellington Rd., Hmptn.	267	329	CD92
Wellington Rd., Har.	215	303	CE55
Wellington Rd., Orp.	291	335	EV100
Wellington Rd., Pnr.	214	303	BZ52
Wellington Rd., Twick.	267	329	CD91
Wellington Rd., Uxb.	240	312	BJ67
Wellington Rd. N., Houns.	258	321	BZ83
Wellington Rd. S., Houns.	258	321	BZ84
Wellington Row E2	39	316	DT69
Wellington Sq. SW3	79	315	DF78
Wellington St. SE18	253	318	EN77
Wellington St. WC2	58/9	316	DL73
Wellington St., Bark.	245	318	EQ67
Wellington Ter. E1	138	317	DV74
Wellington Ter. N8	221	306	DN55
Wellington Ter., Har.	233	313	CD60
Wellington Way E3	130	317	EA69
Wellmeadow Rd. SE6	199	325	EE87
Wellmeadow Rd. SE13	183	325	EE86
Wellmeadow Rd. W7	142	314	CG77
Wellow Wk., Cars.	285	331	DD102
Wells, The N14	208	300	DK45
Wells Clo., Nthlt.	242	313	BW69
Wells Dr. NW9	93	304	CR60
Wells Gdns., Dag.	237	309	FB64
Wells Gdns., Ilf.	234	308	EL59
Wells Gdns., Rain.	237	309	FF65
Wells Ho. Rd. NW10	135	314	CS71
Wells Ms. W1	45	316	DJ71
Wells Pk. Rd. SE26	196	325	DU90
Wells Ri. NW8	19	315	DF67
Wells Rd. W12	146	315	CW75
Wells Rd., Brom.	276	326	EM96
Wells Sq. WC1	35	316	DM69
Wells St. W1	45	316	DJ71
Wells Ter. N4	100	306	DN61
Wells Way SE5	163	316	DS79
Wells Way SW7	66	315	DD76
Wells Yd. N7	116	306	DN64
Wellside Gdns. SW14	170	322	CQ85
Wellsmoor Gdns., Brom.	277	326	EN97
Wellsprings Cres., Wem.	92	304	CP62
Wellstead Ave. N9	210	301	DW45
Wellstead Rd. E6	245	318	EN68
Wellwood Clo., Couls.	294	332	DL114
Wellwood Rd., Ilf.	236	309	EU60
Welsford St. SE1	148	317	DU78
Welsh Clo. E13	244	318	EG69
Welsh Side Wk. NW9	217	304	CS58
Welshpool Ho. E8	128	317	DU67
Welshpool St. E8	128	317	DV67
Weltje Rd. W6	146	315	CU77
Welton Rd. SE18	253	318	ES80
Welwyn Ave., Felt.	257	320	BT86
Welwyn St. E2	128	317	DW69
Welwyn Way, Hayes	241	312	BS70
Wembley Commercial Cen., Wem.	91	304	CK61
Wembley Hill Rd., Wem.	107	304	CM64
Wembley Pk. Bus. Cen., Wem.	92	304	CP62
Wembley Pk. Dr., Wem.	107	304	CM63
Wembley Pt., Wem.	108	304	CP66
Wembley Retail Pk., Wem.	108	304	CP63
Wembley Rd., Hmptn.	267	329	CA94
Wembley Way, Wem.	108	304	CP65
Wemborough Rd., Stan.	216	304	CH53
Wembury Rd. N6	98	306	DH59
Wemyss Rd. SE3	167	317	EF82
Wend, The, Couls.	294	332	DK114
Wendela Ct., Har.	233	313	CE62
Wendell Rd. W12	145	314	CT76
Wendle Ct. SW8	161	316	DL79
Wendling Rd., Sutt.	285	331	DD102
Wendon St. E3	129	317	DZ67
Wendover SE17	86/7	316	DS78
Wendover Clo., Hayes	242	313	BY70
Wendover Dr., N.Mal.	283	330	CT100
Wendover Rd. NW10	125	314	CT68
Wendover Rd. SE9	260	326	EK83
Wendover Rd., Brom.	276	326	EH97
Wendover Way, Horn.	238	310	FJ64
Wendover Way, Orp.	291	335	EU100
Wendover Way, Well.	262	327	EU85
Wendy Clo., Enf.	209	300	DT44
Wendy Way, Wem.	123	314	CL67
Wenlack Clo., Uxb.	230	312	BG62
Wenlock Ct. N1	26	316	DR68
Wenlock Gdns. NW4	218	305	CU56
Wenlock Rd. N1	25	316	DQ68
Wenlock Rd., Edg.	217	304	CP52
Wenlock St. N1	25	316	DQ68
Wennington Rd. E3	129	317	DX68
Wensley Ave., Wdf.Grn.	223	307	EF52
Wensley Clo. SE9	260	326	EM86
Wensley Rd. N18	222	307	DV51
Wensleydale Ave., Ilf.	224	308	EL54
Wensleydale Gdns., Hmptn.	267	329	CB94
Wensleydale Pas., Hmptn.	267	329	CA95
Wensleydale Rd., Hmptn.	267	329	CA93
Wentland Clo. SE6	199	325	ED89
Wentland Rd. SE6	199	325	ED89
Wentworth Ave. N3	219	305	DA52
Wentworth Ave., Borwd.	204	298	CM43
Wentworth Clo. N3	219	305	DB52
Wentworth Clo. SE28	246	319	EX72
Wentworth Clo., Ashf.	265	328	BP91
Wentworth Clo., Brom.	289	334	EG103
Wentworth Clo., Mord.	284	331	DA101
Wentworth Clo., Orp.	291	334	ES106
Wentworth Clo., Surb.	282	330	CK103
Wentworth Cres. SE15	164	317	DU80
Wentworth Cres., Hayes	249	320	BR76
Wentworth Dr., Pnr.	214	303	BU57
Wentworth Gdns. N13	209	300	DP49
Wentworth Hill, Wem.	91	304	CM60
Wentworth Ms. E3	129	317	DZ70
Wentworth Pk. N3	219	305	DA52
Wentworth Pl., Stan.	216	304	CH51
Wentworth Rd. E12	234	308	EK63
Wentworth Rd. NW11	218	305	CZ58
Wentworth Rd., Croy.	286	332	DN101
Wentworth Rd., Sthl.	250	321	BW77
Wentworth St. E1	51	316	DT72
Wentworth Way, Pnr.	214	303	BX56
Wentworth Way, S.Croy.	295	333	DU114
Wenvoe Ave., Bexh.	255	319	FB82
Wernbrook St. SE18	253	318	EQ79
Werndee Rd. SE25	274	325	DU98
Werneth Hall Rd., Ilf.	224	308	EM55
Werrington St. NW1	21	316	DJ68
Werter Rd. SW15	173	323	CY84
Wesley Ave. E16	141	317	EE72
Wesley Ave. NW10	125	314	CR69
Wesley Ave., Houns.	250	321	BY82
Wesley Clo. N7	99	306	DM61
Wesley Clo. SE17	84/5	316	DP77
Wesley Clo., Har.	233	313	CC61
Wesley Clo., Orp.	278	327	EW97
Wesley Rd. E10	104	307	EC59
Wesley Rd. NW10	124	314	CQ67
Wesley Rd. SE17	84/5	316	DP77
Wesley Rd., Hayes	242	313	BU73
Wesley Sq. W11	137	315	CY72
Wesley St. W1	44	316	DG71
Wesleyan Pl. NW5	114	306	DH63
Wessex Ave. SW19	271	323	DA96
Wessex Clo., Ilf.	225	308	ES58
Wessex Clo., Kings.T.	269	322	CP95
Wessex Dr., Erith	255	319	FE82
Wessex Dr., Pnr.	214	303	BY52
Wessex Gdns. NW11	95	305	CY60
Wessex La., Grnf.	243	313	CD68
Wessex Rd., Houns.	256	320	BJ84
Wessex St. E2	128	317	DW69
Wessex Way NW11	95	305	CY60
West App., Orp.	291	334	EQ99
West Arbour St. E1	138	317	DW72
West Ave. E17	223	307	EB56
West Ave. N3	219	305	DA51
West Ave. NW4	218	305	CX57
West Ave., Hayes	249	312	BT73
West Ave., Pnr.	214	303	BZ58
West Ave., Sthl.	242	313	BZ73
West Ave., Wall.	286	332	DL106
West Ave. Rd. E17	223	307	EA56
West Bank N16	101	306	DS59
West Bank, Bark.	245	318	EP67
West Bank, Enf.	202	300	DQ40
West Barnes La. SW20	283	331	CV99
West Barnes La., N.Mal.	270	323	CV97
West Carriage Dr. W2	54	315	DD73
West Cen. St. WC1	46/7	316	DL72
West Chantry, Har.	215	303	CB53
West Clo. N9	209	300	DT48
West Clo., Ashf.	264	328	BL91
West Clo., Barn.	206	299	CV43
West Clo., Grnf.	243	313	CC68
West Clo., Hmptn.	266	329	BY93
West Clo., Wem.	91	304	CM60
West Common Rd., Brom.	289	334	EG103
West Common Rd., Uxb.	240	312	BK64
West Cotts. NW6	112	305	DA64
West Ct. SE18	252	318	EM80
West Ct., Wem.	90	304	CJ61
West Cromwell Rd. SW5	147	315	CZ77
West Cromwell Rd. W14	147	315	CZ78
West Cross Route W10	137	315	CX73
West Cross Route W11	137	315	CX74
West Cross Way, Brent.	152	314	CH79
West Dene, Sutt.	292	331	CY107
West Drayton Pk. Ave., West Dr.	248	320	BL76
West Drayton Rd., Uxb.	248	312	BM72
West Dr. SW16	272	324	DJ91
West Dr., Cars.	293	331	DD110
West Dr., Har.	215	303	CD51
West Dr. (Cheam), Sutt.	292	331	CX109
West Dr. Gdns., Har.	215	303	CD51
West Eaton Pl. SW1	80	316	DG77
West Eaton Pl. Ms. SW1	68	316	DG76
West Ella Rd. NW10	109	304	CS66
West End Ave. E10	223	307	ED57
West End Ave., Pnr.	214	303	BX56
West End Ct., Pnr.	214	303	BX56
West End Gdns., Nthlt.	242	313	BW68
West End La. NW6	112	305	DA64
West End La., Hayes	257	320	BQ80
West End La., Pnr.	214	303	BX55
West End Rd., Nthlt.	232	313	BW66
West End Rd., Ruis.	232	313	BU63
West End Rd., Sthl.	242	313	BY74
West Gdn. Pl. W2	42/3	315	DE72
West Gdns. E1	138	317	DV73
West Gdns. SW17	271	323	DE93
West Gate W5	123	314	CL69
West Grn. Pl., Grnf.	243	313	CD67
West Grn. Rd. N15	221	306	DP56
West Gro. SE10	166	317	EC81
West Gro., Wdf.Grn.	224	308	EJ51
West Halkin St. SW1	68	316	DG76
West Hall Rd., Rich.	154	314	CP81
West Hallowes SE9	260	326	EL88
West Ham La. E15	121	307	ED66
West Ham Pk. E7	121	307	EF66
West Hampstead Ms. NW6	112	305	DB65
West Harding St. EC4	48	316	DN72
West Harold, Swan.	279	327	FD97
West Hatch Manor, Ruis.	231	312	BT60
West Heath Ave. NW11	96	305	DA60
West Heath Clo. NW3	96	305	DA62
West Heath Clo., Dart.	263	327	FF86
West Heath Dr. NW11	96	305	DA60
West Heath Gdns. NW3	96	305	DA61
West Heath Rd. NW3	96	305	DA61
West Heath Rd. SE2	254	319	EW79
West Heath Rd., Dart.	263	327	FF86
West Hendon Bdy. NW9	217	304	CT58
West Hill SW15	189	323	CX87
West Hill SW18	189	323	CX87
West Hill, Har.	233	313	CE61
West Hill, S.Croy.	295	332	DS110
West Hill, Wem.	91	304	CM60
West Hill Ct. N6	98	306	DG62
West Hill Pk. N6	97	305	DF61
West Hill Rd. SW18	173	323	CZ86
West Hill Way N20	207	299	DB46
West Holme, Erith	255	319	FC81
West Ho. Clo. SW19	189	323	CY88
West India Ave. E14	140	317	EA74
West India Dock Rd. E14	139	317	DZ72
West Kentish Town Est. NW5	114	306	DG65
West La. SE16	148	317	DV75
West Lo. Ave. W3	134	314	CN74
West Mall W8	52	315	DA74
West Malling Way, Horn.	238	310	FJ64
West Mead, Ruis.	232	313	BW63
West Ms. N17	222	307	DV51
West Ms. SW1	81	316	DJ77
West Oak, Beck.	275	325	ED95
West Pk. SE9	260	326	EL89
West Pk. Ave., Rich.	154	314	CN81
West Pk. Clo., Houns.	250	321	BZ79
West Pk. Clo., Rom.	226	309	EX57
West Pk. Rd., Rich.	154	314	CN81
West Pk. Rd., Sthl.	243	313	CC74
West Pier E1	138	317	DV74
West Pl. SW19	270	323	CW92
West Poultry Ave. EC1	48/9	316	DP71
West Quarters W12	136	315	CU72
West Quay Dr., Hayes	242	313	BY71
West Ramp, Houns.	257	320	BN81
West Ridge Gdns., Grnf.	243	313	CC68
West Rd. E15	131	317	EF67
West Rd. N17	222	307	DV51
West Rd. SW3	79	315	DF78
West Rd. SW4	177	324	DK85

Woodcote Pk. Ave., Pur.	294	332	DJ112
Woodcote Pl. SE27	273	324	DP92
Woodcote Rd. E11	234	308	EG59
Woodcote Rd., Wall.	293	332	DH107
Woodcote Valley Rd., Pur.	294	332	DK113
Woodcrest Rd., Pur.	294	332	DL113
Woodcroft N21	208	300	DM46
Woodcroft SE9	260	326	EM90
Woodcroft, Grnf.	106	304	CG65
Woodcroft Ave. NW7	217	304	CS52
Woodcroft Ave., Stan.	215	303	CF53
Woodcroft Cres., Uxb.	241	312	BP67
Woodcroft Rd., Th.Hth.	286	332	DP99
Woodedge Clo. E4	211	301	EF46
Woodend SE19	273	324	DQ93
Woodend, Sutt.	285	331	DC103
Woodend, The, Wall.	293	332	DH109
Woodend Rd. E17	223	307	EC54
Wooder Gdns. E7	234	308	EG63
Wooderson Clo. SE25	273	324	DS98
Woodfall Ave., Barn.	206	299	CZ43
Woodfall Dr., Dart.	263	327	FE84
Woodfall Rd. N4	100	306	DN60
Woodfall St. SW3	79	315	DF78
Woodfarrs SE5	179	324	DR84
Woodfield Ave. NW9	217	304	CS56
Woodfield Ave. SW16	193	324	DK90
Woodfield Ave. W5	122	314	CJ70
Woodfield Ave., Cars.	293	332	DG107
Woodfield Ave., Nthwd.	213	302	BS49
Woodfield Ave., Wem.	90	304	CJ62
Woodfield Clo. SE19	273	324	DQ94
Woodfield Clo., Enf.	202	300	DS42
Woodfield Cres. W5	123	314	CK70
Woodfield Dr., Barn.	208	300	DG46
Woodfield Dr., Rom.	228	310	FG56
Woodfield Gdns. W9	137	315	CZ71
Woodfield Gdns., N.Mal.	283	330	CT99
Woodfield Gro. SW16	193	324	DK90
Woodfield La. SW16	193	324	DK90
Woodfield Pl. W9	127	315	CZ70
Woodfield Rd. W5	122	314	CJ70
Woodfield Rd. W9	137	315	CZ71
Woodfield Rd., Houns.	250	321	BV82
Woodfield Ter., Uxb.	212	302	BH54
Woodfield Way N11	220	306	DK52
Woodfield Way, Horn.	238	310	FK60
Woodfields, The, S.Croy.	295	332	DT111
Woodfines, The, Horn.	228	310	FK58
Woodford Ave., Ilf.	224	308	EL55
Woodford Bri. Rd., Ilf.	224	308	EK55
Woodford Ct. W12	147	315	CX75
Woodford Cres., Pnr.	214	303	BV54
Woodford New Rd. E17	223	307	EE56
Woodford New Rd. E18	223	307	EE54
Woodford New Rd., Wdf.Grn.	223	307	EF52
Woodford Pl., Wem.	91	304	CL60
Woodford Rd. E7	234	308	EH63
Woodford Rd. E18	224	308	EG56
Woodford Trd. Est., Wdf.Grn.	224	308	EK54
Woodgate Ave., Chess.	282	330	CK106
Woodgate Cres., Nthwd.	214	303	BU51
Woodgate Dr. SW16	272	324	DK94
Woodger Rd. W12	146	315	CW75
Woodgers Gro., Swan.	279	327	FF96
Woodget Clo. E6	244	318	EL72
Woodgrange Ave. N12	219	305	DD51
Woodgrange Ave. W5	134	314	CN74
Woodgrange Ave., Enf.	210	301	DU44
Woodgrange Ave., Har.	216	304	CJ57
Woodgrange Clo., Har.	216	304	CK57
Woodgrange Gdns., Enf.	210	301	DU44
Woodgrange Rd. E7	234	308	EH64
Woodgrange Ter., Enf.	210	301	DU44
Woodhall Ave. SE21	195	324	DT90
Woodhall Ave., Pnr.	214	303	BY54
Woodhall Clo., Uxb.	240	312	BK64
Woodhall Cres., Horn.	238	311	FM59
Woodhall Dr. SE21	195	324	DT90
Woodhall Dr., Pnr.	214	303	BX53
Woodhall Gate, Pnr.	214	303	BX52
Woodhall Rd., Pnr.	214	303	BX52
Woodham Ct. E18	223	307	EF56
Woodham Rd. SE6	198	325	EC90
Woodhatch Clo. E6	244	318	EL72
Woodhaven Gdns., Ilf.	225	308	EQ55
Woodhayes Rd. SW19	270	323	CW94
Woodhead Dr., Orp.	291	334	ES103
Woodheyes Rd. NW10	109	304	CR64
Woodhill SE18	252	318	EL77
Woodhill Cres., Har.	216	304	CK58
Woodhouse Ave., Grnf.	243	313	CF68
Woodhouse Clo., Grnf.	243	313	CF68
Woodhouse Clo., Hayes	249	320	BS76
Woodhouse Gro. E12	234	308	EL65
Woodhouse Rd. E11	105	307	EF62
Woodhouse Rd. N12	219	305	DC51
Woodhurst Ave., Orp.	291	334	EQ100
Woodhurst Rd. SE2	254	319	EU78
Woodhurst Rd. W3	134	314	CQ73
Woodington Clo. SE9	261	326	EN86
Woodison St. E3	129	317	DY70
Woodknoll Dr., Chis.	276	326	EM95
Woodland Clo. NW9	217	304	CQ58
Woodland Clo. SE19	273	324	DS93
Woodland Clo., Uxb.	231	312	BP61
Woodland Cres. SE10	167	317	EE79
Woodland Gdns. N10	220	306	DH57
Woodland Gdns., Islw.	259	321	CE83
Woodland Gro. SE10	151	317	EE78
Woodland Hill SE19	273	324	DS93
Woodland Ri. N10	220	306	DH56
Woodland Ri., Grnf.	106	304	CG65
Woodland Rd. E4	211	301	EC46
Woodland Rd. N11	208	300	DH50
Woodland Rd. SE19	273	324	DT92
Woodland Rd., Th.Hth.	273	324	DN98
Woodland St. E8	117	306	DT65
Woodland Ter. SE7	252	318	EL77
Woodland Ter. SE18	252	318	EL77
Woodland Wk. NW3	113	305	DE64
Woodland Wk. SE10	151	317	EE78
Woodland Wk., Brom.	275	325	EE91
Woodland Way N21	209	300	DN47
Woodland Way NW7	217	304	CS51
Woodland Way SE2	254	319	EX77
Woodland Way, Croy.	288	333	DY102
Woodland Way, Mitch.	272	324	DG94
Woodland Way, Mord.	270	323	CZ98
Woodland Way, Orp.	277	326	EQ98
Woodland Way, Pur.	294	332	DN113
Woodland Way, Surb.	282	330	CP103
Woodland Way, W.Wick.	288	333	EB105
Woodlands NW11	218	305	CY58
Woodlands SW20	270	323	CW98
Woodlands, Har.	215	303	CA56
Woodlands, The N14	208	300	DH46
Woodlands, The SE13	199	325	ED87
Woodlands, The SE19	273	324	DQ94
Woodlands, The, Islw.	251	321	CF82
Woodlands, The, Wall.	293	332	DH109
Woodlands Ave. E11	234	308	EG60
Woodlands Ave. N3	219	305	DC52
Woodlands Ave. W3	134	314	CP74
Woodlands Ave., Horn.	228	310	FK57
Woodlands Ave., N.Mal.	269	322	CQ95
Woodlands Ave., Rom.	226	309	EY58
Woodlands Ave., Ruis.	232	313	BW59
Woodlands Ave., Sid.	261	326	ES88
Woodlands Ave., Wor.Pk.	283	330	CT103
Woodlands Clo. NW11	218	305	CY57
Woodlands Clo., Brom.	276	326	EM96
Woodlands Clo., Swan.	279	327	FF97
Woodlands Dr., Stan.	215	303	CF51
Woodlands Dr., Sun.	266	329	BW96
Woodlands Gro., Islw.	251	321	CE82
Woodlands Par., Ashf.	265	328	BQ93
Woodlands Pk., Bex.	279	327	FC91
Woodlands Pk. Rd. N15	221	306	DP57
Woodlands Pk. Rd. SE10	167	317	EE79
Woodlands Ri., Swan.	279	327	FF96
Woodlands Rd. E11	105	307	EE61
Woodlands Rd. E17	223	307	EC55
Woodlands Rd. N9	210	301	DW46
Woodlands Rd. SW13	171	322	CT83
Woodlands Rd., Bexh.	262	327	EY83
Woodlands Rd., Brom.	276	326	EL96
Woodlands Rd., Enf.	202	300	DR38
Woodlands Rd., Har.	215	303	CF57
Woodlands Rd., Ilf.	235	308	EQ62
Woodlands Rd., Islw.	259	321	CD83
Woodlands Rd., Rom.	227	309	FF55
Woodlands Rd. (Harold Wd.), Rom.	229	311	FN53
Woodlands Rd., Sthl.	242	313	BX74
Woodlands Rd., Surb.	282	330	CK101
Woodlands St. SE13	199	325	ED87
Woodlands Way SW15	173	323	CZ85
Woodlawn Clo. SW15	173	323	CZ85
Woodlawn Cres., Twick.	259	321	CB89
Woodlawn Dr., Felt.	258	321	BX89
Woodlawn Rd. SW6	157	315	CX80
Woodlea Dr., Brom.	289	333	EE99
Woodlea Gro., Nthwd.	213	302	BQ51
Woodlea Rd. N16	101	306	DS62
Woodleigh Ave. N12	219	305	DE51
Woodleigh Gdns. SW16	193	324	DL90
Woodley Clo. SW17	271	323	DF94
Woodley La., Cars.	285	331	DE104
Woodman La. E4	211	301	EE43
Woodman Path, Chig.	225	308	ES51
Woodman St. E16	245	318	EN74
Woodmans Gro. NW10	109	304	CT64
Woodmans Ms. W12	136	315	CW71
Woodmansterne La., Cars.	293	331	DF112
Woodmansterne La., Wall.	293	332	DH111
Woodmansterne Rd. SW16	272	324	DJ94
Woodmansterne Rd., Cars.	293	331	DF112
Woodmere SE9	260	326	EM87
Woodmere Ave., Croy.	288	333	DW101
Woodmere Clo. SW11	176	324	DG83
Woodmere Clo., Croy.	288	333	DX101
Woodmere Gdns., Croy.	288	333	DW101
Woodmere Way, Beck.	289	333	ED99
Woodnook Rd. SW16	272	324	DH92
Woodpecker Clo. N9	210	301	DV44
Woodpecker Clo., Har.	215	303	CF53
Woodpecker Rd. SE14	165	317	DY79
Woodpecker Rd. SE28	246	319	EW73
Woodquest Ave. SE24	178	324	DQ85
Woodridge Clo., Enf.	202	300	DN39
Woodridge Way, Nthwd.	213	302	BS51
Woodridings Ave., Pnr.	214	303	BZ53
Woodridings Clo., Pnr.	214	303	BZ52
Woodriffe Rd. E11	105	307	ED59
Woodrise, Pnr.	214	303	BU57
Woodrow SE18	252	318	EM77
Woodrow Ave., Hayes	249	312	BT71
Woodrow Clo., Grnf.	106	304	CH66
Woodrow Ct. N17	222	307	DV52
Woodrush Clo. SE14	165	317	DY80
Woodrush Way, Rom.	226	309	EX56
Woods, The, Uxb.	241	312	BP63
Woods Clo. SE19	273	324	DS93
Woods Ms. W1	56	316	DG73
Woods Pl. SE1	74/5	316	DS76
Woods Rd. SE15	164	317	DV81
Woodseer St. E1	51	316	DT71
Woodsford SE17	86	316	DR78
Woodsford Sq. W14	147	315	CY75
Woodshire Rd., Dag.	237	309	FB62
Woodside NW11	219	305	DA57
Woodside SW19	270	323	CZ93
Woodside, Orp.	291	335	EU106
Woodside Ave. N6	219	305	DF57
Woodside Ave. N10	219	305	DF57
Woodside Ave. N12	207	299	DC49
Woodside Ave. SE25	287	333	DV100
Woodside Ave., Chis.	277	326	EQ92
Woodside Ave., Wem.	123	314	CL67
Woodside Clo., Bexh.	263	327	FD84
Woodside Clo., Stan.	204	298	CH50
Woodside Clo., Surb.	283	330	CQ102
Woodside Clo., Wem.	123	314	CL67
Woodside Ct. N12	207	299	DC49
Woodside Ct. Rd., Croy.	287	333	DU101
Woodside Cres., Sid.	261	326	ES90
Woodside Dr., Dart.	279	327	FE91
Woodside End, Wem.	123	314	CL67
Woodside Gdns. E4	211	301	EB50
Woodside Gdns. N17	221	306	DS54
Woodside Gra. Rd. N12	207	299	DB49
Woodside Grn. SE25	287	333	DU100
Woodside Gro. N12	207	299	DC48
Woodside La. N12	207	299	DB48
Woodside La., Bex.	262	327	EX86
Woodside Pk. SE25	287	333	DU99
Woodside Pk. Ave. E17	223	307	ED56
Woodside Pk. Rd. N12	207	299	DB49
Woodside Pl., Wem.	123	314	CL67
Woodside Rd. E13	244	318	EJ70
Woodside Rd. N22	220	306	DM52
Woodside Rd. SE25	287	333	DV100
Woodside Rd., Bexh.	263	327	FD84
Woodside Rd., Brom.	290	334	EL99
Woodside Rd., Kings.T.	268	322	CL94
Woodside Rd., N.Mal.	269	322	CR96
Woodside Rd., Nthwd.	213	302	BT52
Woodside Rd., Pur.	294	332	DK113
Woodside Rd., Sid.	261	326	ES90
Woodside Rd., Sutt.	285	331	DC104
Woodside Way, Croy.	287	333	DV100
Woodside Way, Mitch.	272	324	DH95
Woodsome Rd. NW5	98	306	DG62
Woodspring Rd. SW19	189	323	CY89
Woodstead Gro., Edg.	216	304	CL51
Woodstock Ave. NW11	95	305	CY60
Woodstock Ave. W13	142	314	CG76
Woodstock Ave., Islw.	168	322	CG85
Woodstock Ave., Sthl.	242	313	BZ69
Woodstock Ave., Sutt.	284	331	CZ101
Woodstock Clo., Bex.	262	327	EZ87
Woodstock Clo., Stan.	216	304	CL54
Woodstock Ct. SE12	260	326	EG86
Woodstock Cres. N9	210	301	DV44
Woodstock Dr., Uxb.	240	312	BL63
Woodstock Gdns., Beck.	275	325	EB95
Woodstock Gdns., Hayes	249	312	BT71
Woodstock Gdns., Ilf.	236	309	EU61
Woodstock Gro. W12	147	315	CX75
Woodstock La., Surb.	282	330	CJ103
Woodstock La. S., Chess.	282	330	CJ105
Woodstock Ms. W1	44	316	DG71
Woodstock Ri., Sutt.	284	331	CZ101
Woodstock Rd. E7	234	308	EJ66
Woodstock Rd. E17	223	307	ED54
Woodstock Rd. N4	100	306	DN60
Woodstock Rd. NW11	95	305	CZ59
Woodstock Rd. W4	145	314	CS76
Woodstock Rd., Cars.	285	332	DG106
Woodstock Rd., Croy.	287	332	DR104
Woodstock Rd., Wem.	107	304	CM66
Woodstock St. E16	141	317	EE72
Woodstock St. W1	44/5	316	DH72
Woodstock Ter. E14	140	317	EB73
Woodstock Way, Mitch.	272	324	DH96
Woodstone Ave., Epsom	283	331	CU106
Woodsyre SE26	273	324	DT91
Woodthorpe Rd. SW15	172	323	CV84
Woodthorpe Rd., Ashf.	264	328	BK92
Woodtree Clo. NW4	218	305	CW54
Woodvale Ave. SE25	273	324	DT97
Woodvale Wk. SE27	273	324	DQ92
Woodvale Way NW11	95	305	CX62
Woodview Ave. E4	211	301	EC49
Woodview Clo. N4	100	306	DP59
Woodview Clo. SW15	269	322	CR91
Woodview Clo., Kings.T.	269	322	CR91
Woodview Clo., Orp.	291	334	EQ103
Woodview Clo., S.Croy.	295	333	DV114
Woodview Rd., Swan.	279	327	FC96
Woodville SE3	252	318	EH81
Woodville Clo. SE12	260	326	EG85
Woodville Clo., Tedd.	268	322	CG91
Woodville Gdns. NW11	95	305	CX59
Woodville Gdns. W5	133	314	CL72
Woodville Gdns., Ilf.	225	308	EP55
Woodville Gdns., Ruis.	231	312	BQ59
Woodville Gro., Well.	262	327	EU83
Woodville Rd. E11	105	307	EF60
Woodville Rd. E17	222	307	DY56
Woodville Rd. E18	224	308	EH54
Woodville Rd. N16	117	306	DS64
Woodville Rd. NW6	127	315	CZ68
Woodville Rd. NW11	95	305	CX59
Woodville Rd. W5	133	314	CK72
Woodville Rd., Mord.	271	323	DA98
Woodville Rd., Rich.	184	322	CH90
Woodville Rd., Th.Hth.	273	324	DQ98
Woodville St. SE18	252	318	EL77
Woodward Ave. NW4	218	305	CU57
Woodward Gdns., Dag.	236	309	EW66
Woodward Gdns., Stan.	215	303	CF52
Woodward Rd., Dag.	236	309	EV66
Woodwarde Rd. SE22	179	324	DS86
Woodway Cres., Har.	216	304	CG58
Woodwell St. SW18	174	323	DC85
Woodyard Clo. NW5	114	306	DG64
Woodyard La. SE21	195	324	DS87
Woodyates Rd. SE12	260	326	EG86
Wool Rd. SW20	270	323	CV94
Woolacombe Rd. SE3	252	318	EJ81
Woolacombe Way, Hayes	249	320	BS77
Wooler St. SE17	86	316	DR78
Woolf Clo. SE28	246	319	EV74
Woollaston Rd. N4	221	306	DP58
Woolmead Ave. NW9	94	305	CU59
Woolmer Gdns. N18	222	307	DU51
Woolmer Rd. N18	210	301	DU50
Woolmore St. E14	140	317	EC73
Woolneigh St. SW6	174	323	DB83
Woolstaplers Way SE16	148	317	DU77
Woolston Clo. E17	222	307	DX54
Woolstone Rd. SE23	197	325	DY89
Woolwich Ch. St. SE18	252	318	EL76
Woolwich Common SE18	253	318	EN79
Woolwich Dockyard Ind. Est. SE18	252	318	EL76
Woolwich Ferry Pier E16	253	318	EN75
Woolwich Garrison SE18	253	318	EN78
Woolwich High St. SE18	253	318	EN76
Woolwich Ind. Est. SE28	253	318	ES76
Woolwich Manor Way E6	244	318	EM70
Woolwich Manor Way E16	245	318	EP73
Woolwich New Rd. SE18	253	318	EP77
Woolwich Rd. SE2	254	319	EX79
Woolwich Rd. SE7	252	318	EH78
Woolwich Rd. SE10	151	317	EF78
Woolwich Rd., Belv.	254	319	EZ78
Woolwich Rd., Bexh.	263	327	FA84
Wooster Gdns. E14	141	317	ED72
Wooster Pl. SE1	86	316	DR77
Woosters Ms., Har.	215	303	CC55
Wootton Clo., Horn.	228	310	FK57
Wootton Gro. N3	219	305	DA53
Wootton St. SE1	60	316	DN74
Worbeck Rd. SE20	274	325	DV96
Worcester Ave. N17	222	307	DU52
Worcester Ave., Upmin.	239	311	FT60
Worcester Clo., Croy.	288	333	DZ103
Worcester Clo., Mitch.	272	324	DG96
Worcester Cres. NW7	205	298	CS48
Worcester Dr., Ashf.	265	328	BP92
Worcester Gdns. SW11	175	323	DF85
Worcester Gdns., Grnf.	233	313	CC65
Worcester Gdns., Ilf.	234	308	EL59
Worcester Gdns., Wor.Pk.	283	330	CS103
Worcester Ms. NW6	112	305	DB65
Worcester Pk. Rd., Wor.Pk.	283	330	CQ104
Worcester Rd. E12	234	308	EM63
Worcester Rd. E17	222	307	DX54
Worcester Rd. SW19	270	323	CZ92
Worcester Rd., Sutt.	292	331	DA108
Worcester Rd., Uxb.	248	312	BJ71
Worcesters Ave., Enf.	203	301	DU38
Wordsworth Ave. E12	234	308	EL66
Wordsworth Ave. E18	223	307	EF55
Wordsworth Ave., Grnf.	243	313	CD69
Wordsworth Clo., Rom.	228	310	FJ53
Wordsworth Dr., Sutt.	284	331	CW105
Wordsworth Rd. N16	117	306	DS64
Wordsworth Rd. SE1	87	316	DT77
Wordsworth Rd. SE20	274	325	DX94
Wordsworth Rd., Hmptn.	266	329	BZ91
Wordsworth Rd., Wall.	294	332	DJ107
Wordsworth Rd., Well.	253	318	ES81
Wordsworth Wk. NW11	218	305	CZ56
Wordsworth Way, West Dr.	248	320	BL77
Worfield St. SW11	159	315	DE80
Worgan St. SE11	83	316	DM78
Worgan St. SE16	149	317	DX76
Worland Rd. E15	121	307	EE66
World Trade Cen. E1	63	316	DT73
World's End Est. SW10	158	315	DC80
Worlds End La. N21	208	300	DM43
World's End Pas. SW10	159	315	DD80
World's End Pl. SW10	158	315	DC80
Worlidge St. W6	146	315	CW78
Worlingham Rd. SE22	179	324	DT84
Wormholt Rd. W12	136	315	CU74
Wormwood St. EC2	50/1	316	DS72
Wornington Rd. W10	127	315	CY70
Woronzow Rd. NW8	18	315	DD67
Worple Ave. SW19	270	323	CX94
Worple Ave., Islw.	168	322	CG85
Worple Ave., Stai.	264	328	BH93
Worple Clo., Har.	232	313	BZ60
Worple Rd. SW19	270	323	CY94
Worple Rd. SW20	270	323	CW96
Worple Rd., Islw.	168	322	CG84
Worple Rd., Stai.	264	328	BH94
Worple Rd. Ms. SW19	270	323	CZ93
Worple St. SW14	171	322	CR83
Worple Way, Har.	232	313	BZ60
Worple Way, Rich.	169	322	CL85
Worship St. EC2	38	316	DR70
Worslade Rd. SW17	271	323	DD91
Worsley Bri. Rd. SE26	274	325	DZ91
Worsley Bri. Rd., Beck.	275	325	EA92
Worsley Rd. E11	121	307	EE63
Worsopp Dr. SW4	176	324	DJ85
Worth Clo., Orp.	291	334	ES105
Worth Gro. SE17	86	316	DR78
Worthing Clo. E15	131	317	EE68
Worthing Rd., Houns.	250	321	BZ79
Worthington Clo., Mitch.	272	324	DH98
Worthington Rd., Surb.	282	330	CM102
Worthy Down Ct. SE18	253	318	EN80
Wortley Rd. E6	234	308	EK66
Wortley Rd., Croy.	286	332	DN101
Worton Gdns., Islw.	251	321	CD82
Worton Hall Est., Islw.	259	321	CE84
Worton Pk. Ind. Est., Islw.	259	321	CF83
Worton Rd., Islw.	259	321	CD84
Worton Way, Houns.	251	321	CD82
Worton Way, Islw.	251	321	CD82
Wotton Grn., Orp.	278	327	EX98
Wotton Rd. NW2	94	305	CW62
Wotton Rd. SE8	165	317	DZ79
Wotton Way, Sutt.	292	331	CW110
Wouldham Rd. E16	141	317	EF72
Wrabness Way, Stai.	280	328	BH95
Wragby Rd. E11	105	307	EE62
Wrampling Pl. N9	210	301	DU46
Wrangthorn Wk., Croy.	286	332	DN105
Wray Ave., Ilf.	225	308	EN55
Wray Clo., Horn.	238	310	FJ59
Wray Cres. N4	99	306	DL61
Wray Rd., Sutt.	292	331	CZ109
Wrayfield Rd., Sutt.	284	331	CX104
Wrays Way, Hayes	241	312	BS70
Wraysbury Clo., Houns.	258	321	BY85
Wrekin Rd. SE18	253	318	EQ80
Wren Ave. NW2	110	305	CW64
Wren Ave., Sthl.	250	321	BZ77
Wren Clo. E16	141	317	EF72
Wren Clo. N9	210	301	DX46
Wren Clo., Orp.	278	327	EX97
Wren Dr., West Dr.	248	320	BK76
Wren Gdns., Dag.	236	309	EX64
Wren Gdns., Horn.	237	309	FF60
Wren Landing E14	140	317	EA74
Wren Path SE28	253	318	ER76
Wren Rd. SE5	163	316	DR81
Wren Rd., Dag.	236	309	EX64
Wren Rd., Sid.	278	327	EW91
Wren St. WC1	35	316	DM70
Wrens Ave., Ashf.	265	328	BQ91
Wrentham Ave. NW10	127	315	CX68
Wrenthorpe Rd., Brom.	275	325	EE91
Wrenwood Way, Pnr.	214	303	BV56
Wrestlers Ct. EC3	50/1	316	DS72
Wrexham Rd. E3	130	317	EA68
Wricklemarsh Rd. SE3	252	318	EJ81
Wrigglesworth St. SE14	165	317	DX80
Wright Gdns., Shep.	281	328	BN99
Wright Rd., Houns.	250	321	BW80
Wrights All. SW19	270	323	CW93
Wrights Clo. SE13	183	325	ED84
Wrights Clo., Dag.	237	309	FB63
Wrights Grn. SW4	177	324	DK84
Wrights La. W8	64/5	315	DB76
Wrights Pl. NW10	108	304	CQ65
Wrights Rd. E3	129	317	DZ68
Wrights Rd. SE25	273	324	DS97
Wrights Row, Wall.	285	332	DH105
Wrights Wk. SW14	171	322	CR83
Wrigley Clo. E4	211	301	ED50
Writtle Wk., Rain.	247	319	FE67
Wrotham Rd. NW1	114	306	DJ66
Wrotham Rd. W13	132	314	CH74
Wrotham Rd., Well.	254	319	EW81
Wrottesley Rd. NW10	126	315	CU68
Wrottesley Rd. SE18	253	318	EQ79
Wroughton Rd. SW11	175	323	DF85
Wroughton Ter. NW4	218	305	CV56
Wroxall Rd., Dag.	236	309	EW65
Wroxham Gdns. N11	220	306	DJ52
Wroxham Gdns., Enf.	202	300	DN35
Wroxham Rd. SE28	246	319	EX73
Wroxton Rd. SE15	164	317	DV82
Wrythe Grn., Cars.	285	331	DF104
Wrythe Grn. Rd., Cars.	285	331	DF104
Wrythe La., Cars.	285	331	DC101
Wulfstan St. W12	135	314	CT71
Wyatt Clo. SE16	149	317	DZ75
Wyatt Clo., Felt.	258	321	BX88
Wyatt Clo., Hayes	242	313	BU71
Wyatt Dr. SW13	156	315	CV79
Wyatt Pk. Rd. SW2	193	324	DL89
Wyatt Rd. E7	234	308	EG65
Wyatt Rd. N5	100	306	DQ62
Wyatt Rd., Dart.	263	327	FF83
Wyatt Rd., Stai.	264	328	BG92
Wyatts La. E17	223	307	EC55
Wybert St. NW1	33	316	DJ70
Wyborne Way NW10	108	304	CQ66
Wych Elm Clo., Horn.	239	311	FN59
Wych Elm Dr., Brom.	275	325	EF94
Wych Elm Pas., Kings.T.	268	322	CM95
Wych Elm Rd., Horn.	229	311	FN58
Wyche Gro., S.Croy.	295	332	DR108
Wycherley Clo. SE3	167	317	EF80
Wycherley Cres., Barn.	207	299	DB44
Wychwood Ave., Edg.	216	304	CK51
Wychwood Ave., Th.Hth.	273	324	DQ97
Wychwood Clo., Edg.	216	304	CK51
Wychwood Clo., Sun.	266	329	BU93
Wychwood End N6	98	306	DJ59
Wychwood Gdns., Ilf.	224	308	EM56
Wychwood Way SE19	273	324	DR93
Wychwood Way, Nthwd.	213	302	BT52
Wyclif St. EC1	36/7	316	DP69
Wycliffe Clo., Well.	253	318	ET81
Wycliffe Rd. SW11	160	316	DG82
Wycliffe Rd. SW19	271	323	DB93
Wycombe Gdns. NW11	96	305	DA61
Wycombe Pl. SW18	174	323	DC86
Wycombe Rd. N17	222	307	DU53
Wycombe Rd., Ilf.	224	308	EM57
Wycombe Rd., Wem.	124	314	CN67
Wydehurst Rd., Croy.	287	333	DU101
Wydell Clo., Mord.	284	331	CX100
Wydeville Manor Rd. SE12	276	326	EH91
Wye Clo., Ashf.	265	328	BP91
Wye Clo., Orp.	291	334	ET101
Wye Clo., Ruis.	231	302	BQ58
Wye St. SW11	159	315	DD82
Wyemead Cres. E4	211	301	EE47
Wyevale Clo., Pnr.	214	303	BU55
Wyfields, Ilf.	225	308	EP53
Wyfold Rd. SW6	157	315	CY81
Wyhill Wk., Dag.	237	309	FC65
Wyke Clo., Islw.	251	321	CF79
Wyke Gdns. W7	251	321	CF76
Wyke Rd. E3	120	307	EA66
Wyke Rd. SW20	270	323	CW96
Wykeham Ave., Dag.	236	309	EW65
Wykeham Ave., Horn.	228	310	FK58
Wykeham Clo., West Dr.	249	320	BN78
Wykeham Grn., Dag.	236	309	EW65
Wykeham Hill, Wem.	91	304	CM60
Wykeham Ri. N20	206	299	CY46
Wykeham Rd. NW4	218	305	CW57
Wykeham Rd., Har.	216	304	CH56
Wylchin Clo., Pnr.	231	302	BT56
Wyld Way, Wem.	108	304	CP65
Wyldes Clo. NW11	96	305	DC60
Wyldfield Gdns. N9	209	300	DT47
Wyleu St. SE23	197	325	DY87
Wylie Rd., Sthl.	251	321	CA76
Wyllen Clo. E1	128	317	DW70
Wylo Dr., Barn.	206	299	CU44
Wymering Rd. W9	28	315	DA69
Wymond St. SW15	172	323	CW83
Wynan Rd. E14	150	317	EB78
Wynaud Ct. N22	220	306	DM51
Wyncham Ave., Sid.	261	326	ES88
Wynchgate N14	208	300	DK46
Wynchgate N21	208	300	DL45
Wynchgate, Har.	215	303	CE52
Wyncroft Clo., Brom.	276	326	EM97
Wyndale Ave. NW9	217	304	CN58
Wyndcliff Rd. SE7	252	318	EH79
Wyndcroft Clo., Enf.	202	300	DP41
Wyndham Clo., Orp.	291	334	EQ102
Wyndham Clo., Sutt.	292	331	DA108
Wyndham Cres. N19	98	306	DJ62
Wyndham Cres., Houns.	259	321	CA86
Wyndham Est. SE5	162	316	DQ80
Wyndham Ms. W1	43	315	DF71
Wyndham Pl. W1	43	315	DF71
Wyndham Rd. E6	234	308	EK66
Wyndham Rd. SE5	162	316	DQ80
Wyndham Rd. W13	142	314	CH76
Wyndham Rd., Barn.	207	299	DF46
Wyndham Rd., Kings.T.	268	322	CM94
Wyndham St. W1	43	315	DF71
Wyndham Yd. W1	43	315	DF71
Wyneham Rd. SE24	179	324	DR85
Wynell Rd. SE23	197	325	DX90
Wynford Gro., Orp.	278	327	EV97
Wynford Pl., Belv.	255	319	FA79
Wynford Rd. N1	23	316	DM68
Wynford Way SE9	260	326	EM90
Wynlie Gdns., Pnr.	214	303	BV54
Wynndale Rd. E18	224	308	EH53
Wynne Rd. SW9	162	316	DN82
Wynns Ave., Sid.	262	327	EU85
Wynnstay Gdns. W8	64	315	DA76
Wynter St. SW11	174	323	DC84
Wynton Gdns. SE25	287	332	DS99
Wynton Pl. W3	134	314	CP72
Wynyard Ter. SE11	83	316	DM78
Wynyatt St. EC1	36/7	316	DP69
Wyre Gro., Edg.	205	298	CP48
Wyre Gro., Hayes	250	321	BU77
Wyresdale Cres., Grnf.	243	313	CF69
Wyteleaf Clo., Ruis.	231	302	BQ58
Wythburn Pl. W1	43	315	DF72
Wythens Wk. SE9	261	326	EP86
Wythenshawe Rd., Dag.	237	309	FA62
Wythes Clo., Brom.	276	326	EM96
Wythes Rd. E16	244	318	EL74
Wythfield Rd. SE9	260	326	EM86
Wyvenhoe Rd., Har.	233	313	CC62
Wyvern Clo., Orp.	291	335	EV104
Wyvern Gro., Hayes	257	320	BP80
Wyvern Rd., Pur.	294	332	DP110
Wyvern Way, Uxb.	240	312	BH66
Wyvil Est. SW8	161	316	DL80
Wyvil Rd. SW8	161	316	DL79
Wyvis St. E14	140	317	EB71
Yabsley St. E14	140	317	EC74
Yalding Clo., Orp.	278	327	EX98
Yalding Rd. SE16	148	317	DU76
Yale Clo., Houns.	258	321	BZ85
Yale Way, Horn.	238	310	FG63
Yarborough Rd. SW19	271	323	DD95
Yardbridge Clo., Sutt.	292	331	DB110
Yardley Clo. E4	211	301	EB43
Yardley La. E4	211	301	EB43
Yardley St. WC1	36	316	DN69
Yarmouth Cres. N17	222	307	DV57
Yarmouth Pl. W1	56/7	316	DH74
Yarnfield Sq. SE15	164	317	DU81
Yarnton Way SE2	254	319	EX75
Yarnton Way, Erith	254	319	EX75
Yarrow Cres. E6	244	318	EL71
Yateley St. SE18	252	318	EK76
Yates Ct. NW2	111	305	CX65
Yeading Ave., Har.	232	313	BY61
Yeading Fork, Hayes	242	313	BW71
Yeading Gdns., Hayes	242	313	BV71
Yeading La., Hayes	242	313	BV72
Yeading La., Nthlt.	242	313	BW69
Yeames Clo. W13	132	314	CG72
Yeate St. N1	117	306	DR66
Yeatman Rd. N6	219	305	DF58
Yeats Clo. NW10	109	304	CS65
Yeats Clo. SE13	167	317	ED82
Yeldham Rd. W6	147	315	CX78
Yellow Hammer Ct. NW9	217	304	CS54
Yelverton Clo., Rom.	228	310	FK53
Yelverton Rd. SW11	159	315	DD82
Yenston Clo., Mord.	284	331	DA100
Yeo St. E3	140	317	EB71
Yeoman Clo. E6	245	318	EP72
Yeoman Clo. SE27	194	324	DP90
Yeoman Rd., Nthlt.	232	313	BY66
Yeoman St. SE8	149	317	DY77
Yeomans Acre, Ruis.	214	303	BU58
Yeoman's Ms., Islw.	259	321	CE85
Yeoman's Row SW3	66/7	315	DE76
Yeomans Way, Enf.	203	301	DW40
Yeomans Yd. E1	63	316	DT73
Yeomen Way, Ilf.	225	308	EQ51
Yeovil Clo., Orp.	291	334	ES103
Yeovilton Pl., Kings.T.	268	322	CK92
Yerbury Rd. N19	99	306	DK62
Yester Dr., Chis.	276	326	EL94
Yester Pk., Chis.	276	326	EM94
Yester Rd., Chis.	276	326	EL94
Yevele Way, Horn.	238	311	FL59
Yew Ave., West Dr.	248	312	BL73
Yew Gro. NW2	111	305	CX63
Yew Tree Clo. N21	209	300	DN45
Yew Tree Clo., Well.	254	319	EU81
Yew Tree Clo., Wor.Pk.	283	330	CS102
Yew Tree Ct., Borwd.	204	298	CK44
Yew Tree Gdns., Rom.	227	309	FD57
Yew Tree Gdns. (Chadwell Heath), Rom.	226	309	EY57
Yew Tree Rd. W12	135	314	CT73
Yew Tree Rd., Uxb.	240	312	BM67
Yew Tree Wk., Houns.	258	321	BZ85
Yew Tree Wk., Pur.	295	332	DQ110
Yew Trees, Shep.	280	328	BM98
Yew Wk., Har.	233	313	CE60
Yewdale Clo., Brom.	275	325	EE93
Yewfield Rd. NW10	109	304	CT65
Yews, The, Ashf.	265	328	BP91
Yews Ave., Enf.	203	301	DV36
Yewtree Clo. N22	220	306	DJ53
Yewtree Clo., Har.	215	303	CB56
Yewtree Rd., Beck.	274	325	DZ97
Yoakley Rd. N16	101	306	DS61
Yoke Clo. N7	115	306	DL65
Yolande Gdns. SE9	260	326	EL85
Yonge Pk. N4	100	306	DN62
York Ave. SW14	170	322	CQ85
York Ave. W7	243	313	CE74
York Ave., Hayes	249	312	BQ71
York Ave., Sid.	261	326	ES89
York Ave., Stan.	216	304	CH53
York Bri. NW1	32	316	DG70
York Bldgs. WC2	58/9	316	DL73
York Clo. E6	244	318	EM72
York Clo. W7	243	313	CE74
York Clo., Mord.	271	323	DB98
York Gate N14	208	300	DL45
York Gate NW1	32	316	DG70
York Gro. SE15	164	317	DW81
York Hill SE27	194	324	DP90
York Hill Est. SE27	194	324	DP90
York Ho., Wem.	107	304	CM63
York Ho. Pl. W8	64/5	315	DB75
York Ms. NW5	114	306	DH64
York Ms., Ilf.	235	308	EN62
York Par., Brent.	143	314	CK78
York Pl. SW11	174	323	DC83
York Pl. WC2	58/9	316	DL73
York Pl., Dag.	237	309	FC65
York Pl., Ilf.	235	308	EN61
York Ri. NW5	98	306	DH62
York Ri., Orp.	291	334	ES102
York Rd. E4	211	301	EA50
York Rd. E7	234	308	EG65
York Rd. E10	104	307	EC62
York Rd. E17	222	307	DX57
York Rd. N11	220	306	DK51
York Rd. N18	222	307	DV51
York Rd. N21	209	300	DR45
York Rd. SE1	71	316	DM75
York Rd. SW11	174	323	DC84
York Rd. SW18	174	323	DC84
York Rd. SW19	271	323	DC93
York Rd. W3	134	314	CQ72
York Rd. W5	142	314	CJ76
York Rd., Barn.	207	299	DC43
York Rd., Brent.	143	314	CK78
York Rd., Croy.	286	332	DN101
York Rd., Houns.	259	321	CB83
York Rd., Ilf.	235	308	EN62
York Rd., Kings.T.	268	322	CM94
York Rd., Nthwd.	214	303	BU54
York Rd., Rain.	237	309	FD66
York Rd., Rich.	169	322	CM85
York Rd., Sutt.	292	331	DA107
York Rd., Tedd.	267	329	CE91
York Rd., Uxb.	240	312	BK66
York Sq. E14	139	317	DY72
York St. W1	43	315	DF71
York St., Bark.	245	318	EQ67
York St., Mitch.	285	332	DG101
York St., Twick.	184	322	CG88
York Ter., Enf.	202	300	DQ38
York Ter., Erith	255	319	FC81
York Ter. E. NW1	32	316	DG70
York Ter. W. NW1	32	316	DG70
York Way N1	22/3	316	DL67
York Way N7	115	306	DK65
York Way N20	207	299	DF48
York Way, Felt.	258	321	BZ90
York Way Ct. N1	22/3	316	DL67
York Way Est. N7	115	306	DL65
Yorkland Ave., Well.	261	326	ET83
Yorkshire Clo. N16	101	306	DS62
Yorkshire Gdns. N18	210	301	DV50
Yorkshire Grey Pl. NW3	112	305	DC63
Yorkshire Grey Yd. WC1	47	316	DM71
Yorkshire Rd. E14	139	317	DY72
Yorkshire Rd., Mitch.	286	332	DL99
Yorkton St. E2	128	317	DU68
Young Rd. E16	244	318	EJ72
Young St. W8	64/5	315	DB75
Youngmans Clo., Enf.	202	300	DQ39
Young's Bldgs. EC1	37	316	DQ70
Youngs Rd., Ilf.	225	308	ER57
Yoxley App., Ilf.	225	308	EQ58
Yoxley Dr., Ilf.	225	308	EQ58
Yukon Rd. SW12	192	324	DH87
Yuletide Clo. NW10	109	304	CS66
Yunus Khan Clo. E17	223	307	EA57
Zampa Rd. SE16	148	317	DW78
Zander Ct. E2	128	317	DU68
Zangwill Rd. SE3	252	318	EK81
Zealand Ave., West Dr.	256	320	BK80
Zealand Rd. E3	129	317	DY68
Zelah Rd., Orp.	291	335	EV101
Zennor Rd. SW12	192	324	DJ88
Zenoria St. SE22	179	324	DT84
Zermatt Rd., Th.Hth.	273	324	DQ98
Zetland St. E14	140	317	EB71
Zion Pl., Th.Hth.	273	324	DR98
Zion Rd., Th.Hth.	273	324	DR98
Zoar St. SE1	61	316	DQ74
Zoffany St. N19	99	306	DK61